# FARMERS' ALMANAC

*Calculated for the United States*
*for the year of our Lord*

**2020**

*Being bissextile, or leap year, and until the*
## FOURTH OF JULY
*The 244th Year of the Independence of the*
## UNITED STATES

Containing early America at its best, delightfully threaded through with
a measure of good humor, amusing anecdotes, wise-old weather predictions,
helpful hints, and good reading for every member of the
family done on a high moral plane.

EDITED BY PETER GEIGER, PHILOM.
MANAGING EDITOR, SONDRA DUNCAN, PHILOM.

COPYRIGHT © 2019 BY ALMANAC PUBLISHING COMPANY

ISSN: 0737-6731

FARMERS' ALMANAC P.O. Box 1609, Lewiston, Maine 04241

FarmersAlmanac.com

# We Make It EASIER for You!

## GREAT GIFT IDEAS FOR EVERYONE

### FROM OUR
### FARMERS' ALMANAC® STORE

For the **Gardener**

For the **Weather Watcher**

For the **Recycler**

For the **Homesteader**

For the **Planner**

*Shop anytime. From any device.*
<u>Store.FarmersAlmanac.com</u>

# CONTENTS

 **FarmersAlmanac.com**

*(continued)*

*Is Salt Therapy a Miracle Cure?* **78**

*What is a Super Moon?* **120**

Download our **NEW**
**Full Moon Lore** PDF at
**FarmersAlmanac.com/digital-editions**

# CONTENTS

*Polar Coaster Winter Ahead for 2019-20!*
*65*

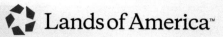

# Take A Closer Look

*Dear Readers,*

It's here! The 2020 edition of the *Farmers' Almanac* and another decade in the new millennium are both upon us. It's hard to believe that twenty years ago we were worried about Y2K and all of our computers crashing. Now, most of us carry high-powered "mini-computers" in our back pockets that allow us to stay connected with each other by voice and text, take beautiful photos, play games, and tune into the latest news or updates on friends and family.

Advances in technology afford us perspectives that we could not have imagined. They allow us to look at things differently and certainly more quickly. But, despite all of these advancements, it's still important to embrace the past and stay connected to our roots. Whether it's the folklore passed down from our ancestors, ways to use natural products for a healthier lifestyle, or tips on digging your hands into garden soil, the *Farmers' Almanac* remains a resource to ensure you remain tethered to important traditions, while also providing you with the tools you need to plan ahead. We invite you to take a closer look at the Almanac—in print and online—and "see clearly" all of the benefits it provides for the past, present, and future.

Our founder David Young was a visionary. He knew that human curiosity of the night sky and dependency on weather predictions mixed with sage advice would be important to readers for years to come. He imagined a printed *Farmers' Almanac* that could, in many ways, predict the future. We have continued his vision by publishing every year for over 200 years. But we didn't stop there: this valuable information can also be found at **FarmersAlmanac.com**. Here you can access what you need to know for the days, weeks, and months ahead—whether it's the best day to fish or quit a bad habit, or to locate a helpful hint for making the most perfect, flaky biscuits.

In this 2020 edition, you'll also find all the fun, entertaining, and engaging information that you expect from the *Farmers' Almanac.* If you're looking to add more plants *(or bugs)* to your diet, eat more local produce, make your own cough drops, move to a place where it snows more than 500 inches a year, or learn the answers to questions such as who invented the first weight loss diet, will winter be as cold and long as it was last year, and how do animals survive extreme weather, you've come to the right place.

*Happy Reading!*

Peter Geiger
*Philom., Editor*

Sandi Duncan
*Philom., Managing Editor*

# DIY *Favorite Fall Flavors*

## *Pumpkin Spice*

3 tablespoons ground cinnamon
2 teaspoons ground ginger
2 teaspoons ground nutmeg
½ teaspoon ground allspice
1½ teaspoons ground cloves

*Mix all ingredients together. Store in an airtight jar or plastic bag.*

## *Mulling Spice Mix*

¼ cup orange peel
¼ cup lemon peel
2 tablespoons Grenadine syrup
3 sticks cinnamon
2 whole nutmegs, crushed, or 2 tablespoons ground nutmeg
6 whole cloves
½ teaspoon cardamom
3 tablespoons brown sugar

*Sprinkle a few tablespoons of this mix over fresh cider before you warm it. Or store in an airtight tin or a tightly closed glass jar as a gift or for later use.*

## Love the *Smell* of *Autumn?*

*Try one or both of these mixtures and use a diffuser for best results:*

4 drops sweet orange essential oil
3 drops lemon essential oil
3 drops fir essential oil

4 drops sweet orange essential oil
2 drops sage essential oil
3 drops of lime essential oil

# FARMERS' ALMANAC
## Helpful Hints

The original source for life-hacks.

### Holiday Tradition

Create a special keepsake this holiday. Have family members sign a tablecloth with washable marker. Then **embroider the names** and add to the tablecloth as the family grows.

### Reusable Storage

Don't throw away the empty, cardboard six-pack bottle carrier. **Use it to store** tools, glue, pencils, and other items in your garage or work room.

### Cup Holder Cleaner

To clean the grime and spills that tend to accumulate in your car's cup holder, **place an old sock over the bottom of a reusable travel cup.** Spray the sock with your favorite cleaner, insert it into the holder, and twist.

*Header illustration by Martina Fugazzotto*

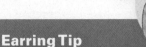

## Earring Tip

Keep your stud earrings together by fastening them onto **a loose button**. Works at home in your jewelry box or when traveling so you don't lose them.

## Bathroom Brainstorm

Add **a second shower curtain rod** on the inside or outside of your shower. Use the second rod to hang towels or clothes that need to be line dried.

## Home Spa

Tie **a bunch of fresh eucalyptus** to your shower head and let the smell turn your shower into an invigorating way to start the day. (Eucalyptus is known for helping open nasal passages.)

## Bug Bite Relief

Soak a cloth in a mixture of **water and Epsom salts** (two tablespoons per cup of water). Ring out excess water and hold the wet cloth on the bite for several minutes.

## Got Moles?

Crush **several cloves of garlic** and stick the mash into the mole tunnels. They don't like the smell.

## Camping Made Easier

Use **a plastic snow sled** with a rope lead to haul your camping gear from the car to your site.

## Balloon Fun & Function

At your next cookout, use **frozen water balloons** to keep beverages cold. Once they melt use them for a refreshing water balloon fight.

## Leftover Wine Corks

Use **corks as plant markers**. Write the name of the plant on the cork with permanent marker, push it onto a metal skewer (or a chopstick), and place in the soil next to the appropriate plant.

*Get more Helpful Hints at [FarmersAlmanac.com](FarmersAlmanac.com), or by signing up for our weekly eNewsletter, and by following us on Pinterest!*

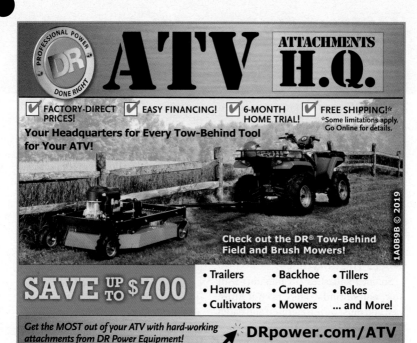

# It's *Winter Squash* Season!
## *Give These Varieties a Try*

One of the oldest known crops to mankind is squash. Squash gets its name from the Narragansett Native American word *askutasquah,* meaning "eaten raw or uncooked." Technically, squash is a fruit, but is considered a vegetable for cooking purposes. There are many varieties of squash, which typically fall into one of two categories: summer squash and winter squash.

### What's The Difference?

Summer squashes are immature with soft, edible rinds. They do not store well and must be refrigerated and eaten within a few days. Summer squashes require short cooking times or may be eaten raw. Varieties include pattypan or "scallop," yellow summer, cousa, yellow crookneck, and zucchini.

Winter squashes are harvested after the fruit and seeds have matured and the rind has hardened. Winter varieties are typically cooked before eating. Unlike summer squashes, winter squashes are best kept at room temperature and may be stored for long periods of time.

Even though many people consider winter squash to be a starchy, high-carb vegetable, you'd be remiss if you avoided these nutrition powerhouses. While winter squash are higher in carbohydrates than summer squash varieties, recent studies have shown they actually help steady blood sugar. And their vivid orange hues (due to the high concentration of carotenoids like beta- and alpha-carotene) make them a great source of vitamin A. Winter squash varieties are also high in pectin, a fiber that helps aid digestion, and is loaded with B vitamins.

Butternut

Spaghetti

Acorn

Buttercup

Kabocha

**Check out our tasty summer and winter squash recipes online: FarmersAlmanac.com/squash-season**

Delicata

Blue Hubbard

Turban

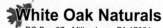

# What's In Season?

## FARMERS' ALMANAC®
## SEASONAL PRODUCE GUIDE*

**S**trawberries in September? Watermelons in winter? Today most fruits and vegetables are available year-round, but that doesn't mean anytime is the best time to buy. For maximum freshness, flavor, and nutritional content, produce should be purchased when it's in season, shortly after farmers have harvested it.

To help you buy the freshest produce possible, we've come up with **an abbreviated list** of which of **our favorite fruits and vegetables** are in season according to the *Farmers' Almanac* weather zone *(see map at right)*.

**FALL** *(Sept., Oct., Nov.)*

**WINTER** *(Dec., Jan., Feb.)*

**SPRING** *(Mar., Apr., May)*

**SUMMER** *(June, July, Aug.)*

*A complete list of available produce per zone and season can be found in our 2020 ebook edition or at FarmersAlmanac.com/produce-guide.*

| ZONE 1: Northeast & New England | ZONE 2: Great Lakes, Ohio Valley, & Midwest |
|---|---|
| Apples, Beets, Grapes, Plums, Squash | Cabbage, Cauliflower, Pears, Pawpaws, Rutabagas |
| Brussels Sprouts, Leeks, Salsify, Parsnips, Horseradish | Chicories, Horseradish, Salsify, Sweet Potatoes, Winter Squash |
| Asparagus, Fiddleheads, Garlic Scapes, Lettuce, Rhubarb | Cabbage, Lettuce/Greens, Peas, Parsnips, Radishes |
| Blueberries, Raspberries, Lima Beans, Melons | Cherries, Gooseberries, Okra, Sunchokes, Turnips |

*Compiled by Tiffany Means*

## ZONE 3:
### Southeast

Grapefruit, Pecans, Summer & Winter Squash, Tangerines, Figs

Beets, Brussels Sprouts, Sweet Potatoes, Kumquats, Radishes

Asparagus, Peas, String Beans, Strawberries, Vidalia Onions

Apricots, Key Limes, Melons, Grapes & Muscadines, Rhubarb

## ZONE 4:
### North Central

Apples, Okra, Radishes, Summer & Winter Squash, Tomatoes

Chicories, Horseradish, Salsify, Winter Squash

Asparagus, Horseradish, Peas, Lettuces/Greens, Parsnips

Boysenberries, Cauliflower, Gooseberries, Rhubarb

## ZONE 5:
### South Central

Apples, Eggplant, Melons, Persimmons, Pomegranates

Kumquats, Mandarins, Grapefruit, Sunchokes, Tangerines

Asparagus, Beets, Cucumbers, Strawberries, Turnips

Apples, Figs, Grapes, Okra, Plums, Sweet Corn

## ZONE 6:
### Northwest

Figs, Grapes, Melons, Pears, Tomatoes

Apples, Horseradish, Leeks, Sunchokes, Winter Squash

Fiddleheads, Lettuce/Greens, Nettles, Radishes, Rhubarb

Apricots, Beets, Blackberries, Strawberries, Sweet Corn

## ZONE 7:
### Southwest

Almonds, Grapes, Walnuts, Dates, Persimmons

Grapefruit, Kumquats, Lettuce/Greens, Rutabagas, Tangerines

Beets, Broccoli, Oranges, Radishes, Strawberries

Apricots, Artichokes, Cherries, Figs, Summer & Winter Squash

# BEST DAYS
## FOR
# GARDENING
## CALENDAR

*Turn to* **Page 188**

# 10 Best Edible Insects

Wildcrafters and survivalists report that many bugs are surprisingly delicious (not to mention an essential source of protein). If you're thinking of giving bugs a try, we recommend that you start with the cooked varieties rather than trying to eat them raw or live.*

**001. Crickets:** Remove legs; dry roast, fry, or stir-fry. *(And be sure to check out our story on cricket flour at FarmersAlmanac.com/cricket-flour)*

**002. Cicadas:** "The shrimp of the land." Delicious roasted over an open fire or deep-fried and tossed with salt and seasonings like chili powder or honey mustard.

**003. Mealworms:** Can be oven roasted and salted or marinated with ginger, garlic, and soy and stir-fried.

**004. Scorpions:** Served skewered and fried in China and Thailand. Reportedly taste similar to soft shell crab.

**005. June Bugs/Beetles:** Fry in oil/butter with shallots.

**006. Grasshoppers:** Remove legs, skewer, and roast over coals. Brush with teriyaki sauce while roasting.

**007. Ants:** Can be roasted in a dry pan and added as a flavoring or crunchy topping to other dishes.

**008. Waxworms:** The flavor is somewhat like pine nuts, and they can be roasted or sautéed.

**009. Termites:** Forage swarming termites from rotten trees in the forest (not house termites). Roast or fry. They are said to taste a bit like carrots.

**010. Pill Bugs (Sow Bugs):** These insects are related to lobster and shrimp. Boil or sauté briefly in butter.

***CAUTION:** Avoid insects with bright yellow, red, or orange markings, as they may be poisonous. Stick to insects that are black, brown, green, or cream/tan colored. And be sure you have a reliable wild source well away from areas sprayed with pesticides.*

by Edward Higgins

# On-the-Go?

The *Farmers' Almanac* digital editions easily go with you!

*Available on Kindle, iPad, Nook, and your phone:*

 FarmersAlmanac.com/digital-editions

# Know Your FROST Types

*A look at some common varieties:*

### Rime Frost

Rime frost looks like sugar sprinkled onto the edges of leaves and flower petals. It occurs whenever damp winds are coupled with extremely low temperatures. The word "rime" means "crust."

### Hoar Frost

Hoar frost is frost that resembles spiky hairs. This type of frost gets its name from the word "hoar," which means "ancient," because it resembles an old man's bushy, white beard. It happens when water vapor freezes instantly after coming into contact with a very cold surface.

### Fern Frost

Fern frost is a kind of frost that appears on windows when there is very cold air on one side and moist air on the other. This causes tiny water droplets to form on the cold glass and freeze into patterns that resemble leaves or ferns.

 **Be sure you're planting at the right time—check out our interactive Average Frost Dates calendar: FarmersAlmanac.com/average-frost-dates**

# FREEZE Your
## *Fresh* **Fruits** and **Vegetables**
### *(And Save Money, Too!)*

In the summertime, nothing is better than fresh food straight from your garden or the local farmers' market. Wouldn't it be great to have these delicious fruits and vegetables available year-round? Well, you can. Save money and eat healthy, tasty meals all winter long by preserving those homegrown fruits and vegetables through freezing. *It's easier than you think!*

Freezing slows food deterioration and stops the growth of bacteria. Food can be frozen in containers such as freezer bags (these are heavier duty than the thinner sandwich bags), plastic containers (butter tubs and whipped topping containers work well), canning jars, aluminum foil, or freezer paper. ***Remember— food expands as it freezes, so do not overfill containers.***

## Freezing *Fruits*

Prevent cut fruits such as apples, peaches, and pears from darkening by first soaking them in a commercial anti-darkening agent, or make your own solution by combining one teaspoonful of lemon juice with one quart of water. For many fruits, it is best to add sugar or a sugar syrup (see recipes below) to enhance taste and help the fruit retain its color.

### Sugar Syrup Recipes
**Light Syrup:** Boil 2 cups sugar and 4 cups water.
*(Makes 5 cups syrup.)*
**Medium Syrup:** Boil 3 cups sugar and 4 cups water.
*(Makes 5 ½ cups syrup.)*
**Heavy Syrup:** Boil 4 ¾ cups sugar and 4 cups water.
*(Makes 6 ½ cups syrup.)*
**Cool syrup, then pour over fruit before freezing.**

Fresh vegetables must be blanched before freezing. Blanching involves submerging vegetables into boiling water for a short period of time and then immersing them into cold water to stop the cooking process. Blanching kills enzymes that age the produce, resulting in fresher-tasting food.

**For more how-to tips on blanching, visit our website: FarmersAlmanac.com/blanching**

## Handy *Blanching* Guide:

**Asparagus:** 2-4 minutes *(depending on size)*
**Beets (whole):** 25-30 minutes *(slice after blanching)*
**Beans (Snap, Green, or Wax):** 3 minutes
**Broccoli:** 3 minutes
**Brussels Sprouts:** 3-5 minutes *(depending on size)*
**Cabbage:** 1 ½ minutes
**Carrots (sliced or diced):** 2 minutes
**Cauliflower (flowerets, 1 inch across):** 3 minutes
**Corn on the Cob (small ears):** 7 minutes
**Eggplant:** 4 minutes
**Greens (Beet Greens, Collard Greens, Kale, Chard, Mustard Greens, Turnip Greens, Spinach):** 2 minutes; collards: 3 minutes
**Lima Beans:** 2-4 minutes *(depending on size)*
**Onions (whole):** 2 ½ minutes; rings: 10-15 seconds
**Parsnips (sliced):** 2 minutes
**Peas (edible pods):** 1 ½ minutes; **(green/shelled):** 1 ½ minutes
**Potatoes (Irish new):** 3-5 minutes
**Rutabagas:** 3 minutes
**Soybeans:** 6 minutes
**Summer Squash (Zucchini, Yellow, White Scallop):** 3 minutes
**Turnips (cubed):** 2 minutes

# Tips from the Pros:
# Tastier Vegetables!

When cooking vegetables, ever wonder if you should boil the water *before* or *after* you add the vegetables to the pot? Here's a *Farmers' Almanac* secret so you'll always remember—

> **Vegetables that grow ABOVE ground: Add to *boiling* water.**
>
> **Vegetables that grow BELOW ground: Start off in *cold* water.**

*What's the reason?* Cooking aboveground vegetables simply entails softening their cell walls to make them more palatable and digestible. Because most green vegetables are small with thin cell walls, that process doesn't take very long. All you need to do is boil water, add the vegetables, and cook until they are just tender.

Root vegetables, on the other hand, contain a great deal of starch, and that starch needs to be dissolved before they can be eaten. The problem, of course, is that most root veggies are quite large and they can get overcooked, as anyone who's overboiled potatoes knows all too well.

Starting potatoes off in cold water creates more even cooking. Throwing cold potatoes into boiling water gelatinizes the starches at the surface of the potato too fast, leaving you with a mushy exterior that falls apart and dissolves into the cooking water before the center cooks through. By starting in cold water, potato temperature rises more gently.

While very few vegetables are "boiled" these days (thanks to clever chefs in the kitchen who come up with the best cooking methods to preserve flavor), this particular method still "holds water" for corn and potatoes!

**P** *"Pin" this tip & many other helpful hints by following at Pinterest.com/farmersalmanac.*

## Want More Flavor?

• Cook vegetables in chicken, beef, or vegetable broth.

• Salt vegetables *(if desired)* cooked in a microwave *after* they are cooked and not before. This prevents liquid from being drawn out and interfering with the microwave.

• Try adding a little garlic salt to fresh veggies.

Veggies that grow **ABOVE GROUND:** Start off in *BOILING* water

# *WHEN* TO
# BOIL
# WATER

Veggies that grow **UNDERGROUND:** Start off in *COLD* water

**FARMERS' ALMANAC** STORE

# *Fall Camping*
# TIPS +
# TRICKS

*C*amping is a popular pastime that's good for both body and soul. Spending time immersed in Mother Nature's beauty can decrease stress and create a sense of connection and well-being while hiking, fishing, and related activities strengthen our bodies.

Though summer is the most popular season for camping, the fun doesn't have to end just because autumn has arrived. Fall can be one of the best times of the year for spending time outdoors. Mosquitoes and other summer pests have mostly disappeared as have droves of other people clogging up your favorite destination and taking the best campsites. Changing leaves are a special treat, and the chill in the air makes nature hikes a little easier.

With a little extra planning, an autumn outing can be as good as, or better than, a summer camping trip. ***Here are some important things to consider:***

### Wear Layers

Autumn temperatures are known to be unpredictable, with summer highs during the day and downright wintry conditions at night. Be prepared for this changeable weather and adjust your wardrobe accordingly.

### Wear a Hat

This is especially important at night, when temperatures can plummet close to freezing, but it is also important for the daytime. No matter how many layers you wear, most of your body heat would still escape through a bare head.

## Check Your Sleeping Bag

Make sure your sleeping bag is rated for cold weather. Being warm enough while sleeping can mean the difference between a happy memory and a miserable night. A mummy bag is the best bet because it keeps in the most warmth. Also bring along a sleeping pad to insulate yourself from the cold ground.

## Consider Cooking Times

Food takes longer to cook when it's cold and daylight is shorter. Allow yourself enough time before it gets dark.

## Be Aware of Wildlife

Bears and other animals can become even more of a concern in autumn. As their food supply begins to die off, they become more determined in their foraging. Be sure to seal any food you have in airtight containers—or in your car—to prevent attracting them. Be on the lookout for bees and wasps, too. They become more active and aggressive at this time of year.

# 5 *Favorite* CAMPING HACKS

**1.** After cooking, fill a pot of water and leave it to warm on the stove or fire for cleanup.

**2.** Bring two coolers—one just for drinks and the other for food. This will help keep the food cooler from being opened too many times.

**3.** Always pack duct tape. It's useful for many things.

**4.** Spice it up. Fill empty Tic Tac™ containers with your favorite seasonings and use a permanent marker to write what's inside.

**5.** To save time on prep work, create a bin of essential camping items to keep packed and ready year-round. Buy an extra set of pots and pans and other similar items at a garage sale or dollar store. Make sure the bin is rain- and rodent-proof before filling it up.

# 9 Reasons to Keep Witch Hazel in Your Home

**W**itch hazel is a plant that is grown throughout North America. But it is also a compound made from the plant's leaf, bark, and twigs. It is sold as a medicinal product that has many health benefits including:

**1. Soothes Razor Burn.** Because of its natural astringent properties, witch hazel is popularly used by both men and women as a soothing post-shave treatment. Just wet your hands with witch hazel, rub together, and tap on affected skin.

**2. Provides Hemorrhoid Relief.** Witch hazel is effective at easing the itching, swelling, and pain of hemorrhoids. Just apply to the area with a cotton pad to get relief.

**3. Treats Skin Irritations.** Because of its drying and anti-itch properties, witch hazel can be used to soothe irritated skin caused by poison ivy, poison oak, and poison sumac.

**4. Heals Bruises.** Witch hazel can help fade discoloration and speed up the healing process of bruises. Just apply to bruises with a cotton ball.

**5. Treats Acne.** Witch hazel's astringent properties help remove impurities from pores and keep skin clear. Apply after cleansing.

**6. Soothes and Heals Eczema.** Applying witch hazel to affected areas helps treat the skin condition.

**7. Treats Varicose Veins.** Soak a soft cloth in witch hazel and lay over varicose veins to temporarily reduce swelling and pain.

**8. Cools Sunburn and Soothes Windburn.** Witch hazel combined with aloe can soothe painful sunburn. Its anti-inflammatory powers aid in healing sunburned and windburned skin. Just apply to affected areas with a cotton ball in a gentle dabbing motion.

**9. Treats Bug Bites.** Applying witch hazel with a cotton pad to insect bites helps reduce swelling, sting, and itch.

## Why the Name?

The word "witch" in witch hazel actually has nothing to do with witches. It comes from the Old English *wiche,* which meant "pliant" or "bendable." The term had been used in the names of several plant species in Europe for hundreds of years before it was applied to the genus *Hamamelis* in North America. Other popular names for witch hazel include "snapping hazel" and "winterbloom."

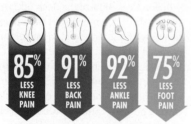

# FAVORITE Pumpkin RECIPES

## Roasted Pumpkin Seeds

### Ingredients:

*2 cups of raw pumpkin seeds straight from the pumpkin*

*Water for cleaning/soaking*

*2 tablespoons salt*

*1 tablespoon melted butter*

### Directions:

Next time you carve a jack-o'-lantern or slice up a pumpkin for pie, save those seeds! First, soak the harvested seeds in a large bowl of water and remove any remaining pumpkin flesh by rubbing them with your fingers. (Don't worry if you don't get 100% of the flesh off.) Dry the seeds on a paper towel then place in a bowl. Coat with melted butter and sprinkle with salt. Spread the seeds on a cookie sheet and bake at 350°F for 30 minutes, or until they reach a light golden brown color, turning occasionally during cooking. Store cooled seeds in an airtight plastic container. Use to top your salads or simply as a snack.

## 🎃 Tips on Cooking Fresh Pumpkin

Remove the stem and cut the pumpkin in half. Scoop out the seeds and stringy mass and rinse. Cook in one of the following ways:

• **Boil or Steam:** Cut the pumpkin into large chunks, and place in a pot with one cup of water. Cover and boil 20-30 minutes or until tender. Alternatively, the pumpkin may be placed in a steamer basket and steamed for 10-12 minutes.

• **Bake:** Place pumpkin halves, skin-side down, on roasting pan with a thin layer of water. Cover and bake at 300°F for one hour or until tender.

• **Microwave:** Place pumpkin halves, skin side down, in microwave-safe bowl with a couple inches of water. Cook on high for 15 minutes. If pumpkin is not done, continue cooking at 1-2 minute intervals until tender.

Allow pumpkin to cool, and then remove peel. Purée in a food processor or blender. Each pound of raw, untrimmed pumpkin will yield approximately one cup of purée. Pumpkin purée may be kept frozen for up to one year.

# Pumpkin Pancakes

**Ingredients:**
*2 egg yolks*
*1 cup pumpkin*
*1 ¼ cups milk*
*2 tablespoons melted shortening*
*2 teaspoons baking powder*
*½ teaspoon salt*
*2 tablespoons sugar*
*1 cup flour*
*2 egg whites, beaten until fluffy*

**Directions:**

Beat egg yolks; add pumpkin, milk, and shortening. Sift baking powder, salt, sugar, and flour. Add to pumpkin mixture and stir. Gently fold in beaten egg whites. Fry on a hot griddle.

# Pumpkin Nog

**Ingredients:**
*1 can (15 oz.) canned pumpkin*
*1 can (12 oz.) evaporated milk*
*2 tablespoons honey*
*1 teaspoon ground cinnamon*
*1 pint vanilla ice cream*
*2-3 tablespoons rum (optional)*
*Ground nutmeg*

**Directions:**

Place pumpkin, evaporated milk, honey, and cinnamon in blender and blend until smooth. Add ice cream (and rum, if desired). Blend again until smooth. Sprinkle with nutmeg.

# Pumpkin Dip

**Ingredients:**
*1 can (29 oz.) pumpkin*
*2 packages (8 oz. each) cream cheese, softened*
*3 cups powdered sugar*
*2 teaspoons vanilla*
*3 teaspoons pumpkin pie spice*

**Directions:**

Mix all ingredients well and serve with gingersnaps.

## Pick A "Pie Pumpkin"

Select one with a stem at least 1-2 inches long (shorter stems hasten decay). Misshapen pumpkins are fine for cooking, but avoid any with soft spots or blemishes.

# Feed a Fever *or a Cold?*

W e've all heard the saying, "feed a fever and starve a cold." Or is it "feed a cold and starve a fever"? While some get confused on the wording, the actual phrase, which dates back to the middle 1500s, advocates starving a fever while feeding a cold.

So is this good advice to follow? It seems there are differing opinions. Some assert the phrase is nothing more than a medical myth, while others believe it may contain at least some truth.

Healthcare proponents against the phrase state that you should continue eating normally whether you are battling a fever or a cold. They argue that starvation only adds additional strain to your body while you are sick.

However, research by Dutch scientists suggests eating boosts the type of immune response needed to fight off the common cold virus, while fasting promotes a type of immune reaction necessary to overcome the bacterial infections that trigger most fevers.

Others also note that a fever is commonly associated with the flu, which requires a larger amount of metabolic activity to battle the invading virus. Since the process of digestion also demands a great deal of energy, fasting

allows the body to divert more of its resources into fighting off the illness. On the other hand, a cold typically takes one to two weeks to run its course, so starving yourself for this long a length of time would be counterproductive.

Overall, it seems the best advice may be a middle-of-the-road solution. For a fever, take in plenty of liquids, such as soup, broth, and fruit juices, and eat if you feel hungry. If you are battling a cold, also consume lots of liquids and eat moderately (including foods rich in Vitamin C) to keep your energy up for the longer recovery period. *As always, consult with your physician for a treatment plan that is right for you.*

(YES, you could get rid of your CPAP!)

## SLEEP APNEA · DIGESTIVE AILMENTS · SINUSITIS · INJURIES · RASHES & ECZEMA

# You can address all of these ailments naturally - WITHOUT DRUGS!

### Sleep Apnea Relief

Ensure deep, steady breathing throughout the night *WITHOUT CPAP*. A natural herbal solution.

### Food Poisoning

Food Poisoning Relief (AKA "The Antidote") *effectively terminates food poisoning* and relieves the condition within an hour.

### Leg Relaxer

Relax cramped muscles and calm irritated nerves. Soothes restless legs so you can sleep peacefully.

### Respiratory Relief

A proven natural solution for relief from bronchitis and pneumonia and for acute or recurring respiratory distress.

### Sinus Infection

Antimicrobial power in either a convenient nasal spray or neti-pot rinse. Don't bathe the germs, kill them.

### Injury Repair

Bruise, Strain & Tear Repair heals damaged tendons and ligaments naturally. Don't mask the pain, heal the damage.

**NATURE'S RITE™**

# Natural products that *work!*

For more products & more savings, visit **MyNaturesRite.com** or call **800-991-7088**

**Use Coupon Code FARM-20 for 20% OFF Entire Order!**

**SATISFACTION GUARANTEED**
100% Money Back Guarantee

**Dear Friends,**

*I developed these natural healthcare products to empower you in your quest for natural healing. They represent the best solutions that I have found through years of laboratory, clinical and experiential research and development.*

*Best of Health,*

**Steven Frank, Founder, Innovative Herbalist Nature's Rite**

37

## MAKE YOUR OWN
## ODOR-MASKING
### *Toilet Spray*

With our easy DIY recipe (below) and an inexpensive spray bottle, you can keep your bathroom fresh for pennies!

### *"Bottom Bouquet"*\*
### Odor-Masking Toilet Spray

**Ingredients:**

*1–4-oz. spray bottle (glass is best)*
*3 oz water*
*15 drops lemongrass essential oil*
*10 drops peppermint essential oil*
*10 drops lavender essential oil*
*1 teaspoon vegetable glycerin (creates the important "barrier")*

**Directions:**

Mix all ingredients in a small bowl, and then funnel into spray bottle. Seal tightly and label.

**To Use:**

Shake well before each use. Spray the surface of the toilet water with 4-5 sprays *before* doing your business.

Gets up to 50 uses!

*\*Congratulations to our Facebook fan Anne Moss for coming up with the winning name of our spray!*

If YOU want to enter the next contest, be sure to follow *Farmers' Almanac* on **Facebook** and subscribe to our weekly enews: **FarmersAlmanac.com/follow**.

*H*ave you noticed? Toilet sprays are suddenly all the rage. Unlike room sprays, these air fresheners prevent odors from escaping at the source—they're sprayed right on the surface of the toilet water and create a barrier so no odors can escape.

We understand this is a sensitive topic for many but, the truth is, we all have to use the restroom; it's just that no one wants anyone to know that they were there. It's a private and delicate function, so we can understand these sprays' popularity.

There are many odor-masking toilet sprays on the market and while they work, they can be pricey. The most popular ones go for $8 or more for a mere 2 ounces. The good news is that they're simple to make at home.

Happy **May 6th**!

We've declared May 6th "Read Your *Farmers' Almanac* in the Bathroom Day!" How come? FarmersAlmanac.com/May6

# 6 Reasons to Eat More BANANAS

Forget the cup of coffee or chocolate bar. Instead, reach for a banana which gives an instant, substantial, and sustained boost of energy. Bananas contain three natural sugars—sucrose, fructose, and glucose—combined with fiber. And research has proven that just two bananas provide enough energy for a strenuous 90-minute workout.

Yet energy isn't the only way bananas can help you keep fit. Eating bananas can also help overcome or prevent a substantial number of illnesses and conditions when added to your daily diet. *Take a look!*

• Bananas are a good source of fiber (an average-size one contains 3 grams), which has a variety of health benefits including keeping your bowels healthy.

• Bananas contain a low acid content. This is good for your stomach and can help ease heartburn.

• This unique tropical fruit is extremely high in potassium, which is beneficial for managing blood pressure and overall heart health.

• Snacking on bananas between meals helps keep blood sugar levels up and can help with morning sickness.

• Bananas are a good source of vitamin B6, which helps with metabolism and brain function.

• They come in their own package (skin) making them easy to travel with and the perfect snack food.

## NEW Recipe Contest!

Turn to page 42 for last year's QUINOA recipe winners!

Our contest is going **BANANAS!** This year we're looking for original, delicious recipes that call for **at least one** banana as an ingredient.

*Win Cash Prizes: The top three winning recipes will earn cash prizes ($250 for 1st place, $200 for 2nd place and $150 for 3rd place) and get their recipes published in the 2021 Farmers' Almanac and online. No professional cooks please. Recipes must be submitted by 2/14/20. All recipes become property of Almanac Publishing Company.*

*To submit:*
*FarmersAlmanac.com/recipe-contest or mail to: Farmers' Almanac Recipe Contest, 70 Mt. Hope Ave, Lewiston, ME 04240, USA.*

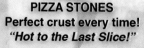

Turn to page 40 for this year's recipe contest ingredient!

# QUINOA
## Recipe Contest *Winners!*

### 1st Place - $250 WINNER
### Superfood Hash with Quinoa, Sweet Potato, Kale, & Avocado

*Laureen Pittman – Riverside, CA*

Photo by Laureen Pittman

#### Ingredients:

*2 medium-sized heads of garlic*

*2 medium sweet potatoes, peeled and cubed*

*2 tablespoons extra virgin olive oil, plus extra if needed*

*1 medium onion, chopped*

*1 medium red bell pepper, chopped*

*2 cloves garlic, minced or pressed*

*5 ounces kale leaves, chopped*

*½ teaspoon apple cider vinegar*

*¼ teaspoon dried red chili flakes (optional)*

*1 cup cooked white quinoa*

*4 large eggs*

*1 large avocado, peeled and sliced*

#### Directions:

Add the potatoes to a large pot of salted boiling water and simmer until tender. Drain and dry completely with paper towels.

Heat olive oil in a large skillet over medium heat. Add the onion and bell pepper and sauté in hot oil until vegetables are soft, about 6-8 minutes. Add the garlic and cook for 1 more minute. Add the cooked sweet potatoes, kale, vinegar, and chili flakes (if using) and stir to combine. Season with salt and pepper. Cover and cook for 5 minutes, stirring occasionally. Add the quinoa and stir to combine. Gently press hash down with a spatula and make four egg-sized wells in the hash with the back of a spoon. Crack eggs into the wells, season with salt and pepper, and cover. Cook until whites are set but yolks are still runny (about 5 minutes). Remove from heat and top with sliced avocados. Serve immediately.

### 2nd Place - $150 WINNER
### Chocolate Banana Quinoa Cake

*Shauna Havey – Roy, UT*

*(continued on facing page)*

# Chocolate Banana Quinoa Cake *(continued)*

## Ingredients:

*2 ripe bananas*

*2 eggs*

*2 tablespoons melted butter*

*1 teaspoon vanilla extract*

*¼ cup maple syrup*

*¼ cup sugar*

*2 cups cooked quinoa*

*1 cup quinoa flakes*

*1 tablespoon black chia seeds*

*½ teaspoon salt*

*1 teaspoon baking powder*

*4 ounces dark chocolate, coarsely chopped*

*1 teaspoon salted butter, softened*

## Directions:

Preheat oven to 350°F. Line an 8-inch square pan with parchment and leave some hanging over the sides. Place the bananas, eggs, melted butter, vanilla, syrup, and sugar into a food processor. Pulse until fully puréed. Pour mixture into a large mixing bowl.

Add the quinoa, quinoa flakes, chia seeds, salt, and baking powder. Gently fold mixture to combine, then pour into baking pan. Bake just until the cake is firm through to the center (30 minutes). Remove and allow to fully cool.

Lift cake from pan by the parchment and cut into squares. Microwave the chocolate on defrost in 30-second increments, stirring in between, until fully melted. Stir softened butter into chocolate. Pour mixture into a zip top bag, snip a small hole in the corner and pipe chocolate onto each square in a cross-hatch pattern. Allow chocolate to set for 5-10 minutes before serving.

3<sup>rd</sup>

## 3ʳᵈ Place - $100 WINNER
## Colorful, Cheesy Quinoa Cups

*Margee Berry – White Salmon, WA*

## Ingredients:

*Nonstick olive oil cooking spray*

*2 cups water*

*1 cup tricolor quinoa (or any other variety)*

*4 large eggs*

*½ cup part-skim ricotta cheese*

*2 tablespoons all-purpose flour*

*½ teaspoon baking powder*

*1 10-ounce package frozen spinach, thawed, chopped, and squeezed dry*

*⅓ cup crumbled feta cheese*

*3 tablespoons sun-dried tomatoes, chopped*

*¼ cup fresh grated Parmesan cheese*

## Directions:

Preheat oven to 375°F. Coat a 12-cup nonstick muffin tin with the cooking spray. In a medium saucepan, bring water to boil, and then stir in quinoa.

Cover with lid, lower heat, and simmer until quinoa is tender and all liquid is absorbed (about 15 minutes). Remove from heat, fluff with fork, and let stand 10 minutes to cool.

In a large bowl, whisk the egg, ricotta cheese, flour, and baking powder until blended. Stir in quinoa, spinach, feta cheese, and sun-dried tomatoes until combined. Divide into muffin cups and sprinkle tops with Parmesan cheese.

Bake until quinoa cups are a little golden on top and have risen (about 20 minutes). Let cool for 5 minutes in the pan on a wire rack. Gently loosen and remove. Makes 12.

# FARMERS' ALMANAC

# HANDY GUIDE TO COMPANION PLANTING

*Plant these vegetables together for best results and to deter pests!*

## CUCUMBERS

Beans, Celery, Corn, Peas, Lettuce, Dill, Radishes

## CARROTS

Tomatoes, Leeks, Sage, Rosemary, Chives

## GREEN BEANS

Corn, Cucumbers, Summer Savory, Radishes, Potatoes, Brussels Sprouts, Peas, Broccoli

## SWEET CORN

Green Beans, Cucumbers, Peas, Pumpkins, Melons, Zucchini

## ONIONS

Carrots, Beets, Cabbage, Carrots, Lettuce, Parsnips, Tomatoes

## PEPPERS

Basil, Onions, Spinach, Tomatoes

## LETTUCE

Mint, Chives, Garlic, Beans, Beets, Broccoli, Carrots, Corn, Peas, Radishes

## SQUASH

Corn, Beans, Peas, Radishes, Dill

## TOMATOES

Basil, Asparagus, Carrots, Celery, Onions, Lettuce, Parsley, Spinach

*Want more tips and tricks from Almanac-approved gardeners?*
Visit FarmersAlmanac.com/home-garden

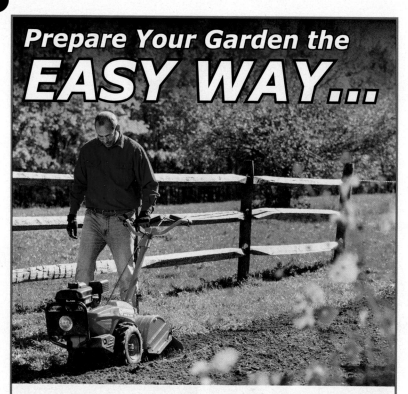

# Prepare Your Garden the EASY WAY...

## ...with Dual Rotating Tines!

**OUR PRO XL ROTOTILLER** lets you choose between forward rotation for cultivating, or counter-rotation for deep soil tilling or sod busting.

**ONE-HAND OPERATION!** Self-propulsion lets you walk to one side while you easily steer with one hand, leaving no footprints in the freshly tilled bed!

**8 TILLER MODELS!** No matter how big or small the job, we've got one for you!

# FRUIT FLIES?
## TRY THIS:

### APPLE CIDER VINEGAR + DISH SOAP

Fill a small bowl with apple cider vinegar + two drops of liquid dish soap. Mix well. Fruit flies will be drawn to the bowl ... *and to their demise!*

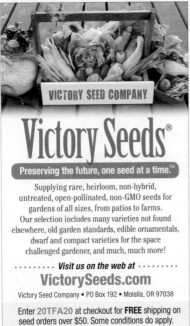
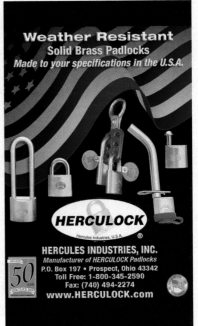

# GARDENING TIP:

## Clever Seed "Pots"

Hollowed out lemon and orange peels, halved empty egg shells, and ice cream cones (flat-bottomed) work well as seed starters. Put soil inside and plant your seeds. When ready for transplanting, simply plant the whole thing, "pot" and all!

# STOP PAIN FAST!

**S**mooth Gator's 60 Second Pain Relief is a topical pain relief cream made with all natural ingredients like ALOE, EUCALYPTUS, LAVENDER, TEA TREE, PEPPERMINT and WINTERGREEN.

This safe, no bad smell, non-greasy formula allows for more flexibility and movement while stopping your pain fast.

> Smooth Gator's 60 Second Pain Relief is the #1 product selected by our customers throughout North America.

Use for arthritis, sprains, strains, aches of the back, neck, knees, shoulders, elbows and much more!

It's easy, just apply a quarter-size amount of 60 Second Pain Relief on area affected by pain; don't rub in, just rub on, and it will absorb on its own. Wait one to two minutes, and your pain goes away.

$44^{95}$
for 8 oz.

Call Smooth Gator today at **727-278-3137** for your pain relief needs or visit **smoothgator.com**

FREE NATURAL LIP BALM
WITH EVERY ORDER!

Smooth Gator | 727-278-3137 | smoothgator.com

50

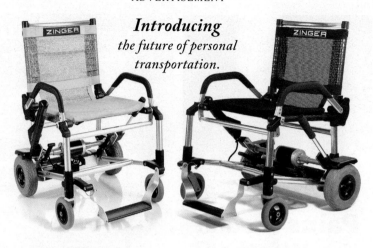

*Introducing*
the future of personal
transportation.

# It's not a Wheelchair...
## It's not a Power Chair...
### It's a Zinger!

Years of work by innovative engineers have resulted in a mobility device that's truly unique. They created a battery that provides powerful energy at a fraction of the weight of most batteries. The *Zinger* features two steering levers, one on either side of the seat. The user pushes both levers down to go forward, pulls them both up to brake, and pushes one while pulling the other to turn to either side. This enables great mobility, the ability to turn on a dime and to pull right up to tables or desks. The controls are right on the steering lever so it's simple to operate and its exclusive footrest swings out of the way when you stand up or sit down. With its rugged yet lightweight aluminum frame, the *Zinger* is sturdy and durable yet convenient and comfortable! What's more, it easily folds up for storage in a car seat or trunk– you can even gate-check it at the airport like a stroller. Think about it, you can take your *Zinger* almost anywhere, so you don't have to let mobility issues rule your life. It folds in seconds without tools and is safe and reliable. It holds up to 275 pounds, and it goes up to 6 mph and operates for up to 8 hours on a single charge.

Why spend another day letting mobility issues hamper your independence and quality of life?

## Zinger Chair

Call now and receive a utility basket absolutely FREE with your order.

# 1-888-544-0005
**Mention code 111285 when ordering.**

83952

Zinger is not a wheelchair or medical device and is not covered by Medicare or Medicaid.

© 2019 *first*STREET for Boomers and Beyond, Inc.

# Can Aches & Pains Predict the *Weather?*

T he idea that body aches can predict the weather comes from an ancient bit of weather lore:

*A coming storm your shooting corns presage,*
*And aches will throb, your hollow tooth will rage.*

While not every piece of weather lore is true, evidence suggests that this one is based in fact. As far back as the 1960s, medical researchers have found that there is a genuine connection between increased pain and cold, wet weather. While the effect is most commonly linked to arthritis sufferers, many have reported feeling increased pain from nerve disorders, migraines, recently healed fractures, toothaches, corns, and scars, when the weather was about to change.

The most likely culprit is the drop in atmospheric pressure that occurs right before a storm begins. This slight shift in air pressure may be enough to dilate blood vessels and stimulate the nerve endings in sensitive areas, like sore feet, creaky knees, or bad teeth.

# How Did a *Fuzzy Caterpillar* Become a *Weather Forecaster?*

By Amber Kanuckle

The banded woolly bear, also known as the woolly worm caterpillar, is one of the "signs of nature" that supposedly foretells what the upcoming winter weather may be like. According to folklore, if the caterpillar's orange band is narrow, the winter will be snowy. If the band is wide, a mild winter is predicted. And fuzzier-than-normal woolly bears mean that winter will be very cold.

## Caterpillar to Weather Forecaster?

These caterpillars and their ability to predict winter weather have been part of American folklore since the colonial era but were popularized by entomologist Dr. Howard C. Curran, curator of insects at the American Museum of Natural History in New York City, when he decided to put them to the test.

In 1948, Curran went to Bear Mountain, New York, to study the woolly bears and found that over half of his test subjects had wide orange bands, meaning the upcoming winter would be milder than average. And it was. He relayed his findings to a reporter, who published the story in the *New York Herald Tribune*. Dr. Curran continued his study for eight more years but was never able to fully conclude whether the caterpillar was a reliable prognosticator.

## All Black Caterpillars?

Some people confuse caterpillars that are all black, all brown, or another color with woolly bears, but they are actually a different species altogether and should not be "consulted" for winter weather predicting.

Even though not everyone subscribes to the woolly bear method of weather forecasting, watching them in the fall is an exciting American tradition that is unlikely to change anytime soon. In fact, there's even a famous Woollybear Festival held annually in Vermilion, Ohio, that celebrates the caterpillar's amazing weather forecasting abilities.

**Learn more about other animals that supposedly can predict the weather:** FarmersAlmanac.com/animal-weather

# Grind Away ANY Size Stump FAST!

The **DR® STUMP GRINDER** uses carbide-tipped cutting teeth (taking 360 "bites" per second) to reduce any stump to a pile of woodchips. Grinds stumps below ground level so they are gone forever!

- Faster, safer and easier than digging, burning, or using chemicals.
- New, more powerful and lower-priced models.
- Now towable with your riding mower or ATV.

*Assembled in the USA using domestic and foreign parts.

*Self-Propelled Model Available!*

1A0B7X © 2019

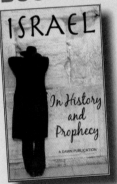

# Easy, Cost Effective WAYS to *Naturally* Melt Ice

While salt is the best-known substance to melt ice, it does have drawbacks. Salt can injure your pets' paws, enter into groundwater, and harm grass and shrubs that are planted nearby. *If you're looking for less harmful ways to melt ice and snow, try some of these:*

## Baking Soda

Sprinkle baking soda over slippery walkways and stairways. Known for lowering the freezing point of ice, baking soda will help accelerate the melting process.

## Vinegar

Mix equal parts of vinegar and water to create a de-icing mixture. Pour on iced surfaces (including frosted windshields) and ice will slowly turn to liquid.

## DIY Ice Melter

- 2 qts warm water
- 6 drops dish soap
- 2 oz. rubbing alcohol

*Transfer solution to a spray bottle and spray over icy, snowy areas for an easier shoveling experience.*

## Grab a Tarp

Before the big freeze, grab a tarp and cover the area you don't want to freeze over. Depending on the type of storm—snow or ice—you can shovel off or shake off the tarp before it gets the chance to freeze solid.

## *Bonus:* Add Extra Traction

Use clean cat litter, birdseed, or wood ash from your fireplace to add grit to slippery, icy walkways near your home. They won't melt the ice, but they will add traction when walking on slippery surfaces.

# START DEAD BATTERIES.™

**ULTRASAFE® LITHIUM JUMP STARTERS.**

**NOCO®**
nocoboost.com

# LOVE IT OR HATE IT?

**When it comes to weather in the United States, there's something for everyone**

### By Caleb Weatherbee

*W*eather. *While it's a state of the atmosphere, it's also a state of mind. And it is very subjective. One person's sunshine is another person's sweater weather. Fortunately, when it comes to weather in the U.S., there's something for everyone. Nowhere else on Earth will you find such a diverse mixture of weather-related events year-round. Are you in the right spot for your weather passions?*

Check out our popular story on the
*5 Snowiest Places in the U.S.*:
FarmersAlmanac.com/snowiest-places

## Seismic Snows

Snow is one of those weather events that can cause great divides—people either love it or hate it. There's no in-between. If snow is your passion, you'll want to head to **Alta, Utah *(pop. 383)***, as it is the snowiest inhabited place in the country, receiving an average of **507.8 inches** annually. It has snowed in every month except July and August.

## Holy Hurricanes!

Hurricanes are defined as tropical cyclones that attain a wind speed of 75 mph or more. The word hurricane may have originated from the Mayan storm god, *Hunraken,* or perhaps from the Carib word, *urican,* for "big wind." They are the deadliest storms on earth. Born over tropical waters, they produce utter chaos as they plow into coastal regions, not so much because of their high winds but because of the enormous waves and high tides that result. If you're passionate about hurricanes, keep the state of Florida on your radar.

**Florida is by far the most hurricane-prone state**, according to the National Oceanic and Atmospheric Administration (NOAA). Based on a survey taken between 1851 to 2017, a total of 117 hurricanes have scored a direct hit on the "Sunshine State." That's almost twice as many as the runner up, Texas, with 64. Louisiana is third with 54, and North Carolina fourth with 51. **Miami and Orlando rank #1 and #2 as the cities that have suffered the most with 22 and 14 hurricanes (respectively) having approached to within 50 miles.** While hurricane season runs from June 1–November 30, the "prime-time" for hurricane activity is mid-August through mid-October.

### Looking for Lightning?

Compared to a hurricane or winter storm, a thunderstorm is a hiccup on the radar system. Typically, a thunderstorm spans only 10-15 miles in width and usually lasts about 20 or 30 minutes. But make no mistake about it,

what thunderstorms lack in size, they more than make up for in violence, and are the second leading cause of weather-related deaths in the country. (The first is floods.) On average our country has 100,000 thunderstorms annually. Of these, about 10,000 attain the category of "severe," producing hail at least ¾-inch in diameter, damaging winds over 58 mph, and sudden "down-bursts" in excess of 100 mph.

**Florida wins this category again, with Tampa the #1 city, averaging 83 thunderstorm days a year.**

**Find out which are the Best Places To Watch A Thunderstorm:**
FarmersAlmanac.com/best-storm-spots

### Terrible Twisters

Tornadoes are generated by severe thunderstorms and can often be seen extending down from the base of a cloud, much like a giant twisting funnel. Tornadoes tend to be located to the southwest of thunderstorms. Wherever they touch down, tornadoes can cause incredible damage because of the tremendous winds and extremely low pressure associated with them. A typical tornado is less than a thousand feet in diameter, and as it moves with the severe thunderstorm, it rarely lasts for more than a minute or two in any one place. But this is plenty of time—with winds that can exceed 200 mph, destruction is almost instantaneous.

*(continued)*

The months of April, May, and June see the highest tornado activity. Most tornadoes develop in a region from South Dakota to the Gulf Coast of Texas known as "Tornado Alley," where cool, dry air from Canada clashes with warm moist air from the Gulf of Mexico. **In parts of northern Texas and central Oklahoma, an average of nine tornadoes per year occurs per 10,000 square miles.**

## Countless Clouds

Are you a fan of cloudy days? Some say cloudy days make them happy. We know clouds are made up of water droplets or ice crystals if the temperature is below freezing. The water droplets that form clouds are very tiny—in fact, it takes a million cloud droplets just to make one single raindrop! So it takes billions of cloud droplets to form one cloud. On their own, water droplets and dust particles simply float inside a cloud because they're so tiny and light. But when there are countless millions of them, the droplets collide with one another, clinging together and becoming bigger and heavier. Eventually, the cloud becomes too heavy, and gravity causes the water droplets to fall back to Earth as rain.

If you're seeking days with endless clouds, the south coast of Alaska has by far the cloudiest weather in the U.S. **Cold Bay** *(pop. 108)* **experiences an average of 304 overcast days each year. On the mainland, Astoria, Oregon, sees 239 days experiencing at least 75% cloud cover.**

## Sunny Spots

Finally, if hot and sunny days make you the happiest, there are plenty of spots in which you can find them. Head for **Yuma, Arizona.** This desert city receives the highest percentage of sunshine of any city in the country. Just be sure you're ready for the heat: **from June through September, the daily high temperatures run above 100° F.** Many cities in southern California also fit the bill.

BEST DAY TO TAKE A VACATION

Page 132

The maps below reflect an overview of the *Farmers' Almanac* general weather outlook for winter (January–March) and summer (June–August) for the United States.

### WINTER 2019-20: *Polar Coaster Winter Ahead!*

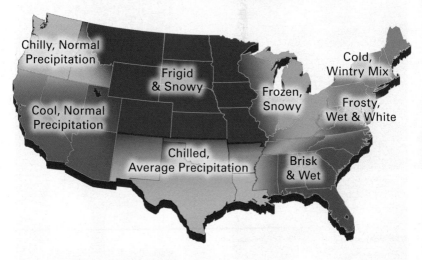

### SUMMER 2020

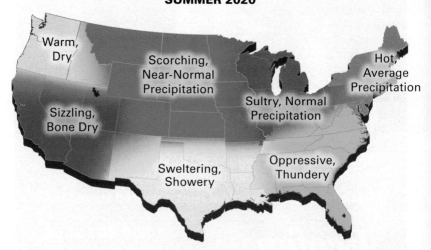

🐓 Get the complete forecast for the year ahead, including spring & fall weather maps, at FarmersAlmanac.com/weather

# FARMERS' ALMANAC ANNUAL
# WEATHER OUTLOOK

**LOOKING AHEAD:**
A Summary of What to Expect
for Winter 2019-20 and Beyond

Every year since 1818, the *Farmers' Almanac* has provided trusted long-range weather predictions that help people plan ahead. We use a mathematical and astronomical formula based on rules established in our very first publication. And while that formula has been altered slightly over the years, it remains true to the one created by our founder for accurately predicting the upcoming weather a year in advance.

Last winter, our teeth-chatteringly cold outlook proved to be quite accurate. *(See page 138 for more insight on how we did last year.)* So it's with great anticipation that we release our official forecast for what's ahead.

## Polar Coaster Winter

Our long-range forecast is calling for yet another freezing, frigid, and frosty winter for two-thirds of the country. The areas east of the Rockies, all the way to the Appalachians, may get the worst of the bitterly cold conditions. The most frigid temperatures will be from the northern Plains into the Great Lakes. The Northeast, including the densely populated corridor running from Washington to Boston, should generally average colder-than-normal temperatures as well. The western third of the country will see near-normal temperatures, which means fewer shivers for them.

The coldest outbreak of the season is predicted to arrive during the final week of January, and last through the beginning of February. Temperatures could possibly drop to 40 below zero across the northern Plains! As the freezing air blows across the Great Lakes, intense bursts of heavy snow showers and squalls could, in the most extreme cases, deposit 30–40 inches in a single day, especially in the snowbelt areas.

## Let It Snow

Above-normal winter precipitation is expected over the eastern third of the country as well as the Great Plains, Midwest, and the Great Lakes. The Pacific Northwest and Southwest should see near-normal precipitation. With colder-than-normal temperatures in the Northeast and above-normal precipitation expected, our outlook forewarns of not only a good amount of snow but also a wintry mix of rain, sleet, and snow, especially along the coast.

*(continued)*

may be the threat of strong to severe weather, with some storms capable of spawning tornado activity. Temperatures will run somewhat cool for most regions, even into June.

## Summer Outlook

Summer starts on a stormy note in most regions. July runs hot for much of the nation, with well-above-normal temperatures predicted. Much of the country will see near-normal precipitation, but the far West will be drier than normal, and it will be wet across the southern Plains and the Gulf Coast through Florida.

## Dates of Interest

We are **"red flagging"** the first part of January over most of the eastern half of the country due to a very active storm track that we expect to deliver frequent bouts of heavy precipitation, as well as strong and gusty winds. Take note that January 4–7 and 12–15 could, depending on where you live, mean copious amounts of snow, rain, sleet, and ice. And for those of you who live northeast of the Texas Panhandle to the western Great Lakes, watch out for what could prove to be a memorable storm producing hefty snows for the Great Plains during the third week of January. This system will push temperatures down, and drag the coldest Arctic air across the rest of the country into the beginning of February.

## Spring Forecast

Again, spring will see a slow start with winter lingering across the Midwest, Great Lakes, Northeast, and New England. Occasional wet snow and unseasonably chilly conditions will hang on into April. Much of the rest of the country will experience frequent and widespread precipitation. During the first week of April across the Plains states and parts of the Southwest, there

## Hurricanes

A hurricane might threaten Florida during the first week of June, just as the season officially begins, and a subtropical disturbance could affect parts of the Atlantic Seaboard during the third week of June. Then things should quiet down during July and August before ramping up again in mid-September with a tropical storm threat along the Gulf Coast. A hurricane threat for the mid-Atlantic and Northeast is predicted at the same time. Typically, tropical cyclone activity over the Atlantic and Caribbean Sea increases exponentially during the second week of August and reaches its peak on September 10.

## Fall

Fall will transition with cooler temperatures slowly moving in during September in all regions. The East will see a cool, dry September and October, with colder and stormier conditions expected for November and December. Over the Plains, possibly extending as far east as the Ohio Valley, there may be outbursts of severe weather capable of spawning a few tornadoes during the second week of September. The rest of the fall season will see successive pushes of stormy, progressively colder air masses. Our first mention of flurries comes during the beginning of October over the northern Rockies. The far West will see alternating periods of fair and unsettled weather in September, but as we progress further into October and especially November, we'll see storm activity from the Pacific increasing, bringing windy and rainy conditions as we approach the end of the year.

Until next year ...

*Caleb Weatherbee*

🐓 *Looking for regional, day-to-day forecasts?* **Turn to page 145!**

*And turn to page 138 to find out how accurate our winter outlook was last year!*

# FARMERS' ALMANAC®
### SINCE 1818

*Plan Your Day. Grow Your Life.*

ORIGINATOR: David Young, Philom. (1781–1852)

EDITOR: Peter Geiger, Philom.

MANAGING EDITOR: Sondra Duncan, Philom.

ART DIRECTOR: Corinne Mockler

WEATHER PROGNOSTICATOR: Caleb Weatherbee

WEB CONTENT EDITOR: Susan Higgins

ASTRONOMICAL CALCULATIONS & FORMATTING:
Q++Studio: www.qppstudio.net

CUSTOMER SERVICE: Patrick Travers

ADMINISTRATIVE SUPPORT: David Marshall

COPYEDITORS/PROOFREADERS:
Shelby Forbes, PhD, Rescue Edit
Tracy Crump Editing Services
Michelle Nati

CONTACT: Questions@FarmersAlmanac.com

PUBLISHER: Almanac Publishing Company
P.O. Box 1609, Lewiston, ME 04241 USA

Phone: 207-755-2000 Fax: 207-755-2622

DISPLAY ADVERTISING:
Fox Associates
adinfo.farmersalmanac@foxrep.com
1-800-440-0231

CLASSIFIEDS:
Bob Farmer - Bob@BobFarmer.com

**www.FarmersAlmanac.com**

# PHILOSOFACTS

### Part Philosophy. Part Fact.

**THOUGHT OF THE YEAR:**

Make your vision so clear that your fears become irrelevant.

A collection of small bits of wit and wisdom from the *Farmers' Almanac*—
**Philosofacts are often big on truth.**

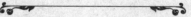

It doesn't require many words to speak the truth.

Some people only like the change that jingles in their pockets.

Nothing makes a fish bigger than almost being caught.

The highway of fear is the shortest route to defeat.

Years may wrinkle the skin, but lack of enthusiasm wrinkles the soul.

Saving for a rainy day shouldn't cloud the sunny ones.

Loving to learn is almost as important as learning to love.

Aspire to inspire before you expire.

You can pretend to be serious, but you can't pretend to be witty.

A snowflake is winter's butterfly.

One generation plants the trees under whose cool shade another generation takes its ease.

Optimism is when a tea kettle can be up to its neck in hot water and still sing.

Spring is when you feel like whistling even when your shoe is full of slush.

Reading gives us someplace to go when we have to stay where we are.

Remember to find joy in the ordinary.

You are never too old to reinvent yourself.

Facts don't change: feelings do.

There's no traffic on the extra mile.

Take the time to enjoy and enjoy the time you take.

# Riddles, Puzzles, & Brainteasers

### 1) A Rose by Any Other Name

What do roses call each other?

### 2) Hey, That's Mine!

What belongs to you, but everyone else uses it more than you do?

### 3) Ba-Dump-Bump

What do you get when you cross a comedian with a warm roll?

### 4) New Tricks

What's more impressive than a talking dog?

### 5) A Peach of a Joke

How many peaches grow on a tree?

### 6) Back and Forth

Forward I am heavy, backwards I am not. *What am I?*

## LETTER QUIZZES:

**A)** What are the next three letters in the following sequence?
J, F, M, A, M, J, J, A, S, __, __, __.

**B)** Guess the next three letters in the series:
G T N T L ...

## RAY'S SIBLINGS

Ray's parents have five children. The name of the first is January, the second is February, the third is called March and the fourth child is April. *What is the name of the fifth child?*

## TONGUE TWISTERS:

*Six sticky skeletons.*

*I saw a kitten eating chicken in the kitchen.*

*There was a minimum of cinnamon in her aluminum pan.*

### ANSWERS

1) **A Rose by Any Other Name:** Bud-dy. 2) **Hey, That's Mine!:** Your name. 3) **Ba-Dump-Bump:** Hot cross puns. 4) **New Tricks:** A spelling bee. 5) **A Peach of a Joke:** All of them. 6) **Back and Forth:** TON. When spelled backwards it does become NOT. **Letter Quizzes: A)** O, N, D. The sequence is first letter of the months of the year: October, November and December are next. **B)** I, T, S. The complete sequence is the first letter of every word in the sentence. **Ray's Siblings:** Ray! The fifth child was Ray himself.

# World's Most Powerful Leaf Vacuum!

### Perfect for YARD CLEAN-UP!

**Starting at just $1099⁹⁹**

Easy Dumping!

Doubles as a utility trailer!

**DR® LEAF VACUUMS** have proven in laboratory testing to achieve the most vacuum power versus competitors. And now, our *PILOT* model combines this same amazing yard clean-up power with an equally amazing new price!

☑ **Rated #1 in Vacuum Power**

☑ **Unloads with Just One Hand**

☑ **Converts to an All-Purpose Trailer**

☑ **Stores Flat in Minutes**

USA ENGINEERED & BUILT*

\* Assembled in the USA using domestic & foreign parts.

1A0BBX © 2019

**FREE SHIPPING**
**6 MONTH TRIAL**
SOME LIMITATIONS APPLY
Go online or call for details.

*Go Online or Call for FREE DVD & Info Kit!*

**DRleafvac.com**
**TOLL FREE 877-201-5019**

PROFESSIONAL POWER DONE RIGHT DR

# FABULOUS FIRSTS

By Jim Kneiszel

W hether it's a lifesaving convenience, a bold invention, or a mystery of the cosmos, we don't often think about how these things came to be. *Here is a smattering of famous firsts and how they came about:*

## FIRST WEIGHT LOSS DIET

It seems as though folks have been fixated on their flab forever. Every year dozens of new diets emerge, all promising to obliterate obesity. But weight loss hasn't always been an obsession, and there was a time when being on the heavier side was considered a sign of prosperity. Until British undertaker to the stars William Banting worried about his porky profile, that is.

Banting, who built coffins for royalty, including King George III and IV and Queen Victoria, tried in vain to trim fat from his 5-foot 5-inch, 202-pound frame. He consulted with a surgeon friend and experimented with exercise regimens and starvation. He finally stumbled on a diet that helped him lose almost 50 pounds. In 1863, he published the first diet pamphlet, *Letter on Corpulence, Addressed to the Public,* which detailed his low-carbohydrate, high-protein diet.

Interestingly, the first diet has many similarities to the popular weight loss programs of today, including ketogenic diets. Banting drastically reduced his intake of breads and pastries, dairy and sugar and replaced them with fish, beef, mutton, and kidneys. He must have enjoyed his daily nip of alcohol, because he still drank his share of gin, whiskey, and brandy and usually enjoyed a glass or two of claret or sherry before bed. The Banting diet made him famous, and he happily kept off the weight and lived to a ripe old age of 81. Diet experts are still tweaking the Banting diet to this day.

# FIRST ELECTRIC CAR

Historians disagree over the builder of the first crude electric car, saying it may have been Scot Robert Anderson (1832), American Thomas Davenport (1834), or Dutch Sibrandus Stratingh (1834). But did you know that 130 years ago, electric cars outsold gas-powered vehicles by 10 to 1? In fact, American manufacturers Oldsmobile and Studebaker started out producing electric cars and the first US car dealership in 1896 sold only electric cars.

In 1907, an illustrated guide to autos listed 69 different electric vehicles produced across the country, including Toledo, Ohio, Chicago, and New York. At that time, it looked as if the electric car would become the new standard as American engineers developed electric vehicles, including the Baker Electric Roadster which traveled up to 200 miles on a single charge. And believe it or not, nearly 100 years before the Toyota Prius, German Ferdinand Porsche developed the first hybrid gas-electric car using the same charging principle of regenerative braking.

*Who killed the electric car?* Experts speculate, but it was likely a combination of cheap gasoline, development of the electric starter for gas-powered cars, improved roads, and perhaps the failure of an electric vehicle joint venture between Henry Ford and Thomas Edison. In 1915, Edison predicted, "I believe that ultimately the electric motor will be universally used for trucking in all large cities and that the electric automobile will be the family carriage of the future." A century later, his prediction may finally come true.

# FIRST BOTTLED WATER

When you reach into the convenience store cooler and select a bottle of water, do you stop to think how the massive bottled water industry was born? The practice of bottling water for sale goes all the way back to 1622 in the Malvern Hills north of London in the U.K. In a valley of granite substrate, the Holy Well

bottling plant was born. Water coming up through cracks in the stone was thought to have healing properties, so

*(continued)*

it was captured in glass bottles and sold across the country.

Poet Robert Bloomfield wrote of the restorative Holy Well: "Boast, Malvern, that thy springs revive, the drooping patient, scarce alive, where as he gathers strength to toil, not e'en they heights his spirits foil." Holy Well water was sold for centuries, and the popularity of bottled water soared after German-Swiss Johann Jacob Schweppe began sucessfully selling carbonated spring water in Geneva, Switzerland, in the late 1700s. Bottled water lost popularity after an English doctor named Alexander Houston used chlorine to kill bacteria in 1905, ending the typhoid epidemic.

But bottled water was revived thanks to the invention of PET (polyethylene terephthalate) plastic by Nathaniel C. Wyeth, a DuPont engineer. This plastic could be fashioned into lightweight and sturdy bottles perfect for the cold drink of water you grab at the store. Americans today consume billions of gallons of bottled water. Interestingly, you can travel back in time and enjoy water like that first bottled at Holy Well. The plant was purchased and restored in 2009 and is back in production.

# FIRST 9-1-1 CALL

On February 16, 1968, the first 9-1-1 call was placed in the small Alabama town of Hayleyville (population 6,000). The persistence of a local independent phone company and local politicians allowed the community to go active with 9-1-1 technology before bigger cities. The ceremonial call between Alabama Speaker of the House Rankin Fite and US Representative Tom Bevill established that the universal number worked. This culminated in a project spearheaded by the Federal Communications Commission and the American Telephone and Telegraph Company (now AT&T).

Before this, callers had to memorize and dial the full numbers for their local police and fire departments. It often required several calls to summon an ambulance or report a fire. That wasn't good enough for the National Association of Fire Chiefs, which called for the creation of a universal emergency number in 1957. Ten years later, President Lyndon Johnson's Commission on Law Enforcement and Administration of Justice concurred, and AT&T recommended using 9-1-1 because the three numbers were easy to remember and quickly dialed on a rotary phone.

Every June, Hayleyville celebrates with the 9-1-1 Festival, which honors police, fire, and rescue personnel with a parade, live music, and a fun run.

# FIRST UFO SIGHTING

Roswell, New Mexico, in the 1950s is ubiquitous in legend and lore for sightings of unidentified flying objects or UFOs. But you have to go back almost 300 years to track the first documented account of someone reporting strange flashes of light in the nighttime sky. Puritan settler John Winthrop, governor of the Massachusetts Bay Colony, wrote in his diary on March 1, 1639, about what several boatmen rowing on the tidal basin Muddy River saw. Winthrop called witness John Everell "a sober, discreet man" when he explained seeing a bright light flash across the sky. "When it stood still, it flamed up and was about three yards square. When it ran, it contracted into the figure of a swine; it ran as swift as an arrow toward Charleston and up and down about two or three hours."

When the strange encounter ended, the men said their boat had been transported about a mile by the tide but was then mysteriously returned to its original location. Some maintain that what the men saw was an *ignis fatuus,* a light caused by combustion of gas from decomposing organic matter over a marsh. Speculation aside, the mysterious sighting spawned similar tales still told today, some unexplained, others hoaxes that play on peoples' imaginations. In 1897 in Texas, a newspaper reporter fabricated a story of dozens of witnesses finding a crashed spacecraft and a dead Martian body in the wreckage. The term *flying saucer* originated in 1947 when a pilot reported seeing nine boomerang-like objects flying through the sky.

*Finding firsts are a fabulously fun way to learn a little more about how things came to be!*

 Find more history and trivia at <u>FarmersAlmanac.com</u>.

# When is the *REAL* First Day of Spring?

Traditionally the first day of spring is celebrated on March 21st, but in actuality, spring can arrive as early as the 19th (as it will this year). There are many interesting reasons why this happens, but spring more often than not starts on the 20th of March, unless it's a leap year, like this year.

 Learn more at <u>FarmersAlmanac.com/first-day-of-spring</u>

# DIY COUGH DROPS

## Soothe and quiet coughs with these delicious, all-natural cough drops

These are a bit time-consuming and require some patience while cooking (if you've ever made candy, you may be familiar with this fact), but the result is a tasty, all-natural lozenge that your whole family will love. The best part is no candy mold is needed!

The ginger in this recipe will give the drops a tiny bit of "heat"—if you don't like ginger you can omit it. *See Variations on next page.*

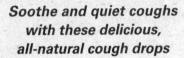

## HONEY LEMON GINGER COUGH DROPS

**Ingredients:**

*1 cup organic honey*

*1 lemon (preferably organic; if not, wash the residue off the exterior), sliced*

*2-inch piece of fresh ginger root (preferably organic), peeled and cut into thin slices*

*2 cups water*

*Powdered sugar*

**Additional Tools:**
*Candy thermometer\**

**Directions:**

In a large saucepan, place lemon and ginger slices in water and bring to a boil. Reduce heat and simmer uncovered for 30 minutes.

While the liquid is simmering, prepare your candy "molds" using the following method: Cover a cookie sheet with parchment paper. Pour enough powdered sugar to create 1-inch thickness and smooth down with a knife or frosting spreader so the surface is smooth.

Then, using the back of a round teaspoon measure, make indentations in the sugar. Set aside. These indentations will be your candy molds.

Take the saucepan off the heat and strain the solids out, reserving liquid to yield about ¾ cup. Add the liquid back to the saucepan and add the honey. Cook over medium heat, stirring frequently so the mixture doesn't boil up the sides. Your mixture is at the hard candy stage when the candy thermometer reaches 300°F. **(NOTE: Honey scorches easily, so do not turn up the heat to speed the process).**

*If you don't have a candy thermometer, you can use the "ice water" method to test if your candy is ready: Drop a small bit of the mixture into a glass of ice water. The candy should form a hard ball. Take it out and test it. It should "crack" when bitten. If it's still soft, keep cooking.*

When your candy mixture is ready, take it off the heat and stir down the bubbles. (Be careful as this mixture is very hot and can burn your skin.) Carefully spoon the mixture into each of the powdered sugar molds (you'll need to work quickly), and let the candy harden completely at room temperature. (Do not refrigerate or freeze to speed up the process—they only take about 20 minutes to cool.) Dust drops completely in the sugar by swirling them around. Now they're ready to enjoy!

This recipe yields approximately 36 cough drops, depending on the size of your individual candy molds. Store in a resealable plastic bag or candy dish.

**Variations:**

You can substitute the lemon and ginger in this recipe with any other herbs you like. Make an herbal tea by boiling 2 cups of water and adding 2 teaspoons of the dried herbs (use organic if possible) of your choice. Some ideas are slippery elm, cinnamon, clove, or chamomile. Simmer for 20 minutes and strain away any solids until you have ¾ to 1 cup of herb-infused tea. Then follow the recipe above, starting from when you add the honey.

***To safely clean your pot:*** Allow to soak in hot tap water until the sugar mixture is completely dissolved and then wash as usual.

# IS SALT THERAPY THE NEXT MIRACLE CURE?

### By Deborah Tukua

Salt is probably in your kitchen but not in your medicine cabinet. Yet most of us are familiar with its antibacterial and healing properties. For generations, a salt water gargle has been a trusted home remedy for a throat infection. But in addition to treating sore throats, salt is also an effective natural remedy for many common ailments.

## SALT-BASED HOME REMEDIES YOU NEED TO TRY

**Sore Throat.** Add 1 teaspoon finely ground sea salt to an 8-oz. glass of warm water and stir until dissolved. Gargle the salt water solution in the back of your throat and spit out. This home remedy kills bacteria, fights infections, and reduces inflammation.

**Heat Exhaustion.** In hot weather, heat exhaustion can be the result of salt depletion or dehydration. If this occurs, stir 1 teaspoon of sea salt into a liter of water and sip. Also, move to a cooler place, loosen clothing, remove shoes, lie down, and apply cool compresses to the face and neck.

**Dehydration.** To replenish fluids lost during sweating, replace electrolytes,

and increase energy, try this DIY sports drink. To 8-ounces of filtered water, add a teaspoon of raw honey, protein powder, and a pinch of Himalayan sea salt. Stir and drink.

**Sore Muscles.** Moist heat therapy has been found to effectively sooth and relieve soreness as it penetrates deep tissues and muscles faster than dry heat therapy. Moist heat is also less apt to dehydrate your skin. An Epsom salt

The recorded use of salt for medicinal purposes dates back thousands of years to ancient Egyptian, Greek, and Roman civilizations. Hippocrates (460 BC), the famous Greek physician considered the father of medicine, used various salt-based healing methods. In fact, he recorded the use of salt in ways that we use today, such as inhaling salt water steam to treat respiratory ailments *(see page 80)*, using it to treat digestive issues, and applying it topically for skin problems.

bath combines the benefits of heat therapy with magnesium sulfate, a known agent for relieving sore muscles from overexertion. Add ½ to 1 cup of Epsom salt (magnesium sulfate) to a tub of very warm, but not hot, water. Sit back in the tub, relax, and soak for about 15 minutes.

**Ear Infection.** One natural, effective way to relieve an earache is with a warm salt sock. This DIY treatment creates a shift in the pressure within the ear, draws fluid out and eases the pain. Salt pillows are available for purchase, but it is easy to make your own salt sock.

### Materials*:
*1 clean, all-white, 100% cotton sock*

*1–1 ½ cups of coarse sea salt*

### Directions:
Pour coarse sea salt into the sock and tie a knot at the end. Heat in a clean, dry skillet over medium-low heat for about 4-6 minutes. To heat the sock evenly, shake it around and flip every 30-60 seconds. Heat until very warm but not burning to the touch. Test on your hand before applying to the ear. Cover the ear and the area behind your jaw bone with the warm sock and relax.

***NOTES:*** *Only use a white sock as dyed threads may melt when heated. Do not substitute regular table salt for the sea salt. Never microwave the salt sock.*

*(continued)*

## Why Doesn't Salt Pour Easily in Damp Weather?

**By Tiffany Means**

*When windows won't open and salt clogs the shaker,*

*The weather will favor the umbrella maker!*

This weather folklore tells us that wood and salt are both hygroscopic, a fancy word that means each likes to absorb moisture from the air. As wood soaks up moisture, it swells and warps, which can make doors and windows harder to open. Similarly, when salt takes on moisture, its individual grains stick together and become too big to fit through the tiny holes in the shaker. This is why you sometimes see grains of dried rice inside salt shakers — the rice absorbs the moisture, freeing up the crystals.

Knowing this, you can assume that whenever salt clumps or wood swells, it's a sign there's a good amount of humidity in the air. And as you know, high humidity points to an increased chance of rain.

# RESPIRATORY ISSUES?

Got allergies, a sinus infection, or a cold? *Release the healing power of salt!*

**Seashore.** The beach is a therapeutic location low in pollen, which makes it an ideal retreat for allergy sufferers. Breathing salty air is also great for healing sinus infections. Plus, there's another curative benefit: swimming in the ocean speeds the healing of minor cuts and pimples.

**Salt Cave/Halotherapy.** For conditions such as asthma, sinusitis, and chronic obstructive pulmonary disease (COPD), visit the nearest salt therapy cave or spa for halotherapy. Clients relax in a controlled microclimate and breathe in the salt-infused air pumped into the room. Other benefits include improving skin conditions such as acne, dermatitis, and eczema.

**Salt Inhalation.** This can be done at home with a dry Himalayan salt inhaler or a fine mist nebulizer using a salt solution. You breathe gently through the mouthpiece and exhale through the nose. By cleansing your entire respiratory system—sinuses, nasal cavities, throat, and lungs—it reduces inflammation and mucus. This is helpful with asthma, bronchitis, hay fever, and other respiratory ailments. Salt inhalers are available online and in stores.

**Saline Nasal Irrigation.** Saline (salt water) nasal sprays and rinses remove pollen and bacteria from your nose, help reduce mucous, inflammation, and postnasal drip, and restore moisture to dry nasal and sinus passages.

Want to make your own? Dissolve ¼ teaspoon of finely ground sea salt in an 8-ounce glass jar of warm, distilled water. Use a clean medicine dropper, a bulb syringe, spray bottle, or neti pot to flush the nostrils with drops of the salty solution.

**Himalayan Salt Lamps.** Breathing clean air is important for good health. These decorative salt lamps emit a soothing glow as the light bulb within warms a block or chunks of pink Himalayan sea salt. It is thought to release negative ions, which reduce the level of electromagnetic radiation in the home caused by cell phones, computers, TVs, etc. It purifies indoor air as it attracts water vapors, trapping any allergens, bacteria, or mold present in the water. Authentic salt lamps are available in retail stores and online.

# STRESSED OUT?

Have you tried float therapy, also known as sensory deprivation floating?

Picture yourself floating with ease in a shallow tank of skin-temperature water. The 1,000-plus pounds of Epsom salt in the tank makes you float effortlessly. The private, quiet atmosphere helps you relax. Floating in salt water

has many therapeutic benefits, including lowering blood pressure and heart rate, providing deep relaxation and stress relief, improving sleep, and reducing chronic pain, anxiety, and PTSD, to name a few. Float tanks aren't practical to install in the home due to the excessive upkeep, but salt flotation centers are a growing wellness trend across the country.

## DID YOU KNOW?

Natural, unrefined sea salt, such as Himalayan sea salt, contains more than 84 essential trace minerals!

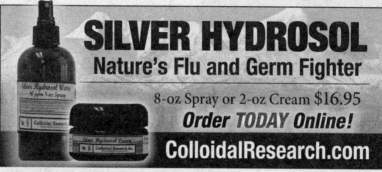

# Natural device stops a cold before it starts

Ｎew research shows you can stop a cold in its tracks if you take one simple step with a new device when you feel a cold about to start.

Colds start after cold viruses get in your nose. Viruses multiply fast. If you don't stop them early, they spread and cause misery.

But scientists have found a quick way to kill a virus - touch it with copper. Researchers at labs and universities agree, copper is "antimicrobial." It kills microbes, such as viruses and bacteria, just by touch.

That's why ancient Greeks and Egyptians used copper to purify water and heal wounds. They didn't know about viruses and bacteria, but now we do.

Scientists say the high conductance of copper disrupts the electrical balance in a microbe cell and destroys the cell in seconds.

Tests by the EPA (Environmental Protection Agency) show germs die fast on copper. So some hospitals tried copper for touch surfaces like faucets and doorknobs. This cut the spread of MRSA and other illnesses by over half, and saved lives.

The strong scientific evidence gave inventor Doug Cornell an idea. When he felt a cold about to start he fashioned a smooth copper probe and rubbed it gently in his nose for 60 seconds.

"It worked!" he exclaimed. "The cold never got going." It worked again every time. He has not had a single cold for 7 years since.

He asked relatives and friends to try it. They said it worked for them, too, so he patented CopperZap™ and put it on the market.

Soon hundreds of people had tried it and given feedback. Nearly 100% said the copper stops colds if used

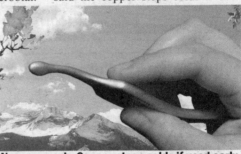

**New research: Copper stops colds if used early.**

within 3 hours after the first sign. Even up to 2 days, if they still get the cold it is milder than usual and they feel better.

Users wrote things like, "It stopped my cold right away," and "Is it supposed to work that fast?"

"What a wonderful thing," wrote Physician's Assistant Julie. "No more colds for me!"

Pat McAllister, age 70, received one for Christmas and called it "one of the best presents ever. This little jewel really works." Now thousands of users have simply stopped getting colds.

People often use CopperZap preventively. Frequent flier Karen Gauci used to get colds after crowded flights. Though skeptical, she tried it several times a day on travel days for 2 months. "Sixteen flights and not a sniffle!" she exclaimed.

Businesswoman Rosaleen says when people are sick around her she uses CopperZap morning and night. "It saved me last holidays," she said. "The kids had colds going round and round, but not me."

Many users say it also helps with sinuses. Attorney Donna Blight had a 2-day sinus headache. When her CopperZap arrived, she tried it. "I am shocked!" she said. "My head cleared, no more headache, no more congestion."

Some users say copper stops nighttime stuffiness if used just before bed. One man said, "Best sleep I've had in years."

Copper can also stop flu if used early and for several days. Lab technicians placed 25 million live flu viruses on a CopperZap. No viruses were found alive soon after.

People have used it on cold sores and say it can completely prevent ugly outbreaks. You can also rub it gently on wounds, cuts, or lesions to combat infections.

The handle is curved and finely textured to improve contact. It kills germs picked up on fingers and hands to protect you and your family.

Copper even kills deadly germs that have become resistant to anti-

**Sinus trouble, cold sores, stuffiness.**

biotics. If you are near sick people, a moment of handling it may keep serious infection away. It may even save a life.

The EPA says copper works even when tarnished. It kills hundreds of different disease germs so it can prevent serious or even fatal illness.

CopperZap is made in the U.S. of pure copper. It has a 90-day full money back guarantee when used as directed to stop a cold. It is $69.95. Get $10 off each CopperZap with code **FMA2** at www.CopperZap.com or call toll-free 1-888-411-6114.

Buy once, use forever.

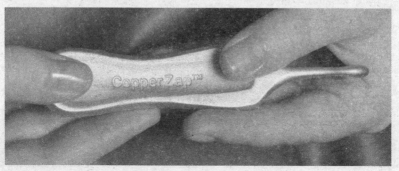

# 20 WAYS TO IMPROVE EYE HEALTH IN 2020

Of our five senses (taste, touch, hearing, smell, and sight), eyesight is one of the most valuable. Experts reveal that humans perceive about 80% of all impressions through our vision. Eyesight is also imperative to your safety, especially if one or a few of your other senses are compromised. To help protect your eyesight now and in the future here are some valuable tips.

by / Bob Farmer

- [ ] Know Your Family's Eye Health History
- [ ] Find the Right Eye Care Provider for You
- [ ] Schedule Yearly Comprehensive Eye Exams
- [ ] Adjust Screen Brightness/Reduce Glare
- [ ] Safely Wear & Care for Contact Lenses
- [ ] Look Away from Oncoming Headlights
- [ ] Use Lubricating Eye Drops
- [ ] Throw Away Old Makeup
- [ ] Spend More Time Outdoors
- [ ] Protect Against UV Rays Year-Round
- [ ] Take a Break from Digital Devices
- [ ] Don't Rely on Online Vision Tests
- [ ] Protect Your Eyes at Work
- [ ] Increase your Water Intake
- [ ] Get Regular Exercise
- [ ] Don't Forget to Blink
- [ ] Eat Your Greens
- [ ] Avoid Dry Air
- [ ] Avoid Smoking
- [ ] Eat More Fish

The American Optometric Association assisted with this article. Learn more about these tips and how to keep your eyes healthy at FarmersAlmanac.com/improve-eyesight

# How to (Easily) Move to a More Plant-Based Diet

By Amy Grisak

Eating less meat and animal products isn't just for vegans. Opting for little, or no meat on your plate is shown to decrease your risk of heart disease, as well as diabetes, obesity, and a slew of similar health issues. Many people also find that reducing or eliminating animal-based foods all together lessens the frequency of gastrointestinal issues, makes them feel better overall, and is an easy switch for a healthier lifestyle.

*Here are some plant-based substitutes for traditional animal-based foods.*

## Meat Substitutes:

**Tempeh** – Tempeh is a soy-based product that is traditionally made with soybeans, but can also be made with any type of bean, such as black beans, black-eyed peas, or chickpeas. Some types of tempeh also include grains, such as brown rice, barley, millet, or seeds. With its nuttier, almost chunky, texture, tempeh works well in chilis and spaghetti in place of ground beef. It is a great way to make "crab" cakes, sans the crab. Tempeh is a good source of not only protein, but manganese, iron, and other trace minerals, and you can usually find it sold in various flavors or plain varieties.

**Tofu** – Sometimes known as bean or soya curd, tofu is a soybean product made from the curds of soymilk. These curds are pressed into blocks and are made into different textures—soft, firm, and extra-firm. High in protein and calcium, this versatile soy product takes on the flavor of whatever you put with it. Press it to create a more meat-like texture, and season it to use in everything from salads to grilled sandwiches.

**Portobello Mushroom** – The substantial portobello mushroom adds a hearty and earthy flavor to meatless dishes. It can be sliced or used whole as a meat stand-in for sandwiches; or, you can add it to pastas or rice dishes for a hearty entree rich in riboflavin, niacin, and B vitamins.

# Butter Substitutes:

Butter is the basis for a lot of baking, as well as for spreading on fresh toast or a stack of pancakes. While one butter might not work for every purpose, there are a number of options out there.

**Applesauce** – For baking, especially cakes, applesauce is a terrific substitute for butter, as it creates a moist and delicious dessert with far fewer calories. Use it in a 1 to 1 ratio.

**Avocado** – Avocado is a great choice if you're looking for a good fat replacement. It does not contain as much fat as dairy butter, has no cholesterol, contains less calories, and can be used in a 1 to 1 ratio in your baked goods (1 cup avocado equals 1 cup butter). It does not have the sweetness of applesauce, but maintains a moist, rich texture.

**Vegan Butter** – Mixing fats from cocoa butter, olive oil, or even cashews, vegan butters are made to be spreadable. Their one drawback is that they typically do not melt quite as well as regular dairy-based butter or margarine.

# Cheese Substitutes:

Dairy cheese is often the most difficult food to replace. But with exceptional commercial preparations, along with simple home creations, you won't miss it a bit.

**Cashews** – Cashews have an almost buttery quality, so when combined with vinegar, nutritional yeast, lemon juice, and seasonings, it not only provides a powerful dose of vitamin B, but it also makes for a delicious cheese-like spread. You can also make a firmer cheese as a solid parmesan replacement *(be sure to visit **FarmersAlmanac.com** for our cashew ricotta recipe)*.

**Potato Provolone** – Using a potato starch base, this sliced cheese is perfect for sandwiches, including grilled cheese where you want that scrumptious melt. You can also use it to make a delicious au gratin potato dish with plenty of stringy cheese.

**Aquafaba Mozzarella** – Aquafaba, the liquid from a can of chickpeas, works as a fantastic binding agent, along with nutritional yeast, lemon juice, and salt to create your own vegan mozzarella.
*(continued)*

## Egg Substitutes:

A staple in the kitchen and on breakfast menus everywhere, people love their eggs. Fortunately, there are a number of ways to replace eggs in baking, as well as in a main course.

**Silken Tofu** – You can use tofu as an easy, protein-packed replacement for eggs in baking, as long as you're making a cake or dessert that requires baking powder and baking soda so that they leaven properly. Replace the egg with ¼ cup silken tofu, and be sure to whip before mixing it into the batter.

**Arrowroot** – Part of what eggs do in baking is bind ingredients together. An alternative is to mix 2 tablespoons of arrowroot with 3 tablespoons of water.

**Chickpea** – Also called gram or besan flour, this pea-based flour creates a great scrambled egg substitute when combined with nutritional yeast and kalanamak, a special salt that imparts an egg-like flavor. Cooked up on its own or with an array of vegetables, you have a hearty breakfast substitute.

**Applesauce** – Substitute ¼ cup of applesauce for 1 egg in baked goods. It helps bind, adds moisture, and doesn't add any cholesterol.

## Dairy Substitutes:

Whether you reach for a non-dairy milk because of lactose intolerance or to reduce calories in your diet, there are a growing number of delicious and nutritious milk options at your fingertips.

**Hemp Milk** – Made from hemp seeds blended with water, it has a slightly sweet, nutty taste, and a texture close to the consistency of 2 percent regular milk. Even though hemp milk has only 2 grams of protein per cup, it is low in carbohydrates and sugar, and rich in omega-3 fatty acids.

**Soy Milk** – With 7 grams of protein (compared to milk's 8 grams) per cup, soy milk is completely lactose-free. Made from ground soy beans, it is low in cholesterol, and a good source of vitamin B-6, iron, manganese, and several other trace minerals.

**Almond Milk** – With only 30 calories per 8 ounce serving, almond milk works well on cereal or whenever you want skim milk. And while it has only 1 gram of protein per cup, it is packed chock full of calcium.

# 10 Common Number Phrases

## and How They Came To Be

**By Richard Lederer**

It is not only the mathematician who is fascinated by numbers. Whether we realize or not, we all speak numbers every day, from zero through ten, and beyond. It's as easy as one-two-three.

From time to time, we hear people say, "That didn't work. I guess we'll have to go back to *ground zero*." *Ground zero* is a fairly new term. It refers to the surface area directly above or below the point of detonation of a nuclear bomb. Thus, one cannot actually go back to *ground zero.*

The more logical phrase is "I guess we'll have to go back to *square one*." Here the metaphor is rooted in a board game like Monopoly or a street game such as hopscotch, where a player has to return to the starting square.

Hidden forms of **two** occur in the words *twilight, zwieback, between, betwixt,* and *combine,* in which *twi, zwie, tween, twixt,* and *bi* all mean two. That's why *twilight* is literally the time of two lights, the fading sunset and the emerging light of the Moon and stars. The root sense of *zwieback* is twice baked, and to *combine* is to join two things.

In **three** *sheets to the wind,* a common expression for the unsteady state of drunkenness, *sheets* refers to the lines attached to the two lower corners of a square sail for control. When both sheets of an old sailing vessel came loose or were allowed to run free, the ship would lurch and stagger like an inebriated person.

Four shows up in a derogatory poker idiom. A **four** *flusher* is a poker player who pretends to hold a hand of five cards of the same suit but in fact owns a worthless four-suit hand and one that doesn't match. It was a short leap for *four flusher* to come to mean a phony, a bluffer.

We easily see that the *quint* in *quintet* and *quintuplets* means the number **five**. Less apparent is the meaning behind *quintessence.* The ancient Greeks held that everything in the world was composed of four elements—Earth, air, fire, and water. To these the philosopher Aristotle added a fifth essence (Latin: *quinta essentia*), the purest and most concentrated of all because it made up the heavenly bodies and the human

God-seeking soul.

Joining three sheets to the wind is another numerical nautical expression, *deep six*. This is an old naval idiom that means to throw overboard, with *six* signifying six fathoms deep. By extension, to *deep six* has come to mean to get rid of someone or something.

Your *sixth sense*—the one beyond sight, hearing, touch, taste, and smell—may be leading you to the *quintessence*, to the very height, of happiness. That would be **seventh** *heaven*. In Islam, as set forth in the Koran, the seventh ring of stars is the highest, the heaven of heavens, and represents supreme bliss.

One of the best known expressions involving the number **eight** is *behind the eight ball*. In one version of Kelly pool, all the balls must be pocketed in numerical order except for the eight, which is saved for last. If another ball touches the eight, the player is penalized. Hence, any pool player whose cue ball or target ball is *behind the eight ball*

is in the perilous position of having to sink another ball without even nicking the eight. *Behind the eight ball* has been generalized to mean any difficult, or troublesome situation.

Hopefully you're in *seventh heaven* and on *cloud* **nine** and not *deep sixed* and *behind the eight ball,* now that you know that the English language always has your number. On *cloud nine* means a state of high euphoria and is a reference to the International Classification of Clouds in which a *cloud nine* may reach the height of 30,000–40,000 feet.

To *decimate (dec* is the Latin root for **ten**, as in *decade* and *decimal)* once described the nasty habit of Romans maiming or slaying one out of every ten captives or mutineers. Nowadays *decimate* means to destroy a large number of living things with no connection to the number ten.

Clearly, the days of our English language have long been numbered, 24/7.

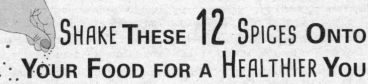

# SHAKE THESE 12 SPICES ONTO YOUR FOOD FOR A HEALTHIER YOU

**By Deborah Tukua**

*Did you know that some common spices double as antioxidants? It's true! A sprinkle of this, a pinch of that, and you could turn a tasty dish or drink into a healthier one.* **Here's how:**

## The Importance of Antioxidants

*What are antioxidants, and why do we need them?* Antioxidants play a key role in disease prevention by ridding the body of harmful free radicals. An excess of cell-damaging free radicals compromises our immune function.

Dark chocolate, berries, tomatoes, sweet potatoes, pecans, carrots, and broccoli are all great sources of antioxidants. Yet, eating antioxidant-rich foods may not be enough. In *Prescription for Nutritional Healing: The A-to-Z Guide to Supplements,* Phyllis A. Blanch, CNC,

states, "Although many antioxidants can be obtained from food sources, it is difficult to get enough of them from these sources to hold back the free radicals constantly being generated in our polluted environment. Antioxidants work synergistically in giving protection against free radical damage, so it is better to take small doses of several different antioxidants rather than a large amount of only one."

*So, where could you look for additional antioxidants?* Think spices and herbs! Certain herbs and spices have been found to be richer, more concentrated sources of antioxidants than the foods mentioned above. And it's easy to incorporate spices into your meals and beverages throughout the day. A little goes a long way to up your intake.

## Top 12 Antioxidant Herbs & Spices by ORAC Value*

| Herbs & Spices | ORAC Value | Herbs & Spices | ORAC Value |
|---|---|---|---|
| Cloves *(ground)* | 314,446 | Basil *(dried)* | 67,553 |
| Cinnamon *(ground)* | 267,537 | Curry Powder | 48,504 |
| Oregano *(dried)* | 159,277 | Sage | 32,004 |
| Turmeric | 102,700 | Ginger *(ground)* | 28,871 |
| Cumin | 76,800 | Black Pepper | 27,618 |
| Parsley *(dried)* | 74,349 | Chili Powder | 23,636 |

*\*ORAC is the abbreviation for Oxygen Radical Absorbance Capacity units, a unit of measurement for antioxidants developed by the National Institutes of Health (NIH). No daily serving quantity has been established.*

**BANANAS**
Make your plants
grow like crazy!

**SHAVING CREAM**
Get rid of that
squeak!

# "VINEGAR Can Do What?!"

## Just put it on your grocery list and put away the plunger, cap the toxic cleaners, AND wipe out weeds naturally!

(By Frank K. Wood)

If you want to boost your Social Security payouts, cut your cable bill, protect your identity, and learn hundreds of ways to live well on a fixed income, then you need *Uncommon Solutions to Common Everyday Problems: Household How-Tos, Fix-Its, and Money-Savers*.

You'll be amazed at how you can lower your utility bills, get the most from Medicare, and spend less on groceries — right now!

▶ Know the law! Only these three must know your Social Security number.
▶ 12 senior discounts you've never heard of, and some retailers hope you don't find out.
▶ Ants hate this scent ... but you will love it and how it keeps them out of your kitchen!
▶ How to stop identity thieves and get rid of a ton of junk mail with one phone call!
▶ The five cleaning products you should never be without ... they cost less than $10!
▶ Secrets to paying less for groceries, utilities, clothes, medications, and more!

▶ Forget monthly satellite or cable bills. Pay this once and watch TV forever!
▶ 9 documents you should never destroy!
▶ How to un-fix your income — hundreds of ways to make extra money ... after you retire!

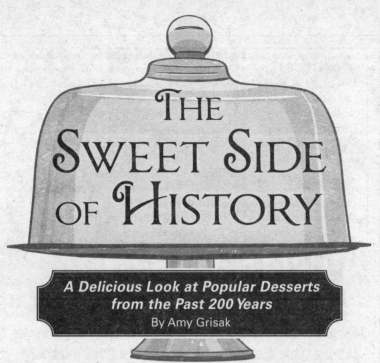

# THE SWEET SIDE OF HISTORY

## A Delicious Look at Popular Desserts from the Past 200 Years
### By Amy Grisak

Food is an exceptional storyteller, and desserts share the sweet side of the evolution of our culture over the past 200 years. Here's a look at some of the most popular sweet treats over the *Farmers' Almanac*'s history:

**1820s** – In these days, home cooks used local ingredients, and what we now consider desserts weren't necessarily relegated to the end of the meal.

"Early on, sugar was expensive and hard to get," explains Libby O'Connell, author of *The American Plate: A Culinary History in 100 Bites,* so many Americans relied on locally sourced ingredients to satisfy their sweet tooth and provide much needed calories.

"One of the more traditional foods was Indian pudding," she says. Made with ground corn, an inherently American food, along with molasses and spices, it was often served with heavy cream. Indian pudding was something

enjoyed right out of the oven as well as throughout the day.

During this time period, the way we cooked changed. "By 1820, most kitchens had a tin kitchen, a reflector oven," she says. "And people on the East Coast often had a wall oven." This meant cakes, which required an even temperature to bake properly, were a possibility.

When it was time to throw a party, whether for an election or community gathering, they baked what was called the "Great Cake." Made with yeast as a leavening agent and combined with an enormous amount of flour, butter, sugar, and dried fruit, along with a considerable amount of alcohol (such as brandy or rum), it was meant to feed the town for an extended period of time.

During this first part of the 1800s, ice cream grew in popularity especially for those who could acquire ice in the summer. And while plain vanilla and strawberry were popular flavors, ice cream also had a savory side. Most notably, Dolley Madison, first lady and wife of President James Madison, was known for serving oyster ice cream at White House dinners.

This frozen treat became even more accessible to the public when, in 1932, Augustus Jackson, an African American cook who worked in the White House, invented the hand-cranked ice cream churn many of us know today. He also opened an ice cream parlor in Washington, D.C.

The most popular dessert brought by the early colonists arriving from Britain was the apple pie, and it was foremost on the table at this time. "Apple pie reigned supreme," says O'Connell.

## As American as Apple Pie

**1870s** – This gilded age of America heralded the growth of industry, along with access to freezers and better baking ingredients and appliances.

O'Connell notes that with the rise of great gourmet restaurants, such as the renowned Delmonico's in New York City, dishes like baked Alaska, an ice cream cake encased in meringue then doused with spirits and set ablaze, came to dazzle guests. She says chemists figured out that egg whites are an excellent insulator, which allowed the creator of baked Alaska, Chef Charles Ranhofer, to combine the frozen center with a flamboyant display fit for the times. More so, as O'Connell points out, Ranhofer named it in a moment of marketing genius as a gesture to the controversial purchase of Alaska.

In contrast to the luxury enjoyed by some, waves of European immigrants brought simple, yet satisfying, desserts. German immigrants were known for apple strudel and shoo-fly pie, made with eggs, molasses, and spices.

"In the 1870s, you start seeing layer cakes," says O'Connell. Reliable baking powder was finally developed so "people could start making cakes at home."

And still, apple pie was the perennial favorite, regardless of status. O'Connell points out that baking, particularly pie baking, was an important skill for many women in America since not everyone could have ice cream (particularly if you lived in a little sod house on the prairie), but everyone could make fruit pies.

## Cans and Store-Bought Convenience

**1920s** – Lots of changes happened in the Roaring Twenties and not just in fashion or social perceptions. The rise of commercial canning harkened the advent of fruit cocktail, which initially

*(continued)*

was served with alcohol until Prohibition. Having this type of fruit in a can was a game changer for this era since people were not used to having fresh fruit when it was out of season.

"Sometimes it was a dessert, but it was served at any time of the day," notes O'Connell.

O'Connell says Nabisco also came along at that time offering Oreos and Fig Newtons. Although we still eat these cookies today, she says store-bought cookies were a gift from heaven for most housewives because they didn't have to bake them.

Packaged cream cheese was new on the scene, and New York-style cheesecake was an instant hit.

"You also had Jell-O. Invented in 1890, it became popular from national advertising," she says. "They marketed it as 'America's Most Famous Dessert.'"

In reality, Jell-O was just becoming well known at this time, but no one wanted to be left out if it was the most popular dessert out there. "Children loved it," says O'Connell. "People just thought it was the cat's pajamas."

As always, apple pie was still the go-to dessert for practically any celebration or mid-week treat.

## Box Desserts and Elegant Flavors

**1970s** – The '70s were a dichotomy. On one hand, people looked for quick convenience, yet more elegant, French-inspired desserts were also gaining popularity.

"This is the rise of the boxed mixes. A lot of households had cake mix," says O'Connell.

On the flip side, Alice Waters and Julia Child influenced American cooking by making seemingly complicated French cuisine possible in the average American kitchen. Chocolate mousse and creme brulee were both easy to make and impressive.

Ice cream continued to be a favorite, but this era brought a twist on flavors. She says, "You have the introduction of gourmet ice cream." The high quality of Haagen Dazs and 31 flavors of Baskin-Robbins completely changed how we enjoyed ice cream.

**2020** – Currently, there's an awareness of how and where food is grown. "There is an increase in the use of seasonal fruit in desserts. People like the local, fresh ingredients," she says.

Also, with gluten being an issue for so many, flourless chocolate cake, which is amazingly delicious beyond being safe for those with a gluten intolerance, is a common staple on many menus.

"And we still have apple pie," she said. While modifying this traditional dessert, like by adding cheese, snazzes up the flavor, it's still the classic flavor that has been around as long as, if not longer than, America.

Desserts shine a light on culture throughout our history. From the time when they were an important source of calories made with local ingredients by necessity to our era when we look again at our local foods, this time by choice; they have always been a sweet way to share special moments together.

 *Check out some of our favorites at FarmersAlmanac.com/desserts*

Have you ever wondered how animals, like squirrels, butterflies, snakes, or birds, or even larger ones, like deer or bison, survive nasty bouts of weather? Luckily, the answer in most cases is "pretty well" as they have developed ingenious ways to take on the worst Mother Nature can throw their way.

*Here are a few examples of how animals protect themselves during extreme weather conditions.*

# 7 WAYS ANIMALS STAY SAFE DURING WILD WEATHER

By Cynthia McMurray

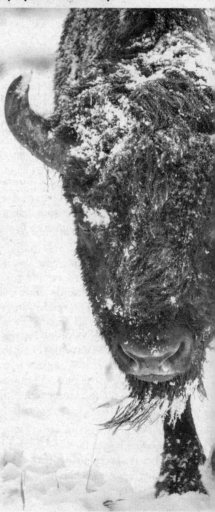

## TAKE SHELTER

Smaller animals have an advantage when it comes to taking shelter from a storm. They can hide out in microhabitats such as thick underbrush or other vegetation. Woodpeckers and chickadees are among some of the birds that will find holes in trees while other animals seek refuge in cavernous rocks or nooks offered by man-made structures. If they are burrowers, such as moles, badgers, groundhogs, some squirrels and snakes, and the burrowing owl, they head underground. Birds will often hide on the leeward side of large trees during extremely windy weather, which not only shelters them from the brunt of gale-force winds but also keeps them fairly dry during severe rains. Low-lying microhabitats are also a great way to stay warm when bitter cold sets in since the temperature is actually several degrees warmer closer to the ground, especially when the sun is out. Animals instinctively know to take advantage of this and go low.

## PUFF UP

There is a reason humans wear down jackets. Feathers, although light, trap air and create excellent insulation. Birds will puff out their feathers, the more the better, and this trick allows them to trap their body heat while keeping even the coldest of Arctic chills out.

## GO HIGH

Most animals sense signs of danger. Birds and some mammals, for instance, notice changes in the smell of the air, feel a drop in barometric pressure, or hear vibrations that warn of an impending storm. These signals cause them to instinctively head to higher ground or hunker down to stay safe during the bad weather. North Carolina's much-loved wild horses, for example, have survived hundreds of years by making it to higher ground prior to a hurricane.

## HEAD FOR THE EYE

While a storm rages on, its eye remains calm, which is why some birds, like pelicans, seagulls, and others in its path, will fly directly into it, where they will be protected until the storm subsides. This can be an exhausting task, however, as they must continuously follow the storm safely within the eye for many hours or even days.

## FATTEN UP

Most animals (hibernators or not) instinctively fatten up prior to winter as a way to both stay warm and survive. This allows them to use energy from the fat they stored when they are unable to find food. However, some researchers found that animals such as honeybees, squirrels, rabbits, deer, and many others instinctively and frantically forage in anticipation of bad weather and the aftermath, which often affects their regular food sources. Extra food also provides them with the energy needed to keep their heart rates stabilized and to shiver, which generates heat in colder temps.

## HUNKER DOWN

As some animals migrate early or head to higher ground when a storm is coming, others simply hunker down and ride it out. For instance, crows, like many perching birds, will pick a safe branch and go into lock down. Perching birds have evolved to have toes that literally lock around a branch when they rest or sleep. So, during a raging storm, it actually takes less energy for them to give in and rest, tethered to the tree by their feet. Alligators are also among those that will typically stay put in their normal habitat even during a hurricane. They will instinctively look for safety on a riverbank where they might find fallen logs (or beneath man-made structures, like your porch—*so watch out!*). Some animals often bed down in groups for warmth and safety. Fun fact: Buffalo, which roam in herds, will actually do the opposite and walk into a snowstorm in hopes of eventually reaching safety on the other side.

*(continued)*

## EVOLVE

Birds, for example, can tolerate bouts of extreme cold because of something called counter-current exchange. Birds' legs are particularly vulnerable as they are thin and unprotected by feathers, so the blood in the veins of their legs cools faster. As this cold blood runs up their legs, however, it passes by arteries, which carry warm blood. This heat is transferred allowing the blood flowing back down to their legs to be cooled, while the blood flowing up to their core is warmed. So, by the time the arterial blood actually reaches their feet, it is already cool and therefore, does not lose a lot of heat.

When a big storm or frigid weather approaches, humans head indoors to the safety of our homes. We bundle up if we have to brave the elements and take the necessary precautions in anticipation of any potential aftermath. Animals survive because they have evolved to adapt. They instinctively know when, where, and how to seek protection in the most severe weather. While these instincts will not always save them, they certainly do give them an advantage.

 Visit FarmersAlmanac.com/winter-animals to learn more about animals in winter!

## BEST DAYS TO SET EGGS

*According to Moon lore and Almanac tradition, for best results you should "set" eggs (place under a hen or in an incubator) during the specific phases of the Moon shown on the dates below. A chick usually takes about **21 days** to hatch.*

| | |
|---|---|
| **JANUARY** 6-8, 16, 17 | **JULY** 7, 8 |
| **FEBRUARY** 3, 4, 12-14 | **AUGUST** 3, 4, 30, 31 |
| **MARCH** 11, 12 | **SEPT.** 8, 9, 27, 28 |
| **APRIL** 7, 8 | **OCT.** 5-7, 25 |
| **MAY** 4-6, 13, 14 | **NOV.** 1-3, 29, 30 |
| **JUNE** 1, 2, 9, 10, 29 | **DEC.** 26-28 |

## ANIMAL GESTATION & INCUBATION

*This table shows the **average** period of time between impregnation and birth of the young, called "incubation" in egg-laying animals.*

| Referred to As | Average # of Young | Gestation in Days |
|---|---|---|
| Elephant | 1 | 640–645 |
| Giraffe | 1 | 395–425 |
| Donkey | 1 | 340–420 |
| Horse | 1 | 340–365 |
| Seal | 3 | 350 |
| Cow | 1 | 284 |
| Human | 1 | 280 |
| Monkey | 1 | 164 |
| Goat | 1–2 | 150 |
| Sheep | 1–2 | 148 |
| Pig | 10 | 114 |
| Lion | 2–4 | 108 |
| Cat | 4–6 | 58–63 |
| Dog | 6–8 | 58–60 |
| Fox | 5–8 | 51–53 |
| Rabbit | 4–8 | 33 |
| Rat | 10 | 22 |
| Mouse | 10 | 22 |
| Goose | 15–18 | 28–35 |
| Turkey | 12–15 | 28 |
| Duck | 9–12 | 26–28 |
| Hen | 12–15 | 21 |

## A Good Reason to RAISE CHICKENS

They—along with Guinea Fowl—will eat almost anything, including ticks! Researchers in South Africa found that in tick-infested areas, chickens will eat as many as 10 ticks per hour. If you have a fenced-in yard or enough space to let them roam, just a few hens will put a massive dent in the tick population while supplying you with farm fresh eggs.

## Our Favorite Uses for EGGSHELLS

*Don't throw out or compost those empty eggshells just yet! Here are some great uses for them:*

• Use crushed eggshells as a calcium- and mineral-rich additive to wild bird feed and chicken feed.

• Add eggshells to ground coffee before brewing. The shells help reduce the bitter taste.

• As a soil additive for houseplants, eggshells add minerals and help keep soil loose and aerated.

• Scatter crushed eggshells around your vegetables and flowers. The smell of the eggs deter deer and repel slugs, snails, and cutworms.

• Use empty shells with soapy water as a natural abrasive for pots and pans, especially when camping.

• Add to your garden to keep cats from using your garden as an outdoor litter box. Cats don't like the sharpness under their tender paws.

# How to Get Rid of
# Fleas
## *Naturally*

**Prevention:**

Wash your pet's bedding and vacuum your home each week to pick up eggs and larvae that have found their way indoors. If possible, scatter a handful of fresh cedar chips in your pet's bedding to help repel fleas.

Make a pet flea collar with essential oils. However, **you should always do your homework** before choosing an oil for your pet. Cedar oil and lavender oil are two pet-friendly options. To use, add 5 drops of oil to a tablespoon of water and then dab the solution on a collar or bandana for your pet to wear. *Note:* **ONLY for external use.**

**Flea Infestation**

If your home has a flea infestation, the key to success is persistence. Fleas lay eggs at an amazing rate—one adult female will lay 20-50 eggs each day for a total of 2,000 eggs over her lifetime. To keep up with the eggs, vacuum your home thoroughly daily and dispose of the vacuum bag after each session.

In hard-to-clean spots, such as carpets or area rugs, scatter salt. Salt dries out fleas and is safe to use indoors.

Borax powder is also effective against fleas and their larvae. Sprinkle borax powder *(not to be confused with boric acid!)* onto carpets and other heavily trafficked areas, work it in with a stiff-bristled broom, and close off the area for the night so pets and children cannot access. Vacuum it up first thing in the morning and dispose of the vacuum bag in a dumpster or trash bin away from your home.

On your pets, a simple soap-and-water bath is the best way to get rid of fleas fast. The fleas will rush toward your pet's face to keep from drowning, so use a flea comb to remove them. Dunk the comb in soapy water to trap the fleas so that you can dispose of them. Add cedar or lavender oil to your pet's bathwater to help prevent a new infestation.

# America's ORIGINAL
## Walk-Behind Brush Mower!

*The DR® FIELD AND BRUSH MOWER is Now Better than Ever!*

**USA ENGINEERED & BUILT***

☑ **FASTER.** Up to 20 HP and 34" wide cut for faster mowing!

☑ **EASIER.** Power steering gives you fingertip control.

☑ **NEW CHOICES:** including PTO and tow-behind models for tractors and ATVs.

*Assembled in the USA using domestic and foreign parts.

**Starting at just $1599⁹⁹**

*Mows and mulches weeds, brush, even saplings up to 3" thick!*

*Own an ATV or Tractor?*
## MOW WHILE YOU RIDE...

*Tow-Behind Models offset to left or right!*

1A0BAX © 2019

PROFESSIONAL POWER
**DR**
DONE RIGHT

# THE MOTHERS OF MODERN GOVERNMENT

## CELEBRATING 100 YEARS OF WOMEN'S RIGHT TO VOTE

**by Jean Grigsby**

This year marks the 100th anniversary of the 19th Amendment, which guarantees all American women the right to vote. It was passed by Congress on June 4, 1919, and ratified on August 18, 1920, after a decades-long struggle.

Some women involved in the Women's Suffrage movement have become household names. **Elizabeth Cady Stanton** *(1815-1902)* and **Lucretia Mott** *(1793-1880)* organized the first meeting dedicated to women's rights, which was held on July 19 and 20, 1848 in Seneca Falls, New York. At what would later become known as the Seneca Falls Convention, the Declaration of Sentiments was read and ultimately adopted.

The Declaration of Sentiments was written by Stanton to echo the preamble of the Declaration of Independence with the word "women" inserted: *"We hold these truths to be self-evident: that all men and women are created equal."*

Stanton's declaration outlined "a history of repeated injuries ... on the part of man toward woman," such as denying the right to own property, obtain an education, and keep earned wages. The Seneca Falls Convention galvanized women to fight for the right to vote and launched the Women's Suffrage movement.

After the convention, Stanton and Mott, along with **Susan B. Anthony** *(1820-1906),* led the effort in the adoption of the 19th Amendment—an effort that would take more than 50 years of struggle. None of them would live to see women achieve the right to vote, but their leadership would live on through the many lesser-known, but no less notable, women who carried on what they had begun.

---

**"If Congress refuse [sic] to listen to and grant what women ask...What is there left for women to do but to become the mothers of the future government?"**

*- Victoria Claflin Woodhull*

---

## Victoria Claflin Woodhull
### (1838 - 1927)

A leader of the suffrage movement, Woodhull was the first woman to be nominated and campaign for the U.S. presidency, running on behalf of the Equal Rights Party in 1872. She was also the first woman to own (along with her sister) a brokerage firm on Wall Street and the first woman to start a weekly newspaper.

The Equal Rights Party was one of many organizations established to lobby for local, state, and national voting rights. After the Civil War ended in 1865, the battle for women's right to vote grew more intense and fractious. A split in the movement occurred over the proposed 15th Amendment, which gave the right to vote to black men. Stanton, Anthony, and others didn't support the amendment because it excluded women. Other suffragists, including Lucy Stone and Julia Ward Howe, did support it, contending that once black men could vote, women would soon follow.

Stanton and Anthony formed the National Woman Suffrage Association to work for suffrage on the federal level and to fight for other changes, such as granting property rights to married women. Lucy Stone created the American Woman Suffrage Association, which aimed to secure the new ballot through state legislation.

## Lucy Stone
### (1818 - 1893)

As an abolitionist and suffragist, Stone dedicated her life to fighting inequality. She was the first woman in Massachusetts to earn a college degree, and she defied gender norms when she famously wrote marriage vows to reflect her egalitarian beliefs, including excluding any reference to wifely obedience. She also refused to take her husband's last name.

In 1890, the National Woman Suffrage Association and the American Woman Suffrage Association united under the common heading of "National American Woman Suffrage Association" (NAWSA). In addition to organizing suffrage groups and rallying at conventions and meetings, suffrage supporters employed a number of other strategies. Suffragists exercised their First Amendment rights

*(continued)*

to "peaceably assemble" and "petition for a government redress of grievances" using traditional strategies, including lobbying lawmakers and challenging laws in the courts.

Some of the activism that now seems tame, such as marching in parades and making street corner speeches, was deemed "unladylike" at the time. One of the more radical suffragists, Alice Paul, was forced to resign from the NAWSA because of her insistence on using militant strategies.

### ALICE PAUL
*(1885 - 1977)*

After college, Paul went to England and was exposed to the more extreme tactics used by British suffragists. She advocated for the use of these tactics in the U.S. to bring attention to the cause. She and Lucy Burns organized what would become the National Woman's Party, which relied on strategies such as mass marches and hunger strikes. Paul was a visionary leader who was the first to organize picketing at the White House.

Militant suffragists also organized parades and silent vigils. Many endured being heckled and harassed in public, and, at times, more brutal opposition, including being jailed and physically abused.

Another key leader of the time was the politically savvy Carrie Chapman Catt, who was named president of the NAWSA in 1915.

### CARRIE CHAPMAN CATT
*(1859 - 1947)*

Involved in women's suffrage since the 1880s, Catt developed her "Winning Plan," a political strategy that coordinated state campaigns in the effort to push for amending the U.S. Constitution. After the 19th Amendment, she went

min Moran. *Cover of program for the National American Women's Suffrage Association, Washington, D.C. March 3, 1913*. Illustration. 1913. Public Domain; Cuerden, Adam (restorer). *Mrs. Carrie Chapman Catt, Speaker at Continental Hall, Joint Suffrage Procession Committee, 1420 F Street Northwest, Washington, D.C.* Photograph. 1913. Public Domain.

on to found the League of Women Voters in 1920 to educate women about and encourage their active participation in politics.

By 1900, more than three million women worked for wages outside the home. Conditions were often unfair and unsafe. Many women joined the movement to gain influence in the making of labor laws. The movement grew even further when the U.S. entered World War I in 1917, and more women entered the workforce. The swelling ranks of activists brought successes at the state level. Wyoming was the first territory and state to grant women the right to vote in 1869 and 1890, respectively.

### JEANNETTE RANKIN
*(1878 - 1920)*

A suffragist and peace activist from Montana, Rankin was the first woman to serve in Congress. She was elected in 1916 to one of her state's at-large congressional seats almost four years before the 19th Amendment was passed.

By the time of Rankin's election, most of the suffragists were behind the goal of a constitutional amendment. Key victories came in 1917 when New York adopted women's suffrage, and in 1918, when President Wilson (a reluctant convert) urged Congress to pass a voting rights amendment.

On May 21, 1919, the House of Representatives passed the amendment, and two weeks later, the Senate followed suit. When Tennessee became the 36th state to ratify the amendment on August 18, 1920, the amendment passed its final hurdle to obtaining the agreement of three-fourths of the states.

When the 19th Amendment went into effect on August 26, 1920, it opened the door for greater roles for women in public life and changed the course of American history forever.

# WIPERS UP OR DOWN?

## The Great Debate.

Once winter storms start, it's not uncommon to see parked cars with their windshield wipers propped up in anticipation of precipitation, namely ice. Is it a smart way to prepare, or does it do damage?

*Here are the two schools of thought:*

**Propping Wipers Up—Pros:**

• Prevents damage to the wiper motor, especially if you start the car and find that the wipers were left on and they are frozen to the windshield.

• Protects the rubber part of the windshield wiper.

• Makes clearing away snow and ice from the windshield easier.

**Leaving Wipers Down—Pros:**

• Prevents damaging the springs inside the blade arm.

• Discourages vandalism.

• Works because defroster releases frozen blades.

**So Which Is Correct?**

Several wiper manufacturers recommend lifting the wipers before things get icy to protect the rubber blade, and the American Automobile Association (AAA) claims that leaving wipers up does not weaken the springs. If you do choose to leave them down, it's important to give your car enough time to warm up. The defroster will release frozen blades from the windshield.

### GREAT WIPER DEBATE: UP OR DOWN?

UP
DOWN
DON'T HAVE SNOW!

Follow us on Facebook so YOU can vote up or down!

### DEICE YOUR WINDSHIELD WITH A POTATO!

The night before freezing temperatures, rub a half of a potato over your car's windshield. The sugar from the potato creates a barrier over the window and prevents ice from forming, so you won't have to scrape in the morning!

# ENERGAIRE® IONIZER CLEARS THE AIR OF SMOKE, POLLEN, POLLUTION.

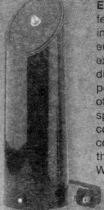

EnergAire continuously purifies up to 4,000 cubic feet (a large room) of air and makes it breathable and invigorating. Restores natural ion balance to unhealthy environments caused by industrial pollution, automobile exhaust, central air-conditioning, and heating, smoke, dust, pollen, animal fur . . . removes microscopic pollution particles not removed by any other method of air purification. EnergAire was rated Number One for speed of removal of cigarette smoke by the leading U.S. consumer protection magazine. It has no noisy fan, no costly filter, and requires no maintenance. Uses less than 2 watts. 9" high. 3" diameter. Weighs less than 1 pound.

### $69.95

# RODAR® ULTRASOUND GETS RID OF RATS, MICE, BATS, ROACHES, OTHER PESTS.

RODAR is the superpowerful professional ultrasonic pest repeller with up to 60 or more times the power of other devices — and power is what makes RODAR so effective. RODAR ultrasound equals a jet engine — noise unbearable to pests but at frequencies humans and pets cannot hear. RODAR units are completely safe. RODAR drives pests out and keeps them from getting in. Handsome simulated walnut cabinet. Uses less than 5 watts. 5-5/8" high. Weight 1-1/2 pounds.

### $99.95

**TO ORDER:** Send cost for unit(s) plus $10.00 each for shipping and handling (in Mass. add 6.25% tax) by check, money order, MasterCard, Visa, or Discover number and expiration date to:

**MICRON CORPORATION**
Dept. 736 • 89 Access Road • Norwood, MA 02062
CALL TOLL-FREE 1-800-456-0734
www.MicronCorp.com/almanac

*90-Day Money-Back Guarantee — 12-Month Warranty!*

# Weather-Dependent Professions

**By Tiffany Means**

*You've experienced it before: you grab your bag and coffee cup and head out the door only to find you need to go back inside for an umbrella! Thanks to the gray weather, you can now expect a soggy, slippery morning commute to the office and a sleepy day once you get there. While the weather may dampen your workday and your mood, for some folks, including those in the following careers, it's a more serious matter. It can mean the difference between a job well done and one not done at all.*

## Viticulturists

One kind of weather can set grape growers on edge, especially at autumn harvest time: rain. Moisture early on in the growing season is a necessity, but once grapes mature, water can dilute sugars and flavors, cause skins to split, and encourage rotting and disease. Vineyard managers intentionally schedule harvest for days and weeks when there's a good stretch of clear, frost-free weather in the fall forecast.

## Beekeepers

Weather doesn't affect beekeepers directly, but it does influence bee behavior, which in turn influences how beekeepers support their hives. Bees are busiest and more even tempered on calm, sunny days when air temperatures are above 70° F, which makes these the best days for disturbing bees with "hive-keeping" chores. However, when temperatures move from mild to miserable (100° F), beekeepers should take action to keep bees cool by creating a nearby water source and even setting up shade umbrellas.

## Confectioners

Candymakers require a cool, dry environment when making sweet treats. Since sugar is hygroscopic (that is, absorbs moisture), it pulls water vapor from the air on muggy days when the outdoor relative humidity is high. The more moisture in the air for sugar to soak up as it cools, the less likely it is to "set" or harden properly.

## Archaeologists

While archaeologists are more concerned with soil than the sky, they do keep a close eye on the weather, especially when planning excavations—the digging up and cataloging of ancient artifacts. Conditions that can postpone digs include extreme cold (the ground can freeze at deep levels, making digging impossible) and rainstorms (these can leave footprints in excavated soil and wash out an excavation site). Dry conditions are ideal, but if the weather is too dry, the soil can bake. If that happens, as archaeologists dig at the earth with their tools, it will crumble and cake away instead of gently loosening a little at a time.

## Astronauts

Before astronauts can blast off into space, they have to fly through Earth's atmosphere—and its weather. To make sure they get the best possible send-off, the National Aeronautics and Space Administration (NASA) will not let a rocket launch unless certain weather conditions—including limits for rain, lightning, clouds, and wind—are met at the launch site at Florida's John F. Kennedy Space Center. And not only do these conditions have to be met in the minutes leading up to the countdown window but days before it, too.

## Construction Workers

Builders depend on fair weather to keep them focused on their jobs rather than their comfort. But even when the weather is less than perfect, their work continues on. About the only weather conditions they won't work in are extreme cold, extreme heat, and heavy rain. Not only do such extremes put workers at greater risk for cold- and heat-related illnesses (such as frostbite and heatstroke), but they can damage building materials, too.

## Ski Instructors

Ten inches of snow might be enough to close your office, but ski instructors need that much snow (and more) for their "offices" (ski slopes and resorts) to open. In fact, local ski seasons don't begin until temperatures are consistently cold enough for natural snow or machine-made snow to fall and create a sufficient snow "base" (height of snow above the ground).

## Painters

Professional painting contractors, especially those who do exterior work, require surfaces to be fully dry before painting and for hours to days after. Rain, snow, fog, high humidity, and low air temperatures (50° F and below) can interrupt the drying or "curing" process. Once moisture from such weather enters in the uncured paint layer, it can cause a myriad of paint job problems, like poor adhesion, mildew growth, and a shortened life span.

*(continued)*

**Lawn Professionals**

While any type of unsettled weather can turn the friendly skies unfriendly, icy, windy, and convective conditions pose the biggest threats to their planes, passengers, and crew.

> **Mother Nature doesn't make for a very good business partner.**

For lawn professionals, rain may be good for business, but it's not so good for working in. Wet grass clippings can make lawns slick to walk on and can stick to mowing equipment, causing blade or vacuum blockages. Blades of grass are also harder to cut when wet and don't slice as clean or as close. Not to mention, doing yard work in a thunderstorm increases one's risk of being struck by lightning. (According to the National Weather Service, of the number of people struck by lightning while performing weekly routine activities, 17% were doing general yard work and 7% were mowing.)

Now, that's something to think about the next time you head out the door and look up at the sky before grabbing an umbrella on your way to work.

**Pilots**

Pilots monitor preflight and in-flight weather conditions to inform them in making a number of decisions. They may choose to reroute and fly around weather-impacted airspace or to divert and land at alternate sites. Sometimes when the weather is severe, they may choose not to operate the aircraft at all.

### BONUS JOB:

**Farmers & Agriculturists**

Farmers require sufficient rain, sun, and temperatures to produce bountiful crop and livestock yields, which is why droughts and freezes are two of their biggest concerns. Hot, dry weather can lead to more pests and diseases and can cause heat stress in animals, while frosts and freezes can damage or even kill young crops before they've had a chance to ripen. Weather not only impacts a farmer's produce, but his or her daily chores. One example? Exceptionally rainy days. These can make soil too wet and muddy for field work, including planting.

# PROTECT YOUR LAND

## PROTECT YOUR FAMILY

# Always call or click **811** and work with pipeline and utility operators to locate underground lines.

Hitting a pipeline or underground utility can impact your family for generations. Underground lines can be located less than 12 inches below the surface due to topsoil removal, erosion and weather. Never assume the location or depth of underground lines.

Always call or click 811 or contact the pipeline or utility line operator to discuss your project and to check the location and depth of underground lines before you deep plow, till, rip, install a fence or drain tiles. Operators will locate the pipeline, perform a depth and safety analysis and work with you to help protect you, your land and the pipeline or underground utility line. Operators will typically request to be on-site during projects directly near the underground line to provide safety guidance regarding clearances and backfilling procedures.

The safety information on the following pages provide general guidance regarding how to safely work near underground pipelines and utility lines. This safety guide is designed to increase awareness regarding the safety risks associated with excavation-type activities near underground pipelines and utility lines, and to facilitate project planning and coordination with pipeline and utility line operators.

Pipeline Operators
for Ag Safety

Get the facts at **PipelineAgSafety.org**

## Land Contour Modifications

Land contour projects near underground pipelines and utility lines, including the installation of ponds, lakes and drainage ditches, require expert engineering in planning and implementation to protect land, water and underground pipeline and utility line infrastructure. A plan should be developed and provided to the pipeline or

utility line operator in advance to initiate discussion regarding potential impact to the integrity and safety of underground pipelines. Call or click 811 to initiate contact with all impacted pipeline and utility line operators and to discuss the land contour modifications you are planning.

When considering land contour modifications, no substantial amount of soil can be removed or added directly near underground pipelines or utility lines. Project requirements should be designed to maintain the current pipeline or utility line depth of cover or as advised by the operator. The edge of a proposed land contour modification should maintain a minimum clearance of at least 25 feet when parallel to a pipeline or utility line.

## Drain Tile Installation

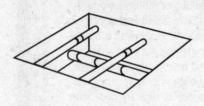

*Maintain minimum clearance. Cross at an angle as close to 90 degrees as possible.*

When planning your field drain tile installation project, call or click 811 to check the location of pipelines and utility lines and to discuss your installation plans with pipeline and utility line operators. Advanced planning is key to allow sufficient  time for operators to review the project design, verify pipeline depths and operational requirements.

Generally, field drain tiles crossing a pipeline or utility line should be as near to 90 degrees (perpendicular to the line) as possible and clear the line by at least 24 inches. Solid tiles and plastic pipe are typically recommended when crossing a pipeline or utility line. Pea gravel is used to prevent settling.

Pipeline Operators
for Ag Safety

Get the facts at **PipelineAgSafety.org**

## Subsoiling, Deep Ripping or Deep Plowing

Due to erosion and topsoil removal, the existing depth of underground pipelines and utility lines may not support deep tillage activities, such as subsoiling, deep ripping or plowing.

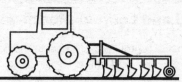

Never assume the location or depth of pipelines or underground utility lines. Call or click 811 to initiate contact with pipeline and utility operators. Operators will locate the pipeline, perform a depth and safety analysis and work with you to ensure that you, your land and the pipeline or utility line stay safe.

# Safety Guidelines

 **Step 1: Call or click 811 before agricultural excavation activities.**

Never rely on pipeline markers to identify the location of pipelines or utility lines. Markers indicate the general, but not exact, location of pipelines or utility lines.

Always call or click 811 at least two to three working days before you deep plow, tile, scrape or dig. 811 is a **free service** in most states that will notify pipeline and underground utility operators of your planned work. For larger projects, contact the operator during the planning phase to allow time to ensure safety for you and the pipeline or utility line.

 **Step 2: Wait for Operators to Mark Lines**

Identify the location where you will be digging using white paint or coordinate a time to meet with the operator to discuss your project. Wait for operators to locate their lines before beginning your project. Operators may request to be on-site when you dig.

 **Step 3: Dig with Hand-Digging Tools Near the Line & Backfill Properly**

Dig with care using appropriate hand digging or vacuum-digging tools near the pipeline. For your safety, backhoes, augers and other mechanical equipment should not be used when digging within 24 inches of the outside edge of pipelines or utility lines. Don't remove flags, stakes or paint marks until you've finished digging. Carefully backfill and compact the soil.

 **Step 4: Notify Operator Regarding Damage or Leaks**

Never operate mechanical equipment in an area where you suspect a leak. Immediately notify operator if you dent, scrape or hit a pipeline while digging so that it can be inspected and repaired, if needed, to prevent future damage. If you suspect a pipeline leak, immediately leave the area in an upwind direction and warn others to stay away. From a safe location, call 911 and the operator.

# 10 COOL FACTS YOU DIDN'T KNOW ABOUT JELLYFISH

## By Glenn Morris

The sight of a jellyfish prompts a reaction that is directly proportional to the observer's interest and exposure. Marine scientists can become transfixed when observing these seemingly delicate, often-multicolored organisms pulsing surreally through the water. Likewise, swimmers, surfers, and snorkelers might stop what they're doing to watch these amazing creatures, but then they scatter. They know that these gelatinous creatures sting.

"Most people here know not to tangle with jellies if they can avoid it," says Terri Kirby Hathaway, marine education specialist with North Carolina Sea Grant on Roanoke Island. "People entangling with jellyfish is almost always a wrong-place, wrong-time encounter... They do what they do," adds Hathaway, "and we get in the way." When that happens, it can result in what can only be described as underwater, long-lasting, wrap-around bee stings.

Nevertheless, these fascinating creatures are marine marvels. Here are 10 fascinating facts about jellies that can take your breath away without laying a tentacle on you!

**1. They are not Fish.** "They are no way, no how fish of any type or description," declares Hathaway. They don't have bones, gills, fins, scales, or any other fish equipment or body parts. "The fish part of the name is wrong," says Hathaway. What should you call them? "Well, jellies."

**2. Greek Monster?** Some jellies look like dainty umbrellas or bells decorated with an elegant fringe suspended from the center or the edge. The billowing main shape is called the medusa, as it resembles Medusa who had serpents for hair according to Greek mythology.

**3. Jellies are Elevators.** "They can only move up and down in the water column," says Hathaway. "They can't go east, west, north, or south intentionally." Jellies move up by collapsing the medusa (like quickly closing an umbrella) which pushes water down and propels them upward. Beyond that, these creatures go where the winds blow and the currents take them. Some jellies travel around the world in the ballast tanks of oceangoing ships to invade waters as non-native species when ships jettison the tanks.

**4. The Sting's the Thing.** Scientists classify jellies in the phylum *Cnidaria* (silent "C"). The name originates from the Greek word "cnidos," meaning stinging nettle for the specialized stinging cells, cnidocytes or nematocysts. This cell "explodes" on contact, launching a harpoon-like organelle containing neu-

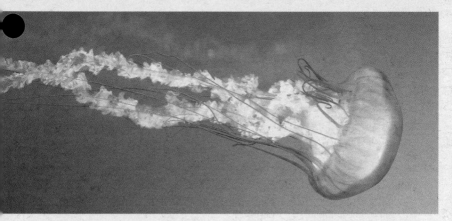

rotoxins into whatever touched it. Jellies feed and defend themselves this way. Most stings are painful but not life-threatening. There are exceptions in Pacific waters. Close relatives like sea anemones and corals, which spend their adult lives attached to the sea bottom, can also sting. Rinsing, not scrubbing, with vinegar is the best antidote.

**5. Simply Simpletons.** Most jellies are simple organisms. Think of them as "bags" made of two cell layers, an outer ectoderm or epidermis (housing the stinging cells) and an inner endoderm or gastrodermis (lining the gut). The filling between the layers is the mesoglea, a layer of jellylike substance that provides volume and weight. Some are transparent, others are colorful and translucent, and some change colors with the salinity of the water.

**6. Water not Jelly.** Jellies are 95% water. That's one reason they look so elegant beneath the surface but look like a blob of goo on the beach.

**7. All Shapes and Sizes.** There are at least 9,000 known species of *Cnidaria* and some inhabit every ocean. Their sizes span from tiny to wow. The smallest medusae are barely visible (but still pack a sting). The largest, the Nomura's jellyfish, can grow from the size of a grain of rice to six feet across

in six months. A single jelly of this species can weigh up to 200 pounds.

**8. Simple yet Complex.** Medusozoa jellies have a two-step procreation plan. First, it involves egg fertilization by free-floating sperm. This produces larvae that sink and attach to a firm surface. Then the larvae grow into polyps that bud and release tiny medusae that grow into the adult form.

**9. Blooms.** Sudden massive reproductive surges, known as "blooms," can deplete local fish supplies, ruin fishing nets, and shut down nuclear plants by clogging the cooling water intakes. The cause of these blooms is still not completely understood.

**10. Colony in One.** A frequenter of our eastern and southern coasts, the surface-living Portuguese man-o'-war, is part of the same species and closely related, but not a true jellyfish. The interesting thing about the Portuguese man-o'-war is that it's not one organism but a colony of specialists that survive together but not apart. The telltale violet sail is one organism; the stinging tentacles are another.

Visit **FarmersAlmanac.com** for more beach safety tips including stings, sand, surf, and sunburns!

## PEAK FOLIAGE DATES FOR THE CONTIGUOUS U.S.

| Location | Dates | Location | Dates |
| --- | --- | --- | --- |
| Alabama *(Northern)* | Oct 19–Nov 4 | Missouri *(Northern)* | Oct 5–21 |
| Arizona | Oct 5–21 | Missouri *(Southern)* | Oct 12–28 |
| Arkansas | Oct 19–Nov 4 | Montana *(Central)* | Sep 28–Oct 9 |
| Arkansas *(Ozarks)* | Oct 12–28 | Montana *(Western)* | Oct 5–21 |
| California *(Northern)* | Oct 15–31 | Nebraska | Oct 5–21 |
| Colorado | Oct 5–14 | Nevada | Oct 12–28 |
| Connecticut | Oct 12–28 | New Hampshire *(Inland)* | Sep 28–Oct 9 |
| Delaware | Oct 19–Nov 4 | New Hampshire *(Coastal)* | Oct 5–21 |
| Florida | Nov 2–11 | New Jersey *(Inland)* | Oct 12–28 |
| Georgia *(Northern)* | Oct 19–Nov 4 | New Jersey *(Coastal)* | Oct 19–Nov 4 |
| Idaho | Oct 5–21 | New Mexico | Sep 28–Oct 9 |
| Illinois *(Northern)* | Oct 5–21 | New York* | Sep 28–Oct 28 |
| Illinois *(Southern)* | Oct 12–28 | North Carolina *(Inland)* | Oct 12–28 |
| Indiana *(Northern)* | Oct 5–21 | North Carolina *(Coastal)* | Oct 19–Nov 4 |
| Indiana *(Southern)* | Oct 12–28 | North Dakota | Oct 5–21 |
| Iowa | Oct 5–21 | Ohio | Oct 5–21 |
| Kansas *(Northern)* | Oct 5–21 | Oklahoma | Oct 26–Nov 4 |
| Kansas *(Southern)* | Oct 12–28 | Oregon | Oct 12–28 |
| Kentucky *(Eastern)* | Oct 5–21 | Pennsylvania | Oct 5–21 |
| Kentucky *(Western)* | Oct 12–28 | Rhode Island | Oct 12–28 |
| Louisiana | Nov 2–11 | South Carolina | Oct 19–Nov 4 |
| Maine *(Inland)* | Oct 1–17 | South Dakota | Oct 5–21 |
| Maine *(Coastal)* | Oct 5–21 | Tennessee | Oct 12–28 |
| Maryland *(Inland)* | Oct 12–28 | Texas | Nov 2–11 |
| Maryland *(Coastal)* | Oct 19–Nov 4 | Utah | Oct 5–21 |
| Massachusetts *(Inland)* | Oct 5–21 | Vermont *(Northern)* | Sep 24–Oct 10 |
| Massachusetts *(Coastal)* | Oct 12–28 | Vermont *(Southern)* | Oct 5–14 |
| Michigan *(Northern)* | Oct 1–17 | Virginia *(Inland)* | Oct 12–28 |
| Michigan *(Southern)* | Oct 5–21 | Virginia *(Coastal)* | Oct 19–Nov 4 |
| Minnesota *(Northern)* | Oct 1–17 | Washington | Oct 12–28 |
| Minnesota *(Southern)* | Oct 5–21 | West Virginia | Oct 5–21 |
| Mississippi *(Northern)* | Oct 19–Nov 4 | Wisconsin | Oct 5–14 |
| | | Wyoming | Oct 5–14 |

*Depending on elevation and distance from the coast. All peak times are usually earlier at higher elevations.*

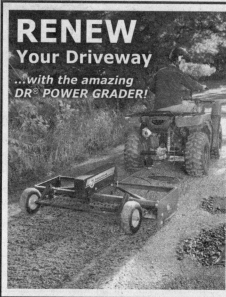

# WHAT MAKES A MOON
## "SUPER?"

*No, it's not a cape or its ability to leap tall buildings. It does have to do with how close the Moon is to the Earth as well as its orbit.*

A Supermoon is caused by the shape of the Moon's orbit, which is not a perfect circle but an ellipse, or oval, shape. As the Moon orbits the Earth each month, it reaches a point farthest from Earth called the *apogee* and a point closest called the *perigee*.

According to how most people define a Supermoon, it occurs when the Moon **is at least 90% of the way to its perigee position at the same time it is in its "full" or "new" phase.** An extreme Supermoon is when a full or new Moon happens at the same time the Moon is at perigee.

### Why New And Full Phases?

The reason these two Moon phases are singled out is because each of them means that the Sun, Earth, and Moon are in alignment. When the Moon is **full**, it sits exactly on the opposite side of the Earth from the Sun. When the Moon is **new**, it sits between the Earth and the Sun. In both cases, the gravitational pull from these two bodies—the Moon and the Sun—combine to create higher-than-normal tides called "spring tides," on Earth. When the Moon is also at perigee at this time, the effect is magnified into what is known as a *proxigean spring tide*.

A new Moon at perigee isn't very exciting to look at because in this phase, the Moon does not reflect the Sun's light, so it is invisible to the naked eye. Therefore, full Supermoons get all the attention.

There are four or five Supermoon events each year, half of which are full Supermoons. Extreme Supermoons are rare and occur at intervals ranging from as little as a year to 20 years or more.

### Not All Supermoons Are Created Equal!

Just as the Moon's orbit isn't a perfect circle, it also varies slightly from month to month and year to year. Its perigee one month may be slightly farther from the Earth than its perigee the next month. The Moon's average distance from the Earth is 235,000 miles, and its average *farthest* distance is 248,000 miles.

### 2020 Super Full Moon Dates: March 9 and April 7

## FULL MOONS

| Year/Month | Date | Full Moon Name | Time (EST/EDT) |
|---|---|---|---|
| **2019**/September | 14th | Full Harvest Moon | 12:33 am |
| **2019**/October | 13th | Full Hunter's Moon | 5:08 pm |
| **2019**/November | 12th | Full Beaver Moon | 8:34 am |
| **2019**/December | 12th | Full Cold Moon | 12:12 am |
| **2020**/January | 10th | Full Wolf Moon | 2:21 pm |
| **2020**/February | 9th | Full Snow Moon | 2:33 am |
| **2020**/March | 9th | Full Worm Moon | 1:48 pm |
| **2020**/April | 7th | Full Pink Moon | 10:35 pm |
| **2020**/May | 7th | Full Flower Moon | 6:45 am |
| **2020**/June | 5th | Full Strawberry Moon | 3:12 pm |
| **2020**/July | 5th | Full Buck Moon | 12:44 am |
| **2020**/August | 3rd | Full Sturgeon Moon | 11:59 am |
| **2020**/September | 2nd | Full Corn Moon | 1:22 am |
| **2020**/October | 1st | Full Harvest Moon | 5:05 pm |
| **2020**/October | 31st | Full Blue Moon | 10:49 am |
| **2020**/November | 30th | Full Beaver Moon | 4:30 am |
| **2020**/December | 29th | Full Cold Moon | 10:28 pm |

## THE LUNAR CYCLE

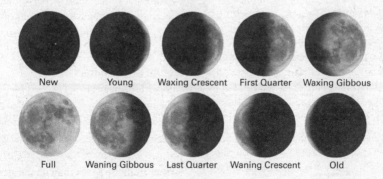

New  Young  Waxing Crescent  First Quarter  Waxing Gibbous

Full  Waning Gibbous  Last Quarter  Waning Crescent  Old

**New Moon** The Moon is not illuminated by direct sunlight.

**Waxing Crescent** The Moon is partly, but less than one-half, illuminated by direct sunlight while the illuminated part is increasing.

**First Quarter** One-half of the Moon appears illuminated by direct sunlight while the illuminated part is increasing.

**Waxing Gibbous** The Moon is more than one-half, but not fully, illuminated by direct sunlight while the illuminated part is increasing.

**Full Moon** The Moon is fully illuminated by direct sunlight.

**Waning Gibbous** The Moon is less than fully, but more than one-half, illuminated by direct sunlight while the illuminated part is decreasing.

**Last Quarter** One-half of the Moon appears illuminated by direct sunlight while the illuminated part is decreasing.

**Waning Crescent** The Moon is partly, but less than one-half, illuminated by direct sunlight while the illuminated part is decreasing.

## ANNUAL METEOR SHOWERS

*This table lists some of the best-known meteor showers. If your location observes Daylight Saving Time, add one hour to the time shown. All times given are listed in Eastern Time.*

| Name | Maximum Activity | Average Hourly Rate | Best Direction and Time to View | Speed |
|------|------------------|---------------------|----------------------------------|-------|
| Quadrantids | Jan 3–4 | 60–120 | Northeast 4–6 am | Medium |
| Lyrids | Apr 21–22 | 10–20 | Overhead 2–4 am | Swift streaks |
| Eta Aquarids | May 4–5 | 20–40 | Southeast 2–4 am | Very swift, long paths |
| Delta Aquarids | Jul 28–29 | 15–25 | South 1–3 am | Slow, long paths |
| Perseids | Aug 11–13 | 50–100 | Northeast 2–4 am | Very swift, rich display |
| Orionids | Oct 21–22 | 15–25 | South 2–4 am | Swift streaks |
| South Taurids | Nov 2–4 | 10–20 | South 1–3 am | Very slow, bright |
| North Taurids | Nov 12–14 | 10–20 | South 12–2 am | Slow fireballs |
| Leonids | Nov 17–18 | 25–50 | S/Southeast 4–6 am | Very swift |
| Geminids | Dec 13–14 | 50–100 | Overhead 1–3 am | Medium |
| Ursids | Dec 22–23 | 15–25 | North All night | Medium |

### METEOR-WATCHING TIPS:

- **Comfortable seating**
- **Warm layers (even in the summer!)**
- **Clear, unobstructed view**
- **Little to no light pollution (including from the gibbous or full Moon)**

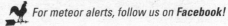

*For meteor alerts, follow us on **Facebook!***

## OBSERVING THE VISIBLE PLANETS

### QUICK-VIEW TABLE FOR 2020

| PLANET | WHEN VISIBLE | | | WHEN BRIGHTEST | |
| | MORNINGS | EVENINGS | FAINT OR INVISIBLE | MORNINGS | EVENINGS |
|---|---|---|---|---|---|
| **Mercury** | Mar. 17 to Apr. 7 / Jul. 15 to Aug. 1 / Nov. 3 to Nov. 22 | Jan. 26 to Feb. 16 / May 21 to Jun. 11 / Sep. 17 to Oct. 8 | Except for periods around the dates listed in the adjacent columns | Nov.3 to Nov. 22* | Jan. 26 to Feb. 16* |
| **Venus** | Jun. 13 to Dec. 31 | Jan. 1 to May 24 | May 25 to Jun. 12 | Jul. 10 to Aug. 13 | Mar. 24 to Apr. 26 |
| **Mars** | Jan. 1 to Oct. 12 | Oct. 13 to Dec. 31 | Not in 2020 | Oct. 4 to Oct. 12 | Oct. 13 to Oct. 17 |
| **Jupiter** | Jan. 15 to Jul. 13 | Jul. 14 to Dec. 31 | Jan.1 to Jan. 14 | Jul. 11 to Jul. 13 | Jul. 14 to Jul. 16 |
| **Saturn** | Jan. 29 to Jul. 19 | Jul. 20 to Dec. 31 | Jan. 1 to Jan. 28 | Jul. 4 to Jul. 19 | Jul. 20 to Aug. 9 |
| **Uranus** | May 12 to Oct. 30 | Jan. 1 to Apr. 8; / Oct. 31 to Dec. 31 | Apr. 9 to May 11 | Aug. 21 to Oct. 30 | Oct. 31 to Dec. 31 |
| **Neptune** | Mar. 24 to Sep. 10 | Jan. 1 to Feb. 20; / Sep. 11 to Dec. 31 | Feb. 21 to Mar. 23 | Jul. 16 to Sep. 10 | Sep. 11 to Nov. 5 |

*Apparitions that are the brightest and easiest to spot.

 **STARRY-EYED?**

Be sure to follow *Farmers' Almanac* on Facebook for easy-to-follow night sky graphics!

And visit **FarmersAlmanac.com** for more information on visible planets.

## ECLIPSES OF THE SUN AND MOON IN 2020

*Times listed are Eastern. Daylight Saving Time is taken into account for Eclipses II, III and IV.*

### I. JANUARY 10 – Penumbral Eclipse of the MOON

The lower portion of the Moon tracks deep into the Earth's outer shadow—the penumbra. This event will be visible solely from the Eastern Hemisphere: Europe, Africa, and Asia. No part of this eclipse will be visible from North America. For some minutes around the time of mid-eclipse, the lower part of the Moon will appear to be noticeably "smudged" or "soiled." Unlike the Earth's umbra which appears much darker and with a sharper edge, the penumbra appears more as a diffuse shading on the lunar disk.

**Penumbral Eclipse Begins:** 12:05 pm • **Mid-Eclipse:** 2:10 pm
**Penumbral Eclipse Ends:** 4:14 pm • **Magnitude of the Eclipse:** 0.921

### II. JUNE 5 – Penumbral Eclipse of the MOON

Once again the Moon encounters the Earth's outer penumbral shadow. But unlike in January where more than nine-tenths of the Moon's diameter became immersed in the penumbra, less than six-tenths of the Moon will penetrate the penumbra. Visibility will be confined to central and east Africa, Eastern Europe, western and central Asia, most of Indonesia and Australia.

**Penumbral Eclipse Begins:** 1:43 pm • **Mid-Eclipse:** 3:25 pm
**Penumbral Eclipse Ends:** 5:06 pm • **Magnitude of the Eclipse:** 0.593

### III. JUNE 20-21 – Annular Eclipse of the SUN

Because at this moment in time the Moon is situated at a distance of 241,000 miles from Earth, its disk will appear slightly smaller than the Sun; four-tenths of one percent smaller to be exact. As such, when the Moon passes squarely in front of the Sun, it will not totally cover it, but instead a narrow ring of sunlight will remain visible. Hence, the term "annular" eclipse, derived from the Latin "annulus" meaning ring-shaped.

The path of annularity is widest and the ring phase lasts longest at the very beginning and end (the sunrise and sunset points) respectively, measuring about 50 miles and lasting roughly 80 seconds. The path is considerably narrower and the ring phase is much shorter at the middle of the path. The path starts in central Africa. Then it moves northeast, cutting through parts of the Democratic Republic of the Congo, Central African Republic, South Sudan, Sudan, Ethiopia, the Red Sea, Yemen, Saudi Arabia, Oman, the Gulf of Oman, Pakistan, and India. Then it turns east and finally southeast over China, Taiwan and then out into the Philippine Sea, passing just south of Guam before coming to an end at sunset over the North Pacific Ocean.

The point of greatest eclipse will occur over Uttarakhand, a state in northern India crossed by the Himalayas. A partial eclipse of varying extent will be visible over much of Africa and Asia, as well as Indonesia. A slice of southeast Europe will catch the opening stages of the eclipse after sunrise and a small section of northernmost Australia will catch the end just prior to sunset.

**Partial Eclipse Begins:** 11:45 pm *(June 20)* • **Annular Eclipse Begins:** 12:48 am *(June 21)* • **Greatest Eclipse:** 2:41 am • **Annular Eclipse Ends:** 4:31 am • **Partial Eclipse Ends:** 5:34 am • **Maximum Duration of Annularity:** 1 min. 22.0 secs.

## IV. JULY 4-5 – Penumbral Eclipse of the MOON

A nonevent. Less than fourth-tenths of the Moon will slide through the southern edge of the Earth's penumbra, not enough to create any kind of noticeable darkening on the Moon's disk.

**Penumbral Eclipse Begins:** 12:05 pm *(July 4)* • **Mid-Eclipse:** 12:30 am *(July 5)* **Penumbral Eclipse Ends:** 1:55 am • **Magnitude of the Eclipse:** 0.380

## V. NOVEMBER 30 – Penumbral Eclipse of the MOON

Most of North America will be able to see this eclipse. With more than four-fifths of the Moon becoming immersed by the penumbral shadow, a noticeable shading effect should be evident over the Moon's upper limb for some minutes around the time of mid-eclipse.

**Penumbral Eclipse Begins:** 2:29 am • **Mid-Eclipse:** 4:42 am **Penumbral Eclipse Ends:** 6:55 am • **Magnitude of the Eclipse:** 0.855

## VI. DECEMBER 14 – Total Eclipse of the SUN

The final eclipse of 2020 will be visible only from the lower two-thirds of South America and a narrow slice of southwestern Africa. North America will not see any part of it. The narrow path of the total eclipse starts over the South Atlantic Ocean, then sweeps southeast through the Patagonia section of Chile and Argentina, then continues out over the South Atlantic Ocean, coming to an end at local sunset about 230 miles southwest off the coast of Namibia.

The point of greatest eclipse is 18 miles northwest of Sierra Colorada, a village and municipality in Río Negro Province in Argentina (pop. 1,300). Here the path width is 55 miles, and the total eclipse will last 2 minutes 9.6 seconds.

Approximately 400 to 500 miles to the north are the big metropolitan areas of Santiago, Buenos Aires, and Montevideo. All three cities will see a fairly large amount of the Sun obscured by the Moon (about 75 to 80 percent). Unfortunately they are all too far away to experience the panoply of amazing sights that accompany that magic word "totality." *¡Qué lástima!*

**Partial Eclipse Begins:** 8:33 am • **Total Eclipse Begins:** 9:32 am • **Greatest Eclipse:** 11:18 am • **Total Eclipse Ends:** 12:54 pm • **Partial Eclipse Ends:** 1:53 pm **Maximum Duration of Totality:** 2 minutes 09.6 seconds

The term retrograde comes from the Latin word *retrogradus,* which literally means "backward step." As the name suggests, retrograde is when a planet appears to go backward in its orbit, as viewed from Earth. Astronomers refer to this as "apparent retrograde motion," because it is an optical illusion.

## Backward Motion?

Every planet in our Solar System travels in the same direction in its journey around the Sun, and none of them ever pause or turn back in the opposite direction. Yet, all of them appear to do just that from time to time.

Because of the Earth's daily rotation, the objects appear to move from east to west through the night sky. While the location of the stars relative to the Earth is fixed, at least from our vantage point, the other planets in our solar system all orbit the Sun at varying speeds. The outer planets—Mars, Jupiter, Saturn, Uranus, and Neptune—all take longer to orbit the Sun than the Earth does, because their orbits are larger. Because of this, the Earth often laps these planets in its journey around the Sun. When the Earth overtakes an outer planet, that planet appears to travel backward, as compared to the stars, for a time. *(Picture two cars on the highway going in the same direction in different lanes. If one car is driving faster than the other, the slower car will appear to go backward from the perspective of a person in the faster car.)*

## Why Dread It?

Astrologers believe that the Moon, stars, planets, and Sun affect events here on Earth, and that each planet in our Solar System rules a different aspect of life. Like the Greek messenger god it was named for, Mercury is said to govern transportation and communication.

Those who dread Mercury's retrograde motion say that, when the planet travels backward, its power to positively influence these domains is stifled, leading to chaos. Believers in the malevolent power of Mercury retrograde blame the phenomenon for everything from arguments to lost mail or luggage to car accidents and warn people to hold back on conducting important business during this time.

Of course, few of us can afford to hide under our beds for three weeks, so for most people, life goes on as usual during Mercury retrograde. And if you choose to be more cautious during this time, well, a little extra caution never hurt anyone.

### Mercury Retrograde in 2020:

February 13–March 9
June 17–July 12
October 13–November 13

# SCIATICA BACK PAIN?

Are radiating pains down the back of your leg, or pain in your lower back or buttocks making it uncomfortable to sit, walk or sleep? Millions of people are suffering unnecessarily because they are not aware of this effective, topical treatment.

MagniLife® Leg & Back Pain Relief Cream combines seven active ingredients, Colocynthis to relieve burning pains and tingling sensations. This product is not intended to *treat or cure* sciatica, but can relieve painful symptoms. *"It provided me with the only relief for my sciatica."* - Mary.

MagniLife® Leg & Back Pain Relief Cream is **sold at Walgreens, CVS, Rite Aid and Amazon**. Order risk free for $19.99 +$5.95 S&H for a 4 oz jar. Get a **FREE** jar when you order two for $39.98 +$5.95 S&H. Send payment to: MagniLife SC-FM2, PO Box 6789, McKinney, TX 75071 or call **1-800-632-1416**. Money back guarantee. Order now at **www.LegBackCream.com**

# STABBING FOOT PAIN?

Are you suffering from burning, tingling, numbing or stabbing pain in your feet or legs? Over 20 million Americans live with these aggravating symptoms and put up with the pain because they are not aware of this topical treatment available without a prescription.

MagniLife® Pain Relieving Foot Cream contains eucalyptus oil and yellow jasmine to relieve tingling and burning pain, while moisturizers restore cracked, damaged, and itchy skin to help keep bacteria out. *"It's the ONLY product that helps relieve the burning, and tingling feeling in my feet!"* - Mable NY.

MagniLife® Pain Relieving Foot Cream is **sold at Walgreens, CVS, Rite Aid, Amazon, Target and Walmart**, in the foot care and diabetes sections. Order risk free for $19.99 +$5.95 S&H for a 4 oz jar. Get a **FREE** jar when you order two for $39.98 +$5.95 S&H. Send payment to: MagniLife NC-FM2, PO Box 6789, McKinney, TX 75071, or call **1-800-632-1416**. Satisfaction guaranteed. Order now at **www.MDFootCream.com**

# AGE SPOTS?

Are unsightly brown spots on your face and body making you uncomfortable? Liver spots, also known as age spots, affect the cosmetic surface of the skin and can add years to your appearance. Millions of people live with the dark spots and try to cover them with makeup, or bleach them with harsh chemicals because they are not aware of this new topical treatment that gently and effectively lightens the shade of the skin.

MagniLife® Age Spot Cream uses botanicals, such as licorice root extract to naturally fade age spots, freckles, and age-associated discolorations. Emollients soften and smooth skin while protecting against harmful external factors. *"It is fading my liver spots. This product actually works!!!"* - Patricia C., NJ.

MagniLife® Age Spot Cream can be ordered risk free for $19.99 +$5.95 S&H for a 2 oz jar. Get a **FREE** jar when you order two for $39.98 +$5.95 S&H. Send payment to: MagniLife AC-FM2, PO Box 6789, McKinney, TX 75071 or call **1-800-632-1416**. Satisfaction guaranteed. Order now at **www.AgeSpotSolution.com**

## ASTROLOGY AND ASTRONOMY EXPLAINED

**ASTROLOGY** interprets the influence that the Sun and Moon have while they are in a specific zodiacal constellation, and is based on the concept that there are 12 signs of the zodiac, measuring 30° each, along the astrological circle.

Because the astrological placement doesn't take into account the precession of the equinoxes (the "wobble" that the Earth's axis experiences over a 26,000-year interval), the Moon's place according to astrology differs from its physical place according to astronomy. For your convenience, we provide both the astrological place of the Moon and the physical, or astronomical, place of the Moon, which is listed on the Calendar Pages under the Moon's Place column.

**ASTRONOMY** is the scientific interpretation of matter in space. The Moon can wander into a few astronomical constellations that are not members of the zodiac. These constellations include: Sextans, the Sextant (SXT); and Ophiuchus, the Serpent Bearer (OPH). Thus, you will see these abbreviations under the Moon's Place listing on the Calendar Pages.

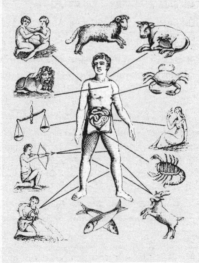

RAM
**ARIES (ARI)**
*Head & Face*
**March 19 at 11:50 pm
to April 19 at 10:45 am**

TWINS
**GEMINI (GEM)**
*Arms*
**May 20 at 9:49 am
to June 20 at 5:44 pm**

LION
**LEO (LEO)**
*Heart*
**July 22 at 4:37 am
to Aug. 22 at 11:45 am**

BALANCE
**LIBRA (LIB)**
*Reins*
**Sept. 22 at 9:31 am
to Oct. 22 at 7:00 pm**

ARCHER
**SAGITTARIUS (SAG)**
*Thighs*
**Nov. 21 at 3:40 pm
to Dec. 21 at 5:02 am**

WATER BEARER
**AQUARIUS (AQU)**
*Legs*
**Jan. 20 at 9:55 am
to Feb. 18 at 11:57 pm**

BULL
**TAURUS (TAU)**
*Neck*
**April 19 at 10:45 am
to May 20 at 9:49 am**

CRAB
**CANCER (CAN)**
*Breast*
**June 20 at 5:44 pm
to July 22 at 4:37 am**

VIRGIN
**VIRGO (VIR)**
*Bowels*
**Aug. 22 at 11:45 am
to Sept. 22 at 9:31 am**

SCORPION
**SCORPIO (SCO)**
*Secrets*
**Oct. 22 at 7:00 pm
to Nov. 21 at 3:40 pm**

GOAT
**CAPRICORN (CAP)**
*Knees*
**Dec. 21 at 5:02 am
to Jan. 19 at 3:40 pm**

FISHES
**PISCES (PSC)**
*Feet*
**Feb. 18 at 11:57 pm
to March 19 at 11:50 pm**

### THE MAN OF MANY SIGNS

Astrologers associate the signs of the zodiac with specific parts of the body, believing that these signs have an effect on those parts. The dates listed on both sides are the Sun's place in each astrological sign.

*This is not to be confused with the Moon's place in the zodiac, which is used for calculating our charts and calendars.*

## MOON'S ASTROLOGICAL PLACE IN THE ZODIAC

**The signs listed below are based on astrological calculations for 2019–2020.
Use these signs for all planting and other Almanac traditions.**

*NOTE: The Moon's Place column on the Calendar Pages gives the astronomical position.*

| | SEP | OCT | NOV | DEC | JAN | FEB | MAR | APR | MAY | JUN | JUL | AUG | SEP | OCT | NOV | DEC |
|---|---|---|---|---|---|---|---|---|---|---|---|---|---|---|---|---|
| 1 | LIB | SCO | CAP | AQU | ARI | TAU | GEM | CAN | LEO | LIB | SAG | CAP | PSC | ARI | TAU | CAN |
| 2 | SCO | SAG | CAP | AQU | ARI | TAU | GEM | LEO | VIR | SCO | SAG | AQU | PSC | ARI | GEM | CAN |
| 3 | SCO | SAG | AQU | PSC | ARI | GEM | CAN | LEO | VIR | SCO | SAG | AQU | ARI | TAU | GEM | CAN |
| 4 | SAG | CAP | AQU | PSC | TAU | GEM | CAN | VIR | LIB | SAG | CAP | PSC | ARI | TAU | CAN | LEO |
| 5 | SAG | CAP | PSC | ARI | TAU | CAN | CAN | VIR | LIB | SAG | CAP | PSC | ARI | TAU | CAN | LEO |
| 6 | SAG | AQU | PSC | ARI | GEM | CAN | LEO | LIB | SCO | CAP | AQU | PSC | TAU | GEM | CAN | VIR |
| 7 | CAP | AQU | PSC | ARI | GEM | LEO | LEO | LIB | SCO | CAP | AQU | ARI | TAU | GEM | LEO | VIR |
| 8 | CAP | AQU | ARI | TAU | GEM | LEO | VIR | SCO | SAG | AQU | PSC | ARI | GEM | CAN | LEO | LIB |
| 9 | AQU | PSC | ARI | TAU | CAN | VIR | VIR | SCO | SAG | AQU | PSC | TAU | GEM | CAN | VIR | LIB |
| 10 | AQU | PSC | TAU | GEM | CAN | VIR | LIB | SAG | CAP | AQU | PSC | TAU | GEM | LEO | VIR | SCO |
| 11 | AQU | PSC | TAU | GEM | LEO | LIB | LIB | SAG | CAP | PSC | ARI | TAU | CAN | LEO | LIB | SCO |
| 12 | PSC | ARI | TAU | CAN | LEO | LIB | SCO | CAP | AQU | PSC | ARI | GEM | CAN | LEO | LIB | SAG |
| 13 | PSC | ARI | GEM | CAN | VIR | SCO | SCO | CAP | AQU | ARI | TAU | GEM | LEO | VIR | SCO | SAG |
| 14 | ARI | TAU | GEM | LEO | VIR | SCO | SAG | CAP | PSC | ARI | TAU | CAN | LEO | VIR | SCO | CAP |
| 15 | ARI | TAU | CAN | LEO | LIB | SAG | SAG | AQU | PSC | ARI | TAU | CAN | VIR | LIB | SAG | CAP |
| 16 | ARI | GEM | CAN | LEO | LIB | SAG | CAP | AQU | PSC | TAU | GEM | CAN | VIR | LIB | SAG | CAP |
| 17 | TAU | GEM | LEO | VIR | SCO | SAG | CAP | PSC | ARI | TAU | GEM | LEO | LIB | SCO | CAP | AQU |
| 18 | TAU | GEM | LEO | VIR | SCO | CAP | AQU | PSC | ARI | GEM | CAN | LEO | LIB | SCO | CAP | AQU |
| 19 | GEM | CAN | VIR | LIB | SAG | CAP | AQU | PSC | TAU | GEM | CAN | VIR | SCO | SAG | AQU | PSC |
| 20 | GEM | CAN | VIR | LIB | SAG | AQU | AQU | ARI | TAU | GEM | LEO | VIR | SCO | SAG | AQU | PSC |
| 21 | GEM | LEO | LIB | SCO | CAP | AQU | PSC | ARI | TAU | CAN | LEO | LIB | SAG | CAP | PSC | ARI |
| 22 | CAN | LEO | LIB | SCO | CAP | AQU | PSC | TAU | GEM | CAN | VIR | LIB | SAG | CAP | PSC | ARI |
| 23 | CAN | VIR | LIB | SAG | CAP | PSC | ARI | TAU | GEM | LEO | VIR | SCO | CAP | AQU | PSC | ARI |
| 24 | LEO | VIR | SCO | SAG | AQU | PSC | ARI | TAU | CAN | LEO | LIB | SCO | CAP | AQU | ARI | TAU |
| 25 | LEO | LIB | SCO | CAP | AQU | ARI | ARI | GEM | CAN | VIR | LIB | SAG | CAP | PSC | ARI | TAU |
| 26 | VIR | LIB | SAG | CAP | PSC | ARI | TAU | GEM | CAN | VIR | LIB | SAG | AQU | PSC | TAU | GEM |
| 27 | VIR | SCO | SAG | CAP | PSC | ARI | TAU | CAN | LEO | LIB | SCO | CAP | AQU | PSC | TAU | GEM |
| 28 | LIB | SCO | CAP | AQU | PSC | TAU | GEM | CAN | LEO | LIB | SCO | CAP | PSC | ARI | TAU | GEM |
| 29 | LIB | SAG | CAP | AQU | ARI | TAU | GEM | LEO | VIR | SCO | SAG | AQU | PSC | ARI | GEM | CAN |
| 30 | SCO | SAG | AQU | PSC | ARI | | GEM | LEO | VIR | SCO | SAG | AQU | ARI | TAU | GEM | CAN |
| 31 | | CAP | | PSC | TAU | | CAN | | LIB | | CAP | AQU | | TAU | | LEO |

## BEST DAYS IN 2020

*The best days listed here are based on both the phase of the Moon and its position in the zodiac. Many people believe that if you do the tasks on the dates listed, you will get the best results possible.*

| | JAN | FEB | MAR | APR | MAY | JUN |
|---|---|---|---|---|---|---|
| **COOKING/BAKING** | | | | | | |
| **Bake** | 1-3, 9, 29, 30 | 5, 6, 25-27 | 3-5, 24, 25, 31 | 1, 6, 27, 28 | 4, 5, 24-26, 31 | 1, 21, 22, 27, 28 |
| **Brew** | 10 | NO GOOD DAYS | 21, 22 | 17-19 | 14-16 | 11, 12 |
| **Can Fruits & Vegetables** | 10, 17, 18 | 13, 14 | 12, 13, 21, 22 | 8, 9, 17-19 | 7, 14-16 | 11, 12 |
| **Dry Fruits & Vegetables** | 11, 12 | NO GOOD DAYS | 14, 15 | 10, 11 | 8, 9 | 5 |
| **Jams/Jellies** | 17, 18 | 13, 14, 20-22 | 12, 13, 18-20 | 8, 9, 15, 16 | 7, 12, 13, 19-21 | 8-10, 16, 17 |
| **HEALTH & BEAUTY** | | | | | | |
| **Cut Hair to Increase Growth** | 4, 5, 9, 26-28, 31 | 1, 2, 5, 6, 23, 24, 28, 29 | 3-5, 26, 27, 31 | 1, 22-24, 27, 28 | 6, 24-26 | 2, 3, 21, 22, 29, 30 |
| **Cut Hair to Slow Growth** | 11, 12, 15, 16, 19, 20 | 11, 12, 15-17, 20-22 | 10, 11, 14, 15, 18-20, 23 | 7, 10, 11, 15, 16, 20, 21 | 8, 9, 12, 13, 17, 18 | 5, 8-10, 13-15, 18-20 |
| **Quit Smoking** | 11-14, 19, 20 | 9, 10, 15-17, 20-22 | 9, 14, 15, 18-20, 23 | 10, 11, 15, 16, 20, 21 | 8, 9, 12, 13, 17, 18 | 5, 8-10, 13-15, 18-20 |
| **Start Diet to Gain Weight** | 9, 26-28 | 5, 6, 23, 24 | 3-5, 31 | 1, 27, 28 | 24-26 | 21, 22 |
| **Start Diet to Lose Weight** | 11-14, 19, 20 | 9, 10, 15-17, 20-22 | 9, 14, 15, 18-20, 23 | 10, 11, 15, 16, 20, 21 | 8, 9, 12, 13, 17, 18 | 5, 8-10, 13-15 |
| **PARENTING** | | | | | | |
| **Potty Train** | 19-28 | 15-24 | 14-22 | 10-19 | 8-16 | 4-12 |
| **Wean Humans or Animals** | 19-28 | 15-24 | 14-22 | 10-19 | 8-16 | 4-12 |
| **HOME MAINTENANCE** | | | | | | |
| **Demolition** | 11, 12, 19, 20 | 15-17 | 14, 15, 23 | 10, 11, 20, 21 | 8, 9, 17, 18 | 5, 13-15 |
| **Paint** | 4, 5, 11, 12, 24, 25, 31 | 1, 2, 7, 8, 20-22, 28, 29 | 6, 7, 18-20, 26, 27 | 2, 3, 15, 16, 22-24, 29, 30 | 1, 12, 13, 19-21, 27, 28 | 8-10, 16, 17, 23, 24 |
| **Wash Windows** | 19, 20 | 15-17 | 14, 15 | 10, 11 | 8, 9 | 4, 5 |
| **Wash Wooden Floors** | 11, 12, 19, 20 | 15-17, 20-22 | 14, 15, 18-20, 23 | 10, 11, 15, 16, 20, 21 | 8, 9, 12, 13, 17, 18 | 5, 8-10, 13-15, 18-20 |
| **Wax Floors** | 4, 5, 9, 26-28, 31 | 1, 2, 5, 6, 23, 24, 28, 29 | 3-5, 8, 26, 27, 31 | 1, 4-6, 22-24, 27, 28 | 2-6, 24-26, 29-31 | 1-3, 21, 22, 25-30 |

## BEST DAYS IN 2020

*The best days listed here are based on both the phase of the Moon and its position in the zodiac. Many people believe that if you do the tasks on the dates listed, you will get the best results possible.*

| JUL | AUG | SEP | OCT | NOV | DEC | |
|---|---|---|---|---|---|---|
| **COOKING/BAKING** | | | | | | |
| 4, 24-26, 31 | 1, 21, 22, 27, 28 | 17, 18, 23-25, 30 | 16, 21, 22, 28, 29 | 17, 18, 24, 25 | 14-16, 21-23 | **BAKE** |
| 8-10, 18, 19 | 4-6, 14-16 | 2, 11, 12 | 8, 9 | 4-6 | 1-3, 29, 30 | **BREW** |
| 8-10, 18, 19 | 4-6, 14-16 | 2, 11, 12 | 8, 9 | 4-6, 13, 14 | 1-3, 10, 11, 29, 30 | **CAN FRUITS & VEGETABLES** |
| 11 | 7, 8 | 3-5 | 1, 2 | 7 | 4, 5, 31 | **DRY FRUITS & VEGETABLES** |
| 6, 7, 13-15 | 3, 9-11 | 6, 7 | 3-5, 31 | 1, 13, 14 | 10, 11 | **JAMS/JELLIES** |
| **HEALTH & BEAUTY** | | | | | | |
| 4, 27, 28, 31 | 1, 23, 24, 27, 28 | 1, 19, 20, 23-25, 28, 29 | 17, 18, 21, 22, 25-27, 30 | 17, 18, 21-23, 26-28 | 14-16, 19, 20, 24, 25 | **CUT HAIR TO INCREASE GROWTH** |
| 6, 7, 11, 12, 16, 17 | 3, 7, 8, 12, 13, 17 | 3-5, 8-10, 13, 14 | 1, 2, 6, 7, 10-12, 15 | 2, 3, 7, 8, 11, 12, 30 | 4, 5, 8, 9, 12, 13, 31 | **CUT HAIR TO SLOW GROWTH** |
| 6, 7, 11, 12, 16, 17 | 3, 7, 8, 12, 13, 17 | 3-5, 8-10, 13-16 | 1, 2, 6, 7, 10-14 | 2, 3, 7-10, 30 | 4-7, 12, 13, 31 | **QUIT SMOKING** |
| NO GOOD DAYS | NO GOOD DAYS | 1, 28, 29 | 25-27 | 21-23 | 19, 20 | **START DIET TO GAIN WEIGHT** |
| 6, 7, 11, 12 | 3, 7, 8, 17 | 3-5, 13-16 | 1, 2, 10-14 | 7-10 | 4-7, 12, 13, 31 | **START DIET TO LOSE WEIGHT** |
| **PARENTING** | | | | | | |
| 1-10, 29-31 | 1-6, 25-31 | 1, 2, 21-29 | 19-27 | 15-23 | 12-20 | **POTTY TRAIN** |
| 1-10, 29-31 | 1-6, 25-31 | 1, 2, 21-29 | 19-27 | 15-23 | 12-20 | **WEAN HUMANS OR ANIMALS** |
| **HOME MAINTENANCE** | | | | | | |
| 11, 12 | 7, 8, 17 | 3-5, 13, 14 | 1, 2, 10-12 | 7, 8 | 4, 5, 12, 13, 31 | **DEMOLITION** |
| 6, 7, 13-15, 20, 21 | 2, 3, 9-11, 17, 18, 29-31 | 6, 7, 13, 14, 26, 27 | 3-5, 10-12, 23, 24, 30, 31 | 1, 7, 8, 19, 20, 26-28 | 4, 5, 17, 18, 24, 25, 31 | **PAINT** |
| 1-3, 29, 30 | 25, 26 | 21, 22 | 19, 20 | 15, 16 | 12, 13 | **WASH WINDOWS** |
| 6, 7, 11, 12, 16, 17 | 3, 7, 8, 12, 13, 17 | 3-5, 8-10, 13, 14 | 1, 2, 6, 7, 10-12 | 2, 3, 7, 8, 30 | 4, 5, 12, 13, 31 | **WASH WOODEN FLOORS** |
| 4, 22-28, 31 | 1, 19-24, 27, 28 | 1, 17-20, 23-25, 28, 29 | 16-18, 21, 22, 25-27, 30 | 17, 18, 21-23, 26-28 | 14-16, 19, 20, 24, 25 | **WAX FLOORS** |

## BEST DAYS IN 2020

*The best days listed here are based on both the phase of the Moon and its position in the zodiac.*
*Many people believe that if you do the tasks on the dates listed, you will get the best results possible.*

| | JAN | FEB | MAR | APR | MAY | JUN |
|---|---|---|---|---|---|---|
| **OUTDOOR CHORES** | | | | | | |
| **CUT FIREWOOD** | 1-9, 24-31 | 1-8, 23-29 | 1-8, 24-31 | 1-6, 22-30 | 1-6, 22-31 | 1-4, 21-30 |
| **DIG HOLES** | 1-9, 24-31 | 1-8, 23-29 | 1-8, 24-31 | 1-6, 22-30 | 1-6, 22-31 | 1-4, 21-30 |
| **DIG POST HOLES** | 11, 12 | 20-22 | 18-20 | 15, 16 | 12, 13, 19-21 | 8-10, 16, 17 |
| **HARVEST** | 19, 20 | 15-17, 20-22 | 18-20, 23 | 15, 16, 20, 21 | 17, 18 | 13-15, 18-20 |
| **KILL PLANT PESTS** | 1-3, 6-8, 11-14, 19, 20, 24, 25, 29, 30 | 3, 4, 7-10, 15-17, 20-22, 25-27 | 1, 2, 6-9, 14, 15, 18-20, 23-25, 28-30 | 2-5, 10, 11, 15, 16, 20, 21, 25, 26, 29, 30 | 1-3, 8, 9, 12, 13, 17, 18, 22, 23, 27-30 | 4, 5, 8-10, 13-15, 18-20, 23-26 |
| **MOW TO INCREASE GROWTH** | 1-9, 24-31 | 1-8, 23-29 | 1-8, 24-31 | 1-6, 22-30 | 1-6, 22-31 | 1-4, 21-30 |
| **MOW TO SLOW GROWTH** | 10-23 | 9-22 | 9-23 | 7-21 | 7-21 | 5-20 |
| **PICK APPLES & PEARS** | 11, 12, 19, 20 | 15-17 | 14, 15, 23 | 10, 11, 20, 21 | 8, 9, 17, 18 | 5, 13-15 |
| **PRUNE TREES** | 17, 18, 21-23 | 13, 14, 18, 19 | 12, 13, 16, 17 | 8, 9, 12-14 | 7, 10, 11 | 6, 7 |
| **FARM/ANIMAL** | | | | | | |
| **CASTRATE FARM ANIMALS** | 19-28 | 15-24 | 14-22 | 10-19 | 8-16 | 4-12 |
| **HUNT** | 10 | 13, 14 | 12, 13 | 8, 9 | 7 | 11, 12 |
| **SLAUGHTER** | 10 | 9-11 | 9-11 | 7-9 | 7-9 | 5-7 |
| **ADVERTISE, TRAVEL, & MORE** | | | | | | |
| **ADVERTISE TO SELL** | 4, 5, 19, 20, 31 | 1, 2, 15-17, 28, 29 | 14, 15, 26, 27 | 10, 11, 22-24 | 8, 9, 19-21 | 4, 5, 16, 17 |
| **ASK FOR A LOAN** | 11, 12 | NO GOOD DAYS | NO GOOD DAYS | NO GOOD DAYS | 19-21 | 16, 17 |
| **BUY A HOME** | 31 | 28, 29 | 26, 27, 31 | 22-24, 27-29 | 24-28 | 21-24 |
| **GET MARRIED** | 4, 5, 9, 26-28, 31 | 1, 2, 5-8, 23, 24, 28, 29 | 3-7, 21, 22, 26, 27, 31 | 1-3, 6, 17-19, 22-24, 27-30 | 1,4,5,14-16, 19-21,24-28,31 | 1, 16, 17, 21-24, 27, 28 |
| **TRAVEL FOR PLEASURE** | 6-8 | 3, 4, 7, 8 | 1, 2, 6, 7, 28-30 | 2, 3, 25, 26, 29, 30 | 1, 22, 23, 27, 28 | 4, 23, 24 |

## BEST DAYS IN 2020

*The best days listed here are based on both the phase of the Moon and its position in the zodiac. Many people believe that if you do the tasks on the dates listed, you will get the best results possible.*

| JUL | AUG | SEP | OCT | NOV | DEC | |
|---|---|---|---|---|---|---|
| **OUTDOOR CHORES** | | | | | | |
| 1-4, 20-31 | 1, 2, 18-31 | 1, 17-30 | 16-30 | 15-29 | 14-28 | **CUT FIREWOOD** |
| 1-4, 20-31 | 1, 2, 18-31 | 1, 17-30 | 16-30 | 15-29 | 14-28 | **DIG HOLES** |
| 6, 7, 13-15 | 3, 9-11, 17 | 6, 7, 13, 14 | 3-5, 10-12, 31 | 1, 7, 8 | 4, 5, 31 | **DIG POST HOLES** |
| 12, 16, 17 | 12, 13, 17 | 10, 13-16 | 10-14 | 8-10 | 7, 12, 13 | **HARVEST** |
| 1-3, 6, 7, 11, 12, 16, 17, 20-23, 29, 30 | 2, 3, 7, 8, 12, 13, 17-20, 25, 26, 29-31 | 3-5, 8-10, 13-16, 21, 22, 26, 27, 30 | 1, 2, 6, 7, 10-14, 19, 20, 23, 24, 28, 29 | 2, 3, 7-10, 15, 16, 19, 20, 24, 25, 29, 30 | 4-7, 12, 13, 17, 18, 21-23, 26-28, 31 | **KILL PLANT PESTS** |
| 1-4, 20-31 | 1, 2, 18-31 | 1, 17-30 | 16-30 | 15-29 | 14-28 | **MOW TO INCREASE GROWTH** |
| 5-19 | 3-17 | 2-16 | 1-15, 31 | 1-14, 30 | 1-13, 29-31 | **MOW TO SLOW GROWTH** |
| 11, 12 | 7, 8, 17 | 3-5, 13, 14 | 1, 2, 10-12 | 7, 8 | 4, 5, 12, 13, 31 | **PICK APPLES & PEARS** |
| 5 | NO GOOD DAYS | NO GOOD DAYS | NO GOOD DAYS | 13, 14 | 10, 11 | **PRUNE TREES** |
| **FARM/ANIMAL** | | | | | | |
| 1-10, 29-31 | 1-6, 25-31 | 1, 2, 21-29 | 19-27 | 15-23 | 12-20 | **CASTRATE FARM ANIMALS** |
| 8-10 | 4-6 | 2 | 8 | 4-6 | 1-3, 29, 30 | **HUNT** |
| 5-7 | 3-5 | 2-4 | 1-3, 31 | 1, 2, 30 | 1, 2, 29, 30 | **SLAUGHTER** |
| **ADVERTISE, TRAVEL, & MORE** | | | | | | |
| 1-3, 13-15, 29, 30 | 9-11, 25, 26 | 6, 7, 21, 22 | 3-5, 19, 20, 30, 31 | 1, 15, 16, 26-28 | 12, 13, 24, 25 | **ADVERTISE TO SELL** |
| 13-15 | 9-11, 17 | 6, 7, 13, 14 | 3-5, 10-12, 31 | 1, 7, 8 | 4, 5, 31 | **ASK FOR A LOAN** |
| 20, 21 | 18 | NO GOOD DAYS | NO GOOD DAYS | NO GOOD DAYS | NO GOOD DAYS | **BUY A HOME** |
| 13-15, 18-21, 24-26 | 11, 14-18, 21, 22 | 1, 11-14, 17, 18, 28, 29 | 9-12, 15, 16, 25-27, 30 | 8, 11, 12, 21-23, 26-28 | 8, 9, 19, 20, 24, 25 | **GET MARRIED** |
| 1-3, 20, 21, 29, 30 | 18, 25, 26 | 21, 22 | 19, 20 | 15, 16, 29 | 26-28 | **TRAVEL FOR PLEASURE** |

## *FARMERS' ALMANAC* 2020 FISHING CALENDAR

### What is the best day to fish?

*Some say that the best day is any day you can cast a line in the water!*

Experience does show that there are certain days and times when fish tend to be more active, making the fishing much better. Our Fishing Calendar is based on the Moon phase, the zodiac sign the Moon is in, and our experience. Local conditions, tides, and weather may affect your fishing success.

| | January Fishing Condition | January Best Time | February Fishing Condition | February Best Time | March Fishing Condition | March Best Time | April Fishing Condition | April Best Time | May Fishing Condition | May Best Time | June Fishing Condition | June Best Time |
|---|---|---|---|---|---|---|---|---|---|---|---|---|
| 1 | P | E | F | M | P | E | B | M | P | M | P | M |
| 2 | P | M | F | M | P | M | P | M | F | M | B | M |
| 3 | P | M | P | M | B | M | P | M | F | M | B | M |
| 4 | F | M | P | M | B | M | G | M | F | M | F | M |
| 5 | F | M | B | M | B | M | G | M | F | M | F | E |
| 6 | P | M | B | M | F | M | F | M | B | M | G | E |
| 7 | F | M | F | M | F | M | F | E | B | E | G | E |
| 8 | F | M | F | M | G | M | B | E | F | E | B | E |
| 9 | B | M | G | E | G | E | B | E | F | E | G | E |
| 10 | B | E | G | E | F | E | F | E | G | E | G | E |
| 11 | F | E | F | E | F | E | P | E | F | E | B | E |
| 12 | F | E | F | E | B | E | F | E | G | E | B | E |
| 13 | G | E | G | E | G | E | F | E | G | E | P | M |
| 14 | F | E | G | E | P | E | F | M | B | M | P | M |
| 15 | P | E | P | M | P | E | G | M | B | M | P | M |
| 16 | P | E | P | M | F | M | G | M | B | M | F | M |
| 17 | G | M | P | M | F | M | B | M | P | M | F | M |
| 18 | G | M | F | M | G | M | B | M | P | M | P | M |
| 19 | P | M | F | M | G | M | B | M | F | M | P | M |
| 20 | P | M | G | M | G | M | P | M | P | M | P | M |
| 21 | F | M | F | M | B | M | P | M | P | M | G | E |
| 22 | P | M | F | M | G | M | P | E | P | E | G | E |
| 23 | P | M | G | E | P | M | P | E | P | E | P | E |
| 24 | F | E | G | E | P | E | P | E | G | E | P | E |
| 25 | F | E | P | E | P | E | P | E | B | E | F | E |
| 26 | G | E | P | E | P | E | P | E | B | E | F | E |
| 27 | B | E | P | E | F | E | B | E | P | E | P | E |
| 28 | B | E | F | E | P | E | B | E | P | E | P | M |
| 29 | P | E | F | E | P | E | P | E | F | M | G | M |
| 30 | P | E | | | P | E | P | M | F | M | G | M |
| 31 | F | E | | | B | E | | | P | M | | |

## FARMERS' ALMANAC 2020 FISHING CALENDAR

**CALENDAR KEY:** *Fishing Condition:* This column lists the overall rating for the entire day, based on our formula. **B=Best** means that you will catch something almost every time you cast your line in the water. **G=Good** means that you will catch enough fish that day to feel gratified. **F=Fair** means that you may catch one or two fish, but you will have to work hard to do so. **P=Poor** means the fish will either steal all your bait or will not even touch your line. *Best Time:* This column lists the best time of the day when fish will be biting: **M=Morning** or **E=Evening**. To view online, visit **FarmersAlmanac.com.**

| | July Fishing Condition | July Best Time | August Fishing Condition | August Best Time | September Fishing Condition | September Best Time | October Fishing Condition | October Best Time | November Fishing Condition | November Best Time | December Fishing Condition | December Best Time |
|---|---|---|---|---|---|---|---|---|---|---|---|---|
| 1 | P | M | G | M | B | M | F | E | G | E | B | E |
| 2 | F | M | B | M | B | E | F | E | F | E | B | E |
| 3 | F | M | B | E | F | E | G | E | F | E | B | E |
| 4 | G | M | B | E | F | E | G | E | B | E | P | E |
| 5 | G | E | B | E | F | E | F | E | B | E | P | E |
| 6 | B | E | B | E | F | E | P | E | B | E | F | E |
| 7 | B | E | P | E | F | E | P | E | P | E | F | M |
| 8 | B | E | P | E | P | E | B | E | P | M | P | M |
| 9 | B | E | F | E | P | E | B | M | F | M | P | M |
| 10 | B | E | F | E | P | M | P | M | F | M | G | M |
| 11 | P | E | F | M | B | M | P | M | P | M | G | M |
| 12 | P | M | P | M | B | M | P | M | P | M | P | M |
| 13 | F | M | P | M | P | M | F | M | F | M | P | M |
| 14 | F | M | B | M | P | M | P | M | F | M | P | E |
| 15 | F | M | B | M | P | M | P | M | P | E | P | E |
| 16 | P | M | G | M | P | M | P | E | P | E | P | E |
| 17 | P | M | P | M | P | E | F | E | P | E | G | E |
| 18 | G | M | P | E | P | E | F | E | F | E | G | E |
| 19 | G | M | P | E | F | E | P | E | G | E | B | E |
| 20 | P | E | P | E | G | E | P | E | G | E | B | E |
| 21 | P | E | P | E | P | E | F | E | B | M | P | M |
| 22 | P | E | P | E | P | E | F | E | B | M | P | M |
| 23 | F | E | G | E | F | M | G | M | B | M | P | M |
| 24 | P | E | G | E | F | M | G | M | P | M | F | M |
| 25 | P | E | P | M | F | M | B | M | P | M | F | M |
| 26 | P | E | P | M | G | M | B | M | F | M | F | M |
| 27 | G | M | F | M | G | M | B | M | G | M | F | M |
| 28 | G | M | F | M | B | M | F | M | G | M | F | M |
| 29 | P | M | G | M | B | M | F | M | F | M | B | E |
| 30 | P | M | B | M | F | M | G | M | F | E | B | E |
| 31 | G | M | B | M | | | G | E | | | F | E |

## EXPLANATION OF THE CALENDAR PAGES

### Times Listed

The astronomical times listed for daily sunrise/sunset, moonrise/moonset, solar noon, length of day, and twilight are based on: northern states 40°N latitude, 75°W longitude (near Philadelphia, PA) and southern states 35°N latitude, 90°W longitude (near Memphis, TN). NOTE: Times listed for the southern states are in Central Time, with adjustments made for Daylight Saving Time.

### Adjustments

The times for the rising and setting of the Sun and Moon are calculated for an observer located exactly on one of the standard meridians (in North America: Eastern–75° West; Central–90° West; Mountain–105° West; Pacific–120° West). If your longitude is very close to one of these, then luck is with you, and you can use the printed times for the rising and setting of the Sun and Moon without any correction.

If your longitude is different from one of these standard meridians, you need to add four minutes to the times listed on the Calendar Page for each degree of longitude that you are west of your time zone meridian. Or subtract four minutes for each degree you are east of it. For example, Boston, Massachusetts (longitude 71°) is 4 degrees east of the Eastern Time meridian. So, for Boston, subtract 16 minutes from the times obtained from the Calendar Pages. The result is in Eastern Standard Time or Eastern Daylight Time, depending on the time of year.

The above calculations will yield approximate local times for the rising and setting of the Sun and Moon, but will ignore the less important difference between your latitude and those of the Calendar Pages (35° and 40° North), as well as the character of your local horizon.

### Earliest Moonrise/Moonset

Times listed in this column of the Calendar Pages are based on the earliest visible moonset or moonrise of the day. Moonrise and moonset are when the upper limb appears or disappears above/below the horizon. The arrow up means the Moon is rising, and the arrow down means it's setting. There are dates when neither moonrise nor moonset occurs during darkness. These dates are identified with the word "None" on the Calendar Pages.

## EXPLANATION OF THE CALENDAR PAGES

### Moon's Place

This column shows the astronomical position of the Moon at 7:00 am EST/DST. As the Moon travels in the night sky, in addition to the 12 well-known zodiac constellations, it will also enter 5 other constellations: Auriga (AUR), located to the north of Taurus; Cetus (CET), a large constellation bordering the southern part of Pisces; Ophiuchus (OPH), a large complex constellation whose lower portion reaches into the zodiac immediately adjacent to Scorpius and Sagittarius; Orion (ORI), a constellation that straddles the celestial equator and whose northern extremities border Gemini and Taurus; and Sextants (SXT), a faint and unimpressive star pattern whose northwest corner comes very close to the ecliptic in Leo.

### Rise, Set, and Culmination Times for Stars and Planets

As with the rising and setting times of the Sun and Moon, use the correction table to convert zone time to local time in order to obtain a greater degree of accuracy. This rule also pertains to the culmination or meridian passage ("mer.") time of a given object for the Moon's southing or meridian passage.

### Twilight and Length of Days

Across the calendars, and even with the Sunday Liturgical Calendar, you will find the average length of day and length of astronomical twilight beginning Sunday. These calendars are calculated for 35 and 40 degrees North latitude, based on the Sun being 8.5 degrees below the horizon, which roughly corresponds to the ambient light from a full Moon on a cloudless night.

*The "Calendar Pages" are across from our monthly weather predictions (starting on page 144). On these pages, you will find many important celestial events, dates, and times.*

# A Look Back at WINTER 2018-19

### LAST YEAR IN REVIEW:
How accurate were our forecasts?

Our prediction of "teeth-chattering cold" for winter 2018-19 brought about a lot of attention and controversy. In our long-range outlook, which we released in August 2018, we called for "unusually snowy and/or wet conditions across the Pacific Northwest, Northeast, and Mid-Atlantic States." We also predicted the coldest temperatures would arrive in February and warned of a stormier-than-normal March, which would push snow totals to above normal for the northern/central Rockies and Plains.

***So what happened?*** Here are some season highlights:

- Late January's Arctic blast resulted in Chicago having subzero temperatures for 52 straight hours. No all-time records were broken in the Windy City, but the low temperature of -23°F was close to breaking the all-time record of -27°F. On January 29th, Chicago's wind chill dipped to -52°F!

- On January 31st, the all-time coldest record for Illinois was reported in Mt. Carroll at -38°F.

- February kicked off on a frigid note from Minnesota and Wisconsin east through the Great Lakes into upstate New York and across to New England.

High temperatures were as much as 30° colder than normal, and low temperatures were subzero or in the single digits for most areas. Strong winds created dangerously low wind chills, causing some schools to close.

- For the first time on record, Los Angeles went an entire February without once hitting 70°F. And the City of Angels registered this past February as its coldest month since 1962, with temperatures averaging about 5 degrees colder than normal.

- And the month of February across the contiguous U.S. averaged nearly 2° below normal, ranking it in the coldest top third in 125 years of record keeping.

### Snowfall?

- Caribou, Maine had its snowiest January ever, with 59.8 inches, and 165 inches total for the winter months!

• Record snowfall and cold temperatures were reported from Washington State to Wisconsin in February. Eau Claire, Wisconsin, set a record for all-time snowiest month with 53.7 inches.

• Sea-Tac Airport (Seattle) saw its snowiest February (20.2 inches) since record-keeping first began in 1945.

• On February 20th, the first measurable snowfall (½ inch) in more than a decade fell in Las Vegas, Nevada. And the very next day, a total of 35.9 inches of snow was measured at Pulliam Airport (just south of Flagstaff, Arizona)—a new 1-day record.

• Omaha, Nebraska, saw its all-time snowiest winter with 46.1 inches.

### Statistically Speaking

*Sounds like a pretty accurate forecast, doesn't it?* You may be surprised to learn that climatologists have indicated that winter 2018-19 turned out to be slightly warmer (1.2°) than normal, statistically speaking.

*The reason?* Taking into account the 90-day interval from December 1st to February 28th (defined as "meteorological winter"), the mean temperature was 33.4°F, or 1.2° above average. Yet, the last week of January through February, and into early March, temperatures averaged more than 2° below normal nationwide. But overall, January was 2.6° above normal, and December was 2.9° above normal.

However, we would contend that the overall 1.2° above-normal winter temperature was of little solace to the folks in the southeast U.S. who were digging out of their big pre-Christmas snowfall, or the folks around the Great Lakes and Plains who were enduring hours of sub-zero temperatures and life-threatening wind chills in late January!

### Wettest Winter on Record

Last winter's precipitation total was 9.01–2.22 inches above average, which was the wettest on record. Out of the 48 contiguous states, 43 had a wetter-than-normal winter; Tennessee had its all-time wettest winter dating back to 1895 (which only reinforces our prediction where we called for a wet winter in many places).

So all in all, our accuracy speaks for itself, but we do remind everyone that our predictions are long-range and are meant to give you a good idea of what should come your way in the next year or so. But we also bow to Mother Nature, who loves to throw us a curveball or two. However, we always stand by our predictions, just as we have for over two centuries.

*Be sure to turn to page 65 for our upcoming winter outlook.*

# HOW DOES THE FARMERS' ALMANAC PREDICT THE WEATHER?

Each and every year since 1818, the *Farmers' Almanac* has been offering long-range weather predictions that are known to be amazingly accurate. In this day and age in which weather is found at a click of a button, the *Farmers' Almanac* continues to offer over a year's worth of weather forecasts in one printed book.

People find the *Almanac's* long-range forecast especially useful when planning their days ahead, particularly when preparing for vacations, special events, weddings, heating bills, and more. Many businesses consult the *Farmers' Almanac's* outlook for their planning as well. And what's really amazing is that these weather predictions are quite accurate.

**So how does the *Farmers' Almanac* do it?**

The editors of the *Farmers' Almanac* firmly deny using any type of computer satellite tracking equipment, weather lore, or groundhogs. What they will admit to is using a specific and reliable set of rules that were developed back in 1818 by David Young, the *Almanac's* first editor. These rules have been altered slightly and turned into a formula that is both mathematical and astronomical. The formula takes things like sunspot activity, position of the planets, tidal action of the Moon, and a variety of other factors into consideration.

The only person who knows the exact formula is the *Farmers' Almanac* weather prognosticator, who goes by the pseudonym "Caleb Weatherbee." To protect this reliable formula and proprietary, the *Almanac* editors prefer to keep both Caleb's true identity and the formula a closely guarded brand secret.

While some may ask how a 200-year-old publication can still make such accurate weather forecasts, the *Farmers' Almanac* editors like to remind everyone that this formula has been time-tested, challenged, and approved for nearly two centuries. The *Farmers' Almanac* is the oldest source of consecutively published weather forecasts, longer than the National Weather Service.

Unlike your local news, government, or commercial weather service, the *Almanac's* forecasts are calculated in advance. Once the latest edition of the *Farmers' Almanac* is printed, the editors never go back to change or update its forecasts the way other local sources do.

Though weather forecasting, and long-range forecasting in particular, remains an inexact science, longtime *Almanac* followers claim that our forecasts are 80%–85% accurate. Check out the "On the Money" page at **FarmersAlmanac.com/on-the-money** to see some of the past weather events the *Farmers' Almanac* has accurately called for.

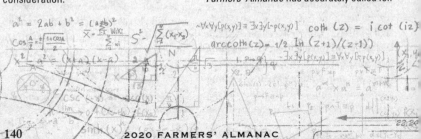

# STOP FOOT & LEG PAIN FAST!

**S**mooth Gator's Foot and Leg Rub is a topical cream made with all natural ingredients like CAMPHOR, ROSEMARY and PEPPERMINT.

This safe, non-greasy formula relieves pain associated with neuropathy, nerve conditions and/or poor circulation in your foot and legs below the knee.

With all natural oils, relieve night-time sensations of numbness, tingling, and burning!

Perfect for increased circulation for your feet and lower legs, to soothe hot/cold and burning sensations, and to desensitize nerve endings.

It's easy! Just apply liberally to feet and lower legs before bedtime, or before and after any long periods of standing. Don't rub in, just rub on, and it will absorb on its own. Experience the dramatic results!

Call Smooth Gator today at **727-278-3137** for your pain relief needs or visit **smoothgator.com**

**FREE NATURAL LIP BALM WITH EVERY ORDER!**

Smooth Gator | 727-278-3137 | smoothgator.com

$**44**⁹⁵
per bottle

141

# 2020

## JANUARY
| S | M | T | W | T | F | S |
|---|---|---|---|---|---|---|
|   |   |   | 1 | 2 | 3 | 4 |
| 5 | 6 | 7 | 8 | 9 | 10 | 11 |
| 12 | 13 | 14 | 15 | 16 | 17 | 18 |
| 19 | 20 | 21 | 22 | 23 | 24 | 25 |
| 26 | 27 | 28 | 29 | 30 | 31 |   |

## FEBRUARY
| S | M | T | W | T | F | S |
|---|---|---|---|---|---|---|
|   |   |   |   |   |   | 1 |
| 2 | 3 | 4 | 5 | 6 | 7 | 8 |
| 9 | 10 | 11 | 12 | 13 | 14 | 15 |
| 16 | 17 | 18 | 19 | 20 | 21 | 22 |
| 23 | 24 | 25 | 26 | 27 | 28 | 29 |

## MARCH
| S | M | T | W | T | F | S |
|---|---|---|---|---|---|---|
| 1 | 2 | 3 | 4 | 5 | 6 | 7 |
| 8 | 9 | 10 | 11 | 12 | 13 | 14 |
| 15 | 16 | 17 | 18 | 19 | 20 | 21 |
| 22 | 23 | 24 | 25 | 26 | 27 | 28 |
| 29 | 30 | 31 |   |   |   |   |

## APRIL
| S | M | T | W | T | F | S |
|---|---|---|---|---|---|---|
|   |   |   | 1 | 2 | 3 | 4 |
| 5 | 6 | 7 | 8 | 9 | 10 | 11 |
| 12 | 13 | 14 | 15 | 16 | 17 | 18 |
| 19 | 20 | 21 | 22 | 23 | 24 | 25 |
| 26 | 27 | 28 | 29 | 30 |   |   |

## MAY
| S | M | T | W | T | F | S |
|---|---|---|---|---|---|---|
|   |   |   |   |   | 1 | 2 |
| 3 | 4 | 5 | 6 | 7 | 8 | 9 |
| 10 | 11 | 12 | 13 | 14 | 15 | 16 |
| 17 | 18 | 19 | 20 | 21 | 22 | 23 |
| 24 | 25 | 26 | 27 | 28 | 29 | 30 |
| 31 |   |   |   |   |   |   |

## JUNE
| S | M | T | W | T | F | S |
|---|---|---|---|---|---|---|
|   | 1 | 2 | 3 | 4 | 5 | 6 |
| 7 | 8 | 9 | 10 | 11 | 12 | 13 |
| 14 | 15 | 16 | 17 | 18 | 19 | 20 |
| 21 | 22 | 23 | 24 | 25 | 26 | 27 |
| 28 | 29 | 30 |   |   |   |   |

## JULY
| S | M | T | W | T | F | S |
|---|---|---|---|---|---|---|
|   |   |   | 1 | 2 | 3 | 4 |
| 5 | 6 | 7 | 8 | 9 | 10 | 11 |
| 12 | 13 | 14 | 15 | 16 | 17 | 18 |
| 19 | 20 | 21 | 22 | 23 | 24 | 25 |
| 26 | 27 | 28 | 29 | 30 | 31 |   |

## AUGUST
| S | M | T | W | T | F | S |
|---|---|---|---|---|---|---|
|   |   |   |   |   |   | 1 |
| 2 | 3 | 4 | 5 | 6 | 7 | 8 |
| 9 | 10 | 11 | 12 | 13 | 14 | 15 |
| 16 | 17 | 18 | 19 | 20 | 21 | 22 |
| 23 | 24 | 25 | 26 | 27 | 28 | 29 |
| 30 | 31 |   |   |   |   |   |

## SEPTEMBER
| S | M | T | W | T | F | S |
|---|---|---|---|---|---|---|
|   |   | 1 | 2 | 3 | 4 | 5 |
| 6 | 7 | 8 | 9 | 10 | 11 | 12 |
| 13 | 14 | 15 | 16 | 17 | 18 | 19 |
| 20 | 21 | 22 | 23 | 24 | 25 | 26 |
| 27 | 28 | 29 | 30 |   |   |   |

## OCTOBER
| S | M | T | W | T | F | S |
|---|---|---|---|---|---|---|
|   |   |   |   | 1 | 2 | 3 |
| 4 | 5 | 6 | 7 | 8 | 9 | 10 |
| 11 | 12 | 13 | 14 | 15 | 16 | 17 |
| 18 | 19 | 20 | 21 | 22 | 23 | 24 |
| 25 | 26 | 27 | 28 | 29 | 30 | 31 |

## NOVEMBER
| S | M | T | W | T | F | S |
|---|---|---|---|---|---|---|
| 1 | 2 | 3 | 4 | 5 | 6 | 7 |
| 8 | 9 | 10 | 11 | 12 | 13 | 14 |
| 15 | 16 | 17 | 18 | 19 | 20 | 21 |
| 22 | 23 | 24 | 25 | 26 | 27 | 28 |
| 29 | 30 |   |   |   |   |   |

## DECEMBER
| S | M | T | W | T | F | S |
|---|---|---|---|---|---|---|
|   |   | 1 | 2 | 3 | 4 | 5 |
| 6 | 7 | 8 | 9 | 10 | 11 | 12 |
| 13 | 14 | 15 | 16 | 17 | 18 | 19 |
| 20 | 21 | 22 | 23 | 24 | 25 | 26 |
| 27 | 28 | 29 | 30 | 31 |   |   |

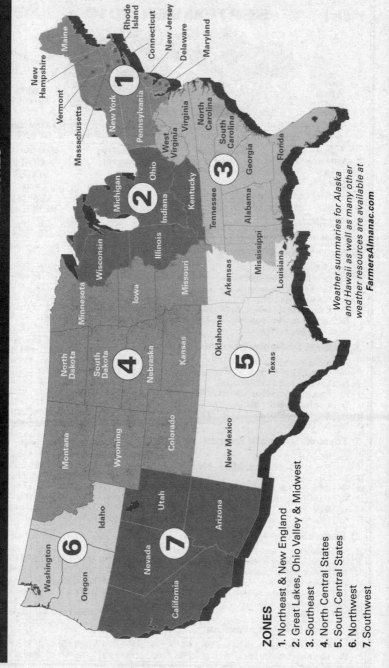

## FARMERS' ALMANAC UNITED STATES WEATHER ZONES

*Weather summaries for Alaska and Hawaii as well as many other weather resources are available at* **FarmersAlmanac.com**

### ZONES

1. Northeast & New England
2. Great Lakes, Ohio Valley & Midwest
3. Southeast
4. North Central States
5. South Central States
6. Northwest
7. Southwest

# SEPTEMBER 2019

9th Month — 30 Days

**VIRGO**
August 23 to September 22

**LIBRA**
September 23 to October 22

NOW AUTUMN'S GOLDEN STORES BEHOLD, WITH FRUIT EACH TREE IS CROWNED;
PEACHES IN SUITS OF RED OR GOLD, EACH TWIG BOWS TOWARD THE GROUND.

**MOON'S PHASES — EASTERN DAYLIGHT TIME**

|  |  |  |
|---|---|---|
| ☽ First Quarter | 5th | 11:10 pm |
| ○ Full Moon | 14th | 12:33 am |
| ☾ Last Quarter | 21st | 10:41 pm |
| ● New Moon | 28th | 2:26 pm |

Subtract 1 hour for CDT, 2 hours for MDT, and 3 hours for PDT.

**SUN ON MERIDIAN CIVIL TIME**

| Day | H:MM:SS |
|---|---|
| 1st | 13:00:31 |
| 8th | 12:58:11 |
| 15th | 12:55:43 |
| 22nd | 12:53:13 |
| 29th | 12:50:49 |

CALENDAR FOR **NORTHERN STATES** (EDT) — 40°N. Lat. 75°W. Long.

CALENDAR FOR **SOUTHERN STATES** (CDT) — 35°N. Lat. 90°W. Long.

| DATE | ASTRONOMY, HOLIDAYS, AND EVENTS | MOON'S PLACE AT 7am ASTRONOMICALLY | SUN RISES | SUN SETS | EARLIEST MOONRISE MOONSET | MOON'S MERIDIAN PASSAGE | SUN RISES | SUN SETS | EARLIEST MOONRISE MOONSET | MOON'S MERIDIAN PASSAGE |
|---|---|---|---|---|---|---|---|---|---|---|
| **35. Twelfth Sunday after Pentecost** | | | Day's Length: 13h 05m · Astron. Twilight: 1h 22m | | | | Day's Length: 12h 35m · Astron. Twilight: 1h 17m | | | |
| 1 Su | Lily Tomlin born, 1939 | VIR | 6:27 | 7:32 | 9:18p̄ | 3:12p | 6:32 | 7:27 | 9:21p̄ | 3:14p |
| 2 Mo | **Labor Day**; Mars in conjunction | VIR | 6:28 | 7:30 | 9:51p̄ | 4:04p | 6:33 | 7:26 | 9:56p̄ | 4:06p |
| 3 Tu | Mercury in superior conjunction | LIB | 6:29 | 7:29 | 10:24p̄ | 4:56p | 6:34 | 7:24 | 10:33p̄ | 4:58p |
| 4 We | Paul Harvey born, 1918 | LIB | 6:30 | 7:27 | 11:00p̄ | 5:48p | 6:35 | 7:23 | 11:12p̄ | 5:50p |
| 5 Th | Moon, Jupiter best visible in the SW 9:33pm | SCO | 6:31 | 7:26 | 11:40p̄ | 6:40p | 6:35 | 7:22 | 11:54p̄ | 6:42p |
| 6 Fr | Carnation processed evaporated milk, 1899 | OPH | 6:32 | 7:24 | None | 7:32p | 6:36 | 7:20 | None | 7:34p |
| 7 Sa | 1st Miss America Pageant, 1921 | SAG | 6:33 | 7:22 | 12:24ã | 8:24p | 6:37 | 7:19 | 12:39ã | 8:26p |
| **36. Thirteenth Sunday after Pentecost** | | | Day's Length: 12h 47m · Astron. Twilight: 1h 21m | | | | Day's Length: 12h 40m · Astron. Twilight: 1h 16m | | | |
| 8 Su | Jupiter in eastern quadrature | SAG | 6:34 | 7:21 | 1:12ã | 9:15p | 6:37 | 7:17 | 1:29ã | 9:17p |
| 9 Mo | Otis Redding born, 1941 | SAG | 6:35 | 7:19 | 2:05ã | 10:05p | 6:38 | 7:16 | 2:21ã | 10:07p |
| 10 Tu | Traditional peak of hurricane season | CAP | 6:36 | 7:18 | 3:00ã | 10:52p | 6:39 | 7:15 | 3:15ã | 10:54p |
| 11 We | Agatha Christie wed Max Mallowan, 1930 | CAP | 6:37 | 7:16 | 3:57ã | 11:38p | 6:40 | 7:13 | 4:11ã | 11:40p |
| 12 Th | 1st practical typewriter sold, 1873 | AQU | 6:38 | 7:14 | 4:55ã | None | 6:40 | 7:12 | 5:07ã | None |
| 13 Fr | Moon at apogee 9:15am | AQU | 6:39 | 7:13 | 5:53ã | 12:22ã | 6:41 | 7:10 | 6:02ã | 12:23ã |
| 14 Sa | Holy Cross Day | AQU | 6:40 | 7:11 | 7:50p̄ | 1:04ã | 6:42 | 7:09 | 7:49p̄ | 1:06ã |
| **37. Fourteenth Sunday after Pentecost** | | | Day's Length: 12h 29m · Astron. Twilight: 1h 20m | | | | Day's Length: 12h 25m · Astron. Twilight: 1h 15m | | | |
| 15 Su | William H. Taft born, 1857 | CET | 6:40 | 7:09 | 8:15p̄ | 1:45ã | 6:43 | 7:07 | 8:16p̄ | 1:47ã |
| 16 Mo | Shawmut changed its name to Boston, 1630 | CET | 6:41 | 7:08 | 8:41p̄ | 2:27ã | 6:43 | 7:06 | 8:45p̄ | 2:28ã |
| 17 Tu | Citizenship Day | PSC | 6:42 | 7:06 | 9:07p̄ | 3:08ã | 6:44 | 7:04 | 9:14p̄ | 3:10ã |
| 18 We | Ember Day; Saturn direct | ARI | 6:43 | 7:04 | 9:37p̄ | 3:52ã | 6:45 | 7:03 | 9:46p̄ | 3:53ã |
| 19 Th | 1st underground nuclear test, 1957 | TAU | 6:44 | 7:03 | 10:10p̄ | 4:37ã | 6:45 | 7:02 | 10:22p̄ | 4:39ã |
| 20 Fr | Ember Day | TAU | 6:45 | 7:01 | 10:49p̄ | 5:25ã | 6:46 | 7:00 | 11:03p̄ | 5:27ã |
| 21 Sa | Ember Day; *The Hobbit* published, 1937 | TAU | 6:46 | 6:59 | 11:35p̄ | 6:16ã | 6:47 | 6:59 | 11:51p̄ | 6:19ã |
| **38. Fifteenth Sunday after Pentecost** | | | Day's Length: 12h 11m · Astron. Twilight: 1h 20m | | | | Day's Length: 12h 10m · Astron. Twilight: 1h 15m | | | |
| 22 Su | Michael Faraday born, 1791 | GEM | 6:47 | 6:58 | None | 7:11ã | 6:48 | 6:57 | None | 7:13ã |
| 23 Mo | Autumnal equinox (1st day of fall) 3:50am | GEM | 6:48 | 6:56 | 12:29ã | 8:08ã | 6:48 | 6:56 | 12:46ã | 8:11ã |
| 24 Tu | US Supreme Court established, 1789 | CAN | 6:49 | 6:54 | 1:32ã | 9:07ã | 6:49 | 6:54 | 1:48ã | 9:10ã |
| 25 We | William Faulkner born, 1897 | CAN | 6:50 | 6:53 | 2:41ã | 10:06ã | 6:50 | 6:53 | 2:56ã | 10:09ã |
| 26 Th | Federal Trade Commission est., 1914 | LEO | 6:51 | 6:51 | 3:55ã | 11:04ã | 6:51 | 6:52 | 4:07ã | 11:06ã |
| 27 Fr | Moon at perigee 10:17pm | LEO | 6:52 | 6:49 | 5:11ã | 12:00p | 6:51 | 6:50 | 5:20ã | 12:03p |
| 28 Sa | Ed Sullivan born, 1902 | VIR | 6:53 | 6:48 | 6:27ã | 12:55p | 6:52 | 6:49 | 6:33ã | 12:57p |
| **39. Sixteenth Sunday after Pentecost** | | | Day's Length: 11h 52m · Astron. Twilight: 1h 20m | | | | Day's Length: 11h 52m · Astron. Twilight: 1h 14m | | | |
| 29 Su | Gold Star Mother's Day; Michaelmas Day | VIR | 6:54 | 6:46 | 7:45p̄ | 1:49p | 6:53 | 6:47 | 7:50p̄ | 1:51p |
| 30 Mo | Rosh Hashanah (New Year 5780) | VIR | 6:55 | 6:45 | 8:19p̄ | 2:42p | 6:54 | 6:46 | 8:27p̄ | 2:45p |

## SEPTEMBER 2019 WEATHER FORECAST

### ZONE 1 Northeast & New England

**1–3:** Unseasonable chill; fair for Labor Day. **4–7:** Clearing; more chilly air shifts into region after rain. **8–11:** Continued chill, dry. **12–15:** Lots of clouds. **16–19:** Showers continue. **20–23:** Scattered showers. **24–27:** Variably cloudy, widely scattered showers. **28–30:** Cloudy.

### ZONE 2 Great Lakes, Ohio Valley & Midwest

**1–3:** Unseasonably chilly temperatures Labor Day holiday. **4–7:** Showers initially, then clearing, with unseasonable chill east from Great Lakes. **8–11:** A strong chill across Great Lakes, then south. Heavy showers sweep east out of Ohio River Valley. **12–15:** Showers, thunderstorms Great Lakes to Kentucky, then quickly cooling. **16–19:** Showery. **20–23:** Light showers. **24–27:** Light rain and showers widely scattered. Cool, then moderating. **28–30:** Developing storm system brings rain to the Great Lakes/Ohio Valley, then early frost.

### ZONE 3 Southeast

**1–3:** Rain, Florida to Gulf of Mexico. **4–7:** Rains end; oppressively hot/humid. **8–11:** Clouds and haze; a few pop-up showers. **12–15:** Cloudy with hurricane threat Carolinas. **16–19:** Clouds linger; scattered showers. **20–23:** Heavy tropical rains Mississippi; hot, oppressively humid Mississippi, Alabama, Georgia, Florida. **24–27:** Heavy rains. **28–30:** Showers diminish.

### ZONE 4 North Central States

**1–3:** Thunderstorms, some heavy, over Rockies, then into Great Plains. **4–7:** Dry, chillier. **8–11:** Unseasonably chilly air sweeps across northern Plains to south. Showery lee slopes of Rockies. **12–15:** Showers slowly diminish, from west to east. **16–19:** Autumnal chill over most of Rockies, Plains. Showers Minnesota, Iowa, Missouri. **20–23:** Light showers northern Great Plains. **24–27:** Widely scattered light rain. **28–30:** Showers, then cold air from Rockies. Developing storm system brings rain to Great Plains east, then early frost/freeze.

### ZONE 5 South Central States

**1–3:** Showers and thunderstorms, some heavy. **4–7:** Showers subside; warm and humid. **8–11:** Showers lee slopes of Rockies, and southern Plains. **12–15:** Texas, Oklahoma, Arkansas, northern Louisiana: thunderstorms and showers, then cooler. Clear/colder New Mexico. **16–19:** Clear to partly cloudy; warm Louisiana. Crisp, chilly over southern Rockies and Plains. Arkansas showers move east. **20–23:** Tropical rains for Louisiana; hot/humid Texas, all points east. **24–27:** Tropical rains, showers continue Deep South. **28–30:** Showers, then cooler/drier air from the north.

### ZONE 6 Northwest

**1–3:** Fair, then turning unsettled. **4–7:** Pleasant. **8–11:** Unsettled conditions return. **12–15:** Generally fair, but chilly. **16–19:** Unsettled. **20–23:** Fair, then very unsettled. **24–27:** Widely scattered light showers, chilly winds. **28–30:** Showers, rain precede a shot of colder air.

### ZONE 7 Southwest

**1–3:** Thunderstorms, some heavy, for Rockies and the southwest states. **4–7:** Threatening skies. **8–11:** Unsettled; windy. **12–15:** Fair. **16–19:** Clear to partly cloudy skies; warm. **20–23:** Southwest hot and dry. **24–27:** Gusty winds, cool. **28–30:** Milder, then turning wet.

# OCTOBER 2019

10th Month · 31 Days

**LIBRA**
September 23 to
October 22

**SCORPIO**
October 23 to
November 21

AND NOW THE FROST IS SEEN IN MORN, OVERSPREADING FIELDS WITH WHITE;
THE FARMER GATHERS IN HIS CORN, WITH PLEASURE AND DELIGHT.

### MOON'S PHASES
**EASTERN DAYLIGHT TIME**

|  |  |  |
|---|---|---|
| ☽ First Quarter | 5th | 12:47 pm |
| ○ Full Moon | 13th | 5:08 pm |
| ☾ Last Quarter | 21st | 8:39 am |
| ● New Moon | 27th | 11:38 pm |

Subtract 1 hour for CDT, 2 hours for MDT, and 3 hours for PDT.

### SUN ON MERIDIAN
**CIVIL TIME**

| Day | H:MM:SS |
|---|---|
| 1st | 12:50:10 |
| 8th | 12:48:03 |
| 15th | 12:46:16 |
| 22nd | 12:44:57 |
| 29th | 12:44:12 |

| DATE | | ASTRONOMY, HOLIDAYS, AND EVENTS | MOON'S PLACE AT 7am ASTRONOMICALLY | NORTHERN STATES (EDT) 40°N. Lat. 75°W. Long. SUN RISES | SUN SETS | EARLIEST MOONRISE MOONSET | MOON'S MERIDIAN PASSAGE | SOUTHERN STATES (CDT) 35°N. Lat. 90°W. Long. SUN RISES | SUN SETS | EARLIEST MOONRISE MOONSET | MOON'S MERIDIAN PASSAGE |
|---|---|---|---|---|---|---|---|---|---|---|---|
| 1 | Tu | 1st "Model T" Ford built, 1908 | LIB | 6:56 | 6:43 | 8:55p̄ | 3:36p | 6:54 | 6:44 | 9:06p̄ | 3:38p |
| 2 | We | Fast of Gedaliah | LIB | 6:57 | 6:41 | 9:34p̄ | 4:30p | 6:55 | 6:43 | 9:47p̄ | 4:32p |
| 3 | Th | Moon, Jupiter best visible in the SW 8:21pm | OPH | 6:58 | 6:40 | 10:17p̄ | 5:24p | 6:56 | 6:42 | 10:33p̄ | 5:26p |
| 4 | Fr | 1st carving began on Mt. Rushmore, 1927 | SAG | 6:59 | 6:38 | 11:05p̄ | 6:17p | 6:57 | 6:40 | 11:22p̄ | 6:20p |
| 5 | Sa | Fall Astronomy Day; Moon/Saturn best visible | SAG | 7:00 | 6:36 | 11:57p̄ | 7:10p | 6:57 | 6:39 | None | 7:12p |

Day's Length: 11h 34m · Astron. Twilight: 1h 20m
Day's Length: 11h 39m · Astron. Twilight: 1h 15m

### 40. Seventeenth Sunday after Pentecost

| DATE | | ASTRONOMY, HOLIDAYS, AND EVENTS | | SUN RISES | SUN SETS | MOONRISE/SET | MERIDIAN | SUN RISES | SUN SETS | MOONRISE/SET | MERIDIAN |
|---|---|---|---|---|---|---|---|---|---|---|---|
| 6 | Su | George Westinghouse born, 1846 | SAG | 7:01 | 6:35 | None | 8:01p | 6:58 | 6:37 | 12:14ã | 8:03p |
| 7 | Mo | Saturn in eastern quadrature | CAP | 7:02 | 6:33 | 12:53ã | 8:49p | 6:59 | 6:36 | 1:09ã | 8:51p |
| 8 | Tu | R.L. Stine born, 1943 | CAP | 7:03 | 6:32 | 1:50ã | 9:36p | 7:00 | 6:35 | 2:05ã | 9:37p |
| 9 | We | Yom Kippur; Fire Prevention Day | AQU | 7:04 | 6:30 | 2:48ã | 10:20p | 7:01 | 6:33 | 3:01ã | 10:22p |
| 10 | Th | Moon at apogee 2:18pm | AQU | 7:05 | 6:29 | 3:46ã | 11:03p | 7:01 | 6:32 | 3:56ã | 11:04p |
| 11 | Fr | Eleanor Roosevelt born, 1884 | AQU | 7:06 | 6:27 | 4:44ã | 11:44p | 7:02 | 6:31 | 4:51ã | 11:46p |
| 12 | Sa | Columbus Day (traditional) | PSC | 7:07 | 6:26 | 5:42ã | None | 7:03 | 6:29 | 5:46ã | None |

Day's Length: 11h 16m · Astron. Twilight: 1h 20m
Day's Length: 11h 24m · Astron. Twilight: 1h 15m

### 41. Eighteenth Sunday after Pentecost

| DATE | | ASTRONOMY, HOLIDAYS, AND EVENTS | | SUN RISES | SUN SETS | MOONRISE/SET | MERIDIAN | SUN RISES | SUN SETS | MOONRISE/SET | MERIDIAN |
|---|---|---|---|---|---|---|---|---|---|---|---|
| 13 | Su | Messier discovered whirlpool galaxy, 1773 | CET | 7:08 | 6:24 | 6:40ã | 12:25a | 7:04 | 6:28 | 6:42ã | 12:27a |
| 14 | Mo | **Columbus Day**; Succot | PSC | 7:09 | 6:22 | 7:41ã | 1:07a | 7:05 | 6:27 | 7:17p̄ | 1:09a |
| 15 | Tu | Emeril Lagasse, American chef, born, 1959 | CET | 7:10 | 6:21 | 7:39p̄ | 1:50a | 7:06 | 6:26 | 7:48p̄ | 1:52a |
| 16 | We | Noah Webster born, 1758 | ARI | 7:11 | 6:20 | 8:11p̄ | 2:35a | 7:06 | 6:24 | 8:23p̄ | 2:37a |
| 17 | Th | Albert Einstein moved to Princeton, NJ, 1933 | TAU | 7:12 | 6:18 | 8:48p̄ | 3:23a | 7:07 | 6:23 | 9:02p̄ | 3:25a |
| 18 | Fr | U.S. govt. banned artificial sweeteners, 1969 | TAU | 7:13 | 6:17 | 9:31p̄ | 4:13a | 7:08 | 6:22 | 9:47p̄ | 4:15a |
| 19 | Sa | Basketball introduced to Olympics, 1933 | ORI | 7:14 | 6:15 | 10:22p̄ | 5:06a | 7:09 | 6:21 | 10:39p̄ | 5:08a |

Day's Length: 10h 58m · Astron. Twilight: 1h 21m
Day's Length: 11h 10m · Astron. Twilight: 1h 15m

### 42. Nineteenth Sunday after Pentecost

| DATE | | ASTRONOMY, HOLIDAYS, AND EVENTS | | SUN RISES | SUN SETS | MOONRISE/SET | MERIDIAN | SUN RISES | SUN SETS | MOONRISE/SET | MERIDIAN |
|---|---|---|---|---|---|---|---|---|---|---|---|
| 20 | Su | Mickey Mantle, baseball great, born, 1931 | GEM | 7:15 | 6:14 | 11:20p̄ | 6:01a | 7:10 | 6:19 | 11:37p̄ | 6:04a |
| 21 | Mo | Daniel Boone born, 1734 | GEM | 7:16 | 6:12 | None | 6:58a | 7:11 | 6:18 | None | 7:01a |
| 22 | Tu | Simchat Torah | CAN | 7:17 | 6:11 | 12:25ã | 7:55a | 7:12 | 6:17 | 12:41ã | 7:58a |
| 23 | We | 1st U.S. horseshoe champ. tourney, 1915 | LEO | 7:19 | 6:10 | 1:35ã | 8:51a | 7:12 | 6:16 | 1:48ã | 8:54a |
| 24 | Th | United Nations Day | LEO | 7:20 | 6:08 | 2:48ã | 9:46a | 7:13 | 6:15 | 2:58ã | 9:49a |
| 25 | Fr | John Steinbeck awarded Nobel Prize, 1962 | VIR | 7:21 | 6:07 | 4:01ã | 10:40a | 7:14 | 6:13 | 4:09ã | 10:42a |
| 26 | Sa | Moon at perigee 6:31am | VIR | 7:22 | 6:06 | 5:16ã | 11:33a | 7:15 | 6:12 | 5:19ã | 11:35a |

Day's Length: 10h 41m · Astron. Twilight: 1h 22m
Day's Length: 10h 55m · Astron. Twilight: 1h 16m

### 43. Twentieth Sunday after Pentecost

| DATE | | ASTRONOMY, HOLIDAYS, AND EVENTS | | SUN RISES | SUN SETS | MOONRISE/SET | MERIDIAN | SUN RISES | SUN SETS | MOONRISE/SET | MERIDIAN |
|---|---|---|---|---|---|---|---|---|---|---|---|
| 27 | Su | 1st newsreel featuring sound released, 1927 | VIR | 7:23 | 6:04 | 6:30ã | 12:26p | 7:16 | 6:11 | 6:30ã | 12:28p |
| 28 | Mo | Jonas Salk born, 1914 | LIB | 7:24 | 6:03 | 6:47p̄ | 1:20p | 7:17 | 6:10 | 6:56p̄ | 1:22p |
| 29 | Tu | NYSE crash, Great Depression began, 1929 | LIB | 7:25 | 6:02 | 7:25p̄ | 2:14p | 7:18 | 6:09 | 7:37p̄ | 2:16p |
| 30 | We | John Adams born, 1735 | SCO | 7:26 | 6:00 | 8:07p̄ | 3:10p | 7:19 | 6:08 | 8:22p̄ | 3:12p |
| 31 | Th | Halloween; Mercury retrograde | OPH | 7:27 | 5:59 | 8:54p̄ | 4:05p | 7:20 | 6:07 | 9:11p̄ | 4:07p |

# OCTOBER 2019 WEATHER FORECAST

## ZONE 1 Northeast & New England

**1–3:** Partly cloudy, possible frost New England. **4–7:** Dry, cool. **8–11:** Heavy rain from west, then clear/cooler. **12–15:** Generally fair Columbus Day weekend. **16–19:** Blustery, cool northerly winds for much of New England. **20–23:** Cold; northerly winds persist New England; a few locally heavy showers by the 23rd. **24–27:** Rainy. **28–31:** Very unsettled for Halloween, especially New England.

## ZONE 2 Great Lakes, Ohio Valley & Midwest

**1–3:** Cold rains Great Lakes. **4–7:** Great Lakes, points south to Kentucky: Many showers, a few thunderstorms. **8–11:** Rains move to east of Great Lakes; then clear/cooler weather from west. **12–15:** Generally fair for Columbus Day. **16–19:** Humid; showery Great Lakes to points south. **20–23:** Showers, then a mix of clouds/sun. **24–27:** Considerable low clouds, areas of fog cover Great Lakes, Ohio River Valley. **28–31:** Generally dry weather in time for Halloween.

## ZONE 3 Southeast

**1–3:** Fair, quite warm. **4–7:** Dry, cooler. **8–11:** Showers, some heavy, especially Tennessee, Alabama; then clear/cooler weather moves in from west. **12–15:** Possible hurricane threat in Carolinas for Columbus Day. Generally fair elsewhere. **16–19:** Muggy/showery. **20–23:** Brief shot of cold. **24–27:** Cloudiness, areas of fog. Rain from Carolinas, south to Florida. **28–31:** Clearing, with drier weather for trick-or-treaters.

## ZONE 4 North Central States

**1–3:** Cold rains over northern Rockies rapidly move east across the northern Plains. **4–7:** Much of Rockies dry, cool. Many showers, a few thunderstorms move east from the Great Plains. **8–11:** Cold, clear Rockies. **12–15:** Mild, widely scattered showers dampen Columbus Day weekend. **16–19:** Rain or wet snow Rockies, south into Colorado. **20–23:** Rapidly warms, then stormy conditions, east into Great Plains. **24–27:** Clouds, scattered showers, steadier rain for Colorado, points south. **28–31:** Gusty winds for Halloween.

## ZONE 5 South Central States

**1–3:** Very warm for southern Rockies, points east. **4–7:** Many showers, a few thunderstorms move east from southern Great Plains to the western Gulf of Mexico. **8–11:** Clear and chilly over the southern Rockies. **12–15:** Mild holiday weekend: Scattered showers. **16–19:** Rain or even wet snow parts of New Mexico. **20–23:** Rapid warm-up, then very unsettled into the southern Great Plains. **24–27:** Rain New Mexico, Texas, parts of Oklahoma. **28–31:** Dry. Watch for dusty wind parts of southern Plains.

## ZONE 6 Northwest

**1–3:** Clearing, chilly. **4–7:** Very unsettled. **8–11:** Light showers along coast. **12–15:** A few passing showers for Columbus Day holiday. **16–19:** Clear initially, then showers. **20–23:** A rapid warm-up, then stormy. **24–27:** Mostly fair, but chilly, then turns unsettled. **28–31:** Boo! More stormy weather for Halloween.

## ZONE 7 Southwest

**1–3:** Clearing skies. **4–7:** Fair, then windy, with some showers. **8–11:** Fair. **12–15:** Mild, a few showers. **16–19:** Fair, then a return to showers. **20–23:** Clear/hot. **24–27:** Mostly fair initially, then turning unsettled. **28–31:** Skies clear.

# NOVEMBER 2019

11th Month     **NOVEMBER 2019**     30 Days

**SCORPIO**
October 23 to
November 21

**SAGITTARIUS**
November 22 to
December 20

*TIME ON HIS WING FAST HASTES AWAY, AND CHILLS EACH WARM SUCCEED;*
*TO CAPRICORN SOL HASTES EACH DAY, SO NIGHTS THE DAY EXCEED.*

### MOON'S PHASES — EASTERN STANDARD TIME

| | | | |
|---|---|---|---|
| ◐ First Quarter | 4th | 5:23 am |
| ○ Full Moon | 12th | 8:34 am |
| ◑ Last Quarter | 19th | 4:11 pm |
| ● New Moon | 26th | 10:06 am |

Subtract 1 hour for CST, 2 hours for MST, and 3 hours for PST.

### SUN ON MERIDIAN CIVIL TIME

| Day | H:MM:SS |
|---|---|
| 1st | 12:44:04 |
| 8th | 11:44:13 |
| 15th | 11:45:02 |
| 22nd | 11:46:34 |
| 29th | 11:48:44 |

### CALENDAR FOR NORTHERN STATES
(EST) — 40°N. Lat. 75°W. Long.

### CALENDAR FOR SOUTHERN STATES
(CST) — 35°N. Lat. 90°W. Long.

| DATE | | ASTRONOMY, HOLIDAYS, AND EVENTS | MOON'S PLACE AT 7am ASTRONOMICALLY | SUN RISES | SUN SETS | EARLIEST MOONRISE MOONSET | MOON'S MERIDIAN PASSAGE | SUN RISES | SUN SETS | EARLIEST MOONRISE MOONSET | MOON'S MERIDIAN PASSAGE |
|---|---|---|---|---|---|---|---|---|---|---|---|
| 1 | Fr | All Saints' Day; Moon, Saturn best visible | SAG | 7:29 | 5:58 | 9:46p̄ | 5:00p | 7:21 | 6:06 | 10:03p̄ | 5:02p |
| 2 | Sa | All Souls' Day; Daniel Boone born, 1734 | SAG | 7:30 | 5:57 | 10:42p̄ | 5:53p | 7:22 | 6:05 | 10:59p̄ | 5:55p |

**44. Twenty-first Sunday after Pentecost**
Day's Length: 10h 25m — Astron. Twilight: 1h 23m
Day's Length: 10h 42m — Astron. Twilight: 1h 17m

| 3 | Su | Daylight Saving Time ends | CAP | 6:31 | 4:56 | 10:40p̄ | 5:43p | 6:22 | 5:04 | 10:55p̄ | 5:46p |
|---|---|---|---|---|---|---|---|---|---|---|---|
| 4 | Mo | 1st air-conditioned car displayed, 1939 | CAP | 6:32 | 4:55 | 11:38p̄ | 6:31p | 6:23 | 5:03 | 11:52p̄ | 6:33p |
| 5 | Tu | **Election Day** (get out and vote!) | CAP | 6:33 | 4:54 | None | 7:17p | 6:24 | 5:02 | None | 7:18p |
| 6 | We | Sally Field, actress, born 1946 | AQU | 6:34 | 4:52 | 12:37ā | 8:00p | 6:25 | 5:02 | 12:48ā | 8:01p |
| 7 | Th | Moon at apogee 3:31am | AQU | 6:35 | 4:51 | 1:35ā | 8:42p | 6:26 | 5:01 | 1:43ā | 8:43p |
| 8 | Fr | Edmond Halley (Halley's Comet) born, 1656 | PSC | 6:37 | 4:50 | 2:33ā | 9:23p | 6:27 | 5:00 | 2:38ā | 9:25p |
| 9 | Sa | Spiro T. Agnew born, 1918 | CET | 6:38 | 4:49 | 3:31ā | 10:04p | 6:28 | 4:59 | 3:34ā | 10:06p |

**45. Twenty-second Sunday after Pentecost**
Day's Length: 10h 10m — Astron. Twilight: 1h 24m
Day's Length: 10h 29m — Astron. Twilight: 1h 18m

| 10 | Su | Windshield wiper patented, 1910 | PSC | 6:39 | 4:48 | 4:30ā | 10:47p | 6:29 | 4:58 | 4:29ā | 10:49p |
|---|---|---|---|---|---|---|---|---|---|---|---|
| 11 | Mo | **Veterans Day;** Mercury transit of the Sun | CET | 6:40 | 4:48 | 5:30ā | 11:32p | 6:30 | 4:57 | 5:27ā | 11:33p |
| 12 | Tu | 1st drive-up bank opened, 1946 | ARI | 6:41 | 4:47 | 6:31ā | None | 6:31 | 4:57 | 6:25ā | None |
| 13 | We | Holland tunnel opened, 1927 | TAU | 6:42 | 4:46 | 5:47p̄ | 12:19a | 6:32 | 4:56 | 6:01p̄ | 12:21a |
| 14 | Th | Sadie Hawkins Day | TAU | 6:43 | 4:45 | 6:29p̄ | 1:09a | 6:33 | 4:55 | 6:44p̄ | 1:11a |
| 15 | Fr | Battery hearing aid patented, 1902 | TAU | 6:45 | 4:44 | 7:17p̄ | 2:02a | 6:34 | 4:55 | 7:34p̄ | 2:04a |
| 16 | Sa | Oklahoma became 46th state, 1907 | GEM | 6:46 | 4:43 | 8:14p̄ | 2:57a | 6:35 | 4:54 | 8:31p̄ | 3:00a |

**46. Twenty-third Sunday after Pentecost**
Day's Length: 9h 56m — Astron. Twilight: 1h 25m
Day's Length: 10h 18m — Astron. Twilight: 1h 19m

| 17 | Su | Gordon Lightfoot born, 1938 | GEM | 6:47 | 4:43 | 9:16p̄ | 3:54a | 6:36 | 4:54 | 9:33p̄ | 3:56a |
|---|---|---|---|---|---|---|---|---|---|---|---|
| 18 | Mo | Nintendo released the GameCube, 2001 | CAN | 6:48 | 4:42 | 10:24p̄ | 4:51a | 6:37 | 4:53 | 10:39p̄ | 4:53a |
| 19 | Tu | James Garfield born, 1831 | LEO | 6:49 | 4:41 | 11:34p̄ | 5:46a | 6:38 | 4:52 | 11:46p̄ | 5:48a |
| 20 | We | Mercury direct; Robert F. Kennedy born, 1925 | LEO | 6:50 | 4:41 | None | 6:40a | 6:39 | 4:52 | None | 6:42a |
| 21 | Th | Rebecca Felton 1st woman Senator, 1922 | LEO | 6:51 | 4:40 | 12:45ā | 7:32a | 6:40 | 4:52 | 12:54ā | 7:34a |
| 22 | Fr | Rodney Dangerfield born, 1921 | VIR | 6:53 | 4:39 | 1:57ā | 8:23a | 6:41 | 4:51 | 2:02ā | 8:25a |
| 23 | Sa | Moon at perigee 2:32am | VIR | 6:54 | 4:39 | 3:09ā | 9:14a | 6:42 | 4:51 | 3:10ā | 9:16a |

**47. Christ the King Sunday**
Day's Length: 9h 44m — Astron. Twilight: 1h 27m
Day's Length: 10h 08m — Astron. Twilight: 1h 20m

| 24 | Su | Moon, Mercury, Mars best visible SE 6:04am | VIR | 6:55 | 4:38 | 4:21ā | 10:06a | 6:43 | 4:50 | 4:19ā | 10:08a |
|---|---|---|---|---|---|---|---|---|---|---|---|
| 25 | Mo | Venus, Jupiter best visible in SW 5:26pm | LIB | 6:56 | 4:38 | 5:33ā | 10:59a | 6:44 | 4:50 | 5:28ā | 11:01a |
| 26 | Tu | Great Appalachian Storm dumped 57", 1950 | SCO | 6:57 | 4:37 | 6:44ā | 11:54a | 6:45 | 4:50 | 6:36ā | 11:56a |
| 27 | We | NYC's Pennsylvania Station opened, 1910 | OPH | 6:58 | 4:37 | 5:42p̄ | 12:49p | 6:46 | 4:49 | 5:58p̄ | 12:52p |
| 28 | Th | **Thanksgiving Day** | SAG | 6:59 | 4:37 | 6:32p̄ | 1:45p | 6:46 | 4:49 | 6:49p̄ | 1:48p |
| 29 | Fr | Moon, Saturn best visible in the SW 6:02pm | SAG | 7:00 | 4:36 | 7:27p̄ | 2:41p | 6:47 | 4:49 | 7:44p̄ | 2:43p |
| 30 | Sa | Hurricane season ends | SAG | 7:01 | 4:36 | 8:25p̄ | 3:34p | 6:48 | 4:49 | 8:42p̄ | 3:36p |

# NOVEMBER 2019 WEATHER FORECAST

## ZONE 1 Northeast & New England

**1–3:** Cold spell, especially New England, down to Mid-Atlantic States. Dry/chilly for New York City Marathon. **4–7:** Clear, crisp Mid-Atlantic, then milder. **8–11:** Rapid temperature changes, with storm intensifying, moving east: Heavy rain/wet snow. Then colder. **12–15:** Clouds linger, spotty precipitation; then colder. **16–19:** Light snow/flurries, cold. **20–23:** Dry, cold. **24–27:** Wet weather. **28–30:** Storm along Atlantic Coast, increasing winds, copious precipitation; not good for Macy's Thanksgiving Day Parade.

## ZONE 2 Great Lakes, Ohio Valley & Midwest

**1–3:** Sun, then increasing clouds. **4–7:** Rain from west; then clear, frosty. **8–11:** Rapid temperature changes from Great Lakes eastward. Strong storm brings heavy rain/wet snow. Then frigid cold. **12–15:** New storm from Great Lakes up to eastern Canada: Heavy rain and wet snow, then clearing; very cold. **16–19:** Very cold Great Lakes. Fast-moving storm, heavy snow, then colder. **20–23:** Rain, thunderstorms, especially Great Lakes. **24–27:** Unsettled, wet. **28–30:** Rain, snow showers for Thanksgiving. Colder.

## ZONE 3 Southeast

**1–3:** Mixed clouds, sun. Turning colder. **4–7:** Clear, crisp, then milder. **8–11:** Violent thunderstorms for Tennessee, points south, moving east to coast; a deep freeze follows. **12–15:** Area fog gives way to clearing, cold from the west. **16–19:** Gulf of Mexico to Florida: late-day rain showers. **20–23:** Fair/dry. **24–27:** Wet. **28–30:** Storm hugs Atlantic Coast, bringing increasing winds and heavy precipitation for Turkey Day.

## ZONE 4 North Central States

**1–3:** Unsettled; rain/snow over Rockies. **4–7:** Rain in Plains spreads east; then clear, frosty. **8–11:** Increasing clouds. **12–15:** Pacific Northwest storm moves east; heavy rain/wet snow. Then clearing and cold. **16–19:** Fast-moving storm crosses northern Rockies with heavy snow, cold air. **20–23:** Thunderstorms for northern tier, especially Rockies. **24–27:** Dry/cold wind northern Rockies, Great Plains. **28–30:** Rain/snow Plains, Rockies for Thanksgiving; then frigid.

## ZONE 5 South Central States

**1–3:** Unsettled. **4–7:** Showers, turning colder. **8–11:** Clouding up. **12–15:** Storm toward Rockies, Great Plains, then east. Heavy precipitation, then clear. Very cold in southern states. **16–19:** Rain showers become snow. **20–23:** Showers, scattered thunderstorms. **24–27:** Dry, colder. **28–30:** Rain/snow for Thanksgiving; then frigid air sweeps south.

## ZONE 6 Northwest

**1–3:** Heavy clouds, showers linger. **4–7:** Showers. **8–11:** Heavy rain and wet snow move inland. **12–15:** Clouds linger, precipitation fades. **16–19:** Fast-moving storm brings heavy snow/rain along coast. **20–23:** More rain, snow. **24–27:** Wet, chilly. **28–30:** Wet Thanksgiving.

## ZONE 7 Southwest

**1–3:** Cloudy. **4–7:** Pacific storm pushes rain east, coastal California to Arizona. **8–11:** Pacific disturbance moves inland; showers. **12–15:** Another storm brings widely scattered showers. **16–19:** The Pacific storms continue. **20–23:** Mix of clouds, sun. **24–27:** Changeable, but dry. **28–30:** Sun, clouds; good forecast for Thanksgiving.

# DECEMBER 2019

**12th Month** — **31 Days**

**SAGITTARIUS**
November 22 to
December 20

**CAPRICORN**
December 21 to
January 19

COLD BLOWS THE WIND, THE FROZEN RAIN AND FLEECY SNOW DESCEND;
FOR, FREEZING WINTER'S COME AGAIN, AND SO THE YEAR DOES END.

| MOON'S PHASES EASTERN STANDARD TIME | | | |
|---|---|---|---|
| ◗ First Quarter | 4th | 1:58 am | |
| ○ Full Moon | 12th | 12:12 am | |
| ◐ Last Quarter | 18th | 11:57 pm | |
| ● New Moon | 26th | 12:13 am | |

Subtract 1 hour for CST, 2 hours for MST, and 3 hours for PST.

| SUN ON MERIDIAN CIVIL TIME | |
|---|---|
| Day | H:MM:SS |
| 1st | 11:49:28 |
| 8th | 11:52:20 |
| 15th | 11:55:33 |
| 22nd | 11:59:00 |
| 29th | 12:02:28 |

MOON'S PLACE AT 7am ASTRONOMICALLY

| | | CALENDAR FOR NORTHERN STATES (EST) 40°N. Lat. 75°W. Long. | | | | CALENDAR FOR SOUTHERN STATES (CST) 35°N. Lat. 90°W. Long. | | | |
|---|---|---|---|---|---|---|---|---|---|
| DATE | ASTRONOMY, HOLIDAYS, AND EVENTS | | SUN RISES | SUN SETS | EARLIEST MOONRISE MOONSET | MOON'S MERIDIAN PASSAGE | SUN RISES | SUN SETS | EARLIEST MOONRISE MOONSET | MOON'S MERIDIAN PASSAGE |

### 48. First Sunday of Advent

Day's Length: 9h 34m — Astron. Twilight: 1h 28m
Day's Length: 9h 59m — Astron. Twilight: 1h 21m

| | | | | | | | | | | | |
|---|---|---|---|---|---|---|---|---|---|---|---|
| 1 | Su | U.S. gas rationing went into effect, 1942 | CAP | 7:02 | 4:36 | 9:25p̄ | 4:24p̄ | 6:49 | 4:49 | 9:40p̄ | 4:26p̄ |
| 2 | Mo | 1st U.S. savings bank opened, 1816 | CAP | 7:03 | 4:35 | 10:25p̄ | 5:11p | 6:50 | 4:48 | 10:37p̄ | 5:12p |
| 3 | Tu | Paul Harvey's 1st national broadcast, 1950 | AQU | 7:04 | 4:35 | 11:24p̄ | 5:55p | 6:51 | 4:48 | 11:33p̄ | 5:57p |
| 4 | We | Moon at apogee 11:07pm | AQU | 7:05 | 4:35 | None | 6:37p | 6:52 | 4:48 | None | 6:39p |
| 5 | Th | Prohibition came to an end, 1933 | AQU | 7:06 | 4:35 | 12:22ã | 7:19p | 6:53 | 4:48 | 12:28ã | 7:20p |
| 6 | Fr | Washington Monument constructed, 1884 | CET | 7:07 | 4:35 | 1:19ã | 8:00p | 6:53 | 4:48 | 1:23ã | 8:01p |
| 7 | Sa | Pearl Harbor Day; Apollo 17 launched, 1972 | CET | 7:08 | 4:35 | 2:17ã | 8:41p | 6:54 | 4:48 | 2:18ã | 8:43p |

### 49. Second Sunday of Advent

Day's Length: 9h 26m — Astron. Twilight: 1h 29m
Day's Length: 9h 53m — Astron. Twilight: 1h 22m

| | | | | | | | | | | | |
|---|---|---|---|---|---|---|---|---|---|---|---|
| 8 | Su | Conception B.V.M.; Earliest sunset of 2019 | PSC | 7:09 | 4:35 | 3:16ã | 9:25p | 6:55 | 4:48 | 3:15ã | 9:27p |
| 9 | Mo | Clarence Birdseye born, 1886 | ARI | 7:10 | 4:35 | 4:17ã | 10:11p | 6:56 | 4:49 | 4:13ã | 10:13p |
| 10 | Tu | Venus, Saturn best visible in the SW 5:38pm | TAU | 7:10 | 4:35 | 5:20ã | 11:00p | 6:57 | 4:49 | 5:13ã | 11:03p |
| 11 | We | Venus, Saturn still visible in the SW 5:39pm | TAU | 7:11 | 4:35 | 6:24ã | 11:53p | 6:57 | 4:49 | 6:15ã | 11:56p |
| 12 | Th | Frank Sinatra born, 1915 | TAU | 7:12 | 4:35 | 5:11p̄ | None | 6:58 | 4:49 | 5:27p̄ | None |
| 13 | Fr | Dick Van Dyke born, 1925 | GEM | 7:13 | 4:35 | 6:05p̄ | 12:49a | 6:59 | 4:49 | 6:23p̄ | 12:52a |
| 14 | Sa | Howard Cosell retired, 1984 | GEM | 7:13 | 4:36 | 7:08p̄ | 1:47a | 7:00 | 4:50 | 7:25p̄ | 1:50a |

### 50. Third Sunday of Advent

Day's Length: 9h 22m — Astron. Twilight: 1h 29m
Day's Length: 9h 50m — Astron. Twilight: 1h 22m

| | | | | | | | | | | | |
|---|---|---|---|---|---|---|---|---|---|---|---|
| 15 | Su | Walter Elias "Walt" Disney died, 1966 | CAN | 7:14 | 4:36 | 8:15p̄ | 2:45a | 7:00 | 4:50 | 8:31p̄ | 2:48a |
| 16 | Mo | Jane Austen born, 1775 | LEO | 7:15 | 4:36 | 9:26p̄ | 3:42a | 7:01 | 4:50 | 9:38p̄ | 3:45a |
| 17 | Tu | Joseph Henry born, 1797 | LEO | 7:16 | 4:36 | 10:37p̄ | 4:37a | 7:01 | 4:51 | 10:46p̄ | 4:39a |
| 18 | We | Ember Day; Moon at perigee 3:28pm | LEO | 7:16 | 4:37 | 11:47p̄ | 5:29a | 7:02 | 4:51 | 11:53p̄ | 5:31a |
| 19 | Th | Corrugated paper patented, 1871 | VIR | 7:17 | 4:37 | None | 6:20a | 7:03 | 4:51 | None | 6:22a |
| 20 | Fr | Ember Day; Sacagawea died, 1812 | VIR | 7:17 | 4:38 | 12:57ã | 7:10a | 7:03 | 4:52 | 1:00ã | 7:12a |
| 21 | Sa | Winter solstice, 11:19pm; Ember Day | VIR | 7:18 | 4:38 | 2:07ã | 7:59a | 7:04 | 4:52 | 2:06ã | 8:02a |

### 51. Fourth Sunday of Advent

Day's Length: 9h 20m — Astron. Twilight: 1h 29m
Day's Length: 9h 49m — Astron. Twilight: 1h 22m

| | | | | | | | | | | | |
|---|---|---|---|---|---|---|---|---|---|---|---|
| 22 | Su | U.S. Golf Association formed, 1894 | LIB | 7:18 | 4:39 | 3:17ã | 8:50a | 7:04 | 4:53 | 3:13ã | 8:52a |
| 23 | Mo | Chanukah; James Gregory born, 1911 | LIB | 7:19 | 4:39 | 4:27ã | 9:42a | 7:05 | 4:53 | 4:20ã | 9:45a |
| 24 | Tu | Ava Gardner born, 1922 | OPH | 7:19 | 4:40 | 5:35ã | 10:37a | 7:05 | 4:54 | 5:26ã | 10:39a |
| 25 | We | **Christmas Day** | OPH | 7:20 | 4:40 | 6:41ã | 11:32a | 7:06 | 4:54 | 6:29ã | 11:34a |
| 26 | Th | Annular Central solar eclipse 12:18am (Asia) | SAG | 7:20 | 4:41 | 5:13p̄ | 12:27p | 7:06 | 4:55 | 5:30p̄ | 12:30p |
| 27 | Fr | Jupiter in conjunction | SAG | 7:20 | 4:42 | 6:10p̄ | 1:22p | 7:06 | 4:56 | 6:27p̄ | 1:24p |
| 28 | Sa | Moon, Venus best visible in the SW 5:56pm | CAP | 7:21 | 4:42 | 7:10p̄ | 2:14p | 7:07 | 4:56 | 7:26p̄ | 2:16p |

### 52. First Sunday after Christmas

Day's Length: 9h 22m — Astron. Twilight: 1h 29m
Day's Length: 9h 50m — Astron. Twilight: 1h 22m

| | | | | | | | | | | | |
|---|---|---|---|---|---|---|---|---|---|---|---|
| 29 | Su | 1st American YMCA, Boston, 1851 | CAP | 7:21 | 4:43 | 8:11p̄ | 3:03p | 7:07 | 4:57 | 8:24p̄ | 3:05p |
| 30 | Mo | California's 1st freeway opened, 1940 | AQU | 7:21 | 4:44 | 9:11p̄ | 3:49p | 7:07 | 4:58 | 9:21p̄ | 3:50p |
| 31 | Tu | New Year's Eve | AQU | 7:21 | 4:45 | 10:09p̄ | 4:32p | 7:07 | 4:59 | 10:17p̄ | 4:34p |

# DECEMBER 2019 WEATHER FORECAST

## ZONE 1 Northeast & New England

**1–3:** Cloudy, rain/wet snow, then clear, cold. **4–7:** Coastal storm along Atlantic Seaboard; mixed precipitation, frigid air. **8–11:** Dry/tranquil. **12–15:** Widespread clouds, showers. **16–19:** Rain/wintery mix, gusty winds. **20–23:** Lingering rain showers, wet snow. **24–27:** Wet/white for Chrstimas: Rain showers (south), wet snow (north). **28–31:** Year ends on blustery, colder note; frequent snow showers, flurries.

## ZONE 2 Great Lakes, Ohio Valley & Midwest

**1–3:** Rain/wet snow shifts east to Great Lakes, points south to Kentucky; clear, cold follows. **4–7:** Storm from Texas moves to Ohio River Valley, depositing heavy rain/wet snow, very cold air. **8–11:** Temperatures still below seasonal norms. **12–15:** Scattered snow showers. **16–19:** Considerable cloud cover, but little precipitation. Nights seasonably cold; days milder. **20–23:** Rain/snow. **24–27:** Sunshine, cold/dry Christmas. **28–31:** Cold, dry end to 2019.

## ZONE 3 Southeast

**1–3:** Rain, wet snow Tennessee, points south, Gulf Coast; clear, cold follows. **4–7:** Coastal storm along Atlantic Seaboard; moderate to heavy rain, strong winds, very cold. Freeze into Florida. **8–11:** Dry. **12–15:** Cloudy, scattered showers. **16–19:** Heavy rain and winds, cloudy. **20–23:** Showers. **24–27:** Possibly soggy Christmas. **28–31:** Blustery. Cold winds fade; sunny.

## ZONE 4 North Central States

**1–3:** Stormy from western slopes of the Rockies, all points east, then clearing, cold. **4–7:** Another storm from Pacific Northwest to northern Rockies. **8–11:** Storm from Rockies brings snow to Plains. **12–15:** Pacific storm brings widespread rain, snow to Rockies. **16–19:** Cloudy, passing snow flurries. **20–23:** Periods of heavy rain/snow. Bitterly cold. **24–27:** Fair, dry, very cold for Christmas. **28–31:** Moisture from Pacific Northwest brings threat of snow.

## ZONE 5 South Central States

**1–3:** Mostly cloudy, windy; showers of rain/wet snow. **4–7:** Storm from Texas moves northeast, bringing widespread rain, wet snow. **8–11:** More rain or wet snow. **12–15:** Unsettled. **16–19:** Cloudy. Passing rain/wet snow shower. **20–23:** Another round of precipitation, then much colder. **24–27:** Fair, dry, cold for the holiday. **28–31:** More rain, wet snow.

## ZONE 6 Northwest

**1–3:** From the Pacific Northwest Coast to the western slopes of the Rockies, stormy conditions prevail: Rain, wet snow, then shifts east. **4–7:** Another storm from Pacific Northwest moves to northern Rockies. **8–11:** Cloudy with showers. **12–15:** Pacific storm brings widespread rain, snow. **16–19:** Cloudy. Lingering showers. **20–23:** Heavy rain/snow as low-pressure disturbances enter Washington, then sweep east. **24–27:** Fair, dry, cold for Christmas. **28–31:** More rain/ mixed precipitation.

## ZONE 7 Southwest

**1–3:** Showers of rain/some wet snow. **4–7:** Scattered precipitation. **8–11:** Mix of sun and clouds, risk of a shower. **12–15:** Unsettled. **16–19:** Clouds/sun. **20–23:** Showery. **24–27:** Fair, dry, very chilly for Christmastime. **28–31:** Dry and chilly end to 2019.

# JANUARY 2020

**1ˢᵗ Month**  **31 Days**

**CAPRICORN**
December 21 to
January 19

**AQUARIUS**
January 20 to
February 17

NOW DREARY WINTER'S PIERCING COLD, FLOATS ON THE NORTHERN GALE,
AND TREES, THOUGH GREEN, LOOK DRY AND OLD; SNOW COVERS HILL AND DALE.

### MOON'S PHASES
**EASTERN STANDARD TIME**

| | | |
|---|---|---|
| ◐ First Quarter | 2ⁿᵈ | 11:45 pm |
| ○ Full Moon | 10ᵗʰ | 2:21 pm |
| ◑ Last Quarter | 17ᵗʰ | 7:58 am |
| ● New Moon | 24ᵗʰ | 4:42 pm |

Subtract 1 hour for CST, 2 hours for MST,
and 3 hours for PST.

### SUN ON MERIDIAN
**CIVIL TIME**

| Day | H:MM:SS |
|---|---|
| 1ˢᵗ | 12:03:55 |
| 8ᵗʰ | 12:07:04 |
| 15ᵗʰ | 12:09:47 |
| 22ⁿᵈ | 12:11:59 |
| 29ᵗʰ | 12:13:33 |

**MOON'S PLACE AT 7am ASTRONOMICALLY**

### CALENDAR FOR NORTHERN STATES
(EST)
**40°N. Lat.**
**75°W. Long.**

### CALENDAR FOR SOUTHERN STATES
(CST)
**35°N. Lat.**
**90°W. Long.**

| DATE | | ASTRONOMY, HOLIDAYS, AND EVENTS | MOON'S PLACE | SUN RISES | SUN SETS | EARLIEST MOONRISE MOONSET | MOON'S MERIDIAN PASSAGE | SUN RISES | SUN SETS | EARLIEST MOONRISE MOONSET | MOON'S MERIDIAN PASSAGE |
|---|---|---|---|---|---|---|---|---|---|---|---|
| 1 | We | New Year's Day; Moon at apogee 8:32pm | AQU | 7:22 | 4:45 | 11:07p̄ | 5:14p | 7:08 | 4:59 | 11:12p̄ | 5:15p |
| 2 | Th | TV cigarette ads banned, 1971 | PSC | 7:22 | 4:46 | None | 5:54p | 7:08 | 5:00 | None | 5:56p |
| 3 | Fr | Alaska admitted 49ᵗʰ U.S. state, 1959 | CET | 7:22 | 4:47 | 12:05ā | 6:35p | 7:08 | 5:01 | 12:07ā | 6:37p |
| 4 | Sa | 1ˢᵗ State of the Union address, 1790 | PSC | 7:22 | 4:48 | 1:03ā | 7:18p | 7:08 | 5:02 | 1:02ā | 7:19p |

Day's Length: 9h 27m
Astron. Twilight: 1h 28m | Day's Length: 9h 54m
Astron. Twilight: 1h 22m

## 1. Epiphany Sunday

| | | | | | | | | | | | |
|---|---|---|---|---|---|---|---|---|---|---|---|
| 5 | Su | Earth at perihelion; Latest sunrise of 2020 | CET | 7:22 | 4:49 | 2:02ā | 8:02p | 7:08 | 5:02 | 1:59ā | 8:04p |
| 6 | Mo | Epiphany; Joan of Arc born, 1412 | ARI | 7:22 | 4:50 | 3:03ā | 8:49p | 7:08 | 5:03 | 2:57ā | 8:51p |
| 7 | Tu | 1ˢᵗ presidential election, 1789 | TAU | 7:22 | 4:51 | 4:06ā | 9:40p | 7:08 | 5:04 | 3:58ā | 9:42p |
| 8 | We | 1ˢᵗ U.S. exhibit of *Mona Lisa*, 1963 | TAU | 7:22 | 4:52 | 5:11ā | 10:35p | 7:08 | 5:05 | 5:00ā | 10:37p |
| 9 | Th | Ice storm paralyzed New England, 1998 | GEM | 7:21 | 4:53 | 6:14ā | 11:33p | 7:08 | 5:06 | 6:02ā | 11:35p |
| 10 | Fr | 1ˢᵗ Texas oil strike, 1901 | GEM | 7:21 | 4:54 | 7:15ā | None | 7:08 | 5:07 | 7:02ā | None |
| 11 | Sa | Alexander Hamilton born, 1789 | CAN | 7:21 | 4:55 | 5:59p̄ | 12:32ā | 7:08 | 5:08 | 6:16p̄ | 12:35ā |

Day's Length: 9h 35m
Astron. Twilight: 1h 28m | Day's Length: 10h 01m
Astron. Twilight: 1h 21m

## 2. First Sunday after Epiphany

| | | | | | | | | | | | |
|---|---|---|---|---|---|---|---|---|---|---|---|
| 12 | Su | Baptism of Jesus; John Hancock born, 1737 | CAN | 7:21 | 4:56 | 7:11p̄ | 1:32ā | 7:08 | 5:09 | 7:25p̄ | 1:34ā |
| 13 | Mo | Moon at perigee 3:30pm | LEO | 7:21 | 4:57 | 8:25p̄ | 2:29ā | 7:08 | 5:10 | 8:35p̄ | 2:32ā |
| 14 | Tu | Benedict Arnold born, 1741 | LEO | 7:20 | 4:58 | 9:37p̄ | 3:24ā | 7:08 | 5:11 | 9:45p̄ | 3:27ā |
| 15 | We | Elizabeth I crowned queen of England, 1559 | VIR | 7:20 | 4:59 | 10:49p̄ | 4:17ā | 7:07 | 5:12 | 10:53p̄ | 4:19ā |
| 16 | Th | Civil Service System est., 1883 | VIR | 7:19 | 5:00 | 11:59p̄ | 5:07ā | 7:07 | 5:12 | 11:59p̄ | 5:09ā |
| 17 | Fr | Captain Cook sailed Antarctic Circle, 1773 | VIR | 7:19 | 5:01 | None | 5:57ā | 7:07 | 5:13 | None | 5:59ā |
| 18 | Sa | A.A. Milne born, 1882 | LIB | 7:19 | 5:02 | 1:08ā | 6:47ā | 7:06 | 5:14 | 1:05ā | 6:49ā |

Day's Length: 9h 45m
Astron. Twilight: 1h 26m | Day's Length: 10h 09m
Astron. Twilight: 1h 20m

## 3. Second Sunday after Epiphany

| | | | | | | | | | | | |
|---|---|---|---|---|---|---|---|---|---|---|---|
| 19 | Su | Robert E. Lee born, 1807 | LIB | 7:18 | 5:03 | 2:17ā | 7:38ā | 7:06 | 5:15 | 2:11ā | 7:40ā |
| 20 | Mo | MLK Jr. Birthday (obs.) | OPH | 7:18 | 5:05 | 3:25ā | 8:30ā | 7:06 | 5:16 | 3:16ā | 8:33ā |
| 21 | Tu | Stonewall Jackson born, 1824 | OPH | 7:17 | 5:06 | 4:30ā | 9:24ā | 7:05 | 5:17 | 4:19ā | 9:26ā |
| 22 | We | Apollo 5 (unmanned) launched, 1968 | SAG | 7:16 | 5:07 | 5:32ā | 10:18ā | 7:05 | 5:18 | 5:19ā | 10:21ā |
| 23 | Th | Moon/Jupiter pair optimal visibility, SE sky | SAG | 7:16 | 5:08 | 6:27ā | 11:12ā | 7:04 | 5:19 | 6:14ā | 11:15ā |
| 24 | Fr | James Marshall found gold, 1848 | CAP | 7:15 | 5:09 | 7:15ā | 12:05p | 7:04 | 5:20 | 7:03ā | 12:07p |
| 25 | Sa | League of Nations founded, 1919 | CAP | 7:14 | 5:10 | 5:58p̄ | 12:55p | 7:03 | 5:21 | 6:12p̄ | 12:57p |

Day's Length: 9h 58m
Astron. Twilight: 1h 25m | Day's Length: 10h 20m
Astron. Twilight: 1h 19m

## 4. Third Sunday after Epiphany

| | | | | | | | | | | | |
|---|---|---|---|---|---|---|---|---|---|---|---|
| 26 | Su | Douglas MacArthur born, 1880 | CAP | 7:14 | 5:12 | 6:59p̄ | 1:42p | 7:03 | 5:22 | 7:10p̄ | 1:44p |
| 27 | Mo | Lewis Carroll born, 1832 | AQU | 7:13 | 5:13 | 7:58p̄ | 2:27p | 7:02 | 5:24 | 8:07p̄ | 2:29p |
| 28 | Tu | Space shuttle exploded, 1986 | AQU | 7:12 | 5:14 | 8:56p̄ | 3:09p | 7:02 | 5:25 | 9:03p̄ | 3:11p |
| 29 | We | Moon at apogee 4:33pm | PSC | 7:11 | 5:15 | 9:54p̄ | 3:50p | 7:01 | 5:26 | 9:57p̄ | 3:52p |
| 30 | Th | Mahatma Gandhi murdered, 1948 | CET | 7:10 | 5:16 | 10:51p̄ | 4:31p | 7:00 | 5:27 | 10:52p̄ | 4:33p |
| 31 | Fr | 1ˢᵗ U.S. satellite launched, 1958 | PSC | 7:10 | 5:18 | 11:49p̄ | 5:12p | 7:00 | 5:28 | 11:47p̄ | 5:14p |

# JANUARY 2020 WEATHER FORECAST

## ZONE 1 Northeast & New England

**1–3:** Cold front brings rain/snow showers. Wet, windy for Mummers Parade in Philadelphia. **4–7:** Storm moving from Mid-Atlantic to Cape Cod brings significant snow (4-8"). **8–11:** A "winterlude." **12–15:** New England: snowy and windy. Windswept rains Maryland, Delaware; everywhere else, a wintry mix. **16–19:** Wet, unseasonably mild. **20–23:** Fair, very cold. **24–27:** Gusty winds; rain changing to snow. **28–31:** Very cold air. Heavy lake-effect snow showers/squalls lee of Great Lakes.

## ZONE 2 Great Lakes, Ohio Valley & Midwest

**1–3:** Sharp cold front brings gusty winds, widespread snow showers. **4–7:** Blustery, cold; flurries. **8–11:** Steady snow spreads in from the west, significant accumulations possible. **12–15:** Snowy, then fair/cold. **16–19:** Blustery winds. **20–23:** Fair, then increasingly cloudy skies, very cold; snow for Wisconsin, U.P. of Michigan. **24–27:** Frigidly cold air plunges south from Canada. Snow showers and squalls to the lee of the Great Lakes. **28–31:** Fair, bitter cold.

## ZONE 3 Southeast

**1–3:** Storm from Gulf of Mexico brings rain showers. **4–7:** A stronger storm evolves over Florida, generates more showery rainfall, scattered thunderstorms. **8–11:** Turning stormy Mississippi Valley. **12–15:** Heavy, windswept rains, then turning fair. **16–19:** Clearing but windy, followed by showers for Alabama/Georgia, points north. **20–23:** Rain, showers. Mild, then colder. **24–27:** Very cold; blustery winds. **28–31:** Fair, but bitterly cold.

## ZONE 4 North Central States

**1–3:** Fair, cold. **4–7:** Milder, then snowy from Rockies, points east. **8–11:** Fair, then unsettled. **12–15:** Fair/cold. **16–19:** Light snow across Plains; windy. **20–23:** Major storm cuts path from northwest Missouri through Wisconsin and U.P. of Michigan. Heavy snows across the Plains; one to two feet possible. **24–27:** Temperatures plummet to as low as 40° below across the northern and central Plains. **28–31:** Fair skies, then turning milder with snow/rain showers.

## ZONE 5 South Central States

**1–3:** Fair, cold. **4–7:** Blustery, light snow southern Rockies. Rain Texas and Gulf Coast, then clearing. **8–11:** Fair, then unsettled. **12–15:** Fair/cold. **16–19:** Light snow Plains. Fair, then showers Texas. **20–23:** A major storm cuts a path from Texas Panhandle to Kansas. Heavy snow across Plains: possibly one foot or more. **24–27:** Frigidly cold. **28–31:** Fair for the West, then unsettled, showers.

## ZONE 6 Northwest

**1–3:** Fair and chilly. **4–7:** Showers for Washington/Oregon, followed by clearing. **8–11:** Fair, then stormy. **12–15:** Fair/chilly. **16–19:** Showers, especially along the coast. **20–23:** Very unsettled, with rain and, over higher terrain, snow (up to one foot). **24–27:** Fair and cold. **28–31:** Fair, then showers.

## ZONE 7 Southwest

**1–3:** Fair, cold. Brisk winds for Tournament of Roses Parade. **4–7:** Milder in west, followed by some rain/snow. **8–11:** Becoming stormy for California, points east. **12–15:** Fair/cold. **16–19:** Showers along Pacific Coast. Otherwise, clearing, windy elsewhere. **20–23:** Milder; few showers. **24–27:** Stormy Utah, points east. Heavy accumulations mountains. Fair elsewhere. **28–31:** Fair, then developing showers.

# FEBRUARY 2020

2nd Month — 29 Days

**AQUARIUS**
January 20 to February 17

**PISCES**
February 18 to March 18

ALTHOUGH THE WINTER GREY WITH AGE, YET REIGNS A SOVEREIGN KING;
SOL'S PLASTIC RAYS WILL SOON ASSUAGE, AND USHER IN THE SPRING.

### MOON'S PHASES — EASTERN STANDARD TIME

| ☽ First Quarter | 1st | 8:42 pm |
| ○ Full Moon | 9th | 2:33 am |
| ☾ Last Quarter | 15th | 5:17 pm |
| ● New Moon | 23rd | 10:32 am |

Subtract 1 hour for CST, 2 hours for MST, and 3 hours for PST.

### SUN ON MERIDIAN CIVIL TIME

| Day | H:MM:SS |
|---|---|
| 1st | 12:14:02 |
| 8th | 12:14:38 |
| 15th | 12:14:37 |
| 22nd | 12:14:00 |
| 29th | 12:12:53 |

**CALENDAR FOR NORTHERN STATES** (EST) — 40°N. Lat. 75°W. Long.

**CALENDAR FOR SOUTHERN STATES** (CST) — 35°N. Lat. 90°W. Long.

| DATE | | ASTRONOMY, HOLIDAYS, AND EVENTS | MOON'S PLACE AT 7am ASTRONOMICALLY | SUN RISES | SUN SETS | EARLIEST MOONRISE MOONSET | MOON'S MERIDIAN PASSAGE | SUN RISES | SUN SETS | EARLIEST MOONRISE MOONSET | MOON'S MERIDIAN PASSAGE |
|---|---|---|---|---|---|---|---|---|---|---|---|
| 1 | Sa | 1st Supreme Court meeting, 1790 | CET | 7:09 | 5:19 | None | 5:54p | 6:59 | 5:29 | None | 5:56p |

**5. Fourth Sunday after Epiphany** — Day's Length: 10h 12m, Astron. Twilight: 1h 24m / Day's Length: 10h 32m, Astron. Twilight: 1h 18m

| 2 | Su | Groundhog Day (Candlemas) | ARI | 7:08 | 5:20 | 12:48ã | 6:39p | 6:58 | 5:30 | 12:43ã | 6:41p |
| 3 | Mo | 15th Amendment ratified, 1870 | TAU | 7:07 | 5:21 | 1:49ã | 7:27p | 6:57 | 5:31 | 1:42ã | 7:29p |
| 4 | Tu | Midpoint of winter | TAU | 7:06 | 5:23 | 2:52ã | 8:19p | 6:57 | 5:32 | 2:42ã | 8:21p |
| 5 | We | U.S. & U.K. sign Panama Canal Treaty, 1900 | TAU | 7:05 | 5:24 | 3:55ã | 9:15p | 6:56 | 5:33 | 3:43ã | 9:17p |
| 6 | Th | Babe Ruth born, 1895 | GEM | 7:04 | 5:25 | 4:56ã | 10:14p | 6:55 | 5:34 | 4:44ã | 10:16p |
| 7 | Fr | Charles Dickens born, 1812 | GEM | 7:03 | 5:26 | 5:54ã | 11:14p | 6:54 | 5:35 | 5:42ã | 11:16p |
| 8 | Sa | Boy Scouts Day | CAN | 7:01 | 5:27 | 6:45ã | None | 6:53 | 5:36 | 6:34ã | None |

**6. Fifth Sunday after Epiphany** — Day's Length: 10h 28m, Astron. Twilight: 1h 23m / Day's Length: 10h 45m, Astron. Twilight: 1h 17m

| 9 | Su | U.S. Weather Bureau est., 1870 | LEO | 7:00 | 5:28 | 6:02p̃ | 12:13a | 6:52 | 5:37 | 6:14p̃ | 12:16a |
| 10 | Mo | Moon at perigee 3:35pm | LEO | 6:59 | 5:30 | 7:18p̃ | 1:11a | 6:51 | 5:38 | 7:27p̃ | 1:13a |
| 11 | Tu | Thomas Edison born, 1847 | VIR | 6:58 | 5:31 | 8:33p̃ | 2:07a | 6:50 | 5:39 | 8:38p̃ | 2:09a |
| 12 | We | Lincoln's Birthday | VIR | 6:57 | 5:32 | 9:46p̃ | 3:00a | 6:49 | 5:40 | 9:48p̃ | 3:02a |
| 13 | Th | Barbie doll went on sale, 1959 | VIR | 6:56 | 5:33 | 10:58p̃ | 3:52a | 6:48 | 5:41 | 10:56p̃ | 3:54a |
| 14 | Fr | Valentine's Day | LIB | 6:54 | 5:34 | None | 4:43a | 6:47 | 5:42 | None | 4:45a |
| 15 | Sa | Susan B. Anthony born, 1820 | LIB | 6:53 | 5:36 | 12:09ã | 5:35a | 6:46 | 5:43 | 12:04ã | 5:37a |

**7. Sixth Sunday after Epiphany** — Day's Length: 10h 45m, Astron. Twilight: 1h 21m / Day's Length: 10h 58m, Astron. Twilight: 1h 16m

| 16 | Su | King Tutankhamun's Tomb unsealed, 1923 | SCO | 6:52 | 5:37 | 1:18ã | 6:27a | 6:45 | 5:44 | 1:10ã | 6:29a |
| 17 | Mo | **Presidents' Day** | OPH | 6:51 | 5:38 | 2:24ã | 7:20a | 6:44 | 5:44 | 2:14ã | 7:23a |
| 18 | Tu | Moon/Mars pair optimal visibility, SE sky | SAG | 6:49 | 5:39 | 3:26ã | 8:14a | 6:43 | 5:45 | 3:14ã | 8:16a |
| 19 | We | Battle of Iwo Jima, 1945 | SAG | 6:48 | 5:40 | 4:23ã | 9:08a | 6:42 | 5:46 | 4:10ã | 9:10a |
| 20 | Th | Moon/Jupiter/Saturn visually close, SE sky | SAG | 6:47 | 5:41 | 5:12ã | 10:00a | 6:41 | 5:47 | 5:00ã | 10:02a |
| 21 | Fr | Nixon 1st US president to visit China, 1972 | CAP | 6:45 | 5:43 | 5:55ã | 10:50a | 6:39 | 5:48 | 5:44ã | 10:52a |
| 22 | Sa | Washington's Birthday (Traditional) | CAP | 6:44 | 5:44 | 6:32ã | 11:38a | 6:38 | 5:49 | 6:22ã | 11:40a |

**8. Seventh Sunday after Epiphany** — Day's Length: 11h 02m, Astron. Twilight: 1h 21m / Day's Length: 11h 13m, Astron. Twilight: 1h 16m

| 23 | Su | Tootsie Roll introduced, 1896 | AQU | 6:42 | 5:45 | 5:49p̃ | 12:23p | 6:37 | 5:50 | 5:59p̃ | 12:25p |
| 24 | Mo | 100-hour snowstorm of 1969 began | AQU | 6:41 | 5:46 | 6:48p̃ | 1:06p | 6:36 | 5:51 | 6:55p̃ | 1:08p |
| 25 | Tu | Shrove Tuesday/Mardi Gras | CET | 6:40 | 5:47 | 7:46p̃ | 1:48p | 6:35 | 5:52 | 7:50p̃ | 1:49p |
| 26 | We | Ash Wednesday; Moon at apogee 6:47am | CET | 6:38 | 5:48 | 8:43p̃ | 2:28p | 6:33 | 5:53 | 8:45p̃ | 2:30p |
| 27 | Th | Henry Wadsworth Longfellow born, 1807 | PSC | 6:37 | 5:49 | 9:41p̃ | 3:09p | 6:32 | 5:54 | 9:39p̃ | 3:11p |
| 28 | Fr | Republican Party founded, 1854 | CET | 6:35 | 5:50 | 10:39p̃ | 3:50p | 6:31 | 5:55 | 10:35p̃ | 3:52p |
| 29 | Sa | Leap Day; Solid helium produced, 1908 | ARI | 6:34 | 5:52 | 11:38p̃ | 4:34p | 6:30 | 5:56 | 11:32p̃ | 4:35p |

## FEBRUARY 2020 WEATHER FORECAST

### ZONE 1 Northeast & New England

**1–3:** Unsettled perhaps a flaky Groundhog Day, then clearing/cold. **4–7:** Storm strengthens south of Long Island and intensifies as it moves northeast. Two to five inches of snow from NYC, points north and east; lesser amounts south and west. **8–11:** Light snow, flurries. **12–15:** Clearing skies; blustery. **16–19:** Fair. **20–23:** Some snow, flurries. **24–29:** Fair, then unsettled with snow and rain.

### ZONE 2 Great Lakes, Ohio Valley & Midwest

**1–3:** Wet, then clearing and cold. **4–7:** Clearing/blustery winds, colder. **8–11:** Light snow, flurries. **12–15:** More snowy weather, especially in and around the Great Lakes. **16–19:** Fair skies. **20–23:** Snowstorm; significant accumulations possible. **24–29:** Sunny to partly cloudy skies/cold.

### ZONE 3 Southeast

**1–3:** Very cold air plunges across the South, bringing frost to Gulf Coast, northern Florida. Fair, but unseasonably chilly Super Bowl LIV at Miami's Hard Rock Stadium. **4–7:** Fair, pleasant. **8–11:** Light snow and rain. **12–15:** Milder and showery. **16–19:** Fair. **20–23:** Light snow and rain. **24–29:** Fair, then unsettled.

### ZONE 4 North Central States

**1–3:** Light snow Colorado, the Plains. **4–7:** A major storm brings heavy snow from the Montana-Idaho area eastward. Accumulations of one foot or more. **8–11:** Clearing and colder. **12–15:** Fair, then flurries over the Plains. **16–19:** Stormy over the Rockies. **20–23:** Snowstorm for Plains; heaviest for Kansas. **24–29:** Fair and cold Plains. Becoming unsettled Rockies.

### ZONE 5 South Central States

**1–3:** Rain Texas and across southern Plains, then clearing, cold. **4–7:** Very unsettled; snow Texas, some localities getting up to a half-foot. **8–11:** Colder. Some snow, then fair. **12–15:** Fair, then flurries Plains. **16–19:** Stormy. **20–23:** Snow/rain. **24–29:** Fair/cold Plains. Becoming unsettled Rockies. Increasingly cloudy for Mardi Gras in New Orleans.

### ZONE 6 Northwest

**1–3:** Pleasant. **4–7:** Major storm brings heavy snow to Bitterroot Range of Idaho, with accumulations possibly exceeding 12 inches. **8–11:** Dry/colder. **12–15:** Fair, then showery. **16–19:** Stormy weather evolves. **20–23:** Fair weather. **24–29:** Skies becoming unsettled.

### ZONE 7 Southwest

**1–3:** Light snow for Utah, then clearing. Tranquil elsewhere. **4–7:** Windy, showery. **8–11:** Clearing/colder. **12–15:** Fair, then showers spread east from Pacific Coast. **16–19:** Turning stormy California, all points east. **20–23:** Fair. **24–29:** Pleasant California, points east, then wet/windy.

# MARCH 2020

**3rd Month** · **31 Days**

**PISCES**
February 18 to
March 18

**ARIES**
March 19 to
April 18

NOW SPRING HAS COME, THE BIRDS REJOICE, AND CHAUNT THE CHEERFUL LAY;
THE FARMER WITH EXULTING JOYS, PREPARES FOR APRIL'S DAY.

| MOON'S PHASES EASTERN DAYLIGHT TIME | | | |
|---|---|---|---|
| ◑ First Quarter | 2nd | 2:57 pm | |
| ○ Full Moon | 9th | 1:48 pm | |
| ◐ Last Quarter | 16th | 5:34 am | |
| ● New Moon | 24th | 5:28 am | |

Subtract 1 hour for CDT, 2 hours for MDT, and 3 hours for PDT.

| SUN ON MERIDIAN CIVIL TIME | |
|---|---|
| Day | H:MM:SS |
| 1st | 12:12:42 |
| 8th | 13:11:06 |
| 15th | 13:09:13 |
| 22nd | 13:07:10 |
| 29th | 13:05:04 |

MOON'S PLACE AT 7am ASTRONOMICALLY

| | CALENDAR FOR NORTHERN STATES (EDT) 40°N. Lat. 75°W. Long. | | | | CALENDAR FOR SOUTHERN STATES (CDT) 35°N. Lat. 90°W. Long. | | | |
|---|---|---|---|---|---|---|---|---|
| DATE — ASTRONOMY, HOLIDAYS, AND EVENTS | SUN RISES | SUN SETS | EARLIEST MOONRISE MOONSET | MOON'S MERIDIAN PASSAGE | SUN RISES | SUN SETS | EARLIEST MOONRISE MOONSET | MOON'S MERIDIAN PASSAGE |

### 9. First Sunday of Lent
Day's Length: 11h 20m · Astron. Twilight: 1h 20m (Northern)
Day's Length: 11h 28m · Astron. Twilight: 1h 15m (Southern)

| 1 | Su | 1st U.S. Bank est., 1780 | TAU | 6:32 | 5:53 | None | 5:19p | 6:28 | 5:56 | None | 5:21p |
| 2 | Mo | Act Prohibiting Importation of Slaves, 1807 | TAU | 6:31 | 5:54 | 12:39ā | 6:08p | 6:27 | 5:57 | 12:30ā | 6:10p |
| 3 | Tu | Florida admitted as the 27th state, 1845 | TAU | 6:29 | 5:55 | 1:40ā | 7:01p | 6:26 | 5:58 | 1:29ā | 7:03p |
| 4 | We | Ember Day; Knute Rockne born, 1888 | GEM | 6:28 | 5:56 | 2:41ā | 7:56p | 6:25 | 5:59 | 2:28ā | 7:59p |
| 5 | Th | School segregation banned, 1956 | GEM | 6:26 | 5:57 | 3:39ā | 8:55p | 6:23 | 6:00 | 3:26ā | 8:57p |
| 6 | Fr | Ember Day; Alamo captured, 1836 | CAN | 6:25 | 5:58 | 4:32ā | 9:53p | 6:22 | 6:01 | 4:20ā | 9:56p |
| 7 | Sa | Ember Day | CAN | 6:23 | 5:59 | 5:19ā | 10:52p | 6:21 | 6:02 | 5:09ā | 10:54p |

### 10. Second Sunday of Lent
Day's Length: 11h 39m · Astron. Twilight: 1h 20m
Day's Length: 11h 43m · Astron. Twilight: 1h 15m

| 8 | Su | Daylight Saving Time begins | LEO | 7:22 | 7:00 | 7:01ā | None | 7:19 | 7:02 | 6:53ā | None |
| 9 | Mo | Fast of Esther; Amerigo Vespucci born, 1454 | LEO | 7:20 | 7:01 | 7:06p̄ | 12:49a | 7:18 | 7:03 | 7:13p̄ | 12:51a |
| 10 | Tu | Purim; Moon at perigee 2:37am | VIR | 7:18 | 7:02 | 8:22p̄ | 1:44a | 7:17 | 7:04 | 8:26p̄ | 1:47a |
| 11 | We | Johnny Appleseed Day | VIR | 7:17 | 7:03 | 9:38p̄ | 2:38a | 7:15 | 7:05 | 9:38p̄ | 2:41a |
| 12 | Th | Girl Scouts Day; Girl Scouts founded, 1912 | VIR | 7:15 | 7:05 | 10:52p̄ | 3:32a | 7:14 | 7:06 | 10:49p̄ | 3:34a |
| 13 | Fr | Standard time adopted in U.S., 1884 | LIB | 7:14 | 7:06 | None | 4:26a | 7:12 | 7:07 | 11:58p̄ | 4:28a |
| 14 | Sa | Albert Einstein born, 1879 | LIB | 7:12 | 7:07 | 12:05ā | 5:20a | 7:11 | 7:08 | None | 5:22a |

### 11. Third Sunday of Lent
Day's Length: 11h 57m · Astron. Twilight: 1h 20m
Day's Length: 11h 59m · Astron. Twilight: 1h 14m

| 15 | Su | Maine admitted as 23rd state, 1820 | OPH | 7:10 | 7:08 | 1:15ā | 6:15a | 7:10 | 7:08 | 1:05ā | 6:17a |
| 16 | Mo | James Madison born, 1751 | SAG | 7:09 | 7:09 | 2:20ā | 7:10a | 7:08 | 7:09 | 2:09ā | 7:12a |
| 17 | Tu | St. Patrick's Day | SAG | 7:07 | 7:10 | 3:20ā | 8:04a | 7:07 | 7:10 | 3:07ā | 8:06a |
| 18 | We | Moon and Mars at same right ascension | SAG | 7:06 | 7:11 | 4:12ā | 8:57a | 7:05 | 7:11 | 3:59ā | 8:59a |
| 19 | Th | Vernal equinox, spring begins 11:50pm | CAP | 7:04 | 7:12 | 4:56ā | 9:48a | 7:04 | 7:12 | 4:44ā | 9:50a |
| 20 | Fr | Mars/Jupiter/Saturn visually close | CAP | 7:02 | 7:13 | 5:34ā | 10:36a | 7:03 | 7:12 | 5:24ā | 10:38a |
| 21 | Sa | Johann Sebastian Bach born, 1685 | AQU | 7:01 | 7:14 | 6:07ā | 11:21a | 7:01 | 7:13 | 5:59ā | 11:23a |

### 12. Fourth Sunday of Lent
Day's Length: 12h 16m · Astron. Twilight: 1h 20m
Day's Length: 12h 14m · Astron. Twilight: 1h 15m

| 22 | Su | Jamestown massacre, 1622 | AQU | 6:59 | 7:15 | 6:36ā | 12:05p | 7:00 | 7:14 | 6:30ā | 12:07p |
| 23 | Mo | "Give me Liberty, or give me Death!," 1775 | AQU | 6:58 | 7:16 | 7:02ā | 12:46p | 6:58 | 7:15 | 6:59ā | 12:48p |
| 24 | Tu | Moon at apogee 11:41am | CET | 6:56 | 7:17 | 7:37p̄ | 1:27p | 6:57 | 7:16 | 7:39p̄ | 1:29p |
| 25 | We | Annunciation Day | CET | 6:54 | 7:18 | 8:34p̄ | 2:08p | 6:56 | 7:16 | 8:34p̄ | 2:09p |
| 26 | Th | Soviet weather satellite Meteor 1, 1969 | PSC | 6:53 | 7:19 | 9:32p̄ | 2:49p | 6:54 | 7:17 | 9:29p̄ | 2:51p |
| 27 | Fr | Farm Credit Administration formed, 1933 | ARI | 6:51 | 7:20 | 10:32p̄ | 3:31p | 6:53 | 7:18 | 10:26p̄ | 3:33p |
| 28 | Sa | Three Mile Island meltdown, 1979 | TAU | 6:49 | 7:21 | 11:32p̄ | 4:16p | 6:51 | 7:19 | 11:23p̄ | 4:18p |

### 13. Fifth Sunday of Lent
Day's Length: 12h 34m · Astron. Twilight: 1h 21m
Day's Length: 12h 30m · Astron. Twilight: 1h 15m

| 29 | Su | U.S. ratified 23rd Amendment, 1961 | TAU | 6:48 | 7:22 | None | 5:03p | 6:50 | 7:20 | None | 5:05p |
| 30 | Mo | Alaska purchased for $7.2 million, 1867 | TAU | 6:46 | 7:23 | 12:32ā | 5:54p | 6:49 | 7:20 | 12:21ā | 5:56p |
| 31 | Tu | Mars/Saturn pair optimal visibility, SE sky | ORI | 6:45 | 7:24 | 1:32ā | 6:47p | 6:47 | 7:21 | 1:20ā | 6:49p |

## MARCH 2020 WEATHER FORECAST

### ZONE 1 Northeast & New England

**1–3:** Wet, then clear/cold. **4–7:** Wet snow upstate New York/New England; snow and/or rain farther south. **8–11:** Stormy, then fair/very mild. **12–15:** Light snow New England; heavy wet snow and/or rain farther south, then fair. **16–19:** Rapidly moving storm brings two to five inches, wet snow north (upstate NY and central/northern New England); wintry mix/rain farther south. **20–23:** A slow-moving storm brings strong winds and heavy precipitation. **24–27:** Fair, then unsettled. **28–31:** Clearing.

### ZONE 2 Great Lakes, Ohio Valley & Midwest

**1–3:** Fair/cold. **4–7:** Unsettled weather. **8–11:** Clearing skies, turning spring-like. **12–15:** Rapidly moving storm brings two to five inches wet snow to Illinois, Indiana, Ohio, and the L.P. of Michigan, a wintry mix/rain to Kentucky. **16–19:** Clearing and blustery. **20–23:** Storms move through Great Lakes, then clear. **24–27:** Fair, followed by unsettled skies. **28–31:** Clearing and pleasant.

### ZONE 3 Southeast

**1–3:** Showers, then fair. **4–7:** Unsettled. **8–11:** Clearing skies, pleasant. **12–15:** Scattered showers, then fair. **16–19:** Showery rains, gusty winds, scattered thunderstorms appear as storm takes shape along Carolinas. **20–23:** Heavy rain upper Mississippi and Tennessee Valley, east to the Carolinas, then fair. **24–27:** Sunny. **28–31:** Showers quickly sweep through, then clearing.

### ZONE 4 North Central States

**1–3:** Fair and cold. **4–7:** Unsettled over Rockies, points east. **8–11:** Fair. **12–15:** Light snow Colorado, eastward across the Plains, then fair. **16–19:** Fair, then stormy weather spreads in from the west over Plains. **20–23:** Cold through Rockies and Plains. **24–27:** Fair skies, then unsettled, with showers. **28–31:** Pleasant spring weather, then becoming stormy over Rockies.

### ZONE 5 South Central States

**1–3:** Fair and cold, showers Texas eastward, then fair. **4–7:** Stormy southern Rockies through Louisiana. **8–11:** Fair. **12–15:** Scattered showers Texas eastward, then fair. Gusty winds, showers Southern Plains. **16–19:** Fair skies, then stormy into the Plains. **20–23:** Cold for Rockies/Plains. Heavy rain Texas and points east, then fair. **24–27:** Fair, then unsettled; showers Rockies and points east. **28–31:** Pleasant spring weather, then stormy for Rockies.

### ZONE 6 Northwest

**1–3:** Fair and quite chilly. **4–7:** Stormy weather. **8–11:** Fair. **12–15:** Showery, then turning fair. **16–19:** Fair weather, then stormy from Washington/Oregon, points east. **20–23:** Quite chilly, but dry. **24–27:** Fair skies, then turning unsettled. **28–31:** Pleasant spring weather, then becoming stormy.

### ZONE 7 Southwest

**1–3:** Fair/cold. **4–7:** Stormy. **8–11:** Fair weather. **12–15:** Light snow Utah, then fair. Elsewhere, quite breezy under a mix of clouds and Sun. **16–19:** Pleasant weather, then windy in California and points east. **20–23:** Cold and dry. **24–27:** Threatening skies, then clearing. **28–31:** Pleasant spring weather, then becoming stormy over West Coast.

# APRIL 2020

4th Month     **APRIL 2020**     30 Days

**ARIES**
March 19 to
April 18

**TAURUS**
April 19 to
May 19

HAIL, APRIL WITH HER SMILING FACE HAS COME TO CHEER THE PLAIN;
THE GRASS IS SEEN TO START APACE, AS DOES THE NEEDFUL GRAIN.

| MOON'S PHASES EASTERN DAYLIGHT TIME | | | SUN ON MERIDIAN CIVIL TIME | | |
|---|---|---|---|---|---|
| ◐ First Quarter | 1st | 6:21 am | Day | H:MM:SS | |
| ○ Full Moon | 7th | 10:35 pm | 1st | 13:04:10 | |
| ◑ Last Quarter | 14th | 6:56 pm | 8th | 13:02:10 | |
| ● New Moon | 22nd | 10:26 pm | 15th | 13:00:22 | |
| ◐ First Quarter | 30th | 4:38 pm | 22nd | 12:58:53 | |
| Subtract 1 hour for CDT, 2 hours for MDT, and 3 hours for PDT. | | | 29th | 12:57:46 | |

| DATE | | ASTRONOMY, HOLIDAYS, AND EVENTS | MOON'S PLACE AT 7am ASTRONOMICALLY | CALENDAR FOR NORTHERN STATES (EDT) 40°N. Lat. 75°W. Long. | | | | CALENDAR FOR SOUTHERN STATES (CDT) 35°N. Lat. 90°W. Long. | | | |
|---|---|---|---|---|---|---|---|---|---|---|---|
| | | | | SUN RISES | SUN SETS | EARLIEST MOONRISE MOONSET | MOON'S MERIDIAN PASSAGE | SUN RISES | SUN SETS | EARLIEST MOONRISE MOONSET | MOON'S MERIDIAN PASSAGE |
| 1 | We | April Fools' Day | GEM | 6:43 | 7:25 | 2:30ă | 7:42p | 6:46 | 7:22 | 2:17ă | 7:44p |
| 2 | Th | 1st U.S. Mint est., 1792 | GEM | 6:41 | 7:26 | 3:23ă | 8:39p | 6:45 | 7:23 | 3:10ă | 8:41p |
| 3 | Fr | Super tornado outbreak, 13 states, 1974 | CAN | 6:40 | 7:27 | 4:11ă | 9:36p | 6:43 | 7:24 | 4:00ă | 9:38p |
| 4 | Sa | Mexico's El Chicon volcano erupted, 1982 | LEO | 6:38 | 7:28 | 4:53ă | 10:32p | 6:42 | 7:24 | 4:44ă | 10:34p |

### 14. Passion/Palm Sunday
Day's Length: 12h 53m   Astron. Twilight: 1h 22m    Day's Length: 12h 45m   Astron. Twilight: 1h 16m

| 5 | Su | 1st presidential veto, 1792 | LEO | 6:37 | 7:29 | 5:31ă | 11:27p | 6:40 | 7:25 | 5:25ă | 11:29p |
|---|---|---|---|---|---|---|---|---|---|---|---|
| 6 | Mo | Celluloid patented, 1869 | VIR | 6:35 | 7:30 | 6:05ă | None | 6:39 | 7:26 | 6:03ă | None |
| 7 | Tu | Moon at perigee 2:15pm; Supermoon | VIR | 6:33 | 7:31 | 6:38ă | 12:21a | 6:38 | 7:27 | 6:39ă | 12:23a |
| 8 | We | Betty Ford born, 1918 | VIR | 6:32 | 7:32 | 8:26p̃ | 1:15a | 6:36 | 7:28 | 8:24p̃ | 1:17a |
| 9 | Th | Holy Thursday; 1st Day of Passover | LIB | 6:30 | 7:33 | 9:42p̃ | 2:09a | 6:35 | 7:28 | 9:36p̃ | 2:12a |
| 10 | Fr | Good Friday; ASPCA founded, 1866 | LIB | 6:29 | 7:34 | 10:56p̃ | 3:05a | 6:34 | 7:29 | 10:47p̃ | 3:07a |
| 11 | Sa | Apollo 13 launched, 1970 | OPH | 6:27 | 7:35 | None | 4:02a | 6:32 | 7:30 | 11:55p̃ | 4:04a |

### 15. Easter Sunday
Day's Length: 13h 11m   Astron. Twilight: 1h 23m    Day's Length: 13h 00m   Astron. Twilight: 1h 17m

| 12 | Su | U.S. Civil War began, 1861 | OPH | 6:26 | 7:36 | 12:07ă | 4:59a | 6:31 | 7:31 | None | 5:01a |
|---|---|---|---|---|---|---|---|---|---|---|---|
| 13 | Mo | Easter Monday; Thomas Jefferson born, 1743 | SAG | 6:24 | 7:37 | 1:11ă | 5:56a | 6:30 | 7:32 | 12:58ă | 5:58a |
| 14 | Tu | Pan-American Day | SAG | 6:23 | 7:38 | 2:08ă | 6:51a | 6:28 | 7:32 | 1:54ă | 6:53a |
| 15 | We | Moon/Saturn visually closest, SE | CAP | 6:21 | 7:39 | 2:56ă | 7:44a | 6:27 | 7:33 | 2:43ă | 7:46a |
| 16 | Th | Mercury farthest south | CAP | 6:20 | 7:40 | 3:36ă | 8:33a | 6:26 | 7:34 | 3:25ă | 8:35a |
| 17 | Fr | "Help Me Rhonda" released, 1965 | AQU | 6:18 | 7:41 | 4:10ă | 9:20a | 6:25 | 7:35 | 4:02ă | 9:22a |
| 18 | Sa | Paul Revere's ride, 1775 | AQU | 6:17 | 7:42 | 4:40ă | 10:04a | 6:23 | 7:36 | 4:34ă | 10:06a |

### 16. Second Sunday of Easter
Day's Length: 13h 28m   Astron. Twilight: 1h 24m    Day's Length: 13h 14m   Astron. Twilight: 1h 18m

| 19 | Su | Orthodox Easter; Revolutionary War, 1775 | AQU | 6:15 | 7:43 | 5:07ă | 10:46a | 6:22 | 7:36 | 5:03ă | 10:48a |
|---|---|---|---|---|---|---|---|---|---|---|---|
| 20 | Mo | Patriot's Day; Moon at apogee 3:14pm | PSC | 6:14 | 7:44 | 5:31ă | 11:27a | 6:21 | 7:37 | 5:30ă | 11:28a |
| 21 | Tu | John Adams 1st U.S. Vice President, 1789 | CET | 6:12 | 7:45 | 5:55ă | 12:07p | 6:20 | 7:38 | 5:56ă | 12:09p |
| 22 | We | Earth Day; 1st Earth Day observed, 1970 | PSC | 6:11 | 7:46 | None | 12:48p | 6:18 | 7:39 | 6:23ă | 12:50p |
| 23 | Th | William Shakespeare born, 1564 | CET | 6:10 | 7:47 | 8:25p̃ | 1:30p | 6:17 | 7:40 | 8:20p̃ | 1:32p |
| 24 | Fr | 1st soda fountain patent granted, 1833 | ARI | 6:08 | 7:48 | 9:26p̃ | 2:14p | 6:16 | 7:40 | 9:18p̃ | 2:16p |
| 25 | Sa | Spacecraft Ranger crashed on Moon, 1962 | TAU | 6:07 | 7:49 | 10:27p̃ | 3:01p | 6:15 | 7:41 | 10:16p̃ | 3:03p |

### 17. Third Sunday of Easter
Day's Length: 13h 45m   Astron. Twilight: 1h 26m    Day's Length: 13h 28m   Astron. Twilight: 1h 20m

| 26 | Su | John James Audubon born, 1785 | TAU | 6:06 | 7:50 | 11:27p̃ | 3:50p | 6:14 | 7:42 | 11:15p̃ | 3:52p |
|---|---|---|---|---|---|---|---|---|---|---|---|
| 27 | Mo | Ulysses S. Grant born, 1822 | TAU | 6:04 | 7:51 | None | 4:42p | 6:13 | 7:43 | None | 4:45p |
| 28 | Tu | League of Nations founded, 1919 | GEM | 6:03 | 7:53 | 12:25ă | 5:36p | 6:12 | 7:44 | 12:12ă | 5:39p |
| 29 | We | Joan of Arc arrived Siege of Orleans, 1429 | GEM | 6:02 | 7:54 | 1:20ă | 6:32p | 6:11 | 7:45 | 1:06ă | 6:34p |
| 30 | Th | George Washington inaugurated, 1789 | CAN | 6:00 | 7:55 | 2:08ă | 7:27p | 6:09 | 7:45 | 1:56ă | 7:29p |

## APRIL 2020 WEATHER FORECAST

### ZONE 1 Northeast & New England

**1–3:** Fair, unseasonably warm. **4–7:** Showers and gusty thunderstorms New England, New York, and all points south, then fair. **8–11:** Showers spread in from west. **12–15:** Fair. Nice for Easter. **16–19:** Thunderstorms, some with heavy rains, then turning fair and pleasant. **20–23:** Pleasant weather. Sunny for Patriots Day and Boston Marathon. **24–27:** Rainy Maine to Mid-Atlantic States, heavy wet snows higher terrain, then fair. **28–30:** Turning stormy; unseasonably warm.

### ZONE 2 Great Lakes, Ohio Valley & Midwest

**1–3:** Sharp Midwest cold front translates into tornado threat for Illinois, Indiana, western Kentucky. **4–7:** Fair, pleasant. **8–11:** Showers across Illinois and Michigan, points east, then fair. **12–15:** Fair skies. Lovely Easter Sunday. **16–19:** Showers, thunderstorms sweep through the Great Lakes area, then fair. **20–23:** Fair skies, then unsettled. **24–27:** Showery, then becoming fair. **28–30:** Turning stormy.

### ZONE 3 Southeast

**1–3:** Fair. **4–7:** Showers and strong-to-severe thunderstorms, then turning fair. **8–11:** Scattered showers. **12–15:** Fair skies. Drying out for final round of the Masters in Augusta and Easter Sunday. **16–19:** Some thunderstorms, then fair and pleasant. **20–23:** Pleasant. **24–27:** Showers, then fair. **28–30:** Stormy.

### ZONE 4 North Central States

**1–3:** Squally over Plains. Strong thunderstorms Colorado. Tornado threat for Kansas/Missouri. **4–7:** Fair, pleasant. **8–11:** Showers Plains, then fair. Windy/showery Colorado. **12–15:** Increasingly cloudy Easter. Fair, then turning stormy; squally Rockies and Plains. **16–19:** Becoming fair. **20–23:** Showers Rockies and Plains. **24–27:** Fair, then thunderstorms over northern Rockies. **28–30:** Stormy through Colorado and across Plains States.

### ZONE 5 South Central States

**1–3:** Strong thunderstorms capable of spawning tornadoes for eastern Texas and Arkansas. **4–7:** Fair, pleasant. **8–11:** Showers across Plains, then fair. Windy, showery New Mexico, then pleasant. Scattered showers Louisiana. **12–15:** Fair, then squally for Rockies. Cloudy southern Plains. Clouding up for Easter Sunday. **16–19:** Clearing skies. **20–23:** Showers for Rockies, Plains. **24–27:** Fair. **28–30:** Gusty winds/showery southern Plains; stormy Texas and Arkansas.

### ZONE 6 Northwest

**1–3:** Clearing. **4–7:** Fair skies, pleasant. **8–11:** Unsettled weather. **12–15:** Fair, then turning stormy. Sunshine Easter. **16–19:** Fair weather. **20–23:** Fair, then unsettled, especially along Pacific Coast. **24–27:** Fair. **28–30:** Unsettled/showery.

### ZONE 7 Southwest

**1–3:** Clearing West Coast. Strong thunderstorms Nevada, Utah, and Arizona. **4–7:** Fair/pleasant. **8–11:** Wind/showers Nevada, Utah, Arizona, then pleasant. **12–15:** Fair weather. Easter Sunday is dry. **16–19:** Fair skies. **20–23:** Fair, then unsettled along West Coast. **24–27:** Fair weather. **28–30:** Stormy Utah. Mixed clouds/Sun, risk of showers elsewhere.

# MAY 2020

**5th Month** | **31 Days**

**TAURUS**
April 19 to
May 19

**GEMINI**
May 20 to
June 19

WITH VERDURE THE WIDE EARTH'S OVERSPREAD, AND TREES ADORNED WITH BLOOMS;
THE PATHS IN MAY BOW SWEET TO TREAD, MID FORESTS OF PERFUME.

### MOON'S PHASES
**EASTERN DAYLIGHT TIME**

| | | |
|---|---|---|
| ○ Full Moon | 7th | 6:45 am |
| ◐ Last Quarter | 14th | 10:03 am |
| ● New Moon | 22nd | 1:39 pm |
| ◑ First Quarter | 29th | 11:30 pm |

Subtract 1 hour for CDT, 2 hours for MDT, and 3 hours for PDT.

### SUN ON MERIDIAN
**CIVIL TIME**

| Day | H:MM:SS |
|---|---|
| 1st | 12:57:32 |
| 8th | 12:56:58 |
| 15th | 12:56:52 |
| 22nd | 12:57:14 |
| 29th | 12:58:01 |

### CALENDAR FOR NORTHERN STATES
(EDT)
40°N. Lat. 75°W. Long.

### CALENDAR FOR SOUTHERN STATES
(CDT)
35°N. Lat. 90°W. Long.

| DATE | | ASTRONOMY, HOLIDAYS, AND EVENTS | MOON'S PLACE AT 7am ASTRONOMICALLY | SUN RISES | SUN SETS | EARLIEST MOONRISE MOONSET | MOON'S MERIDIAN PASSAGE | SUN RISES | SUN SETS | EARLIEST MOONRISE MOONSET | MOON'S MERIDIAN PASSAGE |
|---|---|---|---|---|---|---|---|---|---|---|---|
| 1 | Fr | Law Day; 1st US postal card issued, 1873 | LEO | 5:59 | 7:56 | 2:51ă | 8:21p | 6:08 | 7:46 | 2:41ă | 8:23p |
| 2 | Sa | Kentucky Derby; Spring Astronomy Day | LEO | 5:58 | 7:57 | 3:29ă | 9:14p | 6:07 | 7:47 | 3:21ă | 9:17p |

**18. Fourth Sunday of Easter**
Day's Length: 14h 01m / Astron. Twilight: 1h 28m
Day's Length: 13h 41m / Astron. Twilight: 1h 21m

| 3 | Su | Great San Francisco Fire, 1851 | LEO | 5:57 | 7:58 | 4:03ă | 10:07p | 6:06 | 7:48 | 3:59ă | 10:09p |
|---|---|---|---|---|---|---|---|---|---|---|---|
| 4 | Mo | Panama Canal construction began, 1904 | VIR | 5:56 | 7:59 | 4:35ă | 10:59p | 6:05 | 7:49 | 4:34ă | 11:02p |
| 5 | Tu | Cinco de Mayo; Moon at perigee 11:10pm | VIR | 5:54 | 8:00 | 5:06ă | 11:53p | 6:04 | 7:49 | 5:08ă | 11:55p |
| 6 | We | Read *Farmers' Almanac* in bathroom day | VIR | 5:53 | 8:01 | 5:38ă | None | 6:03 | 7:50 | 5:44ă | None |
| 7 | Th | Pres. Ford declared end Vietnam War, 1975 | LIB | 5:52 | 8:02 | 8:30p̄ | 12:47a | 6:02 | 7:51 | 8:22p̄ | 12:50a |
| 8 | Fr | V. E. Day; Battle of the Coral Sea began, 1942 | LIB | 5:51 | 8:03 | 9:44p̄ | 1:44a | 6:02 | 7:52 | 9:34p̄ | 1:46a |
| 9 | Sa | Kermit the Frog made TV debut, 1955 | OPH | 5:50 | 8:03 | 10:54p̄ | 2:42a | 6:01 | 7:53 | 10:42p̄ | 2:44a |

**19. Fifth Sunday of Easter**
Day's Length: 14h 16m / Astron. Twilight: 1h 30m
Day's Length: 13h 54m / Astron. Twilight: 1h 23m

| 10 | Su | Mother's Day | SAG | 5:49 | 8:04 | 11:56p̄ | 3:41a | 6:00 | 7:53 | 11:43p̄ | 3:43a |
|---|---|---|---|---|---|---|---|---|---|---|---|
| 11 | Mo | F5 tornado strikes Waco, TX, 1953 | SAG | 5:48 | 8:05 | None | 4:39a | 5:59 | 7:54 | None | 4:41a |
| 12 | Tu | Lag B'Omer, Moon/Jupiter/Saturn close | SAG | 5:47 | 8:06 | 12:50ă | 5:35a | 5:58 | 7:55 | 12:37ă | 5:37a |
| 13 | We | Final battle of the Civil War, 1865 | CAP | 5:46 | 8:07 | 1:35ă | 6:27a | 5:57 | 7:56 | 1:23ă | 6:29a |
| 14 | Th | 1st smallpox vaccination, 1796 | CAP | 5:45 | 8:08 | 2:12ă | 7:16a | 5:57 | 7:57 | 2:02ă | 7:18a |
| 15 | Fr | 1st flight attendant anniversary, 1930 | AQU | 5:44 | 8:09 | 2:43ă | 8:01a | 5:56 | 7:57 | 2:36ă | 8:03a |
| 16 | Sa | Armed Forces Day; U.S. nickel created, 1866 | AQU | 5:43 | 8:10 | 3:11ă | 8:44a | 5:55 | 7:58 | 3:06ă | 8:46a |

**20. Sixth Sunday of Easter**
Day's Length: 14h 29m / Astron. Twilight: 1h 33m
Day's Length: 14h 05m / Astron. Twilight: 1h 24m

| 17 | Su | Alaska became US territory, 1884 | PSC | 5:42 | 8:11 | 3:36ă | 9:25a | 5:54 | 7:59 | 3:34ă | 9:27a |
|---|---|---|---|---|---|---|---|---|---|---|---|
| 18 | Mo | United Nations moved to NYC, 1951 | CET | 5:41 | 8:12 | 4:00ă | 10:06a | 5:54 | 8:00 | 4:00ă | 10:07a |
| 19 | Tu | Anne Boleyn beheaded, 1536 | PSC | 5:41 | 8:13 | 4:23ă | 10:46a | 5:53 | 8:00 | 4:26ă | 10:48a |
| 20 | We | Mercury farthest north | CET | 5:40 | 8:14 | 4:48ă | 11:28a | 5:52 | 8:01 | 4:54ă | 11:30a |
| 21 | Th | Ascension Day | ARI | 5:39 | 8:15 | 5:14ă | 12:11p | 5:52 | 8:02 | 5:23ă | 12:13p |
| 22 | Fr | National Maritime Day | TAU | 5:38 | 8:16 | 5:44ă | 12:57p | 5:51 | 8:03 | 5:56ă | 12:59p |
| 23 | Sa | South Carolina became state, 1788 | TAU | 5:38 | 8:16 | 9:21p̄ | 1:46p | 5:51 | 8:03 | 9:09p̄ | 1:49p |

**21. Seventh Sunday of Easter**
Day's Length: 14h 40m / Astron. Twilight: 1h 35m
Day's Length: 14h 14m / Astron. Twilight: 1h 26m

| 24 | Su | Queen Victoria born, 1819 | TAU | 5:37 | 8:17 | 10:21p̄ | 2:38p | 5:50 | 8:04 | 10:08p̄ | 2:41p |
|---|---|---|---|---|---|---|---|---|---|---|---|
| 25 | Mo | **Memorial Day** | GEM | 5:36 | 8:18 | 11:17p̄ | 3:32p | 5:50 | 8:05 | 11:04p̄ | 3:35p |
| 26 | Tu | Montana organized U.S. territory, 1864 | GEM | 5:36 | 8:19 | None | 4:28p | 5:49 | 8:05 | 11:55p̄ | 4:30p |
| 27 | We | Chrysler Building opens in NY, 1930 | CAN | 5:35 | 8:20 | 12:08ă | 5:23p | 5:49 | 8:06 | None | 5:25p |
| 28 | Th | Orthodox Ascension Day | CAN | 5:35 | 8:21 | 12:52ă | 6:17p | 5:48 | 8:07 | 12:41ă | 6:19p |
| 29 | Fr | Shavuot | LEO | 5:34 | 8:21 | 1:31ă | 7:09p | 5:48 | 8:07 | 1:22ă | 7:11p |
| 30 | Sa | Joan of Arc burned, 1431 | LEO | 5:34 | 8:22 | 2:05ă | 8:00p | 5:48 | 8:08 | 1:59ă | 8:03p |

**22. Pentecost Sunday**
Day's Length: 14h 50m / Astron. Twilight: 1h 36m
Day's Length: 14h 22m / Astron. Twilight: 1h 27m

| 31 | Su | Walt Whitman born, 1819 | VIR | 5:33 | 8:23 | 2:36ă | 8:51p | 5:47 | 8:09 | 2:34ă | 8:53p |
|---|---|---|---|---|---|---|---|---|---|---|---|

## MAY 2020 WEATHER FORECAST

### ZONE 1 Northeast & New England

**1–3:** Thunderstorms end; unseasonably chilly, very windy. **4–7:** Warm-to-hot temperatures, then showery. **8–11:** Fair weather. **12–15:** Squally weather moves in. **16–19:** Clearing. Weather improves in time for the Preakness. **20–23:** Heavy rain showers move in from west, then fair. **24–27:** Pleasant, then very breezy with showers. **28–31:** Weather improves slowly: thunderstorms, then turning fair.

### ZONE 2 Great Lakes, Ohio Valley & Midwest

**1–3:** Fair and quite cool. Dry track for Derby Day. **4–7:** Pleasant Great Lakes and points east, then showery. **8–11:** Fair Great Lakes and points east. **12–15:** Squally weather Wisconsin and points east. **16–19:** Clearing. **20–23:** Showers Great Lakes, then fair. **24–27:** Unsettled weather spreads into Ohio Valley. Showery Indy 500. **28–31:** Turning fair.

### ZONE 3 Southeast

**1–3:** Rain along coast, then fair/chilly. **4–7:** Some showers along Gulf Coast. **8–11:** Pleasant skies. **12–15:** Scattered thunderstorms. **16–19:** Clearing skies. **20–23:** Showers Gulf Coast to Florida, followed by clearing. **24–27:** Heavy rains. **28–31:** Clearing skies.

### ZONE 4 North Central States

**1–3:** Fair, quite cool. **4–7:** Showers over Rockies, across Plains, then clear. **8–11:** Fair skies, then turning very unsettled over Rockies and Plains States. **12–15:** Squally weather Minnesota and points east. Clearing skies elsewhere. **16–19:** Fair, then some rain. **20–23:** Clearing for Kansas and Nebraska, then pleasant. **24–27:** Unsettled Colorado and points east. **28–31:** Mostly fair skies.

### ZONE 5 South Central States

**1–3:** Fair and quite cool. **4–7:** Showers Rockies, across the Plains, then clear. Threatening skies for northern New Mexico, Texas, Oklahoma. **8–11:** Becoming very unsettled for Rockies/Plains. **12–15:** Clearing. **16–19:** Fair skies, then unsettled, some rain. **20–23:** Showers Texas, Gulf Coast, followed by clearing. **24–27:** Heavy rains for Texas, Louisiana. **28–31:** Mostly fair skies, quite cool.

### ZONE 6 Northwest

**1–3:** Fair/cool. **4–7:** Unsettled. **8–11:** Changeable skies; Sun and clouds mix, risk of a shower. **12–15:** Clearing skies. **16–19:** Fair, then turning unsettled with some rain. **20–23:** Clearing/pleasant. **24–27:** Unsettled. **28–31:** Mostly fair skies, quite cool.

### ZONE 7 Southwest

**1–3:** Fair, pleasant. **4–7:** Threatening skies. **8–11:** Varying amounts of clouds and Sun. **12–15:** Clearing skies. **16–19:** Fair skies, then unsettled with some rain. **20–23:** Clearing skies. **24–27:** Unsettled weather from the West Coast and points east through Utah; skies threatening over the rest of the southwest. **28–31:** Mostly fair skies and cool.

# JUNE 2020

**6th Month**     **30 Days**

**GEMINI**
May 20 to
June 19

**CANCER**
June 20 to
July 21

SOL'S HEATING RAYS EACH MIST RETRACTS, THAT HOVERS OVER THE PLAIN;
THE CLOUDS OVERHEAD GROW THICK AND BLACK, IN TORRENTS POURS THE RAIN.

| MOON'S PHASES EASTERN DAYLIGHT TIME | | | | SUN ON MERIDIAN CIVIL TIME | | |
|---|---|---|---|---|---|---|
| ○ Full Moon | 5th | 3:12 pm | | Day | H:MM:SS | |
| ◑ Last Quarter | 13th | 2:24 am | | 1st | 12:58:27 | |
| ● New Moon | 21st | 2:41 am | | 8th | 12:59:41 | |
| ◐ First Quarter | 28th | 4:16 am | | 15th | 13:01:08 | |
| Subtract 1 hour for CDT, 2 hours for MDT, and 3 hours for PDT. | | | | 22nd | 13:02:40 | |
| | | | | 29th | 13:04:08 | |

| | | | | CALENDAR FOR NORTHERN STATES (EDT) 40°N. Lat. 75°W. Long. | | | | CALENDAR FOR SOUTHERN STATES (CDT) 35°N. Lat. 90°W. Long. | | | |
|---|---|---|---|---|---|---|---|---|---|---|---|---|
| DATE | ASTRONOMY, HOLIDAYS, AND EVENTS | MOON'S PLACE AT 7am ASTRONOMICALLY | | SUN RISES | SUN SETS | EARLIEST MOONRISE MOONSET | MOON'S MERIDIAN PASSAGE | SUN RISES | SUN SETS | EARLIEST MOONRISE MOONSET | MOON'S MERIDIAN PASSAGE |
| 1 Mo | Hurricane season begins | VIR | | 5:33 | 8:23 | 3:06ã | 9:42p | 5:47 | 8:09 | 3:07ã | 9:44p |
| 2 Tu | Moon at perigee 11:47pm | VIR | | 5:32 | 8:24 | 3:36ã | 10:34p | 5:47 | 8:10 | 3:40ã | 10:36p |
| 3 We | Ember Day | LIB | | 5:32 | 8:25 | 4:08ã | 11:28p | 5:46 | 8:11 | 4:16ã | 11:30p |
| 4 Th | 1st recorded solar eclipse, China, 781 BC | LIB | | 5:32 | 8:25 | 4:43ã | None | 5:46 | 8:11 | 4:55ã | None |
| 5 Fr | Ember Day | OPH | | 5:31 | 8:26 | 5:24ã | 12:25a | 5:46 | 8:12 | 5:38ã | 12:27a |
| 6 Sa | Ember Day | OPH | | 5:31 | 8:27 | 9:39p̃ | 1:23a | 5:46 | 8:12 | 9:26p̃ | 1:26a |

**23. Trinity Sunday** — Day's Length: 14h 56m / Astron. Twilight: 1h 38m — Day's Length: 14h 27m / Astron. Twilight: 1h 28m

| | | | | | | | | | | | |
|---|---|---|---|---|---|---|---|---|---|---|---|
| 7 Su | Orthodox Pentecost; Children's Day | SAG | | 5:31 | 8:27 | 10:38p̃ | 2:22a | 5:46 | 8:13 | 10:24p̃ | 2:25a |
| 8 Mo | *Nineteen Eighty-Four* published, 1949 | SAG | | 5:31 | 8:28 | 11:28p̃ | 3:21a | 5:45 | 8:13 | 11:15p̃ | 3:23a |
| 9 Tu | Moon/Saturn pair optimal visibility, SE sky | CAP | | 5:31 | 8:28 | None | 4:16a | 5:45 | 8:14 | 11:58p̃ | 4:18a |
| 10 We | Alcoholics Anonymous founded, 1935 | CAP | | 5:31 | 8:29 | 12:09ã | 5:07a | 5:45 | 8:14 | None | 5:09a |
| 11 Th | Corpus Christi; End of sugar rationing, 1947 | AQU | | 5:30 | 8:29 | 12:43ã | 5:55a | 5:45 | 8:14 | 12:35ã | 5:57a |
| 12 Fr | Nelson Mandela imprisoned, 1964 | AQU | | 5:30 | 8:30 | 1:13ã | 6:40a | 5:45 | 8:15 | 1:07ã | 6:41a |
| 13 Sa | Earliest sunrise of the year | AQU | | 5:30 | 8:30 | 1:39ã | 7:22a | 5:45 | 8:15 | 1:36ã | 7:24a |

**24. Corpus Christi Sunday** — Day's Length: 15h 00m / Astron. Twilight: 1h 39m — Day's Length: 14h 30m / Astron. Twilight: 1h 29m

| | | | | | | | | | | | |
|---|---|---|---|---|---|---|---|---|---|---|---|
| 14 Su | Flag Day; Moon at apogee 9:00pm | CET | | 5:30 | 8:31 | 2:03ã | 8:03a | 5:45 | 8:16 | 2:03ã | 8:04a |
| 15 Mo | Beatles' *Yesterday & Today* released, 1966 | CET | | 5:30 | 8:31 | 2:27ã | 8:43a | 5:45 | 8:16 | 2:29ã | 8:45a |
| 16 Tu | 772g meteorite near Kilbourn, WI, 1911 | PSC | | 5:30 | 8:31 | 2:51ã | 9:24a | 5:45 | 8:16 | 2:56ã | 9:26a |
| 17 We | Battle of Bunker Hill, 1775 | ARI | | 5:31 | 8:32 | 3:16ã | 10:07a | 5:46 | 8:17 | 3:24ã | 10:08a |
| 18 Th | War of 1812 declared, 1812 | TAU | | 5:31 | 8:32 | 3:45ã | 10:52a | 5:46 | 8:17 | 3:55ã | 10:54a |
| 19 Fr | Moon/Venus at same ecliptic longitude | TAU | | 5:31 | 8:32 | 4:18ã | 11:40a | 5:46 | 8:17 | 4:31ã | 11:42a |
| 20 Sa | Summer solstice 5:44pm; Highest transit Sun | TAU | | 5:31 | 8:32 | 4:56ã | 12:31p | 5:46 | 8:17 | 5:12ã | 12:33p |

**25. Third Sunday after Pentecost** — Day's Length: 15h 01m / Astron. Twilight: 1h 39m — Day's Length: 14h 31m / Astron. Twilight: 1h 29m

| | | | | | | | | | | | |
|---|---|---|---|---|---|---|---|---|---|---|---|
| 21 Su | Father's Day; Martha Washington born, 1731 | GEM | | 5:31 | 8:33 | 9:10p̃ | 1:26p | 5:46 | 8:18 | 8:57p̃ | 1:28p |
| 22 Mo | Hurricane Agnes, 1972 | GEM | | 5:31 | 8:33 | 10:04p̃ | 2:22p | 5:47 | 8:18 | 9:51p̃ | 2:24p |
| 23 Tu | Typewriter patented, 1868 | CAN | | 5:32 | 8:33 | 10:51p̃ | 3:18p | 5:47 | 8:18 | 10:40p̃ | 3:20p |
| 24 We | St. John the Baptist (Midsummer Day) | CAN | | 5:32 | 8:33 | 11:32p̃ | 4:13p | 5:47 | 8:18 | 11:23p̃ | 4:15p |
| 25 Th | Virginia ratified U.S. Constitution, 1788 | LEO | | 5:32 | 8:33 | None | 5:06p | 5:47 | 8:18 | None | 5:09p |
| 26 Fr | Christmas declared federal holiday, 1870 | LEO | | 5:33 | 8:33 | 12:08ã | 5:58p | 5:48 | 8:18 | 12:01ã | 6:00p |
| 27 Sa | Latest sunset of 2020 | VIR | | 5:33 | 8:33 | 12:40ã | 6:48p | 5:48 | 8:18 | 12:36ã | 6:50p |

**26. Fourth Sunday after Pentecost** — Day's Length: 15h 00m / Astron. Twilight: 1h 39m — Day's Length: 14h 30m / Astron. Twilight: 1h 29m

| | | | | | | | | | | | |
|---|---|---|---|---|---|---|---|---|---|---|---|
| 28 Su | Treaty of Versailles signed, 1919 | VIR | | 5:34 | 8:33 | 1:09ã | 7:37p | 5:49 | 8:18 | 1:09ã | 7:40p |
| 29 Mo | National Forest Service organized, 1891 | VIR | | 5:34 | 8:33 | 1:38ã | 8:28p | 5:49 | 8:18 | 1:41ã | 8:30p |
| 30 Tu | 1st publishing of *Gone with the Wind*, 1936 | LIB | | 5:34 | 8:33 | 2:08ã | 9:19p | 5:49 | 8:18 | 2:15ã | 9:22p |

# JUNE 2020 WEATHER FORECAST

## ZONE 1 Northeast & New England

**1–3:** Pleasant, then scattered showers. **4–7:** Dry, pleasant weather; some unseasonably chilly mornings. Sunny for Belmont Stakes. **8–11:** Thunderstorms; local flooding possible. **12–15:** Pleasant conditions. **16–19:** Showery elsewhere; possible severe thunderstorms, then fair. **20–23:** Pleasant and tranquil, but a subtropical disturbance offshore should be watched. **24–27:** Thunderstorms, followed by fair conditions. **28–30:** Scattered showers.

## ZONE 2 Great Lakes, Ohio Valley & Midwest

**1–3:** Pleasant, then scattered showers Ohio River Valley and points east. **4–7:** Pleasant Great Lakes area eastward. **8–11:** Unsettled. **12–15:** Pleasant. **16–19:** Showery, then fair. **20–23:** Dangerous thunderstorms move east into Great Lakes area. **24–27:** Thunderstorms from the Ohio River Valley and points north and east, then fair. **28–30:** More scattered thunderstorms.

## ZONE 3 Southeast

**1–3:** Rain. **4–7:** Early-season hurricane threat Florida. **8–11:** Scattered thunderstorms. **12–15:** Fair, hot. **16–19:** Heat is tempered a bit by scattered showers. Subtropical cyclone threatens northern Florida to the coasts of the Carolinas. **20–23:** Muggy weather throughout the region. **24–27:** Thunderstorms for the Gulf Coast and points north and east, then fair. **28–30:** Scattered showers.

## ZONE 4 North Central States

**1–3:** Scattered showers. **4–7:** Fair, then unsettled weather sweeps through the Rockies. **8–11:** Unsettled Plains, points east. Clearing for Colorado, points west. **12–15:** Hot Rockies, Plains. Showers, Colorado. **16–19:** Clearing Plains and points east. **20–23:** Dangerous thunderstorms Rockies, moving east over the Plains. **24–27:** Fair and hot conditions. **28–30:** Showery.

## ZONE 5 South Central States

**1–3:** Gusty winds, rain Texas. **4–7:** Fair, then unsettled through Rockies. **8–11:** Unsettled Plains, points east; thunderstorms Texas. **12–15:** Hot Rockies and Plains. **16–19:** Clearing Plains, points east. Scattered thunderstorms through Louisiana and Arkansas, followed by clearing. **20–23:** Gusty winds, showery southern Plains, points east. **24–27:** Fair/hot. **28–30:** Showers, windy New Mexico. Scattered showers Texas and points east.

## ZONE 6 Northwest

**1–3:** Scattered showers for Washington/Oregon. **4–7:** Fair skies, then unsettled. **8–11:** Clearing skies. **12–15:** Becoming unsettled Washington/Oregon. **16–19:** Fair skies. **20–23:** Unsettled. **24–27:** Fair, turning warm to hot. **28–30:** Showery.

## ZONE 7 Southwest

**1–3:** Sunshine, gusty winds. **4–7:** Fair, then unsettled/showery. **8–11:** Clearing skies. **12–15:** Hot and dry, then turning cloudy with some scattered showers. **16–19:** Fair. **20–23:** Unsettled. **24–27:** Fair and hot. **28–30:** Scattered showers, gusty winds.

# JULY 2020

**7th Month** — **31 Days**

**CANCER**
June 20 to July 21

**LEO**
July 22 to August 21

THE MOWER WALKS WITH SCYTHE IN HAND, TO YONDER FIELD AWAY;
THE GRASS HE PROSTRATES OVER THE LAND; HOW SWEET THE NEW MADE HAY.

**MOON'S PHASES — EASTERN DAYLIGHT TIME**

|  |  |  |
|---|---|---|
| ○ Full Moon | 5th | 12:44 am |
| ◑ Last Quarter | 12th | 7:29 pm |
| ● New Moon | 20th | 1:33 pm |
| ◐ First Quarter | 27th | 8:33 am |

Subtract 1 hour for CDT, 2 hours for MDT, and 3 hours for PDT.

**SUN ON MERIDIAN CIVIL TIME**

| Day | H:MM:SS |
|---|---|
| 1st | 13:04:31 |
| 8th | 13:05:42 |
| 15th | 13:06:33 |
| 22nd | 13:07:00 |
| 29th | 13:06:58 |

| DATE | | ASTRONOMY, HOLIDAYS, AND EVENTS | MOON'S PLACE AT 7am ASTRONOMICALLY | Northern SUN RISES | Northern SUN SETS | Northern EARLIEST MOONRISE MOONSET | Northern MOON'S MERIDIAN PASSAGE | Southern SUN RISES | Southern SUN SETS | Southern EARLIEST MOONRISE MOONSET | Southern MOON'S MERIDIAN PASSAGE |
|---|---|---|---|---|---|---|---|---|---|---|---|
| 1 | We | The dollar named U.S. monetary unit, 1785 | LIB | 5:35 | 8:33 | 2:41ã | 10:13p | 5:50 | 8:18 | 2:51ã | 10:16p |
| 2 | Th | Midpoint of 2020 | SCO | 5:35 | 8:33 | 3:18ã | 11:10p | 5:50 | 8:18 | 3:32ã | 11:12p |
| 3 | Fr | Dog Days begin | OPH | 5:36 | 8:33 | 4:02ã | None | 5:51 | 8:18 | 4:18ã | None |
| 4 | Sa | **Independence Day**; Earth at aphelion | SAG | 5:37 | 8:32 | 4:52ã | 12:08a | 5:51 | 8:18 | 5:10ã | 12:10a |

**27. Fifth Sunday after Pentecost**
Day's Length: 14h 55m / Astron. Twilight: 1h 38m
Day's Length: 14h 26m / Astron. Twilight: 1h 28m

| DATE | | ASTRONOMY, HOLIDAYS, AND EVENTS | | SUN RISES | SUN SETS | EARLIEST M/M | MOON'S MP | SUN RISES | SUN SETS | EARLIEST M/M | MOON'S MP |
|---|---|---|---|---|---|---|---|---|---|---|---|
| 5 | Su | P.T. Barnum born, 1810 | SAG | 5:37 | 8:32 | 9:18p̃ | 1:06a | 5:52 | 8:18 | 9:05p̃ | 1:08a |
| 6 | Mo | Moon/Jupiter pair optimal visibility, S sky | CAP | 5:38 | 8:32 | 10:03p̃ | 2:03a | 5:52 | 8:17 | 9:51p̃ | 2:05a |
| 7 | Tu | 1st women FBI members sworn in, 1972 | CAP | 5:38 | 8:31 | 10:41p̃ | 2:56a | 5:53 | 8:17 | 10:31p̃ | 2:59a |
| 8 | We | 1st issue of *The Wall Street Journal*, 1889 | CAP | 5:39 | 8:31 | 11:13p̃ | 3:46a | 5:53 | 8:17 | 11:06p̃ | 3:48a |
| 9 | Th | Fast of Tammuz | AQU | 5:40 | 8:31 | 11:40p̃ | 4:33a | 5:54 | 8:17 | 11:36p̃ | 4:35a |
| 10 | Fr | Hurricane Dennis hit Florida, 2005 | AQU | 5:40 | 8:30 | None | 5:17a | 5:54 | 8:16 | None | 5:18a |
| 11 | Sa | E.B. White born, 1899 | PSC | 5:41 | 8:30 | 12:06ã | 5:58a | 5:55 | 8:16 | 12:04ã | 6:00a |

**28. Sixth Sunday after Pentecost**
Day's Length: 14h 48m / Astron. Twilight: 1h 36m
Day's Length: 14h 21m / Astron. Twilight: 1h 27m

| DATE | | ASTRONOMY, HOLIDAYS, AND EVENTS | | SUN RISES | SUN SETS | EARLIEST M/M | MOON'S MP | SUN RISES | SUN SETS | EARLIEST M/M | MOON'S MP |
|---|---|---|---|---|---|---|---|---|---|---|---|
| 12 | Su | Moon at apogee 3:26pm | CET | 5:42 | 8:29 | 12:29ã | 6:39a | 5:56 | 8:16 | 12:30ã | 6:40a |
| 13 | Mo | 1st All-Star Game played outside U.S., 1982 | PSC | 5:42 | 8:29 | 12:53ã | 7:19a | 5:56 | 8:15 | 12:57ã | 7:21a |
| 14 | Tu | 1st major U.S. World's Fair opened, 1853 | CET | 5:43 | 8:28 | 1:18ã | 8:01a | 5:57 | 8:15 | 1:24ã | 8:03a |
| 15 | We | St. Swithin's Day; Rembrandt born, 1606 | ARI | 5:44 | 8:28 | 1:44ã | 8:45a | 5:58 | 8:14 | 1:54ã | 8:47a |
| 16 | Th | District of Columbia authorized, 1790 | TAU | 5:45 | 8:27 | 2:15ã | 9:31a | 5:58 | 8:14 | 2:27ã | 9:33a |
| 17 | Fr | Disneyland opened, 1955 | TAU | 5:46 | 8:26 | 2:51ã | 10:21a | 5:59 | 8:13 | 3:06ã | 10:23a |
| 18 | Sa | Nelson Mandela born, 1918 | TAU | 5:46 | 8:26 | 3:34ã | 11:14a | 6:00 | 8:13 | 3:51ã | 11:17a |

**29. Seventh Sunday after Pentecost**
Day's Length: 14h 38m / Astron. Twilight: 1h 34m
Day's Length: 14h 12m / Astron. Twilight: 1h 26m

| DATE | | ASTRONOMY, HOLIDAYS, AND EVENTS | | SUN RISES | SUN SETS | EARLIEST M/M | MOON'S MP | SUN RISES | SUN SETS | EARLIEST M/M | MOON'S MP |
|---|---|---|---|---|---|---|---|---|---|---|---|
| 19 | Su | Fiberglass sutures used in surgery, 1939 | GEM | 5:47 | 8:25 | 4:25ã | 12:10p | 6:00 | 8:12 | 4:43ã | 12:13p |
| 20 | Mo | U.S. robot spacecraft landed on Mars, 1976 | GEM | 5:48 | 8:24 | 5:25ã | 1:08p | 6:01 | 8:12 | 5:43ã | 1:10p |
| 21 | Tu | Ernest Hemingway born, 1899 | CAN | 5:49 | 8:24 | 9:30p̃ | 2:05p | 6:02 | 8:11 | 9:20p̃ | 2:07p |
| 22 | We | Wiley Post completed 1st solo flight, 1933 | LEO | 5:50 | 8:23 | 10:08p̃ | 3:00p | 6:02 | 8:10 | 10:01p̃ | 3:02p |
| 23 | Th | Salvation Army founded, 1865 | LEO | 5:51 | 8:22 | 10:42p̃ | 3:53p | 6:03 | 8:10 | 10:37p̃ | 3:56p |
| 24 | Fr | Amelia Earhart born, 1897 | LEO | 5:51 | 8:21 | 11:12p̃ | 4:45p | 6:04 | 8:09 | 11:11p̃ | 4:47p |
| 25 | Sa | Moon at perigee 12:53am | VIR | 5:52 | 8:20 | 11:42p̃ | 5:35p | 6:04 | 8:08 | 11:44p̃ | 5:37p |

**30. Eighth Sunday after Pentecost**
Day's Length: 14h 26m / Astron. Twilight: 1h 32m
Day's Length: 14h 02m / Astron. Twilight: 1h 24m

| DATE | | ASTRONOMY, HOLIDAYS, AND EVENTS | | SUN RISES | SUN SETS | EARLIEST M/M | MOON'S MP | SUN RISES | SUN SETS | EARLIEST M/M | MOON'S MP |
|---|---|---|---|---|---|---|---|---|---|---|---|
| 26 | Su | U.S. military desegregated, 1948 | VIR | 5:53 | 8:19 | None | 6:25p | 6:05 | 8:07 | None | 6:27p |
| 27 | Mo | Bugs Bunny made official debut, 1940 | VIR | 5:54 | 8:18 | 12:11ã | 7:16p | 6:06 | 8:07 | 12:17ã | 7:18p |
| 28 | Tu | U.S. passes 14th Amendment, 1868 | LIB | 5:55 | 8:17 | 12:43ã | 8:08p | 6:07 | 8:06 | 12:52ã | 8:10p |
| 29 | We | Dwarf planet Eris discovered, 2005 | LIB | 5:56 | 8:16 | 1:18ã | 9:03p | 6:07 | 8:05 | 1:30ã | 9:05p |
| 30 | Th | Fast of Av; Henry Ford born, 1863 | OPH | 5:57 | 8:15 | 1:58ã | 9:59p | 6:08 | 8:04 | 2:13ã | 10:01p |
| 31 | Fr | 1st U.S. patent issued, 1790 | SAG | 5:58 | 8:14 | 2:45ã | 10:56p | 6:09 | 8:03 | 3:02ã | 10:58p |

**CALENDAR FOR NORTHERN STATES** (EDT) — 40°N. Lat. 75°W. Long.

**CALENDAR FOR SOUTHERN STATES** (CDT) — 35°N. Lat. 90°W. Long.

## JULY 2020 WEATHER FORECAST

### ZONE 1 Northeast & New England
**1–3:** Clearing New England. Fair/hot Maryland and Delaware. **4–7:** Widely scattered showers and thunderstorms could hinder July 4th activities. **8–11:** Widespread thunderstorms, then turning fair. **12–15:** Windy, rainy, followed by clearing. **16–19:** Hot, 90s to near 100. **20–23:** Severe thunderstorms, then fair. **24–27:** Thunderstorms. **28–31:** Hot; perhaps an isolated thunderstorm.

### ZONE 2 Great Lakes, Ohio Valley & Midwest
**1–3:** Hot. **4–7:** Severe thunderstorms sweep in from the west possibly threatening the Fourth of July holiday. **8–11:** Fair, hot. **12–15:** Thunderstorms again sweep in from the west over the Great Lakes. **16–19:** Hot; temperatures will be in the 90s, followed by thunderstorms. **20–23:** Severe thunderstorms Great Lakes and points east, then fair. **24–27:** Thunderstorms. **28–31:** Hot; risk of hit-or-miss thunderstorms.

### ZONE 3 Southeast
**1–3:** Fair, hot weather. **4–7:** Big thunderstorms could mar Independence Day activities for Tennessee, northern portions of Mississippi, Alabama, Georgia, and the Carolinas. **8–11:** Mostly fair/hot. **12–15:** Rainy/windy, then fair. **16–19:** Hot and sultry. **20–23:** Thunderstorms. **24–27:** Showery. **28–31:** Hot with widely scattered showers and thunderstorms.

### ZONE 4 North Central States
**1–3:** Hot. **4–7:** Severe thunderstorms, with possible tornado weather most of Kansas, Missouri, eastern parts of Nebraska, through Iowa. **8–11:** Fair, hot. Temperatures soar to near 100°. **12–15:** Unsettled for Rockies; thunderstorms Plains. **16–19:** Hot, then stormy through Rockies over Plains to Nebraska and Dakotas. **20–23:** Fair. **24–27:** Scattered showers across Rockies, Plains, then clearing. **28–31:** Hot; thunderstorms.

### ZONE 5 South Central States
**1–3:** Hot. **4–7:** Severe thunderstorms; possible tornadoes in Oklahoma; big thunderstorms Texas, northeastward through Arkansas and Louisiana. **8–11:** Mostly fair, hot. **12–15:** Unsettled Rockies; thunderstorms across the Plains. **16–19:** Hot, then stormy. Squally monsoons New Mexico. **20–23:** Fair. **24–27:** Scattered showers, then clearing. Showery Texas, points east. **28–31:** Hot; only widely scattered showers and thunderstorms, chiefly New Mexico.

### ZONE 6 Northwest
**1–3:** Fair. **4–7:** Unsettled conditions for July 4th holiday. **8–11:** Mostly fair with warm-to-hot temperatures. **12–15:** Unsettled. **16–19:** Temperatures warm to hot, then widely scattered showers. **20–23:** Fair. **24–27:** Turning unsettled with scattered showers, followed by clearing. **28–31:** Warm-to-hot temperatures; risk of showers.

### ZONE 7 Southwest
**1–3:** Fair skies. **4–7:** Mixed clouds and Sun; risk of passing shower/thunderstorm. **8–11:** Hot/dry. **12–15:** Variable cloudiness, dry. No weather problems for the MLB All Star Game at Dodger Stadium. **16–19:** Hot. Squally monsoons Arizona. **20–23:** Fair. **24–27:** Turning unsettled West Coast. **28–31:** Hot temperatures; widely scattered showers/thunderstorms, chiefly over Arizona.

# AUGUST 2020

**8th Month** — **31 Days**

**LEO**
July 22 to
August 21

**VIRGO**
August 22 to
September 21

THE GATHERING CLOUDS BESPREAD THE SKY, AND GENTLE SHOWERS DESCEND;
THE RIPENING FRUITS WE JUST DESCRY, AS SUMMER IS AT END.

### MOON'S PHASES — EASTERN DAYLIGHT TIME

| | | |
|---|---|---|
| ○ Full Moon | 3rd | 11:59 am |
| ◑ Last Quarter | 11th | 12:45 pm |
| ● New Moon | 18th | 10:42 pm |
| ◐ First Quarter | 25th | 1:58 pm |

Subtract 1 hour for CDT, 2 hours for MDT, and 3 hours for PDT.

### SUN ON MERIDIAN CIVIL TIME

| Day | H:MM:SS |
|---|---|
| 1st | 13:06:48 |
| 8th | 13:06:03 |
| 15th | 13:04:50 |
| 22nd | 13:03:13 |
| 29th | 13:01:13 |

MOON'S PLACE AT 7am ASTRONOMICALLY

### CALENDAR FOR NORTHERN STATES (EDT) — 40°N. Lat. 75°W. Long.

### CALENDAR FOR SOUTHERN STATES (CDT) — 35°N. Lat. 90°W. Long.

| DATE | | ASTRONOMY, HOLIDAYS, AND EVENTS | MOON'S PLACE | SUN RISES | SUN SETS | EARLIEST MOONRISE MOONSET | MOON'S MERIDIAN PASSAGE | SUN RISES | SUN SETS | EARLIEST MOONRISE MOONSET | MOON'S MERIDIAN PASSAGE |
|---|---|---|---|---|---|---|---|---|---|---|---|
| 1 | Sa | Francis Scott Key born, 1779 | SAG | 5:59 | 8:13 | 3:38ã | 11:52p | 6:10 | 8:02 | 3:56ã | 11:55p |

**31. Ninth Sunday after Pentecost** — Day's Length: 14h 13m / Astron. Twilight: 1h 30m — Day's Length: 13h 51m / Astron. Twilight: 1h 22m

| 2 | Su | "Wild Bill" Hickok shot, 1876 | SAG | 6:00 | 8:12 | 4:37ã | None | 6:10 | 8:02 | 4:55ã | None |
| 3 | Mo | Mars at perihelion | CAP | 6:01 | 8:11 | 5:40ã | 12:47a | 6:11 | 8:01 | 5:56ã | 12:49a |
| 4 | Tu | President Barack Obama born, 1961 | CAP | 6:01 | 8:10 | 9:12p | 1:38a | 6:12 | 8:00 | 9:04p | 1:40a |
| 5 | We | NASA revealed liquid on Mars, 2011 | AQU | 6:02 | 8:09 | 9:41p | 2:26a | 6:13 | 7:59 | 9:36p | 2:28a |
| 6 | Th | Midpoint of summer | AQU | 6:03 | 8:08 | 10:07p | 3:11a | 6:13 | 7:58 | 10:04p | 3:13a |
| 7 | Fr | Creation of Purple Heart, 1782 | PSC | 6:04 | 8:06 | 10:31p | 3:53a | 6:14 | 7:57 | 10:31p | 3:55a |
| 8 | Sa | Dustin Hoffman born, 1937 | CET | 6:05 | 8:05 | 10:55p | 4:34a | 6:15 | 7:56 | 10:58p | 4:36a |

**32. Tenth Sunday after Pentecost** — Day's Length: 13h 58m / Astron. Twilight: 1h 28m — Day's Length: 13h 39m / Astron. Twilight: 1h 21m

| 9 | Su | Moon/Mars pair optimal visibility, SE sky | PSC | 6:06 | 8:04 | 11:19p | 5:15a | 6:16 | 7:55 | 11:24p | 5:17a |
| 10 | Mo | Smithsonian Institution chartered, 1846 | CET | 6:07 | 8:03 | 11:44p | 5:56a | 6:16 | 7:54 | 11:53p | 5:58a |
| 11 | Tu | Dog Days end; 1st roller rink opened, 1866 | ARI | 6:08 | 8:01 | None | 6:38a | 6:17 | 7:52 | None | 6:40a |
| 12 | We | IBM unveiled its 1st PC, 1981 | TAU | 6:09 | 8:00 | 12:13ã | 7:23a | 6:18 | 7:51 | 12:24ã | 7:25a |
| 13 | Th | Annie Oakley born, 1860 | TAU | 6:10 | 7:59 | 12:46ã | 8:11a | 6:19 | 7:50 | 1:00ã | 8:13a |
| 14 | Fr | V. J. Day; Doc Holliday born, 1851 | TAU | 6:11 | 7:57 | 1:25ã | 9:02a | 6:19 | 7:49 | 1:41ã | 9:04a |
| 15 | Sa | Moon/Venus pair optimal visibility, E sky | GEM | 6:12 | 7:56 | 2:12ã | 9:56a | 6:20 | 7:48 | 2:30ã | 9:59a |

**33. Eleventh Sunday after Pentecost** — Day's Length: 13h 42m / Astron. Twilight: 1h 26m — Day's Length: 13h 26m / Astron. Twilight: 1h 19m

| 16 | Su | 1st issue of *Sports Illustrated*, 1954 | GEM | 6:13 | 7:55 | 3:08ã | 10:53a | 6:21 | 7:47 | 3:26ã | 10:55a |
| 17 | Mo | Cat Nights begin | CAN | 6:14 | 7:53 | 4:12ã | 11:51a | 6:22 | 7:46 | 4:29ã | 11:53a |
| 18 | Tu | Shelley Winters born, 1920 | LEO | 6:15 | 7:52 | 5:22ã | 12:48p | 6:23 | 7:44 | 5:37ã | 12:50p |
| 19 | We | Gold discovered in CA, 1848 | LEO | 6:16 | 7:51 | 8:40p | 1:43p | 6:23 | 7:43 | 8:34p | 1:45p |
| 20 | Th | Dial telephone patent filed, 1896 | LEO | 6:17 | 7:49 | 9:12p | 2:37p | 6:24 | 7:42 | 9:10p | 2:39p |
| 21 | Fr | Moon at perigee 6:49am | VIR | 6:18 | 7:48 | 9:43p | 3:29p | 6:25 | 7:41 | 9:44p | 3:31p |
| 22 | Sa | Mona Lisa stolen from Louvre, 1911 | VIR | 6:19 | 7:46 | 10:13p | 4:20p | 6:26 | 7:39 | 10:18p | 4:22p |

**34. Twelfth Sunday after Pentecost** — Day's Length: 13h 25m / Astron. Twilight: 1h 24m — Day's Length: 13h 12m / Astron. Twilight: 1h 18m

| 23 | Su | Oliver Hazard Perry born, 1785 | VIR | 6:20 | 7:45 | 10:44p | 5:12p | 6:26 | 7:38 | 10:52p | 5:14p |
| 24 | Mo | Printing of Gutenberg Bible completed, 1456 | LIB | 6:20 | 7:43 | 11:19p | 6:04p | 6:27 | 7:37 | 11:30p | 6:07p |
| 25 | Tu | Galileo Galilei demonstrated telescope, 1609 | LIB | 6:21 | 7:42 | 11:57p | 6:59p | 6:28 | 7:35 | None | 7:01p |
| 26 | We | The 19th amendment took effect, 1920 | OPH | 6:22 | 7:40 | None | 7:54p | 6:28 | 7:34 | 12:12ã | 7:57p |
| 27 | Th | Lyndon B. Johnson born, 1908 | OPH | 6:23 | 7:39 | 12:42ã | 8:51p | 6:29 | 7:33 | 12:58ã | 8:53p |
| 28 | Fr | Moon/Jupiter/Saturn visually close, S sky | SAG | 6:24 | 7:37 | 1:33ã | 9:47p | 6:30 | 7:32 | 1:51ã | 9:49p |
| 29 | Sa | Oliver Wendell Holmes born, 1841 | SAG | 6:25 | 7:36 | 2:29ã | 10:41p | 6:31 | 7:30 | 2:47ã | 10:43p |

**35. Thirteenth Sunday after Pentecost** — Day's Length: 13h 08m / Astron. Twilight: 1h 23m — Day's Length: 12h 57m / Astron. Twilight: 1h 17m

| 30 | Su | Hurricane Carol killed 68 people, 1954 | CAP | 6:26 | 7:34 | 3:30ã | 11:33p | 6:31 | 7:29 | 3:47ã | 11:35p |
| 31 | Mo | 1st recorded comet-sun collision, 1979 | CAP | 6:27 | 7:32 | 4:33ã | None | 6:32 | 7:27 | 4:48ã | None |

## AUGUST 2020 WEATHER FORECAST

### ZONE 1 Northeast & New England

**1–3:** Fair. **4–7:** Thunderstorms, through New England south to Delmarva Peninsula, then turning mainly fair. **8–11:** Heavy showers; a few isolated severe storms possible, then clearing. **12–15:** Pleasant. **16–19:** Thunderstorms, then turning fair. **20–23:** Fair, then becoming unsettled, showers. **24–27:** Mostly fair, hot. **28–31:** The heat goes on.

### ZONE 2 Great Lakes, Ohio Valley & Midwest

**1–3:** Squally Great Lakes. **4–7:** Mostly fair and hot. **8–11:** Showers Illinois and Michigan, then clearing. **12–15:** Fair, then turning very unsettled. **16–19:** Thunderstorms from Great Lakes and points east, then turning fair. **20–23:** Fair, then showers develop from the west and move into Great Lakes area. **24–27:** Mostly fair, hot. **28–31:** Stormy.

### ZONE 3 Southeast

**1–3:** Mostly fair skies. **4–7:** Showers, thunderstorms, then mostly fair. **8–11:** Scattered thunderstorms, then turning fair. **12–15:** Pleasant weather. **16–19:** Thunderstorms for Tennessee east to Carolinas, then clearing skies. **20–23:** Thunderstorms. **24–27:** Humid/showery. **28–31:** Scattered thunderstorms.

### ZONE 4 North Central States

**1–3:** Squally for Colorado, and across Plains States. **4–7:** Mostly fair, hot. **8–11:** Showers Rockies, Plains. **12–15:** Fair, then very unsettled, with heavy thunderstorms across Colorado, points east.

**16–19:** Pleasant weather. **20–23:** Fair, then showers from Rockies and points east. **24–27:** Fair skies, then unsettled over Rockies. **28–31:** Stormy Plains and points east.

### ZONE 5 South Central States

**1–3:** Gusty winds/showery New Mexico, Texas, parts of Oklahoma. **4–7:** Mostly fair, hot. **8–11:** Rain Texas. Gusty winds over Plains. **12–15:** Fair, then turning unsettled. **16–19:** Pleasant. **20–23:** Fair, then showers from Rockies and points east. **24–27:** Fair weather, then turning unsettled over Rockies. **28–31:** Thunderstorms from Plains move through Texas, all points east.

### ZONE 6 Northwest

**1–3:** Unsettled. **4–7:** Mostly fair. Warm-to-hot temperatures. **8–11:** Showery. **12–15:** Fair skies, then turning unsettled. **16–19:** Pleasant weather. **20–23:** Fair, followed by clouds and some widely scattered showers. **24–27:** Fair, then unsettled. **28–31:** Fair skies return.

### ZONE 7 Southwest

**1–3:** Squally Utah. Gusty winds, showers Nevada/northern Arizona. **4–7:** Mostly fair and hot. **8–11:** Changeable; mixed clouds, sun, risk of a shower. **12–15:** Fair, then very unsettled with heavy thunderstorms across Utah and points east. **16–19:** Pleasant weather. **20–23:** Fair, then cloudiness, gusty winds, and a passing shower possible. **24–27:** Fair skies, then becoming unsettled. **28–31:** Fair weather.

# SEPTEMBER 2020

**9th Month** — **30 Days**

**VIRGO**
August 22 to
September 21

**LIBRA**
September 22 to
October 21

NOW AUTUMN'S GOLDEN STORES BEHOLD, WITH FRUIT EACH TREE IS CROWNED;
PEACHES IN SUITS OF RED OR GOLD, EACH TWIG BOWS TOWARD THE GROUND.

**MOON'S PHASES**
**EASTERN DAYLIGHT TIME**

| | | |
|---|---|---|
| ○ Full Moon | 2nd | 1:22 am |
| ◑ Last Quarter | 10th | 5:26 am |
| ● New Moon | 17th | 7:00 am |
| ◐ First Quarter | 23rd | 9:55 pm |

Subtract 1 hour for CDT, 2 hours for MDT, and 3 hours for PDT.

**SUN ON MERIDIAN**
**CIVIL TIME**

| Day | H:MM:SS |
|---|---|
| 1st | 13:00:16 |
| 8th | 12:57:55 |
| 15th | 12:55:27 |
| 22nd | 12:52:58 |
| 29th | 12:50:34 |

**CALENDAR FOR NORTHERN STATES** (EDT) 40°N. Lat. 75°W. Long.

**CALENDAR FOR SOUTHERN STATES** (CDT) 35°N. Lat. 90°W. Long.

| DATE | | ASTRONOMY, HOLIDAYS, AND EVENTS | MOON'S PLACE AT 7am ASTRONOMICALLY | SUN RISES | SUN SETS | EARLIEST MOONRISE MOONSET | MOON'S MERIDIAN PASSAGE | SUN RISES | SUN SETS | EARLIEST MOONRISE MOONSET | MOON'S MERIDIAN PASSAGE |
|---|---|---|---|---|---|---|---|---|---|---|---|
| 1 | Tu | Pullman sleeping car, 1859 | AQU | 6:28 | 7:31 | 5:36ă | 12:21a | 6:33 | 7:26 | 5:48ă | 12:23a |
| 2 | We | Great Fire of London, 1666 | AQU | 6:29 | 7:29 | 8:09p̄ | 1:07a | 6:34 | 7:25 | 8:06p̄ | 1:08a |
| 3 | Th | ATM machine 1st used, 1969 | AQU | 6:30 | 7:28 | 8:34p̄ | 1:50a | 6:34 | 7:23 | 8:33p̄ | 1:51a |
| 4 | Fr | Los Angeles, CA, founded 1781 | CET | 6:31 | 7:26 | 8:58p̄ | 2:31a | 6:35 | 7:22 | 8:59p̄ | 2:33a |
| 5 | Sa | Jesse James born, 1847 | PSC | 6:32 | 7:24 | 9:21p̄ | 3:12a | 6:36 | 7:21 | 9:26p̄ | 3:13a |

**36. Fourteenth Sunday after Pentecost**
Day's Length: 1h 50m / Astron. Twilight: 1h 21m
Day's Length: 12h 43m / Astron. Twilight: 1h 16m

| 6 | Su | Moon at apogee 2:20am | PSC | 6:33 | 7:23 | 9:46p̄ | 3:52a | 6:37 | 7:19 | 9:53p̄ | 3:54a |
|---|---|---|---|---|---|---|---|---|---|---|---|
| 7 | Mo | **Labor Day** | ARI | 6:34 | 7:21 | 10:13p̄ | 4:34a | 6:37 | 7:18 | 10:23p̄ | 4:36a |
| 8 | Tu | Buddy Holly born, 1936 | TAU | 6:35 | 7:20 | 10:43p̄ | 5:17a | 6:38 | 7:16 | 10:56p̄ | 5:19a |
| 9 | We | Lincoln received law license, 1836 | TAU | 6:36 | 7:18 | 11:19p̄ | 6:03a | 6:39 | 7:15 | 11:35p̄ | 6:05a |
| 10 | Th | Traditional peak of hurricane season | TAU | 6:36 | 7:16 | None | 6:52a | 6:39 | 7:13 | None | 6:54a |
| 11 | Fr | Halley's Comet rediscovered, 1909 | GEM | 6:37 | 7:15 | 12:02ă | 7:44a | 6:40 | 7:12 | 12:19ă | 7:46a |
| 12 | Sa | Canyonlands National Park est., 1964 | GEM | 6:38 | 7:13 | 12:52ă | 8:38a | 6:41 | 7:11 | 1:11ă | 8:41a |

**37. Fifteenth Sunday after Pentecost**
Day's Length: 12h 32m / Astron. Twilight: 1h 21m
Day's Length: 12h 28m / Astron. Twilight: 1h 15m

| 13 | Su | Willie Mays hit 500th HR, 1965 | CAN | 6:39 | 7:11 | 1:51ă | 9:35a | 6:42 | 7:09 | 2:09ă | 9:37a |
|---|---|---|---|---|---|---|---|---|---|---|---|
| 14 | Mo | Holy Cross Day | CAN | 6:40 | 7:10 | 2:58ă | 10:31a | 6:42 | 7:08 | 3:14ă | 10:34a |
| 15 | Tu | Darwin reached Galapagos Islands, 1835 | LEO | 6:41 | 7:08 | 4:10ă | 11:27a | 6:43 | 7:06 | 4:23ă | 11:30a |
| 16 | We | Ember Day; San Felipe Hurricane, 1928 | LEO | 6:42 | 7:06 | 5:24ă | 12:22p | 6:44 | 7:05 | 5:35ă | 12:24p |
| 17 | Th | Citizenship Day | VIR | 6:43 | 7:05 | 6:40ă | 1:16p | 6:45 | 7:03 | 6:47ă | 1:18p |
| 18 | Fr | Ember Day; Moon at perigee 9:41am | VIR | 6:44 | 7:03 | 8:11p̄ | 2:09p | 6:45 | 7:02 | 8:14p̄ | 2:11p |
| 19 | Sa | Rosh Hashanah (New Year 5781); Ember Day | VIR | 6:45 | 7:01 | 8:42p̄ | 3:02p | 6:46 | 7:00 | 8:49p̄ | 3:04p |

**38. Sixteenth Sunday after Pentecost**
Day's Length: 12h 14m / Astron. Twilight: 1h 20m
Day's Length: 12h 12m / Astron. Twilight: 1h 15m

| 20 | Su | Dr. Joyce Brothers born, 1928 | LIB | 6:46 | 7:00 | 9:16p̄ | 3:56p | 6:47 | 6:59 | 9:27p̄ | 3:58p |
|---|---|---|---|---|---|---|---|---|---|---|---|
| 21 | Mo | Fast of Gedaliah | LIB | 6:47 | 6:58 | 9:54p̄ | 4:52p | 6:47 | 6:58 | 10:08p̄ | 4:54p |
| 22 | Tu | Autumnal equinox, fall begins 9:31am | OPH | 6:48 | 6:56 | 10:38p̄ | 5:48p | 6:48 | 6:56 | 10:54p̄ | 5:51p |
| 23 | We | Lewis & Clark completed journey, 1806 | OPH | 6:49 | 6:55 | 11:28p̄ | 6:46p | 6:49 | 6:55 | 11:46p̄ | 6:48p |
| 24 | Th | Moon/Jupiter pair optimal visibility, SW sky | SAG | 6:50 | 6:53 | None | 7:43p | 6:50 | 6:53 | None | 7:45p |
| 25 | Fr | Sequoia National Park est., 1890 | SAG | 6:51 | 6:51 | 12:23ă | 8:38p | 6:50 | 6:52 | 12:42ă | 8:40p |
| 26 | Sa | Fall Astronomy Day | CAP | 6:52 | 6:50 | 1:23ă | 9:30p | 6:51 | 6:50 | 1:41ă | 9:32p |

**39. Seventeenth Sunday after Pentecost**
Day's Length: 11h 56m / Astron. Twilight: 1h 20m
Day's Length: 11h 57m / Astron. Twilight: 1h 14m

| 27 | Su | Gold Star Mother's Day | CAP | 6:53 | 6:48 | 2:26ă | 10:19p | 6:52 | 6:49 | 2:41ă | 10:21p |
|---|---|---|---|---|---|---|---|---|---|---|---|
| 28 | Mo | Yom Kippur | AQU | 6:54 | 6:47 | 3:28ă | 11:05p | 6:53 | 6:48 | 3:41ă | 11:06p |
| 29 | Tu | Michaelmas Day; Michelangelo born, 1571 | AQU | 6:55 | 6:45 | 4:30ă | 11:48p | 6:53 | 6:46 | 4:40ă | 11:50p |
| 30 | We | 1st Edison hydroelectric plant, 1882 | AQU | 6:56 | 6:43 | 5:30ă | None | 6:54 | 6:45 | 5:37ă | None |

## SEPTEMBER 2020 WEATHER FORECAST

### ZONE 1 Northeast & New England

**1–3:** Thunderstorms, then becoming pleasant. **4–7:** Improving weather for Labor Day; scattered showers and thunderstorms, then fair. **8–11:** Clearing, cooler weather. **12–15:** Hurricane threat from Virginia Capes/Delmarva to Cape Cod on to eastern Maine. **16–19:** Fair, then showers. **20–23:** Mostly fair skies developing. **24–27:** Locally heavy showers/thunderstorms. **28–30:** Clear.

### ZONE 2 Great Lakes, Ohio Valley & Midwest

**1–3:** Fair. **4–7:** Showers persist through Labor Day. **8–11:** Severe thunderstorms. Tornado possibility. **12–15:** Thunderstorms in Kentucky and Ohio Valley, followed by clearing. **16–19:** Fair, then scattered showers. **20–23:** Mostly fair. **24–27:** Locally heavy showers and thunderstorms from the Great Lakes, points east. **28–30:** Fair/quite cool.

### ZONE 3 Southeast

**1–3:** Thunderstorms clear the Atlantic Coast, then turning fair. **4–7:** Potentially stormy Labor Day weekend; widespread thunderstorms. **8–11:** Fair skies. **12–15:** Thunderstorms from Tennessee Valley and points east. Hurricane threat for Outer Banks of North Carolina. **16–19:** Rain/showers. **20–23:** Mostly fair skies. **24–27:** Showery and thundery. **28–30:** Gradually clearing.

### ZONE 4 North Central States

**1–3:** Fair. **4–7:** Showers through holiday weekend. **8–11:** Severe thunderstorms Rockies, points east. Possible tornado weather for parts of Kansas/Missouri/Iowa. **12–15:** Clearing skies, pleasant. **16–19:** Turning unsettled Rockies and across Plains, then fair. **20–23:** Fair, then scattered showers/thunderstorms over the Rockies. **24–27:** Colorado, thunderstorms; squalls over the Plains. **28–30:** Fair skies, unseasonably chilly.

### ZONE 5 South Central States

**1–3:** Clearing. **4–7:** Mixed bag for Labor Day; windy in New Mexico. Scattered showers Texas and points east, then fair. **8–11:** Severe thunderstorms from Rockies through the Plains; tornado weather possible. Tropical storm threat Texas and Louisiana Gulf Coast. **12–15:** Clearing and pleasant. **16–19:** Turning unsettled; showers over Rockies and Plains, then fair. **20–23:** Fair, then scattered showers/thunderstorms. **24–27:** Thunderstorms for Colorado; squalls for Plains. Windy, locally heavy showers New Mexico to Texas. Thunder showers Louisiana, Arkansas. **28–30:** Fair and unseasonably chilly.

### ZONE 6 Northwest

**1–3:** Fair. **4–7:** Showery for holiday weekend. **8–11:** Continued unsettled with a few more showers. **12–15:** Clearing, pleasant. **16–19:** Turning unsettled, showers Washington, Oregon. **20–23:** Fair, followed by scattered showers. **24–27:** More scattered showers. **28–30:** Fair skies and quite cool.

### ZONE 7 Southwest

**1–3:** Fair skies. **4–7:** Showers. Windy conditions Arizona. **8–11:** Mixed clouds and Sun; a few showers and possible thunderstorms. **12–15:** Clearing skies, pleasant. **16–19:** Threatening weather; few showers. **20–23:** Fair, then scattered showers/a few thunderstorms; windy with a few showers for California and Nevada. **24–27:** Thunderstorms Utah, then clearing. Fair weather elsewhere. **28–30:** Fair skies, unseasonably chilly.

# OCTOBER 2020

10th Month — 31 Days

**LIBRA**
September 22 to
October 21

**SCORPIO**
October 22 to
November 20

AND NOW THE FROST IS SEEN IN MORN, OVERSPREADING FIELDS WITH WHITE;
THE FARMER GATHERS IN HIS CORN, WITH PLEASURE AND DELIGHT.

### MOON'S PHASES — EASTERN DAYLIGHT TIME

| | | | |
|---|---|---|---|
| ○ Full Moon | 1st | 5:05 pm |
| ◑ Last Quarter | 9th | 8:40 pm |
| ● New Moon | 16th | 3:31 pm |
| ◐ First Quarter | 23rd | 9:23 am |
| ○ Full Moon | 31st | 10:49 am |

Subtract 1 hour for CDT, 2 hours for MDT, and 3 hours for PDT.

### SUN ON MERIDIAN CIVIL TIME

| Day | H:MM:SS |
|---|---|
| 1st | 12:49:55 |
| 8th | 12:47:50 |
| 15th | 12:46:07 |
| 22nd | 12:44:52 |
| 29th | 12:44:10 |

### CALENDAR FOR NORTHERN STATES (EDT)
40°N. Lat. 75°W. Long.

### CALENDAR FOR SOUTHERN STATES (CDT)
35°N. Lat. 90°W. Long.

| DATE | | ASTRONOMY, HOLIDAYS, AND EVENTS | MOON'S PLACE AT 7am ASTRONOMICALLY | SUN RISES | SUN SETS | EARLIEST MOONRISE MOONSET | MOON'S MERIDIAN PASSAGE | SUN RISES | SUN SETS | EARLIEST MOONRISE MOONSET | MOON'S MERIDIAN PASSAGE |
|---|---|---|---|---|---|---|---|---|---|---|---|
| 1 | Th | 1st Mississippi River steamboat, 1911 | PSC | 6:57 | 6:42 | 6:29ă | 12:30a | 6:55 | 6:43 | 6:33ă | 12:31a |
| 2 | Fr | Groucho Marx born, 1890 | CET | 6:58 | 6:40 | 7:25p̂ | 1:10a | 6:56 | 6:42 | 7:29p̂ | 1:12a |
| 3 | Sa | Succot; Moon at apogee 1:07pm | PSC | 6:59 | 6:38 | 7:49p̂ | 1:51a | 6:56 | 6:41 | 7:55p̂ | 1:52a |

#### 40. Eighteenth Sunday after Pentecost
Day's Length: 11h 37m — Astron. Twilight: 1h 20m
Day's Length: 11h 42m — Astron. Twilight: 1h 15m

| | | | | | | | | | | | |
|---|---|---|---|---|---|---|---|---|---|---|---|
| 4 | Su | 1st volunteer fire department, 1648 | ARI | 7:00 | 6:37 | 8:15p̂ | 2:32a | 6:57 | 6:39 | 8:24p̂ | 2:34a |
| 5 | Mo | Ray Kroc born, 1902 | ARI | 7:01 | 6:35 | 8:44p̂ | 3:14a | 6:58 | 6:38 | 8:56p̂ | 3:16a |
| 6 | Tu | Jane Eyre 1st published in London, 1847 | TAU | 7:02 | 6:34 | 9:17p̂ | 3:59a | 6:59 | 6:36 | 9:32p̂ | 4:01a |
| 7 | We | Desmond Tutu born, 1931 | TAU | 7:03 | 6:32 | 9:56p̂ | 4:46a | 7:00 | 6:35 | 10:13p̂ | 4:48a |
| 8 | Th | Cats opened on Broadway, 1982 | TAU | 7:04 | 6:31 | 10:43p̂ | 5:36a | 7:00 | 6:34 | 11:01p̂ | 5:38a |
| 9 | Fr | Fire Prevention Day | GEM | 7:05 | 6:29 | 11:37p̂ | 6:29a | 7:01 | 6:32 | 11:55p̂ | 6:31a |
| 10 | Sa | U.S. Naval Academy est., 1845 | GEM | 7:06 | 6:27 | None | 7:23a | 7:02 | 6:31 | None | 7:25a |

#### 41. Nineteenth Sunday after Pentecost
Day's Length: 11h 19m — Astron. Twilight: 1h 20m
Day's Length: 11h 27m — Astron. Twilight: 1h 15m

| | | | | | | | | | | | |
|---|---|---|---|---|---|---|---|---|---|---|---|
| 11 | Su | Simchat Torah | CAN | 7:07 | 6:26 | 12:38ă | 8:18a | 7:03 | 6:30 | 12:56ă | 8:20a |
| 12 | Mo | **Columbus Day** | LEO | 7:08 | 6:24 | 1:46ă | 9:12a | 7:04 | 6:28 | 2:01ă | 9:14a |
| 13 | Tu | Margaret Thatcher born, 1925 | LEO | 7:09 | 6:23 | 2:58ă | 10:06a | 7:04 | 6:27 | 3:10ă | 10:08a |
| 14 | We | George Eastman patented photo film, 1884 | LEO | 7:10 | 6:21 | 4:12ă | 10:59a | 7:05 | 6:26 | 4:20ă | 11:02a |
| 15 | Th | Virgil born, 70 BC | VIR | 7:11 | 6:20 | 5:27ă | 11:52a | 7:06 | 6:25 | 5:32ă | 11:55a |
| 16 | Fr | Moon at perigee 7:39pm | VIR | 7:12 | 6:18 | 6:43ă | 12:46p | 7:07 | 6:23 | 6:45ă | 12:48p |
| 17 | Sa | Pope John Paul I born, 1912 | VIR | 7:13 | 6:17 | 7:10p̂ | 1:40p | 7:08 | 6:22 | 7:19p̂ | 1:43p |

#### 42. Twentieth Sunday after Pentecost
Day's Length: 11h 02m — Astron. Twilight: 1h 21m
Day's Length: 11h 12m — Astron. Twilight: 1h 15m

| | | | | | | | | | | | |
|---|---|---|---|---|---|---|---|---|---|---|---|
| 18 | Su | Mason-Dixon line est., 1767 | LIB | 7:14 | 6:16 | 7:47p̂ | 2:37p | 7:09 | 6:21 | 8:00p̂ | 2:39p |
| 19 | Mo | John Jay, 1st U.S. Chief Justice, 1789 | SCO | 7:15 | 6:14 | 8:30p̂ | 3:35p | 7:10 | 6:20 | 8:45p̂ | 3:38p |
| 20 | Tu | John Dewey born, 1859 | OPH | 7:16 | 6:13 | 9:18p̂ | 4:35p | 7:10 | 6:18 | 9:36p̂ | 4:38p |
| 21 | We | Guggenheim Museum opened, 1959 | SAG | 7:17 | 6:11 | 10:14p̂ | 5:34p | 7:11 | 6:17 | 10:33p̂ | 5:37p |
| 22 | Th | Moon/Jupiter/Saturn visually close, SW sky | SAG | 7:18 | 6:10 | 11:14p̂ | 6:32p | 7:12 | 6:16 | 11:33p̂ | 6:34p |
| 23 | Fr | 1st use of aircraft in war, 1911 | CAP | 7:19 | 6:09 | None | 7:26p | 7:13 | 6:15 | None | 7:28p |
| 24 | Sa | United Nations Day | CAP | 7:20 | 6:07 | 12:18ă | 8:16p | 7:14 | 6:14 | 12:34ă | 8:19p |

#### 43. Twenty-first Sunday after Pentecost
Day's Length: 10h 44m — Astron. Twilight: 1h 22m
Day's Length: 10h 58m — Astron. Twilight: 1h 16m

| | | | | | | | | | | | |
|---|---|---|---|---|---|---|---|---|---|---|---|
| 25 | Su | Home use of microwaves introduced, 1955 | CAP | 7:22 | 6:06 | 1:21ă | 9:03p | 7:15 | 6:13 | 1:35ă | 9:05p |
| 26 | Mo | 1st electric generator Hoover Dam, 1936 | AQU | 7:23 | 6:05 | 2:23ă | 9:47p | 7:16 | 6:12 | 2:34ă | 9:49p |
| 27 | Tu | Theodore Roosevelt born, 1858 | AQU | 7:24 | 6:03 | 3:24ă | 10:29p | 7:17 | 6:10 | 3:32ă | 10:31p |
| 28 | We | Harvard University founded, 1636 | PSC | 7:25 | 6:02 | 4:23ă | 11:10p | 7:18 | 6:09 | 4:28ă | 11:11p |
| 29 | Th | Statue of Liberty dedicated, 1886 | CET | 7:26 | 6:01 | 5:21ă | 11:50p | 7:19 | 6:08 | 5:23ă | 11:52p |
| 30 | Fr | Moon at apogee 2:28pm | PSC | 7:27 | 6:00 | 6:19ă | None | 7:19 | 6:07 | 6:18ă | None |
| 31 | Sa | Halloween; 1st All Hallows' Eve, 834 | CET | 7:28 | 5:58 | 7:18ă | 12:31a | 7:20 | 6:06 | 7:14ă | 12:32a |

## OCTOBER 2020 WEATHER FORECAST

### ZONE 1 Northeast & New England

**1–3:** Fair, then scattered rain showers. **4–7:** Fair/pleasant; some unseasonably cold mornings. **8–11:** Heavy showers and gusty thunderstorms, followed by clearing, cool weather. **12–15:** Pleasant weather returns. **16–19:** Showers, then clearing. **20–23:** Rainy/milder. **24–27:** Thunderstorms, then becoming clear. **28–31:** Fair skies, followed by showers.

### ZONE 2 Great Lakes, Ohio Valley & Midwest

**1–3:** Gusty showers. **4–7:** Fair/pleasant, followed by increasingly cloudy skies. **8–11:** Heavy showers/thunderstorms. **12–15:** Partly sunny, pleasant. **16–19:** Showers Great Lakes and points east. **20–23:** Gusty winds, showers. **24–27:** Clearing and colder. **28–31:** Fair, then showers Michigan/Ohio, points east.

### ZONE 3 Southeast

**1–3:** Fair, then turning unsettled. **4–7:** Pleasant. **8–11:** Heavy rains, followed by clearing and cool conditions. **12–15:** Pleasant weather. **16–19:** Cold rain, then fair. **20–23:** Pleasant, then rain along the Gulf Coast. **24–27:** Clearing, quite cool. **28–31:** Fair skies.

### ZONE 4 North Central States

**1–3:** Light rain, mixed with snow over mountains of Montana; gusty winds and showers across Plains. **4–7:** Fair, then stormy, rainy Rockies; rain showers/wet flurries Plains to Dakotas and Nebraska. **8–11:** Fair, chilly. **12–15:** Milder, then showers, wet flurries for the Rockies; showers across Plains. **16–19:** Mostly fair. **20–23:** Unsettled Rockies, Plains. **24–27:** Clearing and colder. **28–31:** Wet Rockies/Plains, then turning fair.

### ZONE 5 South Central States

**1–3:** Gusty winds, showery. **4–7:** Fair, then turning stormy, showers. **8–11:** Fair and chilly. **12–15:** Milder, followed by showers. **16–19:** Mostly fair. **20–23:** Unsettled, Rockies and Plains. **24–27:** Clearing, colder. **28–31:** Wet weather, followed by clearing skies.

### ZONE 6 Northwest

**1–3:** Light rain, mixed with snow over the mountains of Idaho. **4–7:** Fair, then turning stormy. **8–11:** Fair and cool. **12–15:** Milder, then showers. **16–19:** Mostly fair weather. **20–23:** Unsettled from the Pacific Coast, spreading east. **24–27:** Clearing/chilly. **28–31:** Unsettled; showers for Washington and Oregon.

### ZONE 7 Southwest

**1–3:** Unsettled conditions. **4–7:** Gusty winds and showery. **8–11:** Fair/chilly. **12–15:** Milder, then showers. **16–19:** Mostly fair skies. **20–23:** Unsettled from West Coast, points east. **24–27:** Clearing and turning colder. **28–31:** Unsettled and showery.

# NOVEMBER 2020

**11ᵗʰ Month** | **30 Days**

**SCORPIO**
October 22 to
November 20

**SAGITTARIUS**
November 21 to
December 20

TIME ON HIS WING FAST HASTES AWAY, AND CHILLS EACH WARM SUCCEED;
TO CAPRICORN SOL HASTES EACH DAY, SO NIGHTS THE DAY EXCEED.

**MOON'S PHASES**
**EASTERN STANDARD TIME**

| | | |
|---|---|---|
| ◐ Last Quarter | 8ᵗʰ | 8:46 am |
| ● New Moon | 15ᵗʰ | 12:07 am |
| ◑ First Quarter | 21ˢᵗ | 11:45 pm |
| ○ Full Moon | 30ᵗʰ | 4:30 am |

Subtract 1 hour for CST, 2 hours for MST,
and 3 hours for PST.

**SUN ON MERIDIAN**
**CIVIL TIME**

| Day | H:MM:SS |
|---|---|
| 1ˢᵗ | 11:44:03 |
| 8ᵗʰ | 11:44:16 |
| 15ᵗʰ | 11:45:11 |
| 22ⁿᵈ | 11:46:47 |
| 29ᵗʰ | 11:49:01 |

| DATE | ASTRONOMY, HOLIDAYS, AND EVENTS | MOON'S PLACE AT 7am ASTRONOMICALLY | CALENDAR FOR NORTHERN STATES (EST) 40°N. Lat. 75°W. Long. | | | | CALENDAR FOR SOUTHERN STATES (CST) 35°N. Lat. 90°W. Long. | | | |
|---|---|---|---|---|---|---|---|---|---|---|
| | | | SUN RISES | SUN SETS | EARLIEST MOONRISE MOONSET | MOON'S MERIDIAN PASSAGE | SUN RISES | SUN SETS | EARLIEST MOONRISE MOONSET | MOON'S MERIDIAN PASSAGE |
| **44. Twenty-second Sunday after Pentecost** | | | Day's Length: 10h 28m Astron. Twilight: 1h 23m | | | | Day's Length: 10h 44m Astron. Twilight: 1h 17m | | | |
| 1 Su | Daylight Saving Time ends; All Saints' Day | ARI | 6:29 | 4:57 | 5:46ꝑ | 1:13a | 6:21 | 5:05 | 5:57ꝑ | 1:15a |
| 2 Mo | All Souls' Day; Daniel Boone born, 1734 | TAU | 6:31 | 4:56 | 6:18ꝑ | 12:57a | 6:22 | 5:04 | 6:32ꝑ | 12:59a |
| 3 Tu | **Election Day** | TAU | 6:32 | 4:55 | 6:55ꝑ | 1:43a | 6:23 | 5:04 | 7:11ꝑ | 1:45a |
| 4 We | Walter Cronkite born, 1916 | TAU | 6:33 | 4:54 | 7:38ꝑ | 2:33a | 6:24 | 5:03 | 7:56ꝑ | 2:35a |
| 5 Th | Guy Fawkes arrested, 1605 | GEM | 6:34 | 4:53 | 8:29ꝑ | 3:24a | 6:25 | 5:02 | 8:48ꝑ | 3:26a |
| 6 Fr | Jacob Schick patented electric shaver, 1923 | GEM | 6:35 | 4:52 | 9:27ꝑ | 4:17a | 6:26 | 5:01 | 9:45ꝑ | 4:19a |
| 7 Sa | 1ˢᵗ airfreight shipment, 1910 | CAN | 6:36 | 4:51 | 10:31ꝑ | 5:10a | 6:27 | 5:00 | 10:47ꝑ | 5:12a |
| **45. Twenty-third Sunday after Pentecost** | | | Day's Length: 10h 12m Astron. Twilight: 1h 24m | | | | Day's Length: 10h 31m Astron. Twilight: 1h 18m | | | |
| 8 Su | X-ray Discovery Day, 1895 | CAN | 6:37 | 4:50 | 11:39ꝑ | 6:03a | 6:28 | 4:59 | 11:53ꝑ | 6:05a |
| 9 Mo | *Mayflower* spotted land, 1620 | LEO | 6:39 | 4:49 | None | 6:56a | 6:29 | 4:58 | None | 6:58a |
| 10 Tu | Wreck of *Edmund Fitzgerald*, 1975 | LEO | 6:40 | 4:48 | 12:49â | 7:47a | 6:30 | 4:58 | 1:00â | 7:49a |
| 11 We | **Veterans Day** | VIR | 6:41 | 4:47 | 2:01â | 8:38a | 6:31 | 4:57 | 2:08â | 8:40a |
| 12 Th | Ellis Island closed, 1954 | VIR | 6:42 | 4:46 | 3:15â | 9:29a | 6:32 | 4:56 | 3:18â | 9:32a |
| 13 Fr | Vietnam War Memorial dedicated, 1982 | VIR | 6:43 | 4:45 | 4:31â | 10:22a | 6:33 | 4:56 | 4:30â | 10:25a |
| 14 Sa | Moon at perigee 6:36am | LIB | 6:44 | 4:44 | 5:48â | 11:18a | 6:34 | 4:55 | 5:44â | 11:20a |
| **46. Twenty-fourth Sunday after Pentecost** | | | Day's Length: 9h 58m Astron. Twilight: 1h 25m | | | | Day's Length: 10h 20m Astron. Twilight: 1h 19m | | | |
| 15 Su | 1ˢᵗ modern Olympics, 1859 | LIB | 6:45 | 4:44 | 5:18ꝑ | 12:16p | 6:35 | 4:54 | 5:32ꝑ | 12:18p |
| 16 Mo | Oklahoma admitted as 46ᵗʰ state, 1907 | OPH | 6:47 | 4:43 | 6:04ꝑ | 1:16p | 6:36 | 4:54 | 6:21ꝑ | 1:19p |
| 17 Tu | 1ˢᵗ steamship through Panama Canal, 1913 | SAG | 6:48 | 4:42 | 6:58ꝑ | 2:18p | 6:37 | 4:53 | 7:17ꝑ | 2:21p |
| 18 We | Moon/Jupiter/Saturn visually close, SW sky | SAG | 6:49 | 4:41 | 7:59ꝑ | 3:19p | 6:38 | 4:53 | 8:18ꝑ | 3:21p |
| 19 Th | Gettysburg Address, 1863 | SAG | 6:50 | 4:41 | 9:03ꝑ | 4:16p | 6:39 | 4:52 | 9:21ꝑ | 4:19p |
| 20 Fr | 1ˢᵗ commercial teletype service, 1931 | CAP | 6:51 | 4:40 | 10:09ꝑ | 5:10p | 6:40 | 4:52 | 10:24ꝑ | 5:12p |
| 21 Sa | Mayflower Compact signed, 1620 | CAP | 6:52 | 4:39 | 11:13ꝑ | 5:59p | 6:41 | 4:51 | 11:25ꝑ | 6:01p |
| **47. Christ the King Sunday** | | | Day's Length: 9h 46m Astron. Twilight: 1h 26m | | | | Day's Length: 10h 09m Astron. Twilight: 1h 20m | | | |
| 22 Su | President JFK assassinated, 1963 | AQU | 6:53 | 4:39 | None | 6:45p | 6:42 | 4:51 | None | 6:47p |
| 23 Mo | 1ˢᵗ jukebox, 1889 | AQU | 6:54 | 4:38 | 12:15â | 7:28p | 6:42 | 4:50 | 12:24â | 7:30p |
| 24 Tu | Darwin's *Origin of Species* published, 1859 | PSC | 6:56 | 4:38 | 1:15â | 8:09p | 6:43 | 4:50 | 1:21â | 8:10p |
| 25 We | Moon/Mars visually closest, SE | CET | 6:57 | 4:37 | 2:14â | 8:49p | 6:44 | 4:50 | 2:17â | 8:51p |
| 26 Th | **Thanksgiving Day**; Moon at apogee 7:18pm | PSC | 6:58 | 4:37 | 3:12â | 9:29p | 6:45 | 4:49 | 3:12â | 9:31p |
| 27 Fr | Anders Celsius born, 1701 | CET | 6:59 | 4:37 | 4:10â | 10:11p | 6:46 | 4:49 | 4:07â | 10:13p |
| 28 Sa | Grand Ole Opry made radio debut, 1925 | ARI | 7:00 | 4:36 | 5:09â | 10:54p | 6:47 | 4:49 | 5:03â | 10:56p |
| **48. First Sunday of Advent** | | | Day's Length: 9h 35m Astron. Twilight: 1h 28m | | | | Day's Length: 10h 01m Astron. Twilight: 1h 21m | | | |
| 29 Su | Central New England's worst ice storm, 1921 | TAU | 7:01 | 4:36 | 6:09â | 11:40p | 6:48 | 4:49 | 6:01â | 11:42p |
| 30 Mo | Hurricane season ends; St. Andrew | TAU | 7:02 | 4:36 | 4:54ꝑ | None | 6:49 | 4:49 | 5:10ꝑ | None |

## NOVEMBER 2020 WEATHER FORECAST

### ZONE 1 Northeast & New England

**1–3:** Fair and cold. Ideal conditions for runners in NYC Marathon. **4–7:** Stormy, heavy rains, perhaps mixed with sleet, wet snow in the mountains. **8–11:** Fair. **12–15:** Rain, then clearing. **16–19:** Increasingly cloudy, with rain and (over mountains) snow. **20–23:** More rain and wet snow, then clearing/colder. **24–27:** Unsettled, light snow, flurries; clearing in time for Thanksgiving. Macy's parade in NYC goes off without a hitch. **28–30:** Mostly fair.

### ZONE 2 Great Lakes, Ohio Valley & Midwest

**1–3:** Rain, wet snow for Great Lakes. **4–7:** Stormy for nation's midsection, which sweeps heavy precipitation up through the Ohio Valley, then fair and cold. **8–11:** Increasingly cloudy, but pleasant. **12–15:** Some rain for Great Lakes, then fair. **16–19:** Storm emerging out of the southwest states dumps snow and rain up through Great Lakes. **20–23:** Fair and cold. **24–27:** Light snow through Great Lakes and Ohio Valley, followed by fair skies for Thanksgiving. **28–30:** Fair, then stormy.

### ZONE 3 Southeast

**1–3:** Fair and pleasant. **4–7:** Unsettled; showery/thundery. **8–11:** Wet weather continues. **12–15:** Rain, then clearing. **16–19:** Breezy/pleasant. **20–23:** Rainy skies, then fair, colder. **24–27:** Quick changes during Thanksgiving holiday: fair, then rain, then quickly followed by clearing. **28–30:** Fair/milder.

### ZONE 4 North Central States

**1–3:** Turning stormy Colorado, Plains. **4–7:** Stormy Missouri, then fair/cold. Clearing, cold elsewhere. **8–11:** Pleasant, then unsettled, with strong winds, heavy precipitation for Rockies/Plains. Some wet snow for parts of Colorado, Kansas. **12–15:** Fair. **16–19:** Windy, with snow for Colorado and Plains. **20–23:** Fair, cold. **24–27:** Light snow Rockies/Plains, points east for Thanksgiving. **28–30:** Fair, then turning stormy.

### ZONE 5 South Central States

**1–3:** Stormy, southern Plains to Texas. **4–7:** Stormy Arkansas, then fair, cold. Clearing/cold elsewhere. **8–11:** Turning unsettled with gusty winds, heavy precipitation; some wet snow northern New Mexico, Texas/Oklahoma. **12–15:** Rain Texas and points east, followed by clearing. Fair elsewhere. **16–19:** Blustery, with snow Plains States. **20–23:** Fair, cold. **24–27:** Generally unsettled for Thanksgiving, light snow Rockies, Plains. Fair, then rain for Texas. **28–30:** Fair, then stormy.

### ZONE 6 Northwest

**1–3:** Mixed Sun, clouds; pleasant. **4–7:** Clearing, chilly. **8–11:** Pleasant, then unsettled. **12–15:** Fair. **16–19:** Blustery, with showers Washington and Oregon. **20–23:** Fair, chilly. **24–27:** Unsettled/showery for Thanksgiving time. **28–30:** Fair at first, then turning stormy.

### ZONE 7 Southwest

**1–3:** Pleasant weather, except stormy for Utah. **4–7:** Clearing and cold. **8–11:** Pleasant, then unsettled; gusty winds and precipitation. Wet snow Nevada, Utah, and parts of Arizona. **12–15:** Fair skies. **16–19:** Gusty winds with heavy precipitation; snow for Utah. **20–23:** Fair, cold. **24–27:** Light snow Nevada, Utah, and parts of Arizona, then fair, cold. **28–30:** Fair, then stormy; snowstorm for Utah; showers and thunderstorms for Arizona.

# DECEMBER 2020

12th Month · 31 Days

**SAGITTARIUS**
November 21 to
December 20

**CAPRICORN**
December 21 to
January 18

COLD BLOWS THE WIND, THE FROZEN RAIN AND FLEECY SNOW DESCEND;
FOR, FREEZING WINTER'S COME AGAIN, AND SO THE YEAR DOES END.

| MOON'S PHASES EASTERN STANDARD TIME | | | SUN ON MERIDIAN CIVIL TIME | |
|---|---|---|---|---|
| ◑ Last Quarter | 7th | 7:37 pm | Day | H:MM:SS |
| ● New Moon | 14th | 11:17 am | 1st | 11:49:45 |
| ◐ First Quarter | 21st | 6:41 pm | 8th | 11:52:39 |
| ○ Full Moon | 29th | 10:28 pm | 15th | 11:55:56 |
| | | | 22nd | 11:59:24 |
| Subtract 1 hour for CST, 2 hours for MST, and 3 hours for PST. | | | 29th | 12:02:50 |

| | | | | | CALENDAR FOR NORTHERN STATES (EST) 40°N. Lat. 75°W. Long. | | | | CALENDAR FOR SOUTHERN STATES (CST) 35°N. Lat. 90°W. Long. | | | |
|---|---|---|---|---|---|---|---|---|---|---|---|---|
| DATE | | ASTRONOMY, HOLIDAYS, AND EVENTS | MOON'S PLACE AT 7am ASTRONOMICALLY | | SUN RISES | SUN SETS | EARLIEST MOONRISE MOONSET | MOON'S MERIDIAN PASSAGE | SUN RISES | SUN SETS | EARLIEST MOONRISE MOONSET | MOON'S MERIDIAN PASSAGE |
| 1 | Tu | Rosa Parks arrested, 1955 | TAU | | 7:03 | 4:35 | 5:36p | 12:29a | 6:50 | 4:49 | 5:54p | 12:31a |
| 2 | We | La Guardia Airport opened, 1939 | GEM | | 7:04 | 4:35 | 6:25p | 1:20a | 6:51 | 4:48 | 6:44p | 1:22a |
| 3 | Th | Alka Seltzer sold for 1st time, 1931 | GEM | | 7:05 | 4:35 | 7:21p | 2:13a | 6:52 | 4:48 | 7:40p | 2:15a |
| 4 | Fr | Edison invented phonograph, 1877 | CAN | | 7:06 | 4:35 | 8:23p | 3:06a | 6:52 | 4:48 | 8:40p | 3:09a |
| 5 | Sa | Walt Disney born, 1901 | CAN | | 7:07 | 4:35 | 9:29p | 3:59a | 6:53 | 4:48 | 9:44p | 4:02a |

**49. Second Sunday of Advent** — Day's Length: 9h 27m, Astron. Twilight: 1h 28m (Northern) · Day's Length: 9h 54m, Astron. Twilight: 1h 22m (Southern)

| 6 | Su | 13th Amendment ratified, ended slavery, 1865 | LEO | | 7:08 | 4:35 | 10:37p | 4:51a | 6:54 | 4:48 | 10:49p | 4:53a |
| 7 | Mo | Pearl Harbor Day; Earliest sunset of 2020 | LEO | | 7:08 | 4:35 | 11:46p | 5:42a | 6:55 | 4:48 | 11:55p | 5:44a |
| 8 | Tu | Conception B.V.M.; Eli Whitney born, 1765 | VIR | | 7:09 | 4:35 | None | 6:31a | 6:56 | 4:49 | None | 6:33a |
| 9 | We | 1st YMCA in North America, 1851 | VIR | | 7:10 | 4:35 | 12:57a | 7:20a | 6:56 | 4:49 | 1:01a | 7:22a |
| 10 | Th | Emily Dickinson born, 1830 | VIR | | 7:11 | 4:35 | 2:08a | 8:10a | 6:57 | 4:49 | 2:09a | 8:12a |
| 11 | Fr | Chanukah | LIB | | 7:12 | 4:35 | 3:22a | 9:02a | 6:58 | 4:49 | 3:19a | 9:04a |
| 12 | Sa | Moon at perigee 3:34pm | LIB | | 7:13 | 4:35 | 4:38a | 9:57a | 6:59 | 4:49 | 4:31a | 9:59a |

**50. Third Sunday of Advent** — Day's Length: 9h 22m, Astron. Twilight: 1h 29m (Northern) · Day's Length: 9h 50m, Astron. Twilight: 1h 22m (Southern)

| 13 | Su | Federal Reserve System est., 1913 | SCO | | 7:13 | 4:36 | 5:54a | 10:55a | 6:59 | 4:50 | 5:45a | 10:58a |
| 14 | Mo | Mariner 2 flew by Venus, 1962 | OPH | | 7:14 | 4:36 | 7:10a | 11:57a | 7:00 | 4:50 | 6:57a | 11:59a |
| 15 | Tu | Prohibition ended, 1933 | SAG | | 7:15 | 4:36 | 5:38p | 12:59p | 7:01 | 4:50 | 5:57p | 1:01p |
| 16 | We | Ember Day; Boston Tea Party, 1773 | SAG | | 7:15 | 4:36 | 6:42p | 2:00p | 7:01 | 4:51 | 7:01p | 2:02p |
| 17 | Th | FCC approved RCA's color TV specs, 1953 | CAP | | 7:16 | 4:37 | 7:50p | 2:57p | 7:02 | 4:51 | 8:06p | 2:59p |
| 18 | Fr | Ember Day; 1st U.S. Thanksgiving, 1777 | CAP | | 7:17 | 4:37 | 8:57p | 3:50p | 7:03 | 4:51 | 9:11p | 3:52p |
| 19 | Sa | Ember Day | AQU | | 7:17 | 4:38 | 10:02p | 4:38p | 7:03 | 4:51 | 10:12p | 4:40p |

**51. Fourth Sunday of Advent** — Day's Length: 9h 20m, Astron. Twilight: 1h 29m (Northern) · Day's Length: 9h 49m, Astron. Twilight: 1h 22m (Southern)

| 20 | Su | Virginia Company set sail for U.S., 1606 | AQU | | 7:18 | 4:38 | 11:04p | 5:23p | 7:04 | 4:52 | 11:11p | 5:25p |
| 21 | Mo | Winter solstice, winter begins 5:02am | AQU | | 7:18 | 4:39 | None | 6:05p | 7:04 | 4:53 | None | 6:07p |
| 22 | Tu | James Oglethorpe born, 1696 | CET | | 7:19 | 4:39 | 12:04a | 6:46p | 7:05 | 4:53 | 12:08a | 6:48p |
| 23 | We | NASA approved to continue Voyager 2, 1981 | CET | | 7:19 | 4:40 | 1:02a | 7:26p | 7:05 | 4:54 | 1:03a | 7:28p |
| 24 | Th | Moon at apogee 11:26am | PSC | | 7:20 | 4:40 | 2:00a | 8:07p | 7:05 | 4:54 | 1:59a | 8:09p |
| 25 | Fr | Christmas Day | ARI | | 7:20 | 4:41 | 2:59a | 8:50p | 7:06 | 4:55 | 2:54a | 8:52p |
| 26 | Sa | Washington crossed the Delaware, 1776 | TAU | | 7:20 | 4:42 | 3:59a | 9:35p | 7:06 | 4:56 | 3:51a | 9:37p |

**52. First Sunday after Christmas** — Day's Length: 9h 22m, Astron. Twilight: 1h 29m (Northern) · Day's Length: 9h 50m, Astron. Twilight: 1h 22m (Southern)

| 27 | Su | Howdy Doody made TV debut, 1947 | TAU | | 7:21 | 4:42 | 4:59a | 10:23p | 7:07 | 4:56 | 4:49a | 10:25p |
| 28 | Mo | Woodrow Wilson born, 1856 | TAU | | 7:21 | 4:43 | 6:00a | 11:13p | 7:07 | 4:57 | 5:48a | 11:16p |
| 29 | Tu | Charles Goodyear born, 1800 | TAU | | 7:21 | 4:44 | 6:59a | None | 7:07 | 4:58 | 6:45a | None |
| 30 | We | Rudyard Kipling born, 1865 | GEM | | 7:21 | 4:44 | 5:14p | 12:07a | 7:07 | 4:58 | 5:32p | 12:09a |
| 31 | Th | New Year's Eve | GEM | | 7:22 | 4:45 | 6:15p | 1:01a | 7:08 | 4:59 | 6:33p | 1:03a |

# DECEMBER 2020 WEATHER FORECAST

## ZONE 1 Northeast & New England

**1–3:** Snow/rain. **4–7:** Mostly fair, cold. **8–11:** Light snow New England; showers Mid-Atlantic States, then clearing. **12–15:** Major East Coast storm. **16–19:** Blustery and cold; scattered flurries. **20–23:** Heavy rains near the coastal plains; ice/snow interior. **24–27:** Fair, cold Christmas. **28–31:** Strong weather front from west brings gusty winds and a wide variety of precipitation to close out the year.

## ZONE 2 Great Lakes, Ohio Valley & Midwest

**1–3:** Snow Great Lakes area, with accumulations of 2-4". **4–7:** Fair/cold. **8–11:** Light snow, then turning fair. **12–15:** Stormy. **16–19:** Dry and turning colder. **20–23:** Light snow east through Ohio Valley, then becoming fair. **24–27:** Increasingly cloudy skies for Christmas. **28–31:** Intense Midwest storm delivers heavy wind, snow/mixed precipitation as 2020 comes to a close.

## ZONE 3 Southeast

**1–3:** Rainy; some wet snow mixes in over higher terrain of Tennessee. **4–7:** Fair, cold. **8–11:** Cold showers, then clearing. **12–15:** Rainy. **16–19:** Rains clear, then fair, cold, with frosts to Florida. **20–23:** Rain/showers, then fair, colder. **24–27:** Fair and unseasonably cold Yuletide. Frosts down to Gulf Coast. **28–31:** Windy and rainy South; wintry mix for the mountains of the Virginias, Carolinas, and Tennessee as the year winds down.

## ZONE 4 North Central States

**1–3:** Big storm clears Dakotas/Nebraska area. **4–7:** Fair at first, then unsettled: wet for Rockies, Plains. **8–11:** Clearing skies Plains. **12–15:** Stormy Rockies, across Plains. **16–19:** Colder weather. **20–23:** Some snow or flurries. **24–27:** Fair, then stormy, with heavy snow over Rockies, Plains. **28–31:** Clearing skies as we make the transition to 2021.

## ZONE 5 South Central States

**1–3:** Gradually clearing skies. **4–7:** Fair at first, then unsettled with showers; wet for Rockies and Plains. **8–11:** Fair skies. **12–15:** Stormy in Rockies, across Plains; rain in Texas. **16–19:** Colder temperatures. **20–23:** Some showers of rain or wet snow. **24–27:** Fair, then stormy. **28–31:** Clearing skies Rockies, points east as we say goodbye to 2020.

## ZONE 6 Northwest

**1–3:** Fair skies. **4–7:** Fair at first, then unsettled with showers. **8–11:** Clearing skies. **12–15:** Changeable; Sun/clouds, risk of a passing shower. **16–19:** Chilly and dry. **20–23:** Showers Washington, Oregon. **24–27:** Very unsettled. **28-31:** Clearing as we ring out the old year and usher in the new.

## ZONE 7 Southwest

**1–3:** Fair skies. **4–7:** Fair at first, then unsettled with showers Pacific Coast. **8–11:** Fair skies for California, points east. **12–15:** Milder under threatening skies. **16–19:** Colder weather moves in. **20–23:** Rain and (over mountainous terrain) snow, then clearing. **24–27:** Fair, then becoming very unsettled. **28–31:** Clearing weather moves in as we close the books on 2020.

# Can COLD WEATHER Ever Be a Good Thing?

By Deborah Tukua

**W**hile winter cold may not be your favorite, there are some health benefits to this cooler time of year.

## Better Sleep • • • • • • • • • • •

Sleeping in a cooler room instead of a warmer one has been found to promote restful sleep. Did you know that your body naturally drops in temperature when asleep? This explains why you may find it difficult to sleep well in a room that is too warm. If you have trouble getting a good night sleep, try making the room a little cooler. In addition, a cooling pillow can be helpful to those suffering from insomnia, hot flashes, or night sweats. Cooling pillows infused with a cooling gel draw heat away from your body and reduce the temperature of your bed, helping you get a good night's sleep.

## • • • • • • • • • • Beauty Benefits

While we may consider cold weather harsh, our skin can actully benefit from exposure to cooler temperatures. Cold enhances blood circulation, which reduces the likelihood of puffy eyes and facial swelling. When exposed to cooler temperatures, the blood vessels in your face react, giving you that fresh, "wholesome" look—clear, bright eyes and rosy-red cheeks. Exposure to cool weather also tightens the pores of your skin and invigorates your face, like a refreshing splash of cold water or a cold shower. Hot water has an opposite effect and can dry the skin. But that's not to say prolonged exposure to very cold air doesn't wreak havoc on your skin (frostbite, etc.). Always protect exposed skin when the temperatures are below freezing.

## Mood and Behavior

Do hot temperatures make you hot-tempered? Or do you find you're cranky when it's cold? Researchers in Poland conducted a study to determine if there was a direct correlation between stress levels and temperatures. They found that the stress hormone, cortisol, is actually lower in your body in winter, and rises along with hotter summer temperatures. Increased levels of cortisol (along with dehydration and being forced to stay indoors during extreme heat) are thought to make us more apt to be irritable or angry. Crime statistics support this research as a rise in reported acts of violence during hot summer weather are the norm. So don't be surprised if, on sweltering summer days, your fuse is short.

## A Break From Pollen Allergies

The good news about cold weather is that pollen counts are low. So if you suffer from seasonal allergies, you may just get a break. Of course, there are other allergens in wintertime you should consider, such as mold and dust mites, but for the most part, you'll get a bit of a reprieve.

## Hot or Cold, Fit or Fat

Cold temperatures may be your friend when it comes to exercise. Exercising outdoors during cooler weather can actually kickstart your efforts to lose excess body fat. The brown fat that your body burns to generate energy is triggered by the cold. Your body burns more calories to keep warm in cold weather then when trying to cool down in hot weather. The difference, however, is that people tend to think they burn more calories than they actually are when exercising in hot weather, due to sweating.

And to bring it back to your mood, while gray skies and shorter days with less sunshine in the winter may bring on the blues, exercising in cold weather can actually make you happier. Hot, humid weather can leave you feeling drained, especially after physical exertion. Experts say taking your workout outdoors in cold weather increases the release of endorphins, those feel-good hormones. So as your body works harder to stay warm, it naturally lifts your mood.

*Ever notice that your electronic devices don't like cold weather either? Learn why at FarmersAlmanac.com/cold-gadgets*

# WEATHER SAYINGS
## You May Not Know

### ONION SNOW

Onion snow originated with the Pennsylvania Dutch culture and language. It refers to a snowfall that occurs right after the spring onions have started sprouting. Some believe this late spring snow is an indicator of a good time to start planting onions. Another spring snow term particular to the Pennsylvania Dutch is a "sapling bender," referring to when it snows heavily in the spring, bending the branches of the new saplings.

### THREE ICE MEN

In Europe's not-too-distant past, parts of the continent remained rather cold through the middle of May, making planting before then risky. German and Swiss lore refers to mid-May as "Iceman Days," while an old French saying states "St. Mammertius, St. Pancratius, and St. Gervatius (the Francophone spelling of the three saints' names) do not pass without a frost." Because the agrarian people of medieval Europe weren't likely to be literate, let alone be aware of dates, they measured time by following the church calendar and by observing nature. Remembering that the last frost of the year generally falls around the feast of Servatius was a useful marker for pre-modern farmers.

In some regions, the lore goes on to note that rain will fall on Feast of St. Sophia, marking the beginning of planting season. For this reason, May 15 is referred to as "Zimna Zoska," or "Cold Sophia" in Poland.

This bit of lore dates back to before the creation of the Gregorian calendar in 1582, at which time most days of the year shifted somewhat. While the feasts of the Three Chilly Saints are still celebrated from May 11-13 on our calendar, these days used to fall a little later in the astronomical year—from May 19-22.

# MOTHER'S DAY RULE

The premise of the Mother's Day Rule is simple—Mother's Day falls on the second Sunday in May which, for many, the threat of frost has passed *(see page 184 for average frost dates)*, and it's considered safe to get your garden started. It's a good rule of thumb because while the calendar may say spring, it doesn't mean we'll have spring temperatures in March and April (especially for those in the Northeast). If your tender plants go in the ground too early, when temperatures are still chilly at night, you're setting yourself up for disaster. Of course, those who live in warmer, arid climates have their own set of rules for when to plant, and much depends on the plant itself and its hardiness.

While this rule is a good one, it's really more of a Mother's Day "guideline." We all know Mother Nature can be fickle, no matter what part of the country you live in, and it's not unheard of to have a freak snowstorm as late as May. But for the most part, the second Sunday in May is a safe time, temperature-wise.

*Folklore aside, successful gardeners know that understanding a plant's hardiness (its ability to withstand cold conditions) is key. Every plant has a different level of hardiness; some grow well in cold weather while others need the soil to be nice and cozy warm. Refer to the growing information on each seed packet (or greenhouse label) before getting started. Check the USDA's Hardiness Zones map for even more good information about when to plant.*

*See our Gardening by the Moon calendar (starting on page 188) for key planting and task dates based on the phases of the Moon.*

# FAVORITE
# SNOW LORE

I f you look up the word "lore" in the dictionary, the official definition is "the body of knowledge, especially of a traditional, anecdotal, or popular nature, on a particular subject." While we here at the *Farmers' Almanac* don't consult or use weather lore when making our famous winter prognostications, we do have a few choice picks that we're sharing here. Wondering if (and when) it will snow? Check out this winter weather lore and make your own predictions:

WEATHER LORE

WHEN PIGS SQUEAL IN THE WINTER, THERE WILL BE A BLIZZARD

*Your Weather Watching Guide. FarmersAlmanac.com*

WEATHER LORE

SNOW LIKE COTTON, SOON FORGOTTEN. SNOW LIKE MEAL, WILL GIVE A GREAT DEAL

*Your Weather Watching Guide. FarmersAlmanac.com*

WEATHER LORE

A *RING* AROUND THE SUN OR MOON MEANS *RAIN* OR *SNOW* IS COMING SOON.

*Your Weather Watching Guide • FarmersAlmanac.com*

WEATHER LORE

SMOKE THAT CURLS DOWNWARD AND LINGERS MEANS A NEARING STORM

*Your Weather Watching Guide. FarmersAlmanac.com*

 *Like Lore? Find more at <u>FarmersAlmanac.com</u> and by following us on Facebook, Twitter, Pinterest, and Instagram*

# SOMETIMES BEING A FOLLOWER *DOES* PAY OFF!

**Follow *Farmers' Almanac* on social media for tips, advice, lore, *and more!***

## 5 PLANTS FOR A BUG-FREE BACK YARD & PATIO

Basil · Lavender · Rosemary · Lemongrass

*Your Gardening Guide · FarmersAlmanac.com*

### WHY ARE THEY CALLED "CLING" PEACHES?

"Clingstone" or "cling" peaches are a variety of peach in which the flesh of the peach will cling to the stone (or pit). These peaches are mostly used in canning. Most fresh peaches sold are "freestone," which separate easily from the pit.

**NOW YOU KNOW!**

## FULL PINK MOON

### APRIL

One of the names for April's full Moon came from the herb moss pink ground phlox, which is one of the earliest flowers of springtime. Among coastal tribes it was known as the Full Fish Moon, because this was the time that the shad swam upstream to spawn.

*Plan Your Day. Grow Your Life. FarmersAlmanac.com  #FollowThePossible*

### How Long Until It's Decomposed?

*Estimated lengths of time items break down in marine environments*

**PLASTIC BOTTLES** 450 YEARS

**DISPOSABLE DIAPER** 450 YEARS

**STYROFOAM CUP** 50-500 YEARS

**6-PACK RINGS** 400 YEARS

**PLASTIC CUTLERY** 100-1000 YEARS

**MYLAR BALLOONS NEVER**

*Source: NOAA, Woods Hole Sea Grant*

## FARMERS' ALMANAC — Helpful Hints for All Seasons!

### PROTECT PAWS!

SALT ON THE SIDEWALK?

PROTECT YOUR PET BY MASSAGING A THIN LAYER OF PETROLEUM JELLY ONTO THE BOTTOM OF YOUR DOG'S FEET BEFORE HEADING OUTSIDE.

## DIY TOILET *Cleaner*

### It's Easy!

- Drop in two Alka-Seltzer tablets.
- Wait for 20 minutes.
- Brush bowl, and flush!

### "THE *LOUDER* THE FROG, THE *MORE* THE RAIN"

## SPRING WEATHER LORE

### YOU MAY NOT KNOW

# UNUSUAL (BUT USEFUL) WAYS TO USE
# POTATOES

**We all know that potatoes are a delicious, budget-friendly food, but did you know they can also perform a multitude of tasks around the home?**

### Gravy Thickener

Instant mashed potatoes are a good thickener for stews and gravies.

### Silverware Cleaner

Use the water from boiling potatoes to clean tarnished silverware. Let the water cool, soak the silverware in it for 30 minutes, and then wash and dry.

### Kitchen Burn Remedy

Rub a potato slice onto the area. The starch neutralizes the burn and helps prevent scarring.

### Eye De-puffer

Slices of raw potatoes will help reduce swelling and puffiness of the eyes. Lay slices over your eyes and relax for 10 minutes.

### Sunburn Soother

For instant relief, combine instant mashed potato mix with crushed ice. Pat onto sunburned areas and leave on for 5–10 minutes. Then rinse off.

### Poison Ivy Treatment

Whip a raw potato into a paste in your blender. Spread onto the affected area and cover loosely with plastic wrap. Leave on for at least 15 minutes. Then rinse off.

### Dry Skin Remedy

Grate one or two small potatoes and soak them in olive oil for 20 minutes. Place the potato/oil mixture on your dry hands and leave on for at least 10 minutes. Then rinse your hands to clean them of the potatoes.

### Splinter Remover

Cut a potato into thin slices. Place one slice on the splinter. (Use the side without the skin.) Varying sources suggest leaving it on the spot from 10–20 minutes to the whole night. If you do decide to leave it overnight, secure the potato slice with two bandages to keep it firmly in place. As you remove the potato slice, it should pull out the entire splinter in one piece.

## Soup Rescuer

If you accidentally over-salt soup or another dish, just drop in a peeled potato—it will absorb the excess salt.

## Rust Remover

You can use a slice of potato to scrub rusted surfaces—this works especially well for knife blades, pots, and pans. Sprinkle a little salt or baking soda onto the potato and then rub it over the rust spot or just insert the knife blade into a potato and let it sit. The oxalic acid in the potato helps to dissolve the rust.

For More Useful Tips Follow Us Online!

# GROW YOUR OWN POTATOES!

Want to grow your own tasty spuds? Here's what you need to know: Small potatoes can be planted whole. For large potatoes like bakers, cut into pieces making sure there are a couple of eyes on each piece. Allowing the pieces to dry out for a day or two may help prevent rotting. Plant the pieces in your garden or a container filled with well-drained potting mix and wait for them to sprout. In a few months you should be able to dig up a whole bunch of new potatoes!

Sweet potatoes are even easier to grow than potatoes, because you don't have to look for any eyes. The easiest method is to plant the entire sweet potato. However, to produce more than one plant, cut a sweet potato in half and suspend it using toothpicks in a shallow container of water. Roots and sprouts will begin to grow in a few days. Once the sprouts are about four inches or so in length, just twist them off and place them in a container of water. When the roots from this container reach about an inch in length, you can plant them in soil in a garden or large container.

**Learn more on our website, at FarmersAlmanac.com/growpotatoes**

## AVERAGE FROST DATES

*The dates listed below are normal averages for a light frost in selected towns. The definition of a light frost is when the temperatures are between 29°–32°F. During a light frost, tender plants may be killed, with little destructive effect on more hardy vegetation.*

*There is a 50% probability that a frost may occur after the spring date and before the fall date listed (as well as a 50% chance one could happen earlier in the spring or later in the fall). Dates are courtesy of the National Climatic Data Center and the National Oceanic and Atmospheric Administration.*

| ALABAMA | FIRST | LAST | CONNECTICUT | FIRST | LAST |
|---|---|---|---|---|---|
| Birmingham | Nov 9 | Apr 2 | Danbury | Oct 9 | May 1 |
| Huntsville | Nov 4 | Mar 30 | Hartford | Oct 9 | Apr 26 |
| Mobile | Nov 29 | Feb 28 | Stamford | Oct 17 | Apr 29 |
| Montgomery | Nov 12 | Mar 11 | **DELAWARE** | **FIRST** | **LAST** |
| **ALASKA** | **FIRST** | **LAST** | Dover | Oct 30 | Apr 8 |
| Anchorage | Sep 23 | May 8 | Lewes | Nov 5 | Apr 6 |
| Fairbanks | Sep 8 | May 15 | Wilmington | Nov 15 | Apr 10 |
| Juneau | Oct 4 | May 8 | **WASHINGTON, DC** | **FIRST** | **LAST** |
| Nome | Aug 31 | Jun 11 | | Nov 15 | |
| **ARIZONA** | **FIRST** | **LAST** | | | Mar 29 |
| Flagstaff | Sep 22 | Jun 9 | **FLORIDA** | **FIRST** | **LAST** |
| Phoenix | Dec 16 | Jan 30 | Jacksonville | Dec 3 | Feb 26 |
| Tucson | Nov 29 | Feb 16 | Orlando | Jan 8 | Jan 30 |
| Yuma | Dec 20 | Jan 24 | Tallahassee | Nov 17 | Mar 22 |
| **ARKANSAS** | **FIRST** | **LAST** | Tampa | Jan 19 | Jan 21 |
| Fort Smith | Oct 31 | Mar 31 | **GEORGIA** | **FIRST** | **LAST** |
| Jonesboro | Nov 4 | Mar 29 | Atlanta | Nov 16 | Mar 24 |
| Little Rock | Nov 12 | Mar 22 | Augusta | Nov 7 | Mar 30 |
| Texarkana | Nov 16 | Mar 13 | Columbus | Nov 19 | Mar 11 |
| **CALIFORNIA** | **FIRST** | **LAST** | Savannah | Nov 25 | Mar 1 |
| Fresno | Dec 3 | Feb 4 | **IDAHO** | **FIRST** | **LAST** |
| Red Bluff | Dec 1 | Feb 22 | Boise | Oct 8 | May 5 |
| Sacramento | Dec 4 | Feb 10 | Idaho Falls | Sep 20 | May 27 |
| San Bernardino | Dec 24 | Jan 21 | Moscow | Sep 20 | May 25 |
| Tahoe City | Sep 19 | Jun 18 | Salmon | Sep 20 | May 25 |
| **COLORADO** | **FIRST** | **LAST** | **ILLINOIS** | **FIRST** | **LAST** |
| Denver | Oct 4 | Apr 30 | Chicago | Oct 24 | Apr 20 |
| Grand Junction | Oct 16 | May 1 | Mt. Vernon | Oct 14 | Apr 14 |
| Julesburg | Sep 24 | May 7 | Quincy | Oct 22 | Apr 10 |
| Pueblo | Oct 5 | Apr 30 | Springfield | Oct 13 | Apr 13 |

*NOTE: Higher elevations in HAWAII do occasionally see at-or-near freezing temperatures but definitive frost dates are not available.*

## AVERAGE FROST DATES

| INDIANA | FIRST | LAST | MASSACHUSETTS (CONT.) | FIRST | LAST |
|---|---|---|---|---|---|
| Evansville | Nov 3 | Apr 3 | Boston | Nov 7 | Apr 7 |
| Indianapolis | Oct 18 | Apr 18 | New Bedford | Nov 2 | Apr 13 |
| South Bend | Oct 19 | Apr 26 | Worcester | Nov 14 | Apr 26 |
| Terre Haute | Oct 15 | Apr 20 | **MICHIGAN** | **FIRST** | **LAST** |
| **IOWA** | **FIRST** | **LAST** | Cheboygan | Oct 10 | May 18 |
| Cedar Rapids | Oct 6 | Apr 25 | Detroit | Oct 17 | Apr 26 |
| Des Moines | Oct 12 | Apr 20 | Grand Rapids | Oct 8 | May 5 |
| Fort Dodge | Oct 4 | Apr 29 | Marquette | Oct 13 | May 11 |
| Sioux City | Oct 3 | Apr 26 | **MINNESOTA** | **FIRST** | **LAST** |
| **KANSAS** | **FIRST** | **LAST** | Baudette | Sep 21 | May 16 |
| Garden City | Oct 11 | Apr 27 | Duluth | Oct 17 | May 15 |
| Great Bend | Oct 19 | Apr 13 | Minneapolis | Oct 5 | Apr 30 |
| Independence | Oct 25 | Apr 8 | Willmar | Oct 1 | Apr 30 |
| Topeka | Oct 11 | Apr 19 | **MISSISSIPPI** | **FIRST** | **LAST** |
| **KENTUCKY** | **FIRST** | **LAST** | Greenville | Nov 17 | Mar 9 |
| Ashland | Oct 13 | May 4 | Hattiesburg | Nov 19 | Mar 12 |
| Lexington | Oct 25 | Apr 15 | Jackson | Nov 9 | Mar 23 |
| Mayfield | Oct 21 | Apr 17 | Tupelo | Oct 28 | Apr 5 |
| Murray | Oct 28 | Apr 5 | **MISSOURI** | **FIRST** | **LAST** |
| **LOUISIANA** | **FIRST** | **LAST** | Jefferson City | Oct 18 | Apr 13 |
| Alexandria | Nov 19 | Mar 6 | Kansas City | Oct 28 | Apr 7 |
| Baton Rouge | Nov 29 | Feb 26 | Poplar Bluff | Oct 28 | Apr 4 |
| Monroe | Nov 15 | Mar 3 | St. Louis | Oct 29 | Apr 7 |
| Shreveport | Nov 18 | Mar 10 | **MONTANA** | **FIRST** | **LAST** |
| **MAINE** | **FIRST** | **LAST** | Billings | Sep 27 | May 8 |
| Augusta | Oct 8 | Apr 27 | Bozeman | Sep 19 | May 26 |
| Bangor | Oct 7 | May 7 | Glendive | Sep 29 | May 2 |
| Portland | Oct 6 | May 2 | Great Falls | Sep 22 | May 17 |
| Presque Isle | Sep 20 | May 21 | Helena | Sep 18 | May 19 |
| **MARYLAND** | **FIRST** | **LAST** | **NEBRASKA** | **FIRST** | **LAST** |
| Baltimore | Oct 29 | Apr 11 | Grand Island | Oct 8 | Apr 26 |
| Frederick | Oct 30 | Apr 9 | North Platte | Oct 4 | May 5 |
| Salisbury | Oct 30 | Apr 5 | Omaha | Oct 12 | Apr 21 |
| **MASSACHUSETTS** | **FIRST** | **LAST** | Scottsbluff | Sep 27 | May 3 |
| Amherst | Oct 29 | Apr 17 | | | |

## AVERAGE FROST DATES

| NEVADA | FIRST | LAST | OHIO | FIRST | LAST |
|---|---|---|---|---|---|
| Elko | Oct 10 | Jun 9 | Cincinnati | Oct 23 | Apr 13 |
| Ely | Sep 6 | Jun 18 | Cleveland | Oct 23 | Apr 30 |
| Las Vegas | Nov 27 | Feb 16 | Columbus | Oct 13 | Apr 26 |
| Reno | Oct 3 | May 21 | Toledo | Oct 8 | May 1 |
| **NEW HAMPSHIRE** | **FIRST** | **LAST** | **OKLAHOMA** | **FIRST** | **LAST** |
| Berlin | Sep 21 | May 20 | Beaver | Oct 14 | Apr 18 |
| Concord | Sep 21 | May 20 | Enid | Nov 3 | Apr 4 |
| Keene | Sep 26 | May 13 | Lawton | Nov 7 | Mar 29 |
| Nashua | Oct 3 | May 7 | Tulsa | Nov 7 | Mar 27 |
| **NEW JERSEY** | **FIRST** | **LAST** | **OREGON** | **FIRST** | **LAST** |
| Atlantic City | Nov 11 | Mar 31 | Baker | Sep 13 | Jun 3 |
| Cape May | Nov 6 | Apr 6 | Eugene | Oct 19 | Apr 22 |
| New Brunswick | Oct 20 | Apr 20 | Klamath Falls | Sep 18 | Jun 7 |
| Newark | Nov 7 | Apr 3 | Portland | Nov 15 | Mar 23 |
| **NEW MEXICO** | **FIRST** | **LAST** | **PENNSYLVANIA** | **FIRST** | **LAST** |
| Albuquerque | Oct 28 | Apr 16 | Erie | Oct 29 | Apr 29 |
| Carlsbad | Nov 3 | Apr 3 | Lebanon | Oct 13 | Apr 27 |
| Santa Rosa | Oct 22 | Apr 19 | Philadelphia | Nov 4 | Apr 6 |
| **NEW YORK** | **FIRST** | **LAST** | Pittsburgh | Oct 17 | Apr 29 |
| Albany | Oct 3 | May 2 | Wilkes Barre | Oct 16 | Apr 26 |
| Buffalo | Oct 19 | Apr 24 | **RHODE ISLAND** | **FIRST** | **LAST** |
| Elmira | Oct 3 | May 9 | Kingston | Oct 3 | May 8 |
| Lake Placid | Sep 11 | Jun 7 | Newport | Nov 7 | Apr 15 |
| New York City | Nov 15 | Apr 1 | Providence | Oct 22 | Apr 16 |
| Syracuse | Oct 13 | Apr 28 | **SOUTH CAROLINA** | **FIRST** | **LAST** |
| **NORTH CAROLINA** | **FIRST** | **LAST** | Charleston | Nov 25 | Mar 9 |
| Asheville | Oct 25 | Apr 12 | Columbia | Nov 1 | Apr 1 |
| Charlotte | Nov 9 | Apr 11 | Florence | Nov 7 | Mar 26 |
| Fayetteville | Nov 5 | Mar 28 | Greenville | Nov 4 | Apr 4 |
| Raleigh-Durham | Oct 28 | Apr 10 | **SOUTH DAKOTA** | **FIRST** | **LAST** |
| **NORTH DAKOTA** | **FIRST** | **LAST** | Hot Springs | Sep 20 | May 16 |
| Bismarck | Sep 21 | May 14 | Pierre | Oct 3 | May 2 |
| Fargo | Sep 27 | May 10 | Sioux Falls | Sep 28 | May 3 |
| Grand Forks | Sep 27 | May 10 | Watertown | Sep 25 | May 10 |
| Minot | Sep 28 | May 9 | | | |

## AVERAGE FROST DATES

| TENNESSEE | FIRST | LAST | VIRGINIA (CONT.) | FIRST | LAST |
|---|---|---|---|---|---|
| Chattanooga | Nov 4 | Apr 1 | Richmond | Oct 30 | Apr 6 |
| Knoxville | Oct 22 | Apr 16 | Roanoke | Oct 22 | Apr 13 |
| Memphis | Nov 13 | Mar 22 | **WASHINGTON** | **FIRST** | **LAST** |
| Nashville | Oct 28 | Apr 6 | Olympia | Oct 6 | May 5 |
| **TEXAS** | **FIRST** | **LAST** | Seattle | Nov 17 | Mar 10 |
| Amarillo | Oct 20 | Apr 18 | Spokane | Oct 3 | May 2 |
| Dallas | Nov 25 | Mar 3 | Vancouver | Oct 15 | Apr 20 |
| Houston | Dec 20 | Feb 8 | **WEST VIRGINIA** | **FIRST** | **LAST** |
| San Antonio | Nov 25 | Feb 28 | Charleston | Oct 21 | Apr 22 |
| **UTAH** | **FIRST** | **LAST** | Martinsburg | Oct 19 | Apr 19 |
| Cedar City | Oct 1 | May 21 | Morgantown | Oct 18 | Apr 30 |
| Logan | Sep 29 | May 14 | **WISCONSIN** | **FIRST** | **LAST** |
| Salt Lake City | Oct 25 | Apr 19 | Appleton | Oct 7 | May 4 |
| **VERMONT** | **FIRST** | **LAST** | Eau Claire | Sep 29 | May 7 |
| Burlington | Oct 3 | May 8 | Madison | Oct 2 | May 10 |
| Montpelier | Oct 1 | May 11 | Milwaukee | Oct 14 | Apr 27 |
| Rutland | Sep 28 | May 13 | **WYOMING** | **FIRST** | **LAST** |
| **VIRGINIA** | **FIRST** | **LAST** | Casper | Sep 19 | May 22 |
| Charlottesville | Oct 31 | Apr 7 | Cheyenne | Sep 26 | May 12 |
| Norfolk | Nov 23 | Mar 20 | Gillette | Sep 4 | May 18 |

## United States Department of Agriculture (USDA) Plant Hardiness Zone Map

Helps gardeners and growers determine which plants are most likely to thrive in a specific area

**Download a detailed, full-color map here:**
http://planthardiness.ars.usda.gov

*Cold- & Frost-Tolerant ANNUALS:* Pot Marigold, Bachelor's Button, Larkspur, Sweet Pea, Sweet Alyssum, Bells of Ireland, Forget-Me-Not, Black-Eyed Susan, Pansy, Viola, Johnny Jump-Up, Snapdragon, Dusty Miller & Phlox.

*Cold- & Frost-Tolerant VEGETABLES:* Beets, Broccoli, Brussels Sprouts, Cabbage, Carrots, Cauliflower, Chard, Collards, Garlic, Kale, Lettuce, Mustard, Onions, Parsley, Spinach & Turnips.

 **GREEN THUMB?**
More gardening tips and how-tos can be found online at **FarmersAlmanac.com**.

## GARDENING ACCORDING TO THE MOON

### QUICK VIEW TABLE FOR 2020

| | Plant Aboveground Crops | Plant Root Crops | Transplant | Plant Seedbeds | Plant Flowers | Kill Plant Pests |
|---|---|---|---|---|---|---|
| **JANUARY** | 4, 5, 9, 26-28, 31 | 10, 15-18, 21-23 | 10, 17, 18 | 9, 10, 17, 18 | 9, 10, 15, 16 | 1-3, 6-8, 11-14, 19, 20, 24, 25, 29, 30 |
| **FEBRUARY** | 1, 2, 5, 6, 23, 24, 28, 29 | 11-14, 18, 19 | 13, 14 | 5, 6, 13, 14 | 5, 6, 11, 12 | 3, 4, 7-10, 15-17, 20-22, 25-27 |
| **MARCH** | 3-5, 26, 27, 31 | 10-13, 16, 17, 21, 22 | 12, 13, 21, 22 | 3-5, 12, 13, 31 | 3-5, 10, 11, 31 | 1, 2, 6-9, 14, 15, 18-20, 23-25, 28-30 |
| **APRIL** | 1, 6, 22-24, 27, 28 | 7-9, 12-14, 17-19 | 8, 9, 17-19 | 1, 8, 9, 27, 28 | 1, 6, 7, 27, 28 | 2-5, 10, 11, 15, 16, 20, 21, 25, 26, 29, 30 |
| **MAY** | 4-6, 24-26, 31 | 7, 10, 11, 14-16, 19-21 | 7, 14-16, 19-21 | 6, 7, 24-26 | 4, 5, 24-26, 31 | 1-3, 8, 9, 12, 13, 17, 18, 22, 23, 27-30 |
| **JUNE** | 1-3, 21, 22, 27-30 | 6, 7, 11, 12, 16, 17 | 11, 12, 16, 17 | 2, 3, 21, 22, 29, 30 | 1, 21, 22, 27, 28 | 4, 5, 8-10, 13-15, 18-20, 23-26 |
| **JULY** | 4, 24-28, 31 | 5, 8-10, 13-15, 18, 19 | 8-10, 13-15, 18, 19 | 18, 19, 27, 28 | 18, 19, 24-26 | 1-3, 6, 7, 11, 12, 16, 17, 20-23, 29, 30 |
| **AUGUST** | 1, 21-24, 27, 28 | 4-6, 9-11, 14-16 | 4-6, 9-11, 14-16 | 14-16, 23, 24 | 14-16, 21, 22 | 2, 3, 7, 8, 12, 13, 17-20, 25, 26, 29-31 |
| **SEPTEMBER** | 1, 17-20, 23-25, 28, 29 | 2, 6, 7, 11, 12 | 2, 6, 7, 11, 12 | 11, 12, 19, 20 | 11, 12, 17, 18 | 3-5, 8-10, 13-16, 21, 22, 26, 27, 30 |
| **OCTOBER** | 16-18, 21, 22, 25-27, 30 | 3-5, 8, 9, 15, 31 | 3-5, 8, 9, 31 | 8, 9, 17, 18 | 8, 9, 15, 16 | 1, 2, 6, 7, 10-14, 19, 20, 23, 24, 28, 29 |
| **NOVEMBER** | 17, 18, 21-23, 26-28 | 1, 4-6, 11-14 | 1, 4-6, 13, 14 | 4-6, 13, 14 | 4-6, 11, 12 | 2, 3, 7-10, 15, 16, 19, 20, 24, 25, 29, 30 |
| **DECEMBER** | 14-16, 19, 20, 24, 25 | 1-3, 8-11, 29, 30 | 1-3, 10, 11, 29, 30 | 1-3, 10, 11, 29, 30 | 1-3, 8, 9, 29, 30 | 4-7, 12, 13, 17, 18, 21-23, 26-28, 31 |

## 2020 GARDENING ACCORDING TO THE MOON

*The most favorable days for planting aboveground vegetables, root and forage crops, and for doing other gardening tasks as determined by the phases of the Moon.*

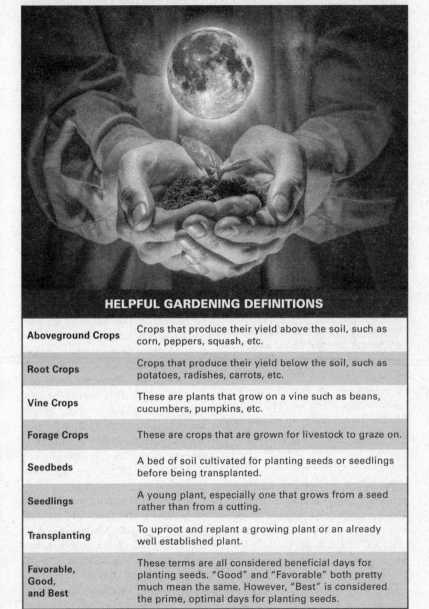

### HELPFUL GARDENING DEFINITIONS

| | |
|---|---|
| **Aboveground Crops** | Crops that produce their yield above the soil, such as corn, peppers, squash, etc. |
| **Root Crops** | Crops that produce their yield below the soil, such as potatoes, radishes, carrots, etc. |
| **Vine Crops** | These are plants that grow on a vine such as beans, cucumbers, pumpkins, etc. |
| **Forage Crops** | These are crops that are grown for livestock to graze on. |
| **Seedbeds** | A bed of soil cultivated for planting seeds or seedlings before being transplanted. |
| **Seedlings** | A young plant, especially one that grows from a seed rather than from a cutting. |
| **Transplanting** | To uproot and replant a growing plant or an already well established plant. |
| **Favorable, Good, and Best** | These terms are all considered beneficial days for planting seeds. "Good" and "Favorable" both pretty much mean the same. However, "Best" is considered the prime, optimal days for planting seeds. |

*(continued)*

**JANUARY 1–3:** Barren, do no planting. **4, 5:** Fine for planting beans, peppers, cucumbers, melons, and other above-ground crops where climate is suitable. **6–8:** Poor days for planting, seeds tend to rot in ground. **9, 10:** Plant seedbeds and flower gardens. First day is best planting day for aboveground crops, especially peas, beans, cucumbers, and squash where suitable. Second day is a good day for transplanting. Second day is most fruitful for planting beets, carrots, onions, and other hardy root crops in the Deep South. **11–14:** Barren time. Best for killing weeds, poison ivy, briars, and other plant pests, and for clearing wood lots and fencerows. **15, 16:** A favorable time for sowing grains, hay, and forage crops. Favorable days for planting flowers and root crops. **17, 18:** Start seedbeds. Good for transplanting. Plant carrots, turnips, onions, beets, Irish potatoes, other root crops in the South. Also good for leafy vegetables. **19, 20:** Do no planting. **21–23:** Good for planting root crops where climate permits. **24, 25:** A good time to kill plant pests or do plowing. Poor planting. **26–28:** Extra good days for peas, peppers, tomatoes, and other vine crops. Fine for planting any aboveground crop where climate permits. **29, 30:** Barren days, do no planting. **31:** Fine for planting beans, peppers, cucumbers, melons, and other aboveground crops where climate is suitable.

**FEBRUARY 1, 2:** Fine for planting beans, peppers, cucumbers, melons, and other aboveground crops where climate is suitable. **3, 4:** Any seed planted now will tend to rot. **5, 6:** Plant seedbeds and flower gardens. Fine for planting beans, tomatoes, corn, cotton, peppers, cucumbers, melons, and other aboveground crops where the climate allows.

**7–10:** Clear ground, turn sod, kill plant pests. **11, 12:** Fine days for sowing hay, grains, and forage crops. Plant flowers. Favorable for planting root crops. **13, 14:** Start seedbeds. Good for transplanting. Plant carrots, turnips, onions, beets, Irish potatoes, and other root crops in the South. Lettuce and other leafy vegetables will do well. **15–17:** Poor planting days. **18, 19:** Any root crops that can be planted now will do well. **20–22:** Barren days. Fine for clearing, plowing, fertilizing, and killing plant pests. **23, 24:** Extra good for cucumbers, peas, cantaloupes, and other vine crops. Set strawberry plants. Plant peppers, sweet corn, tomatoes, peas, and other aboveground crops in southern Florida, California, and Texas. **25–27:** Any seeds planted during this barren time will grow poorly and yield little. **28, 29:** Fine for planting beans, peppers, cucumbers, melons, and other aboveground crops where climate permits.

**MARCH 1, 2:** Seeds planted now tend to rot in ground. **3–5:** Excellent days for sowing seedbeds and flower gardens. Best planting days for aboveground crops, especially peas, beans, cucumbers, and squash where climate permits. **6–9:** A most barren period, best for killing plant pests or doing chores around the farm. **10, 11:** Fine for sowing grains, hay, and forage crops. Plant flowers. Favorable days for planting root crops. **12, 13:** Start seedbeds now. Good days for transplanting. Excellent time for planting root crops that can be planted at this time. Also good for leafy vegetables. **14, 15:** Barren days, do no planting. **16, 17:** Any root crops that can be planted now will do well. **18–20:** A barren period, best for killing plant pests, plowing and cultivating. **21, 22:** Good period for planting cucumbers, melons, pumpkins, peas, and other vine crops and for setting strawberry plants. Good for transplanting. Favorable days for planting beets, carrots, radishes, salsify, turnips, peanuts, and other root crops. **23–25:** Cultivate and spray, do general farm work, but no planting. **26, 27:** Favorable for planting crops yielding aboveground. **28–30:** Any seeds planted now tend to rot in ground. **31:** Excellent day for sowing seedbeds and flower gardens. Best for planting aboveground crops, especially peas, beans, cucumbers, and squash where climate is suitable.

**APRIL 1:** Good day to plant seedbeds and start flower gardens. Plant beans, tomatoes, peppers, corn, cotton, and other aboveground crops on this most fruitful day. **2–5:** Grub out weeds, briars, and other plant pests. **6, 7:** A favorable time for sowing grains, hay, and fodder crops. Plant flowers. On the first day, plant corn, melons, squash, tomatoes, and other aboveground crops. Second day is for planting root crops. **8, 9:** Start seedbeds. Good days for transplanting. Good days for planting beets, carrots, radishes, turnips, peanuts, and other root crops. Also good for leafy vegetables. **10, 11:** Neither plant nor sow during this barren time. **12–14:** Favorable days for planting beets, carrots, turnips, radishes, onions, and other root crops. **15, 16:** Excellent time for killing weeds, briars, poison ivy, and other plant pests. **17–19:** Set strawberry plants. Excellent for vine crops, such as beans, peas, and cucumbers. Good days for transplanting. Favorable for planting root crops. **20, 21:** Break ground or cultivate. Poor planting days. **22–24:** Favorable for planting beans, corn, cotton, tomatoes, peppers, and other aboveground crops. **25, 26:** Poor days for planting, seeds tend to rot in ground. **27, 28:** Start flower gardens and plant seedbeds. Plant tomatoes, beans, peppers, corn, cotton, and any other aboveground crops on these fruitful days. **29, 30:** Grub out weeds, briars, and other plant pests.

**MAY 1-3:** A barren period. Favorable for killing plant pests, cultivating, or taking a short vacation. **4, 5:** Favorable time for sowing grains, fodder crops and hay. Plant flowers. Excellent for planting corn, beans, peppers, and other aboveground crops. **6, 7:** Plant seedbeds. First day is excellent for planting aboveground crops, and planting leafy vegetables. The second day is good for transplanting and for planting carrots, beets, onions, turnips, and other root crops. Also good for leafy vegetables. **8, 9:** Seeds planted now will do poorly and yield little. **10, 11:** Plant late beets, potatoes, onions, carrots, and other root crops. **12, 13:** Kill plant pests on these barren days. **14–16:** Fine for vine crops. Set strawberry plants. Good days for transplanting. Favorable time for planting late root crops. **17, 18:** Poor planting. Fine days for cultivating or spraying. **19–21:** Good for transplanting. Root crops that can be planted now will yield well. **22, 23:** Any seed planted now will tend to rot. **24–26:** Plant seedbeds and flower gardens. A most favorable time for corn, cotton, okra, beans, peppers, eggplant, and other aboveground crops. **27–30:** A barren period. Favorable days for killing plant pests, cultivating, or taking a short vacation. **31:** Favorable time for sowing hay, fodder crops, and grains. Plant flowers. Excellent time for planting corn, beans, peppers, and other aboveground crops where the climate is suitable.

*(continued)*

**JUNE 1:** Sow grains and forage crops. Plant flowers. Favorable day for planting peas, beans, tomatoes, and other fall crops bearing aboveground. **2, 3:** Plant seedbeds. Extra good time for planting cauliflower, cabbage, collards, fall lettuce, and other leafy vegetables. All aboveground crops planted now will do well. **4, 5:** Poor planting days, cut hay or do general farm work. **6, 7:** Plant potatoes, onions, carrots, late beets, and other root crops. **8–10:** Poor days for planting. Kill plant pests, spray, fertilize, do general farm work. **11, 12:** Set strawberry plants. Excellent for any vine crops such as beans, peas, and cucumbers. Good days for transplanting. Favorable time for planting late root crops. **13–15:** Cut hay or do plowing on these barren days. **16, 17:** Good days for transplanting and for planting root crops. **18–20:** Seeds planted now tend to rot in ground. **21, 22:** Excellent for sowing seedbeds and flower gardens. Plant tomatoes, beans, peppers, corn, cotton, and other aboveground crops on these most fruitful days. **23–26:** Poor days for planting. Kill plant pests, clear fencerows, or clear land. **27, 28:** Sow grains and forage crops. Plant flowers. Favorable for planting peas, tomatoes, beans, and any other fall crop bearing aboveground. **29, 30:** Plant seedbeds. Extra good for planting cabbage, fall lettuce, cauliflower, collards, and other leafy vegetables. All aboveground crops planted now will do well.

**JULY 1–3:** Barren, neither plant nor sow. **4, 5:** First day is when any aboveground crops that can be planted now will do well. Second day is a good day for planting beets, carrots, salsify, Irish potatoes, and other root crops. **6, 7:** Good days for killing weeds, briars, and other plant pests, but poor for planting.

**8–10:** Set strawberry plants. Good days for transplanting and for planting beets, carrots, radishes, salsify, turnips, peanuts, and other root crops. Also good for vine crops. **11, 12:** A barren period. **13–15:** Good for transplanting. Root crops that can be planted now will yield well. **16, 17:** Poor for planting, seeds tend to rot in ground at this time. **18, 19:** Good days for planting seedbeds and flower gardens and for transplanting. A most fruitful time for planting root crops. **20–23:** A most barren period. Kill plant pests and do general farm work. **24–26:** Sow grains and forage crops. Plant flowers. Favorable days for planting peas, beans, tomatoes, and other fall crops bearing aboveground. **27, 28:** Start seedbeds. Extra good for fall cabbage, lettuce, mustard greens, cauliflower, and other leafy vegetables. Good for any aboveground crop that can be planted now. **29, 30:** Barren days, neither plant nor sow. **31:** Any aboveground crops that can be planted now will do well.

**AUGUST 1:** A good time to plant aboveground crops. **2, 3:** Barren days, fine for killing plant pests. **4–6:** Excellent for any vine crops such as beans, peas, and cucumbers. Good time period for transplanting. Favorable days for planting root crops. **7, 8:** Neither plant nor sow on these barren days. **9–11:** Good days for transplanting. Root crops that can be planted now will yield well. **12, 13:** Any seed planted now will tend to rot. **14–16:** Plant seedbeds and flower gardens. Good days for transplanting. Most favorable for planting turnips, onions, beets, and other root crops. **17–20:** Best for killing weeds, briars, poison ivy, and other plant pests. Clear wood lots and fencerows. **21, 22:** Excellent days for sowing grains, winter wheat, oats, and rye. Plant flowers. Good days for planting aboveground crops. **23, 24:** Plant seedbeds. Plant tomatoes, peas, peppers, beans, and any other aboveground crop in southern Florida, Texas, and California. Extra good days for leafy vegetables. **25, 26:** Cut winter wood, do clearing and plowing, but no planting. **27, 28:** A good time period for planting aboveground crops. **29–31:** Barren days, fine for killing plant pests

**SEPTEMBER 1, 2:** Extra good for vine crops. First day is favorable for planting aboveground crops. Second day is good for transplanting and for planting root crops. **3–5:** A poor time to plant. **6, 7:** Good days for transplanting and for planting root crops. **8–10:** Seeds planted now tend to rot in ground. **11, 12:** Plant seedbeds and flower gardens. Good for transplanting. Fine planting days for fall potatoes, turnips, onions, carrots, beets, and other root crops. **13–16:** Clear ground, turn sod, or kill plant pests. **17, 18:** Excellent for sowing grains, hay, and forage crops. Plant flowers. Good days for planting peas, beans, tomatoes, peppers, and other aboveground crops in southern Florida, Texas, and California. **19, 20:** Start seedbeds. Excellent time period for planting aboveground crops that can be planted now, including leafy vegetables which will do well. **21, 22:** Clear fencerows, wood lots, and fields, but do no planting. **23-25:** Any aboveground crops that can be planted now will do well. **26, 27:** Poor planting days. Kill plant pests. **28, 29:** Extra good days for vine crops. Favorable time span for planting aboveground crops. **30:** A poor time to plant.

**OCTOBER 1, 2:** Barren days, do no planting. **3–5:** Good for transplanting. Good days for planting beets, carrots, onions, turnips, and other hardy root crops where climate is suitable. **6, 7:** Poor days for planting, seeds tend to rot in ground. **8, 9:** Start seedbeds and flower gardens. Good days for transplanting. Best planting days for turnips, fall potatoes, onions, carrots, beets, and other root crops where climate is suitable. **10–14:** A most barren period, best for doing chores around the farm or killing plant pests. **15, 16:** Fine for sowing grains, hay, and forage crops. Plant flowers. First day is a favorable day for planting root crops. Second day is a favorable day for planting beans, peas, squash, sweet corn, tomatoes, and any other aboveground crops in southern Florida, Texas, and California. **17, 18:** Start seedbeds. Favorable days for planting aboveground crops, and leafy vegetables such as lettuce, kale, cabbage, and celery where climate is suitable. **19, 20:** Do clearing and plowing, but no planting. **21, 22:** Plant peas, tomatoes, beans, and any other aboveground crops, indoors in the North and outdoors in lower South. **23, 24:** Poor planting days. Kill poison ivy, weeds, clear land, but do no planting. **25–27:** Extra good for vine crops. Favorable days for planting aboveground crops where climate is suitable. **28, 29:** Barren days, do no planting. **30, 31:** First day is fine for planting beans, peppers, cucumbers, melons, and other aboveground crops where climate permits. Second day is a good day for transplanting and for planting beets, carrots, onions, turnips, and other hardy root crops where climate is suitable.

**NOVEMBER 1:** A good day for transplanting. Plant root crops where climate permits. **2, 3:** Any seed planted now will tend to rot. **4–6:** Start seedbeds and flower gardens. Good for transplanting. Best for planting fall potatoes, beets,

*(continued)*

turnips, onions, carrots, and other root crops where climate is suitable. **7–10:** Grub out weeds, briars, and other plant pests. **11, 12:** Favorable for sowing hay, grains, and fodder crops. Plant flowers. Also favorable for planting root crops. **13, 14:** Start seedbeds. Good for transplanting. Plant carrots, beets, onions, turnips, Irish potatoes, and other root crops in the South. **15, 16:** Poor planting days. **17, 18:** Good for planting peas, squash, corn, tomatoes, and any other aboveground crops in southern Florida, Texas, and California. **19, 20:** A good time to kill plant pests or do plowing. Poor for planting. **21–23:** Extra good for vine crops. Favorable days for planting aboveground crops where the climate allows. **24, 25:** Seeds planted now will grow poorly and yield little. **26–28:** Fine days for planting beans, peppers, cucumbers, melons, and other aboveground crops where climate is suitable. **29, 30:** Any seed planted now will tend to rot.

**DECEMBER 1-3:** Good days to start seedbeds and flower gardens and for transplanting. Most favorable days for planting beets, onions, turnips, and other root crops where climate allows. **4–7:** A barren period. Favorable for killing plant pests, cultivating, or taking a short vacation. **8, 9:** Plant flowers. Fine for sowing hay, fodder crops, and grains. Favorable time period for planting root crops. **10, 11:** Start seedbeds. Good days for transplanting. Plant beets, carrots, onions, turnips, Irish potatoes, and any other root crops in the South. **12, 13:** Do no planting. **14–16:** Plant sweet corn, beans, peppers, and other aboveground crops where climate is suitable. **17, 18:** Barren days. Fine for clearing, plowing, fertilizing, and killing plant pests. **19, 20:** Extra good for peas,

cucumbers, cantaloupes, and other vine crops. Plant tomatoes, peppers, sweet corn, and other aboveground crops in southern Florida, California, and Texas. **21–23:** Barren period. **24, 25:** Fine for planting beans, peppers, cucumbers, melons, and other aboveground crops where climate permits. **26–28:** Seeds planted now tend to rot in ground. **29, 30:** Start seedbeds and flower gardens. Good for transplanting. A most favorable time for planting beets, onions, turnips, and other root crops where the climate allows. **31:** A barren period. Favorable for killing plant pests, cultivating, or taking a short vacation.

# WHY GOD PERMITS EVIL

*Send for this*

## FREE 32pp BOOKLET

Visit our website
www.dawnbible.com

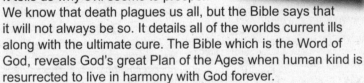

When catastrophe
strikes, the question is asked,
**why doesn't God do
something about it?**

The Bible answers this question.
It tells us why evil seems to prosper.
We know that death plagues us all, but the Bible says that
it will not always be so. It details all of the worlds current ills
along with the ultimate cure. The Bible which is the Word of
God, reveals God's great Plan of the Ages when human kind is
resurrected to live in harmony with God forever.

### WRITE, PHONE or EMAIL for YOUR FREE 32 PAGE COPY
### 1-800-234-DAWN

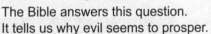

dawnbible@aol.com

DAWN PUBLISHING 199 RAILROAD AVENUE
EAST RUTHERFORD NJ 07073

## Astrologers - Readers

**ANGELIC GUIDANCE**
Psychic Medium Clairvoyant Positive
Energy, Astrology 1-323-466-3684
www.TruePsychicReader.com

**MOTHER JOLEEN SPIRITUAL READER**
Helps all problems. I won't ask why you've
called. I'll Tell You. One call will convince
you! Available 24/7 Call 850-276-4226

**ANGELINA GUARANTEES** Solves Health,
Love, Money and Luck Problems 1 Free
Question 512-470-9147

**ANSWERS ALL QUESTIONS** Solves life's problems. One call will convince you. Rev. Evette
does what others claim. Need help desperately?
Call immediately, 100% money back guarantee.
423-894-6699, PO Box 80322, Chattanooga, TN
37414

**LOVE RELATIONSHIP SPECIALIST** Reuniting
Lovers. Call for a Free Reading 512-521-9804

**MAMA LUCY – LOVE SPECIALIST** Voodoo Spell
Caster Gets Immediate Results 512-586-5912

**MISS GRAY** Has God-Given Powers To Help You
in All Matters of Life. Call Now! 615-584-9881

**MISS MARY** Rootworker, Spellcaster Reunites
Lovers. My Magical Powers Are Beyond Your
Imagination 912-261-9324

**MOTHER BLACK –** Powerful Root Worker Removes Bad Luck Immediate Results 912-996-1438

**NATALIE DOES WHAT OTHERS CLAIM TO
BUT WITHOUT FAILURE** 817-851-6474

**PROPHET R** works with spirits, roots, herbs,
candles, lucky hands, and can remove unnatural
conditions. Lucky mojo's 919-813-8787

**SOPHIA GREEN** Don't tell me. I'll tell you! Help
with all problems. Help reunite lovers. Guaranteed. 956-878-7053

## Books

**FREE BIBLE STUDY GUIDE** "What is This
World Coming To?" Associated Bible Stu-
dents P.O. Box 1783F Wilmington, DE 19899
Info@godspromises.org 888-949-PRAY.

**FREE TRACTS** God loves you. New earth. Why
does a loving God permit Calamities, Bible Stan-

dard (FAJ) 1156 St. Matthews Road, Chester
Springs, PA 19425 www.biblestandard.com

**FREE BOOKLETS:** Life, Immortality, Soul, Pollution Crisis, Judgment Day, Restitution, sample
magazine. Bible Standard (FA), 1156 St. Matthews Road, Chester Springs, PA 19425. www.
biblestandard.com

**WHY WE LIVE AFTER DEATH** and more titles
free booklets, audio books www.GrailForum.com,
888-205-7307, 786 Jones Road, Vestal, NY 13850

## Business Opportunities

**$800 WEEKLY POTENTIAL!** Process HUD/FHA
refunds from home. Free Information available.
Call 860-357-1599

## Garden/Farm Supplies

**CATTLE AND HOG EQUIPMENT** - Farm and
ornamental fencing. Hog Haven confinement
units, poultry, pet supplies, wild game feeders.
See us at www.lucoinc.com or call 888-816-6707,
Luco MFG. Co. Box 385 Strong City, KS 66869

**GREEN HAVEN OPEN POLLINATED CORN
SEED.** Silage, Grain, Wildlife, Available Certified
Organic. Early Varieties visit us online at www.
openpollinated.com 607-566-9253

## Miscellaneous

**www.azuregreen.net** Amulets, Oils, Herbs, Candles, Incense, Statuary, Gemstones, 8,000 items.

## Music/Records/Tapes/CDs

**ACCORDIONS, CONCERTINAS,** Button Boxes,
Rolands. Buy, sell, trade, repair, tune. Catalogues
$5. Castiglione, PO Box 40, Warren, MI 48090.
www.castiglioneaccordions.com 586-755-6050

# UNIQUELY ENGAGE
## New & Existing Customers
### with the *Farmers' Almanac*

### ← GROW

Increase awareness, your client base, and sales by giving your customers a valuable "gift" they'll use all year-long.

### MOTIVATE →

Persuade customers to visit your website, attend a grand opening, or stop by your tradeshow booth with an Almanac featuring a special offer.

### ← THANK

Tell customers you appreciate their loyalty with a customized year-end message of thanks.

## JANUARY

**1** New Year's Day
**5** Epiphany *(Catholic)*
**6** Epiphany *(Episcopal)*
**12** Baptism of Jesus
**19** Robert E. Lee Birthday
**20** Martin Luther King, Jr. Birthday *(obs.)*
**30** Franklin D. Roosevelt Birthday

## FEBRUARY

**2** Purification *(Candlemas)*
**2** Groundhog Day
**8** Boy Scouts Day
**12** Lincoln's Birthday
**14** Valentine's Day
**15** Susan B. Anthony Birthday
**17** Presidents' Day
**22** Washington's Birthday *(traditional)*
**25** Shrove Tuesday Mardi Gras
**26** Ash Wednesday

## MARCH

**1** First Sunday in Lent
**1** St. David
**4** Ember Day
**6** Ember Day
**7** Ember Day
**8** Daylight Saving Time Begins
**9** Fast of Esther
**10** Purim
**12** Girl Scouts Day
**15** Ides of March
**17** St. Patrick's Day
**19** Spring Begins EDT
**25** Annunciation Day

## APRIL

**1** April Fools' Day
**5** Palm Sunday
**9** Holy Thursday
**9** First Day of Passover
**10** Good Friday
**12** Easter
**13** Thomas Jefferson Birthday
**14** Pan-American Day
**19** Orthodox Easter
**20** Patriot's Day *(ME & MA)*
**23** St. George

## MAY

**1** Law Day
**2** Kentucky Derby
**8** V. E. Day
**10** Mother's Day
**12** Lag B'Omer
**16** Armed Forces Day
**17** Rogation Sunday
**21** Ascension Day
**22** National Maritime Day
**25** Memorial Day
**28** Orthodox Ascension Day
**29** Shavuot
**31** Pentecost-Whitsunday

## JUNE

**3** Ember Day
**3** Jefferson Davis Birthday
**5** Ember Day
**6** Ember Day
**7** Trinity Sunday
**7** Orthodox Pentecost
**11** Corpus Christi
**14** Children's Day
**14** Flag Day
**20** Summer Begins EDT
**21** Father's Day
**24** St. John the Baptist *(Midsummer Day)*

## JULY

**3** Dog Days Begin
**4** Independence Day
**9** Fast of Tammuz
**15** St. Swithin's Day
**30** Fast of Av

## AUGUST

**11** Dog Days End
**14** V. J. Day
**15** Assumption B.V.M.

## SEPTEMBER

**7** Labor Day
**13** Grandparents' Day
**14** Holy Cross Day
**16** Ember Day
**17** Citizenship Day
**18** Ember Day
**19** Rosh Hashanah *(New Year 5781)*
**19** Ember Day
**21** Fast of Gedaliah
**22** Autumn Begins EDT
**27** Gold Star Mother's Day
**28** Yom Kippur
**29** Michaelmas Day

## OCTOBER

**1** Harvest Moon
**3** Succot
**9** Fire Prevention Day
**11** Simchat Torah
**12** Columbus Day *(traditional and observed)*
**24** United Nations Day
**31** Halloween

## NOVEMBER

**1** Daylight Saving Time Ends
**1** All Saints' Day
**2** All Souls' Day
**3** Election Day
**11** Veterans Day
**26** Thanksgiving Day
**29** Advent Sunday
**30** St. Andrew

## DECEMBER

**7** Pearl Harbor Day
**8** Conception B.V.M.
**11** Chanukah
**16** Ember Day
**18** Ember Day
**19** Ember Day
**21** Winter Begins EST
**25** Christmas Day
**29** St. Thomas Becket
**31** New Year's Eve

# CONNECTICUT

# RULES OF COURT

## FEDERAL

## 2008

# CONNECTICUT

# RULES OF COURT

FEDERAL

2008

Mat#40514837

**ISBN** 978–0–314–97126–5

# PREFACE

This edition of the *Connecticut Rules of Court, Federal, 2008* pamphlet, replaces the 2007 edition. This volume provides in convenient form court rules governing federal practice in Connecticut and is current with amendments received through October 15, 2007.

THE PUBLISHER

November, 2007

\*

# RELATED PRODUCTS

**Connecticut Rules of Evidence**
Publisher's Editorial Staff

**Unfair Trade Practices**
Langer, Belt and Morgan

**Constitution Law**
Rosengren

**Employment Law**
Harris

---

# CONNECTICUT ESTATES PRACTICE SERIES

**Connecticut Probate Deskbook**
Wilhelm

**Death Taxes in Connecticut**
Wilhelm

**Drafting Trusts in Connecticut**
Folsom and Wilhelm

**Drafting Wills in Connecticut**
Folsom and Wilhelm

**Incapacity, Power of Attorney and Adoption in Connecticut**
Folsom and Wilhelm

**Probate Jurisdiction and Procedure in Connecticut**
Folsom and Wilhelm

**Probate Litigation in Connecticut**
Folsom and Wilhelm

**Revocable Trusts and Trust Administration in Connecticut**
Folsom and Wilhelm

**Settlement of Estates in Connecticut**
Wilhelm

---

Westlaw®

WESTCheck® and WESTMATE®

West CD–ROM Libraries™

---

To order any of these Connecticut practice tools, call
your West Representative or **1–800–328–9352**.

# RELATED PRODUCTS
# FROM WEST

---

Connecticut General Statutes Annotated

Connecticut Reporter

Connecticut Rules of Court, State and Federal

Connecticut Digest

Connecticut Business Organizations Law

Connecticut Estate and Probate Law

Connecticut Family Law

Connecticut Real Estate Law

---

## CONNECTICUT PRACTICE SERIES

Practice Book Annotated—Superior Court Civil Rules
Horton and Knox

Juvenile Law
Horton and Krisch

Practice Book Annotated—Forms
Effron and Kaye

Practice Book Annotated—Criminal Procedure
Borden and Orland

Criminal Jury Instructions
Borden and Orland

Rules of Appellate Procedure
Horton and Bartschi

Trial Practice
Yukes

Family Law and Practice with Forms
Rutkin, Hogan and Oldham

Land Use Law and Practice
Fuller

Criminal Law
Borden and Orland

## RELATED PRODUCTS

## INTERNET ACCESS

Contact the West Editorial Department directly with your questions and suggestions by e-mail at west.editor@thomson.com. Visit West's home page on the World Wide Web at west.thomson.com

\*

# WESTLAW ELECTRONIC
# RESEARCH GUIDE

### Westlaw—Expanding the Reach of Your Library

Westlaw is West's online legal research service. With Westlaw, you experience the same quality and integrity that you have come to expect from West books, plus quick, easy access to West's vast collection of statutes, case law materials, public records, and other legal resources, in addition to current news articles and business information. For the most current and comprehensive legal research, combine the strengths of West books and Westlaw.

When you research with westlaw.com you get the convenience of the Internet combined with comprehensive and accurate Westlaw content, including exclusive editorial enhancements, plus features found only in westlaw.com such as ResultsPlus™ or StatutesPlus.™

### Accessing Databases Using the Westlaw Directory

The Westlaw Directory lists all databases on Westlaw and contains links to detailed information relating to the content of each database. Click **Directory** on the westlaw.com toolbar. There are several ways to access a database even when you don't know the database identifier. Browse a directory view. Scan the directory. Type all or part of a database name in the Search these Databases box. The Find a Database Wizard can help you select relevant databases for your search. You can access up to ten databases at one time for user-defined multibase searching.

### Retrieving a Specific Document

To retrieve a specific document by citation or title on westlaw.com click **Find&Print** on the toolbar to display the Find a Document page. If you are unsure of the correct citation format, type the publication abbreviation, e.g., **xx st** (where xx is a state's two-letter postal abbreviation), in the Find this document by citation box and click **Go** to display a fill-in-the-blank template. To retrieve a specific case when you know one or more parties' names, click **Find a Case by Party Name**.

### KeyCite®

KeyCite, the citation research service on Westlaw, makes it easy to trace the history of your case, statute, administrative decision or regulation to determine if there are recent updates, and to find other documents that cite your document. KeyCite will also find pending legislation relating to federal or state statutes. Access the powerful features of KeyCite from the westlaw.com toolbar, the **Links** tab, or KeyCite flags in a document display. KeyCite's red and yellow warning flags tell you at a glance whether your document has negative history. Depth-of-treatment stars help you focus on the most important citing references. KeyCite Alert allows you to monitor the status of your case, statute or rule, and automatically sends you updates at the frequency you specify.

## WESTLAW GUIDE

### ResultsPlus™

ResultsPlus is a Westlaw technology that automatically suggests additional information related to your search.  The suggested materials are accessible by a set of links that appear to the right of your westlaw.com search results:

- Go directly to relevant ALR® articles and Am Jur® annotations.
- Find on-point resources by key number.
- See information from related treatises and law reviews.

### StatutesPlus™

When you access a statutes database in westlaw.com you are brought to a powerful Search Center which collects, on one toolbar, the tools that are most useful for fast, efficient retrieval of statutes documents:

- Have a few key terms? Click **Statutes Index**.
- Know the common name? Click **Popular Name Table**.
- Familiar with the subject matter? Click **Table of Contents**.
- Have a citation or section number? Click **Find by Citation**.
- Interested in topical surveys providing citations across multiple state statutes? Click **50 State Surveys**.
- Or, simply search with **Natural Language** or **Terms and Connectors**.

When you access a statutes section, click on the **Links** tab for all relevant links for the current document that will also include a KeyCite section with a description of the KeyCite status flag. Depending on your document, links may also include administrative, bill text, and other sources that were previously only available by accessing and searching other databases.

### Additional Information

Westlaw is available on the Web at www.westlaw.com.

For search assistance, call the West Reference Attorneys at
1–800–REF–ATTY (1–800–733–2889).

For technical assistance, call West Customer Technical Support at
1–800–WESTLAW (1–800–937–8529).

# TABLE OF CONTENTS

---

## FEDERAL RULES

\*

# FEDERAL RULES OF CIVIL PROCEDURE

### Effective September 16, 1938

### Including Amendments Effective
### December 1, 2007,
### Absent Contrary Congressional Action

*[Publisher's Note: Set forth below are Rules and Forms currently in effect; for Rules and Forms effective December 1, 2007, absent contrary Congressional action, see page 87.]*

---

## Research Note

*These rules may be searched electronically on WESTLAW in the US–RULES database; updates to these rules may be found on WESTLAW in US–ORDERS or US–RULESUPDATES. For search tips, and a detailed summary of database content, consult the WESTLAW Scope Screen of each database.*

---

## Table of Rules

## PROPOSED
## FEDERAL RULES OF CIVIL PROCEDURE
**[Rules and Forms Effective December 1, 2007, absent contrary Congressional action]**
*[See Separate Table of Contents]*

## SUPPLEMENTAL RULES FOR ADMIRALTY OR MARITIME CLAIMS AND ASSET FORFEITURE ACTIONS

# I.  SCOPE OF RULES—ONE FORM OF ACTION

## RULE 1.  SCOPE AND PURPOSE OF RULES

These rules govern the procedure in the United States district courts in all suits of a civil nature whether cognizable as cases at law or in equity or in admiralty, with the exceptions stated in Rule 81. They shall be construed and administered to secure the just, speedy, and inexpensive determination of every action.

[Amended December 29, 1948, effective October 20, 1949; February 28, 1966, effective July 1, 1966; April 22, 1993, effective December 1, 1993.]

## RULE 2.  ONE FORM OF ACTION

There shall be one form of action to be known as "civil action."

# II.  COMMENCEMENT OF ACTION; SERVICE OF PROCESS, PLEADINGS, MOTIONS, AND ORDERS

## RULE 3.  COMMENCEMENT OF ACTION

A civil action is commenced by filing a complaint with the court.

## RULE 4.  SUMMONS

**(a) Form.** The summons shall be signed by the clerk, bear the seal of the court, identify the court and the parties, be directed to the defendant, and state the name and address of the plaintiff's attorney or, if unrepresented, of the plaintiff. It shall also state the time within which the defendant must appear and defend, and notify the defendant that failure to do so will result in a judgment by default against the defendant for the relief demanded in the complaint. The court may allow a summons to be amended.

**(b) Issuance.** Upon or after filing the complaint, the plaintiff may present a summons to the clerk for signature and seal. If the summons is in proper form, the clerk shall sign, seal, and issue it to the plaintiff for service on the defendant. A summons, or a copy of the summons if addressed to multiple defendants, shall be issued for each defendant to be served.

**(c) Service With Complaint; by Whom Made.**

(1) A summons shall be served together with a copy of the complaint. The plaintiff is responsible for service of a summons and complaint within the time

allowed under subdivision (m) and shall furnish the person effecting service with the necessary copies of the summons and complaint.

(2) Service may be effected by any person who is not a party and who is at least 18 years of age. At the request of the plaintiff, however, the court may direct that service be effected by a United States marshal, deputy United States marshal, or other person or officer specially appointed by the court for that purpose. Such an appointment must be made when the plaintiff is authorized to proceed in forma pauperis pursuant to 28 U.S.C. § 1915 or is authorized to proceed as a seaman under 28 U.S.C. § 1916.

**(d) Waiver of Service; Duty to Save Costs of Service; Request to Waive.**

(1) A defendant who waives service of a summons does not thereby waive any objection to the venue or to the jurisdiction of the court over the person of the defendant.

(2) An individual, corporation, or association that is subject to service under subdivision (e), (f), or (h) and that receives notice of an action in the manner provided in this paragraph has a duty to avoid unnecessary costs of serving the summons. To avoid costs, the plaintiff may notify such a defendant of the commencement of the action and request that the defendant waive service of a summons. The notice and request

(A) shall be in writing and shall be addressed directly to the defendant, if an individual, or else to an officer or managing or general agent (or other agent authorized by appointment or law to receive service of process) of a defendant subject to service under subdivision (h);

(B) shall be dispatched through first-class mail or other reliable means;

(C) shall be accompanied by a copy of the complaint and shall identify the court in which it has been filed;

(D) shall inform the defendant, by means of a text prescribed in an official form promulgated pursuant to Rule 84, of the consequences of compliance and of a failure to comply with the request;

(E) shall set forth the date on which the request is sent;

(F) shall allow the defendant a reasonable time to return the waiver, which shall be at least 30 days from the date on which the request is sent, or 60 days from that date if the defendant is addressed outside any judicial district of the United States; and

(G) shall provide the defendant with an extra copy of the notice and request, as well as a prepaid means of compliance in writing.

If a defendant located within the United States fails to comply with a request for waiver made by a plaintiff located within the United States, the court shall impose the costs subsequently incurred in effecting service on the defendant unless good cause for the failure be shown.

(3) A defendant that, before being served with process, timely returns a waiver so requested is not required to serve an answer to the complaint until 60 days after the date on which the request for waiver of service was sent, or 90 days after that date if the defendant was addressed outside any judicial district of the United States.

(4) When the plaintiff files a waiver of service with the court, the action shall proceed, except as provided in paragraph (3), as if a summons and complaint had been served at the time of filing the waiver, and no proof of service shall be required.

(5) The costs to be imposed on a defendant under paragraph (2) for failure to comply with a request to waive service of a summons shall include the costs subsequently incurred in effecting service under subdivision (e), (f), or (h), together with the costs, including a reasonable attorney's fee, of any motion required to collect the costs of service.

**(e) Service Upon Individuals Within a Judicial District of the United States.** Unless otherwise provided by federal law, service upon an individual from whom a waiver has not been obtained and filed, other than an infant or an incompetent person, may be effected in any judicial district of the United States:

(1) pursuant to the law of the state in which the district court is located, or in which service is effected, for the service of a summons upon the defendant in an action brought in the courts of general jurisdiction of the State; or

(2) by delivering a copy of the summons and of the complaint to the individual personally or by leaving copies thereof at the individual's dwelling house or usual place of abode with some person of suitable age and discretion then residing therein or by delivering a copy of the summons and of the complaint to an agent authorized by appointment or by law to receive service of process.

**(f) Service Upon Individuals in a Foreign Country.** Unless otherwise provided by federal law, service upon an individual from whom a waiver has not been obtained and filed, other than an infant or an incompetent person, may be effected in a place not within any judicial district of the United States:

(1) by any internationally agreed means reasonably calculated to give notice, such as those means authorized by the Hague Convention on the Service Abroad of Judicial and Extrajudicial Documents; or

(2) if there is no internationally agreed means of service or the applicable international agreement allows other means of service, provided that service is reasonably calculated to give notice:

(A) in the manner prescribed by the law of the foreign country for service in that country in an action in any of its courts of general jurisdiction; or

(B) as directed by the foreign authority in response to a letter rogatory or letter of request; or

(C) unless prohibited by the law of the foreign country, by

(i) delivery to the individual personally of a copy of the summons and the complaint; or

(ii) any form of mail requiring a signed receipt, to be addressed and dispatched by the clerk of the court to the party to be served; or

(3) by other means not prohibited by international agreement as may be directed by the court.

(g) **Service Upon Infants and Incompetent Persons.** Service upon an infant or an incompetent person in a judicial district of the United States shall be effected in the manner prescribed by the law of the state in which the service is made for the service of summons or other like process upon any such defendant in an action brought in the courts of general jurisdiction of that state. Service upon an infant or an incompetent person in a place not within any judicial district of the United States shall be effected in the manner prescribed by paragraph (2)(A) or (2)(B) of subdivision (f) or by such means as the court may direct.

(h) **Service Upon Corporations and Associations.** Unless otherwise provided by federal law, service upon a domestic or foreign corporation or upon a partnership or other unincorporated association that is subject to suit under a common name, and from which a waiver of service has not been obtained and filed, shall be effected:

(1) in a judicial district of the United States in the manner prescribed for individuals by subdivision (e)(1), or by delivering a copy of the summons and of the complaint to an officer, a managing or general agent, or to any other agent authorized by appointment or by law to receive service of process and, if the agent is one authorized by statute to receive service and the statute so requires, by also mailing a copy to the defendant, or

(2) in a place not within any judicial district of the United States in any manner prescribed for individuals by subdivision (f) except personal delivery as provided in paragraph (2)(C)(i) thereof.

(i) **Serving the United States, Its Agencies, Corporations, Officers, or Employees.**

(1) Service upon the United States shall be effected

(A) by delivering a copy of the summons and of the complaint to the United States attorney for the district in which the action is brought or to an assistant United States attorney or clerical employee designated by the United States attorney in a writing filed with the clerk of the court or by sending a copy of the summons and of the complaint by registered or certified mail addressed to the civil process clerk at the office of the United States attorney and

(B) by also sending a copy of the summons and of the complaint by registered or certified mail to the Attorney General of the United States at Washington, District of Columbia, and

(C) in any action attacking the validity of an order of an officer or agency of the United States not made a party, by also sending a copy of the summons and of the complaint by registered or certified mail to the officer or agency.

(2)(A) Service on an agency or corporation of the United States, or an officer or employee of the United States sued only in an official capacity, is effected by serving the United States in the manner prescribed by Rule 4(i)(1) and by also sending a copy of the summons and complaint by registered or certified mail to the officer, employee, agency, or corporation.

(B) Service on an officer or employee of the United States sued in an individual capacity for acts or omission occurring in connection with the performance of duties on behalf of the United States— whether or not the officer or employee is sued also in an official capacity—is effected by serving the United States in the manner prescribed by Rule 4(i)(1) and by serving the officer or employee in the manner prescribed by Rule 4(e), (f), or (g).

(3) The court shall allow a reasonable time to serve process under Rule 4(i) for the purpose of curing the failure to serve:

(A) all persons required to be served in an action governed by Rule 4(i)(2)(A), if the plaintiff has served either the United States attorney or the Attorney General of the United States. or

(B) the United States in an action governed by Rule 4(i)(2)(B), if the plaintiff has served an officer or employee of the United State sued in an individual capacity.

(j) **Service Upon Foreign, State, or Local Governments.**

(1) Service upon a foreign state or a political subdivision, agency, or instrumentality thereof shall be effected pursuant to 28 U.S.C. § 1608.

(2) Service upon a state, municipal corporation, or other governmental organization subject to suit shall be effected by delivering a copy of the summons and

of the complaint to its chief executive officer or by serving the summons and complaint in the manner prescribed by the law of that state for the service of summons or other like process upon any such defendant.

**(k) Territorial Limits of Effective Service.**

(1) Service of a summons or filing a waiver of service is effective to establish jurisdiction over the person of a defendant

(A) who could be subjected to the jurisdiction of a court of general jurisdiction in the state in which the district court is located, or

(B) who is a party joined under Rule 14 or Rule 19 and is served at a place within a judicial district of the United States and not more than 100 miles from the place from which the summons issues, or

(C) who is subject to the federal interpleader jurisdiction under 28 U.S.C. § 1335, or

(D) when authorized by a statute of the United States.

(2) If the exercise of jurisdiction is consistent with the Constitution and laws of the United States, serving a summons or filing a waiver of service is also effective, with respect to claims arising under federal law, to establish personal jurisdiction over the person of any defendant who is not subject to the jurisdiction of the courts of general jurisdiction of any state.

**(l) Proof of Service.** If service is not waived, the person effecting service shall make proof thereof to the court. If service is made by a person other than a United States marshal or deputy United States marshal, the person shall make affidavit thereof. Proof of service in a place not within any judicial district of the United States shall, if effected under paragraph (1) of subdivision (f), be made pursuant to the applicable treaty or convention, and shall, if effected under paragraph (2) or (3) thereof, include a receipt signed by the addressee or other evidence of delivery to the addressee satisfactory to the court. Failure to make proof of service does not affect the validity of the service. The court may allow proof of service to be amended.

**(m) Time Limit for Service.** If service of the summons and complaint is not made upon a defendant within 120 days after the filing of the complaint, the court, upon motion or on its own initiative after notice to the plaintiff, shall dismiss the action without prejudice as to that defendant or direct that service be effected within a specified time; provided that if the plaintiff shows good cause for the failure, the court shall extend the time for service for an appropriate period. This subdivision does not apply to service in a foreign country pursuant to subdivision (f) or (j)(1).

**(n) Seizure of Property; Service of Summons Not Feasible.**

(1) If a statute of the United States so provides, the court may assert jurisdiction over property. Notice to claimants of the property shall then be sent in the manner provided by the statute or by service of a summons under this rule.

(2) Upon a showing that personal jurisdiction over a defendant cannot, in the district where the action is brought, be obtained with reasonable efforts by service of summons in any manner authorized by this rule, the court may assert jurisdiction over any of the defendant's assets found within the district by seizing the assets under the circumstances and in the manner provided by the law of the state in which the district court is located.

[Amended January 21, 1963, effective July 1, 1963; February 28, 1966, effective July 1, 1966; April 29, 1980, effective August 1, 1980; amended by Pub.L. 97-462, § 2, January 12, 1983, 96 Stat. 2527, effective 45 days after January 12, 1983; amended March 2, 1987, effective August 1, 1987; April 22, 1993, effective December 1, 1993; April 17, 2000, effective December 1, 2000.]

## RULE 4.1  SERVICE OF OTHER PROCESS

**(a) Generally.** Process other than a summons as provided in Rule 4 or subpoena as provided in Rule 45 shall be served by a United States marshal, a deputy United States marshal, or a person specially appointed for that purpose, who shall make proof of service as provided in Rule 4(l). The process may be served anywhere within the territorial limits of the state in which the district court is located, and, when authorized by a statute of the United States, beyond the territorial limits of that state.

**(b) Enforcement of Orders: Commitment for Civil Contempt.** An order of civil commitment of a person held to be in contempt of a decree or injunction issued to enforce the laws of the United States may be served and enforced in any district. Other orders in civil contempt proceedings shall be served in the state in which the court issuing the order to be enforced is located or elsewhere within the United States if not more than 100 miles from the place at which the order to be enforced was issued.

[Adopted April 22, 1993, effective December 1, 1993.]

## RULE 5.  SERVICE AND FILING OF PLEADINGS AND OTHER PAPERS

**(a) Service: When Required.** Except as otherwise provided in these rules, every order required by its terms to be served, every pleading subsequent to the original complaint unless the court otherwise or-

ders because of numerous defendants, every paper relating to discovery required to be served upon a party unless the court otherwise orders, every written motion other than one which may be heard ex parte, and every written notice, appearance, demand, offer of judgment, designation of record on appeal, and similar paper shall be served upon each of the parties. No service need be made on parties in default for failure to appear except that pleadings asserting new or additional claims for relief against them shall be served upon them in the manner provided for service of summons in Rule 4.

In an action begun by seizure of property, in which no person need be or is named as defendant, any service required to be made prior to the filing of an answer, claim, or appearance shall be made upon the person having custody or possession of the property at the time of its seizure.

**(b) Making Service.**

(1) Service under Rules 5(a) and 77(d) on a party represented by an attorney is made on the attorney unless the court orders service on the party.

(2) Service under Rule 5(a) is made by:

(A) Delivering a copy to the person served by:

(i) handing it to the person;

(ii) leaving it at the person's office with a clerk or other person in charge, or if no one is in charge leaving it in a conspicuous place in the office; or

(iii) if the person has no office or the office is closed, leaving it at the person's dwelling house or usual place of abode with someone of suitable age and discretion residing there.

(B) Mailing a copy to the last known address of the person served. Service by mail is complete on mailing.

(C) If the person served has no known address, leaving a copy with the clerk of the court.

(D) Delivering a copy by any other means, including electronic means, consented to in writing by the person served. Service by electronic means is complete on transmission; service by other consented means is complete when the person making service delivers the copy to the agency designated to make delivery. If authorized by local rule, a party may make service under this subparagraph (D) through the court's transmission facilities.

(3) Service by electronic means under Rule 5(b)(2)(D) is not effective if the party making service learns that the attempted service did not reach the person to be served.

**(c) Same: Numerous Defendants.** In any action in which there are unusually large numbers of defendants, the court, upon motion or of its own initiative, may order that service of the pleadings of the defendants and replies thereto need not be made as between the defendants and that any cross-claim, counterclaim, or matter constituting an avoidance or affirmative defense contained therein shall be deemed to be denied or avoided by all other parties and that the filing of any such pleading and service thereof upon the plaintiff constitutes due notice of it to the parties. A copy of every such order shall be served upon the parties in such manner and form as the court directs.

**(d) Filing; Certificate of Service.** All papers after the complaint required to be served upon a party, together with a certificate of service, must be filed with the court within a reasonable time after service, but disclosures under Rule 26(a)(1) or (2) and the following discovery requests and responses must not be filed until they are used in the proceeding or the court orders filing: (i) depositions, (ii) interrogatories, (iii) requests for documents or to permit entry upon land, and (iv) requests for admission.

**(e) Filing With the Court Defined.** The filing of papers with the court as required by these rules shall be made by filing them with the clerk of court, except that the judge may permit the papers to be filed with the judge, in which event the judge shall note thereon the filing date and forthwith transmit them to the office of the clerk. A court may by local rule permit or require papers to be filed, signed, or verified by electronic means that are consistent with technical standards, if any, that the Judicial Conference of the United States establishes. A local rule may require filing by electronic means only if reasonable exceptions are allowed. A paper filed by electronic means in compliance with a local rule constitutes a written paper for the purpose of applying these rules. The clerk shall not refuse to accept for filing any paper presented for that purpose solely because it is not presented in proper form as required by these rules or any local rules or practices.

[Amended January 21, 1963, effective July 1, 1963; March 30, 1970, effective July 1, 1970; April 29, 1980, effective August 1, 1980; March 2, 1987, effective August 1, 1987; April 30, 1991, effective December 1, 1991; April 22, 1993, effective December 1, 1993; April 23, 1996, effective December 1, 1996; April 17, 2000, effective December 1, 2000; April 23, 2001, effective December 1, 2001; April 12, 2006, effective December 1, 2006.]

## RULE 5.1 CONSTITUTIONAL CHALLENGE TO A STATUTE—NOTICE, CERTIFICATION, AND INTERVENTION

**(a) Notice by a Party.** A party that files a pleading, written motion, or other paper drawing into question the constitutionality of a federal or state statute must promptly:

(1) file a notice of constitutional question stating the question and identifying the paper that raises it, if:

(A) a federal statute is questioned and neither the United States nor any of its agencies, officers, or employees is a party in an official capacity, or

(B) a state statute is questioned and neither the state nor any of its agencies, officers, or employees is a party in an official capacity; and

(2) serve the notice and paper on the Attorney General of the United States if a federal statute is challenged—or on the state attorney general if a state statute is challenged—either by certified or registered mail or by sending it to an electronic address designated by the attorney general for this purpose.

**(b) Certification by the Court.** The court must, under 28 U.S.C. § 2403, certify to the Attorney General of the United States that there is a constitutional challenge to a federal statute, or certify to the state attorney general that there is a constitutional challenge to a state statute.

**(c) Intervention; Final Decision on the Merits.** Unless the court sets a later time, the attorney general may intervene within 60 days after the notice of constitutional question is filed or after the court certifies the challenge, whichever is earlier. Before the time to intervene expires, the court may reject the constitutional challenge, but may not enter a final judgment holding the statute unconstitutional.

**(d) No Forfeiture.** A party's failure to file and serve the notice, or the court's failure to certify, does not forfeit a constitutional claim or defense that is otherwise timely asserted.

[Effective December 1, 2006.]

# RULE 6. TIME

**(a) Computation.** In computing any period of time prescribed or allowed by these rules, by the local rules of any district court, by order of court, or by any applicable statute, the day of the act, event, or default from which the designated period of time begins to run shall not be included. The last day of the period so computed shall be included, unless it is a Saturday, a Sunday, or a legal holiday, or, when the act to be done is the filing of a paper in court, a day on which weather or other conditions have made the office of the clerk of the district court inaccessible, in which event the period runs until the end of the next day which is not one of the aforementioned days. When the period of time prescribed or allowed is less than 11 days, intermediate Saturdays, Sundays, and legal holidays shall be excluded in the computation. As used in this rule and in Rule 77(c), "legal holiday" includes New Year's Day, Birthday of Martin Luther King, Jr., Washington's Birthday, Memorial Day, Independence Day, Labor Day, Columbus Day, Veterans Day, Thanksgiving Day, Christmas Day, and any other day appointed as a holiday by the President or the Congress of the United States, or by the state in which the district court is held.

**(b) Enlargement.** When by these rules or by a notice given thereunder or by order of court an act is required or allowed to be done at or within a specified time, the court for cause shown may at any time in its discretion (1) with or without motion or notice order the period enlarged if request therefor is made before the expiration of the period originally prescribed or as extended by a previous order, or (2) upon motion made after the expiration of the specified period permit the act to be done where the failure to act was the result of excusable neglect; but it may not extend the time for taking any action under Rules 50(b) and (c)(2), 52(b), 59(b), (d) and (e) and 60(b), except to the extent and under the conditions stated in them.

**(c) Unaffected by Expiration of Term [Rescinded].**

**(d) For Motions—Affidavits.** A written motion, other than one which may be heard ex parte, and notice of the hearing thereof shall be served not later than 5 days before the time specified for the hearing, unless a different period is fixed by these rules or by order of the court. Such an order may for cause shown be made on ex parte application. When a motion is supported by affidavit, the affidavit shall be served with the motion; and, except as otherwise provided in Rule 59(c), opposing affidavits may be served not later than 1 day before the hearing, unless the court permits them to be served at some other time.

**(e) Additional Time After Certain Kinds of Service.** Whenever a party must or may act within a prescribed period after service and service is made under Rule 5(b)(2)(B), (C), or (D), 3 days are added after the prescribed period would otherwise expire under subdivision (a).

[Amended December 27, 1946, effective March 19, 1948; January 21, 1963, effective July 1, 1963; February 28, 1966, effective July 1, 1966; December 4, 1967, effective July 1, 1968; March 1, 1971, effective July 1, 1971; April 28, 1983, effective August 1, 1983; April 29, 1985, effective August 1, 1985; March 2, 1987, effective August 1, 1987; April 29, 1999, effective December 1, 1999; April 23, 2001, effective December 1, 2001; April 25, 2005, effective December 1, 2005.]

# III. PLEADINGS AND MOTIONS

## RULE 7. PLEADINGS ALLOWED; FORM OF MOTIONS

**(a) Pleadings.** There shall be a complaint and an answer; a reply to a counterclaim denominated as such; an answer to a cross-claim, if the answer contains a cross-claim; a third-party complaint, if a person who was not an original party is summoned under the provisions of Rule 14; and a third-party answer, if a third-party complaint is served. No other pleading shall be allowed, except that the court may order a reply to an answer or a third-party answer.

**(b) Motions and Other Papers.**

(1) An application to the court for an order shall be by motion which, unless made during a hearing or trial, shall be made in writing, shall state with particularity the grounds therefor, and shall set forth the relief or order sought. The requirement of writing is fulfilled if the motion is stated in a written notice of the hearing of the motion.

(2) The rules applicable to captions and other matters of form of pleadings apply to all motions and other papers provided for by these rules.

(3) All motions shall be signed in accordance with Rule 11.

**(c) Demurrers, Pleas, etc., Abolished.** Demurrers, pleas, and exceptions for insufficiency of a pleading shall not be used.

[Amended December 27, 1946, effective March 19, 1948; January 21, 1963, effective July 1, 1963; April 28, 1983, effective August 1, 1983.]

## RULE 7.1 DISCLOSURE STATEMENT

**(a) Who Must File: Nongovernmental Corporate Party.** A nongovernmental corporate party to an action or proceeding in a district court must file two copies of a statement that identifies any parent corporation and any publicly held corporation that owns 10% or more of its stock or states that there is no such corporation.

**(b) Time for Filing; Supplemental Filing.** A party must:

(1) file the Rule 7.1(a) statement with its first appearance, pleading, petition, motion, response, or other request addressed to the court, and

(2) promptly file a supplemental statement upon any change in the information that the statement requires.

[Adopted April 29, 2002, effective December 1, 2002.]

## RULE 8. GENERAL RULES OF PLEADING

**(a) Claims for Relief.** A pleading which sets forth a claim for relief, whether an original claim, counterclaim, cross-claim, or third-party claim, shall contain (1) a short and plain statement of the grounds upon which the court's jurisdiction depends, unless the court already has jurisdiction and the claim needs no new grounds of jurisdiction to support it, (2) a short and plain statement of the claim showing that the pleader is entitled to relief, and (3) a demand for judgment for the relief the pleader seeks. Relief in the alternative or of several different types may be demanded.

**(b) Defenses; Form of Denials.** A party shall state in short and plain terms the party's defenses to each claim asserted and shall admit or deny the averments upon which the adverse party relies. If a party is without knowledge or information sufficient to form a belief as to the truth of an averment, the party shall so state and this has the effect of a denial. Denials shall fairly meet the substance of the averments denied. When a pleader intends in good faith to deny only a part or a qualification of an averment, the pleader shall specify so much of it as is true and material and shall deny only the remainder. Unless the pleader intends in good faith to controvert all the averments of the preceding pleading, the pleader may make denials as specific denials of designated averments or paragraphs or may generally deny all the averments except such designated averments or paragraphs as the pleader expressly admits; but, when the pleader does so intend to controvert all its averments, including averments of the grounds upon which the court's jurisdiction depends, the pleader may do so by general denial subject to the obligations set forth in Rule 11.

**(c) Affirmative Defenses.** In pleading to a preceding pleading, a party shall set forth affirmatively accord and satisfaction, arbitration and award, assumption of risk, contributory negligence, discharge in bankruptcy, duress, estoppel, failure of consideration, fraud, illegality, injury by fellow servant, laches, license, payment, release, res judicata, statute of frauds, statute of limitations, waiver, and any other matter constituting an avoidance or affirmative defense. When a party has mistakenly designated a defense as a counterclaim or a counterclaim as a defense, the court on terms, if justice so requires, shall treat the pleading as if there had been a proper designation.

**(d) Effect of Failure to Deny.** Averments in a pleading to which a responsive pleading is required, other than those as to the amount of damage, are

admitted when not denied in the responsive pleading. Averments in a pleading to which no responsive pleading is required or permitted shall be taken as denied or avoided.

**(e) Pleading to Be Concise and Direct; Consistency.**

(1) Each averment of a pleading shall be simple, concise, and direct. No technical forms of pleading or motions are required.

(2) A party may set forth two or more statements of a claim or defense alternately or hypothetically, either in one count or defense or in separate counts or defenses. When two or more statements are made in the alternative and one of them if made independently would be sufficient, the pleading is not made insufficient by the insufficiency of one or more of the alternative statements. A party may also state as many separate claims or defenses as the party has regardless of consistency and whether based on legal, equitable, or maritime grounds. All statements shall be made subject to the obligations set forth in Rule 11.

**(f) Construction of Pleadings.** All pleadings shall be so construed as to do substantial justice.

[Amended February 28, 1966, effective July 1, 1966; March 2, 1987, effective August 1, 1987.]

# RULE 9. PLEADING SPECIAL MATTERS

**(a) Capacity.** It is not necessary to aver the capacity of a party to sue or be sued or the authority of a party to sue or be sued in a representative capacity or the legal existence of an organized association of persons that is made a party, except to the extent required to show the jurisdiction of the court. When a party desires to raise an issue as to the legal existence of any party or the capacity of any party to sue or be sued or the authority of a party to sue or be sued in a representative capacity, the party desiring to raise the issue shall do so by specific negative averment, which shall include such supporting particulars as are peculiarly within the pleader's knowledge.

**(b) Fraud, Mistake, Condition of the Mind.** In all averments of fraud or mistake, the circumstances constituting fraud or mistake shall be stated with particularity. Malice, intent, knowledge, and other condition of mind of a person may be averred generally.

**(c) Conditions Precedent.** In pleading the performance or occurrence of conditions precedent, it is sufficient to aver generally that all conditions precedent have been performed or have occurred. A denial of performance or occurrence shall be made specifically and with particularity.

**(d) Official Document or Act.** In pleading an official document or official act it is sufficient to aver

that the document was issued or the act done in compliance with law.

**(e) Judgment.** In pleading a judgment or decision of a domestic or foreign court, judicial or quasi-judicial tribunal, or of a board or officer, it is sufficient to aver the judgment or decision without setting forth matter showing jurisdiction to render it.

**(f) Time and Place.** For the purpose of testing the sufficiency of a pleading, averments of time and place are material and shall be considered like all other averments of material matter.

**(g) Special Damage.** When items of special damage are claimed, they shall be specifically stated.

**(h) Admiralty and Maritime Claims.** A pleading or count setting forth a claim for relief within the admiralty and maritime jurisdiction that is also within the jurisdiction of the district court on some other ground may contain a statement identifying the claim as an admiralty or maritime claim for the purposes of Rules 14(c), 38(e), and 82, and the Supplemental Rules for Admiralty or Maritime Claims and Asset Forfeiture Actions. If the claim is cognizable only in admiralty, it is an admiralty or maritime claim for those purposes whether so identified or not. The amendment of a pleading to add or withdraw an identifying statement is governed by the principles of Rule 15. A case that includes an admiralty or maritime claim within this subdivision is an admiralty case within 28 U.S.C. § 1292(a)(3).

[Amended February 28, 1966, effective July 1, 1966; December 4, 1967, effective July 1, 1968; March 30, 1970, effective July 1, 1970; March 2, 1987, effective August 1, 1987; April 11, 1997, effective December 1, 1997; April 12, 2006, effective December 1, 2006.]

# RULE 10. FORM OF PLEADINGS

**(a) Caption; Names of Parties.** Every pleading shall contain a caption setting forth the name of the court, the title of the action, the file number, and a designation as in Rule 7(a). In the complaint the title of the action shall include the names of all the parties, but in other pleadings it is sufficient to state the name of the first party on each side with an appropriate indication of other parties.

**(b) Paragraphs; Separate Statements.** All averments of claim or defense shall be made in numbered paragraphs, the contents of each of which shall be limited as far as practicable to a statement of a single set of circumstances; and a paragraph may be referred to by number in all succeeding pleadings. Each claim founded upon a separate transaction or occurrence and each defense other than denials shall be stated in a separate count or defense whenever a separation facilitates the clear presentation of the matters set forth.

**(c) Adoption by Reference; Exhibits.** Statements in a pleading may be adopted by reference in a different part of the same pleading or in another pleading or in any motion. A copy of any written instrument which is an exhibit to a pleading is a part thereof for all purposes.

# RULE 11.  SIGNING OF PLEADINGS, MOTIONS, AND OTHER PAPERS; REPRESENTATIONS TO COURT; SANCTIONS

**(a) Signature.** Every pleading, written motion, and other paper shall be signed by at least one attorney of record in the attorney's individual name, or, if the party is not represented by an attorney, shall be signed by the party. Each paper shall state the signer's address and telephone number, if any. Except when otherwise specifically provided by rule or statute, pleadings need not be verified or accompanied by affidavit. An unsigned paper shall be stricken unless omission of the signature is corrected promptly after being called to the attention of the attorney or party.

**(b) Representations to Court.** By presenting to the court (whether by signing, filing, submitting, or later advocating) a pleading, written motion, or other paper, an attorney or unrepresented party is certifying that to the best of the person's knowledge, information, and belief, formed after an inquiry reasonable under the circumstances,—

(1) it is not being presented for any improper purpose, such as to harass or to cause unnecessary delay or needless increase in the cost of litigation;

(2) the claims, defenses, and other legal contentions therein are warranted by existing law or by a nonfrivolous argument for the extension, modification, or reversal of existing law or the establishment of new law;

(3) the allegations and other factual contentions have evidentiary support or, if specifically so identified, are likely to have evidentiary support after a reasonable opportunity for further investigation or discovery; and

(4) the denials of factual contentions are warranted on the evidence or, if specifically so identified, are reasonably based on a lack of information or belief.

**(c) Sanctions.** If, after notice and a reasonable opportunity to respond, the court determines that subdivision (b) has been violated, the court may, subject to the conditions stated below, impose an appropriate sanction upon the attorneys, law firms, or parties that have violated subdivision (b) or are responsible for the violation.

(1) *How Initiated.*

(A) By Motion. A motion for sanctions under this rule shall be made separately from other motions or requests and shall describe the specific conduct alleged to violate subdivision (b). It shall be served as provided in Rule 5, but shall not be filed with or presented to the court unless, within 21 days after service of the motion (or such other period as the court may prescribe), the challenged paper, claim, defense, contention, allegation, or denial is not withdrawn or appropriately corrected. If warranted, the court may award to the party prevailing on the motion the reasonable expenses and attorney's fees incurred in presenting or opposing the motion. Absent exceptional circumstances, a law firm shall be held jointly responsible for violations committed by its partners, associates, and employees.

(B) On Court's Initiative. On its own initiative, the court may enter an order describing the specific conduct that appears to violate subdivision (b) and directing an attorney, law firm, or party to show cause why it has not violated subdivision (b) with respect thereto.

(2) *Nature of Sanction; Limitations.* A sanction imposed for violation of this rule shall be limited to what is sufficient to deter repetition of such conduct or comparable conduct by others similarly situated. Subject to the limitations in subparagraphs (A) and (B), the sanction may consist of, or include, directives of a nonmonetary nature, an order to pay a penalty into court, or, if imposed on motion and warranted for effective deterrence, an order directing payment to the movant of some or all of the reasonable attorneys' fees and other expenses incurred as a direct result of the violation.

(A) Monetary sanctions may not be awarded against a represented party for a violation of subdivision (b)(2).

(B) Monetary sanctions may not be awarded on the court's initiative unless the court issues its order to show cause before a voluntary dismissal or settlement of the claims made by or against the party which is, or whose attorneys are, to be sanctioned.

(3) *Order.* When imposing sanctions, the court shall describe the conduct determined to constitute a violation of this rule and explain the basis for the sanction imposed.

**(d) Inapplicability to Discovery.** Subdivisions (a) through (c) of this rule do not apply to disclosures and discovery requests, responses, objections, and motions that are subject to the provisions of Rules 26 through 37.

[Amended April 28, 1983, effective August 1, 1983; March 2, 1987, effective August 1, 1987; April 22, 1993, effective December 1, 1993.]

# RULE 12. DEFENSES AND OBJECTIONS—WHEN AND HOW PRESENTED—BY PLEADING OR MOTION—MOTION FOR JUDGMENT ON THE PLEADINGS

### (a) When Presented.

(1) Unless a different time is prescribed in a statute of the United States, a defendant shall serve an answer

(A) within 20 days after being served with the summons and complaint, or

(B) if service of the summons has been timely waived on request under Rule 4(d), within 60 days after the date when the request for waiver was sent, or within 90 days after that date if the defendant was addressed outside any judicial district of the United States.

(2) A party served with a pleading stating a cross-claim against that party shall serve an answer thereto within 20 days after being served. The plaintiff shall serve a reply to a counterclaim in the answer within 20 days after service of the answer, or, if a reply is ordered by the court, within 20 days after service of the order, unless the order otherwise directs.

(3)(A) The United States, an agency of the United States, or an officer or employee of the United States sued in an official capacity, shall serve an answer to the complaint or cross-claim—or a reply to a counterclaim—within 60 days after the United States attorney is served with the pleading asserting the claim.

(B) An officer or employee of the United States sued in an individual capacity for acts or omissions occurring in connection with the performance of duties on behalf of the United States shall serve an answer to the complaint or cross-claim—or a reply to a counterclaim—within 60 days after service on the officer or employee, or service on the United States attorney, whichever is later.

(4) Unless a different time is fixed by court order, the service of a motion permitted under this rule alters these periods of time as follows:

(A) if the court denies the motion or postpones its disposition until the trial on the merits, the responsive pleading shall be served within 10 days after notice of the court's action; or

(B) if the court grants a motion for a more definite statement, the responsive pleading shall be served within 10 days after the service of the more definite statement.

### (b) How Presented. 
Every defense, in law or fact, to a claim for relief in any pleading, whether a claim, counterclaim, cross-claim, or third-party claim, shall be asserted in the responsive pleading thereto if one is required, except that the following defenses may at the option of the pleader be made by motion: (1) lack of jurisdiction over the subject matter, (2) lack of jurisdiction over the person, (3) improper venue, (4) insufficiency of process, (5) insufficiency of service of process, (6) failure to state a claim upon which relief can be granted, (7) failure to join a party under Rule 19. A motion making any of these defenses shall be made before pleading if a further pleading is permitted. No defense or objection is waived by being joined with one or more other defenses or objections in a responsive pleading or motion. If a pleading sets forth a claim for relief to which the adverse party is not required to serve a responsive pleading, the adverse party may assert at the trial any defense in law or fact to that claim for relief. If, on a motion asserting the defense numbered (6) to dismiss for failure of the pleading to state a claim upon which relief can be granted, matters outside the pleading are presented to and not excluded by the court, the motion shall be treated as one for summary judgment and disposed of as provided in Rule 56, and all parties shall be given reasonable opportunity to present all material made pertinent to such a motion by Rule 56.

### (c) Motion for Judgment on the Pleadings. 
After the pleadings are closed but within such time as not to delay the trial, any party may move for judgment on the pleadings. If, on a motion for judgment on the pleadings, matters outside the pleadings are presented to and not excluded by the court, the motion shall be treated as one for summary judgment and disposed of as provided in Rule 56, and all parties shall be given reasonable opportunity to present all material made pertinent to such a motion by Rule 56.

### (d) Preliminary Hearings. 
The defenses specifically enumerated (1)–(7) in subdivision (b) of this rule, whether made in a pleading or by motion, and the motion for judgment mentioned in subdivision (c) of this rule shall be heard and determined before trial on application of any party, unless the court orders that the hearing and determination thereof be deferred until the trial.

### (e) Motion for More Definite Statement. 
If a pleading to which a responsive pleading is permitted is so vague or ambiguous that a party cannot reasonably be required to frame a responsive pleading, the party may move for a more definite statement before interposing a responsive pleading. The motion shall point out the defects complained of and the details desired. If the motion is granted and the order of the court is not obeyed within 10 days after notice of the order or within such other time as the court may fix, the court may strike the pleading to which the motion was directed or make such order as it deems just.

### (f) Motion to Strike. 
Upon motion made by a party before responding to a pleading or, if no responsive pleading is permitted by these rules, upon motion

made by a party within 20 days after the service of the pleading upon the party or upon the court's own initiative at any time, the court may order stricken from any pleading any insufficient defense or any redundant, immaterial, impertinent, or scandalous matter.

**(g) Consolidation of Defenses in Motion.** A party who makes a motion under this rule may join with it any other motions herein provided for and then available to the party. If a party makes a motion under this rule but omits therefrom any defense or objection then available to the party which this rule permits to be raised by motion, the party shall not thereafter make a motion based on the defense or objection so omitted, except a motion as provided in subdivision (h)(2) hereof on any of the grounds there stated.

**(h) Waiver or Preservation of Certain Defenses.**

(1) A defense of lack of jurisdiction over the person, improper venue, insufficiency of process, or insufficiency of service of process is waived (A) if omitted from a motion in the circumstances described in subdivision (g), or (B) if it is neither made by motion under this rule nor included in a responsive pleading or an amendment thereof permitted by Rule 15(a) to be made as a matter of course.

(2) A defense of failure to state a claim upon which relief can be granted, a defense of failure to join a party indispensable under Rule 19, and an objection of failure to state a legal defense to a claim may be made in any pleading permitted or ordered under Rule 7(a), or by motion for judgment on the pleadings, or at the trial on the merits.

(3) Whenever it appears by suggestion of the parties or otherwise that the court lacks jurisdiction of the subject matter, the court shall dismiss the action.

[Amended December 27, 1946, effective March 19, 1948; January 21, 1963, effective July 1, 1963; February 28, 1966, effective July 1, 1966; March 2, 1987, effective August 1, 1987; April 22, 1993, effective December 1, 1993; April 17, 2000, effective December 1, 2000.]

# RULE 13.   COUNTERCLAIM AND CROSS–CLAIM

**(a) Compulsory Counterclaims.** A pleading shall state as a counterclaim any claim which at the time of serving the pleading the pleader has against any opposing party, if it arises out of the transaction or occurrence that is the subject matter of the opposing party's claim and does not require for its adjudication the presence of third parties of whom the court cannot acquire jurisdiction. But the pleader need not state the claim if (1) at the time the action was commenced the claim was the subject of another pending action, or (2) the opposing party brought suit upon the claim by attachment or other process by which the court did not acquire jurisdiction to render a personal judgment on that claim, and the pleader is not stating any counterclaim under this Rule 13.

**(b) Permissive Counterclaims.** A pleading may state as a counterclaim any claim against an opposing party not arising out of the transaction or occurrence that is the subject matter of the opposing party's claim.

**(c) Counterclaim Exceeding Opposing Claim.** A counterclaim may or may not diminish or defeat the recovery sought by the opposing party. It may claim relief exceeding in amount or different in kind from that sought in the pleading of the opposing party.

**(d) Counterclaim Against the United States.** These rules shall not be construed to enlarge beyond the limits now fixed by law the right to assert counterclaims or to claim credits against the United States or an officer or agency thereof.

**(e) Counterclaim Maturing or Acquired After Pleading.** A claim which either matured or was acquired by the pleader after serving a pleading may, with the permission of the court, be presented as a counterclaim by supplemental pleading.

**(f) Omitted Counterclaim.** When a pleader fails to set up a counterclaim through oversight, inadvertence, or excusable neglect, or when justice requires, the pleader may by leave of court set up the counterclaim by amendment.

**(g) Cross-Claim Against Co-party.** A pleading may state as a cross-claim any claim by one party against a co-party arising out of the transaction or occurrence that is the subject matter either of the original action or of a counterclaim therein or relating to any property that is the subject matter of the original action. Such cross-claim may include a claim that the party against whom it is asserted is or may be liable to the cross-claimant for all or part of a claim asserted in the action against the cross-claimant.

**(h) Joinder of Additional Parties.** Persons other than those made parties to the original action may be made parties to a counterclaim or cross-claim in accordance with the provisions of Rules 19 and 20.

**(i) Separate Trials; Separate Judgments.** If the court orders separate trials as provided in Rule 42(b), judgment on a counterclaim or cross-claim may be rendered in accordance with the terms of Rule 54(b) when the court has jurisdiction so to do, even if the claims of the opposing party have been dismissed or otherwise disposed of.

[Amended December 27, 1946, effective March 19, 1948; January 21, 1963, effective July 1, 1963; February 28, 1966, effective July 1, 1966; March 2, 1987, effective August 1, 1987.]

# RULE 14.   THIRD–PARTY PRACTICE

**(a) When Defendant May Bring in Third Party.** At any time after commencement of the action a defending party, as a third-party plaintiff, may cause a summons and complaint to be served upon a person not a party to the action who is or may be liable to the third-party plaintiff for all or part of the plaintiff's claim against the third-party plaintiff. The third-party plaintiff need not obtain leave to make the service if the third-party plaintiff files the third-party complaint not later than 10 days after serving the original answer. Otherwise the third-party plaintiff must obtain leave on motion upon notice to all parties to the action. The person served with the summons and third-party complaint, hereinafter called the third-party defendant, shall make any defenses to the third-party plaintiff's claim as provided in Rule 12 and any counterclaims against the third-party plaintiff and cross-claims against other third-party defendants as provided in Rule 13. The third-party defendant may assert against the plaintiff any defenses which the third-party plaintiff has to the plaintiff's claim. The third-party defendant may also assert any claim against the plaintiff arising out of the transaction or occurrence that is the subject matter of the plaintiff's claim against the third-party plaintiff. The plaintiff may assert any claim against the third-party defendant arising out of the transaction or occurrence that is the subject matter of the plaintiff's claim against the third-party plaintiff, and the third-party defendant thereupon shall assert any defenses as provided in Rule 12 and any counterclaims and cross-claims as provided in Rule 13. Any party may move to strike the third-party claim, or for its severance or separate trial. A third-party defendant may proceed under this rule against any person not a party to the action who is or may be liable to the third-party defendant for all or part of the claim made in the action against the third-party defendant. The third-party complaint, if within the admiralty and maritime jurisdiction, may be in rem against a vessel, cargo, or other property subject to admiralty or maritime process in rem, in which case references in this rule to the summons include the warrant of arrest, and references to the third-party plaintiff or defendant include, where appropriate, a person who asserts a right under Supplemental Rule C(6)(a)(i) in the property arrested.

**(b) When Plaintiff May Bring in Third Party.** When a counterclaim is asserted against a plaintiff, the plaintiff may cause a third party to be brought in under circumstances which under this rule would entitle a defendant to do so.

**(c) Admiralty and Maritime Claims.** When a plaintiff asserts an admiralty or maritime claim within the meaning of Rule 9(h), the defendant or person who asserts a right under Supplemental Rule C(6)(a)(1), as a third-party plaintiff, may bring in a third-party defendant who may be wholly or partly liable, either to the plaintiff or to the third-party plaintiff, by way of remedy over, contribution, or otherwise on account of the same transaction, occurrence, or series of transactions or occurrences. In such a case the third-party plaintiff may also demand judgment against the third-party defendant in favor of the plaintiff, in which event the third-party defendant shall make any defenses to the claim of the plaintiff as well as to that of the third-party plaintiff in the manner provided in Rule 12 and the action shall proceed as if the plaintiff had commenced it against the third-party defendant as well as the third-party plaintiff.

[Amended December 27, 1946, effective March 19, 1948; January 21, 1963, effective July 1, 1963; February 28, 1966, effective July 1, 1966; March 2, 1987, effective August 1, 1987; April 17, 2000, effective December 1, 2000; April 12, 2006, effective December 1, 2006.]

# RULE 15.   AMENDED AND SUPPLEMENTAL PLEADINGS

**(a) Amendments.** A party may amend the party's pleading once as a matter of course at any time before a responsive pleading is served or, if the pleading is one to which no responsive pleading is permitted and the action has not been placed upon the trial calendar, the party may so amend it at any time within 20 days after it is served. Otherwise a party may amend the party's pleading only by leave of court or by written consent of the adverse party; and leave shall be freely given when justice so requires. A party shall plead in response to an amended pleading within the time remaining for response to the original pleading or within 10 days after service of the amended pleading, whichever period may be the longer, unless the court otherwise orders.

**(b) Amendments to Conform to the Evidence.** When issues not raised by the pleadings are tried by express or implied consent of the parties, they shall be treated in all respects as if they had been raised in the pleadings. Such amendment of the pleadings as may be necessary to cause them to conform to the evidence and to raise these issues may be made upon motion of any party at any time, even after judgment; but failure so to amend does not affect the result of the trial of these issues. If evidence is objected to at the trial on the ground that it is not within the issues made by the pleadings, the court may allow the pleadings to be amended and shall do so freely when the presentation of the merits of the action will be subserved thereby and the objecting party fails to satisfy the court that the admission of such evidence would prejudice the party in maintaining the party's action or defense upon the merits. The court may grant a continuance to enable the objecting party to meet such evidence.

**(c) Relation Back of Amendments.** An amendment of a pleading relates back to the date of the original pleading when

(1) relation back is permitted by the law that provides the statute of limitations applicable to the action, or

(2) the claim or defense asserted in the amended pleading arose out of the conduct, transaction, or occurrence set forth or attempted to be set forth in the original pleading, or

(3) the amendment changes the party or the naming of the party against whom a claim is asserted if the foregoing provision (2) is satisfied and, within the period provided by Rule 4(m) for service of the summons and complaint, the party to be brought in by amendment (A) has received such notice of the institution of the action that the party will not be prejudiced in maintaining a defense on the merits, and (B) knew or should have known that, but for a mistake concerning the identity of the proper party, the action would have been brought against the party.

The delivery or mailing of process to the United States Attorney, or United States Attorney's designee, or the Attorney General of the United States, or an agency or officer who would have been a proper defendant if named, satisfies the requirement of subparagraphs (A) and (B) of this paragraph (3) with respect to the United States or any agency or officer thereof to be brought into the action as a defendant.

**(d) Supplemental Pleadings.** Upon motion of a party the court may, upon reasonable notice and upon such terms as are just, permit the party to serve a supplemental pleading setting forth transactions or occurrences or events which have happened since the date of the pleading sought to be supplemented. Permission may be granted even though the original pleading is defective in its statement of a claim for relief or defense. If the court deems it advisable that the adverse party plead to the supplemental pleading, it shall so order, specifying the time therefor.

[Amended January 21, 1963, effective July 1, 1963; February 28, 1966, effective July 1, 1966; March 2, 1987, effective August 1, 1987; April 30, 1991, effective December 1, 1991; amended by Pub.L. 102–198, § 11, December 9, 1991, 105 Stat. 1626; amended April 22, 1993, effective December 1, 1993.]

# RULE 16.  PRETRIAL CONFERENCES; SCHEDULING; MANAGEMENT

**(a) Pretrial Conferences; Objectives.** In any action, the court may in its discretion direct the attorneys for the parties and any unrepresented parties to appear before it for a conference or conferences before trial for such purposes as

(1) expediting the disposition of the action;

(2) establishing early and continuing control so that the case will not be protracted because of lack of management;

(3) discouraging wasteful pretrial activities;

(4) improving the quality of the trial through more thorough preparation; and

(5) facilitating the settlement of the case.

**(b) Scheduling and Planning.** Except in categories of actions exempted by district court rule as inappropriate, the district judge, or a magistrate judge when authorized by district court rule, shall, after receiving the report from the parties under Rule 26(f) or after consulting with the attorneys for the parties and any unrepresented parties by a scheduling conference, telephone, mail, or other suitable means, enter a scheduling order that limits the time

(1) to join other parties and to amend the pleadings;

(2) to file motions; and

(3) to complete discovery.

The scheduling order also may include

(4) modifications of the times for disclosures under Rules 26(a) and 26(e)(1) and of the extent of discovery to be permitted;

(5) provisions for disclosure or discovery of electronically stored information;

(6) any agreements the parties reach for asserting claims of privilege or of protection as trial-preparation material after production;

(7) the date or dates for conferences before trial, a final pretrial conference, and trial; and

(8) any other matters appropriate in the circumstances of the case.

The order shall issue as soon as practicable but in any event within 90 days after the appearance of a defendant and within 120 days after the complaint has been served on a defendant. A schedule shall not be modified except upon a showing of good cause and by leave of the district judge or, when authorized by local rule, by a magistrate judge.

**(c) Subjects for Consideration at Pretrial Conferences.** At any conference under this rule consideration may be given, and the court may take appropriate action, with respect to

(1) the formulation and simplification of the issues, including the elimination of frivolous claims or defenses;

(2) the necessity or desirability of amendments to the pleadings;

(3) the possibility of obtaining admissions of fact and of documents which will avoid unnecessary proof,

stipulations regarding the authenticity of documents, and advance rulings from the court on the admissibility of evidence;

(4) the avoidance of unnecessary proof and of cumulative evidence, and limitations or restrictions on the use of testimony under Rule 702 of the Federal Rules of Evidence;

(5) the appropriateness and timing of summary adjudication under Rule 56;

(6) the control and scheduling of discovery, including orders affecting disclosures and discovery pursuant to Rule 26 and Rules 29 through 37;

(7) the identification of witnesses and documents, the need and schedule for filing and exchanging pretrial briefs, and the date or dates for further conferences and for trial;

(8) the advisability of referring matters to a magistrate judge or master;

(9) settlement and the use of special procedures to assist in resolving the dispute when authorized by statute or local rule;

(10) the form and substance of the pretrial order;

(11) the disposition of pending motions;

(12) the need for adopting special procedures for managing potentially difficult or protracted actions that may involve complex issues, multiple parties, difficult legal questions, or unusual proof problems;

(13) an order for a separate trial pursuant to Rule 42(b) with respect to a claim, counterclaim, cross-claim, or third-party claim, or with respect to any particular issue in the case;

(14) an order directing a party or parties to present evidence early in the trial with respect to a manageable issue that could, on the evidence, be the basis for a judgment as a matter of law under Rule 50(a) or a judgment on partial findings under Rule 52(c);

(15) an order establishing a reasonable limit on the time allowed for presenting evidence; and

(16) such other matters as may facilitate the just, speedy, and inexpensive disposition of the action.

At least one of the attorneys for each party participating in any conference before trial shall have authority to enter into stipulations and to make admissions regarding all matters that the participants may reasonably anticipate may be discussed. If appropriate, the court may require that a party or its representative be present or reasonably available by telephone in order to consider possible settlement of the dispute.

**(d) Final Pretrial Conference.** Any final pretrial conference shall be held as close to the time of trial as reasonable under the circumstances. The participants at any such conference shall formulate a plan for trial, including a program for facilitating the admission of evidence. The conference shall be attended by at least one of the attorneys who will conduct the trial for each of the parties and by any unrepresented parties.

**(e) Pretrial Orders.** After any conference held pursuant to this rule, an order shall be entered reciting the action taken. This order shall control the subsequent course of the action unless modified by a subsequent order. The order following a final pretrial conference shall be modified only to prevent manifest injustice.

**(f) Sanctions.** If a party or party's attorney fails to obey a scheduling or pretrial order, or if no appearance is made on behalf of a party at a scheduling or pretrial conference, or if a party or party's attorney is substantially unprepared to participate in the conference, or if a party or party's attorney fails to participate in good faith, the judge, upon motion or the judge's own initiative, may make such orders with regard thereto as are just, and among others any of the orders provided in Rule 37(b)(2)(B), (C), (D). In lieu of or in addition to any other sanction, the judge shall require the party or the attorney representing the party or both to pay the reasonable expenses incurred because of any noncompliance with this rule, including attorney's fees, unless the judge finds that the noncompliance was substantially justified or that other circumstances make an award of expenses unjust.

[Amended April 28, 1983, effective August 1, 1983; March 2, 1987, effective August 1, 1987; April 22, 1993, effective December 1, 1993; April 12, 2006, effective December 1, 2006.]

# IV.  PARTIES

## RULE 17.  PARTIES PLAINTIFF AND DEFENDANT; CAPACITY

**(a) Real Party in Interest.** Every action shall be prosecuted in the name of the real party in interest. An executor, administrator, guardian, bailee, trustee of an express trust, a party with whom or in whose name a contract has been made for the benefit of another, or a party authorized by statute may sue in that person's own name without joining the party for whose benefit the action is brought; and when a statute of the United States so provides, an action for the use or benefit of another shall be brought in the name of the United States. No action shall be dis-

missed on the ground that it is not prosecuted in the name of the real party in interest until a reasonable time has been allowed after objection for ratification of commencement of the action by, or joinder or substitution of, the real party in interest; and such ratification, joinder, or substitution shall have the same effect as if the action had been commenced in the name of the real party in interest.

**(b) Capacity to Sue or Be Sued.** The capacity of an individual, other than one acting in a representative capacity, to sue or be sued shall be determined by the law of the individual's domicile. The capacity of a corporation to sue or be sued shall be determined by the law under which it was organized. In all other cases capacity to sue or be sued shall be determined by the law of the state in which the district court is held, except (1) that a partnership or other unincorporated association, which has no such capacity by the law of such state, may sue or be sued in its common name for the purpose of enforcing for or against it a substantive right existing under the Constitution or laws of the United States, and (2) that the capacity of a receiver appointed by a court of the United States to sue or be sued in a court of the United States is governed by Title 28, U.S.C., Sections 754 and 959(a).

**(c) Infants or Incompetent Persons.** Whenever an infant or incompetent person has a representative, such as a general guardian, committee, conservator, or other like fiduciary, the representative may sue or defend on behalf of the infant or incompetent person. An infant or incompetent person who does not have a duly appointed representative may sue by a next friend or by a guardian ad litem. The court shall appoint a guardian ad litem for an infant or incompetent person not otherwise represented in an action or shall make such other order as it deems proper for the protection of the infant or incompetent person.

[Amended December 27, 1946, effective March 19, 1948; December 29, 1948, effective October 20, 1949; February 28, 1966, effective July 1, 1966; March 2, 1987, effective August 1, 1987; April 25, 1988, effective August 1, 1988; amended by Pub.L. 100–690, Title VII, § 7049, November 18, 1988, 102 Stat. 4401 (although amendment by Pub.L. 100–690 could not be executed due to prior amendment by Court order which made the same change effective August 1, 1988).]

## RULE 18. JOINDER OF CLAIMS AND REMEDIES

**(a) Joinder of Claims.** A party asserting a claim to relief as an original claim, counterclaim, cross-claim, or third-party claim, may join, either as independent or as alternate claims, as many claims, legal, equitable, or maritime, as the party has against an opposing party.

**(b) Joinder of Remedies; Fraudulent Conveyances.** Whenever a claim is one heretofore cognizable only after another claim has been prosecuted to a conclusion, the two claims may be joined in a single action; but the court shall grant relief in that action only in accordance with the relative substantive rights of the parties. In particular, a plaintiff may state a claim for money and a claim to have set aside a conveyance fraudulent as to that plaintiff, without first having obtained a judgment establishing the claim for money.

[Amended February 28, 1966, effective July 1, 1966; March 2, 1987, effective August 1, 1987.]

## RULE 19. JOINDER OF PERSONS NEEDED FOR JUST ADJUDICATION

**(a) Persons to Be Joined if Feasible.** A person who is subject to service of process and whose joinder will not deprive the court of jurisdiction over the subject matter of the action shall be joined as a party in the action if (1) in the person's absence complete relief cannot be accorded among those already parties, or (2) the person claims an interest relating to the subject of the action and is so situated that the disposition of the action in the person's absence may (i) as a practical matter impair or impede the person's ability to protect that interest or (ii) leave any of the persons already parties subject to a substantial risk of incurring double, multiple, or otherwise inconsistent obligations by reason of the claimed interest. If the person has not been so joined, the court shall order that the person be made a party. If the person should join as a plaintiff but refuses to do so, the person may be made a defendant, or, in a proper case, an involuntary plaintiff. If the joined party objects to venue and joinder of that party would render the venue of the action improper, that party shall be dismissed from the action.

**(b) Determination by Court Whenever Joinder Not Feasible.** If a person as described in subdivision (a)(1)–(2) hereof cannot be made a party, the court shall determine whether in equity and good conscience the action should proceed among the parties before it, or should be dismissed, the absent person being thus regarded as indispensable. The factors to be considered by the court include: first, to what extent a judgment rendered in the person's absence might be prejudicial to the person or those already parties; second, the extent to which, by protective provisions in the judgment, by the shaping of relief, or other measures, the prejudice can be lessened or avoided; third, whether a judgment rendered in the person's absence will be adequate; fourth, whether the plaintiff will have an adequate remedy if the action is dismissed for nonjoinder.

**(c) Pleading Reasons for Nonjoinder.** A pleading asserting a claim for relief shall state the names, if known to the pleader, of any persons as described in

subdivision (a)(1)–(2) hereof who are not joined, and the reasons why they are not joined.

**(d) Exception of Class Actions.** This rule is subject to the provisions of Rule 23.

[Amended February 28, 1966, effective July 1, 1966; March 2, 1987, effective August 1, 1987.]

## RULE 20. PERMISSIVE JOINDER OF PARTIES

**(a) Permissive Joinder.** All persons may join in one action as plaintiffs if they assert any right to relief jointly, severally, or in the alternative in respect of or arising out of the same transaction, occurrence, or series of transactions or occurrences and if any question of law or fact common to all these persons will arise in the action. All persons (and any vessel, cargo or other property subject to admiralty process in rem) may be joined in one action as defendants if there is asserted against them jointly, severally, or in the alternative, any right to relief in respect of or arising out of the same transaction, occurrence, or series of transactions or occurrences and if any question of law or fact common to all defendants will arise in the action. A plaintiff or defendant need not be interested in obtaining or defending against all the relief demanded. Judgment may be given for one or more of the plaintiffs according to their respective rights to relief, and against one or more defendants according to their respective liabilities.

**(b) Separate Trials.** The court may make such orders as will prevent a party from being embarrassed, delayed, or put to expense by the inclusion of a party against whom the party asserts no claim and who asserts no claim against the party, and may order separate trials or make other orders to prevent delay or prejudice.

[Amended February 28, 1966, effective July 1, 1966; March 2, 1987, effective August 1, 1987.]

## RULE 21. MISJOINDER AND NON–JOINDER OF PARTIES

Misjoinder of parties is not ground for dismissal of an action. Parties may be dropped or added by order of the court on motion of any party or of its own initiative at any stage of the action and on such terms as are just. Any claim against a party may be severed and proceeded with separately.

## RULE 22. INTERPLEADER

**(1)** Persons having claims against the plaintiff may be joined as defendants and required to interplead when their claims are such that the plaintiff is or may be exposed to double or multiple liability. It is not ground for objection to the joinder that the claims of the several claimants or the titles on which their claims depend do not have a common origin or are not identical but are adverse to and independent of one another, or that the plaintiff avers that the plaintiff is not liable in whole or in part to any or all of the claimants. A defendant exposed to similar liability may obtain such interpleader by way of cross-claim or counterclaim. The provisions of this rule supplement and do not in any way limit the joinder of parties permitted in Rule 20.

**(2)** The remedy herein provided is in addition to and in no way supersedes or limits the remedy provided by Title 28, U.S.C., §§ 1335, 1397, and 2361. Actions under those provisions shall be conducted in accordance with these rules.

[Amended December 29, 1948, effective October 20, 1949; March 2, 1987, effective August 1, 1987.]

## RULE 23. CLASS ACTIONS

**(a) Prerequisites to a Class Action.** One or more members of a class may sue or be sued as representative parties on behalf of all only if (1) the class is so numerous that joinder of all members is impracticable, (2) there are questions of law or fact common to the class, (3) the claims or defenses of the representative parties are typical of the claims or defenses of the class, and (4) the representative parties will fairly and adequately protect the interests of the class.

**(b) Class Actions Maintainable.** An action may be maintained as a class action if the prerequisites of subdivision (a) are satisfied, and in addition:

(1) the prosecution of separate actions by or against individual members of the class would create a risk of

(A) inconsistent or varying adjudications with respect to individual members of the class which would establish incompatible standards of conduct for the party opposing the class, or

(B) adjudications with respect to individual members of the class which would as a practical matter be dispositive of the interests of the other members not parties to the adjudications or substantially impair or impede their ability to protect their interests; or

(2) the party opposing the class has acted or refused to act on grounds generally applicable to the class, thereby making appropriate final injunctive relief or corresponding declaratory relief with respect to the class as a whole; or

(3) the court finds that the questions of law or fact common to the members of the class predominate over any questions affecting only individual members, and that a class action is superior to other available methods for the fair and efficient adjudication of the controversy. The matters pertinent to the findings include: (A) the interest of members of the class in individually controlling the prosecution or defense of

separate actions; (B) the extent and nature of any litigation concerning the controversy already commenced by or against members of the class; (C) the desirability or undesirability of concentrating the litigation of the claims in the particular forum; (D) the difficulties likely to be encountered in the management of a class action.

**(c) Determining by Order Whether to Certify a Class Action; Appointing Class Counsel; Notice and Membership in Class; Judgment; Multiple Classes and Subclasses.**

(1)(A) When a person sues or is sued as a representative of a class, the court must—at an early practicable time—determine by order whether to certify the action as a class action.

(B) An order certifying a class action must define the class and the class claims, issues, or defenses, and must appoint class counsel under Rule 23(g).

(C) An order under Rule 23(c)(1) may be altered or amended before final judgment.

(2)(A) For any class certified under Rule 23(b)(1) or (2), the court may direct appropriate notice to the class.

(B) For any class certified under Rule 23(b)(3), the court must direct to class members the best notice practicable under the circumstances, including individual notice to all members who can be identified through reasonable effort. The notice must concisely and clearly state in plain, easily understood language:

- the nature of the action,
- the definition of the class certified,
- the class claims, issues, or defenses,
- that a class member may enter an appearance through counsel if the member so desires,
- that the court will exclude from the class any member who requests exclusion, stating when and how members may elect to be excluded, and
- the binding effect of a class judgment on class members under Rule 23(c)(3).

(3) The judgment in an action maintained as a class action under subdivision (b)(1) or (b)(2), whether or not favorable to the class, shall include and describe those whom the court finds to be members of the class. The judgment in an action maintained as a class action under subdivision (b)(3), whether or not favorable to the class, shall include and specify or describe those to whom the notice provided in subdivision (c)(2) was directed, and who have not requested exclusion, and whom the court finds to be members of the class.

(4) When appropriate (A) an action may be brought or maintained as a class action with respect to particular issues, or (B) a class may be divided into subclasses and each subclass treated as a class, and the provisions of this rule shall then be construed and applied accordingly.

**(d) Orders in Conduct of Actions.** In the conduct of actions to which this rule applies, the court may make appropriate orders: (1) determining the course of proceedings or prescribing measures to prevent undue repetition or complication in the presentation of evidence or argument; (2) requiring, for the protection of the members of the class or otherwise for the fair conduct of the action, that notice be given in such manner as the court may direct to some or all of the members of any step in the action, or of the proposed extent of the judgment, or of the opportunity of members to signify whether they consider the representation fair and adequate, to intervene and present claims or defenses, or otherwise to come into the action; (3) imposing conditions on the representative parties or on intervenors; (4) requiring that the pleadings be amended to eliminate therefrom allegations as to representation of absent persons, and that the action proceed accordingly; (5) dealing with similar procedural matters. The orders may be combined with an order under Rule 16, and may be altered or amended as may be desirable from time to time.

**(e) Settlement, Voluntary Dismissal, or Compromise.**

(1)(A) The court must approve any settlement, voluntary dismissal, or compromise of the claims, issues, or defenses of a certified class.

(B) The court must direct notice in a reasonable manner to all class members who would be bound by a proposed settlement, voluntary dismissal, or compromise.

(C) The court may approve a settlement, voluntary dismissal, or compromise that would bind class members only after a hearing and on finding that the settlement, voluntary dismissal, or compromise is fair, reasonable, and adequate.

(2) The parties seeking approval of a settlement, voluntary dismissal, or compromise under Rule 23(e)(1) must file a statement identifying any agreement made in connection with the proposed settlement, voluntary dismissal, or compromise.

(3) In an action previously certified as a class action under Rule 23(b)(3), the court may refuse to approve a settlement unless it affords a new opportunity to request exclusion to individual class members who had an earlier opportunity to request exclusion but did not do so.

(4)(A) Any class member may object to a proposed settlement, voluntary dismissal, or compromise that requires court approval under Rule 23(e)(1)(A).

(B) An objection made under Rule 23(e)(4)(A) may be withdrawn only with the court's approval.

**(f) Appeals.** A court of appeals may in its discretion permit an appeal from an order of a district court granting or denying class action certification under this rule if application is made to it within ten days after entry of the order. An appeal does not stay proceedings in the district court unless the district judge or the court of appeals so orders.

**(g) Class Counsel.**

(1) *Appointing Class Counsel.*

(A) Unless a statute provides otherwise, a court that certifies a class must appoint class counsel.

(B) An attorney appointed to serve as class counsel must fairly and adequately represent the interests of the class.

(C) In appointing class counsel, the court

(i) must consider:

• the work counsel has done in identifying or investigating potential claims in the action,

• counsel's experience in handling class actions, other complex litigation, and claims of the type asserted in the action,

• counsel's knowledge of the applicable law, and

• the resources counsel will commit to representing the class;

(ii) may consider any other matter pertinent to counsel's ability to fairly and adequately represent the interests of the class;

(iii) may direct potential class counsel to provide information on any subject pertinent to the appointment and to propose terms for attorney fees and nontaxable costs; and

(iv) may make further orders in connection with the appointment.

(2) *Appointment Procedure.*

(A) The court may designate interim counsel to act on behalf of the putative class before determining whether to certify the action as a class action.

(B) When there is one applicant for appointment as class counsel, the court may appoint that applicant only if the applicant is adequate under Rule 23(g)(1)(B) and (C). If more than one adequate applicant seeks appointment as class counsel, the court must appoint the applicant best able to represent the interests of the class.

(C) The order appointing class counsel may include provisions about the award of attorney fees or nontaxable costs under Rule 23(h).

**(h) Attorney Fees Award.** In an action certified as a class action, the court may award reasonable attorney fees and nontaxable costs authorized by law or by agreement of the parties as follows:

(1) *Motion for Award of Attorney Fees.* A claim for an award of attorney fees and nontaxable costs must be made by motion under Rule 54(d)(2), subject to the provisions of this subdivision, at a time set by the court. Notice of the motion must be served on all parties and, for motions by class counsel, directed to class members in a reasonable manner.

(2) *Objections to Motion.* A class member, or a party from whom payment is sought, may object to the motion.

(3) *Hearing and Findings.* The court may hold a hearing and must find the facts and state its conclusions of law on the motion under Rule 52(a).

(4) *Reference to Special Master or Magistrate Judge.* The court may refer issues related to the amount of the award to a special master or to a magistrate judge as provided in Rule 54(d)(2)(D).

[Amended February 28, 1966, effective July 1, 1966; March 2, 1987, effective August 1, 1987; April 24, 1998, effective December 1, 1998; March 27, 2003, effective December 1, 2003.]

## RULE 23.1  DERIVATIVE ACTIONS BY SHAREHOLDERS

In a derivative action brought by one or more shareholders or members to enforce a right of a corporation or of an unincorporated association, the corporation or association having failed to enforce a right which may properly be asserted by it, the complaint shall be verified and shall allege (1) that the plaintiff was a shareholder or member at the time of the transaction of which the plaintiff complains or that the plaintiff's share or membership thereafter devolved on the plaintiff by operation of law, and (2) that the action is not a collusive one to confer jurisdiction on a court of the United States which it would not otherwise have. The complaint shall also allege with particularity the efforts, if any, made by the plaintiff to obtain the action the plaintiff desires from the directors or comparable authority and, if necessary, from the shareholders or members, and the reasons for the plaintiff's failure to obtain the action or for not making the effort. The derivative action may not be maintained if it appears that the plaintiff does not fairly and adequately represent the interests of the shareholders or members similarly situated in enforcing the right of the corporation or association. The action shall not be dismissed or compromised without the approval of the court, and notice of the proposed dismissal or compromise shall be given to shareholders or members in such manner as the court directs.

[Adopted February 28, 1966, effective July 1, 1966; amended March 2, 1987, effective August 1, 1987.]

---

# RULE 23.2 ACTIONS RELATING TO UNINCORPORATED ASSOCIATIONS

An action brought by or against the members of an unincorporated association as a class by naming certain members as representative parties may be maintained only if it appears that the representative parties will fairly and adequately protect the interests of the association and its members. In the conduct of the action the court may make appropriate orders corresponding with those described in Rule 23(d), and the procedure for dismissal or compromise of the action shall correspond with that provided in Rule 23(e).

[Adopted February 28, 1966, effective July 1, 1966.]

# RULE 24. INTERVENTION

**(a) Intervention of Right.** Upon timely application anyone shall be permitted to intervene in an action: (1) when a statute of the United States confers an unconditional right to intervene; or (2) when the applicant claims an interest relating to the property or transaction which is the subject of the action and the applicant is so situated that the disposition of the action may as a practical matter impair or impede the applicant's ability to protect that interest, unless the applicant's interest is adequately represented by existing parties.

**(b) Permissive Intervention.** Upon timely application anyone may be permitted to intervene in an action: (1) when a statute of the United States confers a conditional right to intervene; or (2) when an applicant's claim or defense and the main action have a question of law or fact in common. When a party to an action relies for ground of claim or defense upon any statute or executive order administered by a federal or state governmental officer or agency or upon any regulation, order, requirement, or agreement issued or made pursuant to the statute or executive order, the officer or agency upon timely application may be permitted to intervene in the action. In exercising its discretion the court shall consider whether the intervention will unduly delay or prejudice the adjudication of the rights of the original parties.

**(c) Procedure.** A person desiring to intervene shall serve a motion to intervene upon the parties as provided in Rule 5. The motion shall state the grounds therefor and shall be accompanied by a pleading setting forth the claim or defense for which intervention is sought. The same procedure shall be followed when a statute of the United States gives a right to intervene.

[Amended December 27, 1946, effective March 19, 1948; December 29, 1948, effective October 20, 1949; January 21, 1963, effective July 1, 1963; February 28, 1966, effective July 1, 1966; March 2, 1987, effective August 1, 1987; April 30, 1991, effective December 1, 1991; April 12, 2006, effective December 1, 2006.]

# RULE 25. SUBSTITUTION OF PARTIES

**(a) Death.**

(1) If a party dies and the claim is not thereby extinguished, the court may order substitution of the proper parties. The motion for substitution may be made by any party or by the successors or representatives of the deceased party and, together with the notice of hearing, shall be served on the parties as provided in Rule 5 and upon persons not parties in the manner provided in Rule 4 for the service of a summons, and may be served in any judicial district. Unless the motion for substitution is made not later than 90 days after the death is suggested upon the record by service of a statement of the fact of the death as provided herein for the service of the motion, the action shall be dismissed as to the deceased party.

(2) In the event of the death of one or more of the plaintiffs or of one or more of the defendants in an action in which the right sought to be enforced survives only to the surviving plaintiffs or only against the surviving defendants, the action does not abate. The death shall be suggested upon the record and the action shall proceed in favor of or against the surviving parties.

**(b) Incompetency.** If a party becomes incompetent, the court upon motion served as provided in subdivision (a) of this rule may allow the action to be continued by or against the party's representative.

**(c) Transfer of Interest.** In case of any transfer of interest, the action may be continued by or against the original party, unless the court upon motion directs the person to whom the interest is transferred to be substituted in the action or joined with the original party. Service of the motion shall be made as provided in subdivision (a) of this rule.

**(d) Public Officers; Death or Separation From Office.**

(1) When a public officer is a party to an action in an official capacity and during its pendency dies, resigns, or otherwise ceases to hold office, the action does not abate and the officer's successor is automatically substituted as a party. Proceedings following the substitution shall be in the name of the substituted party, but any misnomer not affecting the substantial rights of the parties shall be disregarded. An order of substitution may be entered at any time, but the omission to enter such an order shall not affect the substitution.

(2) A public officer who sues or is sued in an official capacity may be described as a party by the officer's

official title rather than by name; but the court may require the officer's name to be added.

[Amended December 29, 1948, effective October 20, 1949; April 17, 1961, effective July 19, 1961; January 21, 1963, effective July 1, 1963; March 2, 1987, effective August 1, 1987.]

# V. DEPOSITIONS AND DISCOVERY

## RULE 26. GENERAL PROVISIONS GOVERNING DISCOVERY; DUTY OF DISCLOSURE

**(a) Required Disclosures; Methods to Discover Additional Matter.**

(1) *Initial Disclosures.* Except in categories of proceedings specified in Rule 26(a)(1)(E), or to the extent otherwise stipulated or directed by order, a party must, without awaiting a discovery request, provide to other parties:

(A) the name and, if known, the address and telephone number of each individual likely to have discoverable information that the disclosing party may use to support its claims or defenses, unless solely for impeachment, identifying the subjects of the information;

(B) a copy of, or a description by category and location of, all documents, electronically stored information, and tangible things that are in the possession, custody, or control of the party and that the disclosing party may use to support its claims or defenses, unless solely for impeachment;

(C) a computation of any category of damages claimed by the disclosing party, making available for inspection and copying as under Rule 34 the documents or other evidentiary material, not privileged or protected from disclosure, on which such computation is based, including materials bearing on the nature and extent of injuries suffered; and

(D) for inspection and copying as under Rule 34 any insurance agreement under which any person carrying on an insurance business may be liable to satisfy part or all of a judgment which may be entered in the action or to indemnify or reimburse for payments made to satisfy the judgment.

(E) The following categories of proceedings are exempt from initial disclosure under Rule 26(a)(1):

(i) an action for review on an administrative record;

(ii) a forfeiture action in rem arising from a federal statute;

(iii) a petition for habeas corpus or other proceeding to challenge a criminal conviction or sentence;

(iv) an action brought without counsel by a person in custody of the United States, a state, or a state subdivision;

(v) an action to enforce or quash an administrative summons or subpoena;

(vi) an action by the United States to recover benefit payments;

(vii) an action by the United States to collect on a student loan guaranteed by the United States;

(viii) a proceeding ancillary to proceedings in other courts; and

(ix) an action to enforce an arbitration award.

These disclosures must be made at or within 14 days after the Rule 26(f) conference unless a different time is set by stipulation or court order, or unless a party objects during the conference that initial disclosures are not appropriate in the circumstances of the action and states the objection in the Rule 26(f) discovery plan. In ruling on the objection, the court must determine what disclosures—if any—are to be made, and set the time for disclosure. Any party first served or otherwise joined after the Rule 26(f) conference must make these disclosures within 30 days after being served or joined unless a different time is set by stipulation or court order. A party must make its initial disclosures based on the information then reasonably available to it and is not excused from making its disclosures because it has not fully completed its investigation of the case or because it challenges the sufficiency of another party's disclosures or because another party has not made its disclosures.

(2) *Disclosure of Expert Testimony.*

(A) In addition to the disclosures required by paragraph (1), a party shall disclose to other parties the identity of any person who may be used at trial to present evidence under Rules 702, 703, or 705 of the Federal Rules of Evidence.

(B) Except as otherwise stipulated or directed by the court, this disclosure shall, with respect to a witness who is retained or specially employed to provide expert testimony in the case or whose duties as an employee of the party regularly involve giving expert testimony, be accompanied by a written report prepared and signed by the witness. The report shall contain a complete statement of all opinions to be expressed and the basis and reasons therefor; the data or other information considered

by the witness in forming the opinions; any exhibits to be used as a summary of or support for the opinions; the qualifications of the witness, including a list of all publications authored by the witness within the preceding ten years; the compensation to be paid for the study and testimony; and a listing of any other cases in which the witness has testified as an expert at trial or by deposition within the preceding four years.

(C) These disclosures shall be made at the times and in the sequence directed by the court. In the absence of other directions from the court or stipulation by the parties, the disclosures shall be made at least 90 days before the trial date or the date the case is to be ready for trial or, if the evidence is intended solely to contradict or rebut evidence on the same subject matter identified by another party under paragraph (2)(B), within 30 days after the disclosure made by the other party. The parties shall supplement these disclosures when required under subdivision (e)(1).

(3) *Pretrial Disclosures.* In addition to the disclosures required by Rule 26(a)(1) and (2), a party must provide to other parties and promptly file with the court the following information regarding the evidence that it may present at trial other than solely for impeachment:

(A) the name and, if not previously provided, the address and telephone number of each witness, separately identifying those whom the party expects to present and those whom the party may call if the need arises;

(B) the designation of those witnesses whose testimony is expected to be presented by means of a deposition and, if not taken stenographically, a transcript of the pertinent portions of the deposition testimony; and

(C) an appropriate identification of each document or other exhibit, including summaries of other evidence, separately identifying those which the party expects to offer and those which the party may offer if the need arises.

Unless otherwise directed by the court, these disclosures must be made at least 30 days before trial. Within 14 days thereafter, unless a different time is specified by the court, a party may serve and promptly file a list disclosing (i) any objections to the use under Rule 32(a) of a deposition designated by another party under Rule 26(a)(3)(B) and (ii) any objection, together with the grounds therefor, that may be made to the admissibility of materials identified under Rule 26(a)(3)(C). Objections not so disclosed, other than objections under Rules 402 and 403 of the Federal Rules of Evidence, are waived unless excused by the court for good cause.

(4) *Form of Disclosures.* Unless the court orders otherwise, all disclosures under Rules 26(a)(1) through (3) must be made in writing, signed, and served.

(5) *Methods to Discover Additional Matter.* Parties may obtain discovery by one or more of the following methods: depositions upon oral examination or written questions; written interrogatories; production of documents or things or permission to enter upon land or other property under Rule 34 or 45(a)(1)(C), for inspection and other purposes; physical and mental examinations; and requests for admission.

**(b) Discovery Scope and Limits.** Unless otherwise limited by order of the court in accordance with these rules, the scope of discovery is as follows:

(1) *In General.* Parties may obtain discovery regarding any matter, not privileged, that is relevant to the claim or defense of any party, including the existence, description, nature, custody, condition, and location of any books, documents, or other tangible things and the identity and location of persons having knowledge of any discoverable matter. For good cause, the court may order discovery of any matter relevant to the subject matter involved in the action. Relevant information need not be admissible at the trial if the discovery appears reasonably calculated to lead to the discovery of admissible evidence. All discovery is subject to the limitations imposed by Rule 26(b)(2)(i), (ii), and (iii).

(2) *Limitations.*

(A) By order, the court may alter the limits in these rules on the number of depositions and interrogatories or the length of depositions under Rule 30. By order or local rule, the court may also limit the number of requests under Rule 36.

(B) A party need not provide discovery of electronically stored information from sources that the party identifies as not reasonably accessible because of undue burden or cost. On motion to compel discovery or for a protective order, the party from whom discovery is sought must show that the information is not reasonably accessible because of undue burden or cost. If that showing is made, the court may nonetheless order discovery from such sources if the requesting party shows good cause, considering the limitations of Rule 26(b)(2)(C). The court may specify conditions for the discovery.

(C) The frequency or extent of use of the discovery methods otherwise permitted under these rules and by any local rule shall be limited by the court if it determines that: (i) the discovery sought is unreasonably cumulative or duplicative, or is obtainable from some other source that is more convenient, less burdensome, or less expensive; (ii) the party seeking discovery has had ample opportunity by discovery in the action to obtain the information

sought; or (iii) the burden or expense of the proposed discovery outweighs its likely benefit, taking into account the needs of the case, the amount in controversy, the parties' resources, the importance of the issues at stake in the litigation, and the importance of the proposed discovery in resolving the issues. The court may act upon its own initiative after reasonable notice or pursuant to a motion under Rule 26(c).

(3) *Trial Preparation: Materials.* Subject to the provisions of subdivision (b)(4) of this rule, a party may obtain discovery of documents and tangible things otherwise discoverable under subdivision (b)(1) of this rule and prepared in anticipation of litigation or for trial by or for another party or by or for that other party's representative (including the other party's attorney, consultant, surety, indemnitor, insurer, or agent) only upon a showing that the party seeking discovery has substantial need of the materials in the preparation of the party's case and that the party is unable without undue hardship to obtain the substantial equivalent of the materials by other means. In ordering discovery of such materials when the required showing has been made, the court shall protect against disclosure of the mental impressions, conclusions, opinions, or legal theories of an attorney or other representative of a party concerning the litigation.

A party may obtain without the required showing a statement concerning the action or its subject matter previously made by that party. Upon request, a person not a party may obtain without the required showing a statement concerning the action or its subject matter previously made by that person. If the request is refused, the person may move for a court order. The provisions of Rule 37(a)(4) apply to the award of expenses incurred in relation to the motion. For purposes of this paragraph, a statement previously made is (A) a written statement signed or otherwise adopted or approved by the person making it, or (B) a stenographic, mechanical, electrical, or other recording, or a transcription thereof, which is a substantially verbatim recital of an oral statement by the person making it and contemporaneously recorded.

(4) *Trial Preparation: Experts.*

(A) A party may depose any person who has been identified as an expert whose opinions may be presented at trial. If a report from the expert is required under subdivision (a)(2)(B), the deposition shall not be conducted until after the report is provided.

(B) A party may, through interrogatories or by deposition, discover facts known or opinions held by an expert who has been retained or specially employed by another party in anticipation of litigation or preparation for trial and who is not expected to

be called as a witness at trial only as provided in Rule 35(b) or upon a showing of exceptional circumstances under which it is impracticable for the party seeking discovery to obtain facts or opinions on the same subject by other means.

(C) Unless manifest injustice would result, (i) the court shall require that the party seeking discovery pay the expert a reasonable fee for time spent in responding to discovery under this subdivision; and (ii) with respect to discovery obtained under subdivision (b)(4)(B) of this rule the court shall require the party seeking discovery to pay the other party a fair portion of the fees and expenses reasonably incurred by the latter party in obtaining facts and opinions from the expert.

(5) *Claims of Privilege or Protection of Trial–Preparation Materials.*

(A) Information Withheld. When a party withholds information otherwise discoverable under these rules by claiming that it is privileged or subject to protection as trial-preparation material, the party shall make the claim expressly and shall describe the nature of the documents, communications, or things not produced or disclosed in a manner that, without revealing information itself privileged or protected, will enable other parties to assess the applicability of the privilege or protection.

(B) Information Produced. If information is produced in discovery that is subject to a claim of privilege or of protection as trial-preparation material, the party making the claim may notify any party that received the information of the claim and the basis for it. After being notified, a party must promptly return, sequester, or destroy the specified information and any copies it has and may not use or disclose the information until the claim is resolved. A receiving party may promptly present the information to the court under seal for a determination of the claim. If the receiving party disclosed the information before being notified, it must take reasonable steps to retrieve it. The producing party must preserve the information until the claim is resolved.

(c) **Protective Orders.** Upon motion by a party or by the person from whom discovery is sought, accompanied by a certification that the movant has in good faith conferred or attempted to confer with other affected parties in an effort to resolve the dispute without court action, and for good cause shown, the court in which the action is pending or alternatively, on matters relating to a deposition, the court in the district where the deposition is to be taken may make any order which justice requires to protect a party or person from annoyance, embarrassment, oppression, or undue burden or expense, including one or more of the following:

(1) that the disclosure or discovery not be had;

(2) that the disclosure or discovery may be had only on specified terms and conditions, including a designation of the time or place;

(3) that the discovery may be had only by a method of discovery other than that selected by the party seeking discovery;

(4) that certain matters not be inquired into, or that the scope of the disclosure or discovery be limited to certain matters;

(5) that discovery be conducted with no one present except persons designated by the court;

(6) that a deposition, after being sealed, be opened only by order of the court;

(7) that a trade secret or other confidential research, development, or commercial information not be revealed or be revealed only in a designated way; and

(8) that the parties simultaneously file specified documents or information enclosed in sealed envelopes to be opened as directed by the court.

If the motion for a protective order is denied in whole or in part, the court may, on such terms and conditions as are just, order that any party or other person provide or permit discovery. The provisions of Rule 37(a)(4) apply to the award of expenses incurred in relation to the motion.

**(d) Timing and Sequence of Discovery.** Except in categories of proceedings exempted from initial disclosure under Rule 26(a)(1)(E), or when authorized under these rules or by order or agreement of the parties, a party may not seek discovery from any source before the parties have conferred as required by Rule 26(f). Unless the court upon motion, for the convenience of parties and witnesses and in the interests of justice, orders otherwise, methods of discovery may be used in any sequence, and the fact that a party is conducting discovery, whether by deposition or otherwise, does not operate to delay any other party's discovery.

**(e) Supplementation of Disclosures and Responses.** A party who has made a disclosure under subdivision (a) or responded to a request for discovery with a disclosure or response is under a duty to supplement or correct the disclosure or response to include information thereafter acquired if ordered by the court or in the following circumstances:

(1) A party is under a duty to supplement at appropriate intervals its disclosures under subdivision (a) if the party learns that in some material respect the information disclosed is incomplete or incorrect and if the additional or corrective information has not otherwise been made known to the other parties during the discovery process or in writing. With respect to

testimony of an expert from whom a report is required under subdivision (a)(2)(B) the duty extends both to information contained in the report and to information provided through a deposition of the expert, and any additions or other changes to this information shall be disclosed by the time the party's disclosures under Rule 26(a)(3) are due.

(2) A party is under a duty seasonably to amend a prior response to an interrogatory, request for production, or request for admission if the party learns that the response is in some material respect incomplete or incorrect and if the additional or corrective information has not otherwise been made known to the other parties during the discovery process or in writing.

**(f) Conference of Parties; Planning for Discovery.** Except in categories of proceedings exempted from initial disclosure under Rule 26(a)(1)(E) or when otherwise ordered, the parties must, as soon as practicable and in any event at least 21 days before a scheduling conference is held or a scheduling order is due under Rule 16(b), confer to consider the nature and basis of their claims and defenses and the possibilities for a prompt settlement or resolution of the case, to make or arrange for the disclosures required by Rule 26(a)(1), to discuss any issues relating to preserving discoverable information, and to develop a proposed discovery plan that indicates the parties' views and proposals concerning:

(1) what changes should be made in the timing, form, or requirement for disclosures under Rule 26(a), including a statement as to when disclosures under Rule 26(a)(1) were made or will be made;

(2) the subjects on which discovery may be needed, when discovery should be completed, and whether discovery should be conducted in phases or be limited to or focused upon particular issues;

(3) any issues relating to disclosure or discovery of electronically stored information, including the form or forms in which it should be produced;

(4) any issues relating to claims of privilege or of protection as trial-preparation material, including—if the parties agree on a procedure to assert such claims after production—whether to ask the court to include their agreement in an order;

(5) what changes should be made in the limitations on discovery imposed under these rules or by local rule, and what other limitations should be imposed; and

(6) any other orders that should be entered by the court under Rule 26(c) or under Rule 16(b) and (c).

The attorneys of record and all unrepresented parties that have appeared in the case are jointly responsible for arranging the conference, for attempting in good faith to agree on the proposed discovery plan, and for

submitting to the court within 14 days after the conference a written report outlining the plan. A court may order that the parties or attorneys attend the conference in person. If necessary to comply with its expedited schedule for Rule 16(b) conferences, a court may by local rule (i) require that the conference between the parties occur fewer than 21 days before the scheduling conference is held or a scheduling order is due under Rule 16(b), and (ii) require that the written report outlining the discovery plan be filed fewer than 14 days after the conference between the parties, or excuse the parties from submitting a written report and permit them to report orally on their discovery plan at the Rule 16(b) conference.

**(g) Signing of Disclosures, Discovery Requests, Responses, and Objections.**

(1) Every disclosure made pursuant to subdivision (a)(1) or subdivision (a)(3) shall be signed by at least one attorney of record in the attorney's individual name, whose address shall be stated. An unrepresented party shall sign the disclosure and state the party's address. The signature of the attorney or party constitutes a certification that to the best of the signer's knowledge, information, and belief, formed after a reasonable inquiry, the disclosure is complete and correct as of the time it is made.

(2) Every discovery request, response, or objection made by a party represented by an attorney shall be signed by at least one attorney of record in the attorney's individual name, whose address shall be stated. An unrepresented party shall sign the request, response, or objection and state the party's address. The signature of the attorney or party constitutes a certification that to the best of the signer's knowledge, information, and belief, formed after a reasonable inquiry, the request, response, or objection is:

(A) consistent with these rules and warranted by existing law or a good faith argument for the extension, modification, or reversal of existing law;

(B) not interposed for any improper purpose, such as to harass or to cause unnecessary delay or needless increase in the cost of litigation; and

(C) not unreasonable or unduly burdensome or expensive, given the needs of the case, the discovery already had in the case, the amount in controversy, and the importance of the issues at stake in the litigation.

If a request, response, or objection is not signed, it shall be stricken unless it is signed promptly after the omission is called to the attention of the party making the request, response, or objection, and a party shall not be obligated to take any action with respect to it until it is signed.

(3) If without substantial justification a certification is made in violation of the rule, the court, upon motion or upon its own initiative, shall impose upon the person who made the certification, the party on whose behalf the disclosure, request, response, or objection is made, or both, an appropriate sanction, which may include an order to pay the amount of the reasonable expenses incurred because of the violation, including a reasonable attorney's fee.

[Amended December 27, 1946, effective March 19, 1948; January 21, 1963, effective July 1, 1963; February 28, 1966, effective July 1, 1966; March 30, 1970, effective July 1, 1970; April 29, 1980, effective August 1, 1980; April 28, 1983, effective August 1, 1983; March 2, 1987, effective August 1, 1987; April 22, 1993, effective December 1, 1993; April 17, 2000, effective December 1, 2000; April 12, 2006, effective December 1, 2006.]

# RULE 27. DEPOSITIONS BEFORE ACTION OR PENDING APPEAL

**(a) Before Action.**

(1) *Petition.* A person who desires to perpetuate testimony regarding any matter that may be cognizable in any court of the United States may file a verified petition in the United States district court in the district of the residence of any expected adverse party. The petition shall be entitled in the name of the petitioner and shall show: 1, that the petitioner expects to be a party to an action cognizable in a court of the United States but is presently unable to bring it or cause it to be brought, 2, the subject matter of the expected action and the petitioner's interest therein, 3, the facts which the petitioner desires to establish by the proposed testimony and the reasons for desiring to perpetuate it, 4, the names or a description of the persons the petitioner expects will be adverse parties and their addresses so far as known, and 5, the names and addresses of the persons to be examined and the substance of the testimony which the petitioner expects to elicit from each, and shall ask for an order authorizing the petitioner to take the depositions of the persons to be examined named in the petition, for the purpose of perpetuating their testimony.

(2) *Notice and Service.* At least 20 days before the hearing date, the petitioner must serve each expected adverse party with a copy of the petition and a notice stating the time and place of the hearing. The notice may be served either inside or outside the district or state in the manner provided in Rule 4. If that service cannot be made with due diligence on an expected adverse party, the court may order service by publication or otherwise. The court must appoint an attorney to represent persons not served in the manner provided by Rule 4 and to cross-examine the deponent if an unserved person is not otherwise represented. Rule 17(c) applies if any expected adverse party is a minor or is incompetent.

(3) *Order and Examination.* If the court is satisfied that the perpetuation of the testimony may prevent a failure or delay of justice, it shall make an order designating or describing the persons whose depositions may be taken and specifying the subject matter of the examination and whether the depositions shall be taken upon oral examination or written interrogatories. The depositions may then be taken in accordance with these rules; and the court may make orders of the character provided for by Rules 34 and 35. For the purpose of applying these rules to depositions for perpetuating testimony, each reference therein to the court in which the action is pending shall be deemed to refer to the court in which the petition for such deposition was filed.

(4) *Use of Deposition.* If a deposition to perpetuate testimony is taken under these rules or if, although not so taken, it would be admissible in evidence in the courts of the state in which it is taken, it may be used in any action involving the same subject matter subsequently brought in a United States district court, in accordance with the provisions of Rule 32(a).

**(b) Pending Appeal.** If an appeal has been taken from a judgment of a district court or before the taking of an appeal if the time therefor has not expired, the district court in which the judgment was rendered may allow the taking of the depositions of witnesses to perpetuate their testimony for use in the event of further proceedings in the district court. In such case the party who desires to perpetuate the testimony may make a motion in the district court for leave to take the depositions, upon the same notice and service thereof as if the action was pending in the district court. The motion shall show (1) the names and addresses of persons to be examined and the substance of the testimony which the party expects to elicit from each; (2) the reasons for perpetuating their testimony. If the court finds that the perpetuation of the testimony is proper to avoid a failure or delay of justice, it may make an order allowing the depositions to be taken and may make orders of the character provided for by Rules 34 and 35, and thereupon the depositions may be taken and used in the same manner and under the same conditions as are prescribed in these rules for depositions taken in actions pending in the district court.

**(c) Perpetuation by Action.** This rule does not limit the power of a court to entertain an action to perpetuate testimony.

[Amended December 27, 1946, effective March 19, 1948; December 29, 1948, effective October 20, 1949; March 1, 1971, effective July 1, 1971; March 2, 1987, effective August 1, 1987; April 25, 2005, effective December 1, 2005.]

## RULE 28. PERSONS BEFORE WHOM DEPOSITIONS MAY BE TAKEN

**(a) Within the United States.** Within the United States or within a territory or insular possession subject to the jurisdiction of the United States, depositions shall be taken before an officer authorized to administer oaths by the laws of the United States or of the place where the examination is held, or before a person appointed by the court in which the action is pending. A person so appointed has power to administer oaths and take testimony. The term officer as used in Rules 30, 31 and 32 includes a person appointed by the court or designated by the parties under Rule 29.

**(b) In Foreign Countries.** Depositions may be taken in a foreign country (1) pursuant to any applicable treaty or convention, or (2) pursuant to a letter of request (whether or not captioned a letter rogatory), or (3) on notice before a person authorized to administer oaths in the place where the examination is held, either by the law thereof or by the law of the United States, or (4) before a person commissioned by the court, and a person so commissioned shall have the power by virtue of the commission to administer any necessary oath and take testimony. A commission or a letter of request shall be issued on application and notice and on terms that are just and appropriate. It is not requisite to the issuance of a commission or a letter of request that the taking of the deposition in any other manner is impracticable or inconvenient; and both a commission and a letter of request may be issued in proper cases. A notice or commission may designate the person before whom the deposition is to be taken either by name or descriptive title. A letter of request may be addressed "To the Appropriate Authority in [here name the country]." When a letter of request or any other device is used pursuant to any applicable treaty or convention, it shall be captioned in the form prescribed by that treaty or convention. Evidence obtained in response to a letter of request need not be excluded merely because it is not a verbatim transcript, because the testimony was not taken under oath, or because of any similar departure from the requirements for depositions taken within the United States under these rules.

**(c) Disqualification for Interest.** No deposition shall be taken before a person who is a relative or employee or attorney or counsel of any of the parties, or is a relative or employee of such attorney or counsel, or is financially interested in the action.

[Amended December 27, 1946, effective March 19, 1948; January 21, 1963, effective July 1, 1963; April 29, 1980, effective August 1, 1980; March 2, 1987, effective August 1, 1987; April 22, 1993, effective December 1, 1993.]

# RULE 29. STIPULATIONS REGARDING DISCOVERY PROCEDURE

Unless otherwise directed by the court, the parties may by written stipulation (1) provide that depositions may be taken before any person, at any time or place, upon any notice, and in any manner and when so taken may be used like other depositions, and (2) modify other procedures governing or limitations placed upon discovery, except that stipulations extending the time provided in Rules 33, 34, and 36 for responses to discovery may, if they would interfere with any time set for completion of discovery, for hearing of a motion, or for trial, be made only with the approval of the court.

[Amended March 30, 1970, effective July 1, 1970; April 22, 1993, effective December 1, 1993.]

# RULE 30. DEPOSITIONS UPON ORAL EXAMINATION

**(a) When Depositions May Be Taken; When Leave Required.**

(1) A party may take the testimony of any person, including a party, by deposition upon oral examination without leave of court except as provided in paragraph (2). The attendance of witnesses may be compelled by subpoena as provided in Rule 45.

(2) A party must obtain leave of court, which shall be granted to the extent consistent with the principles stated in Rule 26(b)(2), if the person to be examined is confined in prison or if, without the written stipulation of the parties,

(A) a proposed deposition would result in more than ten depositions being taken under this rule or Rule 31 by the plaintiffs, or by the defendants, or by third-party defendants;

(B) the person to be examined already has been deposed in the case; or

(C) a party seeks to take a deposition before the time specified in Rule 26(d) unless the notice contains a certification, with supporting facts, that the person to be examined is expected to leave the United States and be unavailable for examination in this country unless deposed before that time.

**(b) Notice of Examination: General Requirements; Method of Recording; Production of Documents and Things; Deposition of Organization; Deposition by Telephone.**

(1) A party desiring to take the deposition of any person upon oral examination shall give reasonable notice in writing to every other party to the action. The notice shall state the time and place for taking the deposition and the name and address of each person to be examined, if known, and, if the name is not known, a general description sufficient to identify the person or the particular class or group to which the person belongs. If a subpoena duces tecum is to be served on the person to be examined, the designation of the materials to be produced as set forth in the subpoena shall be attached to, or included in, the notice.

(2) The party taking the deposition shall state in the notice the method by which the testimony shall be recorded. Unless the court orders otherwise, it may be recorded by sound, sound-and-visual, or stenographic means, and the party taking the deposition shall bear the cost of the recording. Any party may arrange for a transcription to be made from the recording of a deposition taken by nonstenographic means.

(3) With prior notice to the deponent and other parties, any party may designate another method to record the deponent's testimony in addition to the method specified by the person taking the deposition. The additional record or transcript shall be made at that party's expense unless the court otherwise orders.

(4) Unless otherwise agreed by the parties, a deposition shall be conducted before an officer appointed or designated under Rule 28 and shall begin with a statement on the record by the officer that includes (A) the officer's name and business address; (B) the date, time, and place of the deposition; (C) the name of the deponent; (D) the administration of the oath or affirmation to the deponent; and (E) an identification of all persons present. If the deposition is recorded other than stenographically, the officer shall repeat items (A) through (C) at the beginning of each unit of recorded tape or other recording medium. The appearance or demeanor of deponents or attorneys shall not be distorted through camera or sound-recording techniques. At the end of the deposition, the officer shall state on the record that the deposition is complete and shall set forth any stipulations made by counsel concerning the custody of the transcript or recording and the exhibits, or concerning other pertinent matters.

(5) The notice to a party deponent may be accompanied by a request made in compliance with Rule 34 for the production of documents and tangible things at the taking of the deposition. The procedure of Rule 34 shall apply to the request.

(6) A party may in the party's notice and in a subpoena name as the deponent a public or private corporation or a partnership or association or governmental agency and describe with reasonable particularity the matters on which examination is requested. In that event, the organization so named shall designate one or more officers, directors, or managing agents, or other persons who consent to testify on its behalf, and may set forth, for each person designated, the matters on which the person will testify. A

subpoena shall advise a non-party organization of its duty to make such a designation. The persons so designated shall testify as to matters known or reasonably available to the organization. This subdivision (b)(6) does not preclude taking a deposition by any other procedure authorized in these rules.

(7) The parties may stipulate in writing or the court may upon motion order that a deposition be taken by telephone or other remote electronic means. For the purposes of this rule and Rules 28(a), 37(a)(1), and 37(b)(1), a deposition taken by such means is taken in the district and at the place where the deponent is to answer questions.

**(c) Examination and Cross–Examination; Record of Examination; Oath; Objections.** Examination and cross-examination of witnesses may proceed as permitted at the trial under the provisions of the Federal Rules of Evidence except Rules 103 and 615. The officer before whom the deposition is to be taken shall put the witness on oath or affirmation and shall personally, or by someone acting under the officer's direction and in the officer's presence, record the testimony of the witness. The testimony shall be taken stenographically or recorded by any other method authorized by subdivision (b)(2) of this rule. All objections made at the time of the examination to the qualifications of the officer taking the deposition, to the manner of taking it, to the evidence presented, to the conduct of any party, or to any other aspect of the proceedings shall be noted by the officer upon the record of the deposition; but the examination shall proceed, with the testimony being taken subject to the objections. In lieu of participating in the oral examination, parties may serve written questions in a sealed envelope on the party taking the deposition and the party taking the deposition shall transmit them to the officer, who shall propound them to the witness and record the answers verbatim.

**(d) Schedule and Duration; Motion to Terminate or Limit Examination.**

(1) Any objection during a deposition must be stated concisely and in a non-argumentative and non-suggestive manner. A person may instruct a deponent not to answer only when necessary to preserve a privilege, to enforce a limitation directed by the court, or to present a motion under Rule 30(d)(4).

(2) Unless otherwise authorized by the court or stipulated by the parties, a deposition is limited to one day of seven hours. The court must allow additional time consistent with Rule 26(b)(2) if needed for a fair examination of the deponent or if the deponent or another person, or other circumstance, impedes or delays the examination.

(3) If the court finds that any impediment, delay, or other conduct has frustrated the fair examination of the deponent, it may impose upon the persons respon-

sible an appropriate sanction, including the reasonable costs and attorney's fees incurred by any parties as a result thereof.

(4) At any time during a deposition, on motion of a party or of the deponent and upon a showing that the examination is being conducted in bad faith or in such manner as unreasonably to annoy, embarrass, or oppress the deponent or party, the court in which the action is pending or the court in the district where the deposition is being taken may order the officer conducting the examination to cease forthwith from taking the deposition, or may limit the scope and manner of the taking of the deposition as provided in Rule 26(c). If the order made terminates the examination, it may be resumed thereafter only upon the order of the court in which the action is pending. Upon demand of the objecting party or deponent, the taking of the deposition must be suspended for the time necessary to make a motion for an order. The provisions of Rule 37(a)(4) apply to the award of expenses incurred in relation to the motion.

**(e) Review by Witness; Changes; Signing.** If requested by the deponent or a party before completion of the deposition, the deponent shall have 30 days after being notified by the officer that the transcript or recording is available in which to review the transcript or recording and, if there are changes in form or substance, to sign a statement reciting such changes and the reasons given by the deponent for making them. The officer shall indicate in the certificate prescribed by subdivision (f)(1) whether any review was requested and, if so, shall append any changes made by the deponent during the period allowed.

**(f) Certification and Delivery by Officer; Exhibits; Copies.**

(1) The officer must certify that the witness was duly sworn by the officer and that the deposition is a true record of the testimony given by the witness. This certificate must be in writing and accompany the record of the deposition. Unless otherwise ordered by the court, the officer must securely seal the deposition in an envelope or package indorsed with the title of the action and marked "Deposition of [here insert name of witness]" and must promptly send it to the attorney who arranged for the transcript or recording, who must store it under conditions that will protect it against loss, destruction, tampering, or deterioration. Documents and things produced for inspection during the examination of the witness must, upon the request of a party, be marked for identification and annexed to the deposition and may be inspected and copied by any party, except that if the person producing the materials desires to retain them the person may (A) offer copies to be marked for identification and annexed to the deposition and to serve thereafter as originals if the person affords to all parties fair oppor-

tunity to verify the copies by comparison with the originals, or (B) offer the originals to be marked for identification, after giving to each party an opportunity to inspect and copy them, in which event the materials may then be used in the same manner as if annexed to the deposition. Any party may move for an order that the original be annexed to and returned with the deposition to the court, pending final disposition of the case.

(2) Unless otherwise ordered by the court or agreed by the parties, the officer shall retain stenographic notes of any deposition taken stenographically or a copy of the recording of any deposition taken by another method. Upon payment of reasonable charges therefor, the officer shall furnish a copy of the transcript or other recording of the deposition to any party or to the deponent.

(3) The party taking the deposition shall give prompt notice of its filing to all other parties.

(g) **Failure to Attend or to Serve Subpoena; Expenses.**

(1) If the party giving the notice of the taking of a deposition fails to attend and proceed therewith and another party attends in person or by attorney pursuant to the notice, the court may order the party giving the notice to pay to such other party the reasonable expenses incurred by that party and that party's attorney in attending, including reasonable attorney's fees.

(2) If the party giving the notice of the taking of a deposition of a witness fails to serve a subpoena upon the witness and the witness because of such failure does not attend, and if another party attends in person or by attorney because that party expects the deposition of that witness to be taken, the court may order the party giving the notice to pay to such other party the reasonable expenses incurred by that party and that party's attorney in attending, including reasonable attorney's fees.

[Amended January 21, 1963, effective July 1, 1963; March 30, 1970, effective July 1, 1970; March 1, 1971, effective July 1, 1971; November 20, 1972, effective July 1, 1975; April 29, 1980, effective August 1, 1980; March 2, 1987, effective August 1, 1987; April 22, 1993, effective December 1, 1993; April 17, 2000, effective December 1, 2000.]

# RULE 31. DEPOSITIONS UPON WRITTEN QUESTIONS

(a) **Serving Questions; Notice.**

(1) A party may take the testimony of any person, including a party, by deposition upon written questions without leave of court except as provided in paragraph (2). The attendance of witnesses may be compelled by the use of subpoena as provided in Rule 45.

(2) A party must obtain leave of court, which shall be granted to the extent consistent with the principles stated in Rule 26(b)(2), if the person to be examined is confined in prison or if, without the written stipulation of the parties,

(A) a proposed deposition would result in more than ten depositions being taken under this rule or Rule 30 by the plaintiffs, or by the defendants, or by third-party defendants;

(B) the person to be examined has already been deposed in the case; or

(C) a party seeks to take a deposition before the time specified in Rule 26(d).

(3) A party desiring to take a deposition upon written questions shall serve them upon every other party with a notice stating (1) the name and address of the person who is to answer them, if known, and if the name is not known, a general description sufficient to identify the person or the particular class or group to which the person belongs, and (2) the name or descriptive title and address of the officer before whom the deposition is to be taken. A deposition upon written questions may be taken of a public or private corporation or a partnership or association or governmental agency in accordance with the provisions of Rule 30(b)(6).

(4) Within 14 days after the notice and written questions are served, a party may serve cross questions upon all other parties. Within 7 days after being served with cross questions, a party may serve redirect questions upon all other parties. Within 7 days after being served with redirect questions, a party may serve recross questions upon all other parties. The court may for cause shown enlarge or shorten the time.

(b) **Officer to Take Responses and Prepare Record.** A copy of the notice and copies of all questions served shall be delivered by the party taking the deposition to the officer designated in the notice, who shall proceed promptly, in the manner provided by Rule 30(c), (e), and (f), to take the testimony of the witness in response to the questions and to prepare, certify, and file or mail the deposition, attaching thereto the copy of the notice and the questions received by the officer.

(c) **Notice of Filing.** When the deposition is filed the party taking it shall promptly give notice thereof to all other parties.

[Amended March 30, 1970, effective July 1, 1970; March 2, 1987, effective August 1, 1987; April 22, 1993, effective December 1, 1993.]

# RULE 32. USE OF DEPOSITIONS IN COURT PROCEEDINGS

(a) **Use of Depositions.** At the trial or upon the hearing of a motion or an interlocutory proceeding,

any part or all of a deposition, so far as admissible under the rules of evidence applied as though the witness were then present and testifying, may be used against any party who was present or represented at the taking of the deposition or who had reasonable notice thereof, in accordance with any of the following provisions:

(1) Any deposition may be used by any party for the purpose of contradicting or impeaching the testimony of deponent as a witness, or for any other purpose permitted by the Federal Rules of Evidence.

(2) The deposition of a party or of anyone who at the time of taking the deposition was an officer, director, or managing agent, or a person designated under Rule 30(b)(6) or 31(a) to testify on behalf of a public or private corporation, partnership or association or governmental agency which is a party may be used by an adverse party for any purpose.

(3) The deposition of a witness, whether or not a party, may be used by any party for any purpose if the court finds:

(A) that the witness is dead; or

(B) that the witness is at a greater distance than 100 miles from the place of trial or hearing, or is out of the United States, unless it appears that the absence of the witness was procured by the party offering the deposition; or

(C) that the witness is unable to attend or testify because of age, illness, infirmity, or imprisonment; or

(D) that the party offering the deposition has been unable to procure the attendance of the witness by subpoena; or

(E) upon application and notice, that such exceptional circumstances exist as to make it desirable, in the interest of justice and with due regard to the importance of presenting the testimony of witnesses orally in open court, to allow the deposition to be used.

A deposition taken without leave of court pursuant to a notice under Rule 30(a)(2)(C) shall not be used against a party who demonstrates that, when served with the notice, it was unable through the exercise of diligence to obtain counsel to represent it at the taking of the deposition; nor shall a deposition be used against a party who, having received less than 11 days notice of a deposition, has promptly upon receiving such notice filed a motion for a protective order under Rule 26(c)(2) requesting that the deposition not be held or be held at a different time or place and such motion is pending at the time the deposition is held.

(4) If only part of a deposition is offered in evidence by a party, an adverse party may require the offeror to introduce any other part which ought in fairness to be considered with the part introduced, and any party may introduce any other parts.

Substitution of parties pursuant to Rule 25 does not affect the right to use depositions previously taken; and, when an action has been brought in any court of the United States or of any State and another action involving the same subject matter is afterward brought between the same parties or their representatives or successors in interest, all depositions lawfully taken and duly filed in the former action may be used in the latter as if originally taken therefor. A deposition previously taken may also be used as permitted by the Federal Rules of Evidence.

**(b) Objections to Admissibility.** Subject to the provisions of Rule 28(b) and subdivision (d)(3) of this rule, objection may be made at the trial or hearing to receiving in evidence any deposition or part thereof for any reason which would require the exclusion of the evidence if the witness were then present and testifying.

**(c) Form of Presentation.** Except as otherwise directed by the court, a party offering deposition testimony pursuant to this rule may offer it in stenographic or nonstenographic form, but, if in nonstenographic form, the party shall also provide the court with a transcript of the portions so offered. On request of any party in a case tried before a jury, deposition testimony offered other than for impeachment purposes shall be presented in nonstenographic form, if available, unless the court for good cause orders otherwise.

**(d) Effect of Errors and Irregularities in Depositions.**

(1) *As to Notice.* All errors and irregularities in the notice for taking a deposition are waived unless written objection is promptly served upon the party giving the notice.

(2) *As to Disqualification of Officer.* Objection to taking a deposition because of disqualification of the officer before whom it is to be taken is waived unless made before the taking of the deposition begins or as soon thereafter as the disqualification becomes known or could be discovered with reasonable diligence.

(3) *As to Taking of Deposition.*

(A) Objections to the competency of a witness or to the competency, relevancy, or materiality of testimony are not waived by failure to make them before or during the taking of the deposition, unless the ground of the objection is one which might have been obviated or removed if presented at that time.

(B) Errors and irregularities occurring at the oral examination in the manner of taking the deposition, in the form of the questions or answers, in the oath or affirmation, or in the conduct of parties, and errors of any kind which might be obviated,

removed, or cured if promptly presented, are waived unless seasonable objection thereto is made at the taking of the deposition.

(C) Objections to the form of written questions submitted under Rule 31 are waived unless served in writing upon the party propounding them within the time allowed for serving the succeeding cross or other questions and within 5 days after service of the last questions authorized.

(4) *As to Completion and Return of Deposition.* Errors and irregularities in the manner in which the testimony is transcribed or the deposition is prepared, signed, certified, sealed, indorsed, transmitted, filed, or otherwise dealt with by the officer under Rules 30 and 31 are waived unless a motion to suppress the deposition or some part thereof is made with reasonable promptness after such defect is, or with due diligence might have been, ascertained.

[Amended March 30, 1970, effective July 1, 1970; November 20, 1972, effective July 1, 1975; April 29, 1980, effective August 1, 1980; March 2, 1987, effective August 1, 1987; April 22, 1993, effective December 1, 1993.]

# RULE 33.  INTERROGATORIES TO PARTIES

(a) **Availability.**  Without leave of court or written stipulation, any party may serve upon any other party written interrogatories, not exceeding 25 in number including all discrete subparts, to be answered by the party served or, if the party served is a public or private corporation or a partnership or association or governmental agency, by any officer or agent, who shall furnish such information as is available to the party.  Leave to serve additional interrogatories shall be granted to the extent consistent with the principles of Rule 26(b)(2).  Without leave of court or written stipulation, interrogatories may not be served before the time specified in Rule 26(d).

(b) **Answers and Objections.**

(1) Each interrogatory shall be answered separately and fully in writing under oath, unless it is objected to, in which event the objecting party shall state the reasons for objection and shall answer to the extent the interrogatory is not objectionable.

(2) The answers are to be signed by the person making them, and the objections signed by the attorney making them.

(3) The party upon whom the interrogatories have been served shall serve a copy of the answers, and objections if any, within 30 days after the service of the interrogatories.  A shorter or longer time may be directed by the court or, in the absence of such an order, agreed to in writing by the parties subject to Rule 29.

(4) All grounds for an objection to an interrogatory shall be stated with specificity.  Any ground not stated in a timely objection is waived unless the party's failure to object is excused by the court for good cause shown.

(5) The party submitting the interrogatories may move for an order under Rule 37(a) with respect to any objection to or other failure to answer an interrogatory.

(c) **Scope; Use at Trial.**  Interrogatories may relate to any matters which can be inquired into under Rule 26(b)(1), and the answers may be used to the extent permitted by the rules of evidence.

An interrogatory otherwise proper is not necessarily objectionable merely because an answer to the interrogatory involves an opinion or contention that relates to fact or the application of law to fact, but the court may order that such an interrogatory need not be answered until after designated discovery has been completed or until a pre-trial conference or other later time.

(d) **Option to Produce Business Records.**  Where the answer to an interrogatory may be derived or ascertained from the business records, including electronically stored information, of the party upon whom the interrogatory has been served or from an examination, audit or inspection of such business records, including a compilation, abstract or summary thereof, and the burden of deriving or ascertaining the answer is substantially the same for the party serving the interrogatory as for the party served, it is a sufficient answer to such interrogatory to specify the records from which the answer may be derived or ascertained and to afford to the party serving the interrogatory reasonable opportunity to examine, audit or inspect such records and to make copies, compilations, abstracts, or summaries.  A specification shall be in sufficient detail to permit the interrogating party to locate and to identify, as readily as can the party served, the records from which the answer may be ascertained.

[Amended December 27, 1946, effective March 19, 1948; March 30, 1970, effective July 1, 1970; April 29, 1980, effective August 1, 1980; April 22, 1993, effective December 1, 1993; April 12, 2006, effective December 1, 2006.]

# RULE   34.  PRODUCTION   OF   DOCUMENTS, ELECTRONICALLY STORED INFORMATION, AND THINGS AND ENTRY UPON LAND FOR INSPECTION AND OTHER PURPOSES

(a) **Scope.**  Any party may serve on any other party a request (1) to produce and permit the party making the request, or someone acting on the requestor's behalf, to inspect, copy, test, or sample any designated documents or electronically stored information—in-

cluding writings, drawings, graphs, charts, photographs, sound recordings, images, and other data or data compilations stored in any medium from which information can be obtained—translated, if necessary, by the respondent into reasonably usable form, or to inspect, copy, test, or sample any designated tangible things which constitute or contain matters within the scope of Rule 26(b) and which are in the possession, custody or control of the party upon whom the request is served; or (2) to permit entry upon designated land or other property in the possession or control of the party upon whom the request is served for the purpose of inspection and measuring, surveying, photographing, testing, or sampling the property or any designated object or operation thereon, within the scope of Rule 26(b).

**(b) Procedure.** The request shall set forth, either by individual item or by category, the items to be inspected, and describe each with reasonable particularity. The request shall specify a reasonable time, place, and manner of making the inspection and performing the related acts. The request may specify the form or forms in which electronically stored information is to be produced. Without leave of court or written stipulation, a request may not be served before the time specified in Rule 26(d).

The party upon whom the request is served shall serve a written response within 30 days after the service of the request. A shorter or longer time may be directed by the court or, in the absence of such an order, agreed to in writing by the parties, subject to Rule 29. The response shall state, with respect to each item or category, that inspection and related activities will be permitted as requested, unless the request is objected to, including an objection to the requested form or forms for producing electronically stored information, stating the reasons for the objection. If objection is made to part of an item or category, the part shall be specified and inspection permitted of the remaining parts. If objection is made to the requested form or forms for producing electronically stored information—or if no form was specified in the request—the responding party must state the form or forms it intends to use. The party submitting the request may move for an order under Rule 37(a) with respect to any objection to or other failure to respond to the request or any part thereof, or any failure to permit inspection as requested.

Unless the parties otherwise agree, or the court otherwise orders:

(i) a party who produces documents for inspection shall produce them as they are kept in the usual course of business or shall organize and label them to correspond with the categories in the request;

(ii) if a request does not specify the form or forms for producing electronically stored informa-

tion, a responding party must produce the information in a form or forms in which it is ordinarily maintained or in a form or forms that are reasonably usable; and

(iii) a party need not produce the same electronically stored information in more than one form.

**(c) Persons Not Parties.** A person not a party to the action may be compelled to produce documents and things or to submit to an inspection as provided in Rule 45.

[Amended December 27, 1946, effective March 19, 1948; March 30, 1970, effective July 1, 1970; April 29, 1980, effective August 1, 1980; March 2, 1987, effective August 1, 1987; April 30, 1991, effective December 1, 1991; April 22, 1993, effective December 1, 1993; April 12, 2006, effective December 1, 2006.]

# RULE 35. PHYSICAL AND MENTAL EXAMINATIONS OF PERSONS

**(a) Order for Examination.** When the mental or physical condition (including the blood group) of a party or of a person in the custody or under the legal control of a party, is in controversy, the court in which the action is pending may order the party to submit to a physical or mental examination by a suitably licensed or certified examiner or to produce for examination the person in the party's custody or legal control. The order may be made only on motion for good cause shown and upon notice to the person to be examined and to all parties and shall specify the time, place, manner, conditions, and scope of the examination and the person or persons by whom it is to be made.

**(b) Report of Examiner.**

(1) If requested by the party against whom an order is made under Rule 35(a) or the person examined, the party causing the examination to be made shall deliver to the requesting party a copy of the detailed written report of the examiner setting out the examiner's findings, including results of all tests made, diagnoses and conclusions, together with like reports of all earlier examinations of the same condition. After delivery the party causing the examination shall be entitled upon request to receive from the party against whom the order is made a like report of any examination, previously or thereafter made, of the same condition, unless, in the case of a report of examination of a person not a party, the party shows that the party is unable to obtain it. The court on motion may make an order against a party requiring delivery of a report on such terms as are just, and if an examiner fails or refuses to make a report the court may exclude the examiner's testimony if offered at trial.

(2) By requesting and obtaining a report of the examination so ordered or by taking the deposition of

the examiner, the party examined waives any privilege the party may have in that action or any other involving the same controversy, regarding the testimony of every other person who has examined or may thereafter examine the party in respect of the same mental or physical condition.

(3) This subdivision applies to examinations made by agreement of the parties, unless the agreement expressly provides otherwise. This subdivision does not preclude discovery of a report of an examiner or the taking of a deposition of the examiner in accordance with the provisions of any other rule.

[Amended March 30, 1970, effective July 1, 1970; March 2, 1987, effective August 1, 1987; amended by Pub.L. 100–690, Title VII, § 7047(b), November 18, 1988, 102 Stat. 4401; amended April 30, 1991, effective December 1, 1991.]

## RULE 36.  REQUESTS FOR ADMISSION

(a) Request for Admission. A party may serve upon any other party a written request for the admission, for purposes of the pending action only, of the truth of any matters within the scope of Rule 26(b)(1) set forth in the request that relate to statements or opinions of fact or of the application of law to fact, including the genuineness of any documents described in the request. Copies of documents shall be served with the request unless they have been or are otherwise furnished or made available for inspection and copying. Without leave of court or written stipulation, requests for admission may not be served before the time specified in Rule 26(d).

Each matter of which an admission is requested shall be separately set forth. The matter is admitted unless, within 30 days after service of the request, or within such shorter or longer time as the court may allow or as the parties may agree to in writing, subject to Rule 29, the party to whom the request is directed serves upon the party requesting the admission a written answer or objection addressed to the matter, signed by the party or by the party's attorney. If objection is made, the reasons therefor shall be stated. The answer shall specifically deny the matter or set forth in detail the reasons why the answering party cannot truthfully admit or deny the matter. A denial shall fairly meet the substance of the requested admission, and when good faith requires that a party qualify an answer or deny only a part of the matter of which an admission is requested, the party shall specify so much of it as is true and qualify or deny the remainder. An answering party may not give lack of information or knowledge as a reason for failure to admit or deny unless the party states that the party has made reasonable inquiry and that the information known or readily obtainable by the party is insufficient to enable the party to admit or deny. A party who considers that a matter of which an admission has been requested presents a genuine issue for trial may

not, on that ground alone, object to the request; the party may, subject to the provisions of Rule 37(c), deny the matter or set forth reasons why the party cannot admit or deny it.

The party who has requested the admissions may move to determine the sufficiency of the answers or objections. Unless the court determines that an objection is justified, it shall order that an answer be served. If the court determines that an answer does not comply with the requirements of this rule, it may order either that the matter is admitted or that an amended answer be served. The court may, in lieu of these orders, determine that final disposition of the request be made at a pre-trial conference or at a designated time prior to trial. The provisions of Rule 37(a)(4) apply to the award of expenses incurred in relation to the motion.

(b) Effect of Admission. Any matter admitted under this rule is conclusively established unless the court on motion permits withdrawal or amendment of the admission. Subject to the provision of Rule 16 governing amendment of a pre-trial order, the court may permit withdrawal or amendment when the presentation of the merits of the action will be subserved thereby and the party who obtained the admission fails to satisfy the court that withdrawal or amendment will prejudice that party in maintaining the action or defense on the merits. Any admission made by a party under this rule is for the purpose of the pending action only and is not an admission for any other purpose nor may it be used against the party in any other proceeding.

[Amended December 27, 1946, effective March 19, 1948; March 30, 1970, effective July 1, 1970; March 2, 1987, effective August 1, 1987; April 22, 1993, effective December 1, 1993.]

## RULE 37.  FAILURE TO MAKE DISCLOSURE OR COOPERATE IN DISCOVERY; SANCTIONS

(a) Motion for Order Compelling Disclosure or Discovery. A party, upon reasonable notice to other parties and all persons affected thereby, may apply for an order compelling disclosure or discovery as follows:

(1) *Appropriate Court.* An application for an order to a party shall be made to the court in which the action is pending. An application for an order to a person who is not a party shall be made to the court in the district where the discovery is being, or is to be, taken.

(2) *Motion.*

(A) If a party fails to make a disclosure required by Rule 26(a), any other party may move to compel disclosure and for appropriate sanctions. The mo-

tion must include a certification that the movant has in good faith conferred or attempted to confer with the party not making the disclosure in an effort to secure the disclosure without court action.

(B) If a deponent fails to answer a question propounded or submitted under Rules 30 or 31, or a corporation or other entity fails to make a designation under Rule 30(b)(6) or 31(a), or a party fails to answer an interrogatory submitted under Rule 33, or if a party, in response to a request for inspection submitted under Rule 34, fails to respond that inspection will be permitted as requested or fails to permit inspection as requested, the discovering party may move for an order compelling an answer, or a designation, or an order compelling inspection in accordance with the request. The motion must include a certification that the movant has in good faith conferred or attempted to confer with the person or party failing to make the discovery in an effort to secure the information or material without court action. When taking a deposition on oral examination, the proponent of the question may complete or adjourn the examination before applying for an order.

(3) *Evasive or Incomplete Disclosure, Answer, or Response.* For purposes of this subdivision an evasive or incomplete disclosure, answer, or response is to be treated as a failure to disclose, answer, or respond.

(4) *Expenses and Sanctions.*

(A) If the motion is granted or if the disclosure or requested discovery is provided after the motion was filed, the court shall, after affording an opportunity to be heard, require the party or deponent whose conduct necessitated the motion or the party or attorney advising such conduct or both of them to pay to the moving party the reasonable expenses incurred in making the motion, including attorney's fees, unless the court finds that the motion was filed without the movant's first making a good faith effort to obtain the disclosure or discovery without court action, or that the opposing party's nondisclosure, response, or objection was substantially justified, or that other circumstances make an award of expenses unjust.

(B) If the motion is denied, the court may enter any protective order authorized under Rule 26(c) and shall, after affording an opportunity to be heard, require the moving party or the attorney filing the motion or both of them to pay to the party or deponent who opposed the motion the reasonable expenses incurred in opposing the motion, including attorney's fees, unless the court finds that the making of the motion was substantially justified or that other circumstances make an award of expenses unjust.

(C) If the motion is granted in part and denied in part, the court may enter any protective order authorized under Rule 26(c) and may, after affording an opportunity to be heard, apportion the reasonable expenses incurred in relation to the motion among the parties and persons in a just manner.

**(b) Failure to Comply With Order.**

(1) *Sanctions by Court in District Where Deposition Is Taken.* If a deponent fails to be sworn or to answer a question after being directed to do so by the court in the district in which the deposition is being taken, the failure may be considered a contempt of that court.

(2) *Sanctions by Court in Which Action Is Pending.* If a party or an officer, director, or managing agent of a party or a person designated under Rule 30(b)(6) or 31(a) to testify on behalf of a party fails to obey an order to provide or permit discovery, including an order made under subdivision (a) of this rule or Rule 35, or if a party fails to obey an order entered under Rule 26(f), the court in which the action is pending may make such orders in regard to the failure as are just, and among others the following:

(A) An order that the matters regarding which the order was made or any other designated facts shall be taken to be established for the purposes of the action in accordance with the claim of the party obtaining the order;

(B) An order refusing to allow the disobedient party to support or oppose designated claims or defenses, or prohibiting that party from introducing designated matters in evidence;

(C) An order striking out pleadings or parts thereof, or staying further proceedings until the order is obeyed, or dismissing the action or proceeding or any part thereof, or rendering a judgment by default against the disobedient party;

(D) In lieu of any of the foregoing orders or in addition thereto, an order treating as a contempt of court the failure to obey any orders except an order to submit to a physical or mental examination;

(E) Where a party has failed to comply with an order under Rule 35(a) requiring that party to produce another for examination, such orders as are listed in paragraphs (A), (B), and (C) of this subdivision, unless the party failing to comply shows that that party is unable to produce such person for examination.

In lieu of any of the foregoing orders or in addition thereto, the court shall require the party failing to obey the order or the attorney advising that party or both to pay the reasonable expenses, including attorney's fees, caused by the failure, unless the court finds that the failure was substantially justified or that other circumstances make an award of expenses unjust.

## (c) Failure to Disclose; False or Misleading Disclosure; Refusal to Admit.

(1) A party that without substantial justification fails to disclose information required by Rule 26(a) or 26(e)(1) or to amend a prior response to discovery as required by Rule 26(e)(2), is not, unless such failure is harmless, permitted to use as evidence at a trial, at a hearing, or on a motion any witness or information not so disclosed. In addition to or in lieu of this sanction, the court, on motion and after affording an opportunity to be heard, may impose other appropriate sanctions. In addition to requiring payment of reasonable expenses, including attorney's fees, caused by the failure, these sanctions may include any of the actions authorized under Rule 37(b)(2)(A), (B), and (C) and may include informing the jury of the failure to make the disclosure.

(2) If a party fails to admit the genuineness of any document or the truth of any matter as requested under Rule 36, and if the party requesting the admissions thereafter proves the genuineness of the document or the truth of the matter, the requesting party may apply to the court for an order requiring the other party to pay the reasonable expenses incurred in making that proof, including reasonable attorney's fees. The court shall make the order unless it finds that (A) the request was held objectionable pursuant to Rule 36(a), or (B) the admission sought was of no substantial importance, or (C) the party failing to admit had reasonable ground to believe that the party might prevail on the matter, or (D) there was other good reason for the failure to admit.

## (d) Failure of Party to Attend at Own Deposition or Serve Answers to Interrogatories or Respond to Request for Inspection.

If a party or an officer, director, or managing agent of a party or a person designated under Rule 30(b)(6) or 31(a) to testify on behalf of a party fails (1) to appear before the officer who is to take the deposition, after being served with a proper notice, or (2) to serve answers or objections to interrogatories submitted under Rule 33, after proper service of the interrogatories, or (3) to serve a written response to a request for inspection submitted under Rule 34, after proper service of the request, the court in which the action is pending on motion may make such orders in regard to the failure as are just, and among others it may take any action authorized under subparagraphs (A), (B), and (C) of subdivision (b)(2) of this rule. Any motion specifying a failure under clause (2) or (3) of this subdivision shall include a certification that the movant has in good faith conferred or attempted to confer with the party failing to answer or respond in an effort to obtain such answer or response without court action. In lieu of any order or in addition thereto, the court shall require the party failing to act or the attorney advising that party or both to pay the reasonable expenses, including attorney's fees, caused by the failure unless the court finds that the failure was substantially justified or that other circumstances make an award of expenses unjust.

The failure to act described in this subdivision may not be excused on the ground that the discovery sought is objectionable unless the party failing to act has a pending motion for a protective order as provided by Rule 26(c).

## (e) Subpoena of Person in Foreign Country [Abrogated].

## (f) Electronically Stored Information.

Absent exceptional circumstances, a court may not impose sanctions under these rules on a party for failing to provide electronically stored information lost as a result of the routine, good-faith operation of an electronic information system.

## (g) Failure to Participate in the Framing of a Discovery Plan.

If a party or a party's attorney fails to participate in good faith in the development and submission of a proposed discovery plan as required by Rule 26(f), the court may, after opportunity for hearing, require such party or attorney to pay to any other party the reasonable expenses, including attorney's fees, caused by the failure.

[Amended December 29, 1948, effective October 20, 1949; March 30, 1970, effective July 1, 1970; April 29, 1980, effective August 1, 1980; amended by Pub.L. 96–481, Title II, § 205(a), October 21, 1980, 94 Stat. 2330, effective October 1, 1981; amended March 2, 1987, effective August 1, 1987; April 22, 1993, effective December 1, 1993; April 17, 2000, effective December 1, 2000; April 12, 2006, effective December 1, 2006.]

# VI. TRIALS

## RULE 38. JURY TRIAL OF RIGHT

(a) **Right Preserved.** The right of trial by jury as declared by the Seventh Amendment to the Constitution or as given by a statute of the United States shall be preserved to the parties inviolate.

(b) **Demand.** Any party may demand a trial by jury of any issue triable of right by a jury by (1) serving upon the other parties a demand therefor in writing at any time after the commencement of the action and not later than 10 days after the service of the last pleading directed to such issue, and (2) filing the demand as required by Rule 5(d). Such demand may be indorsed upon a pleading of the party.

**(c) Same: Specification of Issues.** In the demand a party may specify the issues which the party wishes so tried; otherwise the party shall be deemed to have demanded trial by jury for all the issues so triable. If the party has demanded trial by jury for only some of the issues, any other party within 10 days after service of the demand or such lesser time as the court may order, may serve a demand for trial by jury of any other or all of the issues of fact in the action.

**(d) Waiver.** The failure of a party to serve and file a demand as required by this rule constitutes a waiver by the party of trial by jury. A demand for trial by jury made as herein provided may not be withdrawn without the consent of the parties.

**(e) Admiralty and Maritime Claims.** These rules shall not be construed to create a right to trial by jury of the issues in an admiralty or maritime claim within the meaning of Rule 9(h).

[Amended February 28, 1966, effective July 1, 1966; March 2, 1987, effective August 1, 1987; April 22, 1993, effective December 1, 1993.]

## RULE 39.　TRIAL BY JURY OR BY THE COURT

**(a) By Jury.** When trial by jury has been demanded as provided in Rule 38, the action shall be designated upon the docket as a jury action. The trial of all issues so demanded shall be by jury, unless (1) the parties or their attorneys of record, by written stipulation filed with the court or by an oral stipulation made in open court and entered in the record, consent to trial by the court sitting without a jury or (2) the court upon motion or of its own initiative finds that a right of trial by jury of some or of all those issues does not exist under the Constitution or statutes of the United States.

**(b) By the Court.** Issues not demanded for trial by jury as provided in Rule 38 shall be tried by the court; but, notwithstanding the failure of a party to demand a jury in an action in which such a demand might have been made of right, the court in its discretion upon motion may order a trial by a jury of any or all issues.

**(c) Advisory Jury and Trial by Consent.** In all actions not triable of right by a jury the court upon motion or of its own initiative may try any issue with an advisory jury or, except in actions against the United States when a statute of the United States provides for trial without a jury, the court, with the consent of both parties, may order a trial with a jury whose verdict has the same effect as if trial by jury had been a matter of right.

## RULE 40.　ASSIGNMENT OF CASES FOR TRIAL

The district courts shall provide by rule for the placing of actions upon the trial calendar (1) without request of the parties or (2) upon request of a party and notice to the other parties or (3) in such other manner as the courts deem expedient. Precedence shall be given to actions entitled thereto by any statute of the United States.

## RULE 41.　DISMISSAL OF ACTIONS

**(a) Voluntary Dismissal: Effect Thereof.**

(1) *By Plaintiff; By Stipulation.* Subject to the provisions of Rule 23(e), of Rule 66, and of any statute of the United States, an action may be dismissed by the plaintiff without order of court (i) by filing a notice of dismissal at any time before service by the adverse party of an answer or of a motion for summary judgment, whichever first occurs, or (ii) by filing a stipulation of dismissal signed by all parties who have appeared in the action. Unless otherwise stated in the notice of dismissal or stipulation, the dismissal is without prejudice, except that a notice of dismissal operates as an adjudication upon the merits when filed by a plaintiff who has once dismissed in any court of the United States or of any state an action based on or including the same claim.

(2) *By Order of Court.* Except as provided in paragraph (1) of this subdivision of this rule, an action shall not be dismissed at the plaintiff's instance save upon order of the court and upon such terms and conditions as the court deems proper. If a counterclaim has been pleaded by a defendant prior to the service upon the defendant of the plaintiff's motion to dismiss, the action shall not be dismissed against the defendant's objection unless the counterclaim can remain pending for independent adjudication by the court. Unless otherwise specified in the order, a dismissal under this paragraph is without prejudice.

**(b) Involuntary Dismissal: Effect Thereof.** For failure of the plaintiff to prosecute or to comply with these rules or any order of court, a defendant may move for dismissal of an action or of any claim against the defendant. Unless the court in its order for dismissal otherwise specifies, a dismissal under this subdivision and any dismissal not provided for in this rule, other than a dismissal for lack of jurisdiction, for improper venue, or for failure to join a party under Rule 19, operates as an adjudication upon the merits.

**(c) Dismissal of Counterclaim, Cross–Claim, or Third–Party Claim.** The provisions of this rule apply to the dismissal of any counterclaim, cross-claim, or third-party claim. A voluntary dismissal by the claimant alone pursuant to paragraph (1) of subdivision (a) of this rule shall be made before a responsive pleading

is served or, if there is none, before the introduction of evidence at the trial or hearing.

**(d) Costs of Previously–Dismissed Action.** If a plaintiff who has once dismissed an action in any court commences an action based upon or including the same claim against the same defendant, the court may make such order for the payment of costs of the action previously dismissed as it may deem proper and may stay the proceedings in the action until the plaintiff has complied with the order.

[Amended December 27, 1946, effective March 19, 1948; January 21, 1963, effective July 1, 1963; February 28, 1966, effective July 1, 1966; December 4, 1967, effective July 1, 1968; March 2, 1987, effective August 1, 1987; April 30, 1991, effective December 1, 1991.]

## RULE 42.  CONSOLIDATION; SEPARATE TRIALS

**(a) Consolidation.** When actions involving a common question of law or fact are pending before the court, it may order a joint hearing or trial of any or all the matters in issue in the actions; it may order all the actions consolidated; and it may make such orders concerning proceedings therein as may tend to avoid unnecessary costs or delay.

**(b) Separate Trials.** The court, in furtherance of convenience or to avoid prejudice, or when separate trials will be conducive to expedition and economy, may order a separate trial of any claim, cross-claim, counterclaim, or third-party claim, or of any separate issue or of any number of claims, cross-claims, counterclaims, third-party claims, or issues, always preserving inviolate the right of trial by jury as declared by the Seventh Amendment to the Constitution or as given by a statute of the United States.

[Amended February 28, 1966, effective July 1, 1966.]

## RULE 43.  TAKING OF TESTIMONY

**(a) Form.** In every trial, the testimony of witnesses shall be taken in open court, unless a federal law, these rules, the Federal Rules of Evidence, or other rules adopted by the Supreme Court provide otherwise. The court may, for good cause shown in compelling circumstances and upon appropriate safeguards, permit presentation of testimony in open court by contemporaneous transmission from a different location.

**(b) Scope of Examination and Cross–Examination [Abrogated].**

**(c) Record of Excluded Evidence [Abrogated].**

**(d) Affirmation in Lieu of Oath.** Whenever under these rules an oath is required to be taken, a solemn affirmation may be accepted in lieu thereof.

**(e) Evidence on Motions.** When a motion is based on facts not appearing of record the court may hear the matter on affidavits presented by the respective parties, but the court may direct that the matter be heard wholly or partly on oral testimony or deposition.

**(f) Interpreters.** The court may appoint an interpreter of its own selection and may fix the interpreter's reasonable compensation. The compensation shall be paid out of funds provided by law or by one or more of the parties as the court may direct, and may be taxed ultimately as costs, in the discretion of the court.

[Amended February 28, 1966, effective July 1, 1966; November 20, 1972, and December 18, 1972, effective July 1, 1975; March 2, 1987, effective August 1, 1987; April 23, 1996, effective December 1, 1996.]

## RULE 44.  PROOF OF OFFICIAL RECORD

**(a) Authentication.**

(1) *Domestic.* An official record kept within the United States, or any state, district, or commonwealth, or within a territory subject to the administrative or judicial jurisdiction of the United States, or an entry therein, when admissible for any purpose, may be evidenced by an official publication thereof or by a copy attested by the officer having the legal custody of the record, or by the officer's deputy, and accompanied by a certificate that such officer has the custody. The certificate may be made by a judge of a court of record of the district or political subdivision in which the record is kept, authenticated by the seal of the court, or may be made by any public officer having a seal of office and having official duties in the district or political subdivision in which the record is kept, authenticated by the seal of the officer's office.

(2) *Foreign.* A foreign official record, or an entry therein, when admissible for any purpose, may be evidenced by an official publication thereof; or a copy thereof, attested by a person authorized to make the attestation, and accompanied by a final certification as to the genuineness of the signature and official position (i) of the attesting person, or (ii) of any foreign official whose certificate of genuineness of signature and official position relates to the attestation or is in a chain of certificates of genuineness of signature and official position relating to the attestation. A final certification may be made by a secretary of embassy or legation, consul general, vice consul, or consular agent of the United States, or a diplomatic or consular official of the foreign country assigned or accredited to the United States. If reasonable opportunity has been given to all parties to investigate the authenticity and accuracy of the documents, the court may, for good cause shown, (i) admit an attested copy without

final certification or (ii) permit the foreign official record to be evidenced by an attested summary with or without a final certification. The final certification is unnecessary if the record and the attestation are certified as provided in a treaty or convention to which the United States and the foreign country in which the official record is located are parties.

**(b) Lack of Record.** A written statement that after diligent search no record or entry of a specified tenor is found to exist in the records designated by the statement, authenticated as provided in subdivision (a)(1) of this rule in the case of a domestic record, or complying with the requirements of subdivision (a)(2) of this rule for a summary in the case of a foreign record, is admissible as evidence that the records contain no such record or entry.

**(c) Other Proof.** This rule does not prevent the proof of official records or of entry or lack of entry therein by any other method authorized by law.

[Amended February 28, 1966, effective July 1, 1966; March 2, 1987, effective August 1, 1987; April 30, 1991, effective December 1, 1991.]

## RULE 44.1    DETERMINATION OF FOREIGN LAW

A party who intends to raise an issue concerning the law of a foreign country shall give notice by pleadings or other reasonable written notice. The court, in determining foreign law, may consider any relevant material or source, including testimony, whether or not submitted by a party or admissible under the Federal Rules of Evidence. The court's determination shall be treated as a ruling on a question of law.

[Adopted February 28, 1966, effective July 1, 1966; amended November 20, 1972, effective July 1, 1975; March 2, 1987, effective August 1, 1987.]

## RULE 45.    SUBPOENA

**(a) Form; Issuance.**

(1) Every subpoena shall

(A) state the name of the court from which it is issued; and

(B) state the title of the action, the name of the court in which it is pending, and its civil action number; and

(C) command each person to whom it is directed to attend and give testimony or to produce and permit inspection, copying, testing, or sampling of designated books, documents, electronically stored information, or tangible things in the possession, custody or control of that person, or to permit inspection of premises, at a time and place therein specified; and

(D) set forth the text of subdivisions (c) and (d) of this rule.

A command to produce evidence or to permit inspection, copying, testing, or sampling may be joined with a command to appear at trial or hearing or at deposition, or may be issued separately. A subpoena may specify the form or forms in which electronically stored information is to be produced.

(2) A subpoena must issue as follows:

(A) for attendance at a trial or hearing, from the court for the district where the trial or hearing is to be held;

(B) for attendance at a deposition, from the court for the district where the deposition is to be taken, stating the method for recording the testimony; and

(C) for production, inspection, copying, testing, or sampling, if separate from a subpoena commanding a person's attendance, from the court for the district where the production or inspection is to be made.

(3) The clerk shall issue a subpoena, signed but otherwise in blank, to a party requesting it, who shall complete it before service. An attorney as officer of the court may also issue and sign a subpoena on behalf of

(A) a court in which the attorney is authorized to practice; or

(B) a court for a district in which a deposition or production is compelled by the subpoena, if the deposition or production pertains to an action pending in a court in which the attorney is authorized to practice.

**(b) Service.**

(1) A subpoena may be served by any person who is not a party and is not less than 18 years of age. Service of a subpoena upon a person named therein shall be made by delivering a copy thereof to such person and, if the person's attendance is commanded, by tendering to that person the fees for one day's attendance and the mileage allowed by law. When the subpoena is issued on behalf of the United States or an officer or agency thereof, fees and mileage need not be tendered. Prior notice of any commanded production of documents and things or inspection of premises before trial shall be served on each party in the manner prescribed by Rule 5(b).

(2) Subject to the provisions of clause (ii) of subparagraph (c)(3)(A) of this rule, a subpoena may be served at any place within the district of the court by which it is issued, or at any place without the district that is within 100 miles of the place of the deposition, hearing, trial, production, inspection, copying, testing, or sampling specified in the subpoena or at any place within the state where a state statute or rule of court

permits service of a subpoena issued by a state court of general jurisdiction sitting in the place of the deposition, hearing, trial, production, inspection, copying, testing, or sampling specified in the subpoena. When a statute of the United States provides therefor, the court upon proper application and cause shown may authorize the service of a subpoena at any other place. A subpoena directed to a witness in a foreign country who is a national or resident of the United States shall issue under the circumstances and in the manner and be served as provided in Title 28, U.S.C. § 1783.

(3) Proof of service when necessary shall be made by filing with the clerk of the court by which the subpoena is issued a statement of the date and manner of service and of the names of the persons served, certified by the person who made the service.

**(c) Protection of Persons Subject to Subpoenas.**

(1) A party or an attorney responsible for the issuance and service of a subpoena shall take reasonable steps to avoid imposing undue burden or expense on a person subject to that subpoena. The court on behalf of which the subpoena was issued shall enforce this duty and impose upon the party or attorney in breach of this duty an appropriate sanction, which may include, but is not limited to, lost earnings and a reasonable attorney's fee.

(2)(A) A person commanded to produce and permit inspection, copying, testing, or sampling of designated electronically stored information, books, papers, documents or tangible things, or inspection of premises need not appear in person at the place of production or inspection unless commanded to appear for deposition, hearing or trial.

(B) Subject to paragraph (d)(2) of this rule, a person commanded to produce and permit inspection, copying, testing, or sampling may, within 14 days after service of the subpoena or before the time specified for compliance if such time is less than 14 days after service, serve upon the party or attorney designated in the subpoena written objection to producing any or all of the designated materials or inspection of the premises—or to producing electronically stored information in the form or forms requested. If objection is made, the party serving the subpoena shall not be entitled to inspect, copy, test, or sample the materials or inspect the premises except pursuant to an order of the court by which the subpoena was issued. If objection has been made, the party serving the subpoena may, upon notice to the person commanded to produce, move at any time for an order to compel the production, inspection, copying, testing, or sampling. Such an order to compel shall protect any person who is not a party or an officer of a party from significant expense resulting from the inspection, copying, testing, or sampling commanded.

(3)(A) On timely motion, the court by which a subpoena was issued shall quash or modify the subpoena if it

(i) fails to allow reasonable time for compliance;

(ii) requires a person who is not a party or an officer of a party to travel to a place more than 100 miles from the place where that person resides, is employed or regularly transacts business in person, except that, subject to the provisions of clause (c)(3)(B)(iii) of this rule, such a person may in order to attend trial be commanded to travel from any such place within the state in which the trial is held;

(iii) requires disclosure of privileged or other protected matter and no exception or waiver applies; or

(iv) subjects a person to undue burden.

(B) If a subpoena

(i) requires disclosure of a trade secret or other confidential research, development, or commercial information, or

(ii) requires disclosure of an unretained expert's opinion or information not describing specific events or occurrences in dispute and resulting from the expert's study made not at the request of any party, or

(iii) requires a person who is not a party or an officer of a party to incur substantial expense to travel more than 100 miles to attend trial, the court may, to protect a person subject to or affected by the subpoena, quash or modify the subpoena or, if the party in whose behalf the subpoena is issued shows a substantial need for the testimony or material that cannot be otherwise met without undue hardship and assures that the person to whom the subpoena is addressed will be reasonably compensated, the court may order appearance or production only upon specified conditions.

**(d) Duties in Responding to Subpoena.**

(1)(A) A person responding to a subpoena to produce documents shall produce them as they are kept in the usual course of business or shall organize and label them to correspond with the categories in the demand.

(B) If a subpoena does not specify the form or forms for producing electronically stored information, a person responding to a subpoena must produce the information in a form or forms in which the person ordinarily maintains it or in a form or forms that are reasonably usable.

(C) A person responding to a subpoena need not produce the same electronically stored information in more than one form.

(D) A person responding to a subpoena need not provide discovery of electronically stored information from sources that the person identifies as not reasonably accessible because of undue burden or cost. On motion to compel discovery or to quash, the person from whom discovery is sought must show that the information sought is not reasonably accessible because of undue burden or cost. If that showing is made, the court may nonetheless order discovery from such sources if the requesting party shows good cause, considering the limitations of Rule 26(b)(2)(C). The court may specify conditions for the discovery.

(2)(A) When information subject to a subpoena is withheld on a claim that it is privileged or subject to protection as trial-preparation materials, the claim shall be made expressly and shall be supported by a description of the nature of the documents, communications, or things not produced that is sufficient to enable the demanding party to contest the claim.

(B) If information is produced in response to a subpoena that is subject to a claim of privilege or of protection as trial-preparation material, the person making the claim may notify any party that received the information of the claim and the basis for it. After being notified, a party must promptly return, sequester, or destroy the specified information and any copies it has and may not use or disclose the information until the claim is resolved. A receiving party may promptly present the information to the court under seal for a determination of the claim. If the receiving party disclosed the information before being notified, it must take reasonable steps to retrieve it. The person who produced the information must preserve the information until the claim is resolved.

(e) **Contempt.** Failure of any person without adequate excuse to obey a subpoena served upon that person may be deemed a contempt of the court from which the subpoena issued. An adequate cause for failure to obey exists when a subpoena purports to require a nonparty to attend or produce at a place not within the limits provided by clause (ii) of subparagraph (c)(3)(A).

[Amended December 27, 1946, effective March 19, 1948; December 29, 1948, effective October 20, 1949; March 30, 1970, effective July 1, 1970; April 29, 1980, effective August 1, 1980; April 29, 1985, effective August 1, 1985; March 2, 1987, effective August 1, 1987; April 30, 1991, effective December 1, 1991; April 25, 2005, effective December 1, 2005; April 12, 2006, effective December 1, 2006.]

## RULE 46.  EXCEPTIONS UNNECESSARY

Formal exceptions to rulings or orders of the court are unnecessary; but for all purposes for which an exception has heretofore been necessary it is sufficient that a party, at the time the ruling or order of the court is made or sought, makes known to the court the action which the party desires the court to take or the party's objection to the action of the court and the grounds therefor; and, if a party has no opportunity to object to a ruling or order at the time it is made, the absence of an objection does not thereafter prejudice the party.

[Amended March 2, 1987, effective August 1, 1987.]

## RULE 47.  SELECTION OF JURORS

(a) **Examination of Jurors.**  The court may permit the parties or their attorneys to conduct the examination of prospective jurors or may itself conduct the examination.  In the latter event, the court shall permit the parties or their attorneys to supplement the examination by such further inquiry as it deems proper or shall itself submit to the prospective jurors such additional questions of the parties or their attorneys as it deems proper.

(b) **Peremptory Challenges.**  The court shall allow the number of peremptory challenges provided by 28 U.S.C. § 1870.

(c) **Excuse.**  The court may for good cause excuse a juror from service during trial or deliberation.

[Amended February 28, 1966, effective July 1, 1966; April 30, 1991, effective December 1, 1991.]

## RULE 48.  NUMBER OF JURORS— PARTICIPATION IN VERDICT

The court shall seat a jury of not fewer than six and not more than twelve members and all jurors shall participate in the verdict unless excused from service by the court pursuant to Rule 47(c).  Unless the parties otherwise stipulate, (1) the verdict shall be unanimous and (2) no verdict shall be taken from a jury reduced in size to fewer than six members.

[Amended April 30, 1991, effective December 1, 1991.]

## RULE 49.  SPECIAL VERDICTS AND INTERROGATORIES

(a) **Special Verdicts.**  The court may require a jury to return only a special verdict in the form of a special written finding upon each issue of fact.  In that event the court may submit to the jury written questions susceptible of categorical or other brief answer or may submit written forms of the several special findings which might properly be made under the pleadings and evidence; or it may use such other method of submitting the issues and requiring the written findings thereon as it deems most appropriate. The court shall give to the jury such explanation and instruction concerning the matter thus submitted as may be necessary to enable the jury to make its findings upon each issue.  If in so doing the court

omits any issue of fact raised by the pleadings or by the evidence, each party waives the right to a trial by jury of the issue so omitted unless before the jury retires the party demands its submission to the jury. As to an issue omitted without such demand the court may make a finding; or, if it fails to do so, it shall be deemed to have made a finding in accord with the judgment on the special verdict.

**(b) General Verdict Accompanied by Answer to Interrogatories.** The court may submit to the jury, together with appropriate forms for a general verdict, written interrogatories upon one or more issues of fact the decision of which is necessary to a verdict. The court shall give such explanation or instruction as may be necessary to enable the jury both to make answers to the interrogatories and to render a general verdict, and the court shall direct the jury both to make written answers and to render a general verdict. When the general verdict and the answers are harmonious, the appropriate judgment upon the verdict and answers shall be entered pursuant to Rule 58. When the answers are consistent with each other but one or more is inconsistent with the general verdict, judgment may be entered pursuant to Rule 58 in accordance with the answers, notwithstanding the general verdict, or the court may return the jury for further consideration of its answers and verdict or may order a new trial. When the answers are inconsistent with each other and one or more is likewise inconsistent with the general verdict, judgment shall not be entered, but the court shall return the jury for further consideration of its answers and verdict or shall order a new trial.

[Amended January 21, 1963, effective July 1, 1963; March 2, 1987, effective August 1, 1987.]

# RULE 50. JUDGMENT AS A MATTER OF LAW IN JURY TRIALS; ALTERNATIVE MOTION FOR NEW TRIAL; CONDITIONAL RULINGS

**(a) Judgment as a Matter of Law.**

(1) *In General.* If a party has been fully heard on an issue during a jury trial and the court finds that a reasonable jury would not have a legally sufficient evidentiary basis to find for the party on that issue, the court may:

(A) resolve the issue against the party; and

(B) grant a motion for judgment as a matter of law against the party on a claim or defense that, under the controlling law, can be maintained or defeated only with a favorable finding on that issue.

(2) *Motion.* A motion for judgment as a matter of law may be made at any time before the case is submitted to the jury. The motion must specify the judgment sought and the law and facts that entitle the movant to the judgment.

**(b) Renewing the Motion After Trial; Alternative Motion for a New Trial.** If the court does not grant a motion for judgment as a matter of law made under subdivision (a), the court is considered to have submitted the action to the jury subject to the court's later deciding the legal questions raised by the motion. The movant may renew its request for judgment as a matter of law by filing a motion no later than 10 days after the entry of judgment or—if the motion addresses a jury issue not decided by a verdict—no later than 10 days after the jury was discharged. The movant may alternatively request a new trial or join a motion for a new trial under Rule 59.

In ruling on a renewed motion, the court may:

(1) if a verdict was returned:

(A) allow the judgment to stand,

(B) order a new trial, or

(C) direct entry of judgment as a matter of law; or

(2) if no verdict was returned:

(A) order a new trial, or

(B) direct entry of judgment as a matter of law.

**(c) Granting Renewed Motion for Judgment as a Matter of Law; Conditional Rulings; New Trial Motion.**

(1) If the renewed motion for judgment as a matter of law is granted, the court shall also rule on the motion for a new trial, if any, by determining whether it should be granted if the judgment is thereafter vacated or reversed, and shall specify the grounds for granting or denying the motion for the new trial. If the motion for a new trial is thus conditionally granted, the order thereon does not affect the finality of the judgment. In case the motion for a new trial has been conditionally granted and the judgment is reversed on appeal, the new trial shall proceed unless the appellate court has otherwise ordered. In case the motion for a new trial has been conditionally denied, the appellee on appeal may assert error in that denial; and if the judgment is reversed on appeal, subsequent proceedings shall be in accordance with the order of the appellate court.

(2) Any motion for a new trial under Rule 59 by a party against whom judgment as a matter of law is rendered shall be filed no later than 10 days after entry of the judgment.

**(d) Same: Denial of Motion for Judgment as a Matter of Law.** If the motion for judgment as a matter of law is denied, the party who prevailed on that motion may, as appellee, assert grounds entitling the party to a new trial in the event the appellate court concludes that the trial court erred in denying

the motion for judgment. If the appellate court reverses the judgment, nothing in this rule precludes it from determining that the appellee is entitled to a new trial, or from directing the trial court to determine whether a new trial shall be granted.

[Amended January 21, 1963, effective July 1, 1963; March 2, 1987, effective August 1, 1987; April 30, 1991, effective December 1, 1991; April 22, 1993, effective December 1, 1993; April 27, 1995, effective December 1, 1995; April 12, 2006, effective December 1, 2006.]

# RULE 51.  INSTRUCTIONS TO JURY; OBJECTIONS; PRESERVING A CLAIM OF ERROR

**(a) Requests.**

(1) A party may, at the close of the evidence or at an earlier reasonable time that the court directs, file and furnish to every other party written requests that the court instruct the jury on the law as set forth in the requests.

(2) After the close of the evidence, a party may:

(A) file requests for instructions on issues that could not reasonably have been anticipated at an earlier time for requests set under Rule 51(a)(1), and

(B) with the court's permission file untimely requests for instructions on any issue.

**(b) Instructions.** The court:

(1) must inform the parties of its proposed instructions and proposed action on the requests before instructing the jury and before final jury arguments;

(2) must give the parties an opportunity to object on the record and out of the jury's hearing to the proposed instructions and actions on requests before the instructions and arguments are delivered; and

(3) may instruct the jury at any time after trial begins and before the jury is discharged.

**(c) Objections.**

(1) A party who objects to an instruction or the failure to give an instruction must do so on the record, stating distinctly the matter objected to and the grounds of the objection.

(2) An objection is timely if:

(A) a party that has been informed of an instruction or action on a request before the jury is instructed and before final jury arguments, as provided by Rule 51(b)(1), objects at the opportunity for objection required by Rule 51(b)(2); or

(B) a party that has not been informed of an instruction or action on a request before the time for objection provided under Rule 51(b)(2) objects promptly after learning that the instruction or request will be, or has been, given or refused.

**(d) Assigning Error; Plain Error.**

(1) A party may assign as error:

(A) an error in an instruction actually given if that party made a proper objection under Rule 51(c), or

(B) a failure to give an instruction if that party made a proper request under Rule 51(a), and—unless the court made a definitive ruling on the record rejecting the request—also made a proper objection under Rule 51(c).

(2) A court may consider a plain error in the instructions affecting substantial rights that has not been preserved as required by Rule 51(d)(1)(A) or (B).

[Amended March 2, 1987, effective August 1, 1987; March 27, 2003, effective December 1, 2003.]

# RULE 52.  FINDINGS BY THE COURT; JUDGMENT ON PARTIAL FINDINGS

**(a) Effect.** In all actions tried upon the facts without a jury or with an advisory jury, the court shall find the facts specially and state separately its conclusions of law thereon, and judgment shall be entered pursuant to Rule 58; and in granting or refusing interlocutory injunctions the court shall similarly set forth the findings of fact and conclusions of law which constitute the grounds of its action. Requests for findings are not necessary for purposes of review. Findings of fact, whether based on oral or documentary evidence, shall not be set aside unless clearly erroneous, and due regard shall be given to the opportunity of the trial court to judge of the credibility of the witnesses. The findings of a master, to the extent that the court adopts them, shall be considered as the findings of the court. It will be sufficient if the findings of fact and conclusions of law are stated orally and recorded in open court following the close of the evidence or appear in an opinion or memorandum of decision filed by the court. Findings of fact and conclusions of law are unnecessary on decisions of motions under Rule 12 or 56 or any other motion except as provided in subdivision (c) of this rule.

**(b) Amendment.** On a party's motion filed no later than 10 days after entry of judgment, the court may amend its findings—or make additional findings—and may amend the judgment accordingly. The motion may accompany a motion for a new trial under Rule 59. When findings of fact are made in actions tried without a jury, the sufficiency of the evidence supporting the findings may be later questioned whether or not in the district court the party raising the question objected to the findings, moved to amend them, or moved for partial findings.

**(c) Judgment on Partial Findings.** If during a trial without a jury a party has been fully heard on an

issue and the court finds against the party on that issue, the court may enter judgment as a matter of law against that party with respect to a claim or defense that cannot under the controlling law be maintained or defeated without a favorable finding on that issue, or the court may decline to render any judgment until the close of all the evidence. Such a judgment shall be supported by findings of fact and conclusions of law as required by subdivision (a) of this rule.

[Amended December 27, 1946, effective March 19, 1948; January 21, 1963, effective July 1, 1963; April 28, 1983, effective August 1, 1983; April 29, 1985, effective August 1, 1985; April 30, 1991, effective December 1, 1991; April 22, 1993, effective December 1, 1993; April 27, 1995, effective December 1, 1995.]

## RULE 53.  MASTERS

### (a) Appointment.

(1) Unless a statute provides otherwise, a court may appoint a master only to:

(A) perform duties consented to by the parties;

(B) hold trial proceedings and make or recommend findings of fact on issues to be decided by the court without a jury if appointment is warranted by

(i) some exceptional condition, or

(ii) the need to perform an accounting or resolve a difficult computation of damages; or

(C) address pretrial and post-trial matters that cannot be addressed effectively and timely by an available district judge or magistrate judge of the district.

(2) A master must not have a relationship to the parties, counsel, action, or court that would require disqualification of a judge under 28 U.S.C. § 455 unless the parties consent with the court's approval to appointment of a particular person after disclosure of any potential grounds for disqualification.

(3) In appointing a master, the court must consider the fairness of imposing the likely expenses on the parties and must protect against unreasonable expense or delay.

### (b) Order Appointing Master.

(1) *Notice.* The court must give the parties notice and an opportunity to be heard before appointing a master. A party may suggest candidates for appointment.

(2) *Contents.* The order appointing a master must direct the master to proceed with all reasonable diligence and must state:

(A) the master's duties, including any investigation or enforcement duties, and any limits on the master's authority under Rule 53(c);

(B) the circumstances—if any—in which the master may communicate ex parte with the court or a party;

(C) the nature of the materials to be preserved and filed as the record of the master's activities;

(D) the time limits, method of filing the record, other procedures, and standards for reviewing the master's orders, findings, and recommendations; and

(E) the basis, terms, and procedure for fixing the master's compensation under Rule 53(h).

(3) *Entry of Order.* The court may enter the order appointing a master only after the master has filed an affidavit disclosing whether there is any ground for disqualification under 28 U.S.C. § 455 and, if a ground for disqualification is disclosed, after the parties have consented with the court's approval to waive the disqualification.

(4) *Amendment.* The order appointing a master may be amended at any time after notice to the parties, and an opportunity to be heard.

### (c) Master's Authority. 
Unless the appointing order expressly directs otherwise, a master has authority to regulate all proceedings and take all appropriate measures to perform fairly and efficiently the assigned duties. The master may by order impose upon a party any non-contempt sanction provided by Rule 37 or 45, and may recommend a contempt sanction against a party and sanctions against a nonparty.

### (d) Evidentiary Hearings. 
Unless the appointing order expressly directs otherwise, a master conducting an evidentiary hearing may exercise the power of the appointing court to compel, take, and record evidence.

### (e) Master's Orders. 
A master who makes an order must file the order and promptly serve a copy on each party. The clerk must enter the order on the docket.

### (f) Master's Reports. 
A master must report to the court as required by the order of appointment. The master must file the report and promptly serve a copy of the report on each party unless the court directs otherwise.

### (g) Action on Master's Order, Report, or Recommendations.

(1) *Action.* In acting on a master's order, report, or recommendations, the court must afford an opportunity to be heard and may receive evidence, and may: adopt or affirm; modify; wholly or partly reject or reverse; or resubmit to the master with instructions.

(2) *Time To Object or Move.* A party may file objections to—or a motion to adopt or modify—the master's order, report, or recommendations no later than 20 days from the time the master's order, report,

or recommendations are served, unless the court sets a different time.

(3) *Fact Findings*. The court must decide de novo all objections to findings of fact made or recommended by a master unless the parties stipulate with the court's consent that:

(A) the master's findings will be reviewed for clear error, or

(B) the findings of a master appointed under Rule 53(a)(1)(A) or (C) will be final.

(4) *Legal Conclusions*. The court must decide de novo all objections to conclusions of law made or recommended by a master.

(5) *Procedural Matters*. Unless the order of appointment establishes a different standard of review, the court may set aside a master's ruling on a procedural matter only for an abuse of discretion.

**(h) Compensation.**

(1) *Fixing Compensation*. The court must fix the master's compensation before or after judgment on the basis and terms stated in the order of appoint-

ment, but the court may set a new basis and terms after notice and an opportunity to be heard.

(2) *Payment*. The compensation fixed under Rule 53(h)(1) must be paid either:

(A) by a party or parties; or

(B) from a fund or subject matter of the action within the court's control.

(3) *Allocation*. The court must allocate payment of the master's compensation among the parties after considering the nature and amount of the controversy, the means of the parties, and the extent to which any party is more responsible than other parties for the reference to a master. An interim allocation may be amended to reflect a decision on the merits.

**(i) Appointment of Magistrate Judge.** A magistrate judge is subject to this rule only when the order referring a matter to the magistrate judge expressly provides that the reference is made under this rule.

[Amended February 28, 1966, effective July 1, 1966; April 28, 1983, effective August 1, 1983; March 2, 1987, effective August 1, 1987; April 30, 1991, effective December 1, 1991; April 22, 1993, effective December 1, 1993; March 27, 2003, effective December 1, 2003.]

# VII. JUDGMENT

### RULE 54. JUDGMENTS; COSTS

**(a) Definition; Form.** "Judgment" as used in these rules includes a decree and any order from which an appeal lies. A judgment shall not contain a recital of pleadings, the report of a master, or the record of prior proceedings.

**(b) Judgment Upon Multiple Claims or Involving Multiple Parties.** When more than one claim for relief is presented in an action, whether as a claim, counterclaim, cross-claim, or third-party claim, or when multiple parties are involved, the court may direct the entry of a final judgment as to one or more but fewer than all of the claims or parties only upon an express determination that there is no just reason for delay and upon an express direction for the entry of judgment. In the absence of such determination and direction, any order or other form of decision, however designated, which adjudicates fewer than all the claims or the rights and liabilities of fewer than all the parties shall not terminate the action as to any of the claims or parties, and the order or other form of decision is subject to revision at any time before the entry of judgment adjudicating all the claims and the rights and liabilities of all the parties.

**(c) Demand for Judgment.** A judgment by default shall not be different in kind from or exceed in amount that prayed for in the demand for judgment. Except as to a party against whom a judgment is entered by default, every final judgment shall grant

the relief to which the party in whose favor it is rendered is entitled, even if the party has not demanded such relief in the party's pleadings.

**(d) Costs; Attorneys' Fees.**

(1) *Costs Other Than Attorneys' Fees*. Except when express provision therefor is made either in a statute of the United States or in these rules, costs other than attorneys' fees shall be allowed as of course to the prevailing party unless the court otherwise directs; but costs against the United States, its officers, and agencies shall be imposed only to the extent permitted by law. Such costs may be taxed by the clerk on one day's notice. On motion served within 5 days thereafter, the action of the clerk may be reviewed by the court.

(2) *Attorneys' Fees*.

(A) Claims for attorneys' fees and related nontaxable expenses shall be made by motion unless the substantive law governing the action provides for the recovery of such fees as an element of damages to be proved at trial.

(B) Unless otherwise provided by statute or order of the court, the motion must be filed no later than 14 days after entry of judgment; must specify the judgment and the statute, rule, or other grounds entitling the moving party to the award; and must state the amount or provide a fair estimate of the amount sought. If directed by the court,

the motion shall also disclose the terms of any agreement with respect to fees to be paid for the services for which claim is made.

(C) On request of a party or class member, the court shall afford an opportunity for adversary submissions with respect to the motion in accordance with Rule 43(e) or Rule 78. The court may determine issues of liability for fees before receiving submissions bearing on issues of evaluation of services for which liability is imposed by the court. The court shall find the facts and state its conclusions of law as provided in Rule 52(a).

(D) By local rule the court may establish special procedures by which issues relating to such fees may be resolved without extensive evidentiary hearings. In addition, the court may refer issues relating to the value of services to a special master under Rule 53 without regard to the provisions of Rule 53(a)(1) and may refer a motion for attorneys' fees to a magistrate judge under Rule 72(b) as if it were a dispositive pretrial matter.

(E) The provisions of subparagraphs (A) through (D) do not apply to claims for fees and expenses as sanctions for violations of these rules or under 28 U.S.C. § 1927.

[Amended December 27, 1946, effective March 19, 1948; April 17, 1961, effective July 19, 1961; March 2, 1987, effective August 1, 1987; April 22, 1993, effective December 1, 1993; April 29, 2002, effective December 1, 2002; March 27, 2003, effective December 1, 2003.]

## RULE 55.  DEFAULT

(a) Entry.  When a party against whom a judgment for affirmative relief is sought has failed to plead or otherwise defend as provided by these rules and that fact is made to appear by affidavit or otherwise, the clerk shall enter the party's default.

(b) Judgment.  Judgment by default may be entered as follows:

(1) *By the Clerk.*  When the plaintiff's claim against a defendant is for a sum certain or for a sum which can by computation be made certain, the clerk upon request of the plaintiff and upon affidavit of the amount due shall enter judgment for that amount and costs against the defendant, if the defendant has been defaulted for failure to appear and is not an infant or incompetent person.

(2) *By the Court.*  In all other cases the party entitled to a judgment by default shall apply to the court therefor; but no judgment by default shall be entered against an infant or incompetent person unless represented in the action by a general guardian, committee, conservator, or other such representative who has appeared therein.  If the party against whom judgment by default is sought has appeared in the action, the party (or, if appearing by representative,

the party's representative) shall be served with written notice of the application for judgment at least 3 days prior to the hearing on such application.  If, in order to enable the court to enter judgment or to carry it into effect, it is necessary to take an account or to determine the amount of damages or to establish the truth of any averment by evidence or to make an investigation of any other matter, the court may conduct such hearings or order such references as it deems necessary and proper and shall accord a right of trial by jury to the parties when and as required by any statute of the United States.

(c) Setting Aside Default.  For good cause shown the court may set aside an entry of default and, if a judgment by default has been entered, may likewise set it aside in accordance with Rule 60(b).

(d) Plaintiffs, Counterclaimants, Cross-Claimants.  The provisions of this rule apply whether the party entitled to the judgment by default is a plaintiff, a third-party plaintiff, or a party who has pleaded a cross-claim or counterclaim.  In all cases a judgment by default is subject to the limitations of Rule 54(c).

(e) Judgment Against the United States.  No judgment by default shall be entered against the United States or an officer or agency thereof unless the claimant establishes a claim or right to relief by evidence satisfactory to the court.

[Amended March 2, 1987, effective August 1, 1987.]

## RULE 56.  SUMMARY JUDGMENT

(a) For Claimant.  A party seeking to recover upon a claim, counterclaim, or cross-claim or to obtain a declaratory judgment may, at any time after the expiration of 20 days from the commencement of the action or after service of a motion for summary judgment by the adverse party, move with or without supporting affidavits for a summary judgment in the party's favor upon all or any part thereof.

(b) For Defending Party.  A party against whom a claim, counterclaim, or cross-claim is asserted or a declaratory judgment is sought may, at any time, move with or without supporting affidavits for a summary judgment in the party's favor as to all or any part thereof.

(c) Motion and Proceedings Thereon.  The motion shall be served at least 10 days before the time fixed for the hearing.  The adverse party prior to the day of hearing may serve opposing affidavits.  The judgment sought shall be rendered forthwith if the pleadings, depositions, answers to interrogatories, and admissions on file, together with the affidavits, if any, show that there is no genuine issue as to any material fact and that the moving party is entitled to a judgment as a matter of law.  A summary judgment, interlocutory in character, may be rendered on the

issue of liability alone although there is a genuine issue as to the amount of damages.

**(d) Case Not Fully Adjudicated on Motion.** If on motion under this rule judgment is not rendered upon the whole case or for all the relief asked and a trial is necessary, the court at the hearing of the motion, by examining the pleadings and the evidence before it and by interrogating counsel, shall if practicable ascertain what material facts exist without substantial controversy and what material facts are actually and in good faith controverted. It shall thereupon make an order specifying the facts that appear without substantial controversy, including the extent to which the amount of damages or other relief is not in controversy, and directing such further proceedings in the action as are just. Upon the trial of the action the facts so specified shall be deemed established, and the trial shall be conducted accordingly.

**(e) Form of Affidavits; Further Testimony; Defense Required.** Supporting and opposing affidavits shall be made on personal knowledge, shall set forth such facts as would be admissible in evidence, and shall show affirmatively that the affiant is competent to testify to the matters stated therein. Sworn or certified copies of all papers or parts thereof referred to in an affidavit shall be attached thereto or served therewith. The court may permit affidavits to be supplemented or opposed by depositions, answers to interrogatories, or further affidavits. When a motion for summary judgment is made and supported as provided in this rule, an adverse party may not rest upon the mere allegations or denials of the adverse party's pleading, but the adverse party's response, by affidavits or as otherwise provided in this rule, must set forth specific facts showing that there is a genuine issue for trial. If the adverse party does not so respond, summary judgment, if appropriate, shall be entered against the adverse party.

**(f) When Affidavits Are Unavailable.** Should it appear from the affidavits of a party opposing the motion that the party cannot for reasons stated present by affidavit facts essential to justify the party's opposition, the court may refuse the application for judgment or may order a continuance to permit affidavits to be obtained or depositions to be taken or discovery to be had or may make such other order as is just.

**(g) Affidavits Made in Bad Faith.** Should it appear to the satisfaction of the court at any time that any of the affidavits presented pursuant to this rule are presented in bad faith or solely for the purpose of delay, the court shall forthwith order the party employing them to pay to the other party the amount of the reasonable expenses which the filing of the affidavits caused the other party to incur, including reasonable attorney's fees, and any offending party or attorney may be adjudged guilty of contempt.

[Amended December 27, 1946, effective March 19, 1948; January 21, 1963, effective July 1, 1963; March 2, 1987, effective August 1, 1987.]

## RULE 57.   DECLARATORY JUDGMENTS

The procedure for obtaining a declaratory judgment pursuant to Title 28, U.S.C., § 2201, shall be in accordance with these rules, and the right to trial by jury may be demanded under the circumstances and in the manner provided in Rules 38 and 39. The existence of another adequate remedy does not preclude a judgment for declaratory relief in cases where it is appropriate. The court may order a speedy hearing of an action for a declaratory judgment and may advance it on the calendar.

[Amended December 29, 1948, effective October 20, 1949.]

## RULE 58.   ENTRY OF JUDGMENT

**(a) Separate Document.**

(1) Every judgment and amended judgment must be set forth on a separate document, but a separate document is not required for an order disposing of a motion:

    (A) for judgment under Rule 50(b);

    (B) to amend or make additional findings of fact under Rule 52(b);

    (C) for attorney fees under Rule 54;

    (D) for a new trial, or to alter or amend the judgment, under Rule 59; or

    (E) for relief under Rule 60.

(2) Subject to Rule 54(b):

    (A) unless the court orders otherwise, the clerk must, without awaiting the court's direction, promptly prepare, sign, and enter the judgment when:

        (i) the jury returns a general verdict,

        (ii) the court awards only costs or a sum certain, or

        (iii) the court denies all relief;

    (B) the court must promptly approve the form of the judgment, which the clerk must promptly enter, when:

        (i) the jury returns a special verdict or a general verdict accompanied by interrogatories, or

        (ii) the court grants other relief not described in Rule 58(a)(2).

**(b) Time of Entry.** Judgment is entered for purposes of these rules:

(1) if Rule 58(a)(1) does not require a separate document, when it is entered in the civil docket under Rule 79(a), and

(2) if Rule 58(a)(1) requires a separate document, when it is entered in the civil docket under Rule 79(a) and when the earlier of these events occurs:

(A) when it is set forth on a separate document, or

(B) when 150 days have run from entry in the civil docket under Rule 79(a).

**(c) Cost or Fee Awards.**

(1) Entry of judgment may not be delayed, nor the time for appeal extended, in order to tax costs or award fees, except as provided in Rule 58(c)(2).

(2) When a timely motion for attorney fees is made under Rule 54(d)(2), the court may act before a notice of appeal has been filed and has become effective to order that the motion have the same effect under Federal Rule of Appellate Procedure 4(a)(4) as a timely motion under Rule 59.

**(d) Request for Entry.** A party may request that judgment be set forth on a separate document as required by Rule 58(a)(1).

[Amended December 27, 1946, effective March 19, 1948; January 21, 1963, effective July 1, 1963; April 22, 1993, effective December 1, 1993; April 29, 2002, effective December 1, 2002.]

# RULE 59. NEW TRIALS; AMENDMENT OF JUDGMENTS

**(a) Grounds.** A new trial may be granted to all or any of the parties and on all or part of the issues (1) in an action in which there has been a trial by jury, for any of the reasons for which new trials have heretofore been granted in actions at law in the courts of the United States; and (2) in an action tried without a jury, for any of the reasons for which rehearings have heretofore been granted in suits in equity in the courts of the United States. On a motion for a new trial in an action tried without a jury, the court may open the judgment if one has been entered, take additional testimony, amend findings of fact and conclusions of law or make new findings and conclusions, and direct the entry of a new judgment.

**(b) Time for Motion.** Any motion for a new trial shall be filed no later than 10 days after entry of the judgment.

**(c) Time for Serving Affidavits.** When a motion for new trial is based on affidavits, they shall be filed with the motion. The opposing party has 10 days after service to file opposing affidavits, but that period may be extended for up to 20 days, either by the court for good cause or by the parties' written stipulation. The court may permit reply affidavits.

**(d) On Court's Initiative; Notice; Specifying Grounds.** No later than 10 days after entry of judgment the court, on its own, may order a new trial for any reason that would justify granting one on a party's motion. After giving the parties notice and an opportunity to be heard, the court may grant a timely motion for a new trial for a reason not stated in the motion. When granting a new trial on its own initiative or for a reason not stated in a motion, the court shall specify the grounds in its order.

**(e) Motion to Alter or Amend Judgment.** Any motion to alter or amend a judgment shall be filed no later than 10 days after entry of the judgment.

[Amended December 27, 1946, effective March 19, 1948; February 28, 1966, effective July 1, 1966; April 27, 1995, effective December 1, 1995.]

# RULE 60. RELIEF FROM JUDGMENT OR ORDER

**(a) Clerical Mistakes.** Clerical mistakes in judgments, orders or other parts of the record and errors therein arising from oversight or omission may be corrected by the court at any time of its own initiative or on the motion of any party and after such notice, if any, as the court orders. During the pendency of an appeal, such mistakes may be so corrected before the appeal is docketed in the appellate court, and thereafter while the appeal is pending may be so corrected with leave of the appellate court.

**(b) Mistakes; Inadvertence; Excusable Neglect; Newly Discovered Evidence; Fraud, etc.** On motion and upon such terms as are just, the court may relieve a party or a party's legal representative from a final judgment, order, or proceeding for the following reasons: (1) mistake, inadvertence, surprise, or excusable neglect; (2) newly discovered evidence which by due diligence could not have been discovered in time to move for a new trial under Rule 59(b); (3) fraud (whether heretofore denominated intrinsic or extrinsic), misrepresentation, or other misconduct of an adverse party; (4) the judgment is void; (5) the judgment has been satisfied, released, or discharged, or a prior judgment upon which it is based has been reversed or otherwise vacated, or it is no longer equitable that the judgment should have prospective application; or (6) any other reason justifying relief from the operation of the judgment. The motion shall be made within a reasonable time, and for reasons (1), (2), and (3) not more than one year after the judgment, order, or proceeding was entered or taken. A motion under this subdivision (b) does not affect the finality of a judgment or suspend its operation. This rule does not limit the power of a court to entertain an independent action to relieve a party from a judg-

ment, order, or proceeding, or to grant relief to a defendant not actually personally notified as provided in Title 28, U.S.C., § 1655, or to set aside a judgment for fraud upon the court. Writs of coram nobis, coram vobis, audita querela, and bills of review and bills in the nature of a bill of review, are abolished, and the procedure for obtaining any relief from a judgment shall be by motion as prescribed in these rules or by an independent action.

[Amended December 27, 1946, effective March 19, 1948; December 29, 1948, effective October 20, 1949; March 2, 1987, effective August 1, 1987.]

## RULE 61. HARMLESS ERROR

No error in either the admission or the exclusion of evidence and no error or defect in any ruling or order or in anything done or omitted by the court or by any of the parties is ground for granting a new trial or for setting aside a verdict or for vacating, modifying, or otherwise disturbing a judgment or order, unless refusal to take such action appears to the court inconsistent with substantial justice. The court at every stage of the proceeding must disregard any error or defect in the proceeding which does not affect the substantial rights of the parties.

## RULE 62. STAY OF PROCEEDINGS TO ENFORCE A JUDGMENT

**(a) Automatic Stay; Exceptions—Injunctions, Receiverships, and Patent Accountings.** Except as stated herein, no execution shall issue upon a judgment nor shall proceedings be taken for its enforcement until the expiration of 10 days after its entry. Unless otherwise ordered by the court, an interlocutory or final judgment in an action for an injunction or in a receivership action, or a judgment or order directing an accounting in an action for infringement of letters patent, shall not be stayed during the period after its entry and until an appeal is taken or during the pendency of an appeal. The provisions of subdivision (c) of this rule govern the suspending, modifying, restoring, or granting of an injunction during the pendency of an appeal.

**(b) Stay on Motion for New Trial or for Judgment.** In its discretion and on such conditions for the security of the adverse party as are proper, the court may stay the execution of or any proceedings to enforce a judgment pending the disposition of a motion for a new trial or to alter or amend a judgment made pursuant to Rule 59, or of a motion for relief from a judgment or order made pursuant to Rule 60, or of a motion for judgment in accordance with a motion for a directed verdict made pursuant to Rule 50, or of a motion for amendment to the findings or for additional findings made pursuant to Rule 52(b).

**(c) Injunction Pending Appeal.** When an appeal is taken from an interlocutory or final judgment granting, dissolving, or denying an injunction, the court in its discretion may suspend, modify, restore, or grant an injunction during the pendency of the appeal upon such terms as to bond or otherwise as it considers proper for the security of the rights of the adverse party. If the judgment appealed from is rendered by a district court of three judges specially constituted pursuant to a statute of the United States, no such order shall be made except (1) by such court sitting in open court or (2) by the assent of all the judges of such court evidenced by their signatures to the order.

**(d) Stay Upon Appeal.** When an appeal is taken the appellant by giving a supersedeas bond may obtain a stay subject to the exceptions contained in subdivision (a) of this rule. The bond may be given at or after the time of filing the notice of appeal or of procuring the order allowing the appeal, as the case may be. The stay is effective when the supersedeas bond is approved by the court.

**(e) Stay in Favor of the United States or Agency Thereof.** When an appeal is taken by the United States or an officer or agency thereof or by direction of any department of the Government of the United States and the operation or enforcement of the judgment is stayed, no bond, obligation, or other security shall be required from the appellant.

**(f) Stay According to State Law.** In any state in which a judgment is a lien upon the property of the judgment debtor and in which the judgment debtor is entitled to a stay of execution, a judgment debtor is entitled, in the district court held therein, to such stay as would be accorded the judgment debtor had the action been maintained in the courts of that state.

**(g) Power of Appellate Court Not Limited.** The provisions in this rule do not limit any power of an appellate court or of a judge or justice thereof to stay proceedings during the pendency of an appeal or to suspend, modify, restore, or grant an injunction during the pendency of an appeal or to make any order appropriate to preserve the status quo or the effectiveness of the judgment subsequently to be entered.

**(h) Stay of Judgment as to Multiple Claims or Multiple Parties.** When a court has ordered a final judgment under the conditions stated in Rule 54(b), the court may stay enforcement of that judgment until the entering of a subsequent judgment or judgments and may prescribe such conditions as are necessary to secure the benefit thereof to the party in whose favor the judgment is entered.

[Amended December 27, 1946, effective March 19, 1948; December 29, 1948, effective October 20, 1949; April 17, 1961, effective July 19, 1961; March 2, 1987, effective August 1, 1987.]

## RULE 63.  INABILITY OF A JUDGE TO PROCEED

If a trial or hearing has been commenced and the judge is unable to proceed, any other judge may proceed with it upon certifying familiarity with the record and determining that the proceedings in the case may be completed without prejudice to the par-ties.  In a hearing or trial without a jury, the successor judge shall at the request of a party recall any witness whose testimony is material and disputed and who is available to testify again without undue burden.  The successor judge may also recall any other witness.

[Amended March 2, 1987, effective August 1, 1987; April 30, 1991, effective December 1, 1991.]

# VIII.   PROVISIONAL AND FINAL REMEDIES

## RULE 64.  SEIZURE OF PERSON OR PROPERTY

At the commencement of and during the course of an action, all remedies providing for seizure of person or property for the purpose of securing satisfaction of the judgment ultimately to be entered in the action are available under the circumstances and in the manner provided by the law of the state in which the district court is held, existing at the time the remedy is sought, subject to the following qualifications: (1) any existing statute of the United States governs to the extent to which it is applicable; (2) the action in which any of the foregoing remedies is used shall be commenced and prosecuted or, if removed from a state court, shall be prosecuted after removal, pursuant to these rules.  The remedies thus available include arrest, attachment, garnishment, replevin, sequestration, and other corresponding or equivalent remedies, however designated and regardless of whether by state procedure the remedy is ancillary to an action or must be obtained by an independent action.

## RULE 65.  INJUNCTIONS

**(a) Preliminary Injunction.**

(1) *Notice.*  No preliminary injunction shall be issued without notice to the adverse party.

(2) *Consolidation of Hearing With Trial on Merits.*  Before or after the commencement of the hearing of an application for a preliminary injunction, the court may order the trial of the action on the merits to be advanced and consolidated with the hearing of the application.  Even when this consolidation is not ordered, any evidence received upon an application for a preliminary injunction which would be admissible upon the trial on the merits becomes part of the record on the trial and need not be repeated upon the trial.  This subdivision (a)(2) shall be so construed and applied as to save to the parties any rights they may have to trial by jury.

**(b) Temporary Restraining Order; Notice; Hearing; Duration.**  A temporary restraining order may be granted without written or oral notice to the adverse party or that party's attorney only if (1) it clearly appears from specific facts shown by affidavit or by the verified complaint that immediate and irreparable injury, loss, or damage will result to the applicant before the adverse party or that party's attorney can be heard in opposition, and (2) the applicant's attorney certifies to the court in writing the efforts, if any, which have been made to give the notice and the reasons supporting the claim that notice should not be required.  Every temporary restraining order granted without notice shall be indorsed with the date and hour of issuance; shall be filed forthwith in the clerk's office and entered of record; shall define the injury and state why it is irreparable and why the order was granted without notice; and shall expire by its terms within such time after entry, not to exceed 10 days, as the court fixes, unless within the time so fixed the order, for good cause shown, is extended for a like period or unless the party against whom the order is directed consents that it may be extended for a longer period.  The reasons for the extension shall be entered of record.  In case a temporary restraining order is granted without notice, the motion for a preliminary injunction shall be set down for hearing at the earliest possible time and takes precedence of all matters except older matters of the same character; and when the motion comes on for hearing the party who obtained the temporary restraining order shall proceed with the application for a preliminary injunction and, if the party does not do so, the court shall dissolve the temporary restraining order.  On 2 days' notice to the party who obtained the temporary restraining order without notice or on such shorter notice to that party as the court may prescribe, the adverse party may appear and move its dissolution or modification and in that event the court shall proceed to hear and determine such motion as expeditiously as the ends of justice require.

**(c) Security.**  No restraining order or preliminary injunction shall issue except upon the giving of security by the applicant, in such sum as the court deems proper, for the payment of such costs and damages as may be incurred or suffered by any party who is found to have been wrongfully enjoined or restrained.  No such security shall be required of the United States or of an officer or agency thereof.

The provisions of Rule 65.1 apply to a surety upon a bond or undertaking under this rule.

**(d) Form and Scope of Injunction or Restraining Order.** Every order granting an injunction and every restraining order shall set forth the reasons for its issuance; shall be specific in terms; shall describe in reasonable detail, and not by reference to the complaint or other document, the act or acts sought to be restrained; and is binding only upon the parties to the action, their officers, agents, servants, employees, and attorneys, and upon those persons in active concert or participation with them who receive actual notice of the order by personal service or otherwise.

**(e) Employer and Employee; Interpleader; Constitutional Cases.** These rules do not modify any statute of the United States relating to temporary restraining orders and preliminary injunctions in actions affecting employer and employee; or the provisions of Title 28, U.S.C., § 2361, relating to preliminary injunctions in actions of interpleader or in the nature of interpleader; or Title 28, U.S.C., § 2284, relating to actions required by Act of Congress to be heard and determined by a district court of three judges.

**(f) Copyright Impoundment.** This rule applies to copyright impoundment proceedings.

[Amended December 27, 1946, effective March 19, 1948; December 29, 1948, effective October 20, 1949; February 28, 1966, effective July 1, 1966; March 2, 1987, effective August 1, 1987; April 23, 2001, effective December 1, 2001.]

## RULE 65.1  SECURITY: PROCEEDINGS AGAINST SURETIES

Whenever these rules, including the Supplemental Rules for Admiralty or Maritime Claims and Asset Forfeiture Actions, require or permit the giving of security by a party, and security is given in the form of a bond or stipulation or other undertaking with one or more sureties, each surety submits to the jurisdiction of the court and irrevocably appoints the clerk of the court as the surety's agent upon whom any papers affecting the surety's liability on the bond or undertaking may be served. The surety's liability may be enforced on motion without the necessity of an independent action. The motion and such notice of the motion as the court prescribes may be served on the clerk of the court, who shall forthwith mail copies to the sureties if their addresses are known.

[Adopted February 28, 1966, effective July 1, 1966; amended March 2, 1987, effective August 1, 1987; April 12, 2006, effective December 1, 2006.]

## RULE 66.  RECEIVERS APPOINTED BY FEDERAL COURTS

An action wherein a receiver has been appointed shall not be dismissed except by order of the court.

The practice in the administration of estates by receivers or by other similar officers appointed by the court shall be in accordance with the practice heretofore followed in the courts of the United States or as provided in rules promulgated by the district courts. In all other respects the action in which the appointment of a receiver is sought or which is brought by or against a receiver is governed by these rules.

[Amended December 27, 1946, effective March 19, 1948; December 29, 1948, effective October 20, 1949.]

## RULE 67.  DEPOSIT IN COURT

In an action in which any part of the relief sought is a judgment for a sum of money or the disposition of a sum of money or the disposition of any other thing capable of delivery, a party, upon notice to every other party, and by leave of court, may deposit with the court all or any part of such sum or thing, whether or not that party claims all or any part of the sum or thing. The party making the deposit shall serve the order permitting deposit on the clerk of the court. Money paid into court under this rule shall be deposited and withdrawn in accordance with the provisions of Title 28, U.S.C., §§ 2041, and 2042; the Act of June 26, 1934, c. 756, § 23, as amended (48 Stat. 1236, 58 Stat. 845), U.S.C., Title 31, § 725v;* or any like statute. The fund shall be deposited in an interest-bearing account or invested in an interest-bearing instrument approved by the court.

  \* Law Revision Counsel Note: Repealed and reenacted as 28 U.S.C. §§ 572a and 2043 by Pub.L. 97–258, §§ 2(g)(3)(B), (4)(E), 5(b), September 13, 1982, 96 Stat. 1061, 1068.

[Amended December 29, 1948, effective October 20, 1949; April 28, 1983, effective August 1, 1983.]

## RULE 68.  OFFER OF JUDGMENT

At any time more than 10 days before the trial begins, a party defending against a claim may serve upon the adverse party an offer to allow judgment to be taken against the defending party for the money or property or to the effect specified in the offer, with costs then accrued. If within 10 days after the service of the offer the adverse party serves written notice that the offer is accepted, either party may then file the offer and notice of acceptance together with proof of service thereof and thereupon the clerk shall enter judgment. An offer not accepted shall be deemed withdrawn and evidence thereof is not admissible except in a proceeding to determine costs. If the judgment finally obtained by the offeree is not more favorable than the offer, the offeree must pay the costs incurred after the making of the offer. The fact that an offer is made but not accepted does not preclude a subsequent offer. When the liability of one party to another has been determined by verdict or order or judgment, but the amount or extent of the

liability remains to be determined by further proceedings, the party adjudged liable may make an offer of judgment, which shall have the same effect as an offer made before trial if it is served within a reasonable time not less than 10 days prior to the commencement of hearings to determine the amount or extent of liability.

[Amended December 27, 1946, effective March 19, 1948; February 28, 1966, effective July 1, 1966; March 2, 1987, effective August 1, 1987.]

## RULE 69.  EXECUTION

(a) **In General.**  Process to enforce a judgment for the payment of money shall be a writ of execution, unless the court directs otherwise.  The procedure on execution, in proceedings supplementary to and in aid of a judgment, and in proceedings on and in aid of execution shall be in accordance with the practice and procedure of the state in which the district court is held, existing at the time the remedy is sought, except that any statute of the United States governs to the extent that it is applicable.  In aid of the judgment or execution, the judgment creditor or a successor in interest when that interest appears of record, may obtain discovery from any person, including the judgment debtor, in the manner provided in these rules or in the manner provided by the practice of the state in which the district court is held.

(b) **Against Certain Public Officers.**  When a judgment has been entered against a collector or other officer of revenue under the circumstances stated in Title 28, U.S.C., § 2006, or against an officer of Congress in an action mentioned in the Act of March 3, 1875, ch. 130, § 8 (18 Stat. 401), U.S.C., Title 2, § 118, and when the court has given the certificate of probable cause for the officer's act as provided in those statutes, execution shall not issue against the officer or the officer's property but the final judgment shall be satisfied as provided in such statutes.

[Amended December 29, 1948, effective October 20, 1949; March 30, 1970, effective July 1, 1970; March 2, 1987 effective August 1, 1987.]

## RULE 70.  JUDGMENT FOR SPECIFIC ACTS; VESTING TITLE

If a judgment directs a party to execute a conveyance of land or to deliver deeds or other documents or to perform any other specific act and the party fails to comply within the time specified, the court may direct the act to be done at the cost of the disobedient party by some other person appointed by the court and the act when so done has like effect as if done by the party.  On application of the party entitled to performance, the clerk shall issue a writ of attachment or sequestration against the property of the disobedient party to compel obedience to the judgment.  The court may also in proper cases adjudge the party in contempt.  If real or personal property is within the district, the court in lieu of directing a conveyance thereof may enter a judgment divesting the title of any party and vesting it in others and such judgment has the effect of a conveyance executed in due form of law.  When any order or judgment is for the delivery of possession, the party in whose favor it is entered is entitled to a writ of execution or assistance upon application to the clerk.

## RULE 71.  PROCESS IN BEHALF OF AND AGAINST PERSONS NOT PARTIES

When an order is made in favor of a person who is not a party to the action, that person may enforce obedience to the order by the same process as if a party; and, when obedience to an order may be lawfully enforced against a person who is not a party, that person is liable to the same process for enforcing obedience to the order as if a party.

[Amended March 2, 1987, effective August 1, 1987.]

# IX.  SPECIAL PROCEEDINGS

## RULE 71A.  CONDEMNATION OF PROPERTY

(a) **Applicability of Other Rules.**  The Rules of Civil Procedure for the United States District Courts govern the procedure for the condemnation of real and personal property under the power of eminent domain, except as otherwise provided in this rule.

(b) **Joinder of Properties.**  The plaintiff may join in the same action one or more separate pieces of property, whether in the same or different ownership and whether or not sought for the same use.

(c) **Complaint.**

(1) *Caption.*  The complaint shall contain a caption as provided in Rule 10(a), except that the plaintiff shall name as defendants the property, designated generally by kind, quantity, and location, and at least one of the owners of some part of or interest in the property.

(2) *Contents.*  The complaint shall contain a short and plain statement of the authority for the taking, the use for which the property is to be taken, a description of the property sufficient for its identification, the interests to be acquired, and as to each separate piece of property a designation of the defendants who have been joined as owners thereof or of

some interest therein. Upon the commencement of the action, the plaintiff need join as defendants only the persons having or claiming an interest in the property whose names are then known, but prior to any hearing involving the compensation to be paid for a piece of property, the plaintiff shall add as defendants all persons having or claiming an interest in that property whose names can be ascertained by a reasonably diligent search of the records, considering the character and value of the property involved and the interests to be acquired, and also those whose names have otherwise been learned. All others may be made defendants under the designation "Unknown Owners." Process shall be served as provided in subdivision (d) of this rule upon all defendants, whether named as defendants at the time of the commencement of the action or subsequently added, and a defendant may answer as provided in subdivision (e) of this rule. The court meanwhile may order such distribution of a deposit as the facts warrant.

(3) *Filing.* In addition to filing the complaint with the court, the plaintiff shall furnish to the clerk at least one copy thereof for the use of the defendants and additional copies at the request of the clerk or of a defendant.

**(d) Process.**

(1) *Notice; Delivery.* Upon the filing of the complaint the plaintiff shall forthwith deliver to the clerk joint or several notices directed to the defendants named or designated in the complaint. Additional notices directed to defendants subsequently added shall be so delivered. The delivery of the notice and its service have the same effect as the delivery and service of the summons under Rule 4.

(2) *Same; Form.* Each notice shall state the court, the title of the action, the name of the defendant to whom it is directed, that the action is to condemn property, a description of the defendant's property sufficient for its identification, the interest to be taken, the authority for the taking, the uses for which the property is to be taken, that the defendant may serve upon the plaintiff's attorney an answer within 20 days after service of the notice, and that the failure so to serve an answer constitutes a consent to the taking and to the authority of the court to proceed to hear the action and to fix the compensation. The notice shall conclude with the name of the plaintiff's attorney and an address within the district in which action is brought where the attorney may be served. The notice need contain a description of no other property than that to be taken from the defendants to whom it is directed.

(3) *Service of Notice.*

(A) Personal Service. Personal service of the notice (but without copies of the complaint) shall be made in accordance with Rule 4 upon a defendant whose residence is known and who resides within the United States or a territory subject to the administrative or judicial jurisdiction of the United States.

(B) Service by Publication. Upon the filing of a certificate of the plaintiff's attorney stating that the attorney believes a defendant cannot be personally served, because after diligent inquiry within the state in which the complaint is filed the defendant's place of residence cannot be ascertained by the plaintiff or, if ascertained, that it is beyond the territorial limits of personal service as provided in this rule, service of the notice shall be made on this defendant by publication in a newspaper published in the county where the property is located, or if there is no such newspaper, then in a newspaper having a general circulation where the property is located, once a week for not less than three successive weeks. Prior to the last publication, a copy of the notice shall also be mailed to a defendant who cannot be personally served as provided in this rule but whose place of residence is then known. Unknown owners may be served by publication in like manner by a notice addressed to "Unknown Owners."

Service by publication is complete upon the date of the last publication. Proof of publication and mailing shall be made by certificate of the plaintiff's attorney, to which shall be attached a printed copy of the published notice with the name and dates of the newspaper marked thereon.

(4) *Return; Amendment.* Proof of service of the notice shall be made and amendment of the notice or proof of its service allowed in the manner provided for the return and amendment of the summons under Rule 4.

**(e) Appearance or Answer.** If a defendant has no objection or defense to the taking of the defendant's property, the defendant may serve a notice of appearance designating the property in which the defendant claims to be interested. Thereafter, the defendant shall receive notice of all proceedings affecting it. If a defendant has any objection or defense to the taking of the property, the defendant shall serve an answer within 20 days after the service of notice upon the defendant. The answer shall identify the property in which the defendant claims to have an interest, state the nature and extent of the interest claimed, and state all the defendant's objections and defenses to the taking of the property. A defendant waives all defenses and objections not so presented, but at the trial of the issue of just compensation, whether or not the defendant has previously appeared or answered, the defendant may present evidence as to the amount of the compensation to be paid for the property, and the defendant may share in the distribution of the award.

No other pleading or motion asserting any additional defense or objection shall be allowed.

**(f) Amendment of Pleadings.** Without leave of court, the plaintiff may amend the complaint at any time before the trial of the issue of compensation and as many times as desired, but no amendment shall be made which will result in a dismissal forbidden by subdivision (i) of this rule. The plaintiff need not serve a copy of an amendment, but shall serve notice of the filing, as provided in Rule 5(b), upon any party affected thereby who has appeared and, in the manner provided in subdivision (d) of this rule, upon any party affected thereby who has not appeared. The plaintiff shall furnish to the clerk of the court for the use of the defendants at least one copy of each amendment and shall furnish additional copies on the request of the clerk or of a defendant. Within the time allowed by subdivision (e) of this rule a defendant may serve an answer to the amended pleading, in the form and manner and with the same effect as there provided.

**(g) Substitution of Parties.** If a defendant dies or becomes incompetent or transfers an interest after the defendant's joinder, the court may order substitution of the proper party upon motion and notice of hearing. If the motion and notice of hearing are to be served upon a person not already a party, service shall be made as provided in subdivision (d)(3) of this rule.

**(h) Trial.** If the action involves the exercise of the power of eminent domain under the law of the United States, any tribunal specially constituted by an Act of Congress governing the case for the trial of the issue of just compensation shall be the tribunal for the determination of that issue; but if there is no such specially constituted tribunal any party may have a trial by jury of the issue of just compensation by filing a demand therefor within the time allowed for answer or within such further time as the court may fix, unless the court in its discretion orders that, because of the character, location, or quantity of the property to be condemned, or for other reasons in the interest of justice, the issue of compensation shall be determined by a commission of three persons appointed by it.

In the event that a commission is appointed the court may direct that not more than two additional persons serve as alternate commissioners to hear the case and replace commissioners who, prior to the time when a decision is filed, are found by the court to be unable or disqualified to perform their duties. An alternate who does not replace a regular commissioner shall be discharged after the commission renders its final decision. Before appointing the members of the commission and alternates the court shall advise the parties of the identity and qualifications of each prospective commissioner and alternate and may permit the parties to examine each such designee. The parties shall not be permitted or required by the court to

suggest nominees. Each party shall have the right to object for valid cause to the appointment of any person as a commissioner or alternate. If a commission is appointed it shall have the authority of a master provided in Rule 53(c) and proceedings before it shall be governed by the provisions of Rule 53(d). Its action and report shall be determined by a majority and its findings and report shall have the effect, and be dealt with by the court in accordance with the practice, prescribed in Rule 53(e), (f), and (g). Trial of all issues shall otherwise be by the court.

**(i) Dismissal of Action.**

(1) *As of Right.* If no hearing has begun to determine the compensation to be paid for a piece of property and the plaintiff has not acquired the title or a lesser interest in or taken possession, the plaintiff may dismiss the action as to that property, without an order of the court, by filing a notice of dismissal setting forth a brief description of the property as to which the action is dismissed.

(2) *By Stipulation.* Before the entry of any judgment vesting the plaintiff with title or a lesser interest in or possession of property, the action may be dismissed in whole or in part, without an order of the court, as to any property by filing a stipulation of dismissal by the plaintiff and the defendant affected thereby; and, if the parties so stipulate, the court may vacate any judgment that has been entered.

(3) *By Order of the Court.* At any time before compensation for a piece of property has been determined and paid and after motion and hearing, the court may dismiss the action as to that property, except that it shall not dismiss the action as to any part of the property of which the plaintiff has taken possession or in which the plaintiff has taken title or a lesser interest, but shall award just compensation for the possession, title or lesser interest so taken. The court at any time may drop a defendant unnecessarily or improperly joined.

(4) *Effect.* Except as otherwise provided in the notice, or stipulation of dismissal, or order of the court, any dismissal is without prejudice.

**(j) Deposit and Its Distribution.** The plaintiff shall deposit with the court any money required by law as a condition to the exercise of the power of eminent domain; and, although not so required, may make a deposit when permitted by statute. In such cases the court and attorneys shall expedite the proceedings for the distribution of the money so deposited and for the ascertainment and payment of just compensation. If the compensation finally awarded to any defendant exceeds the amount which has been paid to that defendant on distribution of the deposit, the court shall enter judgment against the plaintiff and in favor of that defendant for the deficiency. If the compensation finally awarded to any defendant is

less than the amount which has been paid to that defendant, the court shall enter judgment against that defendant and in favor of the plaintiff for the overpayment.

**(k) Condemnation Under a State's Power of Eminent Domain.** The practice as herein prescribed governs in actions involving the exercise of the power of eminent domain under the law of a state, provided that if the state law makes provision for trial of any issue by jury, or for trial of the issue of compensation by jury or commission or both, that provision shall be followed.

**(l) Costs.** Costs are not subject to Rule 54(d).

[Adopted April 30, 1951, effective August 1, 1951; amended January 21, 1963, effective July 1, 1963; April 29, 1985, effective August 1, 1985; March 2, 1987, effective August 1, 1987; April 25, 1988, effective August 1, 1988; amended by Pub.L. 100–690, Title VII, § 7050, November 18, 1988, 102 Stat. 4401 (although amendment by Pub.L. 100–690 could not be executed due to prior amendment by Court order which made the same change effective August 1, 1988); amended April 22, 1993, effective December 1, 1993; March 27, 2003, effective December 1, 2003.]

## RULE 72. MAGISTRATE JUDGES; PRETRIAL ORDERS

**(a) Nondispositive Matters.** A magistrate judge to whom a pretrial matter not dispositive of a claim or defense of a party is referred to hear and determine shall promptly conduct such proceedings as are required and when appropriate enter into the record a written order setting forth the disposition of the matter. Within 10 days after being served with a copy of the magistrate judge's order, a party may serve and file objections to the order; a party may not thereafter assign as error a defect in the magistrate judge's order to which objection was not timely made. The district judge to whom the case is assigned shall consider such objections and shall modify or set aside any portion of the magistrate judge's order found to be clearly erroneous or contrary to law.

**(b) Dispositive Motions and Prisoner Petitions.** A magistrate judge assigned without consent of the parties to hear a pretrial matter dispositive of a claim or defense of a party or a prisoner petition challenging the conditions of confinement shall promptly conduct such proceedings as are required. A record shall be made of all evidentiary proceedings before the magistrate judge, and a record may be made of such other proceedings as the magistrate judge deems necessary. The magistrate judge shall enter into the record a recommendation for disposition of the matter, including proposed findings of fact when appropriate. The clerk shall forthwith mail copies to all parties.

A party objecting to the recommended disposition of the matter shall promptly arrange for the transcription of the record, or portions of it as all parties may agree upon or the magistrate judge deems sufficient, unless the district judge otherwise directs. Within 10 days after being served with a copy of the recommended disposition, a party may serve and file specific, written objections to the proposed findings and recommendations. A party may respond to another party's objections within 10 days after being served with a copy thereof. The district judge to whom the case is assigned shall make a de novo determination upon the record, or after additional evidence, of any portion of the magistrate judge's disposition to which specific written objection has been made in accordance with this rule. The district judge may accept, reject, or modify the recommended decision, receive further evidence, or recommit the matter to the magistrate judge with instructions.

[Former Rule 72 abrogated December 4, 1967, effective July 1, 1968; new Rule 72 adopted April 28, 1983, effective August 1, 1983; amended April 30, 1991, effective December 1, 1991; April 22, 1993, effective December 1, 1993.]

## RULE 73. MAGISTRATE JUDGES; TRIAL BY CONSENT AND APPEAL OPTIONS

**(a) Powers; Procedure.** When specially designated to exercise such jurisdiction by local rule or order of the district court and when all parties consent thereto, a magistrate judge may exercise the authority provided by Title 28, U.S.C. § 636(c) and may conduct any or all proceedings, including a jury or nonjury trial, in a civil case. A record of the proceedings shall be made in accordance with the requirements of Title 28, U.S.C. § 636(c)(5).

**(b) Consent.** When a magistrate judge has been designated to exercise civil trial jurisdiction, the clerk shall give written notice to the parties of their opportunity to consent to the exercise by a magistrate judge of civil jurisdiction over the case, as authorized by Title 28, U.S.C. § 636(c). If, within the period specified by local rule, the parties agree to a magistrate judge's exercise of such authority, they shall execute and file a joint form of consent or separate forms of consent setting forth such election.

A district judge, magistrate judge, or other court official may again advise the parties of the availability of the magistrate judge, but, in so doing, shall also advise the parties that they are free to withhold consent without adverse substantive consequences. A district judge or magistrate judge shall not be informed of a party's response to the clerk's notification, unless all parties have consented to the referral of the matter to a magistrate judge.

The district judge, for good cause shown on the judge's own initiative, or under extraordinary circumstances shown by a party, may vacate a reference of a

civil matter to a magistrate judge under this subdivision.

**(c) Appeal.** In accordance with Title 28, U.S.C. § 636(c)(3), appeal from a judgment entered upon direction of a magistrate judge in proceedings under this rule will lie to the court of appeals as it would from a judgment of the district court.

**(d) Optional Appeal Route [Abrogated].**

[Former Rule 73 abrogated December 4, 1967, effective July 1, 1968; new Rule 73 adopted April 28, 1983, effective August 1, 1983; amended March 2, 1987, effective August 1, 1987; April 22, 1993, effective December 1, 1993; April 11, 1997, effective December 1, 1997.]

## RULE 74. METHOD OF APPEAL FROM MAGISTRATE JUDGE TO DISTRICT JUDGE UNDER TITLE 28, U.S.C. § 636(c)(4) AND RULE 73(d) [ABROGATED]

[Former Rule 74 abrogated December 4, 1967, effective July 1, 1968; new Rule 74 adopted April 28, 1983, effective August

1, 1983; amended April 22, 1993, effective December 1, 1993; abrogated April 11, 1997, effective December 1, 1997.]

## RULE 75. PROCEEDINGS ON APPEAL FROM MAGISTRATE JUDGE TO DISTRICT JUDGE UNDER RULE 73(d) [ABROGATED]

[Former Rule 75 abrogated December 4, 1967, effective July 1, 1968; new Rule 75 adopted April 28, 1983, effective August 1, 1983; amended March 2, 1987, effective August 1, 1987; April 22, 1993, effective December 1, 1993; abrogated April 11, 1997, effective December 1, 1997.]

## RULE 76. JUDGMENT OF THE DISTRICT JUDGE ON THE APPEAL UNDER RULE 73(d) AND COSTS [ABROGATED]

[Former Rule 76 abrogated December 4, 1967, effective July 1, 1968; new Rule 76 adopted April 28, 1983, effective August 1, 1983; amended April 22, 1993, effective December 1, 1993; abrogated April 11, 1997, effective December 1, 1997.]

# X. DISTRICT COURTS AND CLERKS

## RULE 77. DISTRICT COURTS AND CLERKS

**(a) District Courts Always Open.** The district courts shall be deemed always open for the purpose of filing any pleading or other proper paper, of issuing and returning mesne and final process, and of making and directing all interlocutory motions, orders, and rules.

**(b) Trials and Hearings; Orders in Chambers.** All trials upon the merits shall be conducted in open court and so far as convenient in a regular court room. All other acts or proceedings may be done or conducted by a judge in chambers, without the attendance of the clerk or other court officials and at any place either within or without the district; but no hearing, other than one ex parte, shall be conducted outside the district without the consent of all parties affected thereby.

**(c) Clerk's Office and Orders by Clerk.** The clerk's office with the clerk or a deputy in attendance shall be open during business hours on all days except Saturdays, Sundays, and legal holidays, but a district court may provide by local rule or order that its clerk's office shall be open for specified hours on Saturdays or particular legal holidays other than New Year's Day, Birthday of Martin Luther King, Jr., Washington's Birthday, Memorial Day, Independence Day, Labor Day, Columbus Day, Veterans Day, Thanksgiving Day, and Christmas Day. All motions and applications in the clerk's office for issuing mesne

process, for issuing final process to enforce and execute judgments, for entering defaults or judgments by default, and for other proceedings which do not require allowance or order of the court are grantable of course by the clerk; but the clerk's action may be suspended or altered or rescinded by the court upon cause shown.

**(d) Notice of Orders or Judgments.** Immediately upon the entry of an order or judgment the clerk shall serve a notice of the entry in the manner provided for in Rule 5(b) upon each party who is not in default for failure to appear, and shall make a note in the docket of the service. Any party may in addition serve a notice of such entry in the manner provided in Rule 5(b) for the service of papers. Lack of notice of the entry by the clerk does not affect the time to appeal or relieve or authorize the court to relieve a party for failure to appeal within the time allowed, except as permitted in Rule 4(a) of the Federal Rules of Appellate Procedure.

[Amended December 27, 1946, effective March 19, 1948; January 21, 1963, effective July 1, 1963; December 4, 1967, effective July 1, 1968; March 1, 1971, effective July 1, 1971; March 2, 1987, effective August 1, 1987; April 30, 1991, effective December 1, 1991; April 23, 2001, effective December 1, 2001.]

## RULE 78. MOTION DAY

Unless local conditions make it impracticable, each district court shall establish regular times and places, at intervals sufficiently frequent for the prompt dis-

patch of business, at which motions requiring notice and hearing may be heard and disposed of; but the judge at any time or place and on such notice, if any, as the judge considers reasonable may make orders for the advancement, conduct, and hearing of actions.

To expedite its business, the court may make provision by rule or order for the submission and determination of motions without oral hearing upon brief written statements of reasons in support and opposition.

[Amended March 2, 1987, effective August 1, 1987.]

## RULE 79. BOOKS AND RECORDS KEPT BY THE CLERK AND ENTRIES THEREIN

(a) **Civil Docket.** The clerk shall keep a book known as "civil docket" of such form and style as may be prescribed by the Director of the Administrative Office of the United States Courts with the approval of the Judicial Conference of the United States, and shall enter therein each civil action to which these rules are made applicable. Actions shall be assigned consecutive file numbers. The file number of each action shall be noted on the folio of the docket whereon the first entry of the action is made. All papers filed with the clerk, all process issued and returns made thereon, all appearances, orders, verdicts, and judgments shall be entered chronologically in the civil docket on the folio assigned to the action and shall be marked with its file number. These entries shall be brief but shall show the nature of each paper filed or writ issued and the substance of each order or judgment of the court and of the returns showing execution of process. The entry of an order or judgment shall show the date the entry is made. When in an action trial by jury has been properly demanded or ordered the clerk shall enter the word "jury" on the folio assigned to that action.

(b) **Civil Judgments and Orders.** The clerk shall keep, in such form and manner as the Director of the Administrative Office of the United States Courts with the approval of the Judicial Conference of the United States may prescribe, a correct copy of every final judgment or appealable order, or order affecting title to or lien upon real or personal property, and any other order which the court may direct to be kept.

(c) **Indices; Calendars.** Suitable indices of the civil docket and of every civil judgment and order referred to in subdivision (b) of this rule shall be kept by the clerk under the direction of the court. There shall be prepared under the direction of the court calendars of all actions ready for trial, which shall distinguish "jury actions" from "court actions."

(d) **Other Books and Records of the Clerk.** The clerk shall also keep such other books and records as may be required from time to time by the Director of the Administrative Office of the United States Courts with the approval of the Judicial Conference of the United States.

[Amended December 27, 1946, effective March 19, 1948; December 29, 1948, effective October 20, 1949; January 21, 1963, effective July 1, 1963.]

## RULE 80. STENOGRAPHER; STENOGRAPHIC REPORT OR TRANSCRIPT AS EVIDENCE

(a) **Stenographer** [Abrogated].

(b) **Official Stenographer** [Abrogated].

(c) **Stenographic Report or Transcript as Evidence.** Whenever the testimony of a witness at a trial or hearing which was stenographically reported is admissible in evidence at a later trial, it may be proved by the transcript thereof duly certified by the person who reported the testimony.

[Amended December 27, 1946, effective March 19, 1948.]

# XI. GENERAL PROVISIONS

## RULE 81. APPLICABILITY IN GENERAL

(a) **Proceedings to Which the Rules Apply.**

(1) These rules do not apply to prize proceedings in admiralty governed by Title 10, U.S.C., §§ 7651–7681. They do apply to proceedings in bankruptcy to the extent provided by the Federal Rules of Bankruptcy Procedure.

(2) These rules are applicable to proceedings for admission to citizenship, habeas corpus, and quo warranto, to the extent that the practice in such proceedings is not set forth in statutes of the United States, the Rules Governing Section 2254 Cases, or the Rules

Governing Section 2255 Proceedings, and has heretofore conformed to the practice in civil actions.

(3) In proceedings under Title 9, U.S.C., relating to arbitration, or under the Act of May 20, 1926, ch. 347, § 9 (44 Stat. 585), U.S.C., Title 45, § 159, relating to boards of arbitration of railway labor disputes, these rules apply only to the extent that matters of procedure are not provided for in those statutes. These rules apply to proceedings to compel the giving of testimony or production of documents in accordance with a subpoena issued by an officer or agency of the United States under any statute of the United States except as otherwise provided by statute or by rules of

the district court or by order of the court in the proceedings.

(4) These rules do not alter the method prescribed by the Act of February 18, 1922, c. 57, § 2 (42 Stat. 388), U.S.C., Title 7, § 292; or by the Act of June 10, 1930, c. 436, § 7 (46 Stat. 534), as amended, U.S.C., Title 7, § 499g(c), for instituting proceedings in the United States district courts to review orders of the Secretary of Agriculture; or prescribed by the Act of June 25, 1934, c. 742, § 2 (48 Stat. 1214), U.S.C., Title 15, § 522, for instituting proceedings to review orders of the Secretary of the Interior; or prescribed by the Act of February 22, 1935, c. 18, § 5 (49 Stat. 31), U.S.C., Title 15, § 715d(c), as extended, for instituting proceedings to review orders of petroleum control boards; but the conduct of such proceedings in the district courts shall be made to conform to these rules so far as applicable.

(5) These rules do not alter the practice in the United States district courts prescribed in the Act of July 5, 1935, c. 372, §§ 9 and 10 (49 Stat. 453), as amended, U.S.C., Title 29, §§ 159 and 160, for beginning and conducting proceedings to enforce orders of the National Labor Relations Board; and in respects not covered by those statutes, the practice in the district courts shall conform to these rules so far as applicable.

(6) These rules apply to proceedings for enforcement or review of compensation orders under the Longshoremen's and Harbor Workers' Compensation Act, Act of March 4, 1927, c. 509, §§ 18, 21 (44 Stat. 1434, 1436), as amended, U.S.C., Title 33, §§ 918, 921, except to the extent that matters of procedure are provided for in that Act. The provisions for service by publication and for answer in proceedings to cancel certificates of citizenship under the Act of June 27, 1952, c. 477, Title III, c. 2, § 340 (66 Stat. 260), U.S.C., Title 8, § 1451, remain in effect.

(7) [Abrogated].

**(b) Scire Facias and Mandamus.** The writs of scire facias and mandamus are abolished. Relief heretofore available by mandamus or scire facias may be obtained by appropriate action or by appropriate motion under the practice prescribed in these rules.

**(c) Removed Actions.** These rules apply to civil actions removed to the United States district courts from the state courts and govern procedure after removal. Repleading is not necessary unless the court so orders. In a removed action in which the defendant has not answered, the defendant shall answer or present the other defenses or objections available under these rules within 20 days after the receipt through service or otherwise of a copy of the initial pleading setting forth the claim for relief upon which the action or proceeding is based, or within 20 days after the service of summons upon such initial

pleading, then filed, or within 5 days after the filing of the petition for removal, whichever period is longest. If at the time of removal all necessary pleadings have been served, a party entitled to trial by jury under Rule 38 shall be accorded it, if the party's demand therefor is served within 10 days after the petition for removal is filed if the party is the petitioner, or if not the petitioner within 10 days after service on the party of the notice of filing the petition. A party who, prior to removal, has made an express demand for trial by jury in accordance with state law, need not make a demand after removal. If state law applicable in the court from which the case is removed does not require the parties to make express demands in order to claim trial by jury, they need not make demands after removal unless the court directs that they do so within a specified time if they desire to claim trial by jury. The court may make this direction on its own motion and shall do so as a matter of course at the request of any party. The failure of a party to make demand as directed constitutes a waiver by that party of trial by jury.

**(d) District of Columbia; Courts and Judges [Abrogated].**

**(e) Law Applicable.** Whenever in these rules the law of the state in which the district court is held is made applicable, the law applied in the District of Columbia governs proceedings in the United States District Court for the District of Columbia. When the word "state" is used, it includes, if appropriate, the District of Columbia. When the term "statute of the United States" is used, it includes, so far as concerns proceedings in the United States District Court for the District of Columbia, any Act of Congress locally applicable to and in force in the District of Columbia. When the law of a state is referred to, the word "law" includes the statutes of that state and the state judicial decisions construing them.

**(f) References to Officer of the United States.** Under any rule in which reference is made to an officer or agency of the United States, the term "officer" includes a district director of internal revenue, a former district director or collector of internal revenue, or the personal representative of a deceased district director or collector of internal revenue.

[Amended December 28, 1939, effective April 3, 1941; December 27, 1946, effective March 19, 1948; December 29, 1948, effective October 20, 1949; April 30, 1951, effective August 1, 1951; January 21, 1963, effective July 1, 1963; February 28, 1966, effective July 1, 1966; December 4, 1967, effective July 1, 1968; March 1, 1971, effective July 1, 1971; March 2, 1987, effective August 1, 1987; April 23, 2001, effective December 1, 2001; April 29, 2002, effective December 1, 2002.]

# RULE 82. JURISDICTION AND VENUE UNAFFECTED

These rules shall not be construed to extend or limit the jurisdiction of the United States district courts or

the venue of actions therein.  An admiralty or maritime claim within the meaning of Rule 9(h) shall not be treated as a civil action for the purposes of Title 28, U.S.C., §§ 1391–1392.

[Amended December 29, 1948, effective October 20, 1949; February 28, 1966, effective July 1, 1966; April 23, 2001, effective December 1, 2001.]

## RULE 83.  RULES BY DISTRICT COURTS; JUDGE'S DIRECTIVES

**(a) Local Rules.**

(1) Each district court, acting by a majority of its district judges, may, after giving appropriate public notice and an opportunity for comment, make and amend rules governing its practice.  A local rule shall be consistent with—but not duplicative of—Acts of Congress and rules adopted under 28 U.S.C. §§ 2072 and 2075, and shall conform to any uniform numbering system prescribed by the Judicial Conference of the United States.  A local rule takes effect on the date specified by the district court and remains in effect unless amended by the court or abrogated by the judicial council of the circuit.  Copies of rules and amendments shall, upon their promulgation, be furnished to the judicial council and the Administrative Office of the United States Courts and be made available to the public.

(2) A local rule imposing a requirement of form shall not be enforced in a manner that causes a party to lose rights because of a nonwillful failure to comply with the requirement.

**(b) Procedures When There Is No Controlling Law.**  A judge may regulate practice in any manner consistent with federal law, rules adopted under 28 U.S.C. §§ 2072 and 2075, and local rules of the district.  No sanction or other disadvantage may be imposed for noncompliance with any requirement not in federal law, federal rules, or the local district rules unless the alleged violator has been furnished in the particular case with actual notice of the requirement.

[Amended April 29, 1985, effective August 1, 1985; April 27, 1995, effective December 1, 1995.]

## RULE 84.  FORMS

The forms contained in the Appendix of Forms are sufficient under the rules and are intended to indicate the simplicity and brevity of statement which the rules contemplate.

[Amended December 27, 1946, effective March 19, 1948.]

## RULE 85.  TITLE

These rules may be known and cited as the Federal Rules of Civil Procedure.

## RULE 86.  EFFECTIVE DATE

**(a) Effective Date of Original Rules.***  These rules will take effect on the day which is 3 months subsequent to the adjournment of the second regular session of the 75th Congress, but if that day is prior to September 1, 1938, then these rules will take effect on September 1, 1938.  They govern all proceedings in actions brought after they take effect and also all further proceedings in actions then pending, except to the extent that in the opinion of the court their application in a particular action pending when the rules take effect would not be feasible or would work injustice, in which event the former procedure applies.

**(b) Effective Date of Amendments.**  The amendments adopted by the Supreme Court on December 27, 1946, and transmitted to the Attorney General on January 2, 1947, shall take effect on the day which is three months subsequent to the adjournment of the first regular session of the 80th Congress, but, if that day is prior to September 1, 1947, then these amendments shall take effect on September 1, 1947.  They govern all proceedings in actions brought after they take effect and also all further proceedings in actions then pending, except to the extent that in the opinion of the court their application in a particular action pending when the amendments take effect would not be feasible or would work injustice, in which event the former procedure applies.

**(c) Effective Date of Amendments.**  The amendments adopted by the Supreme Court on December 29, 1948, and transmitted to the Attorney General on December 31, 1948, shall take effect on the day following the adjournment of the first regular session of the 81st Congress.

**(d) Effective Date of Amendments.**  The amendments adopted by the Supreme Court on April 17, 1961, and transmitted to the Congress on April 18, 1961, shall take effect on July 19, 1961.  They govern all proceedings in actions brought after they take effect and also all further proceedings in actions then pending, except to the extent that in the opinion of the court their application in a particular action pending when the amendments take effect would not be feasible or would work injustice, in which event the former procedure applies.

**(e) Effective Date of Amendments.**  The amendments adopted by the Supreme Court on January 21, 1963, and transmitted to the Congress on January 21, 1963, shall take effect on July 1, 1963.  They govern all proceedings in actions brought after they take effect and also all further proceedings in actions then pending, except to the extent that in the opinion of the court their application in a particular action pending when the amendments take effect would not be feasi-

ble or would work injustice, in which event the former procedure applies.

[Amended December 27, 1946, effective March 19, 1948; December 29, 1948, effective October 20, 1949; April 17, 1961, effective July 19, 1961; January 21, 1963, and March 18, 1963, effective July 1, 1963.]

* Suggested title added by Publisher.

# APPENDIX OF FORMS

(See Rule 84)

## INTRODUCTORY STATEMENT

1. The following forms are intended for illustration only. They are limited in number. No attempt is made to furnish a manual of forms. Each form assumes the action to be brought in the Southern District of New York. If the district in which an action is brought has divisions, the division should be indicated in the caption.

2. Except where otherwise indicated each pleading, motion, and other paper should have a caption similar to that of the summons, with the designation of the particular paper substituted for the word "Summons". In the caption of the summons and in the caption of the complaint all parties must be named but in other pleadings and papers, it is sufficient to state the name of the first party on either side, with an appropriate indication of other parties. See Rules 4(b), 7(b)(2), and 10(a).

3. In Form 3 and the forms following, the words, "Allegation of jurisdiction," are used to indicate the appropriate allegation in Form 2.

4. Each pleading, motion, and other paper is to be signed in his individual name by at least one attorney of record (Rule 11). The attorney's name is to be followed by his address as indicated in Form 3. In forms following Form 3 the signature and address are not indicated.

5. If a party is not represented by an attorney, the signature and address of the party are required in place of those of the attorney.

## FORM 1.  SUMMONS

United States District Court for the Southern District of New York

Civil Action, File Number _____

A. B., Plaintiff )
     v. ) *Summons*
C. D., Defendant )

*To the above-named Defendant:*

You are hereby summoned and required to serve upon _____, plaintiff's attorney, whose address is _____, an answer to the complaint which is herewith served upon you, within 20 [1] days after service of this summons upon you, exclusive of the day of service. If you fail to do so, judgment by default will be taken against you for the relief demanded in the complaint.

_____
*Clerk of Court.*

[Seal of the U.S. District Court]
Dated _____

(This summons is issued pursuant to Rule 4 of the Federal Rules of Civil Procedure.)

1. If the United States or an officer or agency thereof is a defendant, the time to be inserted as to it is 60 days.

[Amended December 29, 1948, effective October 20, 1949.]

## FORM 1A.  NOTICE OF LAWSUIT AND REQUEST
## FOR WAIVER OF SERVICE OF SUMMONS

TO: _____ (A) _____

[as _____ (B) _____ of _____ (C) _____ ]

A lawsuit has been commenced against you (or the entity on whose behalf you are addressed).  A copy of the complaint is attached to this notice.  It has been filed in the United States District Court for the ___(D)___ and has been assigned docket number ___(E)___ .

This is not a formal summons or notification from the court, but rather my request that you sign and return the enclosed waiver of service in order to save the cost of serving you with a judicial summons and an additional copy of the complaint.  The cost of service will be avoided if I receive a signed copy of the waiver within ___(F)___ days after the date designated below as the date on which this Notice and Request is sent.  I enclose a stamped and addressed envelope (or other means of cost-free return) for your use.  An extra copy of the waiver is also attached for your records.

If you comply with this request and return the signed waiver, it will be filed with the court and no summons will be served on you.  The action will then proceed as if you had been served on the date the waiver is filed, except that you will not be obligated to answer the complaint before 60 days from the date designated below as the date on which this notice is sent (or before 90 days from that date if your address is not in any judicial district of the United States).

If you do not return the signed waiver within the time indicated, I will take appropriate steps to effect formal service in a manner authorized by the Federal Rules of Civil Procedure and will then, to the extent authorized by those Rules, ask the court to require you (or the party on whose behalf you are addressed) to pay the full costs of such service.  In that connection, please read the statement concerning the duty of parties to waive the service of the summons, which is set forth on the reverse side (or at the foot) of the waiver form.

I affirm that this request is being sent to you on behalf of the plaintiff, this ___ day of _____, ___.

_____
Signature of Plaintiff's Attorney or
Unrepresented Plaintiff

Notes:

A—Name of individual defendant (or name of officer or agent of corporate defendant)

B—Title, or other relationship of individual to corporate defendant

C—Name of corporate defendant, if any

D—District

E—Docket number of action

F—Addressee must be given at least 30 days (60 days if located in foreign country) in which to return waiver

[Adopted April 22, 1993, effective December 1, 1993.]


## FORM 1B.  WAIVER OF SERVICE OF SUMMONS

TO: ___(name of plaintiff's attorney or unrepresented plaintiff)___

I acknowledge receipt of your request that I waive service of a summons in the action of ___(caption of action)___ , which is case number ___(docket number)___ in the United States District Court for the ___(district)___ .  I have also received a copy of

the complaint in the action, two copies of this instrument, and a means by which I can return the signed waiver to you without cost to me.

I agree to save the cost of service of a summons and an additional copy of the complaint in this lawsuit by not requiring that I (or the entity on whose behalf I am acting) be served with judicial process in the manner provided by Rule 4.

I (or the entity on whose behalf I am acting) will retain all defenses or objections to the lawsuit or to the jurisdiction or venue of the court except for objections based on a defect in the summons or in the service of the summons.

I understand that a judgment may be entered against me (or the party on whose behalf I am acting) if an answer or motion under Rule 12 is not served upon you within 60 days after ___(date request was sent)___, or within 90 days after that date if the request was sent outside the United States.

_____     _____
Date                                  Signature
                                      Printed/typed name: _____
                                          [as _____ ]
                                          [of _____ ]

*To be printed on reverse side of the waiver form or set forth*
*at the foot of the form:*
Duty to Avoid Unnecessary Costs of Service of Summons

Rule 4 of the Federal Rules of Civil Procedure requires certain parties to cooperate in saving unnecessary costs of service of the summons and complaint. A defendant located in the United States who, after being notified of an action and asked by a plaintiff located in the United States to waive service of a summons, fails to do so will be required to bear the cost of such service unless good cause be shown for its failure to sign and return the waiver.

It is not good cause for a failure to waive service that a party believes that the complaint is unfounded, or that the action has been brought in an improper place or in a court that lacks jurisdiction over the subject matter of the action or over its person or property. A party who waives service of the summons retains all defenses and objections (except any relating to the summons or to the service of the summons), and may later object to the jurisdiction of the court or to the place where the action has been brought.

A defendant who waives service must within the time specified on the waiver form serve on the plaintiff's attorney (or unrepresented plaintiff) a response to the complaint and must also file a signed copy of the response with the court. If the answer or motion is not served within this time, a default judgment may be taken against that defendant. By waiving service, a defendant is allowed more time to answer than if the summons had been actually served when the request for waiver of service was received.

[Adopted April 22, 1993, effective December 1, 1993.]

# FORM 2. ALLEGATION OF JURISDICTION

## (a) Jurisdiction Founded on Diversity of Citizenship and Amount.

Plaintiff is a [citizen of the State of Connecticut] [1] [corporation incorporated under the laws of the State of Connecticut having its principal place of business in the State of Connecticut] and defendant is a corporation incorporated under the laws of the State of New York having its principal place of business in a State other than the State of Connecticut. The matter in controversy exceeds, exclusive of interest and costs, the sum specified by 28 U.S.C. § 1332.

## (b) Jurisdiction Founded on the Existence of a Federal Question.

The action arises under [the Constitution of the United States, Article ____, Section ____]; [the ____ Amendment to the Constitution of the United States, Section ____]; [the Act of ____, ____ Stat. ____; U.S.C., Title ____, § ____]; [the Treaty of the United States (here describe the treaty) ] [2] as hereinafter more fully appears.

**(c) Jurisdiction Founded on the Existence of a Question Arising Under Particular Statutes.**

The action arises under the Act of _____, _____ Stat. _____; U.S.C., Title _____, § _____, as hereinafter more fully appears.

**(d) Jurisdiction Founded on the Admiralty or Maritime Character of the Claim.**

This is a case of admiralty and maritime jurisdiction, as hereinafter more fully appears. [If the pleader wishes to invoke the distinctively maritime procedures referred to in Rule 9(h), add the following or its substantial equivalent: This is an admiralty or maritime claim within the meaning of Rule 9(h).]

1. Form for natural person.

2. Use the appropriate phrase or phrases. The general allegation of the existence of a Federal question is ineffective unless the matters constituting the claim for relief as set forth in the complaint raise a Federal question.

[Amended April 17, 1961, effective July 19, 1961; February 28, 1966, effective July 1, 1966; April 22, 1993, effective December 1, 1993; April 29, 1999, effective December 1, 1999.]

### Notes of Advisory Committee

1. *Diversity of Citizenship.* If the plaintiff is an assignee, he should allege such other facts of citizenship as will show that he is entitled to prosecute his action under U.S.C.A., Title 28, § 1332, formerly § 41(1).

2. *Jurisdiction Founded on Some Fact Other Than Diversity of Citizenship.* The allegation as to the matter in controversy may be omitted in any case where by law no jurisdictional amount is required. See for example, U.S.C.A., Title 28, former § 41(2)–(28).

3. *Pleading Venue.* Since improper venue is an affirmative dilatory defense, it is not necessary for plaintiff to include allegations showing the venue to be proper.

4. It is sufficient to allege that a corporation is incorporated in a particular state, there being, for jurisdictional purposes, a conclusive presumption that all of its members or stockholders are citizens of that State, Marshal v. Baltimore and Ohio R.R. Co., 1853, 16 How. 314; Henderson, Position of Foreign Corporations in American Constitutional Law (1918) 54–64.

## FORM 3. COMPLAINT ON A PROMISSORY NOTE

1. Allegation of jurisdiction.

2. Defendant on or about June 1, 1935, executed and delivered to plaintiff a promissory note [in the following words and figures: (here set out the note verbatim) ]; [a copy of which is hereto annexed as Exhibit A]; [whereby defendant promised to pay to plaintiff or order on June 1, 1936 the sum of _____ dollars with interest thereon at the rate of six percent. per annum].

3. Defendant owes to plaintiff the amount of said note and interest.

Wherefore plaintiff demands judgment against defendant for the sum of _____ dollars, interest, and costs.

Signed: _____

*Attorney for Plaintiff.*

Address: _____

[Amended January 21, 1963, effective July 1, 1963.]

### Notes of Advisory Committee

1. The pleader may use the material in one of the three sets of brackets. His choice will depend upon whether he desires to plead the document verbatim, or by exhibit, or according to its legal effect.

2. Under the rules free joinder of claims is permitted. See Rules 8(e) and 18. Consequently the claims set forth in each and all of the following forms may be joined with this

complaint or with each other. Ordinarily each claim should be stated in a separate division of the complaint, and the divisions should be designated as counts successively numbered. In particular the rules permit alternative and inconsistent pleading. See Form 10.

## FORM 4. COMPLAINT ON AN ACCOUNT

1. Allegation of jurisdiction.

2. Defendant owes plaintiff _____ dollars according to the account hereto annexed as Exhibit A.

Wherefore (etc. as in Form 3).

[Amended January 21, 1963, effective July 1, 1963.]

## FORM 5. COMPLAINT FOR GOODS SOLD AND DELIVERED

1. Allegation of jurisdiction.

2. Defendant owes plaintiff _____ dollars for goods sold and delivered by plaintiff to defendant between June 1, 1936 and December 1, 1936.

Wherefore (etc. as in Form 3).

[Amended January 21, 1963, effective July 1, 1963.]

### Notes of Advisory Committee

This form may be used where the action is for an agreed price or for the reasonable value of the goods.

## FORM 6. COMPLAINT FOR MONEY LENT

1. Allegation of jurisdiction.

2. Defendant owes plaintiff _____ dollars for money lent by plaintiff to defendant on June 1, 1936.

Wherefore (etc. as in Form 3).

[Amended January 21, 1963, effective July 1, 1963.]

## FORM 7. COMPLAINT FOR MONEY PAID BY MISTAKE

1. Allegation of jurisdiction.

2. Defendant owes plaintiff _____ dollars for money paid by plaintiff to defendant by mistake on June 1, 1936, under the following circumstances: [here state the circumstances with particularity—see Rule 9(b)].

Wherefore (etc. as in Form 3).

[Amended January 21, 1963, effective July 1, 1963.]

## FORM 8. COMPLAINT FOR MONEY HAD AND RECEIVED

1. Allegation of jurisdiction.

2. Defendant owes plaintiff _____ dollars for money had and received from one G. H. on June 1, 1936, to be paid by defendant to plaintiff.

Wherefore (etc. as in Form 3).

[Amended January 21, 1963, effective July 1, 1963.]

## FORM 9.  COMPLAINT FOR NEGLIGENCE

1.  Allegation of jurisdiction.

2.  On June 1, 1936, in a public highway called Boylston Street in Boston, Massachusetts, defendant negligently drove a motor vehicle against plaintiff who was then crossing said highway.

3.  As a result plaintiff was thrown down and had his leg broken and was otherwise injured, was prevented from transacting his business, suffered great pain of body and mind, and incurred expenses for medical attention and hospitalization in the sum of one thousand dollars.

Wherefore plaintiff demands judgment against defendant in the sum of _____ dollars and costs.

[Amended January 21, 1963, effective July 1, 1963.]

### Notes of Advisory Committee

Since contributory negligence is an affirmative defense, the complaint need contain no allegation of due care of plaintiff.

## FORM 10.  COMPLAINT FOR NEGLIGENCE WHERE PLAINTIFF IS UNABLE TO DETERMINE DEFINITELY WHETHER THE PERSON RESPONSIBLE IS C. D. OR E. F. OR WHETHER BOTH ARE RESPONSIBLE AND WHERE HIS EVIDENCE MAY JUSTIFY A FINDING OF WILFULNESS OR OF RECKLESSNESS OR OF NEGLIGENCE

| | |
|---|---|
| A. B., Plaintiff | ) |
| v. | ) *Complaint* |
| C. D. and E. F., Defendants | ) |

1.  Allegation of jurisdiction.

2.  On June 1, 1936, in a public highway called Boylston Street in Boston, Massachusetts, defendant C. D. or defendant E. F., or both defendants C. D. and E. F. wilfully or recklessly or negligently drove or caused to be driven a motor vehicle against plaintiff who was then crossing said highway.

3.  As a result plaintiff was thrown down and had his leg broken and was otherwise injured, was prevented from transacting his business, suffered great pain of body and mind, and incurred expenses for medical attention and hospitalization in the sum of one thousand dollars.

Wherefore plaintiff demands judgment against C. D. or against E. F. or against both in the sum of _____ dollars and costs.

[Amended January 21, 1963, effective July 1, 1963.]

## FORM 11.  COMPLAINT FOR CONVERSION

1.  Allegation of jurisdiction.

2.  On or about December 1, 1936, defendant converted to his own use ten bonds of the _____ Company (here insert brief identification as by number and issue) of the value of _____ dollars, the property of plaintiff.

Wherefore plaintiff demands judgment against defendant in the sum of _____ dollars, interest, and costs.

[Amended January 21, 1963, effective July 1, 1963.]

## FORM 12.   COMPLAINT FOR SPECIFIC PERFORMANCE
## OF CONTRACT TO CONVEY LAND

1.   Allegation of jurisdiction.

2.   On or about December 1, 1936, plaintiff and defendant entered into an agreement in writing a copy of which is hereto annexed as Exhibit A.

3.   In accord with the provisions of said agreement plaintiff tendered to defendant the purchase price and requested a conveyance of the land, but defendant refused to accept the tender and refused to make the conveyance.

4.   Plaintiff now offers to pay the purchase price.

Wherefore plaintiff demands (1) that defendant be required specifically to perform said agreement, (2) damages in the sum of one thousand dollars, and (3) that if specific performance is not granted plaintiff have judgment against defendant in the sum of _____ dollars.

[Amended January 21, 1963, effective July 1, 1963.]

### Notes of Advisory Committee

Here, as in Form 3, plaintiff may set forth the contract verbatim in the complaint or plead it, as indicated, by exhibit, or plead it according to its legal effect.  Furthermore, plaintiff may seek legal or equitable relief or both even though this was impossible under the system in operation before these rules.

## FORM 13.   COMPLAINT ON CLAIM FOR DEBT AND TO SET ASIDE
## FRAUDULENT CONVEYANCE UNDER RULE 18(b)

A. B., Plaintiff                          )
            *v.*                          )   *Complaint*
C. D. and E. F., Defendants    )

1.   Allegation of jurisdiction.

2.   Defendant C. D. on or about _____ executed and delivered to plaintiff a promissory note [in the following words and figures: (here set out the note verbatim) ]; [a copy of which is hereto annexed as Exhibit A]; [whereby defendant C. D. promised to pay to plaintiff or order on _____ the sum of five thousand dollars with interest thereon at the rate of _____ percent. per annum].

3.   Defendant C. D. owes to plaintiff the amount of said note and interest.

4.   Defendant C. D. on or about _____ conveyed all his property, real and personal [or specify and describe] to defendant E. F. for the purpose of defrauding plaintiff and hindering and delaying the collection of the indebtedness evidenced by the note above referred to.

Wherefore plaintiff demands:

(1) That plaintiff have judgment against defendant C. D. for _____ dollars and interest; (2) that the aforesaid conveyance to defendant E. F. be declared void and the judgment herein be declared a lien on said property;  (3) that plaintiff have judgment against the defendants for costs.

[Amended January 21, 1963, effective July 1, 1963.]

## FORM 14.   COMPLAINT FOR NEGLIGENCE UNDER
## FEDERAL EMPLOYERS' LIABILITY ACT

1.   Allegation of jurisdiction.

2.   During all the times herein mentioned defendant owned and operated in interstate commerce a railroad which passed through a tunnel located at _____ and known as Tunnel No. _____.

3.   On or about June 1, 1936, defendant was repairing and enlarging the tunnel in order to protect interstate trains and passengers and freight from injury and in order to make the tunnel more conveniently usable for interstate commerce.

4.   In the course of thus repairing and enlarging the tunnel on said day defendant employed plaintiff as one of its workmen, and negligently put plaintiff to work in a portion of the tunnel which defendant had left unprotected and unsupported.

5.   By reason of defendant's negligence in thus putting plaintiff to work in that portion of the tunnel, plaintiff was, while so working pursuant to defendant's orders, struck and crushed by a rock, which fell from the unsupported portion of the tunnel, and was (here describe plaintiff's injuries).

6.   Prior to these injuries, plaintiff was a strong, able-bodied man, capable of earning and actually earning _____ dollars per day.  By these injuries he has been made incapable of any gainful activity, has suffered great physical and mental pain, and has incurred expense in the amount of _____ dollars for medicine, medical attendance, and hospitalization.

Wherefore plaintiff demands judgment against defendant in the sum of _____ dollars and costs.

# FORM 15.   COMPLAINT FOR DAMAGES UNDER MERCHANT MARINE ACT

1.   Allegation of jurisdiction.  [If the pleader wishes to invoke the distinctively maritime procedures referred to in Rule 9(h), add the following or its substantial equivalent: This is an admiralty or maritime claim within the meaning of Rule 9(h).]

2.   During all the times herein mentioned defendant was the owner of the steamship _____ and used it in the transportation of freight for hire by water in interstate and foreign commerce.

3.   During the first part of (month and year) at _____ plaintiff entered the employ of defendant as an able seaman on said steamship under seamen's articles of customary form for a voyage from _____ ports to the Orient and return at a wage of _____ dollars per month and found, which is equal to a wage of _____ dollars per month as a shore worker.

4.   On June 1, 1936, said steamship was about _____ days out of the port of _____ and was being navigated by the master and crew on the return voyage to _____ ports.  (Here describe weather conditions and the condition of the ship and state as in an ordinary complaint for personal injuries the negligent conduct of defendant.)

5.   By reason of defendant's negligence in thus (brief statement of defendant's negligent conduct) and the unseaworthiness of said steamship, plaintiff was (here describe plaintiff's injuries).

6.   Prior to these injuries, plaintiff was a strong, able-bodied man, capable of earning and actually earning _____ dollars per day.  By these injuries he has been made incapable of any gainful activity; has suffered great physical and mental pain, and has incurred expense in the amount of _____ dollars for medicine, medical attendance, and hospitalization.

Wherefore plaintiff demands judgment against defendant in the sum of _____ dollars and costs.

[Amended February 28, 1966, effective July 1, 1966.]

# FORM 16.   COMPLAINT FOR INFRINGEMENT OF PATENT

1.   Allegation of jurisdiction.

2.   On May 16, 1934, United States Letters Patent No. _____ were duly and legally issued to plaintiff for an invention in an electric motor; and since that date plaintiff has been and still is the owner of those Letters Patent.

3. Defendant has for a long time past been and still is infringing those Letters Patent by making, selling, and using electric motors embodying the patented invention, and will continue to do so unless enjoined by this court.

4. Plaintiff has placed the required statutory notice on all electric motors manufactured and sold by him under said Letters Patent, and has given written notice to defendant of his said infringement.

Wherefore plaintiff demands a preliminary and final injunction against continued infringement, an accounting for damages, and an assessment of interest and costs against defendant.

[Amended January 21, 1963, effective July 1, 1963.]

## FORM 17.  COMPLAINT FOR INFRINGEMENT OF COPYRIGHT AND UNFAIR COMPETITION

1. Allegation of jurisdiction.

2. Prior to March, 1936, plaintiff, who then was and ever since has been a citizen of the United States, created and wrote an original book, entitled _____.

3. This book contains a large amount of material wholly original with plaintiff and is copyrightable subject matter under the laws of the United States.

4. Between March 2, 1936, and March 10, 1936, plaintiff complied in all respects with the Act of (give citation) and all other laws governing copyright, and secured the exclusive rights and privileges in and to the copyright of said book, and received from the Register of Copyrights a certificate of registration, dated and identified as follows: "March 10, 1936, Class _____, No. _____."

5. Since March 10, 1936, said book has been published by plaintiff and all copies of it made by plaintiff or under his authority or license have been printed, bound, and published in strict conformity with the provisions of the Act of _____ and all other laws governing copyright.

6. Since March 10, 1936, plaintiff has been and still is the sole proprietor of all rights, title, and interest in and to the copyright in said book.

7. After March 10, 1936, defendant infringed said copyright by publishing and placing upon the market a book entitled _____, which was copied largely from plaintiff's copyrighted book, entitled _____.

8. A copy of plaintiff's copyrighted book is hereto attached as "Exhibit 1"; and a copy of defendant's infringing book is hereto attached as "Exhibit 2."

9. Plaintiff has notified defendant that defendant has infringed the copyright of plaintiff, and defendant has continued to infringe the copyright.

10. After March 10, 1936, and continuously since about _____, defendant has been publishing, selling and otherwise marketing the book entitled _____, and has thereby been engaging in unfair trade practices and unfair competition against plaintiff to plaintiff's irreparable damage.

Wherefore plaintiff demands:

(1) That defendant, his agents, and servants be enjoined during the pendency of this action and permanently from infringing said copyright of said plaintiff in any manner, and from publishing, selling, marketing or otherwise disposing of any copies of the book entitled _____.

(2) That defendant be required to pay to plaintiff such damages as plaintiff has sustained in consequence of defendant's infringement of said copyright and said unfair trade practices and unfair competition and to account for

(a) all gains, profits and advantages derived by defendant by said trade practices and unfair competition and

(b) all gains, profits, and advantages derived by defendant by his infringement of plaintiff's copyright or such damages as to the court shall appear proper within the provisions of the copyright statutes, but not less than two hundred and fifty dollars.

(3) That defendant be required to deliver up to be impounded during the pendency of this action all copies of said book entitled _____ in his possession or under his control and to deliver up for destruction all infringing copies and all plates, molds, and other matter for making such infringing copies.

(4) That defendant pay to plaintiff the costs of this action and reasonable attorney's fees to be allowed to the plaintiff by the court.

(5) That plaintiff have such other and further relief as is just.

[Amended December 27, 1946, effective March 19, 1948.]

# FORM 18.   COMPLAINT FOR INTERPLEADER AND DECLARATORY RELIEF

1.   Allegation of jurisdiction.

2.   On or about June 1, 1935, plaintiff issued to G. H. a policy of life insurance whereby plaintiff promised to pay to K. L. as beneficiary the sum of _____ dollars upon the death of G. H.  The policy required the payment by G. H. of a stipulated premium on June 1, 1936, and annually thereafter as a condition precedent to its continuance in force.

3.   No part of the premium due June 1, 1936, was ever paid and the policy ceased to have any force or effect on July 1, 1936.

4.   Thereafter, on September 1, 1936, G. H. and K. L. died as the result of a collision between a locomotive and the automobile in which G. H. and K. L. were riding.

5.   Defendant C. D. is the duly appointed and acting executor of the will of G. H.; defendant E. F. is the duly appointed and acting executor of the will of K. L.; defendant X. Y. claims to have been duly designated as beneficiary of said policy in place of K. L.

6.   Each of defendants, C. D., E. F., and X. Y. is claiming that the above-mentioned policy was in full force and effect at the time of the death of G. H.; each of them is claiming to be the only person entitled to receive payment of the amount of the policy and has made demand for payment thereof.

7.   By reason of these conflicting claims of the defendants, plaintiff is in great doubt as to which defendant is entitled to be paid the amount of the policy, if it was in force at the death of G. H.

Wherefore plaintiff demands that the court adjudge:

(1) That none of the defendants is entitled to recover from plaintiff the amount of said policy or any part thereof.

(2) That each of the defendants be restrained from instituting any action against plaintiff for the recovery of the amount of said policy or any part thereof.

(3) That, if the court shall determine that said policy was in force at the death of G. H., the defendants be required to interplead and settle between themselves their rights to the money due under said policy, and that plaintiff be discharged from all liability in the premises except to the person whom the court shall adjudge entitled to the amount of said policy.

(4) That plaintiff recover its costs.

[Amended January 21, 1963, effective July 1, 1963.]

## FORM 18–A. NOTICE AND ACKNOWLEDGMENT FOR SERVICE BY MAIL [ABROGATED]

[Abrogated April 22, 1993, effective December 1, 1993.]

## FORM 19. MOTION TO DISMISS, PRESENTING DEFENSES OF FAILURE TO STATE A CLAIM, OF LACK OF SERVICE OF PROCESS, OF IMPROPER VENUE, AND OF LACK OF JURISDICTION UNDER RULE 12(b)

The defendant moves the court as follows:

1. To dismiss the action because the complaint fails to state a claim against defendant upon which relief can be granted.

2. To dismiss the action or in lieu thereof to quash the return of service of summons on the grounds (a) that the defendant is a corporation organized under the laws of Delaware and was not and is not subject to service of process within the Southern District of New York, and (b) that the defendant has not been properly served with process in this action, all of which more clearly appears in the affidavits of M. N. and X. Y. hereto annexed as Exhibit A and Exhibit B respectively.

3. To dismiss the action on the ground that it is in the wrong district because (a) the jurisdiction of this court is invoked solely on the ground that the action arises under the Constitution and laws of the United States and (b) the defendant is a corporation incorporated under the laws of the State of Delaware and is not licensed to do or doing business in the Southern District of New York, all of which more clearly appears in the affidavits of K. L. and V. W. hereto annexed as Exhibits C and D respectively.

4. To dismiss the action on the ground that the court lacks jurisdiction because the amount actually in controversy is less than ten thousand dollars exclusive of interest and costs.*

Signed: _____
*Attorney for Defendant.*

Address: _____

*Notice of Motion*

To: _____
    *Attorney for Plaintiff.*

_____

Please take notice, that the undersigned will bring the above motion on for hearing before this Court at Room _____, United States Court House, Foley Square, City of New York, on the _____ day of _____, 20__, at 10 o'clock in the forenoon of that day or as soon thereafter as counsel can be heard.

Signed: _____
*Attorney for Defendant.*

Address: _____

[Amended December 29, 1948, effective October 20, 1949; April 17, 1961, effective July 19, 1961; March 27, 2003, effective December 1, 2003.]

### Notes of Advisory Committee

1. The above motion and notice of motion may be combined and denominated Notice of Motion. See Rule 7(b).

2. As to paragraph 3, see U.S.C., Title 28, § 1391 (Venue generally), subsections (b) and (c).

3. As to paragraph 4, see U.S.C., Title 28, § 1331 (Federal question; amount in controversy; costs), as amended by P.L. 85–554, 72 Stat. 415, July 25, 1958, requiring that the amount in controversy, exclusive of interest and costs, be in excess of $10,000.*

* Pub. Note: The $10,000 minimum amount in controversy requirement of the federal question jurisdiction statute was repealed in 1980. 28 U.S.C.A. § 1331, as amended by Pub.L. 96–486, § 2(a), December 1, 1980, 94 Stat. 2369. Also note that the amount in controversy required in diversity of citizenship suits under 28 U.S.C.A. § 1332(a) was increased to $75,000 by Pub.L. 104–317, Title II, § 205(a), October 19, 1996, 110 Stat. 385.

# FORM 20. ANSWER PRESENTING DEFENSES UNDER RULE 12(b)

## First Defense

The complaint fails to state a claim against defendant upon which relief can be granted.

## Second Defense

If defendant is indebted to plaintiffs for the goods mentioned in the complaint, he is indebted to them jointly with G. H. G. H. is alive; is a citizen of the State of New York and a resident of this district, is subject to the jurisdiction of this court, as to both service of process and venue; can be made a party without depriving this court of jurisdiction of the present parties, and has not been made a party.

## Third Defense

Defendant admits the allegation contained in paragraphs 1 and 4 of the complaint; alleges that he is without knowledge or information sufficient to form a belief as to the truth of the allegations contained in paragraph 2 of the complaint; and denies each and every other allegation contained in the complaint.

## Fourth Defense

The right of action set forth in the complaint did not accrue within six years next before the commencement of this action.

## Counterclaim

(Here set forth any claim as a counterclaim in the manner in which a claim is pleaded in a complaint. No statement of the grounds on which the court's jurisdiction depends need be made unless the counterclaim requires independent grounds of jurisdiction.)

## Cross-Claim Against Defendant M. N.

(Here set forth the claim constituting a cross-claim against defendant M. N. in the manner in which a claim is pleaded in a complaint. The statement of grounds upon which the court's jurisdiction depends need not be made unless the cross-claim requires independent grounds of jurisdiction.)

### Notes of Advisory Committee

The above form contains examples of certain defenses provided for in Rule 12(b). The first defense challenges the legal sufficiency of the complaint. It is a substitute for a general demurrer or a motion to dismiss.

The second defense embodies the old plea in abatement; the decision thereon, however, may well provide under Rules 19 and 21 for the citing in of the party rather than an abatement of the action.

The third defense is an answer on the merits.

The fourth defense is one of the affirmative defenses provided for in Rule 8(c).

The answer also includes a counterclaim and a cross-claim.

[The Notes incorporate revisions made by the Advisory Committee at the same time amendments to certain other rules were made by Order dated December 27, 1946, effective March 19, 1948.]

# FORM 21.  ANSWER TO COMPLAINT SET FORTH IN FORM 8, WITH COUNTERCLAIM FOR INTERPLEADER

## Defense

Defendant admits the allegations stated in paragraph 1 of the complaint; and denies the allegations stated in paragraph 2 to the extent set forth in the counterclaim herein.

## Counterclaim for Interpleader

1.  Defendant received the sum of _____ dollars as a deposit from E. F.

2.  Plaintiff has demanded the payment of such deposit to him by virtue of an assignment of it which he claims to have received from E. F.

3.  E. F. has notified the defendant that he claims such deposit, that the purported assignment is not valid, and that he holds the defendant responsible for the deposit.

Wherefore defendant demands:

(1) That the court order E. F. to be made a party defendant to respond to the complaint and to this counterclaim.[1]

(2) That the court order the plaintiff and E. F. to interplead their respective claims.

(3) That the court adjudge whether the plaintiff or E. F. is entitled to the sum of money.

(4) That the court discharge defendant from all liability in the premises except to the person it shall adjudge entitled to the sum of money.

(5) That the court award to the defendant its costs and attorney's fees.

1.  Rule 13(h) provides for the court ordering parties to a counterclaim, but who are not parties to the original action, to be brought in as defendants.

[Amended January 21, 1963, effective July 1, 1963.]

# FORM 22.  MOTION TO BRING IN THIRD-PARTY DEFENDANT [SUPERSEDED]

[Superseded by Forms 22–A and 22–B January 21, 1963, effective July 1, 1963.]

## FORM 22–A.  SUMMONS AND COMPLAINT
## AGAINST THIRD–PARTY DEFENDANT

United States District Court for the Southern District of New York

Civil Action, File Number _____

| | |
|---|---|
| A. B., Plaintiff ) | |
| v. ) | |
| C. D., Defendant and ) | |
| Third-Party Plaintiff ) | Summons |
| v. ) | |
| E. F., Third-Party ) | |
| Defendant ) | |

To the above-named Third-Party Defendant:

You are hereby summoned and required to serve upon _____, plaintiff's attorney whose address is _____, and upon _____, who is attorney for C. D., defendant and third-party plaintiff, and whose address is _____, an answer to the third-party complaint which is herewith served upon you within 20 days after the service of this summons upon you exclusive of the day of service.  If you fail to do so, judgment by default will be taken against you for the relief demanded in the third-party complaint.  There is also served upon you herewith a copy of the complaint of the plaintiff which you may but are not required to answer.

_____
*Clerk of Court.*

[Seal of District Court]

Dated _____

---

United States District Court for the Southern District of New York

Civil Action, File Number _____

| | |
|---|---|
| A. B., Plaintiff ) | |
| v. ) | |
| C. D., Defendant and ) | |
| Third-Party Plaintiff ) | Third-Party Complaint |
| v. ) | |
| E. F., Third-Party ) | |
| Defendant ) | |

1.  Plaintiff A. B. has filed against defendant C. D. a complaint, a copy of which is hereto attached as "Exhibit A."

2.  (Here state the grounds upon which C. D. is entitled to recover from E. F., all or part of what A. B. may recover from C. D.  The statement should be framed as in an original complaint.)

Wherefore C. D. demands judgment against third-party defendant E. F. for all sums [1] that may be adjudged against defendant C. D. in favor of plaintiff A. B.

Signed: _____

*Attorney for C. D.,*
*Third-Party Plaintiff.*

Address: _____

1.  Make appropriate change where C. D. is entitled to only partial recovery-over against E. F.

[Adopted January 21, 1963, effective July 1, 1963.]

## FORM 22–B.   MOTION TO BRING IN THIRD–PARTY DEFENDANT

Defendant moves for leave, as third-party plaintiff, to cause to be served upon E. F. a summons and third-party complaint, copies of which are hereto attached as Exhibit X.

Signed: _____

*Attorney for Defendant*
*C. D.*

Address: _____

### Notice of Motion

(Contents the same as in Form 19. The notice should be addressed to all parties to the action.)

### Exhibit X

(Contents the same as in Form 22–A.)

[Adopted January 21, 1963, effective July 1, 1963.]

## FORM 23.   MOTION TO INTERVENE AS A DEFENDANT UNDER RULE 24

(Based upon the complaint, Form 16)

United States District Court for the Southern District of New York
Civil Action, File Number _____

| | |
|---|---|
| A. B., Plaintiff | ) |
| v. | )   *Motion to intervene as* |
| C. D., Defendant | )   *a defendant* |
| E. F., Applicant for | ) |
| Intervention | ) |

E. F. moves for leave to intervene as a defendant in this action, in order to assert the defenses set forth in his proposed answer, of which a copy is hereto attached, on the ground that he is the manufacturer and vendor to the defendant, as well as to others, of the articles alleged in the complaint to be an infringement of plaintiff's patent, and as such has a defense to plaintiff's claim presenting both questions of law and of fact which are common to the main action.[1]

Signed: _____,

*Attorney for E. F.,*
*Applicant for*
*Intervention.*

Address: _____

_____

Notice of Motion
(Contents the same as in Form 19)

United States District Court for the Southern District of New York
Civil Action, File Number _____

|  | |  |
|---|---|---|
| A. B., Plaintiff | ) | |
| v. | ) | *Intervener's Answer* |
| C. D., Defendant | ) | |
| E. F., Intervener | ) | |

First Defense

Intervener admits the allegations stated in paragraphs 1 and 4 of the complaint; denies the allegations in paragraph 3, and denies the allegations in paragraph 2 in so far as they assert the legality of the issuance of the Letters Patent to plaintiff.

Second Defense

Plaintiff is not the first inventor of the articles covered by the Letters Patent specified in his complaint, since articles substantially identical in character were previously patented in Letters Patent granted to intervener on January 5, 1920.

Signed: _____,
*Attorney for E. F.,*
*Intervener.*

Address: _____

1. For other grounds of intervention, either of right or in the discretion of the court, see Rule 24(a) and (b).

[Amended December 29, 1948, effective October 20, 1949.]

## FORM 24.   REQUEST FOR PRODUCTION OF DOCUMENTS, ETC., UNDER RULE 34

Plaintiff A. B. requests defendant C. D. to respond within _____ days to the following requests:

(1) That defendant produce and permit plaintiff to inspect and to copy each of the following documents:

(Here list the documents either individually or by category and describe each of them.)

(Here state the time, place, and manner of making the inspection and performance of any related acts.)

(2) That defendant produce and permit plaintiff to inspect and to copy, test, or sample each of the following objects:

(Here list the objects either individually or by category and describe each of them.)

(Here state the time, place, and manner of making the inspection and performance of any related acts.)

(3) That defendant permit plaintiff to enter (here describe property to be entered) and to inspect and to photograph, test or sample (here describe the portion of the real property and the objects to be inspected).

(Here state the time, place, and manner of making the inspection and performance of any related acts.)

Signed: _____,
*Attorney for Plaintiff.*

Address: _____

[Amended March 30, 1970, effective July 1, 1970.]

## FORM 25.   REQUEST FOR ADMISSION UNDER RULE 36

Plaintiff A. B. requests defendant C. D. within _____ days after service of this request to make the following admissions for the purpose of this action only and subject to all pertinent objections to admissibility which may be interposed at the trial:

1.   That each of the following documents, exhibited with this request, is genuine.

(Here list the documents and describe each document.)

2.   That each of the following statements is true.

(Here list the statements.)

Signed: _____,
*Attorney for Plaintiff.*

Address: _____

[Amended December 27, 1946, effective March 19, 1948.]

## FORM 26.   ALLEGATION OF REASON FOR OMITTING PARTY

When it is necessary, under Rule 19(c), for the pleader to set forth in his pleading the names of persons who ought to be made parties, but who are not so made, there should be an allegation such as the one set out below:

John Doe named in this complaint is not made a party to this action [because he is not subject to the jurisdiction of this court]; [because he cannot be made a party to this action without depriving this court of jurisdiction].

## FORM 27.   NOTICE OF APPEAL TO COURT OF APPEALS UNDER [FORMER] RULE 73(b) [ABROGATED]

[Abrogated December 4, 1967, effective July 1, 1968.]

### Notes of Advisory Committee

The form of notice of appeal is transferred to the Federal Rules of Appellate Procedure as Form 1.

## FORM 28.   NOTICE: CONDEMNATION

United States District Court for the Southern District of New York

Civil Action, File Number _____

UNITED STATES OF AMERICA,          )
            PLAINTIFF               )
                v.                  )
1,000 ACRES OF LAND IN [here insert )
    a general location as "City of  ) *Notice*
_____" or "County of _____"],    )
JOHN DOE ET AL., AND UNKNOWN        )
    OWNERS, DEFENDANTS              )

To (here insert the names of the defendants to whom the notice is directed):

You are hereby notified that a complaint in condemnation has heretofore been filed in the office of the clerk of the United States District Court for the Southern District of New York, in the United States Court House in New York City, New

York, for the taking (here state the interest to be acquired, as "an estate in fee simple") for use (here state briefly the use, "as a site for a post-office building") of the following described property in which you have or claim an interest.

(Here insert brief description of the property in which the defendants, to whom the notice is directed, have or claim an interest.)

The authority for the taking is (here state briefly, as "the Act of _____, _____ Stat. _____, U.S.C., Title _____, § _____".) [1]

You are further notified that if you desire to present any objection or defense to the taking of your property you are required to serve your answer on the plaintiff's attorney at the address herein designated within twenty days after _____.[2]

Your answer shall identify the property in which you claim to have an interest, state the nature and extent of the interest you claim, and state all of your objections and defenses to the taking of your property. All defenses and objections not so presented are waived. And in case of your failure so to answer the complaint, judgment of condemnation of that part of the above-described property in which you have or claim an interest will be rendered.

But without answering, you may serve on the plaintiff's attorney a notice of appearance designating the property in which you claim to be interested. Thereafter you will receive notice of all proceedings affecting it. At the trial of the issue of just compensation, whether or not you have previously appeared or answered, you may present evidence as to the amount of the compensation to be paid for your property, and you may share in the distribution of the award.

_____
                                                        *United States Attorney.*

Address _____

(Here state an address within the district where the United States Attorney may be served as "United States Court House, New York, N. Y.")

Dated _____

1. And where appropriate add a citation to any applicable Executive Order.

2. Here insert the words "personal service of this notice upon you," if personal service is to be made pursuant to subdivision (d)(3)(i) of this rule [Rule 71A]; or, insert the date of the last publication of notice, if service by publication is to be made pursuant to subdivision (d)(3)(ii) of this rule. [*Pub. Note: Subdivisions (d)(3)(i) and (d)(3)(ii) were renumbered as (d)(3)(A) and (d)(3)(B), effective December 1, 1993.*]

[Adopted April 30, 1951, effective August 1, 1951.]

## FORM 29.  COMPLAINT: CONDEMNATION

United States District Court for the Southern District of New York

CIVIL ACTION, FILE NUMBER _____

| | | |
|---|---|---|
| UNITED STATES OF AMERICA, PLAINTIFF *v.* 1,000 ACRES OF LAND IN [here insert a general location as "City of _____" or "County of _____"], JOHN DOE ET AL., AND UNKNOWN OWNERS, DEFENDANTS | ) ) ) ) ) ) ) ) | *Complaint* |

1.  This is an action of a civil nature brought by the United States of America for the taking of property under the power of eminent domain and for the ascertainment and award of just compensation to the owners and parties in interest.[1]

2. The authority for the taking is (here state briefly, as "the Act of _____, _____ Stat. _____, U.S.C., Title _____, § _____").[2]

3. The use for which the property is to be taken is (here state briefly the use, "as a site for a post-office building").

4. The interest to be acquired in the property is (here state the interest as "an estate in fee simple").

5. The property so to be taken is (here set forth a description of the property sufficient for its identification) or (described in Exhibit A hereto attached and made a part hereof).

6. The persons known to the plaintiff to have or claim an interest in the property [3] are:

(Here set forth the names of such persons and the interests claimed.) [4]

7. In addition to the persons named, there are or may be others who have or may claim some interest in the property to be taken, whose names are unknown to the plaintiff and on diligent inquiry have not been ascertained. They are made parties to the action under the designation "Unknown Owners."

Wherefore the plaintiff demands judgment that the property be condemned and that just compensation for the taking be ascertained and awarded and for such other relief as may be lawful and proper.

_____
*United States Attorney.*

Address _____

(Here state an address within the district where the United States Attorney may be served, as "United States Court House, New York, N. Y.")

**1.** If the plaintiff is not the United States, but is, for example, a corporation invoking the power of eminent domain delegated to it by the state, then this paragraph 1 of the complaint should be appropriately modified and should be preceded by a paragraph appropriately alleging federal jurisdiction for the action, such as diversity. See Form 2.

**2.** And where appropriate add a citation to any applicable Executive Order.

**3.** At the commencement of the action the plaintiff need name as defendants only the persons having or claiming an interest in the property whose names are then known, but prior to any hearing involving the compensation to be paid for a particular piece of property the plaintiff must add as defendants all persons having or claiming an interest in that property whose names can be ascertained by an appropriate search of the records and also those whose names have otherwise been learned. See Rule 71A(c)(2).

**4.** The plaintiff should designate, as to each separate piece of property, the defendants who have been joined as owners thereof or of some interest therein. See Rule 71A(c)(2).

[Adopted April 30, 1951, effective August 1, 1951.]

# FORM 30. SUGGESTION OF DEATH UPON THE RECORD UNDER RULE 25(a)(1)

A. B. [describe as a party, or as executor, administrator, or other representative or successor of C. D., the deceased party] suggests upon the record, pursuant to Rule 25(a)(1), the death of C. D. [describe as party] during the pendency of this action.

[Adopted January 21, 1963, effective July 1, 1963.]

# FORM 31.  JUDGMENT ON JURY VERDICT

United States District Court for the Southern District of New York

Civil Action, File Number _____

| A. B., Plaintiff | ) | |
|---|---|---|
| v. | ) | *Judgment* |
| C. D., Defendant | ) | |

This action came on for trial before the Court and a jury, Honorable John Marshall, District Judge, presiding, and the issues having been duly tried and the jury having duly rendered its verdict,

It is Ordered and Adjudged

[that the plaintiff A. B. recover of the defendant C. D. the sum of _____, with interest thereon at the rate of _____ per cent as provided by law, and his costs of action.]

[that the plaintiff take nothing, that the action be dismissed on the merits, and that the defendant C. D. recover of the plaintiff A. B. his costs of action.]

Dated at New York, New York, this _____ day of _____, 20___.

_____
*Clerk of Court.*

[Adopted January 21, 1963, effective July 1 1963;  March 27, 2003, effective December 1, 2003.]

### Notes of Advisory Committee

1.  This Form is illustrative of the judgment to be entered upon the general verdict of a jury.  It deals with the cases where there is a general jury verdict awarding the plaintiff money damages or finding for the defendant, but is adaptable to other situations of jury verdicts.

2.  The clerk, unless the court otherwise orders, is required forthwith to prepare, sign, and enter the judgment upon a general jury verdict without awaiting any direction by the court.  The form of the judgment upon a special verdict or a general verdict accompanied by answers to interrogatories shall be promptly approved by the court, and the clerk shall thereupon enter it.  See Rule 58, as amended.

3.  The Rules contemplate a simple judgment promptly entered.  See Rule 54(a).  Every judgment shall be set forth on a separate document.  See Rule 58, as amended.

4.  Attorneys are not to submit forms of judgment unless directed in exceptional cases to do so by the court.  See Rule 58, as amended.

# FORM 32.  JUDGMENT ON DECISION BY THE COURT

United States District Court for the Southern District of New York

Civil Action, File Number _____

| A. B., Plaintiff | ) | |
|---|---|---|
| v. | ) | *Judgment* |
| C. D., Defendant | ) | |

This action came on for [trial] [hearing] before the Court, Honorable John Marshall, District Judge, presiding, and the issues having been duly [tried] [heard] and a decision having been duly rendered,

It is Ordered and Adjudged

[that the plaintiff A. B. recover of the defendant C. D. the sum of _____, with interest thereon at the rate of _____ per cent as provided by law, and his costs of action.]

[that the plaintiff take nothing, that the action be dismissed on the merits, and that the defendant C. D. recover of the plaintiff A. B. his costs of action.]

Dated at New York, New York, this _____ day of _____, 20___.

_____
*Clerk of Court.*

[Adopted January 21, 1963, effective July 1, 1963;  March 27, 2003, effective December 1, 2003.]

**Effective Until December 1, 2007, Absent Contrary Congressional Action**

### Notes of Advisory Committee

1. This Form is illustrative of the judgment to be entered upon a decision of the court. It deals with the cases of decisions by the court awarding a party only money damages or costs, but is adaptable to other decisions by the court.

2. The clerk, unless the court otherwise orders, is required forthwith, without awaiting any direction by the court, to prepare, sign, and enter the judgment upon a decision by the court that a party shall recover only a sum certain or costs or that all relief shall be denied. The form of the judgment upon a decision by the court granting other relief shall be promptly approved by the court, and the clerk shall thereupon enter it. See Rule 58, as amended.

3. See also paragraphs 3–4 of the Explanatory Note to Form 31.

## FORM 33. NOTICE OF AVAILABILITY OF MAGISTRATE JUDGE TO EXERCISE JURISDICTION

In accordance with the provisions of Title 28, U.S.C. § 636(c), you are hereby notified that a United States magistrate judge of this district court is available to exercise the court's jurisdiction and to conduct any or all proceedings in this case including a jury or nonjury trial, and entry of a final judgment. Exercise of this jurisdiction by a magistrate judge is, however, permitted only if all parties voluntarily consent.

You may, without adverse substantive consequences, withhold your consent, but this will prevent the court's jurisdiction from being exercised by a magistrate judge. If any party withholds consent, the identity of the parties consenting or withholding consent will not be communicated to any magistrate judge or to the district judge to whom the case has been assigned.

An appeal from a judgment entered by a magistrate judge may be taken directly to the United States court of appeals for this judicial circuit in the same manner as an appeal from any other judgment of a district court.

Copies of the Form for the "Consent to Jurisdiction by a United States Magistrate Judge" are available from the clerk of the court.

[Adopted April 28, 1983, effective August 1, 1983; amended April 22, 1993, effective December 1, 1993; April 11, 1997, effective December 1, 1997.]

## FORM 34. CONSENT TO EXERCISE OF JURISDICTION BY A UNITED STATES MAGISTRATE JUDGE

### UNITED STATES DISTRICT COURT
###  _____ DISTRICT OF _____

```
                           )
          Plaintiff,       )
                           )
     vs.                   )   Docket No. _____
                           )
      Defendant.           )
```

CONSENT TO JURISDICTION BY A UNITED STATES MAGISTRATE JUDGE

In accordance with the provisions of Title 28, U.S.C. § 636(c), the undersigned party or parties to the above-captioned civil matter hereby voluntarily consent to have a United States magistrate judge conduct any and all further proceedings in the case, including trial, and order the entry of a final judgment.

_____     _____
        Date                                     Signature

Note: Return this form to the Clerk of the Court if you consent to jurisdiction by a magistrate judge. Do not send a copy of this form to any district judge or magistrate judge.

[Adopted April 28, 1983, effective August 1, 1983; amended April 22, 1993, effective December 1, 1993; April 11, 1997, effective December 1, 1997.]

## FORM 34A.   ORDER OF REFERENCE

UNITED STATES DISTRICT COURT
_____ DISTRICT OF _____

|  |  |
|---|---|
| Plaintiff, | ) |
| | ) |
| vs. | ) Docket No. _____ |
| | ) |
| Defendant. | ) |

### ORDER OF REFERENCE

IT IS HEREBY ORDERED that the above-captioned matter be referred to United States Magistrate Judge _____ for all further proceedings and entry of judgment in accordance with Title 28, U.S.C. § 636(c) and the consent of the parties.

_____
U. S. District Judge

[Adopted April 22, 1993, effective December 1, 1993.]

## FORM 35.   REPORT OF PARTIES' PLANNING MEETING

[Caption and Names of Parties]

1.   Pursuant to Fed.R.Civ.P. 26(f), a meeting was held on __(date)__ at __(place)__ and was attended by:

    __(name)__   for plaintiff(s)
    __(name)__   for defendant(s)  __(party name)__
    __(name)__   for defendant(s)  __(party name)__

2.   **Pre-discovery Disclosures.**  The parties [have exchanged] [will exchange by __(date)__ ] the information required by [Fed.R.Civ.P. 26(a)(1)] [local rule ___].

3.   **Discovery Plan.** The parties jointly propose to the court the following discovery plan: [Use separate paragraphs or subparagraphs as necessary if parties disagree.]

Discovery will be needed on the following subjects: (brief description of subjects on which discovery will be needed)

Disclosure or discovery of electronically stored information should be handled as follows: (brief description of parties' proposals)

The parties have agreed to an order regarding claims of privilege or of protection as trial-preparation material asserted after production, as follows: (brief description of provisions of proposed order).

All discovery commenced in time to be completed by _____(date)_____ . [Discovery on _____(issue for early discovery)_____ to be completed by _____(date)_____ .]

Maximum of ___ interrogatories by each party to any other party.  [Responses due ___ days after service.]

Maximum of ___ requests for admission by each party to any other party. [Responses due ___ days after service.]

Maximum of ___ depositions by plaintiff(s) and ___ by defendant(s).

Each deposition [other than of _____] limited to maximum of ___ hours unless extended by agreement of parties.

Reports from retained experts under Rule 26(a)(2) due:

  from plaintiff(s) by   (date)  

  from defendant(s) by   (date)  

Supplementations under Rule 26(e) due   (time(s) or interval(s))  .

4. **Other Items.** [Use separate paragraphs or subparagraphs as necessary if parties disagree.]

The parties [request] [do not request] a conference with the court before entry of the scheduling order.

The parties request a pretrial conference in   (month and year)  .

Plaintiff(s) should be allowed until   (date)   to join additional parties and until   (date)   to amend the pleadings.

Defendant(s) should be allowed until   (date)   to join additional parties and until   (date)   to amend the pleadings.

All potentially dispositive motions should be filed by   (date)  .

Settlement [is likely] [is unlikely] [cannot be evaluated prior to  (date) ] [ *may be enhanced by use of the following alternative dispute resolution procedure: [_____].

Final lists of witnesses and exhibits under Rule 26(a)(3) should be due

  from plaintiff(s) by   (date)  

  from defendant(s) by   (date)  

Parties should have ___ days after service of final lists of witnesses and exhibits to list objections under Rule 26(a)(3).

The case should be ready for trial by   (date)   [and at this time is expected to take approximately   (length of time)  ].

[Other matters.]

Date: _____

[Adopted April 22, 1993, effective December 1, 1993; April 12, 2006, effective December 1, 2006.]

  * Pub. Note: So in original, without closed bracket.

# PROPOSED
# FEDERAL RULES OF CIVIL PROCEDURE

### Text of Rules and Forms Effective December 1, 2007, Absent Contrary Congressional Action

*[Publisher's Note: Set forth below are Rules and Forms effective on December 1, 2007, absent contrary Congressional action; for Rules and Forms currently effective, see, ante.]*

---

*Table of Contents*

# TITLE I. SCOPE OF RULES; FORM OF ACTION

## RULE 1. SCOPE AND PURPOSE

These rules govern the procedure in all civil actions and proceedings in the United States district courts, except as stated in Rule 81. They should be construed and administered to secure the just, speedy, and inexpensive determination of every action and proceeding.

[Amended December 29, 1948, effective October 20, 1949; February 28, 1966, effective July 1, 1966; April 22, 1993, effective December 1, 1993; April 30, 2007, effective December 1, 2007, absent contrary Congressional action.]

## RULE 2. ONE FORM OF ACTION

There is one form of action—the civil action.

[Amended April 30, 2007, effective December 1, 2007, absent contrary Congressional action.]

# TITLE II. COMMENCING AN ACTION; SERVICE OF PROCESS, PLEADINGS, MOTIONS, AND ORDERS

## RULE 3. COMMENCING AN ACTION

A civil action is commenced by filing a complaint with the court.

[Amended April 30, 2007, effective December 1, 2007, absent contrary Congressional action.]

## RULE 4. SUMMONS

**(a) Contents; Amendments.**

(1) *Contents.* A summons must:

(A) name the court and the parties;

(B) be directed to the defendant;

(C) state the name and address of the plaintiff's attorney or—if unrepresented—of the plaintiff;

(D) state the time within which the defendant must appear and defend;

(E) notify the defendant that a failure to appear and defend will result in a default judgment against the defendant for the relief demanded in the complaint;

(F) be signed by the clerk; and

(G) bear the court's seal.

(2) *Amendments.* The court may permit a summons to be amended.

**(b) Issuance.** On or after filing the complaint, the plaintiff may present a summons to the clerk for signature and seal. If the summons is properly completed, the clerk must sign, seal, and issue it to the plaintiff for service on the defendant. A summons—or a copy of a summons that is addressed to multiple defendants—must be issued for each defendant to be served.

**(c) Service.**

(1) *In General.* A summons must be served with a copy of the complaint. The plaintiff is responsible for having the summons and complaint served within the time allowed by Rule 4(m) and must furnish the necessary copies to the person who makes service.

(2) *By Whom.* Any person who is at least 18 years old and not a party may serve a summons and complaint.

(3) *By a Marshal or Someone Specially Appointed.* At the plaintiff's request, the court may order that service be made by a United States marshal or deputy marshal or by a person specially appointed by the court. The court must so order if the plaintiff is authorized to proceed in forma pauperis under 28 U.S.C. § 1915 or as a seaman under 28 U.S.C. § 1916.

**(d) Waiving Service.**

(1) *Requesting a Waiver.* An individual, corporation, or association that is subject to service under Rule 4(e), (f), or (h) has a duty to avoid unnecessary expenses of serving the summons. The plaintiff may notify such a defendant that an action has been commenced and request that the defendant waive service of a summons. The notice and request must:

(A) be in writing and be addressed:

(i) to the individual defendant; or

(ii) for a defendant subject to service under Rule 4(h), to an officer, a managing or general agent, or any other agent authorized by appointment or by law to receive service of process;

(B) name the court where the complaint was filed;

(C) be accompanied by a copy of the complaint, two copies of a waiver form, and a prepaid means for returning the form;

(D) inform the defendant, using text prescribed in Form 5, of the consequences of waiving and not waiving service;

(E) state the date when the request is sent;

(F) give the defendant a reasonable time of at least 30 days after the request was sent—or at least 60 days if sent to the defendant outside any judicial district of the United States—to return the waiver; and

(G) be sent by first-class mail or other reliable means.

(2) *Failure to Waive.* If a defendant located within the United States fails, without good cause, to sign and return a waiver requested by a plaintiff located within the United States, the court must impose on the defendant:

(A) the expenses later incurred in making service; and

(B) the reasonable expenses, including attorney's fees, of any motion required to collect those service expenses.

(3) *Time to Answer After a Waiver.* A defendant who, before being served with process, timely returns a waiver need not serve an answer to the complaint until 60 days after the request was sent—or until 90 days after it was sent to the defendant outside any judicial district of the United States.

(4) *Results of Filing a Waiver.* When the plaintiff files a waiver, proof of service is not required and these rules apply as if a summons and complaint had been served at the time of filing the waiver.

(5) *Jurisdiction and Venue Not Waived.* Waiving service of a summons does not waive any objection to personal jurisdiction or to venue.

**(e) Serving an Individual Within a Judicial District of the United States.** Unless federal law provides otherwise, an individual—other than a minor, an incompetent person, or a person whose waiver has been filed—may be served in a judicial district of the United States by:

(1) following state law for serving a summons in an action brought in courts of general jurisdiction in the state where the district court is located or where service is made; or

(2) doing any of the following:

(A) delivering a copy of the summons and of the complaint to the individual personally;

(B) leaving a copy of each at the individual's dwelling or usual place of abode with someone of suitable age and discretion who resides there; or

(C) delivering a copy of each to an agent authorized by appointment or by law to receive service of process.

**(f) Serving an Individual in a Foreign Country.** Unless federal law provides otherwise, an individual—other than a minor, an incompetent person, or a person whose waiver has been filed—may be served at a place not within any judicial district of the United States:

(1) by any internationally agreed means of service that is reasonably calculated to give notice, such as those authorized by the Hague Convention on the Service Abroad of Judicial and Extrajudicial Documents;

(2) if there is no internationally agreed means, or if an international agreement allows but does not specify other means, by a method that is reasonably calculated to give notice:

(A) as prescribed by the foreign country's law for service in that country in an action in its courts of general jurisdiction;

(B) as the foreign authority directs in response to a letter rogatory or letter of request; or

(C) unless prohibited by the foreign country's law, by:

(i) delivering a copy of the summons and of the complaint to the individual personally; or

(ii) using any form of mail that the clerk addresses and sends to the individual and that requires a signed receipt; or

(3) by other means not prohibited by international agreement, as the court orders.

**(g) Serving a Minor or an Incompetent Person.** A minor or an incompetent person in a judicial district of the United States must be served by following state law for serving a summons or like process on such a defendant in an action brought in the courts of general jurisdiction of the state where service is made. A minor or an incompetent person who is not within any judicial district of the United States must be served in the manner prescribed by Rule 4(f)(2)(A), (f)(2)(B), or (f)(3).

**(h) Serving a Corporation, Partnership, or Association.** Unless federal law provides otherwise or the defendant's waiver has been filed, a domestic or foreign corporation, or a partnership or other unincorporated association that is subject to suit under a common name, must be served:

(1) in a judicial district of the United States:

(A) in the manner prescribed by Rule 4(e)(1) for serving an individual; or

(B) by delivering a copy of the summons and of the complaint to an officer, a managing or general agent, or any other agent authorized by appointment or by law to receive service of process and—if the agent is one authorized by statute and the statute so requires—by also mailing a copy of each to the defendant; or

(2) at a place not within any judicial district of the United States, in any manner prescribed by Rule 4(f)

for serving an individual, except personal delivery under (f)(2)(C)(i).

**(i) Serving the United States and Its Agencies, Corporations, Officers, or Employees.**

(1) *United States.* To serve the United States, a party must:

(A)(i) deliver a copy of the summons and of the complaint to the United States attorney for the district where the action is brought—or to an assistant United States attorney or clerical employee whom the United States attorney designates in a writing filed with the court clerk—or

(ii) send a copy of each by registered or certified mail to the civil-process clerk at the United States attorney's office;

(B) send a copy of each by registered or certified mail to the Attorney General of the United States at Washington, D.C.; and

(C) if the action challenges an order of a nonparty agency or officer of the United States, send a copy of each by registered or certified mail to the agency or officer.

(2) *Agency; Corporation; Officer or Employee Sued in an Official Capacity.* To serve a United States agency or corporation, or a United States officer or employee sued only in an official capacity, a party must serve the United States and also send a copy of the summons and of the complaint by registered or certified mail to the agency, corporation, officer, or employee.

(3) *Officer or Employee Sued Individually.* To serve a United States officer or employee sued in an individual capacity for an act or omission occurring in connection with duties performed on the United States' behalf (whether or not the officer or employee is also sued in an official capacity), a party must serve the United States and also serve the officer or employee under Rule 4(e), (f), or (g).

(4) *Extending Time.* The court must allow a party a reasonable time to cure its failure to:

(A) serve a person required to be served under Rule 4(i)(2), if the party has served either the United States attorney or the Attorney General of the United States; or

(B) serve the United States under Rule 4(i)(3), if the party has served the United States officer or employee.

**(j) Serving a Foreign, State, or Local Government.**

(1) *Foreign State.* A foreign state or its political subdivision, agency, or instrumentality must be served in accordance with 28 U.S.C. § 1608.

(2) *State or Local Government.* A state, a municipal corporation, or any other state-created governmental organization that is subject to suit must be served by:

(A) delivering a copy of the summons and of the complaint to its chief executive officer; or

(B) serving a copy of each in the manner prescribed by that state's law for serving a summons or like process on such a defendant.

**(k) Territorial Limits of Effective Service.**

(1) *In General.* Serving a summons or filing a waiver of service establishes personal jurisdiction over a defendant:

(A) who is subject to the jurisdiction of a court of general jurisdiction in the state where the district court is located;

(B) who is a party joined under Rule 14 or 19 and is served within a judicial district of the United States and not more than 100 miles from where the summons was issued;

(C) when authorized by a federal statute.

(2) *Federal Claim Outside State–Court Jurisdiction.* For a claim that arises under federal law, serving a summons or filing a waiver of service establishes personal jurisdiction over a defendant if:

(A) the defendant is not subject to jurisdiction in any state's courts of general jurisdiction; and

(B) exercising jurisdiction is consistent with the United States Constitution and laws.

**(*l*) Proving Service.**

(1) *Affidavit Required.* Unless service is waived, proof of service must be made to the court. Except for service by a United States marshal or deputy marshal, proof must be by the server's affidavit.

(2) *Service Outside the United States.* Service not within any judicial district of the United States must be proved as follows:

(A) if made under Rule 4(f)(1), as provided in the applicable treaty or convention; or

(B) if made under Rule 4(f)(2) or (f)(3), by a receipt signed by the addressee, or by other evidence satisfying the court that the summons and complaint were delivered to the addressee.

(3) *Validity of Service; Amending Proof.* Failure to prove service does not affect the validity of service. The court may permit proof of service to be amended.

**(m) Time Limit for Service.** If a defendant is not served within 120 days after the complaint is filed, the court—on motion or on its own after notice to the plaintiff—must dismiss the action without prejudice against that defendant or order that service be made within a specified time. But if the plaintiff shows good cause for the failure, the court must extend the time for service for an appropriate period. This subdivision

(m) does not apply to service in a foreign country under Rule 4(f) or 4(j)(1).

**(n) Asserting Jurisdiction over Property or Assets.**

(1) *Federal Law.* The court may assert jurisdiction over property if authorized by a federal statute. Notice to claimants of the property must be given as provided in the statute or by serving a summons under this rule.

(2) *State Law.* On a showing that personal jurisdiction over a defendant cannot be obtained in the district where the action is brought by reasonable efforts to serve a summons under this rule, the court may assert jurisdiction over the defendant's assets found in the district. Jurisdiction is acquired by seizing the assets under the circumstances and in the manner provided by state law in that district.

[Amended January 21, 1963, effective July 1, 1963; February 28, 1966, effective July 1, 1966; April 29, 1980, effective August 1, 1980; amended by Pub.L. 97-462, § 2, January 12, 1983, 96 Stat. 2527, effective 45 days after January 12, 1983; amended March 2, 1987, effective August 1, 1987; April 22, 1993, effective December 1, 1993; April 17, 2000, effective December 1, 2000; April 30, 2007, effective December 1, 2007, absent contrary Congressional action.]

## RULE 4.1   SERVING OTHER PROCESS

**(a) In General.** Process—other than a summons under Rule 4 or a subpoena under Rule 45—must be served by a United States marshal or deputy marshal or by a person specially appointed for that purpose. It may be served anywhere within the territorial limits of the state where the district court is located and, if authorized by a federal statute, beyond those limits. Proof of service must be made under Rule 4(*l* ).

**(b) Enforcing Orders: Committing for Civil Contempt.** An order committing a person for civil contempt of a decree or injunction issued to enforce federal law may be served and enforced in any district. Any other order in a civil-contempt proceeding may be served only in the state where the issuing court is located or elsewhere in the United States within 100 miles from where the order was issued.

[Adopted April 22, 1993, effective December 1, 1993; amended April 30, 2007, effective December 1, 2007, absent contrary Congressional action.]

## RULE 5.   SERVING AND FILING PLEADINGS AND OTHER PAPERS

**(a) Service: When Required.**

(1) *In General.* Unless these rules provide otherwise, each of the following papers must be served on every party:

(A) an order stating that service is required;

(B) a pleading filed after the original complaint, unless the court orders otherwise under Rule 5(c) because there are numerous defendants;

(C) a discovery paper required to be served on a party, unless the court orders otherwise;

(D) a written motion, except one that may be heard ex parte; and

(E) a written notice, appearance, demand, or offer of judgment, or any similar paper.

(2) *If a Party Fails to Appear.* No service is required on a party who is in default for failing to appear. But a pleading that asserts a new claim for relief against such a party must be served on that party under Rule 4.

(3) *Seizing Property.* If an action is begun by seizing property and no person is or need be named as a defendant, any service required before the filing of an appearance, answer, or claim must be made on the person who had custody or possession of the property when it was seized.

**(b) Service: How Made.**

(1) *Serving an Attorney.* If a party is represented by an attorney, service under this rule must be made on the attorney unless the court orders service on the party.

(2) *Service in General.* A paper is served under this rule by:

(A) handing it to the person;

(B) leaving it:

(i) at the person's office with a clerk or other person in charge or, if no one is in charge, in a conspicuous place in the office; or

(ii) if the person has no office or the office is closed, at the person's dwelling or usual place of abode with someone of suitable age and discretion who resides there;

(C) mailing it to the person's last known address—in which event service is complete upon mailing;

(D) leaving it with the court clerk if the person has no known address;

(E) sending it by electronic means if the person consented in writing—in which event service is complete upon transmission, but is not effective if the serving party learns that it did not reach the person to be served; or

(F) delivering it by any other means that the person consented to in writing—in which event service is complete when the person making service delivers it to the agency designated to make delivery.

(3) *Using Court Facilities.* If a local rule so authorizes, a party may use the court's transmission facilities to make service under Rule 5(b)(2)(E).

**(c) Serving Numerous Defendants.**

(1) *In General.* If an action involves an unusually large number of defendants, the court may, on motion or on its own, order that:

(A) defendants' pleadings and replies to them need not be served on other defendants;

(B) any crossclaim, counterclaim, avoidance, or affirmative defense in those pleadings and replies to them will be treated as denied or avoided by all other parties; and

(C) filing any such pleading and serving it on the plaintiff constitutes notice of the pleading to all parties.

(2) *Notifying Parties.* A copy of every such order must be served on the parties as the court directs.

**(d) Filing.**

(1) *Required Filings; Certificate of Service.* Any paper after the complaint that is required to be served—together with a certificate of service—must be filed within a reasonable time after service. But disclosures under Rule 26(a)(1) or (2) and the following discovery requests and responses must not be filed until they are used in the proceeding or the court orders filing: depositions, interrogatories, requests for documents or tangible things or to permit entry onto land, and requests for admission.

(2) *How Filing Is Made—In General.* A paper is filed by delivering it:

(A) to the clerk; or

(B) to a judge who agrees to accept it for filing, and who must then note the filing date on the paper and promptly send it to the clerk.

(3) *Electronic Filing, Signing, or Verification.* A court may, by local rule, allow papers to be filed, signed, or verified by electronic means that are consistent with any technical standards established by the Judicial Conference of the United States. A local rule may require electronic filing only if reasonable exceptions are allowed. A paper filed electronically in compliance with a local rule is a written paper for purposes of these rules.

(4) *Acceptance by the Clerk.* The clerk must not refuse to file a paper solely because it is not in the form prescribed by these rules or by a local rule or practice.

[Amended January 21, 1963, effective July 1, 1963; March 30, 1970, effective July 1, 1970; April 29, 1980, effective August 1, 1980; March 2, 1987, effective August 1, 1987; April 30, 1991, effective December 1, 1991; April 22, 1993, effective December 1, 1993; April 23, 1996, effective December 1, 1996; April 17, 2000, effective December 1, 2000; April 23, 2001, effective December 1, 2001; April 12, 2006, effective December 1, 2006; April 30, 2007, effective December 1, 2007, absent contrary Congressional action.]

## RULE 5.1 CONSTITUTIONAL CHALLENGE TO A STATUTE—NOTICE, CERTIFICATION, AND INTERVENTION

**(a) Notice by a Party.** A party that files a pleading, written motion, or other paper drawing into question the constitutionality of a federal or state statute must promptly:

(1) file a notice of constitutional question stating the question and identifying the paper that raises it, if:

(A) a federal statute is questioned and the parties do not include the United States, one of its agencies, or one of its officers or employees in an official capacity; or

(B) a state statute is questioned and the parties do not include the state, one of its agencies, or one of its officers or employees in an official capacity; and

(2) serve the notice and paper on the Attorney General of the United States if a federal statute is questioned—or on the state attorney general if a state statute is questioned—either by certified or registered mail or by sending it to an electronic address designated by the attorney general for this purpose.

**(b) Certification by the Court.** The court must, under 28 U.S.C. § 2403, certify to the appropriate attorney general that a statute has been questioned.

**(c) Intervention; Final Decision on the Merits.** Unless the court sets a later time, the attorney general may intervene within 60 days after the notice is filed or after the court certifies the challenge, whichever is earlier. Before the time to intervene expires, the court may reject the constitutional challenge, but may not enter a final judgment holding the statute unconstitutional.

**(d) No Forfeiture.** A party's failure to file and serve the notice, or the court's failure to certify, does not forfeit a constitutional claim or defense that is otherwise timely asserted.

[Effective December 1, 2006; amended April 30, 2007, effective December 1, 2007, absent contrary Congressional action.]

## RULE 5.2 PRIVACY PROTECTION FOR FILINGS MADE WITH THE COURT

**(a) Redacted Filings.** Unless the court orders otherwise, in an electronic or paper filing with the court that contains an individual's social-security number, taxpayer-identification number, or birth date, the name of an individual known to be a minor, or a

financial-account number, a party or nonparty making the filing may include only:

(1) the last four digits of the social-security number and taxpayer-identification number;

(2) the year of the individual's birth;

(3) the minor's initials; and

(4) the last four digits of the financial-account number.

**(b) Exemptions from the Redaction Requirement.** The redaction requirement does not apply to the following:

(1) a financial-account number that identifies the property allegedly subject to forfeiture in a forfeiture proceeding;

(2) the record of an administrative or agency proceeding;

(3) the official record of a state-court proceeding;

(4) the record of a court or tribunal, if that record was not subject to the redaction requirement when originally filed;

(5) a filing covered by Rule 5.2(c) or (d); and

(6) a pro se filing in an action brought under 28 U.S.C. §§ 2241, 2254, or 2255.

**(c) Limitations on Remote Access to Electronic Files; Social–Security Appeals and Immigration Cases.** Unless the court orders otherwise, in an action for benefits under the Social Security Act, and in an action or proceeding relating to an order of removal, to relief from removal, or to immigration benefits or detention, access to an electronic file is authorized as follows:

(1) the parties and their attorneys may have remote electronic access to any part of the case file, including the administrative record;

(2) any other person may have electronic access to the full record at the courthouse, but may have remote electronic access only to:

(A) the docket maintained by the court; and

(B) an opinion, order, judgment, or other disposition of the court, but not any other part of the case file or the administrative record.

**(d) Filings Made Under Seal.** The court may order that a filing be made under seal without redaction. The court may later unseal the filing or order the person who made the filing to file a redacted version for the public record.

**(e) Protective Orders.** For good cause, the court may by order in a case:

(1) require redaction of additional information; or

(2) limit or prohibit a nonparty's remote electronic access to a document filed with the court.

**(f) Option for Additional Unredacted Filing Under Seal.** A person making a redacted filing may also file an unredacted copy under seal. The court must retain the unredacted copy as part of the record.

**(g) Option for Filing a Reference List.** A filing that contains redacted information may be filed together with a reference list that identifies each item of redacted information and specifies an appropriate identifier that uniquely corresponds to each item listed. The list must be filed under seal and may be amended as of right. Any reference in the case to a listed identifier will be construed to refer to the corresponding item of information.

**(h) Waiver of Protection of Identifiers.** A person waives the protection of Rule 5.2(a) as to the person's own information by filing it without redaction and not under seal.

[Adopted April 30, 2007, effective December 1, 2007, absent contrary Congressional action.]

## RULE 6. COMPUTING AND EXTENDING TIME; TIME FOR MOTION PAPERS

**(a) Computing Time.** The following rules apply in computing any time period specified in these rules or in any local rule, court order, or statute:

(1) *Day of the Event Excluded.* Exclude the day of the act, event, or default that begins the period.

(2) *Exclusions from Brief Periods.* Exclude intermediate Saturdays, Sundays, and legal holidays when the period is less than 11 days.

(3) *Last Day.* Include the last day of the period unless it is a Saturday, Sunday, legal holiday, or—if the act to be done is filing a paper in court—a day on which weather or other conditions make the clerk's office inaccessible. When the last day is excluded, the period runs until the end of the next day that is not a Saturday, Sunday, legal holiday, or day when the clerk's office is inaccessible.

(4) *"Legal Holiday" Defined.* As used in these rules, "legal holiday" means:

(A) the day set aside by statute for observing New Year's Day, Martin Luther King Jr.'s Birthday, Washington's Birthday, Memorial Day, Independence Day, Labor Day, Columbus Day, Veterans' Day, Thanksgiving Day, or Christmas Day; and

(B) any other day declared a holiday by the President, Congress, or the state where the district court is located.

**(b) Extending Time.**

(1) *In General.* When an act may or must be done within a specified time, the court may, for good cause, extend the time:

(A) with or without motion or notice if the court acts, or if a request is made, before the original time or its extension expires; or

(B) on motion made after the time has expired if the party failed to act because of excusable neglect.

(2) *Exceptions.* A court must not extend the time to act under Rules 50(b) and (d), 52(b), 59(b), (d), and (e), and 60(b), except as those rules allow.

**(c) Motions, Notices of Hearing, and Affidavits.**

(1) *In General.* A written motion and notice of the hearing must be served at least 5 days before the time specified for the hearing, with the following exceptions:

(A) when the motion may be heard ex parte;

(B) when these rules set a different time; or

(C) when a court order—which a party may, for good cause, apply for ex parte—sets a different time.

(2) *Supporting Affidavit.* Any affidavit supporting a motion must be served with the motion. Except as Rule 59(c) provides otherwise, any opposing affidavit must be served at least 1 day before the hearing, unless the court permits service at another time.

**(d) Additional Time After Certain Kinds of Service.** When a party may or must act within a specified time after service and service is made under Rule 5(b)(2)(C), (D), (E), or (F), 3 days are added after the period would otherwise expire under Rule 6(a).

[Amended December 27, 1946, effective March 19, 1948; January 21, 1963, effective July 1, 1963; February 28, 1966, effective July 1, 1966; December 4, 1967, effective July 1, 1968; March 1, 1971, effective July 1, 1971; April 28, 1983, effective August 1, 1983; April 29, 1985, effective August 1, 1985; March 2, 1987, effective August 1, 1987; April 29, 1999, effective December 1, 1999; April 23, 2001, effective December 1, 2001; April 25, 2005, effective December 1, 2005; April 30, 2007, effective December 1, 2007, absent contrary Congressional action.]

# TITLE III.   PLEADINGS AND MOTIONS

## RULE 7.   PLEADINGS ALLOWED; FORM OF MOTIONS AND OTHER PAPERS

**(a) Pleadings.** Only these pleadings are allowed:

(1) a complaint;

(2) an answer to a complaint;

(3) an answer to a counterclaim designated as a counterclaim;

(4) an answer to a crossclaim;

(5) a third-party complaint;

(6) an answer to a third-party complaint; and

(7) if the court orders one, a reply to an answer.

**(b) Motions and Other Papers.**

(1) *In General.* A request for a court order must be made by motion. The motion must:

(A) be in writing unless made during a hearing or trial;

(B) state with particularity the grounds for seeking the order; and

(C) state the relief sought.

(2) *Form.* The rules governing captions and other matters of form in pleadings apply to motions and other papers.

[Amended December 27, 1946, effective March 19, 1948; January 21, 1963, effective July 1, 1963; April 28, 1983, effective August 1, 1983; April 30, 2007, effective December 1, 2007, absent contrary Congressional action.]

## RULE 7.1   DISCLOSURE STATEMENT

**(a) Who Must File; Contents.** A nongovernmental corporate party must file two copies of a disclosure statement that:

(1) identifies any parent corporation and any publicly held corporation owning 10% or more of its stock; or

(2) states that there is no such corporation.

**(b) Time to File; Supplemental Filing.** A party must:

(1) file the disclosure statement with its first appearance, pleading, petition, motion, response, or other request addressed to the court; and

(2) promptly file a supplemental statement if any required information changes.

[Adopted April 29, 2002, effective December 1, 2002; April 30, 2007, effective December 1, 2007, absent contrary Congressional action.]

## RULE 8.   GENERAL RULES OF PLEADING

**(a) Claim for Relief.** A pleading that states a claim for relief must contain:

(1) a short and plain statement of the grounds for the court's jurisdiction, unless the court already has jurisdiction and the claim needs no new jurisdictional support;

(2) a short and plain statement of the claim showing that the pleader is entitled to relief; and

(3) a demand for the relief sought, which may include relief in the alternative or different types of relief.

**(b) Defenses; Admissions and Denials.**

(1) *In General.* In responding to a pleading, a party must:

(A) state in short and plain terms its defenses to each claim asserted against it; and

(B) admit or deny the allegations asserted against it by an opposing party.

(2) *Denials—Responding to the Substance.* A denial must fairly respond to the substance of the allegation.

(3) *General and Specific Denials.* A party that intends in good faith to deny all the allegations of a pleading—including the jurisdictional grounds—may do so by a general denial. A party that does not intend to deny all the allegations must either specifically deny designated allegations or generally deny all except those specifically admitted.

(4) *Denying Part of an Allegation.* A party that intends in good faith to deny only part of an allegation must admit the part that is true and deny the rest.

(5) *Lacking Knowledge or Information.* A party that lacks knowledge or information sufficient to form a belief about the truth of an allegation must so state, and the statement has the effect of a denial.

(6) *Effect of Failing to Deny.* An allegation—other than one relating to the amount of damages—is admitted if a responsive pleading is required and the allegation is not denied. If a responsive pleading is not required, an allegation is considered denied or avoided.

**(c) Affirmative Defenses.**

(1) *In General.* In responding to a pleading, a party must affirmatively state any avoidance or affirmative defense, including:

- accord and satisfaction;
- arbitration and award;
- assumption of risk;
- contributory negligence;
- discharge in bankruptcy;
- duress;
- estoppel;
- failure of consideration;
- fraud;
- illegality;
- injury by fellow servant;
- laches;
- license;
- payment;

- release;
- res judicata;
- statute of frauds;
- statute of limitations; and
- waiver.

(2) *Mistaken Designation.* If a party mistakenly designates a defense as a counterclaim, or a counterclaim as a defense, the court must, if justice requires, treat the pleading as though it were correctly designated, and may impose terms for doing so.

**(d) Pleading to Be Concise and Direct; Alternative Statements; Inconsistency.**

(1) *In General.* Each allegation must be simple, concise, and direct. No technical form is required.

(2) *Alternative Statements of a Claim or Defense.* A party may set out two or more statements of a claim or defense alternatively or hypothetically, either in a single count or defense or in separate ones. If a party makes alternative statements, the pleading is sufficient if any one of them is sufficient.

(3) *Inconsistent Claims or Defenses.* A party may state as many separate claims or defenses as it has, regardless of consistency.

**(e) Construing Pleadings.** Pleadings must be construed so as to do justice.

[Amended February 28, 1966, effective July 1, 1966; March 2, 1987, effective August 1, 1987; April 30, 2007, effective December 1, 2007, absent contrary Congressional action.]

# RULE 9. PLEADING SPECIAL MATTERS

**(a) Capacity or Authority to Sue; Legal Existence.**

(1) *In General.* Except when required to show that the court has jurisdiction, a pleading need not allege:

(A) a party's capacity to sue or be sued;

(B) a party's authority to sue or be sued in a representative capacity; or

(C) the legal existence of an organized association of persons that is made a party.

(2) *Raising Those Issues.* To raise any of those issues, a party must do so by a specific denial, which must state any supporting facts that are peculiarly within the party's knowledge.

**(b) Fraud or Mistake; Conditions of Mind.** In alleging fraud or mistake, a party must state with particularity the circumstances constituting fraud or mistake. Malice, intent, knowledge, and other conditions of a person's mind may be alleged generally.

**(c) Conditions Precedent.** In pleading conditions precedent, it suffices to allege generally that all conditions precedent have occurred or been performed. But when denying that a condition precedent has occurred

or been performed, a party must do so with particularity.

**(d) Official Document or Act.** In pleading an official document or official act, it suffices to allege that the document was legally issued or the act legally done.

**(e) Judgment.** In pleading a judgment or decision of a domestic or foreign court, a judicial or quasi-judicial tribunal, or a board or officer, it suffices to plead the judgment or decision without showing jurisdiction to render it.

**(f) Time and Place.** An allegation of time or place is material when testing the sufficiency of a pleading.

**(g) Special Damages.** If an item of special damage is claimed, it must be specifically stated.

**(h) Admiralty or Maritime Claim.**

(1) *How Designated.* If a claim for relief is within the admiralty or maritime jurisdiction and also within the court's subject-matter jurisdiction on some other ground, the pleading may designate the claim as an admiralty or maritime claim for purposes of Rules 14(c), 38(e), and 82 and the Supplemental Rules for Admiralty or Maritime Claims and Asset Forfeiture Actions. A claim cognizable only in the admiralty or maritime jurisdiction is an admiralty or maritime claim for those purposes, whether or not so designated.

(2) *Designation for Appeal.* A case that includes an admiralty or maritime claim within this subdivision (h) is an admiralty case within 28 U.S.C. § 1292(a)(3).

[Amended February 28, 1966, effective July 1, 1966; December 4, 1967, effective July 1, 1968; March 30, 1970, effective July 1, 1970; March 2, 1987, effective August 1, 1987; April 11, 1997, effective December 1, 1997; April 12, 2006, effective December 1, 2006; April 30, 2007, effective December 1, 2007, absent contrary Congressional action.]

## RULE 10.  FORM OF PLEADINGS

**(a) Caption; Names of Parties.** Every pleading must have a caption with the court's name, a title, a file number, and a Rule 7(a) designation. The title of the complaint must name all the parties; the title of other pleadings, after naming the first party on each side, may refer generally to other parties.

**(b) Paragraphs; Separate Statements.** A party must state its claims or defenses in numbered paragraphs, each limited as far as practicable to a single set of circumstances. A later pleading may refer by number to a paragraph in an earlier pleading. If doing so would promote clarity, each claim founded on a separate transaction or occurrence—and each defense other than a denial—must be stated in a separate count or defense.

**(c) Adoption by Reference; Exhibits.** A statement in a pleading may be adopted by reference elsewhere in the same pleading or in any other pleading or motion. A copy of a written instrument that is an exhibit to a pleading is a part of the pleading for all purposes.

[Amended April 30, 2007, effective December 1, 2007, absent contrary Congressional action.]

## RULE 11. SIGNING PLEADINGS, MOTIONS, AND OTHER PAPERS; REPRESENTATIONS TO THE COURT; SANCTIONS

**(a) Signature.** Every pleading, written motion, and other paper must be signed by at least one attorney of record in the attorney's name—or by a party personally if the party is unrepresented. The paper must state the signer's address, e-mail address, and telephone number. Unless a rule or statute specifically states otherwise, a pleading need not be verified or accompanied by an affidavit. The court must strike an unsigned paper unless the omission is promptly corrected after being called to the attorney's or party's attention.

**(b) Representations to the Court.** By presenting to the court a pleading, written motion, or other paper—whether by signing, filing, submitting, or later advocating it—an attorney or unrepresented party certifies that to the best of the person's knowledge, information, and belief, formed after an inquiry reasonable under the circumstances:

(1) it is not being presented for any improper purpose, such as to harass, cause unnecessary delay, or needlessly increase the cost of litigation;

(2) the claims, defenses, and other legal contentions are warranted by existing law or by a nonfrivolous argument for extending, modifying, or reversing existing law or for establishing new law;

(3) the factual contentions have evidentiary support or, if specifically so identified, will likely have evidentiary support after a reasonable opportunity for further investigation or discovery; and

(4) the denials of factual contentions are warranted on the evidence or, if specifically so identified, are reasonably based on belief or a lack of information.

**(c) Sanctions.**

(1) *In General.* If, after notice and a reasonable opportunity to respond, the court determines that Rule 11(b) has been violated, the court may impose an appropriate sanction on any attorney, law firm, or party that violated the rule or is responsible for the violation. Absent exceptional circumstances, a law firm must be held jointly responsible for a violation committed by its partner, associate, or employee.

(2) *Motion for Sanctions.* A motion for sanctions must be made separately from any other motion and must describe the specific conduct that allegedly violates Rule 11(b). The motion must be served under Rule 5, but it must not be filed or be presented to the court if the challenged paper, claim, defense, contention, or denial is withdrawn or appropriately corrected within 21 days after service or within another time the court sets. If warranted, the court may award to the prevailing party the reasonable expenses, including attorney's fees, incurred for the motion.

(3) *On the Court's Initiative.* On its own, the court may order an attorney, law firm, or party to show cause why conduct specifically described in the order has not violated Rule 11(b).

(4) *Nature of a Sanction.* A sanction imposed under this rule must be limited to what suffices to deter repetition of the conduct or comparable conduct by others similarly situated. The sanction may include nonmonetary directives; an order to pay a penalty into court; or, if imposed on motion and warranted for effective deterrence, an order directing payment to the movant of part or all of the reasonable attorney's fees and other expenses directly resulting from the violation.

(5) *Limitations on Monetary Sanctions.* The court must not impose a monetary sanction:

(A) against a represented party for violating Rule 11(b)(2); or

(B) on its own, unless it issued the show-cause order under Rule 11(c)(3) before voluntary dismissal or settlement of the claims made by or against the party that is, or whose attorneys are, to be sanctioned.

(6) *Requirements for an Order.* An order imposing a sanction must describe the sanctioned conduct and explain the basis for the sanction.

(d) **Inapplicability to Discovery.** This rule does not apply to disclosures and discovery requests, responses, objections, and motions under Rules 26 through 37.

[Amended April 28, 1983, effective August 1, 1983; March 2, 1987, effective August 1, 1987; April 22, 1993, effective December 1, 1993; April 30, 2007, effective December 1, 2007, absent contrary Congressional action.]

## RULE 12. DEFENSES AND OBJECTIONS: WHEN AND HOW PRESENTED; MOTION FOR JUDGMENT ON THE PLEADINGS; CONSOLIDATING MOTIONS; WAIVING DEFENSES; PRETRIAL HEARING

(a) **Time to Serve a Responsive Pleading.**

(1) *In General.* Unless another time is specified by this rule or a federal statute, the time for serving a responsive pleading is as follows:

(A) A defendant must serve an answer:

(i) within 20 days after being served with the summons and complaint; or

(ii) if it has timely waived service under Rule 4(d), within 60 days after the request for a waiver was sent, or within 90 days after it was sent to the defendant outside any judicial district of the United States.

(B) A party must serve an answer to a counterclaim or crossclaim within 20 days after being served with the pleading that states the counterclaim or crossclaim.

(C) A party must serve a reply to an answer within 20 days after being served with an order to reply, unless the order specifies a different time.

(2) *United States and Its Agencies, Officers, or Employees Sued in an Official Capacity.* The United States, a United States agency, or a United States officer or employee sued only in an official capacity must serve an answer to a complaint, counterclaim, or crossclaim within 60 days after service on the United States attorney.

(3) *United States Officers or Employees Sued in an Individual Capacity.* A United States officer or employee sued in an individual capacity for an act or omission occurring in connection with duties performed on the United States' behalf must serve an answer to a complaint, counterclaim, or crossclaim within 60 days after service on the officer or employee or service on the United States attorney, whichever is later.

(4) *Effect of a Motion.* Unless the court sets a different time, serving a motion under this rule alters these periods as follows:

(A) if the court denies the motion or postpones its disposition until trial, the responsive pleading must be served within 10 days after notice of the court's action; or

(B) if the court grants a motion for a more definite statement, the responsive pleading must be served within 10 days after the more definite statement is served.

(b) **How to Present Defenses.** Every defense to a claim for relief in any pleading must be asserted in the responsive pleading if one is required. But a party may assert the following defenses by motion:

(1) lack of subject-matter jurisdiction;

(2) lack of personal jurisdiction;

(3) improper venue;

(4) insufficient process;

(5) insufficient service of process;

(6) failure to state a claim upon which relief can be granted; and

(7) failure to join a party under Rule 19.

A motion asserting any of these defenses must be made before pleading if a responsive pleading is allowed. If a pleading sets out a claim for relief that does not require a responsive pleading, an opposing party may assert at trial any defense to that claim. No defense or objection is waived by joining it with one or more other defenses or objections in a responsive pleading or in a motion.

**(c) Motion for Judgment on the Pleadings.** After the pleadings are closed—but early enough not to delay trial—a party may move for judgment on the pleadings.

**(d) Result of Presenting Matters Outside the Pleadings.** If, on a motion under Rule 12(b)(6) or 12(c), matters outside the pleadings are presented to and not excluded by the court, the motion must be treated as one for summary judgment under Rule 56. All parties must be given a reasonable opportunity to present all the material that is pertinent to the motion.

**(e) Motion for a More Definite Statement.** A party may move for a more definite statement of a pleading to which a responsive pleading is allowed but which is so vague or ambiguous that the party cannot reasonably prepare a response. The motion must be made before filing a responsive pleading and must point out the defects complained of and the details desired. If the court orders a more definite statement and the order is not obeyed within 10 days after notice of the order or within the time the court sets, the court may strike the pleading or issue any other appropriate order.

**(f) Motion to Strike.** The court may strike from a pleading an insufficient defense or any redundant, immaterial, impertinent, or scandalous matter. The court may act:

(1) on its own; or

(2) on motion made by a party either before responding to the pleading or, if a response is not allowed, within 20 days after being served with the pleading.

**(g) Joining Motions.**

(1) *Right to Join.* A motion under this rule may be joined with any other motion allowed by this rule.

(2) *Limitation on Further Motions.* Except as provided in Rule 12(h)(2) or (3), a party that makes a motion under this rule must not make another motion under this rule raising a defense or objection that was available to the party but omitted from its earlier motion.

**(h) Waiving and Preserving Certain Defenses.**

(1) *When Some Are Waived.* A party waives any defense listed in Rule 12(b)(2)-(5) by:

(A) omitting it from a motion in the circumstances described in Rule 12(g)(2); or

(B) failing to either:

(i) make it by motion under this rule; or

(ii) include it in a responsive pleading or in an amendment allowed by Rule 15(a)(1) as a matter of course.

(2) *When to Raise Others.* Failure to state a claim upon which relief can be granted, to join a person required by Rule 19(b), or to state a legal defense to a claim may be raised:

(A) in any pleading allowed or ordered under Rule 7(a);

(B) by a motion under Rule 12(c); or

(C) at trial.

(3) *Lack of Subject–Matter Jurisdiction.* If the court determines at any time that it lacks subject-matter jurisdiction, the court must dismiss the action.

**(i) Hearing Before Trial.** If a party so moves, any defense listed in Rule 12(b)(1)-(7)—whether made in a pleading or by motion—and a motion under Rule 12(c) must be heard and decided before trial unless the court orders a deferral until trial.

[Amended December 27, 1946, effective March 19, 1948; January 21, 1963, effective July 1, 1963; February 28, 1966, effective July 1, 1966; March 2, 1987, effective August 1, 1987; April 22, 1993, effective December 1, 1993; April 17, 2000, effective December 1, 2000; April 30, 2007, effective December 1, 2007, absent contrary Congressional action.]

# RULE 13.  COUNTERCLAIM AND CROSSCLAIM

**(a) Compulsory Counterclaim.**

(1) *In General.* A pleading must state as a counterclaim any claim that—at the time of its service—the pleader has against an opposing party if the claim:

(A) arises out of the transaction or occurrence that is the subject matter of the opposing party's claim; and

(B) does not require adding another party over whom the court cannot acquire jurisdiction.

(2) *Exceptions.* The pleader need not state the claim if:

(A) when the action was commenced, the claim was the subject of another pending action; or

(B) the opposing party sued on its claim by attachment or other process that did not establish personal jurisdiction over the pleader on that claim,

and the pleader does not assert any counterclaim under this rule.

**(b) Permissive Counterclaim.** A pleading may state as a counterclaim against an opposing party any claim that is not compulsory.

**(c) Relief Sought in a Counterclaim.** A counterclaim need not diminish or defeat the recovery sought by the opposing party. It may request relief that exceeds in amount or differs in kind from the relief sought by the opposing party.

**(d) Counterclaim Against the United States.** These rules do not expand the right to assert a counterclaim—or to claim a credit—against the United States or a United States officer or agency.

**(e) Counterclaim Maturing or Acquired After Pleading.** The court may permit a party to file a supplemental pleading asserting a counterclaim that matured or was acquired by the party after serving an earlier pleading.

**(f) Omitted Counterclaim.** The court may permit a party to amend a pleading to add a counterclaim if it was omitted through oversight, inadvertence, or excusable neglect or if justice so requires.

**(g) Crossclaim Against a Coparty.** A pleading may state as a crossclaim any claim by one party against a coparty if the claim arises out of the transaction or occurrence that is the subject matter of the original action or of a counterclaim, or if the claim relates to any property that is the subject matter of the original action. The crossclaim may include a claim that the coparty is or may be liable to the crossclaimant for all or part of a claim asserted in the action against the cross-claimant.

**(h) Joining Additional Parties.** Rules 19 and 20 govern the addition of a person as a party to a counterclaim or crossclaim.

**(i) Separate Trials; Separate Judgments.** If the court orders separate trials under Rule 42(b), it may enter judgment on a counterclaim or crossclaim under Rule 54(b) when it has jurisdiction to do so, even if the opposing party's claims have been dismissed or otherwise resolved.

[Amended December 27, 1946, effective March 19, 1948; January 21, 1963, effective July 1, 1963; February 28, 1966, effective July 1, 1966; March 2, 1987, effective August 1, 1987; April 30, 2007, effective December 1, 2007, absent contrary Congressional action.]

## RULE 14. THIRD–PARTY PRACTICE

**(a) When a Defending Party May Bring in a Third Party.**

(1) *Timing of the Summons and Complaint.* A defending party may, as third-party plaintiff, serve a summons and complaint on a nonparty who is or may

be liable to it for all or part of the claim against it. But the third-party plaintiff must, by motion, obtain the court's leave if it files the third-party complaint more than 10 days after serving its original answer.

(2) *Third–Party Defendant's Claims and Defenses.* The person served with the summons and third-party complaint—the "third-party defendant":

(A) must assert any defense against the third-party plaintiff's claim under Rule 12;

(B) must assert any counterclaim against the third-party plaintiff under Rule 13(a), and may assert any counterclaim against the third-party plaintiff under Rule 13(b) or any crossclaim against another third-party defendant under Rule 13(g);

(C) may assert against the plaintiff any defense that the third-party plaintiff has to the plaintiff's claim; and

(D) may also assert against the plaintiff any claim arising out of the transaction or occurrence that is the subject matter of the plaintiff's claim against the third-party plaintiff.

(3) *Plaintiff's Claims Against a Third–Party Defendant.* The plaintiff may assert against the third-party defendant any claim arising out of the transaction or occurrence that is the subject matter of the plaintiff's claim against the third-party plaintiff. The third-party defendant must then assert any defense under Rule 12 and any counterclaim under Rule 13(a), and may assert any counterclaim under Rule 13(b) or any crossclaim under Rule 13(g).

(4) *Motion to Strike, Sever, or Try Separately.* Any party may move to strike the third-party claim, to sever it, or to try it separately.

(5) *Third–Party Defendant's Claim Against a Nonparty.* A third-party defendant may proceed under this rule against a nonparty who is or may be liable to the third-party defendant for all or part of any claim against it.

(6) *Third–Party Complaint In Rem.* If it is within the admiralty or maritime jurisdiction, a third-party complaint may be in rem. In that event, a reference in this rule to the "summons" includes the warrant of arrest, and a reference to the defendant or third-party plaintiff includes, when appropriate, a person who asserts a right under Supplemental Rule C(6)(a)(i) in the property arrested.

**(b) When a Plaintiff May Bring in a Third Party.** When a claim is asserted against a plaintiff, the plaintiff may bring in a third party if this rule would allow a defendant to do so.

**(c) Admiralty or Maritime Claim.**

(1) *Scope of Impleader.* If a plaintiff asserts an admiralty or maritime claim under Rule 9(h), the defendant or a person who asserts a right under

Supplemental Rule C(6)(a)(i) may, as a third-party plaintiff, bring in a third-party defendant who may be wholly or partly liable—either to the plaintiff or to the third-party plaintiff—for remedy over, contribution, or otherwise on account of the same transaction, occurrence, or series of transactions or occurrences.

(2) *Defending Against a Demand for Judgment for the Plaintiff.* The third-party plaintiff may demand judgment in the plaintiff's favor against the third-party defendant. In that event, the third-party defendant must defend under Rule 12 against the plaintiff's claim as well as the third-party plaintiff's claim; and the action proceeds as if the plaintiff had sued both the third-party defendant and the third-party plaintiff.

[Amended December 27, 1946, effective March 19, 1948; January 21, 1963, effective July 1, 1963; February 28, 1966, effective July 1, 1966; March 2, 1987, effective August 1, 1987; April 17, 2000, effective December 1, 2000; April 12, 2006, effective December 1, 2006; April 30, 2007, effective December 1, 2007, absent contrary Congressional action.]

## RULE 15.  AMENDED AND SUPPLEMENTAL PLEADINGS

### (a) Amendments Before Trial.

(1) *Amending as a Matter of Course.* A party may amend its pleading once as a matter of course:

(A) before being served with a responsive pleading; or

(B) within 20 days after serving the pleading if a responsive pleading is not allowed and the action is not yet on the trial calendar.

(2) *Other Amendments.* In all other cases, a party may amend its pleading only with the opposing party's written consent or the court's leave. The court should freely give leave when justice so requires.

(3) *Time to Respond.* Unless the court orders otherwise, any required response to an amended pleading must be made within the time remaining to respond to the original pleading or within 10 days after service of the amended pleading, whichever is later.

### (b) Amendments During and After Trial.

(1) *Based on an Objection at Trial.* If, at trial, a party objects that evidence is not within the issues raised in the pleadings, the court may permit the pleadings to be amended. The court should freely permit an amendment when doing so will aid in presenting the merits and the objecting party fails to satisfy the court that the evidence would prejudice that party's action or defense on the merits. The court may grant a continuance to enable the objecting party to meet the evidence.

(2) *For Issues Tried by Consent.* When an issue not raised by the pleadings is tried by the parties' express or implied consent, it must be treated in all respects as if raised in the pleadings. A party may move—at any time, even after judgment—to amend the pleadings to conform them to the evidence and to raise an unpleaded issue. But failure to amend does not affect the result of the trial of that issue.

### (c) Relation Back of Amendments.

(1) *When an Amendment Relates Back.* An amendment to a pleading relates back to the date of the original pleading when:

(A) the law that provides the applicable statute of limitations allows relation back;

(B) the amendment asserts a claim or defense that arose out of the conduct, transaction, or occurrence set out—or attempted to be set out—in the original pleading; or

(C) the amendment changes the party or the naming of the party against whom a claim is asserted, if Rule 15(c)(1)(B) is satisfied and if, within the period provided by Rule 4(m) for serving the summons and complaint, the party to be brought in by amendment:

(i) received such notice of the action that it will not be prejudiced in defending on the merits; and

(ii) knew or should have known that the action would have been brought against it, but for a mistake concerning the proper party's identity.

(2) *Notice to the United States.* When the United States or a United States officer or agency is added as a defendant by amendment, the notice requirements of Rule 15(c)(1)(C)(i) and (ii) are satisfied if, during the stated period, process was delivered or mailed to the United States attorney or the United States attorney's designee, to the Attorney General of the United States, or to the officer or agency.

### (d) Supplemental Pleadings. On motion and reasonable notice, the court may, on just terms, permit a party to serve a supplemental pleading setting out any transaction, occurrence, or event that happened after the date of the pleading to be supplemented. The court may permit supplementation even though the original pleading is defective in stating a claim or defense. The court may order that the opposing party plead to the supplemental pleading within a specified time.

[Amended January 21, 1963, effective July 1, 1963; February 28, 1966, effective July 1, 1966; March 2, 1987, effective August 1, 1987; April 30, 1991, effective December 1, 1991; amended by Pub.L. 102–198, § 11, December 9, 1991, 105 Stat. 1626; amended April 22, 1993, effective December 1, 1993; April 30, 2007, effective December 1, 2007, absent contrary Congressional action.]

# RULE 16. PRETRIAL CONFERENCES; SCHEDULING; MANAGEMENT

**(a) Purposes of a Pretrial Conference.** In any action, the court may order the attorneys and any unrepresented parties to appear for one or more pretrial conferences for such purposes as:

(1) expediting disposition of the action;

(2) establishing early and continuing control so that the case will not be protracted because of lack of management;

(3) discouraging wasteful pretrial activities;

(4) improving the quality of the trial through more thorough preparation; and

(5) facilitating settlement.

**(b) Scheduling.**

(1) *Scheduling Order.* Except in categories of actions exempted by local rule, the district judge—or a magistrate judge when authorized by local rule—must issue a scheduling order:

    (A) after receiving the parties' report under Rule 26(f); or

    (B) after consulting with the parties' attorneys and any unrepresented parties at a scheduling conference or by telephone, mail, or other means.

(2) *Time to Issue.* The judge must issue the scheduling order as soon as practicable, but in any event within the earlier of 120 days after any defendant has been served with the complaint or 90 days after any defendant has appeared.

(3) *Contents of the Order.*

    (A) Required Contents. The scheduling order must limit the time to join other parties, amend the pleadings, complete discovery, and file motions.

    (B) Permitted Contents. The scheduling order may:

        (i) modify the timing of disclosures under Rules 26(a) and 26(e)(1);

        (ii) modify the extent of discovery;

        (iii) provide for disclosure or discovery of electronically stored information;

        (iv) include any agreements the parties reach for asserting claims of privilege or of protection as trial-preparation material after information is produced;

        (v) set dates for pretrial conferences and for trial; and

        (vi) include other appropriate matters.

(4) *Modifying a Schedule.* A schedule may be modified only for good cause and with the judge's consent.

**(c) Attendance and Matters for Consideration at a Pretrial Conference.**

(1) *Attendance.* A represented party must authorize at least one of its attorneys to make stipulations and admissions about all matters that can reasonably be anticipated for discussion at a pretrial conference. If appropriate, the court may require that a party or its representative be present or reasonably available by other means to consider possible settlement.

(2) *Matters for Consideration.* At any pretrial conference, the court may consider and take appropriate action on the following matters:

    (A) formulating and simplifying the issues, and eliminating frivolous claims or defenses;

    (B) amending the pleadings if necessary or desirable;

    (C) obtaining admissions and stipulations about facts and documents to avoid unnecessary proof, and ruling in advance on the admissibility of evidence;

    (D) avoiding unnecessary proof and cumulative evidence, and limiting the use of testimony under Federal Rule of Evidence 702;

    (E) determining the appropriateness and timing of summary adjudication under Rule 56;

    (F) controlling and scheduling discovery, including orders affecting disclosures and discovery under Rule 26 and Rules 29 through 37;

    (G) identifying witnesses and documents, scheduling the filing and exchange of any pretrial briefs, and setting dates for further conferences and for trial;

    (H) referring matters to a magistrate judge or a master;

    (I) settling the case and using special procedures to assist in resolving the dispute when authorized by statute or local rule;

    (J) determining the form and content of the pretrial order;

    (K) disposing of pending motions;

    (L) adopting special procedures for managing potentially difficult or protracted actions that may involve complex issues, multiple parties, difficult legal questions, or unusual proof problems;

    (M) ordering a separate trial under Rule 42(b) of a claim, counterclaim, crossclaim, third-party claim, or particular issue;

    (N) ordering the presentation of evidence early in the trial on a manageable issue that might, on the evidence, be the basis for a judgment as a matter of law under Rule 50(a) or a judgment on partial findings under Rule 52(c);

(O) establishing a reasonable limit on the time allowed to present evidence; and

(P) facilitating in other ways the just, speedy, and inexpensive disposition of the action.

**(d) Pretrial Orders.** After any conference under this rule, the court should issue an order reciting the action taken. This order controls the course of the action unless the court modifies it.

**(e) Final Pretrial Conference and Orders.** The court may hold a final pretrial conference to formulate a trial plan, including a plan to facilitate the admission of evidence. The conference must be held as close to the start of trial as is reasonable, and must be attended by at least one attorney who will conduct the trial for each party and by any unrepresented party. The court may modify the order issued after a final pretrial conference only to prevent manifest injustice.

**(f) Sanctions.**

(1) *In General.* On motion or on its own, the court may issue any just orders, including those authorized by Rule 37(b)(2)(A)(ii)-(vii), if a party or its attorney:

(A) fails to appear at a scheduling or other pretrial conference;

(B) is substantially unprepared to participate—or does not participate in good faith—in the conference; or

(C) fails to obey a scheduling or other pretrial order.

(2) *Imposing Fees and Costs.* Instead of or in addition to any other sanction, the court must order the party, its attorney, or both to pay the reasonable expenses—including attorney's fees—incurred because of any noncompliance with this rule, unless the noncompliance was substantially justified or other circumstances make an award of expenses unjust.

[Amended April 28, 1983, effective August 1, 1983; March 2, 1987, effective August 1, 1987; April 22, 1993, effective December 1, 1993; April 12, 2006, effective December 1, 2006; April 30, 2007, effective December 1, 2007, absent contrary Congressional action.]

# TITLE IV. PARTIES

## RULE 17. PLAINTIFF AND DEFENDANT; CAPACITY; PUBLIC OFFICERS

**(a) Real Party in Interest.**

(1) *Designation in General.* An action must be prosecuted in the name of the real party in interest. The following may sue in their own names without joining the person for whose benefit the action is brought:

(A) an executor;

(B) an administrator;

(C) a guardian;

(D) a bailee;

(E) a trustee of an express trust;

(F) a party with whom or in whose name a contract has been made for another's benefit; and

(G) a party authorized by statute.

(2) *Action in the Name of the United States for Another's Use or Benefit.* When a federal statute so provides, an action for another's use or benefit must be brought in the name of the United States.

(3) *Joinder of the Real Party in Interest.* The court may not dismiss an action for failure to prosecute in the name of the real party in interest until, after an objection, a reasonable time has been allowed for the real party in interest to ratify, join, or be substituted into the action. After ratification, joinder, or substitution, the action proceeds as if it had been originally commenced by the real party in interest.

**(b) Capacity to Sue or Be Sued.** Capacity to sue or be sued is determined as follows:

(1) for an individual who is not acting in a representative capacity, by the law of the individual's domicile;

(2) for a corporation, by the law under which it was organized; and

(3) for all other parties, by the law of the state where the court is located, except that:

(A) a partnership or other unincorporated association with no such capacity under that state's law may sue or be sued in its common name to enforce a substantive right existing under the United States Constitution or laws; and

(B) 28 U.S.C. §§ 754 and 959(a) govern the capacity of a receiver appointed by a United States court to sue or be sued in a United States court.

**(c) Minor or Incompetent Person.**

(1) *With a Representative.* The following representatives may sue or defend on behalf of a minor or an incompetent person:

(A) a general guardian;

(B) a committee;

(C) a conservator; or

(D) a like fiduciary.

(2) *Without a Representative.* A minor or an incompetent person who does not have a duly appointed representative may sue by a next friend or by a guardian ad litem. The court must appoint a guardian ad litem—or issue another appropriate order—to pro-

tect a minor or incompetent person who is unrepresented in an action.

**(d) Public Officer's Title and Name.** A public officer who sues or is sued in an official capacity may be designated by official title rather than by name, but the court may order that the officer's name be added.

[Amended December 27, 1946, effective March 19, 1948; December 29, 1948, effective October 20, 1949; February 28, 1966, effective July 1, 1966; March 2, 1987, effective August 1, 1987; April 25, 1988, effective August 1, 1988; amended by Pub.L. 100–690, Title VII, § 7049, November 18, 1988, 102 Stat. 4401 (although amendment by Pub.L. 100–690 could not be executed due to prior amendment by Court order which made the same change effective August 1, 1988); April 30, 2007, effective December 1, 2007, absent contrary Congressional action.]

# RULE 18. JOINDER OF CLAIMS

**(a) In General.** A party asserting a claim, counterclaim, crossclaim, or third-party claim may join, as independent or alternative claims, as many claims as it has against an opposing party.

**(b) Joinder of Contingent Claims.** A party may join two claims even though one of them is contingent on the disposition of the other; but the court may grant relief only in accordance with the parties' relative substantive rights. In particular, a plaintiff may state a claim for money and a claim to set aside a conveyance that is fraudulent as to that plaintiff, without first obtaining a judgment for the money.

[Amended February 28, 1966, effective July 1, 1966; March 2, 1987, effective August 1, 1987; April 30, 2007, effective December 1, 2007, absent contrary Congressional action.]

# RULE 19. REQUIRED JOINDER OF PARTIES

**(a) Persons Required to Be Joined if Feasible.**

(1) *Required Party.* A person who is subject to service of process and whose joinder will not deprive the court of subject-matter jurisdiction must be joined as a party if:

    (A) in that person's absence, the court cannot accord complete relief among existing parties; or

    (B) that person claims an interest relating to the subject of the action and is so situated that disposing of the action in the person's absence may:

        (i) as a practical matter impair or impede the person's ability to protect the interest; or

        (ii) leave an existing party subject to a substantial risk of incurring double, multiple, or otherwise inconsistent obligations because of the interest.

(2) *Joinder by Court Order.* If a person has not been joined as required, the court must order that the person be made a party. A person who refuses to join as a plaintiff may be made either a defendant or, in a proper case, an involuntary plaintiff.

(3) *Venue.* If a joined party objects to venue and the joinder would make venue improper, the court must dismiss that party.

**(b) When Joinder Is Not Feasible.** If a person who is required to be joined if feasible cannot be joined, the court must determine whether, in equity and good conscience, the action should proceed among the existing parties or should be dismissed. The factors for the court to consider include:

(1) the extent to which a judgment rendered in the person's absence might prejudice that person or the existing parties;

(2) the extent to which any prejudice could be lessened or avoided by:

    (A) protective provisions in the judgment;

    (B) shaping the relief; or

    (C) other measures;

(3) whether a judgment rendered in the person's absence would be adequate; and

(4) whether the plaintiff would have an adequate remedy if the action were dismissed for nonjoinder.

**(c) Pleading the Reasons for Nonjoinder.** When asserting a claim for relief, a party must state:

(1) the name, if known, of any person who is required to be joined if feasible but is not joined; and

(2) the reasons for not joining that person.

**(d) Exception for Class Actions.** This rule is subject to Rule 23.

[Amended February 28, 1966, effective July 1, 1966; March 2, 1987, effective August 1, 1987; April 30, 2007, effective December 1, 2007, absent contrary Congressional action.]

# RULE 20. PERMISSIVE JOINDER OF PARTIES

**(a) Persons Who May Join or Be Joined.**

(1) *Plaintiffs.* Persons may join in one action as plaintiffs if:

    (A) they assert any right to relief jointly, severally, or in the alternative with respect to or arising out of the same transaction, occurrence, or series of transactions or occurrences; and

    (B) any question of law or fact common to all plaintiffs will arise in the action.

(2) *Defendants.* Persons—as well as a vessel, cargo, or other property subject to admiralty process in rem—may be joined in one action as defendants if:

    (A) any right to relief is asserted against them jointly, severally, or in the alternative with respect

to or arising out of the same transaction, occurrence, or series of transactions or occurrences; and

(B) any question of law or fact common to all defendants will arise in the action.

(3) *Extent of Relief.* Neither a plaintiff nor a defendant need be interested in obtaining or defending against all the relief demanded. The court may grant judgment to one or more plaintiffs according to their rights, and against one or more defendants according to their liabilities.

**(b) Protective Measures.** The court may issue orders—including an order for separate trials—to protect a party against embarrassment, delay, expense, or other prejudice that arises from including a person against whom the party asserts no claim and who asserts no claim against the party.

[Amended February 28, 1966, effective July 1, 1966; March 2, 1987, effective August 1, 1987; April 30, 2007, effective December 1, 2007, absent contrary Congressional action.]

## RULE 21.  MISJOINDER AND NONJOINDER OF PARTIES

Misjoinder of parties is not a ground for dismissing an action. On motion or on its own, the court may at any time, on just terms, add or drop a party. The court may also sever any claim against a party.

[Amended April 30, 2007, effective December 1, 2007, absent contrary Congressional action.]

## RULE 22.  INTERPLEADER

**(a) Grounds.**

(1) *By a Plaintiff.* Persons with claims that may expose a plaintiff to double or multiple liability may be joined as defendants and required to interplead. Joinder for interpleader is proper even though:

(A) the claims of the several claimants, or the titles on which their claims depend, lack a common origin or are adverse and independent rather than identical; or

(B) the plaintiff denies liability in whole or in part to any or all of the claimants.

(2) *By a Defendant.* A defendant exposed to similar liability may seek interpleader through a crossclaim or counterclaim.

**(b) Relation to Other Rules and Statutes.** This rule supplements—and does not limit—the joinder of parties allowed by Rule 20. The remedy this rule provides is in addition to—and does not supersede or limit—the remedy provided by 28 U.S.C. §§ 1335,

1397, and 2361. An action under those statutes must be conducted under these rules.

[Amended December 29, 1948, effective October 20, 1949; March 2, 1987, effective August 1, 1987; April 30, 2007, effective December 1, 2007, absent contrary Congressional action.]

## RULE 23.  CLASS ACTIONS

**(a) Prerequisites.** One or more members of a class may sue or be sued as representative parties on behalf of all members only if:

(1) the class is so numerous that joinder of all members is impracticable;

(2) there are questions of law or fact common to the class;

(3) the claims or defenses of the representative parties are typical of the claims or defenses of the class; and

(4) the representative parties will fairly and adequately protect the interests of the class.

**(b) Types of Class Actions.** A class action may be maintained if Rule 23(a) is satisfied and if:

(1) prosecuting separate actions by or against individual class members would create a risk of:

(A) inconsistent or varying adjudications with respect to individual class members that would establish incompatible standards of conduct for the party opposing the class; or

(B) adjudications with respect to individual class members that, as a practical matter, would be dispositive of the interests of the other members not parties to the individual adjudications or would substantially impair or impede their ability to protect their interests;

(2) the party opposing the class has acted or refused to act on grounds that apply generally to the class, so that final injunctive relief or corresponding declaratory relief is appropriate respecting the class as a whole; or

(3) the court finds that the questions of law or fact common to class members predominate over any questions affecting only individual members, and that a class action is superior to other available methods for fairly and efficiently adjudicating the controversy. The matters pertinent to these findings include:

(A) the class members' interests in individually controlling the prosecution or defense of separate actions;

(B) the extent and nature of any litigation concerning the controversy already begun by or against class members;

(C) the desirability or undesirability of concentrating the litigation of the claims in the particular forum; and

(D) the likely difficulties in managing a class action.

**(c) Certification Order; Notice to Class Members; Judgment; Issues Classes; Subclasses.**

(1) *Certification Order.*

(A) Time to Issue. At an early practicable time after a person sues or is sued as a class representative, the court must determine by order whether to certify the action as a class action.

(B) Defining the Class; Appointing Class Counsel. An order that certifies a class action must define the class and the class claims, issues, or defenses, and must appoint class counsel under Rule 23(g).

(C) Altering or Amending the Order. An order that grants or denies class certification may be altered or amended before final judgment.

(2) *Notice.*

(A) For (b)(1) or (b)(2) Classes. For any class certified under Rule 23(b)(1) or (b)(2), the court may direct appropriate notice to the class.

(B) For (b)(3) Classes. For any class certified under Rule 23(b)(3), the court must direct to class members the best notice that is practicable under the circumstances, including individual notice to all members who can be identified through reasonable effort. The notice must clearly and concisely state in plain, easily understood language:

(i) the nature of the action;

(ii) the definition of the class certified;

(iii) the class claims, issues, or defenses;

(iv) that a class member may enter an appearance through an attorney if the member so desires;

(v) that the court will exclude from the class any member who requests exclusion;

(vi) the time and manner for requesting exclusion; and

(vii) the binding effect of a class judgment on members under Rule 23(c)(3).

(3) *Judgment.* Whether or not favorable to the class, the judgment in a class action must:

(A) for any class certified under Rule 23(b)(1) or (b)(2), include and describe those whom the court finds to be class members; and

(B) for any class certified under Rule 23(b)(3), include and specify or describe those to whom the Rule 23(c)(2) notice was directed, who have not requested exclusion, and whom the court finds to be class members.

(4) *Particular Issues.* When appropriate, an action may be brought or maintained as a class action with respect to particular issues.

(5) *Subclasses.* When appropriate, a class may be divided into subclasses that are each treated as a class under this rule.

**(d) Conducting the Action.**

(1) *In General.* In conducting an action under this rule, the court may issue orders that:

(A) determine the course of proceedings or prescribe measures to prevent undue repetition or complication in presenting evidence or argument;

(B) require—to protect class members and fairly conduct the action—giving appropriate notice to some or all class members of:

(i) any step in the action;

(ii) the proposed extent of the judgment; or

(iii) the members' opportunity to signify whether they consider the representation fair and adequate, to intervene and present claims or defenses, or to otherwise come into the action;

(C) impose conditions on the representative parties or on intervenors;

(D) require that the pleadings be amended to eliminate allegations about representation of absent persons and that the action proceed accordingly; or

(E) deal with similar procedural matters.

(2) *Combining and Amending Orders.* An order under Rule 23(d)(1) may be altered or amended from time to time and may be combined with an order under Rule 16.

**(e) Settlement, Voluntary Dismissal, or Compromise.** The claims, issues, or defenses of a certified class may be settled, voluntarily dismissed, or compromised only with the court's approval. The following procedures apply to a proposed settlement, voluntary dismissal, or compromise:

(1) The court must direct notice in a reasonable manner to all class members who would be bound by the proposal.

(2) If the proposal would bind class members, the court may approve it only after a hearing and on finding that it is fair, reasonable, and adequate.

(3) The parties seeking approval must file a statement identifying any agreement made in connection with the proposal.

(4) If the class action was previously certified under Rule 23(b)(3), the court may refuse to approve a settlement unless it affords a new opportunity to request exclusion to individual class members who had an earlier opportunity to request exclusion but did not do so.

(5) Any class member may object to the proposal if it requires court approval under this subdivision (e); the objection may be withdrawn only with the court's approval.

**(f) Appeals.** A court of appeals may permit an appeal from an order granting or denying class-action certification under this rule if a petition for permission to appeal is filed with the circuit clerk within 10 days after the order is entered. An appeal does not stay proceedings in the district court unless the district judge or the court of appeals so orders.

**(g) Class Counsel.**

(1) *Appointing Class Counsel.* Unless a statute provides otherwise, a court that certifies a class must appoint class counsel. In appointing class counsel, the court:

(A) must consider:

(i) the work counsel has done in identifying or investigating potential claims in the action;

(ii) counsel's experience in handling class actions, other complex litigation, and the types of claims asserted in the action;

(iii) counsel's knowledge of the applicable law; and

(iv) the resources that counsel will commit to representing the class;

(B) may consider any other matter pertinent to counsel's ability to fairly and adequately represent the interests of the class;

(C) may order potential class counsel to provide information on any subject pertinent to the appointment and to propose terms for attorney's fees and nontaxable costs;

(D) may include in the appointing order provisions about the award of attorney's fees or nontaxable costs under Rule 23(h); and

(E) may make further orders in connection with the appointment.

(2) *Standard for Appointing Class Counsel.* When one applicant seeks appointment as class counsel, the court may appoint that applicant only if the applicant is adequate under Rule 23(g)(1) and (4). If more than one adequate applicant seeks appointment, the court must appoint the applicant best able to represent the interests of the class.

(3) *Interim Counsel.* The court may designate interim counsel to act on behalf of a putative class before determining whether to certify the action as a class action.

(4) *Duty of Class Counsel.* Class counsel must fairly and adequately represent the interests of the class.

**(h) Attorney's Fees and Nontaxable Costs.** In a certified class action, the court may award reasonable attorney's fees and nontaxable costs that are authorized by law or by the parties' agreement. The following procedures apply:

(1) A claim for an award must be made by motion under Rule 54(d)(2), subject to the provisions of this subdivision (h), at a time the court sets. Notice of the motion must be served on all parties and, for motions by class counsel, directed to class members in a reasonable manner.

(2) A class member, or a party from whom payment is sought, may object to the motion.

(3) The court may hold a hearing and must find the facts and state its legal conclusions under Rule 52(a).

(4) The court may refer issues related to the amount of the award to a special master or a magistrate judge, as provided in Rule 54(d)(2)(D).

[Amended February 28, 1966, effective July 1, 1966; March 2, 1987, effective August 1, 1987; April 24, 1998, effective December 1, 1998; March 27, 2003, effective December 1, 2003; April 30, 2007, effective December 1, 2007, absent contrary Congressional action.]

## RULE 23.1  DERIVATIVE ACTIONS

**(a) Prerequisites.** This rule applies when one or more shareholders or members of a corporation or an unincorporated association bring a derivative action to enforce a right that the corporation or association may properly assert but has failed to enforce. The derivative action may not be maintained if it appears that the plaintiff does not fairly and adequately represent the interests of shareholders or members who are similarly situated in enforcing the right of the corporation or association.

**(b) Pleading Requirements.** The complaint must be verified and must:

(1) allege that the plaintiff was a shareholder or member at the time of the transaction complained of, or that the plaintiff's share or membership later devolved on it by operation of law;

(2) allege that the action is not a collusive one to confer jurisdiction that the court would otherwise lack; and

(3) state with particularity:

(A) any effort by the plaintiff to obtain the desired action from the directors or comparable authority and, if necessary, from the shareholders or members; and

(B) the reasons for not obtaining the action or not making the effort.

**(c) Settlement, Dismissal, and Compromise.** A derivative action may be settled, voluntarily dismissed, or compromised only with the court's approval. Notice of a proposed settlement, voluntary dismissal, or com-

promise must be given to shareholders or members in the manner that the court orders.

[Adopted February 28, 1966, effective July 1, 1966; amended March 2, 1987, effective August 1, 1987; April 30, 2007, effective December 1, 2007, absent contrary Congressional action.]

## RULE 23.2　ACTIONS RELATING TO UNINCORPORATED ASSOCIATIONS

This rule applies to an action brought by or against the members of an unincorporated association as a class by naming certain members as representative parties. The action may be maintained only if it appears that those parties will fairly and adequately protect the interests of the association and its members. In conducting the action, the court may issue any appropriate orders corresponding with those in Rule 23(d), and the procedure for settlement, voluntary dismissal, or compromise must correspond with the procedure in Rule 23(e).

[Adopted February 28, 1966, effective July 1, 1966; amended April 30, 2007, effective December 1, 2007, absent contrary Congressional action.]

## RULE 24.　INTERVENTION

**(a) Intervention of Right.** On timely motion, the court must permit anyone to intervene who:

(1) is given an unconditional right to intervene by a federal statute; or

(2) claims an interest relating to the property or transaction that is the subject of the action, and is so situated that disposing of the action may as a practical matter impair or impede the movant's ability to protect its interest, unless existing parties adequately represent that interest.

**(b) Permissive Intervention.**

(1) *In General.* On timely motion, the court may permit anyone to intervene who:

(A) is given a conditional right to intervene by a federal statute; or

(B) has a claim or defense that shares with the main action a common question of law or fact.

(2) *By a Government Officer or Agency.* On timely motion, the court may permit a federal or state governmental officer or agency to intervene if a party's claim or defense is based on:

(A) a statute or executive order administered by the officer or agency; or

(B) any regulation, order, requirement, or agreement issued or made under the statute or executive order.

(3) *Delay or Prejudice.* In exercising its discretion, the court must consider whether the intervention will unduly delay or prejudice the adjudication of the original parties' rights.

**(c) Notice and Pleading Required.** A motion to intervene must be served on the parties as provided in Rule 5. The motion must state the grounds for intervention and be accompanied by a pleading that sets out the claim or defense for which intervention is sought.

[Amended December 27, 1946, effective March 19, 1948; December 29, 1948, effective October 20, 1949; January 21, 1963, effective July 1, 1963; February 28, 1966, effective July 1, 1966; March 2, 1987, effective August 1, 1987; April 30, 1991, effective December 1, 1991; April 12, 2006, effective December 1, 2006; April 30, 2007, effective December 1, 2007, absent contrary Congressional action.]

## RULE 25.　SUBSTITUTION OF PARTIES

**(a) Death.**

(1) *Substitution if the Claim Is Not Extinguished.* If a party dies and the claim is not extinguished, the court may order substitution of the proper party. A motion for substitution may be made by any party or by the decedent's successor or representative. If the motion is not made within 90 days after service of a statement noting the death, the action by or against the decedent must be dismissed.

(2) *Continuation Among the Remaining Parties.* After a party's death, if the right sought to be enforced survives only to or against the remaining parties, the action does not abate, but proceeds in favor of or against the remaining parties. The death should be noted on the record.

(3) *Service.* A motion to substitute, together with a notice of hearing, must be served on the parties as provided in Rule 5 and on nonparties as provided in Rule 4. A statement noting death must be served in the same manner. Service may be made in any judicial district.

**(b) Incompetency.** If a party becomes incompetent, the court may, on motion, permit the action to be continued by or against the party's representative. The motion must be served as provided in Rule 25(a)(3).

**(c) Transfer of Interest.** If an interest is transferred, the action may be continued by or against the original party unless the court, on motion, orders the transferee to be substituted in the action or joined with the original party. The motion must be served as provided in Rule 25(a)(3).

**(d) Public Officers; Death or Separation from Office.** An action does not abate when a public officer who is a party in an official capacity dies, resigns, or otherwise ceases to hold office while the action is pending. The officer's successor is automatically substituted as a party. Later proceedings should be in the substituted party's name, but any misnomer not af-

fecting the parties' substantial rights must be disregarded. The court may order substitution at any time, but the absence of such an order does not affect the substitution.

[Amended December 29, 1948, effective October 20, 1949; April 17, 1961, effective July 19, 1961; January 21, 1963, effective July 1, 1963; March 2, 1987, effective August 1, 1987; April 30, 2007, effective December 1, 2007, absent contrary Congressional action.]

# TITLE V.  DISCLOSURES AND DISCOVERY

## RULE 26.  DUTY TO DISCLOSE; GENERAL PROVISIONS GOVERNING DISCOVERY

### (a) Required Disclosures.

(1) *Initial Disclosure.*

(A) In General. Except as exempted by Rule 26(a)(1)(B) or as otherwise stipulated or ordered by the court, a party must, without awaiting a discovery request, provide to the other parties:

(i) the name and, if known, the address and telephone number of each individual likely to have discoverable information—along with the subjects of that information—that the disclosing party may use to support its claims or defenses, unless the use would be solely for impeachment;

(ii) a copy—or a description by category and location—of all documents, electronically stored information, and tangible things that the disclosing party has in its possession, custody, or control and may use to support its claims or defenses, unless the use would be solely for impeachment;

(iii) a computation of each category of damages claimed by the disclosing party—who must also make available for inspection and copying as under Rule 34 the documents or other evidentiary material, unless privileged or protected from disclosure, on which each computation is based, including materials bearing on the nature and extent of injuries suffered; and

(iv) for inspection and copying as under Rule 34, any insurance agreement under which an insurance business may be liable to satisfy all or part of a possible judgment in the action or to indemnify or reimburse for payments made to satisfy the judgment.

(B) Proceedings Exempt from Initial Disclosure. The following proceedings are exempt from initial disclosure:

(i) an action for review on an administrative record;

(ii) a forfeiture action in rem arising from a federal statute;

(iii) a petition for habeas corpus or any other proceeding to challenge a criminal conviction or sentence;

(iv) an action brought without an attorney by a person in the custody of the United States, a state, or a state subdivision;

(v) an action to enforce or quash an administrative summons or subpoena;

(vi) an action by the United States to recover benefit payments;

(vii) an action by the United States to collect on a student loan guaranteed by the United States;

(viii) a proceeding ancillary to a proceeding in another court; and

(ix) an action to enforce an arbitration award.

(C) Time for Initial Disclosures—In General. A party must make the initial disclosures at or within 14 days after the parties' Rule 26(f) conference unless a different time is set by stipulation or court order, or unless a party objects during the conference that initial disclosures are not appropriate in this action and states the objection in the proposed discovery plan. In ruling on the objection, the court must determine what disclosures, if any, are to be made and must set the time for disclosure.

(D) Time for Initial Disclosures—For Parties Served or Joined Later. A party that is first served or otherwise joined after the Rule 26(f) conference must make the initial disclosures within 30 days after being served or joined, unless a different time is set by stipulation or court order.

(E) Basis for Initial Disclosure; Unacceptable Excuses. A party must make its initial disclosures based on the information then reasonably available to it. A party is not excused from making its disclosures because it has not fully investigated the case or because it challenges the sufficiency of another party's disclosures or because another party has not made its disclosures.

(2) *Disclosure of Expert Testimony.*

(A) In General. In addition to the disclosures required by Rule 26(a)(1), a party must disclose to the other parties the identity of any witness it may use at trial to present evidence under Federal Rule of Evidence 702, 703, or 705.

(B) Written Report. Unless otherwise stipulated or ordered by the court, this disclosure must be

accompanied by a written report—prepared and signed by the witness—if the witness is one retained or specially employed to provide expert testimony in the case or one whose duties as the party's employee regularly involve giving expert testimony. The report must contain:

(i) a complete statement of all opinions the witness will express and the basis and reasons for them;

(ii) the data or other information considered by the witness in forming them;

(iii) any exhibits that will be used to summarize or support them;

(iv) the witness's qualifications, including a list of all publications authored in the previous ten years;

(v) a list of all other cases in which, during the previous four years, the witness testified as an expert at trial or by deposition; and

(vi) a statement of the compensation to be paid for the study and testimony in the case.

(C) Time to Disclose Expert Testimony. A party must make these disclosures at the times and in the sequence that the court orders. Absent a stipulation or a court order, the disclosures must be made:

(i) at least 90 days before the date set for trial or for the case to be ready for trial; or

(ii) if the evidence is intended solely to contradict or rebut evidence on the same subject matter identified by another party under Rule 26(a)(2)(B), within 30 days after the other party's disclosure.

(D) Supplementing the Disclosure. The parties must supplement these disclosures when required under Rule 26(e).

(3) *Pretrial Disclosures.*

(A) In General. In addition to the disclosures required by Rule 26(a)(1) and (2), a party must provide to the other parties and promptly file the following information about the evidence that it may present at trial other than solely for impeachment:

(i) the name and, if not previously provided, the address and telephone number of each witness—separately identifying those the party expects to present and those it may call if the need arises;

(ii) the designation of those witnesses whose testimony the party expects to present by deposition and, if not taken stenographically, a transcript of the pertinent parts of the deposition; and

(iii) an identification of each document or other exhibit, including summaries of other evidence—separately identifying those items the party ex-

pects to offer and those it may offer if the need arises.

(B) Time for Pretrial Disclosures; Objections. Unless the court orders otherwise, these disclosures must be made at least 30 days before trial. Within 14 days after they are made, unless the court sets a different time, a party may serve and promptly file a list of the following objections: any objections to the use under Rule 32(a) of a deposition designated by another party under Rule 26(a)(3)(A)(ii); and any objection, together with the grounds for it, that may be made to the admissibility of materials identified under Rule 26(a)(3)(A)(iii). An objection not so made—except for one under Federal Rule of Evidence 402 or 403—is waived unless excused by the court for good cause.

(4) *Form of Disclosures.* Unless the court orders otherwise, all disclosures under Rule 26(a) must be in writing, signed, and served.

**(b) Discovery Scope and Limits.**

(1) *Scope in General.* Unless otherwise limited by court order, the scope of discovery is as follows:

Parties may obtain discovery regarding any non-privileged matter that is relevant to any party's claim or defense—including the existence, description, nature, custody, condition, and location of any documents or other tangible things and the identity and location of persons who know of any discoverable matter. For good cause, the court may order discovery of any matter relevant to the subject matter involved in the action. Relevant information need not be admissible at the trial if the discovery appears reasonably calculated to lead to the discovery of admissible evidence. All discovery is subject to the limitations imposed by Rule 26(b)(2)(C).

(2) *Limitations on Frequency and Extent.*

(A) When Permitted. By order, the court may alter the limits in these rules on the number of depositions and interrogatories or on the length of depositions under Rule 30. By order or local rule, the court may also limit the number of requests under Rule 36.

(B) Specific Limitations on Electronically Stored Information. A party need not provide discovery of electronically stored information from sources that the party identifies as not reasonably accessible because of undue burden or cost. On motion to compel discovery or for a protective order, the party from whom discovery is sought must show that the information is not reasonably accessible because of undue burden or cost. If that showing is made, the court may nonetheless order discovery from such sources if the requesting party shows good cause, considering the limitations of Rule 26(b)(2)(C). The court may specify conditions for the discovery.

(C) When Required. On motion or on its own, the court must limit the frequency or extent of discovery otherwise allowed by these rules or by local rule if it determines that:

(i) the discovery sought is unreasonably cumulative or duplicative, or can be obtained from some other source that is more convenient, less burdensome, or less expensive;

(ii) the party seeking discovery has had ample opportunity to obtain the information by discovery in the action; or

(iii) the burden or expense of the proposed discovery outweighs its likely benefit, considering the needs of the case, the amount in controversy, the parties' resources, the importance of the issues at stake in the action, and the importance of the discovery in resolving the issues.

(3) *Trial Preparation: Materials.*

(A) Documents and Tangible Things. Ordinarily, a party may not discover documents and tangible things that are prepared in anticipation of litigation or for trial by or for another party or its representative (including the other party's attorney, consultant, surety, indemnitor, insurer, or agent). But, subject to Rule 26(b)(4), those materials may be discovered if:

(i) they are otherwise discoverable under Rule 26(b)(1); and

(ii) the party shows that it has substantial need for the materials to prepare its case and cannot, without undue hardship, obtain their substantial equivalent by other means.

(B) Protection Against Disclosure. If the court orders discovery of those materials, it must protect against disclosure of the mental impressions, conclusions, opinions, or legal theories of a party's attorney or other representative concerning the litigation.

(C) Previous Statement. Any party or other person may, on request and without the required showing, obtain the person's own previous statement about the action or its subject matter. If the request is refused, the person may move for a court order, and Rule 37(a)(5) applies to the award of expenses. A previous statement is either:

(i) a written statement that the person has signed or otherwise adopted or approved; or

(ii) a contemporaneous stenographic, mechanical, electrical, or other recording—or a transcription of it—that recites substantially verbatim the person's oral statement.

(4) *Trial Preparation: Experts.*

(A) Expert Who May Testify. A party may depose any person who has been identified as an expert whose opinions may be presented at trial. If

Rule 26(a)(2)(B) requires a report from the expert, the deposition may be conducted only after the report is provided.

(B) Expert Employed Only for Trial Preparation. Ordinarily, a party may not, by interrogatories or deposition, discover facts known or opinions held by an expert who has been retained or specially employed by another party in anticipation of litigation or to prepare for trial and who is not expected to be called as a witness at trial. But a party may do so only:

(i) as provided in Rule 35(b); or

(ii) on showing exceptional circumstances under which it is impracticable for the party to obtain facts or opinions on the same subject by other means.

(C) Payment. Unless manifest injustice would result, the court must require that the party seeking discovery:

(i) pay the expert a reasonable fee for time spent in responding to discovery under Rule 26(b)(4)(A) or (B); and

(ii) for discovery under (B), also pay the other party a fair portion of the fees and expenses it reasonably incurred in obtaining the expert's facts and opinions.

(5) *Claiming Privilege or Protecting Trial-Preparation Materials.*

(A) Information Withheld. When a party withholds information otherwise discoverable by claiming that the information is privileged or subject to protection as trial-preparation material, the party must:

(i) expressly make the claim; and

(ii) describe the nature of the documents, communications, or tangible things not produced or disclosed—and do so in a manner that, without revealing information itself privileged or protected, will enable other parties to assess the claim.

(B) Information Produced. If information produced in discovery is subject to a claim of privilege or of protection as trial-preparation material, the party making the claim may notify any party that received the information of the claim and the basis for it. After being notified, a party must promptly return, sequester, or destroy the specified information and any copies it has; must not use or disclose the information until the claim is resolved; must take reasonable steps to retrieve the information if the party disclosed it before being notified; and may promptly present the information to the court under seal for a determination of the claim. The producing party must preserve the information until the claim is resolved.

### (c) Protective Orders.

(1) *In General.* A party or any person from whom discovery is sought may move for a protective order in the court where the action is pending—or as an alternative on matters relating to a deposition, in the court for the district where the deposition will be taken. The motion must include a certification that the movant has in good faith conferred or attempted to confer with other affected parties in an effort to resolve the dispute without court action. The court may, for good cause, issue an order to protect a party or person from annoyance, embarrassment, oppression, or undue burden or expense, including one or more of the following:

(A) forbidding the disclosure or discovery;

(B) specifying terms, including time and place, for the disclosure or discovery;

(C) prescribing a discovery method other than the one selected by the party seeking discovery;

(D) forbidding inquiry into certain matters, or limiting the scope of disclosure or discovery to certain matters;

(E) designating the persons who may be present while the discovery is conducted;

(F) requiring that a deposition be sealed and opened only on court order;

(G) requiring that a trade secret or other confidential research, development, or commercial information not be revealed or be revealed only in a specified way; and

(H) requiring that the parties simultaneously file specified documents or information in sealed envelopes, to be opened as the court directs.

(2) *Ordering Discovery.* If a motion for a protective order is wholly or partly denied, the court may, on just terms, order that any party or person provide or permit discovery.

(3) *Awarding Expenses.* Rule 37(a)(5) applies to the award of expenses.

### (d) Timing and Sequence of Discovery.

(1) *Timing.* A party may not seek discovery from any source before the parties have conferred as required by Rule 26(f), except in a proceeding exempted from initial disclosure under Rule 26(a)(1)(B), or when authorized by these rules, by stipulation, or by court order.

(2) *Sequence.* Unless, on motion, the court orders otherwise for the parties' and witnesses' convenience and in the interests of justice:

(A) methods of discovery may be used in any sequence; and

(B) discovery by one party does not require any other party to delay its discovery.

### (e) Supplementing Disclosures and Responses.

(1) *In General.* A party who has made a disclosure under Rule 26(a)—or who has responded to an interrogatory, request for production, or request for admission—must supplement or correct its disclosure or response:

(A) in a timely manner if the party learns that in some material respect the disclosure or response is incomplete or incorrect, and if the additional or corrective information has not otherwise been made known to the other parties during the discovery process or in writing; or

(B) as ordered by the court.

(2) *Expert Witness.* For an expert whose report must be disclosed under Rule 26(a)(2)(B), the party's duty to supplement extends both to information included in the report and to information given during the expert's deposition. Any additions or changes to this information must be disclosed by the time the party's pretrial disclosures under Rule 26(a)(3) are due.

### (f) Conference of the Parties; Planning for Discovery.

(1) *Conference Timing.* Except in a proceeding exempted from initial disclosure under Rule 26(a)(1)(B) or when the court orders otherwise, the parties must confer as soon as practicable—and in any event at least 21 days before a scheduling conference is to be held or a scheduling order is due under Rule 16(b).

(2) *Conference Content; Parties' Responsibilities.* In conferring, the parties must consider the nature and basis of their claims and defenses and the possibilities for promptly settling or resolving the case; make or arrange for the disclosures required by Rule 26(a)(1); discuss any issues about preserving discoverable information; and develop a proposed discovery plan. The attorneys of record and all unrepresented parties that have appeared in the case are jointly responsible for arranging the conference, for attempting in good faith to agree on the proposed discovery plan, and for submitting to the court within 14 days after the conference a written report outlining the plan. The court may order the parties or attorneys to attend the conference in person.

(3) *Discovery Plan.* A discovery plan must state the parties' views and proposals on:

(A) what changes should be made in the timing, form, or requirement for disclosures under Rule 26(a), including a statement of when initial disclosures were made or will be made;

(B) the subjects on which discovery may be needed, when discovery should be completed, and whether discovery should be conducted in phases or be limited to or focused on particular issues;

(C) any issues about disclosure or discovery of electronically stored information, including the form or forms in which it should be produced;

(D) any issues about claims of privilege or of protection as trial-preparation materials, including—if the parties agree on a procedure to assert these claims after production—whether to ask the court to include their agreement in an order;

(E) what changes should be made in the limitations on discovery imposed under these rules or by local rule, and what other limitations should be imposed; and

(F) any other orders that the court should issue under Rule 26(c) or under Rule 16(b) and (c).

(4) *Expedited Schedule.* If necessary to comply with its expedited schedule for Rule 16(b) conferences, a court may by local rule:

(A) require the parties' conference to occur less than 21 days before the scheduling conference is held or a scheduling order is due under Rule 16(b); and

(B) require the written report outlining the discovery plan to be filed less than 14 days after the parties' conference, or excuse the parties from submitting a written report and permit them to report orally on their discovery plan at the Rule 16(b) conference.

**(g) Signing Disclosures and Discovery Requests, Responses, and Objections.**

(1) *Signature Required; Effect of Signature.* Every disclosure under Rule 26(a)(1) or (a)(3) and every discovery request, response, or objection must be signed by at least one attorney of record in the attorney's own name—or by the party personally, if unrepresented—and must state the signer's address, e-mail address, and telephone number. By signing, an attorney or party certifies that to the best of the person's knowledge, information, and belief formed after a reasonable inquiry:

(A) with respect to a disclosure, it is complete and correct as of the time it is made; and

(B) with respect to a discovery request, response, or objection, it is:

(i) consistent with these rules and warranted by existing law or by a nonfrivolous argument for extending, modifying, or reversing existing law, or for establishing new law;

(ii) not interposed for any improper purpose, such as to harass, cause unnecessary delay, or needlessly increase the cost of litigation; and

(iii) neither unreasonable nor unduly burdensome or expensive, considering the needs of the case, prior discovery in the case, the amount in controversy, and the importance of the issues at stake in the action.

(2) *Failure to Sign.* Other parties have no duty to act on an unsigned disclosure, request, response, or objection until it is signed, and the court must strike it unless a signature is promptly supplied after the omission is called to the attorney's or party's attention.

(3) *Sanction for Improper Certification.* If a certification violates this rule without substantial justification, the court, on motion or on its own, must impose an appropriate sanction on the signer, the party on whose behalf the signer was acting, or both. The sanction may include an order to pay the reasonable expenses, including attorney's fees, caused by the violation.

[Amended December 27, 1946, effective March 19, 1948; January 21, 1963, effective July 1, 1963; February 28, 1966, effective July 1, 1966; March 30, 1970, effective July 1, 1970; April 29, 1980, effective August 1, 1980; April 28, 1983, effective August 1, 1983; March 2, 1987, effective August 1, 1987; April 22, 1993, effective December 1, 1993; April 17, 2000, effective December 1, 2000; April 12, 2006, effective December 1, 2006; April 30, 2007, effective December 1, 2007, absent contrary Congressional action.]

## RULE 27. DEPOSITIONS TO PERPETUATE TESTIMONY

### (a) Before an Action Is Filed.

(1) *Petition.* A person who wants to perpetuate testimony about any matter cognizable in a United States court may file a verified petition in the district court for the district where any expected adverse party resides. The petition must ask for an order authorizing the petitioner to depose the named persons in order to perpetuate their testimony. The petition must be titled in the petitioner's name and must show:

(A) that the petitioner expects to be a party to an action cognizable in a United States court but cannot presently bring it or cause it to be brought;

(B) the subject matter of the expected action and the petitioner's interest;

(C) the facts that the petitioner wants to establish by the proposed testimony and the reasons to perpetuate it;

(D) the names or a description of the persons whom the petitioner expects to be adverse parties and their addresses, so far as known; and

(E) the name, address, and expected substance of the testimony of each deponent.

(2) *Notice and Service.* At least 20 days before the hearing date, the petitioner must serve each expected adverse party with a copy of the petition and a notice stating the time and place of the hearing. The notice

may be served either inside or outside the district or state in the manner provided in Rule 4. If that service cannot be made with reasonable diligence on an expected adverse party, the court may order service by publication or otherwise. The court must appoint an attorney to represent persons not served in the manner provided in Rule 4 and to cross-examine the deponent if an unserved person is not otherwise represented. If any expected adverse party is a minor or is incompetent, Rule 17(c) applies.

(3) *Order and Examination.* If satisfied that perpetuating the testimony may prevent a failure or delay of justice, the court must issue an order that designates or describes the persons whose depositions may be taken, specifies the subject matter of the examinations, and states whether the depositions will be taken orally or by written interrogatories. The depositions may then be taken under these rules, and the court may issue orders like those authorized by Rules 34 and 35. A reference in these rules to the court where an action is pending means, for purposes of this rule, the court where the petition for the deposition was filed.

(4) *Using the Deposition.* A deposition to perpetuate testimony may be used under Rule 32(a) in any later-filed district-court action involving the same subject matter if the deposition either was taken under these rules or, although not so taken, would be admissible in evidence in the courts of the state where it was taken.

**(b) Pending Appeal.**

(1) *In General.* The court where a judgment has been rendered may, if an appeal has been taken or may still be taken, permit a party to depose witnesses to perpetuate their testimony for use in the event of further proceedings in that court.

(2) *Motion.* The party who wants to perpetuate testimony may move for leave to take the depositions, on the same notice and service as if the action were pending in the district court. The motion must show:

(A) the name, address, and expected substance of the testimony of each deponent; and

(B) the reasons for perpetuating the testimony.

(3) *Court Order.* If the court finds that perpetuating the testimony may prevent a failure or delay of justice, the court may permit the depositions to be taken and may issue orders like those authorized by Rules 34 and 35. The depositions may be taken and used as any other deposition taken in a pending district-court action.

**(c) Perpetuation by an Action.** This rule does not limit a court's power to entertain an action to perpetuate testimony.

[Amended December 27, 1946, effective March 19, 1948; December 29, 1948, effective October 20, 1949; March 1,

1971, effective July 1, 1971; March 2, 1987, effective August 1, 1987; April 25, 2005, effective December 1, 2005; April 30, 2007, effective December 1, 2007, absent contrary Congressional action.]

## RULE 28. PERSONS BEFORE WHOM DEPOSITIONS MAY BE TAKEN

**(a) Within the United States.**

(1) *In General.* Within the United States or a territory or insular possession subject to United States jurisdiction, a deposition must be taken before:

(A) an officer authorized to administer oaths either by federal law or by the law in the place of examination; or

(B) a person appointed by the court where the action is pending to administer oaths and take testimony.

(2) *Definition of "Officer".* The term "officer" in Rules 30, 31, and 32 includes a person appointed by the court under this rule or designated by the parties under Rule 29(a).

**(b) In a Foreign Country.**

(1) *In General.* A deposition may be taken in a foreign country:

(A) under an applicable treaty or convention;

(B) under a letter of request, whether or not captioned a "letter rogatory";

(C) on notice, before a person authorized to administer oaths either by federal law or by the law in the place of examination; or

(D) before a person commissioned by the court to administer any necessary oath and take testimony.

(2) *Issuing a Letter of Request or a Commission.* A letter of request, a commission, or both may be issued:

(A) on appropriate terms after an application and notice of it; and

(B) without a showing that taking the deposition in another manner is impracticable or inconvenient.

(3) *Form of a Request, Notice, or Commission.* When a letter of request or any other device is used according to a treaty or convention, it must be captioned in the form prescribed by that treaty or convention. A letter of request may be addressed "To the Appropriate Authority in [name of country]." A deposition notice or a commission must designate by name or descriptive title the person before whom the deposition is to be taken.

(4) *Letter of Request—Admitting Evidence.* Evidence obtained in response to a letter of request need not be excluded merely because it is not a verbatim transcript, because the testimony was not taken under oath, or because of any similar departure from the

requirements for depositions taken within the United States.

**(c) Disqualification.** A deposition must not be taken before a person who is any party's relative, employee, or attorney; who is related to or employed by any party's attorney; or who is financially interested in the action.

[Amended December 27, 1946, effective March 19, 1948; January 21, 1963, effective July 1, 1963; April 29, 1980, effective August 1, 1980; March 2, 1987, effective August 1, 1987; April 22, 1993, effective December 1, 1993; April 30, 2007, effective December 1, 2007, absent contrary Congressional action.]

## RULE 29. STIPULATIONS ABOUT DISCOVERY PROCEDURE

Unless the court orders otherwise, the parties may stipulate that:

**(a)** a deposition may be taken before any person, at any time or place, on any notice, and in the manner specified—in which event it may be used in the same way as any other deposition; and

**(b)** other procedures governing or limiting discovery be modified—but a stipulation extending the time for any form of discovery must have court approval if it would interfere with the time set for completing discovery, for hearing a motion, or for trial.

[Amended March 30, 1970, effective July 1, 1970; April 22, 1993, effective December 1, 1993; April 30, 2007, effective December 1, 2007, absent contrary Congressional action.]

## RULE 30. DEPOSITIONS BY ORAL EXAMINATION

**(a) When a Deposition May Be Taken.**

(1) *Without Leave.* A party may, by oral questions, depose any person, including a party, without leave of court except as provided in Rule 30(a)(2). The deponent's attendance may be compelled by subpoena under Rule 45.

(2) *With Leave.* A party must obtain leave of court, and the court must grant leave to the extent consistent with Rule 26(b)(2):

(A) if the parties have not stipulated to the deposition and:

(i) the deposition would result in more than 10 depositions being taken under this rule or Rule 31 by the plaintiffs, or by the defendants, or by the third-party defendants;

(ii) the deponent has already been deposed in the case; or

(iii) the party seeks to take the deposition before the time specified in Rule 26(d), unless the party certifies in the notice, with supporting facts,

that the deponent is expected to leave the United States and be unavailable for examination in this country after that time; or

(B) if the deponent is confined in prison.

**(b) Notice of the Deposition; Other Formal Requirements.**

(1) *Notice in General.* A party who wants to depose a person by oral questions must give reasonable written notice to every other party. The notice must state the time and place of the deposition and, if known, the deponent's name and address. If the name is unknown, the notice must provide a general description sufficient to identify the person or the particular class or group to which the person belongs.

(2) *Producing Documents.* If a subpoena duces tecum is to be served on the deponent, the materials designated for production, as set out in the subpoena, must be listed in the notice or in an attachment. The notice to a party deponent may be accompanied by a request under Rule 34 to produce documents and tangible things at the deposition.

(3) *Method of Recording.*

(A) Method Stated in the Notice. The party who notices the deposition must state in the notice the method for recording the testimony. Unless the court orders otherwise, testimony may be recorded by audio, audiovisual, or stenographic means. The noticing party bears the recording costs. Any party may arrange to transcribe a deposition.

(B) Additional Method. With prior notice to the deponent and other parties, any party may designate another method for recording the testimony in addition to that specified in the original notice. That party bears the expense of the additional record or transcript unless the court orders otherwise.

(4) *By Remote Means.* The parties may stipulate—or the court may on motion order—that a deposition be taken by telephone or other remote means. For the purpose of this rule and Rules 28(a), 37(a)(2), and 37(b)(1), the deposition takes place where the deponent answers the questions.

(5) *Officer's Duties.*

(A) Before the Deposition. Unless the parties stipulate otherwise, a deposition must be conducted before an officer appointed or designated under Rule 28. The officer must begin the deposition with an on-the-record statement that includes:

(i) the officer's name and business address;

(ii) the date, time, and place of the deposition;

(iii) the deponent's name;

(iv) the officer's administration of the oath or affirmation to the deponent; and

(v) the identity of all persons present.

(B) Conducting the Deposition; Avoiding Distortion. If the deposition is recorded non-stenographically, the officer must repeat the items in Rule 30(b)(5)(A)(i)-(iii) at the beginning of each unit of the recording medium. The deponent's and attorneys' appearance or demeanor must not be distorted through recording techniques.

(C) After the Deposition. At the end of a deposition, the officer must state on the record that the deposition is complete and must set out any stipulations made by the attorneys about custody of the transcript or recording and of the exhibits, or about any other pertinent matters.

(6) *Notice or Subpoena Directed to an Organization.* In its notice or subpoena, a party may name as the deponent a public or private corporation, a partnership, an association, a governmental agency, or other entity and must describe with reasonable particularity the matters for examination. The named organization must then designate one or more officers, directors, or managing agents, or designate other persons who consent to testify on its behalf; and it may set out the matters on which each person designated will testify. A subpoena must advise a nonparty organization of its duty to make this designation. The persons designated must testify about information known or reasonably available to the organization. This paragraph (6) does not preclude a deposition by any other procedure allowed by these rules.

**(c) Examination and Cross–Examination; Record of the Examination; Objections; Written Questions.**

(1) *Examination and Cross–Examination.* The examination and cross-examination of a deponent proceed as they would at trial under the Federal Rules of Evidence, except Rules 103 and 615. After putting the deponent under oath or affirmation, the officer must record the testimony by the method designated under Rule 30(b)(3)(A). The testimony must be recorded by the officer personally or by a person acting in the presence and under the direction of the officer.

(2) *Objections.* An objection at the time of the examination—whether to evidence, to a party's conduct, to the officer's qualifications, to the manner of taking the deposition, or to any other aspect of the deposition—must be noted on the record, but the examination still proceeds; the testimony is taken subject to any objection. An objection must be stated concisely in a nonargumentative and nonsuggestive manner. A person may instruct a deponent not to answer only when necessary to preserve a privilege, to enforce a limitation ordered by the court, or to present a motion under Rule 30(d)(3).

(3) *Participating Through Written Questions.* Instead of participating in the oral examination, a party may serve written questions in a sealed envelope on the party noticing the deposition, who must deliver them to the officer. The officer must ask the deponent those questions and record the answers verbatim.

**(d) Duration; Sanction; Motion to Terminate or Limit.**

(1) *Duration.* Unless otherwise stipulated or ordered by the court, a deposition is limited to 1 day of 7 hours. The court must allow additional time consistent with Rule 26(b)(2) if needed to fairly examine the deponent or if the deponent, another person, or any other circumstance impedes or delays the examination.

(2) *Sanction.* The court may impose an appropriate sanction—including the reasonable expenses and attorney's fees incurred by any party—on a person who impedes, delays, or frustrates the fair examination of the deponent.

(3) *Motion to Terminate or Limit.*

(A) Grounds. At any time during a deposition, the deponent or a party may move to terminate or limit it on the ground that it is being conducted in bad faith or in a manner that unreasonably annoys, embarrasses, or oppresses the deponent or party. The motion may be filed in the court where the action is pending or the deposition is being taken. If the objecting deponent or party so demands, the deposition must be suspended for the time necessary to obtain an order.

(B) Order. The court may order that the deposition be terminated or may limit its scope and manner as provided in Rule 26(c). If terminated, the deposition may be resumed only by order of the court where the action is pending.

(C) Award of Expenses. Rule 37(a)(5) applies to the award of expenses.

**(e) Review by the Witness; Changes.**

(1) *Review; Statement of Changes.* On request by the deponent or a party before the deposition is completed, the deponent must be allowed 30 days after being notified by the officer that the transcript or recording is available in which:

(A) to review the transcript or recording; and

(B) if there are changes in form or substance, to sign a statement listing the changes and the reasons for making them.

(2) *Changes Indicated in the Officer's Certificate.* The officer must note in the certificate prescribed by Rule 30(f)(1) whether a review was requested and, if so, must attach any changes the deponent makes during the 30–day period.

**(f) Certification and Delivery; Exhibits; Copies of the Transcript or Recording; Filing.**

(1) *Certification and Delivery.* The officer must certify in writing that the witness was duly sworn and

that the deposition accurately records the witness's testimony. The certificate must accompany the record of the deposition. Unless the court orders otherwise, the officer must seal the deposition in an envelope or package bearing the title of the action and marked "Deposition of [witness's name]" and must promptly send it to the attorney who arranged for the transcript or recording. The attorney must store it under conditions that will protect it against loss, destruction, tampering, or deterioration.

(2) *Documents and Tangible Things.*

(A) Originals and Copies. Documents and tangible things produced for inspection during a deposition must, on a party's request, be marked for identification and attached to the deposition. Any party may inspect and copy them. But if the person who produced them wants to keep the originals, the person may:

(i) offer copies to be marked, attached to the deposition, and then used as originals—after giving all parties a fair opportunity to verify the copies by comparing them with the originals; or

(ii) give all parties a fair opportunity to inspect and copy the originals after they are marked—in which event the originals may be used as if attached to the deposition.

(B) Order Regarding the Originals. Any party may move for an order that the originals be attached to the deposition pending final disposition of the case.

(3) *Copies of the Transcript or Recording.* Unless otherwise stipulated or ordered by the court, the officer must retain the stenographic notes of a deposition taken stenographically or a copy of the recording of a deposition taken by another method. When paid reasonable charges, the officer must furnish a copy of the transcript or recording to any party or the deponent.

(4) *Notice of Filing.* A party who files the deposition must promptly notify all other parties of the filing.

**(g) Failure to Attend a Deposition or Serve a Subpoena; Expenses.** A party who, expecting a deposition to be taken, attends in person or by an attorney may recover reasonable expenses for attending, including attorney's fees, if the noticing party failed to:

(1) attend and proceed with the deposition; or

(2) serve a subpoena on a nonparty deponent, who consequently did not attend.

[Amended January 21, 1963, effective July 1, 1963; March 30, 1970, effective July 1, 1970; March 1, 1971, effective July 1, 1971; November 20, 1972, effective July 1, 1975; April 29, 1980, effective August 1, 1980; March 2, 1987, effective August 1, 1987; April 22, 1993, effective December 1, 1993; April 17, 2000, effective December 1, 2000; April 30, 2007,

effective December 1, 2007, absent contrary Congressional action.]

# RULE 31. DEPOSITIONS BY WRITTEN QUESTIONS

## (a) When a Deposition May Be Taken.

(1) *Without Leave.* A party may, by written questions, depose any person, including a party, without leave of court except as provided in Rule 31(a)(2). The deponent's attendance may be compelled by subpoena under Rule 45.

(2) *With Leave.* A party must obtain leave of court, and the court must grant leave to the extent consistent with Rule 26(b)(2):

(A) if the parties have not stipulated to the deposition and:

(i) the deposition would result in more than 10 depositions being taken under this rule or Rule 30 by the plaintiffs, or by the defendants, or by the third-party defendants;

(ii) the deponent has already been deposed in the case; or

(iii) the party seeks to take a deposition before the time specified in Rule 26(d); or

(B) if the deponent is confined in prison.

(3) *Service; Required Notice.* A party who wants to depose a person by written questions must serve them on every other party, with a notice stating, if known, the deponent's name and address. If the name is unknown, the notice must provide a general description sufficient to identify the person or the particular class or group to which the person belongs. The notice must also state the name or descriptive title and the address of the officer before whom the deposition will be taken.

(4) *Questions Directed to an Organization.* A public or private corporation, a partnership, an association, or a governmental agency may be deposed by written questions in accordance with Rule 30(b)(6).

(5) *Questions from Other Parties.* Any questions to the deponent from other parties must be served on all parties as follows: cross-questions, within 14 days after being served with the notice and direct questions; redirect questions, within 7 days after being served with cross-questions; and recross-questions, within 7 days after being served with redirect questions. The court may, for good cause, extend or shorten these times.

**(b) Delivery to the Officer; Officer's Duties.** The party who noticed the deposition must deliver to the officer a copy of all the questions served and of the notice. The officer must promptly proceed in the manner provided in Rule 30(c), (e), and (f) to:

(1) take the deponent's testimony in response to the questions;

(2) prepare and certify the deposition; and

(3) send it to the party, attaching a copy of the questions and of the notice.

**(c) Notice of Completion or Filing.**

(1) *Completion.* The party who noticed the deposition must notify all other parties when it is completed.

(2) *Filing.* A party who files the deposition must promptly notify all other parties of the filing.

[Amended March 30, 1970, effective July 1, 1970; March 2, 1987, effective August 1, 1987; April 22, 1993, effective December 1, 1993; April 30, 2007, effective December 1, 2007, absent contrary Congressional action.]

# RULE 32. USING DEPOSITIONS IN COURT PROCEEDINGS

**(a) Using Depositions.**

(1) *In General.* At a hearing or trial, all or part of a deposition may be used against a party on these conditions:

(A) the party was present or represented at the taking of the deposition or had reasonable notice of it;

(B) it is used to the extent it would be admissible under the Federal Rules of Evidence if the deponent were present and testifying; and

(C) the use is allowed by Rule 32(a)(2) through (8).

(2) *Impeachment and Other Uses.* Any party may use a deposition to contradict or impeach the testimony given by the deponent as a witness, or for any other purpose allowed by the Federal Rules of Evidence.

(3) *Deposition of Party, Agent, or Designee.* An adverse party may use for any purpose the deposition of a party or anyone who, when deposed, was the party's officer, director, managing agent, or designee under Rule 30(b)(6) or 31(a)(4).

(4) *Unavailable Witness.* A party may use for any purpose the deposition of a witness, whether or not a party, if the court finds:

(A) that the witness is dead;

(B) that the witness is more than 100 miles from the place of hearing or trial or is outside the United States, unless it appears that the witness's absence was procured by the party offering the deposition;

(C) that the witness cannot attend or testify because of age, illness, infirmity, or imprisonment;

(D) that the party offering the deposition could not procure the witness's attendance by subpoena; or

(E) on motion and notice, that exceptional circumstances make it desirable—in the interest of justice and with due regard to the importance of live testimony in open court—to permit the deposition to be used.

(5) *Limitations on Use.*

(A) Deposition Taken on Short Notice. A deposition must not be used against a party who, having received less than 11 days' notice of the deposition, promptly moved for a protective order under Rule 26(c)(1)(B) requesting that it not be taken or be taken at a different time or place—and this motion was still pending when the deposition was taken.

(B) Unavailable Deponent; Party Could Not Obtain an Attorney. A deposition taken without leave of court under the unavailability provision of Rule 30(a)(2)(A)(iii) must not be used against a party who shows that, when served with the notice, it could not, despite diligent efforts, obtain an attorney to represent it at the deposition.

(6) *Using Part of a Deposition.* If a party offers in evidence only part of a deposition, an adverse party may require the offeror to introduce other parts that in fairness should be considered with the part introduced, and any party may itself introduce any other parts.

(7) *Substituting a Party.* Substituting a party under Rule 25 does not affect the right to use a deposition previously taken.

(8) *Deposition Taken in an Earlier Action.* A deposition lawfully taken and, if required, filed in any federal- or state-court action may be used in a later action involving the same subject matter between the same parties, or their representatives or successors in interest, to the same extent as if taken in the later action. A deposition previously taken may also be used as allowed by the Federal Rules of Evidence.

**(b) Objections to Admissibility.** Subject to Rules 28(b) and 32(d)(3), an objection may be made at a hearing or trial to the admission of any deposition testimony that would be inadmissible if the witness were present and testifying.

**(c) Form of Presentation.** Unless the court orders otherwise, a party must provide a transcript of any deposition testimony the party offers, but may provide the court with the testimony in nontranscript form as well. On any party's request, deposition testimony offered in a jury trial for any purpose other than impeachment must be presented in nontranscript form, if available, unless the court for good cause orders otherwise.

**(d) Waiver of Objections.**

(1) *To the Notice.* An objection to an error or irregularity in a deposition notice is waived unless

promptly served in writing on the party giving the notice.

(2) *To the Officer's Qualification.* An objection based on disqualification of the officer before whom a deposition is to be taken is waived if not made:

(A) before the deposition begins; or

(B) promptly after the basis for disqualification becomes known or, with reasonable diligence, could have been known.

(3) *To the Taking of the Deposition.*

(A) Objection to Competence, Relevance, or Materiality. An objection to a deponent's competence—or to the competence, relevance, or materiality of testimony—is not waived by a failure to make the objection before or during the deposition, unless the ground for it might have been corrected at that time.

(B) Objection to an Error or Irregularity. An objection to an error or irregularity at an oral examination is waived if:

(i) it relates to the manner of taking the deposition, the form of a question or answer, the oath or affirmation, a party's conduct, or other matters that might have been corrected at that time; and

(ii) it is not timely made during the deposition.

(C) Objection to a Written Question. An objection to the form of a written question under Rule 31 is waived if not served in writing on the party submitting the question within the time for serving responsive questions or, if the question is a recross-question, within 5 days after being served with it.

(4) *To Completing and Returning the Deposition.* An objection to how the officer transcribed the testimony—or prepared, signed, certified, sealed, endorsed, sent, or otherwise dealt with the deposition—is waived unless a motion to suppress is made promptly after the error or irregularity becomes known or, with reasonable diligence, could have been known.

[Amended March 30, 1970, effective July 1, 1970; November 20, 1972, effective July 1, 1975; April 29, 1980, effective August 1, 1980; March 2, 1987, effective August 1, 1987; April 22, 1993, effective December 1, 1993; April 30, 2007, effective December 1, 2007, absent contrary Congressional action.]

# RULE 33.  INTERROGATORIES TO PARTIES

**(a) In General.**

(1) *Number.* Unless otherwise stipulated or ordered by the court, a party may serve on any other party no more than 25 written interrogatories, including all discrete subparts. Leave to serve additional interrogatories may be granted to the extent consistent with Rule 26(b)(2).

(2) *Scope.* An interrogatory may relate to any matter that may be inquired into under Rule 26(b). An interrogatory is not objectionable merely because it asks for an opinion or contention that relates to fact or the application of law to fact, but the court may order that the interrogatory need not be answered until designated discovery is complete, or until a pretrial conference or some other time.

**(b) Answers and Objections.**

(1) *Responding Party.* The interrogatories must be answered:

(A) by the party to whom they are directed; or

(B) if that party is a public or private corporation, a partnership, an association, or a governmental agency, by any officer or agent, who must furnish the information available to the party.

(2) *Time to Respond.* The responding party must serve its answers and any objections within 30 days after being served with the interrogatories. A shorter or longer time may be stipulated to under Rule 29 or be ordered by the court.

(3) *Answering Each Interrogatory.* Each interrogatory must, to the extent it is not objected to, be answered separately and fully in writing under oath.

(4) *Objections.* The grounds for objecting to an interrogatory must be stated with specificity. Any ground not stated in a timely objection is waived unless the court, for good cause, excuses the failure.

(5) *Signature.* The person who makes the answers must sign them, and the attorney who objects must sign any objections.

**(c) Use.** An answer to an interrogatory may be used to the extent allowed by the Federal Rules of Evidence.

**(d) Option to Produce Business Records.** If the answer to an interrogatory may be determined by examining, auditing, compiling, abstracting, or summarizing a party's business records (including electronically stored information), and if the burden of deriving or ascertaining the answer will be substantially the same for either party, the responding party may answer by:

(1) specifying the records that must be reviewed, in sufficient detail to enable the interrogating party to locate and identify them as readily as the responding party could; and

(2) giving the interrogating party a reasonable opportunity to examine and audit the records and to make copies, compilations, abstracts, or summaries.

[Amended December 27, 1946, effective March 19, 1948; March 30, 1970, effective July 1, 1970; April 29, 1980, effective August 1, 1980; April 22, 1993, effective December 1, 1993; April 12, 2006, effective December 1, 2006; April 30,

2007, effective December 1, 2007, absent contrary Congressional action.]

# RULE 34. PRODUCING DOCUMENTS, ELECTRONICALLY STORED INFORMATION, AND TANGIBLE THINGS, OR ENTERING ONTO LAND, FOR INSPECTION AND OTHER PURPOSES

**(a) In General.** A party may serve on any other party a request within the scope of Rule 26(b):

(1) to produce and permit the requesting party or its representative to inspect, copy, test, or sample the following items in the responding party's possession, custody, or control:

(A) any designated documents or electronically stored information—including writings, drawings, graphs, charts, photographs, sound recordings, images, and other data or data compilations—stored in any medium from which information can be obtained either directly or, if necessary, after translation by the responding party into a reasonably usable form; or

(B) any designated tangible things; or

(2) to permit entry onto designated land or other property possessed or controlled by the responding party, so that the requesting party may inspect, measure, survey, photograph, test, or sample the property or any designated object or operation on it.

**(b) Procedure.**

(1) *Contents of the Request.* The request:

(A) must describe with reasonable particularity each item or category of items to be inspected;

(B) must specify a reasonable time, place, and manner for the inspection and for performing the related acts; and

(C) may specify the form or forms in which electronically stored information is to be produced.

(2) *Responses and Objections.*

(A) Time to Respond. The party to whom the request is directed must respond in writing within 30 days after being served. A shorter or longer time may be stipulated to under Rule 29 or be ordered by the court.

(B) Responding to Each Item. For each item or category, the response must either state that inspection and related activities will be permitted as requested or state an objection to the request, including the reasons.

(C) Objections. An objection to part of a request must specify the part and permit inspection of the rest.

(D) Responding to a Request for Production of Electronically Stored Information. The response may state an objection to a requested form for producing electronically stored information. If the responding party objects to a requested form—or if no form was specified in the request—the party must state the form or forms it intends to use.

(E) Producing the Documents or Electronically Stored Information. Unless otherwise stipulated or ordered by the court, these procedures apply to producing documents or electronically stored information:

(i) A party must produce documents as they are kept in the usual course of business or must organize and label them to correspond to the categories in the request;

(ii) If a request does not specify a form for producing electronically stored information, a party must produce it in a form or forms in which it is ordinarily maintained or in a reasonably usable form or forms; and

(iii) A party need not produce the same electronically stored information in more than one form.

**(c) Nonparties.** As provided in Rule 45, a nonparty may be compelled to produce documents and tangible things or to permit an inspection.

[Amended December 27, 1946, effective March 19, 1948; March 30, 1970, effective July 1, 1970; April 29, 1980, effective August 1, 1980; March 2, 1987, effective August 1, 1987; April 30, 1991, effective December 1, 1991; April 22, 1993, effective December 1, 1993; April 12, 2006, effective December 1, 2006; April 30, 2007, effective December 1, 2007, absent contrary Congressional action.]

# RULE 35. PHYSICAL AND MENTAL EXAMINATIONS

**(a) Order for an Examination.**

(1) *In General.* The court where the action is pending may order a party whose mental or physical condition—including blood group—is in controversy to submit to a physical or mental examination by a suitably licensed or certified examiner. The court has the same authority to order a party to produce for examination a person who is in its custody or under its legal control.

(2) *Motion and Notice; Contents of the Order.* The order:

(A) may be made only on motion for good cause and on notice to all parties and the person to be examined; and

(B) must specify the time, place, manner, conditions, and scope of the examination, as well as the person or persons who will perform it.

**(b) Examiner's Report.**

(1) *Request by the Party or Person Examined.* The party who moved for the examination must, on request, deliver to the requester a copy of the examiner's report, together with like reports of all earlier examinations of the same condition. The request may be made by the party against whom the examination order was issued or by the person examined.

(2) *Contents.* The examiner's report must be in writing and must set out in detail the examiner's findings, including diagnoses, conclusions, and the results of any tests.

(3) *Request by the Moving Party.* After delivering the reports, the party who moved for the examination may request—and is entitled to receive—from the party against whom the examination order was issued like reports of all earlier or later examinations of the same condition. But those reports need not be delivered by the party with custody or control of the person examined if the party shows that it could not obtain them.

(4) *Waiver of Privilege.* By requesting and obtaining the examiner's report, or by deposing the examiner, the party examined waives any privilege it may have—in that action or any other action involving the same controversy—concerning testimony about all examinations of the same condition.

(5) *Failure to Deliver a Report.* The court on motion may order—on just terms—that a party deliver the report of an examination. If the report is not provided, the court may exclude the examiner's testimony at trial.

(6) *Scope.* This subdivision (b) applies also to an examination made by the parties' agreement, unless the agreement states otherwise. This subdivision does not preclude obtaining an examiner's report or deposing an examiner under other rules.

[Amended March 30, 1970, effective July 1, 1970; March 2, 1987, effective August 1, 1987; amended by Pub.L. 100–690, Title VII, § 7047(b), November 18, 1988, 102 Stat. 4401; amended April 30, 1991, effective December 1, 1991; April 30, 2007, effective December 1, 2007, absent contrary Congressional action.]

# RULE 36. REQUESTS FOR ADMISSION

**(a) Scope and Procedure.**

(1) *Scope.* A party may serve on any other party a written request to admit, for purposes of the pending action only, the truth of any matters within the scope of Rule 26(b)(1) relating to:

    (A) facts, the application of law to fact, or opinions about either; and

    (B) the genuineness of any described documents.

(2) *Form; Copy of a Document.* Each matter must be separately stated. A request to admit the genuineness of a document must be accompanied by a copy of the document unless it is, or has been, otherwise furnished or made available for inspection and copying.

(3) *Time to Respond; Effect of Not Responding.* A matter is admitted unless, within 30 days after being served, the party to whom the request is directed serves on the requesting party a written answer or objection addressed to the matter and signed by the party or its attorney. A shorter or longer time for responding may be stipulated to under Rule 29 or be ordered by the court.

(4) *Answer.* If a matter is not admitted, the answer must specifically deny it or state in detail why the answering party cannot truthfully admit or deny it. A denial must fairly respond to the substance of the matter; and when good faith requires that a party qualify an answer or deny only a part of a matter, the answer must specify the part admitted and qualify or deny the rest. The answering party may assert lack of knowledge or information as a reason for failing to admit or deny only if the party states that it has made reasonable inquiry and that the information it knows or can readily obtain is insufficient to enable it to admit or deny.

(5) *Objections.* The grounds for objecting to a request must be stated. A party must not object solely on the ground that the request presents a genuine issue for trial.

(6) *Motion Regarding the Sufficiency of an Answer or Objection.* The requesting party may move to determine the sufficiency of an answer or objection. Unless the court finds an objection justified, it must order that an answer be served. On finding that an answer does not comply with this rule, the court may order either that the matter is admitted or that an amended answer be served. The court may defer its final decision until a pretrial conference or a specified time before trial. Rule 37(a)(5) applies to an award of expenses.

**(b) Effect of an Admission; Withdrawing or Amending It.** A matter admitted under this rule is conclusively established unless the court, on motion, permits the admission to be withdrawn or amended. Subject to Rule 16(e), the court may permit withdrawal or amendment if it would promote the presentation of the merits of the action and if the court is not persuaded that it would prejudice the requesting party in maintaining or defending the action on the merits. An admission under this rule is not an admission for any other purpose and cannot be used against the party in any other proceeding.

[Amended December 27, 1946, effective March 19, 1948; March 30, 1970, effective July 1, 1970; March 2, 1987, effective August 1, 1987; April 22, 1993, effective December 1, 1993; April 30, 2007, effective December 1, 2007, absent contrary Congressional action.]

# RULE 37. FAILURE TO MAKE DISCLOSURES OR TO COOPERATE IN DISCOVERY; SANCTIONS

## (a) Motion for an Order Compelling Disclosure or Discovery.

(1) *In General.* On notice to other parties and all affected persons, a party may move for an order compelling disclosure or discovery. The motion must include a certification that the movant has in good faith conferred or attempted to confer with the person or party failing to make disclosure or discovery in an effort to obtain it without court action.

(2) *Appropriate Court.* A motion for an order to a party must be made in the court where the action is pending. A motion for an order to a nonparty must be made in the court where the discovery is or will be taken.

(3) *Specific Motions.*

(A) To Compel Disclosure. If a party fails to make a disclosure required by Rule 26(a), any other party may move to compel disclosure and for appropriate sanctions.

(B) To Compel a Discovery Response. A party seeking discovery may move for an order compelling an answer, designation, production, or inspection. This motion may be made if:

(i) a deponent fails to answer a question asked under Rule 30 or 31;

(ii) a corporation or other entity fails to make a designation under Rule 30(b)(6) or 31(a)(4);

(iii) a party fails to answer an interrogatory submitted under Rule 33; or

(iv) a party fails to respond that inspection will be permitted—or fails to permit inspection—as requested under Rule 34.

(C) Related to a Deposition. When taking an oral deposition, the party asking a question may complete or adjourn the examination before moving for an order.

(4) *Evasive or Incomplete Disclosure, Answer, or Response.* For purposes of this subdivision (a), an evasive or incomplete disclosure, answer, or response must be treated as a failure to disclose, answer, or respond.

(5) *Payment of Expenses; Protective Orders.*

(A) If the Motion Is Granted (or Disclosure or Discovery Is Provided After Filing). If the motion is granted—or if the disclosure or requested discovery is provided after the motion was filed—the court must, after giving an opportunity to be heard, require the party or deponent whose conduct necessitated the motion, the party or attorney advising that conduct, or both to pay the movant's reasonable expenses incurred in making the motion, including attorney's fees. But the court must not order this payment if:

(i) the movant filed the motion before attempting in good faith to obtain the disclosure or discovery without court action;

(ii) the opposing party's nondisclosure, response, or objection was substantially justified; or

(iii) other circumstances make an award of expenses unjust.

(B) If the Motion Is Denied. If the motion is denied, the court may issue any protective order authorized under Rule 26(c) and must, after giving an opportunity to be heard, require the movant, the attorney filing the motion, or both to pay the party or deponent who opposed the motion its reasonable expenses incurred in opposing the motion, including attorney's fees. But the court must not order this payment if the motion was substantially justified or other circumstances make an award of expenses unjust.

(C) If the Motion Is Granted in Part and Denied in Part. If the motion is granted in part and denied in part, the court may issue any protective order authorized under Rule 26(c) and may, after giving an opportunity to be heard, apportion the reasonable expenses for the motion.

## (b) Failure to Comply with a Court Order.

(1) *Sanctions in the District Where the Deposition Is Taken.* If the court where the discovery is taken orders a deponent to be sworn or to answer a question and the deponent fails to obey, the failure may be treated as contempt of court.

(2) *Sanctions in the District Where the Action Is Pending.*

(A) For Not Obeying a Discovery Order. If a party or a party's officer, director, or managing agent—or a witness designated under Rule 30(b)(6) or 31(a)(4)—fails to obey an order to provide or permit discovery, including an order under Rule 26(f), 35, or 37(a), the court where the action is pending may issue further just orders. They may include the following:

(i) directing that the matters embraced in the order or other designated facts be taken as established for purposes of the action, as the prevailing party claims;

(ii) prohibiting the disobedient party from supporting or opposing designated claims or defenses, or from introducing designated matters in evidence;

(iii) striking pleadings in whole or in part;

(iv) staying further proceedings until the order is obeyed;

(v) dismissing the action or proceeding in whole or in part;

(vi) rendering a default judgment against the disobedient party; or

(vii) treating as contempt of court the failure to obey any order except an order to submit to a physical or mental examination.

(B) For Not Producing a Person for Examination. If a party fails to comply with an order under Rule 35(a) requiring it to produce another person for examination, the court may issue any of the orders listed in Rule 37(b)(2)(A)(i)-(vi), unless the disobedient party shows that it cannot produce the other person.

(C) Payment of Expenses. Instead of or in addition to the orders above, the court must order the disobedient party, the attorney advising that party, or both to pay the reasonable expenses, including attorney's fees, caused by the failure, unless the failure was substantially justified or other circumstances make an award of expenses unjust.

**(c) Failure to Disclose, to Supplement an Earlier Response, or to Admit.**

(1) *Failure to Disclose or Supplement.* If a party fails to provide information or identify a witness as required by Rule 26(a) or (e), the party is not allowed to use that information or witness to supply evidence on a motion, at a hearing, or at a trial, unless the failure was substantially justified or is harmless. In addition to or instead of this sanction, the court, on motion and after giving an opportunity to be heard:

(A) may order payment of the reasonable expenses, including attorney's fees, caused by the failure;

(B) may inform the jury of the party's failure; and

(C) may impose other appropriate sanctions, including any of the orders listed in Rule 37(b)(2)(A)(i)-(vi).

(2) *Failure to Admit.* If a party fails to admit what is requested under Rule 36 and if the requesting party later proves a document to be genuine or the matter true, the requesting party may move that the party who failed to admit pay the reasonable expenses, including attorney's fees, incurred in making that proof. The court must so order unless:

(A) the request was held objectionable under Rule 36(a);

(B) the admission sought was of no substantial importance;

(C) the party failing to admit had a reasonable ground to believe that it might prevail on the matter; or

(D) there was other good reason for the failure to admit.

**(d) Party's Failure to Attend Its Own Deposition, Serve Answers to Interrogatories, or Respond to a Request for Inspection.**

(1) *In General.*

(A) Motion; Grounds for Sanctions. The court where the action is pending may, on motion, order sanctions if:

(i) a party or a party's officer, director, or managing agent—or a person designated under Rule 30(b)(6) or 31(a)(4)—fails, after being served with proper notice, to appear for that person's deposition; or

(ii) a party, after being properly served with interrogatories under Rule 33 or a request for inspection under Rule 34, fails to serve its answers, objections, or written response.

(B) Certification. A motion for sanctions for failing to answer or respond must include a certification that the movant has in good faith conferred or attempted to confer with the party failing to act in an effort to obtain the answer or response without court action.

(2) *Unacceptable Excuse for Failing to Act.* A failure described in Rule 37(d)(1)(A) is not excused on the ground that the discovery sought was objectionable, unless the party failing to act has a pending motion for a protective order under Rule 26(c).

(3) *Types of Sanctions.* Sanctions may include any of the orders listed in Rule 37(b)(2)(A)(i)-(vi). Instead of or in addition to these sanctions, the court must require the party failing to act, the attorney advising that party, or both to pay the reasonable expenses, including attorney's fees, caused by the failure, unless the failure was substantially justified or other circumstances make an award of expenses unjust.

**(e) Failure to Provide Electronically Stored Information.** Absent exceptional circumstances, a court may not impose sanctions under these rules on a party for failing to provide electronically stored information lost as a result of the routine, good-faith operation of an electronic information system.

**(f) Failure to Participate in Framing a Discovery Plan.** If a party or its attorney fails to participate in good faith in developing and submitting a proposed discovery plan as required by Rule 26(f), the court may, after giving an opportunity to be heard, require that party or attorney to pay to any other party the reasonable expenses, including attorney's fees, caused by the failure.

[Amended December 29, 1948, effective October 20, 1949; March 30, 1970, effective July 1, 1970; April 29, 1980, effective August 1, 1980; amended by Pub.L. 96–481, Title II, § 205(a), October 21, 1980, 94 Stat. 2330, effective Octo-

ber 1, 1981; amended March 2, 1987, effective August 1, 1987; April 22, 1993, effective December 1, 1993; April 17, 2000, effective December 1, 2000; April 12, 2006, effective December 1, 2006; April 30, 2007, effective December 1, 2007, absent contrary Congressional action.]

# TITLE VI.　TRIALS

## RULE 38.　RIGHT TO A JURY TRIAL; DEMAND

**(a) Right Preserved.** The right of trial by jury as declared by the Seventh Amendment to the Constitution—or as provided by a federal statute—is preserved to the parties inviolate.

**(b) Demand.** On any issue triable of right by a jury, a party may demand a jury trial by:

(1) serving the other parties with a written demand—which may be included in a pleading—no later than 10 days after the last pleading directed to the issue is served; and

(2) filing the demand in accordance with Rule 5(d).

**(c) Specifying Issues.** In its demand, a party may specify the issues that it wishes to have tried by a jury; otherwise, it is considered to have demanded a jury trial on all the issues so triable. If the party has demanded a jury trial on only some issues, any other party may—within 10 days after being served with the demand or within a shorter time ordered by the court—serve a demand for a jury trial on any other or all factual issues triable by jury.

**(d) Waiver; Withdrawal.** A party waives a jury trial unless its demand is properly served and filed. A proper demand may be withdrawn only if the parties consent.

**(e) Admiralty and Maritime Claims.** These rules do not create a right to a jury trial on issues in a claim that is an admiralty or maritime claim under Rule 9(h).

[Amended February 28, 1966, effective July 1, 1966; March 2, 1987, effective August 1, 1987; April 22, 1993, effective December 1, 1993; April 30, 2007, effective December 1, 2007, absent contrary Congressional action.]

## RULE 39.　TRIAL BY JURY OR BY THE COURT

**(a) When a Demand Is Made.** When a jury trial has been demanded under Rule 38, the action must be designated on the docket as a jury action. The trial on all issues so demanded must be by jury unless:

(1) the parties or their attorneys file a stipulation to a nonjury trial or so stipulate on the record; or

(2) the court, on motion or on its own, finds that on some or all of those issues there is no federal right to a jury trial.

**(b) When No Demand Is Made.** Issues on which a jury trial is not properly demanded are to be tried by the court. But the court may, on motion, order a jury trial on any issue for which a jury might have been demanded.

**(c) Advisory Jury; Jury Trial by Consent.** In an action not triable of right by a jury, the court, on motion or on its own:

(1) may try any issue with an advisory jury; or

(2) may, with the parties' consent, try any issue by a jury whose verdict has the same effect as if a jury trial had been a matter of right, unless the action is against the United States and a federal statute provides for a nonjury trial.

[Amended April 30, 2007, effective December 1, 2007, absent contrary Congressional action.]

## RULE 40.　SCHEDULING CASES FOR TRIAL

Each court must provide by rule for scheduling trials. The court must give priority to actions entitled to priority by a federal statute.

[Amended April 30, 2007, effective December 1, 2007, absent contrary Congressional action.]

## RULE 41.　DISMISSAL OF ACTIONS

**(a) Voluntary Dismissal.**

(1) *By the Plaintiff.*

(A) Without a Court Order. Subject to Rules 23(e), 23.1(c), 23.2, and 66 and any applicable federal statute, the plaintiff may dismiss an action without a court order by filing:

(i) a notice of dismissal before the opposing party serves either an answer or a motion for summary judgment; or

(ii) a stipulation of dismissal signed by all parties who have appeared.

(B) Effect. Unless the notice or stipulation states otherwise, the dismissal is without prejudice. But if the plaintiff previously dismissed any federal-or state-court action based on or including the same claim, a notice of dismissal operates as an adjudication on the merits.

(2) *By Court Order; Effect.* Except as provided in Rule 41(a)(1), an action may be dismissed at the plaintiff's request only by court order, on terms that

the court considers proper. If a defendant has pleaded a counterclaim before being served with the plaintiff's motion to dismiss, the action may be dismissed over the defendant's objection only if the counterclaim can remain pending for independent adjudication. Unless the order states otherwise, a dismissal under this paragraph (2) is without prejudice.

**(b) Involuntary Dismissal; Effect.** If the plaintiff fails to prosecute or to comply with these rules or a court order, a defendant may move to dismiss the action or any claim against it. Unless the dismissal order states otherwise, a dismissal under this subdivision (b) and any dismissal not under this rule—except one for lack of jurisdiction, improper venue, or failure to join a party under Rule 19—operates as an adjudication on the merits.

**(c) Dismissing a Counterclaim, Crossclaim, or Third–Party Claim.** This rule applies to a dismissal of any counterclaim, crossclaim, or third-party claim. A claimant's voluntary dismissal under Rule 41(a)(1)(A)(i) must be made:

(1) before a responsive pleading is served; or

(2) if there is no responsive pleading, before evidence is introduced at a hearing or trial.

**(d) Costs of a Previously Dismissed Action.** If a plaintiff who previously dismissed an action in any court files an action based on or including the same claim against the same defendant, the court:

(1) may order the plaintiff to pay all or part of the costs of that previous action; and

(2) may stay the proceedings until the plaintiff has complied.

[Amended December 27, 1946, effective March 19, 1948; January 21, 1963, effective July 1, 1963; February 28, 1966, effective July 1, 1966; December 4, 1967, effective July 1, 1968; March 2, 1987, effective August 1, 1987; April 30, 1991, effective December 1, 1991; April 30, 2007, effective December 1, 2007, absent contrary Congressional action.]

## RULE 42.  CONSOLIDATION; SEPARATE TRIALS

**(a) Consolidation.** If actions before the court involve a common question of law or fact, the court may:

(1) join for hearing or trial any or all matters at issue in the actions;

(2) consolidate the actions; or

(3) issue any other orders to avoid unnecessary cost or delay.

**(b) Separate Trials.** For convenience, to avoid prejudice, or to expedite and economize, the court may order a separate trial of one or more separate issues, claims, crossclaims, counterclaims, or third-party claims. When ordering a separate trial, the court must preserve any federal right to a jury trial.

[Amended February 28, 1966, effective July 1, 1966; April 30, 2007, effective December 1, 2007, absent contrary Congressional action.]

## RULE 43.  TAKING TESTIMONY

**(a) In Open Court.** At trial, the witnesses' testimony must be taken in open court unless a federal statute, the Federal Rules of Evidence, these rules, or other rules adopted by the Supreme Court provide otherwise. For good cause in compelling circumstances and with appropriate safeguards, the court may permit testimony in open court by contemporaneous transmission from a different location.

**(b) Affirmation Instead of an Oath.** When these rules require an oath, a solemn affirmation suffices.

**(c) Evidence on a Motion.** When a motion relies on facts outside the record, the court may hear the matter on affidavits or may hear it wholly or partly on oral testimony or on depositions.

**(d) Interpreter.** The court may appoint an interpreter of its choosing; fix reasonable compensation to be paid from funds provided by law or by one or more parties; and tax the compensation as costs.

[Amended February 28, 1966, effective July 1, 1966; November 20, 1972, and December 18, 1972, effective July 1, 1975; March 2, 1987, effective August 1, 1987; April 23, 1996, effective December 1, 1996; April 30, 2007, effective December 1, 2007, absent contrary Congressional action.]

## RULE 44.  PROVING AN OFFICIAL RECORD

**(a) Means of Proving.**

(1) *Domestic Record.* Each of the following evidences an official record—or an entry in it—that is otherwise admissible and is kept within the United States, any state, district, or commonwealth, or any territory subject to the administrative or judicial jurisdiction of the United States:

(A) an official publication of the record; or

(B) a copy attested by the officer with legal custody of the record—or by the officer's deputy—and accompanied by a certificate that the officer has custody. The certificate must be made under seal:

(i) by a judge of a court of record in the district or political subdivision where the record is kept; or

(ii) by any public officer with a seal of office and with official duties in the district or political subdivision where the record is kept.

(2) *Foreign Record.*

(A) In General. Each of the following evidences a foreign official record—or an entry in it—that is otherwise admissible:

(i) an official publication of the record; or

(ii) the record—or a copy—that is attested by an authorized person and is accompanied either by a final certification of genuineness or by a certification under a treaty or convention to which the United States and the country where the record is located are parties.

(B) Final Certification of Genuineness. A final certification must certify the genuineness of the signature and official position of the attester or of any foreign official whose certificate of genuineness relates to the attestation or is in a chain of certificates of genuineness relating to the attestation. A final certification may be made by a secretary of a United States embassy or legation; by a consul general, vice consul, or consular agent of the United States; or by a diplomatic or consular official of the foreign country assigned or accredited to the United States.

(C) Other Means of Proof. If all parties have had a reasonable opportunity to investigate a foreign record's authenticity and accuracy, the court may, for good cause, either:

(i) admit an attested copy without final certification; or

(ii) permit the record to be evidenced by an attested summary with or without a final certification.

**(b) Lack of a Record.** A written statement that a diligent search of designated records revealed no record or entry of a specified tenor is admissible as evidence that the records contain no such record or entry. For domestic records, the statement must be authenticated under Rule 44(a)(1). For foreign records, the statement must comply with (a)(2)(C)(ii).

**(c) Other Proof.** A party may prove an official record—or an entry or lack of an entry in it—by any other method authorized by law.

[Amended February 28, 1966, effective July 1, 1966; March 2, 1987, effective August 1, 1987; April 30, 1991, effective December 1, 1991; April 30, 2007, effective December 1, 2007, absent contrary Congressional action.]

# RULE 44.1   DETERMINING FOREIGN LAW

A party who intends to raise an issue about a foreign country's law must give notice by a pleading or other writing. In determining foreign law, the court may consider any relevant material or source, including testimony, whether or not submitted by a party or admissible under the Federal Rules of Evidence. The court's determination must be treated as a ruling on a question of law.

[Adopted February 28, 1966, effective July 1, 1966; amended November 20, 1972, effective July 1, 1975; March 2, 1987, effective August 1, 1987; April 30, 2007, effective December 1, 2007, absent contrary Congressional action.]

# RULE 45.   SUBPOENA

**(a) In General.**

(1) *Form and Contents.*

(A) Requirements—In General. Every subpoena must:

(i) state the court from which it issued;

(ii) state the title of the action, the court in which it is pending, and its civil-action number;

(iii) command each person to whom it is directed to do the following at a specified time and place: attend and testify; produce designated documents, electronically stored information, or tangible things in that person's possession, custody, or control; or permit the inspection of premises; and

(iv) set out the text of Rule 45(c) and (d).

(B) Command to Attend a Deposition—Notice of the Recording Method. A subpoena commanding attendance at a deposition must state the method for recording the testimony.

(C) Combining or Separating a Command to Produce or to Permit Inspection; Specifying the Form for Electronically Stored Information. A command to produce documents, electronically stored information, or tangible things or to permit the inspection of premises may be included in a subpoena commanding attendance at a deposition, hearing, or trial, or may be set out in a separate subpoena. A subpoena may specify the form or forms in which electronically stored information is to be produced.

(D) Command to Produce; Included Obligations. A command in a subpoena to produce documents, electronically stored information, or tangible things requires the responding party to permit inspection, copying, testing, or sampling of the materials.

(2) *Issued from Which Court.* A subpoena must issue as follows:

(A) for attendance at a hearing or trial, from the court for the district where the hearing or trial is to be held;

(B) for attendance at a deposition, from the court for the district where the deposition is to be taken; and

(C) for production or inspection, if separate from a subpoena commanding a person's attendance, from the court for the district where the production or inspection is to be made.

(3) *Issued by Whom.* The clerk must issue a subpoena, signed but otherwise in blank, to a party who requests it. That party must complete it before service. An attorney also may issue and sign a subpoena as an officer of:

(A) a court in which the attorney is authorized to practice; or

(B) a court for a district where a deposition is to be taken or production is to be made, if the attorney is authorized to practice in the court where the action is pending.

**(b) Service.**

(1) *By Whom; Tendering Fees; Serving a Copy of Certain Subpoenas.* Any person who is at least 18 years old and not a party may serve a subpoena. Serving a subpoena requires delivering a copy to the named person and, if the subpoena requires that person's attendance, tendering the fees for 1 day's attendance and the mileage allowed by law. Fees and mileage need not be tendered when the subpoena issues on behalf of the United States or any of its officers or agencies. If the subpoena commands the production of documents, electronically stored information, or tangible things or the inspection of premises before trial, then before it is served, a notice must be served on each party.

(2) *Service in the United States.* Subject to Rule 45(c)(3)(A)(ii), a subpoena may be served at any place:

(A) within the district of the issuing court;

(B) outside that district but within 100 miles of the place specified for the deposition, hearing, trial, production, or inspection;

(C) within the state of the issuing court if a state statute or court rule allows service at that place of a subpoena issued by a state court of general jurisdiction sitting in the place specified for the deposition, hearing, trial, production, or inspection; or

(D) that the court authorizes on motion and for good cause, if a federal statute so provides.

(3) *Service in a Foreign Country.* 28 U.S.C. § 1783 governs issuing and serving a subpoena directed to a United States national or resident who is in a foreign country.

(4) *Proof of Service.* Proving service, when necessary, requires filing with the issuing court a statement showing the date and manner of service and the names of the persons served. The statement must be certified by the server.

**(c) Protecting a Person Subject to a Subpoena.**

(1) *Avoiding Undue Burden or Expense; Sanctions.* A party or attorney responsible for issuing and serving a subpoena must take reasonable steps to avoid imposing undue burden or expense on a person subject to the subpoena. The issuing court must en-force this duty and impose an appropriate sanction—which may include lost earnings and reasonable attorney's fees—on a party or attorney who fails to comply.

(2) *Command to Produce Materials or Permit Inspection.*

(A) Appearance Not Required. A person commanded to produce documents, electronically stored information, or tangible things, or to permit the inspection of premises, need not appear in person at the place of production or inspection unless also commanded to appear for a deposition, hearing, or trial.

(B) Objections. A person commanded to produce documents or tangible things or to permit inspection may serve on the party or attorney designated in the subpoena a written objection to inspecting, copying, testing or sampling any or all of the materials or to inspecting the premises—or to producing electronically stored information in the form or forms requested. The objection must be served before the earlier of the time specified for compliance or 14 days after the subpoena is served. If an objection is made, the following rules apply:

(i) At any time, on notice to the commanded person, the serving party may move the issuing court for an order compelling production or inspection.

(ii) These acts may be required only as directed in the order, and the order must protect a person who is neither a party nor a party's officer from significant expense resulting from compliance.

(3) *Quashing or Modifying a Subpoena.*

(A) When Required. On timely motion, the issuing court must quash or modify a subpoena that:

(i) fails to allow a reasonable time to comply;

(ii) requires a person who is neither a party nor a party's officer to travel more than 100 miles from where that person resides, is employed, or regularly transacts business in person—except that, subject to Rule 45(c)(3)(B)(iii), the person may be commanded to attend a trial by traveling from any such place within the state where the trial is held;

(iii) requires disclosure of privileged or other protected matter, if no exception or waiver applies; or

(iv) subjects a person to undue burden.

(B) When Permitted. To protect a person subject to or affected by a subpoena, the issuing court may, on motion, quash or modify the subpoena if it requires:

(i) disclosing a trade secret or other confidential research, development, or commercial information;

(ii) disclosing an unretained expert's opinion or information that does not describe specific occurrences in dispute and results from the expert's study that was not requested by a party; or

(iii) a person who is neither a party nor a party's officer to incur substantial expense to travel more than 100 miles to attend trial.

(C) Specifying Conditions as an Alternative. In the circumstances described in Rule 45(c)(3)(B), the court may, instead of quashing or modifying a subpoena, order appearance or production under specified conditions if the serving party:

(i) shows a substantial need for the testimony or material that cannot be otherwise met without undue hardship; and

(ii) ensures that the subpoenaed person will be reasonably compensated.

**(d) Duties in Responding to a Subpoena.**

(1) *Producing Documents or Electronically Stored Information.* These procedures apply to producing documents or electronically stored information:

(A) Documents. A person responding to a subpoena to produce documents must produce them as they are kept in the ordinary course of business or must organize and label them to correspond to the categories in the demand.

(B) Form for Producing Electronically Stored Information Not Specified. If a subpoena does not specify a form for producing electronically stored information, the person responding must produce it in a form or forms in which it is ordinarily maintained or in a reasonably usable form or forms.

(C) Electronically Stored Information Produced in Only One Form. The person responding need not produce the same electronically stored information in more than one form.

(D) Inaccessible Electronically Stored Information. The person responding need not provide discovery of electronically stored information from sources that the person identifies as not reasonably accessible because of undue burden or cost. On motion to compel discovery or for a protective order, the person responding must show that the information is not reasonably accessible because of undue burden or cost. If that showing is made, the court may nonetheless order discovery from such sources if the requesting party shows good cause, considering the limitations of Rule 26(b)(2)(C). The court may specify conditions for the discovery.

(2) *Claiming Privilege or Protection.*

(A) Information Withheld. A person withholding subpoenaed information under a claim that it is privileged or subject to protection as trial-preparation material must:

(i) expressly make the claim; and

(ii) describe the nature of the withheld documents, communications, or tangible things in a manner that, without revealing information itself privileged or protected, will enable the parties to assess the claim.

(B) Information Produced. If information produced in response to a subpoena is subject to a claim of privilege or of protection as trial-preparation material, the person making the claim may notify any party that received the information of the claim and the basis for it. After being notified, a party must promptly return, sequester, or destroy the specified information and any copies it has; must not use or disclose the information until the claim is resolved; must take reasonable steps to retrieve the information if the party disclosed it before being notified; and may promptly present the information to the court under seal for a determination of the claim. The person who produced the information must preserve the information until the claim is resolved.

**(e) Contempt.** The issuing court may hold in contempt a person who, having been served, fails without adequate excuse to obey the subpoena. A nonparty's failure to obey must be excused if the subpoena purports to require the nonparty to attend or produce at a place outside the limits of Rule 45(c)(3)(A)(ii).

[Amended December 27, 1946, effective March 19, 1948; December 29, 1948, effective October 20, 1949; March 30, 1970, effective July 1, 1970; April 29, 1980, effective August 1, 1980; April 29, 1985, effective August 1, 1985; March 2, 1987, effective August 1, 1987; April 30, 1991, effective December 1, 1991; April 25, 2005, effective December 1, 2005; April 12, 2006, effective December 1, 2006; April 30, 2007, effective December 1, 2007, absent contrary Congressional action.]

## RULE 46. OBJECTING TO A RULING OR ORDER

A formal exception to a ruling or order is unnecessary. When the ruling or order is requested or made, a party need only state the action that it wants the court to take or objects to, along with the grounds for the request or objection. Failing to object does not prejudice a party who had no opportunity to do so when the ruling or order was made.

[Amended March 2, 1987, effective August 1, 1987; April 30, 2007, effective December 1, 2007, absent contrary Congressional action.]

## RULE 47. SELECTING JURORS

(a) **Examining Jurors.** The court may permit the parties or their attorneys to examine prospective jurors or may itself do so. If the court examines the jurors, it must permit the parties or their attorneys to make any further inquiry it considers proper, or must itself ask any of their additional questions it considers proper.

(b) **Peremptory Challenges.** The court must allow the number of peremptory challenges provided by 28 U.S.C. § 1870.

(c) **Excusing a Juror.** During trial or deliberation, the court may excuse a juror for good cause.

[Amended February 28, 1966, effective July 1, 1966; April 30, 1991, effective December 1, 1991; April 30, 2007, effective December 1, 2007, absent contrary Congressional action.]

## RULE 48. NUMBER OF JURORS; VERDICT

A jury must initially have at least 6 and no more than 12 members, and each juror must participate in the verdict unless excused under Rule 47(c). Unless the parties stipulate otherwise, the verdict must be unanimous and be returned by a jury of at least 6 members.

[Amended April 30, 1991, effective December 1, 1991; April 30, 2007, effective December 1, 2007, absent contrary Congressional action.]

## RULE 49. SPECIAL VERDICT; GENERAL VERDICT AND QUESTIONS

(a) **Special Verdict.**

(1) *In General.* The court may require a jury to return only a special verdict in the form of a special written finding on each issue of fact. The court may do so by:

(A) submitting written questions susceptible of a categorical or other brief answer;

(B) submitting written forms of the special findings that might properly be made under the pleadings and evidence; or

(C) using any other method that the court considers appropriate.

(2) *Instructions.* The court must give the instructions and explanations necessary to enable the jury to make its findings on each submitted issue.

(3) *Issues Not Submitted.* A party waives the right to a jury trial on any issue of fact raised by the pleadings or evidence but not submitted to the jury unless, before the jury retires, the party demands its submission to the jury. If the party does not demand submission, the court may make a finding on the issue. If the court makes no finding, it is considered to have made a finding consistent with its judgment on the special verdict.

(b) **General Verdict with Answers to Written Questions.**

(1) *In General.* The court may submit to the jury forms for a general verdict, together with written questions on one or more issues of fact that the jury must decide. The court must give the instructions and explanations necessary to enable the jury to render a general verdict and answer the questions in writing, and must direct the jury to do both.

(2) *Verdict and Answers Consistent.* When the general verdict and the answers are consistent, the court must approve, for entry under Rule 58, an appropriate judgment on the verdict and answers.

(3) *Answers Inconsistent with the Verdict.* When the answers are consistent with each other but one or more is inconsistent with the general verdict, the court may:

(A) approve, for entry under Rule 58, an appropriate judgment according to the answers, notwithstanding the general verdict;

(B) direct the jury to further consider its answers and verdict; or

(C) order a new trial.

(4) *Answers Inconsistent with Each Other and the Verdict.* When the answers are inconsistent with each other and one or more is also inconsistent with the general verdict, judgment must not be entered; instead, the court must direct the jury to further consider its answers and verdict, or must order a new trial.

[Amended January 21, 1963, effective July 1, 1963; March 2, 1987, effective August 1, 1987; April 30, 2007, effective December 1, 2007, absent contrary Congressional action.]

## RULE 50. JUDGMENT AS A MATTER OF LAW IN A JURY TRIAL; RELATED MOTION FOR A NEW TRIAL; CONDITIONAL RULING

(a) **Judgment as a Matter of Law.**

(1) *In General.* If a party has been fully heard on an issue during a jury trial and the court finds that a reasonable jury would not have a legally sufficient evidentiary basis to find for the party on that issue, the court may:

(A) resolve the issue against the party; and

(B) grant a motion for judgment as a matter of law against the party on a claim or defense that, under the controlling law, can be maintained or defeated only with a favorable finding on that issue.

(2) *Motion.* A motion for judgment as a matter of law may be made at any time before the case is submitted to the jury. The motion must specify the

judgment sought and the law and facts that entitle the movant to the judgment.

**(b) Renewing the Motion After Trial; Alternative Motion for a New Trial.** If the court does not grant a motion for judgment as a matter of law made under Rule 50(a), the court is considered to have submitted the action to the jury subject to the court's later deciding the legal questions raised by the motion. No later than 10 days after the entry of judgment—or if the motion addresses a jury issue not decided by a verdict, no later than 10 days after the jury was discharged—the movant may file a renewed motion for judgment as a matter of law and may include an alternative or joint request for a new trial under Rule 59. In ruling on the renewed motion, the court may:

(1) allow judgment on the verdict, if the jury returned a verdict;

(2) order a new trial; or

(3) direct the entry of judgment as a matter of law.

**(c) Granting the Renewed Motion; Conditional Ruling on a Motion for a New Trial.**

(1) *In General.* If the court grants a renewed motion for judgment as a matter of law, it must also conditionally rule on any motion for a new trial by determining whether a new trial should be granted if the judgment is later vacated or reversed. The court must state the grounds for conditionally granting or denying the motion for a new trial.

(2) *Effect of a Conditional Ruling.* Conditionally granting the motion for a new trial does not affect the judgment's finality; if the judgment is reversed, the new trial must proceed unless the appellate court orders otherwise. If the motion for a new trial is conditionally denied, the appellee may assert error in that denial; if the judgment is reversed, the case must proceed as the appellate court orders.

**(d) Time for a Losing Party's New–Trial Motion.** Any motion for a new trial under Rule 59 by a party against whom judgment as a matter of law is rendered must be filed no later than 10 days after the entry of the judgment.

**(e) Denying the Motion for Judgment as a Matter of Law; Reversal on Appeal.** If the court denies the motion for judgment as a matter of law, the prevailing party may, as appellee, assert grounds entitling it to a new trial should the appellate court conclude that the trial court erred in denying the motion. If the appellate court reverses the judgment, it may order a new trial, direct the trial court to determine whether a new trial should be granted, or direct the entry of judgment.

[Amended January 21, 1963, effective July 1, 1963; March 2, 1987, effective August 1, 1987; April 30, 1991, effective December 1, 1991; April 22, 1993, effective December 1, 1993; April 27, 1995, effective December 1, 1995; April 12, 2006, effective December 1, 2006; April 30, 2007, effective December 1, 2007, absent contrary Congressional action.]

# RULE 51.  INSTRUCTIONS TO THE JURY; OBJECTIONS; PRESERVING A CLAIM OF ERROR

**(a) Requests.**

(1) *Before or at the Close of the Evidence.* At the close of the evidence or at any earlier reasonable time that the court orders, a party may file and furnish to every other party written requests for the jury instructions it wants the court to give.

(2) *After the Close of the Evidence.* After the close of the evidence, a party may:

(A) file requests for instructions on issues that could not reasonably have been anticipated by an earlier time that the court set for requests; and

(B) with the court's permission, file untimely requests for instructions on any issue.

**(b) Instructions.** The court:

(1) must inform the parties of its proposed instructions and proposed action on the requests before instructing the jury and before final jury arguments;

(2) must give the parties an opportunity to object on the record and out of the jury's hearing before the instructions and arguments are delivered; and

(3) may instruct the jury at any time before the jury is discharged.

**(c) Objections.**

(1) *How to Make.* A party who objects to an instruction or the failure to give an instruction must do so on the record, stating distinctly the matter objected to and the grounds for the objection.

(2) *When to Make.* An objection is timely if:

(A) a party objects at the opportunity provided under Rule 51(b)(2); or

(B) a party was not informed of an instruction or action on a request before that opportunity to object, and the party objects promptly after learning that the instruction or request will be, or has been, given or refused.

**(d) Assigning Error; Plain Error.**

(1) *Assigning Error.* A party may assign as error:

(A) an error in an instruction actually given, if that party properly objected; or

(B) a failure to give an instruction, if that party properly requested it and—unless the court rejected the request in a definitive ruling on the record—also properly objected.

(2) *Plain Error.* A court may consider a plain error in the instructions that has not been preserved as

required by Rule 51(d)(1) if the error affects substantial rights.

[Amended March 2, 1987, effective August 1, 1987; March 27, 2003, effective December 1, 2003; April 30, 2007, effective December 1, 2007, absent contrary Congressional action.]

# RULE 52. FINDINGS AND CONCLUSIONS BY THE COURT; JUDGMENT ON PARTIAL FINDINGS

## (a) Findings and Conclusions.

(1) *In General.* In an action tried on the facts without a jury or with an advisory jury, the court must find the facts specially and state its conclusions of law separately. The findings and conclusions may be stated on the record after the close of the evidence or may appear in an opinion or a memorandum of decision filed by the court. Judgment must be entered under Rule 58.

(2) *For an Interlocutory Injunction.* In granting or refusing an interlocutory injunction, the court must similarly state the findings and conclusions that support its action.

(3) *For a Motion.* The court is not required to state findings or conclusions when ruling on a motion under Rule 12 or 56 or, unless these rules provide otherwise, on any other motion.

(4) *Effect of a Master's Findings.* A master's findings, to the extent adopted by the court, must be considered the court's findings.

(5) *Questioning the Evidentiary Support.* A party may later question the sufficiency of the evidence supporting the findings, whether or not the party requested findings, objected to them, moved to amend them, or moved for partial findings.

(6) *Setting Aside the Findings.* Findings of fact, whether based on oral or other evidence, must not be set aside unless clearly erroneous, and the reviewing court must give due regard to the trial court's opportunity to judge the witnesses' credibility.

## (b) Amended or Additional Findings.
On a party's motion filed no later than 10 days after the entry of judgment, the court may amend its findings—or make additional findings—and may amend the judgment accordingly. The motion may accompany a motion for a new trial under Rule 59.

## (c) Judgment on Partial Findings.
If a party has been fully heard on an issue during a nonjury trial and the court finds against the party on that issue, the court may enter judgment against the party on a claim or defense that, under the controlling law, can be maintained or defeated only with a favorable finding on that issue. The court may, however, decline to render any judgment until the close of the evidence. A judgment on partial findings must be supported by

findings of fact and conclusions of law as required by Rule 52(a).

[Amended December 27, 1946, effective March 19, 1948; January 21, 1963, effective July 1, 1963; April 28, 1983, effective August 1, 1983; April 29, 1985, effective August 1, 1985; April 30, 1991, effective December 1, 1991; April 22, 1993, effective December 1, 1993; April 27, 1995, effective December 1, 1995; April 30, 2007, effective December 1, 2007, absent contrary Congressional action.]

# RULE 53. MASTERS

## (a) Appointment.

(1) *Scope.* Unless a statute provides otherwise, a court may appoint a master only to:

(A) perform duties consented to by the parties;

(B) hold trial proceedings and make or recommend findings of fact on issues to be decided without a jury if appointment is warranted by:

(i) some exceptional condition; or

(ii) the need to perform an accounting or resolve a difficult computation of damages; or

(C) address pretrial and posttrial matters that cannot be effectively and timely addressed by an available district judge or magistrate judge of the district.

(2) *Disqualification.* A master must not have a relationship to the parties, attorneys, action, or court that would require disqualification of a judge under 28 U.S.C. § 455, unless the parties, with the court's approval, consent to the appointment after the master discloses any potential grounds for disqualification.

(3) *Possible Expense or Delay.* In appointing a master, the court must consider the fairness of imposing the likely expenses on the parties and must protect against unreasonable expense or delay.

## (b) Order Appointing a Master.

(1) *Notice.* Before appointing a master, the court must give the parties notice and an opportunity to be heard. Any party may suggest candidates for appointment.

(2) *Contents.* The appointing order must direct the master to proceed with all reasonable diligence and must state:

(A) the master's duties, including any investigation or enforcement duties, and any limits on the master's authority under Rule 53(c);

(B) the circumstances, if any, in which the master may communicate ex parte with the court or a party;

(C) the nature of the materials to be preserved and filed as the record of the master's activities;

(D) the time limits, method of filing the record, other procedures, and standards for reviewing the

master's orders, findings, and recommendations; and

(E) the basis, terms, and procedure for fixing the master's compensation under Rule 53(g).

(3) *Issuing.* The court may issue the order only after:

(A) the master files an affidavit disclosing whether there is any ground for disqualification under 28 U.S.C. § 455; and

(B) if a ground is disclosed, the parties, with the court's approval, waive the disqualification.

(4) *Amending.* The order may be amended at any time after notice to the parties and an opportunity to be heard.

**(c) Master's Authority.**

(1) *In General.* Unless the appointing order directs otherwise, a master may:

(A) regulate all proceedings;

(B) take all appropriate measures to perform the assigned duties fairly and efficiently; and

(C) if conducting an evidentiary hearing, exercise the appointing court's power to compel, take, and record evidence.

(2) *Sanctions.* The master may by order impose on a party any noncontempt sanction provided by Rule 37 or 45, and may recommend a contempt sanction against a party and sanctions against a nonparty.

**(d) Master's Orders.** A master who issues an order must file it and promptly serve a copy on each party. The clerk must enter the order on the docket.

**(e) Master's Reports.** A master must report to the court as required by the appointing order. The master must file the report and promptly serve a copy on each party, unless the court orders otherwise.

**(f) Action on the Master's Order, Report, or Recommendations.**

(1) *Opportunity for a Hearing; Action in General.* In acting on a master's order, report, or recommendations, the court must give the parties notice and an opportunity to be heard; may receive evidence; and may adopt or affirm, modify, wholly or partly reject or reverse, or resubmit to the master with instructions.

(2) *Time to Object or Move to Adopt or Modify.* A party may file objections to—or a motion to adopt or modify—the master's order, report, or recommenda-

tions no later than 20 days after a copy is served, unless the court sets a different time.

(3) *Reviewing Factual Findings.* The court must decide de novo all objections to findings of fact made or recommended by a master, unless the parties, with the court's approval, stipulate that:

(A) the findings will be reviewed for clear error; or

(B) the findings of a master appointed under Rule 53(a)(1)(A) or (C) will be final.

(4) *Reviewing Legal Conclusions.* The court must decide de novo all objections to conclusions of law made or recommended by a master.

(5) *Reviewing Procedural Matters.* Unless the appointing order establishes a different standard of review, the court may set aside a master's ruling on a procedural matter only for an abuse of discretion.

**(g) Compensation.**

(1) *Fixing Compensation.* Before or after judgment, the court must fix the master's compensation on the basis and terms stated in the appointing order, but the court may set a new basis and terms after giving notice and an opportunity to be heard.

(2) *Payment.* The compensation must be paid either:

(A) by a party or parties; or

(B) from a fund or subject matter of the action within the court's control.

(3) *Allocating Payment.* The court must allocate payment among the parties after considering the nature and amount of the controversy, the parties' means, and the extent to which any party is more responsible than other parties for the reference to a master. An interim allocation may be amended to reflect a decision on the merits.

**(h) Appointing a Magistrate Judge.** A magistrate judge is subject to this rule only when the order referring a matter to the magistrate judge states that the reference is made under this rule.

[Amended February 28, 1966, effective July 1, 1966; April 28, 1983, effective August 1, 1983; March 2, 1987, effective August 1, 1987; April 30, 1991, effective December 1, 1991; April 22, 1993, effective December 1, 1993; March 27, 2003, effective December 1, 2003; April 30, 2007, effective December 1, 2007, absent contrary Congressional action.]

# TITLE VII.   JUDGMENT

## RULE 54.   JUDGMENT; COSTS

**(a) Definition; Form.** "Judgment" as used in these rules includes a decree and any order from which an appeal lies. A judgment should not include recitals of

pleadings, a master's report, or a record of prior proceedings.

**(b) Judgment on Multiple Claims or Involving Multiple Parties.** When an action presents more than

one claim for relief—whether as a claim, counterclaim, crossclaim, or third-party claim—or when multiple parties are involved, the court may direct entry of a final judgment as to one or more, but fewer than all, claims or parties only if the court expressly determines that there is no just reason for delay. Otherwise, any order or other decision, however designated, that adjudicates fewer than all the claims or the rights and liabilities of fewer than all the parties does not end the action as to any of the claims or parties and may be revised at any time before the entry of a judgment adjudicating all the claims and all the parties' rights and liabilities.

**(c) Demand for Judgment; Relief to Be Granted.** A default judgment must not differ in kind from, or exceed in amount, what is demanded in the pleadings. Every other final judgment should grant the relief to which each party is entitled, even if the party has not demanded that relief in its pleadings.

**(d) Costs; Attorney's Fees.**

(1) *Costs Other Than Attorney's Fees.* Unless a federal statute, these rules, or a court order provides otherwise, costs—other than attorney's fees—should be allowed to the prevailing party. But costs against the United States, its officers, and its agencies may be imposed only to the extent allowed by law. The clerk may tax costs on 1 day's notice. On motion served within the next 5 days, the court may review the clerk's action.

(2) *Attorney's Fees.*

(A) Claim to Be by Motion. A claim for attorney's fees and related nontaxable expenses must be made by motion unless the substantive law requires those fees to be proved at trial as an element of damages.

(B) Timing and Contents of the Motion. Unless a statute or a court order provides otherwise, the motion must:

(i) be filed no later than 14 days after the entry of judgment;

(ii) specify the judgment and the statute, rule, or other grounds entitling the movant to the award;

(iii) state the amount sought or provide a fair estimate of it; and

(iv) disclose, if the court so orders, the terms of any agreement about fees for the services for which the claim is made.

(C) Proceedings. Subject to Rule 23(h), the court must, on a party's request, give an opportunity for adversary submissions on the motion in accordance with Rule 43(c) or 78. The court may decide issues of liability for fees before receiving submissions on the value of services. The court must find the facts and state its conclusions of law as provided in Rule 52(a).

(D) Special Procedures by Local Rule; Reference to a Master or a Magistrate Judge. By local rule, the court may establish special procedures to resolve fee-related issues without extensive evidentiary hearings. Also, the court may refer issues concerning the value of services to a special master under Rule 53 without regard to the limitations of Rule 53(a)(1), and may refer a motion for attorney's fees to a magistrate judge under Rule 72(b) as if it were a dispositive pretrial matter.

(E) Exceptions. Subparagraphs (A)-(D) do not apply to claims for fees and expenses as sanctions for violating these rules or as sanctions under 28 U.S.C. § 1927.

[Amended December 27, 1946, effective March 19, 1948; April 17, 1961, effective July 19, 1961; March 2, 1987, effective August 1, 1987; April 22, 1993, effective December 1, 1993; April 29, 2002, effective December 1, 2002; March 27, 2003, effective December 1, 2003; April 30, 2007, effective December 1, 2007, absent contrary Congressional action.]

## RULE 55.  DEFAULT; DEFAULT JUDGMENT

**(a) Entering a Default.** When a party against whom a judgment for affirmative relief is sought has failed to plead or otherwise defend, and that failure is shown by affidavit or otherwise, the clerk must enter the party's default.

**(b) Entering a Default Judgment.**

(1) *By the Clerk.* If the plaintiff's claim is for a sum certain or a sum that can be made certain by computation, the clerk—on the plaintiff's request, with an affidavit showing the amount due—must enter judgment for that amount and costs against a defendant who has been defaulted for not appearing and who is neither a minor nor an incompetent person.

(2) *By the Court.* In all other cases, the party must apply to the court for a default judgment. A default judgment may be entered against a minor or incompetent person only if represented by a general guardian, conservator, or other like fiduciary who has appeared. If the party against whom a default judgment is sought has appeared personally or by a representative, that party or its representative must be served with written notice of the application at least 3 days before the hearing. The court may conduct hearings or make referrals—preserving any federal statutory right to a jury trial—when, to enter or effectuate judgment, it needs to:

(A) conduct an accounting;

(B) determine the amount of damages;

(C) establish the truth of any allegation by evidence; or

(D) investigate any other matter.

**(c) Setting Aside a Default or a Default Judgment.** The court may set aside an entry of default for good cause, and it may set aside a default judgment under Rule 60(b).

**(d) Judgment Against the United States.** A default judgment may be entered against the United States, its officers, or its agencies only if the claimant establishes a claim or right to relief by evidence that satisfies the court.

[Amended March 2, 1987, effective August 1, 1987; April 30, 2007, effective December 1, 2007, absent contrary Congressional action.]

## RULE 56. SUMMARY JUDGMENT

**(a) By a Claiming Party.** A party claiming relief may move, with or without supporting affidavits, for summary judgment on all or part of the claim. The motion may be filed at any time after:

(1) 20 days have passed from commencement of the action; or

(2) the opposing party serves a motion for summary judgment.

**(b) By a Defending Party.** A party against whom relief is sought may move at any time, with or without supporting affidavits, for summary judgment on all or part of the claim.

**(c) Serving the Motion; Proceedings.** The motion must be served at least 10 days before the day set for the hearing. An opposing party may serve opposing affidavits before the hearing day. The judgment sought should be rendered if the pleadings, the discovery and disclosure materials on file, and any affidavits show that there is no genuine issue as to any material fact and that the movant is entitled to judgment as a matter of law.

**(d) Case Not Fully Adjudicated on the Motion.**

(1) *Establishing Facts.* If summary judgment is not rendered on the whole action, the court should, to the extent practicable, determine what material facts are not genuinely at issue. The court should so determine by examining the pleadings and evidence before it and by interrogating the attorneys. It should then issue an order specifying what facts—including items of damages or other relief—are not genuinely at issue. The facts so specified must be treated as established in the action.

(2) *Establishing Liability.* An interlocutory summary judgment may be rendered on liability alone, even if there is a genuine issue on the amount of damages.

**(e) Affidavits; Further Testimony.**

(1) *In General.* A supporting or opposing affidavit must be made on personal knowledge, set out facts that would be admissible in evidence, and show that the affiant is competent to testify on the matters stated. If a paper or part of a paper is referred to in an affidavit, a sworn or certified copy must be attached to or served with the affidavit. The court may permit an affidavit to be supplemented or opposed by depositions, answers to interrogatories, or additional affidavits.

(2) *Opposing Party's Obligation to Respond.* When a motion for summary judgment is properly made and supported, an opposing party may not rely merely on allegations or denials in its own pleading; rather, its response must—by affidavits or as otherwise provided in this rule—set out specific facts showing a genuine issue for trial. If the opposing party does not so respond, summary judgment should, if appropriate, be entered against that party.

**(f) When Affidavits Are Unavailable.** If a party opposing the motion shows by affidavit that, for specified reasons, it cannot present facts essential to justify its opposition, the court may:

(1) deny the motion;

(2) order a continuance to enable affidavits to be obtained, depositions to be taken, or other discovery to be undertaken; or

(3) issue any other just order.

**(g) Affidavit Submitted in Bad Faith.** If satisfied that an affidavit under this rule is submitted in bad faith or solely for delay, the court must order the submitting party to pay the other party the reasonable expenses, including attorney's fees, it incurred as a result. An offending party or attorney may also be held in contempt.

[Amended December 27, 1946, effective March 19, 1948; January 21, 1963, effective July 1, 1963; March 2, 1987, effective August 1, 1987; April 30, 2007, effective December 1, 2007, absent contrary Congressional action.]

## RULE 57. DECLARATORY JUDGMENT

These rules govern the procedure for obtaining a declaratory judgment under 28 U.S.C. § 2201. Rules 38 and 39 govern a demand for a jury trial. The existence of another adequate remedy does not preclude a declaratory judgment that is otherwise appropriate. The court may order a speedy hearing of a declaratory-judgment action.

[Amended December 29, 1948, effective October 20, 1949; April 30, 2007, effective December 1, 2007, absent contrary Congressional action.]

## RULE 58. ENTERING JUDGMENT

**(a) Separate Document.** Every judgment and amended judgment must be set out in a separate document, but a separate document is not required for an order disposing of a motion:

(1) for judgment under Rule 50(b);

(2) to amend or make additional findings under Rule 52(b);

(3) for attorney's fees under Rule 54;

(4) for a new trial, or to alter or amend the judgment, under Rule 59; or

(5) for relief under Rule 60.

**(b) Entering Judgment.**

(1) *Without the Court's Direction.* Subject to Rule 54(b) and unless the court orders otherwise, the clerk must, without awaiting the court's direction, promptly prepare, sign, and enter the judgment when:

(A) the jury returns a general verdict;

(B) the court awards only costs or a sum certain; or

(C) the court denies all relief.

(2) *Court's Approval Required.* Subject to Rule 54(b), the court must promptly approve the form of the judgment, which the clerk must promptly enter, when:

(A) the jury returns a special verdict or a general verdict with answers to written questions; or

(B) the court grants other relief not described in this subdivision (b).

**(c) Time of Entry.** For purposes of these rules, judgment is entered at the following times:

(1) if a separate document is not required, when the judgment is entered in the civil docket under Rule 79(a); or

(2) if a separate document is required, when the judgment is entered in the civil docket under Rule 79(a) and the earlier of these events occurs:

(A) it is set out in a separate document; or

(B) 150 days have run from the entry in the civil docket.

**(d) Request for Entry.** A party may request that judgment be set out in a separate document as required by Rule 58(a).

**(e) Cost or Fee Awards.** Ordinarily, the entry of judgment may not be delayed, nor the time for appeal extended, in order to tax costs or award fees. But if a timely motion for attorney's fees is made under Rule 54(d)(2), the court may act before a notice of appeal has been filed and become effective to order that the motion have the same effect under Federal Rule of Appellate Procedure 4(a)(4) as a timely motion under Rule 59.

[Amended December 27, 1946, effective March 19, 1948; January 21, 1963, effective July 1, 1963; April 22, 1993, effective December 1, 1993; April 29, 2002, effective December 1, 2002; April 30, 2007, effective December 1, 2007, absent contrary Congressional action.]

## RULE 59.  NEW TRIAL; ALTERING OR AMENDING A JUDGMENT

**(a) In General.**

(1) *Grounds for New Trial.* The court may, on motion, grant a new trial on all or some of the issues—and to any party—as follows:

(A) after a jury trial, for any reason for which a new trial has heretofore been granted in an action at law in federal court; or

(B) after a nonjury trial, for any reason for which a rehearing has heretofore been granted in a suit in equity in federal court.

(2) *Further Action After a Nonjury Trial.* After a nonjury trial, the court may, on motion for a new trial, open the judgment if one has been entered, take additional testimony, amend findings of fact and conclusions of law or make new ones, and direct the entry of a new judgment.

**(b) Time to File a Motion for a New Trial.** A motion for a new trial must be filed no later than 10 days after the entry of judgment.

**(c) Time to Serve Affidavits.** When a motion for a new trial is based on affidavits, they must be filed with the motion. The opposing party has 10 days after being served to file opposing affidavits; but that period may be extended for up to 20 days, either by the court for good cause or by the parties' stipulation. The court may permit reply affidavits.

**(d) New Trial on the Court's Initiative or for Reasons Not in the Motion.** No later than 10 days after the entry of judgment, the court, on its own, may order a new trial for any reason that would justify granting one on a party's motion. After giving the parties notice and an opportunity to be heard, the court may grant a timely motion for a new trial for a reason not stated in the motion. In either event, the court must specify the reasons in its order.

**(e) Motion to Alter or Amend a Judgment.** A motion to alter or amend a judgment must be filed no later than 10 days after the entry of the judgment.

[Amended December 27, 1946, effective March 19, 1948; February 28, 1966, effective July 1, 1966; April 27, 1995, effective December 1, 1995; April 30, 2007, effective December 1, 2007, absent contrary Congressional action.]

## RULE 60.  RELIEF FROM A JUDGMENT OR ORDER

**(a) Corrections Based on Clerical Mistakes; Oversights and Omissions.** The court may correct a clerical mistake or a mistake arising from oversight or omission whenever one is found in a judgment, order, or other part of the record. The court may do so on motion or on its own, with or without notice. But after an appeal has been docketed in the appellate court

and while it is pending, such a mistake may be corrected only with the appellate court's leave.

**(b) Grounds for Relief from a Final Judgment, Order, or Proceeding.** On motion and just terms, the court may relieve a party or its legal representative from a final judgment, order, or proceeding for the following reasons:

(1) mistake, inadvertence, surprise, or excusable neglect;

(2) newly discovered evidence that, with reasonable diligence, could not have been discovered in time to move for a new trial under Rule 59(b);

(3) fraud (whether previously called intrinsic or extrinsic), misrepresentation, or misconduct by an opposing party;

(4) the judgment is void;

(5) the judgment has been satisfied, released or discharged; it is based on an earlier judgment that has been reversed or vacated; or applying it prospectively is no longer equitable; or

(6) any other reason that justifies relief.

**(c) Timing and Effect of the Motion.**

(1) *Timing.* A motion under Rule 60(b) must be made within a reasonable time—and for reasons (1), (2), and (3) no more than a year after the entry of the judgment or order or the date of the proceeding.

(2) *Effect on Finality.* The motion does not affect the judgment's finality or suspend its operation.

**(d) Other Powers to Grant Relief.** This rule does not limit a court's power to:

(1) entertain an independent action to relieve a party from a judgment, order, or proceeding;

(2) grant relief under 28 U.S.C. § 1655 to a defendant who was not personally notified of the action; or

(3) set aside a judgment for fraud on the court.

**(e) Bills and Writs Abolished.** The following are abolished: bills of review, bills in the nature of bills of review, and writs of coram nobis, coram vobis, and audita querela.

[Amended December 27, 1946, effective March 19, 1948; December 29, 1948, effective October 20, 1949; March 2, 1987, effective August 1, 1987; April 30, 2007, effective December 1, 2007, absent contrary Congressional action.]

# RULE 61.  HARMLESS ERROR

Unless justice requires otherwise, no error in admitting or excluding evidence—or any other error by the court or a party—is ground for granting a new trial, for setting aside a verdict, or for vacating, modifying, or otherwise disturbing a judgment or order. At every stage of the proceeding, the court must disregard all errors and defects that do not affect any party's substantial rights.

[Amended April 30, 2007, effective December 1, 2007, absent contrary Congressional action.]

# RULE 62.  STAY OF PROCEEDINGS TO ENFORCE A JUDGMENT

**(a) Automatic Stay; Exceptions for Injunctions, Receiverships, and Patent Accountings.** Except as stated in this rule, no execution may issue on a judgment, nor may proceedings be taken to enforce it, until 10 days have passed after its entry. But unless the court orders otherwise, the following are not stayed after being entered, even if an appeal is taken:

(1) an interlocutory or final judgment in an action for an injunction or a receivership; or

(2) a judgment or order that directs an accounting in an action for patent infringement.

**(b) Stay Pending the Disposition of a Motion.** On appropriate terms for the opposing party's security, the court may stay the execution of a judgment—or any proceedings to enforce it—pending disposition of any of the following motions:

(1) under Rule 50, for judgment as a matter of law;

(2) under Rule 52(b), to amend the findings or for additional findings;

(3) under Rule 59, for a new trial or to alter or amend a judgment; or

(4) under Rule 60, for relief from a judgment or order.

**(c) Injunction Pending an Appeal.** While an appeal is pending from an interlocutory order or final judgment that grants, dissolves, or denies an injunction, the court may suspend, modify, restore, or grant an injunction on terms for bond or other terms that secure the opposing party's rights. If the judgment appealed from is rendered by a statutory three-judge district court, the order must be made either:

(1) by that court sitting in open session; or

(2) by the assent of all its judges, as evidenced by their signatures.

**(d) Stay with Bond on Appeal.** If an appeal is taken, the appellant may obtain a stay by supersedeas bond, except in an action described in Rule 62(a)(1) or (2). The bond may be given upon or after filing the notice of appeal or after obtaining the order allowing the appeal. The stay takes effect when the court approves the bond.

**(e) Stay Without Bond on an Appeal by the United States, Its Officers, or Its Agencies.** The court must not require a bond, obligation, or other security from the appellant when granting a stay on an appeal by the United States, its officers, or its

agencies or on an appeal directed by a department of the federal government.

**(f) Stay in Favor of a Judgment Debtor Under State Law.** If a judgment is a lien on the judgment debtor's property under the law of the state where the court is located, the judgment debtor is entitled to the same stay of execution the state court would give.

**(g) Appellate Court's Power Not Limited.** This rule does not limit the power of the appellate court or one of its judges or justices:

(1) to stay proceedings—or suspend, modify, restore, or grant an injunction—while an appeal is pending; or

(2) to issue an order to preserve the status quo or the effectiveness of the judgment to be entered.

**(h) Stay with Multiple Claims or Parties.** A court may stay the enforcement of a final judgment entered under Rule 54(b) until it enters a later judgment or judgments, and may prescribe terms necessary to

secure the benefit of the stayed judgment for the party in whose favor it was entered.

[Amended December 27, 1946, effective March 19, 1948; December 29, 1948, effective October 20, 1949; April 17, 1961, effective July 19, 1961; March 2, 1987, effective August 1, 1987; April 30, 2007, effective December 1, 2007, absent contrary Congressional action.]

## RULE 63.   JUDGE'S INABILITY TO PROCEED

If a judge conducting a hearing or trial is unable to proceed, any other judge may proceed upon certifying familiarity with the record and determining that the case may be completed without prejudice to the parties. In a hearing or a nonjury trial, the successor judge must, at a party's request, recall any witness whose testimony is material and disputed and who is available to testify again without undue burden. The successor judge may also recall any other witness.

[Amended March 2, 1987, effective August 1, 1987; April 30, 1991, effective December 1, 1991; April 30, 2007, effective December 1, 2007, absent contrary Congressional action.]

# TITLE VIII.   PROVISIONAL AND FINAL REMEDIES

## RULE 64.   SEIZING A PERSON OR PROPERTY

**(a) Remedies Under State Law—In General.** At the commencement of and throughout an action, every remedy is available that, under the law of the state where the court is located, provides for seizing a person or property to secure satisfaction of the potential judgment. But a federal statute governs to the extent it applies.

**(b) Specific Kinds of Remedies.** The remedies available under this rule include the following—however designated and regardless of whether state procedure requires an independent action:

- arrest;
- attachment;
- garnishment;
- replevin;
- sequestration; and
- other corresponding or equivalent remedies.

[Amended April 30, 2007, effective December 1, 2007, absent contrary Congressional action.]

## RULE 65.   INJUNCTIONS AND RESTRAINING ORDERS

**(a) Preliminary Injunction.**

(1) *Notice.* The court may issue a preliminary injunction only on notice to the adverse party.

(2) *Consolidating the Hearing with the Trial on the Merits.* Before or after beginning the hearing on a motion for a preliminary injunction, the court may advance the trial on the merits and consolidate it with the hearing. Even when consolidation is not ordered, evidence that is received on the motion and that would be admissible at trial becomes part of the trial record and need not be repeated at trial. But the court must preserve any party's right to a jury trial.

**(b) Temporary Restraining Order.**

(1) *Issuing Without Notice.* The court may issue a temporary restraining order without written or oral notice to the adverse party or its attorney only if:

(A) specific facts in an affidavit or a verified complaint clearly show that immediate and irreparable injury, loss, or damage will result to the movant before the adverse party can be heard in opposition; and

(B) the movant's attorney certifies in writing any efforts made to give notice and the reasons why it should not be required.

(2) *Contents; Expiration.* Every temporary restraining order issued without notice must state the date and hour it was issued; describe the injury and state why it is irreparable; state why the order was issued without notice; and be promptly filed in the clerk's office and entered in the record. The order expires at the time after entry—not to exceed 10 days—that the court sets, unless before that time the court, for good cause, extends it for a like period or the adverse party consents to a longer extension. The

reasons for an extension must be entered in the record.

(3) *Expediting the Preliminary–Injunction Hearing.* If the order is issued without notice, the motion for a preliminary injunction must be set for hearing at the earliest possible time, taking precedence over all other matters except hearings on older matters of the same character. At the hearing, the party who obtained the order must proceed with the motion; if the party does not, the court must dissolve the order.

(4) *Motion to Dissolve.* On 2 days' notice to the party who obtained the order without notice—or on shorter notice set by the court—the adverse party may appear and move to dissolve or modify the order. The court must then hear and decide the motion as promptly as justice requires.

**(c) Security.** The court may issue a preliminary injunction or a temporary restraining order only if the movant gives security in an amount that the court considers proper to pay the costs and damages sustained by any party found to have been wrongfully enjoined or restrained. The United States, its officers, and its agencies are not required to give security.

**(d) Contents and Scope of Every Injunction and Restraining Order.**

(1) *Contents.* Every order granting an injunction and every restraining order must:

(A) state the reasons why it issued;

(B) state its terms specifically; and

(C) describe in reasonable detail—and not by referring to the complaint or other document—the act or acts restrained or required.

(2) *Persons Bound.* The order binds only the following who receive actual notice of it by personal service or otherwise:

(A) the parties;

(B) the parties' officers, agents, servants, employees, and attorneys; and

(C) other persons who are in active concert or participation with anyone described in Rule 65(d)(2)(A) or (B).

**(e) Other Laws Not Modified.** These rules do not modify the following:

(1) any federal statute relating to temporary restraining orders or preliminary injunctions in actions affecting employer and employee;

(2) 28 U.S.C. § 2361, which relates to preliminary injunctions in actions of interpleader or in the nature of interpleader; or

(3) 28 U.S.C. § 2284, which relates to actions that must be heard and decided by a three-judge district court.

**(f) Copyright Impoundment.** This rule applies to copyright-impoundment proceedings.

[Amended December 27, 1946, effective March 19, 1948; December 29, 1948, effective October 20, 1949; February 28, 1966, effective July 1, 1966; March 2, 1987, effective August 1, 1987; April 23, 2001, effective December 1, 2001; April 30, 2007, effective December 1, 2007, absent contrary Congressional action.]

# RULE 65.1 PROCEEDINGS AGAINST A SURETY

Whenever these rules (including the Supplemental Rules for Admiralty or Maritime Claims and Asset Forfeiture Actions) require or allow a party to give security, and security is given through a bond or other undertaking with one or more sureties, each surety submits to the court's jurisdiction and irrevocably appoints the court clerk as its agent for receiving service of any papers that affect its liability on the bond or undertaking. The surety's liability may be enforced on motion without an independent action. The motion and any notice that the court orders may be served on the court clerk, who must promptly mail a copy of each to every surety whose address is known.

[Adopted February 28, 1966, effective July 1, 1966; amended March 2, 1987, effective August 1, 1987; April 12, 2006, effective December 1, 2006; April 30, 2007, effective December 1, 2007, absent contrary Congressional action.]

# RULE 66. RECEIVERS

These rules govern an action in which the appointment of a receiver is sought or a receiver sues or is sued. But the practice in administering an estate by a receiver or a similar court-appointed officer must accord with the historical practice in federal courts or with a local rule. An action in which a receiver has been appointed may be dismissed only by court order.

[Amended December 27, 1946, effective March 19, 1948; December 29, 1948, effective October 20, 1949; April 30, 2007, effective December 1, 2007, absent contrary Congressional action.]

# RULE 67. DEPOSIT INTO COURT

**(a) Depositing Property.** If any part of the relief sought is a money judgment or the disposition of a sum of money or some other deliverable thing, a party—on notice to every other party and by leave of court—may deposit with the court all or part of the money or thing, whether or not that party claims any of it. The depositing party must deliver to the clerk a copy of the order permitting deposit.

**(b) Investing and Withdrawing Funds.** Money paid into court under this rule must be deposited and withdrawn in accordance with 28 U.S.C. §§ 2041 and 2042 and any like statute. The money must be deposit-

ed in an interest-bearing account or invested in a court-approved, interest-bearing instrument.

[Amended December 29, 1948, effective October 20, 1949; April 28, 1983, effective August 1, 1983; April 30, 2007, effective December 1, 2007, absent contrary Congressional action.]

## RULE 68. OFFER OF JUDGMENT

**(a) Making an Offer; Judgment on an Accepted Offer.** More than 10 days before the trial begins, a party defending against a claim may serve on an opposing party an offer to allow judgment on specified terms, with the costs then accrued. If, within 10 days after being served, the opposing party serves written notice accepting the offer, either party may then file the offer and notice of acceptance, plus proof of service. The clerk must then enter judgment.

**(b) Unaccepted Offer.** An unaccepted offer is considered withdrawn, but it does not preclude a later offer. Evidence of an unaccepted offer is not admissible except in a proceeding to determine costs.

**(c) Offer After Liability Is Determined.** When one party's liability to another has been determined but the extent of liability remains to be determined by further proceedings, the party held liable may make an offer of judgment. It must be served within a reasonable time—but at least 10 days—before a hearing to determine the extent of liability.

**(d) Paying Costs After an Unaccepted Offer.** If the judgment that the offeree finally obtains is not more favorable than the unaccepted offer, the offeree must pay the costs incurred after the offer was made.

[Amended December 27, 1946, effective March 19, 1948; February 28, 1966, effective July 1, 1966; March 2, 1987, effective August 1, 1987; April 30, 2007, effective December 1, 2007, absent contrary Congressional action.]

## RULE 69. EXECUTION

**(a) In General.**

(1) *Money Judgment; Applicable Procedure.* A money judgment is enforced by a writ of execution, unless the court directs otherwise. The procedure on execution—and in proceedings supplementary to and in aid of judgment or execution—must accord with the procedure of the state where the court is located, but a federal statute governs to the extent it applies.

(2) *Obtaining Discovery.* In aid of the judgment or execution, the judgment creditor or a successor in interest whose interest appears of record may obtain discovery from any person—including the judgment

debtor—as provided in these rules or by the procedure of the state where the court is located.

**(b) Against Certain Public Officers.** When a judgment has been entered against a revenue officer in the circumstances stated in 28 U.S.C. § 2006, or against an officer of Congress in the circumstances stated in 2 U.S.C. § 118, the judgment must be satisfied as those statutes provide.

[Amended December 29, 1948, effective October 20, 1949; March 30, 1970, effective July 1, 1970; March 2, 1987 effective August 1, 1987; April 30, 2007, absent contrary Congressional action.]

## RULE 70. ENFORCING A JUDGMENT FOR A SPECIFIC ACT

**(a) Party's Failure to Act; Ordering Another to Act.** If a judgment requires a party to convey land, to deliver a deed or other document, or to perform any other specific act and the party fails to comply within the time specified, the court may order the act to be done—at the disobedient party's expense—by another person appointed by the court. When done, the act has the same effect as if done by the party.

**(b) Vesting Title.** If the real or personal property is within the district, the court—instead of ordering a conveyance—may enter a judgment divesting any party's title and vesting it in others. That judgment has the effect of a legally executed conveyance.

**(c) Obtaining a Writ of Attachment or Sequestration.** On application by a party entitled to performance of an act, the clerk must issue a writ of attachment or sequestration against the disobedient party's property to compel obedience.

**(d) Obtaining a Writ of Execution or Assistance.** On application by a party who obtains a judgment or order for possession, the clerk must issue a writ of execution or assistance.

**(e) Holding in Contempt.** The court may also hold the disobedient party in contempt.

[Amended April 30, 2007, effective December 1, 2007, absent contrary Congressional action.]

## RULE 71. ENFORCING RELIEF FOR OR AGAINST A NONPARTY

When an order grants relief for a nonparty or may be enforced against a nonparty, the procedure for enforcing the order is the same as for a party.

[Amended March 2, 1987, effective August 1, 1987; April 30, 2007, effective December 1, 2007, absent contrary Congressional action.]

# TITLE IX. SPECIAL PROCEEDINGS

## RULE 71.1 CONDEMNING REAL OR PERSONAL PROPERTY

**(a) Applicability of Other Rules.** These rules govern proceedings to condemn real and personal property by eminent domain, except as this rule provides otherwise.

**(b) Joinder of Properties.** The plaintiff may join separate pieces of property in a single action, no matter whether they are owned by the same persons or sought for the same use.

**(c) Complaint.**

(1) *Caption.* The complaint must contain a caption as provided in Rule 10(a). The plaintiff must, however, name as defendants both the property—designated generally by kind, quantity, and location—and at least one owner of some part of or interest in the property.

(2) *Contents.* The complaint must contain a short and plain statement of the following:

(A) the authority for the taking;

(B) the uses for which the property is to be taken;

(C) a description sufficient to identify the property;

(D) the interests to be acquired; and

(E) for each piece of property, a designation of each defendant who has been joined as an owner or owner of an interest in it.

(3) *Parties.* When the action commences, the plaintiff need join as defendants only those persons who have or claim an interest in the property and whose names are then known. But before any hearing on compensation, the plaintiff must add as defendants all those persons who have or claim an interest and whose names have become known or can be found by a reasonably diligent search of the records, considering both the property's character and value and the interests to be acquired. All others may be made defendants under the designation "Unknown Owners."

(4) *Procedure.* Notice must be served on all defendants as provided in Rule 71.1(d), whether they were named as defendants when the action commenced or were added later. A defendant may answer as provided in Rule 71.1(e). The court, meanwhile, may order any distribution of a deposit that the facts warrant.

(5) *Filing; Additional Copies.* In addition to filing the complaint, the plaintiff must give the clerk at least one copy for the defendants' use and additional copies at the request of the clerk or a defendant.

**(d) Process.**

(1) *Delivering Notice to the Clerk.* On filing a complaint, the plaintiff must promptly deliver to the clerk joint or several notices directed to the named defendants. When adding defendants, the plaintiff must deliver to the clerk additional notices directed to the new defendants.

(2) *Contents of the Notice.*

(A) Main Contents. Each notice must name the court, the title of the action, and the defendant to whom it is directed. It must describe the property sufficiently to identify it, but need not describe any property other than that to be taken from the named defendant. The notice must also state:

(i) that the action is to condemn property;

(ii) the interest to be taken;

(iii) the authority for the taking;

(iv) the uses for which the property is to be taken;

(v) that the defendant may serve an answer on the plaintiff's attorney within 20 days after being served with the notice;

(vi) that the failure to so serve an answer constitutes consent to the taking and to the court's authority to proceed with the action and fix the compensation; and

(vii) that a defendant who does not serve an answer may file a notice of appearance.

(B) Conclusion. The notice must conclude with the name, telephone number, and e-mail address of the plaintiff's attorney and an address within the district in which the action is brought where the attorney may be served.

(3) *Serving the Notice.*

(A) Personal Service. When a defendant whose address is known resides within the United States or a territory subject to the administrative or judicial jurisdiction of the United States, personal service of the notice (without a copy of the complaint) must be made in accordance with Rule 4.

(B) Service by Publication.

(i) A defendant may be served by publication only when the plaintiff's attorney files a certificate stating that the attorney believes the defendant cannot be personally served, because after diligent inquiry within the state where the complaint is filed, the defendant's place of residence is still unknown or, if known, that it is beyond the territorial limits of personal service. Service is then made by publishing the notice—once a week for at least three successive weeks—in a newspa-

per published in the county where the property is located or, if there is no such newspaper, in a newspaper with general circulation where the property is located. Before the last publication, a copy of the notice must also be mailed to every defendant who cannot be personally served but whose place of residence is then known. Unknown owners may be served by publication in the same manner by a notice addressed to "Unknown Owners."

(ii) Service by publication is complete on the date of the last publication. The plaintiff's attorney must prove publication and mailing by a certificate, attach a printed copy of the published notice, and mark on the copy the newspaper's name and the dates of publication.

(4) *Effect of Delivery and Service.* Delivering the notice to the clerk and serving it have the same effect as serving a summons under Rule 4.

(5) *Proof of Service; Amending the Proof or Notice.* Rule 4(*l*) governs proof of service. The court may permit the proof or the notice to be amended.

**(e) Appearance or Answer.**

(1) *Notice of Appearance.* A defendant that has no objection or defense to the taking of its property may serve a notice of appearance designating the property in which it claims an interest. The defendant must then be given notice of all later proceedings affecting the defendant.

(2) *Answer.* A defendant that has an objection or defense to the taking must serve an answer within 20 days after being served with the notice. The answer must:

(A) identify the property in which the defendant claims an interest;

(B) state the nature and extent of the interest; and

(C) state all the defendant's objections and defenses to the taking.

(3) *Waiver of Other Objections and Defenses; Evidence on Compensation.* A defendant waives all objections and defenses not stated in its answer. No other pleading or motion asserting an additional objection or defense is allowed. But at the trial on compensation, a defendant—whether or not it has previously appeared or answered—may present evidence on the amount of compensation to be paid and may share in the award.

**(f) Amending Pleadings.** Without leave of court, the plaintiff may—as often as it wants—amend the complaint at any time before the trial on compensation. But no amendment may be made if it would result in a dismissal inconsistent with Rule 71.1(i)(1) or (2). The plaintiff need not serve a copy of an amendment, but must serve notice of the filing, as provided in Rule 5(b), on every affected party who has appeared and, as provided in Rule 71.1(d), on every affected party who has not appeared. In addition, the plaintiff must give the clerk at least one copy of each amendment for the defendants' use, and additional copies at the request of the clerk or a defendant. A defendant may appear or answer in the time and manner and with the same effect as provided in Rule 71.1(e).

**(g) Substituting Parties.** If a defendant dies, becomes incompetent, or transfers an interest after being joined, the court may, on motion and notice of hearing, order that the proper party be substituted. Service of the motion and notice on a nonparty must be made as provided in Rule 71.1(d)(3).

**(h) Trial of the Issues.**

(1) *Issues Other Than Compensation; Compensation.* In an action involving eminent domain under federal law, the court tries all issues, including compensation, except when compensation must be determined:

(A) by any tribunal specially constituted by a federal statute to determine compensation; or

(B) if there is no such tribunal, by a jury when a party demands one within the time to answer or within any additional time the court sets, unless the court appoints a commission.

(2) *Appointing a Commission; Commission's Powers and Report.*

(A) Reasons for Appointing. If a party has demanded a jury, the court may instead appoint a three-person commission to determine compensation because of the character, location, or quantity of the property to be condemned or for other just reasons.

(B) Alternate Commissioners. The court may appoint up to two additional persons to serve as alternate commissioners to hear the case and replace commissioners who, before a decision is filed, the court finds unable or disqualified to perform their duties. Once the commission renders its final decision, the court must discharge any alternate who has not replaced a commissioner.

(C) Examining the Prospective Commissioners. Before making its appointments, the court must advise the parties of the identity and qualifications of each prospective commissioner and alternate, and may permit the parties to examine them. The parties may not suggest appointees, but for good cause may object to a prospective commissioner or alternate.

(D) Commission's Powers and Report. A commission has the powers of a master under Rule 53(c). Its action and report are determined by a majority. Rule 53(d), (e), and (f) apply to its action and report.

**(i) Dismissal of the Action or a Defendant.**

(1) *Dismissing the Action.*

(A) By the Plaintiff. If no compensation hearing on a piece of property has begun, and if the plaintiff has not acquired title or a lesser interest or taken possession, the plaintiff may, without a court order, dismiss the action as to that property by filing a notice of dismissal briefly describing the property.

(B) By Stipulation. Before a judgment is entered vesting the plaintiff with title or a lesser interest in or possession of property, the plaintiff and affected defendants may, without a court order, dismiss the action in whole or in part by filing a stipulation of dismissal. And if the parties so stipulate, the court may vacate a judgment already entered.

(C) By Court Order. At any time before compensation has been determined and paid, the court may, after a motion and hearing, dismiss the action as to a piece of property. But if the plaintiff has already taken title, a lesser interest, or possession as to any part of it, the court must award compensation for the title, lesser interest, or possession taken.

(2) *Dismissing a Defendant.* The court may at any time dismiss a defendant who was unnecessarily or improperly joined.

(3) *Effect.* A dismissal is without prejudice unless otherwise stated in the notice, stipulation, or court order.

**(j) Deposit and Its Distribution.**

(1) *Deposit.* The plaintiff must deposit with the court any money required by law as a condition to the exercise of eminent domain and may make a deposit when allowed by statute.

(2) *Distribution; Adjusting Distribution.* After a deposit, the court and attorneys must expedite the proceedings so as to distribute the deposit and to determine and pay compensation. If the compensation finally awarded to a defendant exceeds the amount distributed to that defendant, the court must enter judgment against the plaintiff for the deficiency. If the compensation awarded to a defendant is less than the amount distributed to that defendant, the court must enter judgment against that defendant for the overpayment.

**(k) Condemnation Under a State's Power of Eminent Domain.** This rule governs an action involving eminent domain under state law. But if state law provides for trying an issue by jury—or for trying the issue of compensation by jury or commission or both—that law governs.

**(*l*) Costs.** Costs are not subject to Rule 54(d).

[Adopted April 30, 1951, effective August 1, 1951; amended January 21, 1963, effective July 1, 1963; April 29, 1985, effective August 1, 1985; March 2, 1987, effective August 1,

1987; April 25, 1988, effective August 1, 1988; amended by Pub.L. 100–690, Title VII, § 7050, November 18, 1988, 102 Stat. 4401 (although amendment by Pub.L. 100–690 could not be executed due to prior amendment by Court order which made the same change effective August 1, 1988); amended April 22, 1993, effective December 1, 1993; March 27, 2003, effective December 1, 2003; April 30, 2007, effective December 1, 2007, absent contrary Congressional action.]

# RULE 72. MAGISTRATE JUDGES: PRETRIAL ORDER

**(a) Nondispositive Matters.** When a pretrial matter not dispositive of a party's claim or defense is referred to a magistrate judge to hear and decide, the magistrate judge must promptly conduct the required proceedings and, when appropriate, issue a written order stating the decision. A party may serve and file objections to the order within 10 days after being served with a copy. A party may not assign as error a defect in the order not timely objected to. The district judge in the case must consider timely objections and modify or set aside any part of the order that is clearly erroneous or is contrary to law.

**(b) Dispositive Motions and Prisoner Petitions.**

(1) *Findings and Recommendations.* A magistrate judge must promptly conduct the required proceedings when assigned, without the parties' consent, to hear a pretrial matter dispositive of a claim or defense or a prisoner petition challenging the conditions of confinement. A record must be made of all evidentiary proceedings and may, at the magistrate judge's discretion, be made of any other proceedings. The magistrate judge must enter a recommended disposition, including, if appropriate, proposed findings of fact. The clerk must promptly mail a copy to each party.

(2) *Objections.* Within 10 days after being served with a copy of the recommended disposition, a party may serve and file specific written objections to the proposed findings and recommendations. A party may respond to another party's objections within 10 days after being served with a copy. Unless the district judge orders otherwise, the objecting party must promptly arrange for transcribing the record, or whatever portions of it the parties agree to or the magistrate judge considers sufficient.

(3) *Resolving Objections.* The district judge must determine de novo any part of the magistrate judge's disposition that has been properly objected to. The district judge may accept, reject, or modify the recommended disposition; receive further evidence; or return the matter to the magistrate judge with instructions.

[Former Rule 72 abrogated December 4, 1967, effective July 1, 1968; new Rule 72 adopted April 28, 1983, effective August 1, 1983; amended April 30, 1991, effective December 1, 1991; April 22, 1993, effective December 1, 1993; April 30, 2007,

effective December 1, 2007, absent contrary Congressional action.]

# RULE 73. MAGISTRATE JUDGES: TRIAL BY CONSENT; APPEAL

**(a) Trial by Consent.** When authorized under 28 U.S.C. § 636(c), a magistrate judge may, if all parties consent, conduct a civil action or proceeding, including a jury or nonjury trial. A record must be made in accordance with 28 U.S.C. § 636(c)(5).

**(b) Consent Procedure.**

(1) *In General.* When a magistrate judge has been designated to conduct civil actions or proceedings, the clerk must give the parties written notice of their opportunity to consent under 28 U.S.C. § 636(c). To signify their consent, the parties must jointly or separately file a statement consenting to the referral. A district judge or magistrate judge may be informed of a party's response to the clerk's notice only if all parties have consented to the referral.

(2) *Reminding the Parties About Consenting.* A district judge, magistrate judge, or other court official may remind the parties of the magistrate judge's availability, but must also advise them that they are free to withhold consent without adverse substantive consequences.

(3) *Vacating a Referral.* On its own for good cause—or when a party shows extraordinary circumstances—the district judge may vacate a referral to a magistrate judge under this rule.

**(c) Appealing a Judgment.** In accordance with 28 U.S.C. § 636(c)(3), an appeal from a judgment entered at a magistrate judge's direction may be taken to the court of appeals as would any other appeal from a district-court judgment.

[Former Rule 73 abrogated December 4, 1967, effective July 1, 1968; new Rule 73 adopted April 28, 1983, effective August 1, 1983; amended March 2, 1987, effective August 1, 1987;

April 22, 1993, effective December 1, 1993; April 11, 1997, effective December 1, 1997; April 30, 2007, effective December 1, 2007, absent contrary Congressional action.]

# RULE 74. METHOD OF APPEAL FROM MAGISTRATE JUDGE TO DISTRICT JUDGE UNDER TITLE 28, U.S.C. § 636(c)(4) AND RULE 73(d) [ABROGATED]

[Former Rule 74 abrogated December 4, 1967, effective July 1, 1968; new Rule 74 adopted April 28, 1983, effective August 1, 1983; amended April 22, 1993, effective December 1, 1993; abrogated April 11, 1997, effective December 1, 1997; April 30, 2007, effective December 1, 2007, absent contrary Congressional action.]

# RULE 75. PROCEEDINGS ON APPEAL FROM MAGISTRATE JUDGE TO DISTRICT JUDGE UNDER RULE 73(d) [ABROGATED]

[Former Rule 75 abrogated December 4, 1967, effective July 1, 1968; new Rule 75 adopted April 28, 1983, effective August 1, 1983; amended March 2, 1987, effective August 1, 1987; April 22, 1993, effective December 1, 1993; abrogated April 11, 1997, effective December 1, 1997; April 30, 2007, effective December 1, 2007, absent contrary Congressional action.]

# RULE 76. JUDGMENT OF THE DISTRICT JUDGE ON THE APPEAL UNDER RULE 73(d) AND COSTS [ABROGATED]

[Former Rule 76 abrogated December 4, 1967, effective July 1, 1968; new Rule 76 adopted April 28, 1983, effective August 1, 1983; amended April 22, 1993, effective December 1, 1993; abrogated April 11, 1997, effective December 1, 1997; April 30, 2007, effective December 1, 2007, absent contrary Congressional action.]

# TITLE X. DISTRICT COURTS AND CLERKS: CONDUCTING BUSINESS; ISSUING ORDERS

# RULE 77. CONDUCTING BUSINESS; CLERK'S AUTHORITY; NOTICE OF AN ORDER OR JUDGMENT

**(a) When Court Is Open.** Every district court is considered always open for filing any paper, issuing and returning process, making a motion, or entering an order.

**(b) Place for Trial and Other Proceedings.** Every trial on the merits must be conducted in open court and, so far as convenient, in a regular courtroom. Any

other act or proceeding may be done or conducted by a judge in chambers, without the attendance of the clerk or other court official, and anywhere inside or outside the district. But no hearing—other than one ex parte—may be conducted outside the district unless all the affected parties consent.

**(c) Clerk's Office Hours; Clerk's Orders.**

(1) *Hours.* The clerk's office—with a clerk or deputy on duty—must be open during business hours every day except Saturdays, Sundays, and legal holidays. But a court may, by local rule or order, require

that the office be open for specified hours on Saturday or a particular legal holiday other than one listed in Rule 6(a)(4)(A).

(2) *Orders.* Subject to the court's power to suspend, alter, or rescind the clerk's action for good cause, the clerk may:

(A) issue process;

(B) enter a default;

(C) enter a default judgment under Rule 55(b)(1); and

(D) act on any other matter that does not require the court's action.

**(d) Serving Notice of an Order or Judgment.**

(1) *Service.* Immediately after entering an order or judgment, the clerk must serve notice of the entry, as provided in Rule 5(b), on each party who is not in default for failing to appear. The clerk must record the service on the docket. A party also may serve notice of the entry as provided in Rule 5(b).

(2) *Time to Appeal Not Affected by Lack of Notice.* Lack of notice of the entry does not affect the time for appeal or relieve—or authorize the court to relieve—a party for failing to appeal within the time allowed, except as allowed by Federal Rule of Appellate Procedure (4)(a).

[Amended December 27, 1946, effective March 19, 1948; January 21, 1963, effective July 1, 1963; December 4, 1967, effective July 1, 1968; March 1, 1971, effective July 1, 1971; March 2, 1987, effective August 1, 1987; April 30, 1991, effective December 1, 1991; April 23, 2001, effective December 1, 2001; April 30, 2007, effective December 1, 2007, absent contrary Congressional action.]

## RULE 78.  HEARING MOTIONS; SUBMISSION ON BRIEFS

**(a) Providing a Regular Schedule for Oral Hearings.** A court may establish regular times and places for oral hearings on motions.

**(b) Providing for Submission on Briefs.** By rule or order, the court may provide for submitting and determining motions on briefs, without oral hearings.

[Amended March 2, 1987, effective August 1, 1987; April 30, 2007, effective December 1, 2007, absent contrary Congressional action.]

## RULE 79.  RECORDS KEPT BY THE CLERK

**(a) Civil Docket.**

(1) *In General.* The clerk must keep a record known as the "civil docket" in the form and manner prescribed by the Director of the Administrative Office of the United States Courts with the approval of the Judicial Conference of the United States. The clerk must enter each civil action in the docket. Actions must be assigned consecutive file numbers, which must be noted in the docket where the first entry of the action is made.

(2) *Items to be Entered.* The following items must be marked with the file number and entered chronologically in the docket:

(A) papers filed with the clerk;

(B) process issued, and proofs of service or other returns showing execution; and

(C) appearances, orders, verdicts, and judgments.

(3) *Contents of Entries; Jury Trial Demanded.* Each entry must briefly show the nature of the paper filed or writ issued, the substance of each proof of service or other return, and the substance and date of entry of each order and judgment. When a jury trial has been properly demanded or ordered, the clerk must enter the word "jury" in the docket.

**(b) Civil Judgments and Orders.** The clerk must keep a copy of every final judgment and appealable order; of every order affecting title to or a lien on real or personal property; and of any other order that the court directs to be kept. The clerk must keep these in the form and manner prescribed by the Director of the Administrative Office of the United States Courts with the approval of the Judicial Conference of the United States.

**(c) Indexes; Calendars.** Under the court's direction, the clerk must:

(1) keep indexes of the docket and of the judgments and orders described in Rule 79(b); and

(2) prepare calendars of all actions ready for trial, distinguishing jury trials from nonjury trials.

**(d) Other Records.** The clerk must keep any other records required by the Director of the Administrative Office of the United States Courts with the approval of the Judicial Conference of the United States.

[Amended December 27, 1946, effective March 19, 1948; December 29, 1948, effective October 20, 1949; January 21, 1963, effective July 1, 1963; April 30, 2007, effective December 1, 2007, absent contrary Congressional action.]

## RULE 80.  STENOGRAPHIC TRANSCRIPT AS EVIDENCE

If stenographically reported testimony at a hearing or trial is admissible in evidence at a later trial, the testimony may be proved by a transcript certified by the person who reported it.

[Amended December 27, 1946, effective March 19, 1948; April 30, 2007, effective December 1, 2007, absent contrary Congressional action.]

# TITLE XI.  GENERAL PROVISIONS

## RULE 81.  APPLICABILITY OF THE RULES IN GENERAL; REMOVED ACTIONS

### (a) Applicability to Particular Proceedings.

(1) *Prize Proceedings.* These rules do not apply to prize proceedings in admiralty governed by 10 U.S.C. §§ 7651–7681.

(2) *Bankruptcy.* These rules apply to bankruptcy proceedings to the extent provided by the Federal Rules of Bankruptcy Procedure.

(3) *Citizenship.* These rules apply to proceedings for admission to citizenship to the extent that the practice in those proceedings is not specified in federal statutes and has previously conformed to the practice in civil actions. The provisions of 8 U.S.C. § 1451 for service by publication and for answer apply in proceedings to cancel citizenship certificates.

(4) *Special Writs.* These rules apply to proceedings for habeas corpus and for quo warranto to the extent that the practice in those proceedings:

(A) is not specified in a federal statute, the Rules Governing Section 2254 Cases, or the Rules Governing Section 2255 Cases; and

(B) has previously conformed to the practice in civil actions.

(5) *Proceedings Involving a Subpoena.* These rules apply to proceedings to compel testimony or the production of documents through a subpoena issued by a United States officer or agency under a federal statute, except as otherwise provided by statute, by local rule, or by court order in the proceedings.

(6) *Other Proceedings.* These rules, to the extent applicable, govern proceedings under the following laws, except as these laws provide other procedures:

(A) 7 U.S.C. §§ 292, 499g(c), for reviewing an order of the Secretary of Agriculture;

(B) 9 U.S.C., relating to arbitration;

(C) 15 U.S.C. § 522, for reviewing an order of the Secretary of the Interior;

(D) 15 U.S.C. § 715d(c), for reviewing an order denying a certificate of clearance;

(E) 29 U.S.C. §§ 159, 160, for enforcing an order of the National Labor Relations Board;

(F) 33 U.S.C. §§ 918, 921, for enforcing or reviewing a compensation order under the Longshore and Harbor Workers' Compensation Act; and

(G) 45 U.S.C. § 159, for reviewing an arbitration award in a railway-labor dispute.

### (b) Scire Facias and Mandamus. The writs of scire facias and mandamus are abolished. Relief previously available through them may be obtained by appropriate action or motion under these rules.

### (c) Removed Actions.

(1) *Applicability.* These rules apply to a civil action after it is removed from a state court.

(2) *Further Pleading.* After removal, repleading is unnecessary unless the court orders it. A defendant who did not answer before removal must answer or present other defenses or objections under these rules within the longest of these periods:

(A) 20 days after receiving—through service or otherwise—a copy of the initial pleading stating the claim for relief;

(B) 20 days after being served with the summons for an initial pleading on file at the time of service; or

(C) 5 days after the notice of removal is filed.

(3) *Demand for a Jury Trial.*

(A) As Affected by State Law. A party who, before removal, expressly demanded a jury trial in accordance with state law need not renew the demand after removal. If the state law did not require an express demand for a jury trial, a party need not make one after removal unless the court orders the parties to do so within a specified time. The court must so order at a party's request and may so order on its own. A party who fails to make a demand when so ordered waives a jury trial.

(B) Under Rule 38. If all necessary pleadings have been served at the time of removal, a party entitled to a jury trial under Rule 38 must be given one if the party serves a demand within 10 days after:

(i) it files a notice of removal; or

(ii) it is served with a notice of removal filed by another party.

### (d) Law Applicable.

(1) *State Law.* When these rules refer to state law, the term "law" includes the state's statutes and the state's judicial decisions.

(2) *District of Columbia.* The term "state" includes, where appropriate, the District of Columbia. When these rules provide for state law to apply, in the District Court for the District of Columbia:

(A) the law applied in the District governs; and

(B) the term "federal statute" includes any Act of Congress that applies locally to the District.

[Amended December 28, 1939, effective April 3, 1941; December 27, 1946, effective March 19, 1948; December 29, 1948, effective October 20, 1949; April 30, 1951, effective

August 1, 1951; January 21, 1963, effective July 1, 1963; February 28, 1966, effective July 1, 1966; December 4, 1967, effective July 1, 1968; March 1, 1971, effective July 1, 1971; March 2, 1987, effective August 1, 1987; April 23, 2001, effective December 1, 2001; April 29, 2002, effective December 1, 2002; April 30, 2007, effective December 1, 2007, absent contrary Congressional action.]

## RULE 82. JURISDICTION AND VENUE UNAFFECTED

These rules do not extend or limit the jurisdiction of the district courts or the venue of actions in those courts. An admiralty or maritime claim under Rule 9(h) is not a civil action for purposes of 28 U.S.C. §§ 1391–1392.

[Amended December 29, 1948, effective October 20, 1949; February 28, 1966, effective July 1, 1966; April 23, 2001, effective December 1, 2001; April 30, 2007, effective December 1, 2007, absent contrary Congressional action.]

## RULE 83. RULES BY DISTRICT COURTS; JUDGE'S DIRECTIVES

**(a) Local Rules.**

(1) *In General.* After giving public notice and an opportunity for comment, a district court, acting by a majority of its district judges, may adopt and amend rules governing its practice. A local rule must be consistent with—but not duplicate—federal statutes and rules adopted under 28 U.S.C. §§ 2072 and 2075, and must conform to any uniform numbering system prescribed by the Judicial Conference of the United States. A local rule takes effect on the date specified by the district court and remains in effect unless amended by the court or abrogated by the judicial council of the circuit. Copies of rules and amendments must, on their adoption, be furnished to the judicial council and the Administrative Office of the United States Courts and be made available to the public.

(2) *Requirement of Form.* A local rule imposing a requirement of form must not be enforced in a way that causes a party to lose any right because of a nonwillful failure to comply.

**(b) Procedure When There Is No Controlling Law.** A judge may regulate practice in any manner consistent with federal law, rules adopted under 28 U.S.C. §§ 2072 and 2075, and the district's local rules. No sanction or other disadvantage may be imposed for noncompliance with any requirement not in federal law, federal rules, or the local rules unless the alleged violator has been furnished in the particular case with actual notice of the requirement.

[Amended April 29, 1985, effective August 1, 1985; April 27, 1995, effective December 1, 1995; April 30, 2007, effective December 1, 2007, absent contrary Congressional action.]

## RULE 84. FORMS

The forms in the Appendix suffice under these rules and illustrate the simplicity and brevity that these rules contemplate.

[Amended December 27, 1946, effective March 19, 1948; April 30, 2007, effective December 1, 2007, absent contrary Congressional action.]

## RULE 85. TITLE

These rules may be cited as the Federal Rules of Civil Procedure.

[Amended April 30, 2007, effective December 1, 2007, absent contrary Congressional action.]

## RULE 86. EFFECTIVE DATES

**(a) In General.** These rules and any amendments take effect at the time specified by the Supreme Court, subject to 28 U.S.C. § 2074. They govern:

(1) proceedings in an action commenced after their effective date; and

(2) proceedings after that date in an action then pending unless:

(A) the Supreme Court specifies otherwise; or

(B) the court determines that applying them in a particular action would be infeasible or work an injustice.

**(b) December 1, 2007 Amendments.** If any provision in Rules 1–5.1, 6–73, or 77–86 conflicts with another law, priority in time for the purpose of 28 U.S.C. § 2072(b) is not affected by the amendments taking effect on December 1, 2007.

[Amended December 27, 1946, effective March 19, 1948; December 29, 1948, effective October 20, 1949; April 17, 1961, effective July 19, 1961; January 21, 1963, and March 18, 1963, effective July 1, 1963; April 30, 2007, effective December 1, 2007, absent contrary Congressional action.]

# APPENDIX OF FORMS

## FORM 1.   CAPTION

*(Use on every summons, complaint, answer, motion, or other document.)*

United States District Court

for the

————District of ————

| | | |
|---|---|---|
| A B, Plaintiff | ) | |
| | ) | |
| v. | ) | |
| | ) | Civil Action No. ———— |
| C D, Defendant | ) | |
| | ) | |
| v. | ) | |
| | ) | |
| E F, Third–Party Defendant | ) | |
| *(Use if needed.)* | ) | |

*(Name of Document)*

## FORM 2.   DATE, SIGNATURE, ADDRESS, E–MAIL ADDRESS, AND TELEPHONE NUMBER

*(Use at the conclusion of pleadings and other papers that require a signature.)*

Date _____ _____

_____
(Signature of the attorney or unrepresented party)

_____
(Printed name)

_____
(Address)

_____
(E-mail address)

_____
(Telephone number)

## FORM 3.  SUMMONS

(Caption—See Form 1.)

To *name the defendant*:

A lawsuit has been filed against you.

Within 20 days after service of this summons on you (not counting the day you received it), you must serve on the plaintiff an answer to the attached complaint or a motion under Rule 12 of the Federal Rules of Civil Procedure. The answer or motion must be served on the plaintiff's attorney,_____, whose address is _____. If you fail to do so, judgment by default will be entered against you for the relief demanded in the complaint. You also must file your answer or motion with the court.

Date _____

_____
Clerk of Court

(Court Seal)

*(Use 60 days if the defendant is the United States or a United States agency, or is an officer or employee of the United States allowed 60 days by Rule 12(a)(3).)*

## FORM 4.  SUMMONS ON A THIRD–PARTY COMPLAINT

(Caption—See Form 1.)

To *name the third-party defendant*:

A lawsuit has been filed against defendant _____, who as third-party plaintiff is making this claim against you to pay part or all of what [he] may owe to the plaintiff _____.

Within 20 days after service of this summons on you (not counting the day you received it), you must serve on the plaintiff and on the defendant an answer to the attached third-party complaint or a motion under Rule 12 of the Federal Rules of Civil Procedure. The answer or motion must be served on the defendant's attorney, _____, whose address is, _____, and also on the plaintiff's attorney, _____, whose address is, _____. If you fail to do so, judgment by default will be entered against you for the relief demanded in the third-party complaint. You also must file the answer or motion with the court and serve it on any other parties.

A copy of the plaintiff's complaint is also attached. You may–but are not required to–respond to it.

Date _____

                                                 _____
                                                   Clerk of Court

(Court Seal)

# FORM 5.  NOTICE OF A LAWSUIT AND REQUEST TO WAIVE SERVICE OF A SUMMONS

(Caption—See Form 1.)

To (*name the defendant—or if the defendant is a corporation, partnership, or association name an officer or agent authorized to receive service*):

### Why are you getting this?

A lawsuit has been filed against you, or the entity you represent, in this court under the number shown above. A copy of the complaint is attached.

This is not a summons, or an official notice from the court. It is a request that, to avoid expenses, you waive formal service of a summons by signing and returning the enclosed waiver. To avoid these expenses, you must return the signed waiver within (*give at least 30 days or at least 60 days if the defendant is outside any judicial district of the United States*) from the date shown below, which is the date this notice was sent. Two copies of the waiver form are enclosed, along with a stamped, self-addressed envelope or other prepaid means for returning one copy. You may keep the other copy.

### What happens next?

If you return the signed waiver, I will file it with the court. The action will then proceed as if you had been served on the date the waiver is filed, but no summons will be served on you and you will have 60 days from the date this notice is sent (see the date below) to answer the complaint (or 90 days if this notice is sent to you outside any judicial district of the United States).

If you do not return the signed waiver within the time indicated, I will arrange to have the summons and complaint served on you. And I will ask the court to require you, or the entity you represent, to pay the expenses of making service.

Please read the enclosed statement about the duty to avoid unnecessary expenses.

I certify that this request is being sent to you on the date below.

(Date and sign—See Form 2.)

# FORM 6.  WAIVER OF THE SERVICE OF SUMMONS

(Caption—See Form 1.)

To *name the plaintiff's attorney or the unrepresented plaintiff*:

I have received your request to waive service of a summons in this action along with a copy of the complaint, two copies of this waiver form, and a prepaid means of returning one signed copy of the form to you.

I, or the entity I represent, agree to save the expense of serving a summons and complaint in this case.

I understand that I, or the entity I represent, will keep all defenses or objections to the lawsuit, the court's jurisdiction, and the venue of the action, but that I waive any objections to the absence of a summons or of service.

I also understand that I, or the entity I represent, must file and serve an answer or a motion under Rule 12 within 60 days from _____, the date when this request was sent (or 90 days if it was sent outside the United States). If I fail to do so, a default judgment will be entered against me or the entity I represent.

(Date and sign—See Form 2.)

*(Attach the following to Form 6.)*

Duty to Avoid Unnecessary Expenses of Serving a Summons

Rule 4 of the Federal Rules of Civil Procedure requires certain defendants to cooperate in saving unnecessary expenses of serving a summons and complaint. A defendant who is located in the United States and who fails to return a signed waiver of service requested by a plaintiff located in the United States will be required to pay the expenses of service, unless the defendant shows good cause for the failure.

"Good cause" does *not* include a belief that the lawsuit is groundless, or that it has been brought in an improper venue, or that the court has no jurisdiction over this matter or over the defendant or the defendant's property.

If the waiver is signed and returned, you can still make these and all other defenses and objections, but you cannot object to the absence of a summons or of service.

If you waive service, then you must, within the time specified on the waiver form, serve an answer or a motion under Rule 12 on the plaintiff and file a copy with the court. By signing and returning the waiver form, you are allowed more time to respond than if a summons had been served.

## FORM 7.  STATEMENT OF JURISDICTION

a.  (*For diversity-of-citizenship jurisdiction.*) The plaintiff is [a citizen of *Michigan*] [a corporation incorporated under the laws of *Michigan* with its principal place of business in *Michigan*]. The defendant is [a citizen of *New York*] [a corporation incorporated under the laws of *New York* with its principal place of business in *New York*]. The amount in controversy, without interest and costs, exceeds the sum or value specified by 28 U.S.C. § 1332.

b.  (*For federal-question jurisdiction.*) This action arises under [the United States Constitution, *specify the article or amendment and the section*] [a United States treaty *specify*] [a federal statute, ___U.S.C. § _].

c.  (*For a claim in the admiralty or maritime jurisdiction.*) This is a case of admiralty or maritime jurisdiction. *(To invoke admiralty status under Rule 9(h) use the following:* This is an admiralty or maritime claim within the meaning of Rule 9(h).)

## FORM 8.   STATEMENT OF REASONS FOR OMITTING A PARTY

*(If a person who ought to be made a party under Rule 19(a) is not named, include this statement in accordance with Rule 19(c).)*

This complaint does not join as a party *name* who [is not subject to this court's personal jurisdiction] [cannot be made a party without depriving this court of subject-matter jurisdiction] because *state the reason.*

# FORM 9.  STATEMENT NOTING A PARTY'S DEATH

(Caption—See Form 1.)

In accordance with Rule 25(a) *name the person,* who is [a party to this action] [a representative of or successor to the deceased party] notes the death during the pendency of this action of *name,* [*describe as party* in this action].

(Date and sign—See Form 2.)

## FORM 10. COMPLAINT TO RECOVER A SUM CERTAIN

(Caption—See Form 1.)

1. (Statement of Jurisdiction–See Form 7.)

*(Use one or more of the following as appropriate and include a demand for judgment.)*

*(a) On a Promissory Note*

2. On *date*, the defendant executed and delivered a note promising to pay the plaintiff on *date* the sum of $_____ with interest at the rate of __ percent. A copy of the note [is attached as Exhibit A] [is summarized as follows: _____.]

3. The defendant has not paid the amount owed.

*(b) On an Account*

2. The defendant owes the plaintiff $_____ according to the account set out in Exhibit A.

*(c) For Goods Sold and Delivered*

2. The defendant owes the plaintiff $_____ for goods sold and delivered by the plaintiff to the defendant from *date* to *date*.

*(d) For Money Lent*

2. The defendant owes the plaintiff $_____ for money lent by the plaintiff to the defendant on *date*.

*(e) For Money Paid by Mistake*

2. The defendant owes the plaintiff $_____ for money paid by mistake to the defendant on *date* under these circumstances: *describe with particularity in accordance with Rule 9(b).*

*(f) For Money Had and Received*

2. The defendant owes the plaintiff $_____ for money that was received from *name* on *date* to be paid by the defendant to the plaintiff.

*Demand for Judgment*

Therefore, the plaintiff demands judgment against the defendant for $_____, plus interest and costs.

(Date and sign—See Form 2.)

# FORM 11. COMPLAINT FOR NEGLIGENCE

(Caption—See Form 1.)

1. (Statement of Jurisdiction–See Form 7.)

2. On *date*, at *place*, the defendant negligently drove a motor vehicle against the plaintiff.

3. As a result, the plaintiff was physically injured, lost wages or income, suffered physical and mental pain, and incurred medical expenses of $_____.

Therefore, the plaintiff demands judgment against the defendant for $_____, plus costs.

(Date and sign—See Form 2).

## FORM 12.   COMPLAINT FOR NEGLIGENCE WHEN THE PLAINTIFF DOES NOT KNOW WHO IS RESPONSIBLE

(Caption—See Form 1.)

1.   (Statement of Jurisdiction–See Form 7.)

2.   On *date*, at *place*, defendant *name* or defendant *name* or both of them willfully or recklessly or negligently drove, or caused to be driven, a motor vehicle against the plaintiff.

3.   As a result, the plaintiff was physically injured, lost wages or income, suffered mental and physical pain, and incurred medical expenses of $_____.

Therefore, the plaintiff demands judgment against one or both defendants for $_____, plus costs.

(Date and sign—See Form 2.)

## FORM 13.  COMPLAINT FOR NEGLIGENCE UNDER THE FEDERAL EMPLOYERS' LIABILITY ACT

(Caption—See Form 1.)

1.  (Statement of Jurisdiction—See Form 7.)

2.  At the times below, the defendant owned and operated in interstate commerce a railroad line that passed through a tunnel located at _____.

3.  On *date*, the plaintiff was working to repair and enlarge the tunnel to make it convenient and safe for use in interstate commerce.

4.  During this work, the defendant, as the employer, negligently put the plaintiff to work in a section of the tunnel that the defendant had left unprotected and unsupported.

5.  The defendant's negligence caused the plaintiff to be injured by a rock that fell from an unsupported portion of the tunnel.

6.  As a result, the plaintiff was physically injured, lost wages or income, suffered mental and physical pain, and incurred medical expenses of $_____.

Therefore, the plaintiff demands judgment against the defendant for $_____, and costs.

(Date and sign—See Form 2.)

# FORM 14.  COMPLAINT FOR DAMAGES UNDER THE MERCHANT MARINE ACT

(Caption—See Form 1.)

1.  (Statement of Jurisdiction—See Form 7.)

2.  At the times below, the defendant owned and operated the vessel *name* and used it to transport cargo for hire by water in interstate and foreign commerce.

3.  On *date*, at *place*, the defendant hired the plaintiff under seamen's articles of customary form for a voyage from _____ to _____ and return at a wage of $_____ a month and found, which is equal to a shore worker's wage of $_____ a month.

4.  On *date*, the vessel was at sea on the return voyage. (*Describe the weather and the condition of the vessel.*)

5.  (*Describe as in Form 11 the defendant's negligent conduct.*)

6.  As a result of the defendant's negligent conduct and the unseaworthiness of the vessel, the plaintiff was physically injured, has been incapable of any gainful activity, suffered mental and physical pain, and has incurred medical expenses of $_____.

Therefore, the plaintiff demands judgment against the defendant for $, plus costs.

(Date and sign—See Form 2.)

## FORM 15. COMPLAINT FOR THE CONVERSION OF PROPERTY

(Caption—See Form 1.)

1. (Statement of Jurisdiction—See Form 7.)

2. On *date*, at *place*, the defendant converted to the defendant's own use property owned by the plaintiff. The property converted consists of *describe*.

3. The property is worth $_____.

Therefore, the plaintiff demands judgment against the defendant for $_____, plus costs.

(Date and sign—See Form 2.)

# FORM 16.  THIRD–PARTY COMPLAINT

(Caption—See Form 1.)

1.  Plaintiff _name_ has filed against defendant _name_ a complaint, a copy of which is attached.

2.  *(State grounds entitling defendant's name to recover from third-party defendant's name for (all or an identified share) of any judgment for plaintiff's name against defendant's name.)*

Therefore, the defendant demands judgment against *third-party defendant's name* for *all or an identified share* of sums that may be adjudged against the defendant in the plaintiff's favor.

(Date and sign—See Form 2.)

# FORM 17.  COMPLAINT FOR SPECIFIC PERFORMANCE OF A CONTRACT TO CONVEY LAND

(Caption—See Form 1.)

1.  (Statement of Jurisdiction–See Form 7.)

2.  On *date*, the parties agreed to the contract [attached as Exhibit A][summarize the contract].

3.  As agreed, the plaintiff tendered the purchase price and requested a conveyance of the land, but the defendant refused to accept the money or make a conveyance.

4.  The plaintiff now offers to pay the purchase price.

Therefore, the plaintiff demands that:

(a) the defendant be required to specifically perform the agreement and pay damages of $_____, plus interest and costs, or

(b) if specific performance is not ordered, the defendant be required to pay damages of $_____, plus interest and costs.

(Date and sign—See Form 2.)

## FORM 18. COMPLAINT FOR PATENT INFRINGEMENT

(Caption—See Form 1.)

1. (Statement of Jurisdiction—See Form 7.)

2. On *date*, United States Letters Patent No. _____ were issued to the plaintiff for an invention in an *electric motor*. The plaintiff owned the patent throughout the period of the defendant's infringing acts and still owns the patent.

3. The defendant has infringed and is still infringing the Letters Patent by making, selling, and using *electric motors* that embody the patented invention, and the defendant will continue to do so unless enjoined by this court.

4. The plaintiff has complied with the statutory requirement of placing a notice of the Letters Patent on all *electric motors* it manufactures and sells and has given the defendant written notice of the infringement.

Therefore, the plaintiff demands:

(a) a preliminary and final injunction against the continuing infringement;

(b) an accounting for damages; and

(c) interest and costs.

(Date and sign—See Form 2.)

## FORM 19.  COMPLAINT FOR COPYRIGHT INFRINGEMENT
## AND UNFAIR COMPETITION

(Caption—See Form 1.)

1.  (Statement of Jurisdiction–See Form 7.)

2.  Before *date*, the plaintiff, a United States citizen, wrote a book entitled _____.

3.  The book is an original work that may be copyrighted under United States law. A copy of the book is attached as Exhibit A.

4.  Between *date* and *date*, the plaintiff applied to the copyright office and received a certificate of registration dated _____ and identified as *date, class, number*.

5.  Since *date*, the plaintiff has either published or licensed for publication all copies of the book in compliance with the copyright laws and has remained the sole owner of the copyright.

6.  After the copyright was issued, the defendant infringed the copyright by publishing and selling a book entitled _____, which was copied largely from the plaintiff's book. A copy of the defendant's book is attached as Exhibit B.

7.  The plaintiff has notified the defendant in writing of the infringement.

8.  The defendant continues to infringe the copyright by continuing to publish and sell the infringing book in violation of the copyright, and further has engaged in unfair trade practices and unfair competition in connection with its publication and sale of the infringing book, thus causing irreparable damage.

Therefore, the plaintiff demands that:

(a) until this case is decided the defendant and the defendant's agents be enjoined from disposing of any copies of the defendant's book by sale or otherwise;

(b) the defendant account for and pay as damages to the plaintiff all profits and advantages gained from unfair trade practices and unfair competition in selling the defendant's book, and all profits and advantages gained from infringing the plaintiff's copyright (but no less than the statutory minimum);

(c) the defendant deliver for impoundment all copies of the book in the defendant's possession or control and deliver for destruction all infringing copies and all plates, molds, and other materials for making infringing copies;

(d) the defendant pay the plaintiff interest, costs, and reasonable attorney's fees; and

(e) the plaintiff be awarded any other just relief.

(Date and sign—See Form 2.)

# FORM 20. COMPLAINT FOR INTERPLEADER AND DECLARATORY RELIEF

(Caption—See Form 1.)

1. (Statement of Jurisdiction–See Form 7.)

2. On *date*, the plaintiff issued a life insurance policy on the life of *name* with *name* as the named beneficiary.

3. As a condition for keeping the policy in force, the policy required payment of a premium during the first year and then annually.

4. The premium due on *date* was never paid, and the policy lapsed after that date.

5. On *date*, after the policy had lapsed, both the insured and the named beneficiary died in an automobile collision.

6. Defendant *name* claims to be the beneficiary in place of *name* and has filed a claim to be paid the policy's full amount.

7. The other two defendants are representatives of the deceased persons' estates. Each defendant has filed a claim on behalf of each estate to receive payment of the policy's full amount.

8. If the policy was in force at the time of death, the plaintiff is in doubt about who should be paid.

Therefore, the plaintiff demands that:

(a) each defendant be restrained from commencing any action against the plaintiff on the policy;

(b) a judgment be entered that no defendant is entitled to the proceeds of the policy or any part of it, but if the court determines that the policy was in effect at the time of the insured's death, that the defendants be required to interplead and settle among themselves their rights to the proceeds, and that the plaintiff be discharged from all liability except to the defendant determined to be entitled to the proceeds; and

(c) the plaintiff recover its costs.

(Date and sign—See Form 2.)

## FORM 21.   COMPLAINT ON A CLAIM FOR A DEBT AND TO SET ASIDE A FRAUDULENT CONVEYANCE UNDER RULE 18(B)

(Caption—See Form 1.)

1.   (Statement of Jurisdiction—See Form 7.)

2.   On *date*, defendant *name* signed a note promising to pay to the plaintiff on *date* the sum of $_____ with interest at the rate of ___ percent. [The pleader may, but need not, attach a copy or plead the note verbatim.]

3.   Defendant *name* owes the plaintiff the amount of the note and interest.

4.   On *date*, defendant *name* conveyed all defendant's real and personal property *if less than all, describe it fully* to defendant *name* for the purpose of defrauding the plaintiff and hindering or delaying the collection of the debt.

Therefore, the plaintiff demands that:

(a) judgment for $_____, plus costs, be entered against defendant(s) *name(s)*; and

(b) the conveyance to defendant *name* be declared void and any judgment granted be made a lien on the property.

(Date and sign—See Form 2.)

## FORM 30.  ANSWER PRESENTING DEFENSES UNDER RULE 12(B)

(Caption—See Form 1.)

### Responding to Allegations in the Complaint

1.  Defendant admits the allegations in paragraphs _____.

2.  Defendant lacks knowledge or information sufficient to form a belief about the truth of the allegations in paragraphs _____.

3.  Defendant admits *identify part of the allegation* in paragraph _____ and denies or lacks knowledge or information sufficient to form a belief about the truth of the rest of the paragraph.

### Failure to State a Claim

4.  The complaint fails to state a claim upon which relief can be granted.

### Failure to Join a Required Party

5.  If there is a debt, it is owed jointly by the defendant and *name* who is a citizen of _____. This person can be made a party without depriving this court of jurisdiction over the existing parties.

### Affirmative Defense–Statute of Limitations

6.  The plaintiff's claim is barred by the statute of limitations because it arose more than _____ years before this action was commenced.

### Counterclaim

7.  (*Set forth any counterclaim in the same way a claim is pleaded in a complaint. Include a further statement of jurisdiction if needed.*)

### Crossclaim

8.  (*Set forth a crossclaim against a coparty in the same way a claim is pleaded in a complaint. Include a further statement of jurisdiction if needed.*)

(Date and sign—See Form 2.)

# FORM 31.  ANSWER TO A COMPLAINT FOR MONEY HAD AND RECEIVED WITH A COUNTERCLAIM FOR INTERPLEADER

(Caption—See Form 1.)

### Response to the Allegations in the Complaint
(See Form 30)

### Counterclaim for Interpleader

1.  The defendant received from *name* a deposit of $_____.

2.  The plaintiff demands payment of the deposit because of a purported assignment from *name*, who has notified the defendant that the assignment is not valid and who continues to hold the defendant responsible for the deposit.

Therefore, the defendant demands that:

(a)  *name* be made a party to this action;

(b)  the plaintiff and *name* be required to interplead their respective claims;

(c)  the court decide whether the plaintiff or *name* or either of them is entitled to the deposit and discharge the defendant of any liability except to the person entitled to the deposit; and

(d)  the defendant recover costs and attorney's fees.


(Date and sign—See Form 2.)

## FORM 40.   MOTION TO DISMISS UNDER RULE 12(B) FOR LACK OF JURISDICTION, IMPROPER VENUE, INSUFFICIENT SERVICE OF PROCESS, OR FAILURE TO STATE A CLAIM

(Caption—See Form 1.)

The defendant moves to dismiss the action because:

1.   the amount in controversy is less than the sum or value specified by 28 U.S.C. § 1332;

2.   the defendant is not subject to the personal jurisdiction of this court;

3.   venue is improper (this defendant does not reside in this district and no part of the events or omissions giving rise to the claim occurred in the district);

4.   the defendant has not been properly served, as shown by the attached affidavits of _____; or

5.   the complaint fails to state a claim upon which relief can be granted.

(Date and sign—See Form 2.)

## FORM 41.   MOTION TO BRING IN A THIRD–PARTY DEFENDANT

(Caption—See Form 1.)

The defendant, as third-party plaintiff, moves for leave to serve on *name* a summons and third-party complaint, copies of which are attached.

(Date and sign—See Form 2.)

## FORM 42.  MOTION TO INTERVENE AS
## A DEFENDANT UNDER RULE 24

(Caption—See Form 1.)

1.  *name* moves for leave to intervene as a defendant in this action and to file the attached answer.

*(State grounds under Rule 24(a) or (b).)*

2.  The plaintiff alleges patent infringement. We manufacture and sell to the defendant the articles involved, and we have a defense to the plaintiff's claim.

3.  Our defense presents questions of law and fact that are common to this action.

(Date and sign—See Form 2.)

[An Intervener's Answer must be attached. See Form 30.]

# FORM 50.  REQUEST TO PRODUCE DOCUMENTS AND TANGIBLE THINGS, OR TO ENTER ONTO LAND UNDER RULE 34

(Caption—See Form 1.)

The plaintiff *name* requests that the defendant *name* respond within ____ days to the following requests:

1.   To produce and permit the plaintiff to inspect and copy and to test or sample the following documents, including electronically stored information:

*(Describe each document and the electronically stored information, either individually or by category.)*

*(State the time, place, and manner of the inspection and any related acts.)*

2.   To produce and permit the plaintiff to inspect and copy—and to test or sample—the following tangible things:

*(Describe each thing, either individually or by category.)*

*(State the time, place, and manner of the inspection and any related acts.)*

3.   To permit the plaintiff to enter onto the following land to inspect, photograph, test, or sample the property or an object or operation on the property.

*(Describe the property and each object or operation.)*

*(State the time and manner of the inspection and any related acts.)*

(Date and sign—See Form 2.)

## FORM 51.   REQUEST FOR ADMISSIONS UNDER RULE 36

(Caption—See Form 1.)

The plaintiff *name* asks the defendant *name* to respond within 30 days to these requests by admitting, for purposes of this action only and subject to objections to admissibility at trial:

1.   The genuineness of the following documents, copies of which [are attached] [are or have been furnished or made available for inspection and copying].

(*List each document.*)

2.   The truth of each of the following statements:

(*List each statement.*)

(Date and sign—See Form 2.)

## FORM 52.   REPORT OF THE PARTIES' PLANNING MEETING

(Caption—See Form 1.)

1.   The following persons participated in a Rule 26(f) conference on *date* by *state the method of conferring*:

(*e.g.*, *name* representing the plaintiff.)

2.   Initial Disclosures. The parties [have completed] [will complete by *date*] the initial disclosures required by Rule 26(a)(1).

3.   Discovery Plan. The parties propose this discovery plan:

(*Use separate paragraphs or subparagraphs if the parties disagree.*)

(a)  Discovery will be needed on these subjects: (*describe.*)

(b)  (Dates for commencing and completing discovery, including discovery to be commenced or completed before other discovery.)

(c)  (Maximum number of interrogatories by each party to another party, along with the dates the answers are due.)

(d)  (Maximum number of requests for admission, along with the dates responses are due.)

(e)  (Maximum number of depositions by each party.)

(f)  (Limits on the length of depositions, in hours.)

(g)  (Dates for exchanging reports of expert witnesses.)

(h)  (Dates for supplementations under Rule 26(e).)

4.   Other Items:

(a)  (A date if the parties ask to meet with the court before a scheduling order.)

(b)  (Requested dates for pretrial conferences.)

(c)  (Final dates for the plaintiff to amend pleadings or to join parties.)

(d)  (Final dates for the defendant to amend pleadings or to join parties.)

(e)  (Final dates to file dispositive motions.)

(f)  (State the prospects for settlement.)

(g)  (Identify any alternative dispute resolution procedure that may enhance settlement prospects.)

(h)  (Final dates for submitting Rule 26(a)(3) witness lists, designations of witnesses whose testimony will be presented by deposition, and exhibit lists.)

(i)  (Final dates to file objections under Rule 26(a)(3).)

(j)  (Suggested trial date and estimate of trial length.)

(k)  (Other matters.)

(Date and sign—see Form 2.)

# FORM 60.  NOTICE OF CONDEMNATION

(Caption—See Form 1.)

To *name the defendant*.

1.  A complaint in condemnation has been filed in the United States District Court for the _____District of _____, to take property to use for *purpose*. The interest to be taken is *describe*. The court is located in the United States courthouse at this address: _____.

2.  The property to be taken is described below. You have or claim an interest in it.

(*Describe the property.*)

3.  The authority for taking this property is *cite*.

4.  If you want to object or present any defense to the taking you must serve an answer on the plaintiff's attorney within 20 days [after being served with this notice][from (insert the date of the last publication of notice)]. Send your answer to this address: _____.

5.  Your answer must identify the property in which you claim an interest, state the nature and extent of that interest, and state all your objections and defenses to the taking. Objections and defenses not presented are waived.

6.  If you fail to answer you consent to the taking and the court will enter a judgment that takes your described property interest.

7.  Instead of answering, you may serve on the plaintiff's attorney a notice of appearance that designates the property in which you claim an interest. After you do that, you will receive a notice of any proceedings that affect you. Whether or not you have previously appeared or answered, you may present evidence at a trial to determine compensation for the property and share in the overall award.

(Date and sign—See Form 2.)

## FORM 61.  COMPLAINT FOR CONDEMNATION

(Caption—See Form 1; name as defendants the property and at least one owner.)

    1.  (Statement of Jurisdiction—See Form 7.)

    2.  This is an action to take property under the power of eminent domain and to determine just compensation to be paid to the owners and parties in interest.

    3.  The authority for the taking is _____.

    4.  The property is to be used for _____.

    5.  The property to be taken is (*describe in enough detail for identification—or attach the description and state "is described in Exhibit A, attached."*)

    6.  The interest to be acquired is _____.

    7.  The persons known to the plaintiff to have or claim an interest in the property are: _____. (*For each person include the interest claimed.*)

    8.  There may be other persons who have or claim an interest in the property and whose names could not be found after a reasonably diligent search. They are made parties under the designation "Unknown Owners."

Therefore, the plaintiff demands judgment:

    (a)  condemning the property;

    (b)  determining and awarding just compensation; and

    (c)  granting any other lawful and proper relief.

(Date and sign—See Form 2.)

## FORM 70.  JUDGMENT ON A JURY VERDICT

(Caption—See Form 1.)

This action was tried by a jury with Judge _____ presiding, and the jury has rendered a verdict.

It is ordered that:

[the plaintiff *name* recover from the defendant *name* the amount of $_____ with interest at the rate of __%, along with costs.]

[the plaintiff recover nothing, the action be dismissed on the merits, and the defendant *name* recover costs from the plaintiff *name*.]

Date _____ _____

_____

Clerk of Court

# FORM 71.  JUDGMENT BY THE COURT WITHOUT A JURY

(Caption—See Form 1.)

This action was tried by Judge _____ without a jury and the following decision was reached:

It is ordered that [the plaintiff *name* recover from the defendant *name* the amount of $_____, with prejudgment interest at the rate of ___%, postjudgment interest at the rate of _____%, along with costs.] [the plaintiff recover nothing, the action be dismissed on the merits, and the defendant *name* recover costs from the plaintiff *name*.]

Date _____

                                    _____
                                    Clerk of Court

## FORM 80.  NOTICE OF A MAGISTRATE JUDGE'S AVAILABILITY

1.   A magistrate judge is available under title 28 U.S.C. § 636(c) to conduct the proceedings in this case, including a jury or nonjury trial and the entry of final judgment. But a magistrate judge can be assigned only if all parties voluntarily consent.

2.   You may withhold your consent without adverse substantive consequences. The identity of any party consenting or withholding consent will not be disclosed to the judge to whom the case is assigned or to any magistrate judge.

3.   If a magistrate judge does hear your case, you may appeal directly to a United States court of appeals as you would if a district judge heard it.

A form called *Consent to an Assignment to a United States Magistrate Judge* is available from the court clerk's office.

# FORM 81.   CONSENT TO AN ASSIGNMENT
## TO A MAGISTRATE JUDGE

(Caption—See Form 1.)

I voluntarily consent to have a United States magistrate judge conduct all further proceedings in this case, including a trial, and order the entry of final judgment. (Return this form to the court clerk—not to a judge or magistrate judge.)

Date_____

_____
Signature of the Party

## FORM 82.   ORDER OF ASSIGNMENT TO A MAGISTRATE JUDGE

(Caption—See Form 1.)

With the parties' consent it is ordered that this case be assigned to United States Magistrate Judge _____ of this district to conduct all proceedings and enter final judgment in accordance with 28 U.S.C. § 636(c).

Date _____

_____

United States District Judge

# SUPPLEMENTAL RULES FOR ADMIRALTY OR MARITIME CLAIMS AND ASSET FORFEITURE ACTIONS

## Effective July 1, 1966

### Including Amendments Effective December 1, 2006

## RULE A.  SCOPE OF RULES

(1) These Supplemental Rules apply to:

(A) the procedure in admiralty and maritime claims within the meaning of Rule 9(h) with respect to the following remedies:

(i) maritime attachment and garnishment,

(ii) actions in rem,

(iii) possessory, petitory, and partition actions, and

(iv) actions for exoneration from or limitation of liability;

(B) forfeiture actions in rem arising from a federal statute; and

(C) the procedure in statutory condemnation proceedings analogous to maritime actions in rem, whether within the admiralty and maritime jurisdiction or not. Except as otherwise provided, references in these Supplemental Rules to actions in rem include such analogous statutory condemnation proceedings.

(2) The Federal Rules of Civil Procedure also apply to the foregoing proceedings except to the extent that they are inconsistent with these Supplemental Rules.

[Amended effective December 1, 2006.]

## RULE B.  IN PERSONAM ACTIONS; ATTACHMENT AND GARNISHMENT

(1) **When Available; Complaint, Affidavit, Judicial Authorization, and Process.** In an in personam action:

(a) If a defendant is not found within the district when a verified complaint praying for attachment and the affidavit required by Rule B(1)(b) are filed, a verified complaint may contain a prayer for process to attach the defendant's tangible or intangible personal property—up to the amount sued for—in the hands of garnishees named in the process.

(b) The plaintiff or the plaintiff's attorney must sign and file with the complaint an affidavit stating that, to the affiant's knowledge, or on information and belief, the defendant cannot be found within the district. The court must review the complaint and affidavit and, if the conditions of this Rule B appear to exist, enter an order so stating and authorizing process of attachment and garnishment.  The clerk may issue supplemental process enforcing the court's order upon application without further court order.

(c) If the plaintiff or the plaintiff's attorney certifies that exigent circumstances make court review impracticable, the clerk must issue the summons and process of attachment and garnishment. The plaintiff has the burden in any post-attachment hearing under Rule E(4)(f) to show that exigent circumstances existed.

(d)(i) If the property is a vessel or tangible property on board a vessel, the summons, process, and any supplemental process must be delivered to the marshal for service.

(ii) If the property is other tangible or intangible property, the summons, process, and any supplemental process must be delivered to a person or organization authorized to serve it, who may be (A) a marshal; (B) someone under contract with the United States; (C) someone specially appointed by the court for that purpose; or, (D) in an action brought by the United States, any officer or employee of the United States.

(e) The plaintiff may invoke state-law remedies under Rule 64 for seizure of person or property for the purpose of securing satisfaction of the judgment.

(2) **Notice to Defendant.** No default judgment may be entered except upon proof—which may be by affidavit—that:

(a) the complaint, summons, and process of attachment or garnishment have been served on the defendant in a manner authorized by Rule 4;

(b) the plaintiff or the garnishee has mailed to the defendant the complaint, summons, and process of attachment or garnishment, using any form of mail requiring a return receipt; or

(c) the plaintiff or the garnishee has tried diligently to give notice of the action to the defendant but could not do so.

(3) **Answer.**

(a) *By Garnishee.*  The garnishee shall serve an answer, together with answers to any interrogatories served with the complaint, within 20 days after service

of process upon the garnishee. Interrogatories to the garnishee may be served with the complaint without leave of court. If the garnishee refuses or neglects to answer on oath as to the debts, credits, or effects of the defendant in the garnishee's hands, or any interrogatories concerning such debts, credits, and effects that may be propounded by the plaintiff, the court may award compulsory process against the garnishee. If the garnishee admits any debts, credits, or effects, they shall be held in the garnishee's hands or paid into the registry of the court, and shall be held in either case subject to the further order of the court.

(b) *By Defendant.* The defendant shall serve an answer within 30 days after process has been executed, whether by attachment of property or service on the garnishee.

[Amended April 29, 1985, effective August 1, 1985; March 2, 1987, effective August 1, 1987; April 17, 2000, effective December 1, 2000; April 25, 2005, effective December 1, 2005.]

## RULE C.   IN REM ACTIONS: SPECIAL PROVISIONS

**(1) When Available.** An action in rem may be brought:

(a) To enforce any maritime lien;

(b) Whenever a statute of the United States provides for a maritime action in rem or a proceeding analogous thereto.

Except as otherwise provided by law a party who may proceed in rem may also, or in the alternative, proceed in personam against any person who may be liable.

Statutory provisions exempting vessels or other property owned or possessed by or operated by or for the United States from arrest or seizure are not affected by this rule. When a statute so provides, an action against the United States or an instrumentality thereof may proceed on in rem principles.

**(2) Complaint.** In an action in rem the complaint must:

(a) be verified;

(b) describe with reasonable particularity the property that is the subject of the action; and

(c) state that the property is within the district or will be within the district while the action is pending.

**(3) Judicial Authorization and Process.**

(a) *Arrest Warrant.*

(i) The court must review the complaint and any supporting papers. If the conditions for an in rem action appear to exist, the court must issue an order directing the clerk to issue a warrant for the arrest of the vessel or other property that is the subject of the action.

(ii) If the plaintiff or the plaintiff's attorney certifies that exigent circumstances make court review impracticable, the clerk must promptly issue a summons and a warrant for the arrest of the vessel or other property that is the subject of the action. The plaintiff has the burden in any postarrest hearing under Rule E(4)(f) to show that exigent circumstances existed.

(b) *Service.*

(i) If the property that is the subject of the action is a vessel or tangible property on board a vessel, the warrant and any supplemental process must be delivered to the marshal for service.

(ii) If the property that is the subject of the action is other property, tangible or intangible, the warrant and any supplemental process must be delivered to a person or organization authorized to enforce it, who may be: (A) a marshal; (B) someone under contract with the United States; (C) someone specially appointed by the court for that purpose; or, (D) in an action brought by the United States, any officer or employee of the United States.

(c) *Deposit in Court.* If the property that is the subject of the action consists in whole or in part of freight, the proceeds of property sold, or other intangible property, the clerk must issue—in addition to the warrant—a summons directing any person controlling the property to show cause why it should not be deposited in court to abide the judgment.

(d) *Supplemental Process.* The clerk may upon application issue supplemental process to enforce the court's order without further court order.

**(4) Notice.** No notice other than execution of process is required when the property that is the subject of the action has been released under Rule E(5). If the property is not released within 10 days after execution, the plaintiff must promptly—or within the time that the court allows—give public notice of the action and arrest in a newspaper designated by court order and having general circulation in the district, but publication may be terminated if the property is released before publication is completed. The notice must specify the time under Rule C(6) to file a statement of interest in or right against the seized property and to answer. This rule does not affect the notice requirements in an action to foreclose a preferred ship mortgage under 46 U.S.C. §§ 31301 et seq., as amended.

**(5) Ancillary Process.** In any action in rem in which process has been served as provided by this rule, if any part of the property that is the subject of the action has not been brought within the control of the court because it has been removed or sold, or because it is intangible property in the hands of a

person who has not been served with process, the court may, on motion, order any person having possession or control of such property or its proceeds to show cause why it should not be delivered into the custody of the marshal or other person or organization having a warrant for the arrest of the property, or paid into court to abide the judgment; and, after hearing, the court may enter such judgment as law and justice may require.

### (6) Responsive Pleading; Interrogatories.

(a) *Maritime Arrests and Other Proceedings.*

(i) a* person who asserts a right of possession or any ownership interest in the property that is the subject of the action must file a verified statement of right or interest:

(A) within 10 days after the execution of process, or

(B) within the time that the court allows;

(ii) the* statement of right or interest must describe the interest in the property that supports the person's demand for its restitution or right to defend the action;

(iii) an* agent, bailee, or attorney must state the authority to file a statement of right or interest on behalf of another; and

(iv) a* person who asserts a right of possession or any ownership interest must serve an answer within 20 days after filing the statement of interest or right.

(b) *Interrogatories.* Interrogatories may be served with the complaint in an in rem action without leave of court. Answers to the interrogatories must be served with the answer to the complaint.

[Amended April 29, 1985, effective August 1, 1985; March 2, 1987, effective August 1, 1987; April 30, 1991, effective December 1, 1991; April 17, 2000, effective December 1, 2000; April 29, 2002, effective December 1, 2002; April 25, 2005, effective December 1, 2005; April 12, 2006, effective December 1, 2006.]

* So in copy. Beginning of paragraphs should probably now be capitalized.

## RULE D.  POSSESSORY, PETITORY, AND PARTITION ACTIONS

In all actions for possession, partition, and to try title maintainable according to the course of the admiralty practice with respect to a vessel, in all actions so maintainable with respect to the possession of cargo or other maritime property, and in all actions by one or more part owners against the others to obtain security for the return of the vessel from any voyage undertaken without their consent, or by one or more part owners against the others to obtain possession of the vessel for any voyage on giving security for its safe return, the process shall be by a warrant of arrest of the vessel, cargo, or other property, and by notice in the manner provided by Rule B(2) to the adverse party or parties.

## RULE E.  ACTIONS IN REM AND QUASI IN REM: GENERAL PROVISIONS

(1) **Applicability.**  Except as otherwise provided, this rule applies to actions in personam with process of maritime attachment and garnishment, actions in rem, and petitory, possessory, and partition actions, supplementing Rules B, C, and D.

(2) **Complaint; Security.**

(a) *Complaint.*  In actions to which this rule is applicable the complaint shall state the circumstances from which the claim arises with such particularity that the defendant or claimant will be able, without moving for a more definite statement, to commence an investigation of the facts and to frame a responsive pleading.

(b) *Security for Costs.*  Subject to the provisions of Rule 54(d) and of relevant statutes, the court may, on the filing of the complaint or on the appearance of any defendant, claimant, or any other party, or at any later time, require the plaintiff, defendant, claimant, or other party to give security, or additional security, in such sum as the court shall direct to pay all costs and expenses that shall be awarded against the party by any interlocutory order or by the final judgment, or on appeal by any appellate court.

(3) **Process.**

(a) In admiralty and maritime proceedings process in rem or of maritime attachment and garnishment may be served only within the district.

(b) *Issuance and Delivery.*  Issuance and delivery of process in rem, or of maritime attachment and garnishment, shall be held in abeyance if the plaintiff so requests.

(4) **Execution of Process;  Marshal's Return; Custody of Property;  Procedures for Release.**

(a) *In General.*  Upon issuance and delivery of the process, or, in the case of summons with process of attachment and garnishment, when it appears that the defendant cannot be found within the district, the marshal or other person or organization having a warrant shall forthwith execute the process in accordance with this subdivision (4), making due and prompt return.

(b) *Tangible Property.*  If tangible property is to be attached or arrested, the marshal or other person or organization having the warrant shall take it into the marshal's possession for safe custody. If the character or situation of the property is such that the taking of actual possession is impracticable, the marshal or other person executing the process shall affix a

copy thereof to the property in a conspicuous place and leave a copy of the complaint and process with the person having possession or the person's agent. In furtherance of the marshal's custody of any vessel the marshal is authorized to make a written request to the collector of customs not to grant clearance to such vessel until notified by the marshal or deputy marshal or by the clerk that the vessel has been released in accordance with these rules.

(c) *Intangible Property.* If intangible property is to be attached or arrested the marshal or other person or organization having the warrant shall execute the process by leaving with the garnishee or other obligor a copy of the complaint and process requiring the garnishee or other obligor to answer as provided in Rules B(3)(a) and C(6); or the marshal may accept for payment into the registry of the court the amount owed to the extent of the amount claimed by the plaintiff with interest and costs, in which event the garnishee or other obligor shall not be required to answer unless alias process shall be served.

(d) *Directions With Respect to Property in Custody.* The marshal or other person or organization having the warrant may at any time apply to the court for directions with respect to property that has been attached or arrested, and shall give notice of such application to any or all of the parties as the court may direct.

(e) *Expenses of Seizing and Keeping Property; Deposit.* These rules do not alter the provisions of Title 28, U.S.C., § 1921, as amended, relative to the expenses of seizing and keeping property attached or arrested and to the requirement of deposits to cover such expenses.

(f) *Procedure for Release From Arrest or Attachment.* Whenever property is arrested or attached, any person claiming an interest in it shall be entitled to a prompt hearing at which the plaintiff shall be required to show why the arrest or attachment should not be vacated or other relief granted consistent with these rules. This subdivision shall have no application to suits for seamen's wages when process is issued upon a certification of sufficient cause filed pursuant to Title 46, U.S.C. §§ 603 and 604* or to actions by the United States for forfeitures for violation of any statute of the United States.

**(5) Release of Property.**

(a) *Special Bond.* Whenever process of maritime attachment and garnishment or process in rem is issued the execution of such process shall be stayed, or the property released, on the giving of security, to be approved by the court or clerk, or by stipulation of the parties, conditioned to answer the judgment of the court or of any appellate court. The parties may stipulate the amount and nature of such security. In the event of the inability or refusal of the parties so to stipulate the court shall fix the principal sum of the bond or stipulation at an amount sufficient to cover the amount of the plaintiff's claim fairly stated with accrued interest and costs; but the principal sum shall in no event exceed (i) twice the amount of the plaintiff's claim or (ii) the value of the property on due appraisement, whichever is smaller. The bond or stipulation shall be conditioned for the payment of the principal sum and interest thereon at 6 per cent per annum.

(b) *General Bond.* The owner of any vessel may file a general bond or stipulation, with sufficient surety, to be approved by the court, conditioned to answer the judgment of such court in all or any actions that may be brought thereafter in such court in which the vessel is attached or arrested. Thereupon the execution of all such process against such vessel shall be stayed so long as the amount secured by such bond or stipulation is at least double the aggregate amount claimed by plaintiffs in all actions begun and pending in which such vessel has been attached or arrested. Judgments and remedies may be had on such bond or stipulation as if a special bond or stipulation had been filed in each of such actions. The district court may make necessary orders to carry this rule into effect, particularly as to the giving of proper notice of any action against or attachment of a vessel for which a general bond has been filed. Such bond or stipulation shall be indorsed by the clerk with a minute of the actions wherein process is so stayed. Further security may be required by the court at any time.

If a special bond or stipulation is given in a particular case, the liability on the general bond or stipulation shall cease as to that case.

(c) *Release by Consent or Stipulation; Order of Court or Clerk; Costs.* Any vessel, cargo, or other property in the custody of the marshal or other person or organization having the warrant may be released forthwith upon the marshal's acceptance and approval of a stipulation, bond, or other security, signed by the party on whose behalf the property is detained or the party's attorney and expressly authorizing such release, if all costs and charges of the court and its officers shall have first been paid. Otherwise no property in the custody of the marshal, other person or organization having the warrant, or other officer of the court shall be released without an order of the court; but such order may be entered as of course by the clerk, upon the giving of approved security as provided by law and these rules, or upon the dismissal or discontinuance of the action; but the marshal or other person or organization having the warrant shall not deliver any property so released until the costs and charges of the officers of the court shall first have been paid.

(d) *Possessory, Petitory, and Partition Actions.* The foregoing provisions of this subdivision (5) do not

apply to petitory, possessory, and partition actions. In such cases the property arrested shall be released only by order of the court, on such terms and conditions and on the giving of such security as the court may require.

**(6) Reduction or Impairment of Security.** Whenever security is taken the court may, on motion and hearing, for good cause shown, reduce the amount of security given; and if the surety shall be or become insufficient, new or additional sureties may be required on motion and hearing.

**(7) Security on Counterclaim.**

(a) When a person who has given security for damages in the original action asserts a counterclaim that arises from the transaction or occurrence that is the subject of the original action, a plaintiff for whose benefit the security has been given must give security for damages demanded in the counterclaim unless the court, for cause shown, directs otherwise. Proceedings on the original claim must be stayed until this security is given, unless the court directs otherwise.

(b) The plaintiff is required to give security under Rule E(7)(a) when the United States or its corporate instrumentality counterclaims and would have been required to give security to respond in damages if a private party but is relieved by law from giving security.

**(8) Restricted Appearance.** An appearance to defend against an admiralty and maritime claim with respect to which there has issued process in rem, or process of attachment and garnishment, may be expressly restricted to the defense of such claim, and in that event is not an appearance for the purposes of any other claim with respect to which such process is not available or has not been served.

**(9) Disposition of Property; Sales.**

(a) *Interlocutory Sales; Delivery.*

(i) On application of a party, the marshal, or other person having custody of the property, the court may order all or part of the property sold—with the sales proceeds, or as much of them as will satisfy the judgment, paid into court to await further orders of the court—if:

(A) the attached or arrested property is perishable, or liable to deterioration, decay, or injury by being detained in custody pending the action;

(B) the expense of keeping the property is excessive or disproportionate; or

(C) there is an unreasonable delay in securing release of the property.

(ii) In the circumstances described in Rule E(9)(a)(i), the court, on motion by a defendant or a person filing a statement of interest or right under Rule C(6), may order that the property, rather than

being sold, be delivered to the movant upon giving security under these rules.

(b) *Sales, Proceeds.* All sales of property shall be made by the marshal or a deputy marshal, or by other person or organization having the warrant, or by any other person assigned by the court where the marshal or other person or organization having the warrant is a party in interest; and the proceeds of sale shall be forthwith paid into the registry of the court to be disposed of according to law.

**(10) Preservation of Property.** When the owner or another person remains in possession of property attached or arrested under the provisions of Rule E(4)(b) that permit execution of process without taking actual possession, the court, on a party's motion or on its own, may enter any order necessary to preserve the property and to prevent its removal.

\* Law Revision Counsel Note: Repealed by Pub.L. 98–89, § 4(b), August 26, 1983, 97 Stat. 600, section 1 of which enacted Title 46, Shipping.

[Amended April 29, 1985, effective August 1, 1985; March 2, 1987, effective August 1, 1987; April 30, 1991, effective December 1, 1991; April 17, 2000, effective December 1, 2000; April 12, 2006, effective December 1, 2006.]

## RULE F.  LIMITATION OF LIABILITY

**(1) Time for Filing Complaint; Security.** Not later than six months after receipt of a claim in writing, any vessel owner may file a complaint in the appropriate district court, as provided in subdivision (9) of this rule, for limitation of liability pursuant to statute. The owner (a) shall deposit with the court, for the benefit of claimants, a sum equal to the amount or value of the owner's interest in the vessel and pending freight, or approved security therefor, and in addition such sums, or approved security therefor, as the court may from time to time fix as necessary to carry out the provisions of the statutes as amended; or (b) at the owner's option shall transfer to a trustee to be appointed by the court, for the benefit of claimants, the owner's interest in the vessel and pending freight, together with such sums, or approved security therefor, as the court may from time to time fix as necessary to carry out the provisions of the statutes as amended. The plaintiff shall also give security for costs and, if the plaintiff elects to give security, for interest at the rate of 6 percent per annum from the date of the security.

**(2) Complaint.** The complaint shall set forth the facts on the basis of which the right to limit liability is asserted and all facts necessary to enable the court to determine the amount to which the owner's liability shall be limited. The complaint may demand exoneration from as well as limitation of liability. It shall state the voyage if any, on which the demands sought to be limited arose, with the date and place of its termination; the amount of all demands including all

unsatisfied liens or claims of lien, in contract or in tort or otherwise, arising on that voyage, so far as known to the plaintiff, and what actions and proceedings, if any, are pending thereon; whether the vessel was damaged, lost, or abandoned, and, if so, when and where; the value of the vessel at the close of the voyage or, in case of wreck, the value of her wreckage, strippings, or proceeds, if any, and where and in whose possession they are; and the amount of any pending freight recovered or recoverable. If the plaintiff elects to transfer the plaintiff's interest in the vessel to a trustee, the complaint must further show any prior paramount liens thereon, and what voyages or trips, if any, she has made since the voyage or trip on which the claims sought to be limited arose, and any existing liens arising upon any such subsequent voyage or trip, with the amounts and causes thereof, and the names and addresses of the lienors, so far as known; and whether the vessel sustained any injury upon or by reason of such subsequent voyage or trip.

**(3) Claims Against Owner; Injunction.** Upon compliance by the owner with the requirements of subdivision (1) of this rule all claims and proceedings against the owner or the owner's property with respect to the matter in question shall cease. On application of the plaintiff the court shall enjoin the further prosecution of any action or proceeding against the plaintiff or the plaintiff's property with respect to any claim subject to limitation in the action.

**(4) Notice to Claimants.** Upon the owner's compliance with subdivision (1) of this rule the court shall issue a notice to all persons asserting claims with respect to which the complaint seeks limitation, admonishing them to file their respective claims with the clerk of the court and to serve on the attorneys for the plaintiff a copy thereof on or before a date to be named in the notice. The date so fixed shall not be less than 30 days after issuance of the notice. For cause shown, the court may enlarge the time within which claims may be filed. The notice shall be published in such newspaper or newspapers as the court may direct once a week for four successive weeks prior to the date fixed for the filing of claims. The plaintiff not later than the day of second publication shall also mail a copy of the notice to every person known to have made any claim against the vessel or the plaintiff arising out of the voyage or trip on which the claims sought to be limited arose. In cases involving death a copy of such notice shall be mailed to the decedent at the decedent's last known address, and also to any person who shall be known to have made any claim on account of such death.

**(5) Claims and Answer.** Claims shall be filed and served on or before the date specified in the notice provided for in subdivision (4) of this rule. Each claim shall specify the facts upon which the claimant relies in support of the claim, the items thereof, and the dates on which the same accrued. If a claimant desires to contest either the right to exoneration from or the right to limitation of liability the claimant shall file and serve an answer to the complaint unless the claim has included an answer.

**(6) Information to Be Given Claimants.** Within 30 days after the date specified in the notice for filing claims, or within such time as the court thereafter may allow, the plaintiff shall mail to the attorney for each claimant (or if the claimant has no attorney to the claimant) a list setting forth (a) the name of each claimant, (b) the name and address of the claimant's attorney (if the claimant is known to have one), (c) the nature of the claim, i.e., whether property loss, property damage, death, personal injury etc., and (d) the amount thereof.

**(7) Insufficiency of Fund or Security.** Any claimant may by motion demand that the funds deposited in court or the security given by the plaintiff be increased on the ground that they are less than the value of the plaintiff's interest in the vessel and pending freight. Thereupon the court shall cause due appraisement to be made of the value of the plaintiff's interest in the vessel and pending freight; and if the court finds that the deposit or security is either insufficient or excessive it shall order its increase or reduction. In like manner any claimant may demand that the deposit or security be increased on the ground that it is insufficient to carry out the provisions of the statutes relating to claims in respect of loss of life or bodily injury; and, after notice and hearing, the court may similarly order that the deposit or security be increased or reduced.

**(8) Objections to Claims: Distribution of Fund.** Any interested party may question or controvert any claim without filing an objection thereto. Upon determination of liability the fund deposited or secured, or the proceeds of the vessel and pending freight, shall be divided pro rata, subject to all relevant provisions of law, among the several claimants in proportion to the amounts of their respective claims, duly proved, saving, however, to all parties any priority to which they may be legally entitled.

**(9) Venue; Transfer.** The complaint shall be filed in any district in which the vessel has been attached or arrested to answer for any claim with respect to which the plaintiff seeks to limit liability; or, if the vessel has not been attached or arrested, then in any district in which the owner has been sued with respect to any such claim. When the vessel has not been attached or arrested to answer the matters aforesaid, and suit has not been commenced against the owner, the proceedings may be had in the district in which the vessel may be, but if the vessel is not within any district and no suit has been commenced in any district, then the complaint may be filed in any district. For the convenience of parties and witnesses, in the

interest of justice, the court may transfer the action to any district; if venue is wrongly laid the court shall dismiss or, if it be in the interest of justice, transfer the action to any district in which it could have been brought. If the vessel shall have been sold, the proceeds shall represent the vessel for the purposes of these rules.

[Amended March 2, 1987, effective August 1, 1987.]

## RULE G. FORFEITURE ACTIONS IN REM

**(1) Scope.** This rule governs a forfeiture action in rem arising from a federal statute. To the extent that this rule does not address an issue, Supplemental Rules C and E and the Federal Rules of Civil Procedure also apply.

**(2) Complaint.** The complaint must:

(a) be verified;

(b) state the grounds for subject-matter jurisdiction, in rem jurisdiction over the defendant property, and venue;

(c) describe the property with reasonable particularity;

(d) if the property is tangible, state its location when any seizure occurred and—if different—its location when the action is filed;

(e) identify the statute under which the forfeiture action is brought; and

(f) state sufficiently detailed facts to support a reasonable belief that the government will be able to meet its burden of proof at trial.

**(3) Judicial Authorization and Process.**

(a) *Real Property.* If the defendant is real property, the government must proceed under 18 U.S.C. § 985.

(b) *Other Property; Arrest Warrant.* If the defendant is not real property:

(i) the clerk must issue a warrant to arrest the property if it is in the government's possession, custody, or control;

(ii) the court—on finding probable cause—must issue a warrant to arrest the property if it is not in the government's possession, custody, or control and is not subject to a judicial restraining order; and

(iii) a warrant is not necessary if the property is subject to a judicial restraining order.

(c) *Execution of Process.*

(i) The warrant and any supplemental process must be delivered to a person or organization authorized to execute it, who may be: (A) a marshal or any other United States officer or employee; (B) someone under contract with the United States; or

(C) someone specially appointed by the court for that purpose.

(ii) The authorized person or organization must execute the warrant and any supplemental process on property in the United States as soon as practicable unless:

(A) the property is in the government's possession, custody, or control; or

(B) the court orders a different time when the complaint is under seal, the action is stayed before the warrant and supplemental process are executed, or the court finds other good cause.

(iii) The warrant and any supplemental process may be executed within the district or, when authorized by statute, outside the district.

(iv) If executing a warrant on property outside the United States is required, the warrant may be transmitted to an appropriate authority for serving process where the property is located.

**(4) Notice.**

(a) *Notice by Publication.*

(i) When Publication Is Required. A judgment of forfeiture may be entered only if the government has published notice of the action within a reasonable time after filing the complaint or at a time the court orders. But notice need not be published if:

(A) the defendant property is worth less than $1,000 and direct notice is sent under Rule G(4)(b) to every person the government can reasonably identify as a potential claimant; or

(B) the court finds that the cost of publication exceeds the property's value and that other means of notice would satisfy due process.

(ii) Content of the Notice. Unless the court orders otherwise, the notice must:

(A) describe the property with reasonable particularity;

(B) state the times under Rule G(5) to file a claim and to answer; and

(C) name the government attorney to be served with the claim and answer.

(iii) Frequency of Publication. Published notice must appear:

(A) once a week for three consecutive weeks; or

(B) only once if, before the action was filed, notice of nonjudicial forfeiture of the same property was published on an official internet government forfeiture site for at least 30 consecutive days, or in a newspaper of general circulation for three consecutive weeks in a district where publication is authorized under Rule G(4)(a)(iv).

(iv) Means of Publication. The government should select from the following options a means of publication reasonably calculated to notify potential claimants of the action:

(A) if the property is in the United States, publication in a newspaper generally circulated in the district where the action is filed, where the property was seized, or where property that was not seized is located;

(B) if the property is outside the United States, publication in a newspaper generally circulated in a district where the action is filed, in a newspaper generally circulated in the country where the property is located, or in legal notices published and generally circulated in the country where the property is located; or

(C) instead of (A) or (B), posting a notice on an official internet government forfeiture site for at least 30 consecutive days.

(b) *Notice to Known Potential Claimants.*

(i) Direct Notice Required. The government must send notice of the action and a copy of the complaint to any person who reasonably appears to be a potential claimant on the facts known to the government before the end of the time for filing a claim under Rule G(5)(a)(ii)(B).

(ii) Content of the Notice. The notice must state:

(A) the date when the notice is sent;

(B) a deadline for filing a claim, at least 35 days after the notice is sent;

(C) that an answer or a motion under Rule 12 must be filed no later than 20 days after filing the claim; and

(D) the name of the government attorney to be served with the claim and answer.

(iii) Sending Notice.

(A) The notice must be sent by means reasonably calculated to reach the potential claimant.

(B) Notice may be sent to the potential claimant or to the attorney representing the potential claimant with respect to the seizure of the property or in a related investigation, administrative forfeiture proceeding, or criminal case.

(C) Notice sent to a potential claimant who is incarcerated must be sent to the place of incarceration.

(D) Notice to a person arrested in connection with an offense giving rise to the forfeiture who is not incarcerated when notice is sent may be sent to the address that person last gave to the agency that arrested or released the person.

(E) Notice to a person from whom the property was seized who is not incarcerated when notice is sent may be sent to the last address that person gave to the agency that seized the property.

(iv) When Notice Is Sent. Notice by the following means is sent on the date when it is placed in the mail, delivered to a commercial carrier, or sent by electronic mail.

(v) Actual Notice. A potential claimant who had actual notice of a forfeiture action may not oppose or seek relief from forfeiture because of the government's failure to send the required notice.

**(5) Responsive Pleadings.**

(a) *Filing a Claim.*

(i) A person who asserts an interest in the defendant property may contest the forfeiture by filing a claim in the court where the action is pending. The claim must:

(A) identify the specific property claimed;

(B) identify the claimant and state the claimant's interest in the property;

(C) be signed by the claimant under penalty of perjury; and

(D) be served on the government attorney designated under Rule G(4)(a)(ii)(C) or (b)(ii)(D).

(ii) Unless the court for good cause sets a different time, the claim must be filed:

(A) by the time stated in a direct notice sent under Rule G(4)(b);

(B) if notice was published but direct notice was not sent to the claimant or the claimant's attorney, no later than 30 days after final publication of newspaper notice or legal notice under Rule G(4)(a) or no later than 60 days after the first day of publication on an official internet government forfeiture site; or

(C) if notice was not published and direct notice was not sent to the claimant or the claimant's attorney:

(1) if the property was in the government's possession, custody, or control when the complaint was filed, no later than 60 days after the filing, not counting any time when the complaint was under seal or when the action was stayed before execution of a warrant issued under Rule G(3)(b); or

(2) if the property was not in the government's possession, custody, or control when the complaint was filed, no later than 60 days after the government complied with 18 U.S.C. § 985(c) as to real property, or 60 days after process was executed on the property under Rule G(3).

(iii) A claim filed by a person asserting an interest as a bailee must identify the bailor, and if filed on the bailor's behalf must state the authority to do so.

(b) *Answer.* A claimant must serve and file an answer to the complaint or a motion under Rule 12 within 20 days after filing the claim. A claimant waives an objection to in rem jurisdiction or to venue if the objection is not made by motion or stated in the answer.

**(6) Special Interrogatories.**

(a) *Time and Scope.* The government may serve special interrogatories limited to the claimant's identity and relationship to the defendant property without the court's leave at any time after the claim is filed and before discovery is closed. But if the claimant serves a motion to dismiss the action, the government must serve the interrogatories within 20 days after the motion is served.

(b) *Answers or Objections.* Answers or objections to these interrogatories must be served within 20 days after the interrogatories are served.

(c) *Government's Response Deferred.* The government need not respond to a claimant's motion to dismiss the action under Rule G(8)(b) until 20 days after the claimant has answered these interrogatories.

**(7) Preserving, Preventing Criminal Use, and Disposing of Property; Sales.**

(a) *Preserving and Preventing Criminal Use of Property.* When the government does not have actual possession of the defendant property the court, on motion or on its own, may enter any order necessary to preserve the property, to prevent its removal or encumbrance, or to prevent its use in a criminal offense.

(b) *Interlocutory Sale or Delivery.*

(i) Order to Sell. On motion by a party or a person having custody of the property, the court may order all or part of the property sold if:

(A) the property is perishable or at risk of deterioration, decay, or injury by being detained in custody pending the action;

(B) the expense of keeping the property is excessive or is disproportionate to its fair market value;

(C) the property is subject to a mortgage or to taxes on which the owner is in default; or

(D) the court finds other good cause.

(ii) Who Makes the Sale. A sale must be made by a United States agency that has authority to sell the property, by the agency's contractor, or by any person the court designates.

(iii) Sale Procedures. The sale is governed by 28 U.S.C. §§ 2001, 2002, and 2004, unless all parties, with the court's approval, agree to the sale, aspects of the sale, or different procedures.

(iv) Sale Proceeds. Sale proceeds are a substitute res subject to forfeiture in place of the property that was sold. The proceeds must be held in an interest-bearing account maintained by the United States pending the conclusion of the forfeiture action.

(v) Delivery on a Claimant's Motion. The court may order that the property be delivered to the claimant pending the conclusion of the action if the claimant shows circumstances that would permit sale under Rule G(7)(b)(i) and gives security under these rules.

(c) *Disposing of Forfeited Property.* Upon entry of a forfeiture judgment, the property or proceeds from selling the property must be disposed of as provided by law.

**(8) Motions.**

(a) *Motion To Suppress Use of the Property as Evidence.* If the defendant property was seized, a party with standing to contest the lawfulness of the seizure may move to suppress use of the property as evidence. Suppression does not affect forfeiture of the property based on independently derived evidence.

(b) *Motion To Dismiss the Action.*

(i) A claimant who establishes standing to contest forfeiture may move to dismiss the action under Rule 12(b).

(ii) In an action governed by 18 U.S.C. § 983(a)(3)(D) the complaint may not be dismissed on the ground that the government did not have adequate evidence at the time the complaint was filed to establish the forfeitability of the property. The sufficiency of the complaint is governed by Rule G(2).

(c) *Motion To Strike a Claim or Answer.*

(i) At any time before trial, the government may move to strike a claim or answer:

(A) for failing to comply with Rule G(5) or (6), or

(B) because the claimant lacks standing.

(ii) The motion:

(A) must be decided before any motion by the claimant to dismiss the action; and

(B) may be presented as a motion for judgment on the pleadings or as a motion to determine after a hearing or by summary judgment whether the claimant can carry the burden of establishing standing by a preponderance of the evidence.

(d) *Petition To Release Property.*

(i) If a United States agency or an agency's contractor holds property for judicial or nonjudicial forfeiture under a statute governed by 18 U.S.C.

§ 983(f), a person who has filed a claim to the property may petition for its release under § 983(f).

(ii) If a petition for release is filed before a judicial forfeiture action is filed against the property, the petition may be filed either in the district where the property was seized or in the district where a warrant to seize the property issued. If a judicial forfeiture action against the property is later filed in another district—or if the government shows that the action will be filed in another district—the petition may be transferred to that district under 28 U.S.C. § 1404.

(e) *Excessive Fines.* A claimant may seek to mitigate a forfeiture under the Excessive Fines Clause of the Eighth Amendment by motion for summary judgment or by motion made after entry of a forfeiture judgment if:

(i) the claimant has pleaded the defense under Rule 8; and

(ii) the parties have had the opportunity to conduct civil discovery on the defense.

**(9) Trial.** Trial is to the court unless any party demands trial by jury under Rule 38.

[Effective December 1, 2006.]

# INDEX TO
## FEDERAL RULES OF CIVIL PROCEDURE

**COMMITTEES**
Incompetent person, action or defense, **FRCVP 17**

**COMMONWEALTH**
Official record, authentication, **FRCVP 44**

**COMPENSATION AND SALARIES**
Interpreters, **FRCVP 43**
Masters, **FRCVP 53**

**COMPLAINTS**
Pleadings, this index

**COMPLICATED ISSUES**
Reference to master, **FRCVP 53**

**COMPROMISE AND SETTLEMENT**
Class actions, **FRCVP 23**
Derivative actions by shareholders, **FRCVP 23.1**
Unincorporated associations, actions relating, **FRCVP 23.2**

**COMPULSORY COUNTERCLAIMS**
Pleading, **FRCVP 13**

**COMPULSORY PROCESS**
Admiralty and maritime claims, refusal by garnishee to answer, **FRCVP B**

**CONCISENESS**
Pleading, **FRCVP 8**

**CONCLUSIONS OF LAW**
Amendment on motion for new trial, **FRCVP 59**
Findings by court, **FRCVP 52**
Masters, setting forth in report, **FRCVP 53**

**CONDEMNATION OF PROPERTY**
Generally, **FRCVP 71A**
Complaint, **FRCVP Form 29**
Notice, **FRCVP Form 28**

**CONDITIONAL RULINGS**
Grant of motion, judgment as a matter of law, **FRCVP 50**

**CONDITIONS PRECEDENT**
Pleading, **FRCVP 9**

**CONFERENCES**
Pretrial conferences, **FRCVP 16**

**CONFIDENTIAL OR PRIVILEGED INFORMATION**
Discovery, protective orders, **FRCVP 26**

**CONFLICT OF INTEREST**
Depositions, person taking, disqualification, **FRCVP 28**

**CONFLICT OF LAWS**
Capacity to sue or be sued, **FRCVP 17**

**CONSENT**
Parties,
    Order for trial by jury, **FRCVP 39**
    Trial by court, **FRCVP 39**
    Withdrawal of demand for jury trial, **FRCVP 38**
Release, property, admiralty and maritime claims, actions in rem and quasi in rem, **FRCVP E**

**CONSERVATORS AND CONSERVATORSHIP**
Infants or incompetents, action or defense, **FRCVP 17**

**CONSIDERATION**
Pleading, failure of consideration, defenses, **FRCVP 8**

**CONSOLIDATION**
Merger and Consolidation, generally, this index

**CONSTITUTIONALITY**
Generally, **FRCVP 5.1**

**CONSULS AND CONSULAR AGENTS**
Authentication of official record, **FRCVP 44**
Depositions, taking, **FRCVP 28**

**CONTEMPT**
Depositions, refusal to answer, **FRCVP 37(b)**
Discovery, sanction for failure to comply with order compelling, **FRCVP 37(b)**
Service of order, **FRCVP 4.1**
Subpoena, disobedience, **FRCVP 45**
Summary judgment, filing affidavit in bad faith, **FRCVP 56**

**CONTINUANCES**
Pleading, amendment, conforming to evidence, **FRCVP 15**
Summary judgment, continuance to procure opposing affidavit, **FRCVP 56**

**CONTRADICTING TESTIMONY**
Deponents, use of deposition in court proceedings, **FRCVP 32**

**CONTRIBUTION**
Liability, third party practice, admiralty and maritime claims, **FRCVP 14**

**CONTRIBUTORY NEGLIGENCE**
Affirmative defenses, **FRCVP 8**

**CONVERSION**
Complaint in action, form, **FRCVP Form 11**

**COPIES**
Business records, interrogatories, **FRCVP 33**
Documents, service with requests for admission, **FRCVP 36**
Foreign official records, authentication, **FRCVP 44**
Order for copying, **FRCVP 27**
Process, execution, admiralty and maritime claims, actions in rem and quasi in rem, **FRCVP E**
Production of Documents or Things, generally, this index
Written instruments, exhibit as part of pleading, **FRCVP 10**

**COPYRIGHTS**
Complaints, infringement, **FRCVP Form 17**
Inapplicability of rules, **FRCVP 81**
Injunctions, **FRCVP 65**

**CORAM NOBIS**
Writ abolished, **FRCVP 60**

**CORAM VOBIS**
Writ abolished, **FRCVP 60**

**CORPORATIONS**
Admiralty and maritime claims, actions in rem and quasi in rem, security, **FRCVP E**
Capacity to sue or be sued, determination, **FRCVP 17**
Depositions,
    Oral examination,
        Failure of officer or director to attend at own deposition, sanctions, **FRCVP 37(d)**
        Failure to comply with order compelling designation, sanctions, **FRCVP 37(b)**
        Motion for order compelling designation, **FRCVP 37(a)**
    Use in court proceedings, **FRCVP 32**

**ORDERS**—Cont'd

Consolidation, preliminary injunction hearing with trial on merits, **FRCVP 65**

Depositions, **FRCVP 27**

    Failure of party to attend at own deposition, sanctions, **FRCVP 37(d)**

Discovery, this index

Dismissal of action,

    Condemnation of property, **FRCVP 71A**

    Receivers appointment, **FRCVP 66**

Documents, failure to admit genuineness, award of expenses, **FRCVP 37(c)**

Entry upon land, failure of party to respond to request for inspection, sanctions, **FRCVP 37(d)**

Examiners report, physical and mental examinations, delivery, **FRCVP 35**

Exceptions unnecessary, **FRCVP 46**

Fraud, relief from order, **FRCVP 60**

Interrogatories,

    Answers, **FRCVP 33**

    Failure of party to serve answers, sanctions, **FRCVP 37(d)**

    Objections or failure to answer, **FRCVP 33**

Joinder, persons needed for just adjudication, **FRCVP 19**

Judgment includes order, **FRCVP 54**

Magistrate judges, referral of cases, **FRCVP Form 34A**

Masters, **FRCVP 53**

Mental examination, **FRCVP 27**

Misconduct of party, relief from order, **FRCVP 60**

Motions, this index

Multiple claims or involving multiple parties, termination of action, **FRCVP 54**

New trial, **FRCVP 59**

Newly discovered evidence, relief from order, **FRCVP 60**

Notice of entry given by clerk, **FRCVP 77**

Physical and mental examinations, **FRCVP 35**

Pretrial order, after conference, **FRCVP 16**

Production of documents or things, failure of party to respond to request for inspection, sanctions, **FRCVP 37(d)**

Protective Orders, generally, this index

Reference to master, **FRCVP 53**

Sanctions,

    Representations to court, **FRCVP 11**

    Scheduling or pretrial orders, **FRCVP 16**

Scheduling, pretrial conference, **FRCVP 16**

Service, **FRCVP 5(a)**

    Pleading, numerous defendants, **FRCVP 5(c)**

Substitution of parties, public officers ceasing to hold office, **FRCVP 25**

Sufficiency of answers or objections to requests for admission, **FRCVP 36**

Truth of matter, failure to admit, award of expenses, **FRCVP 37(c)**

Unincorporated associations, actions relating, **FRCVP 23.2**

Voluntary dismissal, **FRCVP 41**

## ORIGINAL RULES AND AMENDMENTS

Actions governed, **FRCVP 86**

## OWNERS

Admiralty and maritime claims against limitation of liability, **FRCVP F**

## PAPERS

Books and Papers, generally, this index

## PARAGRAPHS

Pleading, **FRCVP 10**

**PARTIAL FINDINGS**

Judgments, **FRCVP 52**

**PARTIES**

Additional parties, joinder, counterclaim or cross claim, **FRCVP 13**

Admissions, generally, this index

Capacity to sue or be sued, determination, **FRCVP 17**

Changes, pleadings, amendments, relation back, **FRCVP 15**

Class actions, **FRCVP 23**

Compensation of master, payment, **FRCVP 53**

Conference, discovery matters, **FRCVP 26**

Consent, withdrawal of demand for jury trial, **FRCVP 38**

Corporations,

    Capacity to sue or be sued, **FRCVP 17**

    Disclosure statement, owners and ownership, **FRCVP 7.1**

Cross claim against coparty, **FRCVP 13**

Death, substitution, **FRCVP 25**

Defendants, bringing in third party, **FRCVP 14**

Depositions, generally, this index

Disclosure, motion to compel, **FRCVP 37**

Discovery, **FRCVP 26 et seq.**

Dismissal for lack of an indispensable party, **FRCVP 41**

Failure to join, **FRCVP 12**

Inability to protect property interest, intervention, **FRCVP 24**

Incompetency, **FRCVP 17**

    Substitution, **FRCVP 25**

Indispensable party, dismissal for lack, **FRCVP 41**

Infants, **FRCVP 17**

Interpleader, generally, this index

Interrogatories, generally, this index

Intervention, **FRCVP 24**

    Form, **FRCVP Form 23**

Joinder, **FRCVP 19 et seq.**

    Additional parties, counterclaim or cross claim, **FRCVP 13**

    Class actions, impracticability, **FRCVP 23**

    Dismissal for failure to join, **FRCVP 41**

    Misjoinder or nonjoinder, **FRCVP 12, 21**

    Service of summons, establishing personal jurisdiction, **FRCVP 4(k)**

Misjoinder or nonjoinder, **FRCVP 12, 21**

Motions,

    Bringing in third party defendant, form, **FRCVP Form 22-B**

    Defenses, pleadings, defects, **FRCVP 12**

Multiple parties, judgment, **FRCVP 54**

    Stay of enforcement, **FRCVP 62**

Needed for just adjudication,

    Defense, failure to join, **FRCVP 12**

    Joinder, **FRCVP 19**

Notice, generally, this index

Partnership, capacity to sue or to be sued, **FRCVP 17**

Physical and Mental Examinations, generally, this index

Plaintiffs,

    Bringing in third party, **FRCVP 14**

    Default judgment against, **FRCVP 55**

    Real party in interest, **FRCVP 17**

    Voluntary dismissal, **FRCVP 41**

Planning meeting, report, **FRCVP Form 35**

Pleadings,

    Captions, names, **FRCVP 10**

    Reason for omitting, form, **FRCVP Form 26**

Process in behalf of and against persons not parties, **FRCVP 71**

Public officer, substitution, **FRCVP 25**

Real party in interest, prosecution of action, **FRCVP 17**

Receiver, law governing capacity to sue or be sued, **FRCVP 17**

Representations to court, **FRCVP 11**

\*

# FEDERAL RULES OF EVIDENCE

### Effective July 1, 1975

### Including Amendments Effective
### December 1, 2006

---

*Research Note*

*These rules may be searched electronically on WESTLAW in the US–RULES database; updates to these rules may be found on WESTLAW in US–ORDERS or US–RULESUPDATES. For search tips, and a detailed summary of database content, consult the WESTLAW Scope Screen of each database.*

---

*Table of Rules*

# ARTICLE I.  GENERAL PROVISIONS

## RULE 101.  SCOPE

These rules govern proceedings in the courts of the United States and before the United States bankruptcy judges and United States magistrate judges, to the extent and with the exceptions stated in rule 1101.

[Amended March 2, 1987, effective October 1, 1987; April 25, 1988, effective November 1, 1988; April 22, 1993, effective December 1, 1993.]

## RULE 102.  PURPOSE AND CONSTRUCTION

These rules shall be construed to secure fairness in administration, elimination of unjustifiable expense and delay, and promotion of growth and development of the law of evidence to the end that the truth may be ascertained and proceedings justly determined.

## RULE 103.  RULINGS ON EVIDENCE

**(a) Effect of Erroneous Ruling.** Error may not be predicated upon a ruling which admits or excludes evidence unless a substantial right of the party is affected, and

(1) *Objection.* In case the ruling is one admitting evidence, a timely objection or motion to strike appears of record, stating the specific ground of objection, if the specific ground was not apparent from the context; or

(2) *Offer of Proof.* In case the ruling is one excluding evidence, the substance of the evidence was made known to the court by offer or was apparent from the context within which questions were asked.

Once the court makes a definitive ruling on the record admitting or excluding evidence, either at or before trial, a party need not renew an objection or offer of proof to preserve a claim of error for appeal.

**(b) Record of Offer and Ruling.** The court may add any other or further statement which shows the character of the evidence, the form in which it was offered, the objection made, and the ruling thereon.

It may direct the making of an offer in question and answer form.

**(c) Hearing of Jury.** In jury cases, proceedings shall be conducted, to the extent practicable, so as to prevent inadmissible evidence from being suggested to the jury by any means, such as making statements or offers of proof or asking questions in the hearing of the jury.

**(d) Plain Error.** Nothing in this rule precludes taking notice of plain errors affecting substantial rights although they were not brought to the attention of the court.

[Amended April 17, 2000, effective December 1, 2000.]

## RULE 104.  PRELIMINARY QUESTIONS

**(a) Questions of Admissibility Generally.** Preliminary questions concerning the qualification of a person to be a witness, the existence of a privilege, or the admissibility of evidence shall be determined by the court, subject to the provisions of subdivision (b). In making its determination it is not bound by the rules of evidence except those with respect to privileges.

**(b) Relevancy Conditioned on Fact.** When the relevancy of evidence depends upon the fulfillment of a condition of fact, the court shall admit it upon, or subject to, the introduction of evidence sufficient to support a finding of the fulfillment of the condition.

**(c) Hearing of Jury.** Hearings on the admissibility of confessions shall in all cases be conducted out of the hearing of the jury. Hearings on other preliminary matters shall be so conducted when the interests of justice require, or when an accused is a witness and so requests.

**(d) Testimony by Accused.** The accused does not, by testifying upon a preliminary matter, become subject to cross-examination as to other issues in the case.

**(e) Weight and Credibility.** This rule does not limit the right of a party to introduce before the jury evidence relevant to weight or credibility.

[Amended March 2, 1987, effective October 1, 1987.]

## RULE 105.  LIMITED ADMISSIBILITY

When evidence which is admissible as to one party or for one purpose but not admissible as to another party or for another purpose is admitted, the court, upon request, shall restrict the evidence to its proper scope and instruct the jury accordingly.

## RULE 106.  REMAINDER OF OR RELATED WRITINGS OR RECORDED STATEMENTS

When a writing or recorded statement or part thereof is introduced by a party, an adverse party may require the introduction at that time of any other part or any other writing or recorded statement which ought in fairness to be considered contemporaneously with it.

[Amended March 2, 1987, effective October 1, 1987.]

# ARTICLE II.  JUDICIAL NOTICE

## RULE 201.  JUDICIAL NOTICE OF ADJUDICATIVE FACTS

**(a) Scope of Rule.** This rule governs only judicial notice of adjudicative facts.

**(b) Kinds of Facts.** A judicially noticed fact must be one not subject to reasonable dispute in that it is either (1) generally known within the territorial jurisdiction of the trial court or (2) capable of accurate and ready determination by resort to sources whose accuracy cannot reasonably be questioned.

**(c) When Discretionary.** A court may take judicial notice, whether requested or not.

**(d) When Mandatory.** A court shall take judicial notice if requested by a party and supplied with the necessary information.

**(e) Opportunity to Be Heard.** A party is entitled upon timely request to an opportunity to be heard as to the propriety of taking judicial notice and the tenor of the matter noticed. In the absence of prior notification, the request may be made after judicial notice has been taken.

**(f) Time of Taking Notice.** Judicial notice may be taken at any stage of the proceeding.

**(g) Instructing Jury.** In a civil action or proceeding, the court shall instruct the jury to accept as conclusive any fact judicially noticed. In a criminal case, the court shall instruct the jury that it may, but is not required to, accept as conclusive any fact judicially noticed.

# ARTICLE III.  PRESUMPTIONS IN CIVIL ACTIONS AND PROCEEDINGS

## RULE 301.  PRESUMPTIONS IN GENERAL IN CIVIL ACTIONS AND PROCEEDINGS

In all civil actions and proceedings not otherwise provided for by Act of Congress or by these rules, a presumption imposes on the party against whom it is directed the burden of going forward with evidence to rebut or meet the presumption, but does not shift to such party the burden of proof in the sense of the risk of nonpersuasion, which remains throughout the trial upon the party on whom it was originally cast.

## RULE 302.  APPLICABILITY OF STATE LAW IN CIVIL ACTIONS AND PROCEEDINGS

In civil actions and proceedings, the effect of a presumption respecting a fact which is an element of a claim or defense as to which State law supplies the rule of decision is determined in accordance with State law.

# ARTICLE IV.  RELEVANCY AND ITS LIMITS

## RULE 401.  DEFINITION OF "RELEVANT EVIDENCE"

"Relevant evidence" means evidence having any tendency to make the existence of any fact that is of consequence to the determination of the action more probable or less probable than it would be without the evidence.

## RULE 402.  RELEVANT EVIDENCE GENERALLY ADMISSIBLE; IRRELEVANT EVIDENCE INADMISSIBLE

All relevant evidence is admissible, except as otherwise provided by the Constitution of the United States, by Act of Congress, by these rules, or by other

rules prescribed by the Supreme Court pursuant to statutory authority. Evidence which is not relevant is not admissible.

# RULE 403. EXCLUSION OF RELEVANT EVIDENCE ON GROUNDS OF PREJUDICE, CONFUSION, OR WASTE OF TIME

Although relevant, evidence may be excluded if its probative value is substantially outweighed by the danger of unfair prejudice, confusion of the issues, or misleading the jury, or by considerations of undue delay, waste of time, or needless presentation of cumulative evidence.

# RULE 404. CHARACTER EVIDENCE NOT ADMISSIBLE TO PROVE CONDUCT; EXCEPTIONS; OTHER CRIMES

**(a) Character Evidence Generally.** Evidence of a person's character or a trait of character is not admissible for the purpose of proving action in conformity therewith on a particular occasion, except:

(1) *Character of Accused.* In a criminal case, evidence of a pertinent trait of character offered by an accused, or by the prosecution to rebut the same, or if evidence of a trait of character of the alleged victim of the crime is offered by an accused and admitted under Rule 404(a)(2), evidence of the same trait of character of the accused offered by the prosecution;

(2) *Character of Alleged Victim.* In a criminal case, and subject to the limitations imposed by Rule 412, evidence of a pertinent trait of character of the alleged victim of the crime offered by an accused, or by the prosecution to rebut the same, or evidence of a character trait of peacefulness of the alleged victim offered by the prosecution in a homicide case to rebut evidence that the alleged victim was the first aggressor;

(3) *Character of Witness.* Evidence of the character of a witness, as provided in Rules 607, 608, and 609.

**(b) Other Crimes, Wrongs, or Acts.** Evidence of other crimes, wrongs, or acts is not admissible to prove the character of a person in order to show action in conformity therewith. It may, however, be admissible for other purposes, such as proof of motive, opportunity, intent, preparation, plan, knowledge, identity, or absence of mistake or accident, provided that upon request by the accused, the prosecution in a criminal case shall provide reasonable notice in advance of trial, or during trial if the court excuses pretrial notice on good cause shown, of the general nature of any such evidence it intends to introduce at trial.

[Amended March 2, 1987, effective October 1, 1987; April 30, 1991, effective December 1, 1991; April 17, 2000, effective December 1, 2000; April 12, 2006, effective December 1, 2006.]

# RULE 405. METHODS OF PROVING CHARACTER

**(a) Reputation or Opinion.** In all cases in which evidence of character or a trait of character of a person is admissible, proof may be made by testimony as to reputation or by testimony in the form of an opinion. On cross-examination, inquiry is allowable into relevant specific instances of conduct.

**(b) Specific Instances of Conduct.** In cases in which character or a trait of character of a person is an essential element of a charge, claim, or defense, proof may also be made of specific instances of that person's conduct.

[Amended March 2, 1987, effective October 1, 1987.]

# RULE 406. HABIT; ROUTINE PRACTICE

Evidence of the habit of a person or of the routine practice of an organization, whether corroborated or not and regardless of the presence of eyewitnesses, is relevant to prove that the conduct of the person or organization on a particular occasion was in conformity with the habit or routine practice.

# RULE 407. SUBSEQUENT REMEDIAL MEASURES

When, after an injury or harm allegedly caused by an event, measures are taken that, if taken previously, would have made the injury or harm less likely to occur, evidence of the subsequent measures is not admissible to prove negligence, culpable conduct, a defect in a product, a defect in a product's design, or a need for a warning or instruction. This rule does not require the exclusion of evidence of subsequent measures when offered for another purpose, such as proving ownership, control, or feasibility of precautionary measures, if controverted, or impeachment.

[Amended April 11, 1997, effective December 1, 1997.]

# RULE 408. COMPROMISE AND OFFERS TO COMPROMISE

**(a) Prohibited Uses.** Evidence of the following is not admissible on behalf of any party, when offered to prove liability for, invalidity of, or amount of a claim that was disputed as to validity or amount, or to impeach through a prior inconsistent statement or contradiction:

(1) furnishing or offering or promising to furnish—or accepting or offering or promising to accept—a valuable consideration in compromising or attempting to compromise the claim; and

(2) conduct or statements made in compromise negotiations regarding the claim, except when offered in a criminal case and the negotiations related to a claim by a public office or agency in the exercise of regulatory, investigative, or enforcement authority.

**(b) Permitted Uses.** This rule does not require exclusion if the evidence is offered for purposes not prohibited by subdivision (a). Examples of permissible purposes include proving a witness's bias or prejudice; negating a contention of undue delay; and proving an effort to obstruct a criminal investigation or prosecution.

[Amended effective December 1, 2006.]

## RULE 409.  PAYMENT OF MEDICAL AND SIMILAR EXPENSES

Evidence of furnishing or offering or promising to pay medical, hospital, or similar expenses occasioned by an injury is not admissible to prove liability for the injury.

## RULE 410.  INADMISSIBILITY OF PLEAS, PLEA DISCUSSIONS, AND RELATED STATEMENTS

Except as otherwise provided in this rule, evidence of the following is not, in any civil or criminal proceeding, admissible against the defendant who made the plea or was a participant in the plea discussions:

(1) a plea of guilty which was later withdrawn;

(2) a plea of nolo contendere;

(3) any statement made in the course of any proceedings under Rule 11 of the Federal Rules of Criminal Procedure or comparable state procedure regarding either of the foregoing pleas; or

(4) any statement made in the course of plea discussions with an attorney for the prosecuting authority which do not result in a plea of guilty or which result in a plea of guilty later withdrawn.

However, such a statement is admissible (i) in any proceeding wherein another statement made in the course of the same plea or plea discussions has been introduced and the statement ought in fairness be considered contemporaneously with it, or (ii) in a criminal proceeding for perjury or false statement if the statement was made by the defendant under oath, on the record and in the presence of counsel.

[Amended by Pub.L. 94–149, § 1(9), December 12, 1975, 89 Stat. 805; amended April 30, 1979, effective December 1, 1980 (effective date pursuant to Pub.L. 96–42, July 31, 1979, 93 Stat. 326).]

## RULE 411.  LIABILITY INSURANCE

Evidence that a person was or was not insured against liability is not admissible upon the issue whether the person acted negligently or otherwise wrongfully.  This rule does not require the exclusion of evidence of insurance against liability when offered for another purpose, such as proof of agency, ownership, or control, or bias or prejudice of a witness.

[Amended March 2, 1987, effective October 1, 1987.]

## RULE 412.  SEX OFFENSE CASES; RELEVANCE OF ALLEGED VICTIM'S PAST SEXUAL BEHAVIOR OR ALLEGED SEXUAL PREDISPOSITION

**(a) Evidence Generally Inadmissible.**  The following evidence is not admissible in any civil or criminal proceeding involving alleged sexual misconduct except as provided in subdivisions (b) and (c):

(1) Evidence offered to prove that any alleged victim engaged in other sexual behavior.

(2) Evidence offered to prove any alleged victim's sexual predisposition.

**(b) Exceptions.**

(1) In a criminal case, the following evidence is admissible, if otherwise admissible under these rules:

(A) evidence of specific instances of sexual behavior by the alleged victim offered to prove that a person other than the accused was the source of semen, injury or other physical evidence;

(B) evidence of specific instances of sexual behavior by the alleged victim with respect to the person accused of the sexual misconduct offered by the accused to prove consent or by the prosecution; and

(C) evidence the exclusion of which would violate the constitutional rights of the defendant.

(2) In a civil case, evidence offered to prove the sexual behavior or sexual predisposition of any alleged victim is admissible if it is otherwise admissible under these rules and its probative value substantially outweighs the danger of harm to any victim and of unfair prejudice to any party.  Evidence of an alleged victim's reputation is admissible only if it has been placed in controversy by the alleged victim.

**(c) Procedure to Determine Admissibility.**

(1) A party intending to offer evidence under subdivision (b) must—

(A) file a written motion at least 14 days before trial specifically describing the evidence and stating the purpose for which it is offered unless the court, for good cause, requires a different time for filing or permits filing during trial; and

(B) serve the motion on all parties and notify the alleged victim or, when appropriate, the alleged victim's guardian or representative.

(2) Before admitting evidence under this rule the court must conduct a hearing in camera and afford the victim and parties a right to attend and be heard. The motion, related papers, and the record of the

hearing must be sealed and remain under seal unless the court orders otherwise.

[Adopted by Pub.L. 95–540, § 2(a), October 28, 1978, 92 Stat. 2046, applicable to trials that begin more than 30 days after October 28, 1978; amended by Pub.L. 100–690, Title VII, § 7046(a), November 18, 1988, 102 Stat. 4400; amended April 29, 1994, effective December 1, 1994; amended by Pub.L. 103–322, Title IV, § 40141(b), September 13, 1994, 108 Stat. 1919, effective December 1, 1994.]

## RULE 413. EVIDENCE OF SIMILAR CRIMES IN SEXUAL ASSAULT CASES

**(a)** In a criminal case in which the defendant is accused of an offense of sexual assault, evidence of the defendant's commission of another offense or offenses of sexual assault is admissible, and may be considered for its bearing on any matter to which it is relevant.

**(b)** In a case in which the Government intends to offer evidence under this rule, the attorney for the Government shall disclose the evidence to the defendant, including statements of witnesses or a summary of the substance of any testimony that is expected to be offered, at least fifteen days before the scheduled date of trial or at such later time as the court may allow for good cause.

**(c)** This rule shall not be construed to limit the admission or consideration of evidence under any other rule.

**(d)** For purposes of this rule and Rule 415, "offense of sexual assault" means a crime under Federal law or the law of a State (as defined in section 513 of title 18, United States Code) that involved—

(1) any conduct proscribed by chapter 109A of title 18, United States Code;

(2) contact, without consent, between any part of the defendant's body or an object and the genitals or anus of another person;

(3) contact, without consent, between the genitals or anus of the defendant and any part of another person's body;

(4) deriving sexual pleasure or gratification from the infliction of death, bodily injury, or physical pain on another person; or

(5) an attempt or conspiracy to engage in conduct described in paragraphs (1)–(4).

[Adopted by Pub.L. 103–322, Title XXXII, § 320935(a), September 13, 1994, 108 Stat. 2135, applicable to proceedings commenced on or after July 9, 1995, including all trials commenced on or after July 9, 1995 (Pub.L. 103–322, Title XXXII, § 320935(e), September 13, 1994, 108 Stat. 2137, as amended by Pub.L. 104–208, Div. A, Title I, § 101(a) [Title I, § 120], September 30, 1996, 110 Stat. 3009–25).]

## RULE 414. EVIDENCE OF SIMILAR CRIMES IN CHILD MOLESTATION CASES

**(a)** In a criminal case in which the defendant is accused of an offense of child molestation, evidence of the defendant's commission of another offense or offenses of child molestation is admissible, and may be considered for its bearing on any matter to which it is relevant.

**(b)** In a case in which the Government intends to offer evidence under this rule, the attorney for the Government shall disclose the evidence to the defendant, including statements of witnesses or a summary of the substance of any testimony that is expected to be offered, at least fifteen days before the scheduled date of trial or at such later time as the court may allow for good cause.

**(c)** This rule shall not be construed to limit the admission or consideration of evidence under any other rule.

**(d)** For purposes of this rule and Rule 415, "child" means a person below the age of fourteen, and "offense of child molestation" means a crime under Federal law or the law of a State (as defined in section 513 of title 18, United States Code) that involved—

(1) any conduct proscribed by chapter 109A of title 18, United States Code, that was committed in relation to a child;

(2) any conduct proscribed by chapter 110 of title 18, United States Code;

(3) contact between any part of the defendant's body or an object and the genitals or anus of a child;

(4) contact between the genitals or anus of the defendant and any part of the body of a child;

(5) deriving sexual pleasure or gratification from the infliction of death, bodily injury, or physical pain on a child; or

(6) an attempt or conspiracy to engage in conduct described in paragraphs (1)–(5).

[Adopted by Pub.L. 103–322, Title XXXII, § 320935(a), September 13, 1994, 108 Stat. 2135, applicable to proceedings commenced on or after July 9, 1995, including all trials commenced on or after July 9, 1995 (Pub.L. 103–322, Title XXXII, § 320935(e), September 13, 1994, 108 Stat. 2137, as amended by Pub.L. 104–208, Div. A, Title I, § 101(a) [Title I, § 120], September 30, 1996, 110 Stat. 3009–25).]

## RULE 415. EVIDENCE OF SIMILAR ACTS IN CIVIL CASES CONCERNING SEXUAL ASSAULT OR CHILD MOLESTATION

**(a)** In a civil case in which a claim for damages or other relief is predicated on a party's alleged commis-

sion of conduct constituting an offense of sexual assault or child molestation, evidence of that party's commission of another offense or offenses of sexual assault or child molestation is admissible and may be considered as provided in Rule 413 and Rule 414 of these rules.

(b) A party who intends to offer evidence under this Rule shall disclose the evidence to the party against whom it will be offered, including statements of witnesses or a summary of the substance of any testimony that is expected to be offered, at least fifteen days before the scheduled date of trial or at such later time as the court may allow for good cause.

(c) This rule shall not be construed to limit the admission or consideration of evidence under any other rule.

[Adopted by Pub.L. 103–322, Title XXXII, § 320935(a), September 13, 1994, 108 Stat. 2135, applicable to proceedings commenced on or after July 9, 1995, including all trials commenced on or after July 9, 1995 (Pub.L. 103–322, Title XXXII, § 320935(e), September 13, 1994, 108 Stat. 2137, as amended by Pub.L. 104–208, Div. A, Title I, § 101(a) [Title I, § 120], September 30, 1996, 110 Stat. 3009–25).]

# ARTICLE V. PRIVILEGES

## RULE 501. GENERAL RULE

Except as otherwise required by the Constitution of the United States or provided by Act of Congress or in rules prescribed by the Supreme Court pursuant to statutory authority, the privilege of a witness, person, government, State, or political subdivision thereof shall be governed by the principles of the common law as they may be interpreted by the courts of the United States in the light of reason and experience. However, in civil actions and proceedings, with respect to an element of a claim or defense as to which State law supplies the rule of decision, the privilege of a witness, person, government, State, or political subdivision thereof shall be determined in accordance with State law.

# ARTICLE VI. WITNESSES

## RULE 601. GENERAL RULE OF COMPETENCY

Every person is competent to be a witness except as otherwise provided in these rules. However, in civil actions and proceedings, with respect to an element of a claim or defense as to which State law supplies the rule of decision, the competency of a witness shall be determined in accordance with State law.

## RULE 602. LACK OF PERSONAL KNOWLEDGE

A witness may not testify to a matter unless evidence is introduced sufficient to support a finding that the witness has personal knowledge of the matter. Evidence to prove personal knowledge may, but need not, consist of the witness' own testimony. This rule is subject to the provisions of rule 703, relating to opinion testimony by expert witnesses.

[Amended March 2, 1987, effective October 1, 1987; April 25, 1988, effective November 1, 1988.]

## RULE 603. OATH OR AFFIRMATION

Before testifying, every witness shall be required to declare that the witness will testify truthfully, by oath or affirmation administered in a form calculated to awaken the witness' conscience and impress the witness' mind with the duty to do so.

[Amended March 2, 1987, effective October 1, 1987.]

## RULE 604. INTERPRETERS

An interpreter is subject to the provisions of these rules relating to qualification as an expert and the administration of an oath or affirmation to make a true translation.

[Amended March 2, 1987, effective October 1, 1987.]

## RULE 605. COMPETENCY OF JUDGE AS WITNESS

The judge presiding at the trial may not testify in that trial as a witness. No objection need be made in order to preserve the point.

## RULE 606. COMPETENCY OF JUROR AS WITNESS

(a) At the Trial. A member of the jury may not testify as a witness before that jury in the trial of the case in which the juror is sitting. If the juror is called so to testify, the opposing party shall be afforded an opportunity to object out of the presence of the jury.

(b) Inquiry Into Validity of Verdict or Indictment. Upon an inquiry into the validity of a verdict or indictment, a juror may not testify as to any matter or statement occurring during the course of the jury's deliberations or to the effect of anything upon that or any other juror's mind or emotions as influencing the juror to assent to or dissent from the verdict or indictment or concerning the juror's mental processes in connection therewith. But a juror may testify about

(1) whether extraneous prejudicial information was improperly brought to the jury's attention, (2) whether any outside influence was improperly brought to bear upon any juror, or (3) whether there was a mistake in entering the verdict onto the verdict form. A juror's affidavit or evidence of any statement by the juror may not be received on a matter about which the juror would be precluded from testifying.

[Amended by Pub.L. 94–149, § 1(10), December 12, 1975, 89 Stat. 805; amended March 2, 1987, effective October 1, 1987; April 12, 2006, effective December 1, 2006.]

## RULE 607.  WHO MAY IMPEACH

The credibility of a witness may be attacked by any party, including the party calling the witness.

[Amended March 2, 1987, effective October 1, 1987.]

## RULE 608.  EVIDENCE OF CHARACTER AND CONDUCT OF WITNESS

**(a) Opinion and Reputation Evidence of Character.**  The credibility of a witness may be attacked or supported by evidence in the form of opinion or reputation, but subject to these limitations: (1) the evidence may refer only to character for truthfulness or untruthfulness, and (2) evidence of truthful character is admissible only after the character of the witness for truthfulness has been attacked by opinion or reputation evidence or otherwise.

**(b) Specific Instances of Conduct.**  Specific instances of the conduct of a witness, for the purpose of attacking or supporting the witness' character for truthfulness, other than conviction of crime as provided in rule 609, may not be proved by extrinsic evidence. They may, however, in the discretion of the court, if probative of truthfulness or untruthfulness, be inquired into on cross-examination of the witness (1) concerning the witness' character for truthfulness or untruthfulness, or (2) concerning the character for truthfulness or untruthfulness of another witness as to which character the witness being cross-examined has testified.

The giving of testimony, whether by an accused or by any other witness, does not operate as a waiver of the accused's or the witness' privilege against self-incrimination when examined with respect to matters that relate only to character for truthfulness.

[Amended March 2, 1987, effective October 1, 1987; April 25, 1988, effective November 1, 1988; March 27, 2003, effective December 1, 2003.]

## RULE 609.  IMPEACHMENT BY EVIDENCE OF CONVICTION OF CRIME

**(a) General Rule.** For the purpose of attacking the character for truthfulness of a witness,

(1) evidence that a witness other than an accused has been convicted of a crime shall be admitted, subject to Rule 403, if the crime was punishable by death or imprisonment in excess of one year under the law under which the witness was convicted, and evidence that an accused has been convicted of such a crime shall be admitted if the court determines that the probative value of admitting this evidence outweighs its prejudicial effect to the accused; and

(2) evidence that any witness has been convicted of a crime shall be admitted regardless of the punishment, if it readily can be determined that establishing the elements of the crime required proof or admission of an act of dishonesty or false statement by the witness.

**(b) Time Limit.** Evidence of a conviction under this rule is not admissible if a period of more than ten years has elapsed since the date of the conviction or of the release of the witness from the confinement imposed for that conviction, whichever is the later date, unless the court determines, in the interests of justice, that the probative value of the conviction supported by specific facts and circumstances substantially outweighs its prejudicial effect. However, evidence of a conviction more than 10 years old as calculated herein, is not admissible unless the proponent gives to the adverse party sufficient advance written notice of intent to use such evidence to provide the adverse party with a fair opportunity to contest the use of such evidence.

**(c) Effect of Pardon, Annulment, or Certificate of Rehabilitation.** Evidence of a conviction is not admissible under this rule if (1) the conviction has been the subject of a pardon, annulment, certificate of rehabilitation, or other equivalent procedure based on a finding of the rehabilitation of the person convicted, and that person has not been convicted of a subsequent crime that was punishable by death or imprisonment in excess of one year, or (2) the conviction has been the subject of a pardon, annulment, or other equivalent procedure based on a finding of innocence.

**(d) Juvenile Adjudications.** Evidence of juvenile adjudications is generally not admissible under this rule. The court may, however, in a criminal case allow evidence of a juvenile adjudication of a witness other than the accused if conviction of the offense would be admissible to attack the credibility of an adult and the court is satisfied that admission in evidence is necessary for a fair determination of the issue of guilt or innocence.

**(e) Pendency of Appeal.** The pendency of an appeal therefrom does not render evidence of a conviction inadmissible. Evidence of the pendency of an appeal is admissible.

[Amended March 2, 1987, effective October 1, 1987; January 26, 1990, effective December 1, 1990; April 12, 2006, effective December 1, 2006.]

## RULE 610.　RELIGIOUS BELIEFS OR OPINIONS

Evidence of the beliefs or opinions of a witness on matters of religion is not admissible for the purpose of showing that by reason of their nature the witness' credibility is impaired or enhanced.

[Amended March 2, 1987, effective October 1, 1987.]

## RULE 611.　MODE AND ORDER OF INTERROGATION AND PRESENTATION

(a) **Control by Court.** The court shall exercise reasonable control over the mode and order of interrogating witnesses and presenting evidence so as to (1) make the interrogation and presentation effective for the ascertainment of the truth, (2) avoid needless consumption of time, and (3) protect witnesses from harassment or undue embarrassment.

(b) **Scope of Cross-Examination.** Cross-examination should be limited to the subject matter of the direct examination and matters affecting the credibility of the witness. The court may, in the exercise of discretion, permit inquiry into additional matters as if on direct examination.

(c) **Leading Questions.** Leading questions should not be used on the direct examination of a witness except as may be necessary to develop the witness' testimony. Ordinarily leading questions should be permitted on cross-examination. When a party calls a hostile witness, an adverse party, or a witness identified with an adverse party, interrogation may be by leading questions.

[Amended March 2, 1987, effective October 1, 1987.]

## RULE 612.　WRITING USED TO REFRESH MEMORY

Except as otherwise provided in criminal proceedings by section 3500 of title 18, United States Code, if a witness uses a writing to refresh memory for the purpose of testifying, either—

(1) while testifying, or

(2) before testifying, if the court in its discretion determines it is necessary in the interests of justice,

an adverse party is entitled to have the writing produced at the hearing, to inspect it, to cross-examine the witness thereon, and to introduce in evidence those portions which relate to the testimony of the witness. If it is claimed that the writing contains matters not related to the subject matter of the testimony the court shall examine the writing in camera, excise any portions not so related, and order delivery of the remainder to the party entitled thereto. Any portion withheld over objections shall be preserved and made available to the appellate court in the event of an appeal. If a writing is not produced or delivered pursuant to order under this rule, the court shall make any order justice requires, except that in criminal cases when the prosecution elects not to comply, the order shall be one striking the testimony or, if the court in its discretion determines that the interests of justice so require, declaring a mistrial.

[Amended March 2, 1987, effective October 1, 1987.]

## RULE 613.　PRIOR STATEMENTS OF WITNESSES

(a) **Examining Witness Concerning Prior Statement.** In examining a witness concerning a prior statement made by the witness, whether written or not, the statement need not be shown nor its contents disclosed to the witness at that time, but on request the same shall be shown or disclosed to opposing counsel.

(b) **Extrinsic Evidence of Prior Inconsistent Statement of Witness.** Extrinsic evidence of a prior inconsistent statement by a witness is not admissible unless the witness is afforded an opportunity to explain or deny the same and the opposite party is afforded an opportunity to interrogate the witness thereon, or the interests of justice otherwise require. This provision does not apply to admissions of a party-opponent as defined in rule 801(d)(2).

[Amended March 2, 1987, effective October 1, 1987; April 25, 1988, effective November 1, 1988.]

## RULE 614.　CALLING AND INTERROGATION OF WITNESSES BY COURT

(a) **Calling by Court.** The court may, on its own motion or at the suggestion of a party, call witnesses, and all parties are entitled to cross-examine witnesses thus called.

(b) **Interrogation by Court.** The court may interrogate witnesses, whether called by itself or by a party.

(c) **Objections.** Objections to the calling of witnesses by the court or to interrogation by it may be made at the time or at the next available opportunity when the jury is not present.

## RULE 615.　EXCLUSION OF WITNESSES

At the request of a party the court shall order witnesses excluded so that they cannot hear the testimony of other witnesses, and it may make the order of its own motion. This rule does not authorize exclusion of (1) a party who is a natural person, or (2) an officer or employee of a party which is not a natural person designated as its representative by its attorney, or (3) a person whose presence is shown by a party to be

essential to the presentation of the party's cause, or (4) a person authorized by statute to be present.

[Amended March 2, 1987, effective October 1, 1987; April 25, 1988, effective November 1, 1988; amended by Pub.L.

100–690, Title VII, § 7075(a), November 18, 1988, 102 Stat. 4405 (although amendment by Pub.L. 100–690 could not be executed due to prior amendment by Court order which made the same change effective November 1, 1988); amended April 24, 1998, effective December 1, 1998.]

# ARTICLE VII. OPINIONS AND EXPERT TESTIMONY

## RULE 701. OPINION TESTIMONY BY LAY WITNESSES

If the witness is not testifying as an expert, the witness' testimony in the form of opinions or inferences is limited to those opinions or inferences which are (a) rationally based on the perception of the witness, (b) helpful to a clear understanding of the witness' testimony or the determination of a fact in issue, and (c) not based on scientific, technical, or other specialized knowledge within the scope of Rule 702.

[Amended March 2, 1987, effective October 1, 1987; April 17, 2000, effective December 1, 2000.]

## RULE 702. TESTIMONY BY EXPERTS

If scientific, technical, or other specialized knowledge will assist the trier of fact to understand the evidence or to determine a fact in issue, a witness qualified as an expert by knowledge, skill, experience, training, or education, may testify thereto in the form of an opinion or otherwise, if (1) the testimony is based upon sufficient facts or data, (2) the testimony is the product of reliable principles and methods, and (3) the witness has applied the principles and methods reliably to the facts of the case.

[Amended April 17, 2000, effective December 1, 2000.]

## RULE 703. BASES OF OPINION TESTIMONY BY EXPERTS

The facts or data in the particular case upon which an expert bases an opinion or inference may be those perceived by or made known to the expert at or before the hearing. If of a type reasonably relied upon by experts in the particular field in forming opinions or inferences upon the subject, the facts or data need not be admissible in evidence in order for the opinion or inference to be admitted. Facts or data that are otherwise inadmissible shall not be disclosed to the jury by the proponent of the opinion or inference unless the court determines that their probative value in assisting the jury to evaluate the expert's opinion substantially outweighs their prejudicial effect.

[Amended March 2, 1987, effective October 1, 1987; April 17, 2000, effective December 1, 2000.]

## RULE 704. OPINION ON ULTIMATE ISSUE

(a) Except as provided in subdivision (b), testimony in the form of an opinion or inference otherwise admissible is not objectionable because it embraces an ultimate issue to be decided by the trier of fact.

(b) No expert witness testifying with respect to the mental state or condition of a defendant in a criminal case may state an opinion or inference as to whether the defendant did or did not have the mental state or condition constituting an element of the crime charged or of a defense thereto. Such ultimate issues are matters for the trier of fact alone.

[Amended by Pub.L. 98–473, Title II, § 406, October 12, 1984, 98 Stat. 2067.]

## RULE 705. DISCLOSURE OF FACTS OR DATA UNDERLYING EXPERT OPINION

The expert may testify in terms of opinion or inference and give reasons therefor without first testifying to the underlying facts or data, unless the court requires otherwise. The expert may in any event be required to disclose the underlying facts or data on cross-examination.

[Amended March 2, 1987, effective October 1, 1987; April 22, 1993, effective December 1, 1993.]

## RULE 706. COURT APPOINTED EXPERTS

(a) **Appointment.** The court may on its own motion or on the motion of any party enter an order to show cause why expert witnesses should not be appointed, and may request the parties to submit nominations. The court may appoint any expert witnesses agreed upon by the parties, and may appoint expert witnesses of its own selection. An expert witness shall not be appointed by the court unless the witness consents to act. A witness so appointed shall be informed of the witness' duties by the court in writing, a copy of which shall be filed with the clerk, or at a conference in which the parties shall have opportunity to participate. A witness so appointed shall advise the parties of the witness' findings, if any; the witness' deposition may be taken by any party; and the witness may be called to testify by the court or any party. The witness shall be subject to cross-examination by each party, including a party calling the witness.

(b) **Compensation.** Expert witnesses so appointed are entitled to reasonable compensation in whatever

sum the court may allow. The compensation thus fixed is payable from funds which may be provided by law in criminal cases and civil actions and proceedings involving just compensation under the fifth amendment. In other civil actions and proceedings the compensation shall be paid by the parties in such proportion and at such time as the court directs, and thereafter charged in like manner as other costs.

**(c) Disclosure of Appointment.** In the exercise of its discretion, the court may authorize disclosure to the jury of the fact that the court appointed the expert witness.

**(d) Parties' Experts of Own Selection.** Nothing in this rule limits the parties in calling expert witnesses of their own selection.

[Amended March 2, 1987, effective October 1, 1987.]

# ARTICLE VIII.  HEARSAY

## RULE 801.  DEFINITIONS

The following definitions apply under this article:

**(a) Statement.** A "statement" is (1) an oral or written assertion or (2) nonverbal conduct of a person, if it is intended by the person as an assertion.

**(b) Declarant.** A "declarant" is a person who makes a statement.

**(c) Hearsay.** "Hearsay" is a statement, other than one made by the declarant while testifying at the trial or hearing, offered in evidence to prove the truth of the matter asserted.

**(d) Statements Which Are Not Hearsay.** A statement is not hearsay if—

(1) *Prior Statement by Witness.* The declarant testifies at the trial or hearing and is subject to cross-examination concerning the statement, and the statement is (A) inconsistent with the declarant's testimony, and was given under oath subject to the penalty of perjury at a trial, hearing, or other proceeding, or in a deposition, or (B) consistent with the declarant's testimony and is offered to rebut an express or implied charge against the declarant of recent fabrication or improper influence or motive, or (C) one of identification of a person made after perceiving the person; or

(2) *Admission by Party-Opponent.* The statement is offered against a party and is (A) the party's own statement, in either an individual or a representative capacity or (B) a statement of which the party has manifested an adoption or belief in its truth, or (C) a statement by a person authorized by the party to make a statement concerning the subject, or (D) a statement by the party's agent or servant concerning a matter within the scope of the agency or employment, made during the existence of the relationship, or (E) a statement by a coconspirator of a party during the course and in furtherance of the conspiracy. The contents of the statement shall be considered but are not alone sufficient to establish the declarant's authority under subdivision (C), the agency or employment relationship and scope thereof under subdivision (D), or the existence of the conspiracy and the partic-

ipation therein of the declarant and the party against whom the statement is offered under subdivision (E).

[Amended by Pub.L. 94–113, § 1, October 16, 1975, 89 Stat. 576; amended March 2, 1987, effective October 1, 1987; April 11, 1997, effective December 1, 1997.]

## RULE 802.  HEARSAY RULE

Hearsay is not admissible except as provided by these rules or by other rules prescribed by the Supreme Court pursuant to statutory authority or by Act of Congress.

## RULE 803.  HEARSAY EXCEPTIONS; AVAILABILITY OF DECLARANT IMMATERIAL

The following are not excluded by the hearsay rule, even though the declarant is available as a witness:

**(1) Present Sense Impression.** A statement describing or explaining an event or condition made while the declarant was perceiving the event or condition, or immediately thereafter.

**(2) Excited Utterance.** A statement relating to a startling event or condition made while the declarant was under the stress of excitement caused by the event or condition.

**(3) Then Existing Mental, Emotional, or Physical Condition.** A statement of the declarant's then existing state of mind, emotion, sensation, or physical condition (such as intent, plan, motive, design, mental feeling, pain, and bodily health), but not including a statement of memory or belief to prove the fact remembered or believed unless it relates to the execution, revocation, identification, or terms of declarant's will.

**(4) Statements for Purposes of Medical Diagnosis or Treatment.** Statements made for purposes of medical diagnosis or treatment and describing medical history, or past or present symptoms, pain, or sensations, or the inception or general character of the cause or external source thereof insofar as reasonably pertinent to diagnosis or treatment.

**(5) Recorded Recollection.** A memorandum or record concerning a matter about which a witness once had knowledge but now has insufficient recollec-

tion to enable the witness to testify fully and accurately, shown to have been made or adopted by the witness when the matter was fresh in the witness' memory and to reflect that knowledge correctly. If admitted, the memorandum or record may be read into evidence but may not itself be received as an exhibit unless offered by an adverse party.

**(6) Records of Regularly Conducted Activity.** A memorandum, report, record, or data compilation, in any form, of acts, events, conditions, opinions, or diagnoses, made at or near the time by, or from information transmitted by, a person with knowledge, if kept in the course of a regularly conducted business activity, and if it was the regular practice of that business activity to make the memorandum, report, record, or data compilation, all as shown by the testimony of the custodian or other qualified witness, or by certification that complies with Rule 902(11), Rule 902(12), or a statute permitting certification, unless the source of information or the method or circumstances of preparation indicate lack of trustworthiness. The term "business" as used in this paragraph includes business, institution, association, profession, occupation, and calling of every kind, whether or not conducted for profit.

**(7) Absence of Entry in Records Kept in Accordance With the Provisions of Paragraph (6).** Evidence that a matter is not included in the memoranda reports, records, or data compilations, in any form, kept in accordance with the provisions of paragraph (6), to prove the nonoccurrence or nonexistence of the matter, if the matter was of a kind of which a memorandum, report, record, or data compilation was regularly made and preserved, unless the sources of information or other circumstances indicate lack of trustworthiness.

**(8) Public Records and Reports.** Records, reports, statements, or data compilations, in any form, of public offices or agencies, setting forth (A) the activities of the office or agency, or (B) matters observed pursuant to duty imposed by law as to which matters there was a duty to report, excluding, however, in criminal cases matters observed by police officers and other law enforcement personnel, or (C) in civil actions and proceedings and against the Government in criminal cases, factual findings resulting from an investigation made pursuant to authority granted by law, unless the sources of information or other circumstances indicate lack of trustworthiness.

**(9) Records of Vital Statistics.** Records or data compilations, in any form, of births, fetal deaths, deaths, or marriages, if the report thereof was made to a public office pursuant to requirements of law.

**(10) Absence of Public Record or Entry.** To prove the absence of a record, report, statement, or data compilation, in any form, or the nonoccurrence or nonexistence of a matter of which a record, report, statement, or data compilation, in any form, was regu-

larly made and preserved by a public office or agency, evidence in the form of a certification in accordance with rule 902, or testimony, that diligent search failed to disclose the record, report, statement, or data compilation, or entry.

**(11) Records of Religious Organizations.** Statements of births, marriages, divorces, deaths, legitimacy, ancestry, relationship by blood or marriage, or other similar facts of personal or family history, contained in a regularly kept record of a religious organization.

**(12) Marriage, Baptismal, and Similar Certificates.** Statements of fact contained in a certificate that the maker performed a marriage or other ceremony or administered a sacrament, made by a clergyman, public official, or other person authorized by the rules or practices of a religious organization or by law to perform the act certified, and purporting to have been issued at the time of the act or within a reasonable time thereafter.

**(13) Family Records.** Statements of fact concerning personal or family history contained in family Bibles, genealogies, charts, engravings on rings, inscriptions on family portraits, engravings on urns, crypts, or tombstones, or the like.

**(14) Records of Documents Affecting an Interest in Property.** The record of a document purporting to establish or affect an interest in property, as proof of the content of the original recorded document and its execution and delivery by each person by whom it purports to have been executed, if the record is a record of a public office and an applicable statute authorizes the recording of documents of that kind in that office.

**(15) Statements in Documents Affecting an Interest in Property.** A statement contained in a document purporting to establish or affect an interest in property if the matter stated was relevant to the purpose of the document, unless dealings with the property since the document was made have been inconsistent with the truth of the statement or the purport of the document.

**(16) Statements in Ancient Documents.** Statements in a document in existence twenty years or more the authenticity of which is established.

**(17) Market Reports, Commercial Publications.** Market quotations, tabulations, lists, directories, or other published compilations, generally used and relied upon by the public or by persons in particular occupations.

**(18) Learned Treatises.** To the extent called to the attention of an expert witness upon cross-examination or relied upon by the expert witness in direct examination, statements contained in published treatises, periodicals, or pamphlets on a subject of history, medicine, or other science or art, established as a reliable authority by the testimony or admission of the

witness or by other expert testimony or by judicial notice. If admitted, the statements may be read into evidence but may not be received as exhibits.

**(19) Reputation Concerning Personal or Family History.** Reputation among members of a person's family by blood, adoption, or marriage, or among a person's associates, or in the community, concerning a person's birth, adoption, marriage, divorce, death, legitimacy, relationship by blood, adoption, or marriage, ancestry, or other similar fact of personal or family history.

**(20) Reputation Concerning Boundaries or General History.** Reputation in a community, arising before the controversy, as to boundaries of or customs affecting lands in the community, and reputation as to events of general history important to the community or State or nation in which located.

**(21) Reputation as to Character.** Reputation of a person's character among associates or in the community.

**(22) Judgment of Previous Conviction.** Evidence of a final judgment, entered after a trial or upon a plea of guilty (but not upon a plea of nolo contendere), adjudging a person guilty of a crime punishable by death or imprisonment in excess of one year, to prove any fact essential to sustain the judgment, but not including, when offered by the Government in a criminal prosecution for purposes other than impeachment, judgments against persons other than the accused. The pendency of an appeal may be shown but does not affect admissibility.

**(23) Judgment as to Personal, Family, or General History, or Boundaries.** Judgments as proof of matters of personal, family or general history, or boundaries, essential to the judgment, if the same would be provable by evidence of reputation.

**(24) [Transferred to Rule 807.]**

[Amended by Pub.L. 94–149, § 1(11), December 12, 1975, 89 Stat. 805; amended March 2, 1987, effective October 1, 1987; April 11, 1997, effective December 1, 1997; April 17, 2000, effective December 1, 2000.]

## RULE 804. HEARSAY EXCEPTIONS; DECLARANT UNAVAILABLE

**(a) Definition of Unavailability.** "Unavailability as a witness" includes situations in which the declarant—

(1) is exempted by ruling of the court on the ground of privilege from testifying concerning the subject matter of the declarant's statement; or

(2) persists in refusing to testify concerning the subject matter of the declarant's statement despite an order of the court to do so; or

(3) testifies to a lack of memory of the subject matter of the declarant's statement; or

(4) is unable to be present or to testify at the hearing because of death or then existing physical or mental illness or infirmity; or

(5) is absent from the hearing and the proponent of a statement has been unable to procure the declarant's attendance (or in the case of a hearsay exception under subdivision (b)(2), (3), or (4), the declarant's attendance or testimony) by process or other reasonable means.

A declarant is not unavailable as a witness if exemption, refusal, claim of lack of memory, inability, or absence is due to the procurement or wrongdoing of the proponent of a statement for the purpose of preventing the witness from attending or testifying.

**(b) Hearsay Exceptions.** The following are not excluded by the hearsay rule if the declarant is unavailable as a witness:

(1) *Former Testimony.* Testimony given as a witness at another hearing of the same or a different proceeding, or in a deposition taken in compliance with law in the course of the same or another proceeding, if the party against whom the testimony is now offered, or, in a civil action or proceeding, a predecessor in interest, had an opportunity and similar motive to develop the testimony by direct, cross, or redirect examination.

(2) *Statement Under Belief of Impending Death.* In a prosecution for homicide or in a civil action or proceeding, a statement made by a declarant while believing that the declarant's death was imminent, concerning the cause or circumstances of what the declarant believed to be impending death.

(3) *Statement Against Interest.* A statement which was at the time of its making so far contrary to the declarant's pecuniary or proprietary interest, or so far tended to subject the declarant to civil or criminal liability, or to render invalid a claim by the declarant against another, that a reasonable person in the declarant's position would not have made the statement unless believing it to be true. A statement tending to expose the declarant to criminal liability and offered to exculpate the accused is not admissible unless corroborating circumstances clearly indicate the trustworthiness of the statement.

(4) *Statement of Personal or Family History.*

(A) A statement concerning the declarant's own birth, adoption, marriage, divorce, legitimacy, relationship by blood, adoption, or marriage, ancestry, or other similar fact of personal or family history, even though declarant had no means of acquiring personal knowledge of the matter stated; or

(B) a statement concerning the foregoing matters, and death also, of another person, if the declarant was related to the other by blood, adoption, or marriage or was so intimately associated with the other's family as to be likely to have accurate information concerning the matter declared.

(5) *[Transferred to Rule 807.]*

(6) *Forfeiture by Wrongdoing.* A statement offered against a party that has engaged or acquiesced in wrongdoing that was intended to, and did, procure the unavailability of the declarant as a witness.

[Amended by Pub.L. 94–149, § 1(12) and (13), December 12, 1975, 89 Stat. 806; amended March 2, 1987, effective October 1, 1987; amended by Pub.L. 100–690, Title VII, § 7075(b), November 18, 1988, 102 Stat. 4405; amended April 11, 1997, effective December 1, 1997.]

## RULE 805. HEARSAY WITHIN HEARSAY

Hearsay included within hearsay is not excluded under the hearsay rule if each part of the combined statements conforms with an exception to the hearsay rule provided in these rules.

## RULE 806. ATTACKING AND SUPPORTING CREDIBILITY OF DECLARANT

When a hearsay statement, or a statement defined in Rule 801(d)(2)(C), (D), or (E), has been admitted in evidence, the credibility of the declarant may be attacked, and if attacked may be supported, by any evidence which would be admissible for those purposes if declarant had testified as a witness. Evidence of a statement or conduct by the declarant at any time, inconsistent with the declarant's hearsay statement, is not subject to any requirement that the declarant may have been afforded an opportunity to deny or explain. If the party against whom a hearsay statement has been admitted calls the declarant as a witness, the party is entitled to examine the declarant on the statement as if under cross-examination.

[Amended March 2, 1987, effective October 1, 1987; April 11, 1997, effective December 1, 1997.]

## RULE 807. RESIDUAL EXCEPTION

A statement not specifically covered by Rule 803 or 804 but having equivalent circumstantial guarantees of trustworthiness, is not excluded by the hearsay rule, if the court determines that (A) the statement is offered as evidence of a material fact; (B) the statement is more probative on the point for which it is offered than any other evidence which the proponent can procure through reasonable efforts; and (C) the general purposes of these rules and the interests of justice will best be served by admission of the statement into evidence. However, a statement may not be admitted under this exception unless the proponent of it makes known to the adverse party sufficiently in advance of the trial or hearing to provide the adverse party with a fair opportunity to prepare to meet it, the proponent's intention to offer the statement and the particulars of it, including the name and address of the declarant.

[Adopted April 11, 1997, effective December 1, 1997.]

# ARTICLE IX. AUTHENTICATION AND IDENTIFICATION

## RULE 901. REQUIREMENT OF AUTHENTICATION OR IDENTIFICATION

(a) **General Provision.** The requirement of authentication or identification as a condition precedent to admissibility is satisfied by evidence sufficient to support a finding that the matter in question is what its proponent claims.

(b) **Illustrations.** By way of illustration only, and not by way of limitation, the following are examples of authentication or identification conforming with the requirements of this rule:

(1) *Testimony of Witness With Knowledge.* Testimony that a matter is what it is claimed to be.

(2) *Nonexpert Opinion on Handwriting.* Nonexpert opinion as to the genuineness of handwriting, based upon familiarity not acquired for purposes of the litigation.

(3) *Comparison by Trier or Expert Witness.* Comparison by the trier of fact or by expert witnesses with specimens which have been authenticated.

(4) *Distinctive Characteristics and the Like.* Appearance, contents, substance, internal patterns, or other distinctive characteristics, taken in conjunction with circumstances.

(5) *Voice Identification.* Identification of a voice, whether heard firsthand or through mechanical or electronic transmission or recording, by opinion based upon hearing the voice at any time under circumstances connecting it with the alleged speaker.

(6) *Telephone Conversations.* Telephone conversations, by evidence that a call was made to the number assigned at the time by the telephone company to a particular person or business, if (A) in the case of a person, circumstances, including self-identification, show the person answering to be the one called, or (B) in the case of a business, the call was made to a place of business and the conversation related to business reasonably transacted over the telephone.

(7) *Public Records or Reports.* Evidence that a writing authorized by law to be recorded or filed and in fact recorded or filed in a public office, or a purported public record, report, statement, or data compilation, in any form, is from the public office where items of this nature are kept.

(8) *Ancient Documents or Data Compilation.* Evidence that a document or data compilation, in any

form, (A) is in such condition as to create no suspicion concerning its authenticity, (B) was in a place where it, if authentic, would likely be, and (C) has been in existence 20 years or more at the time it is offered.

(9) *Process or System.* Evidence describing a process or system used to produce a result and showing that the process or system produces an accurate result.

(10) *Methods Provided by Statute or Rule.* Any method of authentication or identification provided by Act of Congress or by other rules prescribed by the Supreme Court pursuant to statutory authority.

## RULE 902. SELF–AUTHENTICATION

Extrinsic evidence of authenticity as a condition precedent to admissibility is not required with respect to the following:

(1) **Domestic Public Documents Under Seal.** A document bearing a seal purporting to be that of the United States, or of any State, district, Commonwealth, territory, or insular possession thereof, or the Panama Canal Zone, or the Trust Territory of the Pacific Islands, or of a political subdivision, department, officer, or agency thereof, and a signature purporting to be an attestation or execution.

(2) **Domestic Public Documents Not Under Seal.** A document purporting to bear the signature in the official capacity of an officer or employee of any entity included in paragraph (1) hereof, having no seal, if a public officer having a seal and having official duties in the district or political subdivision of the officer or employee certifies under seal that the signer has the official capacity and that the signature is genuine.

(3) **Foreign Public Documents.** A document purporting to be executed or attested in an official capacity by a person authorized by the laws of a foreign country to make the execution or attestation, and accompanied by a final certification as to the genuineness of the signature and official position (A) of the executing or attesting person, or (B) of any foreign official whose certificate of genuineness of signature and official position relates to the execution or attestation or is in a chain of certificates of genuineness of signature and official position relating to the execution or attestation. A final certification may be made by a secretary of an embassy or legation, consul general, consul, vice consul, or consular agent of the United States, or a diplomatic or consular official of the foreign country assigned or accredited to the United States. If reasonable opportunity has been given to all parties to investigate the authenticity and accuracy of official documents, the court may, for good cause shown, order that they be treated as presumptively authentic without final certification or permit them to be evidenced by an attested summary with or without final certification.

(4) **Certified Copies of Public Records.** A copy of an official record or report or entry therein, or of a document authorized by law to be recorded or filed and actually recorded or filed in a public office, including data compilations in any form, certified as correct by the custodian or other person authorized to make the certification, by certificate complying with paragraph (1), (2), or (3) of this rule or complying with any Act of Congress or rule prescribed by the Supreme Court pursuant to statutory authority.

(5) **Official Publications.** Books, pamphlets, or other publications purporting to be issued by public authority.

(6) **Newspapers and Periodicals.** Printed materials purporting to be newspapers or periodicals.

(7) **Trade Inscriptions and the Like.** Inscriptions, signs, tags, or labels purporting to have been affixed in the course of business and indicating ownership, control, or origin.

(8) **Acknowledged Documents.** Documents accompanied by a certificate of acknowledgment executed in the manner provided by law by a notary public or other officer authorized by law to take acknowledgments.

(9) **Commercial Paper and Related Documents.** Commercial paper, signatures thereon, and documents relating thereto to the extent provided by general commercial law.

(10) **Presumptions Under Acts of Congress.** Any signature, document, or other matter declared by Act of Congress to be presumptively or prima facie genuine or authentic.

(11) **Certified Domestic Records of Regularly Conducted Activity.** The original or a duplicate of a domestic record of regularly conducted activity that would be admissible under Rule 803(6) if accompanied by a written declaration of its custodian or other qualified person, in a manner complying with any Act of Congress or rule prescribed by the Supreme Court pursuant to statutory authority, certifying that the record—

(A) was made at or near the time of the occurrence of the matters set forth by, or from information transmitted by, a person with knowledge of those matters;

(B) was kept in the course of the regularly conducted activity; and

(C) was made by the regularly conducted activity as a regular practice.

A party intending to offer a record into evidence under this paragraph must provide written notice of that intention to all adverse parties, and must make the record and declaration available for inspection sufficiently in advance of their offer into evidence to provide an adverse party with a fair opportunity to challenge them.

**(12) Certified Foreign Records of Regularly Conducted Activity.** In a civil case, the original or a duplicate of a foreign record of regularly conducted activity that would be admissible under Rule 803(6) if accompanied by a written declaration by its custodian or other qualified person certifying that the record—

(A) was made at or near the time of the occurrence of the matters set forth by, or from information transmitted by, a person with knowledge of those matters;

(B) was kept in the course of the regularly conducted activity; and

(C) was made by the regularly conducted activity as a regular practice.

The declaration must be signed in a manner that, if falsely made, would subject the maker to criminal penalty under the laws of the country where the declaration is signed. A party intending to offer a record into evidence under this paragraph must provide written notice of that intention to all adverse parties, and must make the record and declaration available for inspection sufficiently in advance of their offer into evidence to provide an adverse party with a fair opportunity to challenge them.

[Amended March 2, 1987, effective October 1, 1987; April 25, 1988, effective November 1, 1988; April 17, 2000, effective December 1, 2000.]

## RULE 903. SUBSCRIBING WITNESS' TESTIMONY UNNECESSARY

The testimony of a subscribing witness is not necessary to authenticate a writing unless required by the laws of the jurisdiction whose laws govern the validity of the writing.

# ARTICLE X. CONTENTS OF WRITINGS, RECORDINGS, AND PHOTOGRAPHS

## RULE 1001. DEFINITIONS

For purposes of this article the following definitions are applicable:

**(1) Writings and Recordings.** "Writings" and "recordings" consist of letters, words, or numbers, or their equivalent, set down by handwriting, typewriting, printing, photostating, photographing, magnetic impulse, mechanical or electronic recording, or other form of data compilation.

**(2) Photographs.** "Photographs" include still photographs, X-ray films, video tapes, and motion pictures.

**(3) Original.** An "original" of a writing or recording is the writing or recording itself or any counterpart intended to have the same effect by a person executing or issuing it. An "original" of a photograph includes the negative or any print therefrom. If data are stored in a computer or similar device, any printout or other output readable by sight, shown to reflect the data accurately, is an "original".

**(4) Duplicate.** A "duplicate" is a counterpart produced by the same impression as the original, or from the same matrix, or by means of photography, including enlargements and miniatures, or by mechanical or electronic re-recording, or by chemical reproduction, or by other equivalent techniques which accurately reproduces the original.

## RULE 1002. REQUIREMENT OF ORIGINAL

To prove the content of a writing, recording, or photograph, the original writing, recording, or photograph is required, except as otherwise provided in these rules or by Act of Congress.

## RULE 1003. ADMISSIBILITY OF DUPLICATES

A duplicate is admissible to the same extent as an original unless (1) a genuine question is raised as to the authenticity of the original or (2) in the circumstances it would be unfair to admit the duplicate in lieu of the original.

## RULE 1004. ADMISSIBILITY OF OTHER EVIDENCE OF CONTENTS

The original is not required, and other evidence of the contents of a writing, recording, or photograph is admissible if—

**(1) Originals Lost or Destroyed.** All originals are lost or have been destroyed, unless the proponent lost or destroyed them in bad faith; or

**(2) Original Not Obtainable.** No original can be obtained by any available judicial process or procedure; or

**(3) Original in Possession of Opponent.** At a time when an original was under the control of the party against whom offered, that party was put on notice, by the pleadings or otherwise, that the contents would be a subject of proof at the hearing, and that party does not produce the original at the hearing; or

**(4) Collateral Matters.** The writing, recording, or photograph is not closely related to a controlling issue.

[Amended March 2, 1987, effective October 1, 1987.]

## RULE 1005. PUBLIC RECORDS

The contents of an official record, or of a document authorized to be recorded or filed and actually record-

ed or filed, including data compilations in any form, if otherwise admissible, may be proved by copy, certified as correct in accordance with rule 902 or testified to be correct by a witness who has compared it with the original. If a copy which complies with the foregoing cannot be obtained by the exercise of reasonable diligence, then other evidence of the contents may be given.

### RULE 1006. SUMMARIES

The contents of voluminous writings, recordings, or photographs which cannot conveniently be examined in court may be presented in the form of a chart, summary, or calculation. The originals, or duplicates, shall be made available for examination or copying, or both, by other parties at reasonable time and place. The court may order that they be produced in court.

### RULE 1007. TESTIMONY OR WRITTEN ADMISSION OF PARTY

Contents of writings, recordings, or photographs may be proved by the testimony or deposition of the party against whom offered or by that party's written admission, without accounting for the nonproduction of the original.

[Amended March 2, 1987, effective October 1, 1987.]

### RULE 1008. FUNCTIONS OF COURT AND JURY

When the admissibility of other evidence of contents of writings, recordings, or photographs under these rules depends upon the fulfillment of a condition of fact, the question whether the condition has been fulfilled is ordinarily for the court to determine in accordance with the provisions of rule 104. However, when an issue is raised (a) whether the asserted writing ever existed, or (b) whether another writing, recording, or photograph produced at the trial is the original, or (c) whether other evidence of contents correctly reflects the contents, the issue is for the trier of fact to determine as in the case of other issues of fact.

# ARTICLE XI.　MISCELLANEOUS RULES

### RULE 1101. APPLICABILITY OF RULES

**(a) Courts and Judges.** These rules apply to the United States district courts, the District Court of Guam, the District Court of the Virgin Islands, the District Court for the Northern Mariana Islands, the United States courts of appeals, the United States Claims Court, and to United States bankruptcy judges and United States magistrate judges, in the actions, cases, and proceedings and to the extent hereinafter set forth. The terms "judge" and "court" in these rules include United States bankruptcy judges and United States magistrate judges.

**(b) Proceedings Generally.** These rules apply generally to civil actions and proceedings, including admiralty and maritime cases, to criminal cases and proceedings, to contempt proceedings except those in which the court may act summarily, and to proceedings and cases under title 11, United States Code.

**(c) Rule of Privilege.** The rule with respect to privileges applies at all stages of all actions, cases, and proceedings.

**(d) Rules Inapplicable.** The rules (other than with respect to privileges) do not apply in the following situations:

(1) *Preliminary Questions of Fact.* The determination of questions of fact preliminary to admissibility of evidence when the issue is to be determined by the court under rule 104.

(2) *Grand Jury.* Proceedings before grand juries.

(3) *Miscellaneous Proceedings.* Proceedings for extradition or rendition; preliminary examinations in criminal cases; sentencing, or granting or revoking probation; issuance of warrants for arrest, criminal summonses, and search warrants; and proceedings with respect to release on bail or otherwise.

**(e) Rules Applicable in Part.** In the following proceedings these rules apply to the extent that matters of evidence are not provided for in the statutes which govern procedure therein or in other rules prescribed by the Supreme Court pursuant to statutory authority: the trial of misdemeanors and other petty offenses before United States magistrate judges; review of agency actions when the facts are subject to trial de novo under section 706(2)(F) of title 5, United States Code; review of orders of the Secretary of Agriculture under section 2 of the Act entitled "An Act to authorize association of producers of agricultural products" approved February 18, 1922 (7 U.S.C. 292), and under sections 6 and 7(c) of the Perishable Agricultural Commodities Act, 1930 (7 U.S.C. 499f, 499g(c)); naturalization and revocation of naturalization under sections 310–318 of the Immigration and Nationality Act (8 U.S.C. 1421–1429); prize proceedings in admiralty under sections 7651–7681 of title 10, United States Code; review of orders of the Secretary of the Interior under section 2 of the Act entitled "An Act authorizing associations of producers of aquatic products" approved June 25, 1934 (15 U.S.C. 522); review of orders of petroleum control boards under section 5 of the Act entitled "An Act to regulate interstate and foreign commerce in petroleum and its products by prohibiting the shipment in such commerce of petroleum and its products produced in violation of State law, and for other purposes", approved February 22, 1935 (15 U.S.C. 715d); actions for fines, penalties, or forfeitures under part V of title

IV of the Tariff Act of 1930 (19 U.S.C. 1581–1624), or under the Anti-Smuggling Act (19 U.S.C. 1701–1711); criminal libel for condemnation, exclusion of imports, or other proceedings under the Federal Food, Drug, and Cosmetic Act (21 U.S.C. 301–392); disputes between seamen under sections 4079, 4080, and 4081 of the Revised Statutes (22 U.S.C. 256–258); habeas corpus under sections 2241–2254 of title 28, United States Code; motions to vacate, set aside or correct sentence under section 2255 of title 28, United States Code; actions for penalties for refusal to transport destitute seamen under section 4578 of the Revised Statutes (46 U.S.C. 679);* actions against the United States under the Act entitled "An Act authorizing suits against the United States in admiralty for damage caused by and salvage service rendered to public vessels belonging to the United States, and for other purposes", approved March 3, 1925 (46 U.S.C. 781–790), as implemented by section 7730 of title 10, United States Code.

* Law Revision Counsel Note: Repealed and reenacted as 46 U.S.C. 11104(b)-(d) by Pub.L. 98–89, §§ 1, 2(a), 4(b), August 26, 1983, 97 Stat. 500.

[Amended by Pub.L. 94–149, § 1(14), December 12, 1975, 89 Stat. 806; Pub.L. 95–598, Title II, § 251, November 6, 1978,

92 Stat. 2673, effective October 1, 1979; Pub.L. 97–164, Title I, § 142, April 2, 1982, 96 Stat. 45, effective October 1, 1982; amended March 2, 1987, effective October 1, 1987; April 25, 1988, effective November 1, 1988; amended by Pub.L. 100–690, Title VII, § 7075(c)(1), November 18, 1988, 102 Stat. 4405 (although amendment by Pub.L. 100–690 could not be executed due to prior amendment by Court order which made the same change effective November 1, 1988); amended April 22, 1993, effective December 1, 1993.]

## RULE 1102. AMENDMENTS

Amendments to the Federal Rules of Evidence may be made as provided in section 2072 of title 28 of the United States Code.

[Amended April 30, 1991, effective December 1, 1991.]

## RULE 1103. TITLE

These rules may be known and cited as the Federal Rules of Evidence.

# INDEX TO
# FEDERAL RULES OF EVIDENCE

# FEDERAL RULES OF APPELLATE PROCEDURE AND LOCAL RULES OF THE SECOND CIRCUIT

**Federal Rules of Appellate Procedure**
**Adopted Effective July 1, 1968**
**Including Federal Rules of Appellate Procedure Amendments**
**Effective December 1, 2007, Absent Contrary Congressional Action**
**and Second Circuit Amendments Received Through October 15, 2007**

---

*Research Note*

*These rules may be searched electronically on WESTLAW in the US–RULES database; updates to these rules may be found on WESTLAW in US–ORDERS or US–RULESUPDATES. For search tips, and a detailed summary of database content, consult the WESTLAW Scope Screen of each database.*

---

*Table of Rules*

## FORMS

### FEDERAL RULES OF APPELLATE PROCEDURE FORMS

**Form**

1. Notice of Appeal to a Court of Appeals From a Judgment or Order of a District Court.
2. Notice of Appeal to a Court of Appeals From a Decision of the United States Tax Court.
3. Petition for Review of Order of an Agency, Board, Commission or Officer.
4. Affidavit Accompanying Motion for Permission to Appeal In Forma Pauperis.
5. Notice of Appeal to a Court of Appeals From a Judgment or Order of a District Court or a Bankruptcy Appellate Panel.
6. Certificate of Compliance With Rule 32(a).

### SECOND CIRCUIT MISCELLANEOUS FORMS

Notice of Appearance Form.
Application for Fees and Other Expenses Under Equal Access to Justice Act (Form AO 291).
Criminal Notice of Appeal Form.
Criminal Case Information Form (Form A).
Civil Appeal Pre-argument Statement (Form C).
Civil Appeal Transcript Information (Form D).
Agency Appeal Pre-argument Statement (Form C–A).
Notice of Motion (Form T 1080).
Instructions for Bill of Costs and Itemized and Verified Bill of Costs Form.
Law Student Practice Forms.
Application for Leave to File a Second or Successive Motion to Vacate, Set Aside or Correct Sentence, 28 U.S.C. § 2255, By Prisoner in Federal Custody.
Application for Leave to File a Second or Successive Habeas Corpus Petition, 28 U.S.C. § 2244(b), By Prisoner in State Custody.
Certificate of Death Penalty Case.
Electronic Notification Agreement.
Anti-Virus Certification Form.
Non-Compliance with Digital Brief Requirement (To Be Completed Only In Counseled Cases).

## APPENDIX

### PART A.   AMENDED PLAN TO IMPLEMENT THE CRIMINAL JUSTICE ACT OF 1964

# PART 1.  LOCAL RULES RELATING TO THE ORGANIZATION OF THE COURT

## § 0.11  Name

The name of the court, as fixed by 28 U.S.C. §§ 41, 43(a), is "United States Court of Appeals for the Second Circuit."

[December 1, 1994.]

## § 0.12  Seal

The seal of the court shall contain the words "United States" on the upper part of the outer edge; and the words "Court of Appeals" on the lower part of the outer edge, running from left to right; and the words "Second Circuit" in two lines, in the center, with a dash beneath.

[December 1, 1994.]

## § 0.13  Terms

One term of this court shall be held annually at the City of New York commencing on such day in August or September as the court may designate. It shall be adjourned to such times and places as the court may from time to time direct.

[December 1, 1994.]

## § 0.14  Quorum

(a) Two judges shall constitute a quorum. If, at any time, a quorum does not attend on any day appointed for holding a session of the court, any judge who does attend or, in the absence of any judge, the clerk may adjourn the court for such time as may be appropriate. Any judge attending when less than a quorum is present or at any time when the court is in recess may make any necessary procedural order touching any suit or proceeding preparatory to hearing or decision of the merits. (See Part 2, Local Rule 27(f).)

(b) (Interim) Unless directed otherwise, a panel of the court shall consist of three judges. If a judge of a panel of the court shall cease to continue with the consideration of any matter by reason of recusal, death, illness, resignation, incapacity, or other reason, the two remaining judges will determine the matter if

they reach agreement and neither requests the designation of a third judge. If they do not reach agreement or either requests such a designation, another circuit judge will be designated by the Clerk to sit in place of the judge who has been relieved. The parties shall be advised of such designation, but no additional argument will be had or briefs received unless otherwise ordered.

[December 1, 1994; amendments adopted on an interim basis effective November 16, 2004.]

## § 0.15　Disclosure of Interested Parties [Superseded by FRAP 26.1]

## § 0.16　Clerk

(See generally Federal Rule 45 of the Federal Rules of Appellate Procedure.)

(a) The clerk's office shall be kept at the United States Court House, 40 Foley Square, New York City, and shall be open from 9:00 o'clock A.M. until 5:00 o'clock P.M. daily, except Saturdays, Sundays and legal holidays.

(b) The clerk may permit any original record or paper to be taken from the courtroom or from the office upon such statement of need as the clerk may require, and upon receipt for such record or paper.

(c) When it is required that the record be certified to the Supreme Court of the United States, the clerk if possessed of the original papers, exhibits, and transcript of proceedings of the district court or agency and a copy of the docket entries of that court or agency shall certify and transmit them and the original papers filed in this court.

[December 1, 1994.]

## § 0.17　Clerk's Fees

Following are fees to be charged for services provided by the courts of appeals. No fees are to be charged for services rendered on behalf of the United States, with the exception of those specifically prescribed in items 2, 4 and 5. No fees under this schedule shall be charged to federal agencies or programs which are funded from judiciary appropriations, including, but not limited to, agencies, organizations, and individuals providing services authorized by the Criminal Justice Act, 18 U.S.C. § 3006A, and Bankruptcy Administrator programs.

1. For docketing a case on appeal or review, or docketing any other proceeding, $450. A separate fee shall be paid by each party filing a notice of appeal in the district court, but parties filing a joint notice of appeal in the district court are required to pay only one fee. A docketing fee shall not be charged for the docketing of an application for the allowance of an interlocutory appeal under 28 U.S.C. § 1292(b), unless the appeal is allowed.

2. For every search of the records of the court and certifying the results thereof, $26. This fee shall apply to services rendered on behalf of the United States if the information requested is available through electronic access.

3. For certifying any document or paper, whether the certification is made directly on the document, or by separate instrument, $9.

4. For reproducing any record or paper 50 cents per page. This fee shall apply to paper copies made from either (1) original documents, or (2) microfiche or microfilm reproductions of the original records. This fee shall apply to services rendered on behalf of the United States if the record or paper requested is available through electronic access.

5. For reproduction of recordings of proceedings, regardless of the medium, $26, including the cost of materials. This fee shall apply to services rendered on behalf of the United States if the reproduction of the recording is available electronically.

6. For reproduction of the record in any appeal in which the requirement of an appendix is dispensed with by any court of appeals pursuant to Rule 30(f), F.R.A.P., a flat fee of $71.

7. For each microfiche or microfilm copy of any court record, where available, $5.

8. For retrieval of a record from a Federal Records Center, National Archives, or other storage location removed from the place of business of the court, $45.

9. For a check paid into the court which is returned for a lack of funds, $45.

10. Fees to be charged and collected for copies of opinions shall be fixed, from time to time, by each court, commensurate with the cost of printing.

11. The court may charge and collect fees, commensurate with the cost of printing, for copies of the local rules of court. The court may also distribute copies of the local rules without charge.

12. The clerk shall assess a charge for the handling of registry funds deposited with the court, to be assessed from interest earnings and in accordance with the detailed fee schedule issued by the Director of the Administrative Office of the United States Courts.

13. Upon the filing of any separate or joint notice of appeal or application for appeal from the Bankruptcy Appellate Panel, or notice of the allowance of an appeal from the Bankruptcy Appellate Panel, or of a writ of certiorari, $5 shall be paid by the appellant or petitioner.

14. The court may charge and collect a fee of $200 per remote location for counsel's requested use of video-conferencing equipment in connection with each oral argument.

**15.** For original admission of attorneys to practice, $190 each, including a certificate of admission. For a duplicate certificate of admission or certificate of good standing, $15.

[December 1, 1994. Amended October 17, 2005.]

## § 0.18 Entry of Orders by the Clerk

The clerk shall prepare, sign and enter the following without submission to the court or a judge unless otherwise directed:

(1) orders for the dismissal of an appeal under Rule 42(b) or pursuant to an order of the court or a judge;

(2) procedural orders on consent;

(3) orders on mandate from the Supreme Court of the United States;

(4) judgments in appeals from the United States Tax Court based on a stipulation of the parties;

(5) orders and judgments on decisions by the court in motions and appeals (See Rule 36 of Federal Rules of Appellate Procedure);

(6) orders scheduling the docketing of the record and filing of briefs and argument, which may include a provision that, in the event of default by the appellant in docketing the record or filing the appellant's brief, the appeal will be dismissed by the clerk;

(7) orders dismissing appeals in all cases where a brief for the appellant has not been filed within nine months of the docketing of the appeal and no stipulation extending the time for such filing has been filed.

(8) orders of dismissal as provided in Interim Local Rule § 0.29(d).

[December 1, 1994; subsection (8) adopted on an interim basis effective August 25, 2005.]

## § 0.19 Process

All process of this court shall be in the name of the President of the United States, and shall be in like form and tested in the same manner as process of the Supreme Court.

[December 1, 1994.]

## § 0.20 Opinions of the Court

**(a) Delivery.** Opinions will be delivered at any time, whether the court is in session or not, and are delivered by handing them to the clerk to be recorded.

**(b) Preservation of Original Opinions.** The original opinions of the court shall be filed with the clerk for preservation.

[December 1, 1994.]

## § 0.21 Library

The library of this court shall be open to members of any court of the United States and their staffs, to law officers of the Government, and to members of the bar of this court. It shall be open during such hours as reasonable needs require and be governed by such regulations as the librarian, with the approval of the court, may prescribe. Books shall not be removed from the building.

[December 1, 1994.]

## § 0.22 Judicial Conference of the Second Circuit

**1. Purpose.** There shall be held annually, at such time and place as shall be designated by the chief judge of the circuit, a conference of all the circuit, district and bankruptcy judges, and magistrate judges, of the circuit for the purpose of considering the state of business of the courts and ways and means of improving the administration of justice within the circuit. It shall be the duty of each circuit and district judge in the circuit, in active service, and each bankruptcy judge serving for a term pursuant to 28 U.S.C. § 152, to attend the conference unless excused by the chief judge. The circuit justice shall be invited to attend.

**2. Sessions.** A portion of the conference, to be known as the "executive session," shall be for the judges alone and shall be devoted to a discussion of matters affecting the state of the dockets and the administration of justice throughout the circuit. At other sessions of the conference, members of the bar, to be chosen as set forth in the succeeding paragraph, shall be members of the conference and shall participate in its discussions and deliberations.

**3. Members of the Bar.** Members of the conference from the bar shall be selected to reflect a cross-section of lawyers who currently practice before federal courts in this circuit; members should be willing and able to contribute actively to conference purposes. In order to assure that fresh views are represented, no judge may invite the same individual more than two years out of any five. The membership shall be composed of the following:

(a) The presidents of the state bar associations of the three states of the circuit and a member from each of such associations to be designated by their respective presidents with a view to giving appropriate representation to various areas of the state.

(b) Each United States Attorney of the circuit or an Assistant United States Attorney designated by the United States Attorney.

(c) The Public Defender (or an assistant designated by the Public Defender) for any district within the circuit, and a representative of a community defender organization, authorized to act generally in any district, designated by the president of such organization.

(d) Such number of invitees by the circuit justice, and the active and senior circuit and district judges, as

the judicial council may determine for each conference.

(e) Such additional number of lawyers as shall be selected jointly by the chief judge and the conference chairperson in light of their competence and interest in the subject or subjects to be considered at the conference. These conference members also shall be selected to reflect a cross-section of lawyers who currently practice before federal courts in this circuit, and may include:

(i) Members of county and local bar associations in the circuit, selected in consultation with their respective presidents, reflecting the geography and the relative size and activity in federal litigation of those associations;

(ii) The dean, or other representative of the faculty of law schools within the circuit;

(iii) Members of State/Federal Judicial Councils within the circuit (including especially state court chief judges or chief justices);

(iv) Members of the United States Senate and House of Representatives with a particular interest in the work of the federal courts;

(v) Former presidents of the American Bar Association residing or practicing in the Second Circuit; the current member of the Board of Governors of the American Bar Association from the Second Circuit; the current member of the Standing Committee on the Federal Judiciary of the American Bar Association from the circuit; the chairperson of such committee if residing or practicing in the circuit; and the president, former presidents, and the executive director of the American Law Institute if residing or practicing in the circuit;

(vi) Members of the staff of federal courts within the circuit not enumerated elsewhere in this rule.

(f) Any retired Justice of the Supreme Court of the United States residing within the circuit, any present or former Attorney General of the United States residing or practicing within the circuit, and any circuit or district judge of the circuit who has resigned such office.

(g) The Director (or, if the Director is unable to attend, the Director's designee) of the Administrative Office of the United States Courts, and the Director (or designee) of the Federal Judicial Center.

(h) The circuit and district court executives and clerks of the courts within the circuit.

(i) Members of the committee provided for in paragraph 4 of this Rule, and past chairpersons and executive secretaries of such committee.

4. **Committee.** To assist in the conduct of the conference (other than the executive session), the chief judge shall appoint annually, subject to the approval of the judicial council, members of a committee to be known as the Planning and Program Committee. The

committee, whose members shall be appointed to staggered three-year terms, shall include the presidents of the state bar associations of the three states of the circuit and such number of judges and members of the bar of the circuit as the chief judge may determine.

5. **Chairperson.** The chief judge may also appoint a conference chairperson to be selected from among the active judges of the circuit.

6. **Representative to the Judicial Conference of the United States.**

(a) Three months before the date of the Judicial Conference of the Second Circuit at which the district judge member of the Judicial Conference of the United States from the Second Circuit is to be chosen, the chief judges of the district courts of the circuit, acting together as a nominating committee, shall nominate no more than three active district judges of the circuit (not excluding one of their own number) as candidates for the office of district judge member from the Second Circuit. The names of the nominees will be mailed to all the judges of the circuit and to the Clerk of the Court of Appeals, who is the secretary of the conference, at least thirty days before the date of the executive session of the Circuit Judicial Conference.

(b) Additional active district judges may be put in nomination (i) from the floor at the executive session in replacement of any nominee of the chief judges who is disabled or declines to stand, and (ii) from the floor at the executive session by written nomination signed by at least one-fourth of the judges of the circuit. The one-fourth requirement shall not include vacant judgeships or judgeships for which commissions have been signed but the nominees have not been sworn and have not taken office at the time the nominating petition is signed. No judge may sign more than one such nomination and such nomination may not include more than one judge.

(c) The judge receiving a plurality of the votes of the active judges of the circuit will be the circuit's choice. Voting will be by secret, written ballot. Any judge who expects to be absent from the meeting may send in a judge's ballot unsigned and enclosed in an inner, sealed envelope, to the secretary of the conference provided that the ballot reaches the secretary before the executive meeting is convened.

(d) No judge may succeed himself or herself to a second successive term by election and no judge of any district court may succeed a judge from the same district unless at least three years have elapsed since the expiration of such earlier judge's term; however, in the case of a judge who is a member of the Executive Committee of the Judicial Conference of the United States, such judge may be elected to a second successive term in order to continue eligibility to serve on the Executive Committee.

(e) In the event that it is not convenient to conduct at a Judicial Conference the election referred to here-

in, such election may be conducted by mail ballot following action by the nominating committee, according to such procedures as that body may establish.

[December 1, 1994.]

## § 0.24 Complaints With Respect to Conduct of Judges [Superseded]

[Superseded July 1, 1987 by the Rules of Judicial Council of the Second Circuit Governing Complaints against Judicial Officers under 28 U.S.C. § 372(c). See Court's website, Forms Page.]

## § 0.25 Equal Access to Justice Act Fees

Applications authorized by 28 U.S.C. § 2412(d)(1)(B) shall be filed within 30 days of this court's judgment, and petitions for review authorized by 5 U.S.C. § 504(c)(2) shall be filed within 30 days of the agency's fee determination. Applications and petitions shall be filed with the clerk of this court (original and four copies), served on all parties, and submitted on form AO 291. (A T1080 Motion Information Statement is also required.)

[December 1, 1994.]

## § 0.26 Permissive Review After Appeal of a Magistrate's Judgment to the District Court

Petitions for leave to appeal authorized by 28 U.S.C. § 636(c)(5) shall be filed with the clerk of this court (original and four copies) within 30 days of the District Court's judgment and shall be served on all parties.

[December 1, 1994.]

## § 0.27 Certification of Questions of State Law

Where authorized by state law, this Court may certify to the highest court of a state an unsettled and significant question of state law that will control the outcome of a case pending before this Court. Such certification may be made by this Court sua sponte or on motion of a party filed with the clerk of this Court. Certification will be in accordance with the procedures provided by the state's legislature or highest state court rules, e.g., Conn. Public Act No. 85–111; New York Court of Appeals Rule 500.7. Certification may stay the proceedings in this Court pending the state court's decision whether to accept the certification and its decision of the certified question.

[December 1, 1994.]

## § 0.28 Death Penalty Cases

This rule describes the administration of capital cases in this Court. Capital case, as used in this rule, means any application in this Court, to which the person under sentence is a party, that challenges, defends, or otherwise relates to the validity or execution of a death sentence that has been imposed. Capital cases ordinarily will be heard by panels composed in the manner described herein. The Court, however, may deviate from these procedures; their publication does not give any litigant a right to require that they be followed.

(1) **Certificate of Death Penalty Case.** Upon the filing of any proceeding in a district court of this circuit or in this Court challenging a sentence of death imposed pursuant to a federal or state court judgment, each party in such proceeding must file a Certificate of Death Penalty Case with the Clerk of the Court of Appeals. A Certificate of Death Penalty Case must also be filed by the U.S. Attorney upon the return of a verdict recommending a sentence of death in a district court of this circuit. The Certificate must be in the form provided as annexed to these rules, or in substantially similar form, and must set forth the names, telephone numbers and addresses of the parties and counsel; the proposed date of execution of the sentence, if set; and the emergency nature of the proceedings, if applicable.

A special tracking docket is maintained by the Clerk of this Court for all cases in which a district court of this circuit has imposed a sentence of death, and for all proceedings in a district court of this circuit or in this Court challenging a sentence of death imposed pursuant to a federal or state court judgment.

(2) **Preparation and Transmittal of the Record.** Upon the filing of a notice of appeal from an order under 18 U.S.C. § 3731, 28 U.S.C. § 1291, or 28 U.S.C. § 1292(a)(1) in a death penalty case in the district court, the Clerk of the district court and appellant's counsel must immediately prepare the record for the appeal. The record must be transmitted to this Court within five days of the filing of the notice of appeal unless such order is entered within twenty-one (21) days of the date of a scheduled execution, in which case the record must be transmitted immediately by an expedited means of delivery.

(3) **Monitoring of Cases and Lodging of Relevant Documents.** The Clerk of the Court of Appeals is authorized to monitor the status of scheduled executions and pending litigation in connection with any case within the geographical boundaries of this circuit wherein a warrant or order setting an execution date has been entered, and to establish communications with all parties and relevant state and/or federal courts. The Clerk may direct parties to lodge with this Court five copies of (1) all relevant portions of previous state and/or federal court records, or the entire record, and (2) all pleadings, briefs, and transcripts of any ongoing proceedings. The Clerk may docket such materials in advance of this Court's jurisdiction, under a miscellaneous docket, pending receipt of a notice of appeal or application in such case. This miscellaneous docket case is closed upon the opening of a regularly docketed case in this Court, or upon other final disposition of the case without its reaching this Court (for

example, a reversal of the sentence or conviction which is not appealed, or a carrying out of the execution).

**(4) Capital Case Pool and Panels.**

(a) *Capital Case Pool.* The capital case pool of judges consists of all active judges of the Court and those senior judges who have filed with the Clerk a statement of willingness to serve on capital case panels.

(b) *Capital Case Panel.* Upon receipt of a notice of appeal from the district court, an application for a certificate of appealability, or other application to this Court for relief in a capital case, the Clerk dockets the case and assigns it to a capital case panel (except as provided in paragraph 5 of this rule). A capital case panel consists of three judges, of whom at least one is an active judge of the Court.

(c) *Selection.* Judges are assigned to capital case panels by random drawing from the capital case pool. If a judge is unable to serve, that judge's name is returned to the pool after a replacement has been drawn. In the event a random drawing results in the names of three senior judges having been selected, the name of the third such senior judge is set aside and the selection process continues until an active judge's name is drawn; after the active judge's name has been drawn, the third senior judge's name is returned to the pool.

(d) *Rotation.* A judge drawn from the capital case pool to serve on a capital case panel is not returned to the pool until the pool is exhausted. When the pool has been exhausted, the Clerk prepares a new capital case pool and selects capital case panels from the pool in like manner.

(e) *Replacement.* If any judge serving on a capital case panel is unable to continue to serve, a replacement is drawn from the capital case pool, and the judge ceasing to serve on the panel is returned to the pool.

(f) *Duties of Capital Case Panel.* A capital case panel assigned to a particular capital case handles all matters pertaining to that case, including but not limited to the merits of a direct appeal and of all petitions for collateral review, motions for stay of execution, motions to vacate a stay of execution, applications for a certificate of appealability, motions for an order authorizing the district court to consider a second or successive application for habeas corpus, appeals from subsequent petitions, and remands from the United States Supreme Court. When practical, a capital case panel hearing a direct appeal from a death sentence imposed in federal court hears together with it the direct appeals of co-defendants, at least to the extent they involve issues in common with the appeal of the person sentenced to death. Non-common issues in the appeals of co-defendants may be severed and assigned to an ordinary panel.

(g) *Applications for Certificate of Appealability.* Applications for a certificate of appealability are referred initially to a single judge of the capital case panel, who has authority to grant the certificate. If the single judge does not grant the certificate, the application is referred to the full panel for disposition by majority vote.

**(5) Original Petitions.** All original applications for habeas corpus relief filed in the Clerk's office in a capital case are referred to a judge on the capital case panel in accordance with the approved operating procedures of this Court. Such an application ordinarily is transferred to the appropriate district court.

**(6) Ruling on Certificate of Appealability.** This Court may rule on a certificate of appealability whether or not a formal request is made of this Court, either as a preliminary matter or as part of a merits review of the case.

**(7) Stays of Execution and Motions to Vacate Orders Granting Stay of a Federal or State Court Judgment.**

(a) *Limits on Stays of Execution.* Notwithstanding any provision of this paragraph 7, stays of execution are not granted, or maintained, except in accordance with law. Thus, the provisions of this paragraph 7 for a stay are ineffective in any case in which such stay would be inconsistent with the limitations of 28 U.S.C. § 2262, or any other governing statute.

(b) *Emergency Motions.* Emergency motions or applications are filed with the Clerk of the Court of Appeals. If time does not permit the filing of a motion or application in person or by mail, counsel may communicate with the Clerk and obtain the Clerk's permission to file the motion by telefacsimile. Counsel are encouraged to communicate with the Clerk by telephone as soon as it becomes evident that emergency relief will be sought from this Court. The motion or application must contain a brief account of the prior actions, if any, of this Court and the name of the judge or judges involved in such prior actions.

(c) *Documents Required for Motions for Stay or to Vacate Stay.* The party moving for a stay of execution of a sentence of death or to vacate a stay must file the original and four (4) copies (a total of five) of the motion and serve all parties. A copy of the documents listed below must be attached to the original and to each copy of the motion. If time does not permit, the motion may be filed without attachments, but the movant must file the necessary copies as soon as possible. (If the respondent (the State or the U.S. Attorney) has indicated to the petitioner that it does not seek to oppose the stay immediately and the petitioner states this fact in the petition, these documents need not be filed with the application but must be filed within ten (10) days after the application is filed.)

(i) The indictment or other accusatory instrument;

(ii) The judgment of conviction containing the sentence of death;

(iii) The petition or complaint filed in the district court;

(iv) The opinion of the district court setting forth the reasons for granting or denying relief;

(v) The district court judgment granting or denying relief;

(vi) The district court order granting or denying a stay, and the statement of reasons for its action;

(vii) The certificate of appealability or order denying a certificate of appealability;

(viii) A copy of each state or federal court opinion or judgment bearing on the issues presented in the motion in cases in which appellant was a party;

(ix) A copy of the docket entries of the district court; and

(x) A copy of the notice of appeal.

(d) *Automatic Stays.* In any case in which a sentence of death has been imposed by a district court of this circuit, or by a state court within the circuit, execution of the sentence of death is automatically stayed upon the filing of a notice of appeal from the judgment of conviction or a notice of appeal from the denial of the first application in federal court seeking relief from the sentence of death. The clerk must promptly enter an order implementing the stay. Unless vacated or modified, the stay provided by this subparagraph remains in effect until the expiration of all proceedings available to the person sentenced to death (including review by the United States Supreme Court) as part of the direct review of the judgment of conviction or of the denial of such first application. The stay may be modified or vacated by the assigned panel at any time.

(e) *Other Stays.* A stay of any duration up to that specified in subparagraph 7(f)(i) may be ordered in any case by the assigned capital case panel, upon the affirmative vote of any judge of that panel.

(f) *Duration of Stays: Terminology.* Use of the following terminology to specify the duration of a stay denotes the durations specified below:

(i) If, in granting a stay of execution of a sentence of death, the Court or judge indicates that the stay shall be in effect "for the standard duration" under this rule, this signifies that, unless vacated or modified, the stay remains in effect until the expiration of all proceedings available to the person sentenced to death (including review by the United States Supreme Court) as part of the direct review of the judgment of the district court, or of the Court of Appeals in the case of an original petition filed there.

(ii) If, in granting a stay of execution of a sentence of death, the Court or judge indicates that the stay shall be in effect "for the duration of the appeal," this signifies that, unless vacated or modified, the stay remains in effect until the Court's mandate issues. Absent an order to the contrary preceded by timely notice to counsel, the mandate does not issue until the time for filing a petition for rehearing has expired, or, if such a petition has been filed, until the petition and any petition for rehearing in banc have been determined.

(g) *Stays in Relation to Petitions for Rehearing.*

(i) Petitions for rehearing accompanied by petitions for rehearing in banc are circulated to all judges of the capital case pool simultaneously with the circulation of the petition for rehearing to the assigned capital case panel. Judges participating in the petition for rehearing in banc may vote on a stay of execution of a sentence of death immediately, without waiting for the action of the assigned panel as to the petition for rehearing.

(ii) A stay of execution of a sentence of death pending disposition of the petition for rehearing and the petition for rehearing in banc is granted upon the affirmative vote of any two judges eligible to participate in a rehearing in banc.

(h) All stay applications must be filed with the Clerk of the Court. In each case in which the Court orders a stay of execution, the Clerk of the Court issues a written order in the name of the Court specifying the duration of the stay.

(i) During non-business hours, emergency stay applications must be directed to an assigned representative of the Clerk (the duty clerk), whose telephone number is left with the courthouse security officers. The duty clerk must immediately advise the members of the assigned panel of the filing of an emergency stay application.

(j) In the event the members of the assigned panel cannot be reached by the duty clerk, the duty clerk advises the judge of the court assigned at that time to hear emergency applications of the filing of an off-hours emergency stay application. Notwithstanding the provisions of subparagraphs 7(e) and 7(g)(ii), the applications judge may stay an execution until such time as the application can be placed before the assigned panel or the Court in banc.

Effective October 13, 1998. Amended effective December 1, 2002.

## Interim § 0.29  Non–Argument Calendar

(a) The following appeals or petitions for review, and any motions filed thereon, will be initially placed on the Non-Argument Calendar:

An appeal or petition for review, in which a party seeks review of the denial of—

1. A claim for asylum under the Immigration and Nationality Act ("INA").

2. A claim for withholding of removal under the INA:

3. A claim for withholding or deferral of removal under the Convention Against Torture ("CAT"); or

4. A motion to reopen or reconsider an order involving one of the claims listed above.

Proceedings on the Non-Argument Calendar will be disposed of by a three-judge panel without oral argument unless the Court transfers the proceeding to the Regular Argument Calendar.

**(b)** To the extent practicable, the Clerk's Office will promptly identify proceedings to be placed on the Non-Argument Calendar and issue scheduling orders for them upon the receipt of the certified record. The scheduling order will inform the parties that the proceeding has been placed on the Non-Argument Calendar. Any party to a proceeding on the Non-Argument Calendar may request to have the proceeding transferred to the Regular Argument Calendar. Such a request shall not be made by motion but must be included in the party's brief, identified by a separate heading, and will be adjudicated in conformity with Federal Rule of Appellate Procedure 34(a)(2) and Local Rule 34(d)(1). In its discretion, the Court may at any time transfer a proceeding from the Non-Argu-

ment Calendar to the Regular Argument Calendar. Upon the transfer of a case from the Non-Argument Calendar to the Regular Argument Calendar, no briefs may be filed, other than those specified in the scheduling order, unless leave of Court is obtained. The Court may at any time, sua sponte, with notice to the parties, tentatively transfer a proceeding mistakenly placed on the Regular Argument Calendar to the Non-Argument Calendar.

**(c)** The Civil Appeals Management Plan shall not apply mandatorily to proceedings on the Non-Argument Calendar. However, any party to a proceeding on the Non-Argument Calendar may request a conference under the Civil Appeals Management Plan, which will be promptly provided. A request for a conference will not alter a scheduling order.

**(d)** An appeal or petition for review on the Non-Argument Calendar may be dismissed by the Clerk if, 15 days after the due date, the party seeking review has failed to file its brief. The filing of a motion for an extension of time to file a brief does not stay or alter an existing deadline. If the respondent or appellee fails to file its brief by the due date, the Clerk may calendar the proceedings for decision as early as 15 days following the due date.

[Adopted on an interim basis effective August 25, 2005. Amended effective February 23, 2007.]

# PART 2.   FEDERAL RULES OF APPELLATE PROCEDURE AND LOCAL RULES SUPPLEMENTING FEDERAL RULES OF APPELLATE PROCEDURE

## TITLE I.   APPLICABILITY OF RULES

### FRAP 1.   SCOPE OF RULES; TITLE

**(a) Scope of Rules.**

(1) These rules govern procedure in the United States courts of appeals.

(2) When these rules provide for filing a motion or other document in the district court, the procedure must comply with the practice of the district court.

**(b) [Abrogated].**

**(c) Title.**   These rules are to be known as the Federal Rules of Appellate Procedure.

[Amended April 30, 1979, effective August 1, 1979;  April 25, 1989, effective December 1, 1989;  former Rule 48 renumber-

ed as Rule 1(c) April 29, 1994, effective December 1, 1994; April 24, 1998, effective December 1, 1998;  April 29, 2002, effective December 1, 2002.]

### FRAP 2.   SUSPENSION OF RULES

On its own or a party's motion, a court of appeals may—to expedite its decision or for other good cause—suspend any provision of these rules in a particular case and order proceedings as it directs, except as otherwise provided in Rule 26(b).

[Amended April 24, 1998, effective December 1, 1998.]

# TITLE II. APPEAL FROM A JUDGMENT OR ORDER OF A DISTRICT COURT

## FRAP 3. APPEAL AS OF RIGHT— HOW TAKEN

### (a) Filing the Notice of Appeal.

(1) An appeal permitted by law as of right from a district court to a court of appeals may be taken only by filing a notice of appeal with the district clerk within the time allowed by Rule 4. At the time of filing, the appellant must furnish the clerk with enough copies of the notice to enable the clerk to comply with Rule 3(d).

(2) An appellant's failure to take any step other than the timely filing of a notice of appeal does not affect the validity of the appeal, but is ground only for the court of appeals to act as it considers appropriate, including dismissing the appeal.

(3) An appeal from a judgment by a magistrate judge in a civil case is taken in the same way as an appeal from any other district court judgment.

(4) An appeal by permission under 28 U.S.C. § 1292(b) or an appeal in a bankruptcy case may be taken only in the manner prescribed by Rules 5 and 6, respectively.

### (b) Joint or Consolidated Appeals.

(1) When two or more parties are entitled to appeal from a district-court judgment or order, and their interests make joinder practicable, they may file a joint notice of appeal. They may then proceed on appeal as a single appellant.

(2) When the parties have filed separate timely notices of appeal, the appeals may be joined or consolidated by the court of appeals.

### (c) Contents of the Notice of Appeal.

(1) The notice of appeal must:

(A) specify the party or parties taking the appeal by naming each one in the caption or body of the notice, but an attorney representing more than one party may describe those parties with such terms as "all plaintiffs," "the defendants," "the plaintiffs A, B, et al.," or "all defendants except X";

(B) designate the judgment, order, or part thereof being appealed; and

(C) name the court to which the appeal is taken.

(2) A pro se notice of appeal is considered filed on behalf of the signer and the signer's spouse and minor children (if they are parties), unless the notice clearly indicates otherwise.

(3) In a class action, whether or not the class has been certified, the notice of appeal is sufficient if it names one person qualified to bring the appeal as representative of the class.

(4) An appeal must not be dismissed for informality of form or title of the notice of appeal, or for failure to name a party whose intent to appeal is otherwise clear from the notice.

(5) Form 1 in the Appendix of Forms is a suggested form of a notice of appeal.

### (d) Serving the Notice of Appeal.

(1) The district clerk must serve notice of the filing of a notice of appeal by mailing a copy to each party's counsel of record—excluding the appellant's—or, if a party is proceeding pro se, to the party's last known address. When a defendant in a criminal case appeals, the clerk must also serve a copy of the notice of appeal on the defendant, either by personal service or by mail addressed to the defendant. The clerk must promptly send a copy of the notice of appeal and of the docket entries—and any later docket entries—to the clerk of the court of appeals named in the notice. The district clerk must note, on each copy, the date when the notice of appeal was filed.

(2) If an inmate confined in an institution files a notice of appeal in the manner provided by Rule 4(c), the district clerk must also note the date when the clerk docketed the notice.

(3) The district clerk's failure to serve notice does not affect the validity of the appeal. The clerk must note on the docket the names of the parties to whom the clerk mails copies, with the date of mailing. Service is sufficient despite the death of a party or the party's counsel.

### (e) Payment of Fees.
Upon filing a notice of appeal, the appellant must pay the district clerk all required fees. The district clerk receives the appellate docket fee on behalf of the court of appeals.

[Amended April 30, 1979, effective August 1, 1979; March 10, 1986, effective July 1, 1986; April 25, 1989, effective December 1, 1989; April 22, 1993, effective December 1, 1993; April 29, 1994, effective December 1, 1994; April 24, 1998, effective December 1, 1998.]

## LOCAL RULE 3(d). MAILING OF NOTICE OF APPEAL BY CLERKS OF DISTRICT COURTS TO CLERK OF COURT OF APPEALS

*The clerks of the district courts shall mail to the clerk of the court of appeals copies of notices of appeal in all cases and not simply in those described in FRAP 3(d).*

[December 1, 1994.]

# FRAP 3.1   APPEAL FROM A JUDGMENT OF A MAGISTRATE JUDGE IN A CIVIL CASE [ABROGATED]

[Adopted March 10, 1986, effective July 1, 1986; amended April 22, 1993, effective December 1, 1993; abrogated effective December 1, 1998.]

## FRAP 4.   APPEAL AS OF RIGHT— WHEN TAKEN

### (a) Appeal in a Civil Case.

(1) *Time for Filing a Notice of Appeal.*

(A) In a civil case, except as provided in Rules 4(a)(1)(B), 4(a)(4), and 4(c), the notice of appeal required by Rule 3 must be filed with the district clerk within 30 days after the judgment or order appealed from is entered.

(B) When the United States or its officer or agency is a party, the notice of appeal may be filed by any party within 60 days after the judgment or order appealed from is entered.

(C) An appeal from an order granting or denying an application for a writ of error coram nobis is an appeal in a civil case for purposes of Rule 4(a).

(2) *Filing Before Entry of Judgment.* A notice of appeal filed after the court announces a decision or order—but before the entry of the judgment or order—is treated as filed on the date of and after the entry.

(3) *Multiple Appeals.* If one party timely files a notice of appeal, any other party may file a notice of appeal within 14 days after the date when the first notice was filed, or within the time otherwise prescribed by this Rule 4(a), whichever period ends later.

(4) *Effect of a Motion on a Notice of Appeal.*

(A) If a party timely files in the district court any of the following motions under the Federal Rules of Civil Procedure, the time to file an appeal runs for all parties from the entry of the order disposing of the last such remaining motion:

(i) for judgment under Rule 50(b);

(ii) to amend or make additional factual findings under Rule 52(b), whether or not granting the motion would alter the judgment;

(iii) for attorney's fees under Rule 54 if the district court extends the time to appeal under Rule 58;

(iv) to alter or amend the judgment under Rule 59;

(v) for a new trial under Rule 59; or

(vi) for relief under Rule 60 if the motion is filed no later than 10 days after the judgment is entered.

(B)(i) If a party files a notice of appeal after the court announces or enters a judgment—but before it disposes of any motion listed in Rule 4(a)(4)(A)—the notice becomes effective to appeal a judgment or order, in whole or in part, when the order disposing of the last such remaining motion is entered.

(ii) A party intending to challenge an order disposing of any motion listed in Rule 4(a)(4)(A), or a judgment altered or amended upon such a motion, must file a notice of appeal, or an amended notice of appeal—in compliance with Rule 3(c)—within the time prescribed by this Rule measured from the entry of the order disposing of the last such remaining motion.

(iii) No additional fee is required to file an amended notice.

(5) *Motion for Extension of Time.*

(A) The district court may extend the time to file a notice of appeal if:

(i) a party so moves no later than 30 days after the time prescribed by this Rule 4(a) expires; and

(ii) regardless of whether its motion is filed before or during the 30 days after the time prescribed by this Rule 4(a) expires, that party shows excusable neglect or good cause.

(B) A motion filed before the expiration of the time prescribed in Rule 4(a)(1) or (3) may be ex parte unless the court requires otherwise. If the motion is filed after the expiration of the prescribed time, notice must be given to the other parties in accordance with local rules.

(C) No extension under this Rule 4(a)(5) may exceed 30 days after the prescribed time or 10 days after the date when the order granting the motion is entered, whichever is later.

(6) *Reopening the Time to File an Appeal.* The district court may reopen the time to file an appeal for a period of 14 days after the date when its order to reopen is entered, but only if all the following conditions are satisfied:

(A) the court finds that the moving party did not receive notice under Federal Rule of Civil Procedure 77(d) of the entry of the judgment or order sought to be appealed within 21 days after entry;

(B) the motion is filed within 180 days after the judgment or order is entered or within 7 days after the moving party receives notice under Federal Rule of Civil Procedure 77(d) of the entry, whichever is earlier; and

(C) the court finds that no party would be prejudiced.

(7) *Entry Defined.*

(A) A judgment or order is entered for purposes of this Rule 4(a):

(i) if Federal Rule of Civil Procedure 58(a)(1) does not require a separate document, when the judgment or order is entered in the civil docket under Federal Rule of Civil Procedure 79(a); or

(ii) if Federal Rule of Civil Procedure 58(a)(1) requires a separate document, when the judgment or order is entered in the civil docket under Federal Rule of Civil Procedure 79(a) and when the earlier of these events occurs:

- the judgment or order is set forth on a separate document, or

- 150 days have run from entry of the judgment or order in the civil docket under Federal Rule of Civil Procedure 79(a).

(B) A failure to set forth a judgment or order on a separate document when required by Federal Rule of Civil Procedure 58(a)(1) does not affect the validity of an appeal from that judgment or order.

**(b) Appeal in a Criminal Case.**

(1) *Time for Filing a Notice of Appeal.*

(A) In a criminal case, a defendant's notice of appeal must be filed in the district court within 10 days after the later of:

(i) the entry of either the judgment or the order being appealed; or

(ii) the filing of the government's notice of appeal.

(B) When the government is entitled to appeal, its notice of appeal must be filed in the district court within 30 days after the later of:

(i) the entry of the judgment or order being appealed; or

(ii) the filing of a notice of appeal by any defendant.

(2) *Filing Before Entry of Judgment.* A notice of appeal filed after the court announces a decision, sentence, or order—but before the entry of the judgment or order—is treated as filed on the date of and after the entry.

(3) *Effect of a Motion on a Notice of Appeal.*

(A) If a defendant timely makes any of the following motions under the Federal Rules of Criminal Procedure, the notice of appeal from a judgment of conviction must be filed within 10 days after the entry of the order disposing of the last such remaining motion, or within 10 days after the entry of the judgment of conviction, whichever period ends later. This provision applies to a timely motion:

(i) for judgment of acquittal under Rule 29;

(ii) for a new trial under Rule 33, but if based on newly discovered evidence, only if the motion is made no later than 10 days after the entry of the judgment; or

(iii) for arrest of judgment under Rule 34.

(B) A notice of appeal filed after the court announces a decision, sentence, or order—but before it disposes of any of the motions referred to in Rule 4(b)(3)(A)—becomes effective upon the later of the following:

(i) the entry of the order disposing of the last such remaining motion; or

(ii) the entry of the judgment of conviction.

(C) A valid notice of appeal is effective—without amendment—to appeal from an order disposing of any of the motions referred to in Rule 4(b)(3)(A).

(4) *Motion for Extension of Time.* Upon a finding of excusable neglect or good cause, the district court may—before or after the time has expired, with or without motion and notice—extend the time to file a notice of appeal for a period not to exceed 30 days from the expiration of the time otherwise prescribed by this Rule 4(b).

(5) *Jurisdiction.* The filing of a notice of appeal under this Rule 4(b) does not divest a district court of jurisdiction to correct a sentence under Federal Rule of Criminal Procedure 35(a), nor does the filing of a motion under 35(a) affect the validity of a notice of appeal filed before entry of the order disposing of the motion. The filing of a motion under Federal Rule of Criminal Procedure 35(a) does not suspend the time for filing a notice of appeal from a judgment of conviction.

(6) *Entry Defined.* A judgment or order is entered for purposes of this Rule 4(b) when it is entered on the criminal docket.

**(c) Appeal by an Inmate Confined in an Institution.**

(1) If an inmate confined in an institution files a notice of appeal in either a civil or a criminal case, the notice is timely if it is deposited in the institution's internal mail system on or before the last day for filing. If an institution has a system designed for legal mail, the inmate must use that system to receive the benefit of this rule. Timely filing may be shown by a declaration in compliance with 28 U.S.C. § 1746 or by a notarized statement, either of which must set forth the date of deposit and state that first-class postage has been prepaid.

(2) If an inmate files the first notice of appeal in a civil case under this Rule 4(c), the 14–day period provided in Rule 4(a)(3) for another party to file a notice of appeal runs from the date when the district court dockets the first notice.

(3) When a defendant in a criminal case files a notice of appeal under this Rule 4(c), the 30–day period for the government to file its notice of appeal runs from the entry of the judgment or order appealed from or from the district court's docketing of the defendant's notice of appeal, whichever is later.

**(d) Mistaken Filing in the Court of Appeals.** If a notice of appeal in either a civil or a criminal case is mistakenly filed in the court of appeals, the clerk of that court must note on the notice the date when it was received and send it to the district clerk. The notice is then considered filed in the district court on the date so noted.

[Amended April 30, 1979, effective August 1, 1979; amended by Pub.L. 100–690, Title VII, § 7111, November 18, 1988, 102 Stat. 4419; amended April 30, 1991, effective December 1, 1991; April 22, 1993, effective December 1, 1993; April 27, 1995, effective December 1, 1995; April 24, 1998, effective December 1, 1998; April 29, 2002, effective December 1, 2002; April 25, 2005, effective December 1, 2005.]

## LOCAL RULE 4(b). DUTIES OF ALL RETAINED ATTORNEYS IN CRIMINAL CASES AND ALL CRIMINAL JUSTICE ACT–APPOINTED ATTORNEYS; MOTIONS FOR LEAVE TO WITHDRAW AS COUNSEL ON APPEAL WHERE RETAINED IN A CRIMINAL CASE OR APPOINTED UNDER CRIMINAL JUSTICE ACT, DUTIES OF APPELLATE COUNSEL IN THE EVENT OF AFFIRMANCE

*(a)* When a defendant convicted following trial wishes to appeal, trial counsel, whether retained or appointed by the district court, is responsible for representing the defendant until relieved by the Court of Appeals.

*(b)* If trial counsel was appointed under the Criminal Justice Act, 18 U.S.C. § 3006A, and intends to prosecute the appeal, this court may accept the District Court's finding that the defendant is financially unable to employ counsel and no further proof of the defendant's indigency need be submitted unless specifically required.

*(c)* Any counsel wishing to be relieved on appeal shall, before moving to that end, advise the defendant that the defendant must promptly obtain other counsel unless the defendant desires to proceed pro se and that if the defendant is financially unable to obtain counsel, a lawyer may be appointed by this court under the Criminal Justice Act. If the defendant wishes to have a lawyer so appointed on appeal, counsel must see to it that the defendant receives and fills out the appropriate application forms, which are available from the office of the Clerk of this court. If the defendant desires to proceed pro se, counsel must advise the defendant of the requirements concerning the time within which the record must be docketed and the brief filed.

*(d)* A motion to withdraw as counsel on appeal where the attorney is retained in a criminal case or appointed under the Criminal Justice Act must state the reasons for such relief and must be accompanied by one of the following:

*1.* A showing that new counsel has been retained or appointed to represent defendant; or

*2.* The defendant's completed application for appointment of counsel under the Criminal Justice Act or a showing that such application has already been filed in the Court of Appeals; or

*3.* An affidavit or signed statement from the defendant showing that the defendant has been advised that the defendant may retain new counsel or apply for appointment of counsel and expressly stating that the defendant does not wish to be represented by counsel but elects to appear pro se; or

*4.* An affidavit or signed statement from the defendant showing that the defendant has been advised of the defendant's rights with regard to the appeal and expressly stating that the defendant elects to withdraw the defendant's appeal; or

*5.* A showing that exceptional circumstances prevent counsel from meeting any of the requirements stated in subdivisions *(1)* to *(4)* above. Such a motion must be accompanied by proof of service on the defendant and the Government and will be determined, without oral argument, by a single judge. See Local Rule 27.

*(e)* This Local Rule is supplementary to the Amended Plan to Supplement the Plans Adopted by the Several District Courts Within the Circuit, as required by the Criminal Justice Act of 1964, 18 U.S.C. § 3006A, as amended.

[December 1, 1994; amended effective March 27, 1996.]

## FRAP 5. APPEAL BY PERMISSION

### (a) Petition for Permission to Appeal.

(1) To request permission to appeal when an appeal is within the court of appeals' discretion, a party must file a petition for permission to appeal. The petition must be filed with the circuit clerk with proof of service on all other parties to the district-court action.

(2) The petition must be filed within the time specified by the statute or rule authorizing the appeal or, if no such time is specified, within the time provided by Rule 4(a) for filing a notice of appeal.

(3) If a party cannot petition for appeal unless the district court first enters an order granting permission to do so or stating that the necessary conditions are met, the district court may amend its order, either on its own or in response to a party's motion, to include the required permission or statement. In that event, the time to petition runs from entry of the amended order.

### (b) Contents of the Petition; Answer or Cross–Petition; Oral Argument.

(1) The petition must include the following:

(A) the facts necessary to understand the question presented;

(B) the question itself;

(C) the relief sought;

(D) the reasons why the appeal should be allowed and is authorized by a statute or rule; and

(E) an attached copy of:

(i) the order, decree, or judgment complained of and any related opinion or memorandum, and

(ii) any order stating the district court's permission to appeal or finding that the necessary conditions are met.

(2) A party may file an answer in opposition or a cross-petition within 7 days after the petition is served.

(3) The petition and answer will be submitted without oral argument unless the court of appeals orders otherwise.

**(c) Form of Papers; Number of Copies.** All papers must conform to Rule 32(c)(2). Except by the court's permission, a paper must not exceed 20 pages, exclusive of the disclosure statement, the proof of service, and the accompanying documents required by Rule 5(b)(1)(E). An original and 3 copies must be filed unless the court requires a different number by local rule or by order in a particular case.

**(d) Grant of Permission; Fees; Cost Bond; Filing the Record.**

(1) Within 10 days after the entry of the order granting permission to appeal, the appellant must:

(A) pay the district clerk all required fees; and

(B) file a cost bond if required under Rule 7.

(2) A notice of appeal need not be filed. The date when the order granting permission to appeal is entered serves as the date of the notice of appeal for calculating time under these rules.

(3) The district clerk must notify the circuit clerk once the petitioner has paid the fees. Upon receiving this notice, the circuit clerk must enter the appeal on the docket. The record must be forwarded and filed in accordance with Rules 11 and 12(c).

[Amended April 30, 1979, effective August 1, 1979; April 29, 1994, effective December 1, 1994; April 24, 1998, effective December 1, 1998; April 29, 2002, effective December 1, 2002.]

## FRAP 5.1  APPEAL BY PERMISSION UNDER 28 U.S.C. § 636(c)(5) [ABROGATED]

[Adopted March 10, 1986, effective July 1, 1986; amended April 22, 1993, effective December 1, 1993; April 29, 1994, effective December 1, 1994; abrogated effective December 1, 1998.]

## FRAP 6. APPEAL IN A BANKRUPTCY CASE FROM A FINAL JUDGMENT, ORDER, OR DECREE OF A DISTRICT COURT OR BANKRUPTCY APPELLATE PANEL

**(a) Appeal From a Judgment, Order, or Decree of a District Court Exercising Original Jurisdiction in a Bankruptcy Case.** An appeal to a court of appeals from a final judgment, order, or decree of a district court exercising jurisdiction under 28 U.S.C. § 1334 is taken as any other civil appeal under these rules.

**(b) Appeal From a Judgment, Order, or Decree of a District Court or Bankruptcy Appellate Panel Exercising Appellate Jurisdiction in a Bankruptcy Case.**

(1) *Applicability of Other Rules.* These rules apply to an appeal to a court of appeals under 28 U.S.C. § 158(d) from a final judgment, order, or decree of a district court or bankruptcy appellate panel exercising appellate jurisdiction under 28 U.S.C. § 158(a) or (b). But there are 3 exceptions:

(A) Rules 4(a)(4), 4(b), 9, 10, 11, 12(b), 13–20, 22–23, and 24(b) do not apply;

(B) the reference in Rule 3(c) to "Form 1 in the Appendix of Forms" must be read as a reference to Form 5; and

(C) when the appeal is from a bankruptcy appellate panel, the term "district court," as used in any applicable rule, means "appellate panel."

(2) *Additional Rules.* In addition to the rules made applicable by Rule 6(b)(1), the following rules apply:

(A) Motion for rehearing.

(i) If a timely motion for rehearing under Bankruptcy Rule 8015 is filed, the time to appeal for all parties runs from the entry of the order disposing of the motion. A notice of appeal filed after the district court or bankruptcy appellate panel announces or enters a judgment, order, or decree—but before disposition of the motion for rehearing—becomes effective when the order disposing of the motion for rehearing is entered.

(ii) Appellate review of the order disposing of the motion requires the party, in compliance with Rules 3(c) and 6(b)(1)(B), to amend a previously filed notice of appeal. A party intending to challenge an altered or amended judgment, order, or decree must file a notice of appeal or amended notice of appeal within the time prescribed by Rule 4—excluding Rules 4(a)(4) and 4(b)—measured from the entry of the order disposing of the motion.

(iii) No additional fee is required to file an amended notice.

(B) The record on appeal.

(i) Within 10 days after filing the notice of appeal, the appellant must file with the clerk possessing the record assembled in accordance with Bankruptcy Rule 8006—and serve on the appellee—a statement of the issues to be presented on appeal and a designation of the record to be certified and sent to the circuit clerk.

(ii) An appellee who believes that other parts of the record are necessary must, within 10 days after being served with the appellant's designation, file with the clerk and serve on the appellant a designation of additional parts to be included.

(iii) The record on appeal consists of:

● the redesignated record as provided above;

● the proceedings in the district court or bankruptcy appellate panel; and

● a certified copy of the docket entries prepared by the clerk under Rule 3(d).

(C) Forwarding the record.

(i) When the record is complete, the district clerk or bankruptcy appellate panel clerk must number the documents constituting the record and send them promptly to the circuit clerk together with a list of the documents correspondingly numbered and reasonably identified. Unless directed to do so by a party or the circuit clerk, the clerk will not send to the court of appeals documents of unusual bulk or weight, physical exhibits other than documents, or other parts of the record designated for omission by local rule of the court of appeals. If the exhibits are unusually bulky or heavy, a party must arrange with the clerks in advance for their transportation and receipt.

(ii) All parties must do whatever else is necessary to enable the clerk to assemble and forward the record. The court of appeals may provide by rule or order that a certified copy of the docket entries be sent in place of the redesignated record, but any party may request at any time during the pendency of the appeal that the redesignated record be sent.

(D) Filing the record. Upon receiving the record—or a certified copy of the docket entries sent in place of the redesignated record—the circuit clerk must file it and immediately notify all parties of the filing date.

[Former Rule 6 amended April 30, 1979, effective August 1, 1979; repealed and new Rule 6 adopted April 25, 1989, effective December 1, 1989; caption amended April 30, 1991, effective December 1, 1991; caption and text amended April 22, 1993, effective December 1, 1993; April 24, 1998, effective December 1, 1998.]

## FRAP 7. BOND FOR COSTS ON APPEAL IN A CIVIL CASE

In a civil case, the district court may require an appellant to file a bond or provide other security in any form and amount necessary to ensure payment of costs on appeal. Rule 8(b) applies to a surety on a bond given under this rule.

[Amended April 30, 1979, effective August 1, 1979; April 24, 1998, effective December 1, 1998.]

## FRAP 8. STAY OR INJUNCTION PENDING APPEAL

**(a) Motion for Stay.**

(1) *Initial Motion in the District Court.* A party must ordinarily move first in the district court for the following relief:

(A) a stay of the judgment or order of a district court pending appeal;

(B) approval of a supersedeas bond; or

(C) an order suspending, modifying, restoring, or granting an injunction while an appeal is pending.

(2) *Motion in the Court of Appeals; Conditions on Relief.* A motion for the relief mentioned in Rule 8(a)(1) may be made to the court of appeals or to one of its judges.

(A) The motion must:

(i) show that moving first in the district court would be impracticable; or

(ii) state that, a motion having been made, the district court denied the motion or failed to afford the relief requested and state any reasons given by the district court for its action.

(B) The motion must also include:

(i) the reasons for granting the relief requested and the facts relied on;

(ii) originals or copies of affidavits or other sworn statements supporting facts subject to dispute; and

(iii) relevant parts of the record.

(C) The moving party must give reasonable notice of the motion to all parties.

(D) A motion under this Rule 8(a)(2) must be filed with the circuit clerk and normally will be considered by a panel of the court. But in an exceptional case in which time requirements make that procedure impracticable, the motion may be made to and considered by a single judge.

(E) The court may condition relief on a party's filing a bond or other appropriate security in the district court.

**(b) Proceeding Against a Surety.** If a party gives security in the form of a bond or stipulation or other undertaking with one or more sureties, each surety

submits to the jurisdiction of the district court and irrevocably appoints the district clerk as the surety's agent on whom any papers affecting the surety's liability on the bond or undertaking may be served. On motion, a surety's liability may be enforced in the district court without the necessity of an independent action. The motion and any notice that the district court prescribes may be served on the district clerk, who must promptly mail a copy to each surety whose address is known.

**(c) Stay in a Criminal Case.** Rule 38 of the Federal Rules of Criminal Procedure governs a stay in a criminal case.

[Amended March 10, 1986, effective July 1, 1986; April 27, 1995, effective December 1, 1995; April 24, 1998, effective December 1, 1998.]

# FRAP 9. RELEASE IN A CRIMINAL CASE

**(a) Release Before Judgment of Conviction.**

(1) The district court must state in writing, or orally on the record, the reasons for an order regarding the release or detention of a defendant in a criminal case. A party appealing from the order must file with the court of appeals a copy of the district court's order and the court's statement of reasons as soon as practicable after filing the notice of appeal. An appellant who questions the factual basis for the district court's order must file a transcript of the release proceedings or an explanation of why a transcript was not obtained.

(2) After reasonable notice to the appellee, the court of appeals must promptly determine the appeal on the basis of the papers, affidavits, and parts of the record that the parties present or the court requires. Unless the court so orders, briefs need not be filed.

(3) The court of appeals or one of its judges may order the defendant's release pending the disposition of the appeal.

**(b) Release After Judgment of Conviction.** A party entitled to do so may obtain review of a district-court order regarding release after a judgment of conviction by filing a notice of appeal from that order in the district court, or by filing a motion in the court of appeals if the party has already filed a notice of appeal from the judgment of conviction. Both the order and the review are subject to Rule 9(a). The papers filed by the party seeking review must include a copy of the judgment of conviction.

**(c) Criteria for Release.** The court must make its decision regarding release in accordance with the applicable provisions of 18 U.S.C. §§ 3142, 3143, and 3145(c).

[Amended April 24, 1972, effective October 1, 1972; amended by Pub.L. 98–473, Title II, § 210, October 12, 1984, 98 Stat. 1987; April 29, 1994, effective December 1, 1994; April 24, 1998, effective December 1, 1998.]

# LOCAL RULE 9. RELEASE IN CRIMINAL CASES

*An application pursuant to Rule 9(b) shall contain in the following order:*

*1. the name of appellant; the District Court docket number of the case; the offense of which appellant was convicted; the date and terms of sentence; and the place where appellant has been ordered confined;*

*2. the facts with respect to whether application for bail has been made and denied, and the reasons given for the denial, if known; and the facts and reasons why the action by the District Court on the application does not afford the relief to which the applicant considers himself entitled;*

*3. a concise statement of the questions involved on the appeal, with sufficient facts to give the essential background and a showing that the questions on appeal are not frivolous;*

*4. such other matters as may be deemed pertinent;*

*5. a certificate by counsel, or by applicant if acting pro se, that the appeal is not taken for delay.*

[December 1, 1994.]

# FRAP 10. THE RECORD ON APPEAL

**(a) Composition of the Record on Appeal.** The following items constitute the record on appeal:

(1) the original papers and exhibits filed in the district court;

(2) the transcript of proceedings, if any; and

(3) a certified copy of the docket entries prepared by the district clerk.

**(b) The Transcript of Proceedings.**

(1) *Appellant's Duty to Order.* Within 10 days after filing the notice of appeal or entry of an order disposing of the last timely remaining motion of a type specified in Rule 4(a)(4)(A), whichever is later, the appellant must do either of the following:

(A) order from the reporter a transcript of such parts of the proceedings not already on file as the appellant considers necessary, subject to a local rule of the court of appeals and with the following qualifications:

(i) the order must be in writing;

(ii) if the cost of the transcript is to be paid by the United States under the Criminal Justice Act, the order must so state; and

(iii) the appellant must, within the same period, file a copy of the order with the district clerk; or

(B) file a certificate stating that no transcript will be ordered.

(2) *Unsupported Finding or Conclusion.* If the appellant intends to urge on appeal that a finding or

conclusion is unsupported by the evidence or is contrary to the evidence, the appellant must include in the record a transcript of all evidence relevant to that finding or conclusion.

(3) *Partial Transcript.* Unless the entire transcript is ordered:

(A) the appellant must—within the 10 days provided in Rule 10(b)(1)—file a statement of the issues that the appellant intends to present on the appeal and must serve on the appellee a copy of both the order or certificate and the statement;

(B) if the appellee considers it necessary to have a transcript of other parts of the proceedings, the appellee must, within 10 days after the service of the order or certificate and the statement of the issues, file and serve on the appellant a designation of additional parts to be ordered; and

(C) unless within 10 days after service of that designation the appellant has ordered all such parts, and has so notified the appellee, the appellee may within the following 10 days either order the parts or move in the district court for an order requiring the appellant to do so.

(4) *Payment.* At the time of ordering, a party must make satisfactory arrangements with the reporter for paying the cost of the transcript.

**(c) Statement of the Evidence When the Proceedings Were Not Recorded or When a Transcript Is Unavailable.** If the transcript of a hearing or trial is unavailable, the appellant may prepare a statement of the evidence or proceedings from the best available means, including the appellant's recollection. The statement must be served on the appellee, who may serve objections or proposed amendments within 10 days after being served. The statement and any objections or proposed amendments must then be submitted to the district court for settlement and approval. As settled and approved, the statement must be included by the district clerk in the record on appeal.

**(d) Agreed Statement as the Record on Appeal.** In place of the record on appeal as defined in Rule 10(a), the parties may prepare, sign, and submit to the district court a statement of the case showing how the issues presented by the appeal arose and were decided in the district court. The statement must set forth only those facts averred and proved or sought to be proved that are essential to the court's resolution of the issues. If the statement is truthful, it—together with any additions that the district court may consider necessary to a full presentation of the issues on appeal—must be approved by the district court and must then be certified to the court of appeals as the record on appeal. The district clerk must then send it to the circuit clerk within the time provided by Rule 11. A copy of the agreed statement may be filed in place of the appendix required by Rule 30.

**(e) Correction or Modification of the Record.**

(1) If any difference arises about whether the record truly discloses what occurred in the district court, the difference must be submitted to and settled by that court and the record conformed accordingly.

(2) If anything material to either party is omitted from or misstated in the record by error or accident, the omission or misstatement may be corrected and a supplemental record may be certified and forwarded:

(A) on stipulation of the parties;

(B) by the district court before or after the record has been forwarded; or

(C) by the court of appeals.

(3) All other questions as to the form and content of the record must be presented to the court of appeals.

[Amended April 30, 1979, effective August 1, 1979; March 10, 1986, effective July 1, 1986; April 30, 1991, effective December 1, 1991; April 22, 1993, effective December 1, 1993; April 27, 1995, effective December 1, 1995; April 24, 1998, effective December 1, 1998.]

## FRAP 11.  FORWARDING THE RECORD

**(a) Appellant's Duty.** An appellant filing a notice of appeal must comply with Rule 10(b) and must do whatever else is necessary to enable the clerk to assemble and forward the record. If there are multiple appeals from a judgment or order, the clerk must forward a single record.

**(b) Duties of Reporter and District Clerk.**

(1) *Reporter's Duty to Prepare and File a Transcript.* The reporter must prepare and file a transcript as follows:

(A) Upon receiving an order for a transcript, the reporter must enter at the foot of the order the date of its receipt and the expected completion date and send a copy, so endorsed, to the circuit clerk.

(B) If the transcript cannot be completed within 30 days of the reporter's receipt of the order, the reporter may request the circuit clerk to grant additional time to complete it. The clerk must note on the docket the action taken and notify the parties.

(C) When a transcript is complete, the reporter must file it with the district clerk and notify the circuit clerk of the filing.

(D) If the reporter fails to file the transcript on time, the circuit clerk must notify the district judge and do whatever else the court of appeals directs.

(2) *District Clerk's Duty to Forward.* When the record is complete, the district clerk must number the documents constituting the record and send them promptly to the circuit clerk together with a list of the documents correspondingly numbered and reasonably

identified. Unless directed to do so by a party or the circuit clerk, the district clerk will not send to the court of appeals documents of unusual bulk or weight, physical exhibits other than documents, or other parts of the record designated for omission by local rule of the court of appeals. If the exhibits are unusually bulky or heavy, a party must arrange with the clerks in advance for their transportation and receipt.

**(c) Retaining the Record Temporarily in the District Court for Use in Preparing the Appeal.** The parties may stipulate, or the district court on motion may order, that the district clerk retain the record temporarily for the parties to use in preparing the papers on appeal. In that event the district clerk must certify to the circuit clerk that the record on appeal is complete. Upon receipt of the appellee's brief, or earlier if the court orders or the parties agree, the appellant must request the district clerk to forward the record.

**(d) [Abrogated.]**

**(e) Retaining the Record by Court Order.**

(1) The court of appeals may, by order or local rule, provide that a certified copy of the docket entries be forwarded instead of the entire record. But a party may at any time during the appeal request that designated parts of the record be forwarded.

(2) The district court may order the record or some part of it retained if the court needs it while the appeal is pending, subject, however, to call by the court of appeals.

(3) If part or all of the record is ordered retained, the district clerk must send to the court of appeals a copy of the order and the docket entries together with the parts of the original record allowed by the district court and copies of any parts of the record designated by the parties.

**(f) Retaining Parts of the Record in the District Court by Stipulation of the Parties.** The parties may agree by written stipulation filed in the district court that designated parts of the record be retained in the district court subject to call by the court of appeals or request by a party. The parts of the record so designated remain a part of the record on appeal.

**(g) Record for a Preliminary Motion in the Court of Appeals.** If, before the record is forwarded, a party makes any of the following motions in the court of appeals:

- for dismissal;
- for release;
- for a stay pending appeal;

- for additional security on the bond on appeal or on a supersedeas bond; or
- for any other intermediate order—

the district clerk must send the court of appeals any parts of the record designated by any party.

[Amended April 30, 1979, effective August 1, 1979; March 10, 1986, effective July 1, 1986; April 24, 1998, effective December 1, 1998.]

## LOCAL RULE 11. EXHIBITS

*(a) The district court may, by rule or order, direct that any or all exhibits need not be filed with the clerk upon their offer or receipt in evidence but may be retained in the custody of the attorney (or of a party not represented by an attorney) who produced them, unless an appeal is taken, in which event the following provisions of this rule shall apply.*

*(b) The parties are encouraged to agree with respect to which exhibits are "necessary for the determination of the appeal." See Rule 11(a). In the absence of agreement, the appellant shall, not later than 15 days after the filing of the notice of appeal, serve on the appellee a designation of the exhibits the appellant considers to be necessary. If the appellee considers other exhibits to be necessary, the appellee shall serve a cross-designation upon the appellant within 10 days after service of appellant's designation.*

*(c) Except as provided in paragraph (d), it shall be the duty of any attorney or party having possession of an exhibit designated pursuant to paragraph (b) of this rule, promptly to make such exhibit or a true copy thereof available at the office of the clerk of the district court. The clerk of the district court shall transmit all such exhibits to the clerk of the court of appeals as part of the record pursuant to Rule 11(b). Exhibits which have not been designated shall be retained by the clerk of the district court or, if the district court has authorized their retention by an attorney or party pursuant to paragraph (a) of this rule, by such attorney or party, but shall be transmitted to the clerk of the court of appeals on the request of that court acting on the motion of any judge thereof or on the motion of a party showing good cause for failure to include any such exhibit in the attorney's designation.*

*(d) Documents of unusual bulk or weight and physical exhibits other than documents shall remain in the custody of the attorney or party who produced them. The attorney or party retaining custody of the documents shall permit inspection of them by any other party and shall be responsible for having them available at the argument in the court of appeals if*

*they have been designated, and for their later produc-
tion if subsequently requested by the court of appeals
as provided in the last sentence of paragraph (c) of
this rule.*

*(e) This rule does not relieve the parties of their
obligation under Rule 30 to reproduce in an appendix
to their briefs or in a separate volume, see Rule 30(e),
exhibits (other than those described in paragraph (d)
of this rule) to which they "wish to direct the particular attention of the court."*

[December 1, 1994.]

## FRAP 12. DOCKETING THE APPEAL; FILING A REPRESENTATION STATE-MENT; FILING THE RECORD

**(a) Docketing the Appeal.** Upon receiving the
copy of the notice of appeal and the docket entries
from the district clerk under Rule 3(d), the circuit
clerk must docket the appeal under the title of the
district-court action and must identify the appellant,
adding the appellant's name if necessary.

**(b) Filing a Representation Statement.** Unless
the court of appeals designates another time, the
attorney who filed the notice of appeal must, within 10
days after filing the notice, file a statement with the
circuit clerk naming the parties that the attorney
represents on appeal.

**(c) Filing the Record, Partial Record, or Certifi-
cate.** Upon receiving the record, partial record, or
district clerk's certificate as provided in Rule 11, the
circuit clerk must file it and immediately notify all
parties of the filing date.

[Amended April 30, 1979, effective August 1, 1979; March 10,
1986, effective July 1, 1986; April 22, 1993, effective December 1, 1993; April 24, 1998, effective December 1, 1998.]

# TITLE III. REVIEW OF A DECISION OF THE UNITED STATES TAX COURT

## FRAP 13. REVIEW OF A DECISION OF THE TAX COURT

**(a) How Obtained; Time for Filing Notice of
Appeal.**

(1) Review of a decision of the United States Tax
Court is commenced by filing a notice of appeal with
the Tax Court clerk within 90 days after the entry of
the Tax Court's decision. At the time of filing, the
appellant must furnish the clerk with enough copies of
the notice to enable the clerk to comply with Rule
3(d). If one party files a timely notice of appeal, any
other party may file a notice of appeal within 120 days
after the Tax Court's decision is entered.

(2) If, under Tax Court rules, a party makes a
timely motion to vacate or revise the Tax Court's
decision, the time to file a notice of appeal runs from
the entry of the order disposing of the motion or from
the entry of a new decision, whichever is later.

**(b) Notice of Appeal; How Filed.** The notice of
appeal may be filed either at the Tax Court clerk's
office in the District of Columbia or by mail addressed
to the clerk. If sent by mail the notice is considered
filed on the postmark date, subject to § 7502 of the
Internal Revenue Code, as amended, and the applicable regulations.

**(c) Contents of the Notice of Appeal; Service;
Effect of Filing and Service.** Rule 3 prescribes the
contents of a notice of appeal, the manner of service,
and the effect of its filing and service. Form 2 in the
Appendix of Forms is a suggested form of a notice of
appeal.

**(d) The Record on Appeal; Forwarding; Filing.**

(1) An appeal from the Tax Court is governed by
the parts of Rules 10, 11, and 12 regarding the record
on appeal from a district court, the time and manner
of forwarding and filing, and the docketing in the
court of appeals. References in those rules and in
Rule 3 to the district court and district clerk are to be
read as referring to the Tax Court and its clerk.

(2) If an appeal from a Tax Court decision is taken
to more than one court of appeals, the original record
must be sent to the court named in the first notice of
appeal filed. In an appeal to any other court of
appeals, the appellant must apply to that other court
to make provision for the record.

[Amended April 30, 1979, effective August 1, 1979; April 29,
1994, effective December 1, 1994; April 24, 1998, effective
December 1, 1998.]

## FRAP 14. APPLICABILITY OF OTHER RULES TO THE REVIEW OF A TAX COURT DECISION

All provisions of these rules, except Rules 4–9,
15–20, and 22–23, apply to the review of a Tax Court
decision.

[Amended April 24, 1998, effective December 1, 1998.]

# TITLE IV. REVIEW OR ENFORCEMENT OF AN ORDER OF AN ADMINISTRATIVE AGENCY, BOARD, COMMISSION, OR OFFICER

## FRAP 15. REVIEW OR ENFORCEMENT OF AN AGENCY ORDER—HOW OBTAINED; INTERVENTION

**(a) Petition for Review; Joint Petition.**

(1) Review of an agency order is commenced by filing, within the time prescribed by law, a petition for review with the clerk of a court of appeals authorized to review the agency order. If their interests make joinder practicable, two or more persons may join in a petition to the same court to review the same order.

(2) The petition must:

(A) name each party seeking review either in the caption or the body of the petition—using such terms as "et al.," "petitioners," or "respondents" does not effectively name the parties;

(B) name the agency as a respondent (even though not named in the petition, the United States is a respondent if required by statute); and

(C) specify the order or part thereof to be reviewed.

(3) Form 3 in the Appendix of Forms is a suggested form of a petition for review.

(4) In this rule "agency" includes an agency, board, commission, or officer; "petition for review" includes a petition to enjoin, suspend, modify, or otherwise review, or a notice of appeal, whichever form is indicated by the applicable statute.

**(b) Application or Cross–Application to Enforce an Order; Answer; Default.**

(1) An application to enforce an agency order must be filed with the clerk of a court of appeals authorized to enforce the order. If a petition is filed to review an agency order that the court may enforce, a party opposing the petition may file a cross-application for enforcement.

(2) Within 20 days after the application for enforcement is filed, the respondent must serve on the applicant an answer to the application and file it with the clerk. If the respondent fails to answer in time, the court will enter judgment for the relief requested.

(3) The application must contain a concise statement of the proceedings in which the order was entered, the facts upon which venue is based, and the relief requested.

**(c) Service of the Petition or Application.** The circuit clerk must serve a copy of the petition for review, or an application or cross-application to enforce an agency order, on each respondent as prescribed by Rule 3(d), unless a different manner of service is prescribed by statute. At the time of filing, the petitioner must:

(1) serve, or have served, a copy on each party admitted to participate in the agency proceedings, except for the respondents;

(2) file with the clerk a list of those so served; and

(3) give the clerk enough copies of the petition or application to serve each respondent.

**(d) Intervention.** Unless a statute provides another method, a person who wants to intervene in a proceeding under this rule must file a motion for leave to intervene with the circuit clerk and serve a copy on all parties. The motion—or other notice of intervention authorized by statute—must be filed within 30 days after the petition for review is filed and must contain a concise statement of the interest of the moving party and the grounds for intervention.

**(e) Payment of Fees.** When filing any separate or joint petition for review in a court of appeals, the petitioner must pay the circuit clerk all required fees.

[Amended April 22, 1993, effective December 1, 1993; April 24, 1998, effective December 1, 1998.]

## LOCAL RULE 15. APPLICATION BY NATIONAL LABOR RELATIONS BOARD FOR ENFORCEMENT OF ORDER

*In an application for enforcement by the National Labor Relations Board under Rule 15(b), Federal Rules of Appellate Procedure the respondent(s) shall be considered the petitioner(s), and the National Labor Relations Board considered the respondent, for the purposes of briefing and oral argument, unless the court orders otherwise.*

[December 1, 1994.]

## FRAP 15.1 BRIEFS AND ORAL ARGUMENT IN A NATIONAL LABOR RELATIONS BOARD PROCEEDING

In either an enforcement or a review proceeding, a party adverse to the National Labor Relations Board proceeds first on briefing and at oral argument, unless the court orders otherwise.

[Adopted March 10, 1986, effective July 1, 1986; April 24, 1998, effective December 1, 1998.]

## FRAP 16. THE RECORD ON REVIEW OR ENFORCEMENT

**(a) Composition of the Record.** The record on review or enforcement of an agency order consists of:

(1) the order involved;

(2) any findings or report on which it is based; and

(3) the pleadings, evidence, and other parts of the proceedings before the agency.

**(b) Omissions From or Misstatements in the Record.** The parties may at any time, by stipulation, supply any omission from the record or correct a misstatement, or the court may so direct. If necessary, the court may direct that a supplemental record be prepared and filed.

[Amended April 24, 1998, effective December 1, 1998.]

## FRAP 17. FILING THE RECORD

**(a) Agency to File; Time for Filing; Notice of Filing.** The agency must file the record with the circuit clerk within 40 days after being served with a petition for review, unless the statute authorizing review provides otherwise, or within 40 days after it files an application for enforcement unless the respondent fails to answer or the court orders otherwise. The court may shorten or extend the time to file the record. The clerk must notify all parties of the date when the record is filed.

**(b) Filing—What Constitutes.**

(1) The agency must file:

(A) the original or a certified copy of the entire record or parts designated by the parties; or

(B) a certified list adequately describing all documents, transcripts of testimony, exhibits, and other material constituting the record, or describing those parts designated by the parties.

(2) The parties may stipulate in writing that no record or certified list be filed. The date when the stipulation is filed with the circuit clerk is treated as the date when the record is filed.

(3) The agency must retain any portion of the record not filed with the clerk. All parts of the record retained by the agency are a part of the record on review for all purposes and, if the court or a party so requests, must be sent to the court regardless of any prior stipulation.

[Amended April 24, 1998, effective December 1, 1998.]

## FRAP 18. STAY PENDING REVIEW

**(a) Motion for a Stay.**

(1) *Initial Motion Before the Agency.* A petitioner must ordinarily move first before the agency for a stay pending review of its decision or order.

(2) *Motion in the Court of Appeals.* A motion for a stay may be made to the court of appeals or one of its judges.

(A) The motion must:

(i) show that moving first before the agency would be impracticable; or

(ii) state that, a motion having been made, the agency denied the motion or failed to afford the relief requested and state any reasons given by the agency for its action.

(B) The motion must also include:

(i) the reasons for granting the relief requested and the facts relied on;

(ii) originals or copies of affidavits or other sworn statements supporting facts subject to dispute; and

(iii) relevant parts of the record.

(C) The moving party must give reasonable notice of the motion to all parties.

(D) The motion must be filed with the circuit clerk and normally will be considered by a panel of the court. But in an exceptional case in which time requirements make that procedure impracticable, the motion may be made to and considered by a single judge.

**(b) Bond.** The court may condition relief on the filing of a bond or other appropriate security.

[Amended April 24, 1998, effective December 1, 1998.]

## FRAP 19. SETTLEMENT OF A JUDGMENT ENFORCING AN AGENCY ORDER IN PART

When the court files an opinion directing entry of judgment enforcing the agency's order in part, the agency must within 14 days file with the clerk and serve on each other party a proposed judgment conforming to the opinion. A party who disagrees with the agency's proposed judgment must within 7 days file with the clerk and serve the agency with a proposed judgment that the party believes conforms to the opinion. The court will settle the judgment and direct entry without further hearing or argument.

[Amended March 10, 1986, effective July 1, 1986; April 24, 1998, effective December 1, 1998.]

## FRAP 20. APPLICABILITY OF RULES TO THE REVIEW OR ENFORCEMENT OF AN AGENCY ORDER

All provisions of these rules, except Rules 3–14 and 22–23, apply to the review or enforcement of an agency order. In these rules, "appellant" includes a petitioner or applicant, and "appellee" includes a respondent.

[Amended April 24, 1998, effective December 1, 1998.]

# TITLE V.  EXTRAORDINARY WRITS

## FRAP 21.  WRITS OF MANDAMUS AND PROHIBITION, AND OTHER EXTRAORDINARY WRITS

**(a) Mandamus or Prohibition to a Court: Petition, Filing, Service, and Docketing.**

(1) A party petitioning for a writ of mandamus or prohibition directed to a court must file a petition with the circuit clerk with proof of service on all parties to the proceeding in the trial court.  The party must also provide a copy to the trial-court judge.  All parties to the proceeding in the trial court other than the petitioner are respondents for all purposes.

(2)(A) The petition must be titled "In re [name of petitioner]."

(B) The petition must state:

(i) the relief sought;

(ii) the issues presented;

(iii) the facts necessary to understand the issue presented by the petition; and

(iv) the reasons why the writ should issue.

(C) The petition must include a copy of any order or opinion or parts of the record that may be essential to understand the matters set forth in the petition.

(3) Upon receiving the prescribed docket fee, the clerk must docket the petition and submit it to the court.

**(b) Denial; Order Directing Answer; Briefs; Precedence.**

(1) The court may deny the petition without an answer.  Otherwise, it must order the respondent, if any, to answer within a fixed time.

(2) The clerk must serve the order to respond on all persons directed to respond.

(3) Two or more respondents may answer jointly.

(4) The court of appeals may invite or order the trial-court judge to address the petition or may invite an amicus curiae to do so.  The trial-court judge may request permission to address the petition but may not do so unless invited or ordered to do so by the court of appeals.

(5) If briefing or oral argument is required, the clerk must advise the parties, and when appropriate, the trial-court judge or amicus curiae.

(6) The proceeding must be given preference over ordinary civil cases.

(7) The circuit clerk must send a copy of the final disposition to the trial-court judge.

**(c) Other Extraordinary Writs.**  An application for an extraordinary writ other than one provided for in Rule 21(a) must be made by filing a petition with the circuit clerk with proof of service on the respondents.  Proceedings on the application must conform, so far as is practicable, to the procedures prescribed in Rule 21(a) and (b).

**(d) Form of Papers; Number of Copies.**  All papers must conform to Rule 32(c)(2).  Except by the court's permission, a paper must not exceed 30 pages, exclusive of the disclosure statement, the proof of service, and the accompanying documents required by Rule 21(a)(2)(C).  An original and 3 copies must be filed unless the court requires the filing of a different number by local rule or by order in a particular case.

[Amended April 29, 1994, effective December 1, 1994;  April 23, 1996, effective December 1, 1996;  April 24, 1998, effective December 1, 1998;  April 29, 2002, effective December 1, 2002.]

## LOCAL RULE 21.  PETITIONS FOR WRITS OF MANDAMUS AND PROHIBITION

*(a) Caption.  A petition for writ of mandamus or writ of prohibition pursuant to Rule 21 shall not bear the name of the district judge, but shall be entitled simply, "In re _____, Petitioner."  To the extent that relief is requested of a particular judge, unless otherwise ordered, the judge shall be represented pro forma by counsel for the party opposing the relief, who shall appear in the name of the party and not that of the judge.*

*(b) Number of Copies.  Four copies shall be filed with the original.*

[December 1, 1994.]

# TITLE VI.  HABEAS CORPUS; PROCEEDINGS IN FORMA PAUPERIS

## FRAP 22.  HABEAS CORPUS AND SECTION 2255 PROCEEDINGS

**(a) Application for the Original Writ.**  An application for a writ of habeas corpus must be made to the appropriate district court.  If made to a circuit judge, the application must be transferred to the appropriate district court.  If a district court denies an application made or transferred to it, renewal of the application before a circuit judge is not permitted.  The applicant may, under 28 U.S.C. § 2253, appeal to the court of

appeals from the district court's order denying the application.

**(b) Certificate of Appealability.**

(1) In a habeas corpus proceeding in which the detention complained of arises from process issued by a state court, or in a 28 U.S.C. § 2255 proceeding, the applicant cannot take an appeal unless a circuit justice or a circuit or district judge issues a certificate of appealability under 28 U.S.C. § 2253(c). If an applicant files a notice of appeal, the district judge who rendered the judgment must either issue a certificate of appealability or state why a certificate should not issue. The district clerk must send the certificate or statement to the court of appeals with the notice of appeal and the file of the district-court proceedings. If the district judge has denied the certificate, the applicant may request a circuit judge to issue the certificate.

(2) A request addressed to the court of appeals may be considered by a circuit judge or judges, as the court prescribes. If no express request for a certificate is filed, the notice of appeal constitutes a request addressed to the judges of the court of appeals.

(3) A certificate of appealability is not required when a state or its representative or the United States or its representative appeals.

[Amended by Pub.L. 104–32, § 103, April 24, 1996, 110 Stat. 1218; amended April 24, 1998, effective December 1, 1998.]

## LOCAL RULE 22. CERTIFICATE OF APPEALABILITY

*(a) Prompt Application and Contents of Motion. In cases governed by 28 U.S.C. § 2253 and FRAP Rule 22(b), where an appeal has been taken but no certificate of appealability ("COA") has been issued by the district judge or by this court or a judge thereof, the appellant shall promptly move in this court for such a certificate. Such motion shall identify each issue that the appellant intends to raise on appeal and shall state, with respect to each issue, facts and a brief statement of reasons showing a denial of a constitutional right. When an appeal is filed for which a COA is required and a motion that complies with this rule has not been filed within 30 days after filing the notice of appeal, the clerk shall promptly send the appellant a letter enclosing a copy of this rule and informing the appellant that the required motion for a COA must be filed with the court within 21 days and that failure to file the motion may result in denial of a COA. The motion will be submitted without oral argument. The court will ordinarily limit its consideration of the motion to the issues identified therein. Such an appeal may not proceed unless and until a certificate is granted.*

*(b) Time for Filing Appellant's Brief. In cases governed by 28 U.S.C. § 2253 and FRAP Rule 22(b), the period of time for the filing of appellant's brief*

*and appendix shall not begin to run until a certificate of appealability has issued or, when counsel has been assigned, the date of such assignment, whichever is later.*

[December 1, 1994. Amended effective December 1, 2002; paragraph (a) amended on an interim basis effective May 1, 2003.]

## FRAP 23. CUSTODY OR RELEASE OF A PRISONER IN A HABEAS CORPUS PROCEEDING

**(a) Transfer of Custody Pending Review.** Pending review of a decision in a habeas corpus proceeding commenced before a court, justice, or judge of the United States for the release of a prisoner, the person having custody of the prisoner must not transfer custody to another unless a transfer is directed in accordance with this rule. When, upon application, a custodian shows the need for a transfer, the court, justice, or judge rendering the decision under review may authorize the transfer and substitute the successor custodian as a party.

**(b) Detention or Release Pending Review of Decision Not to Release.** While a decision not to release a prisoner is under review, the court or judge rendering the decision, or the court of appeals, or the Supreme Court, or a judge or justice of either court, may order that the prisoner be:

(1) detained in the custody from which release is sought;

(2) detained in other appropriate custody; or

(3) released on personal recognizance, with or without surety.

**(c) Release Pending Review of Decision Ordering Release.** While a decision ordering the release of a prisoner is under review, the prisoner must—unless the court or judge rendering the decision, or the court of appeals, or the Supreme Court, or a judge or justice of either court orders otherwise—be released on personal recognizance, with or without surety.

**(d) Modification of the Initial Order on Custody.** An initial order governing the prisoner's custody or release, including any recognizance or surety, continues in effect pending review unless for special reasons shown to the court of appeals or the Supreme Court, or to a judge or justice of either court, the order is modified or an independent order regarding custody, release, or surety is issued.

[Amended March 10, 1986, effective July 1, 1986; April 24, 1998, effective December 1, 1998.]

## FRAP 24. PROCEEDING IN FORMA PAUPERIS

**(a) Leave to Proceed In Forma Pauperis.**

(1) *Motion in the District Court.* Except as stated in Rule 24(a)(3), a party to a district-court action who

desires to appeal in forma pauperis must file a motion in the district court. The party must attach an affidavit that:

(A) shows in the detail prescribed by Form 4 of the Appendix of Forms the party's inability to pay or to give security for fees and costs;

(B) claims an entitlement to redress; and

(C) states the issues that the party intends to present on appeal.

(2) *Action on the Motion.* If the district court grants the motion, the party may proceed on appeal without prepaying or giving security for fees and costs, unless a statute provides otherwise. If the district court denies the motion, it must state its reasons in writing.

(3) *Prior Approval.* A party who was permitted to proceed in forma pauperis in the district-court action, or who was determined to be financially unable to obtain an adequate defense in a criminal case, may proceed on appeal in forma pauperis without further authorization, unless:

(A) the district court—before or after the notice of appeal is filed—certifies that the appeal is not taken in good faith or finds that the party is not otherwise entitled to proceed in forma pauperis and states in writing its reasons for the certification or finding; or

(B) a statute provides otherwise.

(4) *Notice of District Court's Denial.* The district clerk must immediately notify the parties and the court of appeals when the district court does any of the following:

(A) denies a motion to proceed on appeal in forma pauperis;

(B) certifies that the appeal is not taken in good faith; or

(C) finds that the party is not otherwise entitled to proceed in forma pauperis.

(5) *Motion in the Court of Appeals.* A party may file a motion to proceed on appeal in forma pauperis in the court of appeals within 30 days after service of the notice prescribed in Rule 24(a)(4). The motion must include a copy of the affidavit filed in the district court and the district court's statement of reasons for its action. If no affidavit was filed in the district court, the party must include the affidavit prescribed by Rule 24(a)(1).

**(b) Leave to Proceed In Forma Pauperis on Appeal or Review of an Administrative Agency Proceeding.** When an appeal or review of a proceeding before an administrative agency, board, commission, or officer (including for the purpose of this rule the United States Tax Court) proceeds directly in a court of appeals, a party may file in the court of appeals a motion for leave to proceed on appeal in forma pauperis with an affidavit prescribed by Rule 24(a)(1).

**(c) Leave to Use Original Record.** A party allowed to proceed on appeal in forma pauperis may request that the appeal be heard on the original record without reproducing any part.

[Amended April 30, 1979, effective August 1, 1979; March 10, 1986, effective July 1, 1986; April 24, 1998, effective December 1, 1998; April 29, 2002, effective December 1, 2002.]

# TITLE VII.  GENERAL PROVISIONS

## FRAP 25.  FILING AND SERVICE

**(a) Filing.**

(1) *Filing With the Clerk.* A paper required or permitted to be filed in a court of appeals must be filed with the clerk.

(2) *Filing: Method and Timeliness.*

(A) In General. Filing may be accomplished by mail addressed to the clerk, but filing is not timely unless the clerk receives the papers within the time fixed for filing.

(B) A Brief or Appendix. A brief or appendix is timely filed, however, if on or before the last day for filing, it is:

(i) mailed to the clerk by First–Class Mail, or other class of mail that is at least as expeditious, postage prepaid; or

(ii) dispatched to a third-party commercial carrier for delivery to the clerk within 3 calendar days.

(C) Inmate Filing. A paper filed by an inmate confined in an institution is timely if deposited in the institution's internal mailing system on or before the last day for filing. If an institution has a system designed for legal mail, the inmate must use that system to receive the benefit of this rule. Timely filing may be shown by a declaration in compliance with 28 U.S.C. § 1746 or by a notarized statement, either of which must set forth the date of deposit and state that first-class postage has been prepaid.

(D) Electronic Filing. A court of appeals may by local rule permit or require papers to be filed, signed, or verified by electronic means that are consistent with technical standards, if any, that the Judicial Conference of the United States establishes. A local rule may require filing by electronic means only if reasonable exceptions are allowed. A paper filed by electronic means in compliance with a local rule constitutes a written paper for the purpose of applying these rules.

(3) *Filing a Motion With a Judge.* If a motion requests relief that may be granted by a single judge, the judge may permit the motion to be filed with the judge; the judge must note the filing date on the motion and give it to the clerk.

(4) *Clerk's Refusal of Documents.* The clerk must not refuse to accept for filing any paper presented for that purpose solely because it is not presented in proper form as required by these rules or by any local rule or practice.

*[Text of paragraph (a)(5) effective December 1, 2007, absent contrary Congressional action]*

(5) *Privacy Protection.* An appeal in a case whose privacy protection was governed by Federal Rule of Bankruptcy Procedure 9037, Federal Rule of Civil Procedure 5.2, or Federal Rule of Criminal Procedure 49.1 is governed by the same rule on appeal. In all other proceedings, privacy protection is governed by Federal Rule of Civil Procedure 5.2, except that Federal Rule of Criminal Procedure 49.1 governs when an extraordinary writ is sought in a criminal case.

**(b) Service of All Papers Required.** Unless a rule requires service by the clerk, a party must, at or before the time of filing a paper, serve a copy on the other parties to the appeal or review. Service on a party represented by counsel must be made on the party's counsel.

**(c) Manner of Service.**

(1) Service may be any of the following:

(A) personal, including delivery to a responsible person at the office of counsel;

(B) by mail;

(C) by third-party commercial carrier for delivery within 3 calendar days; or

(D) by electronic means, if the party being served consents in writing.

(2) If authorized by local rule, a party may use the court's transmission equipment to make electronic service under Rule 25(c)(1)(D).

(3) When reasonable considering such factors as the immediacy of the relief sought, distance, and cost, service on a party must be by a manner at least as expeditious as the manner used to file the paper with the court.

(4) Service by mail or by commercial carrier is complete on mailing or delivery to the carrier. Service by electronic means is complete on transmission, unless the party making service is notified that the paper was not received by the party served.

**(d) Proof of Service.**

(1) A paper presented for filing must contain either of the following:

(A) an acknowledgment of service by the person served; or

(B) proof of service consisting of a statement by the person who made service certifying:

(i) the date and manner of service;

(ii) the names of the persons served; and

(iii) their mail or electronic addresses, facsimile numbers, or the addresses of the places of delivery, as appropriate for the manner of service.

(2) When a brief or appendix is filed by mailing or dispatch in accordance with Rule 25(a)(2)(B), the proof of service must also state the date and manner by which the document was mailed or dispatched to the clerk.

(3) Proof of service may appear on or be affixed to the papers filed.

**(e) Number of Copies.** When these rules require the filing or furnishing of a number of copies, a court may require a different number by local rule or by order in a particular case.

[Amended March 10, 1986, effective July 1, 1986; April 30, 1991, effective December 1, 1991; April 22, 1993, effective December 1, 1993; April 29, 1994, effective December 1, 1994; April 23, 1996, effective December 1, 1996; April 24, 1998, effective December 1, 1998; April 29, 2002, effective December 1, 2002; April 12, 2006, effective December 1, 2006; April 30, 2007, effective December 1, 2007, absent contrary Congressional action.]

## LOCAL RULE 25. FILING AND SERVICE

*To facilitate the Clerk's Office's ability to scan documents, any paper filing, except a paper brief accompanied by a PDF brief submitted pursuant to Local Rule 32(a)(1)(A), must include one unbound copy (papers not stapled together or otherwise attached). The use of paper clips and rubber bands is permitted. When only the original document is filed, the original copy must be unbound.*

[Adopted on an interim basis effective December 1, 2005.]

## FRAP 26. COMPUTING AND EXTENDING TIME

**(a) Computing Time.** The following rules apply in computing any period of time specified in these rules or in any local rule, court order, or applicable statute:

(1) Exclude the day of the act, event, or default that begins the period.

(2) Exclude intermediate Saturdays, Sundays, and legal holidays when the period is less than 11 days, unless stated in calendar days.

(3) Include the last day of the period unless it is a Saturday, Sunday, legal holiday, or—if the act to be done is filing a paper in court—a day on which the weather or other conditions make the clerk's office inaccessible.

(4) As used in this rule, "legal holiday" means New Year's Day, Martin Luther King, Jr.'s Birthday,

Washington's Birthday, Memorial Day, Independence Day, Labor Day, Columbus Day, Veterans' Day, Thanksgiving Day, Christmas Day, and any other day declared a holiday by the President, Congress, or the state in which is located either the district court that rendered the challenged judgment or order, or the circuit clerk's principal office.

**(b) Extending Time.** For good cause, the court may extend the time prescribed by these rules or by its order to perform any act, or may permit an act to be done after that time expires. But the court may not extend the time to file:

(1) a notice of appeal (except as authorized in Rule 4) or a petition for permission to appeal; or

(2) a notice of appeal from or a petition to enjoin, set aside, suspend, modify, enforce, or otherwise review an order of an administrative agency, board, commission, or officer of the United States, unless specifically authorized by law.

**(c) Additional Time After Service.** When a party is required or permitted to act within a prescribed period after a paper is served on that party, 3 calendar days are added to the prescribed period unless the paper is delivered on the date of service stated in the proof of service. For purposes of this Rule 26(c), a paper that is served electronically is not treated as delivered on the date of service stated in the proof of service.

[Amended March 1, 1971, effective July 1, 1971; March 10, 1986, effective July 1, 1986; April 25, 1989, effective December 1, 1989; April 30, 1991, effective December 1, 1991; April 23, 1996, effective December 1, 1996; April 24, 1998, effective December 1, 1998; April 29, 2002, effective December 1, 2002; April 25, 2005, effective December 1, 2005.]

# FRAP 26.1  CORPORATE DISCLOSURE STATEMENT

**(a) Who Must File.** Any nongovernmental corporate party to a proceeding in a court of appeals must file a statement that identifies any parent corporation and any publicly held corporation that owns 10% or more of its stock or states that there is no such corporation.

**(b) Time for Filing; Supplemental Filing.** A party must file the Rule 26.1(a) statement with the principal brief or upon filing a motion, response, petition, or answer in the court of appeals, whichever occurs first, unless a local rule requires earlier filing. Even if the statement has already been filed, the party's principal brief must include the statement before the table of contents. A party must supplement its statement whenever the information that must be disclosed under Rule 26.1(a) changes.

**(c) Number of Copies.** If the Rule 26.1(a) statement is filed before the principal brief, or if a supplemental statement is filed, the party must file an original and 3 copies unless the court requires a different number by local rule or by order in a particular case.

[Adopted April 25, 1989, effective December 1, 1989; amended April 30, 1991, effective December 1, 1991; April 29, 1994, effective December 1, 1994; April 24, 1998, effective December 1, 1998; April 29, 2002, effective December 1, 2002.]

# FRAP 27.  MOTIONS

**(a) In General.**

(1) *Application for Relief.* An application for an order or other relief is made by motion unless these rules prescribe another form. A motion must be in writing unless the court permits otherwise.

(2) *Contents of a Motion.*

(A) Grounds and relief sought. A motion must state with particularity the grounds for the motion, the relief sought, and the legal argument necessary to support it.

(B) Accompanying documents.

(i) Any affidavit or other paper necessary to support a motion must be served and filed with the motion.

(ii) An affidavit must contain only factual information, not legal argument.

(iii) A motion seeking substantive relief must include a copy of the trial court's opinion or agency's decision as a separate exhibit.

(C) Documents barred or not required.

(i) A separate brief supporting or responding to a motion must not be filed.

(ii) A notice of motion is not required.

(iii) A proposed order is not required.

(3) *Response.*

(A) Time to file. Any party may file a response to a motion; Rule 27(a)(2) governs its contents. The response must be filed within 8 days after service of the motion unless the court shortens or extends the time. A motion authorized by Rules 8, 9, 18, or 41 may be granted before the 8–day period runs only if the court gives reasonable notice to the parties that it intends to act sooner.

(B) Request for affirmative relief. A response may include a motion for affirmative relief. The time to respond to the new motion, and to reply to that response, are governed by Rule 27(a)(3)(A) and (a)(4). The title of the response must alert the court to the request for relief.

(4) *Reply to Response.* Any reply to a response must be filed within 5 days after service of the response. A reply must not present matters that do not relate to the response.

**(b) Disposition of a Motion for a Procedural Order.** The court may act on a motion for a procedural order—including a motion under Rule 26(b)—at

any time without awaiting a response, and may, by rule or by order in a particular case, authorize its clerk to act on specified types of procedural motions. A party adversely affected by the court's, or the clerk's, action may file a motion to reconsider, vacate, or modify that action. Timely opposition filed after the motion is granted in whole or in part does not constitute a request to reconsider, vacate, or modify the disposition; a motion requesting that relief must be filed.

**(c) Power of a Single Judge to Entertain a Motion.** A circuit judge may act alone on any motion, but may not dismiss or otherwise determine an appeal or other proceeding. A court of appeals may provide by rule or by order in a particular case that only the court may act on any motion or class of motions. The court may review the action of a single judge.

**(d) Form of Papers; Page Limits; and Number of Copies.**

(1) *Format.*

(A) Reproduction. A motion, response, or reply may be reproduced by any process that yields a clear black image on light paper. The paper must be opaque and unglazed. Only one side of the paper may be used.

(B) Cover. A cover is not required, but there must be a caption that includes the case number, the name of the court, the title of the case, and a brief descriptive title indicating the purpose of the motion and identifying the party or parties for whom it is filed. If a cover is used, it must be white.

(C) Binding. The document must be bound in any manner that is secure, does not obscure the text, and permits the document to lie reasonably flat when open.

(D) Paper Size, Line Spacing, and Margins. The document must be on 8½ by 11 inch paper. The text must be double-spaced, but quotations more than two lines long may be indented and single-spaced. Headings and footnotes may be single-spaced. Margins must be at least one inch on all four sides. Page numbers may be placed in the margins, but no text may appear there.

(E) Typeface and Type Styles. The document must comply with the typeface requirements of Rule 32(a)(5) and the type-style requirements of Rule 32(a)(6).

(2) *Page Limits.* A motion or a response to a motion must not exceed 20 pages, exclusive of the corporate disclosure statement and accompanying documents authorized by Rule 27(a)(2)(B), unless the court permits or directs otherwise. A reply to a response must not exceed 10 pages.

(3) *Number of Copies.* An original and 3 copies must be filed unless the court requires a different number by local rule or by order in a particular case.

**(e) Oral Argument.** A motion will be decided without oral argument unless the court orders otherwise.

[Amended April 30, 1979, effective August 1, 1979; April 25, 1989, effective December 1, 1989; April 29, 1994, effective December 1, 1994; April 24, 1998, effective December 1, 1998; April 29, 2002, effective December 1, 2002; April 25, 2005, effective December 1, 2005.]

## LOCAL RULE 27. MOTIONS

*(a) Form of Motion and Supporting Papers for Motion and Opposition Statement.*

*(1) Form of Motion. A motion must be in writing, unless the court otherwise directs, and must conform to the following requirements:*

*A.   The front page of the motion must follow the form of the Motion Information Statement approved by the Court (T–1080) and contain all information required by the form.*

*B.   The Motion Information Statement must be followed by a memorandum which must (i) indicate the relief sought, (ii) set forth the information and legal argument supporting the motion, and (iii) if emergency relief is sought, explain the reasons for the emergency.*

*C.   Formal Requirements of Motion and Opposition Statement.*

*(i) 8½ by 11 inch paper;*

*(ii) Text double spaced, except for quotations, headings and footnotes;*

*(iii) Margins of one inch on all sides;*

*(iv) Pages sequentially numbered (page numbers may be placed in the margins);*

*(v) Bound or stapled in a secure manner that does not obscure text;*

*(vi) Length: no more than 20 pages, not including attachments and the Motion Information Statement;*

*(vii) Number of copies: original plus four copies;*

*(viii) Required attachments to motion:*

*a.   An affidavit (containing only statements of fact, not legal argument);*

*b.   If the motion seeks substantive relief, a copy of lower court opinion or agency decision;*

*c.   Any exhibits necessary to determine the motion;*

*d.   Proof of service.*

*2.   Non-Compliance Sanctions. If the moving party has not complied with this rule, the motion may be dismissed by the clerk without prejudice to renew upon proper papers. If application is promptly made, the action of the clerk may be reviewed by a single judge. The court may impose costs and an appropri-*

ate fine against either party for failure to comply with this rule.

**(b) Motions to Be Heard at Regular Sessions of the Court.** *Motions seeking substantive relief will normally be determined by a panel conducting a regular session of the court. These include, without limitation, motions seeking bail pending appeal (see Rule 9(b)); dismissal or summary affirmance, including summary enforcement of an agency order; stay or injunction pending appeal or review (see Rules 8 and 18); certificates of appealability (see Rule 22); leave to proceed in forma pauperis (see Rule 24) except when a certificate of appealability has been granted by the district court or counsel has been assigned under 18 U.S.C. § 3006A; and assignment of counsel in cases not within subsection (e). Except as provided in subdivision (c) of this Rule, such motions will normally be noticed for a Tuesday when the court is in session, and the court will hear oral argument from any party desiring this. Motions to dismiss appeals of incarcerated prisoners not represented by counsel for untimeliness or lack of timely prosecution shall not be noticed for a date earlier than fifteen days after the date when prison officials shall certify the motion was received by the prisoner. Any party requesting an expedited hearing must set forth in writing the facts which justify the urgency. Upon appropriate showing of urgency, the clerk may set any motion for a hearing on any day the court is in session. When the clerk thus sets a hearing for a time not later than 24 hours after application to the clerk during the period Monday to Thursday, or for Tuesday morning during the period after Thursday, the clerk may endorse on the motion papers a direction that the parties will be expected to maintain the status quo and such direction shall have the effect of a stay, unless a judge on application shall otherwise direct. Except as otherwise provided in these rules or by order of the court, all motions noticed for a Tuesday, with supporting papers, must be filed not later than the Monday of the preceding week, with notice by the movant to the adverse party to be served not later than the Thursday preceding the last date for filing, if served in person, and not later than the Monday preceding the last date for filing, if served by mail; any papers in response must be served and filed not later than seven days after service of a motion served in person, or ten days after service of a motion served by mail, but in no event later than 12 noon on the Thursday preceding the Tuesday for which the motion is noticed.*

**(c) Motions to Be Heard by a Panel Which Has Rendered a Decision.** *Motions addressed to a previous decision or order of the court or for the stay, recall or modification of any mandate or decision of the court or to withdraw or dismiss an appeal argued but not decided shall be referred by the clerk to the judges who heard the appeal, normally without oral argument.*

**(d) Pro Se Motions by Incarcerated Prisoners Under 28 U.S.C. §§ 2253 and 2255.** *Pro se motions by incarcerated prisoners under 28 U.S.C. §§ 2253 and 2255 for certificates of appealability, leave to proceed in forma pauperis, or assignment of counsel shall be made on seven days' notice to the state or the United States, and will be taken on submission, without being calendared, at such time as the material necessary for the court's consideration shall have been assembled by the deputy clerk designated for the purpose.*

**(e) Motions for Leave to Appeal.** *Motions for leave to appeal under 28 U.S.C. § 1292(b) or under § 24 of the Bankruptcy Act, 11 U.S.C. § 47 (see Rules 5 and 6), shall be submitted without oral argument.*

**(f) Motions to Be Determined by a Single Judge.** *(See Rule 27(b) and (c).) Motions for procedural relief will normally be determined by a single judge without oral argument. Notwithstanding the provision of § 27(a) in regard to dismissals, a single judge may include in an order granting an appellant an extension of time a provision for dismissal of the appeal by the clerk in the event of a default. These include, without limitation, motions for extension of time to file records, briefs, appendices or other papers, or for permission to make late filing in the absence of stipulation; to dispense with printing; for assignment of counsel or transcription of the record at the expense of the United States in cases governed by 18 U.S.C. § 3006A (which action shall be deemed to constitute the grant of leave to proceed in forma pauperis); for allowance of compensation and expenses under 18 U.S.C. § 3006A; for assignment of counsel when a certificate of appealability (see Rule 22) has been granted by the district court and for leave to proceed in forma pauperis in such cases; for leave to file a brief as amicus curiae (see Rule 29); for substitutions (see Rule 43); for consolidation; to intervene or to add or drop parties; for a preference; or for postponement of the argument of an appeal. When the court is not in session, certain of the motions normally returnable before a panel as provided in subdivision (a) may be heard and decided by a single judge. Arrangements for such a hearing shall be made through the clerk.*

**(g) Motions for Permission to File Briefs Exceeding Size Provided by Rule 28(g).**

1.   *A motion for permission to file a brief exceeding the size provided by Rule 28(g) shall be accompanied by a statement of reasons therefor and a copy of the page proofs, and will be disposed of by the clerk or referred by the clerk to a judge as standing directions of the court provide.*

2.   *Such a motion shall be made not later than seven days before the brief is due in criminal cases and not later than two weeks before the brief is due in all other cases.*

*(h) Other Motions.* *Any motion not provided for in this rule or in other rules of this court shall be submitted to the clerk, who will assign it for disposition in accordance with standing directions of the court or, if these are inapplicable, as directed by the judge presiding over the panel of the court in session or assigned for the hearing of motions when the court is not in session. The clerk will notify counsel if and when appearance before the court or a judge is required.*

*(i) Suggestions for In Banc Consideration of a Motion.* *A suggestion by a party for in banc consideration in the first instance of a motion shall not be accepted for filing by the clerk unless the motion sought to be considered in banc has previously been ruled on by a panel of this court.*

*(j) Motions by Pro Se Appellant in Civil Appeals (Including Habeas Corpus).* *In any civil appeal, including an appeal in a habeas corpus proceeding or other collateral attack on a criminal conviction, a motion filed by a pro se appellant (including, but not limited to, a motion for a certificate of appealability ("COA") from the denial of a writ of habeas corpus, a motion for leave to appeal in forma pauperis, for appointment of counsel, or for a transcript at public expense) shall identify each issue that the appellant intends to raise on appeal and shall state, with respect to each issue, facts and a brief statement of reasons showing that the issue has likely merit. When a motion filed by a pro se appellant does not comply with this rule, the clerk shall promptly send the appellant a letter enclosing a copy of this rule and informing the appellant that (1) the required identification of issues and supporting facts and reasons must be filed with the court within 21 days, and (2) if the appellant fails to file the required statement, or if the court determines on considering the appellant's statement that the appeal is frivolous, the court may dismiss the appeal. The motion will be submitted without oral argument. The court will ordinarily limit its consideration of the motion to the issues identified therein.*

*This rule was amended on October 31, 1997, to reflect "Certificate of Appealability" rather than Probable Cause.*

[December 1, 1994. Amended effective October 31, 1997; July 1, 2002; December 1, 2002; paragraph (j) adopted on an interim basis effective May 1, 2003.]

# FRAP 28.  BRIEFS

**(a) Appellant's Brief.**  The appellant's brief must contain, under appropriate headings and in the order indicated:

(1) a corporate disclosure statement if required by Rule 26.1;

(2) a table of contents, with page references;

(3) a table of authorities—cases (alphabetically arranged), statutes, and other authorities—with references to the pages of the brief where they are cited;

(4) a jurisdictional statement, including:

(A) the basis for the district court's or agency's subject-matter jurisdiction, with citations to applicable statutory provisions and stating relevant facts establishing jurisdiction;

(B) the basis for the court of appeals' jurisdiction, with citations to applicable statutory provisions and stating relevant facts establishing jurisdiction;

(C) the filing dates establishing the timeliness of the appeal or petition for review; and

(D) an assertion that the appeal is from a final order or judgment that disposes of all parties' claims, or information establishing the court of appeals' jurisdiction on some other basis;

(5) a statement of the issues presented for review;

(6) a statement of the case briefly indicating the nature of the case, the course of proceedings, and the disposition below;

(7) a statement of facts relevant to the issues submitted for review with appropriate references to the record (see Rule 28(e));

(8) a summary of the argument, which must contain a succinct, clear, and accurate statement of the arguments made in the body of the brief, and which must not merely repeat the argument headings;

(9) the argument, which must contain:

(A) appellant's contentions and the reasons for them, with citations to the authorities and parts of the record on which the appellant relies; and

(B) for each issue, a concise statement of the applicable standard of review (which may appear in the discussion of the issue or under a separate heading placed before the discussion of the issues);

(10) a short conclusion stating the precise relief sought; and

(11) the certificate of compliance, if required by Rule 32(a)(7).

**(b) Appellee's Brief.**  The appellee's brief must conform to the requirements of Rule 28(a)(1)–(9) and (11), except that none of the following need appear unless the appellee is dissatisfied with the appellant's statement:

(1) the jurisdictional statement;

(2) the statement of the issues;

(3) the statement of the case;

(4) the statement of the facts; and

(5) the statement of the standard of review.

**(c) Reply Brief.**  The appellant may file a brief in reply to the appellee's brief.  Unless the court per-

mits, no further briefs may be filed. A reply brief must contain a table of contents, with page references, and a table of authorities—cases (alphabetically arranged), statutes, and other authorities—with references to the pages of the reply brief where they are cited.

**(d) References to Parties.** In briefs and at oral argument, counsel should minimize use of the terms "appellant" and "appellee." To make briefs clear, counsel should use the parties' actual names or the designations used in the lower court or agency proceeding, or such descriptive terms as "the employee," "the injured person," "the taxpayer," "the ship," "the stevedore."

**(e) References to the Record.** References to the parts of the record contained in the appendix filed with the appellant's brief must be to the pages of the appendix. If the appendix is prepared after the briefs are filed, a party referring to the record must follow one of the methods detailed in Rule 30(c). If the original record is used under Rule 30(f) and is not consecutively paginated, or if the brief refers to an unreproduced part of the record, any reference must be to the page of the original document. For example:

- Answer p. 7;
- Motion for Judgment p. 2;
- Transcript p. 231.

Only clear abbreviations may be used. A party referring to evidence whose admissibility is in controversy must cite the pages of the appendix or of the transcript at which the evidence was identified, offered, and received or rejected.

**(f) Reproduction of Statutes, Rules, Regulations, etc.** If the court's determination of the issues presented requires the study of statutes, rules, regulations, etc., the relevant parts must be set out in the brief or in an addendum at the end, or may be supplied to the court in pamphlet form.

**(g) [Reserved].**

**(h) [Reserved].**

**(i) Briefs in a Case Involving Multiple Appellants or Appellees.** In a case involving more than one appellant or appellee, including consolidated cases, any number of appellants or appellees may join in a brief, and any party may adopt by reference a part of another's brief. Parties may also join in reply briefs.

**(j) Citation of Supplemental Authorities.** If pertinent and significant authorities come to a party's attention after the party's brief has been filed—or after oral argument but before decision—a party may promptly advise the circuit clerk by letter, with a copy to all other parties, setting forth the citations. The letter must state the reasons for the supplemental citations, referring either to the page of the brief or to

a point argued orally. The body of the letter must not exceed 350 words. Any response must be made promptly and must be similarly limited.

[Amended April 30, 1979, effective August 1, 1979; March 10, 1986, effective July 1, 1986; April 25, 1989, effective December 1, 1989; April 30, 1991, effective December 1, 1991; April 22, 1993, effective December 1, 1993; April 29, 1994, effective December 1, 1994; April 24, 1998, effective December 1, 1998; April 29, 2002, effective December 1, 2002; April 1, 2005, effective December 1, 2005.]

## *LOCAL RULE 28. BRIEFS*

*1. Briefs must be compact, logically arranged with proper headings, concise, and free from burdensome, irrelevant, immaterial, and scandalous matter. Briefs not complying with this rule may be disregarded and stricken by the court.*

*2. Appellant's brief shall include, as a preliminary statement, the name of the judge or agency member who rendered the decision appealed from and, if the judge's decision or supporting opinion is reported, the citation thereof.*

[December 1, 1994.]

## FRAP 28.1 CROSS–APPEALS

**(a) Applicability.** This rule applies to a case in which a cross-appeal is filed. Rules 28(a)–(c), 31(a)(1), 32(a)(2), and 32(a)(7)(A)–(B) do not apply to such a case, except as otherwise provided in this rule.

**(b) Designation of Appellant.** The party who files a notice of appeal first is the appellant for the purposes of this rule and Rules 30 and 34. If notices are filed on the same day, the plaintiff in the proceeding below is the appellant. These designations may be modified by the parties' agreement or by court order.

**(c) Briefs.** In a case involving a cross-appeal:

(1) *Appellant's Principal Brief.* The appellant must file a principal brief in the appeal. That brief must comply with Rule 28(a).

(2) *Appellee's Principal and Response Brief.* The appellee must file a principal brief in the cross-appeal and must, in the same brief, respond to the principal brief in the appeal. That appellee's brief must comply with Rule 28(a), except that the brief need not include a statement of the case or a statement of the facts unless the appellee is dissatisfied with the appellant's statement.

(3) *Appellant's Response and Reply Brief.* The appellant must file a brief that responds to the principal brief in the cross-appeal and may, in the same brief, reply to the response in the appeal. That brief must comply with Rule 28(a)(2)–(9) and (11), except that none of the following need appear unless the appellant is dissatisfied with the appellee's statement in the cross-appeal:

(A) the jurisdictional statement;

(B) the statement of the issues;

(C) the statement of the case;

(D) the statement of the facts; and

(E) the statement of the standard of review.

(4) *Appellee's Reply Brief.* The appellee may file a brief in reply to the response in the cross-appeal. That brief must comply with Rule 28(a)(2)–(3) and (11) and must be limited to the issues presented by the cross-appeal.

(5) *No Further Briefs.* Unless the court permits, no further briefs may be filed in a case involving a cross-appeal.

**(d) Cover.** Except for filings by unrepresented parties, the cover of the appellant's principal brief must be blue; the appellee's principal and response brief, red; the appellant's response and reply brief, yellow; the appellee's reply brief, gray; an intervenor's or amicus curiae's brief, green; and any supplemental brief, tan. The front cover of a brief must contain the information required by Rule 32(a)(2).

**(e) Length.**

(1) *Page Limitation.* Unless it complies with Rule 28.1(e)(2) and (3), the appellant's principal brief must not exceed 30 pages; the appellee's principal and response brief, 35 pages; the appellant's response and reply brief, 30 pages; and the appellee's reply brief, 15 pages.

(2) *Type-Volume Limitation.*

(A) The appellant's principal brief or the appellant's response and reply brief is acceptable if:

(i) it contains no more than 14,000 words; or

(ii) it uses a monospaced face and contains no more than 1,300 lines of text.

(B) The appellee's principal and response brief is acceptable if:

(i) it contains no more than 16,500 words; or

(ii) it uses a monospaced face and contains no more than 1,500 lines of text.

(C) The appellee's reply brief is acceptable if it contains no more than half of the type volume specified in Rule 28.1(e)(2)(A).

(3) *Certificate of Compliance.* A brief submitted under Rule 28.1(e)(2) must comply with Rule 32(a)(7)(C).

**(f) Time to Serve and File a Brief.** Briefs must be served and filed as follows:

(1) the appellant's principal brief, within 40 days after the record is filed;

(2) the appellee's principal and response brief, within 30 days after the appellant's principal brief is served;

(3) the appellant's response and reply brief, within 30 days after the appellee's principal and response brief is served; and

(4) the appellee's reply brief, within 14 days after the appellant's response and reply brief is served, but at least 3 days before argument unless the court, for good cause, allows a later filing.

[Amended April 25, 2005, effective December 1, 2005.]

# FRAP 29. BRIEF OF AN AMICUS CURIAE

**(a) When Permitted.** The United States or its officer or agency, or a State, Territory, Commonwealth, or the District of Columbia may file an amicus-curiae brief without the consent of the parties or leave of court. Any other amicus curiae may file a brief only by leave of court or if the brief states that all parties have consented to its filing.

**(b) Motion for Leave to File.** The motion must be accompanied by the proposed brief and state:

(1) the movant's interest; and

(2) the reason why an amicus brief is desirable and why the matters asserted are relevant to the disposition of the case.

**(c) Contents and Form.** An amicus brief must comply with Rule 32. In addition to the requirements of Rule 32, the cover must identify the party or parties supported and indicate whether the brief supports affirmance or reversal. If an amicus curiae is a corporation, the brief must include a disclosure statement like that required of parties by Rule 26.1. An amicus brief need not comply with Rule 28, but must include the following:

(1) a table of contents, with page references;

(2) a table of authorities—cases (alphabetically arranged), statutes and other authorities—with references to the pages of the brief where they are cited;

(3) a concise statement of the identity of the amicus curiae, its interest in the case, and the source of its authority to file;

(4) an argument, which may be preceded by a summary and which need not include a statement of the applicable standard of review; and

(5) a certificate of compliance, if required by Rule 32(a)(7).

**(d) Length.** Except by the court's permission, an amicus brief may be no more than one-half the maximum length authorized by these rules for a party's principal brief. If the court grants a party permission to file a longer brief, that extension does not affect the length of an amicus brief.

**(e) Time for Filing.** An amicus curiae must file its brief, accompanied by a motion for filing when necessary, no later than 7 days after the principal

brief of the party being supported is filed. An amicus curiae that does not support either party must file its brief no later than 7 days after the appellant's or petitioner's principal brief is filed. A court may grant leave for later filing, specifying the time within which an opposing party may answer.

**(f) Reply Brief.** Except by the court's permission, an amicus curiae may not file a reply brief.

**(g) Oral Argument.** An amicus curiae may participate in oral argument only with the court's permission.

[Amended April 24, 1998, effective December 1, 1998.]

## INTERIM LOCAL RULE 29. BRIEF OF AN AMICUS CURIAE

*The Court ordinarily will deny leave to file a brief for an amicus curiae where, by reason of a relationship between a judge who would hear the proceeding and the amicus or counsel for the amicus, the filing of the brief would cause the recusal of the judge.*

[Adopted on an interim basis, effective February 7, 2005.]

## FRAP 30. APPENDIX TO THE BRIEFS

**(a) Appellant's Responsibility.**

(1) *Contents of the Appendix.* The appellant must prepare and file an appendix to the briefs containing:

(A) the relevant docket entries in the proceeding below;

(B) the relevant portions of the pleadings, charge, findings, or opinion;

(C) the judgment, order, or decision in question; and

(D) other parts of the record to which the parties wish to direct the court's attention.

(2) *Excluded Material.* Memoranda of law in the district court should not be included in the appendix unless they have independent relevance. Parts of the record may be relied on by the court or the parties even though not included in the appendix.

(3) *Time to File; Number of Copies.* Unless filing is deferred under Rule 30(c), the appellant must file 10 copies of the appendix with the brief and must serve one copy on counsel for each party separately represented. An unrepresented party proceeding in forma pauperis must file 4 legible copies with the clerk, and one copy must be served on counsel for each separately represented party. The court may by local rule or by order in a particular case require the filing or service of a different number.

**(b) All Parties' Responsibilities.**

(1) *Determining the Contents of the Appendix.* The parties are encouraged to agree on the contents of the appendix. In the absence of an agreement, the appellant must, within 10 days after the record is filed, serve on the appellee a designation of the parts of the record the appellant intends to include in the appendix and a statement of the issues the appellant intends to present for review. The appellee may, within 10 days after receiving the designation, serve on the appellant a designation of additional parts to which it wishes to direct the court's attention. The appellant must include the designated parts in the appendix. The parties must not engage in unnecessary designation of parts of the record, because the entire record is available to the court. This paragraph applies also to a cross-appellant and a cross-appellee.

(2) *Costs of Appendix.* Unless the parties agree otherwise, the appellant must pay the cost of the appendix. If the appellant considers parts of the record designated by the appellee to be unnecessary, the appellant may advise the appellee, who must then advance the cost of including those parts. The cost of the appendix is a taxable cost. But if any party causes unnecessary parts of the record to be included in the appendix, the court may impose the cost of those parts on that party. Each circuit must, by local rule, provide for sanctions against attorneys who unreasonably and vexatiously increase litigation costs by including unnecessary material in the appendix.

**(c) Deferred Appendix.**

(1) *Deferral Until After Briefs Are Filed.* The court may provide by rule for classes of cases or by order in a particular case that preparation of the appendix may be deferred until after the briefs have been filed and that the appendix may be filed 21 days after the appellee's brief is served. Even though the filing of the appendix may be deferred, Rule 30(b) applies; except that a party must designate the parts of the record it wants included in the appendix when it serves its brief, and need not include a statement of the issues presented.

(2) *References to the Record.*

(A) If the deferred appendix is used, the parties may cite in their briefs the pertinent pages of the record. When the appendix is prepared, the record pages cited in the briefs must be indicated by inserting record page numbers, in brackets, at places in the appendix where those pages of the record appear.

(B) A party who wants to refer directly to pages of the appendix may serve and file copies of the brief within the time required by Rule 31(a), containing appropriate references to pertinent pages of the record. In that event, within 14 days after the appendix is filed, the party must serve and file copies of the brief, containing references to the pages of the appendix in place of or in addition to the references to the pertinent pages of the record. Except for the correction of typographical errors, no other changes may be made to the brief.

**(d) Format of the Appendix.** The appendix must begin with a table of contents identifying the page at which each part begins. The relevant docket entries must follow the table of contents. Other parts of the record must follow chronologically. When pages from the transcript of proceedings are placed in the appendix, the transcript page numbers must be shown in brackets immediately before the included pages. Omissions in the text of papers or of the transcript must be indicated by asterisks. Immaterial formal matters (captions, subscriptions, acknowledgments, etc.) should be omitted.

**(e) Reproduction of Exhibits.** Exhibits designated for inclusion in the appendix may be reproduced in a separate volume, or volumes, suitably indexed. Four copies must be filed with the appendix, and one copy must be served on counsel for each separately represented party. If a transcript of a proceeding before an administrative agency, board, commission, or officer was used in a district-court action and has been designated for inclusion in the appendix, the transcript must be placed in the appendix as an exhibit.

**(f) Appeal on the Original Record Without an Appendix.** The court may, either by rule for all cases or classes of cases or by order in a particular case, dispense with the appendix and permit an appeal to proceed on the original record with any copies of the record, or relevant parts, that the court may order the parties to file.

[Amended March 30, 1970, effective July 1, 1970; March 10, 1986, effective July 1, 1986; April 30, 1991, effective December 1, 1991; April 29, 1994, effective December 1, 1994; April 24, 1998, effective December 1, 1998.]

## LOCAL RULE 30. APPENDIX

*(a) Deferred Appendix. A deferred appendix as provided in Rule 30(c) may be filed in any case where the parties so stipulate or where, on application, a judge of this court so directs.*

*(b) Original Record. The procedure described in Rule 30(f) for hearing appeals on the original record without the necessity of an appendix (other than a copy of an opinion rendered by the district court) is authorized in all appeals conducted under the Criminal Justice Act, 18 U.S.C. § 3006A, in all other proceedings conducted in forma pauperis, and in all appeals involving a social security decision of the Secretary of Health and Human Services. In such cases the appellant shall file along with the appellant's brief five clearly legible copies of the reporter's transcript or of so much thereof as the appellant desires the court to read (or in the case of social security decisions, of the administrative records), and both parties in their briefs shall direct the court's attention to the portions of the transcript or administrative record deemed relevant to each point. If five copies are not available without incurring undue*

expense, application for leave to proceed with a smaller number of copies may be made.

*(c) Index for Exhibits. The index for exhibits required by FRAP 30(e) shall include a description of the exhibit sufficient to inform the court of its nature; designation merely by exhibit number or letter is not a suitable index.*

*(d) Notice of Appeal. The notice of appeal shall be included in the appendix.*

[December 1, 1994.]

## FRAP 31. SERVING AND FILING BRIEFS

**(a) Time to Serve and File a Brief.**

(1) The appellant must serve and file a brief within 40 days after the record is filed. The appellee must serve and file a brief within 30 days after the appellant's brief is served. The appellant may serve and file a reply brief within 14 days after service of the appellee's brief but a reply brief must be filed at least 3 days before argument, unless the court, for good cause, allows a later filing.

(2) A court of appeals that routinely considers cases on the merits promptly after the briefs are filed may shorten the time to serve and file briefs, either by local rule or by order in a particular case.

**(b) Number of Copies.** Twenty-five copies of each brief must be filed with the clerk and 2 copies must be served on each unrepresented party and on counsel for each separately represented party. An unrepresented party proceeding in forma pauperis must file 4 legible copies with the clerk, and one copy must be served on each unrepresented party and on counsel for each separately represented party. The court may by local rule or by order in a particular case require the filing or service of a different number.

**(c) Consequence of Failure to File.** If an appellant fails to file a brief within the time provided by this rule, or within an extended time, an appellee may move to dismiss the appeal. An appellee who fails to file a brief will not be heard at oral argument unless the court grants permission.

[Amended March 30, 1970, effective July 1, 1970; March 10, 1986, effective July 1, 1986; April 29, 1994, effective December 1, 1994; April 24, 1998, effective December 1, 1998; April 29, 2002, effective December 1, 2002.]

## LOCAL RULE 31. NUMBER OF COPIES OF BRIEF TO BE FILED WITH CLERK

*(b) Notwithstanding FRAP Rule 31(b), the number of copies of each brief that must be filed with the clerk is ten.*

[Adopted effective May 24, 2000.]

# FRAP 32. FORM OF BRIEFS, APPENDICES, AND OTHER PAPERS

## (a) Form of a Brief.

(1) *Reproduction.*

(A) A brief may be reproduced by any process that yields a clear black image on light paper. The paper must be opaque and unglazed. Only one side of the paper may be used.

(B) Text must be reproduced with a clarity that equals or exceeds the output of a laser printer.

(C) Photographs, illustrations, and tables may be reproduced by any method that results in a good copy of the original; a glossy finish is acceptable if the original is glossy.

(2) *Cover.* Except for filings by unrepresented parties, the cover of the appellant's brief must be blue; the appellee's, red; an intervenor's or amicus curiae's, green; any reply brief, gray; and any supplemental brief, tan. The front cover of a brief must contain:

(A) the number of the case centered at the top;

(B) the name of the court;

(C) the title of the case (see Rule 12(a));

(D) the nature of the proceeding (e.g., Appeal, Petition for Review) and the name of the court, agency, or board below;

(E) the title of the brief, identifying the party or parties for whom the brief is filed; and

(F) the name, office address, and telephone number of counsel representing the party for whom the brief is filed.

(3) *Binding.* The brief must be bound in any manner that is secure, does not obscure the text, and permits the brief to lie reasonably flat when open.

(4) *Paper Size, Line Spacing, and Margins.* The brief must be on 8½ by 11 inch paper. The text must be double-spaced, but quotations more than two lines long may be indented and single-spaced. Headings and footnotes may be single-spaced. Margins must be at least one inch on all four sides. Page numbers may be placed in the margins, but no text may appear there.

(5) *Typeface.* Either a proportionally spaced or a monospaced face may be used.

(A) A proportionally spaced face must include serifs, but sans-serif type may be used in headings and captions. A proportionally spaced face must be 14–point or larger.

(B) A monospaced face may not contain more than 10½ characters per inch.

(6) *Type Styles.* A brief must be set in a plain, roman style, although italics or boldface may be used for emphasis. Case names must be italicized or underlined.

(7) *Length.*

(A) Page limitation. A principal brief may not exceed 30 pages, or a reply brief 15 pages, unless it complies with Rule 32(a)(7)(B) and (C).

(B) Type-volume limitation.

(i) A principal brief is acceptable if:

• it contains no more than 14,000 words; or

• it uses a monospaced face and contains no more than 1,300 lines of text.

(ii) A reply brief is acceptable if it contains no more than half of the type volume specified in Rule 32(a)(7)(B)(i).

(iii) Headings, footnotes, and quotations count toward the word and line limitations. The corporate disclosure statement, table of contents, table of citations, statement with respect to oral argument, any addendum containing statutes, rules or regulations, and any certificates of counsel do not count toward the limitation.

(C) Certificate of Compliance.

(i) A brief submitted under Rules 28.1(e)(2) or 32(a)(7)(B) must include a certificate by the attorney, or an unrepresented party, that the brief complies with the type-volume limitation. The person preparing the certificate may rely on the word or line count of the word-processing system used to prepare the brief. The certificate must state either:

• the number of words in the brief; or

• the number of lines of monospaced type in the brief.

(ii) Form 6 in the Appendix of Forms is a suggested form of a certificate of compliance. Use of Form 6 must be regarded as sufficient to meet the requirements of Rules 28.1(e)(3) and 32(a)(7)(C)(i).

**(b) Form of an Appendix.** An appendix must comply with Rule 32(a)(1), (2), (3), and (4), with the following exceptions:

(1) The cover of a separately bound appendix must be white.

(2) An appendix may include a legible photocopy of any document found in the record or of a printed judicial or agency decision.

(3) When necessary to facilitate inclusion of odd-sized documents such as technical drawings, an appendix may be a size other than 8½ by 11 inches, and need not lie reasonably flat when opened.

**(c) Form of Other Papers.**

*(1) Motion.* The form of a motion is governed by Rule 27(d).

*(2) Other Papers.* Any other paper, including a petition for panel rehearing and a petition for hearing or rehearing en banc, and any response to such a petition, must be reproduced in the manner prescribed by Rule 32(a), with the following exceptions:

(A) A cover is not necessary if the caption and signature page of the paper together contain the information required by Rule 32(a)(2). If a cover is used, it must be white.

(B) Rule 32(a)(7) does not apply.

**(d) Signature.** Every brief, motion, or other paper filed with the court must be signed by the party filing the paper or, if the party is represented, by one of the party's attorneys.

**(e) Local Variation.** Every court of appeals must accept documents that comply with the form requirements of this rule. By local rule or order in a particular case a court of appeals may accept documents that do not meet all of the form requirements of this rule.

[Amended April 24, 1998, effective December 1, 1998; April 29, 2002, effective December 1, 2002; April 25, 2005, effective December 1, 2005.]

## LOCAL RULE 32. BRIEFS AND APPENDIX

**(a) Form of Brief.**

*(1)* Briefs in Digital Format.

*(A) Filing Requirement. Every brief filed by a party represented by counsel must be submitted in a Portable Document Format (PDF), in addition to the required number of paper copies, unless counsel certifies that submission of a brief as a PDF document is not practical or would constitute hardship. A party not represented by counsel is encouraged, but is not required, to submit a brief as a PDF document, in addition to the required number of paper copies. The PDF version of the brief must be submitted as an e-mail attachment to briefs@ca2. uscourts.gov. Any party, whether represented by counsel or not, who does not provide a brief in PDF format, must file one unbound copy of the paper brief.*

*(B) Content. The PDF document must contain the entire brief, and need not, but may, contain any supplemental material that is bound with the paper brief. A manual signature need not be included on the PDF copy.*

*(C) Format. The digital version of the brief must be in Portable Document Format (also known as PDF or Acrobat format). Converting a document into PDF format by scanning the document does not comply with this rule.*

*(D) Time for Filing. The PDF version of a brief required by this rule must be filed no later than the time for filing the paper copies of a brief.*

*(E) Virus Protection. Each party submitting a PDF brief must provide a signed paper document which certifies that the PDF brief has been scanned for viruses and that no virus has been detected. The signed paper certificate should be filed along with the paper briefs. A PDF version of the certificate, which need not include a manual signature, must accompany a PDF brief.*

*(F) Identifying Information. A party submitting a PDF brief shall provide the following identifying information in the "Subject" or "Re" box of the header of an e-mail that transmits an attachment: the docket number; the name of the party on whose behalf the brief is filed; the nature of the brief, i.e., "appellant's brief," "appellee's brief," "appellant's reply brief," "amicus brief"; and the date the PDF brief is submitted to the Court.*

*(G) Corrections. If a PDF brief is corrected, a new e-mail attachment with the corrected version shall be submitted, and the label, in addition to the Identifying Information required in subsection (a)(1)(F), shall add the date the corrected version is submitted to the Court.*

*(H) E-Mail Service. A copy of the PDF version of a brief must be e-mailed to all parties represented by counsel who have not been exempted from filing a PDF brief, and to those parties not represented by counsel who elected to submit a PDF brief.*

*(2)* Briefs in Paper Format. *Paper Briefs must conform to FRAP Rule 32(a), with a proviso that, if a litigant prefers to file a printed brief in pamphlet format, it must conform to the following specifications:*

*Size of Pages:  6⅛ by 9¼ inches.*
*Sides used:  Both.*
*Margins:  At least one inch on all sides.*
*Font size:  12-point type or larger, for text and footnotes.*
*Spacing:  2-points or more leading between lines. 6-points or more between paragraphs.*
*Other specifications:  Must conform to FRAP Rule 32(a).*

**(b) Form of Appendix.** *Appendices must conform to FRAP Rule 32(b).*

*(1) All appendices must contain:*

*(A) Sequentially numbered pages beginning with A-1.*

*(B) A detailed index referring to the sequential page numbers.*

*(2) Appendices may:*

*(A) Be printed on both sides of the page.*

*(B) Employ tabs to identify documents. (Use of tabs does not eliminate the requirements to number pages sequentially.)*

*(C) Employ the Manuscript form of transcripts.*

**(c) Covers.** *The docket number of the case must be printed in type at least one inch high on the cover of each brief and appendix.*

**(d) Special Appendix.**

1. Contents of the Special Appendix. *If the application or interpretation of any rule of law, including any constitutional provision, treaty, statute, ordinance, regulation, rule, or sentencing guideline, is significant to the resolution of any issue on appeal, or if the Appendix, exclusive of the orders, opinions, and judgments being appealed, would exceed 300 pages, the parties must provide the court with a Special Appendix, including*

*(A) the verbatim text, with appropriate citation, of any such rule of law, and*

*(B) such orders, opinions and judgments being appealed.*

*The inclusion of such materials in a Special Appendix satisfies the obligations established by FRAP Rules 28(f) and 30(a)(1)(C).*

2. Form of the Special Appendix. *The Special Appendix may be presented either as an addendum at the end of a brief, or as a separately bound volume (in which case it must be designated "Special Appendix" on its cover). The Special Appendix must conform to the requirements of Local Rule 32(b) relating to the Form of Appendix, with the exception that its pages must be sequentially numbered beginning with SPA-1.*

[Former Local Rule 32 rescinded, new Local Rule adopted effective May 24, 2000. Amended effective July 1, 2002; amended on an interim basis effective December 1, 2005.]

# FRAP 32.1   CITING JUDICIAL DISPOSITIONS

**(a) Citation Permitted.** A court may not prohibit or restrict the citation of federal judicial opinions, orders, judgments, or other written dispositions that have been:

(i) designated as "unpublished," "not for publication," "non-precedential," "not precedent," or the like; and

(ii) issued on or after January 1, 2007.

**(b) Copies Required.** If a party cites a federal judicial opinion, order, judgment, or other written disposition that is not available in a publicly accessible electronic database, the party must file and serve a copy of that opinion, order, judgment, or disposition with the brief or other paper in which it is cited.

Effective December 1, 2006.

# LOCAL RULE 32.1   DISPOSITIONS BY SUMMARY ORDER

**(a) Use of Summary Orders.** *The demands of contemporary case loads require the court to be conscious of the need to utilize judicial time effectively. Accordingly, in those cases in which decision is unanimous and each judge of the panel believes that no jurisprudential purpose would be served by an opinion (i.e., a ruling having precedential effect), the ruling may be by summary order instead of by opinion.*

**(b) Precedential Effect of Summary Orders.** *Rulings by summary order do not have precedential effect.*

**(c) Citation of Summary Orders.**

*(1) Citation to summary orders filed after January 1, 2007, is permitted.*

*(A) In a brief or other paper in which a litigant cites a summary order, in each paragraph in which a citation appears, at least one citation must either be to the Federal Appendix or be accompanied by the notation: "(summary order)".*

*(B) Service of Summary Orders on Pro Se Parties. A party citing a summary order must serve a copy of that summary order together with the paper in which the summary order is cited on any party not represented by counsel unless the summary order is available in an electronic database which is publicly accessible without payment of fee (such as the database available at http://www.ca2.uscourts.gov/). If no copy is served by reason of the availability of the order on such a database, the citation must include reference to that database and the docket number of the case in which the order was entered.*

**(d) Legend.** *Summary orders filed after January 1, 2007, shall bear the following legend:*

### SUMMARY ORDER

*Rulings by summary order do not have precedential effect. Citation to summary orders filed after January 1, 2007, is permitted and is governed by this court's Local Rule 32.1 and Federal Rule of Appellate Procedure 32.1. In a brief or other paper in which a litigant cites a summary order, in each paragraph in which a citation appears, at least one citation must either be to the Federal Appendix or be accompanied by the notation: "(summary order)". A party citing a summary order must serve a copy of that summary order together with the paper in which the summary order is cited on any party not represented by counsel unless the summary order is available in an electronic database which is publicly accessible without payment of fee (such as the database available at http://www.ca2.uscourts.gov/). If no copy is served by reason of the availability of the order on such a database, the citation must include reference to that database*

*and the docket number of the case in which the order was entered.*

### COMMENT

Summary orders are issued in cases in which a precedential opinion would serve no jurisprudential purpose because the result is dictated by pre-existing precedent. Such orders are prepared chiefly for the guidance and information of counsel and parties, and the district court (or other adjudicator) that issued the ruling from which the appeal is taken, all of whom are familiar with the facts, procedural history, and issues presented for review. Summary orders are therefore often abbreviated, and may omit material required to convey a complete, accurate understanding of the disposition and/or the principles of law upon which it rests. Like the great majority of the circuits, the court has chosen to make summary orders non-precedential. Denying summary orders precedential effect does not mean that the court considers itself free to rule differently in similar cases. Non-precedential summary order are used to avoid the risk that abbreviated explanations in summary orders might result in distortions of case law. Resolving some cases by summary order allows the court to devote more time to opinions whose publication will be jurisprudentially valuable.

Effective June 26, 2007.

## FRAP 33.  APPEAL CONFERENCES

The court may direct the attorneys—and, when appropriate, the parties to participate in one or more conferences to address any matter that may aid in disposing of the proceedings, including simplifying the issues and discussing settlement. A judge or other person designated by the court may preside over the conference, which may be conducted in person or by telephone. Before a settlement conference, the attorneys must consult with their clients and obtain as much authority as feasible to settle the case. The court may, as a result of the conference, enter an order controlling the course of the proceedings or implementing any settlement agreement.

[Amended April 29, 1994, effective December 1, 1994; April 24, 1998, effective December 1, 1998.]

## FRAP 34.  ORAL ARGUMENT

**(a) In General.**

(1) *Party's Statement.* Any party may file, or a court may require by local rule, a statement explaining why oral argument should, or need not, be permitted.

(2) *Standards.* Oral argument must be allowed in every case unless a panel of three judges who have examined the briefs and record unanimously agrees that oral argument is unnecessary for any of the following reasons:

(A) the appeal is frivolous;

(B) the dispositive issue or issues have been authoritatively decided; or

(C) the facts and legal arguments are adequately presented in the briefs and record, and the decisional process would not be significantly aided by oral argument.

**(b) Notice of Argument; Postponement.** The clerk must advise all parties whether oral argument will be scheduled, and, if so, the date, time, and place for it, and the time allowed for each side. A motion to postpone the argument or to allow longer argument must be filed reasonably in advance of the hearing date.

**(c) Order and Contents of Argument.** The appellant opens and concludes the argument. Counsel must not read at length from briefs, records, or authorities.

**(d) Cross-Appeals and Separate Appeals.** If there is a cross-appeal, Rule 28.1(b) determines which party is the appellant and which is the appellee for purposes of oral argument. Unless the court directs otherwise, a cross-appeal or separate appeal must be argued when the initial appeal is argued. Separate parties should avoid duplicative argument.

**(e) Non-Appearance of a Party.** If the appellee fails to appear for argument, the court must hear appellant's argument. If the appellant fails to appear for argument, the court may hear the appellee's argument. If neither party appears, the case will be decided on the briefs, unless the court orders otherwise.

**(f) Submission on Briefs.** The parties may agree to submit a case for decision on the briefs, but the court may direct that the case be argued.

**(g) Use of Physical Exhibits at Argument; Removal.** Counsel intending to use physical exhibits other than documents at the argument must arrange to place them in the courtroom on the day of the argument before the court convenes. After the argument, counsel must remove the exhibits from the courtroom, unless the court directs otherwise. The clerk may destroy or dispose of the exhibits if counsel does not reclaim them within a reasonable time after the clerk gives notice to remove them.

[Amended April 30, 1979, effective August 1, 1979; March 10, 1986, effective July 1, 1986; April 30, 1991, effective December 1, 1991; April 22, 1993, effective December 1, 1993; April 24, 1998, effective December 1, 1998; April 25, 2005, effective December 1, 2005.]

## LOCAL RULE 34.  ORAL ARGUMENT

*(a) Number of Counsel. Only one counsel will be heard for each party on the argument of a case, except by leave of the court.*

*(b) Time Allotments. The judge scheduled to preside over the panel will set the time allowed for argument by each party after considering the appellant's brief and each party's request for argument time. Normally, ten or fifteen minutes will be allot-*

*ted to each side. Parties on the same side of an appeal may be obliged to divide the time allotted to their side. Arguments in pro se appeals are normally five minutes per side. The clerk will notify counsel and pro se parties of all such time allotments.*

*(c) Postponement of Argument. Except in the event of an emergency, such as unforeseen illness of counsel, an application to postpone the date for oral argument will ordinarily not be favorably entertained. Engagement of counsel in courts (other than the Supreme Court of the United States) or administrative hearings will not be considered good cause for postponement. The date for oral argument may not be postponed by stipulation.*

*(d) Determination by Court Not to Hear Oral Argument.*

*1. If the court, acting sua sponte, contemplates deciding an appeal without hearing oral argument, each of the parties will be given an opportunity to file a statement setting forth reasons for hearing oral argument. Oral argument will be allowed in all cases except those in which a panel of three judges, after examination of the briefs and record, shall be of the unanimous view that oral argument is not needed for one of the following reasons:*

*(i) the appeal is frivolous; or*

*(ii) the dispositive issue or set of issues has been recently authoritatively decided; or*

*(iii) the facts and legal arguments are adequately presented in the briefs and record and the decisional process would not be significantly aided by oral argument.*

*2. To prevent undue delay, incarcerated pro se appellants requesting oral argument shall file the above-mentioned statement of reasons at the time they file their briefs.*

[December 1, 1994.]

## FRAP 35. EN BANC DETERMINATION

**(a) When Hearing or Rehearing En Banc May Be Ordered.** A majority of the circuit judges who are in regular active service and who are not disqualified may order that an appeal or other proceeding be heard or reheard by the court of appeals en banc. An en banc hearing or rehearing is not favored and ordinarily will not be ordered unless:

(1) en banc consideration is necessary to secure or maintain uniformity of the court's decisions; or

(2) the proceeding involves a question of exceptional importance.

**(b) Petition for Hearing or Rehearing En Banc.** A party may petition for a hearing or rehearing en banc.

(1) The petition must begin with a statement that either:

(A) the panel decision conflicts with a decision of the United States Supreme Court or of the court to which the petition is addressed (with citation to the conflicting case or cases) and consideration by the full court is therefore necessary to secure and maintain uniformity of the court's decisions; or

(B) the proceeding involves one or more questions of exceptional importance, each of which must be concisely stated; for example, a petition may assert that a proceeding presents a question of exceptional importance if it involves an issue on which the panel decision conflicts with the authoritative decisions of other United States Courts of Appeals that have addressed the issue.

(2) Except by the court's permission, a petition for an en banc hearing or rehearing must not exceed 15 pages, excluding material not counted under Rule 32.

(3) For purposes of the page limit in Rule 35(b)(2), if a party files both a petition for panel rehearing and a petition for rehearing en banc, they are considered a single document even if they are filed separately, unless separate filing is required by local rule.

**(c) Time for Petition for Hearing or Rehearing En Banc.** A petition that an appeal be heard initially en banc must be filed by the date when the appellee's brief is due. A petition for a rehearing en banc must be filed within the time prescribed by Rule 40 for filing a petition for rehearing.

**(d) Number of Copies.** The number of copies to be filed must be prescribed by local rule and may be altered by order in a particular case.

**(e) Response.** No response may be filed to a petition for an en banc consideration unless the court orders a response.

**(f) Call for a Vote.** A vote need not be taken to determine whether the case will be heard or reheard en banc unless a judge calls for a vote.

[Amended April 30, 1979, effective August 1, 1979; April 29, 1994, effective December 1, 1994; April 24, 1998, effective December 1, 1998; April 1, 2005, effective December 1, 2005.]

## *INTERIM LOCAL RULE 35. EN BANC PROCEDURE*

*(a) Copy of Opinion or Summary Order Required. Each petition for rehearing en banc shall include a copy of the opinion or summary order to which the petition relates, unless the opinion or summary order is included in a petition for panel rehearing that has been combined with the petition for rehearing en banc.*

*(b) Judges Eligible to Request an En Banc Poll. Any Judge of the Court in regular active service and any senior judge who is a member of the panel is eligible to request a poll of the judges in regular active service to determine whether a hearing or*

*rehearing en banc should be ordered (see 28 U.S.C. § 46(c)).*

**(c)  Determination of Majority for Ordering En Banc Consideration.**  *Neither vacancies nor disqualified judges shall be counted in determining the base on which "a majority of the circuit judges of the circuit who are in regular active service" shall be calculated, pursuant to 28 U.S.C. § 46(c), for purposes of ordering a hearing or rehearing en banc.*

**(d)  Procedure After Amendment of Court Ruling.**  *If a panel opinion or summary order is amended, a petition for rehearing en banc, or an amended petition, may be filed within the time specified by F.R.A.P. Rule 35(c), counted from the date of the entry of the amendment. A petition for rehearing en banc filed prior to amendment of the court's ruling will continue to be effective and need not be amended.*

[December 1, 1994; amended rule adopted on an interim basis effective November 16, 2004.]

## FRAP 36.  ENTRY OF JUDGMENT; NOTICE

**(a) Entry.**  A judgment is entered when it is noted on the docket.  The clerk must prepare, sign, and enter the judgment:

(1) after receiving the court's opinion—but if settlement of the judgment's form is required, after final settlement; or

(2) if a judgment is rendered without an opinion, as the court instructs.

**(b) Notice.** On the date when judgment is entered, the clerk must serve on all parties a copy of the opinion—or the judgment, if no opinion was written—and a notice of the date when the judgment was entered.

[Amended April 24, 1998, effective December 1, 1998; April 29, 2002, effective December 1, 2002.]

## FRAP 37.  INTEREST ON JUDGMENT

**(a) When the Court Affirms.**  Unless the law provides otherwise, if a money judgment in a civil case is affirmed, whatever interest is allowed by law is payable from the date when the district court's judgment was entered.

**(b) When the Court Reverses.**  If the court modifies or reverses a judgment with a direction that a money judgment be entered in the district court, the mandate must contain instructions about the allowance of interest.

[Amended April 24, 1998, effective December 1, 1998.]

## FRAP 38.  FRIVOLOUS APPEAL— DAMAGES AND COSTS

If a court of appeals determines that an appeal is frivolous, it may, after a separately filed motion or notice from the court and reasonable opportunity to respond, award just damages and single or double costs to the appellee.

[Amended April 29, 1994, effective December 1, 1994; April 24, 1998, effective December 1, 1998.]

## *LOCAL RULE 38.   OTHER SANCTIONS FOR DELAY*

*In the event of failure by a party to file the record, a brief, or the appendix within the time limited by the Federal Rules of Appellate Procedure, or a rule or order of this court, the court, on motion of a party or on its own motion, may impose other sanctions, including amounts to reimburse an opposing party for the expense of making motions, upon the defaulting party or the defaulting party's attorney.*

[December 1, 1994.]

## FRAP 39.   COSTS

**(a) Against Whom Assessed.**  The following rules apply unless the law provides or the court orders otherwise:

(1) if an appeal is dismissed, costs are taxed against the appellant, unless the parties agree otherwise;

(2) if a judgment is affirmed, costs are taxed against the appellant;

(3) if a judgment is reversed, costs are taxed against the appellee;

(4) if a judgment is affirmed in part, reversed in part, modified, or vacated, costs are taxed only as the court orders.

**(b) Costs For and Against the United States.**  Costs for or against the United States, its agency, or officer will be assessed under Rule 39(a) only if authorized by law.

**(c) Costs of Copies.**  Each court of appeals must, by local rule, fix the maximum rate for taxing the cost of producing necessary copies of a brief or appendix, or copies of records authorized by Rule 30(f).  The rate must not exceed that generally charged for such work in the area where the clerk's office is located and should encourage economical methods of copying.

**(d) Bill of Costs: Objections; Insertion in Mandate.**

(1) A party who wants costs taxed must—within 14 days after entry of judgment—file with the circuit clerk, with proof of service, an itemized and verified bill of costs.

(2) Objections must be filed within 10 days after service of the bill of costs, unless the court extends the time.

(3) The clerk must prepare and certify an itemized statement of costs for insertion in the mandate, but issuance of the mandate must not be delayed for taxing costs. If the mandate issues before costs are finally determined, the district clerk must—upon the circuit clerk's request—add the statement of costs, or any amendment of it, to the mandate.

**(e) Costs on Appeal Taxable in the District Court.** The following costs on appeal are taxable in the district court for the benefit of the party entitled to costs under this rule:

(1) the preparation and transmission of the record;

(2) the reporter's transcript, if needed to determine the appeal;

(3) premiums paid for a supersedeas bond or other bond to preserve rights pending appeal; and

(4) the fee for filing the notice of appeal.

[Amended April 30, 1979, effective August 1, 1979; March 10, 1986, effective July 1, 1986; April 24, 1998, effective December 1, 1998.]

## LOCAL RULE 39. COSTS

*The cost of reproducing the necessary copies of appendices or record excerpts shall be taxed at a rate not to exceed $0.20 per page (which figure may be increased from time to time by the clerk of the court to reflect prevailing rates of economical duplicating or copying processes), or at actual cost, whichever shall be less.*

[December 1, 1994.]

## FRAP 40. PETITION FOR PANEL REHEARING

**(a) Time to File; Contents; Answer; Action by the Court if Granted.**

(1) *Time.* Unless the time is shortened or extended by order or local rule, a petition for panel rehearing may be filed within 14 days after entry of judgment. But in a civil case, if the United States or its officer or agency is a party, the time within which any party may seek rehearing is 45 days after entry of judgment, unless an order shortens or extends the time.

(2) *Contents.* The petition must state with particularity each point of law or fact that the petitioner believes the court has overlooked or misapprehended and must argue in support of the petition. Oral argument is not permitted.

(3) *Answer.* Unless the court requests, no answer to a petition for panel rehearing is permitted. But

ordinarily rehearing will not be granted in the absence of such a request.

(4) *Action by the Court.* If a petition for panel rehearing is granted, the court may do any of the following:

(A) make a final disposition of the case without reargument;

(B) restore the case to the calendar for reargument or resubmission; or

(C) issue any other appropriate order.

**(b) Form of Petition; Length.** The petition must comply in form with Rule 32. Copies must be served and filed as Rule 31 prescribes. Unless the court permits or a local rule provides otherwise, a petition for panel rehearing must not exceed 15 pages.

[Amended April 30, 1979, effective August 1, 1979; April 29, 1994, effective December 1, 1994; April 24, 1998, effective December 1, 1998.]

## INTERIM LOCAL RULE 40. PANEL REHEARING PROCEDURE

**(a) Copy of Opinion or Summary Order Required.** *Each petition for rehearing shall include a copy of the opinion or summary order to which the petition relates.*

**(b) Procedure After Amendment of Court Ruling.** *If a panel opinion or summary order is amended, a petition for panel rehearing, or an amended petition, may be filed within the times specified by F.R.A.P. Rule 40(a)(1), counted from the date of the entry of the amendment. A petition for panel rehearing filed prior to amendment of the court's ruling will continue to be effective and need not be amended.*

**(c) Sanctions.** *If a petition for rehearing is found to be wholly without merit, vexatious and for delay, the court may tax a sum not exceeding $250 against petitioner in favor of the petitioner's adversary, to be collected with the costs in the case.*

[December 1, 1994; amended rule adopted on an interim basis effective November 16, 2004.]

## FRAP 41. MANDATE: CONTENTS; ISSUANCE AND EFFECTIVE DATE; STAY

**(a) Contents.** Unless the court directs that a formal mandate issue, the mandate consists of a certified copy of the judgment, a copy of the court's opinion, if any, and any direction about costs.

**(b) When Issued.** The court's mandate must issue 7 calendar days after the time to file a petition for rehearing expires, or 7 calendar days after entry of an order denying a timely petition for panel rehearing, petition for rehearing en banc, or motion for stay of mandate, whichever is later. The court may shorten or extend the time.

**(c) Effective Date.** The mandate is effective when issued.

**(d) Staying the Mandate.**

(1) *On Petition for Rehearing or Motion.* The timely filing of a petition for panel rehearing, petition for rehearing en banc, or motion for stay of mandate, stays the mandate until disposition of the petition or motion, unless the court orders otherwise.

(2) *Pending Petition for Certiorari.*

(A) A party may move to stay the mandate pending the filing of a petition for a writ of certiorari in the Supreme Court. The motion must be served on all parties and must show that the certiorari petition would present a substantial question and that there is good cause for a stay.

(B) The stay must not exceed 90 days, unless the period is extended for good cause or unless the party who obtained the stay files a petition for the writ and so notifies the circuit clerk in writing within the period of the stay. In that case, the stay continues until the Supreme Court's final disposition.

(C) The court may require a bond or other security as a condition to granting or continuing a stay of the mandate.

(D) The court of appeals must issue the mandate immediately when a copy of a Supreme Court order denying the petition for writ of certiorari is filed.

[Amended April 29, 1994, effective December 1, 1994; April 24, 1998, effective December 1, 1998; April 29, 2002, effective December 1, 2002.]

## LOCAL RULE 41.   ISSUANCE OF MANDATE

*Unless otherwise ordered by the court, the mandate shall issue forthwith in all cases in which (1) an appeal from an order or judgment of a district court or a petition to review or enforce an order of an agency is decided in open court, (2) a petition for a writ of mandamus or other extraordinary writ is adjudicated, or (3) the clerk enters an order dismissing an appeal or a petition to review or enforce an order of an agency for a default in filings, as directed by an order of the court or a judge.*

[December 1, 1994.]

## FRAP 42.   VOLUNTARY DISMISSAL

**(a) Dismissal in the District Court.** Before an appeal has been docketed by the circuit clerk, the district court may dismiss the appeal on the filing of a stipulation signed by all parties or on the appellant's motion with notice to all parties.

**(b) Dismissal in the Court of Appeals.** The circuit clerk may dismiss a docketed appeal if the parties file a signed dismissal agreement specifying how costs are to be paid and pay any fees that are due. But no mandate or other process may issue without a court order. An appeal may be dismissed on the appellant's motion on terms agreed to by the parties or fixed by the court.

[Amended April 24, 1998, effective December 1, 1998.]

## FRAP 43.   SUBSTITUTION OF PARTIES

**(a) Death of a Party.**

(1) *After Notice of Appeal Is Filed.* If a party dies after a notice of appeal has been filed or while a proceeding is pending in the court of appeals, the decedent's personal representative may be substituted as a party on motion filed with the circuit clerk by the representative or by any party. A party's motion must be served on the representative in accordance with Rule 25. If the decedent has no representative, any party may suggest the death on the record, and the court of appeals may then direct appropriate proceedings.

(2) *Before Notice of Appeal Is Filed—Potential Appellant.* If a party entitled to appeal dies before filing a notice of appeal, the decedent's personal representative—or, if there is no personal representative, the decedent's attorney of record—may file a notice of appeal within the time prescribed by these rules. After the notice of appeal is filed, substitution must be in accordance with Rule 43(a)(1).

(3) *Before Notice of Appeal Is Filed—Potential Appellee.* If a party against whom an appeal may be taken dies after entry of a judgment or order in the district court, but before a notice of appeal is filed, an appellant may proceed as if the death had not occurred. After the notice of appeal is filed, substitution must be in accordance with Rule 43(a)(1).

**(b) Substitution for a Reason Other Than Death.** If a party needs to be substituted for any reason other than death, the procedure prescribed in Rule 43(a) applies.

**(c) Public Officer: Identification; Substitution.**

(1) *Identification of Party.* A public officer who is a party to an appeal or other proceeding in an official capacity may be described as a party by the public officer's official title rather than by name. But the court may require the public officer's name to be added.

(2) *Automatic Substitution of Officeholder.* When a public officer who is a party to an appeal or other proceeding in an official capacity dies, resigns, or otherwise ceases to hold office, the action does not abate. The public officer's successor is automatically substituted as a party. Proceedings following the substitution are to be in the name of the substituted party, but any misnomer that does not affect the substantial rights of the parties may be disregarded. An order of substitution may be entered at any time,

but failure to enter an order does not affect the substitution.

[Amended March 10, 1986, effective July 1, 1986; April 24, 1998, effective December 1, 1998.]

# FRAP 44. CASE INVOLVING A CONSTITUTIONAL QUESTION WHEN THE UNITED STATES OR THE RELEVANT STATE IS NOT A PARTY

**(a) Constitutional Challenge to Federal Statute.** If a party questions the constitutionality of an Act of Congress in a proceeding in which the United States or its agency, officer, or employee is not a party in an official capacity, the questioning party must give written notice to the circuit clerk immediately upon the filing of the record or as soon as the question is raised in the court of appeals. The clerk must then certify that fact to the Attorney General.

**(b) Constitutional Challenge to State Statute.** If a party questions the constitutionality of a statute of a State in a proceeding in which that State or its agency, officer, or employee is not a party in an official capacity, the questioning party must give written notice to the circuit clerk immediately upon the filing of the record or as soon as the question is raised in the court of appeals. The clerk must then certify that fact to the attorney general of the State.

[Amended April 24, 1998, effective December 1, 1998; April 29, 2002, effective December 1, 2002.]

## FRAP 45. CLERK'S DUTIES

**(a) General Provisions.**

(1) *Qualifications.* The circuit clerk must take the oath and post any bond required by law. Neither the clerk nor any deputy clerk may practice as an attorney or counselor in any court while in office.

(2) *When Court Is Open.* The court of appeals is always open for filing any paper, issuing and returning process, making a motion, and entering an order. The clerk's office with the clerk or a deputy in attendance must be open during business hours on all days except Saturdays, Sundays, and legal holidays. A court may provide by local rule or by order that the clerk's office be open for specified hours on Saturdays or on legal holidays other than New Year's Day, Martin Luther King, Jr.'s Birthday, Washington's Birthday, Memorial Day, Independence Day, Labor Day, Columbus Day, Veterans' Day, Thanksgiving Day, and Christmas Day.

**(b) Records.**

(1) *The Docket.* The circuit clerk must maintain a docket and an index of all docketed cases in the manner prescribed by the Director of the Administrative Office of the United States Courts. The clerk must record all papers filed with the clerk and all process, orders, and judgments.

(2) *Calendar.* Under the court's direction, the clerk must prepare a calendar of cases awaiting argument. In placing cases on the calendar for argument, the clerk must give preference to appeals in criminal cases and to other proceedings and appeals entitled to preference by law.

(3) *Other Records.* The clerk must keep other books and records required by the Director of the Administrative Office of the United States Courts, with the approval of the Judicial Conference of the United States, or by the court.

**(c) Notice of an Order or Judgment.** Upon the entry of an order or judgment, the circuit clerk must immediately serve a notice of entry on each party, with a copy of any opinion, and must note the date of service on the docket. Service on a party represented by counsel must be made on counsel.

**(d) Custody of Records and Papers.** The circuit clerk has custody of the court's records and papers. Unless the court orders or instructs otherwise, the clerk must not permit an original record or paper to be taken from the clerk's office. Upon disposition of the case, original papers constituting the record on appeal or review must be returned to the court or agency from which they were received. The clerk must preserve a copy of any brief, appendix, or other paper that has been filed.

[Amended March 1, 1971, effective July 1, 1971; March 10, 1986, effective July 1, 1986; April 24, 1998, effective December 1, 1998; April 29, 2002, effective December 1, 2002; April 25, 2005, effective December 1, 2005.]

## FRAP 46. ATTORNEYS

**(a) Admission to the Bar.**

(1) *Eligibility.* An attorney is eligible for admission to the bar of a court of appeals if that attorney is of good moral and professional character and is admitted to practice before the Supreme Court of the United States, the highest court of a state, another United States court of appeals, or a United States district court (including the district courts for Guam, the Northern Mariana Islands, and the Virgin Islands).

(2) *Application.* An applicant must file an application for admission, on a form approved by the court that contains the applicant's personal statement showing eligibility for membership. The applicant must subscribe to the following oath or affirmation:

"I, _____, do solemnly swear [or affirm] that I will conduct myself as an attorney and counselor of this court, uprightly and according to law; and that I will support the Constitution of the United States."

(3) *Admission Procedures.* On written or oral motion of a member of the court's bar, the court will act on the application. An applicant may be admitted by oral motion in open court. But, unless the court

orders otherwise, an applicant need not appear before the court to be admitted. Upon admission, an applicant must pay the clerk the fee prescribed by local rule or court order.

**(b) Suspension or Disbarment.**

(1) *Standard.* A member of the court's bar is subject to suspension or disbarment by the court if the member:

    (A) has been suspended or disbarred from practice in any other court; or

    (B) is guilty of conduct unbecoming a member of the court's bar.

(2) *Procedure.* The member must be given an opportunity to show good cause, within the time prescribed by the court, why the member should not be suspended or disbarred.

(3) *Order.* The court must enter an appropriate order after the member responds and a hearing is held, if requested, or after the time prescribed for a response expires, if no response is made.

**(c) Discipline.** A court of appeals may discipline an attorney who practices before it for conduct unbecoming a member of the bar or for failure to comply with any court rule. First, however, the court must afford the attorney reasonable notice, an opportunity to show cause to the contrary, and, if requested, a hearing.

[Amended March 10, 1986, effective July 1, 1986; April 24, 1998, effective December 1, 1998.]

## LOCAL RULE 46. ATTORNEYS

*(a) (Interim) An applicant shall file with the clerk of the Court of Appeals, in addition to the material required by F.R.A.P. Rule 46, a certificate in writing on a form approved by the court that the applicant has read and is familiar with the Federal Rules of Appellate Procedure (F.R.A.P.) and the local rules of this court.*

*(b) With the filing required by F.R.A.P. 46 and "(a)" above, a motion for admission may be made in writing, in which event it will be acted upon by a single judge, or orally at the beginning of any session of the Court without presence of the applicant being required. The movant shall represent that the movant has read the certificate filed in accordance with "(a)" above and that it meets the requirements of this Rule.*

*(c) Each applicant upon admission shall pay to the clerk a fee which shall be set by the court, to be held by the court in an appropriate depository and expended upon order of the chief judge for the expenses of the Law Library of the court located in the United States Courthouse, Foley Square, New York City, for out-of-pocket expenses incurred by attorneys or counselors assigned by the court to represent indigent persons not reimbursable under 18 U.S.C.*

§ 3006A or other applicable statute, or for other extraordinary purposes approved by the court.

*(d) Counsel of record for all parties must be admitted to practice before this court. Oral argument may be presented only by attorneys admitted to practice before this court. Under exceptional circumstances an attorney may be admitted to argue an appeal pro hac vice. Such admission will be extended as a matter of course to a member of the Bar of a District Court within the circuit who has represented a criminal defendant at trial and appears for that defendant on an appeal taken pursuant to 18 U.S.C. § 3006A, or who is acting for any party in an appeal taken in forma pauperis.*

*1. A notice of appearance must be filed in each case by counsel of record and, if different, by counsel who will argue the appeal, not later than the date of filing the appellant's brief on a form to be provided by the clerk.*

*2. A corporation may not appear pro se. Papers submitted on behalf of a corporation for whom no counsel has entered an appearance will not be filed.*

*(e) Appearance and Argument by Eligible Law Students.*

*1. An eligible law student acting under a supervising attorney may appear in this Court on behalf of any indigent person, the United States, or a governmental agency, provided the party on whose behalf the student appears has consented thereto in writing.*

*2. The supervising attorney shall be a member of the bar of this Court and, with respect to the law student's proposed appearance upon an appeal or other matter before this Court, shall:*

    *(i) file with this Court the attorney's written consent to supervise the student;*

    *(ii) assume personal professional responsibility for the student's work;*

    *(iii) assist the student to the extent necessary;*

    *(iv) appear with the student in all proceedings before this Court and be prepared to supplement any written or oral statement made by the student to this Court or opposing counsel.*

*3. In order to be eligible to appear, the student shall:*

    *(i) be enrolled in a law school approved by the American Bar Association. The student shall be deemed to continue to meet this requirement as long as, following graduation, the student is preparing to take the first state bar examination, of the state of the student's choice within this circuit, for which the student is eligible or, having taken that examination, the student is awaiting publication of the results or admission to the bar after passing that examination;*

*(ii)* have completed legal studies amounting to at least four semesters, or the equivalent;

*(iii)* be certified, by either the dean or a faculty member of the student's law school designated by the dean, as qualified to provide the legal representation permitted by this rule. This certification may be withdrawn by mailing a notice of withdrawal to the clerk of this court or it may be terminated, by vote of a majority of the panel sitting on a case in which the student is appearing, at any time without notice or hearing and without any showing of cause. The loss of certification by action of this court shall not be considered a reflection on the character or ability of the student. The dean or a faculty member designated by the student may recertify such a student for appearances before other panels;

*(iv)* be introduced to this court by an attorney admitted to practice before this court;

*(v)* neither ask for nor receive any compensation or remuneration of any kind for the student's services from the party on whose behalf the student renders services, but this shall not prevent an attorney, legal aid bureau, law school, public defender agency, or the United States from paying compensation to the eligible law student, nor shall it prevent any agency from making proper charges for its services;

*(vi)* certify in writing that the student is familiar and will comply with the Code of Professional Responsibility of the American Bar Association;

*(vii)* certify in writing that the student is familiar with the Federal Rules of Appellate Procedure, the Rules of this court, and any other federal rules relevant to the appeal in which the student is appearing.

4. Upon filing with the clerk of this court the written consents and certifications required by this rule, an eligible law student supervised in accordance with this rule, may with respect to any appeal or other proceeding for which the student had met the requirements of this rule:

*(i)* engage in the drafting or preparation of briefs, appendices, motions, or other documents;

*(ii)* appear before this court and participate in oral argument.

*(f) Suspension or Disbarment.* Suspension or disbarment shall be governed by Rule 46, Federal Rules of Appellate Procedure.

1. In all cases in which an order disbarring an attorney or suspending the attorney from practice (whether or not on consent) has been entered in any other court of record, federal or state, and a certified copy thereof has been filed in this court, the clerk shall enter an order for the court, to become effective twenty-four days after the date of service upon the attorney unless sooner modified or stayed, disbarring the attorney or suspending the attorney from practice in this court upon terms and conditions comparable to those set forth by the other court of record. A reasonable effort shall be made to locate the attorney's current address, and, if that effort is unsuccessful, mailing a copy of the order to the last-known address shall be deemed proper service. A copy of the order shall also be mailed to the Committee on Admissions and Grievances of the Court of Appeals to be established under subsection (h) hereof (hereafter "Committee").

2. Within twenty days from the date of service of this court's order, a motion may be filed in this court either by such attorney or the Committee for a modification or revocation of the order of this court. Any such motion shall set forth specifically the facts and principles relied on by applicant as showing cause why a different disposition should be ordered by this court. The timely filing of such a motion will stay the effectiveness of this court's order until further order of this court.

3. A motion to modify or revoke an order that has become effective under (1) will not be entertained unless good cause is shown for failure to file a motion timely under (2).

4. The court in any matter disputed under (2) or (3) may refer the matter to a special master to be appointed by the court for hearing and report.

5. The foregoing paragraphs of this subsection shall apply to any attorney who resigns from the bar of any other court of record, federal or state, while under investigation into allegations of misconduct on the attorney's part. Upon resigning under such conditions the attorney shall promptly inform the clerk of this court of such resignation.

*(g) Attorneys Convicted of Crime.*

1. Upon the filing with the court of a certificate, duly signed by the clerk of the court in which the conviction has occurred, demonstrating that an attorney has been convicted of a serious crime as hereinafter defined, the clerk of this court shall immediately enter an order suspending the attorney, whether the conviction resulted from a plea of guilty or nolo contendere, judgment after trial, or otherwise, and regardless of the pendency of an appeal from the conviction, unless the court orders otherwise. A copy of such order shall be served upon the attorney by mail at the attorney's last known address. Such suspension shall remain in effect pending disposition of a disciplinary proceeding to be commenced upon the filing of the certificate of conviction, unless the court orders otherwise.

2. The term "serious crime" shall include any felony, federal or state, and any lesser crime a necessary element of which, as determined by statutory or common law definition of such crime in the jurisdiction where the conviction has occurred, is (a) interfer-

ence with the administration of justice; (b) false swearing; (c) misrepresentation; (d) fraud; (e) willful failure to file income tax returns; (f) deceit; (g) bribery; (h) extortion; (i) misappropriation; (j) theft; or (k) an attempt, or conspiracy, or solicitation of another to commit a serious crime.

3. A certificate of conviction of an attorney for any crime shall be conclusive evidence of the commission of that crime by such attorney in any disciplinary proceeding instituted against the attorney based upon the conviction.

4. Upon receipt of a certificate of conviction of an attorney for a serious crime and if no order has been entered under subparagraph (f) above, the court may, in addition to suspending the attorney in accordance with the provisions of (1), supra, also direct the institution of a formal presentment against the attorney, without any probable cause hearing, before the Committee, in which the sole issue to be determined shall be the extent of the final discipline to be imposed. A proceeding under this subparagraph (g)(4) may be terminated if an order is entered under subparagraph (f) above. A disciplinary proceeding so instituted shall not, however, be brought to hearing until all appeals from the conviction are concluded or the time to take such appeal has expired.

5. Upon receipt of a certificate of conviction of an attorney for a crime not constituting a serious crime, other than a traffic offense, the court shall refer the matter to the said Committee for whatever action the Committee may deem warranted. The court may, however, in its discretion, make no such reference with respect to convictions for minor offenses.

6. An attorney suspended under the provisions of (1), shall be reinstated forthwith upon the filing of a clerk's certificate demonstrating that the underlying conviction for a serious crime has been reversed, but the reinstatement will not terminate any proceeding then pending against the attorney, the disposition of which shall be determined by the court or the Committee on the basis of the available evidence.

#### (h) Committee on Admissions and Grievances.

1. Appointment, Members. The court shall appoint a standing committee of nine members of the bar to be known as the Committee on Admissions and Grievances. Three of those first appointed shall serve for the term of one year; three for two years; and the remainder and all thereafter appointed shall serve for the term of three years. Each member shall serve until a member's successor has been appointed. If a member shall hold over after the expiration of the term for which a member was appointed, the period of the member's hold-over shall be treated as part of the term of the member's successor. The court may vacate any such appointment at any time. In the case of any vacancy caused by death, resignation, or otherwise, any successor appointed shall serve the unexpired term of the successor's predecessor. The court shall designate one of the members to serve as chairman whenever it may for any reason be necessary. Five members of the Committee shall constitute a quorum. The court shall appoint a member of the bar as secretary of the Committee, who shall not be entitled to vote on its proceedings.

2. Reference on Matters of Misconduct. The court may refer to the Committee any accusation or evidence of misconduct in respect to any professional matter before this court that allegedly violates the rules of professional conduct or responsibility in effect in the state or other jurisdiction where the attorney maintains his or her principal office for such investigation, hearing and report as the court deems advisable. Such matters thus referred may include not only acts of affirmative misconduct but negligent conduct of counsel. The Committee may, in its discretion, refer such matters to an appropriate bar association for preliminary investigation.

3. Committee Action. In any matter referred to the Committee under the provisions of these Rules it shall provide the attorney with a statement in writing of the charges against him and it shall hold a hearing, on at least ten days' notice to the attorney, making a record of its proceedings; in the event the attorney does not appear, the Committee may take summary action and shall report its recommendation forthwith to the court; in the event that the attorney does appear, the attorney shall be entitled to be represented by counsel, to present witnesses and other evidence on the attorney's behalf, and to confront and cross-examine under oath any witnesses against the attorney. Except as otherwise ordered by the court the Committee shall in its discretion make and be governed by its own rules of procedure.

4. Committee Recommendation. The Committee shall file the record of its proceedings, its recommendation and a brief statement of the reasons therefor with the Clerk who shall retain them in camera after furnishing the court with copies thereof, and the Clerk shall mail a copy of the Committee's recommendation and statement of its reasons to the affected attorney and make the record of the Committee's proceedings available to the attorney. Within twenty days after filing of the record, report and recommendation the attorney may file with the Clerk a statement, not to exceed ten typewritten pages in length, in opposition to or mitigation of the Committee's recommendation. The court, consisting of the active judges thereof, shall act within a reasonable time thereafter by majority vote.

5. Committee Expense. The Committee may be reimbursed for its reasonable expenses in the discretion of the court from such sources as may be available to the court for such purposes.

[December 1, 1994; amended April 26, 1996; amendments adopted on an interim basis effective November 16, 2004. Amended effective February 23, 2007.]

## FRAP 47. LOCAL RULES BY COURTS OF APPEALS

**(a) Local Rules.**

(1) Each court of appeals acting by a majority of its judges in regular active service may, after giving appropriate public notice and opportunity for comment, make and amend rules governing its practice. A generally applicable direction to parties or lawyers regarding practice before a court must be in a local rule rather than an internal operating procedure or standing order. A local rule must be consistent with—but not duplicative of—Acts of Congress and rules adopted under 28 U.S.C. § 2072 and must conform to any uniform numbering system prescribed by the Judicial Conference of the United States. Each circuit clerk must send the Administrative Office of the United States Courts a copy of each local rule and internal operating procedure when it is promulgated or amended.

(2) A local rule imposing a requirement of form must not be enforced in a manner that causes a party to lose rights because of a nonwillful failure to comply with the requirement.

**(b) Procedure When There Is No Controlling Law.** A court of appeals may regulate practice in a particular case in any manner consistent with federal law, these rules, and local rules of the circuit. No sanction or other disadvantage may be imposed for noncompliance with any requirement not in federal law, federal rules, or the local circuit rules unless the alleged violator has been furnished in the particular case with actual notice of the requirement.

[Amended April 27, 1995, effective December 1, 1995; April 24, 1998, effective December 1, 1998.]

## FRAP 48. MASTERS

**(a) Appointment; Powers.** A court of appeals may appoint a special master to hold hearings, if necessary, and to recommend factual findings and disposition in matters ancillary to proceedings in the court. Unless the order referring a matter to a master specifies or limits the master's powers, those powers include, but are not limited to, the following:

(1) regulating all aspects of a hearing;

(2) taking all appropriate action for the efficient performance of the master's duties under the order;

(3) requiring the production of evidence on all matters embraced in the reference; and

(4) administering oaths and examining witnesses and parties.

**(b) Compensation.** If the master is not a judge or court employee, the court must determine the master's compensation and whether the cost is to be charged to any party.

[Former Rule 48 renumbered as Rule 1(c) and new Rule 48 adopted April 29, 1994, effective December 1, 1994; April 24, 1998, effective December 1, 1998.]

# FORMS

# FEDERAL RULES OF APPELLATE PROCEDURE FORMS

## FORM 1. NOTICE OF APPEAL TO A COURT OF APPEALS FROM A JUDGMENT OR ORDER OF A DISTRICT COURT

United States District Court for the
_____ District of _____

File Number _____

| | | |
|---|---|---|
| A. B., Plaintiff | ) | |
| v. | ) | Notice of Appeal |
| C. D., Defendant | ) | |

Notice is hereby given that   (here name all parties taking the appeal)  , (plaintiffs) (defendants) in the above named case,* hereby appeal to the United States Court of Appeals for the _____ Circuit (from the final judgment) (from an order (describing it)) entered in this action on the \_\_\_\_ day of _____, _____.

(s)_____

Attorney for _____

Address:_____

\* See Rule 3(c) for permissible ways of identifying appellants.

[Amended April 22, 1993, effective December 1, 1993; amended March 27, 2003, effective December 1, 2003.]

## FORM 2. NOTICE OF APPEAL TO A COURT OF APPEALS FROM A DECISION OF THE UNITED STATES TAX COURT

UNITED STATES TAX COURT
Washington, D.C.

| | | |
|---|---|---|
| A.B., Petitioner | ) | |
| | ) | |
| v. | ) | Docket No. _____ |
| | ) | |
| Commissioner of Internal | ) | |
| Revenue, Respondent | ) | |

Notice of Appeal

Notice is hereby given that   (here name all parties taking the appeal) *   hereby appeal to the United States Court of Appeals for the _____ Circuit from (that part of) the decision of this court entered in the above captioned proceeding on the \_\_\_\_ day of _____, \_\_\_\_ (relating to _____).

(s)_____

Counsel for _____

Address:_____

\* See Rule 3(c) for permissible ways of identifying appellants.

[Amended April 22, 1993, effective December 1, 1993; amended March 27, 2003, effective December 1, 2003.]

## FORM 3. PETITION FOR REVIEW OF ORDER OF AN AGENCY, BOARD, COMMISSION OR OFFICER

United States Court of Appeals

for the _____ Circuit

A.B., Petitioner )
)
v. ) Petition for Review
XYZ Commission, )
Respondent )

_____(here name all parties bringing the petition)*_____ hereby petition the court for review of the Order of the XYZ Commission (describe the order) entered on _____, 20___.

(s)_____

Attorney for Petitioners

Address:_____

* See Rule 15.

[Amended April 22, 1993, effective December 1, 1993; amended March 27, 2003, effective December 1, 2003.]

## FORM 4. AFFIDAVIT ACCOMPANYING MOTION FOR PERMISSION TO APPEAL IN FORMA PAUPERIS

United States District Court for the _____ District of _____

v. Appeal No. _____

District Court or Agency No. _____

**Affidavit in Support of Motion**

I swear or affirm under penalty of perjury that, because of my poverty, I cannot prepay the docket fees of my appeal or post a bond for them. I believe I am entitled to redress. I swear or affirm under penalty of perjury under United States laws that my answers on this form are true and correct. (28 U.S.C. § 1746; 18 U.S.C. § 1621.)

Signed: _____

**Instructions**

Complete all questions in this application and then sign it. Do not leave any blanks: if the answer to a question is "0," "none," or "not applicable (N/A)," write in that response. If you need more space to answer a question or to explain your answer, attach a separate sheet of paper identified with your name, your case's docket number, and the question number.

Date: _____

**My issues on appeal are:**

1. *For both you and your spouse estimate the average amount of money received from each of the following sources during the past 12 months. Adjust any amount that was received weekly, biweekly, quarterly, semiannually, or annually to show the monthly rate. Use gross amounts, that is, amounts before any deductions for taxes or otherwise.*

| Income source | Average monthly amount during the past 12 months | | Amount expected next month | |
|---|---|---|---|---|
| | You | Spouse | You | Spouse |
| Employment | $_____ | $_____ | $_____ | $_____ |
| Self-employment | $_____ | $_____ | $_____ | $_____ |
| Income from real property (such as rental income) | $_____ | $_____ | $_____ | $_____ |
| Interest and dividends | $_____ | $_____ | $_____ | $_____ |
| Gifts | $_____ | $_____ | $_____ | $_____ |

Alimony                               $_____  $_____  $_____  $_____
Child support                         $_____  $_____  $_____  $_____
Retirement (such as social
security, pensions, annuities,
insurance)                            $_____  $_____  $_____  $_____
Disability (such as social se-
curity, insurance payments)           $_____  $_____  $_____  $_____
Unemployment payments                 $_____  $_____  $_____  $_____
Public-assistance (such as
welfare)                              $_____  $_____  $_____  $_____
Other (specify): _____             $_____  $_____  $_____  $_____
   **Total monthly income:**          $_____  $_____  $_____  $_____

2. *List your employment history, most recent employer first. (Gross monthly pay is before taxes or other deductions.)*

| Employer | Address | Dates of employment | Gross monthly pay |
|---|---|---|---|
| _____ | _____ | _____ | _____ |
| _____ | _____ | _____ | _____ |
| _____ | _____ | _____ | _____ |

3. *List your spouse's employment history, most recent employer first. (Gross monthly pay is before taxes or other deductions.)*

| Employer | Address | Dates of employment | Gross monthly pay |
|---|---|---|---|
| _____ | _____ | _____ | _____ |
| _____ | _____ | _____ | _____ |

   4. *How much cash do you and your spouse have?* $_____

Below, state any money you or your spouse have in bank accounts or in any other financial institution.

| Financial institution | Type of account | Amount you have | Amount your spouse has |
|---|---|---|---|
| _____ | _____ | $_____ | $_____ |
| _____ | _____ | $_____ | $_____ |
| _____ | _____ | $_____ | $_____ |

**If you are a prisoner, seeking to appeal a judgment in a civil action or proceeding, you must attach a statement certified by the appropriate institutional officer showing all receipts, expenditures, and balances during the last six months in your institutional accounts. If you have multiple accounts, perhaps because you have been in multiple institutions, attach one certified statement of each account.**

5. *List the assets, and their values, which you own or your spouse owns. Do not list clothing and ordinary household furnishings.*

**Home**          (Value)      **Other real estate**   (Value)    **Motor vehicle # 1**   (Value)

                                                                   Make & year: _____
_____      _____      Model: _____
_____      _____      Registration # :_____

**Motor vehicle # 2**  (Value)   **Other assets**   (Value)   **Other assets**   (Value)

Make & year: _____     _____      _____
Model: _____           _____      _____
Registration # :_____  _____      _____

6. *State every person, business, or organization owing you or your spouse money, and the amount owed.*

| Person owing you or your spouse money | Amount owed to you | Amount owed to your spouse |
|---|---|---|
| _____ | _____ | _____ |
| _____ | _____ | _____ |
| _____ | _____ | _____ |

7. *State the persons who rely on you or your spouse for support.*

| Name | Relationship | Age |
|---|---|---|
| _____ | _____ | _____ |
| _____ | _____ | _____ |
| _____ | _____ | _____ |

8. *Estimate the average monthly expenses of you and your family. Show separately the amounts paid by your spouse. Adjust any payments that are made weekly, biweekly, quarterly, semiannually, or annually to show the monthly rate.*

|  | You | Your Spouse |
|---|---|---|
| Rent or home-mortgage payment (include lot rented for mobile home) | $_____ | $_____ |
|     Are real-estate taxes included? ☐ Yes ☐ No | | |
|     Is property insurance included? ☐ Yes ☐ No | | |
| Utilities (electricity, heating fuel, water, sewer, and Telephone) | $_____ | $_____ |
| Home maintenance (repairs and upkeep) | $_____ | $_____ |
| Food | $_____ | $_____ |
| Clothing | $_____ | $_____ |
| Laundry and dry-cleaning | $_____ | $_____ |
| Medical and dental expenses | $_____ | $_____ |
| Transportation (not including motor vehicle payments) | $_____ | $_____ |
| Recreation, entertainment, newspapers, magazines, etc. | $_____ | $_____ |
| Insurance (not deducted from wages or included in Mortgage payments) | | |
|     Homeowner's or renter's | $_____ | $_____ |
|     Life | $_____ | $_____ |
|     Health | $_____ | $_____ |
|     Motor Vehicle | $_____ | $_____ |
|     Other: _____ | $_____ | $_____ |
| Taxes (not deducted from wages or included in Mortgage payments) (specify): _____ | $_____ | $_____ |
| Installment payments | | |
|     Motor Vehicle | $_____ | $_____ |
|     Credit card (name): _____ | $_____ | $_____ |
|     Department store (name): _____ | $_____ | $_____ |
|     Other: _____ | $_____ | $_____ |
| Alimony, maintenance, and support paid to others | $_____ | $_____ |
| Regular expenses for operation of business, profession, or farm (attach detailed statement) | $_____ | $_____ |
| Other (specify): _____ | $_____ | $_____ |
| **Total monthly expenses:** | $_____ | $_____ |

9. *Do you expect any major changes to your monthly income or expenses or in your assets or liabilities during the next 12 months?*
☐ Yes ☐ No      If yes, describe on an attached sheet.

10. *Have you paid—or will you be paying—an attorney any money for services in connection with this case, including the completion of this form?* Yes No
If yes, how much? $_____
If yes, state the attorney's name, address, and telephone number:

_____

_____

11. *Have you paid—or will you be paying—anyone other than an attorney (such as a paralegal or a typist) any money for services in connection with this case, including the completion of this form?*
☐ Yes ☐ No
If yes, how much? $_____
If yes, state the person's name, address, and telephone number:

_____

_____

12. *Provide any other information that will help explain why you cannot pay the docket fees for your appeal.*

13.   State the address of your legal residence.

_____

_____

Your daytime phone number:  (___) _____
Your age:  _____ Your years of schooling:  _____
Your social-security number:  _____

[Amended April 24, 1998, effective December 1, 1998.]

## FORM 5.  NOTICE OF APPEAL TO A COURT OF APPEALS FROM A JUDGMENT OR ORDER OF A DISTRICT COURT OR A BANKRUPTCY APPELLATE PANEL

United States District Court for the
_____ District of _____

In re                                    )
_____ )
              Debtor                     )
_____ )          File No. _____
         A.B., Plaintiff                 )
              v.                         )
_____ )
         C.D., Defendant                 )

Notice of Appeal to
United States Court of Appeals
for the _____ Circuit

_____, the plaintiff [or defendant or other party] appeals to the United States Court of Appeals for the _____ Circuit from the final judgment [or order or decree] of the district court for the district of _____ [or bankruptcy appellate panel of the _____ circuit], entered in this case on _____, 20___ [here describe the judgment, order, or decree] _____.

The parties to the judgment [or order or decree] appealed from and the names and addresses of their respective attorneys are as follows:

Dated _____

Signed _____
                                   *Attorney for Appellant*

Address: _____
_____

[Adopted April 25, 1989, effective December 1, 1989;  amended March 27, 2003, effective December 1, 2003.]

## FORM 6.  CERTIFICATE OF COMPLIANCE WITH RULE 32(a)

Certificate of Compliance With Type–Volume Limitation,
Typeface Requirements, and Type Style Requirements

1.  This brief complies with the type-volume limitation of Fed. R. App. P. 32(a)(7)(B) because:

☐ this brief contains [*state the number of*] words, excluding the parts of the brief exempted by Fed. R. App. P. 32(a)(7)(B)(iii), *or*

☐ this brief uses a monospaced typeface and contains [*state the number of*] lines of text, excluding the parts of the brief exempted by Fed. R. App. P. 32(a)(7)(B)(iii).

2.  This brief complies with the typeface requirements of Fed. R. App. P. 32(a)(5) and the type style requirements of Fed. R. App. P. 32(a)(6) because:

☐ this brief has been prepared in a proportionally spaced typeface using [*state name and version of word processing program*] in [*state font size and name of type style*], *or*

☐ this brief has been prepared in a monospaced typeface using [*state name and version of word processing program*] with [*state number of characters per inch and name of type style*].

(s)_____

Attorney for _____

Dated: _____

[Adopted April 29, 2002, effective December 1, 2002.]

# SECOND CIRCUIT MISCELLANEOUS FORMS

## LOCAL FORM FOR NOTICE OF APPEARANCE

Short Title: _____  Docket No. _____

## NOTICE OF APPEARANCE

Appearance for (provide name of party): _____
Status of Party:
( ) Appellant/Petitioner           ( ) Cross–Appellee/Cross Respondent
( ) Appellee/Respondent               ( ) Intervenor
( ) Cross–Appellant/Cross–Petitioner  ( ) Amicus Curiae
( ) Other (Specify):

( ) An attorney will argue this appeal.
   • Name of attorney who will argue appeal, if other than counsel of record: _____
   • Date of arguing attorney's admission to this Court (month, day, year): _____
   • Other Federal/State Bar admissions: (month, day, year): _____
( ) I am a pro se litigant who is not an attorney.
( ) I am an incarcerated pro se litigant.

## TIME REQUEST

( ) Oral argument is not desired.
( ) Oral argument is desired.  Party requests _____ minutes or multi-co-parties request a
   total of _____ minutes to be apportioned as follows:

   If more than 20 minutes per side is requested, set forth reasons:

## AVAILABILITY OF COUNSEL/PRO SE LITIGANT

I understand that the person who will argue the appeal must be ready at any time during or
after the week of argument which appears on the scheduling order.

( ) I know of no dates which would be inconvenient.
( ) I request that the argument of this appeal not be calendared for the following dates,
   which are inconvenient.  I have included religious holidays.

COUNSEL OR PRO SE LITIGANT MUST ADVISE THE COURT IN WRITING OF ANY
CHANGE IN AVAILABILITY.  FAILURE TO DO SO MAY BE CONSIDERED BY THE
COURT IN DECIDING MOTIONS FOR ADJOURNMENT BASED ON UNAVAILABILI-
TY.

## RELATED CASES

( ) This case has not been before this Court previously.
( ) This case has been before this Court previously.  The short title, docket number and
   citation are: _____
( ) Matters related to this appeal or involving the same issue have been or presently are
   before this Court.  The short titles, docket numbers and citations are:

Signature of counsel of record or pro se      Signature of counsel who will argue the ap-
litigant:                                      peal, if different:


_____            _____
Type or Print Name                 Type or Print Name
Name of Firm:
Address:
Telephone:        Date:            Telephone:        Date:

9/98

# UNITED STATES COURT OF APPEALS

## FOR THE

## SECOND CIRCUIT

## NOTICE OF APPEARANCE INFORMATION AND FORM

The form on the reverse side containing appearance, time request, availability, and related case information must be completed by all parties and returned to this office when appellant's brief is due.

**FAILURE TO SUBMIT THIS FORM ON TIME WILL BE CONSIDERED IN DECIDING ANY MOTIONS FOR ADJOURNMENT BASED ON UNAVAILABILITY.**

Each counsel of record or individual appearing pro se must complete this form. If an attorney other than counsel of record will argue the appeal, counsel of record must provide that attorney's name and date of admission to the bar of this Court in the space provided and indicate the dates, if any, when that attorney will be unavailable to argue the appeal.

Counsel of record and counsel who will argue the appeal must be admitted to the bar of this Court or be otherwise eligible to argue an appeal. The Court encourages and prefers *written* pro hac vice motions, filed as early as possible. Admission pro hac vice will be extended as a matter of course to a member of the bar of a district court within the circuit who has represented a criminal defendant at trial and continues representation on an appeal taken pursuant to the Criminal Justice Act. See Local Rule 46. However, counsel are encouraged to apply for general admission to this Court as soon as they meet the qualifications

For information concerning admissions and admission applications, contact the Clerk's Office at 212–857–8603.

# APPLICATION FOR FEES AND OTHER EXPENSES UNDER EQUAL ACCESS TO JUSTICE ACT (FORM AO 291)

AO291
(10/81)

APPLICATION
FOR FEES AND OTHER EXPENSES UNDER THE EQUAL ACCESS TO JUSTICE ACT
Title 28 U.S.C. Section 2412(d), Title II of Public Law 96–481, 94 STAT 2325

| 1. COURT | 2. DATE FILED | 3. DOCKET NO. |
|---|---|---|

1. COURT
A. ☐ SUPREME COURT    E. ☐ COURT OF APPEALS
B. ☐ CUSTOMS AND PATENT APPEALS    F. ☐ DISTRICT COURT
C. ☐ COURT OF CLAIMS    G. ☐ BANKRUPTCY
D. ☐ INTERNATIONAL TRADE

4. NAME OF APPLICANT (One per form)

5. GOVERNMENT AGENCY INVOLVED IN CLAIM
(Use agency code on reverse side)

6. NATURE OF APPLICATION

A. ☐ Original application under 28 USC 2412(d)(1)(A) after judgment in civil action against U.S.

B. ☐ Appeal of fees and expenses awarded by Lower Court. (If Item 6B is checked go to Item 7.)

C. ☐ Original application under 28 USC 2412(d)(3) after review of agency decision.

D. ☐ Petition for leave to appeal an administrative agency fee determination under 5 USC 504(c)(2).

7. APPEAL FROM:

☐ DISTRICT COURT    ☐ BANKRUPTCY COURT

☐ OTHER: _____

7A. DATE FILED IN LOWER COURT    7B. DOCKET NO.

8. ADMINISTRATIVE AGENCY DOCKET NO.      9. DATE FILED IN ADMINISTRATIVE AGENCY

10. SHOWING OF "PREVAILING PARTY" STATUS (28 U.S.C. § 2412(d)(1)(B)):

IS AGENCY ORDER, COURT ORDER, OR OTHER RELEVANT DOCUMENT ATTACHED?    ☐ YES    ☐ NO

11. SHOWING OF ELIGIBILITY (28 U.S.C. § 2412(d)(2)(B)):

IS NET WORTH INFORMATION ATTACHED?    ☐ YES    ☐ NO

12. ENTER ALLEGATION THAT GOVERNMENT POSITION WAS NOT SUBSTANTIALLY JUSTIFIED (28 U.S.C. § 2412(d)(1)(B)):

13. FOR EACH AMOUNT CLAIMED, PLEASE ATTACH ITEMIZATION INFORMATION INDICATING SERVICE PROVIDED, DATE, HOURS, AND RATE (28 U.S.C. § 2412(d)(2)(A)):

AMOUNT CLAIMED

A. ATTORNEY FEES . . . . . . . . . . . . . . . . . . . . . . . . . . . . . . . . . . . . . . . . . $ _____
B. STUDY . . . . . . . . . . . . . . . . . . . . . . . . . . . . . . . . . . . . . . . . . . . . . . . . _____
C. ANALYSIS . . . . . . . . . . . . . . . . . . . . . . . . . . . . . . . . . . . . . . . . . . . . . _____
D. ENGINEERING REPORT . . . . . . . . . . . . . . . . . . . . . . . . . . . . . . . . . _____
E. TEST . . . . . . . . . . . . . . . . . . . . . . . . . . . . . . . . . . . . . . . . . . . . . . . . . _____
F. PROJECT . . . . . . . . . . . . . . . . . . . . . . . . . . . . . . . . . . . . . . . . . . . . . _____
G. EXPERT WITNESS FEES . . . . . . . . . . . . . . . . . . . . . . . . . . . . . . . . _____
H. OTHER FEES AND EXPENSES—SPECIFY
     (1) _____ . . . . . . . . . . . . . . . . . . . . . . . . . . . _____
     (2) _____ . . . . . . . . . . . . . . . . . . . . . . . . . . . _____
     (3) _____ . . . . . . . . . . . . . . . . . . . . . . . . . . . _____
I. TOTAL FEES AND EXPENSES . . . . . . . . . . . . . . . . . . . . . . . . . . . . . $ _____

14. SIGNATURE      15. DATE

NOTE: THIS FORM SHOULD ACCOMPANY YOUR CLAIM WHEN FILED WITH THE CLERK OF COURT.

Page 2

## ADMINISTRATIVE AGENCY CODES

(Use the following abbreviations for the U.S. Government Agency involved in claim (Item 5))

| | |
|---|---|
| BENEFITS REVIEW BOARD | BRB |
| CIVIL AERONAUTICS BOARD | CAB |
| CIVIL SERVICE COMMISSION (U.S.) | CSC |
| CONSUMER PRODUCTS SAFETY COMMISSION | CPSC |
| COPYRIGHT ROYALTY TRIBUNAL | CRT |
| DEPARTMENT OF AGRICULTURE | AGRI |
| DEPARTMENT OF COMMERCE | COMM |
| DEPARTMENT OF DEFENSE | DOD |
| DEPARTMENT OF EDUCATION | EDUC |
| DEPARTMENT OF ENERGY | DOE |
| DEPARTMENT OF HEALTH, EDUCATION & WELFARE | HEW |
| DEPARTMENT OF HEALTH & HUMAN SERVICES | HHS |
| DEPARTMENT OF HOUSING & URBAN DEVELOPMENT | HUD |
| DEPARTMENT OF INTERIOR | DOI |
| DEPARTMENT OF JUSTICE | DOJ |
| DEPARTMENT OF LABOR (Except OSHA) | LABR |
| DEPARTMENT OF TRANSPORTATION, NATIONAL TRANSPORTATION SAFETY BOARD | TRAN |
| DEPARTMENT OF THE TREASURY (Except IRS) | TREA |
| DRUG ENFORCEMENT AGENCY | DEA |
| ENVIRONMENTAL PROTECTION AGENCY | EPA |
| EQUAL EMPLOYMENT OPPORTUNITY COMMISSION | EEOC |
| FEDERAL AVIATION AGENCY | FAA |
| FEDERAL COAL MINE SAFETY BOARD | FCMS |
| FEDERAL COMMUNICATIONS COMMISSION | FCC |
| FEDERAL DEPOSIT INSURANCE CORPORATION | FDIC |
| FEDERAL ELECTION COMMISSION | FEC |
| FEDERAL ENERGY AGENCY | FEA |
| FEDERAL ENERGY REGULATORY COMMISSION | FERC |
| FEDERAL HOME LOAN BANK BOARD | FHLB |
| FEDERAL LABOR RELATIONS AUTHORITY | FLRA |
| FEDERAL MARITIME BOARD | FMBD |
| FEDERAL MARITIME COMMISSION | FMC |
| FEDERAL MINE SAFETY & HEALTH ADMINISTRATION | MSHA |
| FEDERAL MINE SAFETY & HEALTH REVIEW COMMISSION | MSHR |
| FEDERAL RESERVE SYSTEM | FRS |
| FEDERAL TRADE COMMISSION | FTC |
| FOOD & DRUG ADMINISTRATION | FDA |
| GENERAL SERVICES ADMINISTRATION | GSA |
| IMMIGRATION & NATURALIZATION SERVICE | INS |
| INTERNAL REVENUE SERVICE (Except TAX COURT) | IRS |
| INTERSTATE COMMERCE COMMISSION | ICC |
| MERIT SYSTEMS PROTECTION BOARD | MSPB |
| NATIONAL LABOR RELATIONS BOARD | NLRB |
| NUCLEAR REGULATORY COMMISSION | NRC |
| OCCUPATIONAL SAFETY & HEALTH ADMINISTRATION | OSHA |
| OCCUPATIONAL SAFETY & HEALTH REVIEW COMMISSION | OSHC |
| OFFICE OF MANAGEMENT & BUDGET | OMB |
| OFFICE OF PERSONNEL MANAGEMENT | OPM |
| OFFICE OF WORKERS COMPENSATION PROGRAM | OWCP |
| PATENT OFFICE | PATO |
| POSTAL RATE COMMISSION (U.S.) | PRC |
| POSTAL SERVICE (U.S.) | USPS |
| RR RETIREMENT BOARD | RRRB |
| SECURITIES & EXCHANGE COMMISSION | SEC |
| SMALL BUSINESS ADMINISTRATION | SBA |
| TAX COURT, INTERNAL REVENUE SERVICE | TXC |

# LOCAL CRIMINAL NOTICE OF APPEAL FORM

NOTICE OF APPEAL
UNITED STATES DISTRICT COURT
_____ District of _____

_____     Docket No.:_____

_____
                                    (District Court Judge)

_____

Notice is hereby given that _____
appeals to the United States Court of Appeals for the Second Circuit from the judgment [_____]; other [_____];

                                            (specify)

entered in this action on _____.
                          (date)
Offense occurred after November 1, 1987     Yes [_____]      No [_____]

The appeal concerns:  Conviction only [_____] Sentence only [_____] Conviction and Sentence [_____].

                                    _____
                                    (Counsel for Appellant)
Date _____
TO                                  Address _____

                                            _____

                                            _____

                                    Telephone Number _____

        ADD ADDITIONAL PAGE IF NECESSARY
_____
    TO BE COMPLETED BY ATTORNEY          TRANSCRIPT INFORMATION—FORM B
> **QUESTIONNAIRE**                   > **TRANSCRIPT ORDER**   > DESCRIPTION OF
                                                                 PROCEEDINGS FOR
                                                                 WHICH TRANSCRIPT IS
                                                                 REQUIRED (INCLUDE
                                                                 DATE).
                                                                          Dates
[_____] I am ordering a transcript        Prepare transcript of
[_____] I am not ordering a transcript    _____ Pre-trial proceedings    _____
        Reason:                             _____ Trial                    _____
        [_____] Daily copy is available   _____ Sentencing               _____
        [_____] U.S. Attorney has placed or-  _____ Post-trial proceedings  _____
der
        [_____] Other.  Attach explanation

The attorney certifies that he/she will make satisfactory arrangements with the court reporter for payment of the
cost of the transcript.  (FRAP 10(b))  > Method of payment [___] Funds [___]      CJA Form 24 [___]
ATTORNEY'S SIGNATURE                                DATE

> **COURT REPORTER ACKNOWLEDGEMENT**                To be completed by Court Re-
                                                    porter and forwarded to Court
                                                    of Appeals.

_____      _____        Estimated number of pages.
  Date order received    Estimated completion date  _____

Date _____     Signature _____
                                    (Court Reporter)

        DISTRIBUTE COPIES TO THE FOLLOWING:
1.  Original to U.S. District Court (Appeals Clerk)    4.  U.S. Court of Appeals
2.  Copy U.S. Attorney's Office                        5.  Court Reporter (District Court)
3.  Copy to Defendant's Attorney

Revised October, 2002;  August 1, 2005.

# CRIMINAL CASE INFORMATION FORM
## (FORM A)

FORM A—FOR APPEALS IN CRIMINAL CASES

**CASE AND SENTENCING INFORMATION**   To be completed by courtroom deputy.

| CASE TITLE: | DISTRICT | DOCKET NUMBER | JUDGE |
|---|---|---|---|

Affidavit of Financial Status (CJA 23)
☐ Filed   ☐ Unfiled

**DEFENDANT:** Name and Address

Leave to Appeal in Forma Pauperis
☐ Granted ☐ Denied ☐ Not Sought

DEFENDANT'S ATTORNEY:
Name and Address                         SOCIAL SECURITY NO.

**ASSISTANT U.S. ATTORNEY:**
Name and Telephone

Phone:

☐ Appointed
☐ Retained

| Date of Sentence | Bail/Jail disposition ☐ Committed ☐ Not Committed | Defendant found guilty by ☐ Plea ☐ Trial |
|---|---|---|

Number of other co-defendants found guilty: _____

**TRANSCRIPT INFORMATION**   To be completed by courtroom deputy.

Court Reporter in Charge: (Name, Telephone)

Was daily copy prepared?                                    YES   NO

Did Assistant U.S. Attorney order trial minutes?           YES   NO

Did attorney for the defendant order trial minutes?        YES   NO

**COUNSEL AND TRANSCRIPT INFORMATION ON APPEAL**   To be completed by sentencing judge

1. Does defendant's financial status warrant appointment of counsel on appeal?   YES   NO

2. If so, should trial counsel be appointed on appeal?   YES   NO

3. Should trial minutes be transcribed at the expense of the United States pursuant to CJA?   YES   NO

SIGNATURE OF JUDGE                                    DATE

NAME OF COURTROOM DEPUTY                 DATE NOTICE OF APPEAL FILED

### DISTRIBUTE COPIES TO THE FOLLOWING:
1. Original to U.S. District Court (Appeals Clerk).
2. Copy to U.S. Court of Appeals.
3. Copy to U.S. Attorney's Office.
4. Copy to Probation Office.

USCA–2
FORM A Rev. 10–02

# CIVIL APPEAL PRE–ARGUMENT STATEMENT
## (FORM C)

### UNITED STATES COURT OF APPEALS FOR THE SECOND CIRCUIT
### AGENCY APPEAL PRE-ARGUMENT STATEMENT (FORM C-A)

☐ APPLICATION FOR ENFORCEMENT        ☐ PETITION FOR REVIEW

1. SEE NOTICE ON REVERSE.     2. PLEASE TYPE OR PRINT.     3. STAPLE ALL ADDITIONAL PAGES

| CAPTION: | AGENCY NAME: | AGENCY NO.: |
|---|---|---|
| | DATE THE ORDER UPON WHICH REVIEW OR ENFORCEMENT IS SOUGHT WAS ENTERED BELOW: | ALIEN NO : (Immigration Only) |
| | DATE THE PETITION OR APPLICATION WAS FILED: | Is this a cross-petition for review / cross-application for enforcement?<br><br>☐ YES     ☐ NO |

| Contact Information for Petitioner(s) Attorney: | Counsel's Name: | Address: | Telephone No.: | Fax No.: | E-mail: |
|---|---|---|---|---|---|
| Contact Information for Respondent(s) Attorney: | Counsel's Name: | Address: | Telephone No.: | Fax No.: | E-mail: |

| JURISDICTION OF THE COURT OF APPEALS (provide U.S.C. title and section): | APPROX. NUMBER OF PAGES IN THE RECORD: | APPROX. NUMBER OF EXHIBITS IN THE RECORD: | Has this matter been before this Circuit previously? ☐ Yes ☐ No<br><br>If Yes, provide the following:<br><br>Case Name:<br><br>2d Cir. Docket No.:     Reporter Citation: (*i.e.*, F.3d or Fed. App.) |
|---|---|---|---|

*ADDENDUM "A"*: COUNSEL MUST ATTACH TO THIS FORM: (1) A BRIEF, BUT NOT PERFUNCTORY, DESCRIPTION OF THE NATURE OF THE ACTION; (2) THE RESULT BELOW; AND (3) A COPY OF ALL RELEVANT OPINIONS/ORDERS FORMING THE BASIS FOR THIS PETITION FOR REVIEW OR APPLICATION FOR ENFORCEMENT.

*ADDENDUM "B"*: COUNSEL MUST ATTACH TO THIS FORM: (1) THE RELIEF REQUESTED; (2) A LIST OF THE PROPOSED ISSUES; AND (3) THE APPLICABLE APPELLATE STANDARD OF REVIEW FOR EACH PROPOSED ISSUE.

### PART A: STANDING AND VENUE

| STANDING | VENUE |
|---|---|
| PETITIONER / APPLICANT IS:<br><br>☐ AGENCY     ☐ OTHER PARTY<br><br>☐ NON-PARTY (SPECIFY STANDING): | COUNSEL MUST PROVIDE IN THE SPACE BELOW THE FACTS OR CIRCUMSTANCES UPON WHICH VENUE IS BASED: |

**IMPORTANT. COMPLETE AND SIGN REVERSE SIDE OF THIS FORM.**

**FORM C-A** (Rev. April 2006)        Page 1 of 2

| PART B: NATURE OF ORDER UPON WHICH REVIEW OR ENFORCEMENT IS SOUGHT |
|---|
| (Check as many as apply) |

**TYPE OF CASE:**

| | | | |
|---|---|---|---|
| _____ ADMINISTRATIVE REGULATION/ RULEMAKING | | _____ IMMIGRATION-includes denial of an asylum claim |
| _____ BENEFITS REVIEW | | _____ IMMIGRATION-does NOT include denial of an asylum claim |
| _____ UNFAIR LABOR | | _____ TARIFFS |
| _____ HEALTH & SAFETY | | _____ OTHER: |
| _____ COMMERCE | | (SPECIFY) |
| _____ ENERGY | | |

---

1. Is any matter relative to this petition or application still pending below?  ☐ Yes, specify: _____  ☐ No

2. To your knowledge, is there any case presently pending or about to be brought before this Court or another court or administrative agency which:

    (A)    Arises from substantially the same case or controversy as this petition or application ?    ☐ Yes    ☐ No

    (B)    Involves an issue that is substantially similar or related to an issue in this petition or application ?    ☐ Yes    ☐ No

If yes, state whether ☐ "A," or ☐ "B," or ☐ both are applicable, and provide in the spaces below the following information on the *other* action(s):

| Case Name: | Docket No. | Citation: | Court or Agency: |
|---|---|---|---|
| Name of Petitioner or Applicant: | | | |

| Date: | Signature of Counsel of Record: |
|---|---|

## NOTICE TO COUNSEL

**Once you have filed your Petition for Review or Application for Enforcement, you have only ten (10) calendar days in which to complete the following important steps:**

1. Complete this Agency Appeal Pre-Argument Statement (Form C-A); serve it upon your adversary, and file an original and one copy with the Clerk of the Second Circuit.
2. Pay the $450 docketing fee to the Clerk of the Second Circuit, unless you are authorized to prosecute the appeal without payment.

    **PLEASE NOTE: IF YOU DO NOT COMPLY WITH THESE REQUIREMENTS WITHIN TEN (10) CALENDAR DAYS, YOUR PETITION FOR REVIEW OR APPLICATION FOR ENFORCEMENT WILL BE DISMISSED.** *SEE* THE CIVIL APPEALS MANAGEMENT PLAN OF THE UNITED STATES COURT OF APPEALS FOR THE SECOND CIRCUIT.

**FORM C-A** (Rev. April 2006)

Page 2 of 2

[Revised March, 2005; April, 2006.]

# AGENCY APPEAL PRE–ARGUMENT STATEMENT
## (FORM C–A)

### UNITED STATES COURT OF APPEALS FOR THE SECOND CIRCUIT
### CIVIL APPEAL PRE-ARGUMENT STATEMENT (FORM C)

**1. SEE NOTICE ON REVERSE.**　　**2. PLEASE TYPE OR PRINT.**　　**3. STAPLE ALL ADDITIONAL PAGES**

| Case Caption: | District Court or Agency: | Judge: |
|---|---|---|
| | Date the Order or Judgment Appealed from was Entered on the Docket: | District Court Docket No.: |
| | Date the Notice of Appeal was Filed: | Is this a Cross Appeal?  ☐ Yes  ☐ No |

| Attorney(s) for Appellant(s): ☐ Plaintiff ☐ Defendant | Counsel's Name: | Address: | Telephone No.: | Fax No.: | E-mail: |
|---|---|---|---|---|---|
| Attorney(s) for Appellee(s): ☐ Plaintiff ☐ Defendant | Counsel's Name: | Address: | Telephone No.: | Fax No.: | E-mail: |

| Has Transcript Been Prepared? | Approx. Number of Transcript Pages: | Number of Exhibits Appended to Transcript: | Has this matter been before this Circuit previously?  ☐ Yes  ☐ No |
|---|---|---|---|
| | | | If Yes, provide the following: |
| | | | Case Name: |
| | | | 2d Cir. Docket No.:　　　Reporter Citation: (i.e., F.3d or Fed. App.) |

**ADDENDUM "A":** COUNSEL MUST ATTACH TO THIS FORM: (1) A BRIEF, BUT NOT PERFUNCTORY, DESCRIPTION OF THE NATURE OF THE ACTION; (2) THE RESULT BELOW; (3) A COPY OF THE NOTICE OF APPEAL AND A CURRENT COPY OF THE LOWER COURT DOCKET SHEET; AND (4) A COPY OF ALL RELEVANT OPINIONS/ORDERS FORMING THE BASIS FOR THIS APPEAL, INCLUDING TRANSCRIPTS OF ORDERS ISSUED FROM THE BENCH OR IN CHAMBERS.

**ADDENDUM "B":** COUNSEL MUST ATTACH TO THIS FORM A LIST OF THE ISSUES PROPOSED TO BE RAISED ON APPEAL, AS WELL AS THE APPLICABLE APPELLATE STANDARD OF REVIEW FOR EACH PROPOSED ISSUE.

### PART A: JURISDICTION

| 1. Federal Jurisdiction | 2. Appellate Jurisdiction |
|---|---|
| ☐ U.S. a party　　☐ Diversity | ☐ Final Decision　　☐ Order Certified by District Judge (i.e., Fed. R. Civ. P. 54(b)) |
| ☐ Federal question (U.S. not a party)　　☐ Other (specify): _____ | ☐ Interlocutory Decision Appealable As of Right　　☐ Other (specify): _____ |

**IMPORTANT.  COMPLETE AND SIGN REVERSE SIDE OF THIS FORM.**

**FORM C** (Rev. April 2006)

**PART B: DISTRICT COURT DISPOSITION** (Check as many as apply)

| 1. Stage of Proceedings | 2. Type of Judgment/Order Appealed | | 3. Relief | |
|---|---|---|---|---|
| ☐ Pre-trial | ☐ Default judgment | ☐ Judgment / Decision | ☐ Damages: | ☐ Injunctions: |
| ☐ During trial | ☐ Dismissal/jurisdiction | of the Court | | |
| ☐ After trial | ☐ Dismissal/merit | ☐ Jury verdict | ___ Sought: $ _____ | ☐ Preliminary |
| | ☐ Summary judgment | ☐ Judgment NOV | ___ Granted: $ _____ | ☐ Permanent |
| | ☐ Declaratory judgment | ☐ Directed verdict | ___ Denied: $ _____ | ☐ Denied |
| | | ☐ Other (specify): | | |

**PART C: NATURE OF SUIT** (Check as many as apply)

| 1. Federal Statutes | | | 2. Torts | 3. Contracts | 4. Prisoner Petitions |
|---|---|---|---|---|---|
| ☐ Antitrust | ☐ Communications | ☐ Freedom of Information Act | ☐ Admiralty/ Maritime | ☐ Admiralty/ Maritime | ☐ Civil Rights |
| ☐ Bankruptcy | ☐ Consumer Protection | ☐ Immigration | ☐ Assault / Defamation | ☐ Arbitration | Habeas Corpus |
| ☐ Banks/Banking | ☐ Copyright ☐ Patent | ☐ Labor | ☐ FELA | ☐ Commercial | ☐ Mandamus |
| ☐ Civil Rights | ☐ Trademark | ☐ OSHA | ☐ Products Liability | ☐ Employment | ☐ Parole |
| ☐ Commerce, | ☐ Election | ☐ Securities | ☐ Other (Specify): | ☐ Insurance | ☐ Vacate Sentence |
| ☐ Energy | ☐ Soc. Security | ☐ Tax | | ☐ Negotiable | ☐ Other |
| ☐ Commodities | ☐ Environmental | | | Instruments | |
| ☐ Other (specify): _____ | | | | ☐ Other Specify | |

| 5. Other | 6. General | 7. Will appeal raise constitutional issue(s)? |
|---|---|---|
| ☐ Forfeiture/Penalty | ☐ Arbitration | ☐ Yes    ☐ No |
| ☐ Real Property | ☐ Attorney Disqualification | |
| ☐ Treaty (specify): _____ | ☐ Class Action | Will appeal raise a matter of first |
| ☐ Other (specify): _____ | ☐ Counsel Fees | impression? |
| | ☐ Shareholder Derivative | |
| | ☐ Transfer | ☐ Yes    ☐ No |

1. Is any matter relative to this appeal still pending below? ☐ Yes, specify: _____ ☐ No

2. To your knowledge, is there any case presently pending or about to be brought before this Court or another court or administrative agency which:

    (A)   Arises from substantially the same case or controversy as this appeal?    ☐ Yes    ☐ No

    (B)   Involves an issue that is substantially similar or related to an issue in this appeal?    ☐ Yes    ☐ No

If yes, state whether ☐ "A," or ☐ "B," or ☐ both are applicable, and provide in the spaces below the following information on the *other* action(s):

| Case Name: | Docket No. | Citation: | Court or Agency: |
|---|---|---|---|
| Name of Appellant: | | | |

| Date: | Signature of Counsel of Record: |
|---|---|

## NOTICE TO COUNSEL

**Once you have filed your Notice of Appeal with the District Court or the Tax Court, you have only ten (10) calendar days in which to complete the following important steps:**

1. Complete this Civil Appeal Pre-Argument Statement (Form C); serve it upon all parties, and file two copies with the Clerk of the Second Circuit.
2. File two copies of the Court of Appeals Transcript Information/Civil Appeal Form (Form D) with the Clerk of the Second Circuit.
3. Pay the $455 docketing fee to the Clerk of the United States District Court, unless you are authorized to prosecute the appeal without payment.

      **PLEASE NOTE: IF YOU DO NOT COMPLY WITH THESE REQUIREMENTS WITHIN TEN (10) CALENDAR DAYS, YOUR APPEAL WILL BE DISMISSED.** *SEE* THE CIVIL APPEALS MANAGEMENT PLAN OF THE UNITED STATES COURT OF APPEALS FOR THE SECOND CIRCUIT.

**FORM C** (Rev. April 2006)

[Revised August, 2005; April, 2006.]

# CIVIL APPEAL TRANSCRIPT INFORMATION
## (FORM D)

### UNITED STATES COURT OF APPEALS
### FOR THE SECOND CIRCUIT

### CIVIL APPEAL TRANSCRIPT INFORMATION (FORM D)

**NOTICE TO COUNSEL:** COUNSEL FOR THE APPELLANT MUST FILE AN ORIGINAL AND ONE COPY OF THIS FORM WITH THE CLERK OF THE SECOND CIRCUIT IN ALL CIVIL APPEALS WITHIN TEN (10) CALENDAR DAYS AFTER FILING A NOTICE OF APPEAL.

| THIS SECTION MUST BE COMPLETED BY COUNSEL FOR APPELLANT | | |
|---|---|---|
| CASE TITLE | DISTRICT | DOCKET NUMBER |
| | JUDGE | APPELLANT |
| | COURT REPORTER | COUNSEL FOR APPELLANT |

Check the applicable provision:

☐ I am ordering a transcript.

☐ I am not ordering a transcript

Reason for not ordering a transcript:

☐ Copy is already available

☐ No transcribed proceedings

☐ Other (Specify in the space below):

PROVIDE A DESCRIPTION, INCLUDING DATES, OF THE PROCEEDINGS FOR WHICH A TRANSCRIPT IS REQUIRED (*i.e.*, oral argument, order from the bench, etc.)

METHOD OF PAYMENT ☐ Funds ☐ CJA Voucher (CJA 21)

INSTRUCTIONS TO COURT REPORTER:

☐ PREPARE TRANSCRIPT OF PRE-TRIAL PROCEEDINGS

☐ PREPARE TRANSCRIPT OF TRIAL

☐ PREPARE TRANSCRIPT OF OTHER POST-TRIAL PROCEEDINGS

☐ OTHER (Specify in the space below):

DELIVER TRANSCRIPT TO: (COUNSEL'S NAME, ADDRESS, TELEPHONE)

I certify that I have made satisfactory arrangements with the court reporter for payment of the cost of the transcript. *See* Fed. R. App. P. 10(b). I understand that unless I have already ordered the transcript, I shall order its preparation at the time required by the Civil Appeals Management Plan, the Fed. R. App. P., and the local rules.

| COUNSEL'S SIGNATURE | DATE |
|---|---|

COURT REPORTER ACKNOWLEDGMENT: This section is to be completed by the court reporter. Return one copy to the Clerk of the Second Circuit.

| DATE ORDER RECEIVED | ESTIMATED COMPLETION DATE | ESTIMATED NUMBER OF PAGES |
|---|---|---|
| SIGNATURE OF COURT REPORTED | | DATE |

FORM D (Rev. April 2005)

[Revised March, 2005.]

## T–1080.  MOTION INFORMATION STATEMENT

### UNITED STATES COURT OF APPEALS
### FOR THE SECOND CIRCUIT
### MOTION INFORMATION STATEMENT
Thurgood Marshall U.S. Courthouse at Foley Square
40 Centre Street, New York, NY 10007
Telephone: 212–857–8500

Caption [use short title]

**Docket Number(s):** _____

**Motion for:** _____

Set forth below precise, complete statement of relief sought:

_____

_____

_____

_____

**MOVING PARTY:** _____    **OPPOSING PARTY:** _____
☐ Plaintiff  ☐ Defendant
☐ Appellant/Petitioner  ☐ Appellee/Respondent

**MOVING ATTORNEY:** _____    **OPPOSING ATTORNEY:** _____
[name of attorney, with firm, address, phone number, and e-mail]    [name of attorney, with firm, address, phone number, and e-mail]

_____    _____

_____    _____

_____    _____

Court–Judge/Agency appealed from: _____

**Please check appropriate boxes:**

**FOR EMERGENCY MOTIONS, MOTIONS
FOR STAYS AND INJUNCTIONS
PENDING APPEAL:**

Has **consent** of opposing counsel:
A.  been sought?                  ☐ Yes ☐ No
B.  been obtained?               ☐ Yes ☐ No

Has request for relief been made **below**? ☐ Yes ☐ No

Has this relief been previously sought in
this Court?                        ☐ Yes ☐ No

Is **oral argument** requested?        ☐ Yes ☐ No
(requests for oral argument will not necessarily be granted)

Requested return date and explanation of emergency:

Has **argument** date of appeal been **set**: ☐ Yes ☐ No
If yes, enter date _____

_____

**Signature of Moving Attorney:**

_____ **Date:** _____    Has **service** been effected?  ☐ Yes ☐ No
[Attach proof of service]

### ORDER

**IT IS HEREBY ORDERED THAT the motion is GRANTED DENIED.**

**FOR THE COURT:**
CATHERINE O'HAGAN WOLFE,
Clerk of Court
By: _____

Date:
Revised July 1, 2002;  October 31, 2002;  November 1, 2006.

## LOCAL INSTRUCTIONS FOR BILL OF COSTS

Docket No. _____          Short Title: _____

Dear Counsel or Pro Se Litigant:

If you desire to file a bill of costs, enclosed is a form which you should use. Your bill of costs must be:

1. Served.
2. Filed within fourteen (14) days after entry of judgment with proof of service.
3. Verified.
4. Clear as to the number of copies which comprise the printer's unit.
5. Accompanied by printer's bills, which must include minimum charge for printer's unit
   a. of a page
   b. of a cover
   c. of footlines by the line
   d. of an index and table of cases by the page
6. Only for the number of necessary copies inserted in enclosed form.
7. For actual costs at rates not higher than those generally charged such work in the area where the Clerk's Office is located, otherwise subject to reduction.
8. Devoid of such items as postage, delivery charges, service charge, overtime and author's alterations.
9. One copy shall be filed with the original.

Very truly yours,

CATHERINE O'HAGAN WOLFE
Clerk of Court

By: _____
            Deputy Clerk

## ITEMIZED AND VERIFIED BILL OF COSTS

United States Court of Appeals
For the Second Circuit
_____

Docket No. _____

_____

Counsel for _____
respectfully submits, pursuant to Rule 39(c) of the Federal Rules of Appellate
Procedure the within bill of costs and requests the Clerk to prepare an itemized
statement of costs taxed against the _____ and in favor of
_____ for insertion in the mandate.

Docketing Action                                        _____

Costs of printing appendix (necessary copies _____)    _____
Costs of printing brief (necessary copies _____)    _____
Costs of printing reply brief (necessary copies _____)    _____


(VERIFICATION HERE)


                                        _____
                                                        (signature)

# LAW STUDENT PRACTICE FORM

Case Docket No.: _____

Form to Be Completed by the Party for Whom the Law Student Is Rendering Services (if the services are rendered for the Government, by the United States Attorney or an Authorized Representative of the Government Agency Represented).

I authorize _____, a law student, to appear in court or other proceedings on my behalf, and to prepare documents on my behalf.

_____     _____
(Date)                              (Signature of Client)

(If more than one client is involved, approvals from each shall be attached.)

**To Be Completed by the Law Student's Supervising Attorney:**

I will carefully supervise all of this student's work. I authorize this student to appear in court or at other proceedings, and to prepare documents. I will accompany the student at such appearances, sign all documents prepared by the student, assume personal responsibility for the student's work and be prepared to supplement, if necessary, any statements made by the student to the Court or opposing counsel.

_____     _____
(Date)                              (Signature of Attorney)

_____


Form for Designating Compliance With Student Practice Rule (LR 46(a)) of the Court of Appeals for the Second Circuit

_____     _____
(Name of Student)                   (Name of Supervising Attorney)
Address & Telephone of Above:       Address and Telephone of Above:
_____     _____
_____     _____
_____     _____

Name of Law School Student is Attending:
_____
_____
_____

**To Be Completed by Law Student:**

I certify that I have completed at least four (4) semesters of law school; that I am familiar and will comply with the Code of Professional Responsibility of the American Bar Association, the Federal Rules of Appellate Procedure, the Rules of this Court, and any other federal rules relevant to this appeal in which I am appearing; and that I am rendering services.

_____      _____
(Date)                                    (Student's Signature)

**To Be Completed by the Dean or a Designated Faculty Member of the Law School Attended by the Student:**

I certify that this student has completed at least four (4) semesters of law school work and is, to the best of my knowledge, of good character and competent legal ability.

_____      _____
(Date)                                    (Signature of Dean or Faculty Member)

_____
(Position of Above)

# APPLICATION FOR LEAVE TO FILE A SECOND OR SUCCESSIVE MOTION TO VACATE, SET ASIDE OR CORRECT SENTENCE 28 U.S.C. § 2255 BY A PRISONER IN FEDERAL CUSTODY

## UNITED STATES COURT OF APPEALS
## FOR THE SECOND CIRCUIT

Name
_____

_____      _____
Place of Confinement                              Prisoner Number

_____      _____

### INSTRUCTIONS—READ CAREFULLY

(1) This application must be legibly handwritten or typewritten and signed by the applicant under penalty of perjury. Any false statement of a material fact may serve as the basis for prosecution and conviction for perjury.

(2) All questions must be answered concisely in the proper space on the form.

(3) The Judicial Conference of the United States has adopted the 8½ x 11 inch paper size for use throughout the federal judiciary and directed the elimination of the use of legal size paper. All pleadings must be on 8½ x 11 inch paper, otherwise we cannot accept them.

(4) All applicants seeking leave to file a second or successive petition are required to use this form, except in capital cases. In capital cases only, the use of this form is optional.

(5) Additional pages are not permitted except with respect to additional grounds for relief and facts which you rely upon to support those grounds. Do not submit separate petitions, motions, briefs, arguments, etc., except in capital cases.

(6) In accordance with the "Antiterrorism and Effective Death Penalty Act of 1996," as codified at 28 U.S.C. § 2255, effective April 24, 1996, before leave to file a second or successive motion can be granted by the United States Court of Appeals, *it is the applicant's burden* to make a prima facie showing that he satisfies either of the two conditions stated below.

A second or successive motion must be certified as provided in [28 U.S.C.] section 2255 by a panel of the appropriate court of appeals to contain—

(1) newly discovered evidence that, if proven and viewed in light of the evidence as a whole, would be sufficient to establish by clear and convincing evidence that no reasonable factfinder would have found the movant guilty of the offense; or

(2) a new rule of constitutional law, made retroactive to cases on collateral review by the Supreme Court, that was previously unavailable.

(7) When this application is fully completed, the original and four copies must be mailed to:

**Clerk of Court**
**United States Court of Appeals for the Second Circuit**
**United States Courthouse**
**40 Foley Square**
**New York, New York 10007**

### APPLICATION

1. (a) State and division of the United States District Court which entered the judgment of conviction under attack _____

      (b)  Case number _____

2.   Date of judgment of conviction _____

3.   Length of sentence _____ Sentencing Judge _____

4.   Nature of offense or offenses for which you were convicted: _____
    _____
    _____
    _____

5.   Have you taken a direct appeal relating to this conviction and sentence in the federal court?
         Yes ( ) No ( ) If "yes", please not below:
    (a)  Name of court _____
    (b)  Case number _____
    (c)  Grounds raised (list all grounds; use extra pages if necessary) _____
    _____
    _____
    _____
    _____

    (d)  Result _____
    (e)  Date of result _____

6.   Related to this conviction and sentence, have you ever filed a motion to vacate in any federal court?
         Yes ( ) No ( ) If "yes", how many times? _____ (if more than one, complete 6 and 7 below as necessary)
    (a)  Name of court _____
    (b)  Case number _____
    (c)  Nature of proceeding _____
    _____

    (d)  Grounds raised (list all grounds; use extra pages if necessary) _____
    _____
    _____
    _____
    _____
    _____

    (e)  Did you receive an evidentiary hearing on your motion? Yes ( ) No ( )
    (f)  Result _____

    (g)  Date of result _____

7.   As to any second federal motion, give the same information:
    (a)  Name of court _____
    (b)  Case number _____
    (c)  Nature of proceeding _____
    _____

    (d)  Grounds raised (list all grounds; use extra pages if necessary) _____
    _____
    _____
    _____
    _____

    (e)  Did you receive an evidentiary hearing on your motion? Yes ( ) No ( )
    (f)  Result _____

    (g)  Date of result _____

8.   As to any third federal motion, give the same information:
    (a)  Name of court _____
    (b)  Case number _____

(c) Nature of proceeding _____

_____

_____

(d) Grounds raised (list _all_ grounds; use extra pages if necessary) _____

_____

_____

_____

(e) Did you receive an evidentiary hearing on your motion? Yes ( ) No ( )

(f) Result _____

_____

(g) Date of result _____

9. Did you appeal the result of any action taken on your federal motions? (Use extra pages to reflect additional federal motions if necessary)

(1) First motion      No ( ) Yes ( ) Appeal No. _____

(2) Second motion     No ( ) Yes ( ) Appeal No. _____

(3) Third motion      No ( ) Yes ( ) Appeal No. _____

10. If you did _not_ appeal from the adverse action on any motion, explain briefly why you did not: _____

_____

_____

_____

11. State _concisely_ every ground on which you _now_ claim that you are being held unlawfully. Summarize _briefly_ the _facts_ supporting each ground.

A. Ground one: _____

Supporting FACTS (tell your story briefly without citing cases or law): _____

_____

_____

_____

_____

Was this claim raised in a prior motion? Yes ( ) No ( )

Does this claim rely on a "new rule of law?" Yes ( ) No ( )

If "yes," state the new rule of law (give case name and citation): _____

_____

Does this claim rely on "newly discovered evidence?" Yes ( ) No ( )

If "yes," briefly state the newly discovered evidence, when it was discovered, and why it was not previously available to you _____

_____

_____

_____

_____

_____

_____

B. Ground two: _____

Supporting FACTS (tell your story briefly without citing cases or law): _____

_____

_____

_____

_____

Was this claim raised in a prior motion? Yes ( ) No ( )

Does this claim rely on a "new rule of law?" Yes ( ) No ( )
If "yes," state the new rule of law (give case name and citation):

_____

Does this claim rely on "newly discovered evidence?" Yes ( ) No ( )
If "yes," briefly state the newly discovered evidence, when it was discovered, and why it was not previously available to you _____

_____
_____
_____
_____
_____

**[Additional grounds may be asserted on additional pages if necessary]**

12.  Do you have any motion or appeal now pending in any court as to the judgment now under attack? Yes ( ) No ( )
If "yes," name of court _____ Case number _____

Wherefore, applicant prays that the United States Court of Appeals for the Second Circuit grant an Order Authorizing the District Court to Consider Applicant's Second or Successive Motion to Vacate under 28 U.S.C. § 2255.

_____
Applicant's Signature

I declare under Penalty of Perjury that my answers to all the questions in this Application are true and correct.

Executed on _____
[date]

_____
Applicant's Signature

## PROOF OF SERVICE

Applicant must send a copy of this application and all attachments to the United States Attorney's office in the district in which you were convicted.

I certify that on _____[date], I mailed a copy of this Application * and all attachments to _____
at the following address:

_____
_____
_____

_____
Applicant's Signature

* Pursuant to Fed.R.App.P.25(a), "Papers filed by an inmate confined in an institution are timely filed if deposited in the institution's internal mail system on or before the last day of filing. Timely filing of papers by an inmate confined in an institution may be shown by a notarized statement or declaration (in compliance with 28 U.S.C. § 1746) setting forth the date of deposit and stating that first-class postage has been prepaid."

# APPLICATION FOR LEAVE TO FILE A SECOND OR SUCCESSIVE HABEAS CORPUS PETITION 28 U.S.C. § 2244(b) BY A PRISONER IN STATE CUSTODY

## UNITED STATES COURT OF APPEALS
## FOR THE SECOND CIRCUIT

Name
_____

_____

Place of Confinement                     Prisoner Number

_____    _____

## INSTRUCTIONS—READ CAREFULLY

(1) This application must be legibly handwritten or typewritten and signed by the applicant under penalty of perjury. Any false statement of a material fact may serve as the basis for prosecution and conviction for perjury.

(2) All questions must be answered concisely in the proper space on the form.

(3) The Judicial Conference of the United States has adopted the 8½ x 11 inch paper size for use throughout the federal judiciary and directed the elimination of the use of legal size paper. All pleadings must be on 8½ x 11 inch paper, otherwise we cannot accept them.

(4) All applicants seeking leave to file a second or successive petition are required to use this form, except in capital cases. In capital cases only, the use of this form is optional.

(5) Additional pages are not permitted except with respect to additional grounds for relief and facts which you rely upon to support those grounds. Do not submit separate petitions, motions, briefs, arguments, etc., except in capital cases.

(6) In accordance with the "Anti–Terrorism and Effective Death Penalty Act of 1996," as codified at 28 U.S.C. § 2244(b), effective April 24, 1996, before leave to file a second or successive petition can be granted by the United States Court of Appeals, *it is the applicant's burden* to make a prima facie showing that he satisfies either of the two conditions stated below and in 28 U.S.C. § 2244(b).

   (b)(1) a claim presented in a second or successive habeas corpus application under [28 U.S.C.] section 2254 that was presented in a prior application shall be dismissed.

   (2) a claim presented in a second or successive habeas corpus application under [28 U.S.C.] section 2254 that was not presented in a prior application shall be dismissed unless—

   (A) the applicant shows that the claim relies on a new rule of constitutional law, made retroactive to cases on collateral review by the Supreme Court, that was previously unavailable; or

   (B)(i) the factual predicate for the claim could not have been discovered previously through the exercise of due diligence; and

   (ii) the facts underlying the claim, if proven and viewed in light of the evidence as a whole, would be sufficient to establish by clear and convincing evidence that, but for constitutional error, no reasonable factfinder would have found the applicant guilty of the underlying offense.

(7) When this application is fully completed, the original and four copies must be mailed to:

Clerk of Court
United States Court of Appeals for the Second Circuit
United States Courthouse
40 Foley Square
New York, New York 10007

## APPLICATION

1. (a) Name and location of court which entered the judgment of conviction
      under attack _____
   (b) Case number _____
2. Date of judgment of conviction _____
3. Length of sentence _____ Sentencing Judge _____
4. Nature of offense or offenses for which you were convicted: _____
   _____
   _____
   _____

5. Have you ever filed a post-conviction petition, application, or motion for
   collateral relief in any federal court related to this conviction and sentence?
      Yes ( ) No ( ) If "Yes", how many times? _____ (if more than one,
      complete 6 and 7 below as necessary)
   (a) Name of court _____
   (b) Case number _____
   (c) Nature of proceeding _____
      _____
      _____

   (d) Grounds raised (list all grounds; use extra pages if necessary) _____
      _____
      _____
      _____
      _____
      _____

   (e) Did you receive an evidentiary hearing on your petition, application, or
      motion?
      Yes ( ) No ( )
   (f) Result _____
      _____
   (g) Date of result _____
6. As to any second federal petition, application, or motion, give the same
   information:
   (a) Name of court _____
   (b) Case number _____
   (c) Nature of proceeding _____
      _____
      _____

   (d) Grounds raised (list all grounds; use extra pages if necessary) _____
      _____
      _____
      _____
      _____
      _____

   (e) Did you receive an evidentiary hearing on your petition, application, or
      motion?
      Yes ( ) No ( )

(f) Result _____

_____

(g) Date of result _____

7. As to any third federal petition, application, or motion, give the same information:
   (a) Name of court _____
   (b) Case number _____
   (c) Nature of proceeding _____

   _____

   (d) Grounds raised (list <u>all</u> grounds; use extra pages if necessary) _____

   _____

   _____

   _____

   (e) Did you receive an evidentiary hearing on your petition, application, or motion?
       Yes ( ) No ( )
   (f) Result _____

   (g) Date of result _____

8. Did you appeal the result of any action taken on your federal petition, application, or motion? (Use extra pages to reflect additional petitions if necessary)
   (1) First petition, etc.       No ( ) Yes ( ) Appeal No. _____
   (2) Second petition, etc.      No ( ) Yes ( ) Appeal No. _____
   (3) Third petition, etc.       No ( ) Yes ( ) Appeal No. _____

9. If you did <u>not</u> appeal from the adverse action on any petition, application, or motion, explain briefly why you did not: _____

   _____

   _____

   _____

   _____

10. State <u>concisely</u> every ground on which you <u>now</u> claim that you are being held unlawfully. Summarize <u>briefly</u> the <u>facts</u> supporting each ground.
    A. Ground one: _____

    Supporting FACTS (tell your story briefly without citing cases or law):

    _____

    _____

    _____

    _____

    _____

    Was this claim raised in a prior federal petition, application, or motion?
    Yes ( ) No ( )

    Does this claim rely on a "new rule of law?" Yes ( ) No ( )
    If "yes," state the new rule of law (give case name and citation):

    _____

    Does this claim rely on "newly discovered evidence?" Yes ( ) No ( )
    If "yes," briefly state the newly discovered evidence, and why it was not previously available to you _____

    _____

    _____

_____
_____
_____
_____

B.  Ground two: _____

Supporting FACTS (tell your story briefly without citing cases or law):
_____
_____
_____
_____
_____

Was this claim raised in a prior federal petition, application, or motion?
Yes ( ) No ( )

Does this claim rely on a "new rule of law?" Yes ( ) No ( )
If "yes," state the new rule of law (give case name and citation): _____
_____
_____

Does this claim rely on "newly discovered evidence?" Yes ( ) No ( )
If "yes," briefly state the newly discovered evidence, and why it was not
previously available to you _____
_____
_____
_____
_____
_____

**[Additional grounds may be asserted on extra pages if necessary]**

11.  Do you have any motion or appeal now pending in any court as to the judgment
now under attack? Yes ( ) No ( )
If yes, name of court _____ Case number _____

Wherefore, applicant prays that the United States Court of Appeals for the
Second Circuit grant an Order Authorizing the District Court to Consider Applicant's Second or Successive Petition for a Writ of Habeas Corpus under 28 U.S.C.
§ 2254.

_____
Applicant's Signature

I declare under Penalty of Perjury that my answers to all the questions in this
Application are true and correct.

Executed on _____
                [date]

_____
Applicant's Signature

## PROOF OF SERVICE

Applicant must send a copy of this application and all attachments to the attorney general of the state in which applicant was convicted.

I certify that on _____[date], I mailed a copy of this Application * and all attachments to _____
at the following address:

_____

_____


_____

Applicant's Signature

   * Pursuant to Fed.R.App.P. 25(a), "Papers filed by an inmate confined in an institution are timely filed if deposited in the institution's internal mail system on or before the last day of filing. Timely filing of papers by an inmate confined in an institution may be shown by a notarized statement or declaration (in compliance with 28 U.S.C. § 1746) setting forth the date of deposit and stating that first-class postage has been prepaid."

# CERTIFICATE OF DEATH PENALTY CASE

## UNITED STATES COURT OF APPEALS for the SECOND CIRCUIT
## CERTIFICATE OF DEATH PENALTY CASE

|  DISTRICT COURT | LOCATION (CITY) |
|---|---|
| U.S.D.C. DOCKET NUMBER | |

DATE PETITION FILED

[CASE CAPTION],

Petitioner,

-v.-

Respondent.

Fee Status

Paid _____ IFP _____

IFP Pending _____

COUNSEL FOR PETITIONER
(Name, Address & Telephone Number)

COUNSEL FOR RESPONDENT
(Name, Address & Telephone Number)

PETITIONER?S NAME, PRISONER I.D. #, INSTITUTION OF INCARCERATION, ADDRESS & TELEPHONE NUMBER

THIS CASE ARISES FROM: State Court Judgment _____    Federal Court Judgment _____

Complete each of the following statements applicable to this case:

1.  EXECUTION HAS BEEN SCHEDULED FOR _____.
    (Date)

2.  A verdict recommending a sentence of death was rendered on _____
    (Date)

EXPLANATION OF EMERGENCY NATURE OF PROCEEDINGS (attach pages, as necessary).

HAS PETITIONER PREVIOUSLY FILED CASES IN FEDERAL COURT?     ____ YES ____ NO
(If yes, give the Court, caption, docket number, filing date, disposition, and disposition date).

DOES PETITIONER HAVE CASES PENDING IN OTHER COURTS?     ____ YES ____ NO
(If yes, give the Court, caption, docket number, filing date, and status.)

I HEREBY CERTIFY UNDER PENALTY OF PERJURY THAT THE FOREGOING IS TRUE AND CORRECT.

_____
Signature

_____
Type or Print Name

NOTE:   THE COURT OF APPEALS PERIODICALLY WILL REQUEST CASE STATUS REPORTS. PARTIES ARE UNDER A CONTINUING AFFIRMATIVE OBLIGATION TO IMMEDIATELY NOTIFY THE UNITED STATES COURT OF APPEALS FOR THE SECOND CIRCUIT OF ANY CHANGES OR ADDITIONS TO THE INFORMATION CONTAINED ON THIS FORM.

[Effective December 1, 2002.]

# ELECTRONIC NOTIFICATION AGREEMENT

United States Court of Appeals for the Second Circuit
Thurgood Marshall United States Courthouse
40 Foley Square
New York, NY 10007

To Those Who Practice in the Second Circuit:

Beginning December 1, 2002, you may elect to receive electronic notification of all summary orders and opinions issued by the court in any case in which you are the attorney of record or a pro se litigant. If you wish to be served electronically, please complete the form below and return it to the Clerk's Office at your earliest convenience. **Please complete a separate form for each case in which you elect to receive electronic notification.**

---

## ELECTRONIC NOTIFICATION AGREEMENT

**I hereby elect and agree to receive electronic notification of all summary orders and opinions produced by or filed in the Office of the Clerk in the appeal listed below. I agree that electronic notice will be the only notice I receive from the Office of the Clerk and, in the event the automated system that produces these documents is not available, the Clerk may deposit copies of these documents in the United States Mail for first class delivery.**

Short Caption: _____

Docket Number: _____

_____          _____
Attorney Name (print)                         Attorney Signature

Firm Name and _____
Address:        _____
                _____
                _____

Voice Number: _____

Fax Number: _____

E-mail Address: _____

**I prefer to receive notice by: ___ Fax     ___ E-mail (pdf (Adobe) format)**

Special Instructions: _____
(if any)              _____
                      _____

**NOTE: Documents longer than fifteen (15) pages will not be faxed.**

# ANTI–VIRUS CERTIFICATION FORM

CASE NAME: _____

DOCKET NUMBER: _____

I, (please print your name) _____, certify that I have scanned for viruses the PDF version of the

    ___ Appellant's Brief
    ___ Appellee's Brief
    ___ Reply Brief
    ___ Amicus Brief

that was submitted in this case as an e-mail attachment to <briefs@ca2.uscourts. gov> and that no viruses were detected.

Please print the **name** and the **version** of the anti-virus detector that you used
_____
_____

If you know, please print the version of revision and/or the anti-virus signature files _____
_____

(Your Signature) _____

Date: _____

Effective December 1, 2005.

## NON–COMPLIANCE WITH DIGITAL BRIEF REQUIREMENT
### (TO BE COMPLETED ONLY IN COUNSELED CASES)

*See* Second Circuit Local Rule 32(a)(1)(A)

CASE NAME: _____

DOCKET NUMBER: _____

    I, (please print your name) _____, certify that I did not submit a digital copy of the

        ___ Appellant's Brief
        ___ Appellee's Brief
        ___ Reply Brief
        ___ Amicus Brief

in this case because (explain why submission of a digital brief was not practical or constituted undue hardship

_____
_____
_____
_____
_____
_____

                       (Your signature) _____

Date: _____
Effective December 1, 2005.

# APPENDIX

## PART A.　AMENDED PLAN TO IMPLEMENT THE CRIMINAL JUSTICE ACT OF 1964

### I.　AUTHORITY

The United States Court of Appeals for the Second Circuit, in accordance with the Criminal Justice Act of 1964, 18 U.S.C. § 3006A, 21 U.S.C. § 848(q), the guidelines for the Administration of the Criminal Justice Act, Vol. VII, Guide to Judiciary Policies and Procedures, and the Federal Rules of Appellate Procedure, hereby adopts this Plan for furnishing representation in the Court of Appeals for eligible persons financially unable to obtain adequate representation in accordance with the Act.

### II.　STATEMENT OF POLICY

The Plan shall be administered so that those accused of criminal conduct and who are financially unable to pay for legal representation will be provided with legal representation before this Court.

The Judicial Council, in promulgating the amended Plan set forth below, recognizes that while the Criminal Justice Act provides for limited compensation, attorneys chosen pursuant to the Plan to represent indigents are rendering a public and social service of the greatest importance. The Bar has traditionally represented with high dedication persons unable to pay any compensation for such representation. Services performed for eligible persons qualifying under the Plan will continue to be rendered by members of the Bar, essentially in their capacity as officers of the Courts and in keeping with the high traditions of the legal profession and its vital role in society. We also recognize that despite the nominal compensation provided by the Act, such services will be performed with devotion and vigor so that the lofty ideal—equality before the law for all persons—will be achieved. With this recognition of the importance of representation for indigents, we are confident that all segments of the Bar will accept as part of their professional obligations the need to render the most competent services in each and every phase of criminal and habeas corpus proceedings and that the organized Bar will be encouraged into increased activity with respect to the administration of criminal justice.

### III.　DEFINITIONS

　**A.　CJA**—the Criminal Justice Act, 18 USC § 3006A.

　**B.　CJA client**—a person for whom counsel has been appointed under the CJA.

　**C.　CJA attorney**—an attorney who is appointed to represent an eligible person under the CJA.

　**D.　CJA Panel member**—an attorney appointed to the CJA Panel of the Second Circuit Court of Appeals.

　**E.　CJA applicant**—a person applying for representation under the CJA.

　**F.　The or This Court**—the United States Court of Appeals for the Second Circuit.

　**G.　The CJA Committee**—the Court's CJA and Pro Bono Committee.

### IV.　DETERMINATION OF NEED FOR APPOINTED COUNSEL

　**A.　Notice to Defendant.** Whenever in forma pauperis status is ordered by the District Court of this Court in either a criminal appeal in which a defendant appears

335

pro se or in a § 2255 habeas appeal in which the petitioner appears pro se, the Clerk of the Court shall forthwith notify the defendant or petitioner that he or she has the right to be represented and that counsel may be appointed for the defendant or petitioner. The foregoing notice shall also be given in all such appeals taken by the United States.

**B. Request for Attorney on Appeal.** In cases where a request for the appointment of an attorney under the Act is made for the first time on appeal, the Chief Judge or the Chief Judge's designee, before making the appointment, shall inquire into and make a finding as to whether the CJA applicant is financially able to employ counsel. In making the determination, such forms as may be prepared and furnished by the Administrative Office of the United States Courts shall be utilized for the purpose of eliciting permanent information.

In cases where the CJA applicant is found by the district court to be financially unable to employ counsel, the Court of Appeals may accept this finding and appoint or continue an attorney without further proof. But see Fed. R. App. P. 24(a).

**C. Partial Payment.** If a CJA applicant's net financial resources are insufficient to pay fully for retained counsel, counsel may be appointed under the Act, and the CJA applicant may be directed to make partial payment of attorney's fees to the Clerk of Court under the guidelines as established by the Judicial Conference.

**D. Re-examination of Financial Status.** The Court may at any time after appointment of counsel, re-examine the financial status of a CJA client. If the Court finds that a CJA client is financially able to obtain counsel or make partial payment for the CJA client's representation, the appointment should be terminated or partial payment required to be made. If a CJA attorney learns any information indicating that a CJA client or someone on the CJA client's behalf can make payment in whole or in part for legal services, it shall be the CJA attorney's duty to report such information promptly to the Court so that appropriate action may be taken.

## V.   CJA ATTORNEY ADVISORY GROUP

**A. Authority and Composition.** A CJA Attorney Advisory Group will be appointed by the Court to assist the Court and the CJA Committee in reviewing applications for membership on the CJA Panel and to otherwise promote the furnishing of representation pursuant to this Plan. The CJA Attorney Advisory Group shall consist of the Attorney-in-Charge of the Appeals Bureau of Federal Defenders of New York, Inc. and 12 other attorneys selected by the Court for terms not to exceed three years who will collectively represent all of the districts in the Circuit. The members of the CJA Attorney Advisory Group must be admitted to practice in this Court and may not be members of the CJA Panel. Appointments to the Panel shall be made so that the terms of approximately one-third of the Panel members expire at the conclusion of each Term of Court.

**B. Meetings, Terms and Duties.** The Attorney Advisory Group shall review applications filed by attorneys seeking to fill vacancies on the CJA Panel. The Advisory Group shall consider the qualifications and experience of the applicants and recommend to the CJA Committee those applicants it deems qualified to fill the vacancies.

**C. Death Penalty Cases.** A CJA Death Penalty Attorney Advisory Group will be appointed by the Court to assist the Court and the CJA Committee in reviewing applications for membership on the Death Penalty CJA Panel.

## VI.   CJA PANEL

**A. Maintaining the CJA Panel List.** The Clerk of Court, under the direction and supervision of the Chief Judge or the Chief Judge's designee, shall maintain the list of the CJA Panel members that will supplement the services of the Federal Public Defender and Community Defender Offices within this Circuit. The list of

CJA Panel members shall include the name of each attorney and the current business address and telephone number of the attorney. Attorneys accepted for service on the CJA Panel must notify the Clerk of Court, in writing, within 48 hours of any changes in business address, business telephone number, e-mail address, or employment.

**B. Appointments.** Appointments to the CJA Panel shall be made by the Court upon appropriate recommendation from the CJA Committee after consultation with the Attorney Advisory Group.

**C. Applications.**

1. *Submission Requirements.* All private attorneys seeking to be included on the CJA Panel must submit to the Clerk of Court an application and a resume. Applications for membership shall be submitted on the Court's form for Application for Appointment to the CJA Panel, available in the Clerk's Office. The Attorney Advisory Group will review these materials. Applicants must be members in good standing of the Bar of this Court, must maintain an office within the Circuit, and must have demonstrated experience in and knowledge of Title 18 and the habeas corpus provisions of Title 28 of the United States Code, the Federal Rules of Appellate Procedure, the Federal Rules of Criminal Procedure, the Federal Rules of Evidence, the Local Rules and the United States Sentencing Guidelines.

The Court will set and publicize an annual application period for appointment to the CJA Panel.

2. *Term of Appointment.* CJA Panel members shall serve for a term not to exceed three years but may be removed by the Court prior to the expiration of their term. See Section D, Removal; See also Section VII, Release of Appointed Counsel. Upon expiration of the term of a CJA Panel member, the CJA Panel member must reapply for membership if he or she wishes to continue as a member of the CJA Panel. Application for renewal shall be made on the Court's form for Application for Renewal of Membership on the CJA Panel, available in the Clerk's Office. Panel members will be selected on the basis of demonstrated qualification, skill and dedication. Because of the limited size of the CJA Panel, the Court will not be able to appoint every qualified applicant to the Panel, but the Court will make an effort to rotate membership on the CJA Panel in order to ensure that new applicants are given an opportunity to serve.

**D. Removal.**

1. *Court's Discretion.* A CJA Panel member may be removed from the CJA Panel whenever the Court, in its discretion, determines that the member has failed to fulfill satisfactorily the obligations of Panel membership, including the duty to afford competent counsel, or has engaged in other conduct that renders inappropriate his or her continued service on the CJA Panel.

2. *Refusal of Assignments.* The Court may remove a CJA Panel member for refusing three times to accept an appointment during the membership term.

3. *Automatic Removal or Suspension.* A CJA Panel member will be suspended automatically if the member is disbarred or suspended by any state or federal bar or arrested for, charged with, or convicted of a crime. A CJA Panel member is obligated to notify the Clerk of Court, in writing, within 24 hours of any such suspension, disbarment, arrest, filing of criminal charges or conviction (See also Local Rule 46(f)–(h)).

Disbarment or suspension by any state or federal bar or conviction of a crime are grounds for automatic removal from the CJA Panel.

4. *Complaints.* All complaints concerning the conduct of a CJA Panel member shall be forwarded to the Clerk of Court. If the CJA Committee determines that a complaint alleges facts that, if true, would warrant consideration of removal of the CJA Panel member, or that other facts exist potentially warranting removal of a Panel member, the Committee may direct the Attorney Advisory Group to review the complaint, or brief, make such inquiry as it deems appropriate, and issue a report of its findings and recommendations to the Court. The Court has the

authority at any time to remove an attorney from the CJA Panel or to take such other action as it deems appropriate.

# VII.  APPOINTMENT OF COUNSEL

**A.  General.** In all cases on appeal in which the appointment of an attorney by the Court of Appeals under the Act is required, the Court shall appoint a CJA Panel member to represent a CJA client. The appointment of counsel shall be made within a reasonable time after the appeal is docketed.

The selection of counsel shall be the sole and exclusive responsibility of the Court, and no CJA applicant or CJA client will be permitted to select his or her own attorney from the Panel or otherwise; and no attorney or CJA Panel member shall have the right to be selected to represent a CJA applicant or CJA client.

**B.  Non–Panel Member Appointments.** When the Court determines that the appointment of an attorney who is not a member of the CJA Panel is appropriate in the interest of justice, judicial economy, or some other compelling circumstance warranting such appointment, the attorney may be admitted to the CJA Panel pro hac vice and appointed to represent the CJA client.

**C.  Retained Counsel.** Retained counsel, whether or not a member of the Panel, may seek to be appointed under the Act. Such application must be supported by financial documentation as specified in Section IV herein.

**D.  Multiple CJA Clients.** In appeals involving more than one CJA client, separate counsel may be appointed to represent each client. Where circumstances warrant, one attorney may be appointed to represent multiple CJA clients.

**E.  Substitution of Counsel.** The Court may, at any point in the appellate proceedings, substitute one appointed counsel for another. Total compensation to all counsel is subject to the maximum permitted by the Act. Appointed counsel replaced by such substitution shall, absent the Court's approval of interim payment, await the final disposition of the appeal before submitting a claim for compensation. See Section X(B), infra.

# VIII.  RELEASE OF APPOINTED COUNSEL

**A.  Appointed CJA Attorneys.** Counsel appointed under the Act to represent a CJA client in the district court shall continue such representation on appeal unless or until relieved by order of the Court of Appeals.

**B.  Relief of Trial Counsel.** If CJA counsel who acted in the district court wishes to be relieved from representing a CJA client on appeal, he or she shall file with the Clerk of the Court of Appeals, and serve upon a CJA client and all other counsel in the case, a motion seeking to be relieved and stating the grounds in support of the motion. Counsel seeking to be relieved nevertheless shall continue to represent the CJA client on appeal unless or until relieved by the Court of Appeals (See Local Rule 4(b)). The district court may also relieve counsel appointed under the Act provided the district court substitutes counsel as provided in the Act. Once the notice of appeal is filed however, only the Court of Appeals may assign or relieve counsel on appeal.

**C.  CJA Client Seeking to Relieve Counsel.** A CJA client seeking to have a CJA attorney relieved and/or the appointment of a substitute CJA attorney must file a typed or legibly handwritten motion, including a sworn affidavit (under penalties of perjury), setting forth compelling reasons for the substitution and giving a detailed account of the facts justifying the request. Such motion shall not be granted absent compelling circumstances.

# IX.  DUTIES OF APPOINTED COUNSEL

**A.  General.** CJA Panel members must be reasonably available, see also § VI(D)(2) supra, to accept assignments. Upon assignment to represent a CJA client, a CJA attorney shall provide representation in accordance with the Canons of Professional Responsibility and the provisions of this Plan.

**B.  Advice of Rights and Filing of Transcript.** In all cases where trial counsel has acted in the district court under the CJA, such trial counsel shall advise the CJA client of the right to appeal to the United States Court of Appeals and of the obligation to file a timely notice of appeal, and shall file such notice of appeal if requested to do so, unless the CJA client states that the notice of appeal should not be filed. Where appropriate, trial counsel shall also file with the district court the CJA Form 24 for the furnishing of the reporter's transcript at the expense of the United States.

**C.  Writ of Certiorari.** In the event of a decision adverse to the CJA client in this Court, the CJA attorney shall promptly transmit to the CJA client a copy of the Court's decision, advise the CJA client in writing of the right to file a petition for writ of certiorari with the United States Supreme Court, inform the CJA client of the CJA attorney's opinion as to the merit and likelihood of success in obtaining such a writ, and if requested to do so, petition the Supreme Court for certiorari. Despite a CJA client's directive to file a writ, if a CJA attorney has reasonable grounds to believe that a petition for certiorari would have no likelihood of success, the CJA attorney may file with this Court a motion to be relieved and serve a copy on the CJA client and other counsel within ten days of the filing of an adverse decision of this Court. If the Court relieves the CJA attorney, he or she shall, within 48 hours after such motion is granted, so advise the CJA client in writing and inform the CJA client concerning the procedures for filing a petition for a writ of certiorari pro se.

If an adverse party petitions for a writ of certiorari to review a judgment of this Court, the CJA attorney shall take all necessary steps to oppose the petition.

**D.  Furnishing Documents.** A CJA attorney must furnish the client with copies of all papers filed in the matter with the Court that relate to the CJA client's appeal, including all opinions and orders of the Court.

**E.  Oral Argument.** The CJA attorney shall appear for oral argument unless excused by the Court. Presentation of oral argument by an associate attorney not appointed under the Act will be allowed only with permission of the Court.

**F.  No Delegation of Authority.** CJA counsel shall not delegate any non-ministerial tasks in connection with representation of a CJA client to any person other than a partner, associate, paralegal, student or regular employee of the law firm or clinical program of which the Panel member is a partner, associate or affiliate without the written consent of the CJA client and the Court.

**G.  Representation Upon Remand.** The CJA attorney must continue to represent a CJA client in the district court upon remand unless relieved. The fact that a CJA attorney limits his or her practice to appellate work, or that proceedings in the district court on remand will be distant from the CJA attorney's office, will ordinarily be adequate grounds justifying the relief of the CJA attorney upon remand.

**H.  Anders.** If a CJA attorney seeks to be relieved on the grounds that there is no nonfrivolous issue to be raised on the appeal, the CJA attorney must follow the procedures of *Anders v California*, 386 U.S. 738 (1967).

**I.  No Other Reimbursement.** No CJA attorney shall accept a payment from or on behalf of the CJA client in this Court without prior authorization by a United States Circuit Judge on the form provided for such purpose. All such authorized payments shall be received subject to the terms contained in such order and pursuant to the provisions of subsection (f) of the Act.

# X.  PAYMENT OF CLAIMS FOR COMPENSATION AND EXPENSES

**A.  What to Submit.** No CJA attorney shall be compensated for the representation of a CJA client in this Court except upon the submission of the attorney's

voucher in accordance with the rules, regulations and forms promulgated by the Administrative Office of the United States Courts. Unless another means for compensation was specifically approved, such voucher must be accompanied by a written statement specifying the time expended, services rendered, and exact expenses for which reimbursement is sought while the case was pending in this Court.

**B. Time to Submit.** Unless a judge of the court so orders, a claim for attorney's fees, expenses, and services must be submitted no later than 45 days after a mandate has issued. If the appeal is from an interlocutory order or results in remand to the district court, the claim shall be timely if submitted within 45 days of the termination of the case in the district court or in the Court of Appeals. In the event of termination of the representation prior to the issuance of the mandate or the termination of the case, a motion for interim payment shall be timely if submitted within 45 days of the termination of the representation. See Section VII(E), supra.

**C. Maximum Hourly Rates.** The maximum hourly rates currently shall be $92.00 for in-court work and out-of-court work.

**D. Maximum Compensation.** For representation of a party on a direct appeal from a judgment of conviction in a felony, misdemeanor or habeas corpus case, **the total compensation allowed, excluding approved expenses, shall not exceed $5,200, except on appeals taken from the Eastern District and Southern District of New York for which the maximum compensation shall not exceed $7,000** except as described in Section E below. Different limits apply to death penalty federal habeas corpus petitions and federal capital prosecutions.

**E. Excess Payments.** Payments for representation on appeal in excess of the above limitations may be made for extended or complex representation whenever a judge of the Court certifies that the amount of such excess payment is necessary to provide fair compensation and such excess payment is also approved by the Chief Judge of the Second Circuit or the Chief Judge's designee.

**F. Interim Payment.** A judge of this Court may authorize interim payment where the judge determines it is appropriate upon the filing of a motion by a CJA attorney. The Chief Judge or the designee of the Chief Judge may arrange for interim payments.

**G. Payment.** The Clerk of Court shall forthwith forward all approved statements to the Administrative Office of the United States Courts for payment.

## XI. CJA COMPENSATION GUIDELINES

**A. Writ of Certiorari.** Where time and expense for preparation of a Petition for a Writ of Certiorari to the United States Supreme Court has been claimed, a copy of the Petition must accompany the voucher. Vouchers for the CJA attorney's time and expenses involved in the preparation of a Petition are subject to separate compensation limits in the same amounts as listed in Section X(D) supra.

**B. Compensation of Associate Attorneys.** Compensation may be provided under the CJA for services furnished by a partner, associate or affiliate of the appointed CJA attorney, but the total compensation provided for the representation of the CJA client shall be within the limits described in Section X(D) supra. Such services shall not be compensated unless the participation of such partner, associate or affiliate has been approved in advance by a judge of this court.

**C. Excess Voucher.** A CJA attorney submitting a voucher in excess of the maximum allowable compensation is required to submit along with a CJA voucher a memorandum detailing how time was spent and why excess payment is warranted.

**D. Maximum Compensation.** The maximum allowable compensation rates are detailed in Section X of this Plan.

A judge of the court who heard the case shall forward a CJA attorney's application for excess compensation to the Chief Judge or Chief Judge's designee,

with a recommendation for approval or denial. Excess compensation will not be paid unless it is approved by the Chief Judge or the Chief Judge's designee.

### E. Reimbursement of Expenses.

1. *Travel and Transportation.* Reimbursement for travel and transportation expenses shall be consistent with section 2.26 of chapter II, volume VII of the Guide to Judiciary Policies and Procedures. See also chapter VI, volume I, part C of the Guide to Judiciary Policies and Procedures (employee travel regulations). Reimbursement shall be limited to the most economical means of travel and transportation reasonably available. Reimbursement may be claimed only for expenses actually incurred. In all cases, a copy of the ticket used or the bill or receipt must be attached to the voucher for compensation. Travel time to and from court (or the place where the service is rendered) may not be claimed if the round trip is less than one hour.

    a. Commercial Carrier. Reimbursement for transportation by commercial carrier will be limited to economy class accommodations unless unavailable in an emergency. If compensation is claimed at a rate exceeding the economy rates, a detailed explanation in writing must be provided.

    b. Automobile Transportation. If travel is by automobile, the total mileage shall not exceed the fare authorized for travel by economy air travel, except in an emergency, or for other unusual circumstances. Travel reimbursement for a privately owned automobile shall not exceed the current government authorized rate for official travel per mile on a straight mileage basis, plus parking fees, ferry, bridge, road, tolls and tunnel fares.

    c. Meals and Lodging. CJA attorneys will be reimbursed for reasonable actual expenses incurred for meals and lodging within allowable limits. CJA attorneys will not be given a fixed per diem sum. Counsel should be guided by prevailing limitations for travel and subsistence expenses of federal employees. The Clerk of Court can advise attorneys of these limitations. A copy of the hotel or motel bill must be attached to the voucher. Attorneys traveling to attend oral argument will be reimbursed for no more than one and one half days of lodging and meals, absent an order of the Court in compelling circumstances.

    d. Photocopying. Actual costs for reasonable printing services for appendices will be paid if a copy of the bill is submitted. For in-house printing or copying, a maximum of $0.20 per page will be paid. The maximum per page limit is subject to periodic change by directive of the Judicial Conference of the United States. Actual costs for printing of briefs and brief covers will be paid for reasonable printing services if a copy of the bill is submitted. The costs of other forms of reproduction will not be reimbursable including typeset printing.

    e. Courier Service. For delivery of items that could be mailed, expenses will be reimbursed only if a satisfactory explanation is given why normal mail service was not utilized. In non-emergency cases, routine documents such as briefs and motions should be prepared early enough to permit use of the regular mail.

    f. Miscellaneous. CJA Panel members will be permitted to incur only the most reasonable rates for postage, telephone calls, and brief supplies. Supporting documentation is required for single item expenses of $50 or more.

## XII.  FORMS

The forms prepared and furnished by the Administrative Office shall be used, where applicable, in all proceedings under this Plan.

## XIII.  RULES AND REPORTS

The Court shall submit a report on the appointment of counsel under the Act to the Administrative Office of the United States Courts in such form and at such times

as the Judicial Conference may specify. This Plan shall be subject to such rules and regulations of the Judicial Conference of the United States governing the operation of such plans under the Act as may be issued from time to time.

## XIV.  OPERATION OF THE PLAN

This Plan incorporates the Guidelines for the Administration of the Criminal Justice Act of 1964 (18 U.S.C. § 3006A) by reference.

## XV.  NO RIGHTS CREATED

This Plan is intended only as a description of the procedures this Court will follow; it does not create any rights as against any individual or institution.

## XVI.  AMENDMENTS

Amendments to this Plan may be made from time to time by the Court, subject to the approval of the Judicial Council of the Second Circuit.

Effective January 29, 2002.  Amended effective January 1, 2006;  January 29, 2007.

# PART B. REVISED SECOND CIRCUIT PLAN TO EXPEDITE THE PROCESSING OF CRIMINAL APPEALS

The United States Court of Appeals for the Second Circuit has adopted the following revision of its plan to expedite the processing of criminal appeals, said revision to supersede the plan promulgated December 7, 1971 and to have the force and effect of a local rule adopted pursuant to Rule 47 of the Federal Rules of Appellate Procedure.

1. At the time of the sentencing hearing of any defendant found guilty after trial, the courtroom deputy shall provide attorneys with appropriate forms and instruction sheets regarding the rules of the Court of Appeals for processing appeals. The district judge shall:

(a) advise the defendant of the defendant's right to appeal and other rights in that connection as set forth in and required by Rule 32(a)(2), F.R.Crim.P.;

(b) complete and transmit to the Clerk of the District Court a form (in the form attached hereto as Form A, with such changes as the Chief Judge of this Court may from time to time direct) listing information needed for the prompt disposition of an appeal;

(c) make a finding to be shown in the appropriate place on Form A:

1. whether defendant is eligible for appointment of counsel on appeal pursuant to the Criminal Justice Act, and

2. whether there is any reason trial counsel should not be continued on appeal;

(d) make a finding, to be shown in the appropriate place on Form A, whether the minutes of the trial and of any proceedings preliminary thereto or such portions thereof as may be needed for the proper disposition of the appeal should be transcribed at the expense of the United States pursuant to the Criminal Justice Act, and if so, enter an appropriate order to that effect. In any case where a full transcript is not already available, the district judge shall encourage counsel to agree to dispense with the transcription of material not necessary for proper disposition of an appeal.

2. The Clerk of the District Court shall transmit forthwith the notice of appeal, together with the required forms, to the Clerk of the Court of Appeals, who shall promptly enter the appeal upon the appropriate records of this Court.

The Clerk of the District Court shall appoint an appeals clerk to coordinate appeals matters in the district court and serve as the contact between the Clerks of the District Courts and the Court of Appeals.

3. At the time of filing the notice of appeal, counsel for appellant shall complete and transmit to the Clerk of the District Court a form (in the form attached hereto as Form B, with such changes as the Chief Judge of the Court may from time to time direct) certifying that, if trial minutes are necessary, they have been ordered and that satisfactory arrangements for payment of the cost of the transcript have been made with the court reporter.

If the district judge directs the Clerk to file the notice of appeal, the district judge shall order counsel for the appellant to file Form B with the Clerk of the Court of Appeals within 7 days after sentencing.

If retained counsel is to be substituted on appeal by other retained counsel, Form B shall be transmitted within seven days after filing the notice of appeal, together with the substitution of counsel notice.

4. Whenever transcription of the minutes (or a portion thereof) has been ordered in a criminal case, the court reporter shall immediately notify the Clerk of the Court of Appeals on the appropriate form of the estimated length of the transcript and the estimated completion date. The number of days shall not exceed thirty (30) days from the order date except under unusual circumstances which first must be approved by the Court of Appeals upon a showing of need.

5. As soon as practicable after the filing of a notice of appeal in a criminal case, a judge of this Court or a judge's delegate shall issue an order (scheduling order) setting forth as hereafter described, the dates on or before which the record on appeal shall be filed, the brief and appendix of the appellant shall be filed, and the brief of the United States shall be filed, designating the week during which argument of the appeal shall be heard, and making such other provisions as justice may require.

(a) *Docketing of the Record.* The scheduling order shall provide that the record on appeal be docketed within twenty days after filing of the notice of appeal. If, at that time, the transcript is still incomplete a partial record shall be docketed which shall be supplemented when the transcript is complete. This Court will not ordinarily grant motions to extend time to docket the record.

(b) *Appellant's Brief and Appendix.* The scheduling order shall provide that the brief and appendix of appellant be filed not later than thirty days after the date on which the transcription of the trial minutes is scheduled to be completed unless for good cause shown it appears a longer or shorter period should be set. This provision does not affect appellant's right to

file a deferred appendix as provided by FRAP 30(c) and § 30(l) of the Rules of this Court.

(c) *Appellee's Brief.* The scheduling order shall provide that the appellee's brief shall be filed not later than 30 days after the date on which appellant's brief and appendix is to be filed, unless for good cause shown it appears a longer or shorter period should be set.

6. At the time a scheduling order is entered, or at any other time the judge or the judge's delegate who signed such order or, if the judge or the judge's delegate is unavailable, any other judge of this Court may enter any other orders desirable to assure the prompt disposition of the appeal. Such orders may include, but are not limited to, orders appointing counsel on appeal pursuant to the Criminal Justice Act, setting deadlines for filing the transcription of the trial minutes, requiring attorneys for co-appellants to share a copy of the transcript, and instructing the Clerk to permit counsel to remove and examine the official copy of the record for such periods as are necessary.

7. Under Rule 4(b)(a) of this Court, when a defendant convicted following trial wishes to appeal, trial counsel, whether retained or appointed by the district court or during the course of the appeal, is responsible for representing the defendant until relieved by the Court of Appeals. Furthermore, it is the policy of this Circuit that, in the absence of good cause shown, counsel appointed under the Criminal Justice Act for the trial shall be continued on appeal.

8. When new counsel is retained on appeal, whether trial counsel was retained or appointed in the district court or during the course of the appeal, new counsel must promptly file a substitution of counsel form endorsed by the defendant and the previous counsel of record. The substitution form must include a statement affirming that the trial minutes have been ordered.

In all cases when trial counsel, whether retained or appointed, wishes to be relieved as counsel on appeal, trial counsel must move pursuant to Rule 4(b) to be relieved. A motion to be relieved as counsel must be made within seven days after filing of a notice of appeal unless exceptional circumstances excusing a delay are shown.

In the event that it is impossible or impractical to obtain the signature of previous counsel of record, counsel on appeal may file the substitution of counsel

form signed by the defendant, accompanied by counsel's signed affidavit detailing efforts made to obtain the previous counsel's signature.

9. Motions for leave to file oversized briefs, to postpone the date on which briefs are required to be filed, or to alter the date on which argument is to be heard, shall be accompanied by an affidavit or other statement and shall be made not less than seven days before the brief is due, or the argument is scheduled, unless exceptional circumstances exist. Motions not conforming to this requirement will be denied. Motions to postpone the dates set for filing briefs or for argument are not viewed with favor and will be granted only under extraordinary circumstances.

10. In the event the district court grants an extension for filing a notice of appeal pursuant to FRAP 4(a)(b) the Clerk of the District Court shall promptly transmit a copy of the order to the Clerk of the Court of Appeals.

11. The Clerk shall, without further notice, dismiss an appeal for failure by the appellant to docket the record or file an appellant's brief within the time limited by a scheduling order or, if the time has been extended as provided by paragraph 9, within the time so extended; or in the event of default in any action required by these rules or any order resulting from these rules.

12. In cases where the Chief Judge may deem this desirable the Chief Judge or a person designated by the Chief Judge may direct attorneys to attend a preargument conference to be held as soon as practicable before the Chief Judge or a person designated by the Chief Judge, to establish a schedule for the filing of briefs and to consider such other matters as may aid in the prompt disposition of the appeal. At the conclusion of the conference an order shall issue which shall control the subsequent course of the proceeding.

13. When an appeal from a criminal conviction is affirmed in open court, the mandate shall issue forthwith unless the Court shall otherwise direct. In all other criminal appeals, the panel shall consider the desirability of providing for issuance of the mandate at a date earlier than provided by FRAP 41(a).

14. The foregoing Revised Plan to Expedite the Processing of Criminal Appeals shall be applicable to all criminal appeals in which notice of appeal is filed on or after November 18, 1974.

[December 1, 1994.]

# PART C.   CIVIL APPEALS MANAGEMENT PLAN

**1.   Notice of Appeal, Transmission of Copy and Entry by Court of Appeals.** Upon the filing of a notice of appeal in a civil case, the Clerk of the District Court shall forthwith transmit a copy of the notice of appeal to the Clerk of the Court of Appeals, who shall promptly enter the appeal upon the appropriate records of the Court of Appeals.

**2.   Appointment of Counsel for Indigent, Advice by District Court Judge.** If the appeal is in an action in which the appellant may be entitled to the discretionary appointment of counsel under 18 U.S.C. § 3006A(g) but has not had such counsel in the district court and there has been an indication that the appellant may be indigent, the judge who heard the case shall advise the Clerk of the Court of Appeals whether in the judge's judgment such appointment would be in the interests of justice.

**3.   Docketing the Appeal; Filing Pre–Argument Statement; Ordering Transcript.** Within ten calendar days (see FRAP 26(a)) after filing the notice of appeal, the appellant shall cause the appeal to be docketed by taking the following actions:

(a) filing with the Clerk of the Court of Appeals an original and one copy of, and serving on other parties a pre-argument statement (Form C or Form C–A, in the case of a petition for review or enforcement of an agency decision, with such changes as the Chief Judge of this Court may from time to time direct) detailing information needed for the prompt disposition of an appeal;

(b) ordering from the court reporter on a form to be provided by the Clerk of the Court of Appeals (Form D), a transcript of the proceedings pursuant to FRAP 10(b). If desirable the transcript production schedule and the portions of the proceedings to be transcribed shall be subject to determination at the preargument conference, if one should be held, unless the appellant directs the court reporter to begin transcribing the proceedings immediately;

(c) certifying that satisfactory arrangements have been or will be made with the court reporter for payment of the cost of the transcript;

(d) paying the docket fee fixed by the Judicial Conference of the United States pursuant to 28 U.S.C. § 1913 (except when the appellant is authorized to prosecute the appeal without payment of fees).

(e) at the time of filing Form C or Form C–A in the case of a petition for review or enforcement of an agency decision and Form D, the appellant shall also file:

(i) a copy of each of the judgments, orders and/or decisions of the U.S. District Court or agency from which review is sought,

(ii) a copy of each written or transcribed oral opinion rendered in the proceeding from which the review is sought addressing the issues raised on appeal,

(iii) in those cases where a decision is initially reviewed in the U.S. District Court, e.g., bankruptcy, social security, etc., a copy of all judgments, decisions, orders and opinions reviewed by the U.S. District Court which address the issues raised on appeal.

**4.   Scheduling Order; Contents.**

(a) In all civil appeals the staff counsel of the Court of Appeals shall issue a scheduling order as soon as practicable after the pre-argument statement has been filed unless a pre-argument conference has been directed in which event the scheduling order may be deferred until the time of the conference in which case the scheduling order may be entered as part of the pre-argument conference order.

(b) The scheduling order shall set forth the dates on or before which the record on appeal, the brief and appendix of the appellant, and the brief of the appellee shall be filed and also shall designate the week during which argument of the appeal shall be ready to be heard.

### 5. Pre–Argument Conference; Pre–Argument Conference Order.

(a) In cases where staff counsel may deem this desirable, the staff counsel may direct the attorneys to attend a pre-argument conference to be held as soon as practicable before staff counselor a judge designated by the Chief Judge to consider the possibility of settlement, the simplification of the issues, and any other matters which the staff counsel determines may aid in the handling or the disposition of the proceeding.

(b) At the conclusion of the conference the staff counsel shall enter a pre-argument conference order which shall control the subsequent course of the proceeding.

### 6. Non–Compliance Sanctions.

(a) If the appellant has not taken each of the actions set forth in paragraphs 3(a), (b), (c), and (d) of this Plan within the time therein specified, the appeal may be dismissed by the Clerk without further notice.

(b) With respect to docketed appeals in which a scheduling order has been entered, the Clerk shall dismiss the appeal upon default of the appellant regarding any provision of the schedule calling for action on the appellant's part, unless extended by the Court. An appellee who fails to file an appellee's brief within the time limited by a scheduling order or, if the time has been extended as provided by paragraphs 6 or 8, within the time as so extended, will be subjected to such sanctions as the Court may deem appropriate, including those provided in FRAP 31(c) or FRAP 39(a) or Rule 38 of the Local Rules of this Court supplementing FRAP or the imposition of a fine.

(c) In the event of default in any action required by a pre-argument conference order not the subject of the scheduling order, the Clerk shall issue a notice to the appellant that the appeal will be dismissed unless, within ten days thereafter, the appellant shall file an affidavit showing good cause for the default and indicating when the required action will be taken. The staff counsel shall thereupon prepare a recommendation on the basis of which the Chief Judge or any other judge of this Court designated by the Chief Judge shall take appropriate action.

### 7. Motions.
Motions for leave to file oversized briefs, to postpone the date on which briefs are required to be filed, or to alter the date on which argument is to be heard, shall be accompanied by an affidavit or other statement and shall be made not later than two weeks before the brief is due or the argument is scheduled unless exceptional circumstances exist. Motions not conforming to this requirement will be denied.

Motions to alter the date of arguments placed on the calendar are not viewed with favor and will be granted only under extraordinary circumstances.

### 8. Submission on Briefs; Assignment to Panel.
When the parties agree to submit the appeal on briefs, they shall promptly notify the Clerk, who will cause the appeal to be assigned to the first panel available after the time fixed for the filing of all briefs.

### 9. Other Proceedings.

(a) *Review of Administrative Agency Orders; Applications for Enforcement.* In a review of an order of an administrative agency, board, commission or officer, or an application for enforcement of an order of an agency,

(i) The Staff Counsel of the Court of Appeals shall issue a scheduling order as soon as practicable setting forth the dates on or before which the record or authorized substitute, the petitioner's brief and the appendix and the brief of the respondent shall be filed and also shall designate the week during which argument of the proceeding shall be ready to be heard;

(ii) Paragraph 5 of this Plan, pertaining to Pre–Argument Conferences, and Pre–Argument Conference Orders, and Paragraphs 7(b) and 7(c) of this Plan, pertaining to noncompliance sanctions, shall be applicable to this subparagraph.

(b) *Appeals from the Tax Court.* In a review of a decision of the Tax Court,

(i) Paragraphs 3(a) and 3(d) of this Plan, pertaining to filing pre-argument statements and payment of the docket fee, shall be applicable to this subpara-

graph. If the appellant has not taken each of the actions set forth in those paragraphs within the time specified in Paragraph 3, the appeal from the tax court may be dismissed by the Clerk of the Court without further notice.

(ii) Paragraph 4 of this Plan, pertaining to scheduling orders, shall also be applicable hereto.

(iii) Paragraph 5 of this Plan, pertaining to Pre–Argument Conferences and Pre–Argument Conference Orders, and Paragraphs 7(b) and 7(c) of this Plan, pertaining to noncompliance sanctions, shall be applicable to this subparagraph.

# PART D.   GUIDELINES FOR CONDUCT OF PRE–ARGUMENT CONFERENCE UNDER THE CIVIL APPEALS MANAGEMENT PLAN

Pre-argument conferences are conducted by Staff Counsel in counseled civil appeals under Federal Rules of Appellate Procedure 33 and Rule of the Civil Appeals Management Plan (C.A.M.P.), Rules of the Second Circuit, Appendix, Part C.  All fully counseled appeals except prisoner and habeas corpus cases are included in the CAMP program.  Participation in pre-argument conferences is mandatory.

**I.  Purpose.** The purpose is to explore the possibility for settlement of the dispute, to prevent unnecessary motions or delay—by attempting to resolve any procedural problems in the appeal, and to identify, clarify and simplify the issues submitted for review.

In an effort to enable the parties to resolve issues, Staff Counsel, who are full-time employees of the Second Circuit with extensive experience in appellate mediation, are ordinarily expected to give them the benefit of their views of the merits or other aspects of the appeal.  The Staff Counsel typically conducts the conference in a series of joint and sometimes separate caucuses to discuss settlement.

**II.  Authority and Attendance**. The success of the conference depends on the attorneys treating it as a serious and effective procedure which can not only save time and expense for the parties, but also provide an outcome better suited to their needs.  All sides should be thoroughly prepared to discuss **in depth** the legal, factual and procedural issues.  Prior to the conference, attorneys should discuss the matter with their clients and ascertain their goals in resolving the litigation.  They should be prepared to negotiate in good faith and express their views on the merits of their case as well as their client's interests. Attorneys who attend the mediation should be those who have the broadest authority from and the greatest influence with the client.   Attorneys should obtain advance authority from their clients to make such commitments as may reasonably be anticipated.

**III.  Client Participation.**  If feasible, counsel should have their clients available by telephone at the time of the mediation. The Court strongly encourages the parties to participate at every stage of the mediation process.  Ordinarily, attorneys are expected to attend the conference without their clients.  However, with the permission of Staff Counsel, or when appropriate—as required by Staff Counsel, clients may attend with their attorneys.  Staff Counsel does NOT talk with clients outside of the presence of their attorneys.

**IV.  Conference Location.**  Conferences are usually in person at the offices of Staff Counsel located in the Woolworth Building, 233 Broadway 6th Floor, New York, NY.  However, where considerable distances or other significant reasons warrant, Staff Counsel will, in their discretion, arrange to conduct the conference over the telephone or by video if available.

**V.  Good Faith Participation.**  The parties are obligated to participate in the mediation process in good faith with a view to resolving differences as to the merits and other issues in the case. This process requires each attorney, regardless of how strong his or her views are, to exercise a degree of objectivity, patience, cooperation and self-control that will permit the attorney to negotiate based upon reason. The conference provides a neutral forum for appraisal of the case and examination of means to expedite the matter.  Staff Counsel may offer their own views and are entitled to the attorney's respect and careful consideration of those views.  They are, of course, the individual views of the mediator and are not those of the court.No attorney or party is obligated to agree with the mediator or under any compulsion to reach an agreement to which they believe in good conscience they cannot agree to.

Mediation is not productive when counsel are not adequately prepared, present extreme positions, maintain fixed positions, and engage in hard, bottom-line bargaining.  Counsel should be realistic in approaching the mediation.  Mediation is most productive when counsel are conversant with the law and the facts in an appeal and

are fully aware of their client's interests, goals and needs. Moreover, they should strive to understand, but not necessarily agree with, the views of opposing counsel on the law and facts and the goals, interests and needs of their clients.

**VI. Mandatory Participation.** Although the mediation sessions are relatively informal, they are official proceedings of the Court. Sanctions may be imposed against any party who fails to appear for the mediation or otherwise participate fully.

**VII. Confidentiality.** All matters discussed at a pre-argument conference, including the views of Staff Counsel as to the merits, are completely confidential and are not communicated to any member of the Court. Nothing said by any participant to the session is to be disclosed to the judges of the court or judges of any other court that might address the appeal's merits. The mediator's notes do not become part of the Court's file nor anything submitted by the attorneys or parties to Staff Counsel pertaining to the merits. Any ex parte communications are also confidential except to the extent disclosure is authorized. The Court strictly enforces this rule. Likewise, parties are also prohibited from advising members of the Court or any unauthorized third parties of discussions or actions taken at the conference (*Calka v. Kucker Kraus & Bruh*, 167 F.3d 144.145 (2d Cir. 1999). Thus, the Court never knows what transpired at a conference.

**VIII. Grievances.** Any grievances regarding the handling of any case in the C.A.M.P. program should be addressed to Elizabeth Cronin, Director of Legal Affairs and Senior Staff Attorney, 40 Foley Square, New York, New York 10007.

Revised effective September 27, 1996; .

# PART E.   RULES OF THE JUDICIAL COUNCIL OF THE SECOND CIRCUIT GOVERNING COMPLAINTS AGAINST JUDICIAL OFFICERS UNDER 28 U.S.C. § 351 et seq.

## Applicable to Complaints Filed On or After November 2, 2002

*Table of Rules*

## PREFACE TO THE RULES

Section 351, et seq., of Title 28 of the United States Code provides a way for any person to complain about a federal judge or magistrate judge who the person believes "has engaged in conduct prejudicial to the effective and expeditious administration of the business of the courts" or "is unable to discharge all the duties of office by reason of mental or physical disability." It also permits the judicial councils of the circuits to adopt rules for the consideration of these complaints. These rules have been adopted under that authority.

Complaints are filed with the clerk of the court of appeals on a form that has been developed for that purpose. Each complaint is referred first to the chief judge of the circuit, who decides whether the complaint raises an issue that should be investigated. (If the complaint is about the chief judge, another judge will make this decision; see rule 18(e).)

The chief judge will dismiss a complaint if it does not properly raise a problem that is appropriate for consideration under § 351. The chief judge may also conclude the complaint proceeding if the problem has been corrected or if intervening events have made action on the complaint unnecessary. If the complaint is not disposed of in any of these ways, the chief judge will appoint a special committee to investigate the complaint. The special committee makes its report to the judicial council of the circuit, which decides what action, if any, should be taken. The judicial council is a body that consists of the chief judge and six other judges of the court of appeals and the chief judge of each of the district courts within the Second Circuit.

The rules provide, in some circumstances, for review of decisions of the chief judge or the judicial council.

## CHAPTER I.   FILING A COMPLAINT

### Rule 1.   When to Use the Complaint Procedure

(a) **The Purpose of the Procedure.** The purpose of the complaint procedure is to improve the adminis-

tration of justice in the federal courts by taking action when judges or magistrate judges have engaged in conduct that does not meet the standards expected of federal judicial officers or are physically or mentally unable to perform their duties. The law's purpose is essentially forward-looking and not punitive. The emphasis is on correction of conditions that interfere with the proper administration of justice in the courts.

**(b) What May Be Complained About.** The law authorizes complaints about judges or magistrate judges who have "engaged in conduct prejudicial to the effective and expeditious administration of the business of the courts" or who are "unable to discharge all the duties of office by reason of mental or physical disability."

"Conduct prejudicial to the effective and expeditious administration of the business of the courts" does not include making wrong decisions—even very wrong decisions—in the course of hearings, trials, or appeals. It does not include conduct engaged in by a judicial officer prior to appointment to the bench. The law provides that a complaint may be dismissed if it is "directly related to the merits of a decision or procedural ruling."

"Mental or physical disability" may include temporary conditions as well as permanent disability.

**(c) Who May Be Complained About.** The complaint procedure applies to judges of the United States courts of appeals, judges of the United States district courts, judges of United States bankruptcy courts, and United States magistrate judges. These rules apply, in particular, only to judges of the Court of Appeals for the Second Circuit and to district judges, bankruptcy judges, and magistrate judges of federal courts within the circuit. The circuit includes Connecticut, New York and Vermont.

Complaints about other officials of federal courts should be made to their supervisors in the various courts. If such a complaint cannot be satisfactorily resolved at lower levels, it may be referred to the chief judge of the court in which the official is employed. The circuit executive, whose address is United States Courthouse, Foley Square, New York, New York 10007, is sometimes able to provide assistance in resolving such complaints. All complaints must be submitted in writing.

**(d) Time for Filing.** Complaints should be filed promptly. A complaint may be dismissed if it is filed so long after the events in question that the delay will make fair consideration of the matter impossible. A complaint may also be dismissed if it does not indicate the existence of a current problem with the administration of the business of the courts.

**(e) Limitations on Use of the Procedure.** The complaint procedure is not intended to provide a means of obtaining review of a judge's or magistrate judge's decision or ruling in a case. The judicial council of the circuit, the body that takes action under the complaint procedure, does not have the power to change a decision or ruling. Only a court can do that.

The complaint procedure may not be used to have a judge or magistrate judge disqualified from sitting on a particular case. A motion for disqualification should be made in the case.

Also, the complaint procedure may not be used to force a ruling on a particular motion or other matter that has been before the judge or magistrate judge too long. A petition for mandamus can sometimes be used for that purpose.

## Rule 2. How to File a Complaint

**(a) Form.** Complaints should be filed on the official form for filing complaints in the Second Circuit, which is reproduced in the appendix to these rules. Forms may be obtained by writing or telephoning the clerk of the Court of Appeals for the Second Circuit, United States Courthouse, Foley Square, New York, New York 10007 (telephone (212) 857–8702). Forms may be picked up in person at the office of the clerk of the court of appeals or any district court or bankruptcy court within the circuit.

**(b) Statement of Facts.** A statement should be attached to the complaint form, setting forth with particularity the facts upon which the claim of misconduct or disability is based. The statement should not be longer than five pages (five sides), and the paper size should not be larger than the paper the form is printed on. Normally, the statement of facts will include—

(1) A statement of what occurred;

(2) The time and place of the occurrence or occurrences;

(3) Any other information that would assist an investigator in checking the facts, such as the presence of a court reporter or other witness and their names and addresses.

**(c) Legibility.** Complaints should be typewritten if possible. If not typewritten, they must be legible.

**(d) Submission of Documents.** Documents such as excerpts from transcripts may be submitted as evidence of the behavior complained about; if they are, the statement of facts should refer to the specific pages in the documents on which relevant material appears.

**(e) Number of Copies.** If the complaint is about a judge of the court of appeals, an original plus three copies of the complaint form and the statement of facts must be filed; if it is about a district judge or magistrate judge, an original plus four copies must be filed; if it is about a bankruptcy judge, an original plus five copies must be filed. One copy of any supporting transcripts, exhibits, or other documents is sufficient. A separate complaint, with the required

number of copies, must be filed with respect to each judge or magistrate judge complained about.

**(f) Signature and Oath.** The form must be signed by the complainant and the truth of the statements verified in writing under oath. As an alternative to taking an oath, the complainant may declare under penalty of perjury that the statements are true. The complainant's address must also be provided.

**(g) Where to File.** Complaints should be sent to

Clerk of Court
United States Court of Appeals
Thurgood Marshall U.S. Courthouse
40 Foley Square
New York, NY 10007

The envelope should be marked "Complaint of Misconduct" or "Complaint of Disability."

**(h) No Fee Required.** There is no filing fee for complaints of misconduct or disability.

Amended effective December, 2002.

## Rule 3. Action by Clerk of Court of Appeals Upon Receipt of a Complaint

### (a) Receipt of Complaint in Proper Form.

(1) Upon receipt of a complaint against a judge or magistrate judge filed in proper form under these rules, the clerk of the court will open a file, assign a docket number, and acknowledge receipt of the complaint. The clerk will promptly send copies of the complaint to the chief judge of the circuit (or the judge authorized to act as chief judge under rule 18(e)) and to the judge or magistrate judge whose conduct is the subject of the complaint. The original of the complaint will be retained by the clerk.

(2) If a district judge or magistrate judge is complained about, the clerk will also send a copy of the complaint to the chief judge of the district court in which the judge or magistrate judge holds appointment. If a bankruptcy judge is complained about, the clerk will send copies to the chief judges of the district court and the bankruptcy court. However, if the chief judge of a district court or bankruptcy court is a subject of the complaint, the chief judge's copy will be sent to the judge eligible to become the next chief judge of such court.

**(b) Receipt of Complaint About Official Other Than a Judge or Magistrate Judge of the Second Circuit.** If the clerk receives a complaint about an official other than a judge or magistrate judge of the Second Circuit, the clerk will not accept the complaint for filing, and will so advise the complainant.

**(c) Receipt of Complaint Not in Proper Form.** If the clerk receives a complaint against a judge or magistrate judge of this circuit that uses a complaint form but does not comply with the requirements of Rule 2, the clerk will normally not accept the complaint for filing and will advise the complainant of the

appropriate procedures. If a complaint against a judge or magistrate judge is received in letter form, the clerk will normally not accept the letter for filing as a complaint, will advise the writer of the right to file a formal complaint under these rules, and will enclose a copy of these rules and the accompanying forms.

## CHAPTER II. REVIEW OF A COMPLAINT BY THE CHIEF JUDGE

## Rule 4. Review By the Chief Judge

**(a) Purpose of Chief Judge's Review.** When a complaint in proper form is sent to the chief judge by the clerk's office, the chief judge will review the complaint to determine whether it should be (1) dismissed, (2) concluded on the ground that corrective action has been taken, (3) concluded because intervening events have made action on the complaint no longer necessary, or (4) referred to a special committee.

**(b) Inquiry by Chief Judge.** In determining what action to take, the chief judge, with such assistance as may be appropriate, may conduct a limited inquiry for the purpose of determining (1) whether appropriate corrective action has been or can be taken without the necessity for a formal investigation, and (2) whether the facts stated in the complaint are either plainly untrue or are incapable of being established through investigation. For this purpose, the chief judge may request the judge or magistrate judge whose conduct is complained of to file a written response to the complaint. The chief judge may also communicate orally or in writing with the complainant, the judge or magistrate judge whose conduct is complained of, and other people who may have knowledge of the matter, and may review any transcripts or other relevant documents. The chief judge will not undertake to make findings of fact about any material matter that is reasonably in dispute.

**(c) Dismissal.** A complaint will be dismissed if the chief judge concludes—

(1) that the claimed conduct, even if the claim is true, is not "conduct prejudicial to the effective and expeditious administration of the business of the courts" and does not indicate a mental or physical disability resulting in inability to discharge the duties of office;

(2) that the complaint is directly related to the merits of a decision or procedural ruling;

(3) that the complaint is frivolous, a term that includes making charges that are wholly unsupported or have been ruled on in previous complaints by the same complainant; or

(4) that, under the statute, the complaint is otherwise not appropriate for consideration.

**(d) Corrective Action.** The complaint proceeding will be concluded if the chief judge determines that appropriate action has been taken to remedy the problem raised by the complaint or that action on the complaint is no longer necessary because of intervening events.

**(e) Appointment of Special Committee.** If the complaint is not dismissed or concluded, the chief judge will promptly appoint a special committee, constituted as provided in Rule 9, to investigate the complaint and make recommendations to the judicial council. However, ordinarily a special committee will not be appointed until the judge or magistrate judge complained about has been invited to respond to the complaint and has been allowed a reasonable time to do so. In the discretion of the chief judge, separate complaints may be joined and assigned to a single special committee.

**(f) Notice of Chief Judge's Action.**

(1) If the complaint is dismissed or the proceeding concluded on the basis of corrective action taken or because intervening events have made action on the complaint unnecessary, the chief judge will prepare a supporting memorandum that sets forth the allegations of the complaint and the reasons for the disposition. The memorandum will not include the name of the complainant or of the judge or magistrate judge whose conduct was complained of. The order and the supporting memorandum, which may be incorporated in one document, will be filed and provided to the complainant, the judge or magistrate judge, and any judge entitled to receive a copy of the complaint pursuant to Rule 3(a)(2). The complainant will be notified of the right to petition the judicial council for review of the decision and of the deadline for filing a petition.

(2) If a special committee is appointed, the chief judge will notify the complainant, the judge or magistrate judge whose conduct is complained of, and any judge entitled to receive a copy of the complaint pursuant to Rule 3(a)(2) that the matter has been referred, and will inform them of the membership of the committee.

**(g) Report to Judicial Council.** The chief judge will from time to time report to the judicial council of the circuit on actions taken under this rule.

# CHAPTER III.  REVIEW OF CHIEF JUDGE'S DISPOSITION OF A COMPLAINT

## Rule 5.  Petition for Review of Chief Judge's Disposition

If the chief judge dismisses a complaint or concludes the proceeding on the ground that corrective action has been taken or that intervening events have made action unnecessary, a petition for review may be addressed to the judicial council of the circuit. The judicial council may deny the petition for review, or grant the petition and either return the matter to the chief judge for further action or, in exceptional cases, take other appropriate action.

## Rule 6.  How to Petition for Review of a Disposition by the Chief Judge

**(a) Time.** A petition for review must be received in the office of the clerk of the court of appeals within 30 days of the date of the clerk's letter to the complainant transmitting the chief judge's order.

**(b) Form.** A petition should be in the form of a letter, addressed to the clerk of the court of appeals, beginning "I hereby petition the judicial council for review of the chief judge's order ..." There is no need to enclose a copy of the original complaint.

**(c) Legibility.** Petitions should be typewritten if possible. If not typewritten, they must be legible.

**(d) Number of Copies.** Only an original is required.

**(e) Statement of Grounds for Petition.** The letter should set forth a *brief* statement of the reasons why the petitioner believes that the chief judge should not have dismissed the complaint or concluded the proceeding. It should not repeat the complaint; the complaint will be available to members of the circuit council considering the petition.

**(f) Signature.** The letter must be signed by the complainant.

**(g) Where to File.** Petition letters should be sent to

Clerk of Court
United States Court of Appeals
Thurgood Marshall U.S. Courthouse
40 Foley Square
New York, NY 10007

The envelope should be marked "Misconduct Petition" or "Disability Petition."

**(h) No Fee Required.** There is no fee for filing a petition under this procedure.

## Rule 7.  Action by Clerk of Court of Appeals Upon Receipt of a Petition for Review

**(a) Receipt of Timely Petition in Proper Form.** Upon receipt of a petition for review filed within the time allowed and in proper form under these rules, the clerk of the court of appeals will acknowledge receipt of the petition. The clerk will promptly cause to be sent to each member of the judicial council, except for any member disqualified under Rule 18, copies of (1) the complaint form and statement of facts, (2) any response filed by the judge or magistrate judge, (3) any record of information received by the chief judge in connection with the chief judge's

consideration of the complaint, (4) the chief judge's order disposing of the complaint, (5) any memorandum in support of the chief judge's order, (6) the petition for review, (7) any other documents in the files of the clerk that appear to the circuit executive to be relevant and material to the petition or a list of such documents, (8) a list of any documents in the clerk's files that are not being sent because they are not considered by the circuit executive relevant and material, (9) a ballot that conforms with Rule 8(a). The clerk will also send the same materials, except for the ballot, to the circuit executive and the judge or magistrate judge whose conduct is at issue, except that materials previously sent to a person may be omitted.

**(b) Receipt of Untimely Petition.** The clerk will not accept for filing a petition that is received after the deadline set forth in Rule 6(a), and will so advise the complainant.

**(c) Receipt of Timely Petition Not in Proper Form.** Upon receipt of a petition filed within the time allowed but not in proper form under these rules (including a document that is ambiguous about whether a petition for review is intended), the clerk will acknowledge receipt of the petition, call the petitioner's attention to the deficiencies, and give the petitioner the opportunity to correct the deficiencies within fifteen days of the date of the clerk's letter or within the original deadline for filing the petition, whichever is later. If the deficiencies are corrected within the time allowed, the clerk will proceed in accordance with paragraph (a) of this rule. If the deficiencies are not corrected, the clerk will reject the petition, and will so advise the complainant.

# Rule 8.  Review by the Judicial Council of a Chief Judge's Order

**(a) Review Panel.** The Chief Judge shall designate six members of the judicial council (other than the chief judge) to serve as a review panel. A review panel shall be composed of three circuit judges and three district judges. Membership on the review panel shall be changed after four months so that all members of the council shall serve on a review panel once each year. A review panel shall act for the judicial council on all petitions for review of a chief judge's dismissal order, except those petitions referred to the full membership of the council pursuant to Rule 8(b).

**(b) Mail Ballot.** Each member of the review panel to whom a ballot was sent will return a signed ballot, or otherwise communicate the member's vote, to the chief judge by the return date listed on the ballot. The ballot form will provide opportunities to vote to (1) deny the petition for review, or (2) refer the petition to the full membership of the judicial council. The form will also provide an opportunity for mem-

bers to indicate that they have disqualified themselves from participating in consideration of the petition.

Any member of the review panel voting to refer the petition to the full membership of the judicial council, or after such referral, any council member voting to place the petition on the agenda of a meeting of the judicial council shall send a brief statement of reasons to all members of the council.

The petition for review shall be referred to the full membership of the judicial council upon the vote of any member of the review panel and shall be placed on the agenda of a council meeting upon the votes of at least two members of the council; otherwise, the petition for review will be denied.

Upon referral of a petition to the full membership of the judicial council, the clerk shall send to each member of the council not then serving on the review panel the materials specified in Rule 7(a).

**(c) Availability of Documents.** Upon request, the clerk will make available to any member of the judicial council or to the judge or magistrate judge complained about any document from the files that was not sent to the council members pursuant to Rule 7(a).

**(d) Quorum and Voting.** If a petition is placed on the agenda of a meeting of the judicial council, a majority of council members eligible to participate (see Rule 18(b)) shall constitute a quorum and is required for any effective council action.

**(e) Rights of Judge or Magistrate Judge Complained About.**

(1) At any time after the filing of a petition for review by a complainant, the judge or magistrate judge complained about may file, and before the judicial council makes any decision unfavorable to the judge or magistrate judge will be invited to file, a written response with the clerk of the court of appeals. The clerk will promptly distribute copies of the response to each member of the judicial council who is not disqualified and to the complainant. The judge or magistrate judge may not communicate with council members individually about the matter, either orally or in writing.

(2) The judge or magistrate judge complained about will be provided with copies of any communications that may be addressed to the members of the judicial council by the complainant.

**(f) Notice of Council Decision.**

(1) The order of the judicial council, together with any accompanying memorandum in support of the order, will be filed and provided to the complainant, the judge or magistrate judge, and any judge entitled to receive a copy of the complaint pursuant to Rule 3(a)(2).

(2) If the decision is unfavorable to the complainant, the complainant will be notified that the law provides for no further review of the decision.

(3) A memorandum supporting a council order will not include the name of the complainant or the judge or magistrate judge whose conduct was complained of. If the order of the council denies a petition for review of the chief judge's disposition, a supporting memorandum will be prepared only if the judicial council concludes that there is a need to supplement the chief judge's explanation.

## CHAPTER IV.  INVESTIGATION AND RECOMMENDATION BY SPECIAL COMMITTEE

### Rule 9.  Appointment of Special Committee

(a) **Membership.**  A special committee appointed pursuant to Rule 4(e) will consist of the chief judge of the circuit and equal numbers of circuit and district judges. If the complaint is about a district judge, bankruptcy judge, or magistrate judge, the district judge members of the committee will be from districts other than the district of the judge or magistrate judge complained about.

(b) **Presiding Officer.**  At the time of appointing the committee, the chief judge will designate one of its members (who may be the chief judge) as the presiding officer. When designating another member of the committee as the presiding officer, the chief judge may also delegate to such member the authority to direct the clerk of the court of appeals to issue subpoenas related to proceedings of the committee.

(c) **Bankruptcy Judge or Magistrate Judge as Adviser.**  If the judicial officer complained about is a bankruptcy judge or magistrate judge, the chief judge may designate a bankruptcy judge or magistrate judge, as the case may be, to serve as an adviser to the committee. The chief judge will designate such an adviser if, within ten days of notification of the appointment of the committee, the bankruptcy judge or magistrate judge complained about requests that an adviser be designated. The adviser will be from a district other than the district of the judge or magistrate judge complained about. The adviser will not vote but will have the other privileges of a member of the committee.

(d) **Provision of Documents.**  The chief judge will send to each other member of the committee and to the adviser, if any, copies of (1) the complaint form and statement of facts, and (2) any other documents on file pertaining to the complaint (or to that portion of the complaint referred to the special committee).

(e) **Continuing Qualification of Committee Members.**  A member of a special committee who was qualified at the time of appointment may continue to serve on the committee even though the member relinquishes the position of chief judge, circuit judge, or district judge, as the case may be, but only if the member continues to hold office under article III, section 1, of the Constitution of the United States.

(f) **Inability of Committee Member to Complete Service.**  If a member of a special committee can no longer serve because of death, disability, disqualification, resignation, retirement from office, or other reason, the chief judge of the circuit will determine whether to appoint a replacement member, either a circuit or district judge as the case may be. However, no special committee appointed under these rules will function with only a single member, and the quorum and voting requirements for a two-member committee will be applied as if the committee had three members.

### Rule 10.  Conduct of an Investigation

(a) **Extent and Methods to Be Determined by Committee.**  Each special committee will determine the extent of the investigation and the methods of conducting it that are appropriate in the light of the allegations of the complaint. If, in the course of investigation, the committee develops reason to believe that the judge or magistrate judge may be engaged in misconduct that is beyond the scope of the complaint, the committee may, with written notice to the judge or magistrate judge, expand the scope of the investigation to encompass such misconduct.

(b) **Criminal Matters.**  If the complaint alleges criminal conduct on the part of a judge or magistrate judge, or in the event that the committee becomes aware of possible criminal conduct, the committee will consult with the appropriate prosecuting authorities to the extent permitted by 28 U.S.C. § 351, et seq., in an effort to avoid compromising any criminal investigation. However, the committee will make its own determination about the timing of its activities, having in mind the importance of ensuring the proper administration of the business of the courts.

(c) **Staff.**  The committee may arrange for staff assistance in the conduct of the investigation. It may use existing staff of the judicial branch or may arrange, through the Administrative Office of the United States Courts, for the hiring of special staff to assist in the investigation.

(d) **Delegation.**  The committee may delegate duties in its discretion to subcommittees, to staff members, to individual committee members, or to an adviser designated under Rule 9(c). The authority to exercise the committee's subpoena powers may be delegated only to the presiding officer. In the case of failure to comply with such subpoena, the judicial council or special committee may institute a contempt proceeding consistent with 28 U.S.C. § 332(d).

(e) **Report.**  The committee will file with the judicial council a comprehensive report of its investigation, including findings of the investigation and the committee's recommendations for council action. Any find-

ings adverse to the judge or magistrate judge will be based on evidence in the record. The report will be accompanied by a statement of the vote by which it was adopted, any separate or dissenting statements of committee members, and the record of any hearings held pursuant to Rule 11.

**(f) Voting.** All actions of the committee will be by vote of a majority of all of the members of the committee.

## Rule 11. Conduct of Hearings by Special Committee

**(a) Purpose of Hearings.** The committee may hold hearings to take testimony and receive other evidence, to hear arguments, or both. If the committee is investigating allegations against more than one judge or magistrate judge it may, in its discretion, hold joint hearings or separate hearings.

**(b) Notice to Judge or Magistrate Judge Complained About.** The judge or magistrate judge complained about will be given adequate notice in writing of any hearing held, its purposes, the names of any witnesses whom the committee intends to call, and the text of any statements that have been taken from such witnesses. The judge or magistrate judge may at any time suggest additional witnesses to the committee.

**(c) Committee Witnesses.** All persons who are believed to have substantial information to offer will be called as committee witnesses. Such witnesses may include the complainant and the judge or magistrate judge complained about. The witnesses will be questioned by committee members, staff, or both. The judge or magistrate judge will be afforded the opportunity to cross-examine committee witnesses, personally or through counsel.

**(d) Witnesses Called by the Judge or Magistrate Judge.** The judge or magistrate judge complained about may also call witnesses and may examine them personally or through counsel. Such witnesses may also be examined by committee members, staff, or both.

**(e) Witness Fees.** Witness fees will be paid as provided in 28 U.S.C. § 1821.

**(f) Rules of Evidence; Oath.** The Federal Rules of Evidence will apply to any evidentiary hearing except to the extent that departures from the adversarial format of a trial make them inappropriate. All testimony taken at such a hearing will be given under oath or affirmation.

**(g) Record and Transcript.** A record and transcript will be made of any hearing held.

## Rule 12. Rights of Judge or Magistrate Judge in Investigation

**(a) Notice.** The judge or magistrate judge complained about is entitled to written notice of the investigation (Rule 4(f)(2)), to written notice of expansion of the scope of an investigation (Rule 10(a)), and to thirty days written notice of any hearing (Rule 11(b)).

**(b) Presentation of Evidence.** The judge or magistrate judge is entitled to a hearing, and has the right to present evidence and to compel the attendance of witnesses and the production of documents at the hearing. Upon request of the judge or magistrate judge, the chief judge or a designee will direct the clerk of the court of appeals to issue a subpoena in accordance with 28 U.S.C. § 332(d)(1).

**(c) Presentation of Argument.** The judge or magistrate judge may submit written argument to the special committee at any time, and will be given a reasonable opportunity to present oral argument at an appropriate stage of the investigation.

**(d) Attendance at Hearings.** The judge or magistrate judge will have the right to attend any hearing held by the special committee and to receive copies of the transcript and any documents introduced, as well as to receive copies of any written arguments submitted by the complainant to the committee.

**(e) Receipt of Committee's Report.** The judge or magistrate judge will have the right to receive the report of the special committee at the time it is filed with the judicial council.

**(f) Representation by Counsel.** The judge or magistrate judge may be represented by counsel in the exercise of any of the rights enumerated in this rule. The costs of such representation may be borne by the United States as provided in Rule 14(h).

## Rule 13. Rights of Complainant in Investigation

**(a) Notice.** The complainant is entitled to written notice of the investigation as provided in Rule 4(f)(2). Upon the filing of the special committee's report to the judicial council, the complainant will be notified that the report has been filed and is before the council for decision. The Judicial Council may, in its discretion release the special committee's report to the complainant.

**(b) Opportunity to Provide Evidence.** The complainant is entitled to be interviewed by a representative of the committee. If it is believed that the complainant has substantial information to offer, the complainant will be called as a witness at a hearing.

**(c) Presentation of Argument.** The complainant may submit written argument to the special committee. In the discretion of the special committee, the complainant may be permitted to offer oral argument.

**(d) Representation by Counsel.** A complainant may submit written argument through counsel and, if permitted to offer oral argument, may do so through counsel.

## CHAPTER V. JUDICIAL COUNCIL CONSIDERATION OF RECOMMENDATIONS OF SPECIAL COMMITTEE

### Rule 14.   Action by Judicial Council

(a) **Purpose of Judicial Council Consideration.** After receipt of a report of a special committee, the judicial council will determine whether to dismiss the complaint, conclude the proceeding on the ground that corrective action has been taken or that intervening events make action unnecessary, refer the complaint to the Judicial Conference of the United States, or order corrective action.

(b) **Basis of Council Action.** Subject to the rights of the judge or magistrate judge to submit argument to the council as provided in Rule 15(a), the council may take action on the basis of the report of the special committee and the record of any hearings held. If the council finds that the report and record provide an inadequate basis for decision, it may (1) order further investigation and a further report by the special committee or (2) conduct such additional investigation as it deems appropriate.

(c) **Dismissal.** The council will dismiss a complaint if it concludes—

(1) that the claimed conduct, even if the claim is true, is not "conduct prejudicial to the effective and expeditious administration of the business of the courts" and does not indicate a mental or physical disability resulting in inability to discharge the duties of office;

(2) that the complaint is directly related to the merits of a decision or procedural ruling;

(3) that the facts on which the complaint is based have not been demonstrated; or

(4) that, under the statute, the complaint is otherwise not appropriate for consideration.

(d) **Conclusion of the Proceeding on the Basis of Corrective Action Taken.** The council will conclude the complaint proceeding if it determines that appropriate action has already been taken to remedy the problem identified in the complaint, or that intervening events make such action unnecessary.

(e) **Referral to Judicial Conference of the United States.** The judicial council may, in its discretion, refer a complaint to the Judicial Conference of the United States with the council's recommendations for action. It is required to refer such a complaint to the Judicial Conference of the United States if the council determines that a circuit judge or district judge may have engaged in conduct—

(1) that might constitute grounds for impeachment; or

(2) that, in the interest of justice, is not amenable to resolution by the judicial council.

(f) **Order of Corrective Action.** If the complaint is not disposed of under paragraphs (c) through (e) of this rule, the judicial council will take such other action as is authorized by law to assure the effective and expeditious administration of the business of the courts.

(g) **Combination of Actions.** Referral of a complaint to the Judicial Conference of the United States under paragraph (e) or to a district court under paragraph (f) of this rule will not preclude the council from simultaneously taking such other action under paragraph (f) as is within its power.

(h) **Recommendation About Fees.** If the complaint has been finally dismissed, the judicial council, upon request of the judicial officer, shall consider whether to recommend that the Director of the Administrative Office reimburse the judicial officer for attorney's fees and expenses.

(i) **Notice of Action of Judicial Council.** Council action will be by written order. Unless the council finds that, for extraordinary reasons, it would be contrary to the interests of justice, the order will be accompanied by a memorandum, which may be incorporated into one document, setting forth the factual determinations on which it is based and the reasons for the council action. The memorandum will not include the name of the complainant or of the judge or magistrate judge whose conduct was complained about. The order and the supporting memorandum will be filed and provided to the complainant, the judge or magistrate judge, and any judge entitled to receive a copy of the complaint pursuant to Rule 3(a)(2). However, if the complaint has been referred to the Judicial Conference of the United States pursuant to paragraph (e) of this rule and the council determines that disclosure would be contrary to the interests of justice, such disclosure need not be made. The complainant and the judge or magistrate judge will be notified of any right to seek review of the judicial council's decision by the Judicial Conference of the United States and of the procedure for filing a petition for review.

(j) **Public Availability of Council Action.** Materials related to the council's action will be made public at the time and in the manner set forth in Rule 17.

### Rule 15.   Procedures for Judicial Council Consideration of a Special Committee's Report

(a) **Rights of Judge or Magistrate Judge Complained About.** Within ten days after the filing of the report of a special committee, the judge or magistrate judge complained about may address a written response to all of the members of the judicial council. The judge or magistrate judge will also be given an opportunity to present oral argument to the council, personally or through counsel. The judge or magis-

trate judge may not communicate with council members individually about the matter, either orally or in writing, except as the judicial council has authorized one or more of its members to engage in such communications on its behalf.

**(b) Conduct of Additional Investigation by the Council.** If the judicial council decides to conduct additional investigation, the judge or magistrate judge complained about will be given adequate prior notice in writing of that decision and of the general scope and purpose of the additional investigation. The conduct of the investigation will be generally in accordance with the procedures set forth in Rules 10 through 13 for the conduct of an investigation by a special committee. However, if hearings are held, the council may limit testimony to avoid unnecessary repetition of testimony presented before the special committee.

**(c) Quorum and Voting.** A majority of council members eligible to participate (see Rule 18(b)) shall constitute a quorum and is required for any effective council action, except that, in accordance with 28 U.S.C. § 152(e), a decision to remove a bankruptcy judge from office requires a majority of all the members of the council.

# CHAPTER VI. MISCELLANEOUS RULES

## Rule 16. Confidentiality

**(a) General Rule.** Consideration of a complaint by the chief judge, a special committee, or the judicial council will be treated as confidential business, and information about such consideration will not be disclosed by any judge, magistrate judge, or employee of the judicial branch or any person who records or transcribes testimony except in accordance with these rules.

**(b) Files.** All files related to complaints of misconduct or disability, whether maintained by the clerk, the chief judge, members of a special committee, members of the judicial council, or staff, and whether or not the complaint was accepted for filing, will be maintained separate and apart from all other files and records, with appropriate security precautions to ensure confidentiality.

**(c) Disclosure of Memoranda of Reasons.** Memoranda supporting orders of the chief judge or the judicial council, and dissenting opinions or separate statements of members of the council, may contain such information and exhibits as the authors deem appropriate.

**(d) Availability to Judicial Conference.** If a complaint is referred under Rule 14(e) to the Judicial Conference of the United States, the clerk will provide the Judicial Conference with copies of the report of the special committee and any other documents and records that were before the judicial council at the

time of its determination. Upon request of the Judicial Conference or its Committee to Review Circuit Council Conduct and Disability Orders, in connection with their consideration of a referred complaint or a petition under 28 U.S.C. § 355 for review of a council order, the clerk will furnish any other records related to the investigation.

**(e) Availability to District Court.** If the judicial council directs the initiation of proceedings for removal of a magistrate judge under Rule 14(f)(3), the clerk will provide to the chief judge of the district court copies of the report of the special committee and any other documents and records that were before the judicial council at the time of its determination. Upon request of the chief judge of the district court, the judicial council may authorize release of any other records relating to the investigation.

**(f) Impeachment Proceedings.** The judicial council may release to the legislative branch any materials that are believed necessary to an impeachment investigation of a judge or a trial on articles of impeachment.

**(g) Consent of Judge or Magistrate Judge Complained About.** Any materials from the files may be disclosed to any person upon the written consent of both the judge or magistrate judge complained about and the chief judge of the circuit. The chief judge may require that the identity of the complainant be shielded in any materials disclosed.

**(h) Disclosure by Judicial Council in Special Circumstances.** The judicial council may authorize disclosure of information about the consideration of a complaint, including the papers, documents, and transcripts relating to the investigation, to the extent that the council concludes that such disclosure is justified by special circumstances and is not prohibited by 28 U.S.C. § 355.

**(i) Disclosure of Identity by Judge or Magistrate Judge Complained About.** Nothing in this rule will preclude the judge or magistrate judge complained about from acknowledging that such judge is the judge or magistrate judge referred to in documents made public pursuant to Rule 17.

## Rule 17. Public Availability of Decisions

**(a) General Rule.** A docket-sheet record of orders of the chief judge and the judicial council and the texts of any memoranda supporting such orders and any dissenting opinions or separate statements by members of the judicial council will be made public when final action on the complaint has been taken and is no longer subject to review.

(1) If the complaint is finally disposed of without appointment of a special committee, or if it is disposed of by council order dismissing the complaint for reasons other than mootness, or because intervening events have made action on the complaint unneces-

sary, the publicly available materials will not disclose the name of the judge or magistrate judge complained about without such judge's consent.

(2) If the complaint is finally disposed of by censure or reprimand by means of private communication, the publicly available materials will not disclose either the name of the judge or magistrate judge complained about or the text of the reprimand.

(3) If the complaint is finally disposed of by any other action taken pursuant to Rule 14(d) or (f) except dismissal because intervening events have made action on the complaint unnecessary, the text of the dispositive order will be included in the materials made public, and the name of the judge or magistrate judge will be disclosed.

(4) If the complaint is dismissed as moot at any time after the appointment of a special committee, the judicial council will determine whether the name of the judge or magistrate judge is to be disclosed.

(5) The name of the complainant will not be disclosed in materials made public under this rule unless the chief judge orders such disclosure.

(b) **Manner of Making Public.** The records referred to in paragraph (a) will be made public by placing them in a publicly accessible file in the office of the clerk of the court of appeals at the United States Courthouse, Foley Square, New York, New York 10007. The clerk will send copies of the publicly available materials to the Administrative Office of the United States Courts, Office of the General Counsel, Thurgood Marshall Federal Judiciary Building, One Columbus Circle, N.E., Washington, DC 20544, where such materials will also be available for public inspection. In cases in which memoranda appear to have precedential value, the chief judge may cause them to be published.

(c) **Decisions of Judicial Conference Standing Committee.** To the extent consistent with the policy of the Judicial Conference Committee to Review Circuit Council Conduct and Disability Orders, opinions of that committee about complaints arising from this circuit will also be made available to the public in the office of the clerk of the court of appeals.

(d) **Special Rule for Decisions of Judicial Council.** When the judicial council has taken final action on the basis of a report of a special committee, and no petition for review has been filed with the Judicial Conference within thirty days of the council's action, the materials referred to in paragraph (a) will be made public in accordance with this rule as if there were no further right of review.

(e) **Complaints Referred to the Judicial Conference of the United States.** If a complaint is referred to the Judicial Conference of the United States pursuant to Rule 14(e), materials relating to the complaint will be made public only as may be ordered by the Judicial Conference.

## Rule 18.   Disqualification

(a) **Complainant.** If the complaint is filed by a judge, that judge will be disqualified from participation in any consideration of the complaint except to the extent that these rules provide for participation by a complainant. If the complaint is filed by a judge, or identified by the chief judge pursuant to 28 U.S.C. § 351(a), that judge will be disqualified from participation in any consideration of the complaint except to the extent that these rules provide for participation by a complainant.

(b) **Judge Complained About.** A judge whose conduct is the subject of a complaint will be disqualified from participating in any consideration of the complaint except to the extent that these rules provide for participation by a judge or magistrate judge who is complained about. This subsection shall not apply where a complainant files complaints against a majority of the members of the judicial council, in which event, the council members, including those complained against, may refer the complaints, with or without a recommendation for appropriate action, to the Judicial Conference of the United States or to the judicial council of another circuit, or may take other appropriate action, including disposition of the complaints on their merits.

(c) **Member of Special Committee Not Disqualified.** A member of the judicial council who is appointed to a special committee will not be disqualified from participating in council consideration of the committee's report.

(d) **Judge or Magistrate Judge Under Investigation.** Upon appointment of a special committee, the judge or magistrate judge complained about will automatically be disqualified from serving on (1) any special committee appointed under Rule 4(e), (2) the judicial council of the circuit, (3) the Judicial Conference of the United States, and (4) the Committee to Review Circuit Council Conduct and Disability Orders of the Judicial Conference of the United States. The disqualification will continue until all proceedings regarding the complaint are finally terminated, with no further right of review. The proceedings will be deemed terminated thirty days after the final action of the judicial council if no petition for review has at that time been filed with the Judicial Conference.

(e) **Substitute for Chief Judge.** If the chief judge of the circuit is disqualified or otherwise unable to participate in consideration of the complaint, the duties and responsibilities of the chief judge under these rules will be assigned to the circuit judge eligible to become the next chief judge of the circuit.

## Rule 19.   Withdrawal of Complaints and Petitions for Review

(a) **Complaint Pending Before Chief Judge.** A complaint that is before the chief judge for a decision

under Rule 4 may be withdrawn by the complainant with the consent of the chief judge.

**(b) Complaint Pending Before Special Committee or Judicial Council.** After a complaint has been referred to a special committee for investigation, the complaint may be withdrawn by the complainant only with the consent of both (1) the judge or magistrate judge complained about and (2) the special committee (before its report has been filed) or the judicial council.

**(c) Petition for Review of Chief Judge's Disposition.** A petition to the judicial council for review of the chief judge's disposition of a complaint may be withdrawn by the petitioner at any time before the judicial council acts on the petition.

## Rule 19A. Abuse of the Complaint Procedure

If a complainant files vexatious, harassing, or scurrilous complaints, or otherwise abuses the complaint procedure, the council, after affording the complainant an opportunity to respond in writing, may restrict or impose conditions upon the complainant's use of the complaint procedure. Any restrictions or conditions imposed upon a complainant shall be reconsidered by the council periodically.

## Rule 20. Availability of Other Procedures

The availability of the complaint procedure under these rules and 28 U.S.C. § 351, et seq., will not preclude the chief judge of the circuit or the judicial council of the circuit from considering any information that may come to their attention suggesting that a judge or magistrate judge has engaged in conduct prejudicial to the effective and expeditious administra-

tion of the business of the courts or is unable to discharge all the duties of office by reason of disability.

## Rule 21. Availability of Rules and Forms

These rules and copies of the complaint form prescribed by Rule 2 will be available without charge in the office of the clerk of the court of appeals, United States Courthouse, Foley Square, New York, New York 10007, and in each office of the clerk of a district court or bankruptcy court within this circuit.

## Rule 21A. No Implication of Constitutionality

The adoption of these rules shall not be construed as indicating any views with respect to the constitutionality of 28 U.S.C. § 351, et seq., or any action taken hereunder.

## Rule 22. Effective Date

These rules apply to complaints filed on or after November 2, 2002. The handling of complaints filed before that date will be governed by the rules previously in effect.

## Rule 23. Advisory Committee

The advisory committee appointed by the Court of Appeals for the Second Circuit for the study of rules of practice and internal operating procedures shall also constitute the advisory committee for the study of these rules, as provided by 28 U.S.C. § 2077(b), and shall make any appropriate recommendations to the circuit judicial council concerning these rules.

## APPENDIX: COMPLAINT FORM

JUDICIAL COUNCIL OF THE SECOND CIRCUIT
COMPLAINT AGAINST JUDICIAL OFFICER
UNDER 28 U.S.C. § 351, et seq.

INSTRUCTIONS:

(a) All questions on this form must be answered.

(b) A separate complaint form must be filled out for each judicial officer complained against.

(c) Submit the correct number of copies of this form and the statement of facts. For a complaint against:

a court of appeals judge—original and 3 copies

a district court judge or magistrate judge—original and 4 copies

a bankruptcy judge—original and 5 copies

(For further information see Rule 2(e)).

(d) Service on the judicial officer will be made by the Clerk's office. (For further information See Rule 3(a)(1)).

(e) Mail this form, the statement of facts and the appropriate number of copies to the Clerk, United States Court of Appeals, Thurgood Marshall U.S. Courthouse, 40 Foley Square, New York, NY 10007.

1. Complainant's Name:

   _____

   Address:

   _____

   _____

   Daytime Telephone No. (include area code): _____

2. Judge or magistrate judge complained about:
   Name: _____
   Court: _____

3. Does this complaint concern the behavior of the judge or magistrate judge in a particular lawsuit or lawsuits?
   [ ] Yes        [ ] No
   If "yes," give the following information about each lawsuit (use the reverse side if there is more than one):
   Court: _____
   Docket number: _____
   Docket numbers of any appeals to the Second Circuit:

   _____

   Did a lawyer represent you?
   [ ] Yes        [ ] No
   If "yes" give the name, address, and telephone number of your lawyer:

4. Have you previously filed any complaints of judicial misconduct or disability against *any* judge or magistrate judge?
   [ ] Yes        [ ] No
   If "Yes," give the docket number of each complaint.

5. You should attach a statement of facts on which your complaint is based, see Rule 2(b), and

EITHER

   (1) check the box and sign the form. You do not need a notary public if you check this box.

   [ ] I declare under penalty of perjury that:

   (i) I have read Rules 1 and 2 of the Rules of the Judicial Council of the Second Circuit Governing Complaints of Judicial Misconduct or Disability, and

(ii) The statements made in this complaint and attached statement of facts are true and correct to the best of my knowledge.

_____
(signature)

Executed on _____
(date)

<u>OR</u>

(2) check the box below and sign this form in the presence of a notary public;

[   ] I swear (affirm) that—

(i) I have read Rules 1 and 2 of the Rules of the Judicial Council of the Second Circuit Governing Complaints of Judicial Misconduct or Disability, and

(ii) The statements made in this complaint and attached statement of facts are true and correct to the best of my knowledge.

_____
(signature)

Executed on _____
(date)

Sworn and subscribed to
before me this ____
day of _____ 200__.

_____
(Notary Public)
My commission expires: _____

# PART F. GUIDELINES OF THE COURT OF APPEALS FOR THE SECOND CIRCUIT CONCERNING CAMERAS IN THE COURTROOM

Pursuant to a resolution of the Judicial Conference of the United States adopted on March 12, 1996, authorizing each court of appeals to "decide for itself whether to permit the taking of photographs and radio and television coverage of appellate arguments, subject to any restrictions in statutes, national and local rules, and such guidelines as the Judicial Conference may adopt," the Court hereby adopts the following Guidelines:

**1. Exercise of Local Option.** From the date of these Guidelines until further order of this Court, proceedings of the Court conducted in open court may be covered by the media using a television camera, sound recording equipment, and a still camera (hereafter referred to as "camera coverage"), subject to these Guidelines.

**2. Applicable Guidelines.** Camera coverage must be conducted in conformity with applicable statutes, national rules, any guidelines that may be issued by the U.S. Judicial Conference, and these Guidelines of the Second Circuit Court of Appeals.

**3. Eligible Proceedings.** Camera coverage is allowed for all proceedings conducted in open court, except for criminal matters. *See* Fed.R.Crim.P. 53, 54(a). For purposes of these Guidelines, "criminal matters" include not only direct appeals of criminal convictions but also any appeal, motion, or petition challenging a ruling made in connection with a criminal case (such as bail motions or appeals from the dismissal of an indictment) and any appeal from a ruling concerning a post-conviction remedy (such as a habeas corpus petition). Camera coverage is not permitted for pro se matters, whether criminal or civil. On any day when camera coverage is to occur, the Clerk's Office will endeavor to schedule civil and non-pro se matters ahead of criminal and pro se matters. Camera coverage operators will remain seated, away from their equipment, and their equipment will be turned off, during criminal and pro se proceedings.

**4. News Media Pooling.** Camera coverage will be permitted by any person or entity regularly engaged in the gathering and dissemination of news (hereinafter "news media"). If coverage is sought by more than one person or entity, a pool system must be used (one for still photography and one for radio and television). It will be the responsibility of the news media to resolve any disputes among them as to which personnel will operate equipment in the courtroom. In the absence of an agreement, camera coverage will not be permitted for that day's proceedings. The television pictures, audio signals, and still photographs of court proceedings made by pool personnel must be made available to any news media requesting them upon payment of a reasonable fee to the employer of the pool personnel to share the costs of the pool personnel.

**5. Educational Institutions.** The Court may also authorize the coverage of court proceedings and access to pooled coverage by educational institutions.

**6. Prior Notification Requirement.** News media interested in camera coverage of any court proceeding must notify the Court's calendar clerk no later than noon two days preceding the day of the proceeding to be covered (*i.e.*, notification must be made by noon on Tuesday to cover a proceeding on Thursday, or by noon Friday for the following Monday). A calendar of the following week's cases is made public by the Court each Thursday. For good cause shown, relief from this notification requirement may be granted by the presiding judge of a panel.

**7. Discretion of Panel.** The panel assigned to hear oral argument will retain the authority, in its sole discretion, to prohibit camera coverage of any proceeding, and will normally exercise this authority upon the request of any member of the panel.

**8. Technical Restrictions.** Only two television cameras and one still camera will be permitted in the courtroom. The television cameras and the still camera must each be mounted on a tripod and remain at a fixed location along a side wall of the courtroom throughout the proceeding. The still camera must either be capable of silent operation (shutter and film advance) or be enclosed in a sound-muffling device (so-called "blimp"). No artificial lighting is permitted. An unobtrusive microphone may be mounted at the attorney's lectern and in front of each judge. A sound technician may be present in the courtroom with unobtrusive sound-mixing equipment. The Clerk's Office will designate a location for a device outside the courtroom to enable news media to obtain "feeds" of video and audio signals. All camera coverage equipment must be set up prior to the opening of a day's proceedings and may not be removed until after the conclusion of the day's proceedings. If done unobtrusively, film used by the still camera operator and film or tape used by the video camera operator may be removed from the courtroom at the conclusion of the oral argument of a particular case. Operators of camera coverage equipment in the courtroom will wear business attire.

When operational, the Court's video-conferencing equipment may be used for purposes of camera coverage.

**9. Authority of Presiding Judge.** The presiding judge of the panel may direct the cessation of camera

coverage or the removal of camera coverage personnel from the courtroom in the event of noncompliance with these Guidelines.

**10. Personnel to Contact.** The calendar clerk is Chandella Gaillard (or an alternate designated in her absence). She can be reached at (212) 791–1067. [Adopted effective March 27, 1996.]

# SELECTED ORDERS

## ORDER. IN THE MATTER OF THE TERMINATION OF THE BANKRUPTCY APPELLATE PANEL SERVICE OF THE SECOND JUDICIAL CIRCUIT

Pursuant to 28 U.S.C. § 158(b)(1)(C) as amended by the Bankruptcy Reform Act of 1994, the Judicial Council of the Second Circuit has determined there are insufficient judicial resources available in the Second Circuit justifying the continuation of the Bankruptcy Appellate Panel Service in the Second Circuit; it is hereby

**ORDERED** that the Bankruptcy Appellate Panel Service of the Second Circuit is terminated and that appeals of final judgments, orders and decrees and of interlocutory orders and decrees of bankruptcy judges entered in cases and proceedings previously referred to the Bankruptcy Appellate Panel and its appointed judges shall henceforth be referred to and heard by the respective United States District Courts in the Second Circuit; and it is hereby

**ORDERED** that the Bankruptcy Appellate Panel Service of the Second Circuit and its authority to hear and determine appeals from judgments, orders and decrees entered by bankruptcy judges from districts within the Second Circuit shall be terminated effective Friday, June 30, 2000.

Dated: June 30, 2000.

# SELECTED NOTICES

## PRIVACY NOTICE

In compliance with the policy of the Judicial Conference of the United States, and the E-Government Act of 2002, and in order to promote electronic access to case files while also protecting personal privacy and other legitimate interests, parties shall refrain from including, or shall partially redact where inclusion is necessary, the following personal data identifiers from all pleadings filed with the court, including exhibits thereto, whether filed electronically or in paper, unless otherwise ordered by the Court.

**a. Social Security Numbers.** If an individual's Social Security number must be included in a pleading, only the last four digits of that number should be used.

**b. Names of Minor Children.** If the involvement of a minor child must be mentioned, only the initials of that child should be used.

**c. Dates of Birth.** If an individual's date of birth must be included in a pleading, only the year should be used.

**d. Financial Account Numbers.** If financial account numbers are relevant, only the last four digits of these numbers should be used.

In compliance with the E–Government Act of 2002, a party wishing to file a document containing the personal data identifiers listed above may

a. file an unredacted version of the document under seal, or

b. file a reference list under seal. The reference list shall contain the complete personal data identifier(s) and the redacted identifier(s) used in its(their) place in the filing. All references in the case to the redacted identifiers included in the reference list will be construed to refer to the corresponding complete personal data identifier. The reference list must be filed under seal, and may be amended as of right.

The unredacted version of the document or the reference list document shall be retained by the court as part of the record. The court may, however, still require the party to file a redacted copy for the public file.

*The responsibility for redacting these personal identifiers rests solely with counsel and the parties. The Clerk will not review each pleading for compliance with this rule.*

# INDEX TO FEDERAL RULES OF APPELLATE PROCEDURE AND LOCAL RULES OF THE SECOND CIRCUIT

### Abbreviations

FRAP . . . . . . . . . . . . . . . . . . . . . . . . . . . . . Federal Rules of Appellate Procedure
Loc.Rule . . . . . . . . . . . . . . . . . . . . . . . . . . . Local Rules of Second Circuit
Cir.Appendix . . . . . . . . . . . . . . . . . . . . . . . Appendix to Local Rules

\*

# RULES OF THE BANKRUPTCY APPELLATE PANEL SERVICE OF THE SECOND CIRCUIT

## Adopted June 14, 1996

## Terminated Effective June 30, 2000

---

---

## ORDER. IN THE MATTER OF THE TERMINATION OF THE BANKRUPTCY APPELLATE PANEL SERVICE OF THE SECOND JUDICIAL CIRCUIT

Pursuant to 28 U.S.C. § 158(b)(1)(C) as amended by the Bankruptcy Reform Act of 1994, the Judicial Council of the Second Circuit has determined there are insufficient judicial resources available in the Second Circuit justifying the continuation of the Bankruptcy Appellate Panel Service in the Second Circuit; it is hereby

**ORDERED** that the Bankruptcy Appellate Panel Service of the Second Circuit is terminated and that appeals of final judgments, orders and decrees and of interlocutory orders and decrees of bankruptcy judges entered in cases and proceedings previously referred to the Bankruptcy Appellate Panel and its appointed judges shall henceforth be referred to and heard by the respective United States District Courts in the Second Circuit; and it is hereby

**ORDERED** that the Bankruptcy Appellate Panel Service of the Second Circuit and its authority to hear and determine appeals from judgments, orders and decrees entered by bankruptcy judges from districts within the Second Circuit shall be terminated effective Friday, June 30, 2000.

Dated: June 30, 2000.

*

# RULES OF THE UNITED STATES DISTRICT COURT FOR THE DISTRICT OF CONNECTICUT

## Effective January 1, 2003

### Including Amendments Received Through October 15, 2007

---

*Research Note*

*These rules may be searched electronically on WESTLAW in the CT-RULES database; updates to these rules may be found on WESTLAW in CT–ORDERS or CT–RULESUPDATES. For search tips, and a detailed summary of database content, consult the WESTLAW Scope Screen of each database.*

---

## Table of Rules

Standing Order in Civil RICO Cases.
Standing Order in Removed Cases.
Order Re Disclosure Statement.

### CIVIL STANDING ORDERS

Standing Order on Scheduling in Civil Cases.
Standing Order Regarding Trial Memoranda in Civil Cases.
Standing Order in Civil RICO Cases.
Standing Order in Removed Cases.

### CIVIL MISCELLANEOUS NOTICES AND ORDERS

Notice to Counsel Re Local Rule 5(a).
Notice Re Planning Conference and Report.
Order Re: Disclosure Statement.
Cellular Telephone Policy for the District of Connecticut.

### LOCAL RULES FOR MAGISTRATE JUDGES

### LOCAL RULES OF CRIMINAL PROCEDURE

APPENDIX. STANDING ORDER ON DISCOVERY

**CIVIL JUSTICE EXPENSE AND
DELAY REDUCTION PLAN**

**ELECTRONIC CASE FILING**

# LOCAL RULES OF CIVIL PROCEDURE

## RULE 1. SCOPE OF RULES

(a) **Title and Citation.** These rules shall be known as the Local Civil Rules of the United States District Court for the District of Connecticut. They may be cited as D. Conn. L. Civ. R.

(b) **Effective Date.** These rules shall govern the conduct of all civil actions pending in the United States District Court for the District of Connecticut on or after May 1, 1985.

(c) **Definitions.** As used herein, "Judge" shall mean a District Judge of this Court or a visiting Circuit or District Judge assigned to duties in this Court or a Magistrate Judge of this Court performing duties authorized or by the District Judges of this Court. As used herein, "Clerk" shall mean the Clerk of the Court or his or her deputies and assistants authorized by him or her to perform the functions specified herein.

[Effective January 1, 2003; amended effective August 1, 2003.]

## RULE 2. (RESERVED)

## RULE 3. COMMENCEMENT OF ACTION

(a) **Complaint.**

1. The complaint may be filed with the Clerk at Bridgeport, Hartford, or New Haven. All other papers shall be filed at the seat of Court where the docket is maintained for the case involved.

2. All civil complaints submitted to the Clerk for filing shall be accompanied by a summons and a Civil Cover Sheet, Form JS 44a or JS 44c. Complaints not accompanied by a summons and these forms may be rejected for filing by the Clerk. Upon request the Clerk's office will furnish these forms. Persons filing civil complaints who are in custody at the time of filing, and persons filing pro se, are exempted from the requirements of this paragraph. A Civil Cover Sheet indicating that a jury trial is desired shall not suffice as a demand for jury trial.

(b) **Place of Filing; Number of Copies.** Petitions for Writs of Habeas Corpus and motions filed pursuant Title 28, U.S. Code Section 2255 shall be addressed to the Court and filed with the Clerk at Bridgeport, New Haven or Hartford. Two copies of each petition, motion or affidavit must be filed with the original.

(c) **Statutory Fee.** When the petitioner or movant has sufficient funds, his or her petition for Writ of Habeas Corpus or motion must be accompanied by the statutory fee.

(d) **In Forma Pauperis Motion.** When a petition for Writ of Habeas Corpus or motion is filed without

payment of the statutory fee, the required in forma pauperis motion and affidavit must be completed and filed.

[Effective January 1, 2003.]

## RULE 4. CIVIL PROCESS

**(a) Issue and Service.** All civil process, including writs of summons, shall be prepared by the party who seeks such process, and, on the application of a party to the Clerk, shall issue out of the Court under its seal.

**(b) Service Copies.** Each party filing a new complaint, third-party complaint or amended complaint, shall file sufficient copies of the complaint to supply one (original impression) for the Court, one for each private party to be served, and five for the United States or an officer or agency thereof, if a party. The Clerk shall sign and seal the appropriate form of the summons to accompany the service copies of the complaint.

**(c) Attachments and Pre–Judgment Remedies.** In addition to remedies otherwise provided by federal law, a party may secure a pre-judgment remedy, as permitted by, and in accordance with, the law of the State of Connecticut. The complaint shall be signed and filed with the Clerk. A date for the hearing shall be fixed by the Court. Upon written request to the Clerk, public inspection and service of the complaint will be withheld until the order for the hearing has been signed. A release or reduction of attachment shall be issued by the Clerk (1) by request of the attaching party; (2) by stipulation of the attaching party and the person whose property is attached; or (3) by order of the Court. It shall be the duty of counsel in all cases to comply with the requirements of the General Statutes of Connecticut regarding filing certificates of discharge of attachments and lis pendens. In appropriate cases, upon request, the Clerk may issue such certificates in the form prescribed by the General Statutes of Connecticut.

[Effective January 1, 2003.]

## RULE 5. SERVING AND FILING PLEADINGS AND OTHER PAPERS

**(a) E-Filing.** In accordance with the Electronic Filing Policies and Procedures incorporated in these Rules, filing in most cases in this District will be by electronic filing. By order of the Court, upon a showing of good cause, a party may be excused from electronic filing.

**(b) Appearance.** Counsel entering a case after the filing of the complaint, whether on behalf of the plaintiff or the defendant, shall file with the Clerk and serve on all parties or their counsel a notice of appearance. The appearance shall include counsel's name, address, zip code, federal bar number, telephone number, fax number and e-mail address, if available.

**(c) Proof of Service.** Proof of service may be made by written acknowledgment of service by the party served, by a certificate of counsel for the party filing the pleading or papers, by a certificate of the pro se party filing the pleading or papers, or by affidavit of the person making the service. Where proof of service is made by certificate or by affidavit, the certificate or affidavit shall list the name and address of each person served or otherwise comply with the Electronic Filing Policies and Procedures.

**(d) United States as a Party.** Except for cases subject to the Electronic Filing Policies and Procedures, in cases in which the United States is a party, three copies of each pleading or other paper filed shall be served upon the United States Attorney or his or her designee in addition to the copies of the summons and complaint required by Rules 4(d)(4) and 4(d)(5), Fed. R. Civ. P.

**(e) Sealed Documents.**

1. Counsel seeking to file a document under seal shall file a redacted version of the document to be sealed, a motion to seal and shall attach to the motion the unredacted document to be sealed. The unredacted document shall be submitted in an unsealed envelope, bearing the caption of the case, the case number, and the caption of the document to be sealed. The Clerk of the Court shall file-stamp and docket only the redacted document and the motion to seal and shall forward the redacted document, the motion to seal, and the unredacted document to be sealed to the Court for consideration. If ordered sealed by the Court, the Clerk shall seal the unredacted document in the envelope provided by counsel, and shall note the date of the sealing order on the envelope and docket sheet. Upon submission by the party seeking a sealing order, the sealing envelope and its contents shall be treated as a sealed document until otherwise directed by the Court. If the Court denies the motion to seal, the unredacted document will be docketed by the Clerk of the Court. In the alternative, counsel can seek advance permission of the Court to file a document under seal without submitting the document to be sealed.

2. Counsel filing documents which are, or may be claimed to be, subject to any protective or impounding order previously entered shall file with the documents, and serve on all parties, a notice that the documents are, or are claimed to be, subject to such order or orders, identifying the particular order or orders by date, and shall submit such documents to the Clerk under seal.

3. Any file or document ordered sealed by the Court upon motion of the parties, by stipulation or by the Court, sua sponte, shall remain sealed pending further order of this Court, or any Court sitting in review. Upon final determination of the action, as

defined in Rule 83.6(c) of the Local Rules of Civil Procedure, counsel shall have ninety (90) days to file a motion pursuant to Rule 83.6(c) for the return of the sealed documents. Any sealed document thereafter remaining may be destroyed by the Clerk pursuant to Rule 83.6(c) or retired by the Clerk with other parts of the file to the Federal Records Center, whereupon they shall be automatically unsealed without notice to counsel.

**(f) Filing of Discovery Material.**

1. Pursuant to Fed. R. Civ. P. 5(d), expert witness reports, computations of damages, depositions, notices of deposition, interrogatories, requests for documents, requests for admissions, and answers and responses shall not be filed with the Clerk's Office except by order of the Court.

2. A party seeking relief under any of the Federal Rules of Civil Procedure shall file only that portion of the deposition, interrogatory, request for documents or request for admissions that is the subject of the dispute.

3. When discovery material not on file is needed for consideration of a motion or for an appeal, upon application to or order of the Court or by stipulation of counsel, the necessary portion of discovery material shall be filed with the Clerk.

**(g) Service by Facsimile Copy.** Copies of pleadings may be served on counsel through use of a facsimile machine, provided that service of a typewritten copy of the identical pleading is made simultaneously by regular mail. Copies of pleadings may not be filed with the Clerk's Office through the use of a facsimile machine or other electronic means.

**(h) Three Judge Court**. In three-judge court cases, the Clerk shall not accept any complaints, petitions, pleadings, briefs or other papers unless the original is accompanied by three copies thereof for the use of the Court. Counsel filing such papers, after service of process has been effected, shall serve one copy thereof on each other party.

[Effective January 1, 2003; amended effective May 1, 2005; amended January 19, 2007, effective January 1, 2007, *nunc pro tunc.*]

# RULE 6. COMPUTATION OF TIME

Except as otherwise specified in these Local Rules, Fed. R. Civ. P. 6 shall govern the computation of time limitations for purposes of computing any period of time prescribed or allowed by the Federal Rules of Civil Procedure, the Local Rules of this Court, any order of this Court, or any applicable statute.

[Effective January 1, 2003.]

# RULE 7. MOTION PROCEDURES

## (a) Procedures.

1. Any motion involving disputed issues of law shall be accompanied by a written memorandum of law and shall indicate in the lower margin of the motion whether oral argument is requested. Failure to submit a memorandum may be deemed sufficient cause to deny the motion. Unless otherwise ordered by the Court, all memoranda in opposition to any motion shall be filed within twenty-one (21) days of the filing of the motion, and shall indicate in the lower margin of the first page of such memorandum whether oral argument is requested. Failure to submit a memorandum in opposition to a motion may be deemed sufficient cause to grant the motion, except where the pleadings provide sufficient grounds to deny the motion. Nothing in this Rule shall require the Judge ruling on the motion to review portions of the record in response to a motion, where the moving papers do not make specific reference to such portions of the record. Notwithstanding that a request for oral argument has been made, the Judge may, in his or her discretion, deny such request. To expedite a decision or for other good cause, the Court may, on notice to all parties, rule on a motion before expiration of the 21–day period ordinarily permitted for filing opposition papers.

2. Except by permission of the Court, briefs or memoranda shall not exceed forty (40) 8 1/2″ by 11″ pages of double spaced standard typographical print, exclusive of pages containing a table of contents, table of statutes, rules or the like. The original of all motions or briefs shall be filed with the Clerk at the seat of Court where the Judge sits.

3. For good cause shown in the motion, a party may request expedited consideration of the motion by the Court by designating the motion as one seeking "emergency" relief.

## (b) Motions for Extensions of Time.

1. Unless otherwise directed by a particular Judge with respect to cases on his or her docket, the Clerk is empowered to grant initial motions for extensions of time, not to exceed 30 days, in civil cases with regard to the following time limitations:

    (a) the date for filing an answer or motion addressed to the complaint, counterclaim or third party complaint; and

    (b) the date for serving responses to discovery requests.

2. All other motions for extensions of time must be decided by a Judge and will not be granted except for good cause. The good cause standard requires a particularized showing that the time limitation in question cannot reasonably be met despite the diligence of the party seeking the extension.

3. All motions for extensions of time, whether for consideration by the Clerk or a Judge, shall include a statement of the moving counsel that (1) he or she has inquired of opposing counsel and there is agreement or objection to the motion, or that (2) despite diligent effort, he or she cannot ascertain opposing counsel's position. All such motions shall also indicate the number of motions for extension of time that have been filed by the moving party with respect to the same limitation. The motion may be granted ex parte notwithstanding a report of objection by opposing counsel. Opposing counsel may move within 5 days of an order granting a motion for extension of time to have the Court set aside the order for good cause. Agreement of counsel as to any extension of time does not of itself extend any time limitation or provide good cause for failing to comply with a deadline established by the federal rules of civil procedure, these rules or the Court.

**(c) Motions for Reconsideration.**

1. Motions for reconsideration shall be filed and served within ten (10) days of the filing of the decision or order from which such relief is sought, and shall be accompanied by a memorandum setting forth concisely the matters or controlling decisions which counsel believes the Court overlooked in the initial decision or order.

2. In all other respects, motions for reconsideration shall proceed in accordance with Rule 7(a)1 of these Local Rules.

**(d) Reply Briefs.** Reply briefs are not required and the absence of a reply brief will not prejudice the moving party. Any reply brief must be filed within 10 days of the filing of the responsive brief to which reply is being made, as computed under Fed. R. Civ. P. 6. A reply brief may not exceed 10 pages, must be strictly confined to a discussion of matters raised by the responsive brief and must contain references to the pages of the responsive brief to which reply is being made.

**(e) Withdrawal of Appearances.** Withdrawal of appearances may be accomplished only by leave of Court on motion duly noticed, and normally shall not be granted except upon a showing that other counsel has appeared or that the party has elected to proceed pro se, and that the party whose counsel seeks to withdraw has received actual notice by personal service or by certified mail of the motion to withdraw. In cases where the party has failed to engage other counsel or file a pro se appearance, where good cause exists for permitting the withdrawal by the appearing counsel, the Court may grant the motion to withdraw the appearance after notice to the party that failure to either engage successor counsel or file a pro se appearance will result in the granting of the motion to withdraw and may result in a dismissal or default being entered against the party.

**(f) Motions to Amend Pleadings.** Any motion to amend a party's pleading under Fed.R.Civ.P. 15(a) that requires leave of court shall include a statement of the moving counsel that: (1) he or she has inquired of opposing counsel and there is agreement or objection to the motion; or (2) despite diligent effort, he or she cannot ascertain opposing counsel's position.

[Effective January 1, 2003; amended January 19, 2007, effective January 1, 2007, nunc pro tunc; amended effective August 1, 2007.]

# RULE 8.   RULES OF PLEADING

**(a) Statement of the Claim.** A petition for writ of habeas corpus or motion filed pursuant to Title 28, U.S.C., § 2255 shall contain a short and plain statement of the claim made and the relief sought. A petition or motion not in compliance with this Rule shall be subject to dismissal without prejudice by the Court on its own motion.

**(b) Petitions Shall be Legible.** Petitions for writs of habeas corpus and motions filed pursuant to Title 28, U.S. Code § 2255, shall be typewritten or in legible handwriting. Such petitions and motions shall be on forms approved by the Court and supplied by the Clerk.

[Effective January 1, 2003.]

# RULE 9.   (RESERVED)

# RULE 10.   PREPARATION OF PLEADINGS

**(a) Preparation of Pleadings.** All pleadings must be prepared in conformity with the Federal Rules of Civil Procedure. Each such pleading shall be punched with two holes, 2–3/4″ apart, each centered 7/16″ from the upper edge, one being 2–7/8″ from the left edge and the other being 2–7/8″ from the right edge, each being 1/4″ in diameter. Pleadings shall be double-spaced, on 8–1/2″ by 11″ paper with a left margin of at least 1″ free from all typewritten or printed material, shall have page numbers in the bottom margin of each page after page 1, and shall have legibly typed, printed or stamped directly beneath the signature the name of the counsel or party who executed such document, the office address, telephone number, fax number and e-mail address, if available. The federal bar number assigned to counsel should appear beneath his/her signature. The complete docket number, including the initials of the Judge to whom the case has been assigned, shall be typed on each pleading. The date of each pleading shall be included in the case caption.

[Effective January 1, 2003.]

# RULE 11.   SANCTIONS

**(a) Motion for Attorneys' Fees and /or Sanctions.** Motions for attorneys' fees or sanctions shall be filed with the Clerk and served on opposing parties within 30 days of the entry of judgment. Any motions not complying with this rule shall be denied.

[Effective January 1, 2003.]

## RULE 12–RULE 15. (RESERVED)

## RULE 16. STATUS AND SETTLEMENT CONFERENCES AND ADR

### (a) Status Conferences.

1. Pursuant to Fed. R. Civ. P. 16 and 26(f) and Local Rule 53, one or more status conferences may be scheduled before a Judge or a parajudicial officer or special master designated by the presiding Judge. Status conferences may be held in person or by telephone.

**(b) Scheduling Orders.** Within 90 days after the appearance of any defendant, the Court, after considering the parties' proposed case management plan under Fed. R. Civ. P. 26(f) and Local Rule 26(f), shall enter a scheduling order that limits the time:

1. to join other parties and to amend the pleadings;

2. to complete discovery;

3. to file dispositive motions; and

4. to file a joint trial memorandum.

The scheduling order will include a date by which the case will be deemed ready for trial and may also include dates for further status conferences, settlement conferences and other matters appropriate in the circumstances of the particular case. The scheduling order may include provisions for (a) disclosure or discovery of electronically stored information and (b) any agreed provisions for assertion of privilege over or protection of trial-preparation material, after production.

The schedule established by the Court for completing discovery, filing dispositive motions and filing a joint trial memorandum shall not be modified except by further order of the Court on a showing of good cause. The good cause standard requires a particularized showing that the schedule cannot reasonably be met, despite the diligence of the party seeking the modification, for reasons that were not reasonably foreseeable when the parties submitted their proposed case management plan. The trial ready date will not be postponed at the request of a party except to prevent manifest injustice.

This Rule does not require the entry of such a tailored scheduling order in the following categories of cases: pro se prisoner cases; habeas corpus proceedings; appeals from decisions of administrative agencies, including social security disability appeals; recovery of defaulted student loans, recovery of overpayment of veterans' benefits, forfeiture actions, petitions to quash Internal Revenue Service summons, appeals from Bankruptcy Court orders, proceedings to compel arbitration or to confirm or set aside arbitration awards and Freedom of Information Act cases.

### (c) Settlement Conferences.

1. In accordance with Fed. R. Civ. P. 16, one or more conferences may be held for the purpose of discussing possibilities for settlement of the case. A mandatory settlement conference will be held at or shortly after the close of discovery. Counsel have a duty to discuss the possibility of settlement during the planning conference required by Fed. R. Civ. P. 26(f) and Local Rule 16 and may request that an early settlement conference be conducted before the parties undertake significant discovery or motion practice.

2. In a case that will be tried to a jury, such conferences shall be held with the presiding Judge, a Magistrate Judge, or a parajudicial officer or special master designated by the presiding Judge. In a case that will be tried to the Court, such conferences shall be held with a Judge other than the one to whom it has been assigned, a Magistrate Judge, or parajudicial officer or special master designated by the presiding Judge.

3. Counsel shall attend any settlement conference fully authorized to make a final demand or offer. Counsel on both sides must be authorized to act promptly on any proposed settlement. The judicial officer, parajudicial officer, or special master before whom a settlement conference is to be held may require that counsel be accompanied by the person or persons authorized and competent to accept or reject any settlement proposal.

**(d) Pretrial Order.** The Court may make an order reciting the action taken at any status or settlement conference and any amendments allowed to the pleadings, any agreements, concessions or admissions made by any party, and limiting the issues for trial to those not thereby disposed of. A pretrial order may be prepared by the Court and sent to counsel for each party subsequent to the conference, or the Court may require counsel for one of the parties to prepare a proposed written order for consideration and entry by the Court. The order shall become part of the record and shall be binding on the parties, unless modified by the Court at or before the trial so as to prevent manifest injustice.

**(e) Trial Briefs.** The Court may require the parties or any of them within such time as it directs to serve and file a trial brief as to any doubtful points of law which may arise at the trial.

**(f) Failure of Compliance.** For failure to appear at a conference or to participate therein, or for failure to comply with the terms of this Rule or any orders issued pursuant to this Rule, the Court in its discretion may impose such sanctions as are authorized by law, including without limitation an order that the case be placed at the bottom of the trial list, an order with respect to the imposition on the party or, where appropriate, on counsel personally, of costs and counsel fees, or such other order with respect to the

continued prosecution or defense of the action as is just and proper.

**(g) Sanctions Against Counsel.**

(1) It shall be the duty of counsel to promote the just, speedy and inexpensive determination of every action. The Court may impose sanctions directly against counsel who disobey an order of the Court or intentionally obstruct the effective and efficient administration of justice.

(2) *Failure to Pay Costs or Sanctions.* The Clerk shall not accept for filing any papers from an attorney or pro se litigant against whom a final order of monetary sanctions has been imposed until the sanctions have been paid in full. Pending payment, such attorney or pro se litigant also may be barred from appearing in court. An order imposing monetary sanctions becomes final for the purposes of this local rule when the Court of Appeals issues its mandate or the time for filing an appeal expires.

**(h) Alternative Dispute Resolution (ADR).**

1. In addition to existing ADR programs (such as Local Rule 53's Special Masters Program) and those promulgated by individual judges (e.g., Parajudicials Program), a case may be referred for voluntary ADR at any stage of the litigation deemed appropriate by the parties and the judge to whom the particular case has been assigned.

2. Before a case is referred to voluntary ADR, the parties must agree upon, subject to the approval of the judge:

(a) The form of the ADR process (e.g., mediation, arbitration, summary jury trial, minitrial, etc.);

(b) The scope of the ADR process (e.g., settlement of all or specified issues, resolution of discovery schedules or disputes, narrowing of issues, etc.);

(c) The ADR provider (e.g., a court-annexed ADR project; a profit or not-for-profit private ADR organization; or any qualified person or panel selected by the parties);

(d) The effect of the ADR process (e.g., binding or nonbinding).

3. When agreement between the parties and the judge for a voluntary ADR referral has been reached, the parties shall file jointly for the judge's endorsement a "Stipulation for Reference to ADR." The Stipulation, subject to the judge's approval, shall specify:

(a) The form of ADR procedure and the name of the ADR provider agreed upon;

(b) The judicial proceedings, if any, to be stayed pending ADR (e.g., discovery matters, filing of motions, trial, etc.);

(c) The procedures, if any, to be completed prior to ADR (e.g., exchange of documents, medical examination, etc.);

(d) The effect of the ADR process (e.g., binding or nonbinding);

(e) The date or dates for the filing of progress reports by the ADR provider with the trial judge or for the completion of the ADR process; and

(f) The special conditions, if any, imposed by the judge upon any aspect of the ADR process (e.g., requiring trial counsel, the parties, and/or representatives of insurers with settlement authority to attend the voluntary ADR session fully prepared to make final demands or offers).

4. Attendance at ADR sessions shall take precedence over all non-judicially assigned matters (depositions, etc.). With respect to court assignments that conflict with a scheduled ADR session, trial judges may excuse trial counsel temporarily to attend the ADR session, consistent with the orderly disposition of judicially assigned matters. In this regard, trial counsel, upon receiving notice of an ADR session, immediately shall inform the trial judge and opposing counsel in matters scheduled for the same date of his or her obligation to appear at the ADR session.

5. All ADR sessions shall be deemed confidential and protected by the provisions of Fed. R. Evid. 408 and Fed. R.Civ. P. 68. No statement made or document produced as part of an ADR proceeding, not otherwise discoverable or obtainable, shall be admissible as evidence or subject to discovery.

6. At the conclusion of the voluntary ADR session(s), the ADR provider's report to the judge shall merely indicate "case settled or not settled," unless the parties agree to a more detailed report (e.g., stipulation of facts, narrowing of issues and discovery procedures, etc.). If a case settles, the parties shall agree upon the appropriate moving papers to be filed for the trial judge's endorsement (Judgment, Stipulation for Dismissal, etc.). If a case does not settle but the parties agree to the narrowing of discovery matters or legal issues, then the ADR provider's report shall set forth those matters for endorsement or amendment by the judge.

[Effective January 1, 2003; amended effective March 1, 2003; amended January 19, 2007, effective January 1, 2007, *nunc pro tunc.*]

## RULE 17–RULE 25. (RESERVED)

## RULE 26. DUTY OF DISCLOSURE

**(a) Definitions Applicable to Discovery Requests.** The full text of the definitions and rules of construction set forth in paragraphs (c) and (d) herein is deemed incorporated by reference into all discovery requests filed in this District, but shall not preclude (i) the definition of other terms specific to the particular litigation, (ii) the use of abbreviations or (iii) a more narrow definition of a term defined in paragraph (c).

**(b)** This Rule is not intended to broaden or narrow the scope of discovery permitted by the Federal Rules of Civil Procedure for the United States District Courts.

**(c)** The following definitions apply to all discovery requests:

(1) *Communication.* The term "communication" means the transmittal of information (in the form of facts, ideas, inquiries or otherwise).

(2) *Document.* The term "document" is defined to be synonymous in meaning and equal in scope to the usage of this term in Federal Rule of Civil Procedure 34(a). A draft or non-identical copy is a separate document within the meaning of this term. A request for production of "documents" shall encompass, and the response shall include, electronically stored information, as included in Federal Rule of Civil Procedure 34, unless otherwise specified by the requesting party.

(3) *Identify (With Respect to Persons).* When referring to a person, to "identify" means to provide, to the extent known, the person's full name, present or last known address, and when referring to a natural person, additionally, the present or last known place of employment. Once a person has been identified in accordance with this subparagraph, only the name of that person need be listed in response to subsequent discovery requesting the identification of that person.

(4) *Identify (With Respect to Documents or Electronically Stored Information).* When referring to documents or electronically stored information, to "identify" means to provide, to the extent known, information about the (i) type of document or electronically stored information; (ii) its general subject matter; (iii) the date of the document or electronically stored information; and (iv) author(s), addressee(s) and recipient(s).

(5) *Parties.* The terms "plaintiff" and "defendant" as well as a party's full or abbreviated name or a pronoun referring to a party mean the party and, where applicable, its officers, directors, employees, partners, corporate parent, subsidiaries or affiliates. This definition is not intended to impose a discovery obligation on any person who is not a party to the litigation.

(6) *Person.* The term "person" is defined as any natural person or any business, legal or governmental entity or association.

(7) *Concerning.* The term "concerning" means relating to, referring to, describing, evidencing or constituting.

**(d)** The following rules of construction apply to all discovery requests:

(1) *All/Each.* The terms "all" and "each" shall both be construed as all and each.

(2) *And/Or.* The connectives "and" and "or" shall be construed either disjunctively or conjunctively as necessary to bring within the scope of the discovery request all responses that might otherwise be construed to be outside its scope.

(3) *Number.* The use of the singular form of any word includes the plural and vice versa.

**(e) Privilege Log.** In accordance with Fed. R. Civ. P. 26(b), when a claim of privilege or work product protection is asserted in response to a discovery request for documents or electronically stored information, the party asserting the privilege or protection shall provide the following information in the form of a privilege log.

(1) The type of document or electronically stored information;

(2) The general subject matter of the document or electronically stored information;

(3) The date of the document or electronically stored information;

(4) The author of the document or electronically stored information; and

(5) Each recipient of the document or electronically stored information.

This rule shall apply only to requests for documents or electronically stored information.

If the information called for by one or more of the foregoing categories is itself privileged, it need not be disclosed. However, the existence of the document and any non-privileged information called for by the other categories must be disclosed.

This rule requires preparation of a privilege log with respect to all documents withheld on the basis of a claim of privilege or work product protection except the following: written or electronic communications between a party and its trial counsel after commencement of the action and the work product material created after the commencement of the action.

**(f) Parties' Planning Conference.**

(1) Within thirty days after the appearance of any defendant, the attorneys of record and any unrepresented parties who have appeared in the case shall confer for the purposes described in Fed. R. Civ. P. 26(f). If a government entity or official is a defendant, the conference shall be held within thirty days after the appearance of any such defendant. The conference shall be initiated by the plaintiff and may be conducted by telephone. Within ten days after the conference, the participants shall jointly complete and file a report in the form prescribed by Form 26(f), which appears in the Appendix to these Rules. A copy of the report shall be mailed to the chambers of the presiding Judge.

(2) After the parties' report is filed, the Court will issue a written scheduling order pursuant to Fed.R.Civ.P. 16(b). Until such a scheduling order is

issued, the case will be governed by the provisions of the Standing Order On Scheduling In Civil Cases.

(3) This rule shall not apply to the following categories of cases: prisoner petitions; review of decisions by administrative agencies, including social security disability matters; recovery of defaulted student loans; recovery of overpayment of veterans' benefits; forfeiture actions; petitions to quash Internal Revenue summons; appeals from Bankruptcy Court orders; proceedings to compel arbitration or to confirm or set aside awards and cases under the Freedom of Information Act.

(4) This rule applies to cases filed on or after June 1, 1995.

[Effective January 1, 2003; amended January 19, 2007, effective January 1, 2007, *nunc pro tunc*.]

## RULE 27–RULE 29.   (RESERVED)

## RULE 30.   DEPOSITIONS

(a) **Attendance.** Depositions on oral examination or on written interrogatories are deemed to constitute private proceedings which the public is not entitled to attend. Any person other than the witness being deposed, the parties to the action, the parent of a minor deponent, counsel for the witness or any party, or any person who has been disclosed by any party as an expert witness in the case shall, at the request of counsel for any party, or the witness, be excluded from the hearing room while the deposition of any person is being taken. Application for an exception to this rule may be made to the presiding Judge.

(b) **Depositions.** Transcripts of depositions and exhibits marked for identification at the depositions shall not be filed with the Clerk, unless the parties are unable to agree as to who shall retain custody of the transcripts and exhibits. If filed with the Clerk, transcripts of all pre-trial depositions in the case and any exhibits marked upon the taking of any deposition shall be withheld from public inspection by the Clerk, but shall be available to any party for any proper use in the case.

(c) **Transcripts and Copies of Taped Depositions.** Where a deposition has been taken, any party is entitled to a copy of the recording made of the testimony, whether that recording is done through stenographic, audiotape or videotape means. Each party shall bear the expense of his or her own copy of the recording of the deposition testimony.

[Effective January 1, 2003.]

## RULE 31–RULE 36.   (RESERVED)

## RULE 37.   DISCOVERY DISPUTES

(a) No motion pursuant to Rules 26 through 37, Fed. R. Civ. P., shall be filed unless counsel making the motion has conferred with opposing counsel and discussed the discovery issues between them in detail in a good faith effort to eliminate or reduce the area of controversy, and to arrive at a mutually satisfactory resolution. In the event the consultations of counsel do not fully resolve the discovery issues, counsel making a discovery motion shall file with the Court, as a part of the motion papers, an affidavit certifying that he or she has conferred with counsel for the opposing party in an effort in good faith to resolve by agreement the issues raised by the motion without the intervention of the Court, and has been unable to reach such an agreement. If some of the issues raised by the motion have been resolved by agreement, the affidavit shall specify the issues so resolved and the issues remaining unresolved.

(b)(1) Memoranda by both sides shall be filed with the Clerk in accordance with Rule 7(a)1 of these Local Rules before any discovery motion is heard by the Court. Each memorandum shall contain a concise statement of the nature of the case and a specific verbatim listing of each of the items of discovery sought or opposed, and immediately following each specification shall set forth the reason why the item should be allowed or disallowed. Where several different items of discovery are in dispute, counsel shall, to the extent possible, group the items into categories in lieu of an individual listing of each item. Every memorandum shall include, as exhibits, copies of the discovery requests in dispute.

(2) Where a discovery motion seeks disclosure of documents or electronically stored information, and the moving party believes in good faith that there is a significant risk that material information will be destroyed before the motion is decided in accordance with normal procedure, the moving party shall have good cause to seek expedited consideration of the motion in accordance with Rule 7(a)(3).

(c) Where a party has sought or opposed discovery which has resulted in the filing of a motion, and that party's position is not warranted under existing law and cannot be supported by good faith argument for extension, modification or reversal of existing law, sanctions will be imposed in accordance with applicable law. If a sanction consists of or includes a reasonable attorney's fee, the amount of such attorney's fee shall be calculated by using the normal hourly rate of the attorney for the party in whose favor a sanction is imposed, unless the party against whom a sanction is imposed can demonstrate that such amount is unreasonable in light of all the circumstances.

(d) Unless a different time is set by the Court, compliance with discovery ordered by the Court shall be made within ten (10) days of the filing of the Court's order.

[Effective January 1, 2003; amended January 19, 2007, effective January 1, 2007, *nunc pro tunc*.]

## RULE 38.   RESERVED

## RULE 39.   DESIGNATION OF BANKRUPTCY JUDGES TO CONDUCT JURY TRIALS

The United States District Court for the District of Connecticut hereby specially designates the bankruptcy judges of this district to conduct jury trials (pursuant to 28 U.S.C. 157(e)).

[Effective January 1, 2003.]

## RULE 40.   ASSIGNMENTS

(a) **Place of Assignment of Cases.** The place of assignment of a case will be determined by the Court in accordance with a general policy on assignments adopted from time to time by the active Judges of the Court in the interest of the effective administration of justice.

(b) **Individual Calendar System.**

1.   All cases will be assigned to a single Judge from filing to termination. In the event that it is subsequently determined that there is pending in this District a related case, or, if one is later filed, such case should normally be assigned to the Judge having the earliest filed case. A case may be reassigned at the discretion of the Chief Judge.

2.   Personnel of the Clerk's office shall not reveal to any person other than a Judge or the Clerk of this Court the order of assignment of cases or the identity of the Judge to be assigned a particular case, until after the case is filed and assigned.

3.   All cases transferred to this Court as multidistrict litigation, pursuant to the provisions of 28 U.S.C. § 1407, shall be assigned to a designated Judge.

(c) **Assignment to Judge upon Remand.** Whenever an appellate Court has remanded a matter to the District Court, and further proceedings not requiring the trial of an issue of fact are appropriate, an application with reference thereto, whether made upon the motion calendar or otherwise, shall be referred for such further proceedings to the Judge who heard the matter below unless the Chief Judge or the appellate Court otherwise directs.

[Effective January 1, 2003.]

## RULE 41.   DISMISSAL OF ACTIONS

(a) **For Failure To Prosecute.** In civil actions in which no action has been taken by the parties for six (6) months or in which deadlines established by the Court pursuant to Rule 16 appear not to have been met, the Clerk shall give notice of proposed dismissal to counsel of record and pro se parties, if any. If such notice has been given and no action has been taken in the action in the meantime and no satisfactory explanation is submitted to the Court within twenty (20) days thereafter, the Clerk shall enter an order of dismissal. Any such order entered by the Clerk under this Rule may be suspended, altered, or rescinded by the Court for cause shown.

(b) **When Reported Settled to the Court.** When counsel of record report to the Court that a civil action pending on its docket has been settled between the parties and no closing papers are filed within thirty (30) days thereafter, the Clerk shall enter an order of dismissal. Said dismissal shall be without costs and without prejudice to the right of any of the parties thereto to move within thirty (30) days thereafter to reopen if settlement has not, in fact, been consummated.

[Effective January 1, 2003; amended effective March 1, 2003.]

## RULE 42.   CONSOLIDATION

(a) **Consolidation of Cases.** Unless the presiding Judge rules otherwise, where two or more cases are consolidated, whether for trial or pretrial purposes, the Clerk shall maintain a separate docket for each case, but the parties shall file all pleadings and other papers in the master docket, which shall be the docket of the earliest filed case, and copies of all pleadings shall be served on all parties in each of the consolidated cases.

[Effective January 1, 2003.]

## RULE 43–RULE 46.   (RESERVED)

## RULE 47.   SELECTION OF JURORS

(a) **Examination of Jurors.** When impaneling a jury, the presiding Judge will ordinarily conduct the examination of the prospective jurors. Prior to the examination, counsel shall file proposed voir dire questions for submission either to the jury panel as a group or to individual members of the panel. At the close of the Judge's examination, counsel will be given a reasonable opportunity to supplement the examination by putting questions to the panel or individual panel members as the Judge in his or her discretion deems proper, or by submitting additional voir dire questions to the Judge.

(b) **Peremptory Challenges.** Unless otherwise ordered by the presiding Judge, counsel shall exercise their peremptory challenges out of the hearing of the jury. (For number of challenges allowed, see 28 U.S.C. § 1870 and Rule 47(b), Fed.R.Civ.P.).

[Effective January 1, 2003; amended effective August 1, 2003.]

## RULE 48.   JURY PANEL

(a) **Number of Jurors.** The jury shall consist of not less than six members and not more than twelve

members and all jurors shall participate in the verdict unless excused from service by the Court.

[Effective January 1, 2003.]

# RULE 49–RULE 52.  (RESERVED)

# RULE 53.  SPECIAL MASTERS

**(a) Creation of Panel of Special Masters.** The active Judges of the District may appoint from among the members of the bar of this Court a panel of special masters for each seat of Court for the purpose of settlement of cases or for any other proper purpose determined by the Judge to whom a particular case has been assigned.

**(b) Appointment of a Master.** The parties to a civil action may stipulate in writing to, or the Judge to whom the case has been assigned may order, the appointment of a master to report upon particular issues in the case including the holding of status or settlement conferences pursuant to L.R. 16(c) of these Local Rules. The Judge may appoint two masters where the purpose of the appointment is the holding of a settlement conference. The stipulation may suggest the master, in which case the Judge may appoint the person named. A master shall not be appointed to any particular case unless he or she consents to such appointment.

**(c) Directives and Calendars of Special Masters .** The Clerk's Office shall issue calendars for hearings or conferences at the direction of the master. Failure to comply with such calendars and other directives of the master shall subject the attorneys and parties to sanctions in accordance with Rules 16(g)1 and 16(g)2 of these Local Rules.

**(d) May Sit Outside District.** A master may sit outside the District. Where he or she is requested to sit outside the District for the convenience of a party and there is opposition thereto by another party, the special master may make an order for the holding of the hearing, or a part thereof, outside the District, upon such terms and conditions as shall be just. Such order may be reviewed by the Court upon motion of any party, served within fifteen (15) days after notice to all parties of the making of the order.

**(e) Filing of Report.** Upon the filing of his or her report the master shall furnish the Clerk with sufficient copies thereof addressed severally to the parties or their attorneys, to enable the Clerk to mail copies to them.

**(f) Confirmation or Rejection of Masters' Report.** Any party objecting to the report of a master shall serve and file an objection, including the reasons therefor, within fifteen (15) days of the filing of the master's report. Opposing memoranda shall be served and filed within fifteen (15) days thereafter. The absence of a timely objection shall be sufficient grounds to confirm the master's report.

**(g) Compensation.** The compensation of masters shall be fixed by the Court in its discretion, including his or her necessary disbursements, unless all interested parties consent to a rate of compensation or the master consents to serve without compensation. Such compensation and disbursements shall be shared equally by the parties and taxed as costs, unless the Court directs otherwise.

[Effective January 1, 2003.]

# RULE 54.  TAXATION OF COSTS

**(a) Procedure for Taxing Costs.**

1.  Any party who seeks costs in the District Court shall, within ten (10) days after the District Court judgment becomes final due to the expiration of the appeal period, as defined by Fed.R.App.P. Rule 4, or within ten (10) days after the issuance of a mandate by a federal appellate Court, file with the Clerk and serve on all other parties a verified bill of costs pursuant to 28 U.S.C. §§ 1821, 1920, 1923 and 1924, setting forth each item of costs that is claimed.

2.  The Clerk shall enter an order allowing costs to the prevailing party unless the Court otherwise directs. No costs shall be allowed to any party if the Court is unable to identify the prevailing party.

3.  In cases where an offer of judgment for a sum certain is made, and a notice of filing has been docketed as proof of the offer, and the offer is not accepted and thereafter the matter goes to trial with the resulting recovery being less than the offer, the party who made the offer of judgment shall be considered the prevailing party for purposes of taxing costs and shall be paid the costs incurred after the making of the offer.

**(b) Objections to the Bill of Costs.** Any objections to the bill of costs shall be filed with the Clerk within ten (10) days of the filing of the bill of costs and shall specify each item to which there is an objection and the reasons for such objection. The Clerk shall rule on any objection to the bill of costs. In the absence of a timely objection, the Clerk shall award costs in accordance with the provisions of this Local Rule.

**(c) Items Taxable As Costs.**

1.  *Fees of the Clerk and Marshal.* Fees of the Clerk and Marshal are taxable as costs and include the filing fees of the complaint, habeas corpus petitions, appeals and fees for the issuance of deposition subpoenas by another district. Service fees for summonses and initial process, subpoenas for nonparty witnesses testifying at trial, subpoenas for depositions and the cost of mailing if service is executed by mail pursuant to Rule 4(d)(2)(C) of the Federal Rules of Civil Procedure, are also recoverable as costs. All claims for service fees by private process servers shall be supported by documentation attached as an exhibit to the bill of costs.

2. *Fees of the Court Reporter.*

(i) The cost of the original and one copy of the trial transcript, transcripts of pre-trial proceedings, and the cost of postage required for the court reporter to file the transcripts with the Court, are taxable if authorized in advance by the Court or are necessarily obtained for use in the case.

(ii) The cost of an original and one copy of deposition transcripts are recoverable as costs, if used at trial in lieu of live testimony, for cross-examination or impeachment, if used in support of a successful motion for summary judgment, or if they are necessarily obtained for the preparation of the case and not for the convenience of counsel. Appearance fees of the court reporter and the notary or other official presiding at the deposition, are taxable as costs, including travel, subsistence and postage for filing if the transcripts are required to be filed with the Court. Fees for nonparty deponents, including mileage and subsistence, are taxable at the same rate as for attendance at trial, where the deposition is a taxable cost under this subsection. A reasonable fee for the necessary use of an interpreter is also taxable.

3. *Fees for Exemplification and Copies of Papers Necessarily Obtained for Use in the Case.*

(i) Costs for exemplifications or copies of papers are taxable only if counsel can demonstrate that such exemplifications or copies were necessarily obtained for use in the case. Costs for one copy of documents admitted into evidence in lieu of the originals, shall be permitted as costs. Copies for the convenience of counsel or additional copies are not taxable unless otherwise directed by the Court. The fee of a translator is taxable if the copy itself is a taxable cost.

(ii) The cost of patent file wrappers and prior art patents are taxable at the rate charged by the patent office. However, expenses for services of persons checking patent office records to determine what should be ordered are not recoverable.

(iii) Copies of pleadings are not allowed as costs. However, the cost of exhibits appended to a successful motion for summary judgment are allowable.

4. *Fees for Witnesses.*

(i) Witness fees are taxable when the witness has actually testified or was necessarily in attendance at trial and whether or not the witness voluntarily attended or was present under subpoena. Witness fees for attendance at a deposition are recoverable if the deposition is a taxable cost. Witness fees for officers of a corporation are taxable provided that such witnesses are not named parties to the action. Fees for expert witnesses are taxable at the same rates as any other witness. Any amounts in excess of the statutory limits are not taxable. Fees for a competent interpreter are taxable if the fees of the witness involved are taxable.

(ii) Fees for subsistence are taxable if the distance from the Court to the residence of the witness is such that mileage fees would be greater than subsistence fees if the witness were to return to the residence every day. Additional claims for subsistence when the witness has testified and remains in attendance for the convenience of counsel shall not be taxable.

(iii) Mileage shall be taxable at the statutory rate. The "100–mile" rule which limits the total taxable mileage of a witness to 200 miles round trip, will not be applied where it has been demonstrated that the witness' testimony was relevant and material and had a bearing on essential issues of the case. Fees of common carriers are also taxable at coach fare rates. Receipts for common carrier expenses shall be appended to the bill of costs. Miscellaneous toll charges, parking fees, taxicab fares between places of lodging and carrier terminals, are also taxable.

5. *Maps, Charts, Models, Photographs, Summaries, Computations and Statistical Summaries.* The cost of maps and charts are taxable as costs only if admitted into evidence and only if they are not greater than 8 1/2 × 11 in size. Costs for enlargements greater than 8 1/2 × 11 or for models, are not taxable unless by order of the Court. Compilations of summaries, computations and statistical comparisons are also not taxable unless by order of the Court.

6. *Other Items Taxable as Costs Are as Follows .*

(i) Fees to masters, receivers and commissioners, unless otherwise ordered by the Court;

(ii) Premiums paid upon all bonds provided pursuant to statute, rule of Court, order of Court, or stipulation of parties, including bonds in lieu of or in release of attachment, may be taxed as costs to the prevailing party, subject to disallowance entirely or in part by the Court in its discretion;

(iii) Fees incurred in removing a case from state Court, including the fees for service of process in the state Court and fees for witnesses attending depositions prior to removal.

7. *Items Not Taxable as Costs.* In addition to any limitations addressed in the preceding sections, the following items are not recoverable as costs, unless by order of the Court:

(i) Filing fees for cases initiated by the United States;

(ii) Service of process fees for discovery subpoenas;

(iii) Copies of trial transcripts in excess of an original plus one copy;

(iv) Costs of an expedited or daily copy transcript produced for the convenience of counsel;

(v) Counsel's fees and expenses in arranging for and traveling to a deposition or trial;

(vi) Fees of any named party to the action;

(vii) Compensation for an expert witness in excess of the statutorily allowed limits;

(viii) Subsistence fees for witnesses in attendance at trial or deposition, beyond the time of testimony by the witness;

(ix) Attorneys' fees incurred in attending depositions, conferences or trial, including expenses for investigations;

(x) Word processing or typing charges;

(xi) Computerized legal research fees;

(xii) Paralegal expenses;

(xiii) Pre-judgment and post-judgment interest;

(xiv) Costs for maps, charts and photographs greater than 8 1/2 × 11 in size, as well as costs for producing models;

(xv) Copies of pleadings retained by counsel or served on opposing counsel;

(xvi) Telephone calls by counsel, general postage expense of counsel, Federal Express or other express mail service costs.

**(d) Review of the Clerk's Ruling.** Any party may, within five (5) days of the entry of the Clerk's ruling, apply to the Judge before whom the case was assigned for review of the Clerk's ruling on the bill of costs. Such application shall specify which portions of the Clerk's ruling are the subject of the objection and shall specify the reasons therefor. Any other party may respond to such objection within five (5) days of the filing of such objection.

[Effective January 1, 2003.]

# RULE 55.   (RESERVED)

# RULE 56.   SUMMARY JUDGMENT

## (a) Motions for Summary Judgment

1.   There shall be annexed to a motion for summary judgment a document entitled "Local Rule 56(a)1 Statement," which sets forth in separately numbered paragraphs meeting the requirements of Local Rule 56(a)3 a concise statement of each material fact as to which the moving party contends there is no genuine issue to be tried. All material facts set forth in said statement and supported by the evidence will be deemed admitted unless controverted by the statement required to be filed and served by the opposing party in accordance with Local Rule 56(a)2.

2.   The papers opposing a motion for summary judgment shall include a document entitled "Local Rule 56(a)2 Statement," which states in separately numbered paragraphs meeting the requirements of Local Rule 56(a)3 and corresponding to the paragraphs contained in the moving party's Local Rule 56(a)1 Statement whether each of the facts asserted by the moving party is admitted or denied. The Local Rule 56(a)2 Statement must also include in a separate section entitled "Disputed Issues of Material Fact" a list of each issue of material fact as to which it is contended there is a genuine issue to be tried.

3.   Each statement of material fact by a movant in a Local Rule 56(a)1 Statement or by an opponent in a Local Rule 56(a)2 Statement, and each denial in an opponent's Local Rule 56(a)2 Statement, must be followed by a specific citation to (1) the affidavit of a witness competent to testify as to the facts at trial and/or (2) evidence that would be admissible at trial. The affidavits, deposition testimony, responses to discovery requests, or other documents containing such evidence shall be filed and served with the Local Rule 56(a)1 and 2 Statements in conformity with Fed. R. Civ. P. 56(e). The "specific citation" obligation of this Local Rule requires counsel and pro se parties to cite to specific paragraphs when citing affidavits or responses to discovery requests, and to cite to specific pages when citing to deposition or other transcripts or to documents longer than a single page in length. Counsel and pro se parties are hereby notified that failure to provide specific citations to evidence in the record as required by this Local Rule may result in the Court deeming certain facts that are supported by the evidence admitted in accordance with Rule 56(a)1 or in the Court imposing sanctions, including, when the movant fails to comply, an order denying the motion for summary judgment, and, when the opponent fails to comply, an order granting the motion if the undisputed facts show that the movant is entitled to judgment as a matter of law.

4.   The Local Rule 56(a)1 and 2 Statements referred to above shall be filed and served along with the motion, memorandum of law and certificate of service required by Local Rule 7 and the Federal Rule of Civil Procedure 56.

**(b) Notice to Pro Se Litigants Regarding Summary Judgment.** Any represented party moving for summary judgment against a party proceeding pro se shall file and serve, as a separate document, in the form set forth below, a "Notice to Pro Se Litigant Opposing Motion for Summary Judgment." If the pro se party is not a plaintiff, or if the case is to be tried to the Court rather than to a jury, the movant will modify the notice accordingly. The movant shall attach to the notice copies of the full text of Rule 56 of the Federal Rules of Civil Procedure and of this Local Civil Rule 56.

[Effective January 1, 2003; amended effective August 1, 2003; May 1, 2005.]

### Notice to Pro Se Litigant Opposing Motion For Summary Judgment As Required by Local Rule of Civil Procedure 56(b)

The purpose of this notice, which is required by the Court, is to notify you that the defendant has filed a motion for summary judgment asking the Court to dismiss all or some of your claims without a trial. The defendant argues that there is no need for a trial with regard to these claims because no reasonable jury could return a verdict in your favor.

THE DEFENDANT'S MOTION MAY BE GRANTED AND YOUR CLAIMS MAY BE DISMISSED WITHOUT FURTHER NOTICE IF YOU DO NOT FILE PAPERS AS REQUIRED BY RULE 56 OF THE FEDERAL RULES OF CIVIL PROCEDURE AND RULE 56 OF THE LOCAL RULES OF CIVIL PROCEDURE AND IF THE DEFENDANT'S MOTION SHOWS THAT THE DEFENDANT IS ENTITLED TO JUDGMENT AS A MATTER OF LAW. COPIES OF THESE RULES ARE ATTACHED TO THIS NOTICE, AND YOU SHOULD REVIEW THEM VERY CAREFULLY.

The papers you file must show that (1) you disagree with the defendant's version of the facts; (2) you have evidence contradicting the defendant's version; and (3) the evidence you rely on, if believed by a jury, would be sufficient to support a verdict in your favor.

To make this showing, you must file one or more affidavits disputing the defendant's version of the facts. An affidavit is a sworn statement by a witness that the facts contained in the affidavit are true to the best of the witness's knowledge and belief. To be considered by the Court, an affidavit must be signed and sworn to in the presence of a notary public or other person authorized to administer oaths. In addition to affidavits, you may also file deposition transcripts, responses to discovery requests, and other evidence that supports your claims. Please be aware that the Local Rule requires counsel and pro se parties to cite to specific paragraphs when citing affidavits or responses to discovery requests and to cite to specific pages when citing to deposition or other transcripts or to documents longer than a single page in length. If you fail to comply and submit evidence contradicting the defendant's version of the facts, your claims may be dismissed if the defendant's motion shows that the defendant is entitled to judgment as a matter of law.

It is therefore very important that you read the defendant's motion, memorandum of law, affidavits, and other evidentiary materials to see if you agree or disagree with the defendant's version of the relevant facts. It is also very important that you review the enclosed copy of Rule 56 of the Local Rules of Civil Procedure carefully. This rule provides detailed instructions concerning the papers you must file in opposition to the defendant's motion, including how you must respond to specific facts the defendant claims are undisputed (see Rule 56(a)(2)) and how you must support your claims with specific references to evidence (see Rule 56(a)(3)). If you fail to follow these instructions, the defendant's motion may be granted if the defendant's motion shows that the defendant is entitled to judgment as a matter of law.

You must file your opposition papers with the Clerk of the Court and mail a copy to the defendant's counsel within 21 days of the filing of the defendant's motion with the Clerk of the Court. This 21–day period is extended an additional three days if any of the conditions of Rule 6(e) of the Federal Rules of Civil Procedure are met (for example, if you received the defendant's motion by mail or overnight delivery service).

## RULE 57–RULE 66.   (RESERVED)

## RULE 67.   DEPOSIT OF FUNDS IN COURT REGISTRY

**(a) Order for Deposit in Interest Bearing Account.** Whenever a party seeks a Court order for money to be deposited by the Clerk in an interest-bearing account, the party shall file the order with the Clerk, who shall inspect the proposed order for proper form and content and compliance with this Rule prior to signature by the Judge for whom the order is prepared.

**(b) Orders Directing Investment of Funds by Clerk.** Any order obtained by a party or parties in an action that directs the Clerk to invest in an interest-bearing account or instrument funds deposited in the registry of the Court pursuant to 28 U.S.C. § 2041 shall include the following: (1) the amount to be invested; (2) the designation of the type of account or instrument in which the funds shall be invested; and (3) a direction that the Clerk deduct from the income earned on the investment a fee of ten percent (10%), whenever such income becomes available for deduction in the investment so held and without further order of the Court.

**(c) Release of Deposited Funds.** Upon final determination of the action or at such other times as may be appropriate, a party or parties may seek a Court order releasing deposited funds, by submitting a proposed order which shall contain the following information: (1) the name, address and taxpayer identification number of any individual(s) or corporation(s) receiving the funds; and (2) the amount of principal and interest to be paid to any individual(s) or corporation(s). Funds cannot be released from the registry account of the Court without a Court order.

**(d) Registry Account.** For the purpose of this Rule, the Registry Account of Court is held in Bank of America, 157 Church Street, New Haven, CT 06510.

[Effective January 1, 2003; amended effective April 1, 2005.]

## RULE 68.   OFFER OF JUDGMENT

When an offer of judgment is filed pursuant to Connecticut General Statute, § 52–192a or § 52–193, the offer of judgment shall be filed in a sealed envelope bearing the caption of the case, the case number and the caption of the document. The document shall remain under seal until (a) the filing of an acceptance of the offer of judgment at which time the clerk shall enter judgment, or (b) after trial to allow the court to decide whether the plaintiff is entitled to additional interest on the amount recovered, or (c) when the clerk retires the record to the Federal Record Center.

[Effective January 1, 2003.]

## RULE 69–RULE 71.   (RESERVED)

## RULES 72 AND 73.   SEE LOCAL RULES FOR UNITED STATES MAGISTRATE JUDGES

## RULE 74–RULE 76.   (RESERVED)

## RULE 77.1   ENTRY OF ORDERS AND JUDGMENTS

**(a) By the Court.**

1.   A memorandum signed by the Judge or Magistrate of the decision of a motion that does not finally determine all claims for relief shall constitute the required order unless such memorandum directs the submission or settlement of an order in more extended form.

2.   The notation in the appropriate docket of an "order," as defined in the previous paragraph, shall constitute the entry of the order.

3.   Unless otherwise directed by the Court, proposed orders, judgments and decrees shall be presented to the Clerk's office, and not directly to the Judge. Unless the form of order, judgment, or decree is consented to in writing, or unless the Court otherwise directs, five (5) days' notice of settlement is required. Three (3) days' notice is required on all counter proposals. Unless adopted by the Court, such proposed orders, judgments or decrees shall not form any part of the record of the action.

**(b) By the Clerk.** In addition to the other orders that the Clerk is authorized to sign and enter pursuant to these Local Rules or the Federal Rules of Civil Procedure, the Clerk is authorized to sign and enter the following orders and judgments without further direction of the Court:

1.   Consent judgments for the payment of money; orders on consent dismissing actions, withdrawing stipulations, exonerating sureties and permitting visiting lawyers to appear; orders setting aside defaults entered under Fed. R. Civ. P. 55(a); and orders entered pursuant to Fed. R. Civ. P. 4.1(a) specially appointing persons to serve process other than a summons or subpoena.

2.   Orders on consent for the substitution of attorneys in cases not assigned for trial.

3.   Subject to the provisions of Fed. R. Civ. P. 54(b) and 58, judgments upon a general verdict of a jury, or upon a decision by the Court unless the Court otherwise directs. Every judgment shall be set forth on a separate document and shall become effective only when its substance is entered in the civil docket pursuant to Fed. R. Civ. P. 79(a).

**(c) Legal Holidays.** For the purpose of Rules 6 and 77(c), Fed.R.Civ.P., and for all other purposes, the following are hereby designated Legal Holidays for the United States District Court for the District of Connecticut:

New Year's Day (January 1), Martin Luther King, Jr. Day (third Monday in January), Presidents' Day (third Monday in February), Memorial Day (last Monday in May), Independence Day (July 4), Labor Day (first Monday in September), Columbus Day (second Monday in October), Veterans' Day (November 11), Thanksgiving Day (fourth Thursday in November), Christmas Day (December 25); or whenever any such day falls on Sunday, the Monday next following such day; or whenever any such day falls on Saturday, the Friday preceding such day; and any other day appointed as a holiday by the President or the Congress of the United States, or by the Governor or General Assembly of the State of Connecticut.

When a particular holiday is celebrated on different days by the Federal government and the State of Connecticut, then the day designated by the Federal government, and not the day designated by the State of Connecticut, shall be observed as a holiday by the United States District Court for the District of Connecticut.

**(d) District Court Library.** The United States District Court Library is established for use by Court personnel. The library is available to attorneys who are admitted to practice in the United States District Court only on the day they appear before the Court on trial, to argue motions, or to participate in chambers conferences, and only for emergency research.

**(e) Order or Judgment of Appellate Court.** Any order or judgment of an appellate Court, when filed in the office of the Clerk of the District Court, shall automatically become the order or judgment of the District Court and shall be entered as such by the Clerk without further order, except that if such order or judgment of the appellate court requires further proceedings in the District Court other than a new trial, an order shall be entered making the order or judgment of the appellate court the order or judgment of the District Court.

[Effective January 1, 2003.]

## RULE 78. (RESERVED)

## RULE 79. DOCKET NUMBERS

Upon the filing of a complaint, a case will be assigned a docket number, consisting of the following:

1. the prefix 3;

2. the last two digits of the year of filing;

3. a designation of "CV" for civil cases and "CR" for criminal cases;

4. the number of the case (with the first case of each calendar year designated as 00001); and

5. the initials of the Judge to whom the case has been assigned.

[Effective January 1, 2003.]

## RULE 80. STENOGRAPHER

(a) **Reporter's Fees.** An official Court reporter shall be entitled to compensation for transcript at rates which may be fixed from time to time by order of the District Judges. Said rates shall be entered in an Order of the Court and shall be available in the Clerk's Office, along with any other Auxiliary Orders which are adopted pursuant to Local Civil Rule 83.12.

[Effective January 1, 2003.]

## RULE 81. PROCEEDINGS TO WHICH THE RULES APPLY

(a) **Naturalization Sessions of Court.** The petitions of aliens to become citizens of the United States shall be heard from time to time at the various seats of Court, as the Chief Judge shall direct.

(b) **Dismissal of Petition or Motion.** Whenever a petition or motion filed pursuant to this Rule is dismissed as provided for in Rule 8 of these rules, the Clerk shall return the petition or motion to the petitioner along with a brief statement of the defect giving rise to the dismissal.

[Effective January 1, 2003.]

## RULE 82. (RESERVED)

## RULE 83.1 ADMISSION OF ATTORNEYS

(a) **Qualifications.** Any attorney of the bar of the State of Connecticut or of the bar of any United States District Court whose professional character is good may be admitted to practice in this Court upon motion of any attorney of this Court and upon taking the proper oath and the entry of said attorney's name in the records of the Court.

(b) **Procedure for Admission.** Each applicant for admission to the bar of this Court shall file with the Clerk of this Court a written petition accompanied by a sworn affidavit setting forth the applicant's residence and office address, by what Courts the applicant has been admitted to practice, the applicant's legal training and experience at the bar, and that the applicant has studied carefully the jurisdictional provisions of Title 28 U.S.C., the Federal Rules of Civil Procedure, the Federal Rules of Criminal Procedure and the Local Rules of this Court. The affidavit shall also state whether the applicant has ever been convicted of any crime, other than minor traffic offenses, and whether the applicant has ever been denied admission to or disciplined by any Court, whether by way of disbarment, suspension from practice, censure or otherwise. If the applicant has been convicted of any crime, other than minor traffic offenses, or has been denied admission to or been disciplined by any Court, the active Judges of this District or their designee shall make such inquiry as they deem appropriate, and it shall take a majority vote of the active Judges of this District to admit such applicant to this bar. For the purpose of this Rule, "minor traffic offenses" shall mean motor vehicle violations which are neither felonies nor misdemeanors. The petition and affidavit of the applicant shall be accompanied by the sworn affidavit of two members of the bar of this Court, stating where and when they were admitted to practice in this Court, how long and under what circumstances they have known the applicant, what they know of the applicant's character and his or her experience as a lawyer. The sponsoring attorney shall certify in the affidavit that he or she knows of no fact which would call into question the integrity or character of the applicant. The Clerk will examine the petition, affidavit and certificates and, if found to be in compliance with this Rule, the petition for admission will be presented to the Court at a time and place selected by the Clerk. When a petition is called, one of the members of the bar of this District shall move the admission of the petitioner. If admitted, the petitioner shall in open Court take an oath to support the Constitution and laws of the United States of America, and to discharge faithfully his or her duties as an attorney according to law and the recognized standards of ethics of the profession. Under the direction of the Clerk, the newly admitted attorney shall sign the roll of attorneys and pay the fee required by law. Additionally, he or she shall pay a fee of $10.00, which shall be placed by the Clerk in a fund to be used for expenses incurred pursuant to Rule 83.2 of these Local Rules of Civil Procedure.

(c) **Local Office.**

1. Unless otherwise ordered by the Court for good cause shown, no visiting lawyer admitted specially under Rule 83.1(d) not having an office for the transaction of business in person within the District of Connecticut shall appear as attorney of record in any cause without specifying on the record a member of the bar of this Court having an office within the District of Connecticut, upon whom service of all papers shall also be made. All communications sent by

the Court to the local office so designated shall have the same force and effect as if said communications were sent to the out of state office of a visiting lawyer who has been admitted pursuant to Rule 83.1(d), even where the sponsoring lawyer has been excused from attendance in Court pursuant to Rule 83.1(d)1 of these Local Rules of Civil Procedure.

2. Any party appearing pro se must give an address within the District of Connecticut where service can be made upon him or her in the same manner as service is made on an attorney.

3. A member of the bar of this Court who changes his or her office address shall notify the Clerk of such change of address within 30 days of such change, and shall at the same time provide the Clerk with a list of all pending cases in which the attorney has filed an appearance.

**(d) Visiting Lawyers.**

1. Lawyers not members of the Bar of this Court who are members in good standing of the bar of another Federal or State Court may be permitted to represent clients in criminal, civil and miscellaneous proceedings in this Court on written motion by a member of the Bar of this Court. The motion shall be accompanied by an affidavit, duly sworn and executed by the proposed visiting lawyer: (1) stating the visiting lawyer's office address, telephone number, fax number, and e-mail address, if any; (2) identifying each court of which said lawyer is a member of the bar; (3) stating that said lawyer has not been denied admission or disciplined by this Court or any other court, or if that is not true, describing in full the circumstances of any such denial or discipline, including the reasons therefor, any penalty imposed, whether the penalty was satisfied, and whether the lawyer is currently in good standing in the jurisdiction that denied admission or imposed discipline; and (4) stating that said lawyer has fully reviewed and is familiar with the Rules of the United States District Court for the District of Connecticut. Said motion shall be made promptly and may be denied if granting the motion would require modification of a scheduling order entered pursuant to Fed. R. Civ. P. 16(b) or the deadlines established by the standing order on scheduling in civil cases. If the motion is granted, the sponsoring lawyer may apply to be excused from attendance in court. A sponsoring lawyer who is excused from attendance in court is not thereby relieved of any other obligation of an appearing attorney.

2. Each such motion filed on behalf of an attorney shall be accompanied by payment to the Clerk of this Court of a fee of $25.00, which shall be placed in a fund by the Clerk to be used for expenses incurred pursuant to Rule 83.2 of these Local Rules.

3. If a visiting lawyer, admitted to participate in a trial in this Court in conformity with paragraph 1 of Rule 83.1(d) of these Local Rules, shall be disciplined in accordance with Rule 83.2 of these Local Rules, the Chief Judge shall address to the presiding Judge of every Court having disciplinary powers over a bar of which said visiting lawyer is a member, a communication specifying the conduct which led to such disciplinary action, supported when feasible by pertinent extracts from the reporter's transcript or by other documentary evidence, for such disciplinary action, if any, as said Court or Courts shall deem appropriate.

[Effective January 1, 2003; amended effective June 1, 2003; March 1, 2007, nunc pro tunc.]

# RULE 83.2 DISCIPLINE OF ATTORNEYS

### (a) Professional Ethics.

1. Other than the specific Rules enumerated in Rule 83.2(a)2 of these Local Rules, this Court recognizes the authority of the "Rules of Professional Conduct," as approved by the Judges of the Connecticut Superior Court as expressing the standards of professional conduct expected of lawyers practicing in the District of Connecticut. Any changes made by the Judges of the Connecticut Superior Court to the Rules of Professional Conduct shall not be binding in the District of Connecticut, unless such changes are expressly adopted by order of the District Judges. The Clerk shall report to the Judges any such changes. The interpretation of said Rules of Professional Responsibility by any authority other than the United States Supreme Court, the United States Court of Appeals for the Second Circuit and the United States District Court for the District of Connecticut shall not be binding on disciplinary proceedings initiated in the United States District Court for the District of Connecticut.

2. Rule 3.6 and 3.7(b) of the Rules of Professional Conduct are not adopted as rules governing professional conduct in the District of Connecticut. The ethical standards governing public statements by counsel in a criminal case are set forth in Local Criminal Rule 57. The ethical standards governing participation as counsel in a case where either the attorney or another attorney in his or her firm may be a witness for both civil and criminal cases are set forth in Local Civil Rule 83.13.

3. The following Local Civil Rules shall apply in grievance proceedings: Rule 83.1 (Admission of Attorneys), Rule 1 (Definitions), Rule 10 (Preparation of Pleadings), Rule 5(a) (Appearance), Rule 5(b) (Proof of Service), Rule 59(f) (Service by Facsimile Copy), Rule 7(a) (Motion Practice Procedures), and Rule 7(b) (Motions for Extensions of Time.)

### (b) Grievance Committee.

1. The Judges of this Court shall appoint a Grievance Committee of the United States District Court for the District of Connecticut consisting of twelve (12) members of the bar of this Court. One member shall be appointed by the judges as the chairperson of the committee for a term of three years.

2. Members shall be appointed for a term of three (3) years, renewable once, for an additional term of three (3) years. In the event that a vacancy arises before the end of a term, a member of the bar of this Court shall be appointed by the Judges of this Court to fill the vacancy for the balance of the term. Anyone filling such a vacancy is eligible for reappointment to a full three-year term. Five (5) members of the Grievance Committee shall constitute a quorum and any action taken by the Grievance Committee shall be by a majority vote of those members present and voting.

3. The judges shall appoint three (3) members of the bar of this court to serve as Counsel to the Grievance Committee. Assignment of cases to each counsel shall be made on the basis of the assigned seat of court, according to administrative procedures approved by the Clerk.

4. The Grievance Committee and Counsel to the Grievance Committee shall have the use of the staff of the Clerk for clerical and record-keeping assistance, shall have the power to issue subpoenas to compel witnesses to testify and produce documents at proceedings, and may incur such expenses as shall be approved by the Chief Judge of this Court. Compulsory process shall be available to the attorney who is the subject of the complaint.

### (c) Proceedings Upon Complaint.

1. Any person may file with the Clerk of the Court a written verified complaint alleging attorney misconduct relating to any matter relevant to an attorney's qualification to practice before the court. Each person filing a complaint shall file sufficient copies of the complaint to supply an original for the Court, one copy for each attorney who is the subject of the complaint, and one copy for each member of the Grievance Committee. The Clerk shall assign a docket number, consisting of the initials "GP," the last two digits of the year of filing, the number of the case (with the first case of each year being designated as number 1), and the initials of the Judge to whom the case has been assigned. Each complaint shall be assigned to a Judge on a random District-wide basis. Any complaint which arises out of conduct witnessed by a particular Judge of this Court shall not be assigned to that Judge. The personnel of the Clerk's office shall not reveal to any person other than a Judge or the Clerk of this Court the order of assignment of such complaints. The Clerk shall forward a copy of the complaint to the Grievance Committee and counsel assigned to the matter. The complaint, and the fact of filing the complaint, shall be considered sealed and shall not be a record open to the public.

2. The Grievance Committee, upon appropriate notice, shall conduct such hearings as it deems appropriate under rules for fair procedure. Such hearings shall be private unless the attorney complained against requests a public proceeding. The Grievance Committee shall decide whether to recommend that the complaint be dismissed or that the attorney complained against be disciplined (1) by private or public censure, (2) by suspension from the practice of law for a fixed period of time, (3) by indefinite suspension, or (4) by disbarment.

3. When any misconduct or allegation of misconduct which would warrant discipline of any attorney admitted to practice before this Court comes to the attention of any Judge of this Court, the Judge may refer the matter to the Grievance Committee for the initiation of a presentment or the formulation of such other recommendation as may be appropriate. Nothing in this Rule 83.2 shall be interpreted to limit the inherent authority of the Judge to enforce the standards of professional conduct by way of appropriate proceedings other than by referral to the Grievance Committee.

### (d) Recommendation of Grievance Committee.

1. The Grievance Committee shall make its recommendation to the court within 180 days of receipt of the complaint or referral for action. If additional time is needed, Counsel to the Committee shall notify the Clerk and up to an additional 180 days shall be allowed.

2. If the recommendation of the Committee is to dismiss the complaint, the recommendation shall be filed with the court. The Judge to whom the complaint has been assigned may hold further hearings on the recommendation to dismiss or may dismiss the complaint on the written record presented by the Committee.

3. If the Judge decides not to dismiss the complaint, an Order to Show Cause shall be issued by the court directing the attorney complained against to show cause why disciplinary action should not be taken.

4. If the Grievance Committee's recommendation is for discipline, the Grievance Committee shall file its recommendation in the form of a presentment, seeking an order to show cause why the attorney complained against should not have disciplinary action taken against him or her as prayed for in the presentment.

5. Within thirty (30) days of service of the order to show cause issued pursuant to Rule 83.2(d)3 or a presentment issued pursuant to Rule 83.2(d)4, the attorney complained against shall file a written answer. Thereafter, a hearing on the issue shall be held before the assigned Judge. At the hearing, the attorney complained against shall have a right to be represented by counsel, shall have the right to confront and cross-examine witnesses, and shall have the right to offer the testimony of witnesses on his or her behalf. Discipline shall not be imposed unless the Court finds, by clear and convincing evidence, that the attorney complained against should be disciplined. Unless requested to be a public proceeding by the attorney

complained against, all proceedings shall be in private and maintained under seal unless and until discipline is ordered. Absent the filing of an answer as provided above, a hearing shall be held on the limited question of appropriate discipline.

6. Upon the imposition of discipline, other than a private reprimand, the court file shall be unsealed and made a matter of public record. In that event, a notation shall be made on the attorney's admission record indicating the date and nature of the discipline imposed.

**(e) Attorneys Convicted of Crimes.**

1. The Grievance Committee shall take such action as is necessary to keep informed of convictions of "serious crimes," as defined in subparagraph 4, of attorneys admitted to practice before this Court and cause certified copies of such convictions to be filed with this Court.

2. Upon the filing with this Court of a certified copy of a judgment of conviction or proof of change of plea or jury verdict of guilty prior to sentencing, demonstrating that any attorney admitted to practice before the Court has been convicted in any Court of the United States, or the District of Columbia, or of any state, territory, commonwealth or possession of the United States or any foreign country, of a serious crime, the Court shall enter an order immediately suspending that attorney from practice before this Court, whether the conviction resulted from a plea of guilty or nolo contendere or from a verdict after trial or otherwise, and regardless of the pendency of any appeal. A copy of such order shall immediately be served upon the attorney. Upon good cause shown, the Court may set aside such order when it is in the interest of justice to do so. An attorney suspended under the provisions of this subparagraph 2 shall be reinstated immediately upon filing of a certificate demonstrating that the underlying conviction of a serious crime has been reversed, but reinstatement will not terminate any disciplinary proceedings against the attorney brought pursuant to this Rule 83.2.

3. Upon the filing of a certified copy of a judgment of conviction or proof of change of plea or jury verdict of guilty prior to sentencing, demonstrating that any attorney admitted to practice before the Court has been convicted of a serious crime, the matter shall automatically be referred to counsel for the Grievance Committee for the institution of a presentment before this Court, in the manner specified in Rule 83.2(d), in which the sole issue to be determined shall be the extent of the final discipline to be imposed as the result of the conduct resulting in the conviction, provided that a disciplinary proceeding so instituted shall not be brought to final hearing until all direct appeals from the conviction are concluded.

4. The term "serious crime" shall include any felony and any lesser crime a necessary element of which, as determined by the statutory or common law defini-

tion of such crime in the jurisdiction where the judgment was entered, involves false swearing, misrepresentation, fraud, moral turpitude, willful failure to file tax returns or currency transaction reports, deceit, bribery, extortion, misappropriation, theft, or an attempt or a conspiracy or solicitation of another to commit, or the aiding and abetting the commission of any of the foregoing crimes.

5. A certified copy of a judgment of conviction of an attorney for any crime shall be conclusive evidence of the commission of that crime in any disciplinary proceeding instituted against that attorney based upon the conviction.

**(f) Discipline or Resignation in Other Courts.**

1. Any attorney receiving disciplinary action against him or her by order of the Courts of Connecticut or any other state or federal Court or any attorney resigning from the bar of the State of Connecticut or any other state or federal Court while disciplinary proceedings are pending, shall promptly inform the Clerk of this Court of such action.

2. Upon the filing of such information pursuant to this paragraph (f) or such information having otherwise come to the attention of this Court or of the Grievance Committee, counsel for the Grievance Committee shall institute a presentment, in the manner specified in paragraph (d) of this Rule 83.2, petitioning the Court to impose the identical discipline upon or require the resignation of the attorney receiving such disciplinary action or so resigning. After hearing, the Court shall require the resignation of the attorney or shall impose the identical discipline against the attorney unless the Court finds that, on the face of the record upon which the discipline in another jurisdiction is predicated, it clearly appears:

 a. that the procedure was so lacking in notice or opportunity to be heard as to constitute a deprivation of due process; or

 b. that there was such an infirmity of proof establishing the misconduct as to give rise to the clear conviction that the Court could not, consistent with its duty, accept as final the discipline imposed; or

 c. that the imposition of the same discipline by the Court would result in grave injustice; or

 d. that the misconduct established is deemed by the Court to warrant substantially different discipline.

Where the Court determines that any such element exists, it shall enter such other order as it deems appropriate.

3. Upon good cause shown, the Court may set aside such order when it is in the interest of justice to do so. An attorney suspended under the provisions of subparagraph (f)2 shall be reinstated immediately upon filing a certificate demonstrating that the disci-

plinary action in the other jurisdiction has been reversed.

### (g) Mental Disability or Incapacity.

1. In the event an attorney is, by a Court of competent jurisdiction, (1) declared to be incompetent of managing his or her affairs or (2) committed involuntarily to a mental hospital for drug dependency, mental illness, or the addictive or excessive use of alcohol, the Court shall issue an order to show cause, requiring the attorney to show cause why he or she should not be suspended immediately from practicing law in this Court. The matter shall be handled by the Grievance Committee, which shall arrange for a copy of such order to be served, in such manner as the Court shall direct, upon such attorney, his or her conservator, if any, and the director of any institution in which he or she may reside. If, after hearing, the Court concludes that the attorney is incapacitated from continuing to practice law, it shall enter an order suspending him or her on the ground of such disability until further order of the Court.

2. Whenever the Grievance Committee shall have reason to believe that an attorney is incapacitated from practicing in this Court by reason of mental infirmity or illness or because of drug dependency or addiction to alcohol, it shall file a presentment in accordance with paragraph (d) of this Rule 83.2(g)*. Whenever a Judge of this Court has reason to believe that an attorney is similarly incapacitated or otherwise impaired, the Judge may refer the matter to the Grievance Committee for the formulation of such recommendation as may be appropriate, including the initiation of a presentment or such other orders as it deems appropriate. The Grievance Committee may take or direct such action as it deems necessary or proper in order to determine whether such attorney is incapacitated or otherwise impaired, including examination of the attorney by such qualified medical expert or experts as the Grievance Committee shall designate. If, after hearing, the Court concludes that the attorney is incapacitated or otherwise impaired from continuing to practice law, it shall enter an order suspending him or her on the ground of such disability until further order of the Court.

3. In the event there are disciplinary proceedings pending against an attorney who is suspended under this rule, those proceedings shall be held in abeyance for as long as the suspension under this rule remains in effect.

**(h) Resignation.** Any attorney may resign from the bar of this Court by submitting a resignation, in writing, properly witnessed and acknowledged to be the attorney's free act and deed, to the Clerk of this Court, which shall be effective upon filing. However, such resignation shall not affect any pending disciplinary proceedings pursuant to this Rule 83.2, unless the attorney's resignation certifies that the attorney waives the privilege of applying for readmission to the bar at any future time, in which case disciplinary proceedings shall be terminated.

### (i) Reinstatement.

1. An attorney suspended for a fixed period of time shall be automatically reinstated at the end of the period of suspension upon his or her filing (1) an affidavit with the Court demonstrating compliance with the provisions of the suspension order and (2) a certificate of good standing showing the attorney is a member in good standing in the Superior Court for the State of Connecticut or other state court.

2. Petitions for reinstatement by a disbarred or suspended attorney whose period of suspension has not expired shall be filed with the Clerk. Upon the filing of the petition, it shall be assigned to the judge previously assigned the original grievance proceeding. Otherwise, it shall be randomly assigned to another judge of the district. The petition shall automatically be referred to counsel for the Grievance Committee, who shall give public notice by newspaper publication of such petition, allowing 30 days for comment. Counsel shall provide notice to the complainant that a petition for reinstatement has been filed.

3. After the close of the public comment period, the Grievance Committee shall promptly schedule a hearing for the purpose of determining whether or not the petitioner should be reinstated. The Grievance Committee shall make a recommendation to the Court, within thirty (30) days of completing its independent investigation, as to the fitness of the petitioner to be reinstated.

4. Within thirty (30) days of receiving the Committee's recommendation, the Judge assigned to the matter shall schedule a hearing at which the petitioner shall have the burden of demonstrating by clear and convincing evidence that he or she has the moral qualifications, competency and learning in the law required for admission to practice law before this Court and that his or her resumption of the practice of law will not be detrimental to the integrity and standing of the bar or to the administration of justice, or injurious to the public interest.

5. In all proceedings upon a petition for reinstatement, counsel for the Grievance Committee may conduct cross-examination of the witnesses of the petitioner attorney and may file objections to the petition.

6. If the petitioner is found unfit to resume the practice of law, the petition shall be denied. If the petitioner is found fit to resume the practice of law, the judge shall reinstate him or her, provided that the judge may make reinstatement conditional upon (1) the payment of all or part of the costs of the proceedings, (2) the making of partial or complete restitution to parties harmed by the conduct of the petitioner which led to the suspension or disbarment, or (3) the furnishing of proof of competency and learning in the law if the petitioner has been suspended or disbarred

for five years or more, which proof may include certification by the bar examiners of a state or other jurisdiction of the attorney's successful completion of an examination for admission to practice subsequent to the date of suspension or disbarment.

7. Absent exceptional circumstances, no petition for reinstatement under this paragraph shall be filed within one year following an adverse judgment upon a petition for reinstatement filed by or on behalf of the same person.

[Effective January 1, 2003; amended effective August 1, 2003.]

   * Publishers note:  So in original. Probably should read "83.2".

## RULE 83.3   SECURITY FOR COSTS

(a) **Security for Costs**. Any time after the commencement of an action, the defendants, or the plaintiffs upon the filing of a counterclaim, are entitled on request to the Clerk to an order to be entered by the Clerk, as of course, for a cash deposit or bond with recognized corporate surety in the sum of $500.00 as security for costs to be given within thirty days from the entry of such order. Parties who are jointly represented by the same counsel will be deemed to be one party for the purposes of this $500 limitation. Additional, substituted, or reduced security, or a justification of financial responsibility by any surety, may be ordered by the Court at any time during the pendency of the action for good cause found by the Court. Noncompliance with an order entered hereunder may be grounds for summary dismissal or default upon application by a party and notice to the noncomplying party.

(b) **Modification and Waiver.** Upon good cause shown, the Court may modify or waive the requirements of this Rule.

[Effective January 1, 2003.]

## RULE 83.4   OPENING STATEMENTS

Unless the presiding Judge directs otherwise, counsel in civil jury trials shall be permitted to make opening statements subject to limitations imposed by the Judge.

[Effective January 1, 2003; amended effective August 1, 2003.]

## RULE 83.5   SECRECY OF JURY DELIBERATIONS

1. **Trial Jurors.**

a. No person, other than the Court or Court personnel, shall contact or communicate with, directly or indirectly, a juror, potential juror or excused juror, or any relative, friend or associate of any such juror, during jury selection or trial, concerning the subject matter of the trial or the juror's participation in the

trial, except with the permission of and under the supervision of the Court.

b. Jurors have no obligation to speak to any person about any case and may refuse all interviews or requests to discuss the case. Jurors may only speak or write about their own participation in the trial. Jurors may not discuss the deliberations of the jury, votes of the jury, or the actions or comments of any other juror. However, jurors shall report to the Court any extraneous prejudicial information improperly brought to the jury's attention, any outside influence improperly brought to bear upon any juror, or whether the verdict reported was the result of a clerical mistake.

c. No party, and no attorney or person acting on behalf of a party or attorney, shall question a juror concerning the deliberations of the jury, votes of the jury or the actions or comments of any other juror.

d. No person may contact, communicate with or interview any juror in any manner which subjects the juror to harassment, misrepresentation, duress or coercion.

2. **Juror Information.**  The Clerk shall make available to counsel and *pro se* parties participating in jury selection the responses to juror questionnaires of those prospective jurors participating in jury selection. Other individuals may request such information in accordance with the District's Jury Plan.

3. **Grand Jurors.**  No person, other than those authorized under Fed. R. Crim. P. 6 or Court personnel, shall contact or communicate with, directly or indirectly, a grand juror, potential grand juror, or excused grand juror at any time concerning the subject matter of the grand jury proceedings or the juror's participation in the grand jury proceedings. Grand jurors shall also comply with Fed. R. Crim. P. 6.

4. **Violations.**  A violation of this rule may be treated as a contempt of Court. The Court shall have continuing supervision over communications with jurors, even after a trial has been completed.

[Effective January 1, 2003; amended effective February 1, 2007.]

## RULE 83.6   REMOVAL OF PAPERS AND EXHIBITS

(a) **Withdrawal of Pleadings, Papers and Exhibits.** After being filed in Court, pleadings or other papers may be withdrawn only upon order of the Court. Exhibits received in evidence may be withdrawn by stipulation of the parties or by order of the Court.

(b) **Pre-marked Exhibits and Exhibit Lists.** Prior to the commencement of trial, counsel or pro se parties shall pre-mark all exhibits to be offered at hearing or trial. Counsel or pro se shall prepare and

submit to the courtroom deputy and the Judge a list of their exhibits, as pre-marked.

**(c) Custody of Exhibits After Trial.** Except in proceedings before a special master, and unless the Court otherwise directs, exhibits shall not be filed with the clerk, but shall be retained in the custody of counsel or pro se parties who produce them in court. Counsel or pro se parties shall retain these exhibits until final determination of the action, including the date when the mandate of the final reviewing court has been filed or until the time for appeal has expired.

**(d) Exhibits on Appeal.** In the case of an appeal or other review by an appellate court, the parties are encouraged to agree with respect to a designation of exhibits to be included in the record on appeal. In the absence of such an agreement, a party, upon the request of any other party, shall make the original exhibits available to the requesting party, or furnish copies, as may be necessary to enable the requesting party to designate or prepare the record on appeal. All exhibits designated as part of the record on appeal, except large or bulky exhibits, shall be filed with the Clerk, who shall transmit them with the record on appeal to the Clerk of the Court of Appeals. Exhibits not so designated shall remain in the custody of the respective attorneys or pro se parties who shall have the responsibility of forwarding same to the Clerk of the Court of Appeals upon request. Large or bulky exhibits designated as part of the record on appeal shall remain in the custody of counsel or the pro se party producing them and shall be responsible for their transportation to the appellate court.

**(e) Disposition of Exhibits in the Custody of the Clerk.** The offering party shall make arrangements for the return of those exhibits remaining with the Clerk within ninety days after final determination of the action. Exhibits not claimed may be destroyed by the Clerk, without notice.

[Effective January 1, 2003.]

## RULE 83.7   TRANSFER OF CASES TO ANOTHER DISTRICT OR UPON REMAND TO A STATE COURT

In a case ordered transferred to another District Court or remanded to the appropriate State Court, the clerk shall mail, on the eleventh day following the order of transfer or remand, to the Court to which the case is transferred or remanded: (1) a certified copy of the Court's opinion directing such action, and its order thereon, and of the docket entries, and (2) the original of all pleadings and other papers on file in the case, provided that no timely motion for reconsideration of the order of transfer or remand has been filed pursuant to Local Civil Rule 7(c). Where a timely motion for reconsideration has been filed, the Clerk shall delay mailing the file until the Court has ruled on the motion for reconsideration and will thereafter take

such action as is consistent with the ruling on the motion for reconsideration.

[Effective January 1, 2003.]

## RULE 83.8   ORDERS FOR EXTENSION OF FILING RECORD ON APPEAL

An extension of the forty (40) day period within which to transmit the record to the United States Court of Appeals, pursuant to Rule 11(d) of the Rules of Appellate Procedure, shall be granted only upon good cause shown and only if such request for extension is made within the time originally prescribed or within an extension previously granted. The District Court is without authority to extend the time to a day more than ninety (90) days from the date of filing the first notice of appeal. Each application for an extension of time under this Rule must show the date on which the notice of appeal was filed and the date when the last extension, if any, will expire. If the application is based upon delay in obtaining the reporter's transcript, it shall state the date on which the transcript was ordered.

[Effective January 1, 2003.]

## RULE 83.9   LAW STUDENT INTERNSHIP RULES

**(a) Appearance of Law Student Intern.** An eligible law student intern may, with the Court's approval, under supervision by a member of the bar, appear on behalf of any person who has consented in writing to the intern's appearance.

**(b) Requirements of Supervising Attorney.** The attorney who supervises an intern shall:

1. be a member of the bar of the United States District Court for the District of Connecticut;

2. assume personal professional responsibility for the student's work;

3. assist the student to the extent necessary;

4. appear with the student in all proceedings before the Court unless the attorney's presence is waived by the Court;

5. indicate in writing his or her consent to supervise the intern under this Rule.

**(c) Requirements of Law Student Intern.** In order to appear pursuant to this Rule, the law student intern shall:

1. be enrolled in good standing in a law school approved by the American Bar Association;

2. have completed legal studies amounting to at least two semesters of credit, or the equivalent if the school is on some basis other than a semester basis;

3. be introduced to the Court in which he or she is appearing by the supervising attorney;

4. not be employed or compensated by a client. This Rule shall not prevent an attorney, legal aid bureau, law school, public defender, or other agency from compensating a law student intern.

**(d) Privileges of Law Student Intern.** The law student intern, supervised in accordance with this Rule, may:

1. appear as counsel in Court or at other proceedings when the consents of the client and supervising attorney referred to in subdivisions (a) and (b) of this Rule have been filed, and the Court has approved the intern's request to appear; and

2. prepare and sign motions, petitions, answers, briefs and other documents in connection with any matter in which the law student intern has met the conditions of Rule 83.9(c). Each such document must also be signed by the supervising attorney.

[Effective January 1, 2003.]

## RULE 83.10 CIVIL PRO BONO PANEL

### (a) List of Attorneys.

1. The Clerk of the Court shall prepare a list of attorneys (Civil Pro Bono Panel) admitted to practice in this Court, to be grouped according to the seat of Court in which the attorney primarily practices. The attorneys so listed shall be eligible for appointment to represent parties in civil actions when such parties lack the resources, or are otherwise unable, to retain counsel.

2. The Clerk shall obtain from each attorney information to be used in assigning counsel from the Civil Pro Bono Panel. A form for this purpose shall be provided by the Clerk of the Court. This information may include, but need not be limited to: (1) the attorney's prior civil trial experience; (2) the attorney's ability to consult and advise in languages other than English; (3) the attorney's preference for appointment among various types of actions (e.g., Social Security appeals, employment discrimination actions, civil rights actions), and (4) the attorney's preference for appointment to the various seats of Court.

3. Any attorney on the Civil Pro Bono Panel may seek to have his or her name stricken from the Panel, either temporarily or permanently. A Judge of this Court may so strike the name of any such attorney from the Panel, upon good cause shown. Reasons which may constitute good cause for the striking of an attorney's name shall include, but are not limited to, infirmity, retirement, practice limited to courts outside the District of Connecticut, lack of experience or expertise, and prior recent appointment(s) from the Civil Pro Bono Panel. If the attorney's name is stricken for a specified period of time, then said attorney's name shall be reinstated at the expiration of that period unless on a further application, a Judge of this Court has ordered to the contrary.

**(b) Appointment Procedure.**

1. The Clerk shall advise and assist any pro se litigant in filing an in forma pauperis affidavit where the party lacks the resources to retain counsel. Upon the filing of such an affidavit, or at such time as a pro se litigant shall inquire of the Clerk concerning representation and appear, despite reasonable efforts, to be unable to obtain counsel, the Clerk shall also inform the party of the opportunity to apply in writing for appointment of counsel from the Civil Pro Bono Panel.

2. A written application for appointed counsel by the pro se party should be made to the assigned Judge within ten (10) days after the party files an in forma pauperis affidavit.

3. Notwithstanding any past ineligibility for appointed counsel, a pro se litigant may apply for appointment of counsel any time circumstances reasonably appear to warrant such application.

4. The presiding Judge shall determine whether a Panel attorney is to be appointed to represent a pro se party as soon as practicable after an application is filed or when the ends of justice appear best served by such an appointment. The factors to be taken into account in making this determination are: (i) the nature and complexity of the action; (ii) the potential merit of the claims as set forth in the pleadings; (iii) the financial or other inability of the pro se party to retain counsel by other means; (iv) the degree to which the interests of justice will be served by appointment of counsel, including the benefit the Court may derive from the assistance of the appointed counsel; and (v) any other relevant factors. Failure of a pro se party to apply for appointment of counsel in writing shall not preclude appointment with the consent of the pro se party. Upon appointment of an attorney for reasons other than the party's financial inability to obtain counsel, the Clerk shall inform the party that the Court may order disclosure of the facts pertinent to the party's ability to pay an attorney's fee and may also order the payment of an attorney's fee commensurate with the services rendered and the party's financial circumstances.

5. Whenever the presiding Judge concludes that appointment of counsel is warranted, an order shall issue to the Clerk directing an appointment from the Civil Pro Bono Panel at the seat of Court where the action is pending to represent the pro se party. The Judge may direct the appointment of a specific attorney on the Panel.

6. When a petition by a pro se party for habeas corpus is involved, any appointment shall be from the Criminal Justice Act Panel of Attorneys.

7. On receipt of an appointment order the Clerk shall select an attorney from the Panel unless the order directs appointment of a specific attorney. Selection by the Clerk shall be made on a rotating basis from the lists of attorneys on the Panel, which shall be

grouped according to the seat of Court and types of actions reflected as preferences, qualifications or specialties on the attorneys' information forms.

8. Before assigning an attorney, the Clerk shall determine whether the litigant has any other case pending before the Court and whether an attorney has been appointed in such case. Where an appointed attorney is already representing the litigant in a prior action, such attorney is encouraged but not required to represent the litigant in the new action. The Clerk shall inquire of the appointed counsel whether he or she will accept the appointment in the new action. If the appointed counsel declines, the Clerk shall appoint another attorney in accordance with this Rule.

9. The Clerk shall immediately send written notice of the appointment, the pleadings filed to date, relevant correspondence and other documents to the appointed attorney who shall forthwith enter an appearance in the action. The Clerk shall also send immediate written notice to the newly represented party and to all other parties.

**(c) Responsibilities of the Appointed Attorney.**

1. The appointed attorney shall promptly communicate with his or her client.

2. If the appointed attorney reasonably perceives the potential applicability of any of the grounds enumerated in this Rule, the attorney shall, before discussing the merits of the case with the client, advise the client of the provisions of this Rule. Where the attorney did not perceive such prior to discussing the merits of the case with the client, the attorney may request the client to execute a limited waiver of the attorney-client privilege permitting the attorney to disclose under seal to the Court information relevant to the applicability of the Rule. The waiver should indicate that the application for relief will be a privileged Court document and may not be used in the litigation. The client's refusal to execute a waiver shall not preclude the attorney from applying for relief.

3. The appointed attorney should discuss fully the merits of the dispute with the party, and explore with the party the possibilities of resolving the dispute in other forums, including but not limited to administrative forums.

4. If the party decides to prosecute or defend the action after consultation with the appointed attorney, the appointed attorney shall proceed to represent the party in the action, unless or until the attorney-client relationship is terminated as provided in this Rule.

5. Once appointed, the attorney shall freely exercise his or her professional judgment, but shall not be required to represent the client in any other matter.

**(d) Relief From Appointment.**

1. A request for relief from appointment will not be considered unless the party has received specific notice of such request by personal service or by certified mail. Absent an appearance of new counsel, an appointed attorney may apply to be relieved of an appointment only on the following grounds: (i) a conflict of interest results from the representation of the party; (ii) the attorney believes that he or she is not competent to represent the party in the particular type of action assigned; (iii) a personal incompatibility or a substantial disagreement on litigation strategy exists between the attorney and the party; (iv) the attorney lacks the time necessary to represent the client because of the temporary burden of other professional commitments; (v) the party appears to be proceeding for purposes of harassment or malicious injury, or the party's claims or defenses are not warranted under existing law and cannot be supported by good faith argument for extension, modification or reversal of existing law; or (vi) for other good cause shown.

2. If an application for relief from an appointment is granted, another attorney may be ordered to represent the party. The Judge shall have the discretion to deny a further appointment, in which case the party may prosecute or defend the action pro se.

3. Whenever an attorney seeks to be relieved of an order of appointment on any of the grounds set forth above, he or she shall file an application for relief with the Clerk within a reasonable period of time not to exceed thirty (30) days after learning of the facts warranting such relief. The application shall set forth in full the factual and legal basis for the request. The application shall be a privileged Court document kept under seal and shall not be available in discovery or otherwise used in the litigation. The attorney appointed shall thereupon be relieved of the order of appointment upon showing any of the grounds set forth above. The Clerk shall then, without revealing the contents of the application to the Judge, forthwith select another attorney to represent the party in accordance with the provisions of this Rule, unless the Judge determines not to order another appointment pursuant to paragraph (d)2 above.

4. An attorney selected pursuant to Rule 83.10(d)3 may seek to be relieved from appointment on any of the grounds in subparagraph (d)1(v) of this Rule 83.10 by filing an application therefor. The Clerk shall thereupon submit the application for relief of the first and any subsequent appointed attorneys to the assigned Judge. The Judge shall either (i) deny the application of the subsequent attorney and direct that attorney to proceed with the representation or (ii) grant the application. In the latter instance, the Judge may choose not to issue a further order of appointment. If so, the Clerk shall inform the party that no further appointments shall be made and upon request of the pro se party the Judge shall recuse himself or herself.

**(e) Discharge.**

1. A party for whom an attorney has been appointed may request the discharge of the appointed attorney and appointment of another attorney. Such requests must be made within thirty (30) days after the party's initial consultation with the appointed attorney, or within such additional period as is warranted by good cause.

2. When good cause is shown (e.g., substantial disagreement between the party and the appointed attorney on litigation strategy), the appointed attorney shall be discharged from further representation of the party. In such cases, another attorney may thereupon be selected by the Clerk to undertake the representation, in accordance with this Rule. The Judge may deny a further appointment in such cases. Where a party requests discharge of a second appointed attorney, no additional appointments shall be made.

3. Where (i) a request for discharge is not supported by good cause, or (ii) discharge of a second appointed attorney is requested, the party may prosecute or defend the action pro se. In either case, the appointed attorney shall be discharged from the representation.

**(f) Expenses.**

1. The appointed attorney shall bear any expenses of the litigation (e.g., discovery expenses, subpoena fees, transcript expenses), unless the attorney has, prior to incurring such expenses, obtained an order from the Court authorizing such expense. Failure to obtain such an order will not bar the appointed attorney from seeking reimbursement pursuant to Rule 83.10(g)1 and 3.

2. Upon appropriate application by the appointed attorney the Clerk shall certify those expenses for which the appointed attorney may be reimbursed, in accordance with the procedures utilized in in forma pauperis proceedings, in proceedings under the Criminal Justice Act or other guidelines issued by the Court. Thereafter, the assigned Judge may order reimbursement of the expenses of the litigation, as authorized by applicable statute, regulation, rule or other provision of law.

**(g) Compensation for Services.**

1. If the action is one for which compensation for legal services, costs and/or expenses may become available to the appointed attorney by statute, the Clerk shall so inform the pro se party at the time of the application for appointed counsel and at the time the appointment is made. The Clerk shall also then inform the party that any statutory fee may be awarded only by the Judge at the conclusion of the case.

2. Pro se litigants in Social Security disability cases shall be specifically advised by the Clerk that a statutory attorney's fee may be awarded to be paid from the award, if any, of retroactive disability benefits.

3. Upon appropriate application by the appointed attorney, the Judge may award attorney's fees, costs and/or expenses to the appointed attorney for services rendered in the action, as authorized by applicable statute, regulation, rule or other provision of law, and as the Judge deems just and proper. In deciding whether to award attorney's fees the Judge shall consider: (i) the relevant statutes and provisions of law; (ii) the source of the fee award; (iii) the services rendered; and (iv) any other factors he or she deems appropriate.

4. If the party is able to pay for legal services, upon application of the appointed attorney, the Judge may thereupon (i) approve a fee arrangement between the party and the attorney, (ii) order a fee to be paid on a specified basis, or (iii) relieve the attorney from the responsibilities of the appointment and permit the party to retain another attorney or to proceed pro se.

5. A fund shall be kept by the Clerk for the purpose of funding expenses that a party is unable to meet, in whole or in part. This fund shall consist of a portion of the fees collected in connection with applications for admission to the Bar of this Court and motions for admission pro hac vice. The Clerk shall review all applications of appointed attorneys for advance approval of part or all of a litigation expense and decide whether to authorize the expense and provide for payment from the fund. An appointed attorney may request the presiding Judge to review the Clerk's decision. If the party is subsequently reimbursed for an expense that had been funded in whole or in part from the Clerk's fund, the party shall be required to reimburse the fund.

**(h) Duration of Representation.**

1. An appointed attorney shall represent the party in the trial court from the date he or she enters an appearance until he or she has been relieved from appointment by the Court or until a final judgment is entered in the District Court.

2. If the party desires to take an appeal from a final judgment or appealable interlocutory order, or if such judgment or order is appealed by another party, or if the matter is remanded to an administrative forum, the appointed attorney is encouraged but not required to represent the party on the appeal, and in any proceeding, judicial or administrative, which may ensue upon an order of remand.

3. Where the appointed attorney elects not to represent the party on an appeal or in a proceeding upon remand, the attorney shall advise the party of all required steps to be taken in perfecting the appeal or appearing in the proceeding on remand. Upon request of the pro se party the attorney shall file the notice of appeal. The trial Judge may thereafter, upon the request of the party, appoint another attorney from the Panel to represent the party on such appeal or

further proceeding, in accordance with the provisions of this Rule.

[Effective January 1, 2003.]

## RULE 83.11   RECORDINGS AND PHOTOGRAPHS

Except for ceremonial occasions, and then only upon the approval of the presiding Judge, the taking of photographs or the broadcasting by means of radio or television or the recording of the proceedings by any person other than the official court reporter in or from the courtroom during the progress of or in connection with judicial proceedings, including proceedings before the Grand Jury or a Magistrate, whether or not the Court is actually in session, is prohibited.

[Effective January 1, 2003.]

## RULE 83.12   AUXILIARY ORDERS

Orders entered by the Court which affect the procedures or policies of practice before the Court but which do not amend or take the form of a Local Rule, shall be designated as Auxiliary Orders and shall be available in the Clerk's Office.

[Effective January 1, 2003.]

## RULE 83.13   PROHIBITION ON COUNSEL AS WITNESS

**(a) Refusing Employment When Counsel May Be Called as a Witness.** A lawyer shall not accept employment in contemplated or pending litigation if he or she knows or it is obvious that he or she or a lawyer in the same firm ought to be called as a witness, except that he or she may undertake the employment and he or she or a lawyer in his or her firm may testify:

1. If the testimony will relate solely to an uncontested matter.

2. If the testimony will relate solely to a matter of formality and there is no reason to believe that substantial evidence will be offered in opposition to the testimony.

3. If the testimony will relate solely to the nature and value of the legal services rendered in the case by the lawyer or the law firm to the client.

**(b) Withdrawal as Counsel When The Lawyer Becomes a Witness.**

1. If, after undertaking employment in contemplated or pending litigation, a lawyer learns or it is obvious that he or she or a lawyer in the same firm ought to be called as a witness on behalf of the client, he or she shall withdraw from the conduct of the trial and the law firm shall not continue representation in the trial, except that the lawyer may continue the representation, and he or she or a lawyer in the law firm may testify in the circumstances enumerated in Rule 83.13(a).

2. If, after undertaking employment in contemplated or pending litigation, a lawyer learns or it is obvious that he or she or a lawyer in the same firm may be called as a witness other than on behalf of his or her client, the lawyer may continue the representation until it is apparent that his or her testimony is or may be prejudicial to the client.

**(c) Discretion of Court To Provide Relief From This Rule When Lawyer In Same Firm Is Likely To Be A Witness.** The court may in the exercise of its sound discretion permit a lawyer to act as an advocate in a trial in which another lawyer in the lawyer's firm is likely to be called as a witness if disqualification of the lawyer would work substantial hardship on the client and permitting the lawyer to act as an advocate would not cause prejudice to opposing parties.

[Effective January 1, 2003.]

# CIVIL APPENDIX

## FORM 26(f).   REPORT OF PARTIES' PLANNING MEETING

Caption of Case
[List all parties]

Date Complaint Filed:

Date Complaint Served:

Date of Defendant's Appearance:

Pursuant to Fed. R. Civ. P. 16(b), 26(f) and D. Conn. L. Civ. R. 16, a conference was held on [date]. The participants were:

_____ for plaintiff [party name]

_____ for defendant [party name]

### I.   Certification.

Undersigned counsel certify that, after consultation with their clients, they have discussed the nature and basis of the parties' claims and defenses and any possibilities for achieving a prompt settlement or other resolution of the case and, in consultation with their clients, have developed the following proposed case management plan. Counsel further certify that they have forwarded a copy of this report to their clients.

### II.   Jurisdiction.

A. *Subject Matter Jurisdiction.* [Provide a statement of the basis for subject matter jurisdiction with appropriate statutory citations. If plaintiff's allegation of subject matter jurisdiction is denied, specify the basis for the denial. In cases where the basis for

subject matter jurisdiction is diversity of citizenship, if any party is a partnership, limited liability partnership, or limited liability company or corporation, provide the citizenship of each partner, general partner, limited partner and member, and if any such partner, general partner, limited partner or member is itself a partnership, limited liability partnership, or limited liability company or corporation, provide the citizenship of each member.]

B. *Personal Jurisdiction.* [State whether personal jurisdiction is contested and, if it is, summarize the parties' competing positions].

## III.  Brief Description of Case.

[Briefly summarize the claims and defenses of all parties and describe the relief sought. If agreement cannot be reached on a joint statement, each party must provide a short separate statement. The requirement that the parties briefly summarize their claims and defenses is not intended to be unduly burdensome. The parties are obliged to discuss and consider the nature of their claims and defenses at the planning conference in order to formulate a meaningful case management plan. Moreover, the presiding judge needs to be informed of the nature of the claims and defenses in order to evaluate the reasonableness of the parties' proposed plan. The statement of the parties' claims and defenses, whether set forth jointly or separately, does not preclude any party from raising new claims and defenses as permitted by other applicable law.

A. *Claims of Plaintiff/s:*

B. *Defenses and Claims (Counterclaims, Third Party Claims, Cross Claims) of Defendant/s:*

C. *Defenses and Claims of Third Party Defendant/s:*

## IV.  Statement of Undisputed Facts:

Counsel certify that they have made a good faith attempt to determine whether there are any material facts that are not in dispute. The parties state that the following material facts are undisputed:

## V.  Case Management Plan:

A. *Standing Order on Scheduling in Civil Cases.* The parties [request] [do not request] modification of the deadlines in the Standing Order on Scheduling in Civil Cases [as follows]:

B. *Scheduling Conference with the Court.* The parties [request] [do not request] a pretrial conference with the Court before entry of a scheduling order pursuant to Fed. R. Civ. P. 16(b). The parties prefer a conference [in person] [by telephone].

C. *Early Settlement Conference.*

1. The parties certify that they have considered the desirability of attempting to settle the case before undertaking significant discovery or motion practice.

Settlement [is likely] [is unlikely at this time] [may be enhanced by use of the following procedure]:_____.

2. The parties [request] [do not request] an early settlement conference.

3. The parties prefer a settlement conference with [the presiding judge] [a magistrate judge] [a parajudicial officer] [special masters].

4. The parties [request] [do not request] a referral for alternative dispute resolution pursuant to D. Conn. L. Civ. R. 16.

E. *Joinder of Parties and Amendment of Pleadings.*

1. Plaintiff(s) should be allowed until [date] to file motions to join additional parties and until [date] to file motions to amend the pleadings.

2. Defendant(s) should be allowed until [date] to file motions to join additional parties and until [date] to file a response to the complaint.

F. *Discovery.*

1. The parties anticipate that discovery will be needed on the following subjects: [list each of the principal issues of fact on which discovery will be needed; a statement that "discovery will be needed on liability and damages" is insufficient].

2. All discovery, including depositions of expert witnesses pursuant to Fed. R. Civ. P. 26(b)(4), will be commenced by [date] and completed (not propounded) by [date].

3. Discovery [will] [will not] be conducted in phases.

4. Discovery on will be completed by [date].

5. The parties anticipate that the plaintiff(s) will require a total of ____ depositions of fact witnesses and that the defendant(s) will require a total of ____ depositions of fact witnesses. The depositions will commence by [date] and be completed by [date].

6. The parties [will] [will not] request permission to serve more than 25 interrogatories.

7. Plaintiff/s [intend] [do not intend] to call expert witnesses at trial. Plaintiff/s will designate all trial experts and provide opposing counsel with reports from retained experts pursuant to Fed. R. Civ. P. 26(a)(2) by [a date not later than 3 months before the deadline for completing all discovery]. Depositions of any such experts will be completed by [a date not later than 2 months before the deadline for completing all discovery].

8. Defendant/s [intend] [do not intend] to call expert witnesses at trial. Defendant/s will designate all trial experts and provide opposing counsel with reports from retained experts pursuant to Fed. R. Civ. P. 26(a)(2) by [a date not later than 1 month before the deadline for completing all discovery]. Depositions

of such experts will be completed by [a date not later than the discovery cutoff date].

9. A damages analysis will be provided by any party who has a claim or counterclaim for damages by [date].

10. Undersigned counsel have discussed the disclosure and preservation of electronically stored information, including, but not limited to, the form in which such data shall be produced, search terms to be applied in connection with the retrieval and production of such information, the location and format of electronically stored information, appropriate steps to preserve electronically stored information, and the allocation of costs of assembling and producing such information. [The parties agree to the following procedures for the preservation, disclosure, and management of electronically stored information *or* the parties have been unable to reach agreement on the procedures for the preservation, disclosure, and management of electronically stored information. Following is the position of each party:]

11. Undersigned counsel have discussed discovery procedures that minimize the risk of waiver of privilege or work-product protection, including procedures for asserting privilege claims after production. [The parties agree to the following procedures for asserting claims of privilege after production *or* the parties have been unable to reach agreement on the procedures for asserting claims of privilege after production. Following is the position of each party:]

G. *Dispositive Motions:*

Dispositive motions will be filed on or before [date].

H. *Joint Trial Memorandum.*

The joint trial memorandum required by the Standing Order on Trial Memoranda in Civil Cases will be filed by [date].

## VI. TRIAL READINESS.

The case will be ready for trial by [date].

As officers of the Court, undersigned counsel agree to cooperate with each other and the Court to promote the just, speedy and inexpensive determination of this action.

Plaintiff

By _____ Date:

Defendant

By _____ Date:

The undersigned pro se parties certify that they will cooperate with all other parties, counsel of record and the Court to promote the just, speedy and inexpensive determination of this action.

Plaintiff _____ Date:

Defendant _____ Date:

[Effective January 1, 2003; revised effective January 1, 2007.]

# CIVIL STANDING ORDERS

## STANDING ORDER ON SCHEDULING IN CIVIL CASES

1. **Order on Pretrial Deadlines.** Except in cases exempted by D. Conn. L. Civ. R. 16, the Clerk, acting pursuant to the authority of the Court, shall enter in each civil action an Order on Pretrial Deadlines, which Order shall contain the deadlines listed in paragraph 2 of this Standing Order. Said Order shall be entered at the time of the filing of the complaint, and will control the course of the action until a further Scheduling Order is issued pursuant to Fed. R. Civ. P. 16(b) and D. Conn. L. Civ. R. 16.

2. **Presumptive Filing Deadlines.** Unless otherwise ordered by the presiding Judge, parties in civil cases will adhere to the following deadlines:

(a) In accordance with D. Conn. L. Civ. R. 16, within thirty days after the appearance of a defendant, the parties shall confer for the purposes described in Fed. R. Civ. P. 26(f). Within ten days thereafter, the parties shall jointly file a report on Form 26(f), which appears in the Appendix to the Local Civil Rules.

(b) All motions relating to joinder of parties, claims or remedies, class certification, and amendment of the pleadings shall be filed within 60 days after the filing of the complaint, the filing of a petition for removal, or the transfer of an action from another District, except that a defendant may file a third-party complaint within 10 days of serving an answer, as permitted by Fed. R. Civ. P. 14(a).

(c) All motions to dismiss based on the pleadings shall be filed within 90 days after the filing of the complaint, the filing of a petition for removal, or the transfer of an action from another District. The filing of a motion to dismiss will not result in a stay of discovery or extend the time for completing discovery.

(d) Formal discovery pursuant to the Federal Rules of Civil Procedure may not commence until the parties have conferred as required by Fed. R. Civ. P. 26(f) and Local Civil Rule 16 but the parties may commence formal discovery immediately thereafter without awaiting entry of a scheduling order pursuant to Fed. R. Civ. P. 16(b). Informal discovery by agreement of the parties is encouraged and may commence at anytime. Unless otherwise ordered, discovery shall be completed within 6 months after the filing of the complaint, the filing of a petition for removal, or the transfer of an action from another District.

(e) Unless otherwise ordered, all motions for summary judgment shall be filed within 7 months after the filing of the complaint, the filing of a petition for removal, or the transfer of an action from another District.

**3. Modification.** This Order may be modified pursuant to a stipulation signed by all parties and approved by the presiding Judge, or on motion by any party for good cause shown or by the presiding Judge acting sua sponte. The good cause standard requires a particularized showing that the schedule established by this order cannot reasonably be met despite the diligence of the party seeking the extension. Unless specifically ordered by the Court, an extension of time to comply with any one of the time limits in this Order does not automatically extend the time to comply with subsequent time limits.

**4. Status and Settlement Conferences.** The Court may schedule the case for a status conference or a settlement conference at any time.

**5. Standing Order Regarding Trial Memoranda in Civil Cases.** Counsel are alerted that, at an appropriate time during the progress of the case, each party may be ordered to prepare and submit, or the parties may be ordered to jointly prepare and submit, a trial memorandum substantially in the form described in the Standing Order Regarding Trial Memoranda in Civil Cases, which is published in the Local Rules. Counsel should familiarize themselves with that Standing Order and with the particular practice of the Judge to whom the case has been assigned.

[Effective January 1, 2003.]

# STANDING ORDER REGARDING TRIAL MEMORANDA IN CIVIL CASES

At the discretion of the presiding Judge, each party may be ordered to prepare and submit, or the parties may be ordered to jointly prepare and submit, a trial memorandum in duplicate which shall contain the following information:

**1. Trial Counsel.** List the names, addresses and telephone numbers of the attorneys who will try the case. Trial counsel must attend the pretrial conference unless excused by the Court.

**2. Jurisdiction.** Set forth the basis for federal jurisdiction.

**3. Jury/Non-jury.** State whether the case is a jury or court case.

**4. Nature of Case.** State separately the nature of each cause of action and relief sought.

**5. Stipulations of Fact and Law.** Prepare a list of stipulations on any issues of fact and/or law as to which the parties have been able to agree.

**6. Plaintiff's Contentions.** State generally the plaintiff's factual contentions with respect to each cause of action.

**7. Defendant's Contentions.** State generally the defendant's factual contentions with respect to defenses, counterclaims and setoffs.

**8. Legal Issues.** List the legal issues presented by the factual contentions of the parties.

**9. Voir Dire Questions.** For jury cases, attach a list of proposed questions to be submitted to the jury panel.

**10. List of Witnesses.** Set forth the name and address of each witness to be called at trial, with a brief statement of the anticipated testimony. Witnesses not listed, except rebuttal and impeachment witnesses, will not be permitted to testify at trial, except for good cause shown.

**11. Exhibits.** Attach a list of all exhibits, with a brief description of each, that each party will offer at trial on the case-in-chief. Exhibits not listed, except rebuttal and impeachment exhibits, will not be admissible at trial except for good cause shown. All objections to designated exhibits, except as to relevance, must be filed in writing, to be resolved between the parties or by Court ruling prior to jury selection.

**12. Deposition Testimony.** List each witness who is expected to testify by deposition at trial. Such list shall include designation by page references of the deposition transcript which each party proposes to read into evidence. Cross-designations shall be listed as provided by Fed. R. Civ. P. 32(a)(4). The lists shall include all objections to deposition designations. These objections must be resolved between the parties or by Court ruling prior to jury selection. After submission, the Court will permit amendment of the lists only for good cause shown. At the time of trial, the Court will permit reading of testimony from a deposition only in the order in which it was taken.

**13. Requests for Jury Instructions.** For jury cases, attach requests for the jury charge.

**14. Anticipated Evidentiary Problems.** Attach memoranda of fact and law concerning evidentiary problems anticipated by the parties.

**15. Proposed Findings and Conclusions.** For non-jury cases, attach proposed findings of fact and conclusions of law.

**16. Trial Time.** Counsel shall set forth a realistic estimate of trial days required.

**17. Further Proceedings.** Specify, with reasons, the necessity of any further proceedings prior to trial.

**18. Election for Trial by Magistrate.** The parties shall indicate whether they have agreed to have the case tried by a United States Magistrate, and if so, indicate whether the parties have elected to have any

appeal heard by the District Court or by the Court of Appeals.

[Effective January 1, 2003.]

# STANDING ORDER IN CIVIL RICO CASES

In all civil actions where the complaint contains a cause of action pursuant to 18 U.S.C. §§ 1961–1968 the plaintiff shall file a RICO Case Statement within twenty (20) days of filing the complaint. Consistent with counsel's obligations under Fed.R.Civ.P. 11 to make a "reasonable inquiry" prior to the filing of the complaint, the RICO Case Statement shall state in detail the following information:

1. The alleged unlawful conduct that is claimed to be in violation of 18 U.S.C. §§ 1962(a), (b), (c) and/or (d).

2. The identity of each defendant and the alleged misconduct and basis of liability of each defendant.

3. The identity of the alleged wrongdoers, other than the defendants listed in response to paragraph 2, and the alleged misconduct of each wrongdoer.

4. The identity of the alleged victims and the manner in which each victim was allegedly injured.

5. A description of the pattern of racketeering activity or collection of unlawful debts alleged for each RICO claim, which shall include the following information:

a. The alleged predicate acts and the specific statutes which were allegedly violated;

b. The dates of the predicate acts, the participants in the predicate acts, and a description of the facts surrounding the predicate acts;

c. If the RICO claim is based on the predicate offenses of wire fraud, mail fraud, or fraud in the sale of securities, the "circumstances constituting fraud or mistake shall be stated with particularity." Fed. R.Civ.P. 9(b). The time, place and contents of the alleged misrepresentations, and the identity of persons to whom and by whom the alleged misrepresentations were made shall be identified;

d. Whether there has been a criminal conviction for violation of the predicate acts;

e. Whether civil litigation has resulted in a judgment in regard to the predicate acts;

f. The manner in which the predicate acts form a "pattern of racketeering activity"; and

g. Whether the alleged predicate acts relate to each other as part of a common plan, and if so, a detailed description of the common plan.

6. A detailed description of the alleged enterprise for each RICO claim, which shall include:

a. The names of the individuals, partnerships, corporations, associations, or other legal entities, which allegedly constitute the enterprise;

b. The structure, purpose, function and course of conduct of the enterprise.

c. Whether any defendants are employees, officers or directors of the alleged enterprise;

d. Whether any defendants are associated with the alleged enterprise;

e. Whether plaintiff contends that the defendants are individuals or entities separate from the alleged enterprise, or that the defendants are the enterprise itself, or members of the enterprise; and

f. If any defendants are alleged to be the enterprise itself, or members of the enterprise, an explanation as to whether such defendants are perpetrators, passive instruments, or victims of the alleged racketeering activity.

7. Whether plaintiff contends that the pattern of racketeering activity and the enterprise are separate or have merged into one entity.

8. The alleged relationship between the activities of the enterprise and the pattern of racketeering activity, including a description of the manner in which the racketeering activity differs, if at all, from the usual and daily activities of the enterprise.

9. The benefits, if any, the alleged enterprise receives or has received from the alleged pattern of racketeering.

10. The effect of the activities of the enterprise on interstate or foreign commerce.

11. If the complaint alleges a violation of 18 U.S.C. § 1962(a), provide the following information:

a. The identity of the individual(s) who received the income derived from the pattern of racketeering activity or through the collection of an unlawful debt; and

b. The use or investment of such income.

12. If the complaint alleges a violation of 18 U.S.C. § 1962(b), describe in detail the acquisition or maintenance of any interest in or control of the alleged enterprise.

13. If the complaint alleges a violation of 18 U.S.C. § 1962(b), provide the following information:

a. The individuals who are employed by or associated with the enterprise; and

b. Whether the same entity is both the liable "person" and the "enterprise" under § 1962(c).

14. If the complaint alleges a violation of 18 U.S.C. § 1962(d), describe in detail the alleged conspiracy.

15. The alleged injury to business or property.

16. The direct casual relationship between the alleged injury and the violation of the RICO statute.

17. The damages sustained for which each defendant is allegedly liable.

18. A description of other federal causes of action alleged in the complaint, if any, and citation to the relevant statutes.

19. A description of all pendent state claims alleged in the complaint, if any.

20. Any additional information plaintiff feels would be helpful to the Court in processing the RICO claim.

[Effective January 1, 2003.]

## STANDING ORDER ON REMOVED CASES

All parties removing actions to this Court pursuant to 28 U.S.C. § 1441 shall, no later than five days after filing a notice of removal, file and serve a signed statement that sets forth the following information:

1. The date on which each defendant first received a copy of the summons and complaint in the state court action.

2. The date on which each defendant was served with a copy of the summons and complaint, if any of those dates are different from the dates set forth in item 1.

3. In diversity cases, whether any defendant who has been served is a citizen of Connecticut. Also, if any party is a partnership, limited liability partnership or limited liability company or corporation, the citizenship of each partner, general partner, limited partner and member, and if any such partner, general partner, limited partner or member is itself a partnership, limited liability partnership or limited liability company or corporation, the citizenship of each member.

4. If removal takes place more than thirty (30) days after any defendant first received a copy of the summons and complaint, the reasons why removal has taken place at this time.

5. The name of any defendant served prior to the filing of the notice of removal who has not formally joined in the notice of removal and the reasons why any such defendant did not join in the notice of removal.

At the time a removal notice is filed with the Clerk of this Court, the removing party shall also file with the Clerk a separate notice, entitled "Notice of Pending Motions," specifying any pending motions that require action by a Judge of this Court and attaching a true and complete copy of each such motion and all supporting and opposition papers.

The removing party shall list in its certificate of service immediately below the name and address of counsel the name of the party or parties represented by said counsel and all parties appearing pro se.

[Effective January 1, 2003.]

# CIVIL MISCELLANEOUS NOTICES AND ORDERS

## NOTICE TO COUNSEL RE LOCAL RULE 7(b)

To ensure that our records are complete and to ensure that you receive notice of hearings and any court rulings, PLEASE FILE AN APPEARANCE with this office in accordance with Local Rule 7(b) of the Local Rules of Civil Procedure for the District of Connecticut.

[Effective January 1, 2003.]

## NOTICE RE PLANNING CONFERENCE AND REPORT

Pursuant to Fed. R. Civ. P. 26 and Local Civil Rule 26, counsel and pro se parties must conduct a case management conference within 30 days of the appearance of the opposing party and must jointly file a planning conference report within 10 days thereafter using form 26(f), which appears in the Appendix to the Local Rules.

Counsel for the removing defendant(s) is responsible for immediately serving a copy of this notice on all counsel of record and all unrepresented parties at their last known address.

[Effective January 1, 2003.]

## ORDER RE: DISCLOSURE STATEMENT

ANY NON–GOVERNMENTAL CORPORATE PARTY TO AN ACTION IN THIS COURT SHALL FILE A STATEMENT IDENTIFYING ALL ITS PARENT CORPORATIONS AND LISTING ANY PUBLICLY HELD COMPANY THAT OWNS 10% OR MORE OF THE PARTY'S STOCK. A PARTY SHALL FILE THE STATEMENT WITH ITS INITIAL PLEADING FILED IN THE COURT AND SHALL SUPPLEMENT THE STATEMENT WITHIN A REASONABLE TIME OF ANY CHANGE IN THE INFORMATION. COUNSEL SHALL APPEND A CERTIFICATE OF SERVICE TO THE STATEMENT IN COMPLIANCE WITH D. CONN. L. CIV. R. 5(b)*.

COUNSEL FOR PLAINTIFF OR REMOVING DEFENDANT SHALL BE RESPONSIBLE FOR SERVING A COPY OF THIS ORDER UPON ALL PARTIES TO THE ACTION.

BY ORDER OF THE COURT

KEVIN F. ROWE, CLERK

[Effective January 1, 2003.]

* Publisher's Note: So in original. Probably should read "5(c)".

## CELLULAR TELEPHONE POLICY FOR THE DISTRICT OF CONNECTICUT

Cellular telephones are prohibited in the federal courthouses in the District of Connecticut, except they may be possessed by:

1. Attorneys who display a state bar photo identification card;

2. Grand Jurors and Jurors who have been selected for a particular case;

3. Individuals attending naturalization sessions of the Court;

4. The United States Attorney, Assistant U.S. Attorneys, the Federal Defender, and Assistant Federal Defenders;

5. Law enforcement personnel and United States Probation Officers;

6. Judges and their chambers staff;

7. Employees of the Clerk's Office; and

8. Other individuals permitted by the Court.

The United States Marshal's Service will maintain a system for collecting and returning cellular telephones in each courthouse.

This policy is effective July 1, 2006.

Effective July 1, 2006.

# UNITED STATES DISTRICT COURT DISTRICT OF CONNECTICUT LOCAL RULES FOR MAGISTRATE JUDGES

## LOCAL RULE 72.1 GENERAL JURISDICTION AND DUTIES OF MAGISTRATE JUDGES

The following general jurisdiction and duties shall be exercised by each Magistrate Judge appointed by the Court:

**(A)** The Magistrate Judge shall have jurisdiction over the entire District, with such official station as is fixed by the order of appointment.

**(B)** The Magistrate Judge shall perform all duties authorized by 28 U.S.C. Section 636(a), including, but not limited to, the exercise of all powers and duties previously conferred or imposed upon United States Commissioners, and may also conduct extradition proceedings, and exercise misdemeanor trial and sentencing jurisdiction under 18 U.S.C. Section 3401.

**(C)** The Magistrate Judge shall have authority to assist the Judges of this Court in the conduct of civil and criminal proceedings in all respects contemplated by 28 U.S.C. Section 636(b)–(c), including, but not limited to, exercise of the following duties:

(1) The review and any necessary hearing of, and issuance of recommended decision on, any motion for injunctive relief, to suppress evidence, to permit or to refuse class action maintenance, to dismiss or for summary judgment, or any other similar application in civil or criminal cases potentially dispositive of a claim or defense;

(2) The review, any necessary hearing, and determination of nondispositive motions, including, but not limited to, those relating to discovery and other matters of procedure;

(3) The review and any necessary hearing of, and issuance of recommended decision on, any prisoner petitions challenging conditions of confinement and any applications for post-conviction relief, such review

process to the extent pertinent to include also the issuance of preliminary orders and the conduct of incidental proceedings;

(4) The conduct of pretrial conferences; and

(5) Service as a special master in any appropriate proceedings on order of reference, and a special master reference may be made by consent of the parties without regard to the limiting provisions of Rule 53(b), Fed.R.Civ.P.; trial or other disposition of a civil case by the Magistrate Judge on consent of the parties is further expressly authorized in accordance with 28 U.S.C. Section 636(c) and L.R. 73 infra.

**(D)** The Magistrate Judge shall have authority to perform such additional miscellaneous duties as are contemplated by the laws of the United States, rules of procedure governing District Courts, and local court rules and plans, and may also be assigned such other additional duties, not inconsistent with the Constitution and laws of the United States, as the Court may hereafter require.

[Effective January 1, 2003.]

## LOCAL RULE 72.2 REVIEW

**(a)** The Magistrate Judge's written ruling, pre-trial conference order, or decision or report including proposed findings of fact and recommended conclusions of law, shall be filed with the Clerk, and the Clerk shall forthwith mail a copy to each party. Any party wishing to object must, within ten (10) days after service of such order or recommended ruling on him, serve on all parties, and file with the Clerk, written objection which shall specifically identify the ruling, order, proposed findings and conclusions, or part thereof to which objection is made and the factual and legal basis for such objection. A party may not thereafter assign as error a defect in the Magistrate Judge's order to which objection was not timely made. For the pur-

poses of this rule, service of the order of the Magistrate Judge or recommended ruling shall be deemed to occur no later than five (5) days after the filing of such order or ruling with the Clerk.

**(b)** In the event of such objection, in matters acted on by the Magistrate Judge in an advisory capacity under Rule 72.1(C)(1) or (3), supra, the Judge ultimately responsible shall make a de novo determination of those portions of the proposed decision to which objection is made, and may accept, reject, or modify the recommended ruling in whole or in part. Such independent determination may be made on the basis of the record developed before the Magistrate Judge, and need not ordinarily involve rehearing, although further evidence may also be received in the reviewing Judge's discretion. Absent such objection, the Judge ultimately responsible may forthwith endorse acceptance of the proposed decision; but the Judge, in his or her discretion, may afford the parties opportunity to object to any contemplated rejection or substantial modification of the proposed decision. In matters determined by the Magistrate Judge under Rule 72.1(C)(2) or (4), supra, the reviewing Judge on timely objection shall set aside any order found to be clearly erroneous or contrary to law, and may, absent such objection, reconsider any matter sua sponte.

**(c)** Review of special master proceedings shall be in accordance with Rule 53, Fed.R.Civ.P., to the extent applicable. In civil cases referred to the Magistrate Judge for trial by the parties' consent, appeals shall be taken as provided by Rule 4, infra, in accordance with 28 U.S.C. Section 636(c). Appeals in misdemeanor cases shall conform to the requirements of 18 U.S.C. Section 3402 and the Rules of Procedure for Trial of Misdemeanors before Magistrate Judges.

[Effective January 1, 2003.]

# LOCAL RULE 73.  CIVIL TRIAL JURISDICTION

**(A)** (1) Each Magistrate Judge may exercise case-dispositive authority in a civil case on the specific written request of all parties, as permitted by 28 U.S.C. § 636(c)(1), provided the District Judge assigned to the case approves.

(2) When a civil action is commenced, the Clerk shall promptly notify the parties that they may request referral of the case to a Magistrate Judge for disposition pursuant to 28 U.S.C. § 636(c), subject to the approval of the District Judge to whom the case is assigned. The Clerk shall inform the parties that their consent to such a referral must be voluntary and that they are free to withhold consent without adverse consequences. The parties' agreement to such a reference is to be communicated in the first instance to the Clerk by written stipulation, which shall be forwarded to the assigned District Judge for discretionary consideration.

**(B)**(1) A direct appeal to the Court of Appeals shall be taken in the same manner as from any other judgment or reviewable order of this Court.

(2) The scope of an appeal to the referring Judge shall be the same as on an appeal from a judgment of this Court to the Court of Appeals; such appeal shall be taken as herein provided, subject on prompt application to such modification of time limits and procedures in a particular case as may be found appropriate by the Judge in the interest of justice. Dismissal of the appeal may be directed for failure to comply with this Rule 73 or related court orders.

(3) Appeal to the referring Judge shall be taken by filing a notice of appeal with the Clerk within thirty (30) days after entry of the Magistrate Judge's judgment, or within sixty (60) days after such judgment's entry if the United States or any officer or agency thereof is a party; if a timely notice of appeal is filed, any other party may file a notice of appeal within fourteen (14) days thereafter. The Clerk shall forthwith mail copies of a notice of appeal to all other parties. Any attendant stay application shall be made to the Magistrate Judge in the first instance. The record on appeal shall consist of the original papers and exhibits filed with the Clerk, the docket and any transcript of proceedings before the Magistrate Judge. Within ten (10) days after filing the notice of appeal, the appellant shall make arrangements in the first instance for the production of any transcript deemed necessary. Within thirty (30) days after the notice of appeal is filed, the appellant's brief shall be served and filed; the appellee's brief shall be served and filed within thirty (30) days thereafter. Absent scheduling of oral argument on the Judge's own initiative, the appeal will be decided on the papers unless good cause for allowance of oral argument is shown by written request submitted with the brief.

**(C)** These provisions shall be construed to promote expeditious, inexpensive and just decision, and are subject to any controlling uniform procedures for such appeals as may be adopted hereafter by rule or statute.

[Effective January 1, 2003.]

# LOCAL RULE 77.2   ASSIGNMENT

All matters to be referred by the Judges to the Magistrate Judges shall be referred in the first instance to the Clerk for appropriate assignment to be made under the supervision of the Chief Judge, bearing in mind such factors as a Magistrate Judge's prior familiarity with proceedings, the seat of court involved and current caseload allocation. With the assistance of the Magistrate Judge's clerical staff, the Clerk shall be responsible for preparation and issuance of all calendars and notices of proceedings necessitated by such assignments.

[Effective January 1, 2003.]

# UNITED STATES DISTRICT COURT
## DISTRICT OF CONNECTICUT
## LOCAL RULES OF CRIMINAL PROCEDURE

## RULE 1.  SCOPE OF RULES

**(a) Title and Citation.** These Rules shall be known as the Local Criminal Rules of the United States District Court for the District of Connecticut. They may be cited as "D. Conn. L. Cr. R. _____."

**(b) Effective Date.** These rules shall apply in all criminal proceedings in the United States District Court for the District of Connecticut commenced on or after May 1, 1985.

**(c) Applicability of Local Civil Rules.** The following Local Civil Rules shall apply in criminal proceedings: Rules 1(c) (Definitions), 5(c) (Proof of Service), 7(a)1 and 2 (Motion Practice), 7(b) (Motions for Extension of Time), 7(c) (Motions for Reconsideration), 7(d) (Reply Briefs), 7(e) (Withdrawal of Appearances), 10(a) (Preparation of Pleadings), 11 (Sanctions Against Counsel), 40(c) (Remand by Appellate Court), 47(a) (Examination of Jurors), 54 (Taxation of Costs), 80 (Reporter's Fees), 83.1 (Admission of Attorneys), 83.2 (Discipline of Attorneys), 83.5 (Secrecy of Jury Deliberations), 83.6 (Removal of Papers and Exhibits), 83.9 (Law Student Internship Rules), 83.11 (Recordings and Photographs), 83.12 (Auxiliary Orders) and 83.13 (Prohibition on Counsel as Witness).

**(d) Types of Proceedings.** All criminal proceedings requiring judicial action which do not commence with an indictment or information shall be denominated special proceedings. Such proceedings shall include, but not be limited to, the determination of all matters relating to proceedings before the grand jury, motions pursuant to Rule 41, Fed. R. Crim. P., made before indictment; and proceedings pursuant to the Omnibus Crime Control and Safe Streets Act, 18 U.S.C. §§ 2510–20.

[Effective January 1, 2003; amended effective August 1, 2003; December 1, 2004.]

## RULE 2–RULE 15.  RESERVED

## RULE 16.  DISCOVERY

**(a) Timing of Discovery.** At arraignment the Court shall set a schedule for the filing of motions and responses for discovery requests made pursuant to Rules 12.1, 12.2, and 16, Fed.R.Crim.P. All pretrial proceedings shall be governed by such schedule and by any standing orders on pretrial procedure as the Judges of the District may from time to time adopt. Said standing orders shall be published as an appendix to these Local Rules of Criminal Procedure.

[Effective January 1, 2003.]

## RULE 17.  ISSUANCE OF SUBPOENAS ON BEHALF OF PUBLIC DEFENDERS

**(a) Within This District.** Any Public Defender, which term shall include both staff members of the Federal Public Defender and counsel specially appointed pursuant to the Criminal Justice Act, may apply to the Clerk for a witness subpoena when the witness involved will be served within the boundaries of this District. The Clerk shall issue such subpoena to said Public Defender in blank, signed but not otherwise filled in. No subpoena so issued in blank may be served outside the boundaries of this District. The filling in of any such subpoena shall constitute a certificate by said Public Defender, that he or she believes the witness in question will be able to provide relevant and material testimony at the trial and that it is the Public Defender's opinion that the attendance of said witness is reasonably necessary to the defense of the charge.

**(b) Outside This District.** Where the witness to be subpoenaed will be served outside this District, an ex parte application for the issuance of such subpoena shall be made to a Judge or Magistrate.

**(c) Service by Marshal.** Service of subpoenas issued by or at the request of a Public Defender shall be made by the United States Marshal or his or her deputies in the same manner as in other cases and the name and address of the person served shall not be disclosed without prior authorization of said Public Defender. No fee will be allowed for the service by anyone other than the United States Marshal or his or her deputies of any subpoena issued by or at the request of a Public Defender, except when such service has been expressly authorized by written order of Court.

[Effective January 1, 2003.]

## RULE 18–RULE 31.  RESERVED

## RULE 32.  DISCLOSURE OF PRESENTENCE REPORTS

**(a) Initial Disclosure of Presentence Reports.** Unless otherwise ordered by the Court, the Probation Officer shall, not more than 6 weeks after the verdict or finding of guilt, disclose the presentence investigation report, including the worksheets utilized to calculate sentencing guideline ranges, to the defendant and to counsel for the defendant and the government. Within 14 days thereafter, counsel shall communicate

in writing to the Probation Officer and to opposing counsel any objections they may have as to any of the following items contained in or omitted from the report:

   (i) factual inaccuracies;

   (ii) other material information;

   (iii) guideline calculations and sentencing ranges;

   (iv) sentencing classifications;

   (v) sentencing options; and

   (vi) bases for departure.

**(b) Revisions to Report.** After receiving counsel's objections, the Probation Officer shall conduct any further investigation and make any revisions to the presentence report that may be necessary. Any counsel or the Probation Officer may request a meeting to discuss unresolved factual and legal issues.

**(c) Submission of Revised Presentence Report.** No later than 7 days after the deadline for counsel's objections, the Probation Officer shall submit the revised presentence report to the sentencing judge and disclose the revised presentence report to the defendant and counsel for the defendant and the government. The report shall be accompanied by an addendum setting forth any objections counsel may have made that have not been resolved, together with the Probation Officer's comments thereon, and shall have attached thereto any written objections submitted to the Probation Officer pursuant to Local Rule 32(b). The Probation Officer shall certify that the contents of the report, including any revisions to the report, have been disclosed to the defendant and to counsel for the defendant and the government, that the content of the addendum and the Probation Officer's comments on unresolved issues have been communicated to counsel, and that the addendum fairly states any remaining objections.

**(d) Objections to Revised Presentence Report.** Except with regard to any objection made under subdivision (a) that has not been resolved, the final presentence report may be accepted as accurate. The Court, however, for good cause shown, may allow a new objection to be raised at any time before the imposition of sentence.

**(e) Scheduling Order.** The Court shall, with the assistance of the Probation Officer and counsel, establish a scheduling order governing the dates for the initial disclosure of the presentence report, objections by counsel, disclosure of the revised report, sentencing memoranda and responses to sentencing memoranda. In accordance with Fed.R.Crim.P. 32(b)(6), initial disclosure of the presentence report must occur not less than 35 days before the sentencing hearing unless the defendant waives this minimum period.

**(f) Modification of Time Limits.** The times set forth in this Rule may be modified by the Court by scheduling order as provided in Local Rule 32(e) or

for good cause shown, except that the 6 week period set forth in subsection (a) may be enlarged only with the consent of the defendant. In cases in which the defendant has agreed to cooperate with the government, and counsel for the government or the defendant wish to toll the timetable provided in Local Rule 32(a), counsel may submit a request under seal for a confidential sentencing conference pursuant to Local Rule 32(*o*). At any such sentencing conference, counsel may request the Court to establish a report date at which point counsel must report back to the Court as to the status of the case. At the report date, the Court can consider whether to set a sentencing date and enter a scheduling order pursuant to Local Rule 32(e) or set another report date.

**(g) Non-disclosable Information.** Any information that the Probation Officer believes, consistent with Fed.R.Crim.P. 32(b)(5), should not be disclosed to the defendant (such as diagnostic opinions, sources of information obtained upon a promise of confidentiality, or other information the disclosure of which might result in harm, physical or otherwise, to the defendant or other persons) shall be submitted on a separate page from the body of the report and marked "confidential." The sentencing Judge in lieu of making the confidential page available, exclusive of the sentencing recommendation, shall summarize in writing the factual information contained therein if it is to be relied on in determining the sentence. The summary may be provided to the parties in camera. The Judge must give the defendant and defendant's counsel a reasonable opportunity to comment on the information. Nothing in this Rule requires disclosure of portions of the presentence report that are not disclosable under Fed.R.Crim.P. 32.

**(h) Date of Disclosure.** The presentence report shall be deemed to have been disclosed (1) when a copy of the report is physically delivered, (2) one day after the report's availability for inspection is orally communicated, or (3) three days after notice of its availability is mailed.

**(i) Limitations on Disclosure by the Government and the Defense.** Disclosure of the presentence report is made to the government and to the defense, subject to the following limitations:

1. The attorney for the government shall not disclose the contents of the presentence report to any person other than the case agent, experts or consultants hired by the government and the Financial Litigation Unit of the United States Attorney's Office when a fine is imposed.

2. The attorney for the defendant shall not disclose the contents of the presentence report to any person other than the defendant or experts or consultants hired by the defense. The defendant shall not disclose the contents of the presentence report to any person other than his or her attorney and spouse.

3.  The defendant or his or her attorney may take notes regarding the contents of the presentence report; however, such notes are subject to the same prohibition against disclosure as applies to the report itself.

4.  The defendant and the attorney for the defendant and the government may retain their copies of the presentence report, subject to the same limitations on disclosure set forth in this rule.

The presentence report shall remain a confidential Court document, disclosure of which is controlled by the Court. A violation of any of the above conditions shall be treated as a contempt of Court and may be punished by any appropriate sanction, including action by the Grievance Committee pursuant to Rule 1 of these Local Rules of Criminal Procedure and Rule 83.2 of the Local Rules of Civil Procedure.

**(j) Appeals.** On the date of sentencing, a copy of the presentence report shall provisionally be made a part of the district court record and shall be placed under seal. If a notice of appeal is not filed in the district court, the Clerk's Office shall return the report to the Probation Office.

**(k) Disclosure to Other Agencies.**

1.  Any copy of a presentence report which the Court makes available, or has made available, to agencies other than the Federal Bureau of Prisons and the U.S. Parole Commission constitutes a confidential Court document and shall be presumed to remain under the continuing control of the Court during the time it is in temporary custody of such other agencies. Such copy shall be lent or made available for inspection only for the purpose of enabling other agencies to carry out their official functions and shall be returned to the Court after such use, or upon request.

2.  The following legend shall be stamped on the face of those reports lent to all agencies except the Bureau of Prisons and U.S. Parole Commission:

CONFIDENTIAL
PROPERTY OF U.S. COURTS
SUBMITTED FOR OFFICIAL USE ONLY.
TO BE RETURNED AFTER USE.

3.  Authorized agencies which may have access to a presentence report or summary thereof include the following:

(i) United States Probation Offices outside this district.

(ii) United States Pretrial Services Officers.

(iii) The Federal Bureau of Prisons.

(iv) The United States Parole Commission.

(v) The United States Sentencing Commission.

4.  The following legend shall be stamped on those reports sent to the Federal Bureau of Prisons and United States Parole Commission:

CONFIDENTIAL
U.S. PROBATION OFFICE

5.  In addition to the above, the Court may authorize disclosure of a presentence report, or a summary thereof, with the written authorization of the defendant, to other agencies that are currently involved in the treatment, rehabilitation or correction of the defendant such as, but not limited to, mental or physical health practitioners, social service and vocational rehabilitation agencies, state or county Courts or probation/parole departments, and correctional institutions.

6.  For situations other than those described above, requests for disclosure shall be handled on an individual basis by the Court, and shall be granted only upon a showing of compelling need for disclosure in order to meet the ends of justice.

**SENTENCING PROCEDURES**

**(l) The Role of Defense Counsel**

1.  Defense counsel shall read the presentence report prior to sentencing and review the report with the defendant prior to submitting objections pursuant to Rule 32(a) of these Local Rules and prior to sentencing.

2.  Defense counsel may submit a "Defendant's Version of the Offense" to the Probation Officer and, in that event, shall serve a copy on the attorney for the government. Subject to the restrictions of Fed. R. Crim. P. 32 and D. Conn. L. Cr. R. 32(g), the attorney for the defendant shall promptly make available to the attorney for the government all documents provided to the Probation Officer that were not provided to the government in discovery, unless otherwise excused by the Court for good cause shown.

**(m) The Role of the United States Attorney.**

1.  The United States Attorney or an Assistant United States Attorney may advise the Judge, on the record or confidentially in writing, of any cooperation rendered by the defendant to the Government. If such information is given in written form, the memorandum shall be submitted by the U.S. Attorney and it shall be revealed to defense counsel unless the United States Attorney or his or her assistant shows good cause for non-disclosure.

2.  The attorney for the government shall not make any agreement with the defendant or defense counsel regarding the information to be included in the presentence report, including the information conveyed to the probation office in the government's version of the offense. The attorney for the government shall state on the record at any change of plea or sentencing proceeding the government's understanding of the amount of possible restitution based upon consultation with, inter alia, the victim.

3.  The attorney for the government may submit a "Government's Version of the Offense" to the Probation Officer and, in that event, shall serve a copy on

counsel for the defendant. Subject to the restrictions of Fed. R. Crim. P. 32 and D. Conn. L. Cr. R. 32(g), the attorney for the government shall promptly make available to the attorney for the defendant all documents that are provided to the Probation Officer that were not provided to the defense in discovery, unless otherwise excused by the Court for good cause shown.

### (n) The Role of the Probation Officer.

1.   In preparing presentence reports, the Probation Officer is responsible to the Court, and is not bound by the terms of any agreement made between the United States Attorney and the defendant or defense counsel.

2.   In connection with the preparation of the presentence report, the Probation Officer shall:

(i) Consider any sentence or correctional proposals that the defendant or defendant's counsel may suggest;

(ii) Consider any specific factual and opinion evidence submitted by the defendant or defense counsel relating to defendant's physical and mental condition;

(iii) Pursuant to 18 U.S.C., Section 3664(b), include in the presentence report information concerning any damage or injury that the defendant caused to any victims of the offense as provided in 18 U.S.C. § 3663, and information concerning the defendant's ability to make restitution, including information about the defendant's family obligations;

(iv) Include the information required by Fed. R.Crim.P. 32(b)(4), including sentencing guideline calculations, the sentencing range, the kinds of sentence available, and an explanation of any aggravating or mitigating factors that may warrant departure.

(v) Notify defense counsel, in advance and without request, of any interview of the defendant or the defendant's spouse, whether in person or by telephone, and provide said counsel with a reasonable opportunity to attend and/or participate in the interview.

(vi) Include in the presentence report all facts known about the offense charged, as related by both the defendant and the government;

(vii) Notify defense counsel and the attorney for the government, without request, of the availability of the presentence report as provided in Local Rule 32;

3.   In regard to presentence hearings and the sentencing hearing itself, the Probation Officer shall:

(i) Attend such hearings when requested by the Judge;

(ii) Consult with the Judge regarding any queries that the latter may have;

(iii) Make specific sentence recommendations to the Judge when requested.

(o) **Sentencing Memoranda.** Counsel for the defense and the government may submit sentencing memoranda to the Court addressing (i) any factual inaccuracy in the presentence report; (ii) the guidelines calculations; (iii) the available sentencing options, including alternatives to incarceration; (iv) any restitution issues; (v) any bases for departure; and (vi) any other factual or legal issue relevant to sentencing. Any sentencing memorandum shall be filed no later than 10 days prior to the sentencing date, and any response to an opposing party's sentencing memorandum shall be filed no later than 3 days prior to the sentencing date, unless the Court has provided other deadlines for these memoranda by scheduling order. The times set forth in this Rule may be modified by the Court for good cause shown.

(p) **Presentence Conference.** In his or her discretion, the sentencing Judge, prior to the sentencing hearing, may confer with the attorney for the government and defense counsel together (and with the Probation Officer, when requested by the Judge):

1.   To be informed of any agreement;

2.   To consider questions regarding the presentence report;

3.   To define contested issues in the presentence report and, in the discretion of the Judge, establish an appropriate procedure for resolving material factual disputes;

4.   To evaluate the significance of data in the presentence report on the issue of whether the data would support a determination to impose probation, home confinement, community confinement, intermittent confinement, or incarceration;

5.   To consider the appropriateness of further study of the defendant, including psychiatric evaluation and/or presentence diagnostic commitment to a correctional facility;

6.   To review the extent and value of defendant's cooperation with authorities; and to

7.   To consider any other matters deemed appropriate or necessary by the Judge.

(q) **Confidentiality of Communications to Sentencing Judge.** In his or her discretion, the sentencing Judge may hold in confidence any oral or written communication directed to any judicial officer regarding any matter relating to sentencing, any matter relating to a motion filed pursuant to Rule 35, Fed. R.Crim.P., and any inquiry from a defendant or other person relating to the status of the defendant, the defendant's custodial conditions, or the defendant's probation or parole. This Rule shall apply whether such communications are made before, during or after sentencing or the making of a motion pursuant to Rule 35, Fed.R.Crim.P. The sentencing Judge may also hold in confidence any communication made at any time by the United States Probation Officer assigned the case.

**(r) Binding Plea Agreements.** The Court may accept a plea of guilty offered by a defendant pursuant to Fed. R. Cr. P. 11(e)(1)(C). The plea agreement shall be reduced to writing and submitted to the Court for its approval. The agreement may provide for a specific sentence or an applicable Guideline sentencing range. The Court may accept or reject the agreement, or may defer its acceptance or rejection until there has been an opportunity to consider the presentence report. If the Court accepts the agreement it shall inform the defendant that it will embody in the judgment and sentence the disposition provided for in the plea agreement or will impose a sentence within the agreed upon range. If the court rejects the plea agreement, it shall inform the parties of this fact on the record; advise the defendant personally in open court or, on a showing of good cause, in camera, that the court is not bound by the agreement; afford the defendant the opportunity to then withdraw the plea; and advise the defendant on the record that if the defendant persists in a guilty plea or plea of nolo contendere, the disposition of the case may be less favorable to the defendant than that contemplated by the plea agreement.

[Effective January 1, 2003.]

## RULE 33–RULE 42.   RESERVED

## RULE 43.   ATTENDANCE OF DEFENDANTS

**(a) Presence Required.** A defendant in a criminal prosecution admitted to bail shall attend before the Court at all times required by the Federal Rules of Criminal Procedure, and at any time required by the Court.

[Effective January 1, 2003.]

## RULE 44–RULE 46.   RESERVED

## RULE 47.   MOTIONS

**(a)** Any party applying to the Court for an order must do so by motion.

**(b)** Motions to adopt are not permitted, although a party may indicate in the body of a motion or supporting memorandum of law that an argument of a co-defendant is incorporated by reference. Any such incorporation by reference must identify the motion or memorandum of law incorporated by specifying the name of the co-defendant, the date of filing, and the document number. Incorporation by reference of motions or memoranda filed in another case is prohibited. The Court will not consider arguments incorporated by reference unless the requirements of this rule are met.

**(c)** Counsel filing an omnibus response to motions filed by the opposing party must identify the motions responded to by the names of the motions, their document numbers, where appropriate, the names of the defendants who filed the motions, and the dates the motions were filed.

[Effective January 1, 2003; amended effective May 1, 2005.]

## RULE 48 AND RULE 49.   RESERVED

## RULE 50.   ASSIGNMENTS

**(a) Assignment of Judges.** Assignment of Judges to criminal matters shall be made in accordance with a general policy on assignments adopted from time to time by the Judges of the Court in the interest of the effective administration of justice. The personnel of the Clerk's office shall not reveal to any person, other than a Judge or the Clerk of this Court, the order of assignment of Judges or the identity of the Judge assigned to a particular case, until such case has been filed and assigned.

**(b) Individual Calendar System.** All cases will be assigned to a single Judge from filing to termination. In the event that it is subsequently determined that there is pending in this District a related case, or, if one is later filed, such case should normally be assigned to the Judge having the earliest filed case. A case may be reassigned at the discretion of the Chief Judge, after due consultation with the transferor and transferee Judge.

**(c) Assignment of Judges to Special Proceedings.** At any given time one Judge may be designated to hear special proceedings for a particular seat of Court. Each such Judge shall be assigned to hear special proceedings for a designated period, on a rotating basis. The personnel of the Clerk's office shall not reveal to any person, other than a Judge or the Clerk of the Court, the identity of the Judge assigned to hear special proceedings or the order of assignment of Judges.

**(d) Substitution.** In the event that justice requires that some action be taken in a case in the absence of the assigned Judge, another Judge may consent to act in his or her behalf.

[Effective January 1, 2003.]

## RULE 51–RULE 54.   RESERVED

## RULE 55.   RECORDS

**(a) Docket Numbers.** Upon the filing of an information or indictment a case will be assigned a criminal docket number followed by the initials of the Judge to whom the case has been assigned.

**(b) Miscellaneous Docket Numbers.** All matters involving special proceedings shall be assigned a miscellaneous civil docket number followed by the initials of the Judge to whom the case has been assigned.

**(c) Subsequent Proceedings.** If a proceeding is brought before the special proceedings Judge pursu-

ant to this Rule 55 and the matter results in the filing of an information or an indictment, the case shall be assigned in the manner provided in Rule 50 of these Local Rules. In all other cases, the Judge to whom a special proceedings matter has been assigned shall normally preside over that matter until it has been concluded.

[Effective January 1, 2003.]

# RULE 56.   RESERVED

# RULE 57.   RULES BY DISTRICT COURTS

(a) **Appearances.** Attorneys representing defendants named in an information or indictment shall file a notice of appearance with the Clerk and serve a copy on the United States Attorney and all other counsel of record. Such appearance shall contain the attorney's name, address, zip code, federal bar number telephone number, fax number and e-mail address, if available.

(b) **Sealed Documents.**

(1) Counsel seeking to file a document under seal shall file a motion to seal, which shall be accompanied by the document and an unsealed envelope (or other appropriate sealing package). The unsealed envelope shall bear the caption of the criminal case or miscellaneous civil matter, the docket number, and a description of the document(s) to be sealed in the form outlined in paragraph (f). The Clerk of Court shall file stamp the motion to seal, the sealing envelope, and the document(s) to be sealed, shall docket the motion and sealing envelope, and shall forward the motion to seal and sealing envelope with the document(s) to be sealed contained therein, to the Court for consideration. If ordered sealed by the Court, the Clerk shall seal the envelope and its contents, and shall note the date of the sealing order on the envelope and docket sheet. Upon submission by the party seeking a sealing order, the sealing envelope and its contents shall be treated as a sealed document until directed otherwise by the Court.

(2) Counsel filing documents that are, or may be claimed to be, subject to any protective or impounding order previously entered shall file with the documents, and serve on all parties, a notice that the documents are, or are claimed to be, subject to such order or orders, identifying the particular order or orders by date, and shall submit such documents to the Clerk under seal.

(3) Any file or document ordered sealed by the Court upon motion of the parties, by stipulation, or by the Court, sua sponte, shall remain sealed pending further order of this Court, or any Court sitting in review.

(4) Any documents submitted to the Clerk under seal shall be kept and maintained by the Office of the Clerk in a separate, locked filing cabinet or other secure location. All sealed materials shall be maintained by docket number and the docket number shall be the same as that of the underlying criminal case or miscellaneous civil matter. The Clerk shall cause the docket card and the Court's file to reflect that a document or documents have been filed and/or are being held under seal. The Clerk shall not keep any sealed document in the Court file, or in any place other than the separate, locked filing cabinets or other secure location used to keep and maintain documents filed under seal.

(5) Upon final determination of the action, as defined in Rule 83.6(c) of the Local Rules of Civil Procedure, the Clerk of Court shall advise counsel that counsel shall have 90 days to file a motion pursuant to Rule 83.6(a) for the return of sealed documents or requesting their destruction. Any sealed document thereafter remaining may be destroyed by the Clerk pursuant to Rule 83.6 or retired by the Clerk with other parts of the file to the Federal Records Center, whereupon they shall be automatically unsealed without notice to counsel.

(6) The unsealed envelope shall be in substantially the following form:

UNITED STATES DISTRICT COURT
DISTRICT OF CONNECTICUT

[CAPTION]

NO. _____

Contents: _____

Judicial Officer: _____

Attorney: _____

Date Sealed: _____

Date Unsealed: _____

The Clerk of the Court is directed to seal the contents of this envelope until further order of the Court.

SO ORDERED this _____ day of _____, 19___, at _____, Connecticut.

## PUBLIC STATEMENTS BY COUNSEL

(c) **Statements Permitted During Investigation.** A lawyer participating in or associated with the investigation of a criminal matter shall not make or participate in making an extrajudicial statement that a reasonable person would expect to be disseminated by means of public communication and that does more than state without elaboration:

1.   Information contained in a public record.

2.   That the investigation is in progress.

3.   The general scope of the investigation including a description of the offense and, if permitted by law, the identity of the victim.

4.　A request for assistance in apprehending a suspect or assistance in other matters and the information necessary thereto.

5.　A warning to the public of any dangers.

**(d) Statements Prohibited After Commencement of Proceedings.** A lawyer associated with the prosecution or defense of a criminal matter shall not, from the time of the filing of a complaint, information, or indictment, the issuance of an arrest warrant, or arrest until the commencement of the trial or disposition without trial, make or participate in making an extrajudicial statement that a reasonable person would expect to be disseminated by means of public communication and that relates to:

1.　The character, reputation, or prior criminal record (including arrests, indictments, or other charges of crime) of the accused.

2.　The possibility of a plea of guilty to the offense charged or to a lesser offense.

3.　The existence or contents of any confession, admission, or statement given by the accused or his refusal or failure to make a statement.

4.　The performance or results of any examinations or tests or the refusal or failure of the accused to submit to examinations or tests.

5.　The identity, testimony, or credibility of a prospective witness.

6.　Any opinion as to the guilt or innocence of the accused, the evidence, or the merits of the case.

**(e) Statements Permitted After Commencement of Proceedings.** Rule 57(c) does not preclude a lawyer during such period from announcing:

1.　The name, age, residence, occupation, and family status of the accused.

2.　If the accused has not been apprehended, any information necessary to aid in his apprehension or to warn the public of any dangers he may present.

3.　A request for assistance in obtaining evidence.

4.　The identity of the victim of the crime, if otherwise permitted by law.

5.　The fact, time and place of arrest, resistance, pursuit, and use of weapons.

6.　The identity of investigating and arresting officers or agencies and the length of the investigation.

7.　At the time of seizure, a description of the physical evidence seized, other than a confession, admission, or statement.

8.　The nature, substance, or text of the charge.

9.　Quotations from or references to public records of the Court in the case.

10.　The scheduling or result of any step in the judicial proceedings.

11.　That the accused denies the charges made against him.

**(f) Statements Prohibited During Jury Selection and Trial.** During the selection of a jury or the trial of a criminal matter, a lawyer associated with the prosecution or defense of a criminal matter shall not make or participate in making an extrajudicial statement that a reasonable person would expect to be disseminated by means of public communication and that relates to the trial, parties, or issues in the trial or other matters that are reasonably likely to interfere with a fair trial, except that he may quote from or refer without comment to public records of the Court in the case.

**(g) Statements Prohibited Prior to Sentencing.** After the completion of a trial or disposition without trial of a criminal matter and prior to the imposition of sentence, a lawyer or law firm associated with the prosecution or defense shall not make or participate in making an extrajudicial statement that a reasonable person would expect to be disseminated by public communication and that is reasonably likely to affect the imposition of sentence.

[Effective January 1, 2003.]

# RULE 58.　APPEALS

**(a) Notice of Appeal.** When an appeal is taken by a defendant in a criminal case, the Clerk shall cause a file-stamped copy of the notice of appeal to be served upon the United States Attorney, the defendant and all counsel of record in the case. The Clerk shall transmit forthwith a copy of the notice of appeal and of the docket entries to the Clerk of the Court of Appeals.

**(b) Bond on Appeal.** The bond of any defendant admitted to bail pending appeal to the Court of Appeals shall be conditioned upon the defendant-appellant's compliance with the Rules of Appellate Procedure and the Rules of the United States Court of Appeals for the Second Circuit concerning the times for filing the record on appeal and briefs. Applications for an extension of time for filing the record on appeal in a criminal case shall be made to the Court of Appeals in accordance with the "Plan to Expedite the Processing of Criminal Appeals" adopted by the United States Court of Appeals for the Second Circuit.

**(c) Transcripts on Appeal.** When an appeal is taken, counsel shall take the necessary steps forthwith to order that portion of the court reporter's transcript which is required for appeal purposes. The court reporter shall notify the Chief Judge of the United States Court of Appeals for the Second Circuit of the date on which such transcript has been completed. When the transcript is completed, a copy thereof shall be filed immediately by the appellant with the Clerk

of the District Court for perfecting the record on appeal.

[Effective January 1, 2003.]

# CRIMINAL APPENDIX

## APPENDIX. STANDING ORDER ON DISCOVERY

In all criminal cases, it is Ordered:

**(A) Disclosure by the Government.** Within ten (10) days from the date of arraignment, government and defense counsel shall meet, at which time the attorney for the government shall furnish copies, or allow defense counsel to inspect or listen to and record items which are impractical to copy, of the following items in the possession, custody or control of the government, the existence of which is known or by the exercise of due diligence may become known to the attorney for the government or to the agents responsible for the investigation of the case:

(1) Written or recorded statements made by the defendant.

(2) The substance of any oral statement made by the defendant before or after his arrest in response to interrogation by a then known government agent which the government intends to offer in evidence at trial.

(3) Recorded grand jury testimony of the defendant relating to the offense charged.

(4) The defendant's prior criminal record.

(5) Books, papers, documents, photographs, tangible objects, buildings or places, or copies or portions thereof, which are within the possession, custody or control of the government, and which are material to the preparation of the defense or are intended for use by the government as evidence in chief at the trial, or were obtained from or belong to the defendant.

(6) Results or reports of physical or mental examinations and of scientific tests or experiments made in connection with this case. The government shall also disclose to the defendant a written summary of testimony the government intends to use under Rules 702, 703 or 705 of the Federal Rules of Evidence during its case in chief. This summary must describe the witness' opinions, the bases and reasons therefor, and the witness' qualifications.

(7) All warrants, applications, with supporting affidavits, testimony under oath, returns, and inventories for the arrest of the defendant and for the search and/or seizure of the defendant's person, property, things, or items with respect to which the defendant has standing to move to suppress.

(8) All authorizations, applications, orders, and returns obtained pursuant to Chapter 119 of Title 18 of the United States Code with respect to which the defendant has standing to move to suppress, and if requested by the defendant and at reasonable cost to the defendant, all inventories, logs, transcripts and recordings obtained pursuant to Chapter 119 of Title 18 of the United States Code with respect to which the defendant has standing to move to suppress.

(9) Unless otherwise ordered by the presiding Judge pursuant to paragraph F of this Standing Order, a list of the names and addresses of all witnesses whom the government intends to call in the presentation of its case-in-chief, together with any record of prior felony convictions and of prior misdemeanor convictions which reflect on the credibility of any such witness.

(10) All information concerning the existence and substance of any payments, promises of immunity, leniency, or preferential treatment, made to prospective government witnesses, within the scope of United States v. Giglio, 405 U.S. 150 (1972) and Napue v. Illinois, 360 U.S. 264 (1959).

(11) All information known to the government which may be favorable to the defendant on the issues of guilt or punishment within the scope of Brady v. Maryland, 373 U.S. 83 (1963).

(12) All information concerning the defendant's identification in any lineup, showup, photospread or similar identification proceedings.

(13) All information relating to other crimes, wrongs or acts of the defendant that will be offered as evidence by the government at trial pursuant to Federal Rule of Evidence 404(b).

**(B) Disclosure by the Defendant.** Within fourteen (14) days after the meeting required by Section A is held, defense counsel shall:

(1) Inform the attorney for the government in writing whether the nature of the defense is entrapment, insanity, duress or coercion, or acting under public authority at the time of the offense.

(2) Permit the government to inspect and copy the following items that are within the possession, custody or control of the defendant, the existence of which is known or by the exercise of due diligence may become known to the defendant: (a) books, papers, documents, photographs or tangible objects that the defendant intends to introduce as evidence in his case-in-chief at trial; (b) results or reports of physical or mental examinations and of scientific tests or experiments made in connection with this case that the defendant

intends to offer as evidence at trial or which were prepared by a defense witness who will testify concerning the contents thereof. The defendant shall also disclose to the government a written summary of testimony the defendant intends to use as evidence at trial under Rules 702, 703 or 705 of the Federal Rules of Evidence. This summary must describe the witness' opinions, the bases and reasons therefor, and the witness' qualifications.

**(C) Other Discovery Motions.** Within twenty (20) days of arraignment, all motions concerning materials or information not covered by this Standing Order must be filed, with supporting papers and a memorandum of law. The party opposing such motion shall file its response within ten (10) days of the filing of the motion. The Court shall refuse to consider any such motions unless the supporting papers contain a certification that counsel have met and that, after good faith efforts to resolve their differences on discovery, they were unable to reach an accord. Unless otherwise directed by the Court, compliance with discovery ordered by the Court shall be made within ten (10) days of the entry of the Court's order.

**(D) Continuing Duty.** It shall be the continuing duty of counsel for both sides to reveal immediately to opposing counsel all newly-discovered information or other material within the scope of this Standing Order.

**(E) Exhibits.** Not less than ten (10) days prior to trial, the parties shall meet, inspect and premark, either for identification or as full exhibits, all exhibits which they reasonably anticipate will be offered into evidence at trial.

**(F) Compliance.** At the time of arraignment or upon motion promptly filed thereafter with supporting moving papers, the Court may, upon a showing of sufficient cause, order the discovery provided under this Standing Order be denied, restricted or deferred, or make such other order as is appropriate.

**(G) Disclosure of Statements of Witnesses.** After a witness other than the defendant has testified on direct examination at a suppression hearing, a sentencing hearing, a hearing to revoke or modify probation or supervised release, or a detention hearing, the party calling said witness shall produce, for examination and use by the other party, any of the statements in its possession and that relates to the subject matter of the witness' testimony. Any party intending to call a witness at any such proceeding shall ensure that all statements of the witness are available for disclosure at the hearing.

[Effective January 1, 2003.]

# CIVIL JUSTICE EXPENSE AND DELAY REDUCTION PLAN

### Effective November 10, 1993

## 1. LIMIT ON INTERROGATORIES

Unless otherwise permitted by the Court for good cause shown, no party shall serve upon any other party more than 30 written interrogatories, including all parts and sub-parts. This limit may not be waived by agreement of counsel. Local Rule 9(d)(1).

## 2. DISCOVERY DEADLINE

All discovery shall be completed within six months after the filing of the complaint, the filing of a petition for removal, or the date of transfer of an action from another District. Standing Order on Scheduling in Civil Cases 2(c).

## 3. MOTION DEADLINES

All motions relating to joinder of parties, claims or remedies, class certification, and amendment of the pleadings shall be filed within 60 days after the filing of the complaint, the filing of a petition for removal, or the date of transfer of an action from another District. Standing Order on Scheduling in Civil Cases 2(a).

All motions to dismiss based on the pleadings shall be filed within 90 days after the filing of the complaint, the filing of a petition for removal, or the date of transfer of an action from another District. Standing Order on Scheduling in Civil Cases 2(b).

All motions for summary judgment shall be filed within seven months after the filing of the complaint, the filing of a petition for removal, or the date of transfer of an action from another District. Standing Order on Scheduling in Civil Cases 2(d).

## 4. DIFFERENTIAL TREATMENT OF CASES

When indicated, the District Judge in his or her discretion shall order the systematic, differential treatment of civil cases so as to tailor the level of case management to the cases' complexity, length, and amount of resources required for their preparation and disposition.

## 5. VOLUNTARY DISCOVERY

The Court encourages all litigants and their attorneys to engage in cost-effective discovery through the voluntary exchange of information and other cooperative discovery devices.

## 6. DISCOVERY MOTIONS

No discovery motions pursuant to Fed.R.Civ.P. 26 through 37 shall be filed unless they are accompanied by certification that the moving counsel has conferred with opposing counsel and made a good faith effort to eliminate or reduce the area of controversy and to arrive at a mutually satisfactory resolution. Such certification shall take the form of an affidavit filed as part of the motion papers confirming that such good faith efforts have been made and specifying the issues that have been resolved and the issues that remain unresolved. Local Rule 9(d)(2).

## 7. ALTERNATIVE DISPUTE RESOLUTION

In addition to existing ADR programs (such as Local Rule 28's Special Masters Program) and those promulgated by individual judges (e.g., Parajudicials Program), a case may be referred for voluntary ADR at any stage of the litigation deemed appropriate by the parties and then judge to whom the particular case has been assigned.

Before a case is referred to voluntary ADR, the parties must agree upon, subject to the approval of the judge:

(a) The form of the ADR program (e.g., mediation, arbitration, summary jury trial, minitrial, etc.);

(b) The scope of the ADR process (e.g., settlement of all or specified issues, resolution of discovery schedules or disputes, narrowing of issues, etc.);

(c) The ADR provider (e.g., a court-annexed ADR project; a profit or not-for-profit private ADR organization; or any qualified person or panel selected by the parties);

(d) The effect of the ADR process (e.g., binding or nonbinding).

When agreement between the parties and the judge for a voluntary ADR referral has been reached, the parties shall file jointly for the judge's endorsement a "Stipulation for Reference to ADR." The Stipulation, subject to the judge's approval, shall specify:

(a) The form of ADR procedure and the name of the ADR provider agreed upon;

(b) The judicial proceedings, if any, to be stayed pending ADR (e.g., discovery matters, filing of motions, trial, etc.);

(c) The procedures, if any, to be completed prior to ADR (e.g., exchange of documents, medical examinations, etc.);

(d) The effect of the ADR process (e.g., binding or nonbinding);

(e) The date or dates for the filing of the progress reports by the ADR provider with the trial judge or for the completion of the ADR process; and

(f) The special conditions, if any, imposed by the judge upon any aspect of the ADR process (e.g., requiring trial counsel, the parties, and/or representatives of insurers with settlement authority to attend the voluntary ADR session fully prepared to make final demands or offers).

Attendance at ADR sessions shall take precedence over all non-judicially assigned matters (depositions, etc.). With respect to court assignments that conflict with a scheduled ADR session, trial judges may excuse trial counsel temporarily to attend the ADR session, consistent with the orderly disposition of judicially assigned matters. In this regard, trial counsel, upon receiving notice of an ADR session, immediately shall inform the trial judge and opposing counsel in matters scheduled for the same date of his or her obligation to appear at the ADR session.

All ADR sessions shall be deemed confidential and protected by the provisions of Fed.R.Evid. 408 and Fed.R.Civ. p. 68. No statement made or document produced as part of an ADR proceeding, not otherwise discoverable or obtainable, shall be admissible as evidence or subject to discovery.

At the conclusion of the voluntary ADR session(s), the ADR provider's report to the judge shall merely indicate "case settled or not settled," unless the parties agree to a more detailed report (e.g., stipulation of facts, narrowing of issues and discovery procedures, etc.). If a case settles, the parties shall agree upon the appropriate moving papers to be filed for the trial judge's endorsement (Judgment, Stipulation for Dismissal, etc.). If a case does not settle but the parties agree to the narrowing of discovery matters or legal issues, then the ADR provider's report shall set forth those matters for endorsement or amendment by the judge. Local Rule 36, adopted pursuant to Civil Justice Advisory Group Report.

## 8. COURT–APPOINTED ADR PROVIDER

Pursuant to Local Rule 36 and a Standing Order dated February 19, 1993, the Court appoints Sta–Fed ADR, Inc. as a court-annexed ADR program. Sta–Fed ADR, Inc. is a not-for-profit corporation whose core group of mediators are members of the state judiciary, and members of the federal judiciary will serve as officers of the corporation and sit on its Board of Directors. Local Rule 36 and Standing Order dated February 19, 1993, adopted pursuant to Civil Justice Advisory Group Report.

## 9. SPECIAL MASTERS

Pursuant to Local Rule 28, District Judges may appoint special masters to report upon particular issues in a case, to hold early status conferences, or to conduct settlement conferences. Local Rule 28.

## 10. PRETRIAL CONFERENCES

Each party will be represented at each pretrial conference by an attorney with authority to bind that party regarding all matters identified by the Court for discussion at the conference as well as all reasonably related matters.

## 11. SETTLEMENT CONFERENCES

Counsel shall attend any settlement conference fully authorized to make a final demand or offer and to act promptly on any proposed settlement. The judicial officer or special master before whom a settlement conference is held may require that counsel be accompanied by the person or person authorized and competent to accept or reject any settlement proposal, or that such persons be available by telephone. Local Rules 11(b)(3) and 36(3)(f).

## 12. MONITORING AND REPORTING

On at least an annual basis (starting one year from the date of the Court's adoption of the Revised Plan), the Group will collect and review all available data (e.g., from the Administrative Office, Clerk's Office, and Sta–Fed ADR, Inc.'s Office) regarding the effect of the Revised Plan. The Group then will draft a report analyzing the effect of the Revised Plan and forward the report to the Court.

[Effective November 10, 1993.]

# ELECTRONIC CASE FILING

## ELECTRONIC FILING POLICIES AND PROCEDURES

**INTRODUCTION.**

The U.S. District Court for the District of Connecticut permits attorneys in selected civil and criminal cases to file documents with the court from their own offices over the internet using the Case Management/Electronic Case Filing System ("CM/ECF System"). The court strongly encourages parties and their counsel to participate in electronic filing. While parties and pro se litigants may register to receive "read only" electronic filing accounts to access documents in the CM/ECF System and receive electronic notice, only registered attorneys, as officers of the court, will be permitted to file electronically at this time.

**I.  THE ELECTRONIC FILING SYSTEM.**

**A.  Authorization for Electronic Filing.** The Electronic Filing Administrative Policies and Procedures, Local Rule of Civil Procedure 5 and Local Rule of Criminal Procedure 1(c) authorize electronic filing in conjunction with Federal Rule of Civil Procedure 5(e) and Federal Rule of Criminal Procedure 49. Pursuant to the Electronic Filing Administrative Policies and Procedures, the following policies and procedures govern electronic filing in this district unless, due to extraordinary circumstances in a particular case, a judicial officer determines that these policies and procedures should be modified in the interest of justice.

**B.  Definitions and Instructions.** The following definitions and instructions shall apply to these Policies and Procedures for Electronic Filing:

1.  The term "document" shall include pleadings, motions, exhibits, declarations, affidavits, memoranda, papers, orders, notices, and any other filing by or with the Court.

2.  The term "party" shall include counsel of record and a pro se litigant.

3.  All hours stated shall be Connecticut time.

4.  A "filing level account" permits access to electronic cases for viewing and filing documents electronically.

5.  A "Read only" level account is restricted to view only access of electronic docket sheets and documents, with certain exceptions.

6.  As used in these administrative procedures, a "conventionally" or "traditionally" filed or submitted document or pleading is one presented to the Court or a party in paper or other non-electronic, tangible format.

7.  As used in these procedures, "electronically filed" is intended to refer to documents filed by counsel over the internet.

**C.  Application of Rules and Orders.** Unless modified by approved stipulation or order of the Court, all Federal Rules of Civil Procedure, Federal Rules of Criminal Procedure, Local Rules, and orders of the Court shall continue to apply to cases selected for electronic filing.

**D.  Designation of Cases.** Electronic filing over the internet will be permitted when the Court, on its own initiative, designates a case as electronically filed or, with Court approval, in cases in which all counsel of record have consented to this method of filing. Electronic filing over the internet by pro se parties will generally not be permitted at this time. Counsel may express their interest as early as the filing of the action by joint notification to the judicial officer as part of the Parties Planning Conference Report filed pursuant to Local Rule 26(f). The judicial officer may designate the case for electronic filing at any time.

**E.  System Requirements.** While the CM/ECF System requirements may be set forth more completely in a User's Manual or other Court publication, it is expected that the following hardware and software will be needed to electronically file, view and retrieve documents in the CM/ECF System:

1. A personal computer running a standard platform such as Windows, Windows 95, Windows 98, Windows 2000, Windows XP or Apple O/S.

2. An internet provider using Point to Point Protocol (PPP).

3. Netscape Navigator version 4.6, 4.7, 7.02 or Internet Explorer Version 5.5, with JavaScript-enabled (128 bit encryption is strongly recommended) [NOTE: Netscape Navigator version 6.0 is not recommended for use with the CM/ECF System].

4. Software to convert documents from a word processor format to portable document format (PDF).

5. Adobe Acrobat Reader for viewing documents using a "read only" account.

6. Access to a scanner if non-computerized documents need to be imaged.

7. A Public Access to Court Electronic Records ("PACER") system account to view docket sheets and electronically filed documents [NOTE: PACER facilitates electronic access and is the primary interface with the CM/ECF System, to view docket sheets and other case information. It also allows access to images of Court documents, if the documents have been electronically filed and are in the category of documents viewable by the public. All electronic public access to case dockets and documents occurs through PACER. Upon receipt of a Notice of Electronic Filing (NEF), users are permitted one free view of the document within 15 days of filing. Beyond the 15 day period, appropriate charges will be billed.

**F. General Format of Documents Filed Electronically or Submitted on Computer Disk.**

1. *Requirements.* Documents filed electronically or submitted on computer disk must meet the requirements of Fed.R.Civ.P. 10 (Form of Pleadings), Local Rule of Civil Procedure 5 (Service and Filing of Pleadings and Other Papers), Local Rule of Civil Procedure 10 (Preparation of Pleadings), and Local Rule of Civil Procedure 40 (Assignments), as if they had been submitted on paper. Documents filed electronically are also subject to any page limitations set forth by Court order or by Local Rule of Civil Procedure 7 (Motion Practice).

2. *Font.* As part of the National Archives and Records Administration's (NARA) electronic government (E–Gov) initiative and to facilitate preservation processing and future access to electronic records, electronic records that have been converted to PDF from other electronic word processing software must include embedded fonts to guarantee the visual reproduction of all text as created. All fonts embedded in PDF records must be publicly identified as legally embeddable (i.e., font license permits embedding) in a file for unlimited, universal viewing and printing. PDF records that reference fonts other than the "base 14 fonts" must have those fonts referenced in the record (i.e., as a minimum, subsets of all referenced fonts) embedded within the PDF file. The base 14 fonts are: Courier (Regular, Bold, Italic, and Bold Italic), Arial MT (Regular, Bold, Oblique, and Bold Oblique), Times New Roman PS MT (Roman, Bold, Italic, and Bold Italic), Symbol, and ZapfDingbats.

3. *Form.* A key objective of the CM/ECF System is to ensure that as much of the case as possible is filed electronically. Documents filed electronically or submitted on computer disk must not exceed 1.5 mb (1500 kb) in size or, if larger, must be broken into multiple parts. For example, most filings include a primary or main document (e.g., motion) and other supporting items (e.g., memorandum and exhibits). The primary document and each of the supporting documents are deemed separate components of the filing, and each component, i.e., document, is uploaded separately in the filing process. Any document having an electronic file size that exceeds 1.5 mb (1500 kb) cannot be filed electronically, either over the internet or on computer disk and must, instead, be filed in paper accompanied by a Notice of Manual Filing. The Notice of Manual Filing must be filed both electronically and in paper, to provide notice that something could not be filed over the internet. The following example illustrates the application of this section. Counsel seeks to file a motion, a memorandum in support and two exhibits. The motion, memorandum and one of the exhibits are text documents, created in a word processor then published to PDF. In their final form, each document is less than 1.5 mb. The second exhibit is

a photograph and when scanned, is 8 mb, which is too large to file electronically. When counsel electronically files the documents over the internet, counsel will file the motion, the memorandum in support, the text exhibit and a Notice of Manual Filing to alert the public that one item (the photograph) is filed in paper, not electronically. Counsel must physically send the Notice of Manual Filing and the photograph to the clerk's office for filing. Counsel must also serve on opposing counsel a copy of the Notice of Electronic Filing (to document that the other pieces were filed electronically), the Notice of Manual Filing and a copy of the photograph.

## II.  CONSEQUENCES OF FILING DOCUMENTS ELECTRONICALLY.

Electronic transmission of a document consistent with the procedures adopted by the Court shall, upon the receipt of the document by the clerk of court, constitute filing of the document for all purposes of the Federal Rules of Civil Procedure, the Federal Rules of Criminal Procedure and the Local Rules of this court, and shall constitute entry of that document onto the docket maintained by the clerk pursuant to Fed. R. Civ. P. 58 and 79, and Fed. R. Crim. P. 49 and 55. When a document has been filed electronically, the official record is the electronic recording of the document as stored by the court, and the filing party is bound by the document as filed. A document filed electronically is deemed filed at the date and time stated on the Notice of Electronic Filing generated from the court. A receipt acknowledging that the document has been filed will be generated by the Court's server. This receipt should be printed as evidence of the date and time of filing. Counsel can verify the filing of documents by inspecting the Court's electronic docket sheet. In the event a document is inappropriately filed, upon proper notification or motion to the court, the clerk's office will make a correction to the docket noting any necessary changes. Notice will be sent to all counsel of record in the event of any material change to an entry submitted by counsel. Documents filed electronically must be submitted in PDF format, except as provided in Section XIII pertaining to proposed orders. Filing documents electronically does not alter any filing deadlines. All electronic transmissions of documents must be completed (i.e., received by the clerk's office as evidenced by a Notice of Electronic Filing) prior to midnight in order to be considered timely filed that day. Although documents can be filed electronically 24 hours a day, counsel are strongly encouraged to file all documents during normal working hours of the clerk's office (9:00 a.m. to 4:00 p.m.) when assistance is available.

## III.  ELECTRONIC DOCKET.

Upon the filing of a document, a docket entry will be created using the information provided by the filing counsel. The clerk of court will, where necessary and appropriate, modify the docket entry description to comply with quality control standards.

**A.  Title of Docket Entries.** The party electronically filing a pleading or other document shall be responsible for designating a docket entry title for the document by using one of the docket event categories prescribed by the court.

**B.  Correcting Docket Entries.**

1.  Once a document is filed and becomes part of the case docket, corrections to the docket are made only by the clerk's office or at the direction of the clerk's office. The CM/ECF System will not permit the filing party to make changes to the documents or docket entry filed in error once the transaction has been accepted.

2.  A document incorrectly filed in a case may be the result of posting the wrong PDF file to a docket entry, or selecting the wrong document type from the menu, or entering the wrong case number and not catching the error before the transaction is completed. The filing party should call the clerk's office for instructions on what steps should be taken to make a correction.

3.  If counsel discover an error before the entry is reviewed by the clerk's office, counsel should contact the clerk's office with the case number and document number of the error. If appropriate, the clerk's office will make an entry indicating that the document was filed in error. The filing party will be advised if the document needs to be refiled.

**C. Privacy.** To address the privacy concerns created by internet access to court documents, litigants should not include sensitive information in any document filed with the court unless such inclusion is necessary and relevant to the case [see Appendix G (civil cases) and Appendix H (criminal cases)]. If sensitive information must be included, the following personal data identifiers must be partially redacted from the pleading whether it is filed traditionally or electronically:

1. Names of minor children to the initials;

2. Financial account numbers to the last four digits;

3. Social Security numbers to the last four digits; and

4. Dates of birth to the year.

In compliance with the E–Government Act of 2002, a party wishing to file a document containing the personal data identifiers specified above may file an unredacted document under seal, which shall be retained by the court as part of the record. In lieu of an unredacted copy filed under seal, a party may file a reference list, which must be filed under seal. The reference list shall contain the complete personal data identifier(s) and the redacted identifier(s) used in its (their) place in the filing. All references in the case to the redacted identifiers included in the reference list will be construed to refer to the corresponding complete identifier. The reference list may be amended as of right. It shall be retained by the court as part of the record. The court may, however, still require the filing party to file a redacted copy of the reference list for the public file. In addition, counsel are encouraged to exercise caution when filing documents that contain the following:

- personal identifying number such as a driver's license number;

- medical records, treatment and diagnosis;

- employment history;

- individual financial information; and

- proprietary or trade secret information.

## IV. SYSTEM AVAILABILITY.

The Court's CM/ECF System is designed to provide service 24 hours a day. Counsel, however, are encouraged to file documents in advance of filing deadlines and during normal business hours. The clerk's office staff has been trained to respond to questions regarding the CM/ECF System and the registration process. Assistance can be provided from 9:00 a.m. to 4:00 p.m. during any day on which the court is open for business. After-hours voice mail messages may be left at Bridgeport (203–579–5585), New Haven (203–773–2415) or Hartford (860–240–3311).

## V. PUBLIC ACCESS TO THE ELECTRONIC DOCKET.

**A. Internet Access Without a Password.** Any person or organization with a PACER login and password may access the CM/ECF System at the Court's internet site at https://ecf.ctd.uscourts.gov/. Such access to the CM/ECF System through the internet site will allow retrieval of the docket sheet and documents on a real-time basis. Unless a user has a CM/ECF System filing level account, access to the CM/ECF System will be on a "read only" basis.

1. Public remote electronic access to the CM/ECF System for read only purposes is limited to subscribers to the Public Access to court Electronic Records ("PACER") system. The Judicial Conference of the United States has ruled that a user fee will be charged for remotely accessing certain detailed case information, such as docket sheets and filed documents in civil cases, but excluding review of calendars and similar general information.[1] Information regarding the current PACER fees is available on the PACER website at http://pacer.psc.uscourts.gov.

1. The access fee does not apply to official recipients of electronic documents, i.e., parties legally required to receive service or to whom service is directed by the filer in the context of service under Federal Rules of Civil Procedure. Official recipients will receive the initial electronic copy of a document free to download as they see fit, but if they remotely access the document again, they will be charged the applicable access fee.

2. The public can access records in criminal cases not filed under seal or ex parte for any documents filed on or after November 1, 2004. Access to criminal case

records filed on or before October 31, 2004 is restricted to counsel of record in the criminal case.

**B. Public Access at the Court.** Public access to electronic documents that are not sealed or filed ex parte, and to the electronic docket is available in the clerk's office between 9:00 a.m. and 4:00 p.m. Monday through Friday.

**C. Copies and Certified Copies.** Traditional copies in paper and certified copies of electronically filed documents may be purchased at the clerk's office during business hours Monday through Friday. The fees for copying and certification will be charged in accordance with 28 U.S.C. § 1914(b).

**D. Technical Failures.** If counsel is unable to file electronically and, as a result, may miss a filing deadline, counsel must immediately contact the appropriate Help Desk to inform the clerk of court of the difficulty. If the problem occurs after hours, a voice message must be left on the appropriate help desk line. If counsel misses a filing deadline due to an inability to file electronically, counsel may electronically submit the untimely filed document, accompanied by a declaration stating the reason(s) for missing the deadline. The document and declaration must be electronically filed no later than 12:00 noon of the first day on which the court is open for business following the original filing deadline. A model form is provided in Appendix A.

## VI. REGISTRATION AND E–MAIL NOTIFICATION.

**A. E–Mail Notification.** As required by this Court's local rules, all counsel and pro se parties are to include an e-mail address, if available, as part of the signature line on filings. E-mail addresses are captured from filings and added to the CM/ECF System to allow the court to provide electronic notice of orders, rulings and docket activity. The use of e-mail addresses for court notifications does not permit a party to e-file in the absence of a registration and court order designating e-filing in a particular case.

**B. Completion of Registration Form.** Counsel seeking to file documents electronically must submit a completed Electronic Filing System Registration form (Appendix B) prior to being assigned a user identification name and password that will serve as that counsel's signature for Fed. R. Civ. P. 11 purposes. The form is available in hard copy at the clerk's office and is also available on the Court's website at www.ctd.uscourts.gov/cmecf. The completed Registration Form must be signed by the registrant and addressed to:

Roberta D. Tabora, Clerk
United States District Court
Attention: Electronic Filing System Registration
141 Church Street
New Haven, Connecticut 06510

**C. Confirmation of E–Mail Address and Password.** To ensure that the clerk's office has correctly entered a registering attorney's internet e-mail address in the CM/ECF System, the clerk's office will send the attorney an internet e-mail message after assigning the attorney a password. The clerk's office will then send the attorney's login and password information to the e-mail address on record or, if requested by the attorney, mail the password information to the attorney by regular, first-class mail or arrange for the attorney to pick up the information at the clerk's office.

**D. Withdrawal from the CM/ECF System.** Once registered, an attorney may withdraw from participating in the CM/ECF System by providing the clerk's office with notice of withdrawal. Such notice must be in writing, and mailed or delivered to the clerk's office in New Haven. Upon receipt, the clerk's office will immediately cancel the attorney's password and delete the attorney's name from any applicable electronic service list.

**E. Passwords.** Each attorney admitted to practice in the District of Connecticut shall be entitled to one CM/ECF System password from the district court. The

password permits the attorney to participate in the electronic retrieval and filing of pleadings and other papers.

1.   The court will issue passwords only to attorneys in good standing. To be in good standing, an attorney must meet the requirements in Local Rule of Civil Procedure 83.1.

2.   After registering, attorneys are not to change their login names; however, they may change their passwords. If an attorney comes to believe that the security of an existing password has been compromised, the attorney must change his or her password and immediately notify the clerk's office by telephone. Counsel may be subject to sanctions for failure to comply with this provision.

3.   No attorney shall knowingly permit or cause to permit his or her password to be utilized by anyone other than an authorized employee of his or her office.

4.   Once registered, the attorney shall be responsible for all documents filed with his or her password.

5.   Registration for a password is governed by Paragraph B.

6.   An attorney admitted pro hac vice may register for a password in accordance with these Administrative Procedures.

## VII.   ELECTRONIC FILING AND SERVICE OF DOCUMENTS.

### A.   Filing—Civil Cases.

1.   Complaints shall be filed, fees paid, and summonses issued and served in the traditional manner on paper rather than electronically.

2.   Any document requiring a filing fee must be filed in paper and be accompanied by a PDF version of the document on computer disk. Documents requiring filing fees may not be filed over the internet.

3.   All documents filed in paper must also be submitted in PDF form on computer disk, unless the document(s) cannot be reduced to the allowable electronic filing size.

4.   If the case is designated as electronically filed, only documents that cannot be reduced to the allowable size may be filed in paper. Any documents filed in paper pursuant to this provision must be accompanied by a Notice of Manual Filing explaining why the document(s) is (are) not filed over the internet.

5.   If an attorney is unable to create or otherwise produce PDF documents on computer disk and must, therefore, file documents in paper, the attorney may apply to the assigned judge for permission to file documents conventionally. Even if the assigned judge initially grants an attorney permission to file documents conventionally, the assigned judge may withdraw that permission at any time during the pendency of a case.

6.   The clerk's office or any judge of this court may deviate from these procedures in specific cases, without prior notice, if deemed appropriate in the exercise of discretion, considering the need for the just, speedy, and inexpensive determination of matters pending before the court. The court may also amend these procedures at any time without prior notice.

7.   A document will be deemed timely filed if filed prior to midnight. However, if the assigned judge so orders, the document shall be filed by a time certain.

8.   The official court record shall be the electronic file maintained on the Court's servers. The official record shall include, however, any conventional documents or exhibits filed in accordance with these procedures or if required by court rules or policies.

### B.   Filing—Criminal Cases.

1.   All charging documents including the complaint, information, indictment and superseding indictment, shall be filed either in the traditional manner in paper accompanied by a computer disk containing a PDF version of the document or a scanned document that contains an image of any legally required signature.

2. Any document requiring a filing fee must be filed in paper and be accompanied by a PDF version of the document on computer disk. Documents requiring filing fees may not be filed over the internet.

3. All documents filed in paper must also be submitted in PDF form on computer disk, unless the document(s) cannot be reduced to the allowable electronic filing size.

4. If the case is designated as electronically filed, only documents that cannot be reduced to the allowable size may be filed in paper. Any documents filed in paper pursuant to this provision must be accompanied by a Notice of Manual Filing explaining why the document(s) is (are) not filed over the internet.

5. Juvenile criminal matters shall not be filed electronically over the internet, unless after hearing, the court rules that the juvenile shall be tried as an adult. Any documents filed in these cases are to be filed in paper, accompanied by a computer disk containing a PDF version of the document being filed.

6. Documents filed under seal or filed in sealed cases are to be submitted in paper accompanied by a computer disk containing a PDF version of the document being filed. Documents filed under seal or filed in sealed cases are not to be filed over the internet.

7. Access to records in criminal cases not filed under seal or ex parte, will be available to the general public for any documents filed on or after November 1, 2004. Access to documents filed on or before October 31, 2004 is restricted to counsel of record in the criminal case.

8. If an attorney is unable to create or otherwise produce PDF documents on computer disk and must, therefore, file documents in paper, the attorney may apply to the assigned judge for permission to file documents conventionally. Even if the assigned judge initially grants an attorney permission to file documents conventionally, the assigned judge may withdraw that permission at any time during the pendency of a case.

9. The clerk's office or any judge of this court may deviate from these procedures in specific cases, without prior notice, if deemed appropriate in the exercise of discretion, considering the need for the just, speedy, and inexpensive determination of matters pending before the court. The court may also amend these procedures at any time without prior notice.

10. A document will be deemed timely filed if filed prior to midnight. However, if the assigned judge so orders, the document shall be filed by a time certain.

11. The official court record shall be the electronic file maintained on the Court's servers. The official record shall include, however, any conventional documents or exhibits filed in accordance with these procedures or if required by court rules or policies.

C. **Service and Notice of Electronically Filed Documents.** The court, through the capture of e-mail addresses provided as required by the local rules, will provide electronic notification of court activity to any party having an e-mail address in the CM/ECF System. Upon registration and the assignment of a login and password, attorneys consent to the electronic notice and service of all documents, and shall make available e-mail addresses for service. (See instructions for Setting Up E-mail Notification in Appendix C.) Pro se litigants may consent to electronic notice from the court or may consent to electronic service by counsel, by completing the required consent form available at the clerk's office [Appendix D]. Upon the electronic filing of a document by counsel, the CM/ECF System will automatically generate a Notice of Electronic Filing at the time the document is filed with the CM/ECF System. The NEF is sent to all parties registered to receive filings electronically and contains an electronic link (hyperlink) to the filed document, allowing anyone receiving the NEF to retrieve the document through a PACER account. The NEF must be served on any party not having an e-mail address on record with the court, by e-mail, by hand, by facsimile, or by first-class mail postage prepaid. In addition to receiving e-mail notifications of filing activity, counsel are strongly encouraged to sign on to the CM/ECF System at regular intervals to check the docket in their case.

To meet the current requirements of Fed.R.Civ.P. 5, a certificate of service, in the form provided below and in Appendix E, must be included with all documents filed electronically. Such certificate shall indicate that counsel has complied with the electronic filing requirements of the court and has served any counsel or parties unable to accept electronic notice and service. Documents filed in cases that have not been designated as e-filed cases, must contain a certificate of service in the form required by this Court's Local Rule 5(b).

Electronic service of the Notice of Electronic Filing constitutes service of the filed document pursuant to Fed.R.Civ.P. 5(b)(2)(d) and Fed.R.Crim.P. 45(c) and entitles counsel being served to the additional 3 days provided by Fed.R.Civ.P. 6(e).

The following certificate of service should be used in cases designated for electronic filing:

### Certificate of Service

I hereby certify that on [insert date here], a copy of foregoing [insert the name of document being filed] was filed electronically and served by mail on anyone unable to accept electronic filing. Notice of this filing will be sent by e-mail to all parties by operation of the court's electronic filing system or by mail to anyone unable to accept electronic filing as indicated on the Notice of Electronic Filing. Parties may access this filing through the court's CM/ECF System.

/s/[Insert Name of Registered Attorney Making Filing]
Name of Attorney [attorney's federal bar number]
Address
City, State, Zip Code
Phone: (xxx)xxx-xxxx
Fax: (xxx) xxx-xxxx
E-mail: xxx@xxx.xxx

## VIII.  MANUAL FILINGS.

Counsel otherwise participating in the CM/ECF System may be excused from electronically filing a particular document under certain limited circumstances, such as when the document cannot be reduced to an electronic format or exceeds the file size limit described in Section I. F. Documents unable to be filed electronically shall be manually filed with the clerk of court and served upon the parties in accordance with the applicable Federal Rules of Civil Procedure and the Local Rules for filing and service of non-electronic documents. Counsel manually filing a document shall electronically file a Notice of Manual Filing in the form provided in Appendix F, identifying the document being filed in paper and setting forth the reason(s) why the document cannot be filed electronically. If the reason for the manual filing is not due to size restrictions, but rather, is because the document is being filed ex parte or under seal, counsel shall submit a computer disk containing a PDF version of the document being filed.

## IX.   EXCEPTIONS TO ELECTRONIC FILING OVER THE INTERNET.

The court has directed that the following types of documents not be filed electronically over the internet but instead that they be filed in paper, without a PDF version on computer disk, and served pursuant to Fed. R. Civ. P. 5(a) in the traditional manner:

A.   Social Security Administrative Records;

B.   Medical Records;

C.   Documents or exhibits that cannot reasonably be converted to the required PDF format;

D.   Documents that exceed 1.5 mb; or

E.   Individual Party Consents to Proceed Before a U.S. Magistrate Judge.

The following documents are to be filed and served in the traditional manner in paper, accompanied by a computer disk containing a PDF version of any document filed, along with any applicable filing fee, unless otherwise directed by the court:

A. Initial Complaint, Petition, Notice of Removal, initial charging documents in criminal cases;

B. Application for Admission Pro Hac Vice (if granted, submit electronically);

C. Notice of Appeal;

D. Sealed and in-camera Documents; or

E. Ex parte Submissions.

## X. TRANSCRIPTS.

Whenever a transcript is filed by a court reporter, a docket entry will be made to provide electronic notice that a transcript has been filed. When the docket entry is viewed, the CM/ECF System will display a message advising the party that the transcript is available through the Exemplaris transcript service, which can be accessed at https://www.exemplaris.com.

## XI. SIGNATURES.

**A. General.** Documents that must contain original signatures, or that require either verification or an unsworn declaration under any rule or statute, shall be filed electronically over the internet or in PDF format on computer disk, with originally executed copies maintained by the filer. The pleading or other document electronically filed shall indicate a signature, e.g., "/s/Jane Doe."

**B. Attorney Signature.** Counsel's identification name and password shall constitute counsel's signature for purposes of Fed. R. Civ. P. 11, the Federal Rules of Criminal Procedure and any other purpose for which a signature is required on a document in connection with proceedings before the court. All documents filed electronically over the internet, or filed on computer disk in PDF format, shall include a signature block in compliance with Local Rule of Civil Procedure 10 and the attorney's typewritten name, address, telephone number, federal bar number and e-mail address.

In addition, the name of the password registrant under whose password the document is submitted should be preceded by a "/s/" or "s/" or "/s" and typed in the space where the signature would otherwise appear, for example:

/s/[Name of Password Registrant]
Name of Password Registrant [attorney's federal bar number]
Address
City, State, Zip Code
Phone: (xxx) xxx-xxxx
Fax: (xxx) xxx-xxxx
E-mail: xxx@xxx.xxx

**C. Other Signatures.** Several documents may require the signature of non-attorneys, such as documents signed by a grand jury foreperson, a defendant or plaintiff, an affiant, a third-party custodian, a United States Marshal, an officer from Probation, or some other federal officer or agent. Counsel may submit these documents, in PDF format, as scanned documents containing the signature or as PDF documents containing a "/s/" signature. In the latter instance, counsel shall retain the originally executed document containing the signature. In cases where counsel cannot create PDF documents, the clerk's office will scan these documents and upload the electronic version, including signatures, to the CM/ECF System.

A document containing the signature of a defendant in a criminal case may at the Court's option be filed either in paper form or in a scanned format that contains an image of the defendant's signature.

**D. Multiple Signatures.** Documents requiring signatures of more than one attorney shall be filed either by submitting a scanned document containing all necessary signatures; by representing the consent of the other attorneys on the document; by filing the document identifying the attorneys whose signatures are

required and by the submission of a notice of endorsement by the other attorneys no later than three business days after filing, or in any other manner approved by the court. In the case of a stipulation or other document to be signed by two or more persons, the filing party or attorney shall retain the hard copy of the document containing the original signature for period of time provided for in Section XV of this administrative order.

## XII. ORDERS.

All orders, decrees, judgments and proceedings of the court will be filed in accordance with these rules, which will constitute entry on the docket kept by the clerk. Any order signed electronically by a judge or by the clerk or the clerk's designee has the same force and effect as if the judge or clerk had affixed the judge's or clerk's signature to a paper copy of the order and it had been entered on the docket in a conventional manner.

**A. Electronic Submission of Proposed Orders.** Electronic submission of proposed orders is to be done in the manner or method as required by the presiding judge. Proposed orders may not be combined with or attached to an electronically filed motion.

**B. Orders Entered by the Court.** If a judge during a hearing enters an order in paper, notice of the order will be distributed electronically after the hearing. If an oral order is entered, an entry will be placed on the docket and distributed electronically.

When mailing paper copies of an electronically filed order to a party who is not a registered participant of the CM/ECF System, the clerk's office will include the Notice of Electronic Filing to provide the non-participant with proof of the filing.

The assigned judge or the clerk's office, if appropriate, may grant routine orders by a text-only entry upon the docket. In such cases, no PDF document will issue; the text-only entry shall constitute the Court's only order on the matter. The CM/ECF System will generate a "Notice of Electronic Filing" as described in Section II of these procedures.

## XIII. SEALED AND EX PARTE DOCUMENTS.

**A. Sealed Documents.** The filing of documents under seal is governed by Local Rule of Civil Procedure 5(d) and Local Rule of Criminal Procedure 57(b) which permits such filings only with prior leave of the judicial officer. Sealed documents are to be filed in paper accompanied by a computer disk containing a PDF version of the document. Counsel are not permitted to file sealed documents electronically over the internet.

If a case is designated for electronic filing, counsel filing a sealed document shall electronically file a Notice of Manual Filing, identifying the document being filed as "SEALED DOCUMENT" or "SEALED MOTION" unless otherwise directed by the court. The sealed document/motion should then be filed in paper, accompanied by a paper copy of the Notice of Manual Filing and a computer disk containing a PDF version of the document being filed under seal.

**B. Ex Parte Documents.** Documents filed ex parte are to be filed in paper, accompanied by a Notice of Manual Filing and a computer disk containing a PDF version of the document. Counsel are not permitted to file ex parte documents over the internet.

If a case is designated for electronic filing, counsel filing an ex parte document shall electronically file a Notice of Manual Filing, identifying the document being filed as "EX PARTE DOCUMENT" or "EX PARTE MOTION" unless otherwise directed by the court. The ex parte document/motion should then be filed in paper, accompanied by a paper copy of the Notice of Manual Filing and a computer disk containing a PDF version of the document being filed ex parte.

## XIV. TRIAL EXHIBITS.

Exhibits filed with the clerk's office pursuant to Local Rule of Civil Procedure 83.6 will not be filed electronically over the internet or on computer disk. Counsel

submitting the exhibits may be required to resubmit the documents in electronic format once they are admitted into the public record.

## XV.  RETENTION OF ORIGINALS OF DOCUMENTS REQUIRING SCANNING.

Originals of documents requiring scanning to be filed electronically must be retained by the filing party and made available, upon request, to the court and other parties for a period of five years following the expiration of all time periods for appeals or statutes of limitation. If and when a record on appeal is requested, until such time as the Second Circuit accepts electronic filings, counsel will be required to produce the record on appeal in paper.

## XVI.  ADDITIONAL INFORMATION.

Additional information regarding electronic filing can be obtained by calling the Help Desks at 203–579–5861 (Bridgeport), 203–773–2140 (New Haven), or 860–240–3200 (Hartford), or by writing to:

Roberta D. Tabora, Clerk
United States District Court
141 Church Street
New Haven, Connecticut 06510

Revised December 1, 2004;  October 1, 2007.

---

## APPENDIX A.  SAMPLE NOTICE OF UNTIMELY FILING DUE TO TECHNICAL DIFFICULTIES

**Instructions: Where noted, counsel should insert the names of the plaintiff(s) and defendant(s), the name of the party filing the Notice, the appropriate case number, the title of the document, the missed deadline and the reasons why the filing could not be made in a timely basis.**

| | |
|---|---|
| Plaintiff [insert name here] | ) Case No. [insert your case number |
| | ) and initials of the presiding judge] |
| v. | ) |
| | ) |
| Defendant [insert name here] | ) **Declaration that Party was Unable to** |
| | ) **File in a Timely Manner** |
| | ) **Due to Technical Difficulties** |

Please take notice that **[insert Name of Party]** was unable to file the attached **[insert Title of Document]** in a timely manner due to technical difficulties. The deadline for filing the **[insert Title of Document]** was **[insert Filing Deadline Date]**. The reason(s) that I was unable to file the **[insert Title of Document]** in a timely manner and the good faith efforts I made prior to the filing deadline to both file in a timely manner and to inform the court and the other parties that I could not do so are set forth below.

**[Insert your explanation here, describing your reasons and good faith efforts to file and to inform of the difficulties in filing (including dates and times)].**

I declare under penalty of perjury that the foregoing is true and correct.

439

Respectfully submitted,

/s/ [Name of Password Registrant]
Name of Password Registrant [attorney's federal bar number]
Address
City, State, Zip Code
Phone: (xxx) xxx-xxxx
Fax: (xxx) xxx-xxxx
E-mail: xxx@xxx.xxx

## APPENDIX B. ELECTRONIC FILING ATTORNEY REGISTRATION FORM

### UNITED STATES DISTRICT COURT
### DISTRICT OF CONNECTICUT

This form is used to register for an account on the District of Connecticut Electronic Filing System (the CM/ECF System). Registered attorneys will have privileges to electronically file documents and, in conjunction with a PACER access account, to view the electronic docket sheets and documents. By registering, attorneys consent to receiving electronic notice of filings through the CM/ECF System. The following information is required for registration:

### PLEASE TYPE

First Name: _____ Middle Name:

Last Name: _____ If appropriate check one: ( )Sr. ( )Jr. ( )II ( )III

Federal Bar Number:

Are you currently in good standing in all courts in which you are admitted to practice? Yes ___ No ___

Firm Name:

Address:

_____

_____

City: _____ State: ___ Zip Code: _____

Voice Telephone Number: (___)_____ Fax Number: (___) _____

E–Mail Address: _____

**Attorneys seeking to file documents electronically must be admitted to practice in the United States District Court for the District of Connecticut pursuant to Local Rule of Civil Procedure 83.1.**

Date admitted to practice in this court: _____

If admitted pro hac vice: Date motion for pro hac vice granted: _____ in case number: _____

If Attorney of Record in MDL action indicate case number: _____

**By submitting this registration form, the undersigned agrees to abide by all court rules, orders and policies and procedures governing the use of the CM/ECF System. The undersigned also consents to receiving notice of filings pursuant to Fed. R. Civ. P. 5(b) and 77(d) via the Court's electronic filing system. The combination of user ID and password will serve as the signature of the attorney filing the documents. Attorneys must protect the security of their**

**passwords and immediately notify the court if they learn that their password has been compromised. Electronic filing is only permissible in cases approved by the court.**

_____

Signature of Registrant

_____

Date

Submit completed Registration Form to:    Roberta D. Tabora, Clerk
                                          United States District Court
                                          **Attention: Electronic Filing System**

**Registration**

141 Church Street
New Haven, CT 06510

Once your registration is complete, you will receive an e-mail confirmation of your internet address. Your user id and password will be provided by e-mail, in person or by U.S. mail. Procedures for using the CM/ECF System can be downloaded from the court's website at www.ctd.uscourts.gov/cmecf. If you have any questions concerning the registration process or the use of the CM/ECF System, please contact the clerk's office.

_____

## APPENDIX C. SETTING UP E–MAIL NOTIFICATION

Users can receive e-mail notification of all electronic filings in cases they are interested in by setting the automatic e-mail notification in their user accounts.

- Access the "Live" CM/ECF System.
- Select "Utilities"
- Select "Maintain Your Account"
- Select "E-mail Information"
- Enter your correct e-mail address in the "Primary e-mail address" box.
- Under "Send the notices specified below", there will be a U next to "to my primary e-mail address." Click on the box "to these additional addresses" to identify any additional e-mail addresses you would like to receive electronic notice (i.e., at your home e-mail address, an associate, paralegal, secretary, supervisor). [NOTE: whoever opens the e-mail first should save the document to a local network for easy retrieval later, without any associated charges.]
- You will find a U next to "Send notices in cases in which I am involved." Leave this setting defaulted as is.
- If you want to receive notices of activity in other cases in which you are not counsel of record, click on the box "Send notices in these additional cases" to activate this feature. CAVEAT: this does not apply in criminal case documents filed on or before 10/31/04 or to Social Security cases because access in those cases is restricted to counsel of record. In the box to the right, enter each case number on a separate line. Please use the format YY-XXXX (ex. 97–1234).
- Select the type of notice you would like to receive. "Please send a notice for each filing" is automatically selected. This selection sends notices to you immediately upon filing. Select "Send a Daily Summary Report" to have a summary of the notices sent to you at the end of the day (usually at midnight). If you seek electronic notice in only a handful of cases, this selection is the preferred method.
- Under Format notices, the format of the notice is defaulted to "html format for Netscape or ISP e-mail service." If you have some other e-mail service, you may

need to select "text format for cc:Mail, GroupWise, other e-mail service." Some experimentation may be required.

- Click on "Return to Account Screen." From the Account Screen, select "Submit." You will receive a confirmation screen listing the cases and e-mail options you have selected.

---

### APPENDIX D.    CONSENT TO ELECTRONIC FILING BY PRO SE LITIGANT

UNITED STATES DISTRICT COURT
DISTRICT OF CONNECTICUT

_____, Plaintiff

V.

_____, Defendant

Case No.
**[Put case number here]**

### CONSENT TO ELECTRONIC NOTICE BY PRO SE LITIGANT

**A.**   **[Complete the first line for electronic notification from the court]**

I,   (name of pro se litigant)   hereby consent to the court using my e-mail address, as listed below, for the purpose of sending me notification of orders and notices issued by the court.

**B.**   [Complete the second line for electronic service from opposing counsel; **DO NOT COMPLETE THIS LINE IF YOU WANT OPPOSING COUNSEL TO SEND PAPERS BY REGULAR MAIL**]

I,   (name of pro se litigant)   hereby consent to opposing counsel using my e-mail address, as listed below, for the purpose of sending me papers filed with the court.

In the event I change my e-mail provider or discontinue my e-mail service, I will notify the court immediately of the address change so my court records may be updated.

_____
(Name of pro se litigant, typed or printed)

_____
Street Address

_____
City, State, Zip Code

_____
Telephone

_____
E-mail address

_____
Date

_____
Signature

<u>**Certificate of Service**</u>

I hereby certify that on __ [date], a copy of foregoing "Consent to Electronic Service By Pro Se Litigant," was filed and served by mail on the following: [insert name and address of every person served]

---

Signature of pro se litigant

---

## APPENDIX E.  SAMPLE CERTIFICATE OF SERVICE

### UNITED STATES DISTRICT COURT
### DISTRICT OF CONNECTICUT

### SAMPLE CERTIFICATE OF SERVICE

**Instructions: Where noted, counsel should insert the names of the plaintiff(s) and defendant(s), the name of the party filing the Certificate, the appropriate case number and the title of the document(s).**

Plaintiff [insert name here]          ) Case No. [insert your case number
                                        ) and initials of the presiding judge]
v.                                               )
                                                  )
Defendant [insert name here]      )

I hereby certify that on **[insert date here]**, a copy of foregoing **[insert the name of document being filed]** was filed electronically and served by mail on anyone unable to accept electronic filing. Notice of this filing will be sent by e-mail to all parties by operation of the Court's electronic filing system or by mail to anyone unable to accept electronic filing as indicated on the Notice of Electronic Filing. Parties may access this filing through the Court's CM/ECF System.

/s/[Insert Name of Registered Attorney Making Filing
Name of Attorney [attorney's federal bar number]
Address
City, State, Zip Code
Phone: (xxx) xxx-xxxx
Fax: (xxx)xxx-xxxx
E-mail: xxx@xxx.xxx

---

## APPENDIX F.  SAMPLE NOTICE OF MANUAL FILING

**Instructions: Where noted, counsel should insert the names of the plaintiff(s) and defendant(s), the name of the party filing the Notice, the appropriate case number and the title of the document. The appropriate box should be checked identifying the reason why the document is being filed in paper. All documents filed in paper pursuant to a Notice of Manual Filing must be accompanied by a computer disk containing a PDF version of the document being filed unless the document falls within the excepted documents list contained in these policies and procedures.**

Plaintiff [insert name here]   ) Case No. [insert your case number
            ) and initials of the presiding judge here]
v.          )
            )
Defendant [insert name here]  ) Notice of Manual Filing

Please take notice that **[insert Name of Party]** has manually filed the **[insert Title of Document or Thing]**.

This document (or thing) **[please note which option applies and delete the other option]** has not been filed electronically because: **[mark all that apply]**

[ ] the document (or thing) cannot be converted to an electronic format

[ ] the electronic file size of the document exceeds 1.5 mb

[ ] The document (or thing) is filed under seal pursuant to Local Rule of Civil Procedure 5(d) or Local Rule of Criminal Procedure 57(b) or is filed ex parte pursuant to court order, statute or regulation allowing ex parte submissions [e.g. Criminal Justice Act Vouchers submitted pursuant to 18 U.S.C. § 3006A]

[ ] Plaintiff/Defendant is excused from electronically filing this document (or thing) by court order.

The document (or thing) **[delete "document" or "thing" depending on which does not apply to this filing]** has been manually served on all parties.

Respectfully submitted,

/s/ [Name of Password Registrant]
Name of Password Registrant [attorney's federal bar number]
Address
City, State, Zip Code
Phone: (xxx) xxx-xxxx
Fax: (xxx) xxx-xxxx
E-mail: xxx@xxx.xxx

---

## APPENDIX G. NOTICE OF ELECTRONIC AVAILABILITY OF CIVIL CASE FILE INFORMATION

CM/ECF IMPLEMENTATION
UNITED STATES DISTRICT COURT
DISTRICT OF CONNECTICUT

The United States District Court for the District of Connecticut implemented electronic filing and case management (CM/ECF) in October 2003. **As of January 5, 2004, when filing original paper documents with the court, all counsel of record are required to supply a PDF formatted version of the document on a computer disk. Disks will be returned to counsel by mail if a return envelope is supplied or counsel may retrieve disks from the clerk's office.** As of August 2004, the court began accepting pleadings filed electronically over the internet in selected cases. The content of electronically filed pleadings are available on the Court's internet website via WebPACER. Any subscriber to WebPACER will be able to read, download, store and print the full content of electronically filed documents. However, the clerk's office will not make available electronically filed documents that have been sealed or otherwise restricted by court order. Attorneys receiving e-mail notification of filings are permitted one free access. For additional access opportunities and for other interested viewers there are minimal charges associated with case access and a WebPACER password is required.

When submitting electronic documents, *you should not include sensitive information in any document filed with the court* unless such inclusion is necessary and relevant to the case. You must remember that any personal information not otherwise protected will be made available over the internet via WebPACER. If sensitive information must be included, the following personal data identifiers must be **partially redacted** from the pleading by the filer, whether it is filed in the conventional manner (in paper) or electronically over the internet: *Social Security numbers to the last four digits, financial account numbers to the last four digits, dates of birth to the year and names of minor children to the initials.*

In compliance with the E–Government Act of 2002, a party wishing to file a document containing the personal data identifiers specified above may file a motion requesting permission to file an unredacted document under seal. This document shall be retained by the court as part of the record. The court may, however, still require the party to file a redacted copy for the public file. In addition, exercise caution when filing documents that contain the following:

A.  Personal identifying number, such as driver's license number;

B.  Medical records, treatment and diagnosis;

C.  Employment history;

D.  Individual financial information; and

E.  Proprietary or trade secret information.

**Counsel are strongly urged to share this notice with all clients** so that an informed decision about the inclusion of certain materials can be made. If a redacted document is filed, it is the **sole responsibility of counsel and the parties** to be sure that all pleadings comply with the rules of this court requiring redaction of personal data identifiers. **THE CLERK WILL NOT REVIEW EACH PLEADING FOR REDACTION.**

## SPECIAL NOTICE TO SOCIAL SECURITY ATTORNEYS

*You should not include sensitive information, including Social Security numbers, in documents filed electronically. It is your responsibility to provide the U.S. Attorney's Office with the Social Security number of the plaintiff upon the filing and service of a new Social Security complaint. This may be accomplished by writing to: AUSA Ann M. Nevins, U.S. Attorney's Office, 915 Lafayette Blvd., Room 309, Bridgeport, CT 06604.*

---

## APPENDIX H.   NOTICE OF ELECTRONIC AVAILABILITY OF CRIMINAL CASE FILE DOCUMENTS

UNITED STATES DISTRICT COURT
DISTRICT OF CONNECTICUT

10/13/04

EFFECTIVE NOVEMBER 1, 2004, DOCUMENTS FILED IN CRIMINAL CASES IN THIS COURT WILL BE AVAILABLE TO THE PUBLIC ELECTRONICALLY.

Electronic access applies to documents filed on or after November 1, 2004, which would have been otherwise available in paper. Documents filed prior to November 1, 2004 continue to be available, as appropriate, in paper but will not be available electronically.

You shall not include sensitive information in any document filed with the court. You must remember that any personal information not otherwise protected will be made available over the internet via WebPACER. The following personal data identifiers must be partially redacted from the document whether it is filed in paper or electronically:

1) Social Security numbers to the last four digits;

2) Financial account numbers to the last four digits;

3) Names of minor children to the initials;

4) Dates of birth to the year; and

5) Home addresses to the city and state.

In compliance with the E–Government Act of 2002, a party wishing to file a document containing the personal data identifiers specified above may file an unredacted document under seal. This document shall be retained by the court as part of the record. The court may, however, also require the party to file a redacted copy for the public file.

Because filings will be remotely, electronically available and may contain information implicating not only privacy but also personal security concerns, exercise caution when filing a document that contains any of the following information and consider accompanying any such filing with a motion to seal. Until the court has ruled on any motion to seal, pursuant to Local Criminal Rule 57(b), no document that is the subject of a motion to seal, nor the motion itself or any response thereto, will be available electronically or in paper form.

1) any personal identifying number, such as driver's license number;

2) medical records, treatment and diagnosis;

3) employment history;

4) individual financial information;

5) proprietary or trade secret information;

6) information regarding an individual's cooperation with the government;

7) information regarding the victim of any criminal activity;

8) national security information; and

9) sensitive security information as described in 49 U.S.C. § 114(s).

All counsel are strongly urged to share this notice with all clients so that an informed decision about the inclusion of certain materials can be made. If a redacted document is filed, it is the sole responsibility of counsel and the parties to be sure that all documents and pleadings comply with the rules of this court requiring redaction of personal data identifiers. The clerk will not review filings for redaction.

# LOCAL RULES OF BANKRUPTCY PROCEDURE FOR THE UNITED STATES BANKRUPTCY COURT FOR THE DISTRICT OF CONNECTICUT

### Effective May 15, 1997

### Including Amendments Received Through October 15, 2007

---

### Research Note

*These rules may be searched electronically on WESTLAW in the CT-RULES database; updates to these rules may be found on WESTLAW in CT–ORDERS or CT–RULESUPDATES. For search tips, and a detailed summary of database content, consult the WESTLAW Scope Screen of each database.*

---

### Table of Rules

### ELECTRONIC CASE FILING

### STANDING ORDERS

\* Suggested title added by Publisher.

## LBR 1001–1. SCOPE OF RULES; SHORT TITLE; INCORPORATION OF DISTRICT COURT RULES

(a) These Local Rules shall govern the practice and procedure to be followed in all cases and proceedings in the United States Bankruptcy Court for the District of Connecticut. These Rules may be referred to as the "Local Rules of Bankruptcy Procedure" and cited as D.Conn. LBR \_\_\_\_–\_\_.

(b) All Local Rules of Civil Procedure of the United States District Court for the District of Connecticut shall apply in cases or proceedings in the Bankruptcy Court insofar as they are relevant and not inconsistent with the Bankruptcy Code, the Federal Rules of Bankruptcy Procedure, these Local Rules of Bankruptcy Procedure, and the case management procedures applicable at the seat of the Bankruptcy Court to which the case or proceeding has been assigned.

Eff. May 15, 1997.

## LBR 1002–1. PLACE FOR FILING PETITION AND OTHER PAPERS

Petitions and other documents filed simultaneously therewith may be filed with the clerk at Bridgeport, New Haven, or Hartford. All other papers shall be filed at the seat of court where the case is assigned as provided by D.Conn. LBR 1073–1.

Eff. May 15, 1997.

## LBR 1004–1. PARTNERSHIP PETITION

A partner filing a petition on behalf of a partnership shall submit, with the petition or within five (5) business days thereafter, documentation evidencing the requisite consent of partners.

Eff. May 15, 1997.

## LBR 1007–1. LISTS, SCHEDULES, AND STATEMENTS

**(a)** In Chapter 7, 12, and 13 cases, an original and two (2) complete copies of the petition and all papers described in Fed.R.Bankr.P. 1007 shall be filed. For Chapter 9 and 11 cases, an original and six (6) complete copies of the petition and all papers described in Fed.R.Bankr.P. 1007 shall be filed. The clerk shall transmit one (1) copy of all papers filed pursuant to Fed.R.Bankr.P. 1007 and subsections (b) and (c) of this Rule to the United States Trustee.

**(b)** In addition to those papers and any others required by the Bankruptcy Code and Federal Rules of Bankruptcy Procedure, non-individual debtors shall file within fifteen (15) days following the filing of a voluntary petition or consent to an involuntary petition, documentation sufficient under applicable law to evidence authority to file on behalf of the entity.

**(c)** Unless excused by the court, whenever, pursuant to Fed.R.Bankr.P. 1007, schedules are not filed with a voluntary petition, the petition shall be accompanied by a statement containing a brief description of the debtor's assets, their location, and the extent to which they are subject to liens or other interests.

Eff. May 15, 1997.

## LBR 1007–2. MAILING MATRIX

Every petition shall be accompanied by a mailing matrix that complies with instructions available from the clerk. Requirements related to the submission of computer-formatted discs shall be excused only upon the submission of an affidavit indicating that the person filing the petition is unable, due to a lack of computer equipment, to comply.

Eff. May 15, 1997.

## LBR 1009–1. AMENDMENTS TO VOLUNTARY PETITIONS, LISTS, SCHEDULES, AND STATEMENTS

Any amendment to a voluntary petition, list, schedule, or statement shall be dated and shall indicate that it is an amendment. Any such amendment to a schedule, list, or statement that results in the addition of any creditor or changes the name or address of any creditor shall be accompanied by an amendment to the mailing matrix, which amendment shall comply with D.Conn. LBR 1007–2. Upon the filing of any amendment adding creditors, the debtor shall serve upon the newly added creditors a copy of the "Notice of Commencement of Case Under Chapter __ of the Bankruptcy Code, Meeting of Creditors and Fixing of Dates," and any other notice establishing any bar date for filing proofs of claim.

Eff. May 15, 1997.

## LBR 1015–1. CONSOLIDATION OR JOINT ADMINISTRATION OF CASES PENDING IN SAME COURT

**(a)** Upon entry of an order directing the consolidation or joint administration of cases, notice thereof shall be served by the debtor on all creditors and other parties in interest.

**(b)** Consolidated or jointly administered cases shall be assigned to the bankruptcy judge to whom the lower numbered case was assigned.

**(c)** All pleadings and other papers filed in jointly administered cases shall bear a combined caption with the words "Jointly Administered." Except as provided in subsection (d) of this Rule, pleadings and other papers shall be docketed and placed in the case file of the lower numbered case only.

**(d)** All proofs of claim filed in a jointly administered case shall be listed in the claims register and placed in the claims file for the specific case to which they pertain.

**(e)** Notwithstanding the joint administration of cases, each debtor shall file schedules of assets and liabilities.

Eff. May 15, 1997.

## LBR 1073–1. ASSIGNMENT AND REASSIGNMENT OF CASES

**(a)** All cases shall be assigned by the clerk to a bankruptcy judge as follows: (i) those cases in which the debtor resides or has its principal place of business in Fairfield County, exclusive of the towns of Monroe, Shelton and Stratford, shall be assigned to the Bridgeport Division; (ii) those cases in which the debtor resides or has its principal place of business in Litchfield, Middlesex, New London, or New Haven Counties, or in the towns of Monroe, Shelton and Stratford shall be assigned to the New Haven Division; and (iii) those cases in which the debtor resides or has its principal place of business in Hartford, Tolland or Windham Counties shall be assigned to the Hartford Division.

**(b)** Upon motion to the judge to whom the case has been assigned and after notice and a hearing, the clerk shall reassign the case to another Division as ordered by that judge upon the findings that such reassignment would be in the best interests of the estate and parties in interest. Upon such reassignment, the clerk shall transmit the case file to the appropriate office of the clerk.

Eff. May 15, 1997. Amended eff. April 1, 1999.

## LBR 2002–1. NOTICES TO PARTIES IN INTEREST WHO HAVE REQUESTED SERVICE

In addition to the requirements of any other applicable rule governing service, and unless otherwise

ordered by the court, a copy of all motions, pleadings, applications, petitions, and other papers filed in a case shall be timely served on any party in interest who has filed in such a case a written demand for such service.

Eff. May 15, 1997.

## LBR 2014–1. EMPLOYMENT OF PROFESSIONAL PERSONS

(a) In addition to the requirements set forth in Fed.R.Bankr.P. 2014, all applications for the employment of professional persons shall state whether or not the person has an interest adverse to the estate and the nature of that interest and whether or not the person is disinterested. All applications for approval of employment shall be accompanied by a proposed order setting forth the terms of the employment.

(b) In addition to the general requirements set forth in paragraph (a) above, an application for the employment of an accountant shall be accompanied by an affidavit of the proposed accountant, setting forth the nature and extent of the services that the accountant proposes to render, the estimated total cost thereof and hourly rate, the basis of such estimate, and the extent to which the accountant is familiar with the books or accounts of the debtor. Any order authorizing the employment of an accountant shall fix the maximum hourly rate and the maximum amount of compensation sought.

Eff. May 15, 1997.

## LBR 2014–2. NON–PROFESSIONAL EMPLOYEES OF THE TRUSTEE

(a) Unless authorized to carry on the business, a trustee shall not employ any non-professional person at the expense of the estate except on order of the court expressly authorizing such employment and fixing the amount of compensation or the rate or measure thereof. The application for such an order shall be made by the trustee who shall set forth the name of the person sought to be employed, the reason for the selection, the necessity for the employment, and whether the United States Trustee has consented to the request. The trustee shall not employ persons at the expense of the estate merely for the purpose of guarding the property when there are other adequate methods of protecting it at less expense.

(b) Before payment, each such person employed by the trustee shall submit a statement setting forth the dates of employment, and also the hours between which he or she was actually present and performing the duties for which he or she was employed. Such statement shall accompany any application for allowance of compensation submitted by the trustee. The sharing of the compensation paid to non-professional

employees of the trustee with any person is prohibited.

Eff. May 15, 1997.

## LBR 2015–3. POST–CONFIRMATION REPORTS

Within 45 days after the order confirming a plan in a Chapter 11 case and, until the entry of final decree, every 90 days thereafter, the debtor-in-possession, trustee, distributor, or plan proponent shall file a report with the court and serve a copy on any committee appointed in the case, and the United States Trustee, which report shall set forth the action taken and progress made in the consummation of the plan pursuant to 11 U.S.C. § 1106(a)(7).

Eff. May 15, 1997.

## LBR 2016–1. COMPENSATION FOR PROFESSIONAL PERSONS

(a) Unless otherwise ordered by the court, all applications for compensation to attorneys, trustees, accountants, or examiners for services rendered or reimbursement of necessary expenses shall, in addition to the requirements set forth in the Bankruptcy Code and Fed.R.Bankr.P. 2016(a), contain the following information:

(1) The date of the order of appointment;

(2) A brief general narrative statement of the nature of the services provided, including the results obtained, the size of the estate, the total amount of compensation sought, and any other factors which will assist the court in determining the reasonable value of such services;

(3) A typed time sheet, based upon records prepared contemporaneously with the services rendered, setting forth:

    a. The dates the services were rendered;

    b. A description of services in sufficient detail to enable the court to find that such services were actual and necessary;

    c. The time spent rendering each service broken down into tenths of an hour;

    d. The identity of the person(s) rendering such services;

    e. The normal billing rate for each person providing services and a total of the amount of time spent by each person; and

    f. The total compensation sought by each person providing the services.

(4) In the case of an accountant, the maximum compensation fixed in the order of appointment;

(5) In all applications for reimbursement of expenses, an itemization as to purpose, amount, and date incurred, accompanied by an invoice, receipt, or other

documentation for each item for which reimbursement is sought. The general costs of doing business, such as regular postage and ordinary telephone expenses will not be allowed; and

(6) Whenever the time sheet required in paragraph (3) above exceeds five pages, each page shall set forth a cumulative total of the times recorded therein and on preceding pages.

(b) All applications of persons other than attorneys, trustees, accountants, or examiners for compensation and reimbursement of expenses in the amount of $500.00 or less shall be governed by the requirements set forth in the Bankruptcy Code and Fed.R.Bankr.P. 2016(a) and contain the following information:

(1) The date of the order of appointment;

(2) A brief general narrative statement of the nature of the services provided;

(3) Based upon records prepared contemporaneously with the services rendered a statement, indicating:

a. The dates the services were rendered;

b. The identity of the person or persons rendering such services; and

c. The total compensation sought by each person providing the services.

Eff. May 15, 1997.

## LBR 2071–1.  COMMITTEES IN CHAPTER 11 AND 12 CASES

Within five (5) days of the appointment of a committee, the United States Trustee shall file with the court a list containing the names, addresses, and telephone numbers of persons serving on such committee. If a creditors' committee is not constituted, a statement to that effect relating briefly the reasons for not appointing a committee shall be filed with the court.

Eff. May 15, 1997.

## LBR 3002–1.  PROOFS OF CLAIM

Any creditor filing a proof of claim shall, contemporaneously with the filing of the original proof of claim, serve a copy, via first class mail, on the debtor-in-possession or any trustee appointed in a Chapter 11 case, and on the trustee in a Chapter 12 or 13 case.

Eff. May 15, 1997.

## LBR 3015–1.  CHAPTER 12 AND 13 PLANS

The debtor shall file the original and three (3) copies of the Chapter 12 or 13 plan.

Eff. May 15, 1997.

## LBR 3017–1.  TRANSMISSION AND NOTICE OF PLAN AND DISCLOSURE STATEMENT

Unless the court otherwise directs, the proponent of a plan shall transmit all notices and other documents required by Fed.R.Bankr.P. 3017(a).

Eff. May 15, 1997.

## LBR 3018–2.  CERTIFICATION OF ACCEPTANCES AND REJECTIONS OF CHAPTER 11 PLANS

Prior to or at the hearing on confirmation, the proponent of a Chapter 11 plan, or other party who receives the ballots accepting or rejecting such plan, shall certify to the court the amount and number of allowed claims or interests in each class accepting or rejecting the plan. A copy of the certification shall be served upon the debtor, debtor-in-possession, trustee, if any, United States Trustee, any committee appointed pursuant to the Bankruptcy Code, and any other entity designated by the court. On the basis of the certification, the court may find that the plan has been accepted or rejected.

Eff. May 15, 1997.

## LBR 3019–1.  MODIFICATION OF CHAPTER 11 PLAN BEFORE ACCEPTANCE

In the event that the proponent of a Chapter 11 plan files a modification of the plan after transmittal of the disclosure statement and before the time specified for acceptance or rejection of the plan, the proponent shall serve a copy of the plan, as modified, on the debtor, debtor-in-possession, trustee, if any, the United States Trustee, any committee appointed pursuant to the Bankruptcy Code, and any other entity designated by the court. On notice to such entities, the court shall determine, after motion and hearing, whether the modification adversely affects the treatment of the claim of any creditor or the interest of any equity security holder who has not accepted the modification in writing. If the modification is not adverse, the plan, as modified, shall be deemed accepted by the creditors and equity security holders who accept the plan. If the modification is adverse, the requirements of Fed.R.Bankr.P. 3017 shall apply to the modified plan and any amendment to the disclosure statement made necessary by the modification.

Eff. May 15, 1997.

## LBR 3022–1.  CLOSING CHAPTER 11 CASES

(a) Unless the court orders otherwise, within thirty (30) days following substantial consummation of a Chapter 11 plan, the debtor-in-possession, trustee,

distributor, or plan proponent shall file with the clerk and the United States Trustee a closing report which shall: (1) contain a breakdown of the disbursements, as applicable from the inception of the case, for fees of the debtor's attorney, other professional fees and expenses, the trustee's fees, and fees for the trustee's attorney; (2) state the percentage of dividend paid and to be paid, or whether the future dividend percentage is not yet determinable; and (3) state the steps taken to consummate the plan and whether the initial plan distribution is complete.

(b) After substantial consummation of the plan, the debtor-in-possession, trustee, distributor, or plan proponent shall file an application for a final decree in accordance with Fed.R.Bankr.P. 3022.

Eff. May 15, 1997.

## LBR 5003-2. INTEGRITY AND EXAMINATION OF FILES

No papers on file in the office of the clerk shall be removed therefrom except with permission of the clerk.

Eff. May 15, 1997.

## LBR 5010-1. REOPENING CASES

A motion to reopen a case pursuant to 11 U.S.C. § 350(b) and Fed.R.Bankr.P. 5010 shall state the reason therefor and shall be filed with the clerk in the court where such case was closed. The court may direct the clerk to obtain any required part of the record of the closed case from wherever it is stored. A filing fee for a case reopened pursuant to 11 U.S.C. § 350(b) and Fed.R.Bankr.P. 5010 shall be required unless the case is reopened to correct an administrative error, or on account of actions relating to the debtor's discharge.

Eff. May 15, 1997.

## LBR 5011-1. WITHDRAWAL OF REFERENCE

A motion for withdrawal of the reference shall be filed with the clerk of the Bankruptcy Court. The clerk of the Bankruptcy Court shall promptly transmit the motion to the clerk of the United States District Court and notify the movant of the transmission. The movant shall notify all other parties of the transmission. Following transmission of the motion to the clerk of the District Court, all further papers with respect to the motion shall be filed with the clerk of the District Court.

Eff. May 15, 1997.

## LBR 5080-1. COURT FEES

The clerk shall not be required to render any service for which a fee is prescribed by statute or by the Judicial Conference of the United States unless the fee for the service is paid in advance.

Eff. May 15, 1997.

## LBR 6004-1. SALE OF ESTATE PROPERTY

(a) Appraisals shall ordinarily be required prior to any sale not in the ordinary course of business unless the trustee or debtor-in-possession determines that such appraisal is not warranted under the facts of the case. Where appropriate, the trustee or debtor-in-possession may determine the value of any property by reference to current price guides used to determine the value of such property, unless otherwise directed by the court.

(b) Appraisals shall be submitted to the court not later than noon on the day prior to the sale of the property in question. Each appraisal shall be kept under seal upon filing and treated as confidential. Access to the appraisal may be had only by the court, the United States Trustee, and such other parties as the court may direct. Unless otherwise authorized by the court, the appraisals shall be unsealed at the conclusion of the case.

(c) No trustee, appraiser, or auctioneer, or officer, director, stockholder, agent, employee or relative of a trustee, appraiser or auctioneer, shall directly or indirectly purchase any of the property of any bankruptcy estate.

(d) Unless otherwise ordered by the court: (1) assets of an estate shall not be sold on a percentage basis, i.e., on terms providing for the payment of a fixed percentage to creditors and expenses of administration; (2) a public sale shall be advertised at least ten (10) days before the sale, although the trustee may require further advertising; (3) the property to be sold shall be open to public inspection for such reasonable period prior to the sale as the trustee may determine; and (4) an auctioneer shall, before receiving bids, announce the terms of sale, including the statement that no sale is final without the approval of the trustee.

(e) A purchaser at any public sale shall not be entitled to a refund on account of discrepancies between the assets offered for sale by the auctioneer and the assets as listed in the inventory. Any property which, because of reclamation proceedings or for other reasons, is not included in the sale, shall be set apart and conspicuously marked "not included in sale," and such fact shall be announced by the auctioneer before the sale. Except upon prior approval of the Court, only items constituting assets of the estate being administered shall be sold at any sale held pursuant to provisions of the Bankruptcy Code, and such sales shall not be conducted in conjunction with any non-bankruptcy sale.

**(f)** When the trustee acts as auctioneer, he or she shall receive no compensation therefor in excess of the amount provided by the Bankruptcy Code for trustees.

**(g)** Unless the court orders otherwise, trustees must be in attendance throughout all auction sales.

**(h)** The sanctions which may be imposed for violation of this Rule, include, but are not limited to, the disqualification of a person from future employment on behalf of bankruptcy estates.

Eff. May 15, 1997.

## LBR 6005–1. EMPLOYMENT OF APPRAISERS AND AUCTIONEERS

**(a)** All applications for the appointment of an appraiser must be filed with the court for approval. Said applications shall contain at a minimum the following information:

(1) A statement setting forth in what manner and by whom the costs of the appraisal will be paid, and if payment is to be made from assets of the estate a statement that the estate has adequate funds with which to pay the appraisal fee;

(2) The name and address of the appraiser and the maximum amount of the appraisal fee;

(3) A statement to the effect that the appraiser does not hold an interest adverse to the estate, is a disinterested person, and a description of the appraiser's general qualifications;

(4) A description of the item(s) to be appraised, their estimated value and the time required for the appraisal; and

(5) If the appraiser sought to be appointed will incur travel expenses in connection with the appraisal, an explanation as to why a local appraiser is unavailable or unsuitable.

**(b)** All applications for allowance of appraiser's fees for services rendered or reimbursement of expenses totaling $500.00 or more, shall, in addition to the requirements set forth in the Bankruptcy Code and Fed.R.Bankr.P. 2016(a), contain the following information:

(1) The date of the order of appointment;

(2) In concise form, a general narrative statement of the nature of the services provided; and

(3) A statement, based upon records prepared contemporaneously with the services rendered, indicating:

    a.   The dates the services were rendered;

    b.   The identity of the person or persons rendering such services; and

    c.   The total compensation sought by each person providing the services.

**(c)** Unless otherwise provided by the order of the court, sections (d) through (m) of this Rule shall apply to the employment of all auctioneers and the conduct of auctions.

**(d)** The employment of an auctioneer shall be submitted to the court for approval upon application setting forth:

(1) The need for an auctioneer's services;

(2) A description of the property to be sold, its estimated value, and the location thereof;

(3) How the auctioneer is to be paid, and, if payment is to be made from assets of the estate, whether the estate will have adequate funds with which to pay the auctioneer's fee;

(4) If the items to be auctioned constitute collateral, entirely or in part, whether or not the party claiming a security interest in such collateral has agreed to pay any or all of the auctioneer's expenses;

(5) How many assistants, if any, will be required to help the auctioneer and why such assistance is required, a statement by the trustee in support of the number required and the expense to be incurred for each assistant, based upon an hourly fee; and

(6) A statement that the auctioneer is enrolled on the list of qualified auctioneers as approved by the court, or a statement pursuant to subsection (e) of this rule.

**(e)** No auctioneer shall have his or her name enrolled upon the list of qualified auctioneers unless he or she shall file with the clerk a verified application for approval as an auctioneer, which application shall contain:

(1) Facts as to the applicant's qualifications and previous experience as an auctioneer;

(2) A description of the business in which he or she has been engaged within the past ten (10) years;

(3) Banking references;

(4) A statement whether he or she has ever been convicted of any criminal offense, other than motor vehicle violations;

(5) A statement whether he or she has been liable in any litigation for the repayment or return of any money or property held by him or her in a fiduciary capacity;

(6) Three (3) letters of recommendation as to the applicant's character, ability, and experience to act as an auctioneer; and

(7) A statement whether he or she has ever been denied coverage under a corporate surety bond.

**(f)** An auctioneer employed with court approval shall not act until he or she gives in each estate, at his or her own expense, a surety bond in favor of the United States of America, to be approved by and in

such sum as may be fixed by the court, conditioned upon:

(1) The faithful and prompt accounting for all monies and property which may come into his or her possession as auctioneer;

(2) Compliance with all rules, orders, and decrees of the court; and

(3) The faithful performance of his or her duties in all respects.

Said bond shall contain a provision that it may not be canceled or terminated without sixty (60) days notice being given to the clerk and the United States Trustee. In lieu of a bond in each case, an auctioneer may be permitted to file a blanket bond covering all cases in which he or she may act. Such blanket bond shall be in favor of the United States of America, shall be in the sum of one million dollars ($1,000,000.00), and shall be conditioned for each estate on the same terms as bonds in separate estates.

(g) The name of any auctioneer may be removed from the list of qualified auctioneers at any time by the court, in its sole discretion. Notice of such removal shall be sent forthwith to such auctioneer and to his or her bonding or surety company.

(h) In the event that the employment of a particular auctioneer, other than an auctioneer on the list of qualified auctioneers, is required, an application for such employment shall specify the reasons and necessity for such employment. Such auctioneer, before such employment, shall qualify by filing a bond in such amount as is set by the court, unless excused by the court.

(i) Compensation and Expenses:

(1) An auctioneer appointed by the court may be allowed, as compensation on the sale of personal property, a sum equivalent to 10% of the first $50,000.00; 8% of the next $25,000.00; 6% of the next $25,000.00; 4% of the next $50,000.00 and 2% of all amounts over $150,000.00. On real property, an auctioneer may be allowed up to 5% commission on the sale price of the property. Any allowance of compensation and reimbursement of expenses to an auctioneer shall be paid only upon proper application and subject to the approval of the court.

(2) An auctioneer shall be reimbursed for reasonable and necessary expenses directly related to the sale, including printing, advertising, insurance, and bond costs. Where the auctioneer has a blanket bond, the auctioneer may be reimbursed a proportionate amount of the costs, based upon the value of the assets sold by the auctioneer in the particular estate. When directed by the trustee to transport goods, the auctioneer shall be reimbursed for expenditures related thereto. No travel expenses shall be allowed except as ordered by the court. The auctioneer may be reimbursed for his or her expenses only if the application for reimbursement is supported by a sworn affidavit, setting forth the specific expenses incurred and the necessity for such. Vouchers, invoices, receipts, or other appropriate supporting documentation shall accompany the application. Where disbursements were made for advertising, copies of the actual advertisements shall be attached to the affidavit.

(j) A person shall not at any time, directly or indirectly, designate or refer to himself or herself as "Official United States Auctioneer," or as "Official Bankruptcy Auctioneer," or use any similar title or designation which states expressly or by implication that such person is an officer of the United States District Court or Bankruptcy Court, or that such person holds any permanent designation by the court as an auctioneer.

(k) Every auctioneer acting hereunder shall at all times keep proper records of all transactions and shall submit a report of each sale which shall include the following information:

(1) The time and place of sale;

(2) The gross amount of the sale and when property is sold in lots, the items in each lot and the amount received for each lot, with the name of the purchaser, as well as any bulk bid;

(3) An itemized statement of the expenditures, disbursements, and commissions allowable under this Rule, together with appropriate vouchers as described in paragraph (i)(2) above; and

(4) Whenever articles are sold free and clear of liens, with the liens to attach to the proceeds, the articles and liens shall be itemized separately.

(l) The trustee shall not delegate any of his or her fiduciary responsibilities to an auctioneer.

(m) The sanctions that may be imposed for violation of this Rule, include, but are not limited to, the disqualification of the person from future employment on behalf of bankruptcy estates.

Eff. May 15, 1997.

## LBR 7024–2. NOTICE OF CLAIM OF UNCONSTITUTIONALITY

To enable the Court to comply with the requirements of 28 U.S.C. 2403, if at any time prior to the trial of any adversary proceeding or contested matter to which neither the United States, an individual state, nor any agency, officer, or employee of either is a party, a party draws in question the constitutionality of an Act of Congress or a state statute affecting the public interest, such party shall give written notice to the court of the existence of such question and specifically identify the statute and the respects in which it is claimed to be unconstitutional. Copies of the notice shall be served upon all parties to the matter or proceeding, the United States Trustee, and the United States Attorney for the District of Connecticut and/or

the chief legal officer of the State whose statute is claimed to be unconstitutional.

Eff. May 15, 1997.

## LBR 7041–1. ACTIONS TO DETERMINE DISCHARGE AND DISCHARGEABILITY

**(a)** No adversary proceeding to deny a discharge shall be withdrawn, dismissed, or settled except upon an order of the court after notice to the trustee, all creditors, and other parties in interest and a hearing.

**(b)** In the event of a dismissal of an adversary proceeding to deny the discharge of a debtor, no discharge shall be granted unless the debtor shall file an affidavit and the debtor's attorney shall sign and file a statement that no consideration has been promised or given, directly or indirectly, for any such dismissal.

**(c)** No adversary proceeding to determine the dischargeability of a debt shall be settled except upon the order of the court after full disclosure of the terms of any agreement entered into between the parties relating to the payment of the debt in whole or in part.

Eff. May 15, 1997.

## LBR 8004–1. COPIES OF NOTICE OF APPEAL

Upon the filing of a notice of appeal, the appellant shall provide the clerk with sufficient copies of the notice of appeal to permit the clerk to comply with Fed.R.Bankr.P. 8004.

Eff. May 15, 1997.

## LBR 9001–1. DEFINITIONS

The definition provisions of 11 U.S.C. § 101 and Fed.R.Bankr.P. 9001 shall be applicable to these Local Rules.

Eff. May 15, 1997.

## LBR 9004–1. REQUIREMENTS OF FORM

In addition to the requirements of the applicable Local District Court Rule, all petitions, statements, schedules, pleadings, reports, and other papers shall be written, typewritten, printed, or reproduced on durable white paper of good quality on one side of a page only; shall be without erasures or interlineations materially defacing them; and, except for trial or hearing exhibits, shall be punched with two (2) holes two and three-quarters (2¾) inches apart, each centered seven-sixteenths (⁷⁄₁₆) of an inch from the upper edge, one being two and seven-eighths (2⅞) inches from the left-hand edge and the other being the same distance from the right-hand edge, and each one-quarter (¼) of an inch in diameter.

Eff. May 15, 1997.

## LBR 9010–1. APPEARANCES

**(a)** The signature of an attorney for a petitioner on a bankruptcy petition or the signature of an attorney on a complaint or a motion in a bankruptcy case constitutes a notice of appearance pursuant to Fed. R.Bankr.P. 9010(b), and constitutes a certification that the attorney is authorized to practice in the United States Bankruptcy Court for the District of Connecticut.

**(b)** An attorney entering a case under the Bankruptcy Code, or any matter commenced by a complaint or motion, shall first file an appearance with the court and serve the same upon the debtor or the debtor-in-possession, any trustee, any committee or its counsel, the United States Trustee, and, if an adversary proceeding, any party to such proceeding.

Eff. May 15, 1997.

## LBR 9013–1. FORMS OF PLEADINGS APPLYING TO CERTAIN CONTESTED MATTERS

Motions seeking relief under the following listed sections of the Bankruptcy Code shall comply with the requirements of Fed.R.Bankr.P. 7010:

| | |
|---|---|
| Section 362(d) | – Relief from stay; |
| Section 363(c) | – Use of cash collateral; |
| Section 363(f) | – Sale free and clear of interests in property; |
| Section 364(d) | – Obtain or incur debt secured by a senior or equal lien; |
| Section 365(a), (f) | – Assumption or rejection of executory contracts and unexpired leases; |
| Section 506 | – Determination of secured status; and |
| Section 522(f) | – Avoidance of fixing of liens. |

Eff. May 15, 1997.

## LBR 9015–1. JURY TRIALS

**(a)** Fed.R.Civ.P. 38, 39, 47–51, and 81(c) (insofar as it applies to jury trials) apply in cases and proceedings, except that a demand made under Fed.R.Civ.P. 38(b) shall be filed in accordance with Fed.R.Bankr.P. 5005.

**(b)** If the right to a jury trial applies, a timely demand has been filed under Fed.R.Civ.P. 38(b), and the bankruptcy judge has been specially designated to conduct the jury trial, the parties may consent to have a jury trial conducted by a bankruptcy judge under 28 U.S.C. § 157(e) by jointly or separately filing a statement of consent no later than thirty (30) days following the jury trial demand.

Eff. May 15, 1997.

## LBR 9019–2.  ALTERNATIVE DISPUTE RESOLUTION (ADR)

**(a)** An adversary proceeding or a contested matter may be referred for voluntary ADR at any stage of the bankruptcy litigation deemed appropriate by the parties and the judge to whom the adversary proceeding or a contested matter has been assigned.

**(b)** Before an adversary proceeding or a contested matter is referred to voluntary ADR, the parties must agree upon, subject to the approval of the judge:

(1) The form of the ADR process (e.g., mediation, arbitration, summary trial, minitrial, etc.);

(2) The scope of the ADR process (e.g., settlement of all or specified issues, resolution of discovery schedules or disputes, narrowing of issues, etc.);

(3) The ADR provider;  and

(4) The effect of the ADR process (e.g., binding or non-binding).

**(c)** When an agreement between the parties and the judge for a voluntary ADR referral has been reached, the parties shall file jointly for the judge's endorsement a "Stipulation for Reference to ADR." The Stipulation, subject to the judge's approval, shall specify:

(1) The form of the ADR procedure and the name of the ADR provider agreed upon;

(2) The judicial proceedings, if any, to be stayed pending ADR;

(3) The procedures, if any, to be completed prior to ADR (e.g., appraisal, expert opinions, etc.);

(4) The effect of the ADR process;

(5) The date or dates for the filing of progress reports by the ADR provider with the trial judge or for completion of the ADR process;  and

(6) The special conditions, if any, imposed by the judge upon any aspect of the ADR process.

**(d)** All ADR sessions shall be deemed confidential and protected by the provisions of Fed.R.Evid. 408 and Fed.R.Civ.P. 68.  No statement made or document produced as part of an ADR proceeding, not otherwise discoverable or obtainable, shall be admissible as evidence or subject to discovery.

**(e)** At the conclusion of the voluntary ADR session(s), the ADR provider's report to the judge shall merely indicate "matter settled or not settled," unless the parties agree to a more detailed report (e.g., stipulation of facts, narrowing of issues and discovery procedures, etc.).  If a matter settles, the parties shall agree upon the appropriate moving papers to be filed for the judge's endorsement.  If a matter does not settle but the parties agree to a narrowing of discovery or legal issues, then the ADR provider's report shall set forth those matters for endorsement or amendment by the judge.

Eff. May 15, 1997.

## LBR 9029–2.  ADMINISTRATIVE ORDERS

The clerk shall maintain an administrative order book, containing all currently effective administrative orders of the court that are applicable throughout the district, dated and numbered chronologically.  Copies of such administrative orders shall be available upon request at the office of the clerk.

Eff. May 15, 1997.

# ELECTRONIC CASE FILING

## STANDING ORDER NO. 7. IN RE: ELECTRONIC CASE FILING AND CASE MANAGEMENT PROCEDURES

Federal Rule of Civil Procedure (FRCP) 83 and Federal Rules of Bankruptcy Procedure (FRBP) 5005(a)(2), 9011, and 9029, authorize this Court to establish practices and procedures for the filing, signing, maintaining, and verification of pleadings and papers by electronic means; and The Administrative Procedures for Electronic Case Filing (appended hereto and hereafter referred to as Administrative Procedures) have been reviewed by the Court; and here consistent with all applicable rules, statutes, and judicial conference policy; and

IT IS HEREBY ORDERED that:

**1. Electronic Filing is Authorized.** The Court will accept the electronic filing of documents effective August 1, 2005, by way of the Court's Electronic Case Filing System (ECF System). Electronic filing will become mandatory for all attorneys on that date, consistent with the Administrative Procedures. The Court may, from time to time, and only in exceptional circumstances, relieve attorneys from the electronic filing requirement.

**2. Official Record.** Except as otherwise ordered, the official record of the Court for all documents filed on or after August 1, 2005, is the electronic record maintained by the Clerk. All documents submitted in a hard copy format by any person on or after August 1, 2005, including those from *pro se* persons, will be imaged (or otherwise converted) into an electronic form. Once imaged, all such documents will be destroyed in accordance with the procedure authorized by the Court and the clerk will not maintain hard copies of any documents filed in connection with any case or proceeding with the exception of hard copy

filings submitted by *pro se* filers, documents ordered sealed by the Court, or documents required by statute or rule to be maintained in hard copy. Documents filed before August 1, 2005, that have been imaged or otherwise converted to an electronic format will be retained by the clerk's office in accordance with current archiving requirements, unless otherwise ordered by the Court, but the official record will be the electronic file.

**3. Administrative Procedures.** The Administrative Procedures attached hereto constitute the requirements for electronic filing of documents in and by this Court. The procedures may from time to time be amended with the oversight of the Court, and will be available from the Clerk. If provisions of the *Administrative Procedures for Electronic Case Filing* are inconsistent with Local Bankruptcy Rules for the District of Connecticut, the *Administrative Procedures* will control for electronically-filed documents.

**4. Signature.** The electronic filing of any document by an attorney/participant shall constitute the signature of that attorney/participant under the Bankruptcy Rules, Local Rules, and Rules of Civil Procedure. Attorneys/participants filing documents in electronic format that require the signature of any non-attorney/participant shall retain in their office the documents containing the original signature of that person for five years following the conclusion of the case, in accordance with the *Administrative Procedures*.

**5. Notice and Service.** Participation in the Electronic Case Filing System by receipt of a password and login from the Court shall constitute a request for and acceptance of service and notice electronically pursuant to FRBP 9036.

Dated effective August 1, 2005.

## ADMINISTRATIVE PROCEDURES FOR ELECTRONIC CASE FILING

### 1. Scope of Electronic Filing.

(a) *Short Title.* The Administrative Procedures for Electronic Case Filing may be abbreviated and referred to as the "Administrative Procedures" or if addressed individually, as "ECF Procedure #___" and are available in their current version on the Court's website: www.ctb.uscourts.gov

(b) *Definitions.* "Electronic Case Filing" (ECF) refers to documents filed in electronic format. "Conventional Filing" refers to documents filed in paper format. "Filer" refers to any entity with an approved login and password, registered for full use of the ECF system in compliance with these Administrative Procedures. "User" refers to any entity with an approved login and password, registered for limited use of the ECF system in compliance with ECF Procedure #2(b).

(c) *Electronic Case Filing Effective Dates.* Beginning August 1, 2005, the Court will only accept documents filed in electronic format in compliance with these Administrative Procedures, unless authorized by order of the court, and as excepted

in paragraph (d) below. Failure to file electronically, except as authorized in subsections (d) and (e) below, will result in the issuance of a Court's Motion to Dismiss or Strike, and may result in the eventual dismissal or striking of the non-compliant document. Persistent non-compliance with these procedures may result in referral for disciplinary action.

(d) *Conventional Filing Authorized.* The following documents shall be filed conventionally:

(1) documents under seal in compliance with ECF Procedure #8;

(2) documents filed pro se;

(3) court hearing transcripts;

(4) proofs of claim filed by entities who are neither Filers nor Users, or for which a creditor must be entered by the court;

(5) motions to proceed pro hac vice;

(6) other limited documents or filings, as ordered by the Court.

(e) *Exemption from Electronic Filing.* Exemption from electronic filing is available only in exceptional circumstances, and attorneys seeking an exemption must follow the instructions appended hereto in seeking such relief.

## 2. Registration and Training.

(a) *Required Registration Procedure for Filers.*

1. Eligibility for Registration as a Filer. The following persons or entities are eligible to register as Filers in the Court's ECF system: (a) attorneys admitted to practice in the United States Bankruptcy Court for the District of Connecticut, including those admitted pro hac vice; (b) case trustees; (c) Assistant United States Trustees; (d) Assistant United States Attorneys; and (e) other entities the Court determines appropriate. In order to register as a Filer, an entity must complete a registration form (ECF Form 1–Filer Registration or ECF Form 1a–Pro Hac Vice Filer Registration). Registration will be made in a form prescribed by the clerk and requires the Filing User's name, bar number, address, telephone number, Internet e-mail address and, in the case of an attorney, a declaration that the attorney is authorized to practice in this Court. Members of a Filer's staff are encouraged to participate in either on-site or on-line ECF training tutorial, but will not receive a separate login and password.

2. Training for Filers. Filers will be required to complete training as required by the clerk. Applicants my choose either training on-site or through the court's on-line ECF Training Tutorial for Filers. All applicants will be required to successfully complete the Court's On-line Test for Filers in order to be assigned a filer login and password. Onsite training may be scheduled through the court's website, or the clerk's office. On-line training may be accessed at any time. Applicants with a current and valid ECF registration and login issued by another U.S. Bankruptcy Court may, in the discretion of the clerk, be issued a login and password without completing ECF training, upon successful completion of the on-line test. If the on-line test is not satisfactorily completed, the clerk, in her discretion, may require the applicant to attend on-site training. The on-line test, and proof of current registration and valid login from the other bankruptcy court must be submitted with the Registration Form.

3. Submission of Registration Forms. The original signed Registration Form (1 and 1a on pages 16 and 18) must be submitted to the Clerk of Court, 450 Main St., Hartford, CT 06103, ATTN: ECF Registration Desk. A paper copy of the on-line test must be submitted with the registration form. Attorneys who are acting trustees must register and will receive different logins for use as either an attorney and or a trustee.

4. Address changes. Registered Filers shall immediately notify the Court of any changes in the Filer's e-mail address.

(b) *Required Registration Procedure for Users.*

1. Eligibility to Register as User. Except as provided in ECF Procedure 1(d)("Conventional Filing Authorized"), the following persons or entities are eligible to register as Users in the Court's ECF system: Any entity, including entities who file proofs of claim and/or requests for notice but are not appearing as parties in the case. In order to register as a User, an entity must complete a registration form (ECF Form 2). Users shall consult the court's "CM/ECF Users Manual" (available on the court's Internet site) for instructional material on how to file proofs of claim, requests for notice, etc.

2. Training for Users. Users will be required to complete the court's on-line ECF training tutorial for Users and successfully complete on-line test for Users in order to be assigned a User login and password. The original signed User registration form (ECF Form 2, on page 20) and a complete copy of the on-line test, must be submitted to the Clerk of Court, 450 Main St., Hartford, CT 06103, ATTN: ECF Registration Desk. Registered Users shall immediately notify the Court of any changes in the User's e-mail address.

(c) *Suspension or Revocation of Use.* The Court may, for cause, enter an order suspending or revoking a Filer's or User's access to the ECF system. Further, the clerk, upon information received, which indicates potential risk or harm to the ECF system may, without prior notice, temporarily suspend participation in ECF system by any Filer or User, and shall provide prompt notification of such action to the Filer or User. In the event of suspension or revocation the Filer or User will be required to correct any condition that led to the suspension or revocation, and may be required to attend training classes in order to have access to the system restored.

### 3. Logins, Passwords and Security.

(a) *Login and Password.* Once the registration and training are complete for the Filer or User, the Court will send an e-mail message notifying the Filer or User of the login and password assigned. The e-mail message ensures that the Filer or User has a properly functioning e-mail address which will be used by the Court's ECF system.

(b) *Password Security.* Every Filer or User is required to protect the security of the assigned password. If there is any reason to believe the security of the assigned password may have been compromised, the Filer or User must immediately notify the Court's Information Technology Department by e-mail to CTB_ECF_Help@ctb.uscourts.gov A Filer or User may be subject to civil liability, court sanctions or other consequences for failure to take required action in connection with the security of the assigned password. Members of a Filer's or User's staff are encouraged to participate in either on-site or on-line ECF training, but will not receive a separate login and password; Filers or Users are responsible for the entries made by any person using that Filer's or User's password and login.

### 4. Electronic Notice and Service.

(a) *Request, Waiver and Consent.* Registration as a Filer constitutes waiver of the right to personal service or first class mail service. Registration as a Filer also constitutes a written request for, and consent to, electronic service via receipt of a "Notice of Electronic Filing" from ECF of all filed documents, including Orders and Judgments, to which the Filer is entitled. The "Notice of Electronic Filing" that is automatically generated by the court's Electronic Filing System constitutes service or notice of the filed document on Filers. Parties who are not Filers must be provided notice or service of any pleading or other document electronically filed in accordance with the Federal Rules of Civil Procedure, Federal Rules of Bankruptcy Procedure and the Local Rules.

(b) *Certificates of Service.* Except with regard to the method of service authorized by these Procedures, the provisions of the Federal Rules of Bankruptcy Procedure continue to govern the content of a certificate of service. A certificate of service must be included with all documents filed electronically, indicating that service was accomplished through the Notice of Electronic Filing for parties or counsel who are

registered Filers[1] or how service was made if the party or counsel being served is not a registered Filer.

1. A Registered Filers List is available on the Court's website listing the names of parties and attorneys who will receive notice through the Notice of Electronic Filing.

(c) *Personal Service Requirements Not Abrogated.* Nothing contained in this procedure relieves counsel of the burden of providing personal service under Fed. R. Bankr. P. 7004, 9014 or Fed. R. Civ. P. 4.

(d) *Rule 9006(f).* When there is a right or requirement to do some act or undertake some proceeding within a prescribed period after service, the additional three days created by Fed.R.Bankr.P. 9006(f) shall apply.

## 5. Consequences of Electronic Filing.

(a) *Filing and Entry on the Docket.* Once an electronic transmission of a document is made in accordance with these administrative procedures, and has been received by the Court, the document shall be considered filed for all purposes as required by the Federal Rules of Bankruptcy Procedure and the Local Rules of this Court and will be entered on the court docket kept by the clerk pursuant to Rule 5003.

(b) *Official Record.* When a document has been filed through ECF, the official record is the electronic recording of the document as stored by the Court, and the filing party is bound by the document as filed. A document filed through ECF is deemed filed at the date and time stated on the Notice of Electronic Filing from the Court. Documents filed pursuant to these procedures as a conventional paper filing will be scanned or otherwise converted to electronic format and stored in the ECF system and the electronic version will become the official record.

(c) *Filing Date and Time.* Filing a document electronically does not alter the filing deadline for that document. Unless otherwise ordered, filing must be completed before midnight local time where the Court is located in order to be considered timely filed that day. Conventional paper filings will be deemed filed as of the date and time they are file stamped by the clerk.

(d) *Appropriate Title of ECF Documents.* A Filer or User electronically filing a pleading or other document shall be responsible for designating the appropriate title for that pleading or other document by selecting among the categories provided through the ECF system.

(e) *Corrections.* In the event that a docket entry must be corrected, the clerk's office will notify the Filer or User of the error and whether the error will be corrected by the clerk's office or the filing party.

(f) *Payments of Required Fees.*

(1) Fees to be paid using Internet Credit Card Procedure. All required fees, with the exception of those listed in section (2) below, must be promptly paid via the internet credit card process. In the event that internet credit card processing is not available at the time of filing, payment must be made within 48 hours by going to the CM/ECF Utilities Menu—"Internet Payments Due".

(2) Fees to be paid by mail or at the clerk's office. The following fees must be paid by mail, or over the counter at the clerk's office:

    a. Installment payments after the case has been filed

    b. Subpoena Fee

    c. Sanctions

    d. Treasury (small dividends)

    e. Treasury (registry funds)

    f. Any replacement check for a filing fee

    g. Inter-district Index fee

    h. Pro hac vice fee (payable to District Court)

### 6. Court Orders.

(a) *Entry of Orders.* The clerk shall enter all orders and judgments in ECF, which shall constitute entry on the docket kept by the clerk under Rules 5003 and 9021. The electronic signature of the Court or the entry of the order on the docket shall have the same force and effect as if manually signed and docketed as a conventional filing.

(b) *Submission of Proposed Orders.* Unless otherwise ordered by the Court, all proposed orders shall be submitted in WordPerfect or Word compatible format, via e-mail as set out in the Administrative Procedure Number 14 herein. The submission requirements may change from time to time, and Filers should consult these procedures, and the court's CM/ECF website for any amendments.

(c) *Notice to Filers of Orders.* Immediately upon the entry of an order or judgment in a case, including an adversary proceeding, the clerk shall electronically transmit to all Filers who represent the contesting parties and to such other Filers and Users as the Court shall direct, a Notice of Electronic Filing. Electronic transmission of the Notice of Electronic Filing constitutes the notice required by Rule 9022 and service shall be deemed complete upon transmission.

(d) *Notice to Others of Orders.* Immediately upon the entry of an order or judgment in a case, including an adversary proceeding, the clerk or such others as the court shall direct, shall give notice to contesting parties who are neither Filers nor Users, and to such other entities as the Court shall direct, in accordance with the Federal Rules of Bankruptcy Procedure.

### 7. Filing Format Requirements.

(a) *Definitions.* "Electronically Generated Text" is electronic text generated by converting or printing to Portable Document Format (PDF) from the original word processing file, so that the text of the document may be electronically searched and copied. "Scanned Material" is an electronic image of text or other material in PDF format produced by a scanning or imaging process.

(b) *PDF Requirements.* All documents transmitted via the ECF system shall be in Electronically Generated text, in PDF format, so that the text of the document may be searched and copied, except as provided in subsection (c) below.

(c) *Attachments, Exhibits and Other Documents.* All attachments, exhibits and other documents not available as Electronically Generated Text (i.e., those that must be scanned) shall be transmitted to the ECF system, as Scanned Material in PDF format.

(d) *Size Limitations Per Transmission.* Each transmission to the ECF system shall not exceed two (2) megabytes total file size. Files which exceed two (2) megabytes shall be broken into smaller files and transmitted to the ECF system as attachments to the main document.

### 8. Filing of Documents Under Seal.

(a) *Definition.* A document may be filed under seal only upon a court order or pursuant to statute or rule.

(b) *Filing Requirements.* Unless otherwise ordered by the Court, a motion to file a document under seal shall be filed electronically. The motion shall not contain confidential or privileged information. The order authorizing the filing of a document under seal shall be filed electronically unless otherwise ordered by the court. A document ordered to be filed under seal shall be filed with the clerk in paper format and accompanied by the order authorizing the filing of a sealed document.

(c) *Protection of Privacy Interests.* Any entity may file a motion seeking an order limiting electronic access to or prohibiting the electronic filing of certain specifically identified materials on the grounds that such material is subject to protected privacy interests and that electronic access or electronic filing of those materials is likely to prejudice those privacy interests. If the Court determines that access should be limited or that electronic filing would unduly prejudice those privacy interests, then the materials shall be filed as ordered by the Court. Unless otherwise directed, the Court order determining access to or prohibiting the electronic filing shall be filed electronically.

### 9. Retention Requirements.

(a) *Retention of Original Signatures.* Petitions, lists, schedules, statements, amendments, pleadings, affidavits, and other documents that must contain original signatures or that require verification under Rule 1008 or an unsworn declaration as provided in 28 U.S.C. § 1746 shall be filed electronically by Filers and Users. The documents containing the original signature must be retained by the Filer or User who files such a pleading, document, or other matter for five (5) years after the closing of the case or proceeding. This retention does not affect or replace any other retention period required by other applicable laws or rules. Paper documents containing original signatures or verification received by the court from pro se filers, or as otherwise ordered by the court, will be retained and/or disposed of by the court pursuant to procedures as established by the director of the Administrative Office of the United States Courts.

(b) *Production of Documents.* On the request of the court or other authorized entities the Filer or User must provide original documents for review.

(c) *Sanctions.* Failure to maintain such documents for the specified period shall subject the Filer or User to sanctions.

### 10. Signatures.

(a) *Electronic Filing Constitutes Signature.* The transmission by a Filer or User to the ECF system of any document constitutes any required signature of that Filer or User on such document. The Filer need not manually sign a transmitted document. The transmission is the equivalent of a signed paper for all purposes, including, without limitation, the Federal Rules of Bankruptcy Procedure, including Rule 9011, the Bankruptcy Code, and the Local Bankruptcy Rules of this Court.

(b) *Electronic Filing Constitutes Certification.* The transmission by a Filer or User of any document constitutes certification by the Filer or User that all persons indicated on such document have signed the document and have executed an original prior to electronic filing with the Court.

(c) *Form of Electronic Signatures.*

(1) Required Information for Filers and Users. A document transmitted via ECF shall include a signature block setting forth the Filer's or User's name, complete address, telephone number, fax number, e-mail address, and the Filer's federal court bar registration number and firm affiliation, if applicable, preceded by a signature line on which is typed "/s/ Name" where the Filer's or User's signature would otherwise appear in a signed document.

(2) Required Information for Other Entities. A document transmitted via ECF requiring or containing signatures of entities who are not Filers or Users shall either (a) show an image of such signature as it appears in the original signed document, or (b) bear the name of the signatory preceded by "/s/ Name" typed in the space where the signature would otherwise appear in a signed document, accompanied by the signature block information recited in subsection (c)(1) above. When an original signature is required, or has been executed, it must be maintained in accordance with Procedure 9(a) above.

(3) Multiple Attorney/Party Signatures. A document requiring or containing signatures of more than one entity or counsel shall contain the signature information recited in subsections (c)(1) and/or (c)(2) above.

**11. Technical Failure.** A Filer or User whose ECF filing is made untimely as a result of technical failure may through motion seek appropriate redress from the Court. Filers and Users are responsible for consulting the court's website to determine any scheduled system unavailability due to maintenance. Technical difficulties should be reported to the clerk's ECF Help desk immediately. Conventional filings may be authorized by the clerk's office in the event of recurrent or persistent ECF system failure or other technical failure, if time is of the essence.

**12. Public Access.**

(a) *Public Access at the Court.* The public may view all documents in the ECF System at no charge at the clerk's offices in Hartford, New Haven and Bridgeport during regular business hours.

(b) *Internet Access.* Internet access to the ECF system is limited to Public Access to Court Electronic Records ("PACER") system subscribers. Filers and Users may take advantage of the "one free look"[2] provided with the Notice of Electronic Filing to download documents referenced in each Notice of Electronic Filing. In accordance with the Bankruptcy Court Fee Schedule established pursuant to 28 U.S.C. § 1930, User fees are charged for accessing certain detailed case information. Information regarding subscribing to PACER is available on the Court's web site at www.ctb. uscourts.gov and at the clerk's offices.

2. The one free look is available for fifteen (15) days from the date the document was entered on the docket.

(c) *Copies and Certified Copies.* Copies and certified copies of electronically filed documents may be purchased at the office of the clerk. The fee for copying and certification will be in accordance with 28 U.S.C. § 1930 and Judicial Conference Policy.

**13. Privacy.** In compliance with the policy of the Judicial Conference of the United States, and the E–Government Act of 2002, and in order to promote electronic access to case files while also protecting personal privacy and other legitimate interests, parties shall refrain from including, or shall partially redact where inclusion is necessary, the following personal data identifiers from all documents and pleadings filed with the Court, including exhibits thereto, whether filed electronically or conventionally, unless otherwise ordered by the Court or required by statute, the Federal Rules of Bankruptcy Procedure, or the Official Bankruptcy Forms:

(a) *Social Security Numbers.* If an individual's social security number must be included in a pleading, only the last four digits of that number should be used, with the exception of the Statement of Social Security Number Form B–21;

(b) *Names of Minor Children.* If the involvement of a minor child must be mentioned, only the initials of that child should be used. On Schedule I of Official Bankruptcy Form 6, list the relationship and age of the debtor's dependents (e.g., Son, Age 6);

(c) *Dates of Birth.* If an individual's date of birth must be included in a pleading, only the year should be used. On Schedule I of Official Bankruptcy Form 6, list the age of each of the debtor's dependents;

(d) *Financial Account Numbers.* If financial account numbers are relevant, only the last four digits of these numbers should be used. On Schedules D, E, and F of Official Bankruptcy Form 6, debtors, if they so choose, may include their full account numbers to assist the trustee and creditors.

NOTE: *In compliance with the E–Government Act of 2002, a party wishing to file a document containing the personal data identifiers listed above may file an un-redacted document under seal. This document shall be retained by the Court as part of the record. The Court may, however, still require the party to file a redacted copy for the public file. The responsibility for redacting personal identifiers rests solely with counsel and the parties. The Clerk will not review documents for compliance with this procedure.*

**14. Instructions for Submission of Proposed Orders.** All proposed orders must be submitted for the judge's signature via e-mail to the court consistent with the instructions below. Proposed Orders should also be submitted as a PDF attachment to motions or applications to which they relate. The proposed orders so attached will not be processed by the court as having been submitted for judicial signature, but are intended only for viewing and review by those parties served with the underlying motion/application. All proposed orders submitted for the judge's signature via e-mail must be in Word or WordPerfect compatible format, not as a PDF file. All proposed orders must have complete captions, including the name of the debtor(s), case number, the number of the document to which it refers, full title preceded by the words Proposed Order, certificate of service, etc., and must comply with any other requirement specified in the categories below. Any discrepancy between the

proposed order attached to the motion and the order submitted for signature via e-mail, should be clearly noted and explained in a Request for Entry of Order. In addition, proposed orders should not contain a signature line, the name of the judge, or a date line. The e-mail should be in the following format:

(a) *Proposed Orders for Matters That Will Have a Hearing, (not prosecuted pursuant to the Contested Matters/Bar Date Procedure).* Proposed orders on matters that require a hearing must be submitted after receipt of the notice of hearing but, at least three days prior to the scheduled hearing date. The e-mail should be submitted in the following format:

(1) The **subject line** must contain the debtor's name, case number and hearing date. For example: *03–30001 Daniel—hearing date March 15, 2005*

(2) **Attach** the proposed order which *must be in Word or WordPerfect format*, and not as a PDF file. In the body of the e-mail you must reference the document number of the pleading that the attached order relates to.

(3) Submit the proposed order to the following E-mail address:

Judge Dabrowski— ctbecf_ asd hearing@ ctb. uscourts. gov
Judge Krechevsky— ctbecf _ rlk hearing@ ctb. uscourts. gov
Judge Shiff— ctbecf _ ahw shearing @ctb. uscourts. gov
Judge Weil— ctbecf _ lmw hearing@ ctb. uscourts. gov

(b) *Proposed Orders on Motions or Applications That Have Followed the Contested Matters/Bar Date Procedure.*[3] Proposed orders submitted for matters following the contested matters/bar date procedure, must be included as an attachment to the motion to which they relate, and served on all necessary parties. The attachment should be clearly marked as a Proposed Order. The identical order should be submitted consistent with the instructions in this section by e-mail submission after the objection bar date has passed and must be submitted contemporaneously[4] with electronic filing of the Request for Entry of Order. Please note: Any discrepancy between the proposed order attached to the motion and the order submitted for signature subsequent to the bar date should be clearly noted and explained in the Request for Entry of Order. The e-mail should be in the following format:

3.  Please note that at present Judge Krechevsky does not utilize this procedure.

4.  Contemporaneously in this Procedure means as soon as possible after the completion of the electronic filing, and recognizes the different modes of transmission.

(a) The subject line must contain the debtor's name, case number and must indicate that the Request for Entry of Order has been filed. For example: 03–30001 Daniel—request filed.

(b) Attach the proposed order which must be in Word or WordPerfect format, and not as a PDF file. In the body of the e-mail provide the document number of the pleading that the proposed order relates to.

(c) Submit the proposed order to the following **E-mail address:**

Judge Dabrowski— ctbecf _ asd short calendar@ ctb. uscourts. gov
Judge Shiff— ctbecf_ ahws short calendar @ctb. uscourts. gov
Judge Weil— ctbecf_l mw short calendar @ctb. uscourts. gov

(c) *Proposed Orders That Were Returned for Modification after a Hearing or Were Never Submitted Prior to a Hearing.* Proposed orders to which modification is required after a hearing or which are proffered for the first time after the hearing shall be submitted in the following format:

(a) The **subject line** must contain the debtor's name, the case number and must indicate the day the hearing was held. For example: *03–30001 Daniel—hearing held 12/1/04*

(b) **Attach** the proposed order which *must be in Word or WordPerfect format*, and not as a PDF file. In the body of the e-mail provide the document number of the pleading that the proposed order relates to.

(c) Submit the proposed order to the following **E-mail address**:

Judge Dabrowski— ctbecf_ asdtobe submitted@ ctb.uscourts.gov
Judge Krechevsky— ctbecf_ rlktobe submitted@ ctb.uscourts.gov
Judge Shiff— ctbecf_ ahws tobesubmitted@ ctb.uscourts.gov
Judge Weil— ctbecf_ lmwtobe submitted@ ctb.uscourts.gov

(d) *Proposed Orders for Ex Parte Matters.* Proposed orders pertaining to ex parte matters shall be submitted contemporaneously with the electronic filing of the ex parte matter and must be in the following format.

(a) The **subject line** must contain the debtor's name, case number and the words "ex parte".

(b) **Attach** the proposed order which must be in Word or WordPerfect format, and not as a PDF file. In the body of the e-mail provide name of the ex-parte document the proposed order relates to.

(c) Submit the proposed order to the following **E-mail address**:

Judge Dabrowski— ctbecf_ asd exparte@ ctb.uscourts.gov
Judge Krechevsky— ctbecf_ rlk exparte@ ctb.uscourts.gov
Judge Shiff— ctbecf_ ahws exparte@ ctb.uscourts.gov
Judge Weil— ctbecf_ lmw exparte@ ctb.uscourts.gov

(e) *Proposed Orders for Expedited Matters.* Proposed orders pertaining to matters in which expedited action has been requested and proposed orders relating to the motion requesting expedited treatment shall be submitted contemporaneously with the electronic filing of the expedited matter and/or motion for expedited treatment and must be in the following format.

(a) The **subject line** must contain the debtor's name, case number and the word "expedited".

(b) **Attach** the proposed order to which *must be in Word or WordPerfect format*, and not as a PDF file. In the body of the e-mail provide reference to the name of document the proposed order relates to.

(c) Submit the proposed order to the following **E-mail address**:

Judge Dabrowski— ctbecf_ asd expedited@ ctb.uscourts.gov
Judge Krechevsky— ctbecf_ rlk expedited@ ctb.uscourts.gov
Judge Shiff— ctbecf_ ahws expedited@ ctb.uscourts.gov
Judge Weil— ctbecf_ lmw expedited@ ctb.uscourts.gov

Effective August 1, 2005.

---

## ECF FORM NO. 1.   FILER REGISTRATION

Filer Registration, Application for Password, Waiver of Notice And Service by Mail and Consent to Electronic Notice For Electronic Case Filing System

Please complete the following form and the on-line test found on the Training section of the court's website. Return them, by mail, to the Office of the Bankruptcy Court Clerk, 450 Main Street, Hartford, CT 06103, Attn: ECF Registration. We will contact you regarding your registration and password after review of the information herein.

NAME _____

ADDRESS _____

FIRM NAME _____

BAR I.D. _____

E–MAIL ADDRESS _____

PHONE NUMBER(s)

  Office _____

  Cell _____

  Fax _____

Are you an EDI participant? yes \_\_\_ no \_\_\_

E-mail Notice to be sent: After each Filing \_\_\_ End of Day Summary \_\_\_

I declare, under penalty of perjury, the following is true:

1. I am admitted to practice in the United States Bankruptcy Court for the District of Connecticut and that the information set forth above is true and correct;

2. I agree that use of the password to be obtained pursuant to this registration (my password) to file a document in the record of a bankruptcy case or proceeding will constitute my signature upon and my signing of any petitions, schedules, statements, matrices, declarations, verifications, motions, briefs, pleadings or other papers or documents filed by use of my password, for all purposes authorized and required by law, including, without limitation, the United States Code, Federal Rules of Civil Procedure, Federal Rules of Bankruptcy Procedure, Federal Rules of Criminal Procedure, and any applicable local rules and non-bankruptcy law;

3. I agree that it is my responsibility to maintain in my records all documents bearing original signatures filed using my password for a period of five (5) years after the case or proceeding in which the documents have been filed has been closed.

4. I agree that it is my responsibility to protect and secure the confidentiality of my password, and that if I allow my password to be used by anyone other than myself that I do so at my own risk. If I believe that my password has been compromised, it is my responsibility to immediately notify the Court in accordance with ECF Procedure 2.

5. I agree that it is my responsibility to notify the Court, immediately, of any change in my address, telephone number, fax number, or e-mail address.

6. I agree that by registering as a Filer, I waive the right to personal service or first class mail service, and I request and consent to electronic service via receipt of a "Notice of Electronic Filing" from ECF of all filed documents to which I am entitled, except with regard to a summons and complaint under Rule 7004 or an initial motion under Rule 9014.

7. I agree to adhere to the United States Bankruptcy Court for the District of Connecticut Administrative Procedures for Electronic Case Filing. I understand that it is my responsibility to learn and use any and all updates to the Court's Administrative Procedures for Electronic Case Filing, and acknowledge that I have reviewed those Procedures prior to issuance of my password.

_____

ATTORNEY SIGNATURE

_____

DATE

*For Court Use Only:*

 *Approved By:* _____

 *Password:* _____ *Date:* _____

_____

## ECF FORM NO. 1a. PRO HAC VICE FILER REGISTRATION

Filer Registration, Application for Password, Waiver of Notice And Service by Mail and Consent to Electronic Notice For Electronic Case Filing System

Please complete the following form and the on-line test found on the Training section of the court's website. Return them, by mail, to the Office of the Bankruptcy Court Clerk, 450 Main Street, Hartford, CT 06103, Attn: ECF Registration. We will

contact you regarding your registration and password after review of the information herein.

NAME _____

ADDRESS _____

FIRM NAME _____

BAR I.D. _____

E–MAIL ADDRESS _____

PHONE NUMBER(s)
    Office _____
    Cell _____
    Fax _____

Are you an EDI participant? yes ___ no ___

E-mail Notice to be sent: After each Filing ___ End of Day Summary ___

I declare, under penalty of perjury, the following is true:

1.  I am seeking or have been granted permission to appear pro hac vice in the United States Bankruptcy Court for the District of Connecticut and that the information set forth above is true and correct.

2.  I agree that use of the password to be obtained pursuant to this registration (my password) to file a document in the record of a bankruptcy case or proceeding will constitute my signature upon and my signing of any petitions, schedules, statements, matrices, declarations, verifications, motions, briefs, pleadings or other papers or documents filed by use of my password, for all purposes authorized and required by law, including, without limitation, the United States Code, Federal Rules of Civil Procedure, Federal Rules of Bankruptcy Procedure, Federal Rules of Criminal Procedure, and any applicable local rules and non-bankruptcy law.

3.  I agree that it is my responsibility to maintain in my records all documents bearing original signatures filed using my password for a period of five (5) years after the case or proceeding in which the documents have been filed has been closed.

4.  I agree that it is my responsibility to protect and secure the confidentiality of my password, and that if I allow my password to be used by anyone other than myself that I do so at my own risk. If I believe that my password has been compromised, it is my responsibility to immediately notify the Court in accordance with ECF Procedure 2.

5.  I agree that it is my responsibility to notify the Court, immediately, of any change in my address, telephone number, fax number, or e-mail address.

6.  I agree that by registering as a Filer, I waive the right to personal service or first class mail service, and I request and consent to electronic service via receipt of a "Notice of Electronic Filing" from ECF of all filed documents to which I am entitled, except with regard to a summons and complaint under Rule 7004 or an initial motion under Rule 9014.

7.  I agree to adhere to the United States Bankruptcy Court for the District of Connecticut Administrative Procedures for Electronic Case Filing. I understand that it is my responsibility to learn and use any and all updates to the Court's Administrative Procedures for Electronic Case Filing, and acknowledge that I have reviewed those Procedures prior to issuance of my password.

_____

ATTORNEY SIGNATURE

_____

DATE

*For Court Use Only:*

*Approved By:* _____

*Password:* _____ *Date:* _____

ECF FORM NO. 2.   USER REGISTRATION

User Registration and Application for Limited Password for Electric Case Filing System

Please complete the following form, for each entity you are authorized to file on behalf of and return it, by mail with a copy of the on-line test, to the Office of the Bankruptcy Court Clerk, 450 Main Street, Hartford, CT 06103, Attn: ECF Registration. We will contact you regarding your registration and password after review of the information herein.

Name _____

Address _____

Firm Name _____

Entity for Which you are authorized to file _____

Bar I.D. & State _____

Basis for Use (i.e. claims filing) _____

Phone Number _____

Fax Number _____

E–Mail address for use in Electronic Filing _____

I declare, under penalty of perjury, the flowing is true:

1.   Claims or Other Limited Use Application: I am authorized to prepare and file:

☐ proofs of claim

☐ requests for notice

☐ notices of assignment of claims

2.   I agree that use of the password to be obtained pursuant to this registration (my password) to file a document in the record of a bankruptcy case or proceeding will constitute my signature upon and my signing of any proofs of claim, request for notices and assignments of claims, or other papers or documents filed by use of my password, for all purposes authorized and required by law, including, without limitation, the United States Code, Federal Rules of Civil Procedure, Federal Rules of Bankruptcy Procedure, Federal Rules of Criminal Procedure, and any applicable local rules and non-bankruptcy law.

3.   I agree that it is my responsibility to maintain in my records all documents bearing my original signature that are filed using my password, and all documents bearing the original signature of any signer on whose behalf I file documents using my password, for a period of five (5) years after the case or proceeding in which the papers are filed has been closed.

4.   I agree that it is my responsibility to protect and secure the confidentiality of my password. If I believe that my password has been compromised, it is my responsibility to immediately notify the Court in accordance with this Court's ECF Procedures. I agree that it is my responsibility to notify the Court, immediately, of any change in my address, telephone number, fax number, or e-mail address.

5. I agree to adhere to the Court's for the Administrative Procedures for Electronic Case Filing. I understand that it is my responsibility to learn and use any and all updates to the Administrative Procedures for Electronic Case Filing, and acknowledge I have undergone training by the office of the Clerk of the Bankruptcy Court or otherwise qualified as a User prior to issuance of my password.

_____

APPLICANT SIGNATURE

_____

DATE

*For Court Use Only:*

*Approved By:* _____

*Password:* _____ *Date:* _____

---

## INSTRUCTIONS FOR SEEKING EXEMPTION FROM ELECTRONIC FILING

**Summary.** All documents filed in any case or adversary proceeding after August 1, 2005 must be filed electronically, unless exempted by the court. The court will not refuse any document for filing, but attorneys who file paper documents without obtaining an exemption risk dismissal or striking of the document, and may be subject to sanctions. Pro se litigants who are not attorneys are not subject to mandatory electronic filing.

**Procedure for Applying for Exemption.** No blanket exemptions will be granted to attorneys. Exemption from Electronic Filing must be sought on a case by case basis. A Motion for Exemption should be submitted to the Court using the attached standard form Motion for Exemption from Electronic Filing. The form should be completed and submitted in paper form with the first paper document submitted for filing. Documents submitted without the completed motion will not be refused for filing, but will be result in the issuance of a Court's Motion to Dismiss or Strike, which will be set for hearing before the assigned judge.

**Not-Yet-Trained Exemption.** To invoke this exemption, the attorney must schedule a date for ECF training and include a reference to that date in the motion for exemption. If the attorney does not select a date, the clerk will assign a training date. A list of Available ECF Training Dates is posted on the court's web site, www.ctb.uscourts.gov.

**Trained-But-No-Login Exemption.** Attorneys who have completed ECF training but who have not yet obtained a login and password will be granted an exemption good for 15 days to complete their preparation for ECF filing.

**Other-Circumstances Exemption.** In addition to the exemptions listed above, the court may grant exemptions from electronic filing where exceptional circumstances justify such relief. The circumstances should be described in detail in the motion. Exemptions for exceptional circumstances will be made on a case by case basis, and orders granting the exemption will apply only in the particular case in which the order was entered.

**Procedure for Filing Subsequent Paper Documents.** After a Motion for Exemption has been filed, the court will grant or deny the motion and return a copy of the motion and order to the attorney. If granted, the attorney should include a copy of the order with each paper document thereafter submitted for filing. Not-yet-trained, and trained-but-no-login exemptions cover all documents submitted for filing in any division of this court during the time period of the exemption. When filing conventionally documentation of the exemption for exemptions based on pending training or login should accompany the document to be filed. An exemption granted for other reasons is limited to the case in which the Order was granted.

**Out-of-District Attorneys.** The court's electronic filing requirements and the exemptions thereto apply to all attorneys, whether or not located in the district, and whether or not admitted to practice in the district.

**Sanctions.** Any attorney who files documents in paper form, who fails to submit a motion for exemption, or who continues to file documents in paper form after a motion for exemption has been denied or after an exemption has expired, may risk striking of the document or dismissal of the case, and ultimately be subject to disciplinary action.

When an attorney attempts a filing in violation of the above requirements, the following procedure will be followed:

1.   The document will be filed, imaged and docketed by the Clerk.

2.   The Clerk will issue a Court's Motion to Dismiss or Strike for Failure to Comply with the Court's Administrative Procedures, refer the matter to the assigned judge, and set the matter for hearing at the earliest practicable date. The hearing date will be scheduled for the most expedient calendar which is more than five days from the issuance of the Court's Motion to Dismiss or Strike. Except on order of the court, in exceptional circumstances, no telephonic appearances will be allowed.

3.   If the court disallows the filing, an order may be issued striking the pleading from the record, dismissing the case, and/or requiring such other remedial action as the court may deem appropriate.

4.   Except on Order of the Court in exceptional circumstances, no action will be taken by the court with regard to the document pending the hearing on the Court's Motion to Dismiss or Strike.

---

## MOTION FOR EXEMPTION FROM ELECTRONIC FILING

In re:                                          Case No.
        Debtor

## MOTION FOR EXEMPTION FROM ELECTRONIC FILING

I, _____(name & bar no.) hereby apply for exemption from this court's requirement that all documents to be filed in any case or adversary proceeding on or after August 1, 2005, be submitted for filing in electronic form. I have read the instructions issued by this court for completion of this motion, and request exemption on the following ground(s):

(  )   Not–Yet–Trained (in house). I have not yet received Electronic Court Filing (ECF) training. I am scheduled to attend ECF training on ___. I agree to appear on the designated date, to complete my ECF "required assignment," and to file all documents electronically no later than 15 days after the training date.

(  )   Not–Yet–Trained (on-line). I have not yet received Electronic Court Filing (ECF) training. I will complete the ECF on-line training and submit my registration by ___ (date must not be more than 14 days from the filing of this motion). I agree to file all documents electronically no later than 15 days after I complete the on-line training and submit my registration.

(  )   Other. (Provide a detailed explanation of your reasons for requesting an exemption in the space below. Any additional information may be attached, but must be signed, under penalty of perjury ).

_____
_____
_____
_____
_____
_____

I declare under penalty of perjury that the statements in this motion are true. I understand that if I do not complete ECF training as scheduled, or otherwise file documents in paper form without further exemption, any documents I have filed or will file in paper format may be stricken or dismissed, and I may be subject to referral by the court for disciplinary action.

Date:_____   Signature: _____

Print name and Bar Number: _____ Phone Number: _____

Address: _____

_____

# STANDING ORDERS

## AMENDED STANDING ORDER
## 1. INTEREST–BEARING ACCOUNTS *

Pursuant to Rule 67 F.R.Civ.P., it is hereby ORDERED that:

### 1. ORDER FOR DEPOSIT—INTEREST BEARING ACCOUNT

Whenever a party seeks a court order for money to be deposited by the clerk in an interest-bearing account or instrument, the party shall cause the proposed order to be delivered to the clerk or financial administrator who will inspect the proposed order for proper form and content and compliance with this rule prior to signature by the judge for whom the order is prepared.

### 2. ORDERS DIRECTING INVESTMENT OF FUNDS BY CLERK

Any order obtained by a party or parties in an action that directs the clerk to invest in an interest-bearing account or instrument funds deposited in the registry of the court pursuant to 28 U.S.C. § 2041 shall include the following:

(a) the amount to be involved;

(b) the name of the depository approved by the Treasurer of the United States as a depository in which funds may be deposited;

(c) a designation of the type of account or instrument in which the funds shall be invested;

(d) the name of the party entitled to the interest to be earned less the Registry Fee;

(e) wording which directs the Clerk to collect a Registry Fee from the interest earned on the account or instrument (29 U.S.C. § 1914, Item 13—Registry Fee Funds); and a designation of the time the fee shall be collected (e.g., upon closing the account).

Dated at Bridgeport, Connecticut this 18th day of September, 1997.

Alan H. W. Shiff
Chief Bankruptcy Judge

Dated at Hartford, Connecticut this 29th day of September, 1997.

Robert L. Krechevsky
Bankruptcy Judge

Dated at New Haven, Connecticut this 18th day of September, 1997.

Albert S. Dabrowski
Bankruptcy Judge

* Suggested title added by Publisher.

## STANDING ORDER 2. SECURITIES MAINTAINED IN BANKRUPTCY COLLATERAL ACCOUNT

In Conformity with The 1986 Amendment to 11 U.S.C. Sec. 345

It is ordered that any securities now maintained in any bankruptcy collateral account for the Bankruptcy Court for the District of Connecticut with the Federal Reserve Bank of New York or with the Federal Reserve Bank of Boston, with the exception of any collateral account maintained to secure the Clerk's Registry Funds pursuant to Treasury Circulation No. 176, shall henceforth be subject to the direction of the United States Trustee for this district.

Date May 17, 1990

Honorable Robert L. Krechevsky
Chief Judge

Date May 21, 1990

Honorable Alan H.W. Shiff
Bankruptcy Judge

## STANDING ORDER 3. CLERK'S DEPUTIES *

It is hereby

ORDERED that the Clerk of the Bankruptcy Court shall appoint and remove the Clerk's deputies and need not secure the prior approval of the Bankruptcy Judges in connection therewith.

Dated at Hartford, Connecticut, this 26th day of November, 1990.

Robert L. Krechevsky
Chief Bankruptcy Judge

Dated at Hartford, Connecticut this 26th day of November, 1990.

Alan H.W. Shiff
United States Bankruptcy Judge

* Suggested title added by Publisher.

## STANDING ORDER 4.   IN RE TAX PROCEDURES

It appears that because of the automatic stay provision of 11 U.S.C. § 362 the Internal Revenue Service is not assessing tax returns, is not setting off overpayments against balances due, and is withholding tax refunds due debtors in Chapter 7, 11 and 13 cases under the Bankruptcy Code.  In the judgment of the Court, this action of the Internal Revenue Service hinders and delays administration of bankruptcy cases in this District.  Moreover, this action causes debtors undue hardship.  The Internal Revenue Service agrees with this conclusion.  It now also appears that the State of Connecticut has enacted tax legislation which will similarly impact on debtors.  It is therefore

ORDERED that the Internal Revenue Service and the Connecticut Department of Revenue Service be and hereby are each authorized and directed to assess voluntarily filed tax returns and make refunds in the ordinary course of business to debtors who have cases filed in this District, and the Internal Revenue Service and Connecticut Department of Revenue Services are each hereby authorized to offset against any refund due a debtor any taxes due the United States Government and State of Connecticut and it is

FURTHER ORDERED that the stay afforded 11 U.S.C. § 362 be, and it hereby is, automatically modified as provided herein in any case filed in this District, unless otherwise ordered by the Court and it is

FURTHER ORDERED that Standing Order # 5, entered on November 5, 1980, Re: Termination of Stay As To The U.S. Internal Revenue Service Only, and Standing Order # 10, entered on March 2, 1982 Re: Tax Procedures are hereby revoked.

Dated at Hartford, Connecticut, this 17th day of June 1992.

Robert L. Krechevsky
Chief Bankruptcy Judge

Dated at Hartford, Connecticut, this 17th day of June 1992.

Alan H.W. Shiff
United States Bankruptcy Judge

## AMENDED STANDING ORDER 5.  AUTHORIZING CLERK TO SIGN DISCHARGE ORDERS

It is hereby

ORDERED that the Clerk of the Bankruptcy Court is authorized and delegated the ministerial function of signing Orders of Discharge granted in the District of Connecticut and Orders closing chapter 7, 12 and 13 cases.

Dated at Bridgeport, Connecticut, this 22nd day of May, 1997.

Alan H.W. Shiff
Chief Bankruptcy Judge

Dated at Bridgeport Connecticut, this 22nd day of May, 1997.

Robert L. Krechevsky
United States Bankruptcy Judge

Dated at Bridgeport, Connecticut, this 22nd day of May, 1997.

Albert S. Dabrowski
United States Bankruptcy Judge

## STANDING ORDER 6.   IN RE: DISPOSITION OF UNCLAIMED FUNDS

It appearing that all unclaimed funds paid into the court pursuant to 11 U.S.C. section 347(a) shall be deposited into the United States Treasury, and

It further appearing that withdrawal of these funds is governed by 28 U.S.C. Section 2041.  It is therefore

ORDERED that every application shall comply with the Requirements for Filing an Application for Payment of Unclaimed Funds available from the clerk.

Dated at Bridgeport, Connecticut this 21st day of September, 1998.

Alan H.W. Shiff
Chief Bankruptcy Judge

Dated at Hartford, Connecticut this 24th day of September, 1998.

Robert L. Krechevsky
United States Bankruptcy Judge

Dated at New Haven, Connecticut this 22nd day of September, 1998.

Albert S. Dabrowski
United States Bankruptcy Judge

## STANDING ORDER NO. 8.   ADOPTION OF INTERIM BANKRUPTCY RULES

WHEREAS, on April 20, 2005 the Bankruptcy Abuse Prevention and Consumer Protection Act of 2005 (the Act) was enacted into law; and

**WHEREAS,** most provisions of the Act are effective on October 17, 2005; and

**WHEREAS,** the Advisory Committee on Bankruptcy Rules has prepared Interim Rules designed to implement the substantive and procedural changes mandated by the Act; and

**WHEREAS,** the Committee on Rules of Practice and Procedure of the Judicial Conference of the United States has also approved the Interim Rules and recommends the adoption of the Interim Rules to provide uniform procedures for implementing the Act; and

**WHEREAS,** the general effective date of the Act has not provided sufficient time to promulgate rules after appropriate public notice and an opportunity for comment;

**NOW THEREFORE, IT IS ORDERED,** pursuant to 28 U.S.C. section 2071, Rule 83 of the Federal Rules of Civil Procedure and Rule 9029 of the Federal Rules of Bankruptcy Procedure, that the attached Interim Rules* are adopted in their entirety without change by a unanimous vote of the judges of this Court, to be effective October 17, 2005 to conform with the Act. For cases and proceedings not governed by the Act, the Federal Rules of Bankruptcy Procedure and the Local Rules of this Court other than the Interim Rules, shall apply. The Interim Rules shall remain in effect until further order of the court.

Dated this 17th day of October, 2005.

* The Interim Bankruptcy Rules appear, in their entirety, following the Standing Orders of this court.

## STANDING ORDER NO. 13. ADOPTING AMENDMENT TO INTERIM BANKRUPTCY RULE 1007(B), AND REVISIONS TO OFFICIAL FORMS AS APPROVED BY THE JUDICIAL CONFERENCE OF THE UNITED STATES ON SEPTEMBER 19, 2006

WHEREAS, the Judicial Conference of the United States, on September 19, 2006, approved the amendment of Bankruptcy Rule 1007(b), and the amendment of Official Forms 1, 5, 6, 9, 22A, 22C, and 23, and approved new Exhibit D to Official Form 1, it is hereby

ORDERED, that effective October 1, 2006, the above-referenced amendments and new Exhibit D to Official Form 1, are adopted in full by this Court.*

Dated effective October 1, 2006.

* **Publishers note:** The Official Forms do not appear in this publication. Amendments to Interim Bankruptcy Rule 1007, adopted by this Court pursuant to Standing Order No. 13, are set forth below.

## RULE 1007. LISTS, SCHEDULES, STATEMENTS, AND OTHER DOCUMENTS; TIME LIMITS

\* \* \* \* \*

**(B) Schedules, Statements, and Other Documents Required.**

\* \* \* \* \*

(3) Unless the United States trustee has determined that the credit counseling requirement of § 109(h) does not apply in the district, an individual debtor must file a statement of compliance with the credit counseling requirement, prepared as prescribed by the appropriate Official Form which must include one of the following:

(A) an attached certificate and debt repayment plan, if any, required by § 521(b);

(B) a statement that the debtor has received the credit counseling briefing required by § 109(h)(1) but does not have the certificate required by § 521(b);

(C) a certification under § 109(h)(3); or

(D) a request for a determination by the court under § 109(h)(4).

\* \* \* \* \*

**(c) Time Limits.** In a voluntary case, the schedules, statements, and other documents required by subdivision (b)(1), (4), (5), and (6) shall be filed with the petition or within 15 days thereafter, except as otherwise provided in subdivisions (d), (e), (f), and (h) of this rule. In an involuntary case, the list in subdivision (a)(2), and the schedules, statements, and other documents required by subdivision (b)(1) shall be filed by the debtor within 15 days of the entry of the order for relief. In a voluntary case, the documents required by paragraphs (A), (C), and (D) of subdivision (b)(3) shall be filed with the petition. Unless the court orders otherwise, if the debtor has filed a statement under subdivision (b)(3)(B), the documents required by subdivision (b)(3)(A) shall be filed within 15 days of the order for relief. In a chapter 7 case, the debtor shall file the statement required by subdivision (b)(7) within 45 days after the first date set for the meeting of creditors under § 341 of the Code, and in a chapter 13 case no later than the date when the last payment was made by the debtor as required by the plan or the filing of a motion for a discharge under § 1328(b). The debtor shall file the statement required by subdivision (b)(8) no earlier than the date of the last payment made under the plan or the date of the filing of a motion for a discharge under §§ 1141(d)(5)(B), 1228(b), or 1328(b) of the Code. Lists, schedules, statements, and other documents filed prior to the conversion of a case to another chapter shall be deemed filed in the converted case unless the court

directs otherwise. Except as provided in § 1116(3), any extension of time for the filing of the schedules, statements, and other documents required under this rule may be granted only on motion for cause shown and on notice to the United States trustee, any committee elected under § 705 or appointed under § 1102 of the Code, trustee, examiner, or other party as the court may direct. Notice of an extension shall be given to the United States trustee and to any committee, trustee, or other party as the court may direct.

\* \* \* \* \*

### COMMITTEE NOTE

Subdivision (b)(3) of the rule is amended to require the debtor to file an Official Form relating to the credit counseling requirement provided by the 2005 amendments to § 109. Official Form 1 includes statements that warn the debtor of the consequences of failing to comply with the credit counseling requirement. The rule also provides that the debtor may file a statement that the debtor has received credit counseling but has not yet received a certificate from the credit counseling provider. Subdivision (c) is amended to permit the debtor to file the certificate and debt repayment plan within 15 days after the filing of the petition if a Rule 1007(b)(3)(B) statement is filed.

Other changes are stylistic.

## STANDING ORDER 22. MASTER MAILING LIST *

\* Suggested title added by Publisher.

It is hereby Ordered that, effective January 2, 1996, Bankruptcy Standing Order 22 is amended as follows:

Master Mailing List (Matrix) as required by Local Bankruptcy Rule 5(a) shall conform to the following.

### 1. General Requirements.

(A) At the time of filing a voluntary petition or within 15 days following the entry of an order for relief on an involuntary petition, the debtor (or petitioning creditor or partner, upon order of the Court) shall file a separate master mailing list on floppy disk if the petition has more than ten (10) creditors and equity security holders. The master mailing list shall be filed in addition to the list or schedules included within the petition. The disk shall be filed in a sealed 8½″ × 11″ envelope and shall contain names and post office addresses, including zip code and account number where applicable, for every scheduled creditor. The floppy disk shall be filed in accordance with the format and specifications annexed as Exhibit "A".

An attorney who is filing several petitions simultaneously, including one or more petitions with more than ten (10) creditors and equity security holders, in lieu of providing an additional, individual disk list for each petition, may submit a single floppy disk. The floppy disk shall be filed in accordance with the format and specifications annexed as Exhibit "B".

The foregoing requirements are waived for pro se debtors and may be waived only upon submission of a written affidavit by an attorney, attesting to a lack of capacity to comply with the requirement. The waiver request shall be accompanied by a matrix filed in accordance with the format and specifications annexed as Exhibit "C".

(B) The master mailing list shall also include those agencies and officers of the United States in Bankruptcy Rule 2002(j) required to receive notice. In addition to the agency address, the address for the United States Attorney shall be included:

United States Attorney
(re: creditor agency)
P.O. Box 1824
New Haven, CT. 06508

(C) Where a federal tax debt is owed, all lists shall include the address of the Internal Revenue Service office having responsibility for monitoring the case.

IRS—SPECIAL PROCEDURES
135 High Street—Stop 155
Hartford, CT. 06103

(D) All lists shall also include the U.S. Trustee whose address is:

UNITED STATES TRUSTEE
James English Building
105 Court Street, Suite 402
New Haven, CT. 06510

(E) The Tax Collector of the town in which the debtor lives.

2. If the debtor is a partnership, the master mailing list shall contain the names and current mailing addresses of each general and limited partner.

3. If the debtor is a corporation, the master mailing list shall contain the names and current mailing addresses of the present officers and directors, or if none, the immediate past officers and past directors.

4. **Accuracy of Information Provided.** The debtor and debtor's attorney shall be responsible for the preparation of the master mailing lists required by this Standing Order. The debtor shall sign and verify the list attesting to the accuracy and completeness of the information to the best of the debtor's ability.

5. **Amendment of Master Mailing Lists.** Whenever amendments to schedules add new entities or make corrections to mailing addresses, the debtor shall file with the document an amended master mailing list on floppy disk if more than ten (10) creditors are amended. The floppy disk shall be filed in accordance with the format and specifications annexed as Exhibit "A". If less than ten (10) creditors are amended the amended master mailing list may be filed in accordance with the format and specifications annexed as Exhibit "C". The amended master mailing list shall include only the names and addresses of the entities added, deleted or corrected. The amend-

ed list shall clearly indicate the nature of the amendment.

Dated at Hartford, Connecticut this 5th day of December, 1995.

> Honorable Robert L. Krechevsky
> Chief, U.S. Bankruptcy Judge

Dated at Bridgeport, Connecticut this 5th day of December, 1995.

> Honorable Alan H.W. Shiff
> U.S. Bankruptcy Judge

Dated at New Haven, Connecticut this 5th day of December, 1995.

> Honorable Albert S. Dabrowski
> U.S. Bankruptcy Judge

Anyone who needs technical assistance in complying with this order is directed to contact Bob Plourde, Assistant Systems Manager at (203) 240–2610.

December 5, 1995

> Bernardine A. Gordon
> Clerk of Court

---

### EXHIBIT "A"

Floppy Disk: Single Case (More than 10 creditors)

The additional list of creditors on floppy disk shall be filed in a sealed 8½″ × 11″ envelope. The debtor's name and address, social security/taxpayer identification number, chapter filed under and attorney name, address and telephone number shall appear on the envelope. Do NOT include the debtor(s) or the attorney for the debtor(s) on the disk. This is a master mailing list for creditors only. The disk should be in the following format:

1. Must be 3.5″ or 5.25″;
2. Must be formatted for use on an IBM or compatible PC;
3. Contain one ASCII file;
4. One case per file;
5. One file per disk;
6. File must be named "creditor.scn";
7. The first line of the file must be the name of the debtor. If the disk is not filed with the petition, then the case number must be substituted for the debtor name (***94–21323***); use three asterisks before and after the case number;
8. The second line must be blank;
9. Start the list of creditors on the third line;
10. The address must be 4 lines or less;
11. Each line of the address must contain no more than 30 characters;
12. Each address must be separated by two blank lines;
13. The state name can be either two characters or written out fully, however the state name cannot contain periods (i.e. "CT." is invalid but "CT" and "Connecticut" are valid) and,
14. There should be no trailing blanks after the zip code.

---

### EXHIBIT "B"

Floppy disk: Multiple Cases (lists of creditors with more than 10 creditors per case)

The disk must be filed in a sealed 8½″ × 11″ envelope. The debtors' names and addresses, social security/taxpayer identification numbers, chapter filed under and the attorney name, address and telephone number shall appear on the envelope. The floppy disk shall be segmented by individual debtor and shall conform to the following format and specifications:

1. Must be 3.5″ or 5.25″;
2. Must be formatted for use on an IBM or compatible PC;
3. Contain one ASCII file;
4. One file per disk;
5. File must be named "creditor.scn";
6. The first line for each case on the file must be the name of the debtor. If the disk is not filed with the petitions, then the case numbers must be substituted for the debtors' names (***94–22345***); use three asterisks before and after each case number;
7. The second line must be blank;
8. Start the list of creditors on the third line;
9. The address must be 4 lines or less;
10. Each line of the address must not contain more than 30 characters;
11. Each address must be separated by two blank lines;
12. State name can be either two characters or written out fully, however the state name cannot contain periods (i.e. "Conn." is invalid but "CT" and "Connecticut" are valid);
13. There should be no trailing blanks after the zip code;
14. No more than 1000 creditors should be listed;

15. After the last creditor for each case, there should be five blank lines before listing the name (or case number) of the next debtor, and

16. Follow instructions B6–12.

---

EXHIBIT "C"

MATRIX (Must be filed with Affidavit of Lack of Capacity to Prepare a Disk unless Pro Se)

The matrix shall be filed in a sealed envelope, unfolded and unstapled, with the debtor's name and address, social security/taxpayer identification number and attorney name, address, telephone number and chapter of filing affixed to the envelope. The matrix should be in the following format:

1. Printed on clean white plain 8½″ × 11″ paper;
2. Must be typewritten using only one of the following standard typefaces or print styles:

COURIER 10 PITCH
PRESTIGE ELITE
LETTER GOTHIC

DO NOT use proportional typefaces or print styles.

3. Contain no more than 10 addresses to a page;
4. Must be single column;

5. No more than 5 lines per address;
6. No more than 40 characters per line;
7. No type within ½ inch of any edge of paper;
8. States must be abbreviated in 2 characters, capital letters;
9. Never type matrix in all capital letters;
10. Never use the % sign in place of c/o;
11. Minimum of one blank line between addresses;
12. DO NOT include the debtor(s) or the attorney for the debtor(s). This is a matrix of creditors only;
13. Zip codes must be on the last line. Nine digit zip codes should be typed with a hyphen separating the two groups of digits;
14. Must be an original document and not a copy;
15. Contain absolutely NO headers, footers, page numbers, or other extraneous marks that are not directly material to a creditor name or address.

example:

Jerry & Jane Barnes
P.O. Box 102
Elkins, NH 03233

Norwich Savings Society
Attn: Lynn Clapproot
1585 Boston Road
Springfield, MA 01129

# INTERIM BANKRUPTCY RULES

## FEDERAL RULES OF BANKRUPTCY PROCEDURE
## INTERIM BANKRUPTCY RULES

### INTERIM RULE 1006. FILING FEE

**(a) General Requirement.** Every petition shall be accompanied by the filing fee except as provided in subdivisions (b) and (c) of this rule. For the purpose of this rule, "filing fee" means the filing fee prescribed by 28 U.S.C. § 1930(a)(1)-(a)(5) and any other fee prescribed by the Judicial Conference of the United States under 28 U.S.C. § 1930(b) that is payable to the clerk upon the commencement of a case under the Code.

**(b) Payment of Filing Fee in Installments.**

(1) *Application to Pay Filing Fee in Installments.* A voluntary petition by an individual shall be accepted for filing if accompanied by the debtor's signed application, prepared as prescribed by the appropriate Official Form, stating that the debtor is unable to pay the filing fee except in installments.

\* \* \* \* \*

(3) *Postponement of Attorney's Fees.* All installments of the filing fee must be paid in full before the debtor or chapter 13 trustee may make further payments to an attorney or any other person who renders services to the debtor in connection with the case.

**(c) Waiver of Filing Fee.** A voluntary chapter 7 petition filed by an individual shall be accepted for filing if accompanied by the debtor's application requesting a waiver under 28 U.S.C. § 1930(f), prepared as prescribed by the appropriate Official Form.

**COMMITTEE NOTE**
**October 17, 2005**

Subdivision (a) is amended to include a reference to new subdivision (c), which deals with fee waivers under 28 U.S.C. § 1930(f), which was added in 2005.

Subdivision (b)(1) is amended to delete the sentence requiring a disclosure that the debtor has not paid an attorney or other person in connection with the case. Inability to pay the filing fee in installments is one of the requirements for a fee waiver under the 2005 revisions to 28 U.S.C. § 1930(f). If the attorney payment prohibition were retained, payment of an attorney's fee would render many debtors ineligible for installment payments and thus enhance their eligibility for the fee waiver. The deletion of this prohibition from the rule, which was not statutorily required, ensures that debtors who have the financial ability to pay the fee in installments will do so rather than request a waiver.

Subdivision (b)(3) is amended in conformance with the changes to (b)(1) to reflect the 2005 amendments. The change is meant to clarify that (b)(3) refers to payments made after the debtor has filed the bankruptcy case and after the debtor has received permission to pay the fee in installments. Otherwise, the subdivision may conflict with intent and effect of the amendments to subdivision (b)(1).

Amended, on an interim basis, effective October 17, 2005.

## INTERIM RULE 1007. LISTS, SCHEDULES, STATEMENTS, AND OTHER DOCUMENTS; TIME LIMITS

**(A) List of Creditors and Equity Security Holders, and Corporate Ownership Statement.**

\* \* \* \* \*

(4) *Chapter 15 Case.* Unless the court orders otherwise, a foreign representative filing a petition for recognition under chapter 15 shall file with the petition a list containing the name and address of all administrators in foreign proceedings of the debtor, all parties to any litigation in which the debtor is a party and that is pending in the United States at the time of the filing of the petition, and all entities against whom provisional relief is being sought under § 1519 of the Code.

(5) *Extension of Time.* Any extension of time for the filing of lists required by this subdivision may be granted only on motion for cause shown and on notice to the United States trustee and to any trustee, committee elected under § 705 or appointed under § 1102 of the Code, or other party as the court may direct.

**(B) Schedules, Statements, and Other Documents Required.**

(1) Except in a chapter 9 municipality case, the debtor, unless the court orders otherwise, shall file the following schedules, statements, and other documents, prepared as prescribed by the appropriate Official Forms, if any:

(A) schedules of assets and liabilities;

(B) a schedule of current income and expenditures;

(C) a schedule of executory contracts and unexpired leases;

(D) a statement of financial affairs;

(E) copies of all payment advices or other evidence of payment, if any, with all but the last four digits of the debtor's social security number redacted, received

478

by the debtor from an employer within 60 days before the filing of the petition; and

(F) a record of any interest that the debtor has in an account or program of the type specified in § 521(c) of the Code.

(2) An individual debtor in a chapter 7 case shall file a statement of intention as required by § 521(a) of the Code, prepared as prescribed by the appropriate Official Form. A copy of the statement of intention shall be served on the trustee and the creditors named in the statement on or before the filing of the statement.

(3) Unless the United States trustee has determined that the credit counseling requirement of § 109(h) does not apply in the district, an individual debtor must file a statement of compliance with the credit counseling requirement, prepared as prescribed by the appropriate Official Form which must include one of the following:

(A) an attached certificate and debt repayment plan, if any, required by § 521(b);

(B) a statement that the debtor has received the credit counseling briefing required by § 109(h)(1) but does not have the certificate required by § 521(b);

(C) a certification under § 109(h)(3); or

(D) a request for a determination by the court under § 109(h)(4).

(4) Unless § 707(b)(2)(D) applies, an individual debtor in a chapter 7 case with primarily consumer debts shall file a statement of current monthly income prepared as prescribed by the appropriate Official Form, and, if the debtor has current monthly income greater than the applicable median family income for the applicable state and household size, the calculations in accordance with § 707(b), prepared as prescribed by the appropriate Official Form.

(5) An individual debtor in a chapter 11 case shall file a statement of current monthly income, prepared as prescribed by the appropriate Official Form.

(6) A debtor in a chapter 13 case shall file a statement of current monthly income, prepared as prescribed by the appropriate Official Form, and, if the debtor has current monthly income greater than the median family income for the applicable state and family size, a calculation of disposable income in accordance with § 1325(b)(3), prepared as prescribed by the appropriate Official Form.

(7) An individual debtor in a chapter 7 or chapter 13 case shall file a statement regarding completion of a course in personal financial management, prepared as prescribed by the appropriate Official Form.

(8) If an individual debtor in a chapter 11, 12, or 13 case has claimed an exemption under § 522(b)(3)(A) in an amount in excess of the amount set out in § 522(q)(1) in property of the kind described in § 522(p)(1), the debtor shall file a statement as to whether there is pending a proceeding in which the debtor may be found guilty of a felony of a kind described in § 522(q)(1)(A) or found liable for a debt of the kind described in § 522(q)(1)(B).

(c) **Time Limits.** In a voluntary case, the schedules, statements, and other documents required by subdivision (b)(1), (4), (5), and (6) shall be filed with the petition or within 15 days thereafter, except as otherwise provided in subdivisions (d), (e), (f), and (h) of this rule. In an involuntary case, the list in subdivision (a)(2), and the schedules, statements, and other documents required by subdivision (b)(1) shall be filed by the debtor within 15 days of the entry of the order for relief. In a voluntary case, the documents required by paragraphs (A), (C), and (D) of subdivision (b)(3) shall be filed with the petition. Unless the court orders otherwise, if the debtor has filed a statement under subdivision (b)(3)(B), the documents required by subdivision (b)(3)(A) shall be filed within 15 days of the order for relief. In a chapter 7 case, the debtor shall file the statement required by subdivision (b)(7) within 45 days after the first date set for the meeting of creditors under § 341 of the Code, and in a chapter 13 case no later than the date when the last payment was made by the debtor as required by the plan or the filing of a motion for a discharge under § 1328(b). The debtor shall file the statement required by subdivision (b)(8) no earlier than the date of the last payment made under the plan or the date of the filing of a motion for a discharge under §§ 1141(d)(5)(B), 1228(b), or 1328(b) of the

Code. Lists, schedules, statements, and other documents filed prior to the conversion of a case to another chapter shall be deemed filed in the converted case unless the court directs otherwise. Except as provided in § 1116(3), any extension of time for the filing of the schedules, statements, and other documents required under this rule may be granted only on motion for cause shown and on notice to the United States trustee, any committee elected under § 705 or appointed under § 1102 of the Code, trustee, examiner, or other party as the court may direct. Notice of an extension shall be given to the United States trustee and to any committee, trustee, or other party as the court may direct.

* * * * *

## COMMITTEE NOTE
### October 17, 2005

The title of this rule is expanded to refer to "documents" in conformity with the 2005 amendments to § 521 and related provisions of the Bankruptcy Code that include a wider range of documentary requirements.

Subdivision (a) is amended to require that any foreign representative filing a petition for recognition to commence a case under chapter 15, which was added to the Code in 2005, file a list of entities with whom the debtor is engaged in litigation in the United States. The foreign representative filing the petition for recognition also must list any entities against whom provisional relief is being sought as well as all administrators in foreign proceedings of the debtor. This should ensure that the entities most interested in the case, or their representatives, will receive notice of the petition under Rule 2002(q).

Subdivision (b)(1) addresses schedules, statements, and other documents that the debtor must file unless the court orders otherwise and other than in a case under Chapter 9. This subdivision is amended to include documentary requirements added by the 2005 amendments to § 521 that apply to the same group of debtors and have the same time limits as the existing requirements of (b)(1). Consistent with the E–Government Act of 2002, Pub. L. No. 107–347, 116 Stat. 2921 (2002), the payment advices should be redacted before they are filed.

Subdivision (b)(2) is amended to conform the renumbering of the subsections of § 521.

Subdivisions (b)(3) through (b)(7) are new. They implement the 2005 amendments to the Bankruptcy Code. Subdivision (b)(3) provides a procedure for filing documents relating to the nonprofit credit counseling requirement provided by the 2005 amendments to § 109.

Subdivision (b)(4) addresses the filing of information about current monthly income, as defined in § 101, for certain chapter 7 debtors and, if required, additional calculations of expenses required by the 2005 revisions to § 707(b).

Subdivision (b)(5) addresses the filing of information about current monthly income, as defined in § 101, for individual chapter 11 debtors. The 2005 amendments to § 1129(a)(15) condition plan confirmation for individual debtors on the commitment of disposable income as defined in § 1325(b)(2), which is based on current monthly income.

Subdivision (b)(6) addresses the filing of information about current monthly income, as defined in § 101, for chapter 13 debtors and, if required, additional calculations of expenses. These changes are necessary because the 2005 amendments to § 1325 require that determinations of disposable income start with current monthly income.

Subdivision (b)(7) reflects the 2005 amendments to §§ 727 and 1328 that condition the receipt of a discharge on the completion of a personal financial management course, with certain exceptions.

Subdivision (b)(8) is amended to require an individual debtor in a case under chapter 11, 12, and 13 to file a statement that there are no reasonable grounds to believe that the restrictions on a homestead exemption as set out in § 522(q) of the Code are applicable. Sections 1141(d)(5)(C), 1228(f), and 1328(h) each provide that the court shall not enter a discharge order unless it finds that there is no reasonable cause to believe that § 522(q) applies. Requiring the debtor to submit a statement to that effect in cases under chapters 11, 12, and 13 in which an exemption is claimed in excess of the amount allowed under § 522(q)(1) provides the court with a basis to conclude, in the absence of any contrary information, that § 522(q) does not apply. Creditors receive notice under Rule 2002(f)(11) of the time to request postponement of the entry of the discharge so that they can challenge the debtor's assertions in the Rule 1007(b)(8) statement in appropriate cases.

Subdivision (c) is amended to include time limits for the filing requirements added to subdivision (b) due to the 2005 amendments to the Bankruptcy Code, and to make conforming amendments. Separate time limits are provided for the documentation of credit counseling and for the statement of the completion of the financial management course.

Subdivision (c) of the rule is also amended to recognize the limitation on the extension of time to file schedules and statements when the debtor is a small business debtor. Section 1116(3), added to the Bankruptcy Code in 2005, establishes a specific standard for courts to apply in the event that the debtor in possession or the trustee seeks an extension for filing these forms for a period beyond 30 days after the order for relief.

### October 1, 2006

Subdivision (b)(3) of the rule is amended to require the debtor to file an Official Form relating to the credit counseling requirement provided by the 2005 amendments to § 109. Official Form 1 includes statements that warn the debtor of the consequences of failing to comply with the credit counseling requirement. The rule also provides that the debtor may file a statement that the debtor has received credit counseling but has not yet received a certificate from the credit counseling provider. Subdivision (c) is amended to permit the debtor to file the certificate and debt repayment plan within 15 days after the filing of the petition if a Rule 1007(b)(3)(B) statement is filed.

Other changes are stylistic.

Amended, on an interim basis, effective October 17, 2005;  October 1, 2006.

## INTERIM RULE 1009.  AMENDMENTS OF VOLUNTARY PETITIONS, LISTS, SCHEDULES AND STATEMENTS

* * * * *

**(b) Statement of Intention.** The statement of intention may be amended by the debtor at any time before the expiration of the period provided in § 521(a) of the Code. The debtor shall give notice of the amendment to the trustee and to any entity affected thereby.

* * * * *

### COMMITTEE NOTE
#### October 17, 2005

Subdivision (b) is amended to conform to the 2005 amendments to § 521 of the Code.

Amended, on an interim basis, effective October 17, 2005.

## INTERIM RULE 1010.  SERVICE OF INVOLUNTARY PETITION AND SUMMONS; PETITION FOR RECOGNITION OF A FOREIGN NONMAIN PROCEEDING

On the filing of an involuntary petition or a petition for recognition of a foreign nonmain proceeding the clerk shall forthwith issue a summons for service. When an involuntary petition is filed, service shall be made on the debtor. When a petition for recognition of a foreign nonmain proceeding is filed, service shall be made on the debtor, any entity against whom provisional relief is sought under § 1519 of the Code, and on any other parties as the court may direct. The summons shall be served with a copy of the petition in the manner provided for service of a summons and complaint by Rule 7004(a) or (b). If service cannot be so made, the court may order that the summons and petition be served by mailing copies to the party's last known address, and by at least one publication in a manner and form directed by the court. The summons and petition may be served on the party anywhere. Rule 7004 (e) and Rule 4 (*l*) F.R.Civ.P. apply when service is made or attempted under this rule.

### COMMITTEE NOTE
#### October 17, 2005

This rule is amended to implement the 2005 amendments to the Bankruptcy Code, which repealed § 304 of the Code and replaced it with chapter 15 governing ancillary and other cross-

border cases. Under chapter 15, a foreign representative commences a case by filing a petition for recognition of a pending foreign nonmain proceeding. The amendment requires service of the summons and petition on the debtor and any entity against whom the representative is seeking provisional relief. Until the court enters a recognition order under § 1517, no stay is in effect unless the court enters some form of provisional relief under § 1519. Thus, there is no need to serve all creditors of the debtor upon filing the petition for recognition. Only those entities against whom specific provisional relief is sought need to be served. The court may direct that service be made on additional entities as appropriate.

This rule does not apply to a petition for recognition of a foreign main proceeding.

Amended, on an interim basis, effective October 17, 2005.

## INTERIM RULE 1011. RESPONSIVE PLEADING OR MOTION IN INVOLUNTARY AND CROSS–BORDER CASES

(a) **Who May Contest Petition.** The debtor named in an involuntary petition or a party in interest to a petition for recognition of a foreign proceeding may contest the petition. In the case of a petition against a partnership under Rule 1004, a nonpetitioning general partner, or a person who is alleged to be a general partner but denies the allegation, may contest the petition.

\* \* \* \* \*

### COMMITTEE NOTE
October 17, 2005

The rule is amended to reflect the 2005 amendments to the Bankruptcy Code, which repealed § 304 of the Code and added chapter 15. Section 304 covered cases ancillary to foreign proceedings, while chapter 15 of the Code governs ancillary and other cross-border cases and introduces the concept of a petition for recognition of a foreign proceeding.

Amended, on an interim basis, effective October 17, 2005.

## INTERIM RULE 1017. DISMISSAL OR CONVERSION OF CASE; SUSPENSION

\* \* \* \* \*

(e) **Dismissal of an Individual Debtor's Chapter 7 Case or Conversion to a Case Under Chapter 11 or 13 for Abuse.** The court may dismiss or, with the debtor's consent, convert an individual debtor's case for abuse under § 707(b) only on motion and after a hearing on notice to the debtor, the trustee, the United States trustee, and any other entities as the court directs. (1) Except as otherwise provided in § 704(b)(2), a motion to dismiss a case for abuse under § 707(b) or (c) may be filed only within 60 days after the first date set for the meeting of creditors under § 341(a), unless, on request filed before the time has expired, the court for cause extends the time for filing the motion to dismiss. The party filing the motion shall set forth in the motion all matters to be considered at the hearing. A motion to dismiss under § 707(b)(1) and (3) shall state with particularity the circumstances alleged to constitute abuse.

\* \* \* \* \*

### COMMITTEE NOTE
October 17, 2005

Subdivisions (e) and (e)(1) are amended to implement the 2005 revisions to § 707 of the Code. These revisions permit conversion of a chapter 7 case to a case under chapter 11 or 13, change the basis for dismissal or conversion from "substantial abuse" to "abuse," authorize parties other than the United States trustee to bring motions under § 707(b) under certain

circumstances, and add § 707(c) to create an explicit ground for dismissal based on the request of a victim of a crime of violence or drug trafficking. The conforming amendments to subdivision (e) preserve the time limits already in place for § 707(b) motions, except to the extent that § 704(b)(2) sets the deadline for the United States trustee to act. In contrast to the grounds for a motion to dismiss under § 707(b)(2), which are quite specific, the grounds under § 707(b)(1) and (3) are very general. Subdivision (e) therefore requires that motions to dismiss under §§ 707(b)(1) and (3) state with particularity the circumstances alleged to constitute abuse to enable the debtor to respond.

Amended, on an interim basis, effective October 17, 2005.

# INTERIM RULE 1019. CONVERSION OF CHAPTER 11 REORGANIZATION CASE, CHAPTER 12 FAMILY FARMER'S DEBT ADJUSTMENT CASE, OR CHAPTER 13 INDIVIDUAL'S DEBT ADJUSTMENT CASE TO A CHAPTER 7 LIQUIDATION CASE

\* \* \* \* \*

**(2) New Filing Periods.** A new time period for filing a motion under § 707(b) or (c), a claim, a complaint objecting to discharge, or a complaint to obtain a determination of dischargeability of any debt shall commence under Rules 1017, 3002, 4004, or 4007, provided that a new time period shall not commence if a chapter 7 case had been converted to a chapter 11, 12, or 13 case and thereafter reconverted to a chapter 7 case and the time for filing a motion under § 707(b) or (c), a claim, a complaint objecting to discharge, or a complaint to obtain a determination of the dischargeability of any debt, or any extension thereof, expired in the original chapter 7 case.

\* \* \* \* \*

### COMMITTEE NOTE
### October 17, 2005

Subdivision (2) is amended to provide a new filing period for motions under § 707(b) and (c) of the Code when a case is converted to chapter 7.

Amended, on an interim basis, effective October 17, 2005.

# INTERIM RULE 1020. SMALL BUSINESS CHAPTER 11 REORGANIZATION CASE

**(a) Small Business Debtor Designation.** In a voluntary chapter 11 case, the debtor shall state in the petition whether the debtor is a small business debtor. In an involuntary chapter 11 case, the debtor shall file within 15 days after entry of the order for relief a statement as to whether the debtor is a small business debtor. Except as provided in subdivision (c), the status of the case with respect to whether it is a small business case shall be in accordance with the debtor's statement under this subdivision, unless and until the court enters an order finding that the debtor's statement is incorrect.

**(b) Objecting To Designation.** Except as provided in subdivision (c), the United States trustee or a party in interest may file an objection to the debtor's statement under subdivision (a) not later than 30 days after the conclusion of the meeting of creditors held under § 341(a) of the Code, or within 30 days after any amendment to the statement, whichever is later.

**(c) Appointment of Committee of Unsecured Creditors.** If the United States trustee has appointed a committee of unsecured creditors under § 1102(a)(1), the case shall proceed as a small business case only if, and from the time when, the court enters an order determining that the committee has not been sufficiently active and representative to provide effective oversight of the debtor and that the debtor

satisfies all the other requirements for being a small business. A request for a determination under this subdivision may be filed by the United States trustee or a party in interest only within a reasonable time after the failure of the committee to be sufficiently active and representative. The debtor may file a request for a determination at any time as to whether the committee has been sufficiently active and representative.

**(d) Procedure for Objection or Determination.** Any objection or request for a determination under this rule shall be governed by Rule 9014 and served on the debtor, the debtor's attorney, the United States trustee, the trustee, any committee appointed under § 1102 or its authorized agent, or, if no committee of unsecured creditors has been appointed under § 1102, on the creditors included on the list filed under Rule 1007(d), and on such other entities as the court may direct.

**COMMITTEE NOTE**
October 17, 2005

Under the Bankruptcy Code, as amended in 2005, there are no provisions permitting or requiring a small business debtor to elect to be treated as a small business. Therefore, there is no longer any need for a rule on elections to be considered a small business.

The 2005 amendments to the Code include several provisions relating to small business cases under chapter 11. Section 101 of the Code includes definitions of "small business debtor" and "small business case." The purpose of the new language in this rule is to provide a procedure for informing the parties, the United States trustee, and the court of whether the debtor is a small business debtor, and to provide procedures for resolving disputes regarding the proper characterization of the debtor. Because it is important to resolve such disputes early in the case, a time limit for objecting to the debtor's self-designation is imposed. Rule 9006(b)(1), which governs enlargement of time, is applicable to the time limits set forth in this rule.

An important factor in determining whether the debtor is a small business debtor is whether the United States trustee has appointed a committee of unsecured creditors under § 1102 of the Code, and whether such a committee is sufficiently active and representative. Subdivision (c), relating to the appointment and activity of a committee of unsecured creditors, is designed to be consistent with the Code's definition of "small business debtor."

Amended, on an interim basis, effective October 17, 2005.

## INTERIM RULE 1021.   HEALTH CARE BUSINESS CASE

**(a) Health Care Business Designation.** Unless the court orders otherwise, if a petition in a case under chapter 7, chapter 9, or chapter 11 states that the debtor is a health care business, the case shall proceed as a case in which the debtor is a health care business.

**(b) Motion.** The United States trustee or a party in interest may file a motion for a determination as to whether the debtor is a health care business. The motion shall be transmitted to the United States trustee and served on the debtor, the trustee, any committee elected under § 705 or appointed under § 1102 of the Code or its authorized agent, or, if the case is a chapter 9 municipality case or a chapter 11 reorganization case and no committee of unsecured creditors has been appointed under § 1102, on the creditors included on the list filed under Rule 1007(d), and such other entities as the court may direct. The motion shall be governed by Rule 9014.

**COMMITTEE NOTE**
October 17, 2005

Section 101(27A) of the Code, added in 2005, defines a health care business. This rule provides procedures for identifying the debtor as a health care business. The debtor in a voluntary case, or petitioning creditors in an involuntary case, will usually make the identification by checking the appropriate box on the petition. If a party in interest or the United States trustee disagrees with the determination by the debtor or the petitioning creditors as to whether the debtor is a health care business, this rule provides procedures for resolving the dispute.

Amended, on an interim basis, effective October 17, 2005.

## INTERIM RULE 2002. NOTICES TO CREDITORS, EQUITY SECURITY HOLDERS, ADMINISTRATORS IN FOREIGN PROCEEDINGS, PERSONS AGAINST WHOM PROVISIONAL RELIEF IS SOUGHT IN ANCILLARY AND OTHER CROSS–BORDER CASES, UNITED STATES, AND UNITED STATES TRUSTEE

(a) **Twenty–Day Notices to Parties in Interest.** Except as provided in subdivisions (h), (i), (*l*), (p), and (q) of this rule, the clerk, or some other person as the court may direct, shall give the debtor, the trustee, all creditors and indenture trustees at least 20 days' notice by mail of:

\* \* \* \* \*

(b) **Twenty–Five–Day Notices to Parties in Interest.** Except as provided in subdivision (*l*) of this rule, the clerk, or some other person as the court may direct, shall give the debtor, the trustee, all creditors and indenture trustees not less than 25 days notice by mail of (1) the time fixed for filing objections and the hearing to consider approval of a disclosure statement or, under § 1125(f), to make a final determination whether the plan provides adequate information so that a separate disclosure statement is not necessary; and (2) the time fixed for filing objections and the hearing to consider confirmation of a chapter 9, chapter 11, or chapter 13 plan.

(c) **Content of Notice.**

(1) *Proposed Use, Sale, or Lease of Property.* Subject to Rule 6004 the notice of a proposed use, sale, or lease of property required by subdivision (a)(2) of this rule shall include the time and place of any public sale, the terms and conditions of any private sale and the time fixed for filing objections. The notice of a proposed use, sale, or lease of property, including real estate, is sufficient if it generally describes the property. The notice of a proposed sale or lease of personally identifiable information under § 363(b)(1)(A) or (B) of the Code shall state whether the sale is consistent with a policy prohibiting the transfer of the information.

\* \* \* \* \*

(f) **Other Notices.** Except as provided in subdivision (*l*) of this rule, the clerk, or some other person as the court may direct, shall give the debtor, all creditors, and indenture trustees notice by mail of: (1) the order for relief; (2) the dismissal or the conversion of the case to another chapter, or the suspension of proceedings under § 305; (3) the time allowed for filing claims pursuant to Rule 3002; (4) the time fixed for filing a complaint objecting to the debtor's discharge pursuant to § 727 of the Code as provided in Rule 4004; (5) the time fixed for filing a complaint to determine the dischargeability of a debt pursuant to § 523 of the Code as provided in Rule 4007; (6) the waiver, denial, or revocation of a discharge as provided in Rule 4006; (7) entry of an order confirming a chapter 9, 11, or 12 plan; (8) a summary of the trustee's final report in a chapter 7 case if the net proceeds realized exceed $1,500; (9) a notice under Rule 5008 regarding the presumption of abuse; (10) a statement under § 704(b)(1) as to whether the debtor's case would be presumed to be an abuse under § 707(b); and (11) the time to request a delay in the entry of the discharge under §§ 1141(d)(5)(C), 1228(f), and 1328(h). Notice of the time fixed for accepting or rejecting a plan pursuant to Rule 3017(c) shall be given in accordance with Rule 3017(d).

\* \* \* \* \*

(g) **Addressing Notices.**

\* \* \* \* \*

(2) Except as provided in § 342(f) of the Code, if a creditor or indenture trustee has not filed a request designating a mailing address under Rule 2002(g)(1), the notices shall be mailed to the address shown on the list of creditors or schedule of liabilities, whichever is filed later. If an equity security holder has not filed a request designating a mailing address under Rule 2002(g)(1), the notices shall be mailed to the address shown on the list of equity security holders.

\* \* \* \* \*

### (p) Notice to a Foreign Creditor.

(1) If, at the request of a party in interest or the United States trustee, or on its own initiative, the court finds that a notice mailed within the time prescribed by these rules would not be sufficient to give a creditor with a foreign address to which notices under these rules are mailed reasonable notice under the circumstances, the court may order that the notice be supplemented with notice by other means or that the time prescribed for the notice by mail be enlarged.

(2) Unless the court for cause orders otherwise, a creditor with a foreign address to which notices under this rule are mailed shall be given at least 30 days' notice of the time fixed for filing a proof of claim under Rule 3002(c) or Rule 3003(c).

### (q) Notice of Petition for Recognition of Foreign Proceeding and of Court's Intention to Communicate with Foreign Courts and Foreign Representatives.

(1) *Notice of Petition for Recognition.* The clerk, or some other person as the court may direct, shall forthwith give the debtor, all administrators in foreign proceedings of the debtor, all entities against whom provisional relief is being sought under § 1519 of the Code, all parties to any litigation in which the debtor is a party and that is pending in the United States at the time of the filing of the petition, and such other entities as the court may direct, at least 20 days' notice by mail of the hearing on the petition for recognition of a foreign proceeding. The notice shall state whether the petition seeks recognition as a foreign main proceeding or foreign nonmain proceeding.

(2) *Notice of Court's Intention to Communicate with Foreign Courts and Foreign Representatives.* The clerk, or some other person as the court may direct, shall give the debtor, all administrators in foreign proceedings of the debtor, all entities against whom provisional relief is being sought under § 1519 of the Code, all parties to any litigation in which the debtor is a party and that is pending in the United States at the time of the filing of the petition, and such other entities as the court may direct, notice by mail of the court's intention to communicate with a foreign court or foreign representative as prescribed by Rule 5012.

### COMMITTEE NOTE
#### October 17, 2005

Subdivision (b) is amended to provide for 25 days' notice of the time for the court to make a final determination whether the plan in a small business case can serve as a disclosure statement. Conditional approval of a disclosure statement in a small business case is governed by Rule 3017.1 and does not require 25 days' notice. The court may consider this matter in a hearing combined with the confirmation hearing in a small business case.

Subdivision (c)(1) is amended to require that a trustee leasing or selling personally identifiable information under § 363(b)(1)(A) or (B) of the Code, as amended in 2005, include in the notice of the lease or sale transaction a statement as to whether the lease or sale is consistent with a policy prohibiting the transfer of the information.

Section 1514(d) of the Code, added in 2005, requires that such additional time as is reasonable under the circumstances be given to creditors with foreign addresses with respect to notices and the filing of a proof of claim. Thus, subdivision (p)(1) is added to the rule to give the court flexibility to direct that notice by other means shall supplement notice by mail, or to enlarge the notice period, for creditors with foreign addresses. If cause exists, such as likely delays in the delivery of mailed notices in particular locations, the court may order that notice also be given by e-mail, facsimile, or private courier. Alternatively, the court may enlarge the

notice period for a creditor with a foreign address. It is expected that in most situations involving foreign creditors, fairness will not require any additional notice or extension of the notice period. This rule recognizes that the court has discretion to establish procedures to determine, on its own initiative, whether relief under subdivision (p) is appropriate, but that the court is not required to establish such procedures and may decide to act only on request of a party in interest.

Subdivisions (f)(9) and (10) are new. They reflect the 2005 amendments to §§ 342(d) and 704(b) of the Bankruptcy Code. Section 342(d) requires the clerk to give notice to creditors shortly after the commencement of the case as to whether a presumption of abuse exists. Subdivision (f)(9) adds this notice to the list of notices that the clerk must give. Subdivision (f)(10) implements the amendment to § 704(b) which requires the court to provide a copy to all creditors of a statement by the United States trustee or bankruptcy administrator as to whether the debtor's case would be presumed to be an abuse under § 707(b) not later than five days after receiving it.

Subdivision (f)(11) is also added to provide notice to creditors of the debtor's filing of a statement in a chapter 11, 12, or 13 case that there is no reasonable cause to believe that § 522(q) applies in the case. If a creditor disputes that assertion, the creditor can request a delay of the entry of the discharge in the case.

Subdivision (g)(2) of the rule is amended because the 2005 amendments to § 342(f) of the Code permit creditors in chapter 7 and 13 individual debtor cases to file a notice with any bankruptcy court of the address to which the creditor wishes all notices to be sent. This provision does not apply in cases of nonindividuals in chapter 7 and in cases under chapters 11 and 12, so Rule 2002(g)(2) still operates in those circumstances. It also continues to apply in cases under chapters 7 and 13 if the creditor has not filed a notice under § 342(f). The amendment to Rule 2002(g)(2) therefore only limits that subdivision when a creditor files a notice under § 342(f).

Subdivision (p)(2) is added to the rule to grant creditors with a foreign address to which notices are mailed at least 30 days' notice of the time within which to file proofs of claims if notice is mailed to the foreign address, unless the court orders otherwise. If cause exists, such as likely delays in the delivery of notices in particular locations, the court may extend the notice period for creditors with foreign addresses. The court may also shorten the additional notice time if circumstances so warrant. For example, if the court in a chapter 11 case determines that supplementing the notice to a foreign creditor with notice by electronic means, such as e-mail or facsimile, would give the creditor reasonable notice, the court may order that the creditor be given only 20 days' notice in accordance with Rule 2002(a)(7).

Subdivision (q) is added to require that notice of the hearing on the petition for recognition of a foreign proceeding be given to the debtor, all administrators in foreign proceedings of the debtor, entities against whom provisional relief is sought, and entities with whom the debtor is engaged in litigation at the time of the commencement of the case. There is no need at this stage of the proceedings to provide notice to all creditors. If the foreign representative should take action to commence a case under another chapter of the Code, the rules governing those proceedings will operate to provide that notice is given to all creditors.

The rule also requires notice of the court's intention to communicate with a foreign court or foreign representative under Rule 5012.

Amended, on an interim basis, effective October 17, 2005.

## INTERIM RULE 2003.  MEETING OF CREDITORS OR EQUITY SECURITY HOLDERS

   (a) **Date and Place**. Except as provided in § 341(e) of the Code, in a chapter 7 liquidation or a chapter 11 reorganization case, the United States trustee shall call a meeting of creditors to be held no fewer than 20 and no more than 40 days after the order for relief. In a chapter 12 family farmer debt adjustment case, the United States trustee shall call a meeting of creditors to be held no fewer than 20 and no more than 35 days after the order for relief. In a chapter 13 individual's debt adjustment case, the United States trustee shall call a meeting of creditors to be held no fewer than 20 and no more than 50 days after the order for relief. If there is an appeal from or a motion to vacate the order for relief, or if there is a motion to dismiss the case, the United States trustee may set a later date for the meeting. The meeting may be held at a regular place for holding court or at any other place designated by the United States trustee within the district convenient for the parties

in interest. If the United States trustee designates a place for the meeting which is not regularly staffed by the United States trustee or an assistant who may preside at the meeting, the meeting may be held not more than 60 days after the order for relief.

\* \* \* \* \*

**COMMITTEE NOTE**
**October 17, 2005**

If the debtor has solicited acceptances to a plan before commencement of the case, § 341(e), which was added to the Bankruptcy Code in 2005, authorizes the court, on request of a party in interest and after notice and a hearing, to order that a meeting of creditors not be convened. The rule is amended to recognize that a meeting of creditors might not be held in those cases.

Amended, on an interim basis, effective October 17, 2005.

## INTERIM RULE 2007.1   APPOINTMENT OF TRUSTEE OR EXAMINER IN A CHAPTER 11 REORGANIZATION CASE

\* \* \* \* \*

**(b) Election of Trustee.**

\* \* \* \* \*

(3) *Report of Election and Resolution of Disputes.*

(A) Report of Undisputed Election. If no dispute arises out of the election, the United States trustee shall promptly file a report certifying the election, including the name and address of the person elected and a statement that the election is undisputed. The report shall be accompanied by a verified statement of the person elected setting forth the person's connections with the debtor, creditors, any other party in interest, their respective attorneys and accountants, the United States trustee, or any person employed in the office of the United States trustee.

(B) Dispute Arising Out of an Election. If a dispute arises out of an election, the United States trustee shall promptly file a report stating that the election is disputed, informing the court of the nature of the dispute, and listing the name and address of any candidate elected under any alternative presented by the dispute. The report shall be accompanied by a verified statement by each candidate elected under each alternative presented by the dispute, setting forth the person's connections with the debtor, creditors, any other party in interest, their respective attorneys and accountants, the United States trustee, or any person employed in the office of the United States trustee. Not later than the date on which the report of the disputed election is filed, the United States trustee shall mail a copy of the report and each verified statement to any party in interest that has made a request to convene a meeting under § 1104(b) or to receive a copy of the report, and to any committee appointed under § 1102 of the Code.

**(c) Approval of Appointment.** An order approving the appointment of a trustee or an examiner under § 1104(d) of the Code, shall be made on application of the United States trustee. The application shall state the name of the person appointed and, to the best of the applicant's knowledge, all the person's connections with the debtor, creditors, any other parties in interest, their respective attorneys and accountants, the United States trustee, or persons employed in the office of the United States trustee. The application shall state the names of the parties in interest with whom the United States trustee consulted regarding the appointment. The application shall be accompanied by a verified statement of the person appointed setting forth the person's connections with the debtor, creditors, any other party in interest, their respective attorneys and accountants, the United States trustee, or any person employed in the office of the United States trustee.

**COMMITTEE NOTE**
**October 17, 2005**

Under § 1104(b)(2) of the Code, as amended in 2005, if an eligible, disinterested person is elected to serve as trustee in a chapter 11 case, the United States trustee is directed to file a

report certifying the election. The person elected does not have to be appointed to the position. Rather, the filing of the report certifying the election itself constitutes the appointment. The section further provides that in the event of a dispute in the election of a trustee, the court must resolve the matter. The rule is amended to be consistent with § 1104(b)(2).

When the United States trustee files a report certifying the election of a trustee, the person elected must provide a verified statement, similar to the statement required of professional persons under Rule 2014, disclosing connections with parties in interest and certain other persons connected with the case. Although court approval of the person elected is not required, the disclosure of the person's connections will enable parties in interest to determine whether the person is disinterested.

Amended, on an interim basis, effective October 17, 2005.

## INTERIM RULE 2007.2  APPOINTMENT OF PATIENT CARE OMBUDSMAN IN A HEALTH CARE BUSINESS CASE

**(a) Order to Appoint Patient Care Ombudsman.** In a chapter 7, chapter 9, or chapter 11 case in which the debtor is a health care business, the court shall order the appointment of a patient care ombudsman under § 333 of the Code, unless the court, on motion of the United States trustee or a party in interest filed not later than 20 days after the commencement of the case or within another time fixed by the court, finds that the appointment of a patient care ombudsman is not necessary for the protection of patients under the specific circumstances of the case.

**(b) Motion for Order to Appoint Ombudsman.** If the court has ordered that the appointment of an ombudsman is not necessary, or has ordered the termination of the appointment of an ombudsman, the court, on motion of the United States trustee or a party in interest, may order the appointment at any time during the case if the court finds that the appointment of an ombudsman has become necessary to protect patients.

**(c) Appointment of Ombudsman.** If a patient care ombudsman is appointed under § 333, the United States trustee shall promptly file a notice of the appointment, including the name and address of the person appointed. Unless the person appointed is a State Long–Term Care Ombudsman, the notice shall be accompanied by a verified statement of the person appointed setting forth the person's connections with the debtor, creditors, patients, any other party in interest, their respective attorneys and accountants, the United States trustee, and any person employed in the office of the United States trustee.

**(d) Termination of Appointment.** On motion of the United States trustee or a party in interest, the court may terminate the appointment of a patient care ombudsman if the court finds that the appointment is not necessary for the protection of patients.

**(e) Motion.** A motion under this rule shall be governed by Rule 9014. The motion shall be transmitted to the United States trustee and served on the debtor, the trustee, any committee elected under § 705 or appointed under § 1102 of the Code or its authorized agent, or, if the case is a chapter 9 municipality case or a chapter 11 reorganization case and no committee of unsecured creditors has been appointed under § 1102, on the creditors included on the list filed under Rule 1007(d), and such other entities as the court may direct.

### COMMITTEE NOTE
#### October 17, 2005

Section 333 of the Code, added in 2005, requires the court to order the appointment of a health care ombudsman within the first 30 days of a health care business case, unless the court finds that the appointment is not necessary for the protection of patients. The rule recognizes this requirement and provides a procedure by which a party may obtain a court order finding that the appointment of a patient care ombudsman is unnecessary. In the absence of a timely motion under subdivision (a) of this rule, the court will enter an order directing the United States trustee to appoint the ombudsman.

Subdivision (b) recognizes that, despite a previous order finding that a patient care ombudsman is not necessary, circumstances of the case may change or newly discovered

evidence may demonstrate the necessity of an ombudsman to protect the interests of patients. In that event, a party may move the court for an order directing the appointment of an ombudsman.

When the appointment of a patient care ombudsman is ordered, the United States trustee is required to appoint a disinterested person to serve in that capacity. Court approval of the appointment is not required, but subdivision (c) requires the person appointed, if not a State Long–Term Care Ombudsman, to file a verified statement similar to the statement filed by professional persons under Rule 2014 so that parties in interest will have information relevant to disinterestedness. If a party believes that the person appointed is not disinterested, it may file a motion asking the court to find that the person is not eligible to serve.

Subdivision (d) permits parties in interest to move for the termination of the appointment of a patient care ombudsman. If the movant can show that there no longer is any need for the ombudsman, the court may order the termination of the appointment.

Amended, on an interim basis, effective October 17, 2005.

## INTERIM RULE 2015. DUTY TO KEEP RECORDS, MAKE REPORTS, AND GIVE NOTICE OF CASE OR CHANGE OF STATUS

\* \* \* \* \*

(d) **Foreign Representative.** In a case in which the court has granted recognition of a foreign proceeding under chapter 15, the foreign representative shall file any notice required under § 1518 of the Code within 15 days after the date when the representative becomes aware of the subsequent information.

(e) **Transmission of Reports.** In a chapter 11 case the court may direct that copies or summaries of annual reports and copies or summaries of other reports shall be mailed to the creditors, equity security holders, and indenture trustees. The court may also direct the publication of summaries of any such reports. A copy of every report or summary mailed or published pursuant to this subdivision shall be transmitted to the United States trustee.

### COMMITTEE NOTE
#### October 17, 2005

The rule is amended to fix the time for the filing of notices under § 1519 which was added to the Code in 2005. Former subdivision (d) is renumbered as subdivision (e).

Amended, on an interim basis, effective October 17, 2005.

## INTERIM RULE 2015.1 PATIENT CARE OMBUDSMAN

(a) **Reports.** Unless the court orders otherwise, a patient care ombudsman, at least 10 days before making a report under § 333(b)(2) of the Code, shall give notice that the report will be made to the court. The notice shall be transmitted to the United States trustee, posted conspicuously at the health care facility that is the subject of the report, and served on the debtor, the trustee, all patients, and any committee elected under § 705 or appointed under § 1102 of the Code or its authorized agent, or, if the case is a chapter 9 municipality case or a chapter 11 reorganization case and no committee of unsecured creditors has been appointed under § 1102, on the creditors included on the list filed under Rule 1007(d), and such other entities as the court may direct. The notice shall state the date and time when the report will be made, the manner in which the report will be made, and, if the report is in writing, the name, address, telephone number, e-mail address, and website, if any, of the person from whom a copy of the report may be obtained at the debtor's expense.

(b) **Authorization to Review Confidential Patient Records.** A motion by a health care ombudsman under § 333(c) to review confidential patient records shall be governed by Rule 9014, served on the patient and any family member or other contact person whose name and address has been given to the trustee or the debtor for the purpose of providing information regarding the patient's health care, and

transmitted to the United States trustee subject to applicable nonbankruptcy law relating to patient privacy. Unless the court orders otherwise, a hearing on the motion may be commenced no earlier than 15 days after service of the motion.

## COMMITTEE NOTE
### October 17, 2005

This rule is new. It implements § 333, added to the Code in 2005. Subdivision (a) is designed to give parties in interest, including patients or their representatives, sufficient notice so that they will be able to review written reports or attend hearings at which reports are made. The rule permits a notice to relate to a single report or to periodic reports to be given during the case. For example, the ombudsman may give notice that reports will be made at specified intervals or dates during the case.

Subdivision (a) of the rule requires that the notice be posted conspicuously at the health care facility in a place where it will be seen by patients and their families or others visiting the patient. This may require posting in common areas and patient rooms within the facility. Because health care facilities and the patients they serve can vary greatly, the locations of the posted notice should be tailored to the specific facility that is the subject of the report.

Subdivision (b) requires the ombudsman to notify the patient and the United States trustee that the ombudsman is seeking access to confidential patient records so that they will be able to appear and be heard on the matter. This procedure should assist the court in reaching its decision both as to access to the records and appropriate restrictions on that access to ensure continued confidentiality. Notices given under this rule are subject to provisions under applicable federal and state law that relate to the protection of patients' privacy, such as the Health Insurance Portability and Accountability Act of 1996, Pub. L. No. 104–191 (HIPAA).

Amended, on an interim basis, effective October 17, 2005.

## INTERIM RULE 2015.2   TRANSFER OF PATIENT IN HEALTH CARE BUSINESS CASE

Unless the court orders otherwise, if the debtor is a health care business, the trustee may not transfer a patient to another health care business under § 704(a)(12) of the Code unless the trustee gives at least 10 days' notice of the transfer to the patient care ombudsman, if any, and to the patient and any family member or other contact person whose name and address has been given to the trustee or the debtor for the purpose of providing information regarding the patient's health care subject to applicable nonbankruptcy law relating to patient privacy.

## COMMITTEE NOTE
### October 17, 2005

This rule is new. Section 704(a)(12), added to the Code in 2005, authorizes the trustee to relocate patients when a health care business debtor's facility is in the process of being closed. The Code permits the trustee to take this action without the need for any court order, but the notice required by this rule will enable a patient care ombudsman appointed under § 333, or a patient who contends that the trustee's actions violate § 704(a)(12), to have those issues resolved before the patient is transferred.

This rule also permits the court to enter an order dispensing with or altering the notice requirement in proper circumstances. The facility could be closed immediately, or very quickly, such that 10 days' notice would not be possible in some instances. In that event, the court may shorten the time required for notice.

Notices given under this rule are subject to provisions under applicable federal and state law that relate to the protection of patients' privacy, such as the Health Insurance Portability and Accountability Act of 1996, Pub. L. No. 104–191 (HIPAA).

Amended, on an interim basis, effective October 17, 2005.

## INTERIM RULE 3002.   FILING PROOF OF CLAIM OR INTEREST

* * * * *

(c) **Time for Filing.** In a chapter 7 liquidation, chapter 12 family farmer's debt adjustment, or chapter 13 individual's debt adjustment case, a proof of claim is

timely filed if it is filed not later than 90 days after the first date set for the meeting of creditors called under § 341(a) of the Code, except as follows:

(1) A proof of claim filed by a governmental unit, other than for a claim resulting from a tax return filed under § 1308, is timely filed if it is filed not later than 180 days after the date of the order for relief. On motion of a governmental unit before the expiration of such period and for cause shown, the court may extend the time for filing of a claim by the governmental unit. A proof of claim filed by a governmental unit for a claim resulting from a tax return filed under § 1308 is timely filed if it is filed not later than 180 days after the date of the order for relief or 60 days after the date of the filing of the tax return, whichever is later.

\* \* \* \* \*

(6) If notice of the time for filing a proof of claim has been mailed to a creditor at a foreign address, on motion filed by the creditor before or after the expiration of the time, the court may extend the time by not more than 60 days if the court finds that the notice was not sufficient under the circumstances to give the creditor a reasonable time to file a proof of claim.

**COMMITTEE NOTE**
**October 17, 2005**

Subdivision (c)(1) is amended to reflect the addition of § 1308 to the Bankruptcy Code in 2005. This provision requires that chapter 13 debtors file tax returns during the pendency of the case, and imposes bankruptcy-related consequences if debtors fail to do so. Subdivision (c)(1) provides additional time for governmental units to file a proof of claim for tax obligations with respect to tax returns filed during the pendency of a chapter 13 case.

Paragraph (c)(6) is added to give the court discretion to extend the time for filing a proof of claim for a creditor who received notice of the time to file the claim at a foreign address, if the court finds that the notice was not sufficient, under the particular circumstances, to give the foreign creditor a reasonable time to file a proof of claim. This amendment is designed to comply with § 1514(d), which was added to the Code in 2005 and requires that the rules and orders of the court provide such additional time as is reasonable under the circumstances for foreign creditors to file claims in cases under all chapters of the Code.

Amended, on an interim basis, effective October 17, 2005.

# INTERIM RULE 3003. FILING PROOF OF CLAIM OR EQUITY SECURITY INTEREST IN CHAPTER 9 MUNICIPALITY OR CHAPTER 11 REORGANIZATION CASES

\* \* \* \* \*

### (c) Filing Proof of Claim.

(1) *Who May File.* Any creditor or indenture trustee may file a proof of claim within the time prescribed by subdivision (c)(3) of this rule.

(2) *Who Must File.* Any creditor or equity security holder whose claim or interest is not scheduled or scheduled as disputed, contingent, or unliquidated shall file a proof of claim or interest within the time prescribed by subdivision (c)(3) of this rule; any creditor who fails to do so shall not be treated as a creditor with respect to such claim for the purposes of voting and distribution.

(3) *Time for Filing.* The court shall fix and for cause shown may extend the time within which proofs of claim or interest may be filed. Notwithstanding the expiration of such time, a proof of claim may be filed to the extent and under the conditions stated in Rule 3002(c)(2), (c)(3), (c)(4), and (c)(6).

(4) *Effect of Filing Claim or Interest.* A proof of claim or interest executed and filed in accordance with this subdivision shall supersede any scheduling of that claim or interest pursuant to § 521(a)(1) of the Code.

(5) *Filing by Indenture Trustee.* An indenture trustee may file a claim on behalf of all known or unknown holders of securities issued pursuant to the trust instrument under which it is trustee.

\* \* \* \* \*

### COMMITTEE NOTE
### October 17, 2005

The rule is amended to implement § 1514(d), which was added to the Code in 2005, by making the new Rule 3002(c)(6) applicable in chapter 9 and chapter 11 cases. Section 1514(d) requires that creditors with foreign addresses be provided such additional time as is reasonable under the circumstances to file proofs of claims.

Amended, on an interim basis, effective October 17, 2005.

## INTERIM RULE 3016.   FILING OF PLAN AND DISCLOSURE STATEMENT IN A CHAPTER 9 MUNICIPALITY OR CHAPTER 11 REORGANIZATION CASE

\* \* \* \* \*

**(b) Disclosure Statement.** In a chapter 9 or 11 case, a disclosure statement under § 1125 or evidence showing compliance with § 1126(b) of the Code shall be filed with the plan or within a time fixed by the court, unless the plan is intended to provide adequate information under § 1125(f)(1). If the plan is intended to provide adequate information under § 1125(f)(1), it shall be so designated and Rule 3017.1 shall apply as if the plan is a disclosure statement.

\* \* \* \* \*

### COMMITTEE NOTE
### October 17, 2005

Subdivision (b) is amended to recognize that, in 2005, § 1125(f)(1) was added to the Code to provide that the plan proponent in a small business case need not file a disclosure statement if the plan itself includes adequate information and the court finds that a separate disclosure statement is unnecessary. If the plan is intended to provide adequate information in a small business case, it may be conditionally approved as a disclosure statement under Rule 3017.1 and is subject to all other rules applicable to disclosure statements in small business cases.

Amended, on an interim basis, effective October 17, 2005.

## INTERIM RULE 3017.1   COURT CONSIDERATION OF DISCLOSURE STATEMENT IN A SMALL BUSINESS CASE

**(a) Conditional Approval of Disclosure Statement.** In a small business case, the court may, on application of the plan proponent or on its own initiative, conditionally approve a disclosure statement filed in accordance with Rule 3016. On or before conditional approval of the disclosure statement, the court shall:

(1) fix a time within which the holders of claims and interests may accept or reject the plan;

(2) fix a time for filing objections to the disclosure statement;

(3) fix a date for the hearing on final approval of the disclosure statement to be held if a timely objection is filed; and

(4) fix a date for the hearing on confirmation.

**(b) Application of Rule 3017.** Rule 3017(a), (b), (c), and (e) do not apply to a conditionally approved disclosure statement. Rule 3017(d) applies to a conditionally

approved disclosure statement, except that conditional approval is considered approval of the disclosure statement for the purpose of applying Rule 3017(d).

**(c) Final Approval.**

(1) *Notice.* Notice of the time fixed for filing objections and the hearing to consider final approval of the disclosure statement shall be given in accordance with Rule 2002 and may be combined with notice of the hearing on confirmation of the plan.

(2) *Objections.* Objections to the disclosure statement shall be filed, transmitted to the United States trustee, and served on the debtor, the trustee, any committee appointed under the Code and any other entity designated by the court at any time before final approval of the disclosure statement or by an earlier date as the court may fix.

(3) *Hearing.* If a timely objection to the disclosure statement is filed, the court shall hold a hearing to consider final approval before or combined with the hearing on confirmation of the plan.

**COMMITTEE NOTE**
October 17, 2005

Section 101 of the Code, as amended in 2005, defines a "small business case" and "small business debtor,"and eliminates any need to elect that status. Therefore, the reference in the rule to an election is deleted.

As provided in the amendment to Rule 3016(b), a plan intended to provide adequate information in a small business case under § 1125(f)(1) may be conditionally approved and is otherwise treated as a disclosure statement under this rule.

Amended, on an interim basis, effective October 17, 2005.

**INTERIM RULE 3019. MODIFICATION OF ACCEPTED PLAN BEFORE OR AFTER CONFIRMATION IN A CHAPTER 9 MUNICIPALITY OR CHAPTER 11 REORGANIZATION CASE**

**(a)** In a chapter 9 or chapter 11 case, after a plan has been accepted and before its confirmation, the proponent may file a modification of the plan. If the court finds after hearing on notice to the trustee, any committee appointed under the Code, and any other entity designated by the court that the proposed modification does not adversely change the treatment of the claim of any creditor or the interest of any equity security holder who has not accepted in writing the modification, it shall be deemed accepted by all creditors and equity security holders who have previously accepted the plan.

**(b)** If the debtor is an individual, a request to modify the plan under § 1127(e) of the Code shall identify the proponent and shall be filed together with the proposed modification. The clerk, or some other person as the court may direct, shall give the debtor, the trustee, and all creditors not less than 20 days' notice by mail of the time fixed for filing objections and, if an objection is filed, the hearing to consider the proposed modification, unless the court orders otherwise with respect to creditors who are not affected by the proposed modification. A copy of the notice shall be transmitted to the United States trustee. A copy of the proposed modification shall be included with the notice. Any objection to the proposed modification shall be filed and served on the debtor, the proponent of the modification, the trustee, and any other entity designated by the court, and shall be transmitted to the United States trustee. An objection to a proposed modification is governed by Rule 9014.

**COMMITTEE NOTE**
October 17, 2005

Section 1127 was amended in 2005 to provide for modification of a confirmed plan in a chapter 11 case of an individual debtor. The rule is amended to establish the procedure for filing and objecting to a proposed modification of a confirmed plan.

Amended, on an interim basis, effective October 17, 2005.

## INTERIM RULE 4002.   DUTIES OF DEBTOR

**(a) In General.** In addition to performing other duties prescribed by the Code and rules, the debtor shall:

(1) attend and submit to an examination at the times ordered by the court;

(2) attend the hearing on a complaint objecting to discharge and testify, if called as a witness;

(3) inform the trustee immediately in writing as to the location of real property in which the debtor has an interest and the name and address of every person holding money or property subject to the debtor's withdrawal or order if a schedule of property has not yet been filed pursuant to Rule 1007;

(4) cooperate with the trustee in the preparation of an inventory, the examination of proofs of claim, and the administration of the estate; and

(5) file a statement of any change of the debtor's address.

**(b) Individual Debtor's Duty to Provide Documentation.**

(1) *Personal Identification.* Every individual debtor shall bring to the meeting of creditors under § 341:

(A) a picture identification issued by a governmental unit, or other personal identifying information that establishes the debtor's identity; and

(B) evidence of social security number(s), or a written statement that such documentation does not exist.

(2) *Financial Information.* Every individual debtor shall bring to the meeting of creditors under § 341 and make available to the trustee the following documents or copies of them, or provide a written statement that the documentation does not exist or is not in the debtor's possession:

(A) evidence of current income such as the most recent payment advice;

(B) unless the trustee or the United States trustee instructs otherwise, statements for each of the debtor's depository and investment accounts, including checking, savings, and money market accounts, mutual funds and brokerage accounts for the time period that includes the date of the filing of the petition; and

(C) documentation of monthly expenses claimed by the debtor when required by § 707(b)(2)(A) or (B).

(3) *Tax Return.* At least 7 days before the first date set for the meeting of creditors under § 341, the debtor shall provide to the trustee a copy of the debtor's Federal income tax return for the most recent tax year ending immediately before the commencement of the case and for which a return was filed, including any attachments, or a transcript of the tax return, or provide a written statement that the documentation does not exist.

(4) *Tax Returns Provided to Creditors.* If a creditor, at least 15 days before the first date set for the meeting of creditors under § 341, requests a copy of the debtor's tax return that is to be provided to the trustee under subdivision (b)(3), the debtor shall provide to the requesting creditor a copy of the return, including any attachments, or a transcript of the tax return, or provide a written statement that the documentation does not exist at least 7 days before the first date set for the meeting of creditors under § 341.

(5) The debtor's obligation to provide tax returns under Rule 4002(b)(3) and (b)(4) is subject to procedures for safeguarding the confidentiality of tax information established by the Director of the Administrative Office of the United States Courts.

**COMMITTEE NOTE**
October 17, 2005

This rule is amended to implement the directives of § 521(a) (1)(B)(iv) and (e)(2) of the Code, which were added by the 2005 amendments. These Code amendments expressly require the debtor to file with the court, or provide to the trustee, specific documents. The amendments to the rule implement these obligations and establish a time frame for creditors to make requests

for a copy of the debtor's Federal income tax return. The rule also requires the debtor to provide documentation in support of claimed expenses under § 707(b)(2)(A) and (B).

Subdivision (b) is also amended to require the debtor to cooperate with the trustee by providing materials and documents necessary to assist the trustee in the performance of the trustee's duties. Nothing in the rule, however, is intended to limit or restrict the debtor's duties under § 521, or to limit the access of the Attorney General to any information provided by the debtor in the case. The rule does not require that the debtor create documents or obtain documents from third parties; rather, the debtor's obligation is to bring to the meeting of creditors under § 341 the documents which the debtor possesses. Any written statement that the debtor provides indicating either that documents do not exist or are not in the debtor's possession must be verified or contain an unsworn declaration as required under Rule 1008.

Because the amendment implements the debtor's duty to cooperate with the trustee, the materials provided to the trustee would not be made available to any other party in interest at the § 341 meeting of creditors other than the Attorney General. Some of the documents may contain otherwise private information that should not be disseminated. For example, pay stubs and financial account statements might include the social security numbers of the debtor and the debtor's spouse and dependents, as well as the names of the debtor's children. The debtor should redact all but the last four digits of all social security numbers and the names of any minors when they appear in these documents. This type of information would not usually be needed by creditors and others who may be attending the meeting. If a creditor perceives a need to review specific documents or other evidence, the creditor may proceed under Rule 2004.

Tax information produced under this rule is subject to procedures for safeguarding confidentiality established by the Director of the Administrative Office of the United States Courts.

Amended, on an interim basis, effective October 17, 2005.

# INTERIM RULE 4003. EXEMPTIONS

\* \* \* \* \*

### (b) Objecting to a Claim of Exemptions.

(1) Except as provided in paragraph (2), a party in interest may file an objection to the list of property claimed as exempt within 30 days after the meeting of creditors held under § 341(a) is concluded or within 30 days after any amendment to the list or supplemental schedules is filed, whichever is later. The court may, for cause, extend the time for filing objections if, before the time to object expires, a party in interest files a request for an extension.

(2) An objection to a claim of exemption based on § 522(q) shall be filed before the closing of the case. If an exemption is first claimed after a case is reopened, an objection shall be filed before the reopened case is closed.

(3) Copies of the objections shall be delivered or mailed to the trustee, the person filing the list, and the attorney for that person.

\* \* \* \* \*

### COMMITTEE NOTE
#### October 17, 2005

Subdivision (b) is amended to reflect the 2005 addition of subsection (q) to § 522 of the Bankruptcy Code. Section 522(q) imposes a $125,000 limit on a state homestead exemption if the debtor has been convicted of a felony or owes a debt arising from certain causes of action. Other revised provisions of the Bankruptcy Code, such as § 727(a)(12) and § 1328(h), suggest that the court may consider issues relating to § 522 late in the case, and the 30–day period for objections would not be appropriate for this provision. A new subdivision (b)(2) is added to provide a separate time limit for this provision.

Amended, on an interim basis, effective October 17, 2005.

## INTERIM RULE 4004. GRANT OR DENIAL OF DISCHARGE

\* \* \* \* \*

### (c) Grant of Discharge.

(1) In a chapter 7 case, on expiration of the time fixed for filing a complaint objecting to discharge and the time fixed for filing a motion to dismiss the case under Rule 1017(e), the court shall forthwith grant the discharge unless:

\* \* \* \* \*

(F) a motion to extend the time for filing a motion to dismiss the case under Rule 1017(e) is pending,

(G) the debtor has not paid in full the filing fee prescribed by 28 U.S.C. § 1930(a) and any other fee prescribed by the Judicial Conference of the United States under 28 U.S.C. § 1930(b) that is payable to the clerk upon the commencement of a case under the Code, unless the court has waived the fees under 28 U.S.C. § 1930(f);

(H) the debtor has not filed with the court a statement regarding completion of a course in personal financial management as required by Rule 1007(b)(7);

(I) a motion to delay or postpone discharge under § 727(a)(12) is pending; or

(J) a presumption that a reaffirmation agreement is an undue hardship has arisen under § 524(m); or

(K) a motion to delay discharge, alleging that the debtor has not filed with the court all tax documents required to be filed under § 521(f), is pending.

\* \* \* \* \*

(3) If the debtor is required to file a statement under Rule 1007(b)(8), the court shall not grant a discharge earlier than 30 days after the filing of the statement.

### COMMITTEE NOTE
### October 17, 2005

Subdivision (c)(1)(G) is amended to reflect the fee waiver provision added in 2005 to 28 U.S.C. § 1930.

Subdivision (c)(1)(H) is new. It reflects the 2005 addition to the Bankruptcy Code of §§ 727(a)(11) and 1328(g), which require that individual debtors complete a course in personal financial management as a condition to the entry of a discharge. Including this requirement in the rule helps prevent the inadvertent entry of a discharge when the debtor has not complied with this requirement. If a debtor fails to file the required statement regarding a personal financial management course, the clerk will close the bankruptcy case without the entry of a discharge.

Subdivision (c)(1)(I) is new. It reflects the 2005 addition to the Bankruptcy Code of § 727(a)(12). This provision is linked to § 522(q). Section 522(q) limits the availability of the homestead exemption for individuals who have been convicted of a felony or who owe a debt arising from certain causes of action within a particular time frame. The existence of reasonable cause to believe that § 522(q) may be applicable to the debtor constitutes grounds for withholding the discharge.

Subdivision (c)(1)(J) is new. It reflects the 2005 revisions to § 524 of the Bankruptcy Code that alter the requirements for approval of reaffirmation agreements. Section 524(m) sets forth circumstances under which a reaffirmation agreement is presumed to be an undue hardship. This triggers an obligation to review the presumption and may require notice and a hearing. Subdivision (c)(1)(J) has been added to prevent the discharge from being entered until the court approves or disapproves the reaffirmation agreement in accordance with § 524(m).

Subdivision (c)(1)(K) is new. It implements § 1228(a) of Public Law No. 109–8.

The rule is also amended by adding subdivision (c)(3) that postpones the entry of the discharge of an individual debtor in a case under chapter 11, 12, or 13 if there is a question as

to the applicability of § 522(q) of the Code. The postponement provides an opportunity for a creditor to file a motion to limit the debtor's exemption under that provision.

Amended, on an interim basis, effective October 17, 2005.

## INTERIM RULE 4006.  NOTICE OF NO DISCHARGE

If an order is entered denying or revoking a discharge or if a waiver of discharge is filed, the clerk, after the order becomes final or the waiver is filed, or, in the case of an individual, if the case is closed without the entry of an order of discharge, shall promptly give notice thereof to all parties in interest in the manner provided in Rule 2002.

### COMMITTEE NOTE
### October 17, 2005

Rule 4006 is amended to reflect the 2005 revisions to the Bankruptcy Code requiring that individual debtors complete a course in personal financial management as a condition to the entry of a discharge. If the debtor fails to complete the course, no discharge will be entered, but the case may be closed. The amended rule provides notice to parties in interest, including the debtor, that no discharge was entered.

Amended, on an interim basis, effective October 17, 2005.

## INTERIM RULE 4007.  DETERMINATION OF DISCHARGEABILITY OF A DEBT

\* \* \* \* \*

(c) **Time for Filing Complaint Under § 523(C) in a Chapter 7 Liquidation, Chapter 11 Reorganization, Chapter 12 Family Farmer's Debt Adjustment Case, or Chapter 13 Individual's Debt Adjustment Case; Notice of Time Fixed.** Except as provided in subdivision (d), a complaint to determine the dischargeability of a debt under § 523(c) shall be filed no later than 60 days after the first date set for the meeting of creditors under § 341(a). The court shall give all creditors no less than 30 days' notice of the time so fixed in the manner provided in Rule 2002. On motion of a party in interest, after hearing on notice, the court may for cause extend the time fixed under this subdivision. The motion shall be filed before the time has expired.

(d) **Time for Filing Complaint Under § 523(A)(6) in Chapter 13 Individual's Debt Adjustment Case; Notice of Time Fixed.** On motion by a debtor for a discharge under § 1328(b), the court shall enter an order fixing the time to file a complaint to determine the dischargeability of any debt under § 523(a)(6) and shall give no less than 30 days' notice of the time fixed to all creditors in the manner provided in Rule 2002. On motion of any party in interest after hearing on notice the court may for cause extend the time fixed under this subdivision. The motion shall be filed before the time has expired.

\* \* \* \* \*

### COMMITTEE NOTE
### October 17, 2005

Subdivision (c) is amended to reflect the 2005 amendments to § 1328(a) of the Bankruptcy Code. This revision expands the exceptions to discharge upon completion of a chapter 13 plan. Subdivision (c) extends to chapter 13 the same time limits applicable to other chapters of the Code with respect to the two exceptions to discharge that have been added to § 1328(a) and that are within § 523(c).

The amendment to subdivision (d) reflects the 2005 amendments to § 1328(a) that expands the exceptions to discharge upon completion of a chapter 13 plan, including two out of three of the provisions that fall within § 523(c). However, the 2005 revisions to § 1328(a) do not include a reference to § 523(a)(6), which is the third provision to which § 523(c) refers. Thus, the need for subdivision (d) is now limited to that provision.

Amended, on an interim basis, effective October 17, 2005.

# INTERIM RULE 4008.   DISCHARGE AND REAFFIRMATION HEARING

Not more than 30 days following the entry of an order granting or denying a discharge, or confirming a plan in a chapter 11 reorganization case concerning an individual debtor and on not less than 10 days' notice to the debtor and the trustee, the court may hold a hearing as provided in § 524(d) of the Code. A motion by the debtor for approval of a reaffirmation agreement shall be filed before or at the hearing. The debtor's statement required under § 524(k) shall be accompanied by a statement of the total income and total expense amounts stated on schedules I and J. If there is a difference between the income and expense amounts stated on schedules I and J and the statement required under § 524(k), the accompanying statement shall include an explanation of any difference.

## COMMITTEE NOTE
### October 17, 2005

Rule 4008 is amended to reflect the 2005 addition of §§ 524(k)(6)(A) and 524(m) to the Bankruptcy Code. These provisions require that a debtor file a signed statement in support of a reaffirmation agreement, and authorize a court to review the agreement if, based on the assertions on the statement, the agreement is presumed to be an undue hardship. The rule revision requires that an accompanying statement show the total income and expense amounts stated on schedules I and J and an explanation of any discrepancies. This will allow the court to evaluate the reaffirmation for undue hardship as § 524(m) requires. A corresponding change has been made to Rule 4004(c) to prevent the entry of a discharge until the court has approved or disapproved the reaffirmation agreement in accordance with § 524(m).

Amended, on an interim basis, effective October 17, 2005.

# INTERIM RULE 5003.   RECORDS KEPT BY THE CLERK

\* \* \* \* \*

(e) **Register of Mailing Addresses of Federal and State Governmental Units and Certain Taxing Authorities.** The United States or the state or territory in which the court is located may file a statement designating its mailing address. The United States, state, territory, or local governmental unit responsible for the collection of taxes within the district in which the case is pending may file a statement designating an address for service of requests under § 505(b) of the Code, and the designation shall describe where further information concerning additional requirements for filing such requests may be found. The clerk shall keep, in the form and manner as the Director of the Administrative Office of the United States Courts may prescribe, a register that includes the mailing addresses designated under this subdivision, but the clerk is not required to include in the register more than one mailing address for each department, agency, or instrumentality of the United States or the state or territory. If more than one address for a department, agency, or instrumentality is included in the register, the clerk shall also include information that would enable a user of the register to determine the circumstances when each address is applicable, and mailing notice to only one applicable address is sufficient to provide effective notice. The clerk shall update the register annually, effective January 2 of each year. The mailing address in the register is conclusively presumed to be a proper address for the governmental unit, but the failure to use that mailing address does not invalidate any notice that is otherwise effective under applicable law.

\* \* \* \* \*

## COMMITTEE NOTE
### October 17, 2005

The rule is amended to implement the addition of § 505(b)(1) to the Code in 2005, which allows taxing authorities to designate addresses to use for the service of a request under that subsection.

Amended, on an interim basis, effective October 17, 2005.

## INTERIM RULE 5008.  NOTICE REGARDING PRESUMPTION OF ABUSE IN CHAPTER 7 CASES OF INDIVIDUAL DEBTORS

In a chapter 7 case of an individual with primarily consumer debts in which a presumption of abuse has arisen under § 707(b), the clerk shall give to creditors notice of the presumption of abuse in accordance with Rule 2002 within 10 days after the date of the filing of the petition. If the debtor has not filed a statement indicating whether a presumption of abuse has arisen, the clerk shall give notice to creditors within 10 days after the date of the filing of the petition that the debtor has not filed the statement and that further notice will be given if a later filed statement indicates that a presumption of abuse has arisen. If a debtor later files a statement indicating that a presumption of abuse has arisen, the clerk shall give notice to creditors of the presumption of abuse as promptly as practicable.

### COMMITTEE NOTE
#### October 17, 2005

This rule is new. The 2005 revisions to § 342 of the Bankruptcy Code require that clerks give written notice to all creditors not later than 10 days after the date of the filing of the petition that a presumption of abuse has arisen under § 707(b). A statement filed by the debtor will be the source of the clerk's information about the presumption of abuse. This rule enables the clerk to meet its obligation to send the notice within the statutory time period set forth in § 342. In the event that the court receives the debtor's statement after the clerk has sent the first notice, and the debtor's statement indicates a presumption of abuse, this rule requires that the clerk send a second notice.

Amended, on an interim basis, effective October 17, 2005.

## INTERIM RULE 5012.  COMMUNICATION AND COOPERATION WITH FOREIGN COURTS AND FOREIGN REPRESENTATIVES

Except for communications for scheduling and administrative purposes, the court in any case commenced by a foreign representative shall give at least 20 days' notice of its intent to communicate with a foreign court or a foreign representative. The notice shall identify the subject of the anticipated communication and shall be given in the manner provided by Rule 2002(q). Any entity that wishes to participate in the communication shall notify the court of its intention not later than 5 days before the scheduled communication.

### COMMITTEE NOTE
#### October 17, 2005

This rule is new. It implements § 1525 which was added to the Code in 2005. The rule provides an opportunity for parties in the case to take appropriate action prior to the communication between courts or between the court and a foreign representative to establish procedures for the manner of the communication and the right to participate in the communication. Participation in the communication includes both active and passive participation. Parties wishing to participate must notify the court at least 5 days before the hearing so that ample time exists to make arrangements necessary to permit the participation.

Amended, on an interim basis, effective October 17, 2005.

## INTERIM RULE 6004.  USE, SALE, OR LEASE OF PROPERTY

\* \* \* \* \*

### (g) Sale of Personally Identifiable Information.

(1) *Motion.* A motion for authority to sell or lease personally identifiable information under § 363(b)(1)(B) shall include a request for an order directing the United States trustee to appoint a consumer privacy ombudsman under § 332. The motion shall be governed by Rule 9014 and shall be served on any committee elected under § 705 or appointed under § 1102 of the Code, or if the case is a chapter 11

reorganization case and no committee of unsecured creditors has been appointed under § 1102, on the creditors included on the list of creditors filed under Rule 1007(d), and on such other entities as the court may direct. The motion shall be transmitted to the United States trustee.

(2) *Appointment.* If a consumer privacy ombudsman is appointed under § 332, no later than 5 days before the hearing on the motion under § 363(b)(1)(B), the United States trustee shall file a notice of the appointment, including the name and address of the person appointed. The United States trustee's notice shall be accompanied by a verified statement of the person appointed setting forth the person's connections with the debtor, creditors, any other party in interest, their respective attorneys and accountants, the United States trustee, or any person employed in the office of the United States trustee.

**(h) Stay of Order Authorizing Use, Sale, or Lease of Property.** An order authorizing the use, sale, or lease of property other than cash collateral is stayed until the expiration of 10 days after entry of the order, unless the court orders otherwise.

**COMMITTEE NOTE**
October 17, 2005

This rule is amended to implement §§ 332 and 363(b)(1)(B), which were added to the Code in 2005.

Amended, on an interim basis, effective October 17, 2005.

## INTERIM RULE 6011. DISPOSAL OF PATIENT RECORDS IN HEALTH CARE BUSINESS CASE

**(a) Notice by Publication Under § 351(1)(A).** A notice regarding the claiming or disposing of patient records under § 351(1)(A) shall not identify patients by name or other identifying information, but shall:

(1) identify with particularity the health care facility whose patient records the trustee proposes to destroy;

(2) state the name, address, telephone number, e-mail address, and website, if any, of a person from whom information about the patient records may be obtained and how those records may be claimed; and

(3) state the date by which patient records must be claimed, and that if they are not so claimed the records will be destroyed.

**(b) Notice by Mail Under § 351(1)(B).** Subject to applicable nonbankruptcy law relating to patient privacy, a notice regarding the claiming or disposing of patient records under § 351(1) (B) shall, in addition to including the information in subdivision (a), direct that a patient's family member or other representative who receives the notice inform the patient of the notice, and be mailed to the patient and any family member or other contact person whose name and address have been given to the trustee or the debtor for the purpose of providing information regarding the patient's health care, and to insurance companies known to have provided health care insurance to the patient.

**(c) Proof of Compliance With Notice Requirement.** Unless the court orders the trustee to file proof of compliance with § 351(1)(B) under seal, the trustee shall not file, but shall maintain, the proof of compliance for a reasonable time.

**(d) Report of Destruction of Records.** The trustee shall file, not later than 30 days after the destruction of patient records under § 351(3), a report certifying that the unclaimed records have been destroyed and explaining the method used to effect the destruction. The report shall not identify patients by name or other identifying information.

**COMMITTEE NOTE**
October 17, 2005

This rule is new. It implements § 351(1), which was added to the Code in 2005. That provision requires the trustee to notify patients that their patient records will be destroyed if

501

they remain unclaimed for one year after the publication of a notice in an appropriate newspaper. The Code provision also requires that individualized notice be sent to each patient and to the patient's family member or other contact person.

The variety of health care businesses and the range of current and former patients present the need for flexibility in the creation and publication of the notices that will be given. Nevertheless, there are some matters that must be included in any notice being given to patients, their family members, and contact persons to ensure that sufficient information is provided to these persons regarding the trustee's intent to dispose of patient records. Subdivision (a) of this rule lists the minimum requirements for notices given under § 351(1)(A), and subdivision (b) governs the form of notices under § 351(1)(B). Notices given under this rule are subject to provisions under applicable federal and state law that relate to the protection of patients' privacy, such as the Health Insurance Portability and Accountability Act of 1996, Pub. L. No. 104–191 (HIPAA).

Subdivision (c) directs the trustee to maintain proof of compliance with § 351(1)(B), but it prohibits filing the proof of compliance unless the court orders the trustee to file it under seal because the proof of compliance may contain patient names that should or must remain confidential.

Subdivision (d) requires the trustee to file a report with the court regarding the destruction of patient records. This certification is intended to ensure that the trustee properly completed the destruction process. However, because the report will be filed with the court and ordinarily will be available to the public under § 107, the names, addresses, and other identifying information of the patient shall not be included in the report to protect patient privacy.

Amended, on an interim basis, effective October 17, 2005.

## INTERIM RULE 8001.  MANNER OF TAKING APPEAL; VOLUNTARY DISMISSAL; CERTIFICATION TO COURT OF APPEALS

* * * * *

### (f) Certification for Direct Appeal to Court of Appeals.

(1) *Timely Appeal Required.* A certification of a judgment, order, or decree of a bankruptcy court to a court of appeals under 28 U.S.C. § 158(d)(2) shall not be treated as a certification entered on the docket within the meaning of § 1233(b)(4)(A) of Public Law No. 109–8 until a timely appeal has been taken in the manner required by subdivisions (a) or (b) of this rule and the notice of appeal has become effective under Rule 8002.

(2) *Court Where Made.* A certification that a circumstance specified in 28 U.S.C. § 158(d)(2)(A)(i)-(iii) exists shall be filed in the court in which a matter is pending for purposes of 28 U.S.C. § 158(d)(2) and this rule. A matter is pending in a bankruptcy court until the docketing, in accordance with Rule 8007(b), of an appeal taken under 28 U.S.C. § 158(a)(1) or (2), or the grant of leave to appeal under 28 U.S.C. § 158(a)(3). A matter is pending in a district court or bankruptcy appellate panel after the docketing, in accordance with Rule 8007(b), of an appeal taken under 28 U.S.C. § 158(a)(1) or (2), or the grant of leave to appeal under 28 U.S.C. § 158(a)(3).

(A) Certification by Court on Request or Court's Own Initiative.

(i) Before Docketing or Grant of Leave to Appeal. Only a bankruptcy court may make a certification on request or on its own initiative while the matter is pending in the bankruptcy court.

(ii) After Docketing or Grant of Leave to Appeal. Only the district court or bankruptcy appellate panel involved may make a certification on request of the parties or on its own initiative while the matter is pending in the district court or bankruptcy appellate panel.

(B) Certification by All Appellants and Appellees Acting Jointly. A certification by all the appellants and appellees, if any, acting jointly may be made by filing the appropriate Official Form with the clerk of the court in which the matter is pending. The certification may be accompanied by a short statement of the basis for the certification, which may include the information listed in subdivision (f)(3)(C) of this rule.

(3) *Request for Certification; Filing; Service; Contents.*

(A) A request for certification shall be filed, within the time specified by 28 U.S.C. § 158(d)(2), with the clerk of the court in which the matter is pending.

(B) Notice of the filing of a request for certification shall be served in the manner required for service of a notice of appeal under Rule 8004.

(C) A request for certification shall include the following:

(i) the facts necessary to understand the question presented;

(ii) the question itself;

(iii) the relief sought;

(iv) the reasons why the appeal should be allowed and is authorized by statute or rule, including why a circumstance specified in 28 U.S.C. § 158(d)(2)(A)(i)-(iii) exists; and

(v) an attached copy of the judgment, order, or decree complained of and any related opinion or memorandum.

(D) A party may file a response to a request for certification or a cross-request within 10 days after the notice of the request is served, or another time fixed by the court.

(E) The request, cross request, and any response shall not be governed by Rule 9014 and shall be submitted without oral argument unless the court otherwise directs.

(F) A certification of an appeal under 28 U.S.C. § 158(d)(2) shall be made in a separate document served on the parties.

(4) *Certification on Court's Own Initiative.*

(A) A certification of an appeal on the court's own initiative under 28 U.S.C. § 158(d)(2) shall be made in a separate document served on the parties in the manner required for service of a notice of appeal under Rule 8004. The certification shall be accompanied by an opinion or memorandum that contains the information required by subdivision (f)(3)(C)(i)-(iv) of this rule.

(B) A party may file a supplementary short statement of the basis for certification within 10 days after the certification.

**COMMITTEE NOTE**
October 17, 2005

Subdivision (f) is added to the rule to implement the 2005 amendments to 28 U.S.C. § 158(d). That section authorizes appeals directly to the court of appeals, with that court's consent, upon certification that a ground for the appeal exists under § 158(d)(2)(A)(i)-(iii). Certification can be made by the court on its own initiative or in response to a request of a party. Certification also can be made by all of the appellants and appellees. An uncodified provision in Public Law No. 109–8, § 1233(b)(4), requires that, not later than 10 days after a certification is entered on the docket, there must be filed with the circuit clerk a petition requesting permission to appeal. Given the short time limit to file the petition with the circuit clerk, subdivision (f)(1) provides that entry of a certification on the docket does not occur until an effective appeal is taken under Rule 8003(a) or (b).

The rule adopts a bright-line test for identifying the court in which a matter is pending. Under subdivision (f)(2), the bright-line chosen is the "docketing" under Rule 8007(b) of an appeal of an interlocutory order or decree under 28 U.S.C. § 158(a)(2) or a final judgment, order or decree under 28 U.S.C. § 158(a)(1), or the granting of leave to appeal any other interlocutory judgment, order or decree under 28 U.S.C. § 158(a)(3), whichever is earlier.

To ensure that parties are aware of a certification, the rule requires either that it be made on the Official Form (if being made by all of the parties to the appeal) or on a separate document (whether the certification is made on the court's own initiative or in response to a request by a party). This is particularly important because the rule adopts the bankruptcy practice established by Rule 8001(a) and (b) of requiring a notice of appeal in every instance, including interlocutory orders, of appeals from bankruptcy court orders, judgments, and decrees. Because this requirement is satisfied by filing the notice of appeal that takes the appeal to the district court or bankruptcy appellate panel in the first instance, the rule does not require a

503

separate notice of appeal if a certification occurs after a district court or bankruptcy appellate panel decision.

Amended, on an interim basis, effective October 17, 2005.

## INTERIM RULE 8003.   LEAVE TO APPEAL

\* \* \* \* \*

**(d)** If leave to appeal is required by 28 U.S.C. § 158(a) and has not earlier been granted, the authorization of a direct appeal by a court of appeals under 28 U.S.C. § 158(d)(2) shall be deemed to satisfy the requirement for leave to appeal.

### COMMITTEE NOTE
### October 17, 2005

The rule is amended to add subdivision (d) to solve the jurisdictional problem that could otherwise ensue when a district court or bankruptcy appellate panel has not granted leave to appeal under 28 U.S.C. § 158(a)(3). If the court of appeals accepts the appeal, the requirement of leave to appeal is deemed satisfied. However, if the court of appeals does not authorize a direct appeal, the question of whether to grant leave to appeal remains a matter to be resolved by the district court or the bankruptcy appellate panel.

Amended, on an interim basis, effective October 17, 2005.

## INTERIM RULE 9006.   TIME

\* \* \* \* \*

**(b) Enlargement.**

(1) *In General.* Except as provided in paragraphs (2) and (3) of this subdivision, when an act is required or allowed to be done at or within a specified period by these rules or by a notice given thereunder or by order of court, the court for cause shown may at any time in its discretion (1) with or without motion or notice order the period enlarged if the request therefor is made before the expiration of the period originally prescribed or as extended by a previous order or (2) on motion made after the expiration of the specified period permit the act to be done where the failure to act was the result of excusable neglect.

(2) *Enlargement Not Permitted.* The court may not enlarge the time for taking action under Rules 1007(d), 2003(a) and (d), 7052, 9023, and 9024.

(3) *Enlargement Limited.* The court may enlarge the time for taking action under Rules 1006(b)(2), 1007(c) with respect to the time to file schedules and statements in a small business case, 1017(e), 3002(c), 4003(b), 4004(a), 4007(c), 8002 and 9033, only to the extent and under the conditions stated in those rules.

\* \* \* \* \*

### COMMITTEE NOTE
### October 17, 2005

Section 1116(3) of the Code, as amended in 2005, places specific limits on the time for filing schedules and a statement of affairs in small business cases. The rule is amended to recognize that extensions of time for filing these documents are governed by Rule 1007(c), which is amended to recognize restrictions on expanding the time to file these documents in small business cases.

Amended, on an interim basis, effective October 17, 2005.

## INTERIM RULE 9009.   FORMS

The Official Forms prescribed by the Judicial Conference of the United States shall be observed and used with alterations as may be appropriate. Forms may be

combined and their contents rearranged to permit economies in their use. The Director of the Administrative Office of the United States Courts may issue additional forms for use under the Code. The forms shall be construed to be consistent with these rules and the Code. References in the Official Forms to these rules shall include the Interim Rules approved by the Committee on Rules of Practice and Procedure to implement Public Law No. 109–8.

**COMMITTEE NOTE**
**October 17, 2005**

The Official Forms refer to the Federal Rules of Bankruptcy Procedure. This rule is amended so that the reference to rules in the Official Forms includes the Interim Rules that implement the provisions of the Bankruptcy Abuse Prevention and Consumer Protection Act of 2005 (Public Law Number 109–8).

Amended, on an interim basis, effective October 17, 2005.

*

# RULES OF PROCEDURE OF
# THE JUDICIAL PANEL ON
# MULTIDISTRICT LITIGATION

### Effective July 1, 1993

### Renumbered and Amended Effective November 2, 1998

### Including Amendments Effective July 30, 2007

---

*Research Note*

*These rules may be searched electronically on WESTLAW® in the US–RULES database; updates to these rules may be found on WESTLAW® in US–ORDERS or US–RULESUPDATES. For search tips, and a detailed summary of database content, consult the WESTLAW® Scope Screen of each database.*

---

*Table of Rules*

---

# I. GENERAL RULES/RULES FOR MULTIDISTRICT LITIGATION UNDER 28 U.S.C. § 1407

## RULE 1.1 DEFINITIONS

As used in these Rules "Panel" means the members of the Judicial Panel on Multidistrict Litigation appointed by the Chief Justice of the United States pursuant to Section 1407, Title 28, United States Code.

"Clerk of the Panel" means the official appointed by the Panel to act as Clerk of the Panel and shall

include those deputized by the Clerk of the Panel to perform or assist in the performance of the duties of the Clerk of the Panel.

"Chairman" means the Chairman of the Judicial Panel on Multidistrict Litigation appointed by the Chief Justice of the United States pursuant to Section 1407, or the member of the Panel designated by the Panel to act as Chairman in the absence or inability of the appointed Chairman.

A "tag-along action" refers to a civil action pending in a district court and involving common questions of fact with actions previously transferred under Section 1407.

Former Rule 1 adopted May 3, 1993, effective July 1, 1993; renumbered Rule 1.1 September 1, 1998, effective November 2, 1998.

## RULE 1.2   PRACTICE

Where not fixed by statute or rule, the practice shall be that heretofore customarily followed by the Panel.

Former Rule 5 adopted May 3, 1993, effective July 1, 1993; renumbered Rule 1.2 September 1, 1998, effective November 2, 1998.

## RULE 1.3   FAILURE TO COMPLY WITH RULES

The Clerk of the Panel may, when a paper submitted for filing is not in compliance with the provisions of these Rules, advise counsel of the deficiencies and a date for full compliance. If full compliance is not accomplished within the established time, the non-complying paper shall nonetheless be filed by the Clerk of the Panel but it may be stricken by order of the Chairman of the Panel.

Former Rule 4 adopted May 3, 1993, effective July 1, 1993; renumbered Rule 1.3 and amended September 1, 1998, effective November 2, 1998.

## RULE 1.4   ADMISSION TO PRACTICE BEFORE THE PANEL AND REPRESENTATION IN TRANSFERRED ACTIONS

Every member in good standing of the Bar of any district court of the United States is entitled without condition to practice before the Judicial Panel on Multidistrict Litigation. Any attorney of record in any action transferred under Section 1407 may continue to represent his or her client in any district court of the United States to which such action is transferred. Parties to any action transferred under Section 1407 are not required to obtain local counsel in the district to which such action is transferred.

Former Rule 6 adopted May 3, 1993, effective July 1, 1993; renumbered Rule 1.4 September 1, 1998, effective November 2, 1998.

## RULE 1.5   EFFECT OF THE PENDENCY OF AN ACTION BEFORE THE PANEL

The pendency of a motion, order to show cause, conditional transfer order or conditional remand order before the Panel concerning transfer or remand of an action pursuant to 28 U.S.C. § 1407 does not affect or suspend orders and pretrial proceedings in the district court in which the action is pending and does not in any way limit the pretrial jurisdiction of that court. A transfer or remand pursuant to 28 U.S.C. § 1407 shall be effective when the transfer or remand order is filed in the office of the clerk of the district court of the transferee district.

Former Rule 18 adopted May 3, 1993, effective July 1, 1993; renumbered Rule 1.5 September 1, 1998, effective November 2, 1998.

## RULE 1.6   TRANSFER OF FILES

(a) Upon receipt of a certified copy of a transfer order from the clerk of the transferee district court, the clerk of the transferor district court shall forward to the clerk of the transferee district court the complete original file and a certified copy of the docket sheet for each transferred action.

(b) If an appeal is pending, or a notice of appeal has been filed, or leave to appeal has been sought under 28 U.S.C. § 1292(b) or a petition for an extraordinary writ is pending, in any action included in an order of transfer under 28 U.S.C. § 1407, and the original file or parts thereof have been forwarded to the court of appeals, the clerk of the transferor district court shall notify the clerk of the court of appeals of the order of transfer and secure the original file long enough to prepare and transmit to the clerk of the transferee district court a certified copy of all papers contained in the original file and a certified copy of the docket sheet.

(c) If the transfer order provides for the separation and simultaneous remand of any claim, cross-claim, counterclaim, or third-party claim, the clerk of the transferor district court shall retain the original file and shall prepare and transmit to the clerk of the transferee district court a certified copy of the docket sheet and copies of all papers except those relating exclusively to separated and remanded claims.

(d) Upon receipt of an order to remand from the Clerk of the Panel, the transferee district court shall prepare and send to the clerk of the transferor district court the following:

(i) a certified copy of the individual docket sheet for each action being remanded;

(ii) a certified copy of the master docket sheet, if applicable;

(iii) the entire file for each action being remanded, as originally received from the transferor district court and augmented as set out in this rule;

(iv) a certified copy of the final pretrial order, if applicable; and

(v) a "record on remand" to be composed of those parts of the files and records produced during coordinated or consolidated pretrial proceedings which have been stipulated to or designated by counsel as being necessary for any or all proceedings to be conducted following remand. It shall be the responsibility of counsel originally preparing or filing any document to be included in the "record on remand" to furnish on request sufficient copies to the clerk of the transferee district court.

**(e)** The Clerk of the Panel shall be notified when any files have been transmitted pursuant to this Rule.

Former Rule 19 adopted May 3, 1993, effective July 1, 1993; renumbered Rule 1.6 and amended September 1, 1998, effective November 2, 1998.

## RULE 5.1   KEEPING RECORDS AND FILES

**(a)** The records and files of the Panel shall be kept by the Clerk of the Panel at the offices of the Panel. Records and files may be temporarily or permanently removed to such places at such times as the Panel or the Chairman of the Panel shall direct. The Clerk of the Panel may charge fees, as prescribed by the Judicial Conference of the United States, for duplicating records and files. Records and files may be transferred whenever appropriate to the Federal Records Center.

**(b)** In order to assist the Panel in carrying out its functions, the Clerk of the Panel shall obtain the complaints and docket sheets in all actions under consideration for transfer under 28 U.S.C. § 1407 from the clerk of each district court wherein such actions are pending. The Clerk of the Panel shall similarly obtain any other pleadings and orders that could affect the Panel's decision under 28 U.S.C. § 1407.

Former Rule 2 adopted May 3, 1993, effective July 1, 1993; renumbered Rule 5.1 and amended September 1, 1998, effective November 2, 1998.

## RULE 5.11   PLACE OF FILING OF PAPERS

All papers for consideration by the Panel shall be submitted for filing to the Clerk of the Panel by mailing or delivering to:

Clerk of the Panel
Judicial Panel on Multidistrict Litigation
Thurgood Marshall Federal Judiciary Building
One Columbus Circle, N.E., Room G–255, North

Lobby
Washington, D.C. 20002–8004

No papers shall be left with or mailed to a Judge of the panel.

Former Rule 3 adopted May 3, 1993, effective July 1, 1993; renumbered Rule 5.11 and amended September 1, 1998, effective November 2, 1998.

## RULE 5.12   MANNER OF FILING OF PAPERS

**(a)** An original of the following papers shall be submitted for filing to the Clerk of the Panel: a proof of service pursuant to Rule 5.2(a) and (b) of these Rules, a notice of appearance pursuant to Rule 5.2(c) and (d) of these Rules, a corporate disclosure statement pursuant to Rule 5.3 of these Rules, a status notice pursuant to Rules 7.2(f), 7.3(e) and 7.4(b) of these Rules, a notice of opposition pursuant to Rules 7.4(c) and 7.6(f)(ii) of these Rules, a notice of related action pursuant to Rules 7.2(i), 7.3(a) and 7.5(e) of these Rules, an application for extension of time pursuant to Rule 6.2 of these Rules, or a notice of presentation or waiver of oral argument pursuant to Rule 16.1(d) of these Rules. An original and ~~eleven~~ four* copies of all other papers shall be submitted for filing to the Clerk of the Panel. The Clerk of the Panel may require that additional copies also be submitted for filing.

**(b)** When papers are submitted for filing, the Clerk of the Panel shall endorse thereon the date for filing.

**(c)** Copies of motions for transfer of an action or actions pursuant to 28 U.S.C. § 1407 shall be filed in each district court in which an action is pending that will be affected by the motion. Copies of a motion for remand pursuant to 28 U.S.C. § 1407 shall be filed in the Section 1407 transferee district court in which any action affected by the motion is pending.

**(d)** Papers requiring only an original may be faxed to the Panel office with prior approval of the Clerk of the Panel. No papers requiring multiple copies shall be accepted via fax.

Former Rule 7 adopted May 3, 1993, effective July 1, 1993; renumbered Rule 5.12 and amended September 1, 1998, effective November 2, 1998; amended effective April 2, 2001; paragraph (a) suspended in part by Order filed April 19, 2005.

[Publisher's Note: April 19, 2005, the Judicial Panel on Multidistrict Litigation issued an Order reducing the number of copies from eleven to four. The Order reads as follows:

IT IS HEREBY ORDERED that, because the Panel is utilizing filed papers and electronic distribution of those papers, Panel Rule 5.12(a), Manner of Filing Papers, R.P.J.P.M.L., 199 F.R.D. 425, 429 (2001), is partially suspended insofar as papers submitted for filing requiring an original and eleven copies shall be reduced to four copies along with an original.]

## RULE 5.13 FILING OF PAPERS: COMPUTER GENERATED DISK REQUIRED

(a) Whenever an original paper and eleven copies is required to be submitted for filing to the Clerk of the Panel pursuant to Rule 5.12(a) of these Rules, and where a party is represented by counsel, one copy of that paper must also be submitted on a computer readable disk and shall be filed at the time the party's paper is filed. The disk shall contain the entire paper exclusive of computer non-generated exhibits. The label of the disk shall include i) "MDL #___," ii) an abbreviated version of the MDL descriptive title, or other appropriate descriptive title, if not yet designated by the Panel, iii) the identity of the type of paper being filed (i.e. motion, response, reply, etc.), iv) the name of the counsel who signed the paper, and v) the first named represented party on the paper.

(b) The paper must be on a disk in Adobe Acrobat (PDF) format.

(c) One copy of the disk may be served on each party separately represented by counsel. If a party chooses to serve a copy of the disk, the proof of service, as required by Rule 5.2 of these Rules, must indicate service of the paper in both paper and electronic format.

(d) A party may be relieved from the requirements of this Rule by submitting a written application for a waiver, in a timely manner in advance of submission of the paper, certifying that compliance with the Rule would impose undue hardship, that the text of the paper is not available on disk, or that other unusual circumstances preclude compliance with this Rule. The requirements of this Rule shall not apply to parties appearing pro se. Papers embraced by this Rule and submitted by counsel after June 1, 2000 without a computer disk copy or Panel-approved waiver of the requirements of this Rule shall be governed by Rule 1.3 of these Rules.

Effective June 1, 2000; amended effective July 30, 2007.

## RULE 5.2 SERVICE OF PAPERS FILED

(a) All papers filed with the Clerk of the Panel shall be accompanied by proof of previous or simultaneous service on all other parties in all actions involved in the litigation. Service and proof of service shall be made as provided in Rules 5 and 6 of the Federal Rules of Civil Procedure. The proof of service shall indicate the name and complete address of each person served and shall indicate the party represented by each. If a party is not represented by counsel, the proof of service shall indicate the name of the party and the party's last known address. The proof of service shall indicate why any person named as a party in a constituent complaint was not served with the Section 1407 pleading. The original proof of service shall be filed with the Clerk of the Panel and copies thereof shall be sent to each person included within the proof of service. After the "Panel Service List" described in subsection (d) of this Rule has been received from the Clerk of the Panel, the "Panel Service List" shall be utilized for service of responses to motions and all other filings. In such instances, the "Panel Service List" shall be attached to the proof of service and shall be supplemented in the proof of service in the event of the presence of additional parties or subsequent corrections relating to any party, counsel or address already on the "Panel Service List."

(b) The proof of service pertaining to motions for transfer of actions pursuant to 28 U.S.C. § 1407 shall certify that copies of the motions have been mailed or otherwise delivered for filing to the clerk of each district court in which an action is pending that will be affected by the motion. The proof of service pertaining to a motion for remand pursuant to 28 U.S.C. § 1407 shall certify that a copy of the motion has been mailed or otherwise delivered for filing to the clerk of the Section 1407 transferee district court in which any action affected by the motion is pending.

(c) Within eleven days of filing of a motion to transfer, an order to show cause or a conditional transfer order, each party or designated attorney shall notify the Clerk of the Panel, in writing, of the name and address of the attorney designated to receive service of all pleadings, notices, orders and other papers relating to practice before the Judicial Panel on Multidistrict Litigation. Only one attorney shall be designated for each party. Any party not represented by counsel shall be served by mailing such pleadings to the party's last known address. Requests for an extension of time to file the designation of attorney shall not be granted except in extraordinary circumstances.

(d) In order to facilitate compliance with subsection (a) of this Rule, the Clerk of the Panel shall prepare and serve on all counsel and parties not represented by counsel, a "Panel Service List" containing the names and addresses of the designated attorneys and the party or parties they represent in the actions under consideration by the Panel and the names and addresses of the parties not represented by counsel in the actions under consideration by the Panel. After the "Panel Service List" has been received from the Clerk of the Panel, notice of subsequent corrections relating to any party, counsel or address on the "Panel Service List" shall be served on all other parties in all actions involved in the litigation.

(e) If following transfer of any group of multidistrict litigation, the transferee district court appoints liaison counsel, this Rule shall be satisfied by serving each party in each affected action and all liaison counsel. Liaison counsel designated by the transferee district court shall receive copies of all Panel orders concerning their particular litigation and shall be re-

sponsible for distribution to the parties for whom he or she serves as liaison counsel.

Former Rule 8 adopted May 3, 1993, effective July 1, 1993; renumbered Rule 5.2 and amended September 1, 1998, effective November 2, 1998.

## RULE 5.3   CORPORATE DISCLOSURE STATEMENT

**(a)** Any nongovernmental corporate party to a matter before the Panel shall file a statement identifying all its parent corporations and listing any publicly held company that owns 10% or more of the party's stock.

**(b)** A party shall file the corporate disclosure statement within eleven days of the filing of a motion to transfer or remand, an order to show cause, or a motion to vacate a conditional transfer order or a conditional remand order.

**(c)** Once a corporate disclosure statement by a party has been filed in an MDL docket pursuant to subsection (b) of this Rule, such a party is required to update the statement to reflect any change in the information therein i) until the matter before the Panel is decided, and ii) within eleven days of the filing of any subsequent motion to transfer or remand, order to show cause, or motion to vacate a conditional transfer order or a conditional remand order in that docket.

Effective April 2, 2001.

## RULE 6.2   APPLICATIONS FOR EXTENSIONS OF TIME

Any application for an extension of time to file a pleading or perform an act required by these Rules must be in writing, must request a specific number of additional days and may be acted upon by the Clerk of the Panel. Such an application will be evaluated in relation to the impact on the Panel's calendar as well as on the basis of the reasons set forth in support of the application. Any party aggrieved by the Clerk of the Panel's action on such application may submit its objections to the Panel for consideration. Absent exceptional circumstances, no extensions of time shall be granted to file a notice of opposition to either a conditional transfer order or a conditional remand order. All applications for extensions of time shall be filed and served in conformity with Rules 5.12, 5.2 and 7.1 of these Rules.

Former Rule 15 adopted May 3, 1993, effective July 1, 1993; renumbered Rule 6.2 and amended September 1, 1998, effective November 2, 1998.

## RULE 7.1   FORM OF PAPERS FILED

**(a)** Averments in any motion seeking action by the Panel shall be made in numbered paragraphs, each of which shall be limited, as far as practicable, to a statement of a single factual averment.

**(b)** Responses to averments in motions shall be made in numbered paragraphs, each of which shall correspond to the number of the paragraph of the motion to which the responsive paragraph is directed. Each responsive paragraph shall admit or deny wholly or in part the averment of the motion, and shall contain the respondent's version of the subject matter when the averment or the motion is not wholly admitted.

**(c)** Each pleading filed shall be:

(i) flat and unfolded;

(ii) plainly written, typed in double space, printed or prepared by means of a duplicating process, without erasures or interlineations which materially deface it;

(iii) on opaque, unglazed, white paper (not onionskin);

(iv) approximately 8–1/2 x 11 inches in size; and

(v) fastened at the top-left corner without side binding or front or back covers.

**(d)** The heading on the first page of each pleading shall commence not less than three inches from the top of the page. Each pleading shall bear the heading "Before the Judicial Panel on Multidistrict Litigation," the identification "MDL Docket No.___" and the descriptive title designated by the Panel for the litigation involved. If the Panel has not yet designated a title, an appropriate descriptive title shall be used.

**(e)** The final page of each pleading shall contain the name, address and telephone number of the attorney or party in active charge of the case. Each attorney shall also include the name of each party represented.

**(f)** Except with the approval of the Panel, each brief submitted for filing with the Panel shall be limited to twenty pages, exclusive of exhibits. Absent exceptional circumstances, motions to exceed page limits shall not be granted.

**(g)** Exhibits exceeding a cumulative total of 50 pages shall be fastened separately from the accompanying pleading.

**(h)** Proposed Panel orders shall not be submitted with papers for filing.

Former Rule 9 adopted May 3, 1993, effective July 1, 1993; renumbered Rule 7.1 and amended September 1, 1998, effective November 2, 1998; amended effective April 2, 2001.

## RULE 7.2   MOTION PRACTICE

**(a)** All requests for action by the Panel under 28 U.S.C. § 1407 shall be made by written motion. Every motion shall be accompanied by:

(i) a brief in support thereof in which the background of the litigation and factual and legal contentions of the movant shall be concisely stated in sepa-

rate portions of the brief with citation of applicable authorities; and

(ii) a schedule giving

(A) the complete name of each action involved, listing the full name of each party included as such on the district court's docket sheet, not shortened by the use of references such as "et al." or "etc.";

(B) the district court and division in which each action is pending;

(C) the civil action number of each action; and

(D) the name of the judge assigned each action, if known.

**(b)** The Clerk of the Panel shall notify recipients of a motion of the filing date, caption, MDL docket number, briefing schedule and pertinent Panel policies.

**(c)** Within twenty days after filing of a motion, all other parties shall file a response thereto. Failure of a party to respond to a motion shall be treated as that party's acquiescence to the action requested in the motion.

**(d)** The movant may, within five days after the lapse of the time period for filing responsive briefs, file a single brief in reply to any opposition.

**(e)** Motions, their accompaniments, responses, and replies shall also be governed by Rules 5.12, 5.2 and 7.1 of these Rules.

**(f)** With respect to any action that is the subject of Panel consideration, counsel shall promptly notify the Clerk of the Panel of any development that would partially or completely moot the matter before the Panel.

**(g)** A joinder in a motion shall not add any action to the previous motion.

**(h)** Once a motion is filed, any other pleading that purports to be a "motion" in the docket shall be filed by the Clerk of the Panel as a response unless the "motion" adds an action. The Clerk of the Panel, upon designating such a pleading as a motion, shall acknowledge that designation by the distribution of a briefing schedule to all parties in the docket. Response time resulting from an additional motion shall ordinarily be extended only to those parties directly affected by the additional motion. An accelerated briefing schedule for the additional motion may be set by the Clerk of the Panel to conform with the hearing session schedule established by the Chairman.

**(i)** Any party or counsel in a new group of actions under consideration by the Panel for transfer under Section 1407 shall promptly notify the Clerk of the Panel of any potential tag-along action in which that party is also named or in which that counsel appears.

Former Rule 10 adopted May 3, 1993, effective July 1, 1993; renumbered Rule 7.2 and amended September 1, 1998, effective November 2, 1998; amended effective April 2, 2001.

## RULE 7.3 SHOW CAUSE ORDERS

**(a)** When transfer of multidistrict litigation is being considered on the initiative of the Panel pursuant to 28 U.S.C. § 1407(c)(i), an order shall be filed by the Clerk of the Panel directing the parties to show cause why the action or actions should not be transferred for coordinated or consolidated pretrial proceedings. Any party or counsel in such actions shall promptly notify the Clerk of the Panel of any other federal district court actions related to the litigation encompassed by the show cause order. Such notification shall be made for additional actions pending at the time of the issuance of the show cause order and whenever new actions are filed.

**(b)** Any party may file a response to the show cause order within twenty days of the filing of said order unless otherwise provided for in the order. Failure of a party to respond to a show cause order shall be treated as that party's acquiescence to the Panel action contemplated in the order.

**(c)** Within five days after the lapse of the time period for filing a response, any party may file a reply limited to new matters.

**(d)** Responses and replies shall be filed and served in conformity with Rules 5.12, 5.2 and 7.1 of these Rules.

**(e)** With respect to any action that is the subject of Panel consideration, counsel shall promptly notify the Clerk of the Panel of any development that would partially or completely moot the matter before the Panel.

Former Rule 11 adopted May 3, 1993, effective July 1, 1993; renumbered Rule 7.3 and amended September 1, 1998, effective November 2, 1998.

## RULE 7.4 CONDITIONAL TRANSFER ORDERS FOR "TAG–ALONG ACTIONS"

**(a)** Upon learning of the pendency of a potential "tag-along action," as defined in Rule 1.1 of these Rules, an order may be entered by the Clerk of the Panel transferring that action to the previously designated transferee district court on the basis of the prior hearing session(s) and for the reasons expressed in previous opinions and orders of the Panel in the litigation. The Clerk of the Panel shall serve this order on each party to the litigation but, in order to afford all parties the opportunity to oppose transfer, shall not send the order to the clerk of the transferee district court for fifteen days from the entry thereof.

**(b)** Parties to an action subject to a conditional transfer order shall notify the Clerk of the Panel within the fifteen-day period if that action is no longer pending in its transferor district court.

**(c)** Any party opposing the transfer shall file a notice of opposition with the Clerk of the Panel within

the fifteen-day period. If a notice of opposition is received by the Clerk of the Panel within this fifteen-day period, the Clerk of the Panel shall not transmit said order to the clerk of the transferee district court until further order of the Panel. The Clerk of the Panel shall notify the parties of the briefing schedule.

**(d)** Within fifteen days of the filing of its notice of opposition, the party opposing transfer shall file a motion to vacate the conditional transfer order and brief in support thereof. The Chairman of the Panel shall set the motion for the next appropriate hearing session of the Panel. Failure to file and serve a motion and brief shall be treated as withdrawal of the opposition and the Clerk of the Panel shall forthwith transmit the order to the clerk of the transferee district court.

**(e)** Conditional transfer orders do not become effective unless and until they are filed with the clerk of the transferee district court.

**(f)** Notices of opposition and motions to vacate such orders of the Panel and responses thereto shall be governed by Rules 5.12, 5.2, 7.1 and 7.2 of these Rules.

Former Rule 12 adopted May 3, 1993, effective July 1, 1993; renumbered Rule 7.4 and amended September 1, 1998, effective November 2, 1998; amended effective April 2, 2001.

## RULE 7.5   MISCELLANEOUS PROVISIONS CONCERNING "TAG–ALONG ACTIONS"

**(a)** Potential "tag-along actions" filed in the transferee district require no action on the part of the Panel and requests for assignment of such actions to the Section 1407 transferee judge should be made in accordance with local rules for the assignment of related actions.

**(b)** Upon learning of the pendency of a potential "tag-along action" and having reasonable anticipation of opposition to transfer of that action, the Panel may direct the Clerk of the Panel to file a show cause order, in accordance with Rule 7.3 of these Rules, instead of a conditional transfer order.

**(c)** Failure to serve one or more of the defendants in a potential "tag-along action" with the complaint and summons as required by Rule 4 of the Federal Rules of Civil Procedure does not preclude transfer of such action under Section 1407. Such failure, however, may be submitted by such a defendant as a basis for opposing the proposed transfer if prejudice can be shown. The inability of the Clerk of the Panel to serve a conditional transfer order on all plaintiffs or defendants or their counsel shall not render the transfer of the action void but can be submitted by such a party as a basis for moving to remand as to such party if prejudice can be shown.

**(d)** A civil action apparently involving common questions of fact with actions under consideration by

the Panel for transfer under Section 1407, which was either not included in a motion under Rule 7.2 of these Rules, or was included in such a motion that was filed too late to be included in the initial hearing session, will ordinarily be treated by the Panel as a potential "tag-along action."

**(e)** Any party or counsel in actions previously transferred under Section 1407 or under consideration by the Panel for transfer under Section 1407 shall promptly notify the Clerk of the Panel of any potential "tag-along actions" in which that party is also named or in which that counsel appears.

Former Rule 13 adopted May 3, 1993, effective July 1, 1993; renumbered Rule 7.5 and amended September 1, 1998, effective November 2, 1998; amended effective April 2, 2001.

## RULE 7.6   TERMINATION AND REMAND

In the absence of unusual circumstances—

**(a)** Actions terminated in the transferee district court by valid judgment, including but not limited to summary judgment, judgment of dismissal and judgment upon stipulation, shall not be remanded by the Panel and shall be dismissed by the transferee district court. The clerk of the transferee district court shall send a copy of the order terminating the action to the Clerk of the Panel but shall retain the original files and records unless otherwise directed by the transferee judge or by the Panel.

**(b)** Each action transferred only for coordinated or consolidated pretrial proceedings that has not been terminated in the transferee district court shall be remanded by the Panel to the transferor district for trial. Actions that were originally filed in the transferee district require no action by the Panel to be reassigned to another judge in the transferee district at the conclusion of the coordinated or consolidated pretrial proceedings affecting those actions.

**(c)** The Panel shall consider remand of each transferred action or any separable claim, cross-claim, counterclaim or third-party claim at or before the conclusion of coordinated or consolidated pretrial proceedings on

(i) motion of any party,

(ii) suggestion of the transferee district court, or

(iii) the Panel's own initiative, by entry of an order to show cause, a conditional remand order or other appropriate order.

**(d)** The Panel is reluctant to order remand absent a suggestion of remand from the transferee district court. If remand is sought by motion of a party, the motion shall be accompanied by:

(i) an affidavit reciting

(A) whether the movant has requested a suggestion of remand from the transferee district court,

how the court responded to any request, and, if no such request was made, why;

(B) whether all common discovery and other pretrial proceedings have been completed in the action sought to be remanded, and if not, what remains to be done; and

(C) whether all orders of the transferee district court have been satisfactorily complied with, and if not, what remains to be done; and

(ii) a copy of the transferee district court's final pretrial order, where such order has been entered.

Motions to remand and responses thereto shall be governed by Rules 5.12, 5.2, 7.1 and 7.2 of these Rules.

(e) When an order to show cause why an action or actions should not be remanded is entered pursuant to subsection (c), paragraph (iii) of this Rule, any party may file a response within twenty days of the filing of said order unless otherwise provided for in the order. Within five days of filing of a party's response, any party may file a reply brief limited to new matters. Failure of a party to respond to a show cause order regarding remand shall be treated as that party's acquiescence to the remand. Responses and replies shall be filed and served in conformity with Rules 5.12, 5.2 and 7.1 of these Rules.

**(f) Conditional Remand Orders.**

(i) When the Panel has been advised by the transferee district judge, or otherwise has reason to believe, that pretrial proceedings in the litigation assigned to the transferee district judge are concluded or that remand of an action or actions is otherwise appropriate, an order may be entered by the Clerk of the Panel remanding the action or actions to the transferor district court. The Clerk of the Panel shall serve this order on each party to the litigation but, in order to afford all parties the opportunity to oppose remand, shall not send the order to the clerk of the transferee district court for fifteen days from the entry thereof.

(ii) Any party opposing the remand shall file a notice of opposition with the Clerk of the Panel within the fifteen-day period. If a notice of opposition is received by the Clerk of the Panel within this fifteen-day period, the Clerk of the Panel shall not transmit said order to the clerk of the transferee district court until further order of the Panel. The Clerk of the Panel shall notify the parties of the briefing schedule.

(iii) Within fifteen days of the filing of its notice of opposition, the party opposing remand shall file a motion to vacate the conditional remand order and brief in support thereof. The Chairman of the Panel shall set the motion for the next appropriate hearing session of the Panel. Failure to file and serve a motion and brief shall be treated as a withdrawal of the opposition and the Clerk of the Panel shall forthwith transmit the order to the clerk of the transferee district court.

(iv) Conditional remand orders do not become effective unless and until they are filed with the clerk of the transferee district court.

(v) Notices of opposition and motions to vacate such orders of the Panel and responses thereto shall be governed by Rules 5.12, 5.2, 7.1 and 7.2 of these Rules.

(g) Upon receipt of an order to remand from the Clerk of the Panel, the parties shall furnish forthwith to the transferee district clerk a stipulation or designation of the contents of the record or part thereof to be remanded and furnish the transferee district clerk all necessary copies of any pleading or other matter filed so as to enable the transferee district clerk to comply with the order of remand.

Former Rule 14 adopted May 3, 1993, effective July 1, 1993; renumbered Rule 7.6 and amended September 1, 1998, effective November 2, 1998; amended effective April 2, 2001.

## RULE 16.1  HEARING SESSIONS AND ORAL ARGUMENT

(a) Hearing sessions of the Panel for the presentation of oral argument and consideration of matters taken under submission without oral argument shall be held as ordered by the Panel. The Panel shall convene whenever and wherever desirable or necessary in the judgment of the Chairman. The Chairman shall determine which matters shall be considered at each hearing session and the Clerk of the Panel shall give notice to counsel for all parties involved in the litigation to be so considered of the time, place and subject matter of such hearing session.

(b) Each party filing a motion or a response to a motion or order of the Panel under Rules 7.2, 7.3, 7.4 or 7.6 of these Rules may file simultaneously therewith a separate statement limited to one page setting forth reasons why oral argument should, or need not, be heard. Such statements shall be captioned "Reasons Why Oral Argument Should [Need Not] Be Heard," and shall be filed and served in conformity with Rules 5.12 and 5.2 of these Rules.

(c) No transfer or remand determination regarding any action pending in the district court shall be made by the Panel when any party timely opposes such transfer or remand unless a hearing session has been held for the presentation of oral argument except that the Panel may dispense with oral argument if it determines that:

(i) the dispositive issue(s) have been authoritatively decided; or

(ii) the facts and legal arguments are adequately presented in the briefs and record, and the decisional process would not be significantly aided by oral argument.

Unless otherwise ordered by the Panel, all other matters before the Panel, such as a motion for recon-

sideration, shall be considered and determined upon the basis of the papers filed.

**(d)** In those matters in which oral argument is not scheduled by the Panel, counsel shall be promptly advised. If oral argument is scheduled in a matter the Clerk of the Panel may require counsel for all parties who wish to make or to waive oral argument to file and serve notice to that effect within a stated time in conformity with Rules 5.12 and 5.2 of these Rules. Failure to do so shall be deemed a waiver of oral argument by that party. If oral argument is scheduled but not attended by a party, the matter shall not be rescheduled and that party's position shall be treated as submitted for decision by the Panel on the basis of the papers filed.

**(e)** Except for leave of the Panel on a showing of good cause, only those parties to actions scheduled for oral argument who have filed a motion or written response to a motion or order shall be permitted to appear before the Panel and present oral argument.

**(f)** Counsel for those supporting transfer or remand under Section 1407 and counsel for those opposing such transfer or remand are to confer separately prior to the oral argument for the purpose of organizing their arguments and selecting representatives to present all views without duplication.

**(g)** Unless otherwise ordered by the Panel, a maximum of twenty minutes shall be allotted for oral argument in each matter. The time shall be divided equally among those with varying viewpoints. Counsel for the moving party or parties shall generally be heard first.

**(h)** So far as practicable and consistent with the purposes of Section 1407, the offering of oral testimony before the Panel shall be avoided. Accordingly, oral testimony shall not be received except upon notice, motion and order of the Panel expressly providing for it.

**(i)** After an action or group of actions has been set for a hearing session, consideration of such action(s) may be continued only by order of the Panel on good cause shown.

Former Rule 16 adopted May 3, 1993, effective July 1, 1993; renumbered Rule 16.1 and amended September 1, 1998, effective November 2, 1998; amended effective April 2, 2001.

## RULE 16.2 NOTICE OF PRESENTATION OR WAIVER OF ORAL ARGUMENT, AND MATTERS SUBMITTED ON THE BRIEFS [REPEALED]

Former Rule 17 adopted May 3, 1993, effective July 1, 1993; renumbered Rule 16.2 and amended September 1, 1998, effective November 2, 1998; repealed effective April 2, 2001.

# II.  RULES FOR MULTICIRCUIT PETITIONS FOR REVIEW UNDER 28 U.S.C. § 2112(a)(3)

## RULE 17.1 RANDOM SELECTION

**(a)** Upon filing a notice of multicircuit petitions for review, the Clerk of the Panel or designated deputy shall randomly select a circuit court of appeals from a drum containing an entry for each circuit wherein a constituent petition for review is pending. Multiple petitions for review pending in a single circuit shall be allotted only a single entry in the drum. This random selection shall be witnessed by the Clerk of the Panel or a designated deputy other than the random selector. Thereafter, an order on behalf of the Panel shall be issued, signed by the random selector and the witness,

(i) consolidating the petitions for review in the court of appeals for the circuit that was randomly selected; and

(ii) designating that circuit as the one in which the record is to be filed pursuant to Rules 16 and 17 of the Federal Rules of Appellate Procedure.

**(b)** A consolidation of petitions for review shall be effective when the Panel's consolidation order is filed at the offices of the Panel by the Clerk of the Panel.

Former Rule 24 adopted May 3, 1993, effective July 1, 1993; renumbered Rule 17.1 September 1, 1998, effective November 2, 1998.

## RULE 25.1 FILING OF NOTICES

**(a)** An original of a notice of multicircuit petitions for review pursuant to 28 U.S.C. § 2112(a)(3) shall be submitted for filing to the Clerk of the Panel by the affected agency, board, commission or officer. The term "agency" as used in Section II of these Rules shall include agency, board, commission or officer.

**(b)** All notices of multicircuit petitions for review submitted by the affected agency for filing with the Clerk of the Panel shall embrace exclusively petitions for review filed in the courts of appeals within ten days after issuance of an agency order and received by the affected agency from the petitioners within that ten-day period.

**(c)** When a notice of multicircuit petitions for review is submitted for filing to the Clerk of the Panel, the Clerk of the Panel shall file the notice and endorse thereon the date of filing.

**(d)** Copies of notices of multicircuit petitions for review shall be filed by the affected agency with the clerk of each circuit court of appeals in which a petition for review is pending that is included in the notice.

Former Rule 20 adopted May 3, 1993, effective July 1, 1993; renumbered Rule 25.1 and amended September 1, 1998, effective November 2, 1998.

## RULE 25.2   ACCOMPANIMENTS TO NOTICES

**(a)** All notices of multicircuit petitions for review shall be accompanied by:

(i) a copy of each involved petition for review as the petition for review is defined in 28 U.S.C. § 2112(a)(2); and

(ii) a schedule giving

(A) the date of the relevant agency order;

(B) the case name of each petition for review involved;

(C) the circuit court of appeals in which each petition for review is pending;

(D) the appellate docket number of each petition for review;

(E) the date of filing by the court of appeals of each petition for review; and

(F) the date of receipt by the agency of each petition for review.

**(b)** The schedule in Subsection (a)(ii) of this Rule shall also be governed by Rules 25.1, 25.3 and 25.4(a) of these Rules.

Former Rule 21 adopted May 3, 1993, effective July 1, 1993; renumbered Rule 25.2 and amended September 1, 1998, effective November 2, 1998.

## RULE 25.3   SERVICE OF NOTICES

**(a)** All notices of multicircuit petitions for review shall be accompanied by proof of service by the affected agency on all other parties in all petitions for review included in the notice. Service and proof of service shall be made as provided in Rule 25 of the Federal Rules of Appellate Procedure. The proof of service shall state the name and address of each person served and shall indicate the party represented by each. If a party is not represented by counsel, the proof of service shall indicate the name of the party and his or her last known address. The original proof of service shall be submitted by the affected agency for filing with the Clerk of the Panel and copies thereof shall be sent by the affected agency to each person included within the proof of service.

**(b)** The proof of service pertaining to notices of multicircuit petitions for review shall certify that copies of the notices have been mailed or otherwise delivered by the affected agency for filing to the clerk of each circuit court of appeals in which a petition for review is pending that is included in the notice.

Former Rule 22 adopted May 3, 1993, effective July 1, 1993; renumbered Rule 25.3 September 1, 1998, effective November 2, 1998.

## RULE 25.4   FORM OF NOTICES

**(a)** Each notice of multicircuit petitions for review shall be

(i) flat and unfolded;

(ii) plainly written, typed in double space, printed or prepared by means of a duplicating process, without erasures or interlineations which materially deface it;

(iii) on opaque, unglazed white paper (not onionskin);

(iv) approximately 8–1/2 x 11 inches in size; and

(v) fastened at the top-left corner without side binding or front or back covers.

**(b)** The heading on the first page of each notice of multicircuit petitions for review shall commence not less that three inches from the top of the page. Each notice shall bear the heading "Notice to the Judicial Panel on Multidistrict Litigation of Multicircuit Petitions for Review," followed by a brief caption identifying the involved agency, the relevant agency order, and the date of the order.

**(c)** The final page of each notice of multicircuit petitions for review shall contain the name, address and telephone number of the individual or individuals who submitted the notice on behalf of the agency.

Former Rule 23 adopted May 3, 1993, effective July 1, 1993; renumbered Rule 25.4and amended September 1, 1998, effective November 2, 1998.

## RULE 25.5   SERVICE OF PANEL CONSOLIDATION ORDER

**(a)** The Clerk of the Panel shall serve the Panel's consolidation order on the affected agency through the individual or individuals, as identified in Rule 25.4(c) of these Rules, who submitted the notice of multicircuit petitions for review on behalf of the agency.

**(b)** That individual or individuals, or anyone else designated by the agency, shall promptly serve the Panel's consolidation order on all other parties in all petitions for review included in the Panel's consolidation order, and shall promptly submit a proof of that service to the Clerk of the Panel. Service and proof of that service shall also be governed by Rule 25.3 of these Rules.

**(c)** The Clerk of the Panel shall serve the Panel's consolidation order on the clerks of all circuit courts of appeals that were among the candidates for the Panel's random selection.

Former Rule 25 adopted May 3, 1993, effective July 1, 1993; renumbered Rule 25.5 and amended September 1, 1998, effective November 2, 1998.

## CONVERSION TABLE

| Renumbered Rule | Previous Rule |
|---|---|
| 1.1 | 1 |
| 1.2 | 5 |
| 1.3 | 4 |
| 1.4 | 6 |
| 1.5 | 18 |
| 1.6 | 19 |
| 5.1 | 2 |
| 5.11 | 3 |
| 5.12 | 7 |
| 5.13 | — |
| 5.2 | 8 |
| 5.3 | — |

| Renumbered Rule | Previous Rule |
|---|---|
| 6.2 | 15 |
| 7.1 | 9 |
| 7.2 | 10 |
| 7.3 | 11 |
| 7.4 | 12 |
| 7.5 | 13 |
| 7.6 | 14 |
| 16.1 | 16, 16.2 & 17 |
| 17.1 | 24 |
| 25.1 | 20 |
| 25.2 | 21 |
| 25.3 | 22 |
| 25.4 | 23 |
| 25.5 | 25 |

*

# FEDERAL COURTS MISCELLANEOUS FEE SCHEDULES

## COURT OF APPEALS FEE SCHEDULE

### Issued in Accordance With 28 U.S.C. § 1913
### Effective October 1, 1979

### Including Amendments Effective January 1, 2007

The following are fees to be charged for services provided by the courts of appeals. No fees are to be charged for services rendered on behalf of the United States, with the exception of those specifically prescribed in items 2, 4 and 5. No fees under this schedule shall be charged to federal agencies or programs which are funded from judiciary appropriations, including, but not limited to, agencies, organizations, and individuals providing services authorized by the Criminal Justice Act, 18 U.S.C. § 3006A, and Bankruptcy Administrator programs.

(1) For docketing a case on appeal or review, or docketing any other proceeding, $450. A separate fee shall be paid by each party filing a notice of appeal in the district court, but parties filing a joint notice of appeal in the district court are required to pay only one fee. A docketing fee shall not be charged for the docketing of an application for the allowance of an interlocutory appeal under 28 U.S.C. § 1292(b), unless the appeal is allowed. A docketing fee shall not be charged for the docketing of a direct bankruptcy appeal or a direct bankruptcy cross appeal when the fee has been collected by the bankruptcy court in accordance with Item 15 or Item 21 of the Bankruptcy Court Miscellaneous Fee Schedule.

(2) For every search of the records of the court and certifying the results thereof, $26. This fee shall apply to services rendered on behalf of the United States if the information requested is available through electronic access.

(3) For certifying any document or paper, whether the certification is made directly on the document, or by separate instrument, $9.

(4) For reproducing any record or paper, 50 cents per page. This fee shall apply to paper copies made from either: (1) original documents; or (2) microfiche or microfilm reproductions of the original records. This fee shall apply to services rendered on behalf of the United States if the record or paper requested is available through electronic access.

(5) For reproduction of recordings of proceedings, regardless of the medium, $26, including the cost of materials. This fee shall apply to services rendered on behalf of the United States if the reproduction of the recording is available electronically.

(6) For reproduction of the record in any appeal in which the requirement of an appendix is dispensed with by any court of appeals pursuant to Rule 30(f), F.R.A.P., a flat fee of $71.

(7) For each microfiche or microfilm copy of any court record, where available, $5.

(8) For retrieval of a record from a Federal Records Center, National Archives, or other storage location removed from the place of business of the court, $45.

(9) For a check paid into the court which is returned for lack of funds, $45.

(10) Fees to be charged and collected for copies of opinions shall be fixed, from time to time, by each court, commensurate with the cost of printing.

(11) The court may charge and collect fees commensurate with the cost of providing copies of the local rules of court. The court may also distribute copies of the local rules without charge.

(12) The clerk shall assess a charge for the handling of registry funds deposited with the court, to be assessed from interest earnings and in accordance with the detailed fee schedule issued by the Director of the Administrative Office of the United States Courts.

(13) Upon the filing of any separate or joint notice of appeal or application for appeal from the Bankruptcy Appellate Panel, or notice of the allowance of an appeal from the Bankruptcy Appellate Panel, or of a writ of certiorari, $5 shall be paid by the appellant or petitioner.

(14) The court may charge and collect a fee of $200 per remote location for counsel's requested use of videoconferencing equipment in connection with each oral argument.

(15) For original admission of attorneys to practice, $150 each, including a certificate of admission. For a duplicate certificate of admission or certificate of good standing, $15.

# DISTRICT COURT FEE SCHEDULE

### Issued in Accordance With 28 U.S.C. § 1914(b)
### Effective October 1, 1979

### Including Amendments Effective June 1, 2004

Following are fees to be charged for services provided by the district courts. No fees are to be charged for services rendered on behalf of the United States, with the exception of those specifically prescribed in items 2, 4 and 5. No fees under this schedule shall be charged to federal agencies or programs which are funded from judiciary appropriations, including, but not limited to, agencies, organizations, and individuals providing services authorized by the Criminal Justice Act, 18 U.S.C. § 3006A, and Bankruptcy Administrator programs.

(1) For filing or indexing any document not in a case or proceeding for which a filing fee has been paid, $39.

(2) For every search of the records of the district court conducted by the clerk of the district court or a deputy clerk, $26 per name or item searched. This fee shall apply to services rendered on behalf of the United States if the information requested is available through electronic access.

(3) For certification of any document or paper, whether the certification is made directly on the document or by separate instrument, $9. For exemplification of any document or paper, twice the amount of the fee for certification.

(4) For reproducing any record or paper, $.50 per page. This fee shall apply to paper copies made from either: (1) original documents; or (2) microfiche or microfilm reproductions of the original records. This fee shall apply to services rendered on behalf of the United States if the record or paper requested is available through electronic access.

(5) For reproduction of recordings of proceedings, regardless of the medium, $26, including the cost of materials. This fee shall apply to services rendered on behalf of the United States, if the reproduction of the recording is available electronically.

(6) For each microfiche sheet of film or microfilm jacket copy of any court record, where available, $5.

(7) For retrieval of a record from a Federal Records Center, National Archives, or other storage location removed from the place of business of the court, $45.

(8) For a check paid into the court which is returned for lack of funds, $45.

(9) For an appeal to a district judge from a judgment of conviction by a magistrate in a misdemeanor case, $32.

(10) For original admission of attorneys to practice, $150 each, including a certificate of admission. For a duplicate certificate of admission or certificate of good standing, $15.

(11) The court may charge and collect fees commensurate with the cost of providing copies of the local rules of court. The court may also distribute copies of the local rules without charge.

(12) The clerk shall assess a charge for the handling of registry funds deposited with the court, to be assessed from interest earnings and in accordance with the detailed fee schedule issued by the Director of the Administrative Office of the United States Courts.

(13) For filing an action brought under Title III of the Cuban Liberty and Democratic Solidarity (LIBERTAD) Act of 1996, P.L. 104–114, 110 Stat. 785 (1996), $5,431. (This fee is in addition to the filing fee prescribed in 28 U.S.C. § 1914(a) for instituting any civil action other than a writ of habeas corpus.)

# BANKRUPTCY COURT FEE SCHEDULE

### Issued in Accordance With 28 U.S.C. § 1930(b)
### Effective October 1, 1979

### Including Amendments Effective January 1, 2007

Following are fees to be charged for services provided by the bankruptcy courts. No fees are to be charged for services rendered on behalf of the United States, with the exception of those specifically prescribed in items 1, 3, and 5, or to bankruptcy administrators appointed under Public Law No. 99–554, § 302(d)(3)(I). No fees under this schedule shall be charged to federal agencies or programs which are funded from judiciary appropriations, including, but not limited to, agencies, organizations, and individuals providing services authorized by the Criminal Justice Act, 18 U.S.C. § 3006A.

(1) For reproducing any record or paper, $.50 per page. This fee shall apply to paper copies made from either: (1) original documents; or (2) microfiche or microfilm reproductions of the original records. This fee shall apply to services rendered on behalf of the United States if the record or paper requested is available through electronic access.

(2) For certification of any document or paper, whether the certification is made directly on the document or by separate instrument, $9. For exemplification of any document or paper, twice the amount of the charge for certification.

(3) For reproduction of recordings of proceedings, regardless of the medium, $26, including the cost of materials. This fee shall apply to services rendered on behalf of the United States, if the reproduction of the recording is available electronically.

(4) For amendments to a debtor's schedules of creditors, lists of creditors, matrix, or mailing lists, $26 for each amendment, provided the bankruptcy judge may, for good cause, waive the charge in any case. No fee is required when the nature of the amendment is to change the address of a creditor or an attorney for a creditor listed on the schedules or to add the name and address of an attorney for a listed creditor.

(5) For every search of the records of the bankruptcy court conducted by the clerk of the bankruptcy court or a deputy clerk, $26 per name or item searched. This fee shall apply to services rendered on behalf of the United States if the information requested is available through electronic access.

(6) For filing a complaint, $250. If the United States, other than a United States trustee acting as a trustee in a case under Title 11, or a debtor is the plaintiff, no fee is required. If a trustee or debtor in possession is the plaintiff, the fee should be payable only from the estate and to the extent there is any estate realized. If a child support creditor or its representative is the plaintiff, and if such plaintiff files the form required by § 304(g) of the Bankruptcy Reform Act of 1994, no fee is required.

(7) For filing or indexing any document not in a case or proceeding for which a filing fee has been paid, $39.

(8) In all cases filed under title 11, the clerk shall collect from the debtor or the petitioner a miscellaneous administrative fee of $39. This fee may be paid in installments in the same manner that the filing fee may be paid in installments, consistent with the procedure set forth in Federal Rule of Bankruptcy Procedure 1006.

(9) Upon the filing of a petition under Chapter 7 of the Bankruptcy Code, the petitioner shall pay $15 to the clerk of the court for payment to trustees serving in cases as provided in 11 U.S.C. § 330(b)(2). An application to pay the fee in installments may be filed in the manner set forth in Federal Rule of Bankruptcy Procedure 1006(b).

(10) Upon the filing of a motion to convert a case to Chapter 7 of the Bankruptcy Code, the movant shall pay $15 to the clerk of court for payment to trustees serving in cases as provided in 11 U.S.C. § 330(b)(2). Upon the filing of a notice of conversion pursuant to Section 1208(a) or Section 1307(a) of the Code, $15 shall be paid to the clerk of the court for payment to trustees serving in cases as provided in 11 U.S.C. § 330(b)(2). If the trustee serving in the case before the conversion is the movant, the fee shall be payable only from the estate that exists prior to conversion. For filing a motion to convert or a notice of conversion, a fee shall be charged in the amount of the difference between the current filing fee for the chapter under which the case was originally commenced and the current filing fee for the chapter to which the case is requested to be converted. If the filing fee for the chapter to which the case is requested to be converted is less than the fee paid at the commencement of the case, no refund shall be provided. A fee shall not be assessed under this item for converting a Chapter 7 or 13 case to a Chapter 11 case as the fee for these actions is collected pursuant to statute under 28 U.S.C. § 1930(a).

(11) For filing a motion to reopen a Bankruptcy Code case, a fee shall be collected in the same amount as the filing fee prescribed by 28 U.S.C. § 1930(a) for commencing a new case on the date of reopening. The

reopening fee should be charged when a case is closed without a discharge being entered. If the motion to reopen is made for a Chapter 7 case, an additional fee of $15 shall be paid to the clerk of the court for payment to trustees serving in cases as provided in 11 U.S.C. § 330(b)(2). For filing a motion to reopen a Chapter 15 case, a fee shall be charged in the same amount as the filing fee required under Item 16 of this schedule for commencing a new case on the date of reopening. The reopening fee will not be charged if the reopening is necessary: (1) to permit a party to file a complaint to obtain a determination under Rule 4007(b), or, (2) when a creditor is violating the terms of the discharge under 11 U.S.C. § 524. The court may waive this fee under appropriate circumstances or may defer payment of the fee from trustees pending discovery of additional assets. If payment is deferred, the fee shall be waived if no additional assets are discovered.

(12) For each microfiche sheet of film or microfilm jacket copy of any court record, where available, $5.

(13) For retrieval of a record from a Federal Records Center, National Archives, or other storage location removed from the place of business of the court, $45.

(14) For a check paid into the court which is returned for lack of funds, $45.

(15) For docketing a proceeding on appeal or review from a final judgment of a bankruptcy judge pursuant to 28 U.S.C. § 158(a) and (b), $250. A separate fee shall be paid by each party filing a notice of appeal in the bankruptcy court, but parties filing a joint notice of appeal in the bankruptcy court are required to pay only one fee. If a trustee or debtor in possession is the appellant, the fee should be payable only from the estate and to the extent there is any estate realized. Upon notice from the court of appeals that a direct appeal from the bankruptcy court has been authorized, the appellant shall pay an additional $200.

(16) For filing a Chapter 15 proceeding, the fee shall be the same amount as the fee for a case commenced under Chapter 11 of Title 11 as required by 28 U.S.C. § 1930(a)(3).

(17) The court may charge and collect fees commensurate with the cost of providing copies of the local rules of court. The court may also distribute copies of the local rules without charge.

(18) The clerk shall assess a charge for the handling of registry funds deposited with the court, to be assessed from interest earnings and in accordance with the detailed fee schedule issued by the Director of the Administrative Office of the United States Courts.

(19) When a joint case filed under § 302 of Title 11 is divided into two separate cases at the request of the debtor(s), a fee shall be charged equal to the current filing fee for the chapter under which the joint case was commenced. If the motion to divide the case is made for a Chapter 7 case, an additional fee of $15 shall be paid to the clerk of the court for payment to trustees serving in cases as provided in 11 U.S.C. § 330(b)(2).

(20) For filing a motion to terminate, annul, modify, or condition the automatic stay provided under § 362(a) of Title 11, a motion to compel abandonment of property of the estate pursuant to Rule 6007(b) of the Federal Rules of Bankruptcy Procedure, or a motion to withdraw the reference of a case or proceeding under 28 U.S.C. § 157(d), $150. No fee is required for a motion for relief from the co-debtor stay or for a stipulation for court approval of an agreement for relief from a stay. If a child support creditor or its representative is the movant, and if such movant files the form required by § 304(g) of the Bankruptcy Reform Act of 1994, no fee is required.

(21) For docketing a cross appeal from a bankruptcy court determination, $250. If a trustee or debtor in possession is the appellant, the fee should be payable only from the estate and to the extent there is any estate realized. Upon notice from the court of appeals that a direct cross from the bankruptcy court has been authorized, the cross appellant shall pay an additional $200.

# JUDICIAL PANEL ON MULTIDISTRICT LITIGATION FEE SCHEDULE

### Issued in Accordance With 28 U.S.C. § 1932
### Effective October 1, 1979
### Including Amendments Effective June 1, 2004

Following are fees to be charged for services provided by the Judicial Panel on Multidistrict Litigation. No fees are to be charged for services rendered on behalf of the United States, with the exception of those specifically prescribed in items 1 and 3. No fees under this schedule shall be charged to federal agencies or programs which are funded from judiciary appropriations, including, but not limited to, agencies, organizations, and individuals providing services authorized by the Criminal Justice Act, 18 U.S.C. § 3006A.

(1) For every search of the records of the court conducted by the clerk of the court or a deputy clerk, $26 per name or item searched. This fee shall apply to services rendered on behalf of the United States if the information requested is available through electronic access.

(2) For certification of any document or paper, whether the certification is made directly on the document or by separate instrument, $9.

(3) For reproducing any record or paper, $.50 per page. This fee shall apply to paper copies made from either: (1) original documents; or (2) microfiche or microfilm reproductions of the original records. This fee shall apply to services rendered on behalf of the United States if the record or paper requested is available through electronic access.

(4) For retrieval of a record from a Federal Records Center, National Archives, or other storage location removed from the place of business of the court, $45.

(5) For a check paid into the Panel which is returned for lack of funds, $45.

# ELECTRONIC PUBLIC ACCESS FEE SCHEDULE

## Including Amendments Effective September 18, 2007

As directed by Congress, the Judicial Conference has determined that the following fees are necessary to reimburse expenses incurred by the judiciary in providing electronic public access to court records. These fees shall apply to the United States unless otherwise stated. No fees under this schedule shall be charged to federal agencies or programs which are funded from judiciary appropriations, including, but not limited to, agencies, organizations, and individuals providing services authorized by the Criminal Justice Act, 18 U.S.C. § 3006A, and bankruptcy administrator programs.

I.   For electronic access to court data via dial-up service: 60 cents per minute. For electronic access to court data via a federal judiciary Internet site: eight cents per page, with the total for any document, docket sheet, or case-specific report not to exceed the fee for thirty pages—provided however that transcripts of federal court proceedings shall not be subject to the thirty-page fee limit. Attorneys of record and parties in a case (including pro se litigants) receive one free electronic copy of all documents filed electronically, if receipt is required by law or directed by the filer. No fee is owed under this provision until an account holder accrues charges of more than $10 in a calendar year. Consistent with Judicial Conference policy, courts may, upon a showing of cause, exempt indigents, bankruptcy case trustees, individual researchers associated with educational institutions, courts, section 501(c)(3) not-for-profit organizations, court appointed pro bono attorneys, and pro bono ADR neutrals from payment of these fees. Courts must find that parties from the classes of persons or entities listed above seeking exemption have demonstrated that an exemption is necessary in order to avoid unreasonable burdens and to promote public access to information. Any user granted an exemption agrees not to sell for profit the data obtained as a result. Any transfer of data obtained as the result of a fee exemption is prohibited unless expressly authorized by the court. Exemptions may be granted for a definite period of time and may be revoked at the discretion of the court granting the exemption.

II.   For printing copies of any record or document accessed electronically at a public terminal in the courthouse: ten cents per page. This fee shall apply to services rendered on behalf of the United States if the record requested is remotely available through electronic access.

III.   For every search of court records conducted by the PACER Service Center, $26 per name or item searched.

IV.   For the PACER Service Center to reproduce on paper any record pertaining to a PACER account, if this information is remotely available through electronic access, 50 cents per page.

V.   For a check paid to the PACER Service Center which is returned for lack of funds, $45.

### JUDICIAL CONFERENCE POLICY NOTES

Courts should not exempt local, state or federal government agencies, members of the media, attorneys or others not members of one of the groups listed above. Exemptions should be granted as the exception, not the rule. A court may not use this exemption language to exempt all users. An exemption applies only to access related to the case or purpose for which it was given. The prohibition on transfer of information received without fee is not intended to bar a quote or reference to information received as a result of a fee exemption in a scholarly or other similar work.

The electronic public access fee applies to electronic court data viewed remotely from the public records of individual cases in the court, including filed documents and the docket sheet. Electronic court data may be viewed free at public terminals at the courthouse and courts may provide other local court information at no cost. Examples of information that can be provided at no cost include: local rules, court forms, news items, court calendars, opinions, and other information—such as court hours, court location, telephone listings—determined locally to benefit the public and the court.

†